The United States Government Manual 1998/1999

Office of the Federal Register
National Archives and Records Administration

Revised June 2, 1998

Raymond A. Mosley,
Director of the Federal Register.

John W. Carlin,
Archivist of the United States.

On the Cover: "Plan of A Projected Castle for Charleston Harbor, So. Carolina" (from the holdings of the National Archives and Records Administration, Records of the Office of the Chief of Engineers).

This undated ink and watercolor design for an octagonal two-story "castle" or fortified enclosure was proposed as part of the defenses guarding the harbor at Charleston, SC. The plans for the upper and lower stories indicate the locations of the embrasures or flared wall openings through which the guns were to be fired. The upper part of the drawing shows the front and rear facades, and the interior space arrangements can be seen near the bottom. This plan, by an unknown artist, was not approved.

The plan is one of nearly 100 drawings on display in "Designs for Democracy: 200 Years of Drawings from the National Archives," a major exhibition in the Circular Gallery of the National Archives Building in Washington, DC, which highlights some of the essential evidence representing 200 years of Federal design. Prepared, commissioned, received, or approved by the U.S. Government, the designs were originally created to support military objectives, provide civilian services, and facilitate the conduct of Government business. They include elegant watercolors, exquisite ink and wash drawings, bold charcoal and pencil sketches, and finely executed engineering details that were created by professional artists, engineers, inventors, draftsmen, or graphic artists, as well as a few inspired citizens. "Designs for Democracy" is on display through January 10, 1999.

For information on NARA's holdings, exhibits, and publications, visit the National Archives Internet site at http://www.nara.gov/.

For sale by the U.S. Government Printing Office
Superintendent of Documents, Mail Stop: SSOP, Washington, DC 20402-9328
ISBN 0-16-049690-X

Preface

As the official handbook of the Federal Government, *The United States Government Manual* provides comprehensive information on the agencies of the legislative, judicial, and executive branches. The *Manual* also includes information on quasi-official agencies; international organizations in which the United States participates; and boards, commissions, and committees.

A typical agency description includes a list of principal officials, a summary statement of the agency's purpose and role in the Federal Government, a brief history of the agency, including its legislative or executive authority, a description of its programs and activities, and a "Sources of Information" section. This last section provides information on consumer activities, contracts and grants, employment, publications, and many other areas of public interest.

The 1998/99 *Manual* was prepared by the Presidential and Legislative Publications Unit, Office of the Federal Register. Maxine L. Hill was Team Leader, and Karen L. Ashlin was Managing Editor, assisted by Scott Andreae, Brad Brooks, Anna Glover, Margaret A. Hemmig, Michael Hoover, Alfred Jones, and Jennifer Mangum.

THE FEDERAL REGISTER AND ITS SPECIAL EDITIONS

The *Manual* is published as a special edition of the *Federal Register* (see 1 CFR 9.1). Its focus is on programs and activities. Persons interested in detailed organizational structure, the regulatory documents of an agency, or Presidential documents should refer to the *Federal Register* or one of its other special editions, described below.

Issued each Federal working day, the *Federal Register* provides a uniform system for publishing Presidential documents, regulatory documents with general applicability and legal effect, proposed rules, notices, and documents required to be published by statute.

The *Code of Federal Regulations* is an annual codification of the general and permanent rules published in the *Federal Register*. The *Code* is divided into 50 titles that represent broad areas subject to Federal regulation. The *Code* is kept up to date by the individual issues of the *Federal Register*.

The *Weekly Compilation of Presidential Documents* serves as a timely, up-to-date reference source for the public policies and activities of the President. It contains remarks, news conferences, messages, statements, and other Presidential material of a public nature issued by the White House during the week reported.

A companion publication to the *Weekly Compilation* is the *Public Papers of the Presidents*, which contains public Presidential documents and speeches in convenient book form. Volumes of the *Public Papers* have been published for every President since Herbert Hoover, with the exception of Franklin D. Roosevelt, whose papers were published privately.

OTHER OFFICE OF THE FEDERAL REGISTER PUBLICATIONS

The Office of the Federal Register publishes slip laws, which are pamphlet prints of each public and private law enacted by Congress. Slip laws are compiled annually as the *United States Statutes at Large*. The *Statutes* volumes contain all public and private laws and concurrent resolutions enacted during a session of Congress;

iii

recommendations for executive, legislative, and judicial salaries; reorganization plans; proposed and ratified amendments to the Constitution; and Presidential proclamations. Included with many of these documents are sidenotes, U.S. Code and statutes citations, and a summary of their legislative histories.

PUBLICATION AVAILABILITY

The publications of the Office of the Federal Register are available for sale by writing:

Superintendent of Documents
P.O. Box 371954
Pittsburgh, PA 15250–7954

and are also sold at Government Printing Office bookstores located in several major cities. Telephone inquiries should be directed to 202–512–1800.

ELECTRONIC SERVICES

The Office of the Federal Register maintains an Internet site for public law numbers, the Federal Register's public inspection list, and information on the Office and its activities at http://www.nara.gov/fedreg/. This site also contains links to the texts of *The United States Government Manual*, Public Laws, the *Weekly Compilation of Presidential Documents*, the *Federal Register*, and the *Code of Federal Regulations* in electronic format through *GPO Access*. For more information, contact Electronic Information Dissemination Services, U.S. Government Printing Office. Phone, 202–512–1530, or 888–293–6498 (toll-free). E-mail, gpoaccess@gpo.gov. Internet, http://www.access.gpo.gov/su_docs/.

FURTHER INFORMATION

Information on *The United States Government Manual* and other publications of the Office of the Federal Register may be obtained by writing:

Office of the Federal Register
National Archives and Records Administration
Washington, DC 20408

Inquiries should be directed by phone to 202–523–5227, faxed to 202–523–6866, or E-mailed to info@fedreg.nara.gov.

Contents

v

The Declaration of Independence

IN CONGRESS, JULY 4, 1776.

THE UNANIMOUS DECLARATION of the thirteen united STATES OF AMERICA,

WHEN in the Course of human events, it becomes necessary for one people to dissolve the political bands which have connected them with another, and to assume among the powers of the earth, the separate and equal station to which the Laws of Nature and of Nature's God entitle them, a decent respect to the opinions of mankind requires that they should declare the causes which impel them to the separation.—We hold these truths to be self-evident, that all men are created equal, that they are endowed by their Creator with certain unalienable Rights, that among these are Life, Liberty and the pursuit of Happiness.—That to secure these rights, Governments are instituted among Men, deriving their just powers from the consent of the governed,—That whenever any Form of Government becomes destructive of these ends, it is the Right of the People to alter or to abolish it, and to institute new Government, laying its foundation on such principles and organizing its powers in such form, as to them shall seem most likely to effect their Safety and Happiness. Prudence, indeed, will dictate that Governments long established should not be changed for light and transient causes; and accordingly all experience hath shown, that mankind are more disposed to suffer, while evils are sufferable, than to right themselves by abolishing the forms to which they are accustomed. But when a long train of abuses and usurpations, pursuing invariably the same Object evinces a design to reduce them under absolute Despotism, it is their right, it is their duty, to throw off such Government, and to provide new Guards for their future security.— Such has been the patient sufferance of these Colonies; and such is now the necessity which constrains them to alter their former Systems of Government. The history of the present King of Great Britain is a history of repeated injuries and usurpations, all having in direct object the establishment of an absolute Tyranny over these States. To prove this, let Facts be submitted to a candid world.—He has refused his Assent to Laws, the most wholesome and necessary for the public good.—He has forbidden his Governors to pass Laws of immediate and pressing importance, unless suspended in their operation till his Assent should be obtained; and when so suspended, he has utterly neglected to attend to them.—He has refused to pass other Laws for the accommodation of large districts of people, unless those people would relinquish the right of Representation in the Legislature, a right inestimable to them and formidable to tyrants only.—He has called together legislative bodies at places unusual, uncomfortable, and distant from the depository of their public Records, for the sole purpose of fatiguing them into compliance with his measures.—He has dissolved Representative Houses repeatedly, for opposing with manly firmness his invasions on the rights of the people.—He has refused for a long time, after such dissolutions, to cause others to be elected; whereby the Legislative powers, incapable of Annihilation, have returned to the People at large for their exercise; the State

1

remaining in the mean time exposed to all the dangers of invasion from without, and convulsions within.—He has endeavored to prevent the population of these States; for that purpose obstructing the Laws for Naturalization of Foreigners; refusing to pass others to encourage their migration hither, and raising the conditions of new Appropriations of Lands.—He has obstructed the Administration of Justice, by refusing his Assent to Laws for establishing Judiciary powers.—He has made Judges dependent on his Will alone, for the tenure of their offices, and the amount and payment of their salaries.—He has erected a multitude of New Offices, and sent hither swarms of Officers to harrass our people, and eat out their substance.—He has kept among us, in times of peace, Standing Armies, without the Consent of our legislatures.—He has affected to render the Military independent of and superior to the Civil power.—He has combined with others to subject us to a jurisdiction foreign to our constitution, and unacknowledged by our laws; giving his Assent to their Acts of pretended Legislation:—For quartering large bodies of armed troops among us:—For protecting them, by a mock Trial, from punishment for any Murders which they should commit on the Inhabitants of these States:—For cutting off our Trade with all parts of the world:—For imposing Taxes on us without our Consent:—For depriving us in many cases, of the benefits of Trial by Jury:—For transporting us beyond Seas to be tried for pretended offences:—For abolishing the free System of English Laws in a neighbouring Province, establishing therein an Arbitrary government, and enlarging its Boundaries so as to render it at once an example and fit instrument for introducing the same absolute rule into these Colonies:—For taking away our Charters, abolishing our most valuable Laws, and altering fundamentally the Forms of our Governments:—For suspending our own Legislatures, and declaring themselves invested with power to legislate for us in all cases whatsoever.—He has abdicated Government here, by declaring us out of his Protection and waging War against us.—He has plundered our seas, ravaged our Coasts, burnt our towns, and destroyed the lives of our people.—He is at this time transporting large Armies of foreign Mercenaries to compleat the works of death, desolation and tyranny, already begun with circumstances of Cruelty & perfidy scarcely paralleled in the most barbarous ages, and totally unworthy the Head of a civilized nation.—He has constrained our fellow Citizens taken Captive on the high Seas to bear Arms against their Country, to become the executioners of their friends and Brethren, or to fall themselves by their Hands.—He has excited domestic insurrections amongst us, and has endeavoured to bring on the inhabitants of our frontiers, the merciless Indian Savages, whose known rule of warfare, is an undistinguished destruction of all ages, sexes and conditions. In every stage of these Oppressions We have Petitioned for Redress in the most humble terms: Our repeated Petitions have been answered only by repeated injury. A Prince, whose character is thus marked by every act which may define a Tyrant, is unfit to be the ruler of a free people. Nor have We been wanting in attentions to our Brittish brethren. We have warned them from time to time of attempts by their legislature to extend an unwarrantable jurisdiction over us. We have reminded them of the circumstances of our emigration and settlement here. We have appealed to their native justice and magnanimity, and we have conjured them by the ties of our common kindred to disavow these usurpations, which, would inevitably interrupt our connections and correspondence. They too have been deaf to the voice of justice and of consanguinity. We must, therefore, acquiesce in the necessity, which denounces our Separation, and hold them, as we hold the rest of mankind, Enemies in War, in Peace Friends.—

WE, THEREFORE, the Representatives of the UNITED STATES OF AMERICA, in General Congress, Assembled, appealing to the Supreme Judge of the world for the rectitude of our intentions, do, in the Name, and by Authority of the good People of these Colonies, solemnly publish and declare, That these United Colonies are, and of Right ought to be FREE AND INDEPENDENT STATES; that they are Absolved from all Allegiance to the British Crown, and that all political connection between them and the State of Great Britain, is and ought to be totally disolved; and that as Free and

Independent States, they have full Power to levy War, conclude Peace, contract Alliances, establish Commerce, and to do all other Acts and Things which Independent States may of right do.—And for the support of this Declaration, with a firm reliance on the protection of Divine Providence, we mutually pledge to each other our Lives, our Fortunes and our sacred Honor.

John Hancock	Benj. Harrison	Lewis Morris
Button Gwinnett	Thos. Nelson, Jr.	Richd. Stockton
Lyman Hall	Francis Lightfoot Lee	Jno. Witherspoon
Geo. Walton	Carter Braxton	Fras. Hopkinson
Wm. Hooper	Robt. Morris	John Hart
Joseph Hewes	Benjamin Rush	Abra. Clark
John Penn	Benj. Franklin	Josiah Bartlett
Edward Rutledge	John Morton	Wm. Whipple
Thos. Heyward, Jr.	Geo. Clymer	Saml. Adams
Thomas Lynch, Jr.	Jas. Smith	John Adams
Arthur Middleton	Geo. Taylor	Robt. Treat Paine
Samuel Chase	James Wilson	Elbridge Gerry
Wm. Paca	Geo. Ross	Step. Hopkins
Thos. Stone	Caesar Rodney	William Ellery
Charles Carroll of	Geo. Read	Roger Sherman
Carrollton	Tho. M: Kean	Sam. Huntington
George Wythe	Wm. Floyd	Wm. Williams
Richard Henry Lee	Phil. Livingston	Oliver Wolcott
Th. Jefferson	Frans. Lewis	Matthew Thornton
Wm. Paca	Geo. Ross	Step. Hopkins
Thos. Stone	Caesar Rodney	William Ellery
Charles Carroll of	Geo. Read	Roger Sherman
Carrollton	Tho. M: Kean	Sam. Huntington
George Wythe	Wm. Floyd	Wm. Williams
Richard Henry Lee	Phil. Livingston	Oliver Wolcott
Th. Jefferson	Frans. Lewis	Matthew Thornton

The Constitution of the United States

WE THE PEOPLE of the United States, in Order to form a more perfect Union, establish Justice, insure domestic Tranquility, provide for the common defence, promote the general Welfare, and secure the Blessings of Liberty to ourselves and our Posterity, do ordain and establish this Constitution for the United States of America.

Article I

Section 1. All legislative Powers herein granted shall be vested in a Congress of the United States, which shall consist of a Senate and House of Representatives.

Section 2. The House of Representatives shall be composed of Members chosen every second Year by the People of the several States, and the Electors in each State shall have the Qualifications requisite for Electors of the most numerous Branch of the State Legislature.

No Person shall be a Representative who shall not have attained to the Age of twenty five Years, and been seven Years a Citizen of the United States, and who shall not, when elected, be an Inhabitant of that State in which he shall be chosen.

Representatives and direct Taxes shall be apportioned among the several States which may be included within this Union, according to their respective Numbers, which shall be determined by adding to the whole Number of free Persons, including those bound to Service for a Term of Years, and excluding Indians not taxed, three fifths of all other Persons. The actual Enumeration shall be made within three Years after the first Meeting of the Congress of the United States, and within every subsequent Term of ten Years, in such Manner as they shall by Law direct. The Number of Representatives shall not exceed one for every thirty Thousand, but each State shall have at Least one Representative; and until such enumerations shall be made, the State of New Hampshire shall be entitled to chuse three, Massachusetts eight, Rhode-Island and Providence Plantations one, Connecticut five, New-York six, New Jersey four, Pennsylvania eight, Delaware one, Maryland six, Virginia ten, North Carolina five, South Carolina five, and Georgia three.

When vacancies happen in the Representation from any State, the Executive Authority thereof shall issue Writs of Election to fill such Vacancies.

The House of Representatives shall chuse their speaker and other Officers; and shall have the sole Power of Impeachment.

Section 3. The Senate of the United States shall be composed of two Senators from each State, chosen by the Legislature thereof, for six Years; and each Senator shall have one Vote.

Immediately after they shall be assembled in Consequence of the first Election, they shall be divided as equally as may be into three Classes. The Seats of the

Senators of the first Class shall be vacated at the Expiration of the second Year, of the second Class at the Expiration of the fourth Year, and of the third Class at the Expiration of the sixth Year, so that one third may be chosen every second Year; and if Vacancies happen by Resignation, or otherwise, during the Recess of the Legislature of any State, the Executive thereof may make temporary Appointments until the next Meeting of the Legislature, which shall then fill such Vacancies.

No Person shall be a Senator who shall not have attained to the Age of thirty Years, and been nine Years a Citizen of the United States, and who shall not, when elected, be an Inhabitant of that State for which he shall be chosen.

The Vice President of the United States shall be President of the Senate, but shall have no Vote, unless they be equally divided.

The Senate shall chuse their other Officers, and also a President pro tempore, in the Absence of the Vice President, or when he shall exercise the Office of President of the United States.

The Senate shall have the sole Power to try all Impeachments. When sitting for that Purpose, they shall be on Oath or Affirmation. When the President of the United States is tried, the Chief Justice shall preside: And no Person shall be convicted without the concurrence of two thirds of the Members present. Judgment in Cases of Impeachment shall not extend further than to removal from Office, and disqualification to hold and enjoy any Office of honor, Trust or Profit under the United States: but the Party convicted shall nevertheless be liable and subject to Indictment, Trial, Judgment and Punishment, according to law.

Section 4. The Times, Places and Manner of holding Elections for Senators and Representatives, shall be prescribed in each State by the Legislature thereof; but the Congress may at any time by Law make or alter such Regulations, except as to the Places of chusing Senators.

The Congress shall assemble at least once in every Year, and such Meeting shall be on the first Monday in December, unless they shall by Law appoint a different Day.

Section 5. Each House shall be the Judge of the Elections, Returns and Qualifications of its own Members, and a Majority of each shall constitute a Quorum to do business; but a smaller Number may adjourn from day to day, and may be authorized to compel the Attendance of absent Members, in such Manner, and under such Penalties as each House may provide.

Each House may determine the Rules of its Proceedings, punish its Members for disorderly Behaviour, and, with the Concurrence of two thirds, expel a Member.

Each House shall keep a Journal of its Proceedings, and from time to time publish the same, excepting such Parts as may in their Judgment require Secrecy; and the yeas and Nays of the Members of either House on any question shall, at the Desire of one fifth of those Present, be entered on the Journal.

Neither House, during the Session of Congress, shall, without the Consent of the other, adjourn for more than three days, nor to any other place than that in which the two Houses shall be sitting.

Section 6. The Senators and Representatives shall receive a Compensation for their Services, to be ascertained by Law, and paid out of the Treasury of the United States. They shall in all Cases, except Treason, Felony and Breach of the Peace, be privileged from Arrest during their Attendance at the Session of their respective Houses, and in going to and returning from the same; and for any Speech or Debate in either House, they shall not be questioned in any other Place.

No Senator or Representative shall, during the Time for which he was elected, be appointed to any civil Office under the Authority of the United States, which shall have been created, or the Emoluments whereof shall have been encreased during such time; and no Person holding any Office under the United States, shall be a Member of either House during his Continuance in Office.

Section 7. All Bills for raising Revenue shall originate in the House of Representatives; but the Senate may propose or concur with Amendments as on other Bills.

Every Bill which shall have passed the House of Representatives and the Senate, shall, before it become a Law, be presented to the President of the United States; If he approve he shall sign it, but if not he shall return it, with his Objections to that House in which it shall have originated, who shall enter the Objections at large on their Journal, and proceed to reconsider it. If after such Reconsideration two thirds of that House shall agree to pass the Bill, it shall be sent, together with the Objections, to the other House, by which it shall likewise be reconsidered, and if approved by two thirds of that House, it shall become a Law. But in all such Cases the Votes of both Houses shall be determined by yeas and Nays, and the Names of the Persons voting for and against the Bill shall be entered on the Journal of each House respectively. If any Bill shall not be returned by the President within ten Days (Sundays excepted) after it shall have been presented to him, the Same shall be a Law, in like Manner as if he had signed it, unless the Congress by their Adjournment prevent its Return, in which Case it shall not be a Law.

Every Order, Resolution, or Vote to which the Concurrence of the Senate and House of Representatives may be necessary (except on a question of Adjournment) shall be presented to the President of the United States; and before the Same shall take Effect, shall be approved by him, or being disapproved by him, shall be repassed by two thirds of the Senate and House of Representatives, according to the Rules and Limitations prescribed in the Case of a Bill.

Section 8. The Congress shall have Power To lay and collect Taxes, Duties, Imposts and Excises, to pay the Debts and provide for the common Defence and general Welfare of the United States; but all duties, Imposts and Excises shall be uniform throughout the United States;

To borrow Money on the Credit of the United States;

To regulate Commerce with foreign Nations, and among the several States, and with the Indian Tribes;

To establish an uniform Rule of Naturalization, and uniform Laws on the subject of Bankruptcies throughout the United States;

To coin Money, regulate the Value thereof, and of foreign Coin, and fix the Standard of Weights and Measures;

To provide for the Punishment of counterfeiting the Securities and current Coin of the United States;

To establish Post Offices and post Roads;

To promote the Progress of Science and useful Arts, by securing for limited Times to Authors and Inventors exclusive Right to their respective Writings and Discoveries;

To constitute Tribunals inferior to the supreme Court;

To define and punish Piracies and Felonies committed on the high Seas, and Offences against the Law of Nations;

To declare War, grant Letters of Marque and Reprisal, and make rules concerning Captures on Land and Water;

To raise and support Armies, but no Appropriation of Money to that Use shall be for a longer Term than two Years;

To provide and maintain a Navy;

To make rules for the Government and Regulation of the land and naval Forces;

To provide for calling forth the Militia to execute the Laws of the Union, suppress Insurrections and repel Invasions;

To provide for organizing, arming, and disciplining, the Militia, and for governing such Part of them as may be employed in the Service of the United States, reserving to the States respectively, the Appointment of the Officers, and the Authority of training the Militia according to the discipline prescribed by Congress;

To exercise exclusive Legislation in all Cases whatsoever, over such District (not exceeding ten Miles square), as may, by Cession of particular States, and the Acceptance of Congress, become the Seat of the Government of the United States, and to exercise like Authority over all Places purchased by the Consent of the Legislature of the State in which the Same shall be for the Erection of Forts, Magazines, Arsenals, dock-Yards, and other needful Buildings;—And

To make all Laws which shall be necessary and proper for carrying into Execution the foregoing Powers, and all other Powers vested by this Constitution in the Government of the United States, or in any Department or Officer thereof.

Section 9. The Migration or Importation of such Persons as any of the States now existing shall think proper to admit, shall not be prohibited by the Congress prior to the Year one thousand eight hundred and eight, but a Tax or duty may be imposed on such Importation, not exceeding ten dollars for each Person.

The Privilege of the Writ of Habeas Corpus shall not be suspended, unless when in Cases of Rebellion or Invasion the public Safety may require it.

No Bill of Attainder or ex post facto Law shall be passed.

No Capitation, or other direct, Tax shall be laid, unless in Proportion to the Census or Enumeration herein before directed to be taken.

No Tax or Duty shall be laid on Articles exported from any State.

No Preference shall be given by any Regulation of Commerce or Revenue to the Ports of one State over those of another: nor shall Vessels bound to, or from, one State, be obliged to enter, clear, or pay Duties in another.

No money shall be drawn from the Treasury, but in Consequence of Appropriations made by Law; and a regular Statement and Account of the Receipts and Expenditures of all public Money shall be published from time to time.

No Title of Nobility shall be granted by the United States: And no Person holding any Office of Profit or Trust under them, shall, without the Consent of the Congress, accept of any present, Emolument, Office, or Title, of any kind whatever, from any King, Prince, or foreign State.

Section 10. No State shall enter into any Treaty, Alliance, or Confederation; grant Letters of Marque and Reprisal; coin Money; emit Bills of Credit; make any Thing but gold and silver Coin a Tender in Payment of Debts; pass any Bill of Attainder, ex post facto Law, or Law impairing the Obligation of Contracts, or grant any Title of Nobility.

No State shall, without the Consent of the Congress, lay any Imposts or Duties on Imports or Exports, except what may be absolutely necessary for executing it's inspection Laws: and the net Produce of all Duties and Imposts, laid by any State on Imports or Exports, shall be for the Use of the Treasury of the United States; and all such Laws shall be subject to the Revision and Controul of the Congress.

No State shall, without the Consent of Congress, lay any Duty of Tonnage, keep Troops, or Ships of War in time of Peace, enter into any Agreement or Compact with another State, or with a foreign Power, or engage in War, unless actually invaded, or in such imminent Danger as will not admit of delay.

Article II

Section 1. The executive Power shall be vested in a President of the United States of America. He shall hold his Office during the Term of four Years, and, together with the Vice President, chosen for the same Term, be elected, as follows

Each State shall appoint, in such Manner as the Legislature thereof may direct, a Number of Electors, equal to the whole Number of Senators and Representatives to which the State may be entitled in the Congress: but no Senator or Representative, or Person holding an Office of Trust or Profit under the United States, shall be appointed an Elector.

The Electors shall meet in their respective States, and vote by Ballot for two Persons, of whom one at least shall not be an Inhabitant of the same State with themselves. And they shall make a List of all the Persons voted for, and of the Number of Votes for each; which List they shall sign and certify, and transmit sealed to the Seat of the Government of the United States, directed to the President of the Senate. The President of the Senate shall, in the Presence of the Senate and House of Representatives, open all the Certificates, and the Votes shall then be counted. The Person having the greatest Number of Votes shall be the President, if such Number be a Majority of the whole Number of Electors appointed; and if there be more than one who have such Majority, and have an equal Number of Votes, then the House of Representatives shall immediately chuse by Ballot one of them for President: and if no Person have a Majority, then from the five highest on the List the said House shall in like Manner chuse the President. But in chusing the President, the Votes shall be taken by States, the Representation from each State having one Vote; A quorum for this Purpose shall consist of a Member or Members from two thirds of the States, and a Majority of all the States shall be necessary to a Choice. In every Case, after the Choice of the President, the Person having the greatest Number of Votes of the Electors shall be the Vice President. But if there should remain two or more who have equal Votes, the Senate shall chuse from them by Ballot the Vice President.

The Congress may determine the Time of chusing the Electors, and the Day on which they shall give their Votes; which Day shall be the same throughout the United States.

No Person except a natural born Citizen, or a Citizen of the United States, at the time of the Adoption of this Constitution, shall be eligible to the Office of President; neither shall any Person be eligible to that Office who shall not have attained to the Age of thirty five Years, and been fourteen Years a Resident within the United States.

In Case of the Removal of the President from Office, or of his Death, Resignation, or Inability to discharge the Powers and Duties of the said Office, the Same shall devolve on the Vice President, and the Congress may by Law provide for the Case of Removal, Death, Resignation or Inability, both of the President and Vice President, declaring what Officer shall then act as President, and such Officer shall act accordingly, until the Disability be removed, or a President shall be elected.

The President shall, at stated Times, receive for his Services, a Compensation, which shall neither be increased nor diminished during the Period for which he shall have been elected, and he shall not receive within that Period any other Emolument from the United States, or any of them.

Before he enter on the Execution of his Office, he shall take the following Oath or Affirmation:—"I do solemnly swear (or affirm) that I will faithfully execute the Office of President of the United States, and will to the best of my Ability, preserve, protect and defend the Constitution of the United States."

Section 2. The President shall be Commander in Chief of the Army and Navy of the United States, and of the Militia of the several States, when called into the actual

Service of the United States; he may require the Opinion, in writing, of the principal Officer in each of the executive Departments, upon any Subject relating to the Duties of their respective Offices, and he shall have Power to grant Reprieves and Pardons for Offences against the United States, except in Cases of Impeachment.

He shall have Power, by and with the Advice and Consent of the Senate, to make Treaties, provided two thirds of the Senators present concur; and he shall nominate, and by and with the Advice and Consent of the Senate, shall appoint Ambassadors, other public Ministers and Consuls, Judges of the supreme Court, and all other Officers of the United States, whose Appointments are not herein otherwise provided for, and which shall be established by Law: but the Congress may by Law vest the Appointment of such inferior Officers, as they think proper, in the President alone, in the Courts of Law, or in the Heads of Departments.

The President shall have Power to fill up all Vacancies that may happen during the Recess of the Senate, by granting Commissions which shall expire at the End of their next Session.

Section 3. He shall from time to time give to the Congress Information of the State of the Union, and recommend to their Consideration such Measures as he shall judge necessary and expedient; he may, on extraordinary Occasions, convene both Houses, or either of them, and in Case of Disagreement between them, with Respect to the Time of Adjournment, he may adjourn them to such Time as he shall think proper; he shall receive Ambassadors and other public Ministers; he shall take Care that the Laws be faithfully executed, and shall Commission all the Officers of the United States.

Section 4. The President, Vice President and all civil Officers of the United States, shall be removed from Office on Impeachment for, and Conviction of, Treason, Bribery, or other High Crimes and Misdemeanors.

Article III

Section 1. The judicial Power of the United States, shall be vested in one supreme Court, and in such inferior Courts as the Congress may from time to time ordain and establish. The Judges, both of the supreme and inferior Courts, shall hold their Offices during good Behaviour, and shall, at stated Times, receive for their Services, a Compensation, which shall not be diminished during their Continuance in Office.

Section 2. The judicial Power shall extend to all Cases, in Law and Equity, arising under this Constitution, the Laws of the United States, and Treaties made, or which shall be made, under their Authority;—to all Cases affecting Ambassadors, other public Ministers and Consuls;—to all Cases of admiralty and maritime Jurisdiction;—to Controversies to which the United States shall be a Party;—to Controversies between two or more States; between a State and Citizens of another State;—between Citizens of different States;—between Citizens of the same State claiming Lands under Grants of different States, and between a State, or the Citizens thereof, and foreign States, Citizens or Subjects.

In all Cases affecting Ambassadors, other public Ministers and Consuls, and those in which a State shall be Party, the supreme Court shall have original Jurisdiction. In all the other Cases before mentioned, the supreme Court shall have appellate Jurisdiction, both as to Law and Fact, with such Exceptions, and under such Regulations as the Congress shall make.

The Trial of all Crimes, except in Cases of Impeachment, shall be by Jury; and such Trial shall be held in the State where the said Crimes shall have been committed; but when not committed within any State, the Trial shall be at such Place or Places as the Congress may by Law have directed.

Section 3. Treason against the United States, shall consist only in levying War against them, or in adhering to their Enemies, giving them Aid and Comfort. No Person shall be convicted of Treason unless on the Testimony of two Witnesses to the same overt Act, or on Confession in open Court.

The Congress shall have Power to declare the Punishment of Treason, but no Attainder of Treason shall work Corruption of Blood, or Forfeiture except during the Life of the Person attainted.

Article IV

Section 1. Full Faith and Credit shall be given in each State to the public Acts, Records, and judicial Proceedings of every other State. And the Congress may by general Laws prescribe the Manner in which such Acts, Records and Proceedings shall be proved, and the Effect thereof.

Section 2. The Citizens of each State shall be entitled to all Privileges and Immunities of Citizens in the several States.

A Person charged in any State with Treason, Felony, or other Crime, who shall flee from Justice, and be found in another State, shall on Demand of the executive Authority of the State from which he fled, be delivered up, to be removed to the State having Jurisdiction of the Crime.

No person held to Service or Labour in one State, under the Laws thereof, escaping into another, shall, in Consequence of any Law or Regulation therein, be discharged from such Service or Labour, but shall be delivered up on Claim of the Party to whom such Service or Labour may be due.

Section 3. New States may be admitted by the Congress into this Union; but no new State shall be formed or erected within the Jurisdiction of any other State; nor any State be formed by the Junction of two or more States, or Parts of States, without the Consent of the Legislatures of the States concerned as well as of the Congress.

The Congress shall have Power to dispose of and make all needful Rules and Regulations respecting the Territory or other Property belonging to the United States; and nothing in this Constitution shall be so construed as to Prejudice any Claims of the United States, or of any particular State.

Section 4. The United States shall guarantee to every State in this Union a Republican Form of Government, and shall protect each of them against Invasion; and on Application of the Legislature, or of the Executive (when the Legislature cannot be convened) against domestic Violence.

Article V

The Congress, whenever two thirds of both Houses shall deem it necessary, shall propose Amendments to this Constitution, or, on the Application of the Legislatures of two thirds of the several States, shall call a Convention for proposing Amendments, which, in either Case, shall be valid to all Intents and Purposes, as Part of this Constitution, when ratified by the Legislatures of three fourths of the several States, or by Conventions in three fourths thereof, as the one or the other Mode of Ratification may be proposed by the Congress; Provided that no Amendment which may be made prior to the Year One thousand eight hundred and eight shall in any Manner affect the first and fourth Clauses in the Ninth Section of the first Article; and that no State, without its Consent, shall be deprived of its equal Suffrage in the Senate.

Article VI

All Debts contracted and Engagements entered into, before the Adoption of this Constitution, shall be as valid against the United States under this Constitution, as under the Confederation.

This Constitution, and the Laws of the United States which shall be made in Pursuance thereof; and all Treaties made, or which shall be made, under the Authority of the United States, shall be the supreme Law of the Land; and the Judges in every State shall be bound thereby, any Thing in the Constitution or Laws of any State to the Contrary notwithstanding.

The Senators and Representatives before mentioned, and the Members of the several State Legislatures, and all executive and judicial Officers, both of the United States and of the several States, shall be bound by Oath or Affirmation, to support this Constitution; but no religious Test shall ever be required as a Qualification to any Office or public Trust under the United States.

Article VII

The Ratification of the Conventions of nine States, shall be sufficient for the Establishment of this Constitution between the States so ratifying the Same.

done in Convention by the Unanimous Consent of the States present the Seventeenth Day of September in the Year of our Lord one thousand seven hundred and Eighty seven and of the Independence of the United States of America the Twelfth *In witness whereof We have hereunto subscribed our Names,*

Gº Washington—Presidᵗ
and deputy from Virginia

New Hampshire	John Langdon Nicholas Gilman
Massachusetts	Nathaniel Gorham Rufus King
Connecticut	Wᵐ Samˡ Johnson Roger Sherman
New York New Jersey	Alexander Hamilton Wil: Livingston David Brearley. Wᵐ Paterson. Jona: Dayton
Pennsylvania ¹	B Franklin Thomas Mifflin Robᵗ Morris Geo. Clymer Thoˢ FitzSimons Jared Ingersoll

---

¹ Spelled with one "n" on the original document.

	James Wilson Gouv Morris
Delaware	Geo: Read Gunning Bedford jun John Dickinson Richard Bassett Jaco: Broom
Maryland	James McHenry Dan of St Thos Jenifer Danl Carroll
Virginia	John Blair— James Madison Jr.
North Carolina	Wm Blount Richd Dobbs Spaight. Hu Williamson
South Carolina	J. Rutledge Charles Cotesworth Pinckney Charles Pinckney Pierce Butler.
Georgia	William Few Abr Baldwin

Amendments

(The first 10 Amendments were ratified December 15, 1791, and form what is known as the Bill of Rights)

Amendment 1

Congress shall make no law respecting an establishment of religion, or prohibiting the free exercise thereof; or abridging the freedom of speech, or of the press; or the right of the people peaceably to assemble, and to petition the Government for a redress of grievances.

Amendment 2

A well regulated Militia, being necessary to the security of a free State, the right of the people to keep and bear Arms, shall not be infringed.

Amendment 3

No Soldier shall, in time of peace be quartered in any house, without the consent of the Owner, nor in time of war, but in a manner to be prescribed by law.

Amendment 4

The right of the people to be secure in their persons, houses, papers, and effects, against unreasonable searches and seizures, shall not be violated, and no Warrants shall issue, but upon probable cause, supported by Oath or affirmation, and particularly describing the place to be searched, and the persons or things to be seized.

Amendment 5

No person shall be held to answer for a capital, or otherwise infamous crime, unless on a presentment or indictment of a Grand Jury, except in cases arising in the land or naval forces, or in the Militia, when in actual service in time of War or public danger; nor shall any person be subject for the same offence to be twice put in jeopardy of life or limb; nor shall be compelled in any criminal case to be a witness against himself, nor be deprived of life, liberty, or property, without due process of law; nor shall private property be taken for public use, without just compensation.

Amendment 6

In all criminal prosecutions, the accused shall enjoy the right to a speedy and public trial, by an impartial jury of the State and district wherein the crime shall have been committed, which district shall have been previously ascertained by law, and to be informed of the nature and cause of the accusation; to be confronted with the witnesses against him; to have compulsory process for obtaining witnesses in his favor, and to have the Assistance of Counsel for his defence.

Amendment 7

In Suits at common law, where the value in controversy shall exceed twenty dollars, the right of trial by jury shall be preserved, and no fact tried by a jury, shall be otherwise re-examined in any Court of the United States, than according to the rules of the common law.

Amendment 8

Excessive bail shall not be required, nor excessive fines imposed, nor cruel and unusual punishments inflicted.

Amendment 9

The enumeration in the Constitution, of certain rights, shall not be construed to deny or disparage others retained by the people.

Amendment 10

The powers not delegated to the United States by the Constitution, nor prohibited by it to the States, are reserved to the States respectively, or to the people.

Amendment 11

(Ratified February 7, 1795)

The Judicial power of the United States shall not be construed to extend to any suit in law or equity, commenced or prosecuted against one of the United States by Citizens of another State, or by Citizens or Subjects of any Foreign State.

Amendment 12

(Ratified July 27, 1804)

The Electors shall meet in their respective states, and vote by ballot for President and Vice-President, one of whom, at least, shall not be an inhabitant of the same state with themselves; they shall name in their ballots the person voted for as President, and in distinct ballots the person voted for as Vice-President, and they shall make distinct lists of all persons voted for as President, and of all persons voted for as Vice-President, and of the number of votes for each, which lists they shall sign and certify, and transmit sealed to the seat of the government of the United States, directed to the President of the Senate;—The President of the Senate shall, in the presence of the Senate and House of Representatives, open all the certificates and the votes shall then be counted;—The person having the greatest number of votes for President, shall be the President, if such number be a majority of the whole number of Electors appointed; and if no person have such majority, then from the persons having the highest numbers not exceeding three on the list of those voted for as President, the House of Representatives shall choose immediately, by ballot, the President. But in choosing the President, the votes shall be taken by states, the representation from each state having one vote; a quorum for this purpose shall consist of a member or members from two-thirds of the states, and a majority of all the states shall be necessary to a choice. And if the House of Representatives shall not choose a President whenever the right of choice shall devolve upon them, before the fourth day of March next following, then the Vice-President shall act as President, as in the case of the death or other constitutional disability of the President.—The person having the greatest number of votes as Vice-President, shall be the Vice-President, if such number be a majority of the whole number of Electors appointed, and if no person have a majority, then from the two highest numbers on the list, the Senate shall choose the Vice-President; a quorum for the purpose shall consist of two-thirds of the whole number of Senators, and a majority of the whole number shall be necessary to a choice. But no person constitutionally ineligible to the office of President shall be eligible to that of Vice-President of the United States.

Amendment 13

(Ratified December 6, 1865)

Section 1. Neither slavery nor involuntary servitude, except as a punishment for crime whereof the party shall have been duly convicted, shall exist within the United States, or any place subject to their jurisdiction.

Section 2. Congress shall have power to enforce this article by appropriate legislation.

Amendment 14

(Ratified July 9, 1868)

Section 1. All persons born or naturalized in the United States, and subject to the jurisdiction thereof, are citizens of the United States and of the State wherein they reside. No State shall make or enforce any law which shall abridge the privileges or immunities of citizens of the United States; nor shall any State deprive any person of life, liberty, or property, without due process of law; nor deny to any person within its jurisdiction the equal protection of the laws.

Section 2. Representatives shall be apportioned among the several States according to their respective numbers, counting the whole number of persons in each State, excluding Indians not taxed. But when the right to vote at any election for the choice of electors for President and Vice President of the United States, Representatives in Congress, the Executive and Judicial officers of a State, or the members of the Legislature thereof, is denied to any of the male inhabitants of such State, being twenty-one years of age, and citizens of the United States, or in any way abridged, except for participation in rebellion, or other crime, the basis of representation therein shall be reduced in the proportion which the number of such male citizens shall bear to the whole number of male citizens twenty-one years of age in such State.

Section 3. No person shall be a Senator or Representative in Congress, or elector of President and Vice President, or hold any office, civil or military, under the United States, or under any State, who, having previously taken an oath, as a member of Congress, or as an officer of the United States, or as a member of any State legislature, or as an executive or judicial officer of any State, to support the Constitution of the United States, shall have engaged in insurrection or rebellion against the same, or given aid or comfort to the enemies thereof. But Congress may by a vote of two-thirds of each House, remove such disability.

Section 4. The validity of the public debt of the United States, authorized by law, including debts incurred for payment of pensions and bounties for services in suppressing insurrection or rebellion, shall not be questioned. But neither the United States nor any State shall assume or pay any debt or obligation incurred in aid of insurrection or rebellion against the United States, or any claim for the loss or emancipation of any slave; but all such debts, obligations and claims shall be held illegal and void.

Section 5. The Congress shall have power to enforce, by appropriate legislation, the provisions of this article.

Amendment 15

(Ratified February 3, 1870)

Section 1. The right of citizens of the United States to vote shall not be denied or abridged by the United States or by any State on account of race, color, or previous condition of servitude.

Section 2. The Congress shall have power to enforce this article by appropriate legislation.

Amendment 16

(Ratified February 3, 1913)

The Congress shall have power to lay and collect taxes on incomes, from whatever source derived, without apportionment among the several States, and without regard to any census or enumeration.

Amendment 17

(Ratified April 8, 1913)

The Senate of the United States shall be composed of two Senators from each State, elected by the people thereof for six years; and each Senator shall have one vote. The electors in each State shall have the qualifications requisite for electors of the most numerous branch of the State legislatures.

When vacancies happen in the representation of any State in the Senate, the executive authority of such State shall issue writs of election to fill such vacancies: *Provided,* That the legislature of any State may empower the executive thereof to make temporary appointments until the people fill the vacancies by election as the legislature may direct.

This amendment shall not be so construed as to affect the election or term of any Senator chosen before it becomes valid as part of the Constitution.

Amendment 18

(Ratified January 16, 1919. Repealed December 5, 1933 by Amendment 21)

Section 1. After one year from the ratification of this article the manufacture, sale, or transportation of intoxicating liquors within, the importation thereof into, or the exportation thereof from the United States and all territory subject to the jurisdiction thereof for beverage purposes is hereby prohibited.

Section 2. The Congress and the several States shall have concurrent power to enforce this article by appropriate legislation.

Section 3. This article shall be inoperative unless it shall have been ratified as an amendment to the Constitution by the legislatures of the several States as provided in the Constitution, within seven years from the date of the submission hereof to the States by the Congress.

Amendment 19

(Ratified August 18, 1920)

The right of citizens of the United States to vote shall not be denied or abridged by the United States or by any State on account of sex.

Congress shall have power to enforce this article by appropriate legislation.

Amendment 20

(Ratified January 23, 1933)

Section 1. The terms of the President and Vice President shall end at noon on the 20th day of January, and the terms of Senators and Representatives at noon on the 3d day of January, of the years in which such terms would have ended if this article had not been ratified; and the terms of their successors shall then begin.

Section 2. The Congress shall assemble at least once in every year, and such meeting shall begin at noon on the 3d day of January, unless they shall by law appoint a different day.

Section 3. If, at the time fixed for the beginning of the term of the President, the President elect shall have died, the Vice President elect shall become President. If a President shall not have been chosen before the time fixed for the beginning of his term, or if the President elect shall have failed to qualify, then the Vice President elect shall act as President until a President shall have qualified; and the Congress may by law provide for the case wherein neither a President elect nor a Vice President elect shall have qualified, declaring who shall then act as President, or the manner in which one who is to act shall be selected, and such person shall act accordingly until a President or Vice President shall have qualified.

Section 4. The Congress may by law provide for the case of the death of any of the persons from whom the House of Representatives may choose a President whenever the right of choice shall have devolved upon them, and for the case of the death of any of the persons from whom the Senate may choose a Vice President whenever the right of choice shall have devolved upon them.

Section 5. Sections 1 and 2 shall take effect on the 15th day of October following the ratification of this article.

Section 6. This article shall be inoperative unless it shall have been ratified as an amendment to the Constitution by the legislatures of three-fourths of the several States within seven years from the date of its submission.

Amendment 21

(Ratified December 5, 1933)

Section 1. The eighteenth article of amendment to the Constitution of the United States is hereby repealed.

Section 2. The transportation or importation into any State, Territory, or possession of the United States for delivery or use therein of intoxicating liquors, in violation of the laws thereof, is hereby prohibited.

Section 3. This article shall be inoperative unless it shall have been ratified as an amendment to the Constitution by conventions in the several States, as provided in the Constitution, within seven years from the date of the submission hereof to the States by the Congress.

Amendment 22

(Ratified February 27, 1951)

Section 1. No person shall be elected to the office of the President more than twice, and no person who has held the office of President, or acted as President, for more than two years of a term to which some other person was elected President shall be elected to the office of the President more than once. But this Article shall not apply to any person holding the office of President when this Article was proposed by the Congress, and shall not prevent any person who may be holding the office of President, or acting as President, during the term within which this Article becomes operative from holding the office of President or acting as President during the remainder of such term.

Section 2. This article shall be inoperative unless it shall have been ratified as an amendment to the Constitution by the legislatures of three-fourths of the several States within seven years from the date of its submission to the States by the Congress.

Amendment 23

(Ratified March 29, 1961)

Section 1. The District constituting the seat of Government of the United States shall appoint in such manner as the Congress may direct:
A number of electors of President and Vice President equal to the whole number of Senators and Representatives in Congress to which the District would be entitled if it were a State, but in no event more than the least populous State; they shall be in addition to those appointed by the States, but they shall be considered, for the purposes of the election of President and Vice President, to be electors appointed by a State; and they shall meet in the District and perform such duties as provided by the twelfth article of amendment.

Section 2. The Congress shall have power to enforce this article by appropriate legislation.

Amendment 24

(Ratified January 23, 1964)

Section 1. The right of citizens of the United States to vote in any primary or other election for President or Vice President, for electors for President or Vice President, or for Senator or Representative in Congress, shall not be denied or abridged by the United States or any State by reason of failure to pay any poll tax or other tax.

Section 2. The Congress shall have power to enforce this article by appropriate legislation.

Amendment 25

(Ratified February 10, 1967)

Section 1. In case of the removal of the President from office or of his death or resignation, the Vice President shall become President.

Section 2. Whenever there is a vacancy in the office of the Vice President, the President shall nominate a Vice President who shall take office upon confirmation by a majority vote of both Houses of Congress.

Section 3. Whenever the President transmits to the President pro tempore of the Senate and the Speaker of the House of Representatives his written declaration that he is unable to discharge the powers and duties of his office, and until he transmits to them a written declaration to the contrary, such powers and duties shall be discharged by the Vice President as Acting President.

Section 4. Whenever the Vice President and a majority of either the principal officers of the executive departments or of such other body as Congress may by law provide, transmit to the President pro tempore of the Senate and the Speaker of the House of Representatives their written declaration that the President is unable to discharge the powers and duties of his office, the Vice President shall immediately assume the powers and duties of the office as Acting President.

Thereafter, when the President transmits to the President pro tempore of the Senate and the Speaker of the House of Representatives his written declaration that no inability exists, he shall resume the powers and duties of his office unless the Vice President and a majority of either the principal officers of the executive department or of such other body as Congress may by law provide, transmit within four days to the President pro tempore of the Senate and the Speaker of the House of Representatives their written declaration that the President is unable to discharge the powers and duties of his office. Thereupon Congress shall decide the issue, assembling within forty-eight hours for that purpose if not in session. If the Congress, within twenty-one days after receipt of the latter written declaration, or, if Congress is not in session, within twenty-one days after Congress is required to assemble, determines by two-thirds vote of both Houses that the President is unable to discharge the powers and duties of his office, the Vice President shall continue to discharge the same as Acting President; otherwise, the President shall resume the powers and duties of his office.

Amendment 26

(Ratified July 1, 1971)

Section 1. The right of citizens of the United States, who are eighteen years of age or older, to vote shall not be denied or abridged by the United States or by any State on account of age.

Section 2. The Congress shall have the power to enforce this article by appropriate legislation.

Amendment 27

(*Ratified May 7, 1992*)

No law, varying the compensation for the services of the Senators and Representatives, shall take effect, until an election of Representatives shall have intervened.

THE GOVERNMENT OF THE UNITED STATES

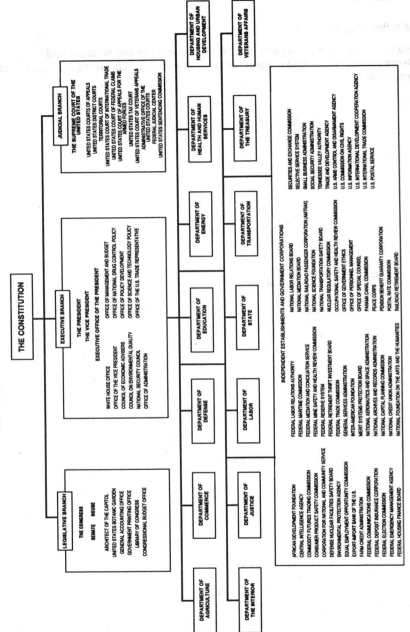

THE CONSTITUTION

LEGISLATIVE BRANCH

THE CONGRESS

SENATE   HOUSE

ARCHITECT OF THE CAPITOL
UNITED STATES BOTANIC GARDEN
GENERAL ACCOUNTING OFFICE
GOVERNMENT PRINTING OFFICE
LIBRARY OF CONGRESS
CONGRESSIONAL BUDGET OFFICE

EXECUTIVE BRANCH

THE PRESIDENT
THE VICE PRESIDENT

EXECUTIVE OFFICE OF THE PRESIDENT

WHITE HOUSE OFFICE
OFFICE OF THE VICE PRESIDENT
COUNCIL OF ECONOMIC ADVISERS
COUNCIL ON ENVIRONMENTAL QUALITY
NATIONAL SECURITY COUNCIL
OFFICE OF ADMINISTRATION

OFFICE OF MANAGEMENT AND BUDGET
OFFICE OF NATIONAL DRUG CONTROL POLICY
OFFICE OF POLICY DEVELOPMENT
OFFICE OF SCIENCE AND TECHNOLOGY POLICY
OFFICE OF THE U.S. TRADE REPRESENTATIVE

JUDICIAL BRANCH

THE SUPREME COURT OF THE UNITED STATES

UNITED STATES COURTS OF APPEALS
UNITED STATES DISTRICT COURTS
TERRITORIAL COURTS
UNITED STATES COURT OF INTERNATIONAL TRADE
UNITED STATES COURT OF FEDERAL CLAIMS
UNITED STATES COURT OF APPEALS FOR THE ARMED FORCES
UNITED STATES TAX COURT
UNITED STATES COURT OF VETERANS APPEALS
ADMINISTRATIVE OFFICE OF THE UNITED STATES COURTS
FEDERAL JUDICIAL CENTER
UNITED STATES SENTENCING COMMISSION

DEPARTMENT OF AGRICULTURE

DEPARTMENT OF COMMERCE

DEPARTMENT OF DEFENSE

DEPARTMENT OF EDUCATION

DEPARTMENT OF ENERGY

DEPARTMENT OF HEALTH AND HUMAN SERVICES

DEPARTMENT OF HOUSING AND URBAN DEVELOPMENT

DEPARTMENT OF THE INTERIOR

DEPARTMENT OF JUSTICE

DEPARTMENT OF LABOR

DEPARTMENT OF STATE

DEPARTMENT OF TRANSPORTATION

DEPARTMENT OF THE TREASURY

DEPARTMENT OF VETERANS AFFAIRS

INDEPENDENT ESTABLISHMENTS AND GOVERNMENT CORPORATIONS

AFRICAN DEVELOPMENT FOUNDATION
CENTRAL INTELLIGENCE AGENCY
COMMODITY FUTURES TRADING COMMISSION
CONSUMER PRODUCT SAFETY COMMISSION
CORPORATION FOR NATIONAL AND COMMUNITY SERVICE
DEFENSE NUCLEAR FACILITIES SAFETY BOARD
ENVIRONMENTAL PROTECTION AGENCY
EQUAL EMPLOYMENT OPPORTUNITY COMMISSION
EXPORT-IMPORT BANK OF THE U.S.
FARM CREDIT ADMINISTRATION
FEDERAL COMMUNICATIONS COMMISSION
FEDERAL DEPOSIT INSURANCE CORPORATION
FEDERAL ELECTION COMMISSION
FEDERAL EMERGENCY MANAGEMENT AGENCY
FEDERAL HOUSING FINANCE BOARD

FEDERAL LABOR RELATIONS AUTHORITY
FEDERAL MARITIME COMMISSION
FEDERAL MEDIATION AND CONCILIATION SERVICE
FEDERAL MINE SAFETY AND HEALTH REVIEW COMMISSION
FEDERAL RESERVE SYSTEM
FEDERAL RETIREMENT THRIFT INVESTMENT BOARD
FEDERAL TRADE COMMISSION
GENERAL SERVICES ADMINISTRATION
INTER-AMERICAN FOUNDATION
MERIT SYSTEMS PROTECTION BOARD
NATIONAL AERONAUTICS AND SPACE ADMINISTRATION
NATIONAL ARCHIVES AND RECORDS ADMINISTRATION
NATIONAL CAPITAL PLANNING COMMISSION
NATIONAL CREDIT UNION ADMINISTRATION
NATIONAL FOUNDATION ON THE ARTS AND THE HUMANITIES

NATIONAL LABOR RELATIONS BOARD
NATIONAL MEDIATION BOARD
NATIONAL RAILROAD PASSENGER CORPORATION (AMTRAK)
NATIONAL SCIENCE FOUNDATION
NATIONAL TRANSPORTATION SAFETY BOARD
NUCLEAR REGULATORY COMMISSION
OCCUPATIONAL SAFETY AND HEALTH REVIEW COMMISSION
OFFICE OF GOVERNMENT ETHICS
OFFICE OF PERSONNEL MANAGEMENT
OFFICE OF SPECIAL COUNSEL
PANAMA CANAL COMMISSION
PEACE CORPS
PENSION BENEFIT GUARANTY CORPORATION
POSTAL RATE COMMISSION
RAILROAD RETIREMENT BOARD

SECURITIES AND EXCHANGE COMMISSION
SELECTIVE SERVICE SYSTEM
SMALL BUSINESS ADMINISTRATION
SOCIAL SECURITY ADMINISTRATION
TENNESSEE VALLEY AUTHORITY
TRADE AND DEVELOPMENT AGENCY
U.S. ARMS CONTROL AND DISARMAMENT AGENCY
U.S. COMMISSION ON CIVIL RIGHTS
U.S. INFORMATION AGENCY
U.S. INTERNATIONAL DEVELOPMENT COOPERATION AGENCY
U.S. INTERNATIONAL TRADE COMMISSION
U.S. POSTAL SERVICE

Legislative Branch

LEGISLATIVE BRANCH

CONGRESS
One Hundred and Fifth Congress, Second Session

The Senate

The Capitol, Washington, DC 20510
Phone, 202–224–3121. Internet, http://www.senate.gov/.

President of the Senate (Vice President of the United States)	AL GORE
President pro tempore	STROM THURMOND
Majority Leader	TRENT LOTT
Minority Leader	THOMAS A. DASCHLE
Secretary of the Senate	GARY SISCO
Sergeant at Arms	GREGORY S. CASEY
Secretary for the Majority	ELIZABETH B. GREENE
Secretary for the Minority	MARTIN P. PAONE
Chaplain	LLOYD J. OGILVIE

The House of Representatives

The Capitol, Washington, DC 20515
Phone, 202–225–3121. Internet, http://www.house.gov/.

The Speaker	NEWT GINGRICH
Clerk	ROBIN H. CARLE
Sergeant at Arms	WILSON L. LIVINGOOD
Chief Administrative Officer	JAMES M. EAGEN III
Chaplain	REV. JAMES DAVID FORD

The Congress of the United States was created by Article I, section 1, of the Constitution, adopted by the Constitutional Convention on September 17, 1787, providing that "All legislative Powers herein granted shall be vested in a Congress of the United States, which shall consist of a Senate and House of Representatives."

The first Congress under the Constitution met on March 4, 1789, in the Federal Hall in New York City. The membership then consisted of 20 [1] Senators and 59 Representatives.

---

[1] New York ratified the Constitution on July 26, 1788, but did not elect its Senators until July 15 and 16, 1789. North Carolina did not ratify the Constitution until November 21, 1789; Rhode Island ratified it on May 29, 1790.

177-653 98 - 2 : QL 3

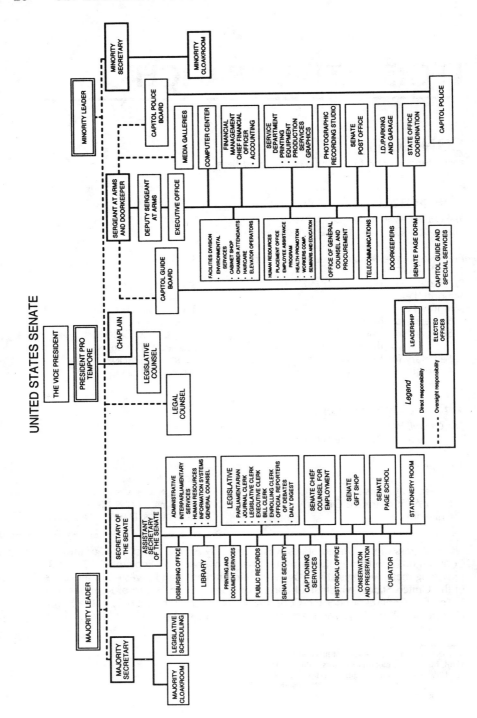

UNITED STATES SENATE

The Senate is composed of 100 Members, 2 from each State, who are elected to serve for a term of 6 years. Senators were originally chosen by the State legislatures. This procedure was changed by the 17th amendment to the Constitution, adopted in 1913, which made the election of Senators a function of the people. There are three classes of Senators, and a new class is elected every 2 years.

The House of Representatives comprises 435 Representatives. The number representing each State is determined by population, but every State is entitled to at least one Representative. Members are elected by the people for 2-year terms, all terms running for the same period.

Both the Senators and the Representatives must be residents of the State from which they are chosen. In addition, a Senator must be at least 30 years of age and must have been a citizen of the United States for at least 9 years; a Representative must be at least 25 years of age and must have been a citizen for at least 7 years.

A Resident Commissioner from Puerto Rico (elected for a 4-year term) and Delegates from American Samoa, the District of Columbia, Guam, and the Virgin Islands complete the composition of the Congress of the United States. Delegates are elected for a term of 2 years. The Resident Commissioner and Delegates may take part in the floor discussions but have no vote in the full House or in the Committee of the Whole House on the State of the Union. They do, however, vote in the committees to which they are assigned.

Officers   The Vice President of the United States is the Presiding Officer of the Senate; in his absence the duties are taken over by a President pro tempore, elected by that body, or someone designated by him. The Presiding Officer of the House of Representatives, the Speaker, is elected by the House; he may designate any Member of the House to act in his absence.

The positions of Senate majority and minority leader have been in existence only since the early years of the 20th century. Leaders are elected at the beginning of each new Congress by a majority vote of the Senators in their political party. In cooperation with their party organizations, leaders are responsible for the design and achievement of a legislative program. This involves managing the flow of legislation, expediting noncontroversial measures, and keeping Members informed regarding proposed action on pending business. Each leader serves as an *ex officio* member of his party's policymaking and organizational bodies and is aided by an assistant floor leader (whip) and a party secretary.

The House leadership is structured essentially the same as the Senate, with the Members in the political parties responsible for the election of their respective leader and whips.

The Secretary of the Senate, elected by vote of the Senate, performs the duties of the Presiding Officer of the Senate in the absence of the Vice President and pending the election of a President pro tempore. The Secretary is the custodian of the seal of the Senate, draws requisitions on the Secretary of the Treasury for moneys appropriated for the compensation of Senators, officers, and employees, and for the contingent expenses of the Senate, and is empowered to administer oaths to any officer of the Senate and to any witness produced before it. The Secretary's executive duties include certification of extracts from the Journal of the Senate; the attestation of bills and joint, concurrent, and Senate resolutions; in impeachment trials, issuance, under the authority of the Presiding Officer, of all orders, mandates, writs, and precepts authorized by the Senate; and certification to the President of the United States of the advice and consent of the Senate to ratification of treaties and the names of persons confirmed or rejected upon the nomination of the President.

The Sergeant at Arms of the Senate is elected by and serves as the Executive Officer of that body. He directs and supervises the various departments and facilities under his jurisdiction. He is

HOUSE OF REPRESENTATIVES

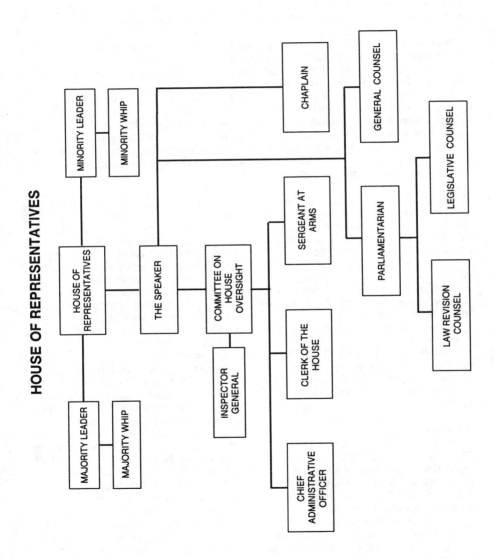

also the Law Enforcement and Protocol Officer. As Law Enforcement Officer, he has statutory power to make arrests; to locate absentee Senators for a quorum; to enforce Senate rules and regulations as they pertain to the Senate Chamber, the Senate wing of the Capitol, and the Senate Office Buildings. He serves as a member of the Capitol Police Board and as its chairman each odd year; and, subject to the Presiding Officer, maintains order in the Senate Chamber. As Protocol Officer, he is responsible for many aspects of ceremonial functions, including the inauguration of the President of the United States; arranging funerals of Senators who die in office; escorting the President when he addresses a Joint Session of Congress or attends any function in the Senate; and escorting heads of state when they visit the Senate.

The elected officers of the House of Representatives include the Clerk, the Sergeant at Arms, the Chief Administrative Officer, and the Chaplain.

The Clerk is custodian of the seal of the House and administers the primary legislative activities of the House. These duties include: accepting the credentials of the Members-elect and calling the Members to order at the commencement of the first session of each Congress; keeping the Journal; taking all votes and certifying the passage of bills; and processing all legislation. Through various departments, the Clerk is also responsible for floor and committee reporting services; legislative information and reference services; the administration of House reports pursuant to House rules and certain legislation including the Ethics in Government Act and the Lobbying Disclosure Act of 1995; the distribution of House documents; and administration of the House Page Program. The Clerk is also charged with supervision of the offices vacated by Members due to death, resignation, or expulsion.

The Sergeant at Arms maintains the order of the House under the direction of the Speaker and is the keeper of the Mace. As a member of the U.S. Capitol Police Board, the Sergeant at Arms is the chief law enforcement officer for the House and serves as Board Chairman each even year. The ceremonial and protocol duties parallel those of the Senate Sergeant at Arms and include arranging the inauguration of the President of the United States, Joint Sessions of Congress, visits to the House of heads of state, and funerals of Members of Congress.

The Sergeant at Arms enforces the rules relating to the privileges of the Hall of the House, including admission to the galleries.

The Chief Administrative Officer is charged with the administration of other House support services, including: payroll, benefits, postal operations and internal mail distribution, computer and telephone service, office furnishings, office equipment, office supplies, and the administration of the House televised floor proceedings.

Committees The work of preparing and considering legislation is done largely by committees of both Houses of Congress. There are 16 standing committees in the Senate and 19 in the House of Representatives. The standing committees of the Senate and the House of Representatives are shown in the list below. In addition, there are select committees in each House (one in the House of Representatives), and various congressional commissions and joint committees composed of Members of both Houses. Each House may also appoint special investigating committees.

The membership of the standing committees of each House is chosen by a vote of the entire body; members of other committees are appointed under the provisions of the measure establishing them.

Each bill and resolution is usually referred to the appropriate committee, which may report a bill out in its original form, favorably or unfavorably, recommend amendments, report original measures, or allow the proposed legislation to die in committee without action.

Standing Committees of the Congress

House Committee	Room[1]	Senate Committee	Room[2]
Agriculture	1301	Agriculture, Nutrition, and Forestry	SR–328A
Appropriations	H218	Appropriations	S–128
Banking and Financial Services	2129	Armed Services	SR–228
Budget	309	Banking, Housing, and Urban Affairs	SD–534
Commerce	2125	Budget	SD–621
Education and the Workforce	2181	Commerce, Science, and Transportation	SD–508
Government Reform and Oversight	2157	Energy and Natural Resources	SD–304
House Oversight	1309	Environment and Public Works	SD–410
Franking Commission:			
Majority	140		
Minority	1338		
International Relations	2170	Finance	SD–219
Judiciary	2138	Foreign Relations	SD–450
Publications	B29		
National Security	2120	Governmental Affairs	SD–340
Resources	1324	Judiciary	SD–224
Rules	H312	Labor and Human Resources	SD–428
Minority	234		
Science	2320	Rules and Administration	SR–305
Small Business	2361	Small Business	SR–428A
Standards of Official Conduct	HT2	Veterans' Affairs	SR–412
Office of Advice and Education	HT2		
Transportation and Infrastructure	2165		
Veterans' Affairs	335		
Ways and Means	1102		

[1] Room numbers with three digits are in the Cannon House Office Building, four digits beginning with 1 are in the Longworth House Office Building, and four digits beginning with 2 are in the Rayburn House Office Building. Room numbers preceded by H or HT are in the House wing of the Capitol Building.
[2] Room numbers preceded by S are in the Senate wing of the Capitol Building; those preceded by SD are in the Dirksen Office Building; and those preceded by SR are in the Russell Office Building.

Congressional Record   Proceedings of Congress are published in the *Congressional Record,* which is issued each day when Congress is in session. Publication of the *Record* began March 4, 1873; it was the first record of debate officially reported, printed, and published directly by the Federal Government. The Daily Digest of the *Congressional Record,* printed in the back of each issue of the *Record,* summarizes the proceedings of that day in each House, and each of their committees and subcommittees, respectively. The Digest also presents the legislative program for each day and, at the end of the week, gives the program for the following week. Its publication was begun March 17, 1947.

Sessions   Section 4 of Article I of the Constitution makes it mandatory that "The Congress shall assemble at least once in every Year. . . ." Under this provision, also, the date for convening Congress was designated originally as the first Monday in December, "unless they shall by Law appoint a different Day." Eighteen acts were passed, up to 1820, providing for the meeting of Congress on other days of the year. From 1820 to 1934, however, Congress met regularly on the first Monday in December. In 1934 the Twentieth Amendment changed the convening of Congress to January 3, unless Congress "shall by law appoint a different day." In addition, the President, according to Article II, section 3, of the Constitution "may, on extraordinary Occasions, convene both Houses, or either of them, and in Case of Disagreement between them, with Respect to the Time of Adjournment, he may adjourn them to such Time as he shall think proper. . . ."

Powers of Congress   Article I, section 8, of the Constitution defines the powers of Congress. Included are the powers to assess and collect taxes—called the chief power; to regulate commerce, both interstate and foreign; to coin money; to establish post offices and post roads; to establish courts inferior to the Supreme Court; to declare war; and to raise and maintain an army and navy. Congress is further empowered "To provide for calling forth the Militia to execute the Laws of the Union, suppress Insurrections and repel Invasions;" and "To make all Laws which shall be necessary and proper for carrying into Execution the foregoing Powers, and all other Powers vested by this Constitution in the Government of the United States, or in any Department or Officer thereof."

Amendments to the Constitution Another power vested in the Congress is the right to propose amendments to the Constitution, whenever two-thirds of both Houses shall deem it necessary. Should two-thirds of the State legislatures demand changes in the Constitution, it is the duty of Congress to call a constitutional convention. Proposed amendments shall be valid as part of the Constitution when ratified by the legislatures or by conventions of three-fourths of the States, as one or the other mode of ratification may be proposed by Congress.

Special Powers of the Senate Under the Constitution, the Senate is granted certain powers not accorded to the House of Representatives. The Senate approves or disapproves certain Presidential appointments by majority vote, and treaties must be concurred in by a two-thirds vote.

Special Powers of the House of Representatives The House of Representatives is granted the power of originating all bills for the raising of revenue.

Both Houses of Congress act in impeachment proceedings, which, according to the Constitution, may be instituted against the President, Vice President, and all civil officers of the United States. The House of Representatives has the sole power of impeachment, and the Senate has the sole power to try impeachments.

Prohibitions Upon Congress Section 9 of Article I of the Constitution also imposes prohibitions upon Congress. "The Privilege of the Writ of Habeas Corpus shall not be suspended, unless when in Cases of Rebellion or Invasion the public Safety may require it." A bill of attainder or an ex post facto law cannot be passed. No export duty can be imposed. Ports of one State cannot be given preference over those of another State. "No money shall be drawn from the Treasury, but in Consequence of Appropriations made by Law. . . ." No title of nobility may be granted.

Rights of Members According to section 6 of Article I, Members of Congress are granted certain privileges. In no case, except in treason, felony, and breach of the peace, can Members be arrested while attending sessions of Congress "and in going to and returning from the same. . . ." Furthermore, the Members cannot be questioned in any other place for remarks made in Congress. Each House may expel a Member of its body by a two-thirds vote.

Enactment of Laws All bills and joint resolutions must pass both the House of Representatives and the Senate and must be signed by the President, except those proposing a constitutional amendment, in order to become law, or be passed over the President's veto by a two-thirds vote of both Houses of Congress. Section 7 of Article I states: "If any Bill shall not be returned by the President within ten Days (Sundays excepted) after it shall have been presented to him, the Same shall be a Law, in like Manner as if he had signed it, unless the Congress by their Adjournment prevent its Return, in which Case it shall not be a Law."

When a bill or joint resolution is introduced in the House, the usual procedure for its enactment into law is as follows:

—assignment to House committee having jurisdiction;

—if favorably considered, it is reported to the House either in its original form or with recommended amendments;

—if the bill or resolution is passed by the House, it is messaged to the Senate and referred to the committee having jurisdiction;

—in the Senate committee the bill, if favorably considered, may be reported in the form as received from the House, or with recommended amendments;

—the approved bill or resolution is reported to the Senate, and if passed by that body, is returned to the House;

—if one body does not accept the amendments to a bill by the other body, a conference committee comprised of

Members of both bodies is usually appointed to effect a compromise;
— when the bill or joint resolution is finally approved by both Houses, it is signed by the Speaker (or Speaker pro tempore) and the Vice President (or President pro tempore or acting President pro tempore) and is presented to the President; and
— once the President's signature is affixed, the measure becomes a law. If the President vetoes the bill, it cannot become a law unless it is re-passed by a two-thirds vote of both Houses.

Publications The *Congressional Directory*, the *Senate Manual*, and the *House Rules* and *Manual* may be obtained from the Superintendent of Documents, Government Printing Office, Washington, DC 20402.

Senators

[Republicans in roman (55); Democrats in italic (45); total, 100]

Room numbers preceded by SR are in the Russell Office Building (Delaware and Constitution Avenues); those preceded by SD are in the Dirksen Office Building (First Street and Constitution Avenue); and those preceded by SH are in the Hart Office Building (Second and C Streets). Members' offices may be reached by phone at 202–224–3121.

Name	State	Room
Abraham, Spencer	Michigan	SD–329
Akaka, Daniel K	Hawaii	SH–720
Allard, Wayne	Colorado	SH–513
Ashcroft, John	Missouri	SH–316
Baucus, Max	Montana	SH–511
Bennett, Robert F	Utah	SD–431
Biden, Joseph R., Jr	Delaware	SR–221
Bingaman, Jeff	New Mexico	SH–703
Bond, Christopher S	Missouri	SR–274
Boxer, Barbara	California	SH–112
Breaux, John B	Louisiana	SH–516
Brownback, Sam	Kansas	SH–303
Bryan, Richard H	Nevada	SR–269
Bumpers, Dale	Arkansas	SD–229
Burns, Conrad R	Montana	SD–187
Byrd, Robert C	West Virginia	SH–311
Campbell, Ben Nighthorse	Colorado	SR–380
Chafee, John H	Rhode Island	SD–505
Cleland, Max	Georgia	SD–461
Coats, Dan	Indiana	SR–404
Cochran, Thad	Mississippi	SR–326
Collins, Susan M	Maine	SR–172
Conrad, Kent	North Dakota	SH–530
Coverdell, Paul	Georgia	SR–200
Craig, Larry E	Idaho	SH–313
D'Amato, Alfonse M	New York	SH–520
Daschle, Thomas A	South Dakota	SH–509
DeWine, Mike	Ohio	SR–140
Dodd, Christopher J	Connecticut	SR–444
Domenici, Pete V	New Mexico	SH–328
Dorgan, Byron L	North Dakota	SH–713
Durbin, Richard J	Illinois	SR–364
Enzi, Michael B	Wyoming	SR–290
Faircloth, Lauch	North Carolina	SH–317
Feingold, Russell D	Wisconsin	SH–716
Feinstein, Dianne	California	SH–331
Ford, Wendell H	Kentucky	SR–173A
Frist, Bill	Tennessee	SD–567
Glenn, John	Ohio	SH–503
Gorton, Slade	Washington	SH–730

Senators—Continued

[Republicans in roman (55); Democrats in italic (45); total, 100]

Room numbers preceded by SR are in the Russell Office Building (Delaware and Constitution Avenues); those preceded by SD are in the Dirksen Office Building (First Street and Constitution Avenue); and those preceded by SH are in the Hart Office Building (Second and C Streets). Members' offices may be reached by phone at 202–224–3121.

Name	State	Room
Graham, Bob	Florida	SH–524
Gramm, Phil	Texas	SR–370
Grams, Rod	Minnesota	SD–257
Grassley, Charles E	Iowa	SH–135
Gregg, Judd	New Hampshire	SR–393
Hagel, Chuck	Nebraska	SR–346
Harkin, Tom	Iowa	SH–731
Hatch, Orrin G	Utah	SR–131
Helms, Jesse	North Carolina	SD–403
Hollings, Ernest F	South Carolina	SR–125
Hutchinson, Y. Tim	Arkansas	SD–245
Hutchison, Kay Bailey	Texas	SR–284
Inhofe, James M	Oklahoma	SR–453
Inouye, Daniel K	Hawaii	SH–722
Jeffords, James M	Vermont	SH–728
Johnson, Tim	South Dakota	SH–502
Kempthorne, Dirk	Idaho	SR–304
Kennedy, Edward M	Massachusetts	SR–315
Kerrey, J. Robert	Nebraska	SH–141
Kerry, John F	Massachusetts	SR–421
Kohl, Herb	Wisconsin	SH–330
Kyl, Jon	Arizona	SH–724
Landrieu, Mary L	Louisiana	SH–702
Lautenberg, Frank R	New Jersey	SH–506
Leahy, Patrick J	Vermont	SR–433
Levin, Carl	Michigan	SR–459
Lieberman, Joseph I	Connecticut	SH–706
Lott, Trent	Mississippi	SR–487
Lugar, Richard G	Indiana	SH–306
Mack, Connie	Florida	SH–517
McCain, John	Arizona	SR–241
McConnell, Mitch	Kentucky	SR–361A
Mikulski, Barbara A	Maryland	SH–709
Moseley-Braun, Carol	Illinois	SH–324
Moynihan, Daniel Patrick	New York	SR–464
Murkowski, Frank H	Alaska	SH–322
Murray, Patty	Washington	SR–111
Nickles, Don	Oklahoma	SH–133
Reed, Jack	Rhode Island	SH–320
Reid, Harry	Nevada	SH–528
Robb, Charles S	Virginia	SR–154
Roberts, Pat	Kansas	SH–302
Rockefeller, John D., IV	West Virginia	SH–531
Roth, William V., Jr	Delaware	SH–104
Santorum, Rick	Pennsylvania	SR–120
Sarbanes, Paul S	Maryland	SH–309
Sessions, Jeff	Alabama	SR–495
Shelby, Richard C	Alabama	SH–110
Smith, Bob	New Hampshire	SD–307
Smith, Gordon	Oregon	SD–359
Snowe, Olympia J	Maine	SR–250
Specter, Arlen	Pennsylvania	SH–711
Stevens, Ted	Alaska	SH–522

Senators—Continued

[Republicans in roman (55); Democrats in italic (45); total, 100]

Room numbers preceded by SR are in the Russell Office Building (Delaware and Constitution Avenues); those preceded by SD are in the Dirksen Office Building (First Street and Constitution Avenue); and those preceded by SH are in the Hart Office Building (Second and C Streets). Members' offices may be reached by phone at 202–224–3121.

Name	State	Room
Thomas, Craig	Wyoming	SH–109
Thompson, Fred	Tennessee	SD–523
Thurmond, Strom	South Carolina	SR–217
Torricelli, Robert G	New Jersey	SD–113
Warner, John W	Virginia	SR–225
Wellstone, Paul D	Minnesota	SH–136
Wyden, Ron	Oregon	SH–717

Representatives

[Republicans in roman (228); Democrats in italic (206); Independents in bold (1); total, 435]

Room numbers with three digits are in the Cannon House Office Building (New Jersey and Independence Avenues), four digits beginning with 1 are in the Longworth House Office Building (between South Capitol Street and New Jersey Avenue on Independence Avenue), and four digits beginning with 2 are in the Rayburn House Office Building (between First and South Capitol Streets on Independence Avenue). Members' offices may be reached by phone at 202–225–3121. The most current listing of House Members can be found on the Internet at http://clerkweb.house.gov/.

Name	State (District)	Room
Abercrombie, Neil	Hawaii (1)	1233
Ackerman, Gary L	New York (5)	2243
Aderholt, Robert B	Alabama (4)	1007
Allen, Thomas H	Maine (1)	1630
Andrews, Robert E	New Jersey (1)	2439
Archer, Bill	Texas (7)	1236
Armey, Richard K	Texas (26)	301
Bachus, Spencer	Alabama (6)	442
Baesler, Scotty	Kentucky (6)	2463
Baker, Richard H	Louisiana (6)	434
Baldacci, John Elias	Maine (2)	1740
Ballenger, Cass	North Carolina (10)	2182
Barcia, James A	Michigan (5)	2419
Barr, Bob	Georgia (7)	1130
Barrett, Bill	Nebraska (3)	2458
Barrett, Thomas M	Wisconsin (5)	1224
Bartlett, Roscoe G	Maryland (6)	322
Barton, Joe	Texas (6)	2264
Bass, Charles F	New Hampshire (2)	218
Bateman, Herbert H	Virginia (1)	2350
Becerra, Xavier	California (30)	1119
Bentsen, Ken	Texas (25)	128
Bereuter, Doug	Nebraska (1)	2184
Berman, Howard L	California (26)	2330
Berry, Marion	Arkansas (1)	1407
Bilbray, Brian P	California (49)	1530
Bilirakis, Michael	Florida (9)	2369
Bishop, Sanford D., Jr	Georgia (2)	1433
Blagojevich, Rod R	Illinois (5)	501
Bliley, Tom	Virginia (7)	2409
Blumenauer, Earl	Oregon (3)	1113
Blunt, Roy	Missouri (7)	508
Boehlert, Sherwood L	New York (23)	2246
Boehner, John A	Ohio (8)	1011

Representatives—Continued

[Republicans in roman (228); Democrats in italic (206); Independents in bold (1); total, 435]

Room numbers with three digits are in the Cannon House Office Building (New Jersey and Independence Avenues), four digits beginning with 1 are in the Longworth House Office Building (between South Capitol Street and New Jersey Avenue on Independence Avenue), and four digits beginning with 2 are in the Rayburn House Office Building (between First and South Capitol Streets on Independence Avenue). Members' offices may be reached by phone at 202–225–3121. The most current listing of House Members can be found on the Internet at http://clerkweb.house.gov/.

Name	State (District)	Room
Bonilla, Henry	Texas (23)	1427
Bonior, David E	Michigan (10)	2207
Bono, Mary	California (44)	324
Borski, Robert A	Pennsylvania (3)	2267
Boswell, Leonard L	Iowa (3)	1029
Boucher, Rick	Virginia (9)	2329
Boyd, Allen	Florida (2)	1237
Brady, Kevin	Texas (8)	1531
Brady, Robert A	Pennsylvania (1)	242
Brown, Corrine	Florida (3)	1610
Brown, George E., Jr	California (42)	2300
Brown, Sherrod	Ohio (13)	328
Bryant, Ed	Tennessee (7)	408
Bunning, Jim	Kentucky (4)	2437
Burr, Richard	North Carolina (5)	1513
Burton, Dan	Indiana (6)	2185
Buyer, Stephen E	Indiana (5)	326
Callahan, Sonny	Alabama (1)	2418
Calvert, Ken	California (43)	1034
Camp, Dave	Michigan (4)	137
Campbell, Tom	California (15)	2442
Canady, Charles T	Florida (12)	2432
Cannon, Chris	Utah (3)	118
Capps, Lois	California (22)	1118
Cardin, Benjamin L	Maryland (3)	104
Carson, Julia	Indiana (10)	1541
Castle, Michael N	Delaware (At Large)	1227
Chabot, Steve	Ohio (1)	129
Chambliss, Saxby	Georgia (8)	1019
Chenoweth, Helen	Idaho (1)	1727
Christensen, Jon	Nebraska (2)	413
Clay, William (Bill)	Missouri (1)	2306
Clayton, Eva M	North Carolina (1)	2440
Clement, Bob	Tennessee (5)	2229
Clyburn, James E	South Carolina (6)	319
Coble, Howard	North Carolina (6)	2239
Coburn, Tom A	Oklahoma (2)	429
Collins, Mac	Georgia (3)	1131
Combest, Larry	Texas (19)	1026
Condit, Gary A	California (18)	2245
Conyers, John, Jr	Michigan (14)	2426
Cook, Merrill	Utah (2)	1431
Cooksey, John	Louisiana (5)	317
Costello, Jerry F	Illinois (12)	2454
Cox, Christopher	California (47)	2402
Coyne, William J	Pennsylvania (14)	2455
Cramer, Robert E. (Bud), Jr	Alabama (5)	2416
Crane, Philip M	Illinois (8)	233
Crapo, Michael D	Idaho (2)	437
Cubin, Barbara	Wyoming (At Large)	1114
Cummings, Elijah E	Maryland (7)	1632

Representatives—Continued

[Republicans in roman (228); Democrats in italic (206); Independents in bold (1); total, 435]

Room numbers with three digits are in the Cannon House Office Building (New Jersey and Independence Avenues), four digits beginning with 1 are in the Longworth House Office Building (between South Capitol Street and New Jersey Avenue on Independence Avenue), and four digits beginning with 2 are in the Rayburn House Office Building (between First and South Capitol Streets on Independence Avenue). Members' offices may be reached by phone at 202–225–3121. The most current listing of House Members can be found on the Internet at http://clerkweb.house.gov/.

Name	State (District)	Room
Cunningham, Randy (Duke)	California (51)	2238
Danner, Pat	Missouri (6)	1207
Davis, Danny K	Illinois (7)	1218
Davis, Jim	Florida (11)	327
Davis, Thomas M	Virginia (11)	224
Deal, Nathan	Georgia (9)	1406
DeFazio, Peter A	Oregon (4)	2134
DeGette, Diana	Colorado (1)	1404
Delahunt, William D	Massachusetts (10)	1517
DeLauro, Rosa L	Connecticut (3)	436
DeLay, Tom	Texas (22)	341
Deutsch, Peter	Florida (20)	204
Diaz-Balart, Lincoln	Florida (21)	404
Dickey, Jay	Arkansas (4)	2453
Dicks, Norman D	Washington (6)	2467
Dingell, John D	Michigan (16)	2328
Dixon, Julian C	California (32)	2252
Doggett, Lloyd	Texas (10)	126
Dooley, Calvin M	California (20)	1201
Doolittle, John T	California (4)	1526
Doyle, Michael F	Pennsylvania (18)	133
Dreier, David	California (28)	237
Duncan, John J., Jr	Tennessee (2)	2400
Dunn, Jennifer	Washington (8)	432
Edwards, Chet	Texas (11)	2459
Ehlers, Vernon J	Michigan (3)	1717
Ehrlich, Robert L., Jr	Maryland (2)	315
Emerson, Jo Ann	Missouri (8)	132
Engel, Eliot L	New York (17)	2303
English, Phil	Pennsylvania (21)	1721
Ensign, John E	Nevada (1)	414
Eshoo, Anna G	California (14)	308
Etheridge, Bob	North Carolina (2)	1641
Evans, Lane	Illinois (17)	2335
Everett, Terry	Alabama (2)	208
Ewing, Thomas W	Illinois (15)	2417
Farr, Sam	California (17)	1117
Fattah, Chaka	Pennsylvania (2)	1205
Fawell, Harris W	Illinois (13)	2368
Fazio, Vic	California (3)	2113
Filner, Bob	California (50)	330
Foley, Mark	Florida (16)	113
Forbes, Michael P	New York (1)	416
Ford, Harold E., Jr	Tennessee (9)	1523
Fossella, Vito	New York (13)	2411
Fowler, Tillie K	Florida (4)	109
Fox, Jon D	Pennsylvania (13)	435
Frank, Barney	Massachusetts (4)	2210
Franks, Bob	New Jersey (7)	225
Frelinghuysen, Rodney P	New Jersey (11)	228
Frost, Martin	Texas (24)	2256

Representatives—Continued

[Republicans in roman (228); Democrats in italic (206); Independents in bold (1); total, 435]

Room numbers with three digits are in the Cannon House Office Building (New Jersey and Independence Avenues), four digits beginning with 1 are in the Longworth House Office Building (between South Capitol Street and New Jersey Avenue on Independence Avenue), and four digits beginning with 2 are in the Rayburn House Office Building (between First and South Capitol Streets on Independence Avenue). Members' offices may be reached by phone at 202–225–3121. The most current listing of House Members can be found on the Internet at http://clerkweb.house.gov/.

Name	State (District)	Room
Furse, Elizabeth	Oregon (1)	316
Gallegly, Elton	California (23)	2427
Ganske, Greg	Iowa (4)	1108
Gejdenson, Sam	Connecticut (2)	1401
Gekas, George W	Pennsylvania (17)	2410
Gephardt, Richard A	Missouri (3)	1226
Gibbons, Jim	Nevada (2)	100
Gilchrest, Wayne T	Maryland (1)	332
Gillmor, Paul E	Ohio (5)	1203
Gilman, Benjamin A	New York (20)	2449
Gingrich, Newt	Georgia (6)	2428
Gonzalez, Henry B	Texas (20)	2413
Goode, Virgil H., Jr	Virginia (5)	1520
Goodlatte, Bob	Virginia (6)	123
Goodling, William F	Pennsylvania (19)	2263
Gordon, Bart	Tennessee (6)	2201
Goss, Porter J	Florida (14)	108
Graham, Lindsey O	South Carolina (3)	1429
Granger, Kay	Texas (12)	515
Green, Gene	Texas (29)	2429
Greenwood, James C	Pennsylvania (8)	2436
Gutierrez, Luis V	Illinois (4)	2438
Gutknecht, Gil	Minnesota (1)	425
Hall, Ralph M	Texas (4)	2221
Hall, Tony P	Ohio (3)	1432
Hamilton, Lee H	Indiana (9)	2314
Hansen, James V	Utah (1)	2466
Harman, Jane	California (36)	325
Hastert, J. Dennis	Illinois (14)	2241
Hastings, Alcee L	Florida (23)	1039
Hastings, Doc	Washington (4)	1323
Hayworth, J.D	Arizona (6)	1023
Hefley, Joel	Colorado (5)	2230
Hefner, W.G. (Bill)	North Carolina (8)	2470
Herger, Wally	California (2)	2433
Hill, Rick	Montana (At Large)	1037
Hilleary, Van	Tennessee (4)	114
Hilliard, Earl F	Alabama (7)	1314
Hinchey, Maurice D	New York (26)	2431
Hinojosa, Rubén	Texas (15)	1032
Hobson, David L	Ohio (7)	1514
Hoekstra, Peter	Michigan (2)	1122
Holden, Tim	Pennsylvania (6)	1421
Hooley, Darlene	Oregon (5)	1419
Horn, Stephen	California (38)	438
Hostettler, John N	Indiana (8)	431
Houghton, Amo	New York (31)	1110
Hoyer, Steny H	Maryland (5)	1705
Hulshof, Kenny C	Missouri (9)	1728
Hunter, Duncan	California (52)	2265
Hutchinson, Asa	Arkansas (3)	1535

Representatives—Continued

[Republicans in roman (228); Democrats in italic (206); Independents in bold (1); total, 435]
Room numbers with three digits are in the Cannon House Office Building (New Jersey and Independence Avenues), four digits beginning with 1 are in the Longworth House Office Building (between South Capitol Street and New Jersey Avenue on Independence Avenue), and four digits beginning with 2 are in the Rayburn House Office Building (between First and South Capitol Streets on Independence Avenue). Members' offices may be reached by phone at 202–225–3121. The most current listing of House Members can be found on the Internet at http://clerkweb.house.gov/.

Name	State (District)	Room
Hyde, Henry J	Illinois (6)	2110
Inglis, Bob	South Carolina (4)	320
Istook, Ernest J., Jr	Oklahoma (5)	119
Jackson, Jesse L., Jr	Illinois (2)	313
Jackson Lee, Sheila	Texas (18)	410
Jefferson, William J	Louisiana (2)	240
Jenkins, William L	Tennessee (1)	1708
John, Christopher	Louisiana (7)	1504
Johnson, Eddie Bernice	Texas (30)	1123
Johnson, Jay W	Wisconsin (8)	1313
Johnson, Nancy L	Connecticut (6)	343
Johnson, Sam	Texas (3)	1030
Jones, Walter B	North Carolina (3)	422
Kanjorski, Paul E	Pennsylvania (11)	2353
Kaptur, Marcy	Ohio (9)	2311
Kasich, John R	Ohio (12)	1111
Kelly, Sue W	New York (19)	1222
Kennedy, Joseph P., II	Massachusetts (8)	2242
Kennedy, Patrick J	Rhode Island (1)	312
Kennelly, Barbara B	Connecticut (1)	201
Kildee, Dale E	Michigan (9)	2187
Kilpatrick, Carolyn C	Michigan (15)	503
Kim, Jay	California (41)	227
Kind, Ron	Wisconsin (3)	1713
King, Peter T	New York (3)	403
Kingston, Jack	Georgia (1)	1507
Kleczka, Gerald D	Wisconsin (4)	2301
Klink, Ron	Pennsylvania (4)	125
Klug, Scott L	Wisconsin (2)	2331
Knollenberg, Joe	Michigan (11)	1511
Kolbe, Jim	Arizona (5)	205
Kucinich, Dennis J	Ohio (10)	1730
LaFalce, John J	New York (29)	2310
LaHood, Ray	Illinois (18)	329
Lampson, Nick	Texas (9)	417
Lantos, Tom	California (12)	2217
Largent, Steve	Oklahoma (1)	426
Latham, Tom	Iowa (5)	516
LaTourette, Steven C	Ohio (19)	1239
Lazio, Rick	New York (2)	2444
Leach, James A	Iowa (1)	2186
Lee, Barbara	California (9)	2108
Levin, Sander M	Michigan (12)	2209
Lewis, Jerry	California (40)	2112
Lewis, John	Georgia (5)	229
Lewis, Ron	Kentucky (2)	223
Linder, John	Georgia (11)	1005
Lipinski, William O	Illinois (3)	1501
Livingston, Bob	Louisiana (1)	2406
LoBiondo, Frank A	New Jersey (2)	222
Lofgren, Zoe	California (16)	318

Representatives—Continued

[Republicans in roman (228); Democrats in italic (206); Independents in bold (1); total, 435]

Room numbers with three digits are in the Cannon House Office Building (New Jersey and Independence Avenues), four digits beginning with 1 are in the Longworth House Office Building (between South Capitol Street and New Jersey Avenue on Independence Avenue), and four digits beginning with 2 are in the Rayburn House Office Building (between First and South Capitol Streets on Independence Avenue). Members' offices may be reached by phone at 202–225–3121. The most current listing of House Members can be found on the Internet at http://clerkweb.house.gov/.

Name	State (District)	Room
Lowey, Nita M	New York (18)	2421
Lucas, Frank D	Oklahoma (6)	107
Luther, Bill	Minnesota (6)	117
McCarthy, Carolyn	New York (4)	1725
McCarthy, Karen	Missouri (5)	1232
McCollum, Bill	Florida (8)	2266
McCrery, Jim	Louisiana (4)	2104
McDade, Joseph M	Pennsylvania (10)	2107
McDermott, Jim	Washington (7)	2349
McGovern, James P	Massachusetts (3)	512
McHale, Paul	Pennsylvania (15)	217
McHugh, John M	New York (24)	2441
McInnis, Scott	Colorado (3)	215
McIntosh, David M	Indiana (2)	1208
McIntyre, Mike	North Carolina (7)	1605
McKeon, Howard P. (Buck)	California (25)	307
McKinney, Cynthia A	Georgia (4)	124
McNulty, Michael R	New York (21)	2161
Maloney, Carolyn B	New York (14)	1330
Maloney, James H	Connecticut (5)	1213
Manton, Thomas J	New York (7)	2235
Manzullo, Donald A	Illinois (16)	409
Markey, Edward J	Massachusetts (7)	2133
Martinez, Matthew G	California (31)	2234
Mascara, Frank	Pennsylvania (20)	314
Matsui, Robert T	California (5)	2308
Meehan, Martin T	Massachusetts (5)	2434
Meek, Carrie P	Florida (17)	401
Meeks, Gregory W	New York (6)	1035
Menendez, Robert	New Jersey (13)	405
Metcalf, Jack	Washington (2)	1510
Mica, John L	Florida (7)	106
Millender-McDonald, Juanita	California (37)	419
Miller, Dan	Florida (13)	102
Miller, George	California (7)	2205
Minge, David	Minnesota (2)	1415
Mink, Patsy T	Hawaii (2)	2135
Moakley, John Joseph	Massachusetts (9)	235
Mollohan, Alan B	West Virginia (1)	2346
Moran, James P	Virginia (8)	1214
Moran, Jerry	Kansas (1)	1217
Morella, Constance A	Maryland (8)	2228
Murtha, John P	Pennsylvania (12)	2423
Myrick, Sue	North Carolina (9)	230
Nadler, Jerrold	New York (8)	2448
Neal, Richard E	Massachusetts (2)	2236
Nethercutt, George R., Jr	Washington (5)	1527
Neumann, Mark W	Wisconsin (1)	415
Ney, Robert W	Ohio (18)	1024
Northup, Anne M	Kentucky (3)	1004
Norwood, Charlie	Georgia (10)	1707

Representatives—Continued

[Republicans in roman (228); Democrats in italic (206); Independents in bold (1); total, 435]
Room numbers with three digits are in the Cannon House Office Building (New Jersey and Independence Avenues), four digits beginning with 1 are in the Longworth House Office Building (between South Capitol Street and New Jersey Avenue on Independence Avenue), and four digits beginning with 2 are in the Rayburn House Office Building (between First and South Capitol Streets on Independence Avenue). Members' offices may be reached by phone at 202–225–3121. The most current listing of House Members can be found on the Internet at http://clerkweb.house.gov/.

Name	State (District)	Room
Nussle, Jim	Iowa (2)	303
Oberstar, James L	Minnesota (8)	2366
Obey, David R	Wisconsin (7)	2462
Olver, John W	Massachusetts (1)	1027
Ortiz, Solomon P	Texas (27)	2136
Owens, Major R	New York (11)	2305
Oxley, Michael G	Ohio (4)	2233
Packard, Ron	California (48)	2372
Pallone, Frank, Jr	New Jersey (6)	420
Pappas, Michael	New Jersey (12)	1710
Parker, Mike	Mississippi (4)	2445
Pascrell, Bill, Jr	New Jersey (8)	1722
Pastor, Ed	Arizona (2)	2465
Paul, Ron	Texas (14)	203
Paxon, Bill	New York (27)	2412
Payne, Donald M	New Jersey (10)	2244
Pease, Edward A	Indiana (7)	226
Pelosi, Nancy	California (8)	2457
Peterson, Collin C	Minnesota (7)	2159
Peterson, John E	Pennsylvania (5)	1020
Petri, Thomas E	Wisconsin (6)	2262
Pickering, Charles W. (Chip)	Mississippi (3)	427
Pickett, Owen B	Virginia (2)	2430
Pitts, Joseph R	Pennsylvania (16)	504
Pombo, Richard W	California (11)	1519
Pomeroy, Earl	North Dakota (At Large)	1533
Porter, John Edward	Illinois (10)	2373
Portman, Rob	Ohio (2)	238
Poshard, Glenn	Illinois (19)	2334
Price, David E	North Carolina (4)	2162
Pryce, Deborah	Ohio (15)	221
Quinn, Jack	New York (30)	331
Radanovich, George P	California (19)	213
Rahall, Nick J., II	West Virginia (3)	2307
Ramstad, Jim	Minnesota (3)	103
Rangel, Charles B	New York (15)	2354
Redmond, Bill	New Mexico (3)	2268
Regula, Ralph	Ohio (16)	2309
Reyes, Silvestre	Texas (16)	514
Riggs, Frank	California (1)	1714
Riley, Bob	Alabama (3)	510
Rivers, Lynn N	Michigan (13)	1724
Rodriguez, Ciro D	Texas (28)	323
Roemer, Tim	Indiana (3)	2348
Rogan, James E	California (27)	502
Rogers, Harold	Kentucky (5)	2468
Rohrabacher, Dana	California (45)	2338
Ros-Lehtinen, Ileana	Florida (18)	2240
Rothman, Steven R	New Jersey (9)	1607
Roukema, Marge	New Jersey (5)	2469
Roybal-Allard, Lucille	California (33)	2435

Representatives—Continued

[Republicans in roman (228); Democrats in italic (206); Independents in bold (1); total, 435]

Room numbers with three digits are in the Cannon House Office Building (New Jersey and Independence Avenues), four digits beginning with 1 are in the Longworth House Office Building (between South Capitol Street and New Jersey Avenue on Independence Avenue), and four digits beginning with 2 are in the Rayburn House Office Building (between First and South Capitol Streets on Independence Avenue). Members' offices may be reached by phone at 202–225–3121. The most current listing of House Members can be found on the Internet at http://clerkweb.house.gov/.

Name	State (District)	Room
Royce, Edward R	California (39)	1133
Rush, Bobby L	*Illinois (1)*	131
Ryun, Jim	Kansas (2)	511
Sabo, Martin Olav	*Minnesota (5)*	2336
Salmon, Matt	Arizona (1)	115
Sanchez, Loretta	*California (46)*	1529
Sanders, Bernard	Vermont (At Large)	2202
Sandlin, Max	*Texas (1)*	214
Sanford, Marshall (Mark)	South Carolina (1)	1223
Sawyer, Thomas C	*Ohio (14)*	1414
Saxton, Jim	New Jersey (3)	339
Scarborough, Joe	Florida (1)	127
Schaefer, Dan	Colorado (6)	2160
Schaffer, Bob	Colorado (4)	212
Schumer, Charles E	*New York (9)*	2211
Scott, Robert C	*Virginia (3)*	2464
Sensenbrenner, F. James, Jr	Wisconsin (9)	2332
Serrano, José E	*New York (16)*	2342
Sessions, Pete	Texas (5)	1318
Shadegg, John B	Arizona (4)	430
Shaw, E. Clay, Jr	Florida (22)	2408
Shays, Christopher	Connecticut (4)	1502
Sherman, Brad	*California (24)*	1524
Shimkus, John	Illinois (20)	513
Shuster, Bud	Pennsylvania (9)	2188
Sisisky, Norman	*Virginia (4)*	2371
Skaggs, David E	*Colorado (2)*	1124
Skeen, Joe	New Mexico (2)	2302
Skelton, Ike	*Missouri (4)*	2227
Slaughter, Louise McIntosh	*New York (28)*	2347
Smith, Adam	*Washington (9)*	1505
Smith, Christopher H	New Jersey (4)	2370
Smith, Lamar S	Texas (21)	2231
Smith, Linda	*Washington (3)*	1317
Smith, Nick	*Michigan (7)*	306
Smith, Robert F	Oregon (2)	1126
Snowbarger, Vince	Kansas (3)	509
Snyder, Vic	*Arkansas (2)*	1319
Solomon, Gerald B.H	New York (22)	2206
Souder, Mark E	Indiana (4)	418
Spence, Floyd	South Carolina (2)	2405
Spratt, John M., Jr	*South Carolina (5)*	1536
Stabenow, Debbie	*Michigan (8)*	1516
Stark, Fortney Pete	*California (13)*	239
Stearns, Cliff	Florida (6)	2352
Stenholm, Charles W	*Texas (17)*	1211
Stokes, Louis	*Ohio (11)*	2365
Strickland, Ted	*Ohio (6)*	336
Stump, Bob	Arizona (3)	211
Stupak, Bart	*Michigan (1)*	1410
Sununu, John E	New Hampshire (1)	1229

Representatives—Continued

[Republicans in roman (228); Democrats in italic (206); Independents in bold (1); total, 435]

Room numbers with three digits are in the Cannon House Office Building (New Jersey and Independence Avenues), four digits beginning with 1 are in the Longworth House Office Building (between South Capitol Street and New Jersey Avenue on Independence Avenue), and four digits beginning with 2 are in the Rayburn House Office Building (between First and South Capitol Streets on Independence Avenue). Members' offices may be reached by phone at 202–225–3121. The most current listing of House Members can be found on the Internet at http://clerkweb.house.gov/.

Name	State (District)	Room
Talent, James M	Missouri (2)	1022
Tanner, John S	Tennessee (8)	1127
Tauscher, Ellen O	California (10)	1440
Tauzin, W.J. (Billy)	Louisiana (3)	2183
Taylor, Charles H	North Carolina (11)	231
Taylor, Gene	Mississippi (5)	2447
Thomas, William M	California (21)	2208
Thompson, Bennie G	Mississippi (2)	1408
Thornberry, William M. (Mac)	Texas (13)	412
Thune, John R	South Dakota (At Large)	506
Thurman, Karen L	Florida (5)	440
Tiahrt, Todd	Kansas (4)	428
Tierney, John F	Massachusetts (6)	120
Torres, Esteban Edward	California (34)	2269
Towns, Edolphus	New York (10)	2232
Traficant, James A., Jr	Ohio (17)	2446
Turner, Jim	Texas (2)	1508
Upton, Fred	Michigan (6)	2333
Velázquez, Nydia M	New York (12)	1221
Vento, Bruce F	Minnesota (4)	2304
Visclosky, Peter J	Indiana (1)	2313
Walsh, James T	New York (25)	2351
Wamp, Zach	Tennessee (3)	423
Waters, Maxine	California (35)	2344
Watkins, Wes	Oklahoma (3)	2312
Watt, Melvin L	North Carolina (12)	1230
Watts, J.C., Jr	Oklahoma (4)	1210
Waxman, Henry A	California (29)	2204
Weldon, Curt	Pennsylvania (7)	2452
Weldon, Dave	Florida (15)	216
Weller, Jerry	Illinois (11)	130
Wexler, Robert	Florida (19)	1609
Weygand, Robert A	Rhode Island (2)	507
White, Rick	Washington (1)	116
Whitfield, Ed	Kentucky (1)	236
Wicker, Roger F	Mississippi (1)	206
Wilson, Heather	New Mexico (1)	2404
Wise, Robert E., Jr	West Virginia (2)	2367
Wolf, Frank R	Virginia (10)	241
Woolsey, Lynn C	California (6)	439
Wynn, Albert Russell	Maryland (4)	407
Yates, Sidney R	Illinois (9)	2109
Young, C.W. Bill	Florida (10)	2407
Young, Don	Alaska (At Large)	2111

Delegates

Christian-Green, Donna M	Virgin Islands	1711
Faleomavaega, Eni F.H	American Samoa	2422
Norton, Eleanor Holmes	District of Columbia	1424
Underwood, Robert A	Guam	424

Representatives—Continued

[Republicans in roman (228); Democrats in italic (206); Independents in bold (1); total, 435]

Room numbers with three digits are in the Cannon House Office Building (New Jersey and Independence Avenues), four digits beginning with 1 are in the Longworth House Office Building (between South Capitol Street and New Jersey Avenue on Independence Avenue), and four digits beginning with 2 are in the Rayburn House Office Building (between First and South Capitol Streets on Independence Avenue). Members' offices may be reached by phone at 202–225–3121. The most current listing of House Members can be found on the Internet at http://clerkweb.house.gov/.

Name	State (District)	Room
Resident Commissioner		
Romero-Barceló, Carlos A	Puerto Rico	2443

For further information concerning the United States Senate, contact the Secretary of the Senate, The Capitol, Washington, DC 20510. Phone, 202–224–2115. Internet, http://www.senate.gov/. For further information concerning the House of Representatives, contact the Clerk, The Capitol, Washington, DC 20515. Phone, 202–225–7000. Internet, http://www.house.gov/. Specific information and legislation can be found on the Internet at http://thomas.loc.gov/. Telephone directories for the United States Senate and the House of Representatives are available for sale by the Superintendent of Documents, Government Printing Office, Washington, DC 20402.

ARCHITECT OF THE CAPITOL

U.S. Capitol Building, Washington, DC 20515
Phone, 202–228–1793. Internet, http://www.aoc.gov/.

Architect of the Capitol	ALAN M. HANTMAN
Assistant Architect of the Capitol	(VACANCY)
Head, Architecture Division	BRUCE ARTHUR
Special Assistant	JAMES E. ELLISON
Superintendent of Construction	WILLIAM B. HOLMES
Administrative Assistant	HERBERT M. FRANKLIN
Director, Human Resources Management Division	HECTOR E. SUAREZ
Director, Equal Employment Opportunity	KATHLEEN GAUSE
Director, Information Resources Management	RICK KASHURBA
Employment Counsel	KEVIN MULSHINE
Curator	BARBARA WOLANIN
Inspector General	ARTHUR L. McINTYE
Director of Engineering	DAN E. HANLON
Assistant Director of Engineering	SCOTT BIRKHEAD
Executive Officer	LYNNE THEISS
Head, Procurement Division	RICHARD N. MUELLER
Budget Officer/Director of Financial Services	W. STUART PREGNALL III
Assistant Budget Officer	JOHN T. BORTLEIN, JR.
Accounting Officer	ELLIOTT BURNHAM
General Counsel	CHARLES K. TYLER
Senior Labor-Management Counsel	MARGARET COX
Senior Landscape Architect	MATTHEW EVANS
Superintendent, House Office Buildings	ROBERT MILEY
Supervising Engineer, Library of Congress	DONALD PARRY
Supervising Engineer of the U.S. Capitol	AMITA N. POOLE
Superintendent, Senate Office Buildings	LAWRENCE R. STOFFEL

The Architect of the Capitol is responsible for the care and maintenance of the U.S. Capitol, nearby buildings, and grounds and for implementing construction, renovation, conservation, and landscape improvement projects as authorized by the Congress.

The Architect of the Capitol is charged with operating and maintaining the buildings of the Capitol complex committed to his care by Congress. Permanent authority for the care and maintenance of the Capitol was established by the act of August 15, 1876 (40 U.S.C. 162, 163). The Architect's duties include the mechanical and structural maintenance of the Capitol, the conservation and care of works of art in the building, the upkeep and improvement of the Capitol grounds, and the arrangement of inaugural and other ceremonies held in the building or on the grounds. Legislation has been enacted from time to time to provide for additional buildings and grounds placed under the jurisdiction of the Architect of the Capitol.

In addition to the Capitol, the Architect is responsible for the upkeep of all of the congressional office buildings, the Library of Congress buildings, the U.S. Supreme Court building, the Thurgood Marshall Federal Judiciary Building, the Capitol Power Plant, the Capitol Police headquarters, and the Robert A. Taft Memorial. The Architect performs his duties in connection with the Senate side of the Capitol, the Senate office buildings, and the operation of the Senate restaurants subject to the approval of the Senate Committee on Rules and Administration. In matters of general policy in connection with the House office buildings and the Capitol Power Plant, his activities are subject to the approval and direction of the House Office Building Commission. The Architect is under the direction of the Speaker in matters concerning the House side of the Capitol. In addition, the Architect of the Capitol serves as the Acting Director of the U.S. Botanic Garden under the Joint Committee on the Library.

Until 1989, the position of Architect of the Capitol was filled by Presidential appointment for an indefinite term. Legislation enacted in 1989 provides that the Architect is to be appointed for a term of 10 years by the President, with the advice and consent of the Senate, from a list of 3 candidates recommended by a congressional commission. Upon confirmation by the Senate, the Architect becomes an official of the legislative branch as an officer and agent of Congress; he is eligible for reappointment after completion of his term. The present Architect, Alan M. Hantman, is the 10th to hold this position and the first to be appointed in accordance with the new procedure.

The Architect, whose original duties were limited to designing and supervising the construction of the Capitol, has assumed additional responsibilities for activities that have been assigned to the office by Congress. Today, in light of the widespread activities under the jurisdiction of the Architect of the Capitol, the administrative function competes heavily with the architectural and engineering functions of the office.

Recent and ongoing projects carried out by the Architect of the Capitol include the renovation, restoration, and modification of the interiors and exteriors of the Thomas Jefferson and John Adams Buildings of the Library of Congress; repair of the Capitol terraces; conversion of the Capitol courtyards into meeting rooms; replacement of worn Minton tile in the Senate corridors of the Capitol; conservation of the Statue of Freedom atop the Capitol dome; completion of the murals in the first-floor House corridors; improvement of speech-reinforcement, electrical, and fire-protection systems in the Capitol and congressional office buildings; removal of architectural barriers throughout the Capitol complex; development of publications and exhibits for the bicentennial of the Capitol; installation of an improved Senate subway system; preparation of a telecommunication plan for the legislative branch agencies; leasing of space in Postal Square for various Senate support services; work on security improvements within the Capitol complex; management oversight of the Thurgood Marshall Federal Judiciary Building; the design and construction of the National Garden adjacent to the Botanic Garden Conservatory; restoration of the U.S. Botanic Garden Conservatory; planning for the proposed Capitol Visitor Center; and direction of the master plan for the future development of the Capitol complex.

The Architect of the Capitol serves as a member of the following bodies: Capitol Police Board, Capitol Guide Board, District of Columbia Zoning Commission, Advisory Council on Historic Preservation, National Capital Memorial Commission, Art Advisory Committee to the Washington Metropolitan Area Transit Authority, and Heritage Preservation. He is also an ex-officio member of the United States Capitol Preservation Commission and the Commission on the Bicentennial of the United States Capitol. In addition, he serves as the Coordinator of Civil Defense for the Capitol complex.

For further information, contact the Office of the Architect of the Capitol, U.S. Capitol Building, Washington, DC 20515. Phone, 202–228–1793. Internet, http://www.aoc.gov/.

UNITED STATES BOTANIC GARDEN

Office of Executive Director, 245 First Street SW., Washington, DC 20024
Phone, 202–225–8333. Internet, http://www.aoc.gov/.
Conservatory, Maryland Avenue, First to Second Streets SW., Washington, DC 20024
Phone, 202–225–6647
Production Facility, 4700 Shepherd Parkway SW., Washington, DC 20032
Phone, 202–563–2220

Director (Architect of the Capitol)	ALAN M. HANTMAN
Executive Director	JEFFREY P. COOPER-SMITH

The United States Botanic Garden informs visitors about the aesthetic, cultural, economic, therapeutic, and ecological importance of plants to the well-being of humankind.

The U.S. Botanic Garden carries out its mission by presenting artistic displays of plants, exhibits, and a program of educational activities; promoting botanical knowledge through the cultivation of an ordered collection of plants; fostering plant conservation by acting as a repository for endangered species; and growing plants for the beautification of the Capitol complex. Uniquely situated at the heart of the U.S. Government, the Botanic Garden seeks to promote the exchange of ideas and information relevant to this mission among national and international visitors and policymakers.

The Conservatory, one of the largest structures of its kind in this country, features both indoor exhibits and two outdoor courtyard gardens. Collections in this facility attract many visitors annually, including botanists, horticulturists, ecologists, students, and garden club members. The permanent collections include orchids, epiphytes, bromeliads, carnivorous plants, ferns, cycads, cacti, succulents, medicinal plants, rare and endangered plants, and plants valued as sources of food, beverages, fibers, and other industrial products. Specialty exhibits range from artwork inspired by plants to seasonal flower shows highlighting the beauty of chrysanthemums, poinsettias, spring flowers, and attractive summer terrace arrangements.

Outdoor plantings are showcased in Bartholdi Park. Also located in this park is Bartholdi Fountain, created by Frederic-Auguste Bartholdi (1834–1904), sculptor of the Statue of Liberty. To the west of the Conservatory, a rose garden marks the border of a 3-acre tract that is the future site of the National Garden.

The Botanic Garden offers educational facilities by making available for study to students, botanists, and floriculturists many rare and interesting botanical specimens. Every year botanical specimens are received from all over the world with requests for identification, and one of the services rendered by the Garden to the public is the identification of such specimens and the furnishing of information relating to the proper methods of growing them.

The U.S. Botanic Garden was founded in 1820 under the auspices of the Columbian Institute for the Promotion of Arts and Sciences, an organization that was the outgrowth of an association known as the Metropolitan Society and that received its charter from Congress on April 20, 1818. The Garden continued under the direction of this Institute until 1837, when the Institute ceased to exist as an active organization.

The Botanic Garden remained abandoned until 1842, when it became necessary for the Government to provide accommodations for the botanical collections brought to Washington, DC, from the South Seas by the U.S. Exploring Expedition of 1838–42, under the leadership of Capt. Charles Wilkes.

The collections were placed temporarily on exhibition at the Patent Office upon return of the expedition in June 1842. The first greenhouse for this purpose was constructed in 1842 on a lot behind the Patent Office Building under the direction and control of the Joint Committee of Congress on the Library, from funds appropriated by Congress.

The act of May 15, 1850 (9 Stat. 427), provided for the relocation of the Botanic Garden under the direction of the Joint Committee on the Library. The site selected was on The Mall at the west end of the Capitol Grounds, practically the same site the Garden occupied during the period it functioned under the Columbia Institute. This site was later enlarged, and the main area continued to serve as the principal Botanic Garden site from 1850 to 1933, when the Garden was relocated to its present site.

Although the Botanic Garden began functioning as a Government-owned institution in 1842, the records indicate that it was not until 1856 that the maintenance of the Garden was specifically placed under the direction of the Joint Committee on the Library and a regular, annual appropriation was provided by Congress (11 Stat. 104).

At the present time the Joint Committee exercises its supervision through the Architect of the Capitol, who has been serving as Acting Director since 1934.

The Botanic Garden's Conservatory closed to the public on September 2, 1997, for major renovations. It is expected to reopen in the year 2000. Bartholdi Park is open from 9 a.m. to 5 p.m. daily.

For further information concerning the United States Botanic Garden, contact the Office of the Architect of the Capitol, U.S. Capitol Building, Washington, DC 20515. Phone, 202–228–1793. Internet, http://www.aoc.gov/.

GENERAL ACCOUNTING OFFICE

441 G Street NW., Washington, DC 20548
Phone, 202–512–3000. Internet, http://www.gao.gov/.

Comptroller General of the United States	JAMES F. HINCHMAN, *Acting*
Deputy Comptroller General of the United States	(VACANCY)
Principal Assistant Comptroller General	JAMES F. HINCHMAN
Assistant Comptroller General for Planning and Reporting	BRIAN P. CROWLEY
Assistant Comptroller General for Operations	JOAN M. DODARO
Assistant Comptroller General for Policy	THOMAS J. BREW, *Acting*
Assistant Comptroller General, General Government Division	NANCY KINGSBURY, *Acting*
Assistant Comptroller General, Health, Education, and Human Services Division	RICHARD L. HEMBRA
Assistant Comptroller General, Office of Information Management and Communications	JOHN HARMAN
Assistant Comptroller General, National Security and International Affairs Division	HENRY L. HINTON, JR.
Assistant Comptroller General, Resources, Community, and Economic Development Division	KEITH O. FULTZ
Assistant Comptroller General, Accounting and Information Management Division	GENE L. DODARO
General Counsel	ROBERT P. MURPHY
Chief Accountant	PHILIP CALDER
Assistant Comptroller General for Special Investigations	ELJAY BOWRON
Support Functions:	
Chief Economist	LOREN YAGER, *Acting*
Director, Affirmative Action/Civil Rights Office	NILDA I. APONTE
Director, Office of Congressional Relations	HELEN H. HSING
Director, Office of Counseling and Career Development	HOWARD N. JOHNSON
Inspector General	FRANCES GARCIA
Director, Office of International Liaison	LINDA L. WEEKS
Director, Personnel	PATRICIA M. RODGERS
Director, Office of Public Affairs	CLEVE E. CORLETT
Director, Office of Recruitment	PAUL JONES
Director, Training Institute	ANNE K. KLEIN
Chair, Personnel Appeals Board	LEROY D. CLARK

The General Accounting Office is the investigative arm of the Congress and is charged with examining all matters relating to the receipt and disbursement of public funds.

The General Accounting Office (GAO) was established by the Budget and Accounting Act of 1921 (31 U.S.C. 702), to independently audit Government

GENERAL ACCOUNTING OFFICE

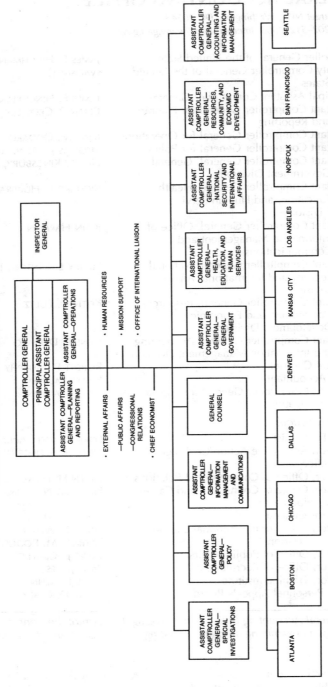

agencies. Over the years, the Congress has expanded GAO's audit authority, added new responsibilities and duties, and strengthened GAO's ability to perform independently.

The Office is under the control and direction of the Comptroller General of the United States, who is appointed by the President with the advice and consent of the Senate for a term of 15 years.

Activities

Audits and Evaluations Supporting the Congress is GAO's fundamental responsibility. In meeting this objective, GAO performs a variety of services, the most prominent of which are audits and evaluations of Government programs and activities. The majority of these reviews are made in response to specific congressional requests. The Office is required to perform work requested by committee chairpersons and, as a matter of policy, assigns equal status to requests from Ranking Minority Members. The Office also responds to individual Member requests, as possible. Other assignments are initiated pursuant to standing commitments to congressional committees, and some reviews are specifically required by law. Finally, some assignments are independently undertaken in accordance with GAO's basic legislative responsibilities.

The ability to review practically any Government function requires a multidisciplined staff able to conduct assignments wherever needed. The Office's staff has expertise in a variety of disciplines, including accounting, law, public and business administration, economics, the social and physical sciences, and others.

The Office is organized so that staff members concentrate on specific subject areas, enabling them to develop a detailed level of knowledge. When an assignment requires specialized experience not available within GAO, outside experts assist the permanent staff. Staff members go wherever necessary on assignments, working onsite to gather data, test transactions, and observe firsthand how Government programs and activities are carried out.

Accounting and Information Management Policy The Office ensures that the Congress has available for its use current, accurate, and complete financial management data. To do this, GAO:

—prescribes accounting principles and standards for the executive branch;

—advises other Federal agencies on fiscal and related policies and procedures; and

—prescribes standards for auditing and evaluating Government programs.

In addition, the Comptroller General, the Secretary of the Treasury, and the Director of the Office of Management and Budget develop standardized information and data processing systems. This includes standard terminology, definitions, classifications, and codes for fiscal, budgetary, and program-related data and information.

Legal Services The Office provides various legal services to the Congress. In response to inquiries from committees and Members, the Comptroller General provides advice on legal issues involving Government programs and activities. The Office is also available to assist in drafting legislation and reviewing legislative proposals before the Congress. In addition, it reviews and reports to the Congress on proposed rescissions and deferrals of Government funds.

Other legal services include resolving bid protests that challenge Government contract awards and assisting Government agencies in interpreting the laws governing the expenditure of public funds.

In addition, GAO's staff of trained investigators conducts special investigations and assists auditors and evaluators when they encounter possible criminal and civil misconduct. When warranted, GAO refers the results of its investigations to the Department of Justice and other law enforcement authorities.

Reporting The Office offers a range of products to communicate the results of its work. The type of product depends on the assignment's objectives and the needs of the intended user. Product types include testimony, oral briefings, and written reports. Virtually all of GAO's reports are available to the public.

A list of GAO reports issued or released during the previous month is furnished monthly to the Congress, its Members, and committees. Copies of GAO reports are also furnished to interested congressional parties; Federal, State, local, and foreign governments; members of the press; college faculty, students, and libraries; and nonprofit organizations.

Copies of unclassified reports are available from the U.S. General Accounting Office, P.O. Box 6015, Gaithersburg, MD 20884–6015. Phone, 202–512–6000. The first copy of each report is free; additional copies are $2 each. There is a 25-percent discount on orders of 100 or more copies mailed to a single address. Orders must be prepaid by cash, check, or money order payable to the Superintendent of Documents.

Electronic Access   Reports, Comptroller General decisions, and GAO special publications may be obtained on the Internet at http://www.gao.gov/.

For further information, contact the Office of Public Affairs, General Accounting Office, 441 G Street NW., Washington, DC 20548. Phone, 202–512–4800.

GOVERNMENT PRINTING OFFICE

732 North Capitol Street NW., Washington, DC 20401
Phone, 202–512–0000. Internet, http://www.access.gpo.gov/.

Public Printer	MICHAEL F. DIMARIO
Deputy Public Printer	ROBERT T. MANSKER
Superintendent of Documents	FRANCIS J. BUCKLEY, JR.
Director, Documents Sales Service	JAMES D. YOUNG
Director, Electronic Information Dissemination	(VACANCY)
Director, Library Programs Service	JAMES D. YOUNG, *Acting*
Chief, Technical Support Group	MITCHELL E. PHELAN
Director, Customer Services	JAMES C. BRADLEY
Superintendent, Congressional Printing Management Division	CHARLES C. COOK, SR.
Superintendent, Departmental Accounts Representative Division	ROBERT G. COX
Superintendent, Typography and Design Division	JOHN W. SAPP
Director, Institute for Federal Printing and Electronic Publishing	LOIS SCHUTTE
Manager, Printing Procurement Department	MEREDITH L. ARNESON
Manager, Production Department	DONALD L. LADD
Manager, Quality Control and Technical Department	ROBERT H. THOMAS
Comptroller	R. BRUCE HOLSTEIN
Director, Engineering Service	JOSEPH A. PALANK
Director, Materials Management Service	THOMAS M. HUGHES
Director, Occupational Health and Environmental Services	WILLIAM T. HARRIS
Director, Office of Administrative Support	RAYMOND J. GARVEY
Director, Office of Budget	WILLIAM M. GUY

Director, Office of Congressional, Legislative, and Public Affairs	ANDREW M. SHERMAN
Director, Office of Equal Employment Opportunity	NADINE L. ELZY
Director, Office of Information Resources Management	PATRICIA R. GARDNER
Director, Office of Labor and Employee Relations	NEAL H. FINE
Director, Office of Personnel	EDWARD A. BLATT
Director, Office of Planning	THOMAS J. MULDOON
Director, Office of Policy Coordination	VINCENT F. ARENDES
Administrative Law Judge	(VACANCY)
General Counsel	ANTHONY J. ZAGAMI
Inspector General	ROBERT G. ANDARY

The mission of the Government Printing Office is to inform the Nation by producing, procuring, and disseminating printed and electronic publications of the Congress as well as the executive departments and establishments of the Federal Government.

The Government Printing Office (GPO) began operations in accordance with Congressional Joint Resolution 25 of June 23, 1860. The activities of GPO are defined in the public printing and documents chapters of title 44 of the U.S. Code.

The Public Printer, who serves as the head of GPO, is appointed by the President with the advice and consent of the Senate.

Activities

The Government Printing Office produces and procures printed and electronic publications for Congress and the departments and establishments of the Federal Government. It furnishes printing supplies to all governmental activities on order. It catalogs, distributes, and sells Government publications in printed and electronic formats.

GPO invites bids from commercial suppliers on a wide variety of printing and reproduction services, awards and administers contracts, and maintains liaison between ordering agencies and contractors.

Printing processes used are electronic prepress, including networked on-demand printing systems; offset presswork, featuring direct-to-plate technology; and bookbinding. Electronic databases prepared for printing are premastered for CD–ROM replication and are used to provide online access.

GPO sells approximately 12,000 different printed and electronic publications that originate in various Government agencies. It administers the depository library program through which a comprehensive range of Government publications are made available for the free use of the public in 1,400 libraries throughout the country. GPO also provides online access to more than 70 databases of Federal Government publications, including the *Congressional Record* and the *Federal Register*. GPO's online information service, GPO Access, may be reached at http://www.access.gpo.gov/.

Sources of Information

Congressional, Legislative, and Public Affairs General inquiries about GPO should be directed to the Office of Congressional, Legislative, and Public Affairs. Phone, 202–512–1991. Fax, 202–512–1293.

Contracts Commercial printers interested in Government printing contract opportunities should direct inquiries to the Manager, Printing Procurement Department, Government Printing Office, Washington, DC 20401. Phone, 202–512–0327. Contract opportunities are also posted on GPO's web site at http://www.access.gpo.gov/, or contact one of the GPO Regional

U.S. GOVERNMENT PRINTING OFFICE

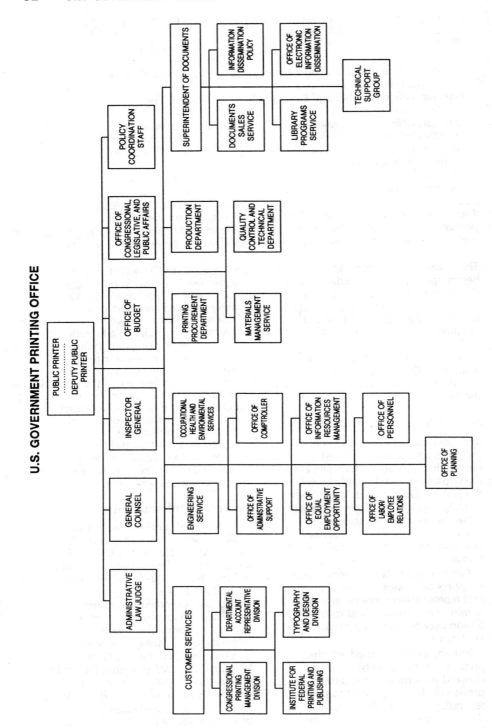

Printing Procurement Offices listed below.

Regional Printing and Procurement Offices—Government Printing Office

(R: Regional Printing Procurement Office; S: Satellite Printing Procurement Office)

Office	Address	Telephone
ATLANTA, GA (R)	Suite 110, 1888 Emery St., 30318–2542	404–605–9160
Charleston, SC (S)	Rm. 122, 334 Meeting St., 29403–6417	803–723–9379
BOSTON, MA (R)	28 Court Square, 02108–2504	617–720–3680
CHICAGO, IL (R)	Suite 810, 200 N. LaSalle St., 60601–1055	312–353–3916
COLUMBUS, OH (R)	Suite 112–B, 1335 Dublin Rd., 43215–7034	614–488–4616
DALLAS, TX (R)	Rm. 3D4, 1100 Commerce St., 75242–0395	214–767–0451
New Orleans, LA (S)	Rm. 310, 423 Canal St., 70130–2352	504–589–2538
Oklahoma City, OK (S)	Suite 100, 3420 D Ave., Tinker AFB, OK 73145–9188	405–231–4146
San Antonio, TX (S)	Bldg. 1552, Door 2, Kelly AFB, TX 78241–5000	210–924–4245
DENVER, CO (R)	Rm. D–1010, Bldg. 53, Denver Federal Center, 80225–0347	303–236–5292
HAMPTON, VA (R)	Suite 400, 11836 Canon Blvd., Newport News, VA 23606–2555	757–873–2800
LOS ANGELES, CA (R)	Suite 110, 12501 E. Imperial Hwy., Norwalk, CA 90650–3136	562–863–1708
San Diego, CA (S)	Suite 109, 2221 Camino Del Rio S., 92108–3609	619–497–6050
NEW YORK, NY (R)	Rm. 709, 201 Varick St., 10014–4879	212–620–3321
PHILADELPHIA, PA (R)	Suite A–190, 928 Jaymore Rd., Southampton, PA 18966–3820	215–364–6465
Pittsburgh, PA (S)	Rm. 501, 1000 Liberty Ave., 15222–4000	412–395–4858
RAPID RESPONSE CENTER	Bldg. 136, Washington Navy Yard, First and N Sts. SE., Washington, DC 20403.	202–755–2110
ST. LOUIS, MO (R)	Rm. 328, 815 Olive St., 63101–1597	314–241–0349
SAN FRANCISCO, CA (R)	Suite I, 536 Stone Rd., Benicia, CA 94510–1170	707–748–1970
SEATTLE, WA (R)	4735 E. Marginal Way S., Federal Center South, 98134–2397	206–764–3726

Suppliers of paper products and printing equipment and supplies; purchasers of surplus printing equipment, waste, and salvage materials; and freight carriers should contact the Director of Materials Management, Government Printing Office, Washington, DC 20401. Phone, 202–512–0935.

The booklet *How To Do Business With the Government Printing Office, A Guide for Contractors* is available upon request from the GPO Central Office or any GPO Regional Printing Procurement Office.

Employment Office of Personnel Management registers are used in filling administrative, technical, crafts, and clerical positions. Inquiries should be directed to the Chief, Employment Branch, Government Printing Office, Washington, DC 20401. Phone, 202–512–1124.

Government Publications Orders and inquiries concerning publications and subscriptions for sale by GPO should be directed to the Superintendent of Documents, Government Printing Office, Washington, DC 20402. Orders may be phoned in to 202–512–1800, or faxed to 202–512–2250. Orders also may be placed via the Internet at http://www.access.gpo.gov/.

To locate Government publications, the public is offered various lists for sale by the Superintendent of Documents, or they may be viewed via the Internet at http://www.access.gpo.gov/.

The *GPO Sales Publications Reference File (PRF)* provides author, title, and subject access to Government publications available for sale through the Superintendent of Documents.

The *Monthly Catalog of U.S. Government Publications* is the most comprehensive listing of Government publications issued by Federal departments and agencies.

There also are two free catalogs of new or popular publications available: *U.S. Government Books,* which lists hundreds of best-selling titles, and *New Books,* a bimonthly list of all Government publications placed on sale in the preceding 2 months. These publications can be obtained by calling the Superintendent of Documents at 202–512–1800.

Remittance for all publications ordered from the Superintendent of Documents must be received in advance of shipment by check or money order payable to the Superintendent of Documents. Orders also may be charged to MasterCard or VISA accounts or a GPO deposit account.

Depository Libraries GPO distributes printed and electronic publications to approximately 1,400 depository libraries nationwide where they may be used by the public free of charge. A list of depository libraries is available from the Superintendent of Documents. Phone, 202–512–1119. It may also be accessed on-line at http://www.access.gpo.gov/.

Electronic Access GPO Access provides online access to key Government publications through the Internet at http://www.access.gpo.gov/. For information about this service, contact the GPO Access support team at 202–512–1530, or E-mail at gpoaccess@gpo.gov.

Bookstores Popular Government publications may be purchased at the GPO bookstores listed below.

Bookstores—Government Printing Office

City	Address	Telephone
Washington, DC, area:		
Main Bookstore	710 N. Capitol St. NW.	202–512–0132
McPherson Square	1510 H St. NW.	202–653–5075
Retail Sales Outlet	8660 Cherry Ln., Laurel, MD	301–953–7974
Atlanta, GA	Suite 120, 999 Peachtree St. NE.	404–347–1900
Birmingham, AL	2021 3d Ave. N.	205–731–1056
Boston, MA	Rm. 169, 10 Causeway St.	617–720–4180
Chicago, IL	Rm. 124, 401 S. State St.	312–353–5133
Cleveland, OH	Rm. 1653, 1240 E. 9th St.	216–522–4922
Columbus, OH	Rm. 207, 200 N. High St.	614–469–6956
Dallas, TX	Rm. 1C50, 1100 Commerce St.	214–767–0076
Denver, CO	Suite 130, 1660 Wyncoop St.	303–844–3964
Detroit, MI	Suite 160, 477 Michigan Ave.	313–226–7816
Houston, TX	801 Travis St.	713–228–1187
Jacksonville, FL	Rm. 100, 100 W. Bay St.	904–353–0569
Kansas City, MO	120 Bannister Mall, 5600 E. Bannister Rd.	816–767–2256
Los Angeles, CA	C–Level, 505 S. Flower St.	213–239–9844
Milwaukee, WI	Rm. 150, 310 W. Wisconsin Ave.	414–297–1304
New York, NY	Rm. 110, 26 Federal Plz.	212–264–3825
Philadelphia, PA	100 N. 17th St.	215–636–1900
Pittsburgh, PA	Rm. 118, 1000 Liberty Ave.	412–395–5021
Portland, OR	1305 SW. 1st St.	503–221–6217
Pueblo, CO	201 W. 8th St.	719–544–3142
San Francisco, CA	Rm. 141–S, 303 2d St.	415–512–2770
Seattle, WA	Rm. 194, 915 2d Ave.	206–553–4270

For further information, contact the Office of Congressional, Legislative, and Public Affairs, Government Printing Office, 732 North Capitol Street NW., Washington, DC 20401. Phone, 202–512–1991. Fax, 202–512–1293. Internet, http://www.access.gpo.gov/.

LIBRARY OF CONGRESS

101 Independence Avenue SE., Washington, DC 20540
Phone, 202–707–5000. Internet, http://www.loc.gov/.

Librarian of Congress	JAMES H. BILLINGTON
Deputy Librarian of Congress	DONALD L. SCOTT
Chief of Staff	JOANN JENKINS
Associate Librarian for Library Services	WINSTON TABB
Associate Librarian for Human Resources Services	LLOYD A. PAULS
Director, Congressional Research Service	DANIEL MULHOLLAN
Register of Copyrights and Associate Librarian for Copyright Services	MARYBETH PETERS
Law Librarian	RUBENS MEDINA
General Counsel	ELIZABETH PUGH

Inspector General
Chief, Loan Division

JOHN W. RENSBARGER
L. CHRISTOPHER WRIGHT

Library of Congress Trust Fund Board
Chairman (Librarian of Congress)
(Secretary of the Treasury)
(U.S. Representative from California and
    Chairman, Joint Committee on the Library)
Appointive Members

JAMES H. BILLINGTON
ROBERT E. RUBIN
WILLIAM M. THOMAS

EDWIN L. COX, PATRICIA DUFF,
JULIE FINLEY, THOMAS S. FOLEY,
ADELE HALL, JOHN KLUGE, PETER
LYNCH, ARTHUR ORTENBERG,
CECILLE PULITZER, LAURENCE
TISCH

The Library of Congress is the national library of the United States, offering diverse materials for research including the world's most extensive collections in many areas such as American history, music, and law.

The Library of Congress was established by act of April 24, 1800 (2 Stat. 56), appropriating $5,000 "for the purchase of such books as may be necessary for the use of Congress . . . ." The Library's scope of responsibility has been widened by subsequent legislation (2 U.S.C. 131–168d). The Librarian, appointed by the President with the advice and consent of the Senate, directs the Library.

Supported mainly by the appropriations of Congress, the Library also uses income from funds received from foundations and other private sources and administered by the Library of Congress Trust Fund Board, as well as monetary gifts presented for direct application (2 U.S.C. 154–163).

Under the organic law, the Library's first responsibility is service to Congress. As the Library has developed, its range of service has come to include the entire governmental establishment and the public at large, making it a national library for the United States.

Activities

Collections   The Library's extensive collections are universal in scope. They include books, serials, and pamphlets on every subject and in a multitude of languages, and research materials in many formats, including maps, photographs, manuscripts, motion pictures, and sound recordings. Among them are the most comprehensive collections of Chinese, Japanese, and Russian language books outside Asia and the former Soviet Union; volumes relating to science and legal materials outstanding for American and foreign law; the world's largest collection of published aeronautical literature; and the most extensive collection in the Western Hemisphere of books printed before 1501 A.D.

The manuscript collections relate to manifold aspects of American history and civilization, and include the personal papers of most of the Presidents from George Washington through Calvin Coolidge. The music collections contain volumes and pieces—manuscript and published—from classic works to the newest popular compositions. Other materials available for research include maps and views; photographic records from the daguerreotype to the latest news photo; recordings, including folksongs and other music, speeches, and poetry readings; prints, drawings, and posters; government documents, newspapers, and periodicals from all over the world; and motion pictures, microforms, and audio and video tapes.

Reference Resources   Admission to the various research facilities of the Library is free. No introduction or credentials are required for persons over high school age. Readers must submit appropriate photo identification with a current

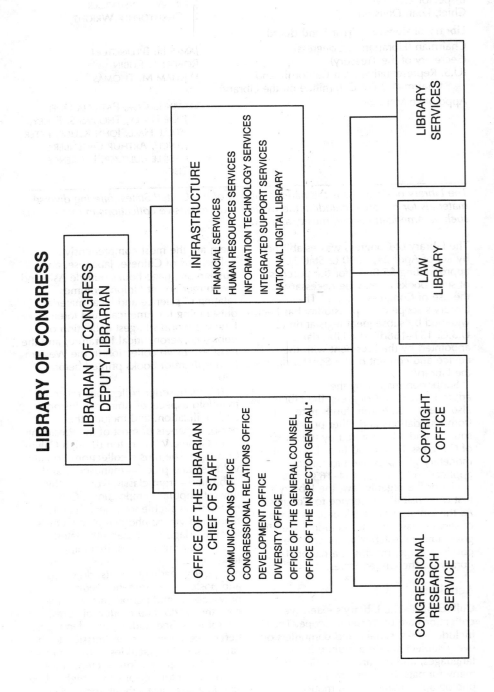

LIBRARY OF CONGRESS

LIBRARIAN OF CONGRESS
DEPUTY LIBRARIAN

OFFICE OF THE LIBRARIAN
CHIEF OF STAFF

COMMUNICATIONS OFFICE
CONGRESSIONAL RELATIONS OFFICE
DEVELOPMENT OFFICE
DIVERSITY OFFICE
OFFICE OF THE GENERAL COUNSEL
OFFICE OF THE INSPECTOR GENERAL*

INFRASTRUCTURE

FINANCIAL SERVICES
HUMAN RESOURCES SERVICES
INFORMATION TECHNOLOGY SERVICES
INTEGRATED SUPPORT SERVICES
NATIONAL DIGITAL LIBRARY

CONGRESSIONAL
RESEARCH
SERVICE

COPYRIGHT
OFFICE

LAW
LIBRARY

LIBRARY
SERVICES

address and, for certain collections, like those of the Manuscript, Rare Book and Special Collections, and Motion Picture, Broadcasting and Recorded Sound Divisions, there are additional requirements. As demands for service to Congress and Federal Government agencies increase, reference service available through correspondence has become limited. The Library must decline some requests and refer correspondents to a library within their area that can provide satisfactory assistance. While priority is given to inquiries pertaining to its holdings of special materials or to subjects in which its resources are unique, the Library does attempt to provide helpful responses to all inquirers.

Copyrights With the enactment of the second general revision of the U.S. copyright law by Act of July 8, 1870 (16 Stat. 212–217), all activities relating to copyright, including deposit and registration, were centralized in the Library of Congress. The Copyright Act of 1976 (90 Stat. 2541), as amended and codified, brought all forms of copyrightable authorship, both published and unpublished, under a single statutory system which gives authors protection immediately upon creation of their works. Exclusive rights granted to authors under the statute include the right to reproduce and prepare derivative works, distribute copies or phonorecords, perform and display the work publicly, and in the case of sound recordings, to perform the work publicly by means of a digital audio transmission. Works eligible for copyright include literary works (books and periodicals), musical works, dramatic works, pantomimes and choreographic works, pictorial, graphic, and sculptural works, motion pictures, sound recordings, and architectural works. Serving in its capacity as a national registry for creative works, the Copyright Office registers nearly 600,000 claims to copyright annually and is a major source of acquisitions for the universal collections of the Library of Congress.

Extension of Service The Library extends its service through:

—an interlibrary loan system;

—the photoduplication, at reasonable cost, of books, manuscripts, maps, newspapers, and prints in its collections;

—the sale of sound recordings, which are released by its Recording Laboratory;

—the exchange of duplicates with other institutions;

—the sale of CD–ROM cataloging tools and magnetic tapes and the publication in book format or microform of cumulative catalogs, which make available the results of the expert bibliographical and cataloging work of its technical personnel;

—a centralized cataloging program whereby the Library of Congress acquires material published all over the world, catalogs it promptly, and distributes cataloging information in machine-readable form as well as by printed cards and other means to the Nation's libraries;

—a cooperative cataloging program whereby the cataloging of data, by name authority and bibliographic records, prepared by other libraries becomes part of the Library of Congress data base and is distributed through the MARC Distribution Service;

—a cataloging-in-publication program in cooperation with American publishers for printing cataloging information in current books;

—the National Serials Data Program, a national center that maintains a record of serial titles to which International Standard Serial Numbers have been assigned and serves, with this file, as the United States Register; and

—the development of general schemes of classification (Library of Congress and Dewey Decimal), subject headings, and cataloging, embracing the entire field of printed matter.

Furthermore, the Library provides for:

—the preparation of bibliographical lists responsive to the needs of Government and research;

—the maintenance and the publication of cooperative publications;

—the publication of catalogs, bibliographical guides, and lists, and of texts of original manuscripts and rare books in the Library of Congress;

—the circulation in traveling exhibitions of items from the Library's collections;

—the provision of books in braille and "talking book" records, as well as books on tape, for the blind and the physically handicapped through 143 cooperating libraries throughout the United States;

—the distribution of its electronic materials via the Internet, including more than 40 million bibliographic records, summaries of congressional bills, copyright registrations, bibliographies and research guides, summaries of foreign laws, an index of Southeast Asian POW/MIA documents, and selections from the Library's unique historical collections—the Library's major contribution to the National Digital Library—via *LC WEB* (http://www.loc.gov/); online public legislative information through *Thomas* (http://thomas.loc.gov/); major exhibits; the Library's catalog; the Library's digitized collection of unique American materials; pointers to external Internet resources including extensive international, national, State, and local government information; and an international electronic library of resources; and

—the provision of research and analytical services on a fee-for-service basis to agencies in the executive and judicial branches.

Congressional Research Service The mission of the Congressional Research Service (CRS) is to provide to the Congress, throughout the legislative process, comprehensive and reliable legislative research, analysis, and information services that are timely, objective, nonpartisan, and confidential, thereby contributing to an informed national legislature. In the last several years, CRS has responded to more than 500,000 requests for services from the Congress annually.

CRS evolved from the Legislative Reference Service, established in 1914 by an act of Congress. The statutory authority for CRS in its current form dates back to the Legislative Reorganization Act of 1946, as amended (2 U.S.C. 72a note), and the Legislative Reorganization Act of 1970, as amended (2 U.S.C. 166). The 1970 act authorized

increased emphasis on in-depth research and analysis. The function and capabilities of CRS have grown over the years in response to the increasing scope of public policy issues on the congressional agenda.

CRS provides multidisciplinary assistance to the Congress at every stage of the legislative process concerning subject areas relevant to policy issues before the Congress. Its Director, assisted by a management team, oversees and coordinates the work of seven research divisions which span the range of public policy subjects and disciplines: American Law; Economics; Environment and Natural Resources Policy; Foreign Affairs and National Defense; Government; and Science, Technology, and Medicine. The Service has two information divisions: the Congressional Reference Division and the Library Services Division. These divisions provide reference, bibliographic, and other information services to the Congress and CRS staff using both traditional techniques and automated systems. The Service's administrative offices are Finance and Administration; Policy Compliance; Research; and the Director's Office.

In addition to responding to individual requests for information and analysis, CRS prepares products and services in anticipation of topics that likely will be on the legislative agenda, and develops and presents seminars that provide a forum for discussion among Members of Congress and their staffs, CRS specialists, and nationally recognized experts on important legislative issues.

The CRS' Internet home page provides Members and their staff with access to CRS products and services and links to public policy, legislative, legal, and reference information. CRS and the Library of Congress contribute to the Legislative Information System, an electronic retrieval system that provides the Congress with the most current and comprehensive legislative information available, including bill summaries and status, full text of legislation, and committee reports.

For further information, call 202–707–5700.

American Folklife Center The Center, which was established in the Library of Congress by Act of January 2, 1976 (20 U.S.C. 2102 *et seq.*), has a coordinative function both in and outside the Federal Establishment to carry out appropriate programs to support, preserve, and present American folklife through such activities as receiving and maintaining folklife collections, scholarly research, field projects, performances, exhibitions, festivals, workshops, publications, and audiovisual presentations. The Center is directed by a Board of Trustees consisting of four members appointed by the President from Federal agencies; four each appointed by the President pro tempore of the Senate and the Speaker of the House from private life; and five *ex officio* members, including: the Librarian of Congress, the Secretary of the Smithsonian Institution, the Chairmen of the National Endowment for the Arts and the National Endowment for the Humanities, and the Director of the Center.

The Center has conducted projects in many locations across the country, such as the ethnic communities of Chicago, IL; southern Georgia; a ranching community in northern Nevada; the Blue Ridge Parkway in southern Virginia and northern North Carolina; and the States of New Jersey, Rhode Island, and Montana. The projects have provided large collections of recordings and photographs for the Archive of Folk Culture. The Center administers the Federal Cylinder Project, which is charged with preserving and disseminating music and oral traditions recorded on wax cylinders dating from the late 1800's to the early 1940's. A cultural conservation study was developed at the Center, in cooperation with the Department of the Interior, pursuant to a congressional mandate. Various conferences, workshops, and symposia are given throughout the year.

The *Folklife Center News,* a quarterly newsletter, and other informational publications are available upon request. The Government Printing Office sells additional Center publications.

The American Folklife Center maintains and administers the Archive of Folk Culture, an extensive collection of ethnographic materials from this country and around the world. It is the national repository for folk-related recordings, manuscripts, and other unpublished materials. The Center's reading room contains over 3,500 books and periodicals; a sizable collection of magazines, newsletters, unpublished theses, and dissertations; field notes; and many textual and some musical transcriptions and recordings.

For further information, call 202–707–6590.

Center for the Book The Center was established in the Library of Congress by act of October 13, 1977 (2 U.S.C. 171 *et seq.*), to stimulate public interest in books, reading, and libraries, and to encourage the study of books and print culture. The Center is a catalyst for promoting and exploring the vital role of books, reading, and libraries—nationally and internationally. As a partnership between the Government and the private sector, the Center for the Book depends on tax-deductible contributions from individuals and corporations to support its programs.

The Center's activities are directed toward the general public and scholars. The overall program includes reading and promotion projects with television and radio networks, symposia, lectures, exhibitions, special events, and publications. More than 50 national educational and civic organizations participate in the Center's annual reading promotion campaign.

Since 1984, 35 States have established statewide book centers that are affiliated with the Center for the Book in the Library of Congress. State centers plan and fund their own projects, involving members of the State's "community of the book," including authors, readers, prominent citizens, and public officials who serve as honorary advisers.

For further information, call 202–707–5221.

National Preservation Program The Library provides technical information related to the preservation of library and archival material. A series of handouts on various preservation and conservation topics has been prepared by the

Preservation Office. Information and publications are available from the Library of Congress, Office of the Director for Preservation, Washington, DC 20540–4500. Phone, 202–707–1840.

National Film Preservation Board   The National Film Preservation Board, presently authorized by the National Film Preservation Act of 1996 (2 U.S.C. 179), serves as a public advisory group to the Librarian of Congress. The Board consists of 40 members and alternates representing the many parts of the diverse American film industry, film archives, scholars, and others. As its primary mission, the Board works to ensure the survival, conservation, and increased public availability of America's film heritage, including advising the Librarian on the annual selection of films to the National Film Registry and counseling the Librarian on development and implementation of the national film preservation plan. Key publications are *Film Preservation 1993: A Study of the Current State of American Film Preservation* (4 volumes, 748 pages) and *Redefining Film Preservation: A National Plan* (79 pages).

For further information, call 202–707–5912.

Sources of Information

Books for the Blind and Physically Handicapped   Talking and braille books and magazines are distributed through 142 regional and subregional libraries to blind and physically handicapped residents of the United States and its territories. Information is available at public libraries throughout the United States and from the headquarters office, Library of Congress, National Library Service for the Blind and Physically Handicapped, 1291 Taylor Street NW., Washington, DC 20542–4960. Phone, 202–707–5100.

Cataloging Data Distribution   Cataloging and bibliographic information in the form of microfiche catalogs, book catalogs, magnetic tapes, CD–ROM cataloging tools, bibliographies, and other technical publications is distributed to libraries and other institutions.

Information about ordering materials is available from the Library of Congress, Cataloging Distribution Service, Washington, DC 20541–4910. Phone, 202–707–6100. TDD, 202–707–0012. Fax, 202–707–1334. E-mail, cdsinfo@mail.loc.gov.

Library of Congress card numbers for new publications are assigned by the Cataloging in Publication Division. Direct inquiries to Library of Congress, CIP Division, Washington, DC 20540–4320. Phone, 202–707–6372.

Contracts   Persons seeking to do business with the Library of Congress should contact the Library of Congress, Contracts and Logistics Services, Landover Center Annex, 1701 Brightseat Road, Landover, MD 20785. Phone, 202–707–8717.

Copyright Services   Information about the copyright law (title 17 of the U.S. Code), the method of securing copyright, and registration procedures may be obtained by writing to the Library of Congress, Copyright Office, Washington, DC 20559–6000. Phone, 202–707–3000. Copyright information is also available through the Internet, at http://www.loc.gov/. Registration application forms may be ordered by calling the forms hotline at 202–707–9100. Reports on copyright facts found in the records of the Copyright Office may be obtained for a fee of $20 an hour; any member of the public, however, may use without charge the Copyright Card Catalog in the Copyright Office. Copyright Office records in machine-readable form cataloged from January 1, 1978, to the present are available through the Internet, at http://www.loc.gov/. The Copyright Information Office is located in Room LM–401, James Madison Memorial Building, 101 Independence Avenue SE., Washington, DC 20559–6000, and is open to the public Monday through Friday, 8:30 a.m. to 5 p.m. eastern time, except Federal holidays.

Employment   Employment inquiries and applications (on SF–171, OF–612, or Federal-format résumé) should be directed to the Library of Congress, Directorate of Personnel, Washington, DC 20540–2200. Potential applicants are encouraged to visit the Employment Office, Room LM–107, 101 Independence Avenue SE., where current vacancy announcements and application forms are available. The personnel hotline provides recorded information on career opportunities. Phone, 202–707–4315. Internet, http://www.loc.gov/.

Photoduplication Service Copies of manuscripts, prints, photographs, maps, and book material not subject to copyright and other restrictions are available for a fee. Order forms for photoreproduction and price schedules are available from the Library of Congress, Photoduplication Service, Washington, DC 20540–4570. Phone, 202–707–5640.

Publications A list of Library of Congress publications, many of which are of interest to the general public, is available through the Internet, at http://www.loc.gov/. A monthly *Calendar of Events,* listing programs and exhibitions at the Library of Congress, can be mailed regularly to persons within 100 miles of Washington, DC. Make requests to the Library of Congress, Office Systems Services, Washington, DC 20540–9440.

Reference and Bibliographic Services Guidance is offered to readers in the identification and use of the material in the Library's collections, and reference service in answer to inquiries is offered to those who have exhausted local, State, and regional resources. Persons requiring services that cannot be performed by the Library staff can be supplied with names of private researchers who work on a fee basis. Requests for information should be directed to the Library of Congress, National Reference Service, Washington, DC 20540–4720. Phone, 202–707–5522. Fax, 202–707–1389.

Research and Reference Services in Science and Technology Reference specialists in the Science and Technology Division answer without charge brief technical inquiries entailing a bibliographic response. Of special interest is a technical report and standards collection exceeding 3.6 million titles. Most of these are in microform and are readily accessible for viewing in the Science Reading Room. Requests for reference service should be directed to the Library of Congress, Science and Technology Division, Washington, DC 20540–4750. Phone, 202–707–5639.

An informal series of reference guides is issued by the Science and Technology Division under the general title *LC Science Tracer Bullet.* These guides are designed to help a reader locate published material on a subject about which he or she has only general knowledge. For a list of available titles, write to the Library of Congress, Science and Technology Division, Reference Section, Washington, DC 20540–4751. Phone, 202–707–5639.

Research Services in General Topics Federal Government agencies can procure directed research and analytical products on foreign and domestic topics using the collections of the Library of Congress through the Federal Research Division. Science, technology, humanities, and social science topics of research are conducted by staff specialists exclusively on behalf of Federal agencies on a fee-for-service basis. Requests for service should be directed to Library of Congress, Federal Research Division, Marketing Office, Washington, DC 20540–4840. Phone, 202–707–3909. Fax, 202–245–3920.

For further information, contact the Public Affairs Office, Library of Congress, 101 Independence Avenue SE., Washington, DC 20540–8610. Phone, 202–707–2905. Fax, 202–707–9199. Internet, http://www.loc.gov/.

CONGRESSIONAL BUDGET OFFICE

Second and D Streets SW., Washington, DC 20515
Phone, 202–226–2621. Internet, http://www.cbo.gov/.

Director	JUNE E. O'NEILL
Deputy Director	JAMES L. BLUM
General Counsel	GAIL DEL BALZO
Assistant Director for Administration and Information	DAVID M. DELQUADRO
Assistant Director for Budget Analysis	PAUL N. VAN DE WATER
Assistant Director for Macroeconomic Analysis	ROBERT A. DENNIS
Assistant Director for Tax Analysis	FRANK SAMMARTINO, *Acting*
Assistant Director for Natural Resources and Commerce	JAN PAUL ACTON
Assistant Director for Health and Human Resources	JOSEPH R. ANTOS
Assistant Director for National Security	CHRISTOPHER JEHN
Assistant Director for Special Studies	ARLENE HOLEN

The Congressional Budget Office provides the Congress with assessments of the economic impact of the Federal budget.

The Congressional Budget Office (CBO) was established by the Congressional Budget Act of 1974 (2 U.S.C. 601), which also created a procedure by which the United States Congress considers and acts upon the annual Federal budget. This process enables the Congress to have an overview of the Federal budget and to make overall decisions regarding spending and taxing levels and the deficit or surplus these levels incur.

The Office provides Congress with basic budget data and with analyses of alternative fiscal, budgetary, and programmatic policy issues.

Activities

Economic Forecasting and Fiscal Policy Analysis The Federal budget affects and is affected by the national economy. The Congressional Budget Office provides Congress with biannual forecasts of the economy and analyses of economic trends and alternative fiscal policies.

Scorekeeping Under the budget process the Congress establishes, by concurrent resolution, targets (or ceilings) for overall expenditures, budget authority and budget outlays, and for broad functional categories. The Congress also establishes targets (or

ceilings) for the levels of revenues, the deficit, and the public debt. The Office "keeps score" for the Congress by monitoring the results of congressional action on individual authorization, appropriation, and revenue bills against the targets (or ceilings) specified in the concurrent resolution.

Cost Projections The Office prepares multiyear cost estimates for carrying out any public bill or resolution reported by congressional committees. As soon as practicable after the beginning of each fiscal year, CBO also provides multiyear projections on the costs of continuing current Federal spending and taxation policies.

Annual Report on the Budget The Office is responsible for submitting to the House and Senate Budget Committees each year a report with respect to fiscal policy that includes alternative spending and revenue levels and 5-year baseline projections of the Federal budget.

Federal Mandates To better assess the impact of laws on State, local, and tribal governments and the private sector, the Congress passed the Unfunded Mandates Reform Act of 1995. The act amends the Congressional Budget Act to require CBO to give authorizing committees a

CONGRESSIONAL BUDGET OFFICE

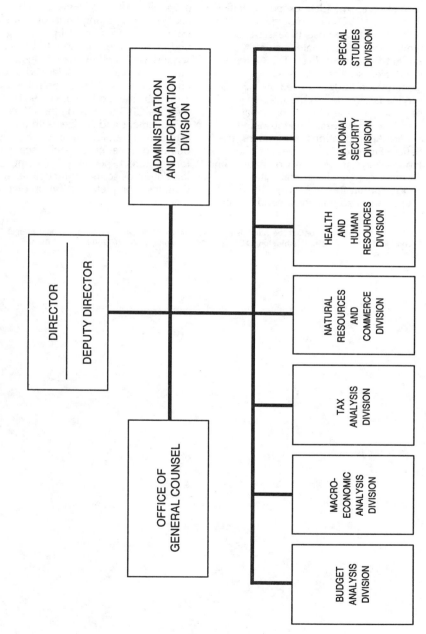

statement about whether reported bills contain Federal mandates. If the 5-year direct costs of an intergovernmental or private-sector mandate exceed specified thresholds, CBO must provide an estimate of those costs (if feasible) and the basis of the estimate.

Budget-Related Studies The Office undertakes studies requested by the Congress on budget-related areas. This service is provided in the following order of priority to: the House and Senate Budget Committees; the House and Senate Appropriations Committees, the Senate Finance Committee, and the House Ways and Means Committee; and all other congressional committees.

Sequestration Reports The Office prepares advisory reports mandated by the Balanced Budget and Emergency Deficit Control Act of 1985, as amended (2 U.S.C. 901), to estimate whether proposed spending levels breach categorical spending limits and, if so, to estimate the amount and percentage of budget resources that should be sequestered to eliminate any excesses.

Pay-As-You-Go The Balanced Budget and Emergency Deficit Control Act of 1985, as amended (2 U.S.C. 901), requires CBO to provide the Office of Management and Budget with an estimate of the amount of change in outlays or receipts for each fiscal year for any direct spending or receipts legislation as soon as practicable after Congress completes action on that legislation.

For further information, contact the Administration and Information Division, Congressional Budget Office, Second and D Streets SW., Washington, DC 20515. Phone, 202–226–2600. Internet, http://www.cbo.gov/.

Judicial Branch

JUDICIAL BRANCH

THE SUPREME COURT OF THE UNITED STATES

United States Supreme Court Building
One First Street NE., Washington, DC 20543
Phone, 202–479–3000

Members:

Chief Justice of the United States	WILLIAM H. REHNQUIST
Associate Justices	JOHN PAUL STEVENS, SANDRA DAY O'CONNOR, ANTONIN SCALIA, ANTHONY M. KENNEDY, DAVID H. SOUTER, CLARENCE THOMAS, RUTH BADER GINSBURG, STEPHEN G. BREYER

Officers:

Clerk	WILLIAM K. SUTER
Reporter of Decisions	FRANK D. WAGNER
Librarian	SHELLEY L. DOWLING
Marshal	DALE E. BOSLEY

Article III, section 1, of the Constitution of the United States provides that "[t]he judicial Power of the United States, shall be vested in one supreme Court, and in such inferior Courts as the Congress may from time to time ordain and establish." The Supreme Court of the United States was created in accordance with this provision and by authority of the Judiciary Act of September 24, 1789 (1 Stat. 73). It was organized on February 2, 1790.

The Supreme Court comprises the Chief Justice of the United States and such number of Associate Justices as may be fixed by Congress. Under that authority, and by virtue of act of June 25, 1948 (28 U.S.C. 1), the number of Associate Justices is eight. Power to nominate the Justices is vested in the President of the United States, and appointments are made with the advice and consent of the Senate. Article III, section 1, of the Constitution further provides that "[t]he Judges, both of the supreme and inferior Courts, shall hold their Offices during good Behaviour, and shall, at stated Times, receive for their Services, a Compensation, which shall not be diminished during their Continuance in Office." A Justice may, if so desired, retire at the age of 70 after serving for 10 years as a Federal judge or at age 65 after 15 years of service.

The Clerk, the Reporter of Decisions, the Librarian, and the Marshal are appointed by the Court to assist in the performance of its functions. Other Court officers, including the Administrative Assistant, the Court Counsel, the Curator, the Director of Data Systems, and the Public Information Officer, are appointed by the Chief Justice to assist him with the administrative aspects of his position.

The library is open to members of the bar of the Court, attorneys for the various Federal departments and agencies, and Members of Congress. Only members of the bar of the Court may practice before the Supreme Court.

The term of the Court begins, by law, the first Monday in October of each year and continues as long as the business before the Court requires, usually until about the end of June. Six members constitute a quorum. Approximately 7,000 cases are passed upon in the course of a term. In addition, some 1,200 applications of various kinds are filed each year that can be acted upon by a single Justice.

Jurisdiction   According to the Constitution (art. III, sec. 2), "[t]he judicial Power shall extend to all Cases, in Law and Equity, arising under this Constitution, the Laws of the United States, and Treaties made, or which shall be made, under their Authority;—to all Cases affecting Ambassadors, other public Ministers and Consuls;—to all Cases of admiralty and maritime Jurisdiction;—to Controversies to which the United States shall be a Party;—to Controversies between two or more States;—between a State and Citizens of another State;—between Citizens of different States;—between Citizens of the same State claiming Lands under Grants of different States, and between a State, or the Citizens thereof, and foreign States, Citizens or Subjects.

"In all Cases affecting Ambassadors, other public Ministers and Consuls, and those in which a State shall be Party, the supreme Court shall have original Jurisdiction. In all the other Cases before mentioned, the supreme Court shall have appellate Jurisdiction, both as to Law and Fact, with such Exceptions, and under such Regulations as the Congress shall make."

Appellate jurisdiction has been conferred upon the Supreme Court by various statutes, under the authority given Congress by the Constitution. The basic statute effective at this time in conferring and controlling jurisdiction of the Supreme Court may be found in 28 U.S.C. 1251, 1253, 1254, 1257–1259, and various special statutes. Congress has no authority to change the original jurisdiction of this Court.

Rulemaking Power   Congress has from time to time conferred upon the Supreme Court power to prescribe rules of procedure to be followed by the lower courts of the United States. Pursuant to these statutes there are now in force rules promulgated by the Court to govern civil and criminal cases in the district courts, bankruptcy proceedings, admiralty cases, appellate proceedings, and the trial of misdemeanors before U.S. magistrate judges.

For further information concerning the Supreme Court, contact the Public Information Office, United States Supreme Court Building, One First Street NE., Washington, DC 20543. Phone, 202–479–3211.

Lower Courts

Article III of the Constitution declares, in section 1, that the judicial power of the United States shall be invested in one Supreme Court and in "such inferior Courts as the Congress may from time to time ordain and establish." The Supreme Court has held that these constitutional courts ". . . share in the exercise of the judicial power defined in that section, can be invested with no other jurisdiction, and have judges who hold office during good behavior, with no power in Congress to provide otherwise."

United States Courts of Appeals   The courts of appeals are intermediate appellate courts created by act of March 3, 1891 (28 U.S.C. ch. 3), to relieve the Supreme Court of considering all appeals in cases originally decided by the Federal trial courts. They are empowered to review all final decisions and certain interlocutory decisions (18 U.S.C. 3731; 28 U.S.C. 1291, 1292) of district courts. They also are empowered to review and enforce orders of many Federal administrative bodies. The decisions of the courts of appeals are final except as they are subject to review on writ of certiorari by the Supreme Court.

The United States is divided geographically into 12 judicial circuits, including the District of Columbia. Each circuit has a court of appeals (28 U.S.C. 41, 1294). Each of the 50 States is assigned to one of the circuits, and the Territories are assigned variously to the first, third, and ninth circuits. There is also a Court of Appeals for the Federal Circuit, which has nationwide jurisdiction defined by subject matter. At present each court of appeals has from 6 to 28 permanent circuit judgeships (179 in all), depending upon the amount of judicial work in the circuit. Circuit judges hold their offices during good behavior as provided by Article III, section 1, of the Constitution. The judge senior in commission who is under 70 years of age (65 at inception of term), has been in office at least 1 year, and has not previously been chief judge, serves as the chief judge of the circuit for a 7-year term. One of the justices of the Supreme Court is assigned as circuit justice for each of the 13 judicial circuits. Each court of appeals normally hears cases in panels consisting of three judges but may sit *en banc* with all judges present.

The judges of each circuit (except the Federal Circuit) by vote determine the size of the judicial council for the circuit, which consists of the chief judge and an equal number of circuit and district judges. The council considers the state of Federal judicial business in the circuit and may "make all necessary and appropriate orders for [its] effective and expeditious administration . . ." (28 U.S.C. 332). The chief judge of each circuit may summon periodically a judicial conference of all judges of the circuit, including members of the bar, to discuss the business of the Federal courts of the circuit (28 U.S.C. 333). The chief

judge of each circuit and a district judge elected from each of the 12 geographical circuits, together with the chief judge of the Court of International Trade, serve as members of the Judicial Conference of the United States, over which the Chief Justice of the United States presides. This is the governing body for the administration of the Federal judicial system as a whole (28 U.S.C. 331).

United States Court of Appeals for the Federal Circuit This court was established under Article III of the Constitution pursuant to the Federal Courts Improvement Act of 1982 (28 U.S.C. 41, 44, 48), as successor to the former United States Court of Customs and Patent Appeals and the United States Court of Claims. The jurisdiction of the court is nationwide (as provided by 28 U.S.C. 1295) and includes appeals from the district courts in patent cases; appeals from the district courts in contract, and certain other civil actions in which the United States is a defendant; and appeals from final decisions of the U.S. Court of International Trade, the U.S. Court of Federal Claims, and the U.S. Court of Veterans Appeals. The jurisdiction of the court also includes the review of administrative rulings by the Patent and Trademark Office, U.S. International Trade Commission, Secretary of Commerce, agency boards of contract appeals, and the Merit Systems Protection Board, as well as rulemaking of the Department of Veterans Affairs; review of decisions of the U.S. Senate Select Committee on Ethics concerning discrimination claims of Senate employees; and review of a final order of an entity to be designated by the President concerning discrimination claims of Presidential appointees.

The court consists of 12 circuit judges. It sits in panels of three or more on each case and may also hear or rehear a case *en banc*. The court sits principally in Washington, DC, and may hold court wherever any court of appeals sits (28 U.S.C. 48).

Judicial Circuits—United States Courts of Appeals

Circuit	Judges	Official Station
	District of Columbia Circuit	
(*Clerk*: Mark J. Langer; *Circuit Executive*: Jill C. Sayenga; Washington, DC)	*Circuit Justice* Chief Justice William H. Rehnquist	
	Circuit Judges Harry T. Edwards, *Chief Judge* Patricia M. Wald Laurence H. Silberman Stephen F. Williams Douglas H. Ginsburg David Bryan Sentelle Karen LeCraft Henderson A. Raymond Randolph Judith W. Rogers David S. Tatel Merrick B. Garland (Vacancy)	Washington, DC Washington, DC Washington, DC Washington, DC Washington, DC Washington, DC Washington, DC Washington, DC Washington, DC Washington, DC Washington, DC
	First Circuit	
Districts of Maine, New Hampshire, Massachusetts, Rhode Island, and Puerto Rico (*Clerk*: Phoebe Morse; *Circuit Executive*: Vincent F. Flanagan; Boston, MA)	*Circuit Justice* Justice David H. Souter	
	Circuit Judges Juan R. Torruella, *Chief Judge* Bruce M. Selya Michael Boudin Norman H. Stahl Sandra L. Lynch (Vacancy)	Hato Rey, PR Providence, RI Boston, MA Concord, NH Boston, MA
	Second Circuit	
Districts of Vermont, Connecticut, northern New York, southern New York, eastern New York, and western New York (*Clerk*: George Lange III; *Circuit Executive*: George Lange III, *Acting* ;New York, NY)	*Circuit Justice* Justice Ruth Bader Ginsburg	
	Circuit Judges Ralph K. Winter, Jr., *Chief Judge* Amalya Lyle Kearse John M. Walker, Jr. Dennis G. Jacobs Pierre N. Leval Guido Calabresi Jose A. Cabranes Fred I. Parker (5 vacancies)	New Haven, CT New York, NY New York, NY New York, NY New York, NY New Haven, CT New Haven, CT Burlington, VT
	Third Circuit	
Districts of New Jersey, eastern Pennsylvania, middle Pennsylvania, western Pennsylvania, Delaware, and the Virgin Islands (*Clerk*: P. Douglas Sisk; *Circuit Executive*: Toby D. Slawsky; Philadelphia, PA)	*Circuit Justice* Justice David H. Souter	
	Circuit Judges Edward R. Becker, *Chief Judge* Dolores Korman Sloviter Walter K. Stapleton Carol Los Mansmann Morton I. Greenberg Anthony J. Scirica Robert E. Cowen Richard Lowell Nygaard Samuel A. Alito, Jr. Jane R. Roth Timothy K. Lewis Theodore A. McKee Marjorie O. Rendell (Vacancy)	Philadelphia, PA Philadelphia, PA Wilmington, DE Pittsburgh, PA Trenton, NJ Philadelphia, PA Trenton, NJ Erie, PA Newark, NJ Wilmington, DE Pittsburgh, PA Philadelphia, PA Philadelphia, PA
	Fourth Circuit	
Districts of Maryland, northern West Virginia,	*Circuit Justice* Chief Justice William H. Rehnquist	

Judicial Circuits—United States Courts of Appeals—Continued

Circuit	Judges	Official Station
southern West Virginia, eastern Virginia, western Virginia, eastern North Carolina, middle North Carolina, western North Carolina, and South Carolina (*Clerk*: Patricia S. Connor; *Circuit Executive*: Samuel W. Phillips; Richmond, VA)	*Circuit Judges* James Harvie Wilkinson III, *Chief Judge* Sam J. Ervin III H. Emory Widener, Jr. Francis D. Murnaghan, Jr. William W. Wilkins, Jr. Paul V. Niemeyer Clyde H. Hamilton J. Michael Luttig Karen J. Williams M. Blane Michael Diana Gribbon Motz (4 vacancies)	Charlottesville, VA Morganton, NC Abingdon, VA Baltimore, MD Greenville, SC Baltimore, MD Columbia, SC Alexandria, VA Orangeburg, SC Charleston, WV Baltimore, MD

Fifth Circuit

Circuit	Judges	Official Station
Districts of northern Mississippi, southern Mississippi, eastern Louisiana, middle Louisiana, western Louisiana, northern Texas, southern Texas, eastern Texas, and western Texas (*Clerk*: Charles R. Fulbruge III; *Circuit Executive*: Gregory A. Nussel; New Orleans, LA)	*Circuit Justice* Justice Antonin Scalia *Circuit Judges* Henry A. Politz, *Chief Judge* Carolyn Dineen King E. Grady Jolly Patrick E. Higginbotham W. Eugene Davis Edith H. Jones Jerry Edwin Smith John M. Duhe, Jr. Rhesa H. Barksdale Jacques L. Wiener, Jr. Emilio M. Garza Harold R. Demoss, Jr. Fortunado P. Benavides Carl E. Stewart Robert M. Parker James L. Dennis (Vacancy)	Shreveport, LA Houston, TX Jackson, MS Dallas, TX Lafayette, LA Houston, TX Houston, TX Lafayette, LA Jackson, MS Shreveport, LA San Antonio, TX Houston, TX Austin, TX Shreveport, LA Tyler, TX New Orleans, LA

Sixth Circuit

Circuit	Judges	Official Station
Districts of northern Ohio, southern Ohio, eastern Michigan, western Michigan, eastern Kentucky, western Kentucky, eastern Tennessee, middle Tennessee, and western Tennessee (*Clerk*: Leonard Green; *Circuit Executive*: James A. Higgins; Cincinnati, OH)	*Circuit Justice* Justice John Paul Stevens *Circuit Judges* Boyce F. Martin, Jr., *Chief Judge* Gilbert S. Merritt Cornelia G. Kennedy David A. Nelson James L. Ryan Danny J. Boggs Alan E. Norris Richard F. Suhrheinrich Eugene E. Siler, Jr. Alice M. Batchelder Martha Craig Daughtrey Karen Nelson Moore Ransey Guy Cole, Jr. Eric L. Clay Ronald Lee Gilman (Vacancy)	Louisville, KY Nashville, TN Detroit, MI Cincinnati, OH Detroit, MI Louisville, KY Columbus, OH Lansing, MI London, KY Medina, OH Nashville, TN Cleveland, OH Columbus, OH Detroit, MI Memphis, TN

Seventh Circuit

Circuit	Judges	Official Station
Districts of northern Indiana, southern Indiana, northern Illinois, central Illinois, southern Illinois, eastern Wisconsin, and western Wisconsin (*Clerk*: Gino J. Agnello; *Circuit Executive*: Collins T. Fitzpatrick;	*Circuit Justice* Justice John Paul Stevens *Circuit Judges* Richard A. Posner, *Chief Judge* Walter J. Cummings John L. Coffey Joel M. Flaum Frank H. Easterbrook	Chicago, IL Chicago, IL Milwaukee, WI Chicago, IL Chicago, IL

Judicial Circuits—United States Courts of Appeals—Continued

Circuit	Judges	Official Station
Chicago, IL)	Kenneth F. Ripple	South Bend, IN
	Daniel A. Manion	South Bend, IN
	Michael S. Kanne	Lafayette, IN
	Ilana Diamond Rovner	Chicago, IL
	Diane P. Wood	Chicago, IL
	Terence T. Evans	Milwaukee, WI

Eighth Circuit

Districts of Minnesota, northern Iowa, southern Iowa, eastern Missouri, western Missouri, eastern Arkansas, western Arkansas, Nebraska, North Dakota, and South Dakota (*Clerk:* Michael Ellis Gans; *Circuit Executive:* Millie B. Adams; St. Louis, MO)	*Circuit Justice* Justice Clarence Thomas	
	Circuit Judges	
	Pasco M. Bowman II, *Chief Judge*	Kansas City, MO
	Richard S. Arnold	Little Rock, AR
	Theodore McMillian	St. Louis, MO
	George G. Fagg	Des Moines, IA
	Roger L. Wollman	Sioux Falls, SD
	Frank J. Magill	Fargo, ND
	Clarence Arlen Beam	Lincoln, NE
	James B. Loken	St. Paul, MN
	David R. Hansen	Cedar Rapids, IA
	Morris S. Arnold	Little Rock, AR
	Diana E. Murphy	Minneapolis, MN

Ninth Circuit

Districts of northern California, eastern California, central California, southern California, Oregon, Nevada, Montana, eastern Washington, western Washington, Idaho, Arizona, Alaska, Hawaii, Territory of Guam, and District Court for the Northern Mariana Islands (*Clerk:* Cathy A. Catterson; *Circuit Executive:* Gregory B. Walters; San Francisco, CA)	*Circuit Justice* Justice Sandra Day O'Connor	
	Circuit Judges	
	Procter Hug, Jr., *Chief Judge*	Reno, NV
	James R. Browning	San Francisco, CA
	Mary M. Schroeder	Phoenix, AZ
	Betty B. Fletcher	Seattle, WA
	Harry Pregerson	Woodland Hills, CA
	Stephan Reinhardt	Los Angeles, CA
	Melvin Brunetti	Reno, NV
	Alex Kozinski	Pasadena, CA
	David R. Thompson	San Diego, CA
	Diarmuid F. O'Scannlain	Portland, OR
	Stephen S. Trott	Boise, ID
	Ferdinand F. Fernandez	Pasadena, CA
	Pamela A. Rymer	Pasadena, CA
	Thomas G. Nelson	Boise, ID
	Andrew J. Kleinfeld	Fairbanks, AK
	Michael D. Hawkins	Phoenix, AZ
	A. Wallace Tashima	Pasadena, CA
	Sidney R. Thomas	Billings, MT
	Barry G. Silverman	Phoenix, AZ
	(9 vacancies)	

Tenth Circuit

Districts of Colorado, Wyoming, Utah, Kansas, eastern Oklahoma, western Oklahoma, northern Oklahoma, and New Mexico (*Clerk:* Patrick J. Fisher; *Circuit Executive:* Robert L. Hoecker; Denver, CO)	*Circuit Justice* Justice Stephen G. Breyer	
	Circuit Judges	
	Stephanie K. Seymour, *Chief Judge*	Tulsa, OK
	John C. Porfilio	Denver, CO
	Stephen H. Anderson	Salt Lake City, UT
	Deanell Reece Tacha	Lawrence, KS
	Bobby R. Baldock	Roswell, NM
	Wade Brorby	Cheyenne, WY
	David M. Ebel	Denver, CO
	Paul J. Kelly, Jr.	Santa Fe, NM
	Robert H. Henry	Oklahoma City, OK
	Mary Beck Briscoe	Topeka, KS
	Carlos F. Lucero	Denver, CO
	Michael R. Murphy	Salt Lake City, UT

Judicial Circuits—United States Courts of Appeals—Continued

Circuit	Judges	Official Station
	Eleventh Circuit	
Districts of northern Georgia, middle Georgia, southern Georgia, northern Florida, middle Florida, southern Florida, northern Alabama, middle Alabama, southern Alabama (*Clerk:* Thomas Kahn; *Circuit Executive:* Norman E. Zoller; Atlanta, GA)	*Circuit Justice* Justice Anthony M. Kennedy *Circuit Judges* Joseph Woodrow Hatchett, *Chief Judge* Gerald B. Tjoflat R. Lanier Anderson III J.L. Edmondson Emmett Ripley Cox Stanley F. Birch, Jr. Joel F. Dubina Susan H. Black Edward E. Carnes Rosemary Barkett Frank Mays Hull Stanley Marcus	Tallahassee, FL Jacksonville, FL Macon, GA Atlanta, GA Mobile, AL Atlanta, GA Montgomery, AL Jacksonville, FL Montgomery, AL Miami, FL Atlanta, GA Miami, FL

Federal Circuit—Washington, DC

Circuit Justice
   Chief Justice William H. Rehnquist

Chief Judge
   Haldane Robert Mayer

Judges
   Giles S. Rich
   Pauline Newman
   Paul R. Michel
   S. Jay Plager
   Alan D. Lourie
   Raymond C. Clevenger III
   Randall R. Rader
   Alvin A. Schall
   William C. Bryson
   Arthur J. Gajarsa
   (Vacancy)

   Clerk: Jan Horbaly
   Administrative Services Officer: Ruth A. Butler

United States District Courts The district courts are the trial courts of general Federal jurisdiction. Each State has at least one district court, while the larger States have as many as four. Altogether there are 89 district courts in the 50 States, plus the one in the District of Columbia. In addition, the Commonwealth of Puerto Rico has a district court with jurisdiction corresponding to that of district courts in the various States.

At present, each district court has from 2 to 28 Federal district judgeships, depending upon the amount of judicial work within its territory. Only one judge is usually required to hear and decide a case in a district court, but in some limited cases it is required that three judges be called together to comprise the court (28 U.S.C. 2284). The judge senior in commission who is under 70 years of age (65 at inception of term),

has been in office for at least 1 year, and has not previously been chief judge, serves as chief judge for a 7-year term. There are altogether 610 permanent district judgeships in the 50 States and 15 in the District of Columbia. There are 7 district judgeships in Puerto Rico. District judges hold their offices during good behavior as provided by Article III, section 1, of the Constitution. However, Congress may create temporary judgeships for a court with the provision that when a vacancy occurs in that district, such vacancy shall not be filled. Each district court has one or more United States magistrate judges and bankruptcy judges, a clerk, a United States attorney, a United States marshal, probation officers, court reporters, and their staffs. The jurisdiction of the district courts is set forth in title 28, chapter 85, of the United States Code and at 18 U.S.C. 3231.

Cases from the district courts are reviewable on appeal by the applicable court of appeals.

Territorial Courts Pursuant to its authority to govern the Territories (art. IV, sec. 3, clause 2, of the Constitution), Congress has established district courts in the territories of Guam and the Virgin Islands. The District Court of the Canal Zone was abolished on April 1, 1982, pursuant to the Panama Canal Act of 1979 (22 U.S.C. 3601 note). Congress has also established a district court in the Northern Mariana Islands, which presently is administered by the United States under a trusteeship agreement with the United Nations. These Territorial courts have jurisdiction not only over the subjects described in the judicial article of the Constitution but also over many local matters that, within the States, are decided in State courts. The district court of Puerto Rico, by contrast, is established under Article III, is classified like other "district courts," and is called a "court of the United States" (28 U.S.C. 451). There is one judge each in Guam and the Northern Mariana Islands, and two in the Virgin Islands. The judges in these courts are appointed for terms of 10 years.

For further information concerning the lower courts, contact the Administrative Office of the United States Courts, Thurgood Marshall Federal Judiciary Building, One Columbus Circle NE., Washington, DC 20544. Phone, 202–273–0107.

United States Court of International Trade This court was originally established as the Board of United States General Appraisers by act of June 10, 1890, which conferred upon it jurisdiction theretofore held by the district and circuit courts in actions arising under the tariff acts (19 U.S.C. ch. 4). The act of May 28, 1926 (19 U.S.C. 405a), created the United States Customs Court to supersede the Board; by acts of August 7, 1939, and June 25, 1948 (28 U.S.C. 1582, 1583), the court was integrated into the United States court structure, organization, and procedure. The act of July 14, 1956 (28 U.S.C. 251), established the court as a court of record of the United States under Article III of the Constitution.

The Customs Courts Act of 1980 (28 U.S.C. 251) constituted the court as the United States Court of International Trade and revised provisions relating to its jurisdiction. The Court of International Trade has all the powers in law and equity of a district court.

The Court of International Trade has jurisdiction over any civil action against the United States arising from Federal laws governing import transactions. This includes classification and valuation cases, as well as authority to review certain agency determinations under the Trade Agreements Act of 1979 (19 U.S.C. 2501) involving antidumping and countervailing duty matters. In addition, it has exclusive jurisdiction of civil actions to review determinations as to the eligibility of workers, firms, and communities for adjustment assistance under the Trade Act of 1974 (19 U.S.C. 2101). Civil actions commenced by the United States to recover customs duties, to recover on a customs bond, or for certain civil penalties alleging fraud or negligence are also within the exclusive jurisdiction of the court.

The court is composed of a chief judge and eight judges, not more than five of whom may belong to any one political party. Any of its judges may be temporarily designated and assigned by the Chief Justice of the United States to sit as a court of appeals or district court judge in any circuit or district. The court has a clerk and deputy clerks, a librarian, court reporters, and other supporting personnel. Cases before the court may be tried before a jury. Under the Federal Courts Improvement Act of 1982 (28 U.S.C. 1295), appeals are taken to the U.S. Court of Appeals for the Federal Circuit, and ultimately review may be sought in appropriate cases in the Supreme Court of the United States.

The principal offices are located in New York, NY, but the court is empowered to hear and determine cases arising at any port or place within the jurisdiction of the United States.

For further information, contact the Clerk, United States Court of International Trade, One Federal Plaza, New York, NY 10007. Phone, 212–264–2814.

Judicial Panel on Multidistrict Litigation The Panel, created by act of April 29, 1968 (28 U.S.C. 1407), and consisting of seven Federal judges designated by the Chief Justice from the courts of appeals and district courts, is authorized to temporarily transfer to a single district, for coordinated or consolidated pretrial proceedings, civil actions pending in different districts that involve one or more common questions of fact.

For further information, contact the Clerk, Judicial Panel on Multidistrict Litigation, Room G–255, Thurgood Marshall Federal Judiciary Building, One Columbus Circle NE., Washington, DC 20002. Phone, 202–273–2800.

Special Courts

The Supreme Court has held that ". . . Article III [of the Constitution] does not express the full authority of Congress to create courts, and that other Articles invest Congress with powers in the exertion of which it may create inferior courts and clothe them with functions deemed essential or helpful in carrying those powers into execution." Such courts, known as legislative courts, have functions which ". . . are directed to the execution of one or more of such powers and are prescribed by Congress independently of section 2 of Article III; and their judges hold office for such term as Congress prescribes, whether it be a fixed period of years or during good behavior." Appeals from the decisions of these courts, with the exception of the U.S. Tax Court and the U.S. Court of Appeals for the Armed Forces, may be taken to the U.S. Court of Appeals for the Federal Circuit. Appeals from the decisions of the Tax Court may be taken to the court of appeals in which judicial circuit the case was initially heard. Certain decisions of the U.S. Court of Appeals for the Armed Forces are reviewable by writ of certiorari in the Supreme Court.

United States Court of Federal Claims The Claims Court was established on October 1, 1982, as an Article I court (28 U.S.C. 171, Article I, U.S. Constitution). The Claims Court succeeds to the original trial jurisdiction of the former Court of Claims, as provided for in 28 U.S.C. 1491 *et seq.* Its name was changed to the United States Court of Federal Claims by the Federal Courts Administration Act of 1992 (28 U.S.C. 1 note, 106 Stat. 4516). The court is composed of a chief judge, designated by the President, and 15 associate judges. All judges are appointed for 15-year terms by the President with the advice and consent of the Senate.

The court has jurisdiction over claims seeking money judgments against the United States. A claim must be founded upon either: the United States Constitution; an act of Congress; the regulation of an executive department;

an express or implied-in-fact contract with the United States; or damages, liquidated or unliquidated, in cases not sounding in tort.

If a bidder files a claim with the court either before or after the award of a Government contract, it has jurisdiction to grant declaratory judgments and equitable relief. Under the Contract Disputes Act (41 U.S.C. 601 *et seq.*), the court may render judgments upon a claim by or against a contractor, or any dispute between a contractor and the United States Government arising under the act.

The Congress, from time to time, also grants the court jurisdiction over specific types of claims against the United States. The National Vaccine Injury Compensation Program, established by 42 U.S.C. 300aa–10 (the Vaccine Act), is an example of such special jurisdiction.

The court also reports to Congress on bills referred by either the House of Representatives or the Senate. Judgments of the court are final and conclusive on both the claimant and the United States. All judgments are subject to appeal to the U.S. Court of Appeals for the Federal Circuit. Collateral to any judgment, the court may issue orders directing the restoration to office or status of any claimant or the correction of applicable records.

The court's jurisdiction is nationwide. Trials are conducted before individual judges at locations most convenient and least expensive to citizens.

For further information, contact the Clerk, United States Court of Federal Claims, 717 Madison Place NW., Washington, DC 20005. Phone, 202–219–9657.

United States Court of Appeals for the Armed Forces This court was established under Article I of the Constitution of the United States pursuant to act of May 5, 1950, as amended (10 U.S.C. 867). Subject only to certiorari review by the Supreme Court of the United States in a limited number of cases, the court serves as the final appellate tribunal to review court-martial convictions of all the Armed

Forces. It is exclusively an appellate criminal court, consisting of five civilian judges who are appointed for 15-year terms by the President with the advice and consent of the Senate. The court is called upon to exercise jurisdiction to review the record in all cases:

—extending to death;

—certified to the court by a Judge Advocate General of an armed force or by the General Counsel of the Department of Transportation, acting for the Coast Guard; or

—petitioned by accused who have received a sentence of confinement for 1 year or more, and/or a punitive discharge.

The court also exercises authority under the All Writs Act (28 U.S.C. 1651 (a)).

In addition, the judges of the court are required by law to work jointly with the senior uniformed lawyer from each armed force, the Chief Counsel of the Coast Guard, and two members of the public appointed by the Secretary of Defense, to make an annual comprehensive survey and to report annually to the Congress on the operation and progress of the military justice system under the Uniform Code of Military Justice, and to recommend improvements wherever necessary.

For further information, contact the Clerk, United States Court of Appeals for the Armed Forces, 450 E Street NW., Washington, DC 20442–0001. Phone, 202–761–1448. Fax, 202–761–4672.

United States Tax Court This is a court of record under Article I of the Constitution of the United States (26 U.S.C. 7441). Currently an independent judicial body in the legislative branch, the court was originally created as the United States Board of Tax Appeals, an independent agency in the executive branch, by the Revenue Act of 1924 (43 Stat. 336) and continued by the Revenue Act of 1926 (44 Stat. 105), the Internal Revenue Codes of 1939, 1954, and 1986. The name was changed to the Tax Court of the United States by the Revenue Act of 1942 (56 Stat. 957), and the Article I status and change in name to United States Tax Court were effected

by the Tax Reform Act of 1969 (83 Stat. 730).

The court is composed of 19 judges. Its strength is augmented by senior judges who may be recalled by the chief judge to perform further judicial duties and by 14 special trial judges who are appointed by the chief judge and serve at the pleasure of the court. The chief judge is elected biennially from among the 19 judges of the court.

The Tax Court tries and adjudicates controversies involving the existence of deficiencies or overpayments in income, estate, gift, and generation-skipping transfer taxes in cases where deficiencies have been determined by the Commissioner of Internal Revenue. It also hears cases commenced by transferees and fiduciaries who have been issued notices of liability by the Commissioner.

The Tax Court has jurisdiction to redetermine excise taxes and penalties imposed on private foundations. Similar jurisdiction over excise taxes has been conferred with regard to public charities, qualified pension plans, and real estate investment trusts.

At the option of the individual taxpayer, simplified procedures may be utilized for the trials of small tax cases, provided that in a case conducted under these procedures the decision of the court would be final and not subject to review by any court. The jurisdictional maximum for such cases is $10,000 for any disputed year.

In disputes relating to public inspection of written determinations by the Internal Revenue Service, the Tax Court has jurisdiction to restrain disclosure or to obtain additional disclosure of written determinations or background file documents and, at the request of any person, to order disclosure of the identity of any person to whom the written determination pertains, if there has been a third party contact noted on the determination made public.

The Tax Court has jurisdiction to render declaratory judgments relating to the qualification of retirement plans, including pension, profit-sharing, stock bonus, annuity, and bond purchase plans; the tax-exempt status of a charitable organization, qualified charitable donee, private foundation, or private operating foundation; and the status of interest on certain governmental obligations. Additional jurisdiction was conferred on the Tax Court by the Technical and Miscellaneous Revenue Act of 1988 (102 Stat. 3342). Such jurisdiction includes injunctive authority over certain procedure assessments, authority to review certain jeopardy assessments and jeopardy levies, and authority to hear and decide appeals by taxpayers from the denial of administrative costs by the Internal Revenue Service.

All decisions, other than small tax case decisions, are subject to review by the courts of appeals and thereafter by the Supreme Court of the United States upon the granting of a writ of certiorari.

The office of the court and all of its judges are located in Washington, DC, with the exception of a field office located in Los Angeles, CA. The court conducts trial sessions at various locations within the United States as reasonably convenient to taxpayers as practicable. Each trial session is conducted by a single judge or a special trial judge. All proceedings are public and are conducted judicially in accordance with the court's Rules of Practice and the rules of evidence applicable in trials without a jury in the U.S. District Court for the District of Columbia. A fee of $60 is prescribed for the filing of a petition. Practice before the court is limited to practitioners admitted under the court's Rules.

For further information, contact the Administrative Office, United States Tax Court, 400 Second Street NW., Washington, DC 20217. Phone, 202–606–8751.

United States Court of Veterans Appeals

The United States Court of Veterans Appeals was established on November 18, 1988 (102 Stat. 4105, 38 U.S.C. 7251) pursuant to Article I of the Constitution, and given exclusive jurisdiction to review decisions of the Board of Veterans Appeals. However, the court may not review the schedule of ratings for disabilities or actions of the Secretary in adopting or revising that schedule. Decisions of the Court of Veterans Appeals may be appealed to the United States Court of Appeals for the Federal Circuit.

The court consists of a chief judge and at least two, but not more than six, associate judges. All judges are appointed by the President with the advice and consent of the Senate for terms of 15 years.

The court's principal office is in the District of Columbia, but the court can also act at any place within the United States.

For further information, contact the Clerk, United States Court of Veterans Appeals, Suite 900, 625 Indiana Avenue NW., Washington, DC 20004–2950. Phone, 202–501–5970.

Other Courts   There have also been created two courts of local jurisdiction for the District of Columbia: the District of Columbia Court of Appeals and the Superior Court.

Business of the Federal Courts

The business of all the Federal courts described here, except the Court of Military Appeals, the Tax Court, the Court of Veterans Appeals, and the District of Columbia courts, is discussed in detail in the text and tables of the *Annual Report of the Director of the Administrative Office of the United States Courts (1940–95).*

ADMINISTRATIVE OFFICE OF THE UNITED STATES COURTS

One Columbus Circle NE., Washington, DC 20544
Phone, 202–273–0107

Director	LEONIDAS RALPH MECHAM
Deputy Director	(VACANCY)
Associate Director, Management and Operations	CLARENCE A. (PETE) LEE, JR.
Chief, Office of Audit	DAVID L. GELLMAN
Chief, Office of Management Coordination	CATHY A. MCCARTHY
Chief, Office of Program Assessment	DUANE REX LEE
Associate Director and General Counsel	WILLIAM R. BURCHILL, JR.
Assistant Director, Office of Judicial Conference Executive Secretariat	KAREN K. SIEGEL
Assistant Director, Office of Legislative Affairs	MICHAEL W. BLOMMER
Deputy Assistant Director	ARTHUR E. WHITE
Assistant Director, Office of Public Affairs	CHARLES D. CONNOR
Deputy Assistant Director	DAVID A. SELLERS
Assistant Director, Office of Court Programs	NOEL J. AUGUSTYN
Deputy Assistant Director for Court Administration	ROBERT LOWNEY
Chief, Court Administration Policy Staff	ABEL J. MATTOS
Chief, Appellate Court and Circuit Administration Division	JOHN P. HEHMAN
Chief, Bankruptcy Court Administration Division	GLEN K. PALMAN
Chief, Defender Services Division	THEODORE J. LIDZ
Chief, District Court Administration Division	GEORGE A. RAY
Chief, Federal Corrections and Supervision Division	EUNICE HOLT JONES
Assistant Director, Office of Facilities, Security, and Administrative Services	P. GERALD THACKER
Deputy Assistant Director	WILLIAM J. LEHMAN
Chief, Policy and Resource Management Staff	ROSS EISENMAN
Chief, Administrative Office Personnel Office	NANCY LEE BRADSHAW
Chief, Administrative Services Office	LAURA C. MINOR
Chief, Court Security Office	DENNIS P. CHAPAS
Chief, Relocation and Travel Management Office	JOHN R. BRESLIN
Chief, Contracts Division	FRED MCBRIDE
Chief, Space and Facilities Division	WILLIAM J. LEHMAN
Assistant Director, Office of Finance and Budget	JOSEPH J. BOBEK
Deputy Assistant Director	GEORGE H. SCHAFER
Chief, Economy Subcommittee Support Office	DIANE VANDENBERG
Financial Liaison Officer	PENNY JACOBS FLEMING
Chief, Accounting and Financial Systems Division	PHILIP L. MCKINNEY
Chief, Budget Division	GREGORY D. CUMMINGS
Assistant Director, Office of Human Resources and Statistics	MYRA HOWZE SHIPLETT

Deputy Assistant Director	R. TOWNSEND ROBINSON
Chief, Analytical Services Office	DAVID L. COOK
Chief, Employee Relations Office	TRUDI M. MORRISON
Chief, Human Resources Division	CHARLOTTE G. PEDDICORD
Chief, Program and Workforce Development Division	MAURICE E. WHITE
Chief, Statistics Division	STEVEN R. SCHLESINGER
Assistant Director, Office of Information Technology	PAMELA B. WHITE
Chief, Computer Security and Independent Testing Office	FRANK S. DOZIER
Chief, Customer Relations Office	DENNIS E. MOREY
Chief, Technology Enhancement Office	RICHARD D. FENNELL
Chief, Technology Policy, Planning, and Acquisitions Office	MELVIN J. BRYSON
Chief, Applications Management and Development Division	GARY L. BOCKWEG
Chief, Networks and Systems Integration Division	CHARLES M. MAYER
Chief, Technology Training and Support Division	CHARLES W. VAGNER
Assistant Director, Office of Judges Programs	PETER G. MCCABE
Special Counsel	JEFFREY A. HENNEMUTH
Chief, Long Range Planning Office	WILLIAM M. LUCIANOVIC, *Acting*
Chief, Rules Committee Support Office	JOHN K. RABIEJ
Chief, Article III Judges Division	JOHN E. HOWELL
Chief, Bankruptcy Judges Division	FRANCIS F. SZCZEBAK
Chief, Magistrate Judges Division	THOMAS C. HNATOWSKI

The Administrative Office of the United States Courts is charged with the nonjudicial, administrative business of the United States Courts, including the maintenance of workload statistics and the disbursement of funds appropriated for the maintenance of the U.S. judicial system.

The Administrative Office of the United States Courts was created by act of August 7, 1939 (28 U.S.C. 601). The Office was established November 6, 1939. Its Director and Deputy Director are appointed by the Chief Justice of the United States after consultation with the Judicial Conference.

Administering the Courts The Director is the administrative officer of the courts of the United States (except the Supreme Court). Under the guidance of the Judicial Conference of the United States the Director is required, among other things, to:

—supervise all administrative matters relating to the offices of clerks and other clerical and administrative personnel of the courts;

—examine the state of the dockets of the courts, secure information as to the courts' need of assistance, and prepare and transmit quarterly to the chief judges of the circuits statistical data and reports as to the business of the courts;

—submit to the annual meeting of the Judicial Conference of the United States, at least 2 weeks prior thereto, a report of the activities of the Administrative Office and the state of the business of the courts;

—fix the compensation of employees of the courts whose compensation is not otherwise fixed by law;

—regulate and pay annuities to widows and surviving dependent children of judges;

—disburse moneys appropriated for the maintenance and operation of the courts;

—examine accounts of court officers;

—regulate travel of judicial personnel;

ADMINISTRATIVE OFFICE OF THE UNITED STATES COURTS

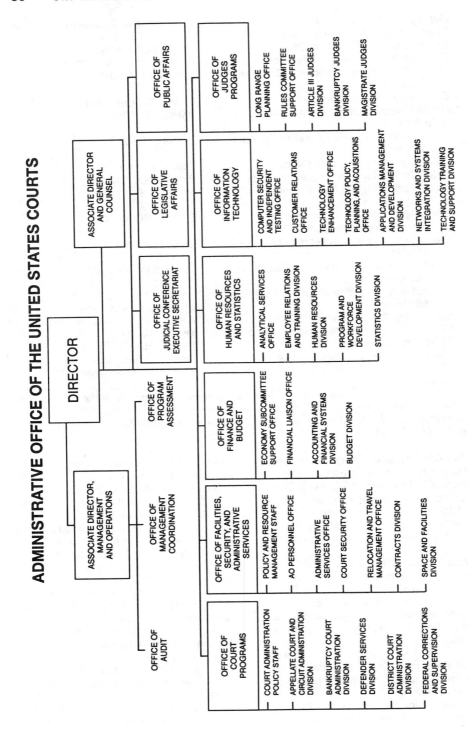

—provide accommodations and supplies for the courts and their clerical and administrative personnel;

—establish and maintain programs for the certification and utilization of court interpreters and the provision of special interpretation services in the courts; and

—perform such other duties as may be assigned to him by the Supreme Court or the Judicial Conference of the United States.

The Director is also responsible for the preparation and submission of the budget of the courts, which shall be transmitted by the Office of Management and Budget to Congress without change.

Probation Officers The Administrative Office exercises general supervision of the accounts and practices of the Federal probation offices, subject to primary control by the respective district courts that they serve. The Office publishes quarterly, in cooperation with the Bureau of Prisons of the Department of Justice, a magazine entitled *Federal Probation,* which is a journal "of correctional philosophy and practice."

The Director also has responsibility with respect to the establishment of pretrial services in the district courts under the Pretrial Services Act of 1982 (18 U.S.C. 3152). These offices report to their respective courts information concerning pretrial release of persons charged with Federal offenses and supervise such persons who are released to their custody.

Bankruptcy The Bankruptcy Amendments and Federal Judgeship Act of 1984 (28 U.S.C. 151) provided that the bankruptcy judges for each judicial district shall constitute a unit of the district court to be known as the bankruptcy court. Bankruptcy judges are appointed by the courts of appeals in such numbers as authorized by Congress and serve for a term of 14 years as judicial officers of the district courts.

This act placed jurisdiction in the district courts over all cases under title 11, United States Code, and all proceedings arising in or related to cases under that title (28 U.S.C. 1334). The district court may provide for such cases and proceedings to be referred to its

bankruptcy judges (as authorized by 28 U.S.C. 157).

The Director of the Administrative Office recommends to the Judicial Conference the official duty stations and places of holding court of bankruptcy judges, surveys the need for additional bankruptcy judgeships to be recommended to Congress, and determines the staff needs of bankruptcy judges and the clerks of the bankruptcy courts.

Federal Magistrate Judges Under the Federal Magistrates Act, as amended (28 U.S.C. 631), the Director of the Administrative Office, under the supervision and direction of the Judicial Conference, exercises general supervision over administrative matters in offices of United States magistrate judges, compiles and evaluates statistical data relating to such offices, and submits reports thereon to the Conference. The Director reports annually to Congress on the business that has come before United States magistrate judges and also prepares legal and administrative manuals for the use of the magistrate judges. The act provides for surveys to be conducted by the Administrative Office of the conditions in the judicial districts in order to make recommendations as to the number, location, and salaries of magistrate judges, which are determined by the Conference subject to the availability of appropriated funds.

Federal Defenders The Criminal Justice Act (18 U.S.C. 3006A) establishes the procedure for the appointment of counsel in Federal criminal cases for individuals who are unable to afford adequate representation under plans adopted by each district court. The act also permits the establishment of Federal public defender or Federal community defender organizations by the district courts in districts where at least 200 persons annually require the appointment of counsel. Two adjacent districts may be combined to reach this total.

Each defender organization submits to the Director of the Administrative Office an annual report of its activities along with a proposed budget or, in the case of community defender organizations, a proposed grant for the coming year. The Director is responsible for the submission of the proposed budgets and grants to the Judicial Conference for approval. The Director also makes payments to the defender organizations out of appropriations in accordance with the approved budgets and grants, as well as compensating private counsel appointed to defend criminal cases in the United States courts.

Sources of Information

Information may be obtained from the following offices:

Bankruptcy Judges Division. Phone, 202–273–1900.

Budget Division. Phone, 202–273–2100.

Defender Services Division. Phone, 202–273–1670.

Federal Corrections and Supervision Division. Phone, 202–273–1600.

General Counsel. Phone, 202–273–1100.

Human Resources Division. Phone, 202–273–1270.

Judicial Conference Executive Secretariat. Phone, 202–273–1140.

Legislative Affairs Office. Phone, 202–273–1120.

Magistrate Judges Division. Phone, 202–273–1830.

Public Affairs Office. Phone, 202–273–0107.

Statistics Division. Phone, 202–273–2240.

For further information, contact one of the offices listed above, Administrative Office of the United States Courts, Thurgood Marshall Federal Judiciary Building, One Columbus Circle NE., Washington, DC 20544.

FEDERAL JUDICIAL CENTER

Thurgood Marshall Federal Judiciary Building,
One Columbus Circle NE., Washington, DC 20002–8003
Phone, 202–273–4000. Internet, http://www.fjc.gov/.

Director	RYA W. ZOBEL
Deputy Director	RUSSELL R. WHEELER
Director of Research	JAMES B. EAGLIN
Director of Judicial Education	CHARLES ARBERG, *Acting*
Director of Court Education	EMILY Z. HUEBNER
Director of Publications and Media	SYLVAN A. SOBEL

The Federal Judicial Center is the judicial branch's agency for policy research and continuing education.

The Federal Judicial Center was created by act of December 20, 1967 (28 U.S.C. 620), to further the development and adoption of improved judicial administration in the courts of the United States.

The Center's basic policies and activities are determined by its Board, which is composed of the Chief Justice of the United States, who is permanent Chairman of the Board by statute, and two judges of the U.S. courts of appeals, three judges of the U.S. district courts, one bankruptcy judge, and one magistrate judge, all of whom are

elected for 4-year terms by the Judicial Conference of the United States. The Director of the Administrative Office of the United States Courts is also a permanent member of the Board.

Pursuant to statute the Center:

—develops and administers orientation and continuing education programs for Federal judges, Federal defenders, and nonjudicial court personnel, including probation officers, pretrial services officers, and clerks' office employees;

—conducts empirical and exploratory research and evaluation on Federal judicial processes, court management, and sentencing and its consequences, usually for the committees of the Judicial Conference or the courts themselves;

—produces research reports, training manuals, video programs, and periodicals about the Federal courts;

—provides guidance and advice and maintains data and records to assist those interested in documenting and conserving the history of the Federal courts; and

—cooperates with and assists other agencies and organizations in providing advice to improve the administration of justice in the courts of foreign countries.

Sources of Information

Information may be obtained from the following offices:

Office of the Director and Deputy Director. Phone, 202–273–4160, or 202–273–4164. Fax, 202–273–4019.

Research Division. Phone, 202–273–4070. Fax, 202–273–4021.

Judicial Education Division. Phone, 202–273–4052. Fax, 202–273–4023.

Court Education Division. Phone, 202–273–4110. Fax, 202–273–4020.

Publications and Media Division. Phone, 202–273–4140. Fax, 202–273–4025.

Federal Judicial History Office. Phone, 202–273–4180. Fax, 202–273–4025.

Interjudicial Affairs Office. Phone, 202–273–4161. Fax, 202–273–4019.

Office of Personnel. Phone, 202–273–4165. Fax, 202–273–4019.

Systems Innovations and Development Office. Phone, 202–273–4200. Fax, 202–273–4024.

Electronic Access Selected Federal Judicial Center publications are available in electronic form through the Internet, at http://www.fjc.gov/.

Publications Single copies of most Federal Judicial Center publications are available free of charge. Phone, 202–273–4153. Fax, 202–273–4025.

For further information, contact the Federal Judicial Center, Thurgood Marshall Federal Judiciary Building, One Columbus Circle NE., Washington, DC 20002–8003. For a recorded message and office directory, dial 202–273–4000 on a touch-tone phone.

UNITED STATES SENTENCING COMMISSION

Suite 2–500, South Lobby, One Columbus Circle NE., Washington, DC 20002–8002
Phone, 202–273–4500. Internet, http://www.ussc.gov/.

Chairman	RICHARD P. CONABOY
Vice Chairman	MICHAEL S. GELACAK
Commissioners	MICHAEL GOLDSMITH, DEANELL R. TACHA, (3 VACANCIES)
Commissioners (*ex officio*)	MICHAEL J. GAINES, MARY FRANCES HARKENRIDER
Staff Director	JOHN H. KRAMER
Deputy Staff Director	PAUL K. MARTIN
General Counsel	JOHN R. STEER
Network Administrator	JOYCE BOUWKAMP
Public Information Specialist	MICHAEL COURLANDER
Director of Training and Technical Assistance	SHARON O. HENEGAN
Director of Policy Analysis	LINDA D. MAXFIELD, *Acting*
Executive Assistant to the Chairman	TIMOTHY B. MCGRATH
Chief Deputy General Counsel	DONALD A. PURDY, JR.
Deputy Director of Training and Technical Assistance	SUSAN WINARSKY
Director of Legislative and Public Affairs	JONATHAN J. WROBLEWSKI

The United States Sentencing Commission develops sentencing policies and practices for the Federal criminal justice system.

The United States Sentencing Commission was established as an independent agency in the judicial branch of the Federal Government by the Sentencing Reform Act of 1984 (28 U.S.C. 991 *et seq.* and 18 U.S.C. 3551 *et seq.*). The Commission establishes sentencing policies and practices for the Federal courts, including guidelines prescribing the appropriate form and severity of punishment for offenders convicted of Federal crimes.

The Commission is composed of seven voting members appointed by the President with the advice and consent of the Senate for 6-year terms, and two nonvoting members. One of the voting members is appointed Chairman.

The Commission evaluates the effects of the sentencing guidelines on the criminal justice system, advises Congress regarding the modification or enactment of statutes relating to criminal law and sentencing matters, establishes a research and development program on sentencing issues, and performs other related duties.

In executing its duties, the Commission promulgates and distributes to Federal courts and to the U.S. Probation System guidelines to be used in determining sentences to be imposed in criminal cases, general policy statements regarding the application of guidelines, and policy statements on the appropriate use of probation and supervised release revocation provisions. These sentencing guidelines and policy statements are designed to further the purposes of just punishment, deterrence, incapacitation, and rehabilitation; provide fairness in meeting the purposes of sentencing; avoid unwarranted disparity; and reflect advancement in the knowledge of human behavior as it relates to the criminal justice process.

In addition, the Commission provides training, conducts research on sentencing-related issues, and serves as an information resource for Congress, criminal justice practitioners, and the public.

Sources of Information

Electronic Access Commission information and materials may be obtained electronically. Internet, http://www.ussc.gov/.
Guideline Application Assistance Helpline Phone, 202–273–4545.
Public Information Information concerning Commission activities is available from the Office of Legislative and Public Affairs. Phone, 202–273–4590.

For further information, contact the Office of Legislative and Public Affairs, United States Sentencing Commission, Suite 2–500, South Lobby, One Columbus Circle NE., Washington, DC 20002–8002. Phone, 202–273–4590.

UNITED STATES SENTENCING COMMISSION

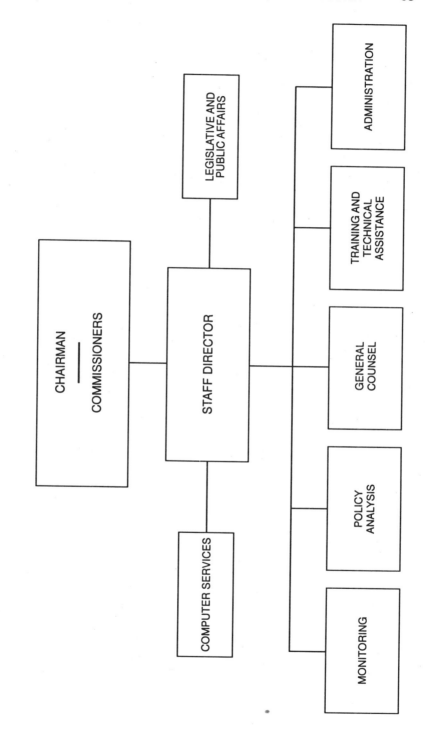

Executive Branch

EXECUTIVE BRANCH

THE PRESIDENT OF THE UNITED STATES

THE PRESIDENT OF THE UNITED STATES   WILLIAM J. CLINTON

Article II, section 1, of the Constitution provides that "[t]he executive Power shall be vested in a President of the United States of America. He shall hold his Office during the Term of four Years, . . . together with the Vice President, chosen for the same Term . . . ." In addition to the powers set forth in the Constitution, the statutes have conferred upon the President specific authority and responsibility covering a wide range of matters (United States Code Index).

The President is the administrative head of the executive branch of the Government, which includes numerous agencies, both temporary and permanent, as well as the 14 executive departments.

THE CABINET

The Cabinet, a creation of custom and tradition dating back to George Washington's administration, functions at the pleasure of the President. Its purpose is to advise the President upon any subject, relating to the duties of the respective offices, on which he requests information (pursuant to Article II, section 2, of the Constitution).

The Cabinet is composed of the heads of the 14 executive departments—the Secretaries of Agriculture, Commerce, Defense, Education, Energy, Health and Human Services, Housing and Urban Development, Interior, Labor, State, Transportation, Treasury, and Veterans Affairs, and the Attorney General. Additionally, in the Clinton administration, Cabinet-level rank has been accorded to: the Chief of Staff to the President; the Director of Central Intelligence; the Chairman, Council of Economic Advisers; the Counselor to the President; the Administrator, Environmental Protection Agency; the Director, Federal Emergency Management Agency; the Director, Office of Management and Budget; the Director, Office of National Drug Control Policy; the Administrator, Small Business Administration; the U.S. Representative to the United Nations; and the U.S. Trade Representative. The Vice President also participates in Cabinet meetings, and from time to time, other individuals are invited to participate in discussions of particular subjects. A Secretary to the Cabinet is designated to provide for the orderly handling and followup of matters brought before the Cabinet.

177-653 98 - 4 : QL 3

THE VICE PRESIDENT OF THE UNITED STATES

THE VICE PRESIDENT   AL GORE

Article II, section I, of the Constitution provides that the President "shall hold his Office during the Term of four Years . . . together with the Vice President . . . ." In addition to his role as President of the Senate, the Vice President is empowered to succeed to the Presidency, pursuant to Article II and the 20th and 25th amendments to the Constitution.

The executive functions of the Vice President include participation in Cabinet meetings and, by statute, membership on the National Security Council and the Board of Regents of the Smithsonian Institution.

EXECUTIVE OFFICE OF THE PRESIDENT

Under authority of the Reorganization Act of 1939 (5 U.S.C. 133–133r, 133t note), various agencies were transferred to the Executive Office of the President by the President's Reorganization Plans I and II of 1939 (5 U.S.C. app.), effective July 1, 1939. Executive Order 8248 of September 8, 1939, established the divisions of the Executive Office and defined their functions. Subsequently, Presidents have used Executive orders, reorganization plans, and legislative initiatives to reorganize the Executive Office to make its composition compatible with the goals of their administrations.

The White House Office

1600 Pennsylvania Avenue NW., Washington, DC 20500
Phone, 202–456–1414

Chief of Staff to the President	ERSKINE B. BOWLES
Assistants to the President and Deputy Chiefs of Staff	MARIA ECHAVESTE, JOHN D. PODESTA
Assistant to the President	SIDNEY BLUMENTHAL
Assistant to the President and Cabinet Secretary	THURGOOD MARSHALL, JR.
Assistant to the President and Chief of Staff to the First Lady	MELANNE VERVEER
Assistant to the President and Deputy Counsel to the President	BRUCE LINDSEY
Assistant to the President and Director of Communications	ANN LEWIS
Assistant to the President and Director of Intergovernmental Affairs	MICKEY IBARRA
Assistant to the President and Director of Legislative Affairs	LAWRENCE J. STEIN
Assistant to the President and Director of Political Affairs	CRAIG T. SMITH
Assistant to the President and Director of Presidential Personnel	BOB NASH
Assistant to the President and Director of Public Liaison	MINYON MOORE

Assistant to the President and Director of Scheduling	STEPHANIE STREETT
Assistant to the President and Director of Special Projects	TODD STERN
Assistant to the President and Director of Speechwriting	MICHAEL A. WALDMAN
Assistant to the President and Press Secretary	MICHAEL MCCURRY
Assistant to the President and Staff Secretary	PHILLIP M. CAPLAN
Assistant to the President for Domestic Policy and Director of the Domestic Policy Council	BRUCE N. REED
Assistant to the President for Economic Policy and Director of the National Economic Council	GENE SPERLING
Assistant to the President for Management and Administration	VIRGINIA M. APUZZO
Assistant to the President for National Security Affairs	SAMUEL R. BERGER
Counsel to the President	CHARLES F. RUFF
Counselor to the President and Special Envoy for the Americas	THOMAS F. MCLARTY III
Counselors to the President	PAUL BEGALA, DOUGLAS B. SOSNIK
Senior Advisor to the President for Policy and Strategy and Executive Assistant to the Chief of Staff for Policy	RAHM I. EMANUEL
Senior Advisor to the President for Policy Development	IRA MAGAZINER
Deputy Assistant to the President and Advisor to the First Lady for the Millennium Program	ELLEN LOVELL
Deputy Assistant to the President and Counsel to the Office of the Chief of Staff	KAREN TRAMONTANO
Deputy Assistant to the President and Deputy Cabinet Secretary	KRIS M. BALDERSTON
Deputy Assistant to the President and Deputy Chief of Staff to the First Lady	ROBERTA GREENE
Deputy Assistant to the President and Deputy Counsel to the President	CHERYL MILLS
Deputy Assistant to the President and Deputy Director of Communications	STACIE SPECTOR
Deputy Assistant to the President and Deputy Director of Legislative Affairs	JANET MURGUIA
Deputy Assistant to the President and Director of Advance	DAN K. ROSENTHAL
Deputy Assistant to the President and Director of Communications	MARSHA BERRY
Deputy Assistant to the President and Director of Oval Office Operations	NANCY HERNREICH
Deputy Assistant to the President and Director of Scheduling for the First Lady	PATRICIA SOLIS DOYLE
Deputy Assistant to the President and Director of the White House Military Office	(VACANCY)
Deputy Assistant to the President and Director of the White House Office for Women's Initiatives and Outreach	(VACANCY)

Deputy Assistant to the President and Social Secretary	CAPRICIA MARSHALL
Deputy Assistant to the President for Domestic Policy	ELENA KAGAN
Deputy Assistant to the President for Economic Policy and Deputy Director of the National Economic Council	SALLY KATZEN
Deputy Assistant to the President for Health Policy	CHRISTOPHER C. JENNINGS
Deputy Assistant to the President for Legislative Affairs and Senate Liaison	TRACEY THORNTON
Deputy Assistant to the President for Management and Administration	MICHAEL D. MALONE
Deputy Assistant to the President for National Security Affairs	DONALD L. KERRICK
Deputy Assistants to the President and Deputy Directors of Intergovernmental Affairs	LYNN CUTLER, FRED DUVAL
Deputy Assistants to the President and Deputy Directors of Political Affairs	LINDA L. MOORE, KAREN SKELTON
Deputy Assistants to the President and Deputy Directors of Presidential Personnel	MARSHA SCOTT, D. VANESSA WEAVER
Deputy Assistants to the President and Deputy Directors of Public Liaison	ROBERT B. JOHNSON, DORIS O. MATSUI
Deputy Assistants to the President and Deputy Press Secretaries	BEVERLY BARNES, JOSEPH LOCKHART, AMY WEISS TOBE, BARRY J. TOIV
Deputy Assistants to the President for Legislative Affairs	CHARLES BRAIN, ALPHONSO MALDON
Deputy National Security Advisor and Deputy Assistant to the President for National Security Affairs	JAMES B. STEINBERG
Special Assistant to the President and Associate Director of Public Liaison	DANIEL WEXLER
Special Assistant to the President and Deputy Director of Presidential Advance	CHRISTOPHER WAYNE
Special Assistant to the President and Deputy Director of Scheduling	JENNIFER PALMIERI
Special Assistant to the President and Deputy Staff Secretary	SEAN MALONEY
Special Assistant to the President and Director of Advance for the First Lady	KELLY CRAIGHEAD
Special Assistant to the President and Director of Correspondence and Presidential Messages	DANIEL BURKHARDT
Special Assistant to the President and Director of Personal Correspondence	ANN MCCOY
Special Assistant to the President and Director of Press Advance	ANNE M. EDWARDS
Special Assistant to the President and Director of Special Projects	ANN F. WALKER
Special Assistant to the President and Director of White House Operations	JOHN DANKOWSKI
Special Assistant to the President and Director, Visitors Office	MELINDA BATES
Special Assistant to the President and Presidential Speechwriter	LISA JORDAN TAMAGNI

Special Assistant to the President and Records Manager	JANIS F. KEARNEY
Special Assistant to the President and Senior Advisor for Public Liaison	RICHARD SOCARIDES
Special Assistant to the President and Senior Presidential Speechwriter	JEFFREY SHESOL
Special Assistant to the President and Senior Speechwriter	LAURA SCHILLER
Special Assistant to the President and Trip Director	KIRK HANLIN
Special Assistant to the President for Cabinet Affairs	ANNE E. MCGUIRE
Special Assistant to the President for Domestic Policy	CYNTHIA RICE
Special Assistant to the President for Intergovernmental Affairs	WILLIAM WHITE
Special Assistant to the President for Legislative Affairs	DONALD F. GOLDBERG
Special Assistant to the President for Legislative Affairs and Staff Director	JEFFREY FORBES
Special Assistant to the President for Policy Planning	THOMAS FREEDMAN
Special Assistant to the President for Public Liaison and Staff Director	CHERYL M. CARTER
Special Assistants to the President and Associate Directors of Presidential Personnel	MARIE TERESE DOMINGUEZ, CHARLES DUNCAN, HEATHER MARABETI
Special Assistants to the President for Legislative Affairs (House)	ROGER BALLENTINE, PETER JACOBY, LISA KOUNTOUPES
Associate Counsels to the President	MEREDITH CABE, VIRGINIA CANTER, DAWN CHIRWA, MICHAEL IMBROSCIO, WILLIAM P. MARSHALL, DIMITRI NIONAKIS, MICHELLE PETERSON, KAREN POPP, KARL RACINE, SARAH WILSON, LISA WINSTON
Senior Counsel	ROBERT WEINER
Special Associate Counsels to the President	ADAM GOLDBERG, SALLY PAXTON
Special Counsel to the President	LANNY BREUER
Special Counsel to the President for Civil Rights	EDWARD CORREIA
Special Counsel to the President for Nominations	MARK CHILDRESS

The White House Office serves the President in the performance of the many detailed activities incident to his immediate office.

The staff of the President facilitates and maintains communication with the Congress, the individual Members of the Congress, the heads of executive agencies, the press and other information media, and the general public.

The various Assistants to the President assist the President in such matters as he may direct.

Office of the Vice President of the United States

Old Executive Office Building, Washington, DC 20501
Phone, 202–456–2326

Assistant to the President and Chief of Staff and Counselor to the Vice President	RONALD A. KLAIN
Deputy Chiefs of Staff	MONICA MAPLES DIXON, PATRICIA EWING
Communications Director	LAWRENCE HAAS
Counsel to the Vice President	CHARLES BURSON
National Security Advisor for the Vice President	LEON S. FUERTH
Director of Legislative Affairs for the Vice President	KAY CASSTEVENS
Executive Assistant to the Vice President	PATRICIA MCHUGH
Chief of Staff to Mrs. Gore	AUDREY HAYNES
Chief Domestic Policy Advisor for the Vice President	DONALD GIPS
Senior Advisor to the Vice President	MICHAEL FELDMAN
Senior Policy Advisor for the Vice President	MORLEY WINOGRAD
Director of Correspondence for the Vice President	BILL MASON
Director of Scheduling and Advance for the Vice President	LISA BERG
Political Director	MAURICE DANIEL

The Office of the Vice President serves the Vice President in the performance of the many detailed activities incident to his immediate office.

Council of Economic Advisers

Old Executive Office Building, Washington, DC 20502
Phone, 202–395–5084. Internet, http://www.whitehouse.gov/WH/EOP/CEA/html/.

Chairman	JANET L. YELLEN
Members	JEFFREY A. FRANKEL, (VACANCY)
Chief of Staff	MICHELE M. JOLIN

The Council of Economic Advisers primarily performs an analysis and appraisal of the national economy for the purpose of providing policy recommendations to the President.

The Council of Economic Advisers (CEA) was established in the Executive Office of the President by the Employment Act of 1946 (15 U.S.C. 1023). It now functions under that statute and Reorganization Plan No. 9 of 1953 (5 U.S.C. app.), effective August 1, 1953.

The Council consists of three members appointed by the President with the advice and consent of the Senate. One of the members is designated by the President as Chairman.

The Council analyzes the national economy and its various segments; advises the President on economic developments; appraises the economic programs and policies of the Federal Government; recommends to the President policies for economic growth and stability; assists in the preparation of the economic reports of the President to the Congress; and prepares the Annual Report of the Council of Economic Advisers.

For further information, contact the Council of Economic Advisers, Old Executive Office Building, Washington, DC 20502. Phone, 202–395–5084. Internet, http:// www.whitehouse.gov/WH/EOP/CEA/html/.

Council on Environmental Quality

Room 360, Old Executive Office Building, Washington, DC 20501
Phone, 202–456–6224

722 Jackson Place NW., Washington, DC 20503
Phone, 202–395–5750. Internet, http://www.whitehouse.gov/ceq/.

Chair	KATHLEEN A. McGINTY
Chief of Staff	WESLEY WARREN
General Counsel	DINAH BEAR
Deputy General Counsel	ELLEN ATHAS
Associate General Counsel	ELISABETH BLAUG
Associate Director for Communications	ELLIOT DIRINGER
Associate Director for Congressional Relations	JUDY JABLOW
Associate Director for the Global Environment	DAVID SANDALOW
Associate Director for Land Management and Transportation	LINDA LANCE
Associate Director for Natural Resources	SALLY ERICSSON
Associate Director for NEPA	RAY CLARK
Associate Director for Outreach and Strategic Planning	BETH VIOLA
Associate Director for Sustainable Development	KEITH LAUGHLIN
Associate Director for Toxins and Environmental Protection	BRAD CAMPBELL
Special Assistant to the Chair for Outreach and Strategic Planning	MICHAEL TERRELL
Special Assistants to the Chair	ROBERT KAPLA, NANCY MARLOW
Administrative Officer	CAROLYN MOSLEY

The Council on Environmental Quality formulates and recommends national policies to promote the improvement of the quality of the environment.

The Council on Environmental Quality (CEQ) was established within the Executive Office of the President by the National Environmental Policy Act of 1969 (NEPA) (42 U.S.C. 4321 *et seq.*). The Environmental Quality Improvement Act of 1970 (42 U.S.C. 4371 *et seq.*) established the Office of Environmental Quality (OEQ) to provide professional and administrative support for the Council. The Council and OEQ are collectively referred to as the Council on Environmental Quality, and the CEQ

Chair, who is appointed by the President, serves as the Director of OEQ.

The Council develops policies which bring into productive harmony the Nation's social, economic, and environmental priorities, with the goal of improving the quality of Federal decisionmaking. As required by NEPA, CEQ evaluates, coordinates, and mediates Federal activities; advises and assists the President on both national and international environmental policy matters; and prepares the President's annual environmental quality report to Congress. In addition, it oversees Federal agency and department implementation of NEPA.

For further information, contact the Information Office, Council on Environmental Quality, 722 Jackson Place NW., Washington, DC 20503. Phone, 202–395–5750. Fax, 202–456–2710. Internet, http:// www.whitehouse.gov/ceq/.

National Security Council

Old Executive Office Building, Washington, DC 20506
Phone, 202–456–1414

Members:

The President	WILLIAM J. CLINTON
The Vice President	AL GORE
The Secretary of State	MADELEINE K. ALBRIGHT
The Secretary of Defense	WILLIAM S. COHEN

Statutory Advisers:

Director of Central Intelligence	GEORGE J. TENET
Chairman, Joint Chiefs of Staff	GEN. HENRY H. SHELTON, USA

Standing Participants:

The Secretary of the Treasury	ROBERT E. RUBIN
U.S. Representative to the United Nations	BILL RICHARDSON
Chief of Staff to the President	ERSKINE B. BOWLES
Assistant to the President for National Security Affairs	SAMUEL R. BERGER
Assistant to the President for Economic Policy	GENE SPERLING

Officials:

Assistant to the President for National Security Affairs	SAMUEL R. BERGER
Deputy Assistants to the President for National Security Affairs	DONALD L. KERRICK, JAMES B. STEINBERG
Executive Secretary	GLYN T. DAVIES

The National Security Council was established by the National Security Act of 1947, as amended (50 U.S.C. 402). The Council was placed in the Executive Office of the President by Reorganization Plan No. 4 of 1949 (5 U.S.C. app.).

The National Security Council is chaired by the President. Its statutory members, in addition to the President, are the Vice President and the Secretaries of State and Defense. The Chairman of the Joint Chiefs of Staff is the statutory military adviser to the Council, and the Director of Central Intelligence is its intelligence adviser. The Secretary of the Treasury, the U.S.

Representative to the United Nations, the Assistant to the President for National Security Affairs, the Assistant to the President for Economic Policy, and the Chief of Staff to the President are invited to all meetings of the Council. The Attorney General and the Director of National Drug Control Policy are invited to attend meetings pertaining to their jurisdictions; other officials are invited, as appropriate.

The Council advises and assists the President in integrating all aspects of national security policy as it affects the United States—domestic, foreign, military, intelligence, and economic—in conjunction with the National Economic Council.

For further information, contact the National Security Council, Old Executive Office Building, Washington, DC 20506. Phone, 202–456–1414.

Office of Administration

Old Executive Office Building
725 Seventeenth Street NW., Washington, DC 20503
Phone, 202–395–6963

Director	ADA L. POSEY
General Counsel and Chief of Staff	MARK LINDSAY
Deputy Director for Administrative Operations and Associate Director for General Services	JOSEPH KEN BRYAN
Deputy Director for Finance and Information Management	PAULETTE CICHON
Associate Director for Facilities Management	(VACANCY)
Associate Director for Financial Management	JURG HOCHULI
Associate Director for Human Resources	MARY COUTTS BECK
Associate Director for Information Systems and Technology	KATHLEEN GALLANT
Associate Director for Library and Research Services	MARY ANN NOWELL
Senior Financial Manager	CHARLES SIGMAN

The Office of Administration was established within the Executive Office of the President by Reorganization Plan No. 1 of 1977 (5 U.S.C. app.). The Office was activated, effective December 4, 1977, by Executive Order 12028 of December 12, 1977.

The Office of Administration provides administrative support services to all units within the Executive Office of the President. The services provided include information, personnel, and financial management; data processing; library services; records maintenance; and general office operations, such as mail, messenger, printing, procurement, and supply services.

For further information, contact the Office of the Director, Office of Administration, Washington, DC 20503. Phone, 202–456–2861.

OFFICE OF ADMINISTRATION

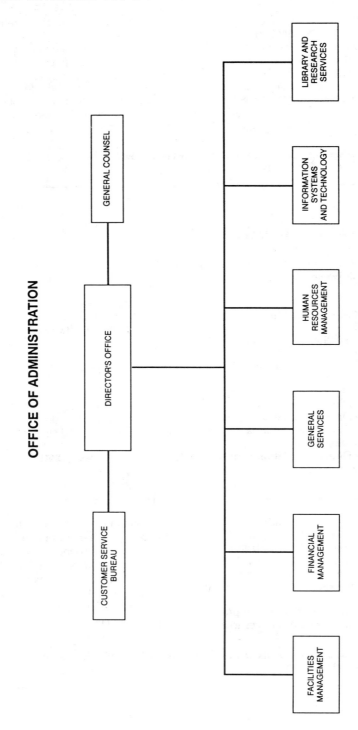

Office of Management and Budget

Executive Office Building, Washington, DC`20503
Phone, 202–395–3080

Director	(VACANCY)
Deputy Director	JACOB J. LEW
Deputy Director for Management	(VACANCY)
Executive Associate Director	JOSHUA GOTBAUM
Associate Director for Legislative Affairs	CHARLES KIEFFER, *Acting*
Associate Director for Administration	CLARENCE C. CRAWFORD
Senior Advisor to the Deputy Director	JILL BLICKSTEIN
Senior Advisor to the Deputy Director for Management	WILLIAM HALTER
General Counsel	ROBERT DAMUS
Associate Director for Communications	LARRY HAAS
Associate Director for Economic Policy	JOSEPH MINARIK
Assistant Director for Budget	(VACANCY)
Deputy Assistant Director for Budget Analysis and Systems	PHIL DAME
Deputy Assistant Director for Budget Review and Concepts	DICK EMERY
Assistant Director for Legislative Reference	JAMES C. MURR
Associate Director for National Security and International Affairs	(VACANCY)
Deputy Associate Director, National Security Division	DAVID MORRISON
Deputy Associate Director, International Affairs Division	PHILIP DUSAULT
Associate Director for Human Resources	BARBARA CHOW
Deputy Associate Director for Human Resources	BARRY WHITE
Associate Director for Health and Personnel	(VACANCY)
Deputy Associate Director for Health	BARRY CLENDENIN
Deputy Associate Director for VA/Personnel	BRUCE LONG
Associate Director for General Government	MICHAEL DEICH
Deputy Associate Director, Transportation, Commerce, Justice, and Services Division	KENNETH SCHWARTZ
Deputy Associate Director, Housing, Treasury, and Finance Division	ALAN RHINESMITH
Associate Director for Natural Resources, Energy, and Science	T.J. GLAUTHIER
Deputy Associate Director, Natural Resources Division	RONALD COGSWELL
Deputy Associate Director, Energy and Science Division	KATHY PEROFF
Administrator, Office of Information and Regulatory Affairs	(VACANCY)
Deputy Administrator for Information and Regulatory Management	DONALD R. ARBUCKLE
Controller	EDWARD DESEVE
Deputy Controller	NORWOOD JACKSON
Administrator, Office of Federal Procurement Policy	(VACANCY)

Associate Administrator for Procurement Policy Development	ALLAN BROWN
Associate Administrator for Procurement Law Development	STEVEN SCHOONER

The Office of Management and Budget evaluates, formulates, and coordinates management procedures and program objectives within and among Federal departments and agencies. It also controls the administration of the Federal budget, while routinely providing the President with recommendations regarding budget proposals and relevant legislative enactments.

The Office of Management and Budget (OMB), formerly the Bureau of the Budget, was established in the Executive Office of the President pursuant to Reorganization Plan No. 1 of 1939 (5 U.S.C. app.), effective July 1, 1939.

By Executive Order 11541 of July 1, 1970, all functions transferred to the President of the United States by part I of Reorganization Plan No. 2 of 1970 (5 U.S.C. app.) were delegated to the Director of the Office of Management and Budget, to be carried out by the Director under the direction of the President. Reorganization Plan No. 1 of 1977 (5 U.S.C. app.) and Executive orders issued pursuant to that plan further amended the functions of OMB.

The Office's primary functions are:

—to assist the President in developing and maintaining effective government by reviewing the organizational structure and management procedures of the executive branch to ensure that the intended results are achieved;

—to assist in developing efficient coordinating mechanisms to implement Government activities and to expand interagency cooperation;

—to assist the President in preparing the budget and in formulating the Government's fiscal program;

—to supervise and control the administration of the budget;

—to assist the President by clearing and coordinating departmental advice on proposed legislation and by making recommendations effecting Presidential action on legislative enactments, in accordance with past practice;

—to assist in developing regulatory reform proposals and programs for paperwork reduction, especially reporting burdens of the public;

—to assist in considering, clearing, and, where necessary, preparing proposed Executive orders and proclamations;

—to plan and develop information systems that provide the President with program performance data;

—to plan, conduct, and promote evaluation efforts that assist the President in assessing program objectives, performance, and efficiency;

—to keep the President informed of the progress of activities by Government agencies with respect to work proposed, initiated, and completed, together with the relative timing of work between the several agencies of the Government, all to the end that the work programs of the several agencies of the executive branch of the Government may be coordinated and that the moneys appropriated by the Congress may be expended in the most economical manner, barring overlapping and duplication of effort; and

—to improve the economy, efficiency, and effectiveness of the procurement processes by providing overall direction of procurement policies, regulations, procedures, and forms.

Sources of Information

Employment   Various civil service examinations and registers are used for filling positions, such as economist, budget examiner, and management analyst. Inquiries on employment should be directed to the Human Resources Division, Office of Administration, Washington, DC 20500. Phone, 202–395–1088.

Inquiries   Contact the Office of Administration, Office of Management and Budget, New Executive Office

OFFICE OF MANAGEMENT AND BUDGET

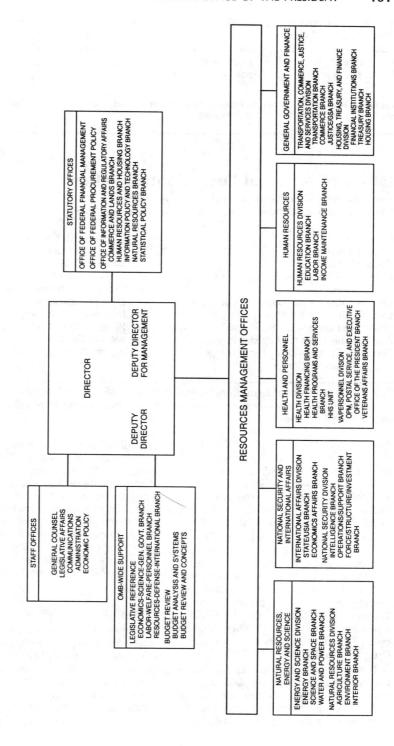

Building, Washington, DC 20503.
Phone, 202–395–3080.
Publications   *The Budget of the U.S.*
Government, The Budget System and
Concepts, and *Catalog of Federal*

Domestic Assistance are for sale by the
Superintendent of Documents,
Government Printing Office,
Washington, DC 20402.

For further information, contact the Office of Management and Budget, Executive Office Building, Washington, DC 20503. Phone, 202–395–3080.

Office of National Drug Control Policy

Executive Office of the President, Washington, DC 20503
Phone, 202–395–6700. Internet, http://www.whitehousedrugpolicy.gov/.

Director	BARRY R. MCCAFFREY
Deputy Director	HOOVER ADGER
Chief of Staff	JANET L. CRIST
Director of Programs, Budget, and Evaluation	JOHN CARNEVALE
Legal Counsel	CHARLES A. BLANCHARD
Deputy Director for Demand Reduction	DAN SCHECTER, *Acting*
Deputy Director for Supply Reduction	BOB BROWN, *Acting*
Associate Director for State and Local Affairs	ROBERT WARSHAW
Assistant Director for Legislative Affairs	MELVIN DUBEE
Director, Counter-Drug Technology Assessment Center	ALBERT BRANDENSTEIN

The Office of National Drug Control Policy coordinates Federal, State, and local efforts to control illegal drug abuse and devises national strategies to effectively carry out antidrug activities.

The Office of National Drug Control Policy was established by the National Narcotics Leadership Act of 1988 (21 U.S.C. 1501 *et seq.*), effective January 29, 1989, as amended by the Violent Crime Control and Law Enforcement Act of 1994 (21 U.S.C. 1502, 1506, 1508).

The Director of National Drug Control Policy is appointed by the President with the advice and consent of the Senate. The Director is assisted by the Deputy Director for Demand Reduction and the Deputy Director for Supply Reduction. The Bureau of State and Local Affairs is a separate division of the Office, headed by an Associate Director for National Drug Control Policy.

The Director of National Drug Control Policy is responsible for establishing policies, objectives, and priorities for the National Drug Control Program, and for annually promulgating a National Drug

Control Strategy to be submitted to the Congress by the President. The Director advises the President regarding necessary changes in the organization, management, budgeting, and personnel allocation of Federal agencies involved in drug enforcement activities, and is also responsible for notifying Federal agencies if their policies are not in compliance with their responsibilities under the National Drug Control Strategy.

Sources of Information

Employment   Inquiries regarding employment should be directed to the Personnel Section, Office of National Drug Control Policy (phone, 202–395–6748) or the Executive Office, Office of Administration (phone, 202–395–5892).
Publications   To receive ONDCP publications about drugs and crime, to

OFFICE OF NATIONAL DRUG CONTROL POLICY

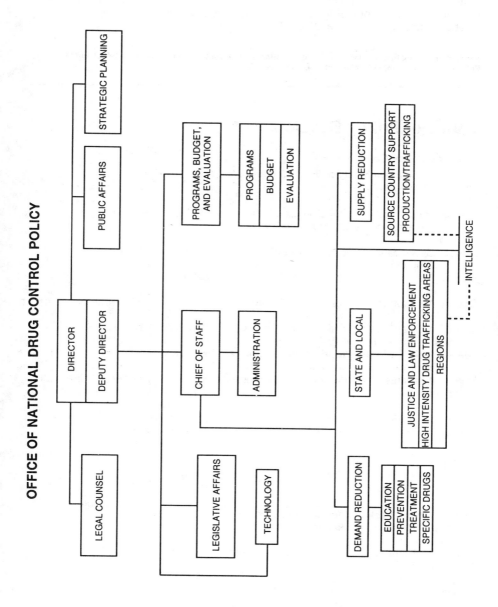

get specific drug-related data, to obtain customized bibliographic searches, and to find out about data availability and other information resources that may meet your needs, contact the ONDCP

Drugs and Crime Clearinghouse. Phone, 800–666–3332. Fax, 301–251–5212. E-mail, askncjrs@aspensys.com. Internet, http://www.whitehousedrugpolicy.gov/.

For further information, contact the Office of National Drug Control Policy, Executive Office of the President, Washington, DC 20503. Phone, 202–395–6700.

Office of Policy Development

Domestic Policy Council
Room 216, Old Executive Office Building, Washington, DC 20502
Phone, 202–456–2216

Assistant to the President for Domestic Policy and Director of the Domestic Policy Council	BRUCE N. REED
Senior Advisor to the President for Policy Development	IRA MAGAZINER
Deputy Assistant to the President for Domestic Policy	ELENA KAGAN
Deputy Assistant to the President for Health Policy	CHRISTOPHER C. JENNINGS
Special Assistant to the President and Chief of Staff to the Domestic Policy Council	PAUL WEINSTEIN, JR.
Special Assistant to the President and Senior Director for Policy Planning	THOMAS FREEDMAN
Special Assistants to the President for Domestic Policy	JOSE CERDA, MICHAEL COHEN, JULIE FERNANDES, JENNIFER KLEIN, CYNTHIA RICE
Director of National AIDS Policy	SANDRA THURMAN
Deputy Director of National AIDS Policy	TODD SUMMERS

National Economic Council
Room 235, Old Executive Office Building, Washington, DC 20502
Phone, 202–456–6630

Assistant to the President for Economic Policy and Director of the National Economic Council	GENE SPERLING
Deputy Assistant to the President for Economic Policy and Deputy Director of the National Economic Council	SALLY KATZEN
Special Assistant to the President and Senior Director of International Economic Affairs	ROBERT KYLE
Special Assistant to the President	PETER ORSZAG
Special Assistant to the President for International Economic Policy	LAEL BRAINARD
Special Assistants to the President for Economic Policy	ANNE LEWIS, DOROTHY ROBYN, CECILIA ROUSE, JAKE SIEWERT

The Office of Policy Development is comprised of the Domestic Policy Council and the National Economic Council, which are responsible for advising and assisting the President in the formulation, coordination, and implementation of domestic and economic policy. The Office of Policy Development also provides support for other policy development and implementation activities as directed by the President.

Domestic Policy Council

The Domestic Policy Council was established on August 16, 1993, by Executive Order 12859. The Council oversees development and implementation of the President's domestic policy agenda and ensures coordination and communication among the heads of relevant Federal offices and agencies.

National Economic Council

The National Economic Council was created on January 25, 1993, by Executive Order 12835, to coordinate the economic policymaking process and provide economic policy advice to the President. The Council also ensures that economic policy decisions and programs are consistent with the President's stated goals, and monitors the implementation of the President's economic goals.

Office of Science and Technology Policy

Old Executive Office Building, Washington, DC 20502
Phone, 202–395–7347. Fax, 202–456–6022. Internet, http://www.whitehouse.gov/ostp.html.

Assistant to the President for Science and Technology, and Director	JOHN H. GIBBONS
Associate Director for Environment	ROSINA BIERBAUM, *Acting*
Associate Director for National Security and International Affairs	KERRI-ANN JONES
Associate Director for Science	ARTHUR BIENENSTOCK
Associate Director for Technology	DUNCAN MOORE
Executive Secretary for the National Science and Technology Council and the President's Committee of Advisors on Science and Technology	(VACANCY)

The Office of Science and Technology Policy was established within the Executive Office of the President by the National Science and Technology Policy, Organization, and Priorities Act of 1976 (42 U.S.C. 6611).

The Office serves as a source of scientific, engineering, and technological analysis and judgment for the President with respect to major policies, plans, and programs of the Federal Government. In carrying out this mission, the Office advises the President of scientific and technological considerations involved in areas of national concern, including the economy, national security, health, foreign relations, and the environment; evaluates the scale, quality, and effectiveness of the Federal effort in science and technology; provides advice and assistance to the President, the Office of Management and Budget, and Federal agencies throughout the Federal budget development process; and assists the President in providing leadership and coordination for the research and development programs of the Federal Government.

For further information, contact the Office of Science and Technology Policy, Old Executive Office Building, Washington, DC 20502. Phone, 202–395–7347. Fax, 202–456–6022. Internet, http://www.whitehouse.gov/ostp.html.

Office of the United States Trade Representative

600 Seventeenth Street NW., Washington, DC 20508
Phone, 202–395–3230

United States Trade Representative	CHARLENE BARSHEFSKY
Deputy U.S. Trade Representative (Washington)	(VACANCY)
Deputy U.S. Trade Representative (Geneva)	RITA HAYES
Chief of Staff	NANCY LEAMOND
Special Trade Negotiator	PETER SCHER
Counselor to the U.S. Trade Representative	ROBERT NOVICK
General Counsel	SUSAN ESSERMAN
Chief Textile Negotiator	C. DONALD JOHNSON
Assistant U.S. Trade Representative for Intergovernmental Affairs and Public Liaison	J. PATE FELTS
Assistant U.S. Trade Representative for Monitoring and Enforcement	JANE BRADLEY
Assistant U.S. Trade Representative for Public/Media Affairs	JAY ZIEGLER
Assistant U.S. Trade Representative for Congressional Affairs	ELIZABETH ARKY
Assistant U.S. Trade Representative for Economic Affairs	DAVID WALTERS
Assistant U.S. Trade Representative for Policy Coordination	FRED MONTGOMERY
Assistant U.S. Trade Representative for Agricultural Affairs	JAMES MURPHY
Assistant U.S. Trade Representative for Trade and Development	JON ROSENBAUM
Assistant U.S. Trade Representative for World Trade Organization (WTO) and Multilateral Affairs	DOROTHY DWOSKIN
Assistant U.S. Trade Representative for Industry	JOSEPH PAPOVICH
Assistant U.S. Trade Representative for China	ROBERT CASSIDY
Assistant U.S. Trade Representative for Asia and the Pacific	DONALD PHILLIPS

Assistant U.S. Trade Representative for Europe and the Mediterranean	CATHY NOVELLI
Assistant U.S. Trade Representative for Environment and Natural Resources	JENNIFER HAVERKAMP
Associate U.S. Trade Representative for Western Hemisphere	PETER ALLGEIER
Assistant U.S. Trade Representative for North American Affairs	JONATHAN HUENEMAN
Assistant U.S. Trade Representative for Japan	WENDY CUTLER
Assistant U.S. Trade Representative for Administration	JOHN HOPKINS

The United States Trade Representative is responsible for directing all trade negotiations of and formulating trade policy for the United States.

The Office of the United States Trade Representative was created as the Office of the Special Representative for Trade Negotiations by Executive Order 11075 of January 15, 1963. The Trade Act of 1974 (19 U.S.C. 2171) established the Office as an agency of the Executive Office of the President charged with administering the trade agreements program under the Tariff Act of 1930 (19 U.S.C. 1654), the Trade Expansion Act of 1962 (19 U.S.C. 1801), and the Trade Act of 1974 (19 U.S.C. 2101). Other powers and responsibilities for coordinating trade policy were assigned to the Office by the Trade Act of 1974 and by the President in Executive Order 11846 of March 27, 1975, as amended.

Reorganization Plan No. 3 of 1979 (5 U.S.C. app.), implemented by Executive Order 12188 of January 4, 1980, charged the Office with responsibility for setting and administering overall trade policy. It also provides that the United States Trade Representative shall be chief representative of the United States for:

—all activities concerning the General Agreement on Tariffs and Trade;

—discussions, meetings, and negotiations in the Organization for Economic Cooperation and Development when such activities deal primarily with trade and commodity issues;

—negotiations in the United Nations Conference on Trade and Development and other multilateral institutions when such negotiations deal primarily with trade and commodity issues;

—other bilateral and multilateral negotiations when trade, including East-West trade, or commodities is the primary issue;

—negotiations under sections 704 and 734 of the Tariff Act of 1930 (19 U.S.C. 1671c and 1673c); and

—negotiations concerning direct investment incentives and disincentives and bilateral investment issues concerning barriers to investment.

The Omnibus Trade and Competitiveness Act of 1988 codified these prior authorities and added additional authority, including the implementation of section 301 actions (regarding enforcement of U.S. rights under international trade agreements).

The Office is headed by the United States Trade Representative, a Cabinet-level official with the rank of Ambassador, who is directly responsible to the President. There are three Deputy United States Trade Representatives, who also hold the rank of Ambassador, two located in Washington and one in Geneva. The Chief Textile Negotiator also holds the rank of Ambassador.

The United States Trade Representative serves as an *ex officio* member of the Boards of Directors of the Export-Import Bank and the Overseas Private Investment Corporation, and serves on the National Advisory Council for International Monetary and Financial Policy.

For further information, contact the Office of Public Affairs, Office of the United States Trade Representative, 600 Seventeenth Street NW., Washington, DC 20506. Phone, 202–395–3230.

Departments

DEPARTMENT OF AGRICULTURE

Fourteenth Street and Independence Avenue SW., Washington, DC 20250
Phone, 202–720–2791. Internet, http://www.usda.gov/.

SECRETARY OF AGRICULTURE	DAN GLICKMAN
Deputy Secretary	RICHARD ROMINGER
Under Secretary for Farm and Foreign Agricultural Services	AUGUST SCHUMACHER
Deputy Under Secretaries	DALLAS SMITH
	JAMES SCHROEDER
Administrator, Farm Service Agency	KEITH KELLY
Administrator, Foreign Agricultural Service	LON HATAMIYA
Administrator, Risk Management Agency	KEN ACKERMAN
Under Secretary for Food, Nutrition, and Consumer Services	SHIRLEY WATKINS
Deputy Under Secretary	JULIE PARADIS
Administrator, Food and Nutrition Service	YVETTE JACKSON
Under Secretary for Food Safety	CATHERINE WOTEKI
Administrator, Food Safety and Inspection Service	THOMAS BILLY
Under Secretary for Natural Resources and Environment	JAMES LYONS
Deputy Under Secretary for Forestry	BRIAN E. BURKE
Deputy Under Secretary for Conservation	CRAIG COX, *Acting*
Chief, Forest Service	MIKE DOMBECK
Chief, Natural Resources Conservation Service	PEARLIE S. REED
Under Secretary for Research, Education, and Economics	MILEY GONZALEZ
Deputy Under Secretary	EILEEN KENNEDY, *Acting*
Administrator, Agricultural Research Service	EDWARD B. KNIPLING, *Acting*
Administrator, Cooperative State Research, Education, and Extension Service	BOBBY H. ROBINSON
Administrator, Economic Research Service	SUSAN E. OFFUTT
Administrator, National Agricultural Statistics Service	DONALD BAY
Under Secretary for Rural Development	JILL LONG-THOMPSON
Deputy Under Secretaries	ARTHUR C. CAMPBELL
	INGA SMULKSTYS
	DAYTON WATKINS
Administrator, Rural Business-Cooperative Service	JAN SHADBURN
Administrator, Rural Housing Service	JAN SHADBURN
Administrator, Rural Utilities Service	WALLY BEYER

Assistant Secretary for Congressional Relations	J. DAVID CARLIN
Assistant Secretary for Marketing and Regulatory Programs	MICHAEL DUNN
Deputy Assistant Secretary	ISI SIDDIQUI, *Acting*
Administrator, Agricultural Marketing Service	ENRIQUE FIGUEROA
Administrator, Animal and Plant Health Inspection Service	TERRY MEDLEY
Administrator, Grain Inspection, Packers, and Stockyards Administration	JAMES R. BAKER
Assistant Secretary for Administration	REBA P. EVANS, *Acting*
Deputy Assistant Secretary	DEBBIE MATZ
Chairman, Board of Contract Appeals	EDWARD HOURY
Judicial Officer	WILLIAM G. JENSON
Chief Judge, Administrative Law Judges	VICTOR PALMER
Director, Office of Operations	PRISCILLA CAREY, *Acting*
Director, Civil Rights	LLOYD E. WRIGHT, *Acting*
Director, Human Resources Management	ROGER L. BENSEY
Director, Procurement and Property Management	W.R. ASHWORTH
Chief Information Officer	ANNE F. THOMSON REED
Deputy Chief Information Officer	IRA L. HOBBS
Chief Financial Officer	SALLY THOMPSON
Deputy Chief Financial Officer	IRWIN T. DAVID
General Counsel	CHARLES RAWLS, *Acting*
Inspector General	ROGER C. VIADERO
Deputy Inspector General	JOYCE N. FLEISCHMAN
Director, Office of Communications	THOMAS S. AMONTREE
Chief Economist	KEITH COLLINS
Director, Office of Risk Assessment and Cost-Benefit Analysis	ALWYNELLE S. AHL
Chairman, World Agricultural Outlook Board	GERALD BANGE
Director, Office of Budget and Program Analysis	STEPHEN B. DEWHURST
Director, Office of Outreach	SAMUEL E. THORNTON
Director, National Appeals Division	NORMAN COOPER
Director, Office of Small and Disadvantaged Business Utilization	SHARRON HARRIS
Director, Office of the Executive Secretariat	LYNNE FINNERTY

[For the Department of Agriculture statement of organization, see the *Code of Federal Regulations*, Title 7, Part 2]

The Department of Agriculture works to improve and maintain farm income and to develop and expand markets abroad for agricultural products. The Department helps to curb and to cure poverty, hunger, and malnutrition. It works to enhance the environment and to maintain production capacity by helping landowners protect the soil, water, forests, and other natural resources. Rural development, credit, and conservation programs are key resources for carrying out national growth policies. Department research findings directly or indirectly benefit all Americans. The Department, through inspection and grading services, safeguards and ensures standards of quality in the daily food supply.

The Department of Agriculture (USDA) was created by act of May 15, 1862 (7 U.S.C. 2201), and was administered by a Commissioner of Agriculture until 1889

DEPARTMENT OF AGRICULTURE

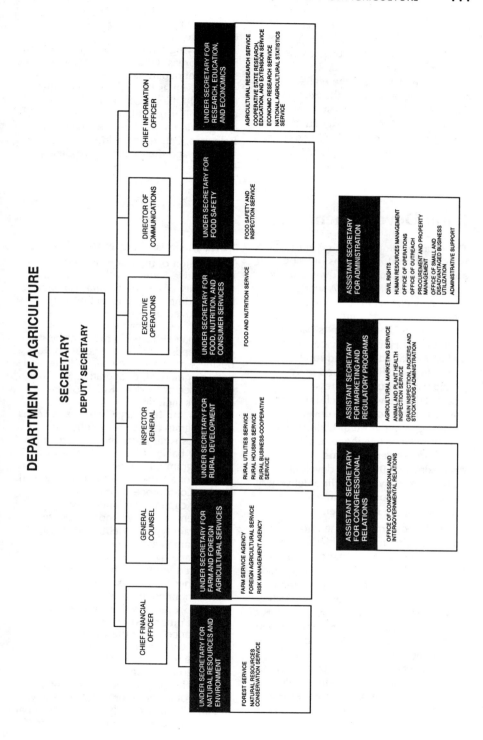

(5 U.S.C. 511, 514, 516). By act of February 9, 1889 (7 U.S.C. 2202, 2208, 2212), the powers and duties of the Department were enlarged. The Department was made the eighth executive department in the Federal Government, and the Commissioner became the Secretary of Agriculture. The Department was reorganized under the Federal Crop Insurance Reform and Department of Agriculture Reorganization Act of 1994 (7 U.S.C. 6901 note).

In carrying out its work in the program mission areas, USDA relies on the support of departmental administration staff, as well as the Office of the Chief Financial Officer, Office of Communications, Office of Congressional and Intergovernmental Relations, Office of the Inspector General, and the Office of the General Counsel.

Rural Development

The rural development mission of USDA is to assist rural Americans in using their abilities to improve their quality of life. To accomplish this, USDA works to foster new cooperative relationships among Government, industry, and communities. The mission is carried out by the Rural Housing Service, which includes rural housing and rural community facility loan and grant programs; the Rural Business-Cooperative Service, which includes business and cooperative development programs; and the Rural Utilities Service, which includes telephone, electric, water, and sewer programs. Approximately 900 rural development field offices provide frontline delivery of all rural development loan and grant programs at the local level.

The Empowerment Zone and Enterprise Community Initiative Office provides technical assistance, training, monitoring, and support to USDA field staff and communities participating in the initiative. Focusing on communities of greatest need, with severe problems of long-term endemic poverty, the program works with other USDA agencies, Federal agencies, State and local governments, and private organizations and universities in a combined effort to develop and promote comprehensive community and economic development in rural America.

Rural Business-Cooperative Service

The mission of the Rural Business-Cooperative Service (RBS) is to enhance the quality of life for all rural Americans by providing leadership in building competitive businesses and sustainable cooperatives that can prosper in the global marketplace. To meet business credit needs in under-served areas, RBS business programs are usually leveraged with commercial, cooperative, or other private sector lenders. RBS business programs include:

Business and Industry Guaranteed Loans This program helps create jobs and stimulates rural economies by providing financial backing for rural businesses. The program guarantees up to 80 percent of a loan made by a commercial lender. Loan proceeds may be used for working capital, machinery and equipment, buildings and real estate, and certain types of debt refinancing. Loan guarantees can be extended to loans made by commercial or other authorized lenders in rural areas (all areas other than cities and unincorporated areas of more than 50,000 people and their immediately adjacent urbanized areas).

Assistance under the Business and Industry Guaranteed Loan Program is available to virtually any legally organized entity, including a cooperative, corporation, partnership, trust, or other profit or nonprofit entity, Indian tribe or federally recognized tribal group, municipality, county, or other political subdivision of a State. Applicants need not have been denied credit elsewhere to apply for this program. The maximum aggregate guaranteed loan(s) amount that can be offered to any one borrower under this program is $25 million.

Business and Industry Direct Loans This program provides loans to public entities and private parties who cannot obtain credit from other sources. Loans to private parties can be made for improving, developing, or financing business and industry, creating jobs, and improving the economic and environmental climate in rural communities, including pollution abatement. Assistance is available in rural areas (all areas other than cities or unincorporated areas of more than 50,000 people and their immediately adjacent urbanized areas).

Eligible applicants include any legally organized entity, including a cooperative, corporation, partnership, trust, or other profit or nonprofit entity, Indian tribe or federally recognized tribal group, municipality, county, any other political subdivision of a State, or individuals. Loans are available to those who cannot obtain credit elsewhere and for public bodies. The maximum aggregate loan amount that can be offered to any one borrower is $10 million.

Intermediary Relending Program Loans These loans finance business facilities and community development projects in rural areas, including cities with populations of less than 25,000. The Service lends these funds to intermediaries, which in turn provide loans to recipients who are developing business facilities or community development projects. Eligible intermediaries include public bodies, nonprofit corporations, Indian tribes, and cooperatives.

Rural Venture Capital Demonstration Program To demonstrate the usefulness of guarantees to attract increased investment in private business enterprises in rural areas, this program designates up to 10 community development venture capital organizations to establish a rural

business private investment pool to make equity investments in rural private business enterprises. The program is available in rural areas (all areas other than cities or unincorporated areas of more than 50,000 people and their immediately adjacent urbanized areas).

Rural Business Enterprise Grants These grants help public bodies, nonprofit corporations, and federally recognized Indian tribal groups finance and facilitate development of small and emerging private business enterprises located in rural areas (all areas other than cities or unincorporated areas of more than 50,000 people and their immediately adjacent urbanized areas). Grant funds can pay for the acquisition and development of land and the construction of buildings, plants, equipment, access streets and roads, parking areas, utility and service extensions, refinancing, and fees for professional services, as well as technical assistance and related training, startup costs and working capital, financial assistance to a third party, production of television programs targeted to rural residents, and rural distance learning networks.

Rural Business Opportunity Grants This program promotes sustainable economic development in rural communities with exceptional needs. Funds are provided for technical assistance, training, and planning activities that improve economic conditions. Applicants must be located in rural areas (all areas other than cities or unincorporated areas of more than 50,000 people and their immediately adjacent urbanized areas). Nonprofit corporations and public bodies, Indian tribes, and cooperatives are eligible for a maximum of $1.5 million per grant.

Rural Economic Development Loans and Grants These loans and grants finance economic development and job creation projects based on sound economic plans in rural areas having a population of less than 2,500 residents. Loans and grants are available to any Rural Utilities Service electric or telecommunications borrower to assist in developing rural areas from an economic standpoint, to create new job opportunities, and to help retain existing employment. Loans at zero interest are made primarily to finance business startup ventures and business expansion projects. Grants are made to telephone and electric utilities to establish revolving loan programs operated at the local level. The revolving loan program provides capital to nonprofit entities and municipal organizations to finance community facilities which promote job creation in rural areas; for facilities which extend or improve medical care to rural residents; and for facilities which promote education and training to enhance marketable job skills for rural residents.

Cooperative Services This program helps farmers and rural communities become self-reliant through the use of cooperative organizations. Studies are conducted to support cooperatives that market farm products, purchase production supplies, and perform related business services. These studies concentrate on the financial, organizational, legal, social, and economic aspects of cooperative activity. Technical assistance and research is provided to improve cooperative performance in organizing new cooperatives, merging existing cooperatives, changing business structures, and developing strategies for growth. Applied research is conducted to give farmers and rural communities expert assistance pertaining to their cooperatives. The program also collects and publishes statistics regarding the role and scope of cooperative activity in U.S. agriculture. The Service's bimonthly magazine, *Rural Cooperatives*, reports current developments and research for cooperative management leadership.

Rural Cooperative Development Grants These grants finance the establishment and operation of centers for cooperative development. The primary purpose of this program is to enhance the economic condition of rural areas through the development of new cooperatives and improving operations of existing cooperatives. Eligible applicants are nonprofit organizations, including institutions of higher education.

Appropriate Technology Transfer for Rural Areas This program provides information to farmers and other rural users on a variety of sustainable agricultural practices that include both cropping and livestock operations. It offers reliable, practical information on production techniques and practices that reduce costs and that are environmentally friendly. Farmers can request such information by telephone at 800–346–9140 (toll-free).

National Sheep Industry Improvement Center The Center promotes strategic development activities to strengthen and enhance the production and marketing of sheep and goat products in the United States. It works to improve infrastructure development, business development, and market and environmental research and designs unique responses to the needs of the industries for their long-term sustainable development. The Center's board of directors oversees its activities and operates a revolving fund for loans and grants.

For further information, contact Rural Development, Office of Communication, Public Affairs, Room 5037–S, Department of Agriculture, Fourteenth Street and Independence Avenue SW., Washington, DC 20250–0320. Phone, 202–720–6903.

Rural Housing Service

The Rural Housing Service (RHS) provides loans to rural residents and communities unable to obtain credit from commercial sources at reasonable rates and terms. These borrowers must have a reasonable chance for success. The Service guarantees loans made by commercial lenders for modest rural housing. It also makes direct loans to low-income rural residents. Rural residents and communities may apply for these loans at approximately 900 local Rural Development offices.

The Service operates under Title V of the Housing Act of 1949 (42 U.S.C. 1471) and the Consolidated Farm and Rural Development Act (7 U.S.C. 1921). It seeks to do business as the lender of first opportunity rather than the lender of last resort.

The Service provides financial and management assistance through the following types of loans:

Guaranteed Single-Family Housing (SFH) Loan Programs The Service guarantees loans made by commercial lenders to moderate-income (up to 115 percent median income for an area) rural residents. Eligible applicants must have sufficient income and acceptable credit but lack the downpayment to secure a loan without assistance. The Service provides up to 100 percent financing for eligible borrowers and guarantees participating lenders against most losses.

Direct Single-Family Housing Loan Program Section 502 loans are made to very low (under 50 percent median income for the area) and low (under 80 percent median income for the area) income families for housing in rural areas. Loans can be made to build, purchase, repair, and refinance homes. The maximum term is 38 years. Loans may be made for 100 percent of the appraised value. The basic interest rate is determined periodically, based on the cost of money. Borrowers may qualify for annual subsidy on the loan, which can reduce the interest rate to as low as 1 percent. Cosigners on promissory notes may be permitted for applicants who may lack repayment ability.

Builders may obtain "conditional commitments" as assurances to a builder or seller that if their houses meet RHS lending requirements, RHS may make loans to qualified applicants.

Home Improvement and Repair Loans and Grants An owner-occupant may obtain a section 504 loan of up to $15,000, or in the case of senior citizens 62 years of age or older, a grant of up to $7,500, to remove health and safety hazards from a home. These loans, available to very low income families, are made at 1 percent interest.

Self-Help Housing Loans Self-help direct SFH loans assist groups of six to eight very low and low income families to build their own home by providing "sweat equity" which reduces the families' mortgage. The families must agree to work together on each other's homes until they are complete. In most cases, self-help participants use the Section 502 Direct program for mortgage financing.

Rural Housing Site Loans Loans are also available to private or public nonprofit organizations to purchase sites for the development of housing for very low and low income families. Loans are repayable in 2 years.

Direct and Guaranteed Multi-Family Housing Loans Loans are made to private, nonprofit corporations, consumer cooperatives, State or local public agencies, and individuals or organizations operating on a profit or limited profit basis to provide rental or cooperative housing in rural areas for persons of very low, low, and moderate income. For direct loans, no downpayment is required from nonprofit organizations. A 3 or 5 percent downpayment is required from other applicants. The maximum term is 50 years, with a 30-year repayment option, and the interest rate may be reduced to 1 percent to make rents affordable to very low and low income families. Rental assistance may be available to defray rent paid by very low income families. Guaranteed loans bear an interest rate negotiated by the lender and borrower. Interest credit is available on a small number of loans to assist with affordability to very low income families.

Farm Labor Housing Loans and Grants Farm labor housing loans and grants enable farmers, public or private nonprofit organizations, or units of local government to build, buy, or rehabilitate farm labor housing. The interest rate is 1 percent and is repaid over 33 years. Grants may be made in connection with a loan to a public/private nonprofit organization or unit of government to ensure affordability of the units to farm workers.

Housing Preservation Grants These grants are made to a public body or public/private nonprofit organization to provide assistance to homeowners and landlords to repair and rehabilitate housing for very low and low income families in rural areas. Financial assistance provided by grantees may include loans, grants, interest reduction on loans, or similar assistance. Up to 20 percent of the grant may be used for program administration.

Housing the Homeless   The Service offers SFH real-estate-owned property to nonprofit organizations or public bodies for transitional housing for the homeless. Qualifying organizations may lease nonprogram property if they can show a documented need in the community for the type of housing use proposed and the financial ability to meet proposed housing costs.

Community Program Loans   Direct and guaranteed loans and grants are authorized to public and quasi-public bodies, nonprofit associations, and certain Indian tribes for essential community facilities such as health care, public safety, and public services. Necessary related equipment may also be purchased. The interest rate is set quarterly for direct loans and is based on yields of municipal bonds. Guaranteed loans bear an interest rate negotiated by the lender and the borrower. The Service guarantees a lender against losses up to 90 percent of principal and interest. Community facility assistance may be provided to towns populated up to 50,000. Nondiscrimination in employment and occupancy is required.

For further information, contact Rural Development, Office of Communication, Public Affairs, Room 5037–S, Department of Agriculture, Fourteenth Street and Independence Avenue SW., Washington, DC 20250–0320. Phone, 202–720–6903.

Rural Utilities Service

The Rural Utilities Service (RUS) is a credit agency that assists rural electric and telephone utilities in obtaining financing and administers a nationwide water and waste loan and grant program to improve the quality of life and promote economic development in rural America. A total of 890 rural electric and 900 rural telephone utilities in 47 States, Puerto Rico, the Virgin Islands, Guam, the Republic of the Marshall Islands, the Northern Mariana Islands, and the Federated States of Micronesia have received financial assistance. Approximately 7,200 rural communities are currently served through financial

assistance received from water and waste loans and grants.

Electric Program   The Rural Electrification Act of 1936, as amended (7 U.S.C. 901–950b), authorizes RUS to provide loans for improving electric service to persons in rural areas, as defined by the Bureau of the Census. Preference is given to nonprofit and cooperative associations and to public bodies. With RUS assistance, rural electric utilities have obtained financing to construct electric generating plants and transmission and distribution lines to provide reliable electric service.

Telecommunications Program   In 1949, RUS (then the Rural Electrification Administration) was authorized to make loans to provide telephone service in rural areas. Congress directed that the rural telephone program be conducted to "assure the availability of adequate telephone service to the widest practicable number of rural users of such service." About 75 percent of the telephone systems financed by the agency are commercial companies, and about 25 percent are subscriber-owned cooperatives.

Loans   Loans are made in accordance with the Act and are subject to the provisions of the Federal Credit Reform Act of 1991. By law, RUS direct loans are made or insured at a municipal rate, but not greater than 7 percent. In cases of hardship, the Administrator may approve loans at an interest rate of 5 percent.

The Service also obtains funds from the Department of the Treasury's Federal Financing Bank (FFB), which it lends to borrowers, primarily for large-scale electric and telecommunication facilities, at an interest rate equal to the cost of money paid by FFB, plus one-eighth of 1 percent.

Supplemental Financing   A 1973 statement of congressional policy—not part of the law—said, in part, ". . . that rural electric and telephone systems should be encouraged and assisted in developing their resources and ability to achieve the financial strength needed to enable them to satisfy their credit needs from their own financial organizations and other sources at reasonable rates and terms consistent with the loan applicant's ability to pay and achievement of the act's objectives."

When RUS approves electric loans, it requires most borrowers to obtain 30 percent of their loan needs from nonagency sources without an agency guarantee. These nonagency sources include the National Rural Utilities Cooperative Finance Corporation, which is owned by electric cooperatives, and the National Bank for Cooperatives.

Telecommunications borrowers obtain supplemental financing from the Rural Telephone Bank (RTB), a U.S. agency established in 1971. Loans are made to telecommunications systems able to meet RTB requirements. Bank loans are made for the same purposes as loans made to RUS but bear interest at a rate consistent with the Bank's cost of money.

The Rural Telephone Bank is managed by a 13-member board of directors. The Administrator of RUS serves as Governor of the Bank until conversion to private ownership, control, and operation. This will take place when 51 percent of the class A stock issued to the United States and outstanding at any time after September 30, 1995, has been fully redeemed and retired. The Bank board holds at least four regularly scheduled meetings a year. Activities of RTB are carried out by RUS employees and the Department's Office of the General Counsel.

Water and Waste Direct and Guaranteed Loan Program   Direct loans may be made to develop water and wastewater systems, including solid waste disposal and storm drainage, in rural areas, cities, and towns with a population of 10,000 or less.

Funds are available to public entities, such as municipalities, counties, special-purpose districts, and Indian tribes. In addition, funds may be made available. to nonprofit corporations. Priority is given to public entities in areas with less than 5,500 people to restore a deteriorating water supply or to improve, enlarge, or modify a water facility or an inadequate waste facility. Preference is given to requests which involve the

merging of small facilities and those serving low-income communities. Applicants must be unable to obtain funds from other sources at reasonable rates and terms. The maximum term for all loans is 40 years. However, no repayment period will exceed State statutes or the useful life of the facility. Interest rates may be obtained from USDA Rural Development field offices.

Guaranteed loans may be made for the same purpose as direct loans. They are made and serviced by lenders such as banks and savings and loan associations. Normally, guarantees will not exceed 80 percent on any loss of interest or principal on the loan.

Water and Waste Disposal Grants Grants may be made to reduce water and waste disposal costs to a reasonable level for users of the system. Grants may be made, in some instances, up to 75 percent of eligible project costs. Requirements for applicants are the same as for loans.

Emergency Community Water Assistance Grants   Grants may be made up to 100 percent of project costs to assist rural communities experiencing a significant decline in quantity or quality of drinking water. Grants can be made to rural cities or towns with populations not exceeding the State's nonmetropolitan median household income requirement.

Technical Assistance and Training Grants   Grants are available for nonprofit organizations to provide rural water and waste system officials with technical assistance and training on a wide range of issues relating to the delivery of water and waste service to rural residents. Legislation requires that at least 1 percent but no more than 3 percent of the funds appropriated for water and waste disposal grants be set aside for these grants.

Solid Waste Management Grants Grants are available for nonprofit organizations and public bodies to provide technical assistance and training to rural areas and towns with populations under 10,000 to reduce or eliminate pollution of water resources and improve planning and management of solid waste facilities.

Rural Water Circuit Rider Technical Assistance Program   Since 1980, the National Rural Water Association has provided, by contract, technical assistance to rural water systems. Circuit riders assist rural water districts with solving operational, financial, and management problems. The assistance may be requested by rural water systems or by RUS. When circuit riders are not working on specific requests, they call on rural water systems to offer assistance. The program complements RUS water and waste loan supervision responsibilities.

Distance Learning and Medical Link Grant Program   The 1990 farm bill authorized the Distance Learning and Telemedicine Grant Program to provide grants to rural schools and health care providers. The 1996 farm bill reauthorized the grant program and established a new loan component. The program helps rural schools and health care providers invest in telecommunications facilities and equipment to bring to rural areas educational and medical resources that otherwise might be unavailable.

For further information, contact the Rural Utilities Service, Department of Agriculture, Room 4051–S, Fourteenth Street and Independence Avenue SW., Washington, DC 20250–0320. Phone, 202–720–1255.

Alternative Agricultural Research and Commercialization Corporation

As an independent entity within USDA, the Alternative Agricultural Research and Commercialization Corporation (AARCC) provides and monitors financial assistance for the development and commercialization of new nonfood and nonfeed products made from agricultural/forestry commodities. By law, AARCC is administered by an 11-member board comprising representatives for processing, financial, producer, and scientific interests.

The Corporation's mission is to assist the private sector in closing the gap between research results and commercialization of industrial nonfood and nonfeed products made from farm and forestry materials. It also seeks to expand market opportunities through development of value-added industrial products and promotion of environmentally friendly products. Any private individual or firm may apply for assistance. While most of the Corporation's clients are small firms, nonprofit organizations and large businesses have also been successful

applicants. Universities and similar institutions may participate as well.

The Corporation can supply financial assistance at the precommercialization stage of a project—that point in a project when the costs are the greatest and the ability to obtain lending from traditional sources is the most difficult. Financial assistance is in the form of a repayable cooperative agreement and includes a repayment portion that recognizes the investment risk taken by AARCC. Applicants are expected to provide at least a 1:1 match when seeking funding from AARCC. The Corporation receives an annual appropriation from Congress and operates under a revolving fund. As Corporation-funded projects become profitable and reimburse AARCC, the money will be returned to the fund to help finance future projects.

For further information, contact the Alternative Agricultural Research and Commercialization Corporation, Room 0156, 1400 Independence Avenue SW., Washington, DC 20250–0401. Phone, 202–690–1633.

Marketing and Regulatory Programs

This mission area includes marketing and regulatory programs other than those concerned with food safety.

Agricultural Marketing Service

The Agricultural Marketing Service (AMS) was established by the Secretary of Agriculture on April 2, 1972, under the authority of Reorganization Plan No. 2 of 1953 (5 U.S.C. app.) and other authorities. The Service administers standardization, grading, certification, market news, marketing orders, research and promotion, and regulatory programs.

Market News   The Service provides current, unbiased information to producers, processors, distributors, and others to assist them in the orderly marketing and distribution of farm commodities. Information is collected on supplies, demand, prices, movement, location, quality, condition, and other market data on farm products in specific markets and marketing areas. The data is disseminated nationally via a modern satellite system and is shared with several countries. The Service also assists countries in developing their own marketing information systems.

Standardization, Grading, and Classing   Grade standards have been established for about 230 agricultural commodities to help buyers and sellers trade on agreed-upon quality levels. Standards are developed with the benefit of views from those in the industries directly affected and others interested. The Service also participates in developing international standards to facilitate trade.

Grading and classing services are provided to certify the grade and quality of products. These grading services are provided to buyers and sellers of live cattle, swine, sheep, meat, poultry, eggs, rabbits, fruits, vegetables, tree nuts, peanuts, dairy products, and tobacco. Classing services are provided to buyers and sellers of cotton and cotton products. These services are mainly voluntary and are provided upon request and for a fee. The Service also is responsible for the certification of turpentine and other naval stores products, and the testing of seed.

Laboratory Testing   The Service provides scientific and laboratory support to its commodity programs relating to testing of microbiological and chemical factors in food products through grading, certification, acceptance, and regulatory programs; testing of peanuts for aflatoxin; testing of imported flue-cured and burley tobacco for pesticide residues; and testing seeds for germination and purity. The agency also carries out quality assurance and safety oversight activities with respect to the Service's commodity division laboratory and testing activities relating to milk market administrators, resident grading programs, and State and private laboratory programs.

The Service also administers the Pesticide Data Program which, in cooperation with States, samples and analyzes fresh fruits and vegetables for pesticide residues. It shares residue test results with the Environmental Protection Agency and other public agencies.

Food Quality Assurance   Under a governmentwide quality assurance program, AMS is responsible for the development and revision of specifications used by Federal agencies in procuring food for military and civilian uses. The Service coordinates and approves certification programs designed to ensure that purchased products conform to the specification requirements.

Section 32 Programs   Under section 32 of the act of August 24, 1935, as amended (7 U.S.C. 612c), 30 percent of customs receipts collected during each calendar year are automatically appropriated for expanding outlets for various commodities. Portions of these funds are transferred to the Food and Nutrition Service of USDA and to the Department of Commerce. Remaining funds are used to purchase commodities for the National School Lunch Program and other feeding programs, for diversion to other outlets, and for administering agreement and order programs.

Regulatory Programs The Service administers several regulatory programs designed collectively to protect producers, handlers, and consumers of agricultural commodities from financial loss or personal injury resulting from careless, deceptive, or fraudulent marketing practices. Such regulatory programs encourage fair trading practices in the marketing of fruits and vegetables, require truth in seed labeling and in advertising.

Under the Egg Products Inspection Act (21 U.S.C. 1031–1056), the Service provides voluntary laboratory analyses of egg products, and monitors the disposition of restricted shell eggs—eggs that are a potential health hazard.

Marketing Agreements and Orders These programs, under authority of the Agricultural Marketing Agreement Act of 1937 (7 U.S.C. 601 *et seq.*), help to establish and maintain orderly marketing conditions for certain commodities. Milk marketing orders establish minimum prices that handlers or distributors are required to pay producers. Programs for fruits, vegetables, and related specialty crops like nuts and spearmint oil help stabilize supplies and market prices. In some cases, they also authorize research and market development activities, including advertising supported by assessments that handlers pay. Through orderly marketing, adjusting the supply to demand, and avoiding unreasonable fluctuations during the marketing season, the income of producers is increased by normal market forces, and consumer interests are protected through quality and quantity control.

Federal marketing orders originate with a request from a producer group to the Secretary of Agriculture. The Secretary can conduct hearings and referenda based on the producer group's proposal for a marketing order. Producer and handler assessments finance their operations.

In carrying out the Government role, the Service ensures that persons interested in the development and operation of the programs have a fair hearing and that each marketing order

works according to Federal law and established rules and guidelines.

Plant Variety Protection Program Under authority of the Plant Variety Protection Act (7 U.S.C. 2321 *et seq.*), the Service administers a program that provides for the issuance of "certificates of plant variety protection." These certificates afford developers of novel varieties of sexually reproduced plants exclusive rights to sell, reproduce, import, or export such varieties, or use them in the production of hybrids or different varieties for a period of 20 years for non-woody plants and 25 years for woody plants.

Research and Promotion Programs The Service monitors certain industry-sponsored research, promotion, and information programs authorized by Federal laws. These programs provide farmers with a means to finance and operate various research, promotion, and information activities for cotton, potatoes, eggs, milk and dairy products, beef, pork, honey, watermelon, mushrooms, soybeans, fresh cut flowers, popcorn, and kiwi fruit.

Transportation Programs The Service is also responsible for the development of an efficient transportation system for rural America that begins at the farm gate and moves agricultural and other rural products through the Nation's highways, railroads, airports, and waterways, and into the domestic and international marketplace. To accomplish this, AMS conducts economic studies and analyses of these systems, and represents agricultural and rural transportation interests in policy and regulatory forums. To provide direct assistance to the transportation community, AMS supplies research and technical information to producers, producer groups, shippers, exporters, rural communities, carriers, governmental agencies, and universities.

The Service carries out responsibilities of USDA's former Office of Transportation under the Agricultural Adjustment Act of 1938 (7 U.S.C. 1281), the Agricultural Marketing Act of 1946 (7 U.S.C. 1621), the Agricultural Trade Development and Assistance Act of

1954 (7 U.S.C. 1691), the Rural Development Act of 1972 (7 U.S.C. 1921 note), the International Carriage of Perishable Foodstuffs Act (7 U.S.C. 4401), and the Cooperative Marketing Act of 1926 (7 U.S.C. 451–457).

Organic Standards Under the Organic Foods Production Act of 1990 (7 U.S.C. 501–522), the Service assists a National Organic Standards Board in developing national organic standards.

Other Programs Other marketing service activities include financial grants to States for marketing improvement projects. The agency also has responsibility for the conduct of studies of the facilities and methods used in the physical distribution of food and other farm products; for research designed to improve the handling of all agricultural products as they move from farm to consumers; and for increasing marketing efficiency by developing improved operating methods, facilities, and equipment for processing, handling, and distributing dairy, poultry, and meat products.

The Agricultural Marketing Service manages the Pesticide Recordkeeping Program in coordination with the National Agricultural Statistics Service and the Environmental Protection Agency. The Service has developed educational programs and assists State agencies in inspecting applicator records.

Field Organization Programs and activities in the field are carried out through a variety of different types of organizations reporting to their respective Washington components.

For further information, contact the Information Staff, Agricultural Marketing Service, Department of Agriculture, P.O. Box 96456, Washington, DC 20250. Phone, 202–720–8999.

Animal and Plant Health Inspection Service

[For the Animal and Plant Health Inspection Service statement of organization, see the *Code of Federal Regulations,* Title 7, Part 371]

The Animal and Plant Health Inspection Service (APHIS) was reestablished by the Secretary of Agriculture on March 14, 1977, pursuant to authority contained in

5 U.S.C. 301 and Reorganization Plan No. 2 of 1953 (5 U.S.C. app.).

The Service was established to conduct regulatory and control programs to protect and improve animal and plant health for the benefit of man and the environment. In cooperation with State governments, the agency administers Federal laws and regulations pertaining to animal and plant health and quarantine, humane treatment of animals, and the control and eradication of pests and diseases. Regulations to prevent the introduction or interstate spread of certain animal or plant pests or diseases are also enforced by the Service. It also carries out research and operational activities to reduce crop and livestock depredations caused by birds, rodents, and predators.

Plant Protection and Quarantine Programs Plant protection officials are responsible for programs to control or eradicate plant pests and diseases. These programs are carried out in cooperation with the States involved, other Federal agencies, farmers, and private organizations. Pest control programs use a single tool or a combination of pest control techniques, both chemical and nonchemical, which are both effective and safe.

Agricultural quarantine inspection officials administer Federal regulations that prohibit or restrict the entry of foreign pests and plants, plant products, animal products and byproducts, and other materials that may harbor pests or diseases. Inspection service is maintained at all major sea, air, border, and interior ports of entry in the continental United States ar.d in Hawaii, Alaska, Puerto Rico, U.S. Virgin Islands, Bahamas, and Bermuda. Services also are provided on a regular or on-call basis at some 500 outlying ports and military installations throughout the country.

Other responsibilities include the inspection and certification of domestic commodities for export; regulation of the import and export of endangered plant species and of genetically engineered organisms and products that present a plant pest risk; and ensuring that imported seed is free of noxious weeds.

Veterinary Services Animal health officials are responsible for programs to protect and improve the health, quality, and marketability of U.S. animals and animal products. The programs are carried out through cooperative links with States, foreign governments, livestock producers, and other Federal Agencies.

Service officials exclude, control, and eradicate animal pests and diseases by carrying out eradication and control programs for certain diseases, providing diagnostic services, and gathering and disseminating information regarding animal health in the United States through land, air, and ocean ports. They also certify as to the health status of animals and animal products being exported to other countries and respond to animal disease incursions or epidemics which threaten the health status of U.S. livestock and poultry.

The Service also administers a Federal law intended to ensure that all veterinary biological products, whether developed by conventional or new biotechnological procedures, used in the diagnosis, prevention, and treatment of animal disease are safe, pure, potent, and effective. The Service regulates firms that manufacture veterinary biological products subject to the act, including licensing the manufacturing establishment and its products, inspecting production facilities and production methods, and testing products under a surveillance program.

Animal Care The Service administers Federal laws concerned with the humane care and handling of all warm-blooded animals bought, sold, and transported—including common carriers—in commerce and used or intended for use as pets at the wholesale level, or used or intended for use in exhibitions or for research purposes. The agency also enforces the Horse Protection Act of 1970, which prohibits the soring of horses at shows and sales.

International Services Service activities in the international arena include conducting cooperative plant and animal pest and disease control, eradication, and surveillance programs in foreign countries. These programs provide a first line of defense for the United States against threats such as screwworm, medfly, foot-and-mouth disease, and other exotic diseases and pests. The Service also provides international representation concerning sanitary and phytosanitary technical trade issues, and manages programs for overseas preclearance of commodities, passengers, and U.S. military activities.

Wildlife Services Wildlife Services officials cooperate with States, counties, local communities, and agricultural producer groups to reduce crop and livestock depredations caused by birds, rodents, and predators. Using methods and techniques that are biologically sound, environmentally acceptable, and economically feasible, they participate in efforts to educate and advise farmers and ranchers on proper uses of control methods and techniques; they suppress serious nuisances and threats to public health and safety caused by birds, rodents, and other wildlife in urban and rural communities; and they work with airport managers to reduce risks of bird strikes. In addition, they conduct research into predator-prey relationships, new control methods, and more efficient and safe uses of present methods such as toxicants, repellants and attractants, biological controls, scare devices, and habitat alteration.

For further information, contact Legislative and Public Affairs, Animal and Plant Health Inspection Service, Department of Agriculture, Washington, DC 20250. Phone, 202–720–2511.

Grain Inspection, Packers, and Stockyards Administration

The Grain Inspection, Packers, and Stockyards Administration (GIPSA) comprises the former Federal Grain Inspection Service and the former Packers and Stockyards Administration.

The primary task of GIPSA is to carry out the provisions of the United States Grain Standards Act (7 U.S.C. 71 et seq.), the Packers and Stockyards Act of 1921, as amended (7 U.S.C. 181–229), the Truth in Lending and Fair Credit Billing Acts (15 U.S.C. 1601 et seq.), and the Equal Credit Opportunity Act (15 U.S.C. 1691 et seq.) with respect to firms subject to GIPSA. The Administration also manages the provisions of section 1324 of the Food Security Act of 1985 (7 U.S.C. 1631), certifying State central filing systems for notification of liens against farm products and ensures integrity in the inspection, weighing, and handling of U.S. grain.

The Administration is responsible for establishing official U.S. standards for grain and other assigned commodities, and for administrating a nationwide official inspection and weighing system. It may, in response to formal application, authorize private and State agencies to perform official services under the authority contained in the act.

Two of GIPSA's three grain inspection divisions are located in Washington, DC; the third is located in Kansas City, MO. Most employees work in field offices around the Nation.

Inspection The United States Grain Standards Act requires that, with some exceptions, all U.S. export grain be officially inspected. At export port locations, inspection is performed by GIPSA or by State agencies that have been delegated export inspection authority by the Administrator. For domestic grain, marketed at inland locations, the Administrator designates private and State agencies to provide official inspection services upon request. Both export and domestic services are provided on a fee basis.

To ensure that the official U.S. grain standards are applied uniformly nationwide, GIPSA's field offices provide oversight, guidance, and assistance to non-Federal agencies performing inspection activities, both at export and inland inspection points.

Buyers and sellers may request appeal inspections of original inspection results, first from a field office and then, if desired, from GIPSA's Board of Appeals and Review. The Administration maintains a quality control program to monitor the national inspection system and to ensure that all field locations accurately and uniformly apply the U.S. grain standards.

Weighing Official weighing of U.S. export grain is performed at port locations by GIPSA or by State agencies

that have been delegated export weighing authority by the Administrator. For domestic grain marketed at inland locations, the weighing services may be provided by GIPSA or by designated private or State agencies. Weighing services are provided on a fee basis, upon request.

As with inspection activities, GIPSA field offices provide oversight, guidance, and assistance to non-Federal agencies performing official weighing services. With the support of the Association of American Railroads and user fees, it conducts a railroad track scale-testing program which includes an annual testing service for all State and railroad company-owned master scales. The Administration is the only entity, public or private, which connects all railroad track scales to the national standards.

Standardization The Administration is responsible for establishing, maintaining, and, as needed, revising official U.S. standards. Such standards exist for corn, wheat, rye, oats, barley, flaxseed, sorghum, soybeans, triticale, sunflower seed, canola, and mixed grain. It is authorized to perform applied research to develop methods of improving accuracy and uniformity in grading grain.

It is also responsible for standardization and inspection activities for rice, dry beans, peas, lentils, hay, straw, hops, and related processed grain commodities under the Agricultural Marketing Act of 1946, as amended (7 U.S.C. 1621). Although standards no longer exist for hay, straw, and hops, GIPSA maintains inspection procedures for and retains authority to inspect these commodities.

Methods Development The Administration's methods development activities include applied research or tests that produce new or improved techniques for measuring grain quality. Examples include new knowledge gained through study of how to establish the framework for real-time grain inspection and develop reference methods to maintain consistency and standardization in the grain inspection system, and the comparison of different techniques for evaluation of end use quality in wheat. Included in this program area are also the development of a new wheat classification system, evaluation of prototype wheat hardness meters, and adapting measurement techniques for pesticides, mycotoxins, heavy metals, vitamins, and grain odor for use in the official grain inspection system.

Compliance   The Administration's compliance activities ensure accurate and uniform implementation of the act, applicable provisions of the Agricultural Marketing Act of 1946, and related regulations—including designating States and private agencies to carry out official inspection and weighing functions and monitoring, and overseeing and reviewing the operations of such agencies to ensure adequate performance.

The agency administers a registration program for all firms that export grain from the United States. In conjunction with the Office of the Inspector General, it carries out a program for investigating reported violations, and initiates followup and corrective actions when appropriate. The total compliance program ensures the integrity of the national inspection and weighing system.

Packers and Stockyards Activities   The Packers and Stockyards Act is an antitrust, trade practice, and financial protection law. Its principal purpose is to maintain effective competition and fair trade practices in the marketing of livestock, meat, and poultry for the protection of livestock and poultry producers. Members of the livestock, poultry, and meat industries are also protected against unfair or monopolistic practices of competitors. The act also protects consumers against unfair business practices in the marketing of meats and poultry and against restrictions of competition that could unduly affect meat and poultry prices.

The provisions of the Packers and Stockyards Act are enforced by investigations of violations of the act with emphasis on payment protection; detecting instances of commercial bribery, fraud in livestock marketing, and false weighing; requiring adequate bond coverage for commission firms, dealers, and packers; and the surveillance of marketing methods at public markets and in geographical market areas of the country.

For further information, contact the Grain Inspection, Packers, and Stockyards Administration, Department of Agriculture, Washington, DC 20250. Phone, 202–720–0219.

Food Safety

Food Safety and Inspection Service

The Food Safety and Inspection Service (FSIS) was established by the Secretary of Agriculture on June 17, 1981, pursuant to authority contained in 5 U.S.C. 301 and Reorganization Plan No. 2 of 1953 (5 U.S.C. app.). At that time, the Service was delegated authority for regulating the meat and poultry industry to ensure that meat and poultry, and meat and poultry products moving in interstate and foreign commerce were safe, wholesome, unadulterated, and accurately labeled. Under the Secretary's Memorandum No. 1010–1, dated October 23, 1994, the Service's authority was extended to include the inspection of egg products.

Meat, Poultry, and Egg Products Inspection   Federal meat and poultry inspection is mandatory for the following animals and birds used for human food: cattle, calves, swine, goats, sheep, lambs, horses (and other equines), chickens, turkeys, ducks, geese, and guineas. The work includes inspection of each animal or bird at slaughter, and inspection of processed products during various stages of production. Under the Egg Products Inspection Act (21 U.S.C. 1031–1056), the Service conducts mandatory, continuous inspection of the production of liquid, dried, and frozen egg products, to ensure that egg products are safe, wholesome, unadulterated, and accurately labeled. The Service tests samples of egg products, and meat and poultry products for microbial and chemical contaminants to monitor trends for enforcement purposes.

Each product label must be approved by the agency before products can be sold. The agency monitors meat and poultry products in storage, distribution, and retail channels; and takes necessary compliance actions to protect the public, including detention of products, voluntary product recalls, court-ordered seizures of products, administrative withdrawal of inspection, and referral for criminal prosecution. The Service also conducts State programs for the inspection of meat and poultry products sold in intrastate commerce.

The Service monitors livestock upon arrival at federally inspected facilities to ensure compliance with the Humane Slaughter Act (7 U.S.C. 1901–1906); conducts voluntary reimbursed inspection for rabbits, other domestic food animals, bison, other exotic food animals (9 U.S.C. 3521), ratites, and certain egg products not covered by the inspection law (7 U.S.C. 1621–1627); and ensures that inedible egg products and inedible products from meat or poultry, such as offal rendered for animal feed, are properly identified and isolated from edible products (21 U.S.C. 1031–1056 and 7 U.S.C. 1624, respectively).

The Service maintains a toll-free meat and poultry hotline (800–535–4555; in the Washington metropolitan area, 202–720–5604) to answer questions about labeling and safe handling of meat and poultry, meat and poultry products, and egg products. The hotline is also accessible (on the same extension) by TDD.

For further information, contact the Director, Food Safety Education and Communications Staff, Food Safety and Inspection Service, Department of Agriculture, Washington, DC 20250. Phone, 202–720–7943. Fax, 202–720–1843. Internet, http://www.usda.gov/agency/fsis/homepage.htm/.

Food, Nutrition, and Consumer Services

In order to reduce hunger, the Food and Nutrition Service, in partnership with cooperative organizations, provides children and needy families access to food, a healthful diet, and nutrition education in a manner that supports American agriculture and inspires public confidence.

Food and Nutrition Service

[For the Food and Nutrition Service statement of organization, see the *Federal Register* of June 6, 1970, 35 FR 8835]

The Food and Nutrition Service (FNS) administers the USDA food assistance programs. These programs, which serve one in six Americans, provide a Federal safety net to people in need and represent our Nation's commitment to the principle that no one in this country should fear hunger or experience want. The goals of the programs are to provide needy persons with access to a more nutritious diet, to improve the eating habits of the Nation's children, and to help America's farmers by providing an outlet for distribution of foods purchased under farmer assistance authorities.

Many of the food programs administered by FNS originated long before the agency was established in 1969. The Food Stamp Program, now the cornerstone of USDA food assistance, began in its modern form in 1961, but it originated as the Food Stamp Plan to help those in need in the 1930's. The National School Lunch Program also has it roots in Depression-era efforts to help low-income children. Today, its mission encompasses teaching children about nutrition and improving the nutrition standards of school meals. The Needy Family Program, which has evolved into the Food Distribution Program on Indian reservations, was the primary means of food assistance during the Great Depression.

The Service works in partnership with the States in all its programs. State and local agencies determine most administrative details regarding distribution of food benefits and eligibility of participants, and FNS provides commodities and funding for additional food and to cover administrative costs. FNS administers the following food assistance programs:

—The Food Stamp Program provides food benefits through State and local welfare agencies to needy persons to increase their food purchasing power. The benefits are used by program participants to buy food in retail stores approved by the Food and Nutrition Service to accept and redeem the benefits.

—The Special Supplemental Nutrition Program for Women, Infants, and Children (WIC) improves the health of low-income pregnant, breastfeeding, and nonbreastfeeding postpartum women, and infants and children up to 5 years of age by providing them with specific nutritious food supplements, nutrition education, and health care referrals.

—The WIC Farmers' Market Nutrition Program provides WIC participants with increased access to fresh produce at farmers' markets, which promotes the local farm economy. Participants receive coupons to purchase fresh fruits and vegetables from authorized farmers.

—The Commodity Supplemental Food Program provides a package of foods monthly to low-income pregnant, postpartum, and breastfeeding women, their infants and children under age 6, and the elderly. Nutrition education is also provided through this program.

—The National School Lunch Program supports nonprofit food services in elementary and secondary schools and in residential child-care institutions to improve the health and nutrition of the Nation's children. More than half the meals served through these institutions are free or at reduced cost.

—The School Breakfast Program supplements the National School Lunch Program by supporting schools in providing needy children with free or low cost breakfasts that meet established nutritional standards.

—The Special Milk Program for Children provides milk for children in those schools, summer camps, and child-care institutions that have no federally supported meal programs.

—The Child and Adult Care Food Program provides cash and commodities for meals for preschool and school-aged children in child-care facilities and for functionally impaired adults in facilities that provide nonresidential care for such individuals.

—The Summer Food Service Program for Children helps various organizations get nutritious meals to needy preschool and school-aged children during the summer months and during school vacations.

—The Emergency Food Assistance Program provides State agencies with commodities for distribution to food banks, food pantries, soup kitchens, and other charitable institutions throughout the country, with administrative funds to assist in distribution.

—The Food Distribution Program on Indian Reservations provides an extensive package of commodities monthly to low-income households on or near Indian reservations in lieu of food stamps. This program is administered at the local level by Indian tribal organizations or State agencies.

—The Nutrition Program for the Elderly provides cash and commodities to States for meals for senior citizens. The food is delivered through senior citizen centers or meals-on-wheels programs.

—The Nutrition Assistance Program, Puerto Rico, American Samoa, and the Commonwealth of the Northern Mariana Islands is a block grant program that provides cash and coupons to participants in three territories.

—The Homeless Children Nutrition Program reimburses providers for nutritious meals served to homeless preschool children in emergency shelters.

—The Nutrition Education and Training Program grants funds to States for the development and dissemination of nutrition information and materials to children and for inservice training of food service and teaching personnel.

No person may be discriminated against because of race, color, sex, creed, national origin, or handicap in the programs administered by the Food and Consumer Service.

For further information, contact the Public Information Officer, Food and Nutrition Service, Department of Agriculture, Alexandria, VA 22302. Phone, 703–305–2286. Internet, http://www.usda.gov/fns.htm.

Center for Nutrition Policy and Promotion

The Center coordinates nutrition policy in USDA and provides overall leadership in nutrition education for the American public. It also coordinates with the Department of Health and Human Services in the review, revision, and dissemination of the *Dietary Guidelines for Americans*, the Federal Government's statement of nutrition policy formed by a consensus of scientific and medical professionals.

For further information, contact the Office of Public Information, Center for Nutrition Policy and Promotion, Suite 200, 1120 20th Street NW., Washington, DC 20036–3406. Phone, 202–418–2312. Internet, http://www.usda.gov/fns/cnpp.htm.

Farm and Foreign Agricultural Services

Through the Farm Service Agency (FSA), this mission area administers farm commodity, crop insurance, and resource conservation programs for farmers, and makes loans through a network of State and county offices. Agency programs are directed at agricultural producers or, in the case of loans, at those with farming experience.

Farm Service Agency

The Federal Agriculture Improvement and Reform Act of 1996 (110 Stat. 888) significantly changed U.S. agricultural policy by removing the link between income support payments and farm prices. The law provided that farmers who participated in the wheat, feed grains, cotton, and rice programs in any one of the previous 5 years could enter into 7-year production flexibility contracts and receive a series of fixed payments. These payments are independent of farm prices and specific crop production, in contrast to the past, when deficiency payments were based on farm prices and the production of specific crops. The Federal Government no longer requires land to be idled or denies payments if farmers switch from their historical crop. The contract, however, requires participating producers to comply with existing conservation plans for the farm, wetland provisions, and planting flexibility provisions, as well as to keep the land in agricultural uses.

The law provided for a one-time signup which ended August 1, 1996. There will be no additional signups except for land coming out of the Conservation Reserve Program.

Farm Service Agency (FSA) programs are described below.

Commodity Loan Programs The Agency administers commodity loan programs for wheat, rice, corn, grain sorghum, barley, oats, oilseeds, tobacco, peanuts, upland and extra-long-staple cotton, and sugar. It provides operating personnel for the Commodity Credit Corporation (CCC), which supports the prices of some agricultural commodities through loans and purchases. This provides farmers with interim financing and helps maintain balanced and adequate supplies of farm commodities, and their orderly distribution, throughout the year and during times of surplus and scarcity. Instead of immediately selling the crop after harvest, a farmer who grows one or more of most field crops can store the produce and take out a "nonrecourse" loan for its value, pledging the crop itself as collateral. "Nonrecourse" means that the producer can discharge debts in full by forfeiting or delivering the commodity to the Government.

A producer must have entered into a production flexibility contract to be eligible for nonrecourse marketing assistance loans for wheat, feed grains, rice, and upland cotton. Any production of a contract commodity by a producer who has entered into a production flexibility contract is eligible for loans.

Nonrecourse loans are also available for oilseeds, tobacco, peanuts, extra-long-staple cotton, raw cane sugar, and refined beet sugar, regardless of whether the producer has entered into a production flexibility contract. Price support for the marketing quota crops—tobacco and peanuts—is made available through producer loan associations. By law, these programs must operate at no net cost to the U.S. Treasury, and no-net cost and marketing assessments are applied to both producers and purchasers.

Commodity Purchase Programs Under the dairy price support program, CCC buys surplus butter, cheese, and nonfat dry milk from processors at announced prices to support the price of milk. These purchases help maintain market prices at the legislated support level, and the commodities are used for hunger relief both in the United States and in foreign countries.

Emergency Assistance In the aftermath of a natural disaster, FSA makes available a variety of emergency assistance programs to farmers in counties that have been designated or declared disaster areas, including cost-share assistance to producers who do not have enough feed to maintain livestock because of a loss of a substantial amount of their normal feed production. Emergency loans are also available. In the event of a national emergency, FSA is responsible for ensuring adequate food production and distribution, as well as the continued availability of feed, seed, fertilizer, and farm machinery.

Farm Loans The Agency offers direct and guaranteed farm ownership and operating loan programs to farmers who are temporarily unable to obtain private commercial credit. Often, these are beginning farmers who can't qualify for

conventional loans because they have insufficient net worth. The Agency also helps established farmers who have suffered financial setbacks from natural disasters or whose resources are too limited to maintain profitable farming operations.

Under the guaranteed loan program, the Agency guarantees qualifying loans made by conventional agricultural lenders for up to 90 percent of principal. Farmers must apply to a conventional lender, who then arranges for the guarantee.

For those unable to qualify for a guaranteed loan, FSA also lends directly to borrowers. To qualify for a direct farm ownership or operating loan, the applicant must be able to show sufficient repayment ability and pledge enough collateral to fully secure the loan. Funding authorities for direct loans are limited, and applicants may have to wait until funds become available.

Conservation Programs The Conservation Reserve Program protects the Nation's most fragile farmland by encouraging farmers to stop growing crops on highly erodible and other environmentally sensitive acreage. In return for planting a protective cover of grass or trees on vulnerable property, the owner receives a rental payment each year of a multi-year contract. Cost-share payments are also available to help establish permanent areas of grass, legumes, trees, windbreaks, or plants that improve water quality and give shelter and food to wildlife.

The Agency also works with other USDA agencies to deliver conservation programs, including the Environmental Quality Incentives Program, which helps farmers and ranchers improve their property to protect the environment and conserve soil and water resources.

For further information, contact the Public Affairs Staff, Farm Service Agency, Department of Agriculture, Stop 0506, 1400 Independence Avenue SW., Washington, DC 20250. Phone, 202–720–5237. Internet, http://www.fsa.usda.gov/.

Commodity Credit Corporation

The Commodity Credit Corporation was organized October 17, 1933, pursuant to Executive Order 6340 of October 16,

1933, under the laws of the State of Delaware, as an agency of the United States. From October 17, 1933, to July 1, 1939, the Corporation was managed and operated in close affiliation with the Reconstruction Finance Corporation. On July 1, 1939, the agency was transferred to the Department of Agriculture by the President's Reorganization Plan No. I of 1939 (5 U.S.C. app.). Approval of the Commodity Credit Corporation Charter Act on June 29, 1948 (15 U.S.C. 714), subsequently amended, established the Corporation, effective July 1, 1948, as an agency and instrumentality of the United States under a permanent Federal charter.

The Corporation stabilizes, supports, and protects farm income and prices, assists in maintaining balanced and adequate supplies of agricultural commodities and their products, and facilitates the orderly distribution of commodities.

The Corporation is managed by a Board of Directors, subject to the general supervision and direction of the Secretary of Agriculture, who is an *ex officio* Director and Chairman of the Board. The Board consists of seven members (in addition to the Secretary of Agriculture), who are appointed by the President of the United States.

The Corporation is capitalized at $100 million and has statutory authority to borrow up to $30 billion from the U.S. Treasury. It utilizes the personnel and facilities of the Farm Service Agency and, in certain foreign assistance operations, the Foreign Agricultural Service to carry out its activities.

A commodity office in Kansas City, MO, has specific responsibilities for the acquisition, handling, storage, and disposal of commodities and products held by the Corporation.

Foreign Assistance Under Public Law 480, the Agricultural Trade Development and Assistance Act of 1954, as amended (7 U.S.C. 1691), the Corporation carries out assigned foreign assistance activities, such as guaranteeing the credit sale of U.S. agricultural commodities abroad. Major emphasis is also being directed toward meeting the needs of developing nations under the Food for Peace Act of 1966 (7 U.S.C. 1691), which further amends the Agricultural Trade Development and Assistance Act of 1954. Under these authorities, agricultural commodities are supplied and exported to combat hunger and malnutrition and to encourage economic development in developing countries. In addition, the Corporation supplies commodities under the Food for Progress Program to provide assistance to developing democracies.

The Corporation encourages U.S. financial institutions to provide financing to developing countries under the Export Credit Guarantee Programs administered by the Foreign Agricultural Service.

For further information, contact the Public Affairs Staff, Farm Service Agency, Department of Agriculture, Stop 0506, 1400 Independence Avenue SW., Washington, DC 20250. Phone, 202–720–5237. Internet, http://www.fsa.usda.gov/. For information about Commodity Credit Corporation export programs, contact the Information Division, Foreign Agricultural Service, Department of Agriculture. Phone, 202–720–3448.

Risk Management Agency

The Risk Management Agency (RMA) helps to stabilize the agricultural economy by providing a sound system of crop insurance. Mandated by the Federal Agriculture Improvement and Reform Act (7 U.S.C. 6933), RMA administers the programs of the Federal Crop Insurance Corporation (FCIC), authorized by the Federal Crop Insurance Act (7 U.S.C. 1501 *et seq.*), and has oversight for other programs related to the risk management of U.S. crops and commodities.

The Under Secretary for Farm and Foreign Agricultural Services serves as Chairman of the seven-member FCIC Board of Directors. Other members of the Board are the Under Secretary for Research Education and Economics, the RMA Administrator, and four non-Government members: three active farmers and one expert on crop insurance. The Board's primary purpose is to oversee the administration of the Federal crop insurance program.

FCIC reinsures 18 insurance companies and a program in Puerto Rico. RMA's national offices are located in Washington, DC, and Kansas City,

MO. Field offices include 10 Regional Service Offices and 6 Compliance Field Offices.

Coverage is now available on over 75 percent of the value of total U.S. crop production. Generally, multiple peril crop insurance (MPCI) policies insure farmers and ranchers against unexpected production losses from natural causes, including drought, excessive moisture, hail, wind, flooding, hurricanes, tornadoes, and lightning. Policies do not cover losses resulting from neglect, poor farming practices, or theft. Standard MPCI policies are based on the producers' actual production history. To make coverage affordable, premiums are subsidized.

RMA also reinsures several revenue based plans of insurance. Generally, revenue insurance provides protection against loss of income due to low yields, prices, or both. One plan, Crop Revenue Coverage, is widely available on corn, grain sorghum, cotton, soybeans, and wheat. Producers must purchase crop insurance by the sales closing date established for the crop they wish to insure. Policies are sold and serviced by private crop insurance agents and companies.

For further information, contact the Office of the Administrator, Risk Management Agency, Department of Agriculture, 1400 Independence Avenue SW., Washington, DC 20250. Phone, 202–690–2803. For information about Federal crop insurance programs, contact the Research and Development Division, 9435 Holmes Road, Kansas City, MO 64131. Phone, 816–926–7394. Internet, http://act.fcic.usda.gov/. For information about the Risk Management Education outreach initiative, contact the Risk Management Education Division, Risk Management Agency, Department of Agriculture, 1400 Independence Avenue SW., Washington, DC 20250. Phone, 202–690–2957. Internet, http://www.usda.gov/rma/rme.

Foreign Agricultural Service

The Foreign Agricultural Service (FAS) has primary responsibility for USDA's overseas market information, access, and development programs. It also administers USDA's export assistance and foreign food assistance programs. The Service carries out its tasks through its network of agricultural counselors, attachés, and trade officers stationed overseas and its U.S.-based team of analysts, marketing specialists, negotiators, and other professionals.

The Foreign Agricultural Service maintains a worldwide agricultural intelligence and reporting system through its attaché service with staff posted in more than 75 countries around the world. They represent the Department of Agriculture and provide information and data on foreign government agricultural policies, analyses of supply and demand conditions, commercial trade relationships, and market opportunities. They report on more than 100 farm commodities, weather, economic factors, and related subjects that affect agriculture and agricultural trade.

At the Foreign Agricultural Service in Washington, DC, agricultural economists and marketing specialists analyze these and other reports. These analyses are supplemented by accumulated background information and by the Crop Condition Assessment system, which analyzes Landsat satellite weather and other data.

To improve access for U.S. farm products abroad, FAS international trade policy specialists coordinate and direct USDA's responsibilities in international trade agreement programs and negotiations. They maintain an ongoing effort to reduce foreign trade barriers and practices that discourage the export of U.S. farm products.

To follow foreign governmental actions that affect the market for U.S. agricultural commodities, FAS relies on its agricultural counselors and attachés. In Washington, a staff of international trade specialists analyzes the trade policies and practices of foreign governments to ensure conduct in conformance with international treaty obligations. During international negotiations, FAS provides staff and support for U.S. agricultural representation.

The Service has a continuing market development program to create, maintain, and expand commercial export markets for U.S. agricultural products. It carries out programs with nonprofit commodity groups, trade associations, and State agriculture departments and their regional associations. It manages market opportunity referral services and organizes trade fairs and sales teams.

The Service's Office of the General Sales Manager also oversees agricultural functions under the Public Law 480 Food for Peace Program, title I (7 U.S.C. 1701); section 416(b) of the Agricultural Act of 1949 (7 U.S.C. 1431); the Food for Progress Program authorized by the Food for Progress Act of 1985; and the Commodity Credit Corporation's (CCC) Export Credit Guarantee Program, Intermediate Export Credit Guarantee Program, Supplier Credit Guarantee Program, Facility Guarantee Program, and Emerging Markets Program.

The Export Credit Guarantee Program (GSM–102) and the Intermediate Export Credit Guarantee Program (GSM–103) encourage the development or expansion of overseas markets for U.S. agricultural commodities by providing guarantees on private financing of U.S. exports to foreign buyers purchasing on credit terms. The foreign buyer contracts for the purchase of U.S. commodities on a deferred-payment basis of 3 years or fewer under GSM–102, or between 3 and 7 years under GSM–103. The foreign buyer's bank issues a letter of credit to guarantee payment to the U.S. exporter or an assignee U.S. lending institution. To receive the payment guarantee, the exporter registers the sale with CCC prior to export and pays a guarantee fee. The payment guarantee is implemented only if the foreign bank fails to pay the exporter or the assignee U.S. lending institution.

The CCC considers coverage on sales of any U.S. agricultural commodity that has the potential of expanding U.S. export markets. A U.S. exporter, private foreign buyer, or foreign government may submit requests that may result in authorized guarantee coverage.

Under the Supplier Credit Guarantee Program, CCC guarantees a portion of a payment due from an importer under short-term financing (up to 180 days) that an exporter has extended directly to the importer for the purchase of U.S. agricultural commodities and products. This direct credit must be secured by a promissory note signed by the importer.

Regulations for this program are found in 7 CFR part 1493, subpart D.

Under the Facility Guarantee Program, CCC guarantees to facilitate the financing of manufactured goods and services exported from the United States to improve or establish agriculture-related facilities in emerging markets. The Facility Guarantee Program is designed to enhance sales of U.S. agricultural commodities and products to emerging markets where the demand for such commodities and products may be constricted due to inadequate storage, processing, or handling capabilities. Facility Guarantee Program regulations are a subpart of the GSM–102 and GSM–103 regulations (7 CFR part 1493).

The Emerging Markets Program was authorized by the Food, Agriculture, Conservation, and Trade Act of 1990 and amended by the Federal Agriculture Improvement and Reform Act of 1996 to promote agricultural exports to emerging markets through the sharing of U.S. agricultural expertise by technical assistance. Technical assistance must develop, maintain, or expand markets for U.S. agricultural exports in emerging markets; improve the effectiveness of food and rural business systems in emerging markets, including potential reductions in trade barriers; and increase prospects for U.S. trade and investment in these countries.

Several export assistance programs are designed to counter or offset the adverse effects from competitors' unfair trade practices on U.S. agriculture. These programs include the Export Enhancement Program (EEP) and the Dairy Export Incentive Program (DEIP).

Under EEP, USDA provides CCC-owned commodities or cash as export bonuses to make U.S. commodities more competitive in the world marketplace. The DEIP and EEP programs are similar, but DEIP is restricted to dairy products.

The Foreign Agricultural Service is also responsible for sales of CCC-owned surplus commodities to private traders, foreign governments, and nonprofit organizations. However, surplus commodities have not been available since fiscal year 1995.

The Market Access Program, provides cost-share assistance to trade promotion organizations, cooperatives, and small businesses to help fund their market development activities overseas.

The Service helps other USDA agencies, U.S. universities, and others enhance America's agricultural competitiveness globally; and increases income and food availability in developing nations by mobilizing expertise for agriculturally led economic growth.

The Service's programs enhance U.S. agriculture's competitiveness by providing U.S. agriculturalists and scientists with linkages to world resources. These linkages often produce new germplasm and technologies that can be vital to improving our current agricultural base and producing new and alternative products. They also foster relationships and understandings that result in trade opportunities and strengthened strategic and political ties.

The Service is a link between the technical expertise of the U.S. agricultural community and Third World nations. By sharing agricultural knowledge with less-developed nations, the United States provides tools to help build stable economies and a more prosperous world. In the process, less-developed nations overcome the barriers of hunger and poverty and gain the economic means to buy needed goods and services in the world marketplace.

The Service also manages programs to exchange visits, germplasm, and technologies between U.S. and international scientists; supports collaborative research projects of mutual interest to the United States and other nations; taps the U.S. agricultural community to provide technical assistance and professional development and training programs to assist economic development in lower income nations; serves as U.S. liaison with international organizations; and organizes overseas trade and investment missions.

These activities serve the needs of other USDA agencies, the Agency for International Development, other public and private institutions, foreign nations, development banks, and the U.S. university and agricultural communities.

For further information, contact the Information Division, Foreign Agricultural Service, Ag Stop 1004, 1400 Independence Avenue SW., Department of Agriculture, Washington, DC 20250–1004. Phone, 202–720–7115. Fax, 202–720–1727. Internet, http://www.fas.usda.gov/.

Research, Education, and Economics

This mission area's main focus is to create, apply, and transfer knowledge and technology to provide affordable food and fiber, ensure food safety and nutrition, and support rural development and natural resource needs of people by conducting integrated national and international research, information, education, and statistical programs and services that are in the national interest.

Agricultural Research Service

The Agricultural Research Service conducts research to develop and transfer solutions to agricultural problems of high national priority. It provides information access and dissemination to ensure high-quality, safe food and other agricultural products; assess the nutritional needs of Americans; sustain a competitive agricultural economy; enhance the natural resource base and the environment; and provide economic opportunities for rural citizens, communities, and society as a whole.

All administrative and management responsibilities of the four Research, Education, and Economic agencies— Agricultural Research Service (ARS), Cooperative State Research, Education, and Extension Service (CSREES), Economic Research Service (ERS), and National Agricultural Statistics Service (NASS)—are administered by the ARS Administrative and Financial

Management Unit headquartered in Washington, DC.

Research activities are carried out at 105 domestic locations (including Puerto Rico) and 3 overseas locations. Much of this research is conducted in cooperation with partners in State universities and experiment stations, other Federal

agencies, and private organizations. A national program staff, headquartered in Beltsville, MD, is the focal point in the overall planning and coordination of ARS' research programs. Day-to-day management of the respective programs for specific field locations is assigned to eight area offices.

Area Offices—Agricultural Research Service

Office	Address
BELTSVILLE AREA—Beltsville Agricultural Research Center, National Arboretum, Washington, DC	Bldg. 003, Beltsville Agricultural Research Ctr. W., Beltsville, MD 20705
MIDSOUTH AREA—AL, KY, LA, MS, TN	P.O. Box 225, Stoneville, MS 38776
MIDWEST AREA—IA, IL, IN, MI, MN, MO, OH, WI	1815 N. University St., Peoria, IL 61804
NORTHERN PLAINS AREA—CO, KS, MT, ND, NE, SD, UT, WY	Suite 150, 1201 Oakridge Rd., Fort Collins, CO 80525–5562
NORTH ATLANTIC AREA—CT, DE, MA, MD, ME, NH, NJ, NY, PA, RI, VT, WV	600 E. Mermaid Ln., Philadelphia, PA 19118
PACIFIC WEST AREA—AK, AZ, CA, HI, ID, NV, OR, WA	800 Buchanan St., Albany, CA 94710
SOUTH ATLANTIC AREA—FL, GA, NC, PR, SC, VI, VA	P.O. Box 5677, Athens, GA 30613
SOUTHERN PLAINS AREA—AR, NM, OK, TX	Suite 230, 7607 Eastmark Dr., College Station, TX 77840

The National Agricultural Library (NAL), administered by ARS, provides information services over a broad range of agricultural interests to a wide cross-section of users, from research scientists to the general public. The Library assists its users through a variety of specialized information centers. Its staff uses advanced information technologies to generate new information products, creating an electronic library as it improves access to the knowledge stored in its multimedia collection of more than 2 million items.

Information is made available through loans, photocopies, reference services, and literature searches. A subject profiling system for selective searches of agricultural data bases is available for USDA scientists. Citations to the agricultural literature are stored in the Agricultural Online Access (AGRICOLA) data base, available through online computer systems and on compact disc. The Library also distributes in the United States the AGRIS data base of citations to the agricultural literature prepared by centers in various parts of the world and coordinated by the Food and Agriculture Organization of the United Nations.

For further information, contact the Information Staff, Agricultural Research Service, Department of Agriculture, 6303 Ivy Lane, Room 450, Greenbelt, MD 20770. Phone, 301–344–2340.

Cooperative State Research, Education, and Extension Service

The Cooperative State Research, Education, and Extension Service (CSREES) expands the research and higher education functions of the former Cooperative State Research Service and the education and outreach functions of the former Extension Service. The result is better customer service and an enhanced ability to respond to national priorities.

The Service links the research and education resources and activities of USDA and works with the following institutions: land-grant institutions in each State, territory, and the District of Columbia; more than 130 colleges of agriculture; 59 agricultural experiment stations; 57 cooperative extension services; 63 schools of forestry; sixteen 1890 historically Black land-grant institutions and Tuskegee University; 27 colleges of veterinary medicine; 42 schools and colleges of family and consumer services; twenty-nine 1994 Native American land-grant institutions; and 127 Hispanic-serving institutions, including 81 members and 45 associate members of the Hispanic Association of Colleges and Universities.

In cooperation with its partners and customers, CSREES provides the focus to advance a global system of research, extension, and higher education in the food and agricultural sciences and related environmental and human sciences to benefit people, communities, and the Nation.

The Service's mission emphasizes partnerships with the public and private sectors to maximize the effectiveness of limited resources. Its programs increase and provide access to scientific knowledge; strengthen the capabilities of land-grant and other institutions in research, extension, and higher education; increase access to and use of improved communication and network systems; and promote informed decisionmaking by producers, families, and social conditions in the United States and globally. These conditions include improved agricultural and other economic enterprises; safer, cleaner water, food, and air; enhanced stewardship and management of natural resources; healthier, more responsible and more productive individuals, families, and communities; and a stable, secure, diverse, and affordable national food supply.

The Service provides research, extension, and education leadership through programs in Plant and Animal Systems; Natural Resources and Environment; Economic and Community Systems; Families, 4–H, and Nutrition; Partnerships; Competitive Research Grants and Awards Management; Science and Education Resources Development; and Communications, Technology, Distance Education, and Special Programs.

The Service's partnership with the land-grant universities and their representatives is critical to the effective shared planning, delivery, and accountability for research, higher education, and extension programs.

As a recognized leader in the design, organization, and application of advanced communication technologies and in meeting the growing demand for enhanced distance education capabilities, CSREES provides essential community access to research and education knowledge and connects the private citizen to other Federal Government information.

For further information, contact the Communications, Technology, and Distance Education Office, Cooperative State Research, Education, and Extension Service, Department of Agriculture, Washington, DC 20250–0906. Phone, 202–720–4651. Fax, 202–690–0289. TDD, 202–690–1899. E-mail, CSREES@reeusda.gov. Internet, http://www.reeusda.gov/.

Economic Research Service

The mission of the Economic Research Service (ERS) is to provide economic and other social science information and analysis for public and private decisions on agriculture, food, natural resources, and rural America. The Service produces such information for use by the general public and to help the executive and legislative branches develop, administer, and evaluate agricultural and rural policies and programs.

The Service produces economic information through a program of research and analysis on: domestic and international agricultural developments; statistical indicators of food and consumer issues and concerns, including nutrition education and food assistance, food safety regulation, determinants of consumer demand for quality and safety, and food marketing trends and developments; agricultural resource and environmental issues; and the effect of public and private actions and policies on national rural and agricultural conditions, including the transformation of the rural economy, the financial performance of the farm sector, and the implications of changing farm credit and financial market structures.

For further information, contact the Information Services Division, Economics Research Service, Department of Agriculture, Washington, DC 20036–5831. Phone, 202–694–5050.

Office of Energy   The Office of Energy serves as the focal point for all energy-related matters within the Department. The Office is responsible for developing and coordinating all USDA energy policies; reviewing and evaluating all USDA energy and energy-related programs; evaluating the economics of new nonfood uses for agricultural crops; serving as economic liaison on new uses issues; and providing liaison with the Department of Energy and other Federal agencies and departments on energy activities that may affect agriculture and rural America. A major component of this is the responsibility for the coordination and evaluation of the departmental Biofuels Program.

The Office also represents the Department in meetings with agriculture, industry, and consumer groups to discuss effects of departmental energy policies, programs, and proposals on the agricultural sector and rural economy.

For further information, contact the Information Services Division, Economic Research Service, Department of Agriculture, Washington, DC 20036–5831. Phone, 202–694–5050.

National Agricultural Statistics Service

The National Agricultural Statistics Service (NASS) prepares estimates and reports on production, supply, price, chemical use, and other items necessary for the orderly operation of the U.S. agricultural economy.

The reports include statistics on field crops, fruits and vegetables, dairy, cattle, hogs, sheep, poultry, aquaculture, and related commodities or processed products. Other estimates concern farm numbers, farm production expenditures, agricultural chemical use, prices received by farmers for products sold, prices paid for commodities and services, indexes of prices received and paid, parity prices, farm employment, and farm wage rates.

The Service prepares these estimates through a complex system of sample surveys of producers, processors, buyers, and others associated with agriculture. Information is gathered by mail, telephone, personal interviews, and field visits.

Beginning in fiscal year 1997 NASS is responsible for conducting the census of agriculture, formerly conducted by the Bureau of the Census, Commerce Department. The census of agriculture is taken every 5 years and provides comprehensive data on the agricultural economy down to the county level. Periodic reports are also issued on irrigation and horticultural specialities.

The 45 State-Federal offices, serving all 50 States, and the national office prepare weekly, monthly, annual, and other periodic reports for free distribution to the news media, Congress; and survey respondents. The reports are available to others free on the Internet, or on a subscription basis. Information on crop and livestock products appears in about 400 reports issued annually. Cooperative agreements with State agencies also permit preparation and publication of estimates of individual crops and livestock by counties in most States.

The Service performs reimbursable survey work and statistical consulting services for other Federal and State agencies and provides technical assistance for developing agricultural data systems in other countries.

For further information, contact the Executive Assistant to the Administrator, National Agricultural Statistics Service, Department of Agriculture, Washington, DC 20250–2000. Phone, 202–720–2707.

Natural Resources and Environment

This mission area is responsible for fostering sound stewardship of 75 percent of the Nation's total land area. Ecosystems are the underpinning for the Department's operating philosophy in this area, in order to maximize stewardship of our natural resources.

This approach ensures that products, values, services, and uses desired by people are produced in ways that sustain healthy, productive ecosystems.

Forest Service

[For the Forest Service statement of organization, see the *Code of Federal Regulations*, Title 36, Part 200.1]

The Forest Service was created by the Transfer Act of February 1, 1905 (16 U.S.C. 472), which transferred the Federal forest reserves and the responsibility for their management from the Department of the Interior to the Department of Agriculture. The forest reserves were established by the President from the public domain under authority of the Creative Act of March 3, 1891 (26 Stat. 1103). The protection and development of the reserves (which became the national forests in 1907) are governed by the Organic Act of June 4, 1897, as amended (16 U.S.C. 473–478); the Multiple Use-Sustained Yield Act of June 12, 1960 (16 U.S.C. 528–531); the Forest and Rangeland Renewable Resources Planning Act of 1974 (16 U.S.C. 1601–1610); and the National Forest Management Act of 1976 (90 Stat. 2947). The Weeks Law of March 1, 1911, as amended (16 U.S.C. 480), allowed the Government to purchase and exchange land for national forests.

Objectives The Forest Service has the Federal responsibility for national leadership in forestry. As set forth in law, its mission is to achieve quality land management under the sustainable, multiple-use management concept to meet the diverse needs of people. To accomplish this goal, it has adopted objectives which include:

—advocating a conservation ethic in promoting the health, productivity, diversity, and beauty of forests and associated lands;

—listening to people and responding to their diverse needs in making decisions;

—protecting and managing the national forests and grasslands to best demonstrate the sustainable, multiple-use management concept;

—providing technical and financial assistance to State and private forest landowners, encouraging them toward active stewardship and quality land management in meeting their specific objectives;

—providing technical and financial assistance to cities and communities to improve their natural environment by planting trees and caring for their forests;

—providing international technical assistance and scientific exchanges to sustain and enhance global resources and to encourage quality land management;

—assisting States and communities in using the forests wisely to promote rural economic development and a quality rural environment;

—developing and providing scientific and technical knowledge, improving our capability to protect, manage, and use forests and rangelands; and

—providing work, training, and education to the unemployed, underemployed, elderly, youth, and the disadvantaged.

National Forest System The Service manages 155 national forests, 20 national grasslands, and 8 land utilization projects on over 191 million acres in 44 States, the Virgin Islands, and Puerto Rico under the principles of multiple-use and sustained yield. The Nation's tremendous need for wood and paper products is balanced with the other vital, renewable resources or benefits that the national forests and grasslands provide: recreation and natural beauty, wildlife habitat, livestock forage, and water supplies. The guiding principle is the greatest good to the greatest number in the long run.

These lands are protected as much as possible from wildfire, epidemics of disease and insect pests, erosion, floods, and water and air pollution. Burned areas get emergency seeding treatment to prevent massive erosion and stream siltation. Roads and trails are built where needed to allow for closely regulated timber harvesting and to give the public access to outdoor recreation areas and provide scenic drives and hikes. Picnic, camping, water-sport, skiing, and other areas are provided with facilities for public convenience and enjoyment. Timber harvesting methods are used that will protect the land and streams, assure rapid renewal of the forest, provide food and cover for wildlife and fish, and have minimum impact on scenic and recreation values. Local communities benefit from the logging and milling activities. These lands also provide needed oil, gas, and minerals. Rangelands are improved for millions of livestock and game animals. The national forests provide a refuge for many species of endangered birds, animals, and fish. Some 34.6 million acres are set aside as wilderness and 175,000 acres as primitive areas where timber will not be harvested.

Cooperation With the States The Service provides national leadership and financial and technical assistance to non-Federal forest landowners, operators, processors of forest products, and urban forestry interests. Through its cooperative State and private forestry programs, the Service protects and improves the quality of air, water, soil, and open space and encourages uses of natural resources on non-Federal lands that best meet the needs of the Nation, while protecting the environment.

Cooperative programs are carried out through the State foresters or equivalent State officials, who receive grant funding under the Cooperative Forestry Assistance Act of 1978 (16 U.S.C. 2101). Cooperators at the State and local levels provide the delivery system for most State and private forestry programs.

Grant funds and technical assistance are available for rural forestry assistance, forestry incentives, insect and disease control, urban forestry assistance, rural fire prevention and control, organization management assistance, State forest resource planning, and technology implementation.

The Service also cooperates with other USDA agencies in providing leadership and technical assistance for the forestry aspects of conservation programs.

The Service's State and private forestry program staff also ensure that the Service and its cooperators keep abreast of the best knowledge and technology in carrying out its programs, and they help to develop technology transfer plans for implementing research results for a broad range of potential users.

Forest Research The Service performs basic and applied research to develop the scientific information and technology needed to protect, manage, use, and sustain the natural resources of the Nation's 1.6 billion acres of forests and rangelands. This research is conducted through a network of 7 forest experiment stations, a Forest Products Laboratory, and the International Institute of Tropical Forestry, including research work units at 77 project locations throughout the United States, Puerto Rico, and the Pacific Trust Islands. Under the authority of the McSweeny-McNary Act of May 22, 1928, as amended and supplemented (45 Stat. 699), research is often performed in cooperation with many of the State agricultural colleges. The Forest Research Service's strategy focuses on three major program components: understanding the structure and functions of forest and range ecosystems; understanding how people perceive and value the protection, management, and use of natural resources; and determining which protection, management, and utilization practices are most suitable for sustainable production and use of the world's natural resources.

International Forestry In response to the U.S. commitment to support natural resource conservation around the world, Congress established the International Forestry Division within the USDA's Forest Service. Its mandate is to provide assistance that promotes sustainable development and global environmental stability, particularly in key countries important in global climate change. This mandate includes a national goal for sustainable management of all forests by the year 2000, investigating research topics with implications for global forest management, and sharing resource management experience with colleagues around the world.

Responsibility for global stewardship is shared by the entire Forest Service. The Forest Service's Office of International Forestry mobilizes support of all Forest Service units—Research, National Forest System, State and Private Forestry, Administration, and Programs and Legislation—to work with other governmental agencies, nongovernmental groups, and international organizations in four major international areas: strategic planning and policy development, training and technical assistance, research and scientific exchange, and disaster relief.

Human Resource Programs The Service operates the Youth Conservation Corps and the Volunteers in the National Forests programs and participates with the Department of Labor on several human resource programs that involve the Nation's citizens, both young and old, in forestry-related activities. Included in these programs are the Job Corps and the Senior Community Service Employment Program. These programs annually accomplish millions of dollars worth of conservation work, while providing participants with such benefits as training, paid employment, and meaningful outdoor experience.

Field Offices—Forest Service

Region/Station/Area	Address
National Forest System Regions [1]—Regional Forester	
1. Northern	Federal Bldg. (P.O. Box 7669), Missoula, MT 59807
2. Rocky Mountain	740 Simms St. (P.O. Box 25127), Lakewood, CO 80225
3. Southwestern	517 Gold Ave. SW., Albuquerque, NM 87102
4. Intermountain	324 25th St., Ogden, UT 84401
5. Pacific Southwest	630 Sansome St., San Francisco, CA 94111
6. Pacific Northwest	333 SW. 1st Ave. (P.O. Box 3623), Portland, OR 97208
8. Southern	1720 Peachtree Rd. NW., Atlanta, GA 30367
9. Eastern	310 W. Wisconsin Ave., Milwaukee, WI 53203
10. Alaska	Federal Office Bldg. (P.O. Box 21628), Juneau, AK 99802
Forest and Range Experiment Stations—Director	
Intermountain	324 25th St., Ogden, UT 84401
North Central	1992 Folwell Ave., St. Paul, MN 55108
Northeastern	Suite 200, 100 Matson Ford Rd. (P.O. Box 6775), Radnor, PA 19087–4585
Pacific Northwest	333 SW. 1st Ave. (P.O. Box 3890), Portland, OR 97208
Pacific Southwest	800 Buchanan St. (P.O. Box 245), Albany, CA 94710
Rocky Mountain	240 W. Prospect Ave., Fort Collins, CO 80526
Southern	200 Weaver Blvd. (P.O. Box 2860), Asheville, NC 28802
Forest Products Laboratory	One Gifford Pinchot Dr., Madison, WI 53705
State and Private Forestry Areas [2]—Director	
Northeastern	Suite 200, 100 Matson Ford Rd. (P.O. Box 6775), Radnor, PA 19087–4585
International Institute of Tropical Forestry	UPR Experimental Station Grounds, Botanical Garden (Call Box 25000), Rio Piedras, PR 00928

[1] There is no Region 7.
[2] In Regions 1 through 6, 8, and 10, State and private forestry activities are directed from regional headquarters.

For further information, contact the Office of Communications, Forest Service, Department of Agriculture, P.O. Box 96090, Washington, DC 20090–6090. Phone, 202–205–8333.

Natural Resources Conservation Service

[For the Natural Resources Conservation Service statement of organization, see the *Code of Federal Regulations*, Title 7, Parts 600 and 601]

The Natural Resources Conservation Service (NRCS), formerly the Soil Conservation Service, has national responsibility for helping America's farmers, ranchers, and other private landowners develop and carry out voluntary efforts to conserve and protect our natural resources. The Service is USDA's technical delivery arm for conservation.

Conservation Technical Assistance This is the foundation program of NRCS. Under this program, NRCS provides technical assistance to land users and units of government for the purpose of sustaining agricultural productivity and protecting and enhancing the natural resource base. This assistance is based on the voluntary cooperation of private landowners and involves comprehensive approaches to reduce soil erosion, improve soil and water quantity and quality, improve and conserve wetlands, enhance fish and wildlife habitat, improve air quality, improve pasture and range condition, reduce upstream flooding, and improve woodlands. Every year, more than 1 million land users receive these technical services, which are channeled through nearly 3,000 conservation districts across the United States and its territories.

Natural Resources Inventory The Natural Resources Inventory (NRI) is a report issued every 5 years on how well the Nation is sustaining natural resources on non-Federal land. This report contains the most comprehensive and statistically reliable data of its kind in the world. The Inventory provides data on the kind and amount of soil, water, vegetation, and related resources; the effects of current land use and management practices on the present and future supply and condition of soil, water, and vegetation; and the changes and trends in the use, extent, and condition of these resources. Inventory data and analytical software are available to the public on CD–ROM.

National Cooperative Soil Survey The National Cooperative Soil Survey provides the public with local information on the uses and capabilities of their soils. The published soil survey for a county or other designated area includes maps and interpretations that are the foundation for farm planning and other private land use decisions as well as for resource planning and policy by Federal, State, and local governments. The surveys are conducted cooperatively with other Federal, State, and local agencies and land grant universities. The Service is the national and world leader in soil classification and soil mapping, and is now expanding its work in soil quality.

Snow Survey and Water Supply Forecasting Program This program collects snowpack moisture data and forecasts seasonal water supplies for streams that derive most of their water from snowmelt. It helps farm operators, rural communities, and municipalities manage water resources through water supply forecasts. It also provides hydrometeorological data for regulating reservoir storage and managing streamflow. The Snow Supply Program is conducted in 11 Western States and Alaska.

Plant Materials Program At 26 plant materials centers across the country, NRCS tests, selects, and ensures the commercial availability of new and improved conservation plants for erosion reduction, wetland restoration, water quality improvement, streambank and riparian area protection, coastal dune stabilization, biomass production, carbon sequestration, and other needs. The Plant Materials Program is a cooperative effort with conservation districts, other Federal and State agencies, commercial businesses, and seed and nursery associations.

River Basin Surveys and Investigations This program involves NRCS with Federal, State, and local agencies in river basin surveys and investigations, flood hazard analysis, and floodplain management assistance. It addresses a variety of natural resource concerns: water quality, water conservation, wetlands protection, agricultural drought, rural development, municipal and industrial water needs, and fish and wildlife habitat.

Small Watersheds Program The Small Watersheds Program helps local sponsoring groups to voluntarily plan and install watershed protection projects on private lands. These projects include flood prevention, water quality improvement, soil erosion and sediment reduction, rural and municipal water supply, irrigation water management, fish and wildlife habitat enhancement, and wetlands restoration. The Service helps local community groups, government entities, and private landowners working together using an integrated, comprehensive watershed approach to natural resource planning.

Flood Prevention Program This program applies to 11 specific flood prevention projects covering about 35 million acres in 11 States. It provides help in flood prevention, water management, and reduction of erosion sedimentation. It also can help in developing recreational facilities and improving fish and wildlife habitat.

Emergency Watershed Protection Program This program provides emergency assistance to safeguard lives and property in jeopardy due to sudden watershed impairment by natural disasters. Emergency work includes quickly establishing a protective plant cover on denuded land and stream banks; opening dangerously restricted channels; and repairing diversions and levees. An emergency area need not be declared a national disaster area to be eligible for help under this program.

Great Plains Conservation Program
This program (GPCP) helps bring about long-term solutions to natural resource problems in the 10 Great Plains States. It is aimed at total conservation treatment of entire farms or ranches. Participation in GPCP is voluntary and provides technical assistance and a long-term cost-share contract between the participant and NRCS. The program has been effective in addressing the needs of socially disadvantaged farmers and ranchers and the needs of American Indian farmers and ranchers. In addition to providing significant erosion and sediment reduction benefits, it addresses problems related to water quality, wildlife habitat protection, and other environmental concerns.

Resource Conservation and Development Program   This program (RC&D) is a locally driven program—an opportunity for civic-oriented groups to work together sharing knowledge and resources in solving common problems facing their region. The program offers aid in balancing the environmental, economic, and social needs of an area. A USDA coordinator helps each designated RC&D council plan, develop, and carry out programs for resource conservation, water management, community development, and environmental enhancement.

Rural Abandoned Mine Program   This program (RAMP) helps protect people and the environment from the adverse effects of past coal-mining practices and promotes the development of soil and water resources on unreclaimed mine land. It provides technical and financial assistance to land users who voluntarily enter into 5- to 10-year contracts for the reclamation of eligible land and water.

Wetlands Reserve Program   Under this program, USDA purchases easements from agricultural land owners who voluntarily agree to restore and protect wetlands. Service employees help these owners develop plans to retire critical wetland habitat from crop production. The primary objectives are to preserve and restore wetlands, improve wildlife habitat, and protect migratory waterfowl.

Water Bank Program   The Service helps landowners protect, improve, or restore wetlands by identifying eligible lands, helping owners develop conservation plans, and implementing necessary land treatments. Through 10-year rental agreements between USDA and landowners, the Water Bank Program protects important nesting, breeding, and feeding areas for migratory waterfowl. Other benefits of the program include water conservation, erosion control, flood control, and landscape beautification.

Colorado River Basin Salinity Control Program   This voluntary incentive program supports the Nation's commitment to water quality in the Colorado River, which provides water to more than 18 million people in parts of seven Western States and Mexico. The Service provides financial and technical assistance to control salt loading to the Colorado River from both natural and human-caused sources. Among the remedies used are management practices to prevent irrigation-induced erosion.

Forestry Incentives Program   This program helps to increase the Nation's supply of products from nonindustrial private forest lands. This also ensures more effective use of existing forest lands and, over time, helps to prevent shortages and price increases for forest products. The program shares the cost incurred by landowners for tree planting and timberstand improvement.

Farmland Protection Program (FPP)
This new program protects soil by encouraging landowners to limit conversion of their farmland to nonagricultural uses. States, Indian tribes, or local governments administer all aspects of acquiring lands that are in FPP except when it is more effective and efficient for the Federal Government to do so. Funds for FPP come from the Commodity Credit Corporation. The Program is authorized by the Federal

Agriculture Improvement and Reform Act of 1996 to protect between 170,000 and 340,000 acres of farmland.

Environmental Quality Incentive Program (EQIP) This Program assists producers with environmental and natural resource conservation improvements on their agricultural lands. One-half of the available funds are for conservation activities related to livestock production. Technical assistance, cost-share payments, incentive payments, and education focus on priority areas and natural resource concerns identified in cooperation with State technical committees. The program uses 5- to 10-year contracts based on conservation plans, as well as a priority evaluation process to maximize environmental benefits per dollar expended. The Secretary of Agriculture, through the rulemaking process, establishes criteria for EQIP assistance, including determining standards for large livestock operations which will be ineligible for cost sharing to construct animal waste management facilities.

Conservation Farm Option This pilot program for producers of wheat, feed grains, cotton, and rice is open to owners or operators of farms that have a production flexibility contract. Under the program, producers may receive one consolidated USDA program payment in lieu of a list of specified payments. The producers must implement a conservation plan that addresses soil, water, and related resources; water quality; wetlands; and wildlife habitat. Participation is voluntary and is based on a 10-year contract.

Farms-for-the-Future Program This program guarantees USDA loans and subsidizes interest on State loans to purchase agricultural land or development rights to preserve vital farmland resources for future generations. The money also can be reinvested by the States to generate earnings for future farmland protection efforts.

For further information, contact the Management Services Division, Natural Resources Conservation Service, Department of Agriculture, P.O. Box 2890, Washington, DC 20013. Phone, 202–690–4811.

Graduate School, U.S. Department of Agriculture

Fourteenth Street and Independence Avenue SW., Washington, DC 20250
Phone, 202–314–3300

Director	PHILIP H. HUDSON
Deputy Director	LYNN EDWARDS
Associate Director	ROBERT BROWN
Program Director, Center for Applied Technology	NAT HOPKINS
Program Director, Correspondence Study	NORMA HARWOOD
Program Director, Evening and Saturday	RONALD MACNAB
Program Director, Government Audit Training Institute	DONALD SMULAND
Program Director, International Institute	JACK MAYKOSKI, *Acting*
Director of Communications	(VACANCY)
Director of Administration	ROBERT KIES
Director, Career Development Programs	LEW TAYLOR
Director, Technology Enabled Learning	DAVID LAMP
Director, National Independent Study Center	MIKE ALLEN
Director, Regional Training Centers	TONY GUTIERREZ
Director, Midwest Training Center	CYNTHIA RUDMANN
Director, National Capital Training Center	NANCY RANDA
Director, Northeast Training Center	FRANK BAUER
Director, Southeast Training Center	DAVID HITT

Director, Southwest Training Center	JOE MATA, *Acting*
Director, Western Training Center	MAUREEN HETZEL
Registrar	CAROLYN NELSON

The Graduate School, U.S. Department of Agriculture, is a continuing education school offering career-related training to adults. It is self-supporting and does not receive direct appropriated funds from Congress or the Department of Agriculture. Fees charged individuals and Government agencies are nominal. Courses are planned with the assistance of Government professionals and specialists.

The faculty is mostly part-time and is drawn from throughout Government and the community at large. They are selected because of their professional and specialized knowledge and experience and thus bring a practicality and experience to their classrooms. Faculty holding regular Government positions take annual leave or leave without pay when teaching during their normal work hours.

The school does not grant degrees but does provide planned sequences of courses leading to certificates of accomplishment in a number of occupational and career fields important to government. Training areas include management, auditing, computer science, communications, foreign language, procurement, financial management, and others.

The Graduate School's objective is to improve Government services by providing needed continuing education and training opportunities for Government employees and agencies.

The Graduate School, administered by a Director and governed by a General Administration Board appointed by the Secretary of Agriculture, was established by the Secretary of Agriculture on September 2, 1921, pursuant to act of May 15, 1862 (7 U.S.C. 2201); joint resolution of April 12, 1892 (27 Stat. 395); and the Deficiencies Appropriation Act of March 3, 1901 (20 U.S.C. 91).

In July 1995, through a memorandum of understanding between the U.S. Office of Personnel Management and the Department of Agriculture, the Graduate School acquired many of the training offices formerly operated by the Office of Personnel Management.

For further information, contact the Communications Office, Graduate School, U.S. Department of Agriculture, Room 160, 600 Maryland Avenue SW., Washington, DC 20024. Phone, 202–401–9129.

Sources of Information

Consumer Activities Educational, organizational, and financial assistance is offered to consumers and their families in such fields as rural housing and farm operating programs, improved nutrition, family living and recreation, food stamp, school lunch, donated foods, and other food programs. Contact the Office of Public Affairs, Department of Agriculture, Washington, DC 20250. Phone, 202–720–2791.

Contracts and Small Business Activities To obtain information about contracting or subcontracting opportunities, attending small business outreach activities, or how to do business with USDA, contact the Office of Small and Disadvantaged Business Utilization. Phone, 202–720–7117. Internet, http://www.usda.gov/da/smallbus.html.

Employment Most jobs in the Department are in the competitive service and are filled by applicants who have established eligibility under an appropriate examination administered by the Office of Personnel Management or Department Special Examining Units.

General employment inquiries should be directed to the agencies.

Persons interested in employment in the Food and Consumer Service should contact the regional offices located in Atlanta, Boston, Chicago, Dallas, Denver, San Francisco, and Robbinsville, NJ, or the national headquarters in Alexandria, VA. Phone, 703–305–2351.

Persons interested in employment in the Office of the Inspector General should contact the USDA Office of Personnel, Room 31–W, Jamie L. Whitten Building, Washington, DC 20250. Phone, 202–720–5781.

In addition, all Forest Service field offices (addresses indicated in the preceding text) accept employment applications.

Environment Educational, organizational, technical, and financial assistance is offered to local citizens, organizations, and communities in such fields as watershed protection, flood prevention, soil and water conservation practices to reduce erosion and sedimentation, community water and waste disposal systems, safe use of pesticides, and the development of pesticide alternatives.

Contact the nearest county extension agent or USDA office, or write to the Office of Communications, Department of Agriculture, Washington, DC 20250. Phone, 202–720–2791.

Films Motion pictures on a variety of agricultural subjects are available for loan through various State Extension Service film libraries. Contact the Video, Teleconference, and Radio Center, Office of Communications, Department of Agriculture, Washington, DC 20250, for a listing of cooperating film libraries. Phone, 202–720–6072.

Color filmstrips and slide sets on a variety of subjects are available for purchase. For a listing of titles and prices, contact the Photography Center, Office of Communications, Department of Agriculture, Washington, DC 20250. Phone, 202–720–6633.

Whistleblower Hotline Persons wishing to register complaints of alleged improprieties concerning the Department should contact one of the regional offices or the Inspector General's whistleblower hotline. Phone, 800–424–9121 (toll-free, outside Washington, DC); 202–690–1622 (within the Washington, DC, metropolitan area); or 202–690–1202 (TDD). Fax, 202–690–2474.

Reading Rooms Located at each USDA agency at addresses indicated in the preceding text.

Speakers Contact the nearest Department of Agriculture office or county Extension agent. In the District of Columbia, contact the Office of Public Liaison, Office of Communications, Department of Agriculture, Washington, DC 20250. Phone, 202–720–2798.

For further information concerning the Department of Agriculture, contact the Office of Communications, Department of Agriculture, Washington, DC 20250. Phone, 202–720–2791. Internet, http://www.usda.gov/.

DEPARTMENT OF COMMERCE

Fourteenth Street between Constitution and Pennsylvania Avenues NW.,
Washington, DC 20230
Phone, 202–482–2000. Internet, http://www.doc.gov/.

SECRETARY OF COMMERCE	WILLIAM M. DALEY
Chief of Staff	DAVID J. LANE
Counselor to the Secretary	(VACANCY)
Assistant to the Secretary and Director, Office of Policy and Strategic Planning	ERIC BIEL, *Acting*
Executive Assistant to the Secretary	SHIRLEY ROTHLISBERGER
Director, Office of White House Liaison	PARNICE GREEN
Executive Secretary	JAMES A. DORSKIND
Deputy Secretary of Commerce	ROBERT L. MALLETT
Senior Advisor and Counselor to the Deputy Secretary	ERIAS A. HYMAN
Associate Deputy Secretary	KENT HUGHES
Director, Office of Small and Disadvantaged Business Utilization	BRENDA BLACK, *Acting*
General Counsel	ANDREW J. PINCUS
Deputy General Counsel	KATHRYN R. LUNNEY
Counselor to the General Counsel	(VACANCY)
Assistant General Counsel for Administration	BARBARA S. FREDERICKS
Assistant General Counsel for Legislation and Regulation	MICHAEL A. LEVITT
Assistant General Counsel for Finance and Litigation	ALDEN F. ABBOTT
Chief Counsel for Economics and Statistics Administration	ROXIE JONES
Chief Counsel for Export Administration	HOYT H. ZIA
Chief Counsel for Import Administration	STEPHEN J. POWELL
Chief Counsel for International Commerce	ELEANOR ROBERTS LEWIS
Chief Counsel for Minority Business Development	DINAH FLYNN, *Acting*
Chief Counsel for Technology Administration	MARK BOHANNON
Director, Commercial Law Development Program	LINDA A. WELLS
Assistant Secretary for Legislative and Intergovernmental Affairs	(VACANCY)
Deputy Assistant Secretary for Legislative and Intergovernmental Affairs	(VACANCY)
Deputy Assistant Secretary for Intergovernmental Affairs	MARK T. JURKOVICH
Inspector General	JOHNNIE E. FRAZIER, *Acting*
Deputy Inspector General	(VACANCY)
Counsel to the Inspector General	ELIZABETH T. BARLOW
Assistant Inspector General for Auditing	GEORGE E. ROSS
Assistant Inspector General for Investigations	STEPHEN E. GARMON

144

Assistant Inspector General for Systems Evaluation	JUDITH J. GORDON
Assistant Inspector General for Inspections and Program Evaluations	JOHNNIE E. FRAZIER
Assistant Inspector General for Compliance and Administration	ALLAN M. FISHER
Director, Office of Public Affairs	MARY F. HANLEY
Press Secretary, Office of the Press Secretary	MARIA T. CARDONA
Director, Office of Business Liaison	LUCIE F. NAPHIN
Director, Office of Consumer Affairs	LAJUAN M. JOHNSON
Chief Financial Officer and Assistant Secretary for Administration	W. SCOTT GOULD
Deputy Assistant Secretary for Administration	LINDA J. BILMES
Chief Information Officer	(VACANCY)
Deputy Assistant Secretary for Security	K. DAVID HOLMES, JR.
Director for Budget, Management, and Information and Deputy Chief Information Officer	ALAN P. BALUTIS
Director, Office of Budget	MARK E. BROWN
Director, Office of Management and Organization	STEPHEN C. BROWNING
Director, Office of Information Policy and Technology	JAMES MCNAMEE
Director, Office of Information Planning and Review	LISA A. WESTERBACK
Director, Office of Computer Services	PATRICK F. SMITH
Director, Office of Civil Rights	KIMBERLY H. WALTON, *Acting*
Director for Executive Budgeting and Assistance Management	SONYA G. STEWART
Director, Office of Executive Assistance Management	JOHN J. PHELAN III
Director, Office of Executive Budgeting	JAMES D. LAWLER
Director for Financial Management and Deputy Chief Financial Officer	ANTHONY MUSICK
Deputy Director	DOUGLAS K. DAY
Director, Office of Financial Policy and Assistance	THEODORE A. JOHNSON
Director, Office of Financial Management Systems	(VACANCY)
Director for Human Resources Management	DEBRA M. TOMCHEK
Executive Resources Program Director	DEBORAH A. JEFFERSON
Personnel Oversight Program Manager	JAMES W. GALLO
Deputy Director	(VACANCY)
Human Resources Manager, Office of Personnel Operations	ANTHONY CALZA, *Acting*
Director, Office of Programs and Policies	PAMELA E. RANKIN
Director, Office of Automated Systems and Pay Policy	DIANE ATCHINSON
Director for Administrative Services	HUGH L. BRENNAN
Director, Office of Safety and Building Management	ROBERT B. HEINEMANN
Director, Office of Real Estate Policy and Major Programs	JAMES M. ANDREWS
Director, Office of Administrative Operations	(VACANCY)

Director for Acquisition Management	ROBERT A. WELCH
Director for Systems and Telecommunications Management	RONALD P. HACK
Director, Office of Telecommunications Management	JUDY L. CUDDEHE
Director, Office of Information Systems	DALE M. LANSER
Director, Office of Technical Support	GEORGE H. IMBER
Under Secretary for Economic Affairs and Administrator, Economics and Statistics Administration	ROBERT SHAPIRO
Deputy Under Secretary	(VACANCY)
Associate Under Secretary	JOHN GRAY
Executive Director	KIM WHITE
Chief Economist	LEE PRICE
Director, Bureau of the Census	(VACANCY)
Deputy Director	BRADFORD R. HUTHER
Associate Director for Communications	(VACANCY)
Principal Associate Director and Chief Financial Officer	NANCY A. POTOK
Principal Associate Director for Programs	PAULA J. SCHNEIDER
Associate Director for Administration/ Comptroller	MICHAEL S. MCKAY, *Acting*
Associate Director for Information Technology	KAREN F. GREGORY
Associate Director for Field Operations	MARVIN D. RAINES
Associate Director for Economic Programs	FREDERICK T. KNICKERBOCKER
Assistant Director for Economic Programs	THOMAS L. MESENBOURG
Associate Director for Decennial Census	JOHN H. THOMPSON
Associate Director for Demographic Programs	NANCY M. GORDON
Associate Director for Methodology and Standards	CYNTHIA Z.F. CLARK
Director, Bureau of Economic Analysis	J. STEPHEN LANDEFELD
Deputy Director	BETTY L. BARKER
Associate Director for National Income Expenditures and Wealth Accounts	GERALD F. DONAHOE
Associate Director for Regional Economics	HUGH W. KNOX
Associate Director for International Economics	GERALD A. POLLACK
Associate Director for Industry Accounts	(VACANCY)
Chief Economist	JACK E. TRIPLETT
Chief Statistician	ROBERT P. PARKER
Under Secretary for Export Administration	WILLIAM A. REINSCH
Deputy Under Secretary	(VACANCY)
Director of Administration	MIRIAM L. COHEN, *Acting*
Director of Congressional and Public Affairs	ROSEMARY WARREN
Assistant Secretary for Export Administration	ROGER R. MAJAK
Deputy Assistant Secretary	IAIN S. BAIRD
Assistant Secretary for Export Enforcement	AMANDA F. DEBUSK
Deputy Assistant Secretary	FRANK DELIBERTI
Assistant Secretary for Economic Development	PHILLIP A. SINGERMAN
Deputy Assistant Secretary	(VACANCY)
Chief Financial Officer	MITCHELL L. LAINE
Deputy Assistant Secretary for Program Operations	CHESTER J. STRAUB, JR.

Deputy Assistant Secretary for Program Research and Evaluation	AWILDA R. MARQUEZ
Chief Counsel	EDWARD LEVIN
Under Secretary for International Trade	DAVID L. AARON
Deputy Under Secretary	TIMOTHY J. HAUSER
Counselor to the Department	JAN H. KALICKI
Chief Financial Officer and Director of Administration	ALAN NEUSCHATZ
Assistant Secretary for Market Access and Compliance	FRANKLIN J. VARGO, *Acting*
Deputy Assistant Secretary for the Western Hemisphere	REGINA VARGO
Deputy Assistant Secretary for Europe	FRANKLIN J. VARGO
Deputy Assistant Secretary for Africa and the Near East	JUDITH BARNETT
Deputy Assistant Secretary for Asia and the Pacific	(VACANCY)
Deputy Assistant Secretary for Japan	MARJORY SEARING
Deputy Assistant Secretary for Agreements Compliance	(VACANCY)
Assistant Secretary for Import Administration	ROBERT S. LaRUSSA
Deputy Assistant Secretary for Antidumping Countervailing Enforcement I	RICHARD W. MORELAND
Deputy Assistant Secretary for Antidumping Countervailing Enforcement II	RICHARD W. MORELAND, *Acting*
Deputy Assistant Secretary for Antidumping Countervailing Enforcement III	JOSEPH A. SPETRINI
Assistant Secretary for Trade Development	ELLIS R. MOTTUR, *Acting*
Deputy Assistant Secretary for Basic Industries	MICHAEL J. COPPS
Deputy Assistant Secretary for Technology and Aerospace Industries	ELLIS R. MOTTUR
Deputy Assistant Secretary for Service Industries and Finance	A. EVERETT JAMES
Deputy Assistant Secretary for Textiles, Apparel, and Consumer Goods Industries	TROY H. CRIBB
Deputy Assistant Secretary for Environmental Technologies Exports	ANNE L. ALONZO
Deputy Assistant Secretary for Tourism Industries	LESLIE R. DOGGETT
Assistant Secretary and Director General of the U.S. and Foreign Commercial Service	MARJORY SEARING, *Acting*
Deputy Assistant Secretary for Domestic Operations	DANIEL J. MCLAUGHLIN
Deputy Assistant Secretary for International Operations	DELORES F. HARROD
Deputy Assistant Secretary for Export Promotion Services	MARY FRAN KIRCHNER
Director, Minority Business Development Agency	COURTLAND V. COX
Deputy Director	PAUL R. WEBBER IV, *Acting*
Assistant Director for External Affairs	BARBARA MADDOX, *Acting*
Associate Director	PAUL R. WEBBER IV, *Acting*

Under Secretary for Oceans and Atmosphere and Administrator, National Oceanic and Atmospheric Administration	D. JAMES BAKER
Counselor to the Under Secretary	SUSAN B. FRUCHTER
Assistant Secretary for Oceans and Atmosphere and Deputy Administrator	TERRY D. GARCIA
Deputy Under Secretary for Oceans and Atmosphere	WILLIAM O. MEHURON, *Acting*
Associate Deputy Under Secretary	JOHN J. CAREY
Chief Scientist	(VACANCY)
Deputy Assistant Secretary for International Affairs	(VACANCY)
Deputy Assistant Secretary for Oceans and Atmosphere	SALLY J. YOZELL
Assistant Administrator for Fisheries	ROLLAND A. SCHMITTEN
Assistant Administrator for Ocean Services and Coastal Zone Management	NANCY FOSTER
Assistant Administrator for Oceanic and Atmospheric Research	ELBERT W. FRIDAY, JR.
Assistant Administrator for Weather Services	JOHN J. KELLY, JR.
Assistant Administrator for Satellite and Information Services	ROBERT S. WINOKUR
Director, Global Programs	J. MICHAEL HALL
Director, Coastal Ocean Program	DONALD SCAVIA
Director, Public and Constituent Affairs	LORI ANN ARGUELLES
Director, Sustainable Development and Intergovernmental Affairs	(VACANCY)
Director, Policy and Strategic Planning	SUSAN B. FRUCHTER
Director, Legislative Affairs	BRIAN WHEELER
Director, International Affairs	(VACANCY)
General Counsel	MONICA P. MEDINA
Director, National Oceanic and Atmospheric Administration Corps Operations	WILLIAM L. STUBBLEFIELD
Chief Financial Officer/Chief Administrative Officer	ANDREW MOXAM, *Acting*
Director, High Performance Computing and Communications	THOMAS N. PYKE, JR.
Director, Systems Acquisition	WILLIAM O. MEHURON
Assistant Secretary for Communications and Information	LARRY IRVING
Deputy Assistant Secretary	SHIRL G. KINNEY
Chief Counsel	KATHY D. SMITH, *Acting*
Director, Policy Coordination and Management	(VACANCY)
Associate Administrator for Spectrum Management	WILLIAM T. HATCH, *Acting*
Associate Administrator for Policy Analysis and Development	KATHRYN C. BROWN
Associate Administrator for International Affairs	J. BECKWITH BURR, *Acting*
Associate Administrator for Telecommunications and Information Applications	BERNADETTE A. MCGUIRE-RIVERA
Assistant Secretary and Commissioner of Patents and Trademarks	BRUCE A. LEHMAN

Deputy Assistant Secretary and Deputy Commissioner	LAWRENCE J. GOFFNEY, JR., *Acting*
Assistant Commissioner for Patents	(VACANCY)
Assistant Commissioner for Trademarks	PHILIP G. HAMPTON
Associate Commissioner and Chief Financial Officer	(VACANCY)
Chief Information Officer	DENNIS SHAW
Under Secretary for Technology	GARY R. BACHULA, *Acting*
Deputy Under Secretary	GARY R. BACHULA
Staff Director for Technology	JOYCE S. HASTY
Chief Counsel	MARK BOHANNON
Assistant Secretary for Technology Policy	(VACANCY)
Deputy Assistant Secretary for Technology Policy	KELLY H. CARNES
Director, Office of International Policy	PHYLLIS GENTHER YOSHIDA, *Acting*
Director, Office of Manufacturing Competitiveness	CARY GRAVATT
Director, Office of Space Commerce	KEITH CALHOUN-SENGHOR
Director, Office of Technology Competitiveness	JON PAUGH
Director, National Institute of Standards and Technology	RAYMOND G. KAMMER, JR.
Deputy Director	ROBERT E. HEBNER, *Acting*
Director of Administration	JORGE R. URRUTIA
Director, Technology Services	PETER L.M. HEYDEMANN
Chief Financial Officer	ROBERT E. HEBNER, *Acting*
Director, Electronics and Electrical Engineering Laboratory	JUDSON C. FRENCH
Director, Chemical Science and Technology Laboratory	HRATCH G. SEMERJIAN
Director, Physics Laboratory	KATHERINE B. GEBBIE
Director, Materials Science and Engineering Laboratory	DALE E. HALL, *Acting*
Director, Building and Fire Research Laboratory	RICHARD N. WRIGHT
Director, Information Technology Laboratory	SHUKRI WAKID
Director, Advanced Technology Program	LURA J. POWELL
Director, Manufacturing Extension Partnership Program	KEVIN M. CARR
Director, National Quality Program	HARRY S. HERTZ
Director, National Technical Information Service	DONALD W. CORRIGAN, *Acting*
Deputy Director	DONALD W. CORRIGAN

The Department of Commerce encourages, serves, and promotes the Nation's international trade, economic growth, and technological advancement. The Department provides a wide variety of programs through the competitive free enterprise system. It offers assistance and information to increase America's competitiveness in the world economy; administers programs to prevent unfair foreign trade competition; provides social and economic statistics and analyses for business and government planners; provides research and support for the increased use of scientific, engineering, and technological development; works to improve our understanding and benefits of the Earth's physical environment and oceanic resources; grants patents and registers trademarks; develops policies and conducts research on telecommunications; provides assistance to promote domestic economic development; and assists in the growth of minority businesses.

The Department was designated as such by act of March 4, 1913 (15 U.S.C. 1501), which reorganized the Department of Commerce and Labor, created by act of February 14, 1903 (15 U.S.C. 1501), by transferring all labor activities into a new, separate Department of Labor. The Department of Commerce (DOC) is composed of the Office of the Secretary and the operating units.

Office of the Secretary

Secretary The Secretary is responsible for the administration of all functions and authorities assigned to the Department of Commerce and for advising the President on Federal policy and programs affecting the industrial and commercial segments of the national economy. The Secretary is served by the offices of Deputy Secretary, Inspector General, General Counsel, and the Assistant Secretaries of Administration, Legislative and Intergovernmental Affairs, and Public Affairs. Other offices whose public purposes are widely administered are detailed below.

Business Liaison This office develops and promotes a cooperative working relationship and ensures effective communication between the Department of Commerce and the business community. The Office's objectives are to keep the business community aware of Department and administration resources, policies, and programs, and to keep Department and administration officials aware of issues of concern to business. The Office also promotes business involvement in departmental policymaking and program development, and provides technical assistance to businesses that desire help in dealing with the Government.

For further information, call 202–482–3942.

Consumer Affairs This office seeks to promote a better understanding between businesses and consumers, to help business improve the quality of their services, to educate consumers to make wise purchasing decisions, and to provide the consumer viewpoint in the development of economic policy. Through a variety of programs, the Office works with businesses, consumers, Government agencies, and international organizations to develop innovative ways to encourage American businesses to become more competitive both in the United States and in the global marketplace.

For further information, contact the Office of Consumer Affairs, U.S. Department of Commerce, Room H5718, Washington, DC 20230. Phone, 202–482–5001. Fax, 202–482–6007. E-mail, caffairs@doc.gov.

Small and Disadvantaged Business Utilization The Office of Small and Disadvantaged Business Utilization (OSDBU) serves as the principal departmental advocate for small, minority, and women business owners. It assures that small firms fully participate in Commerce programs and receive the maximum amount of Commerce contract and subcontract dollars.

The Office is the focal point of the Department's constant efforts to increase awards to small firms by searching for opportunities to match with the capabilities of small, minority, and women-owned firms.

It informs the small business community about Commerce opportunities by publishing the *Annual Forecast of Contracts,* by individual counseling, and by participating with other Federal agencies and trade associations at procurement fairs.

The Office of Small and Disadvantaged Business Utilization was established by the Small Business Act, as amended (15 U.S.C. 644).

For further information, call 202–482–1472.

DEPARTMENT OF COMMERCE

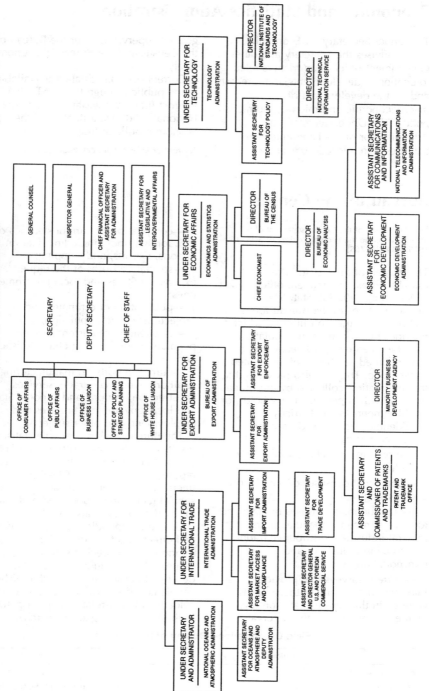

Economics and Statistics Administration

The Under Secretary for Economic Affairs advises the Secretary and other Government officials on matters relating to economic developments and forecasts and on the development of macroeconomic and microeconomic policy. The Under Secretary, as Administrator of the Economics and Statistics Administration, exercises general supervision over the Bureau of the Census and the Bureau of Economic Analysis.

Current economic data are available to the public through the STAT–USA Internet (http://www.stat-usa.gov), the National Trade Data Bank, and the Economic Bulletin Board.

For further information, call 800–782–8872.

Bureau of the Census

[For the Bureau of the Census statement of organization, see the *Federal Register* of Sept. 16, 1975, 40 FR 42765]

The Bureau of the Census was established as a permanent office by act of March 6, 1902 (32 Stat. 51). The major functions of the Bureau are authorized by the Constitution, which provides that a census of population shall be taken every 10 years, and by laws codified as title 13 of the United States Code. The law also provides that the information collected by the Bureau from individual persons, households, or establishments be kept strictly confidential and be used only for statistical purposes.

The principal functions of the Bureau include:

—decennial censuses of population and housing;

—quinquennial censuses of State and local governments, manufacturers, mineral industries, distributive trades, construction industries, and transportation;

—current surveys that provide information on many of the subjects covered in the censuses at monthly, quarterly, annual, or other intervals;

—compilation of current statistics on U.S. foreign trade, including data on imports, exports, and shipping;

—special censuses at the request and expense of States and local government units;

—publication of estimates and projections of the population;

—publication of current data on population and housing characteristics; and

—current reports on manufacturing, retail and wholesale trade, services, construction, imports and exports, State and local government finances and employment, and other subjects.

The Bureau makes available statistical results of its censuses, surveys, and other programs to the public through printed reports, computer tape, CD–ROM's, the Internet, and other media and prepares special tabulations sponsored and paid for by data users. It also produces statistical compendia, catalogs, guides, and directories that are useful in locating information on specific subjects. Upon request, the Bureau makes searches of decennial census records and furnishes certificates to individuals for use as evidence of age, relationship, or place of birth. A fee is charged for searches.

Field Organization—Bureau of the Census

Office	Address
REGIONAL OFFICES:	
ATLANTA—AL, FL, GA	Suite 3200, 101 Marietta St. NW., Atlanta, GA 30303–2700

Field Organization—Bureau of the Census—Continued

Office	Address
BOSTON—CT, MA, ME, NH, NY (all counties not listed under the New York Regional Office), RI, and VT	Suite 301, 2 Copley Pl., P.O. Box 9108, Boston, MA 02117–9108
CHARLOTTE—KY, NC, SC, TN, VA	Suite 106, 901 Center Park Dr., Charlotte, NC 28217–2935
CHICAGO—IL, IN, WI	Suite 5501, 2255 Enterprise Dr., Westchester, IL 60154–5800
DALLAS—LA, MS, TX	Suite 210, 6303 Harry Hines Blvd., Dallas, TX 75235–5269
DENVER—AZ, CO, MT, NE, ND, NM, NV, SD, UT, and WY	Suite 100, 6900 W. Jefferson Ave., Denver, CO 80235–2032
DETROIT—MI, OH, WV	P.O. Box 33405, 1395 Brewery Park Blvd., Detroit, MI 48232–5405
KANSAS CITY—AR, IA, KS, MN, MO, OK	Suite 600, 400 State Ave., Kansas City, KS 66101–2410
LOS ANGELES—CA (counties of Fresno, Imperial, Inyo, Kern, Kings, Los Angeles, Madera, Mariposa, Merced, Monterey, Orange, Riverside, San Benito, San Bernadino, San Diego, San Luis Obispo, Santa Barbara, Tulare, and Ventura), HI	Suite 300, 15350 Sherman Way, Van Nuys, CA 91406–4224
NEW YORK—NJ (counties of Bergen, Essex, Hudson, Middlesex, Morris, Passaic, Somerset, Sussex, Union, and Warren), NY (counties of Bronx, Kings, Nassau, New York, Queens, Richmond, Rockland, Suffolk, and Westchester)	Rm. 37–100, 26 Federal Plz., New York, NY 10278–0044
PHILADELPHIA—DC, DE, MD, NJ (all counties not listed under the New York Regional Office), PA	21st Fl., 1601 Market St., Philadelphia, PA 19103–2395
SEATTLE—AK, CA (all counties not listed under the Los Angeles Regional Office), ID, OR, WA	Rm. 5100, 700 5th Ave., Seattle, WA 98104–5018

For further information, contact the Public Information Office, Bureau of the Census, Department of Commerce, Washington, DC 20233. Phone, 301–457–2804. Fax, 301–457–3670.

Bureau of Economic Analysis

[For the Bureau of Economic Analysis statement of organization, see the *Federal Register* of Dec. 29, 1980, 45 FR 85496]

The Bureau of Economic Analysis (BEA) is the Nation's economic accountant—integrating and interpreting a variety of source data to draw a complete and consistent picture of the U.S. economy. Its economic accounts provide information on such key issues as economic growth, regional development, and the Nation's position in the world economy.

The national income and product accounts—featuring gross domestic product—provide a quantitative view of the production, distribution, and use of the Nation's output. The Bureau also prepares estimates of the Nation's tangible wealth and input-output tables that show how industries interact.

The regional economic accounts provide estimates of personal income, population, and employment for regions, States, and metropolitan areas. The Bureau prepares estimates of gross state product and projections of regional economic activity.

The international economic accounts encompass U.S. international transactions (balance of payments) with foreign countries and the international investment position of the United States. The Bureau provides survey-based data on foreign direct investment in the U.S. and U.S. direct investment abroad.

For further information, contact the Public Information Office, Bureau of Economic Analysis, Department of Commerce, Washington, DC 20230. Phone, 202–606–9900. Fax, 202–606–5310.

Bureau of Export Administration

[For the Bureau of Export Administration statement of organization, see the *Federal Register* of June 7, 1988, 53 FR 20881]

The Bureau of Export Administration was established as a separate agency within the Department of Commerce on October 1, 1987, to separate the functions of export promotion and export control as mandated by the Export Administration Act, as amended (50 U.S.C. app. 2401 *et seq.*).

The Bureau directs the Nation's export control policy. Major functions include processing license applications, conducting foreign availability studies to determine when products should be decontrolled, and enforcing U.S. export control laws.

Export Administration   This office oversees export licensing, technology and policy analysis, economic security and nonproliferation issues, and foreign availability determinations. These activities are instrumental in reducing processing time for granting export licenses and in keeping the list of controlled technology consistent with current risks. This office also works with our allies in seeking stronger, more uniform ways of controlling strategic exports.

Export Enforcement   This office investigates breaches of U.S. export control laws and analyzes export intelligence to assess diversion risks. In addition, this office administers and enforces the antiboycott provisions of the Export Administration Act.

Field Offices—Bureau of Export Administration

Field Area	Address
Boston, MA	Rm. 350, 10 Causeway St., 02222
Dallas, TX	Rm. 622, 525 Griffin St., 75202
Des Plaines, IL	Suite 300, 2400 E. Devon Ave., 60018
Fort Lauderdale, FL	200 E. Lasolas Blvd., 33301
Irvine, CA	Suite 310, 2601 Main St., 92714
Newport Beach, CA	Suite 345, 3300 Irvine Ave., 92660
San Jose, CA	Suite 250, 96 N. 3d St., 95112–5519
Santa Clara, CA	Suite 333, 5201 Great America Pkwy., 95054
Springfield, VA	Rm. 201, 8001 Forbes Pl., P.O. Box 1838, 22151
Staten Island, NY	2 Teleport Dr., 10311

For further information, contact the Bureau of Export Administration, Office of Public Affairs, Room 3897, Fourteenth Street and Constitution Avenue NW., Washington, DC 20230. Phone, 202–482–2721.

Economic Development Administration

The Economic Development Administration (EDA) was created in 1965 under the Public Works and Economic Development Act (42 U.S.C. 3121) as part of an effort to target Federal resources to economically distressed areas and to help develop local economies in the United States. It was mandated to assist rural and urban communities that were outside the mainstream economy and that, as a result, lagged in economic development, industrial growth, and personal income.

The Administration's economic development assistance programs (EDAP's) are carried out through a network of headquarters and regional personnel. It provides grants for public works and development facilities, planning and coordination, defense conversion, and other financial assistance that help to reduce substantial and persistent unemployment in economically distressed areas.

Public works and development facilities grants support infrastructure projects that foster the establishment or expansion of industrial and commercial businesses, supporting the retention and creation of jobs.

Planning grants support the design and implementation of effective economic development policies and programs, by local development organizations, in States and communities.

Technical assistance grants provide for local feasibility and industry studies, management and operational assistance, natural resource development, and export promotion. In addition, EDA funds a network of university centers that provides technical assistance.

Research, evaluation, and demonstration funds are used to support studies about the causes of economic distress and to seek solutions to counteract and prevent such problems.

Economic readjustment grants help communities adjust to a gradual erosion or sudden dislocation of their local economic structure.

Defense conversion grants assist communities adversely affected by Department of Defense base closures and defense contract cutbacks, as well as Department of Energy realignments, by providing development tools that can be effectively and easily implemented.

The Trade Adjustment Assistance Program provides technical assistance to certified firms and industries which have been economically injured by the impact of decreased imports. Comprehensive technical assistance is provided through the Department's wide-ranging network of assistance centers.

Regional Offices—Economic Development Administration

Region	Address
Atlanta, GA	Suite 1820, 401 W. Peachtree St. NW., 30308–3510
Alabama	Contact Atlanta Regional Office
Florida	Contact Atlanta Regional Office
Georgia	Contact Atlanta Regional Office
Kentucky	Suite 200, 771 Corporate Dr., Lexington, KY 40503–5477
Mississippi	Contact Atlanta Regional Office
North Carolina and South Carolina	Rm. 840, 1835 Assembly St., Columbia, SC 29201
Tennessee	Suite 200, 771 Corporate Dr., Lexington, KY 40503–5477
Austin, TX	Suite 121, 903 San Jacinto Blvd., Austin, TX 78701
Arkansas	Rm. 2509, 700 W. Capitol St., Little Rock, AR 72201
Louisiana	Rm. 1025, 501 Magazine St., New Orleans, LA 70130
New Mexico	Contact Austin Regional Office
Oklahoma	Contact Austin Regional Office
Texas	Contact Austin Regional Office
Chicago, IL	Suite 855, 111 N. Canal, 60606–7204
Illinois	104 Federal Bldg., 515 W. 1st St., Duluth, MN 55802
Indiana	Rm. 607, 200 N. High St., Columbus, OH 43214
Michigan	Contact Chicago Regional Office
Minnesota	Rm. 104, 515 W. 1st St., Duluth, MN 55802
Ohio	Rm. 607, 200 N. High St., Columbus, OH 43214
Wisconsin	Contact Chicago Regional Office
Denver, CO	Suite 670, 1244 Speer Blvd., 80204
Colorado and Kansas	Rm. 632, 1244 Speer Blvd., Denver, CO 80204
Iowa	Rm. 593A, 210 Walnut St., Des Moines, IA 50309
Missouri	Rm. B–2, 608 E. Cherry St., Columbia, MO 65201
Montana	Rm. 196, Federal Bldg., Helena, MT 59626
North Dakota and South Dakota	Rm. 216, 102 4th Ave. SE., Aberdeen, SD 57401
Nebraska	Rm. 593A, 210 Walnut St., Des Moines, IA 50309
Utah and Wyoming	125 S. State St., Salt Lake City, UT 84138
Philadelphia, PA	Suite 140 South, Independence Sq. West, Philadelphia, PA 19106
Connecticut	Contact Philadelphia Regional Office
District of Columbia	Contact Philadelphia Regional Office
Delaware	Contact Philadelphia Regional Office
Maine	Contact Philadelphia Regional Office
Maryland and Virginia	Rm. 474, 400 N. 8th St., Richmond, VA 23240
Massachusetts	Contact Philadelphia Regional Office
New Jersey	Contact Philadelphia Regional Office
New Hampshire and Vermont	Suite 209, 143 N. Main St., Concord, NH 03301
New York	Suite 104, 620 Erie Blvd. W., Syracuse, NY 13204
Pennsylvania	1933A New Bernick Hwy., Bloomsburg, PA 17815
Puerto Rico and Virgin Islands	Suite 602, 654 Munoz Rivera Ave., Hato Rey, PR 00918–1738
Rhode Island	Contact Philadelphia Regional Office
West Virginia	Rm. 141, 405 Capital St., Charleston, WV 25301
Seattle, WA	Rm. 1856, 915 2d Ave., 98174
Alaska	Rm. G–80, 605 W. 4th Ave., Anchorage, AK 99501–7594
Arizona	Rm. 441, 304 N. 8th St., Boise, ID 83702

Regional Offices—Economic Development Administration—Continued

Region	Address
California	Suite 244, 121 SW. Salmon St., Portland, OR 97204
....	Rm. 135B, 280 1st St., San Jose, CA 95112
....	Suite 411, 801 I St., Sacramento, CA 95814
....	Suite 205, 283 S. Lake Ave., Pasadena, CA 91101
Hawaii, Guam, American Samoa, Marshall Islands, Micronesia, and Northern Marianas.	P.O. Box 50264, Honolulu, HI 96850
Idaho	Rm. 441, 304 N. 8th St., Boise, ID 83702
Oregon	Suite 244, 121 SW. Salmon St., Portland, OR 97204
Washington	Contact Seattle Regional Office

For further information, contact the Economic Development Administration, Department of Commerce, Washington, DC 20230. Phone, 202–482–5314. Fax, 202–482–0995.

International Trade Administration

[For the International Trade Administration statement of organization, see the *Federal Register* of Jan. 25, 1980, 45 FR 6148]

The International Trade Administration was established on January 2, 1980, by the Secretary of Commerce to promote world trade and to strengthen the international trade and investment position of the United States.

The Administration is headed by the Under Secretary for International Trade, who coordinates all issues concerning trade promotion, international commercial policy, market access, and trade law enforcement. The Administration is responsible for nonagricultural trade operations of the U.S. Government and supports the trade policy negotiation efforts of the U.S. Trade Representative.

Import Administration   The Office of the Assistant Secretary for Import Administration defends American industry against injurious and unfair trade practices by administering efficiently, fairly, and in a manner consistent with U.S. international trade obligations the antidumping and countervailing duty laws of the United States; the machine tool arrangements with Japan and Taiwan under the President's Machine Tool Program. The Office ensures the proper administration of foreign trade zones and advises the Secretary on establishment of new zones; and administers programs

governing watch assemblies, and other statutory import programs.

Market Access and Compliance   The Office of the Assistant Secretary for Market Access and Compliance advises on the analysis, formulation, and implementation of U.S. international economic policies and carries out programs to promote international trade, improve access by U.S. companies to overseas markets, and strengthen the international trade and investment position of the United States. Through the five regional Deputy Assistant Secretaries (Europe; Western Hemisphere; Asia and the Pacific; Africa and the Near East; and Japan), the Office analyzes and develops recommendations for region- and country-specific international economic, trade, and investment policy strategies and objectives. In addition, the Office is responsible for implementing, monitoring, and enforcing foreign compliance with bilateral and multilateral trade agreements.

Trade Development   The Office of the Assistant Secretary for Trade Development advises on international trade and investment policies pertaining to U.S. industrial sectors, carries out programs to strengthen domestic export competitiveness, and promotes U.S. industry participation in international markets. The Office manages an integrated trade development program that includes industry analysis and trade promotion organized by industry sectors, including technology and aerospace; basic industries; service industries and finance; textiles, apparel, and consumer goods; environmental technologies; and tourism.

U.S. and Foreign Commercial Service

The U.S. and Foreign Commercial Service develops, produces, markets, and manages an effective line of high-quality products and services geared to the marketing information needs of the U.S. exporting and international business community. The Service delivers programs through 100 U.S. export assistance centers located in the United States, and 141 posts located in 76 countries throughout the world. It supports overseas trade promotion events; manages a variety of export promotion services and products; promotes U.S. products and services throughout the world market; conducts conferences and seminars in the United States; and assists State and private-sector organizations on export financing.

Domestic Offices—International Trade Administration

Address	Director/Manager	Telephone	Fax
Alabama (Rm. 707, 950 22d St. N., Birmingham, 35203)	George Norton	205–731–1331	205–731–0076
Alaska (Suite 700, 3601 C St., Anchorage, 99503)	Charles Becker	907–271–6237	907–271–6242
Arizona (Suite 970, 2901 N. Central Ave., Phoenix, 85012) ...	Frank Woods	602–640–2513	602–640–2518
Arkansas (Suite 700, 425 W. Capitol Ave., Little Rock, 72201).	Lon J. Hardin	501–324–5794	501–324–7380
California			
Fresno (390–B Fir Ave., Clovis, 93611)	Arlene Mayeda	209–325–1619	209–325–1647
Long Beach (Suite 1670, One World Trade Ctr., 90831)	Joe Sachs	562–980–4550	562–980–4561
Los Angeles (Suite 172, 350 S. Figueroa St., 90071)	Jim Cunningham	213–894–8784	213–894–8790
Monterey (Suite 200, 411 Pacific St., 93940)	Dao Le	408–641–9850	408–641–9849
Newport Beach (Suite 305, 3300 Irvine Ave., 92660)	Paul Tambakis	714–660–1688	714–660–8039
Novato (Suite 102, 330 Ignacio Blvd., 94949)	Elizabeth Krauth	415–883–1966	415–883–2711
Oakland (Suite 740, 530 Water St., 94607)	Raj Shea	510–273–7350	510–251–7352
Ontario (Suite 121, 2940 Inland Empire Blvd., 91764)	Fred Latuperissa	909–466–4134	909–466–4140
Oxnard (Suite 2090, 300 Esplanade Dr., 93030)	Gerald Vaughn	805–981–8150	805–981–1855
Sacramento (2d Fl., 917 7th St., 95814)	Brooks Ohlson	916–498–5155	916–498–5923
San Diego (Suite 230, 6363 Greenwich Dr., 92122)	Mary Delmage	619–557–5395	619–557–6176
San Francisco (14th Fl. 250 Montgomery St., 94104)	(Vacancy)	415–705–2300	415–705–2297
San Jose (Suite 1001, 101 Park Center Plz., 95113)	James S. Kennedy	408–271–7300	408–271–7307
Santa Clara (Rm. 456, 5201 Great America Pkwy., 95054)	James Rigassio	408–970–4610	408–970–4618
West Los Angeles (Suite 975, 11150 Olympic Blvd., 90064)	Sherwin Chen	310–235–7104	310–235–7220
Colorado (Suite 680, 1625 Broadway, Denver, 80202)	Nancy Charles-Parker	303–844–6622	303–844–5651
Connecticut (Suite 903, 213 Court St., Middletown, 06457–3346).	Carl Jacobsen	860–638–6950	860–638–6970
Delaware (Suite 1501, 615 Chestnut St., Philadelphia, PA 19106).	Maria Galindo	215–597–6101	215–597–6123
Florida			
Clearwater (1130 Cleveland St., 34615)	George Martinez	813–461–0011	813–449–2889
Miami (Suite 617, 5600 NW. 36th St., 33166)	John McCartney	305–526–7425	305–526–7434
Orlando (Suite 1270, 200 E. Robinson St., 32801)	Philip A. Ouzts	407–648–6235	407–648–6756
Tallahassee (Suite 2001, The Capitol, 32399–0001)	Michael Higgins	850–488–6469	850–487–3014
Georgia			
Atlanta (Suite 200, 285 Peachtree Ctr. Ave. NE., 30303–1229).	Samuel P. Troy	404–657–1900	404–657–1970
Savannah (Suite 100, 6001 Chatham Ctr. Dr., 31405)	Barbara Prieto	912–652–4204	912–652–4241
Hawaii (Rm. 4106, 300 Ala Moana Blvd., Honolulu, 96850) ...	Amer Kayani	808–541–1782	808–541–3435
Idaho (2d Fl., 700 W. State St., Boise, 83720)	Steve Thompson	208–334–3857	208–334–2783
Illinois			
Chicago (Suite 2440, 55 W. Monroe St., 60603)	Mary N. Joyce	312–353–8040	312–353–8098
Highland Park (Suite 150, 610 Central Ave., 60035)	Robin F. Mugford	847–681–8010	847–681–8012
Rockford (515 N. Court St., 61110)	James Mied	815–987–8123	815–963–7943
Wheaton (201 E. Loop Rd., 60187)	(Vacancy)	312–353–4332	312–353–4336
Indiana (Suite 106, 11405 N. Pennsylvania St., Carmel, 46032).	Dan Swart	317–582–2300	317–582–2301
Iowa (Rm. 817, 210 Walnut St., Des Moines, 50309)	Allen Patch	515–284–4222	515–284–4021
Kansas (151 N. Volutsia, Wichita, 67214)	George D. Lavid	316–269–6160	316–683–7326
Kentucky			
Louisville (Rm. 634B, 601 W. Broadway, 40202)	John Autin	502–582–5066	502–582–6573
Somerset (Suite 320, 2292 S. Hwy. 27, 42501)	Sara Melton	606–677–6160	606–677–6161
Louisiana			
New Orleans (Suite 2150, 365 Canal St., 70130)	David Spann	504–589–6546	504–589–2337
Shreveport (5210 Hollywood Ave. Annex, 71109	Norbert O. Gannon	318–676–3064	318–676–3063
Maine (511 Congress St., Portland, 04101)	Jeffrey Porter	207–541–7400	207–541–7420
Maryland (Suite 2432, 401 E. Pratt St., Baltimore, 21202)	Michael Keaveny	410–962–4539	410–962–4529
Massachusetts			
Boston (Suite 307, 164 Northern Ave., 02210)	Frank J. O'Connor	617–424–5990	617–424–5992

Domestic Offices—International Trade Administration—Continued

Address	Director/Manager	Telephone	Fax
Marlborough (Unit 102, 100 Granger Blvd., 01752)	William Davis	508–624–6000	508–624–7145
Michigan			
Ann Arbor (Suite 103, 425 S. Main St., 48104)	Paul Litton	313–741–2430	313–741–2432
Detroit (Suite 2220, 211 W. Fort St., 48226)	Neil Hesse	313–226–3650	313–226–3657
Grand Rapids (Suite 718–S, 301 W. Fulton St., 49504)	Thomas Maguire	616–458–3564	616–458–3872
Pontiac (250 Elizabeth Lake Rd., 48341)	Richard Corson	248–975–9600	248–975–9606
Minnesota (Rm. 108, 110 S. 4th St., Minneapolis, 55401)	Ronald E. Kramer	612–348–1638	612–348–1650
Mississippi (704 E. Main St., Raymond, 39154)	Harrison Ford	601–857–0128	601–857–0026
Missouri			
Kansas City (Suite 650, 2345 Grand, 64108)	Thomas A. Strauss	816–410–9201	816–410–9208
St. Louis (Suite 303, 8182 Maryland Ave., 63105)	Randall J. LaBounty	314–425–3302	314–425–3381
Montana (2d Fl., 700 W. State St., Boise, ID 83720)	Steve Thompson	208–334–3857	208–334–2783
Nebraska (11135 "O" St., Omaha, 68137)	(Vacancy)	402–221–3664	402–221–3668
Nevada (Suite 152, 1755 E. Plumb La., Reno, 89502)	Jere Dabbs	702–784–5203	702–784–5343
New Hampshire (17 New Hampshire Ave., Portsmouth, 03801–2838).	Susan Berry	603–334–6074	603–334–6110
New Jersey			
Newark (9th Fl., One Gateway Center, 07102)	William Spitler	201–645–4682	201–645–4783
Trenton (Suite 100, Bldg. 6, 3131 Princeton Pk., 08648)	Rod Stuart	609–989–2100	609–989–2395
New Mexico (P.O. Box 20003, Santa Fe, 87504–5003)	Sandra Necessary	505–827–0350	505–827–0263
New York			
Buffalo (Rm. 1304, 111 W. Huron St., 14202)	George Buchanan	716–551–4191	716–551–5290
Harlem (Suite 904, 163 W. 125th St., New York, 10027)	K. L. Fredericks	212–860–6200	212–860–6203
Long Island (Rm. 207, 1550 Franklin Ave., Mineola 11501)	George Soteros	516–739–1765	516–739–3310
New York (Rm. 635, 6 World Trade Ctr., 10048)	Joel W. Barkan, *Acting*	212–466–5222	212–264–1356
Westchester (707 W. Chester Ave., White Plains, 10604)	Joan Kanlian	914–682–6218	914–682–6698
North Carolina			
Charlotte (Suite 435, 521 E. Morehead St., 28202)	Roger Fortner	704–333–4886	704–332–2681
Greensboro (Suite 400, 400 W. Market St., 27401)	Linda Jones, *Acting*	910–333–5345	910–333–5158
North Dakota (Rm. 108, 110 S. 4th St., Minneapolis, MN 55401).	Ronald E. Kramer	612–348–1638	612–348–1650
Ohio			
Cincinnati (Suite 2650, 36 E. 7th St., 45202)	Michael Miller	513–684–2944	513–684–3227
Cleveland (Suite 700, 600 Superior Ave. E., 44114)	Clem von Koschembahr, *Acting.*	216–522–4750	216–522–2235
Columbus (4th Fl., 37 N. High St., 43215)	Mary Beth Double	614–365–9510	614–365–9598
Toledo (300 Madison Ave., 43604)	Robert Abrahams	419–241–0683	419–241–0684
Oklahoma			
Oklahoma City (Suite 330, 301 NW. 63d St., 73116)	Ronald L. Wilson	405–231–5302	405–231–4211
Tulsa (Suite 1400, 700 N. Greenwood Ave., 74106)	(Vacancy)	918–581–7650	918–594–8413
Oregon			
Eugene (Suite 13, 1445 Willamette St., 97401–4003)	Pamela Ward	541–465–6575	541–465–6704
Portland (Suite 242, 121 SW. Salmon St., 97204)	Scott Goddin	503–326–3001	503–326–6351
Pennsylvania			
Harrisburg (3d Fl., 417 Walnut St., 17101)	Deborah Doherty	717–232–0051	717–232–0054
Philadelphia (Suite 1501, 615 Chestnut St., 19106)	Maria Galindo	215–597–6101	215–597–6123
Pittsburgh (2002 Federal Bldg, 1000 Liberty Ave., 15222)	Ted Amn	412–395–5050	412–395–4875
Scranton (Suite B, One Montage Mt. Rd., Moosic, 18507)	Henry LaBlanc	717–969–2530	717–969–2539
Puerto Rico (Rm. G–55, Chardon Ave., San Juan (Hato Rey), 00918).	J. Enrique Vilella	787–766–5555	787–766–5692
Rhode Island (One W. Exchange St., Providence, 02903)	Raimond Meerbach	401–528–5104	401–528–5067
South Carolina			
Charleston (81 Mary St., 29403)	David Kuhlmeier	803–727–4051	803–727–4052
Columbia (Suite 172, 1835 Assembly St., 29201)	Ann Watts	803–765–5345	803–253–3614
Greenville (Suite 109, Bldg. 1, 555 N. Pleasantburg Dr., 29607).	Denis Csizmadia	864–271–1976	864–271–4171
South Dakota (Rm. SS–29A, 2001 S. Summit Ave., Sioux Falls, 57197).	(Vacancy)	605–330–4264	605–330–4266
Tennessee			
Knoxville (301 E. Church Ave., 37915)	Thomas McGinty	423–545–4637	423–545–4435
Memphis (Suite 200, 22 N. Front St., 38103)	Ree Russell	901–544–4137	901–544–3646
Nashville (Suite 114, 404 James Robertson Pkwy, 37219)	Michael Speck	615–736–5161	615–736–2454
Texas			
Austin (2d Fl., 1700 Congress, 78701)	Karen Parker	512–916–5939	512–916–5940
Dallas (Suite 170, 2050 N. Stemmons Fwy., 75207)	Bill Schrage	214–767–0542	214–767–8240
Fort Worth (711 Houston St., 76102)	Vavie Sellschopp	817–212–2673	817–978–0178
Houston (Suite 1160, 500 Dallas, 77002)	James D. Cook	713–718–3062	713–718–3060
San Antonio (Suite 450, 1222 N. Main, 78212)	Mitchel Auerbach	210–228–9878	210–228–9874
Utah (Suite 221, 324 S. State St., Salt Lake City, 84111)	Stephen P. Smoot	801–524–5116	801–524–5886
Vermont (National Life Building, Drawer 20, Montpelier, 05620–0501).	James Cox	802–828–4508	802–828–3258
Virginia			
Arlington (Suite 1300, 1616 N. Fort Myer Dr., 22209)	Sylvia Burns	703–524–2885	703–524–2649
Richmond (Suite 550, 704 E. Franklin St., 23219)	William D. Coale, Jr.	804–771–2246	804–771–2390
Washington			
Seattle (Suite 650, 2001 6th Ave., 98121)	Lisa Kjaer-Schade	206–553–5615	206–553–7253

Domestic Offices—International Trade Administration—Continued

Address	Director/Manager	Telephone	Fax
Spokane (Suite 400, 801 W. Riverside Ave., 99201) .... West Virginia	James K. Hellwig	509–353–2625	509–353–2449
Charleston (Suite 807, 405 Capitol St., 25301)	Harvey Timberlake	304–347–5123	304–347–5408
Wheeling (2d Fl., 1310 Market St., 26003)	Martha Butwin	304–233–7472	304–233–7492
Wisconsin (Rm. 596, 517 E. Wisconsin Ave., Milwaukee, 53202).	Paul D. Churchill	414–297–3473	414–297–3470
Wyoming (Suite 680, 1625 Broadway, Denver, 80202)	Nancy Charles-Parker	303–844–6622	303–844–5651
EASTERN REGION (Suite 2450, 401 E. Pratt St., Baltimore, MD 21202).	Thomas Cox	410–962–2805	410–962–2799
MID-EASTERN REGION (Suite 2025, 36 E. 7th St., Cincinnati, OH 45202).	Gordon B. Thomas	513–684–2947	513–684–3200
MID-WESTERN REGION (Suite 1011, 8182 Maryland Ave., St. Louis, MO 63105).	Sandra Gerley	314–425–3300	314–425–3375
WESTERN REGION (14th Fl., 250 Montgomery St., San Francisco, CA 94104).	Keith Bovetti	415–705–2310	415–705–2299

For further information, contact the International Trade Administration, Department of Commerce, Washington, DC 20230. Phone, 202–482–3809.

Minority Business Development Agency

[For the Minority Business Development Agency statement of organization, see the *Federal Register* of Mar. 17, 1972, 37 FR 5650, as amended]

The Minority Business Development Agency, formerly the Office of Minority Business Enterprise, was established by the Secretary of Commerce on November 1, 1979, and operates under the authority of Executive Order 11625 of October 13, 1971. The Agency develops and coordinates a national program for minority business enterprise.

The Agency was created to assist minority businesses in achieving effective and equitable participation in the American free enterprise system and in overcoming social and economic disadvantages that have limited their participation in the past. The Agency provides national policies and leadership in forming and strengthening a partnership of business, industry, and government with the Nation's minority businesses.

Business development services are provided to the minority business community through three vehicles: the Minority Business Opportunity Committees which disseminate information on business opportunities; the Minority Business Development Centers that provide management and technical assistance and other business development services; and Electronic Commerce which includes a Web page on the Internet that will show how to start a business and use of the Electronic Commerce to electronically match business with contract opportunities.

The Agency promotes and coordinates the efforts of other Federal agencies in assisting or providing market opportunities for minority business. It coordinates opportunities for minority firms in the private sector. Through such public and private cooperative activities, the Agency promotes the participation of Federal, State, and local governments, and business and industry in directing resources for the development of strong minority businesses.

Regional Offices—Minority Business Development Agency

Region	Address	Director	Telephone
Atlanta, GA	Suite 1715, 401 W. Peachtree St. NW., 30308–3516 ...	Robert Henderson	404–730–3300
Chicago, IL	Suite 1406, 55 E. Monroe St., 60603	David Vega	312–353–0182
Dallas, TX	Suite 7B23, 1100 Commerce St., 75242	John Iglehart	214–767–8001
New York, NY	Suite 37–20, 26 Federal Plz., 10278	Heyward Davenport	212–264–3262
San Francisco, CA	Rm. 1280, 221 Main St., 94105	Melda Cabrera	415–744–3001

District Offices—Minority Business Development Agency

District	Address	Officer	Telephone
Boston, MA	Rm. 418, 10 Causeway St., 02222–1041	Rochelle K. Schwartz	617–565–6850
El Monte, CA	Suite 455, 9660 Flair Dr., 91713	Rodolfo Guerra	818–453–8636
Miami, FL	Rm. 1314, 51 SW. 1st Ave., 33130	Rodolfo Suarez	305–536–5054
Philadelphia, PA	Rm. 10128, 600 Arch St., 19106	Alfonso C. Jackson	215–597–9236

For further information, contact the Office of the Director, Minority Business Development Agency, Department of Commerce, Washington, DC 20230. Phone, 202–482–5061. Internet, http://www.mbda.gov/.

National Oceanic and Atmospheric Administration

U.S. Department of Commerce, Washington, DC 20230
Phone, 202–482–2985. Internet, http://www.noaa.gov/.

[For the National Oceanic and Atmospheric Administration statement of organization, see the *Federal Register* of Feb. 13, 1978, 43 FR 6128]

The National Oceanic and Atmospheric Administration (NOAA) was formed on October 3, 1970, by Reorganization Plan No. 4 of 1970 (5 U.S.C. app.). Its principal functions are authorized by Title 15, Chapter 9, United States Code (National Weather Service); Title 33, Chapter 17, United States Code (National Ocean survey), and Title 16, Chapter 9, United States Code (National Marine Fisheries Service).

NOAA is the largest bureau within the Department of Commerce and is integral to providing the Department with an environmental perspective on issues having an impact on the Nation's resources and its economy. NOAA's mission entails environmental assessment, prediction, and stewardship. It is dedicated to monitoring and assessing the state of the environment in order to make accurate and timely forecasts to protect life, property, and natural resources, as well as to promote the economic well-being of the United States and to enhance its environmental security. As the Nation's premier environmental steward, NOAA is committed to protecting America's ocean, coastal, and living marine resources while promoting sustainable economic development.

In order to undertake its mission, NOAA has a strategic plan of seven interrelated goals falling under two broad themes of (1) environmental assessment and prediction with the goals of advancing short-term warnings and forecasts, implement seasonal to interannual climate forecasts, predict and assess decadal-to-centennial climate change, and promote safe navigation, and (2) environmental stewardship, comprised of the goals to build sustainable fisheries, recover protected species, and sustain healthy coastal ecosystems.

NOAA is structured into five primary, component line offices. These are the National Weather Service, the National Environmental Satellite, Data, and Information Service, the National Marine Fisheries Service, the National Ocean Service, and the Office of Oceanic and Atmospheric Research.

National Weather Service

The National Weather Service (NWS) provides daily forecasts and warnings for severe weather events such as hurricanes, tornadoes, winter storms, flooding, and tsunamis. With its modernization program, NWS will be able to maximize its use of advanced computer technology to capture, integrate, and analyze Doppler radar imagery and data from satellites and automated surface instruments, and to speed up the dissemination of its forecasts and warnings. This will allow NWS to provide the public with more localized, timely, and accurate forecasts, increasing the lead time it has to prepare for severe weather events. NWS also provides services in support of aviation and marine activities, agriculture, forestry, and urban air quality control.

For further information, contact the National Weather Service, 1325 East-West Highway, Silver Spring, MD 20910–3283. Phone, 301–713–0689. Fax, 301–713–0610. Internet, http:// www.nws.noaa.gov/.

National Environmental Satellite, Data, and Information Service

The National Environmental Satellite, Data, and Information Service (NESDIS) operates the Nation's civilian geostationary and polar-orbiting environmental satellites. It also manages the largest collection of atmospheric, geophysical, and oceanographic data in the world. From these sources, NESDIS develops and provides, through various media, environmental data for forecasts, national security, and weather warnings to protect life and property. This data is also used to assist in energy distribution, the development of global food supplies, the management of natural resources, and in the recovery of downed pilots and mariners in distress.

For further information, contact the National Environmental Satellite, Data, and Information Service, Room 2069, 4401 Suitland Road, Suitland, MD 20233. Phone, 301–457–5115. Fax, 301–457–5276. Internet, http://www.noaa.gov/nesdis/ nesdis.html/.

National Marine Fisheries Service

The National Marine Fisheries Service (NMFS) supports the management, conservation, and sustainable development of domestic and international living marine resources. NMFS is involved in the stock assessment of the Nation's multi-billion dollar marine fisheries, protecting marine mammals and threatened species, habitat conservation operations, trade and industry assistance, and fishery enforcement activities.

For further information, contact the National Marine Fisheries Service, 1315 East-West Highway, Silver Spring, MD 20910. Phone, 301–713–2239. Fax, 301–713–2258. Internet, http:// kingfish.ssp.nmfs.gov/.

National Ocean Service

The National Ocean Service (NOS), growing out of the Nation's oldest scientific agency, Survey of the Coast, established in 1807 by President Thomas Jefferson, has responsibility to chart the Nation's coastlines and airways to ensure safe navigation, as well as managing and protecting coastal and ocean resources. Through its Coastal Zone Management Program, NOS monitors the health of U.S. coasts by examining how use of the near shore impacts on its ecosystem, striving to protect wetlands, water quality, beaches, and wildlife. NOS is also involved in the assessment of hazardous material spills and works to restore or replace areas damaged by such contamination.

For further information, contact the National Ocean Service, Room 13632, 1305 East-West Highway, Silver Spring, MD 20910. Phone, 301–713–3074. Fax, 301–713–4269. Internet, http:// www.nos.noaa.gov/.

Office of Oceanic and Atmospheric Research

The Office of Oceanic and Atmospheric Research (OAR) carries out research into such phenomena as El Niño, global warming, ozone depletion, solar storms that can disrupt telecommunications and electrical power systems, and coastal and Great Lakes ecosystems. OAR conducts and directs its research programs in coastal, marine, atmospheric, and space sciences through its own laboratories and offices, as well as through networks of university-based programs across the country.

For further information, contact the Office of Oceanic and Atmospheric Research, Room 11627, 1315 East-West Highway, Silver Spring, MD 20910. Phone, 301–713–2458. Fax, 301–713–0163. Internet, http://www.oar.noaa.gov/.

Office of NOAA Corps Operations

NOAA also maintains a fleet of ships and aircraft under the auspices of its Office of NOAA Corps Operations. These are used for scientific, engineering, and technical services, as well as to serve as research platforms for gathering critical marine and atmospheric data in support of a number of NOAA's research programs. This includes flying "hurricane hunter" aircraft into nature's most turbulent storms to collect data critical to hurricane research.

For further information, contact the Office of NOAA Corps Operations, Room 12857, 1315 East-West Highway, Silver Spring, MD 20910–3282. Phone, 301–713–1045.

Field Organization—National Oceanic and Atmospheric Administration

Organization	Address/Telephone	Director
National Weather Service		
Headquarters	1325 East-West Hwy., Silver Spring, MD 20910–3283. Phone, 301–713–0689. Fax, 301–713–0610.	John J. Kelly, Jr.
Office of Meteorology	1325 East-West Hwy., Silver Spring, MD 20910–3283. Phone, 301–713–0700. Fax, 301–713–1598.	Louis W. Uccellini
Office of Hydrology	1325 East-West Hwy., Silver Spring, MD 20910–3283. Phone, 301–713–1658. Fax, 301–713–0963.	Danny L. Fread
National Centers for Environmental Prediction.	5200 Auth Rd., Camp Springs, MD 20746–4304. Phone, 301–763–8016. Fax, 301–763–8434.	Ronald D. McPherson
Office of Systems Development	1325 East-West Hwy., Silver Spring, MD 20910–3283. Phone, 301–713–0745. Fax, 301–713–0003.	Douglas H. Sargeant
Office of Systems Operations	1325 East-West Hwy., Silver Spring, MD 20910–3283. Phone, 301–713–0165. Fax, 301–713–0657.	Walter Telesetsky
National Data Buoy Center	Rm. 344, Bldg. 1100, Stennis Space Center, MS 39529–6000. Phone, 601–688–2800. Fax, 601–688–3153.	Jerry C. McCall
Eastern region	630 Johnson Ave., Bohemia, NY 11716–2626. Phone, 516–244–0100. Fax, 516–244–0109.	John T. Forsing
Southern region	Rm. 10A26, 819 Taylor St., Fort Worth, TX 76102–6171. Phone, 817–978–2651. Fax, 817–334–4187.	X. William Proenza, *Acting*
Central region	Rm. 1836, 601 E. 12th St., Kansas City, MO 64106–2897. Phone, 816–426–5400. Fax, 816–426–3270.	Richard P. Augulis
Training center	Rm. 116, 617 Hardesty St., Kansas City, MO 64124–3097. Phone, 816–374–6238. Fax, 816–374–6726.	John L. Vogel
Western region	Rm. 1210, 125 S. State St., Salt Lake City, UT 84138–1102. Phone, 801–524–6295. Fax, 801–524–5270.	Thomas D. Potter
Alaska region	Rm. 517, 222 W. 7th Ave., Anchorage, AK 99513–7575. Phone, 907–271–5136. Fax, 907–271–3711.	Richard J. Hutcheon
Pacific region	Suite 2200, 737 Bishop St., Honolulu, HI 96813. Phone, 808–532–6416. Fax, 808–532–5569.	Richard H. Hagemeyer
Office of the Federal Coordinator for Meteorological Services and Supporting Research.	1500 Ctr., 8455 Colesville Rd., Silver Spring, MD 20910–3315. Phone, 301–427–2002.	Julian (Skip) Wright, Jr.
National Marine Fisheries Service		
Headquarters	1315 East-West Hwy., Silver Spring, MD 20910. Phone, 301–713–2239. Fax, 301–713–2258.	Rolland A. Schmitten
Alaska region	P.O. Box 21668, Juneau, AK 99802–1668. Phone, 907–586–7221. Fax, 907–586–7249.	Steven Pennoyer
Alaska Fisheries Science Center	Bin C15700, Bldg. 4, 7600 Sand Point Way NE., Seattle, WA 98115. Phone, 206–526–4000. Fax, 206–526–4004.	James W. Balsiger
Northwest region	Bin C15700, Bldg. 1, 7600 Sand Point Way NE., Seattle, WA 98115–0070. Phone, 206–526–6150. Fax, 206–526–6426.	William W. Stelle, Jr.
Northwest Fisheries Science Center ..	2725 Montlake Blvd. E., Seattle, WA 98112. Phone, 206–860–3200. Fax, 206–860–3217.	Usha Varanasi
Northeast region	1 Blackburn Dr., Gloucester, MA 01930. Phone, 978–281–9250. Fax, 978–281–9371.	Andrew Rosenberg
Northeast Fisheries Science Center ..	166 Water St., Woods Hole, MA 02543. Phone, 508–548–5123. Fax, 508–495–2232.	Michael Sissenwine
Southeast region	9721 Executive Ctr. Dr. N., St. Petersburg, FL 33702. Phone, 813–570–5301. Fax, 813–570–5300.	Andrew J. Kammerer
Southeast Fisheries Science Center ..	75 Virginia Beach Dr., Miami, FL 33149. Phone, 305–361–5761. Fax, 305–361–4219.	Brad Brown

Field Organization—National Oceanic and Atmospheric Administration—Continued

Organization	Address/Telephone	Director
Southwest region	Suite 4200, 501 W. Ocean Blvd., Long Beach, CA 90802. Phone, 562–980–4001. Fax, 562–980–4018.	William T. Hogarth, *Acting*
Southwest Fisheries Science Center	P.O. Box 271, 8604 La Jolla Shores Dr., La Jolla, CA 92038. Phone, 619–546–7067. Fax, 619–546–5655.	Michael Tillman
National Environmental Satellite, Data, and Information Service		
Headquarters	Rm. 2069, 4401 Suitland Rd., Suitland, MD 20233. Phone, 301–457–5115. Fax, 301–457–5276.	Robert S. Winokur
Satellite operations	Rm. 0135, 4401 Suitland Rd., Suitland, MD 20233. Phone, 301–457–5130. Fax, 301–457–5175.	Gary K. Davis
Satellite data processing and distribution.	Rm. 1069, 4401 Suitland Rd., Suitland, MD 20233. Phone, 301–457–5120. Fax, 301–457–5184.	Helen M. Wood
Research and applications	NOAA Science Center, 5200 Auth Rd., Camp Springs, MD 20233. Phone, 301–763–8127. Fax, 301–763–8108.	James Purdom
Systems development	Rm. 3301C, 4401 Suitland Rd., Suitland, MD 20233. Phone, 301–457–5277. Fax, 301–420–0932.	Gary K. Davis, *Acting*
National Climatic Data Center	151 Patton Ave., Asheville, NC 28801–5001. Phone, 704–271–4476. Fax, 704–271–4246.	Ken Davidson, *Acting*
National Geophysical Data Center	RL–3, 325 Broadway, Boulder, CO 80303–3328. Phone, 303–497–6215. Fax, 303–497–6513.	Michael S. Loughridge
National Oceanographic Data Center	1315 East-West Hwy., Silver Spring, MD 20910. Phone, 301–713–3267. Fax, 301–713–3300.	Henry Frey
National Ocean Service		
Headquarters	Rm. 13632, 1305 East-West Hwy., Silver Spring, MD 20910. Phone, 301–713–3074. Fax, 301–713–4269.	Nancy Foster
NOAA Coastal Services Center	2234 S. Hobson Ave., Charleston, SC 29405–2409. Phone, 843–740–1200. Fax 843–740–1224.	Margaret Davidson
Hazardous Materials Response Assessment.	Bin C15700, 7600 Sand Point Way NE., Seattle, WA 98115. Phone, 206–526–6317. Fax, 206–526–6329.	David M. Kennedy
Coast survey	Rm. 6147, 1315 East-West Hwy., Silver Spring, MD 20910. Phone, 301–713–2770. Fax, 301–713–4019.	Capt. Nicholas A. Prahl, *Acting*
Aeronautical charting	Rm. 3426, 1305 East-West Hwy., Silver Spring, MD 20910. Phone, 301–713–2619. Fax, 301–713–4587.	Terry M. Laydom
National Geodetic Survey	Rm. 8657, 1315 East-West Hwy., Silver Spring, MD 20910. Phone, 301–713–3222. Fax, 301–713–4175.	Charles W. Challstrom, *Acting*
Ocean resources conservation and assessment.	Rm. 10409, 1305 East-West Hwy., Silver Spring, MD 20910. Phone, 301–713–2989. Fax, 301–713–4389.	Charles N. Ehler
Ocean and coastal resource management.	Rm. 11523, 1305 East-West Hwy., Silver Spring, MD 20910. Phone, 301–713–3155. Fax, 301–713–4012.	Jeffrey R. Benoit
Marine sanctuaries and reserves	Rm. 12520, 1305 East-West Hwy., Silver Spring, MD 20910. Phone, 301–713–3125. Fax, 301–713–0404.	Stephanie Thornton
Office of Oceanic and Atmospheric Research		
Headquarters	Rm. 11627, 1315 East-West Hwy., Silver Spring, MD 20910. Phone, 301–713–2458. Fax, 301–713–0163.	Elbert W. Friday, Jr.
Environmental Research Laboratories	Rm. 11618, 1315 East-West Hwy., Silver Spring, MD 20910. Phone, 301–713–2458. Fax, 301–713–0163.	James L. Rasmussen
Aeronomy Laboratory	Rm. 2204, Bldg. 24, 325 Broadway, Boulder, CO 80303. Phone, 303–497–3134. Fax, 303–497–5340.	Daniel L. Albritton
Air Resources Laboratory	Rm. 3151, 1315 East-West Hwy., Silver Spring, MD 20910. Phone, 301–713–0684, ext. 100. Fax, 301–713–0295.	Bruce Hicks
Atlantic Oceanographic and Meteorological Laboratory.	4301 Rickenbacker Causeway, Miami, FL 33149. Phone, 305–361–4300. Fax, 305–361–4449.	Kristina Katsaros
Climate Diagnostics Center	Rm. 247, RL3, 325 Broadway, Boulder, CO 80303. Phone, 303–497–6878. Fax, 303–497–7013.	Randall Dole

Field Organization—National Oceanic and Atmospheric Administration—Continued

Organization	Address/Telephone	Director
Climate Monitoring and Diagnostics Laboratory.	Rm. A336, RL3, 325 Broadway, Boulder, CO 80303. Phone, 303–497–6074. Fax, 303–497–6975.	David Hofmann
Environmental Technology Laboratory	Rm. A450, RL3, 325 Broadway, Boulder, CO 80303. Phone, 303–497–6291. Fax, 303–497–6020.	Steven Clifford
Forecast Systems Laboratory	Rm. 615, RL3, 325 Broadway, Boulder, CO 80303. Phone, 303–497–6818. Fax, 303–497–6821.	Sandy MacDonald
Geophysical Fluid Dynamics Laboratory.	P.O. Box 308, Princeton University Forrestal Campus, Princeton, NJ 08452. Phone, 609–452–6503. Fax, 609–987–5070.	Jerry Mahlman
Great Lakes Environmental Research Laboratory.	2205 Commonwealth Blvd., Ann Arbor, MI 48105. Phone, 734–741–2244. Fax, 734–741–2003.	Stephen Brandt
National Severe Storms Laboratory ...	1313 Halley Circle, Norman, OK 73069. Phone, 405–366–0426. Fax, 405–366–0472.	James Kimpel
Pacific Marine Environmental Laboratory.	Bldg. 3, Bin C 15700, 7600 Sand Point Way NE., Seattle, WA 98115. Phone, 206–526–6800. Fax, 206–526–6815.	Eddie N. Bernard
Space Environment Center	Rm. 3050, Bldg. 1, 325 Broadway, Boulder, CO 80303. Phone, 303–497–3314. Fax, 303–497–3645.	Ernest G. Hildner
National Undersea Research Program.	Rm. 11350, 1315 East-West Hwy., Silver Spring, MD 20910. Phone, 301–713–2427. Fax, 301–713–1967.	Barbara S.P. Moore
National Sea Grant College Program	Rm. 11716, 1315 East-West Hwy., Silver Spring, MD 20910. Phone, 301–713–2448. Fax, 301–713–0799.	Ronald Baird
Office of Research and Technology Applications.	Rm. 11464, 1315 East-West Hwy., Silver Spring, MD 20910. Phone, 301–713–3565. Fax, 301–713–4100.	Joe Bishop
Office of Finance and Administration		
Headquarters	Rm. 6811, 14th St. and Constitution Ave. NW., Washington, DC 20230. Phone, 202–482–2291.	Joseph Kammerer
Chief Financial Officer/Chief Administrative Officer.	Rm. 6811, 14th St. and Constitution Ave. NW., Washington, DC 20230. Phone, 202–482–2291. Fax, 202–482–4823.	Andrew Moxam, *Acting*
Office of Civil Rights	Rm. 13356, 1315 East-West Hwy., Silver Spring, MD 20910. Phone, 301–713–0500.	Al Corea
Diversity Program Office	Rm. 12122, 1305 East-West Hwy., Silver Spring, MD 20910. Phone, 301–713–1966.	Barbara Marshall-Bailey
Audit and Internal Control Branch	Rm. 8419, 1305 East-West Hwy., Silver Spring, MD 20910. Phone, 301–713–1150.	Barbara Martin
Management and Budget	Rm. 6863, 14th St. and Constitution Ave. NW., Washington, DC 20230. Phone, 202–482–6226.	Tyra D. Smith
Budget Office	Rm. 6114, 14th St. and Constitution Ave. NW., Washington, DC 20230. Phone, 202–482–4600.	(Vacancy)
Finance Office	Rm. 3110, Century 21 Bldg., Germantown, MD 20874–1143. Phone, 301–413–8795.	R.J. Dominic
Environmental Compliance Staff	Rm. 10148, 1305 East-West Hwy., Silver Spring, MD 20910. Phone, 301–713–0845.	Susan A. Kennedy
Human Resources Management Office.	Rm. 12434, 1305 East-West Hwy., Silver Spring, MD 20910. Phone, 301–713–0530.	Stewart Remer
Information Systems Office	Rm. 724, 6100 Executive Blvd., Rockville, MD 20852–3809. Phone, 301–713–3555.	Frank DiGialleonardo
Acquisition, Grants, and Facilities Services Office.	Rm. 4131, 1305 East-West Hwy., Silver Spring, MD 20910. Phone, 301–713–0836.	Michael Nelson, *Acting*
Mountain Administrative Support Center.	325 Broadway, Boulder, CO 80303–3228. Phone, 303–497–6431.	Richard Przywitowski, *Acting*
Eastern Administrative Support Center.	Suite 201, 200 World Trade Ctr., Norfolk, VA 23510–1624. Phone, 757–441–6864.	Gerald R. Lucas
Western Administrative Support Center.	Bldg. 1, 7600 Sand Point Way NE., Seattle, WA 98115–0070. Phone, 206–526–6026. Fax, 206–526–6660.	Kelly C. Sandy
Central Administrative Support Center	Rm. 1736, 601 E. 12th St., Kansas City, MO 64106–2897. Phone, 816–426–2050. Fax, 816–426–7459.	Martha R. Lumpkin
NOAA Corps Operations		
Headquarters	Rm. 12857, 1315 East-West Hwy., Silver Spring, MD 20910–3282. Phone, 301–713–1045.	Rear Adm. William L. Stubblefield

Field Organization—National Oceanic and Atmospheric Administration—Continued

Organization	Address/Telephone	Director
Atlantic Marine Center	439 W. York St., Norfolk, VA 23510–1114. Phone, 757–441–6776.	Rear Adm. John Cialbright
Commissioned Personnel Center	1315 East-West Hwy., Silver Spring, MD 20910. Phone, 301–713–3475.	Capt. Evelyn Fields
Pacific Marine Center	1801 Fairview Ave. E., Seattle, WA 98102–3767. Phone, 206–553–7656.	Rear Adm. John C. Albright
Aircraft Operations Center	7917 Hangar Loop Dr., MacDill AFB, FL 33621–5401. Phone, 813–828–3310.	Capt. George C. Player III

For further information, contact the Office of Public Affairs, National Oceanic and Atmospheric Administration, Department of Commerce, Washington, DC 20230. Phone, 202–482–4190.

National Telecommunications and Information Administration

[For the National Telecommunications and Information Administration statement of organization, see the *Federal Register* of June 5, 1978, 43 FR 24348]

The National Telecommunications and Information Administration (NTIA) was established in 1978 pursuant to Reorganization Plan No. 1 of 1977 (5 U.S.C. app.) and Executive Order 12046 of March 27, 1978 (3 CFR, 1978 Comp., p. 158), by combining the Office of Telecommunications Policy, Executive Office of the President, and the Department of Commerce's Office of Telecommunications to form a new agency reporting to the Secretary of Commerce. Its functions are detailed in the National Telecommunications and Information Administration Organization Act (47 U.S.C. 901 *et seq.*).

The Public Telecommunications Facilities Program (PTFP) was transferred to NTIA in 1979 from the Department of Health, Education, and Welfare pursuant to the Public Telecommunications Financing Act of 1978 (47 U.S.C. 390 *et seq.*), to take advantage of NTIA's technical and policy expertise. Also, NTIA administers the National Endowment for Children's Educational Television under title 47 United States Code, section 394.

The Administration's principal responsibilities and functions include:

—serving as the principal executive branch adviser to the President on telecommunications and information policy;

—developing and presenting U.S. plans and policies at international communications conferences and related meetings;

—prescribing policies for and managing Federal use of the radio frequency spectrum, in accordance with Executive Order 12046, issued under section 305 of the Communications Act of 1934, as amended (47 U.S.C. 305);

—serving as the principal Federal telecommunications research and engineering laboratory, through NTIA's Institute for Telecommunication Sciences (ITS), headquartered in Boulder, Colorado;

—providing grants through the Telecommunications and Information Infrastructure Assistance Program for planning and demonstration projects to promote the goals of the development and widespread availability of advanced telecommunications technologies, to enhance the delivery of social services and generally serve the public interest, to promote access to government information and increase civic participation, and to support the development of an advanced nationwide telecommunications and information infrastructure;

—providing grants through the Public Telecommunications Facilities Program to extend delivery of public telecommunications services to U.S. citizens, to increase ownership and management by women and minorities, and to strengthen the capabilities of existing public broadcasting stations to provide telecommunications services; and

—monitoring grants awarded through the National Endowment for Children's Educational Television to enhance the creation and production of educational television programming for children to develop fundamental intellectual skills.

For further information, contact the National Telecommunications and Information Administration, Department of Commerce, Washington, DC 20230. Phone, 202–482–1551.

Patent and Trademark Office

[For the Patent and Trademark Office statement of organization, see the *Federal Register* of Apr. 14, 1975, 40 FR 16707]

The patent system was established by Congress ". . . to promote the progress of . . . the useful arts. . ." under Article I, section 8, U.S. Constitution (title 35, United States Code: Patents). The registration of trademarks is based on the commerce clause of the U.S. Constitution (title 15, United States Code, chapter 22: Trademarks). The Patent and Trademark Office (PTO) grants patents and registers trademarks to qualified applicants.

The Office examines applications for patents to determine if the applicants are entitled to patents under the law and grants the patents when they are so entitled. The patent law provides for the granting of patents in three major categories: utility patents, design patents, and plant patents. The term of a design patent is 14 years from the date of grant. The term of utility and plant patents is 20 years measured from the earliest effective U.S. filing date, if the application for patent was filed on or after June 8, 1995.For utility or plant patents that were in force on June 8, 1995, or that result from an application filed prior to June 8, 1995, the term shall be the longer of 17 years measured from the date of grant or 20 years measured from the earliest effective U.S. filing date.

All utility patents are subject to the payment of maintenance fees. Effective June 8, 1995, applicants may file provisional applications for patents in the PTO. Provisional applications are available for utility and plant inventions but not design inventions. Provisional applications are not examined and will become abandoned by operation of law within one year of the filing date of the provisional application. The provisional application itself cannot mature into a patent. However, if applicants wish to obtain a patent on the invention disclosed in a provisional application, applicants must file a nonprovisional application not later than 12 months from the filing date of the provisional application.

The Office also issues Statutory Invention Registrations, which have the defensive but not the enforceable attributes of a patent. It also processes international applications for patents under the provisions of the Patent Cooperation Treaty as an International Searching Authority under Chapter I of the Treaty and as an International Preliminary Examining Authority under Chapter II of the Treaty.

Over 122,977 patents providing inventors with exclusive rights were issued for the fiscal year of 1997. Effective January 1, 1996, patentees have the right to exclude others from making, using, offering for sale, or selling the invention throughout the U.S. or importing the invention into the U.S. during the term of their patent. Patents and trademarks may be reviewed and searched in the PTO and in over 80 patent and trademark depository libraries throughout the country. The patent system fosters innovation, investment in developing and marketing inventions, and prompt disclosure of technological information.

About 112,509 trademarks were registered for fiscal year 1997, and 7,389 trademark registrations were renewed. A trademark includes any distinctive word, name, symbol, device, or any combination thereof adopted and used, or intended to be used, by a manufacturer or merchant to identify his goods or services and distinguish them from those manufactured or sold by others. Trademarks, registered for 10 years, with renewal rights of equal term, are examined by the Office for compliance with various statutory requirements to prevent unfair competition and consumer deception.

In addition to the examination of patent and trademark applications, issuance of patents, and registration of trademarks, the Patent and Trademark Office:

—sells printed copies of issued patents and trademark registrations;

—records and indexes documents transferring ownership;

—maintains a scientific library and search files containing over 30 million documents, including U.S. and foreign patents and U.S. trademarks;

—provides search rooms for the public to research their applications;

—hears and decides appeals from prospective inventors and trademark applicants;

—participates in legal proceedings involving the issue of patents or registration of trademarks;

—advocates strengthening intellectual property protection worldwide;

—compiles the *Official Gazettes*, a weekly notice of patents issued and trademarks registered by the Office, including other information; and

—maintains a roster of patent agents and attorneys qualified and recognized to practice before the Office.

For further information, contact the Office of Public Affairs, Patent and Trademark Office, Washington, DC 20231. Phone, 703–305–8341. The Office's operations are located at 2121 Crystal Drive, Arlington, VA 22202.

Technology Administration

The Technology Administration was established by Congress in 1988 (15 U.S.C. 3704). It is headed by the Under Secretary for Technology, who serves as a principal adviser to the Secretary of Commerce and as the Department's spokesperson for science and technology issues.

The Technology Administration serves as the premier technology agency working with U.S. industry in addressing competitiveness and in exercising leadership both within the Department of Commerce and governmentwide. It discharges this role through the Office of Technology Policy (OTP) by advocating coherent policies for maximizing the impact of technology on economic growth; through the National Institute of Standards and Technology (NIST) by carrying out technology programs with U.S. industry; and through the National

Technical Information Service (NTIS) by disseminating technology information. The Office of Air and Space Commercialization, in the Office of the Under Secretary, develops policies fostering the competitiveness of the U.S. commercial space sector.

For further information, call 202–482–1575.

Office of Technology Policy

The primary role of the Office of Technology Policy is to offer assistance to private sector and government communities in advocating and pursuing policies that maximize the impact of technology on economic growth, and by exercising leadership to define the role of government in supporting U.S. industrial competitiveness in the post-cold war environment. The Office serves as a liaison to the private sector, identifying barriers to the rapid commercialization of technology, eliciting support for Administration civilian technology policies, and ensuring that industry's interests are reflected in standards and technology agreements and civilian technology policy. It also assists Federal, State, and local officials, industry, and academic institutions in promoting the technological growth and competitiveness of the U.S. economy.

For further information, call 202–482–5687.

National Institute of Standards and Technology

The National Institute of Standards and Technology (NIST) assists industry in developing technology to improve product quality, modernize manufacturing processes, ensure product reliability, and facilitate rapid commercialization of products based on new scientific discoveries.

The Institute's primary mission is to promote U.S. economic growth by working with industry to develop and apply technology, measurements, and standards. It carries out this mission through four major programs:

—measurement and standards laboratories that provide technical leadership for vital components of the Nation's technology infrastructure needed by U.S. industry to continually improve its products and services. Research is mainly performed in the areas of electronics and electrical engineering, manufacturing engineering, chemical science and technology, physics, materials science and engineering, building and fire research, and information technology;

—a rigorously competitive Advanced Technology Program that provides cost-shared awards to industry to develop high-risk enabling technologies with broad economic potential;

—a Manufacturing Extension Partnership, a nationwide network of extension centers and experts offering technical and business assistance to smaller manufacturers in adopting new technologies and business practices; and

—a highly visible quality outreach program associated with the Malcolm Baldrige National Quality Award that recognizes continuous improvements in quality management by U.S. manufacturers and service companies.

For further information, call 301–975–3058. Fax, 301–926–1630. E-mail, inquiries@nist.gov. Internet, http://www.nist.gov/.

National Technical Information Service

The National Technical Information Service (NTIS) is the Nation's largest central clearinghouse and governmentwide resource for scientific, technical, engineering, and other business-related information. NTIS is a self-supporting agency, using revenue earned from the sale of its products and services to cover its costs. It acquires information from U.S. Government agencies and their contractors and grantees, as well as from foreign, primarily governmental, sources. Under the American Technology Preeminence Act, all Federal agencies are required to transfer unclassified scientific, technical, and engineering information resulting from federally funded research and development activities to NTIS.

The NTIS collection of nearly 3 million works covers a broad array of subjects and includes reports on the results of research and development and scientific studies on manufacturing processes, current events, and foreign and domestic trade; business and management studies; social, economic, and trade statistics; computer software and databases; health care reports, manuals, and data; environmental handbooks, regulations, economic studies, and applied technologies; directories to Federal laboratory and technical resources; and global competitive intelligence. The collection also includes audiovisual training materials in such areas as foreign languages, workplace safety and health, law enforcement, and fire services.

Information products in the NTIS collection are cataloged in the *NTIS Bibliographic Database*, which is available on-line through commercial vendors, on CD–ROM from NTIS, and for recently acquired materials, via FedWorld, NTIS' on-line information network. FedWorld also provides public access to thousands of Government documents, connects to dozens of Federal on-line systems, and offers instant electronic delivery of selected NTIS products.

In addition to its information product offerings to the public, NTIS offers a broad range of services to assist Federal agencies in meeting their information dissemination needs. Services include Web site development, hosting, and interactive communications;

development and replications of diskette and CD–ROM products; duplication of audio, visual, and multimedia materials; and warehousing and distribution of information items in virtually any format. NTIS also operates a joint venture program. Through partnership agreements with private individuals, firms, and other organizations, NTIS seeks to develop new information products and to open new channels of sales and distribution for its materials.

For further information, contact the National Technical Information Service, 5285 Port Royal Road, Springfield, VA 22161. Phone, 800–553– NTIS. Internet, http://www.ntis.gov/.

Sources of Information

Age and Citizenship   Age search and citizenship information is available from the Personal Census Search Unit, Bureau of the Census, Data Preparation Division, P.O. Box 1545, Jeffersonville, IN 47131. Phone, 812–218–3046.

Consumer Affairs   Information is available to businesses and consumers regarding good business practices and resolving consumer complaints. Tip sheets, in English and Spanish, on how to resolve complaints and consumer bulletins, describing programs in the Department of Commerce, are available. Many publications are available on the Internet at http://www.doc.gov/. Phone, 202–482–5001. Fax, 202–482–6007. Consumer response line, 202–482–8021. E-mail, caffairs@doc.gov. For further information, contact the Office of Consumer Affairs, U.S. Department of Commerce, Rm. H5718, Washington, DC 20230.

Economic Conversion Information   The Office of Economic Conversion Information (OECI) is a clearinghouse for communities, businesses, and workers seeking to obtain information regarding defense adjustment and economic development. The Office's database contains descriptions and contact numbers of Federal, State, and local programs; guides and models for economic development; and many other

related items. For further information, contact the Office of Economic Conversion Information, Economic Development Administration, Department of Commerce, Washington, DC 20230. Phone, 800–345–1222. Internet, http://ecix.doc.gov/. Electronic bulletin board (by modem), 800–352– 2949.

Employment   Information is available electronically through the Internet, at http://nets.te.esa.doc.gov/ohrm/. Phone, 202–482–5138.

The National Oceanic and Atmospheric Administration has field employment offices at the Western Administrative Support Center, Bin C15700, 7600 Sand Point Way NE., Seattle, WA 98115 (phone, 206–526– 6294); the Mountain Administrative Support Center, 325 Broadway, Boulder, CO 80303 (phone, 303–497–6332); the Central Administrative Support Center, 601 East Twelfth Street, Kansas City, MO 64106 (phone, 816–426–2056); and the Eastern Administrative Support Center, 200 World Trade Center, Norfolk, VA 23510–1624 (phone, 757–441–6516).

Environment   The National Oceanic and Atmospheric Administration conducts research and gathers data about the oceans, atmosphere, space, and Sun, and applies this knowledge to science and service in ways that touch the lives of all Americans, including warning of dangerous weather, charting seas and skies, guiding our use and protection of ocean and coastal resources, and improving our understanding and stewardship of the environment which sustains us all. For further information, contact the Office of Public and Constituent Affairs, National Oceanic and Atmospheric Administration, Room 6013, 14th Street and Constitution Avenue NW., Washington, DC 20230. Phone, 202–482–6090. Fax, 202–482–3154. Internet, http://www.noaa.gov/.

The Patent and Trademark Office has priority programs for advancement of examination of certain patent applications where the invention could materially enhance the quality of the environment of mankind. For further information, contact the Assistant Commissioner for Patents, Office of Petitions, Washington, DC 20231. Phone, 703–305–9282.

Inspector General Hotline The Office of Inspector General works to promote economy, efficiency, and effectiveness and to prevent and detect fraud, waste, abuse, and mismanagement in departmental programs and operations. To reach the OIG Hotline, call 202–482–2495, or 800–424–5197 (toll-free). E-mail, oighotline@doc.gov. Fax, 202–789–0522. Internet, http://www.oig.doc.gov/.

Publications The titles of selected publications are printed below with the operating units responsible for their issuance. These and other publications dealing with a wide range of business, economic, environmental, scientific, and technical matters are announced in the weekly *Business Service Checklist,* which may be purchased from the Superintendent of Documents, Government Printing Office, Washington, DC 20402. Phone, 202–512–1800.

The Secretary's *Annual Report to Congress* and *Serving the Nation,* two publications which describe the missions, functions, and accomplishments of Commerce agencies and offices, are available by writing the Department of Commerce, Office of Public Affairs, Pennsylvania Avenue and 14th Street NW., Room 5610, Washington, DC, or by calling 202–219–3605 for the *Annual Report* and 202–482–4901 for *Serving the Nation.*

Further information on Commerce publications is available at any of the Department's International Trade Administration export assistance centers.

Lists of Other Documents Individuals with access to fax machines can dial 202–501–1191 *(Flash Facts)* to obtain lists of other publication contacts, Secretarial speeches and biographies, press releases, audiovisuals, Commerce bureau public affairs contacts, and Department programs by subject.

Bureau of the Census The following publications are available from the Government Printing Office: *Census Catalog and Guide; Statistical Abstract of the U.S.; Historical Statistics of the United States, Colonial Times to 1970; County and City Data Book, 1994;* and *State and Metropolitan Area Data Book, 1998.*

Employment opportunites, data highlights, large data files, access tools, and other material are available on the World Wide Web. Internet, http://www.census.gov/. E-mail, webmaster@census.gov.

Bureau of Economic Analysis Publications available from the Government Printing Office include the following: *Survey of Current Business; State Personal Income, 1929–93; Benchmark Input-Output Accounts of the United States, 1987;* and *Foreign Direct Investment in the United States, 1992 Benchmark.* Summary statistics and general information are available on the Internet, at http://www.bea.doc.gov/. To obtain more detailed economic data and press releases, subscribe to the Department of Commerce's Electronic Bulletin Board, by calling 202–482–1986, or by sending E-mail to stat-usa@doc.gov. Additional information on BEA programs, products, and services is available in the *User's Guide to BEA Information,* which may be obtained through the Internet, or by contacting the Public Information Office, BE–53,

Bureau of Economic Analysis, Department of Commerce, Washington, DC 20230. Phone, 202–606–9900.

International Trade Administration *Business America,* which is published biweekly, is available from the Government Printing Office and at ITA export assistance centers.

The Administration maintains an Internet site, at http://www.ita.doc.gov/, which offers the single best place for individuals or firms seeking reports, documents, import case/regulations, texts of international agreements like NAFTA and GATT, market research, and points of contact for assistance in exporting or obtaining remedies from unfair trading practices. Customers are able to review comprehensive information on how to export, search for trade information by either industry or by country, learn how to petition against unfairly priced imports, and obtain information on a number of useful international trade related products like overseas trade leads and agent distributor reports. The Internet site also features E-mail addresses and locations for trade contacts in Washington, overseas, in major exporting centers in the U.S., and in other parts of the Federal Government.

Minority Business Development Agency *Minority Business Today, Federal Resource Guide, BDC Directory, MBDA Annual Business Assistance Report (ABAR),* and *Federal Agency Performance for Minority Business Development* are available from MBDA, Communications Division, Department of Commerce, Washington, DC 20230. Phone, 202–482–1936.

National Institute of Standards and Technology *Journal of Research; Publications of the Advanced Technology Program and Manufacturing Extension Partnership Program; Handbook of Mathematical Functions; Experimental Statistics; International System of Units (SI); Standard Reference Materials Catalog; Specifications, Tolerances, and Other Technical Requirements for Weighing and Measuring Devices Handbook;* and *Uniform Laws and Regulations*

Handbook are available from the Government Printing Office.

National Technical Information Service To place an order, request the *Catalog of NTIS Products and Services,* or other general inquiries, contact the NTIS Sales Desk from 8 a.m. to 8 p.m. (eastern time) at 800–553–NTIS or fax 703–321–8547. TDD, 703–605–6043.

To access the NTIS home page and the FedWorld on-line information network, point Web browser to http://www.ntis.gov/.

To inquire about NTIS information services for other Federal agencies, call 703–605–6540.

National Oceanic and Atmospheric Administration The Administration provides technical memoranda, technical reports, monographs, nautical and aeronautical charts, coastal zone maps, data tapes, and a wide variety of raw and processed environmental data. Information on NOAA products is available through the Internet, at http://www.noaa.gov/; or contact the Office of Public and Constituent Affairs, 14th Street and Constitution Avenue NW., Washington, DC 20230. Phone, 202–482–6090. Fax, 202–482–3154.

National Telecommunications and Information Administration Several hundred Technical Reports, Technical Memoranda, Special Publications, Contractor Reports, and other information products have been published by NTIA or its predecessor agency since 1970. The publications are available from the National Telecommunications and Information Administration, Department of Commerce, Washington, DC 20230 (phone, 202–482–1551); or the National Telecommunications and Information Administration, Institute for Telecommunication Sciences, Department of Commerce, Boulder, CO 80302 (phone, 303–497–3572). Electronic information can be obtained from the NTIA General Bulletin Board (modem, 202–482–1199); or the Information Infrastructure Task Force Bulletin Board (modem, 202–501–1920).

Patent and Trademark Office *General Information Concerning Patents, Basic*

Facts About Trademarks, Official Gazette of the United States Patent and Trademark Office, and *Attorneys and Agents Registered To Practice Before the U.S. Patent and Trademark Office* are available from the Government Printing Office. Publications can be accessed through the Internet, at http://www.uspto.gov/. File transfer protocol, ftp.uspto.gov. Electronic bulletin board (by modem), 703–305–8950. Phone, 703–308–HELP, or 800–PTO–9199.

Small Business and Minority Business Activities Contact the Office of Small and Disadvantaged Business Utilization (phone, 202–482–1472) or the Office of External Affairs, Minority Business Development Agency, Department of Commerce, Washington, DC 20230 (phone, 202–482–4547).

Telephone Directory The Department of Commerce telephone directory is available for sale by the Superintendent of Documents, Government Printing Office, Washington, DC 20402. Phone, 202–512–1800.

For further information concerning the Department of Commerce, contact the Office of Public Affairs, Department of Commerce, Fourteenth Street between Constitution and Pennsylvania Avenues NW., Washington, DC 20230. Phone, 202–219–3605. Internet, http://www.doc.gov/.

DEPARTMENT OF DEFENSE

Office of the Secretary, The Pentagon, Washington, DC 20301–1155
Phone, 703–545–6700. Internet, http://www.defenselink.mil/.

SECRETARY OF DEFENSE	WILLIAM S. COHEN
Deputy Secretary of Defense	JOHN J. HAMRE
Chief of Staff	ROBERT S. TYRER
The Special Assistants to the Secretary and Deputy Secretary of Defense	JAMES M. BODNER, PHEBE NOVAKOVIC
Special Assistant to the Secretary of Defense for Intelligence Policy	CHRISTOPHER K. MELLON
Special Assistant to the Secretary of Defense for Policy and Personnel	PAMELA BERKOWSKY
Special Assistant to the Secretary of Defense for White House Liaison	LIZ BAILEY
Special Assistant to the Deputy Secretary of Defense for Gulf War Illnesses	BERNARD ROSTKER
Director, Defense Reform Initiative	WILLIAM P. HOULEY
Executive Secretary	COL. JAMES N. MATTIS, USMC
Under Secretary of Defense for Acquisition and Technology	JACQUES S. GANSLER
Principal Deputy Under Secretary of Defense for Acquisition and Technology	DAVID R. OLIVER, JR.
Director, Defense Research and Engineering	(VACANCY)
Assistant to the Secretary of Defense for Nuclear and Chemical and Biological (NCB) Defense Programs	(VACANCY)
Deputy Under Secretary of Defense (Advanced Technology)	JOSEPH J. EASH III
Deputy Under Secretary of Defense (Environmental Security)	SHERRI W. GOODMAN
Deputy Under Secretary of Defense (Logistics)	ROY WILLIS, *Acting*
Deputy Under Secretary of Defense (Acquisition Reform)	DONNA S. RICHBOURG
Deputy Under Secretary of Defense (Industrial Affairs and Installations)	JOHN B. GOODMAN
Director, Small and Disadvantaged Business Utilization	ROBERT L. NEAL, JR.
Under Secretary of Defense for Policy	WALTER B. SLOCOMBE
Principal Deputy Under Secretary of Defense for Policy	JAN M. LODAL
Assistant Secretary of Defense (International Security Affairs)	FRANKLIN D. KRAMER
Assistant Secretary of Defense (Strategy and Threat Reduction)	EDWARD L. WARNER III
Director of Net Assessment	ANDREW W. MARSHALL
Assistant Secretary of Defense (Special Operations and Low-Intensity Conflict)	H. ALLEN HOLMES

Defense Adviser, U.S. Mission NATO	ROBERT B. HALL
Deputy Under Secretary of Defense (Policy Support)	(VACANCY)
Under Secretary of Defense for Personnel and Readiness	RUDY F. DE LEON
Assistant Secretary of Defense (Force Management Policy)	(VACANCY)
Assistant Secretary of Defense (Health Affairs)	(VACANCY)
Assistant Secretary of Defense (Reserve Affairs)	CHARLES L. CRAGIN, *Acting*
Deputy Under Secretary of Defense (Readiness)	(VACANCY)
Deputy Under Secretary of Defense (Program Integration)	JEANNE FITES
Under Secretary of Defense (Comptroller)/Chief Financial Officer	WILLIAM J. LYNN III
Principal Deputy Under Secretary (Comptroller)	ALICE C. MARONI
Director, Program Analysis and Evaluation	ROBERT R. SOULE, *Acting*
Assistant Secretary of Defense (Command, Control, Communications, and Intelligence)	ARTHUR L. MONEY, *Acting*
Assistant Secretary of Defense (Legislative Affairs)	SANDRA K. STUART
Assistant Secretary of Defense (Public Affairs)	KENNETH H. BACON
General Counsel	JUDITH A. MILLER
Director, Operational Test and Evaluation	PHILIP E. COYLE III
Inspector General	ELEANOR HILL
Director of Administration and Management	D.O. COOKE

Joint Chiefs of Staff

Chairman	GEN. HENRY H. SHELTON, USA
Vice Chairman	GEN. JOSEPH W. RALSTON, USAF
Chief of Staff, Army	GEN. DENNIS J. REIMER, USA
Chief of Naval Operations	ADM. JAY L. JOHNSON, USN
Chief of Staff, Air Force	GEN. MICHAEL E. RYAN, USAF
Commandant, Marine Corps	GEN. CHARLES C. KRULAK, USMC

Joint Staff

Director	VICE ADM. DENNIS C. BLAIR, USN
Vice Director	MAJ. GEN. STEPHEN T. RIPPE, USA
Director for Manpower and Personnel—J–1	BRIG. GEN. PATRICK O. ADAMS, USAF
Director, Intelligence—J–2	REAR ADM. THOMAS R. WILSON, USN
Director for Operations—J–3	VICE ADM. VERNON E. CLARK, USN
Director for Logistics—J–4	LT. GEN. JOHN M. MCDUFFIE, USA
Director for Strategic Plans and Policy—J–5	VICE ADM. JOHN S. REDD, USN
Director for Command, Control, Communications, and Computer Systems—J–6	LT. GEN. DOUGLAS D. BUCHHOLZ, USA
Director for Operational Plans and Interoperability—J–7	MAJ. GEN. GEORGE F. CLOSE, JR., USA

Director for Force Structure, Resources, and Assessment—J–8   LT. GEN. FRANK B. CAMPBELL, USAF

[For the Department of Defense statement of organization, see the *Code of Federal Regulations*, Title 32, Chapter I, Subchapter R]

The Department of Defense is responsible for providing the military forces needed to deter war and protect the security of our country.

The major elements of these forces are the Army, Navy, Marine Corps, and Air Force, consisting of about 1.5 million men and women on active duty. They are backed, in case of emergency, by the 1.5 million members of the Reserve and National Guard. In addition, there are about 770,000 civilian employees in the Defense Department.

Under the President, who is also Commander in Chief, the Secretary of Defense exercises authority, direction, and control over the Department, which includes the separately organized military departments of Army, Navy, and Air Force, the Joint Chiefs of Staff providing military advice, the combatant commands, and various defense agencies established for specific purposes.

The National Security Act Amendments of 1949 redesignated the National Military Establishment as the Department of Defense and established it as an executive department (10 U.S.C. 111), with the Secretary of Defense as its head. Since that time, many legislative and administrative changes have occurred, evolving the Department into the structure under which it currently operates.

Structure

The Department of Defense is composed of the Office of the Secretary of Defense; the military departments and the military services within those departments; the Chairman of the Joint Chiefs of Staff and the Joint Staff; the combatant commands; the Defense agencies; DOD field activities; and such other offices, agencies, activities, and commands as may be established or designated by law, or by the President or the Secretary of Defense.

In providing immediate staff assistance and advice to the Secretary of Defense, the Office of the Secretary of Defense and the Chairman of the Joint Chiefs of Staff, and the Joint Staff, though separately identified and organized, function in full coordination and cooperation.

The Office of the Secretary of Defense includes the offices of the Deputy Secretary of Defense; the Under Secretary of Defense for Acquisition and Technology; the Under Secretary of Defense for Policy; the Under Secretary of Defense (Comptroller)/Chief Financial Officer; the Under Secretary of Defense for Personnel and Readiness; the Director of Defense Research and Engineering; Assistant Secretaries of Defense; the General Counsel; the Inspector General; the Director of Operational Test and Evaluation; and such other staff offices as the Secretary of Defense establishes to assist him in carrying out his duties and responsibilities. The heads of these offices are staff advisers to the Secretary and perform such functions as he assigns to them.

The Joint Chiefs of Staff consist of the Chairman; the Vice Chairman; the Chief of Staff, U.S. Army; the Chief of Naval Operations; the Chief of Staff, U.S. Air Force; and the Commandant of the Marine Corps. Supported, subject to the authority of the Chairman, by the Joint Staff, they constitute the immediate military staff of the Secretary of Defense. The Chairman is the principal military adviser to the President, the National Security Council, and the Secretary of Defense. The other members of the Joint Chiefs of Staff are the senior military officers of their respective services and are military advisers to the President, the National Security Council, and the Secretary of Defense. The Vice Chairman

DEPARTMENT OF DEFENSE

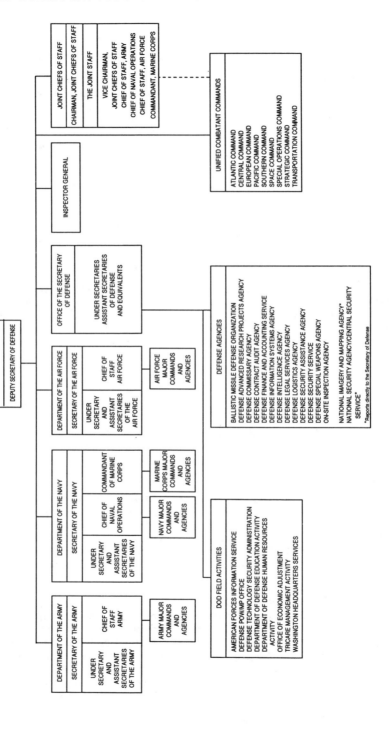

of the Joint Chiefs acts as Chairman in the absence of the Chairman.

Each military department (the Department of the Navy includes naval aviation and the United States Marine Corps) is separately organized under its own Secretary and functions under the authority, direction, and control of the Secretary of Defense. The Secretary of each military department is responsible to the Secretary of Defense for the operation and efficiency of his department. Orders to the military departments are issued through the Secretaries of these departments, or their designees, by the Secretary of Defense or under authority specifically delegated in writing by the Secretary of Defense or provided by law.

The commanders of combatant commands are responsible to the President and the Secretary of Defense for accomplishing the military missions assigned to them and exercising command authority over forces assigned to them. The operational chain of command runs from the President to the Secretary of Defense to the commanders of the combatant commands. The Chairman of the Joint Chiefs of Staff functions within the chain of command by transmitting the orders of the President or the Secretary of Defense to the commanders of the combatant commands.

Office of the Secretary of Defense

Secretary of Defense   The Secretary of Defense is the principal defense policy adviser to the President and is responsible for the formulation of general defense policy and policy related to DOD, and for the execution of approved policy. Under the direction of the President, the Secretary exercises authority, direction, and control over the Department of Defense.

Deputy Secretary of Defense   The Deputy Secretary of Defense is delegated full power and authority to act for the Secretary of Defense and to exercise the powers of the Secretary on any and all matters for which the Secretary is authorized to act pursuant to law.

Acquisition and Technology   The Under Secretary of Defense for Acquisition and Technology is the principal staff assistant and adviser to the Secretary of Defense for all matters relating to the acquisition system, research and development, test and evaluation, production, logistics, military construction, procurement, and economic affairs. The Under Secretary serves as the Defense acquisition executive with responsibility for supervising the performance of the entire Department acquisition system and chairing the Defense Acquisition Board.

Command, Control, Communications, and Intelligence   The Assistant Secretary of Defense (Command, Control, Communications, and Intelligence (C^3I)) is the principal staff assistant and adviser to the Secretary and Deputy Secretary of Defense for C^3I, information management, counterintelligence, and security countermeasures matters, including warning reconnaissance and intelligence and intelligence-related activities conducted by the Department of Defense.

Financial Management   The Under Secretary of Defense (Comptroller)/Chief Financial Officer is the principal adviser and assistant to the Secretary of Defense for budget and fiscal matters, including financial management, accounting policy and systems, budget formulation and execution, contract audit administration and organization, and analyses of force planning and programming as a part of the process upon which DOD force structure, system acquisition, and other resource allocation actions are based. Through the Under Secretary, resource management information is collected, analyzed, and reported to the Office of Management and Budget, the Congress, the General Accounting Office, and other agencies. Supervision, direction, and review of the preparation and execution of the defense budget is provided.

Operational Test and Evaluation The Director of Operational Test and Evaluation serves as the principal staff assistant and adviser to the Secretary of Defense on operational test and evaluation in the Department of Defense and is the principal test and evaluation official within the senior management of the Department.

Personnel and Readiness The Under Secretary of Defense for Personnel and Readiness is the principal staff assistant and adviser to the Secretary of Defense for policy matters relating to the structure and readiness of the Total Force. Functional areas include: readiness; civilian and military personnel policies, programs, and systems; civilian and military equal opportunity programs; health policies, programs, and activities; Reserve Component programs, policies, and activities; family policy, dependent's education, and personnel support programs; and mobilization planning and requirements.

Policy The Under Secretary of Defense for Policy is the principal staff assistant to the Secretary of Defense for policy matters relating to overall international security policy and political-military affairs. Functional areas include NATO affairs; net assessments; foreign military sales; arms limitation agreements; international trade and technology; regional security affairs; special operations and low-intensity conflict; integration of departmental plans and policies with overall national security objectives; drug control policy, requirements, priorities, systems, resources, and programs; and issuance of policy guidance affecting departmental programs.

In addition, the Secretary and Deputy Secretary of Defense are assisted by a special staff of assistants to include the Assistant Secretary of Defense for Legislative Affairs; the General Counsel; the Inspector General; the Assistant Secretary of Defense for Public Affairs; the Director of Administration and Management; and such other officers as the Secretary of Defense establishes to assist him in carrying out his duties and responsibilities.

Joint Chiefs of Staff

Joint Chiefs of Staff

The Joint Chiefs of Staff consist of the Chairman; the Vice Chairman; the Chief of Staff of the Army; the Chief of Naval Operations; the Chief of Staff of the Air Force; and the Commandant of the Marine Corps.

The Chairman of the Joint Chiefs of Staff is the principal military adviser to the President, the National Security Council, and the Secretary of Defense. The other members of the Joint Chiefs of Staff are military advisers who may provide additional information upon request from the President, the National Security Council, or the Secretary of Defense. They may also submit their advice when it does not agree with that of the Chairman.

Subject to the authority of the President and the Secretary of Defense, the Chairman of the Joint Chiefs of Staff is responsible for:

—assisting the President and the Secretary of Defense in providing for the strategic direction and planning of the Armed Forces;

—allocating resources to fulfill strategic plans;

—making recommendations for the assignment of responsibilities within the Armed Forces in accordance with and in support of those logistic and mobility plans;

—comparing the capabilities of American and allied Armed Forces with those of potential adversaries;

—preparing and reviewing contingency plans that conform to policy guidance from the President and the Secretary of Defense;

—preparing joint logistic and mobility plans to support contingency plans; and

—recommending assignment of logistic and mobility responsibilities to the Armed Forces to fulfill logistic and mobility plans.

The Chairman advises the Secretary of Defense on critical deficiencies and strengths in force capabilities (including manpower, logistic, and mobility support) and assesses the effect of such deficiencies and strengths on meeting national security objectives and policy and on strategic plans. He establishes and maintains a uniform system for evaluating the preparedness of each combatant command to carry out assigned missions.

The Chairman advises the Secretary of Defense on the priorities of the requirements identified by the commanders of the combatant commands and on the extent to which program recommendations and budget proposals of the military departments and other DOD components for a fiscal year conform with priorities established in requirements of the combatant commands. He is responsible for submitting to the Secretary alternative program recommendations and budget proposals with guidance provided by the Secretary, in order to achieve greater conformance with priorities established by the combatant commands. The Chairman also advises the Secretary on the extent to which major programs and policies of the Armed Forces in the area of manpower conform with strategic plans and assesses military requirements for defense acquisition programs.

Additionally, the Chairman:

—formulates doctrine and training policies and coordinates military education and training;

—represents the United States on the Military Staff Committee of the United Nations;

—performs such other duties as may be prescribed by law or by the President and the Secretary of Defense;

—convenes and presides over regular meetings of the Joint Chiefs of Staff;

—assists the Joint Chiefs in carrying on their business as promptly as practicable; and

—schedules issues for consideration by the Joint Chiefs.

The Chairman, while so serving, holds the grade of general or admiral and outranks all other officers of the Armed Forces.

The Vice Chairman of the Joint Chiefs performs duties assigned by the Chairman, with the approval of the Secretary of Defense. The Vice Chairman acts as Chairman when there is a vacancy in the office of the Chairman, or in the absence or disability of the Chairman. The Vice Chairman, while so serving, holds the grade of general or admiral and outranks all other officers of the Armed Forces except the Chairman of the Joint Chiefs of Staff.

Joint Staff

The Joint Staff under the Chairman of the Joint Chiefs of Staff assists the Chairman and, subject to the authority of the Chairman, the other members of the Joint Chiefs of Staff, in carrying out their responsibilities.

The Joint Staff is headed by a Director who is selected by the Chairman in consultation with the other members of the Joint Chiefs of Staff, and with the approval of the Secretary of Defense. Officers assigned to serve on the Joint Staff are selected by the Chairman in approximate equal numbers from the Army, Navy, Marine Corps, and Air Force. The Joint Staff is composed of all members of the Armed Forces and civilian employees assigned or detailed to permanent duty to perform the functions assigned to the Chairman of the Joint Chiefs of Staff.

Sources of Information

Audiovisual Products Certain Department of Defense productions on film and videotapes, CD–ROM's, and other audiovisual products such as stock footage and still photographs are available to the public. Usually, they are created by the Department to support training, documentation, and internal information objectives. No admission or any other fees may be charged for exhibition of the productions, and they must be exhibited in their entirety, including all titles at the beginning and end. No portion may be reproduced, edited, or cut in any manner. An up-to-date, full-text searchable listing of the Department's inventory of film and videotape titles is available on the Internet, at http://www.redstone.army.mil/davis/. Persons without Internet access and those interested in obtaining productions may contact the following sources:

—For newer productions, contact the National Technical Information Service, 5285 Port Royal Road, Springfield, VA 22161. Phone, 703–605–6000.

—For older productions, contact the Motion Picture, Sound, and Video Branch (NWDNM), National Archives and Records Administration, 8601 Adelphi Road, College Park, MD 20740–6001. Phone, 301–713–7050.

—For CD–ROM's, stock footage, and still photographs, contact the Defense Visual Information Center, 1363 Z Street, Building 2730, March Air Reserve Base, CA 92518–2717. Phone, 909–413–2515.

There is usually a fee charged for the Department's audiovisual products.

Contracts and Small Business Activities Contact the Director, Small and Disadvantaged Business Utilization, Office of the Secretary of Defense, Room 2A338, 3061 Defense Pentagon, Washington, DC 20301–3061. Phone, 703–697–9383.

DOD Directives and Instructions Correspondence and Directives Directorate, Washington Headquarters Services, Room 2A286, 1155 Defense Pentagon, Washington, DC 20301–1155. Phone, 703–697–4111.

Employment Almost all positions are in the competitive service and are filled from civil service registers. College recruiting requirements are limited primarily to management intern positions at the B.S. and M.S. levels. For additional information, inquiries should be addressed to the Human Resource Services Center, Washington Headquarters Services, Room 2E22, AMC Building, Alexandria, VA 22233–0001. Phone, 703–617–7211. Internet, http://www.hrsc.osd.mil/.

Pentagon Tours Guided tours of the Pentagon are available Monday through Friday, from 9:30 a.m. through 3:30 p.m., excluding Federal holidays. The 75-minute tour starts at the Metro entrance to the Pentagon and is approximately one mile long. Groups of more than 100 should schedule the tour 2 weeks in advance. Wheelchairs are available at no cost. For further information or reservations, contact Pentagon Tours, Director for Programs and Community Relations, 1400 Defense Pentagon, Room 1E776, Washington, DC 20301–1400. Phone, 703–695–1776.

Speakers Civilian and military representatives of the Department of Defense are available to speak on a variety of defense subjects in response to invitations, usually at no cost to the local sponsor. However, speakers may accept transportation, meals, and lodging, if offered by the sponsor of the public event in which they are to participate. Written requests for speakers should be addressed to the Director for Programs and Community Relations, Office of the Assistant Secretary of Defense for Public Affairs, 1400 Defense Pentagon, Washington, DC 20301–1400 (phone, 703–695–3845); or to the public affairs officer of the nearest military installation.

Telephone Directory The Department of Defense telephone directory is available for sale by the Superintendent of Documents, Government Printing Office, Washington, DC 20402. Phone, 202–512–1800.

For further information concerning the Department of Defense, contact the Director, Directorate for Public Communication, Office of the Assistant Secretary of Defense for Public Affairs, 1400 Defense Pentagon, Washington, DC 20301–1400. Phone, 703–697–5737. Internet, http://www.defenselink.mil/.

DOD FIELD ACTIVITIES

American Forces Information Service The American Forces Information Service, established in 1977 under the supervision of the Assistant Secretary of Defense for Public Affairs, is responsible for the Department's internal information program, visual information policy, and visual information and public affairs training. The Armed Forces Radio and Television Service, the Print Media Directorate (which includes among its many products the *Current News Early Bird*), the Armed Forces Radio and Television Service Broadcast Center, the Television-Audio Support Activity, the Defense Information School, the Defense Visual Information Center, and the worldwide operations of the *Stars and Stripes* newspapers function under the Director of American Forces Information Service. In addition, the Service provides policy guidance and oversight for departmental periodicals and pamphlets, military command newspapers, the broadcast elements of the military departments, and departmental audiovisual matters.

(American Forces Information Service, Department of Defense, Suite 311, 601 North Fairfax Street, Alexandria, VA 22314–2007. Phone, 703–428–0597.)

Department of Defense Education Activity The Department of Defense Education Activity (DODEA) was established in 1992 under the authority, direction, and control of the Assistant Secretary of Defense for Force Management Policy. It consists of two subordinate organizational entities: the Department of Defense Dependents Schools and the Department of Defense Domestic Dependent Elementary and Secondary Schools.

The mission of DODEA is to serve as the principal staff adviser to the Assistant Secretary of Defense for Force Management Policy on all Defense education matters relative to overseas and stateside education activities and programs; formulate, develop, and implement policies, technical guidance, and standards for the effective management of Defense education activities and programs; plan, direct, coordinate, and manage the education programs for eligible dependents of U.S. military and civilian personnel stationed overseas and stateside; evaluate the programmatic and operational policies and procedures for the DOD Dependent Schools, and DOD Domestic Dependent Elementary and Secondary Schools; and provide education activity representation at meetings and deliberations of educational panels and advisory groups.

(Department of Defense Education Activity, 4040 North Fairfax Drive, Arlington, VA 22203–1635. Phone, 703–696–4236.)

Department of Defense Human Resources Activity The Department of Defense Human Resources Activity was formed through the merger of the Defense Manpower Data Center with the Civilian Personnel Management Service. This field activity falls under the authority, direction, and control of the Under Secretary of Defense for Personnel and Readiness. The mission of DHRA includes supporting the OUSD (P&R) in planning and formulating civilian personnel programs; providing policy support; developing and managing DOD civilian personnel information systems and civilian personnel administrative services for the Office of the Secretary of Defense, the Military Departments, and Defense Agencies; collecting and maintaining an archive of automated manpower, personnel, training, and financial data bases for DOD to support the information requirements of the OUSD (P&R) and other members of the DOD manpower, personnel, and training communities; conducting large-scale surveys of DOD personnel; developing and managing selection tests used for entry into the military; and maintaining data and systems used to determine entitlements for DOD benefits such as medical, exchange, and commissary.

(Department of Defense Human Resources Activity-Headquarters, Suite B200, 1400 Key Boulevard, Arlington, VA 22209–5144. Phone, 703–696–1720.)

Defense Prisoner of War/Missing Personnel Office   The Defense Prisoner of War/Missing Personnel Office (DPMO) was established July 16, 1993, under the authority, direction, and control of the Assistant Secretary of Defense for International Security Affairs and provides centralized management of prisoner of war/missing personnel affairs within the Department of Defense. DPMO's responsibilities include leadership and policy oversight for all efforts to reach an accounting for Americans still unaccounted for as a result of U.S. involvement in past conflicts since World War II as well as the recovery and accounting of those Americans isolated in harm's way in future conflicts.

DPMO is the lead proponent for prisoner of war/missing personnel matters, including policy and oversight within the Department of Defense of the entire process for investigation and recovery related to missing persons (which includes matters related to search, rescue, escape, and evasion), and the procedures to be followed by Department of Defense boards of inquiry relating to missing persons and by officials reviewing the reports of such boards. The Office represents the Department of Defense in negotiations with officials of foreign governments regarding efforts to achieve the fullest possible accounting of missing American service members and other designated civilian personnel; assembles and maintains data bases on U.S. military and civilian personnel who are or were prisoners of war or missing as a result of a hostile action; prescribes uniform procedures for determination of the status of missing personnel and for systematic, comprehensive, and timely

collection, analysis, review, dissemination, and periodic update of information related to missing personnel; declassifies Department of Defense documents for disclosure and release in accordance with section 1082 of Public Law 102–190 (50 U.S.C. 435 note), Executive Order 12812, and Executive Order 12958; and maintains channels of communication on prisoner of war/missing personnel matters between the Department of Defense and the Congress, prisoner of war/missing personnel families, and the American public through periodic consultations and other appropriate measures.

DPMO coordinates with the interagency community, the Joint Staff, services, and combatant commands to provide policy, control, and oversight over all personnel recovery matters. The Office promulgates policy and oversees implementation of these policies throughout the Department. DPMO is also responsible for policy oversight of Code of Conduct training throughout the Department of Defense and represents the Department at the Interagency Committee on Search and Rescue.

(Defense Prisoner of War/Missing Personnel Office, Department of Defense, OASD/ISA, The Pentagon, Washington, DC 20301–2400. Phone, 703–602–2102. Fax, 703–602–1890.)

Defense Technology Security Administration   The Defense Technology Security Administration (DTSA) was established by the Deputy Secretary of Defense on May 10, 1985, under the authority, direction, and control of the Assistant Secretary of Defense for International Security Policy. The mission of DTSA is to develop and implement DOD policies on international transfers of defense–related goods, services, and technologies to ensure that: critical U.S. military technological advantages are preserved; transfers of defense-related technology which could prove detrimental to U.S. security interests are controlled and limited; proliferation of weapons of mass destruction and their means of delivery is prevented; and legitimate defense cooperation with foreign allies and friends is supported.

(Defense Technology Security Administration, Department of Defense, Suite 300, 400 Army Navy Drive, Arlington, VA 22202–2884. Phone, 703–604–5215.)

Office of Economic Adjustment The Office of Economic Adjustment is responsible for planning and managing the Department's defense economic adjustment programs and for assisting Federal, State, and local officials in cooperative efforts to alleviate any serious social and economic side effects resulting from major departmental realignments or other actions.

(Office of Economic Adjustment, Department of Defense, 400 Army Navy Drive, Suite 200, Arlington, VA 22202–2884. Phone, 703–604–6020.)

TRICARE Management Activity The TRICARE Management Activity (TMA) was formed on February 10, 1998, from the consolidation of the TRICARE Support Office (formerly Civilian Health and Medical Program of the Uniformed Services (CHAMPUS) headquarters), the Defense Medical Programs Activity (DMPA), and the integration of health management program functions formerly located in the Office of the Assistant Secretary of Defense for Health Affairs (OASD(HA)). The TMA mission is to manage TRICARE; administer and manage the Defense Health Program appropriation; provide operational direction and support to the Uniformed Services in the management and administration of the TRICARE program; and administer CHAMPUS.

(TRICARE Management Activity, Suite 810, Skyline 5, 5111 Leesburg Pike, Falls Church, VA 22041–3206. Phone, 703–681–6909. Fax, 703–681–8706.)

Washington Headquarters Services The Director of Administration and Management serves in a dual capacity as the Director of Washington Headquarters Services. The agency's mission is to provide administrative and operational support to certain Department of Defense activities in the National Capital region. Such support includes budget and accounting, personnel management, office services, security, correspondence, directives and records management, travel, building administration, information and data systems, voting assistance program, and other administrative support as required.

(Washington Headquarters Services, Department of Defense, Room 3D972, The Pentagon, Washington, DC 20301–1155. Phone, 703–695–4436.)

DEPARTMENT OF THE AIR FORCE

1670 Air Force Pentagon, Washington, DC 20330–1670

SECRETARY OF THE AIR FORCE	F. WHITTEN PETERS, *Acting*
Confidential Assistant	(VACANCY)
Staff Assistant	(VACANCY)
Military Assistant	(VACANCY)
Under Secretary of the Air Force	F. WHITTEN PETERS
Confidential Assistant	ELIANG BROCK
Deputy Under Secretary (International Affairs)	ROBERT D. BAUERLEIN
Principal Assistant Deputy Under Secretary (International Affairs)	MAJ. GEN. CLINTON V. HORN
Assistant Deputy Under Secretary (International Affairs)	BRIG. GEN. WILLIAM E. STEVENS
Director, Small and Disadvantaged Business Utilization	ANTHONY J. DELUCA
Assistant Secretary (Manpower, Reserve Affairs, Installations, and Environment)	RODNEY A. COLEMAN
Executive Director, Air Force Board for Correction of Military Records	MACK M. BURTON
Director, Air Force Personnel Council	COL. CHERYL M. HARRIS
Director, Air Force Civilian Appellate Review Office	SOPHIE A. CLARK
Principal Deputy Assistant Secretary (Manpower, Reserve Affairs, Installations, and Environment)	PHILLIP P. UPSCHULTE
Deputy Assistant Secretary (Force Management and Personnel)	RUBY B. DEMESME
Deputy Assistant Secretary (Reserve Affairs)	BRYAN E. SHARRATT
Deputy Assistant Secretary (Installations)	JIMMY G. DISHNER
Deputy Assistant Secretary (Environment, Safety, and Occupational Health)	THOMAS W.L. MCCALL, JR.
Deputy Assistant Secretary (Equal Opportunity)	DENNIS M. COLLINS
Assistant Secretary (Financial Management and Comptroller of the Air Force)	ROBERT F. HALE
Principal Deputy Assistant Secretary (Financial Management)	JAMES R. SPEER
Superintendent, Executive Services	SR. M. SGT. PRESTON DUNN
Deputy Assistant Secretary (Budget)	MAJ. GEN. GEORGE T. STRINGER
Director, Budget and Appropriations Liaison	COL. PHILIP E. RUTER
Director, Budget Management and Execution	ROBERT W. ZOOK
Director, Budget Investment	MICHAEL J. NOVEL, *Acting*
Director, Budget Operations and Personnel	BRIG. GEN. EVERETT G. ODGERS
Director, Budget Programs	COL. GORDON KAGE

184

Deputy Assistant Secretary (Cost and Economics)	LEROY T. BASEMAN
Deputy Assistant Secretary (Management Systems)	A. ERNEST FITZGERALD
Deputy Assistant Secretary (Financial Operations)	JOHN J. NETHERY
Assistant Secretary (Acquisition)	ARTHUR L. MONEY
Principal Deputy Assistant Secretary (Acquisition)	LT. GEN. GEORGE K. MUELLNER
Principal Deputy Assistant Secretary (Acquisition and Management)	DARLENE A. DRUYUN
Mission Area Director, Information Dominance	BRIG. GEN. DAVID A. NAGY
Deputy Assistant Secretary (Contracting)	BRIG. GEN. FRANK J. ANDERSON, JR.
Deputy Assistant Secretary (Management Policy and Program Integration)	BLAISE J. DURANTE
Mission Area Director, Global Reach	BRIG. GEN. TOME H. WALTERS, JR.
Director, Special Programs	COL. NEIL G. KACENA
Mission Area Director, Global Power	BRIG. GEN. BRUCE A. CARLSON
Mission Area Director, Space and Nuclear Deterrence	BRIG. GEN. JAMES R. BEALE
Deputy Assistant Secretary (Science, Technology, and Engineering)	HELMUT HELLWIG
Air Force Program Executive Officers:	
Airlift and Trainers	BRIG. GEN. RICHARD V. REYNOLDS
Battle Management Programs	JOHN M. GILLIGAN
Command, Control, and Communications Systems	BRIG. GEN. CRAIG P. WESTON
Fighter and Bomber Programs	MAJ. GEN. ROBERT F. RAGGIO
Joint Logistics Systems	OSCAR A. GOLDFARB
Space Programs	BRENT R. COLLINS
Weapons	HARRY E. SHULTE
Director, Joint Strike Fighter Technology Program	BRIG. GEN. LESLIE F. KENNE
Assistant Secretary (Space)	KEITH R. HALL
Principal Deputy Assistant Secretary (Space)	DAVID A. KIER
Deputy Assistant Secretary (Space Plans and Policy)	RICHARD M. MCCORMICK
Director, Special Projects	BRIG. GEN. ROBERT E. LARNED
Director, Space Systems	BRIG. GEN. HOWARD J. MITCHELL
General Counsel	SHEILA C. CHESTON
Inspector General of the Air Force	LT. GEN. RICHARD T. SWOPE
Administrative Assistant to the Secretary	WILLIAM A. DAVIDSON
Chief, Civilian Personnel Division	PEGGY S. PARK
Director, Plans, Programs, and Budget	LT. COL. L.E. HURLBUT
Chief, Military Personnel Division	LT. COL. KEN JAMES
Director, Security and Special Programs Oversight	GENE BOESCH
Auditor General of the Air Force	JACKIE R. CRAWFORD
Director, Legislative Liaison	MAJ. GEN. PAUL V. HESTER
Chief, Congressional Inquiry Division	COL. NICKI WATTS
Director, Public Affairs	BRIG. GEN. RONALD T. SCONYERS

Air Staff

Chief of Staff	GEN. MICHAEL E. RYAN
Vice Chief of Staff	GEN. RALPH E. EBERHART

Assistant Vice Chief of Staff	LT. GEN. DAVID L. VESELY
Deputy Chief of Staff (Plans and Programs)	LT. GEN. LAWRENCE P. FARRELL, JR.
Deputy Chief of Staff (Personnel)	LT. GEN. MICHAEL D. MCGINTY
Deputy Chief of Staff (Air and Space Operations)	LT. GEN. JOHN P. JUMPER
Deputy Chief of Staff (Installations and Logistics)	LT. GEN. WILLIAM P. HALLIN
Director of Communications and Information	LT. GEN. WILLIAM J. DONAHUE
Chief Master Sergeant of the Air Force	CH. M. SGT. ERIC BENKEN
Chief, Safety/Director, Air Force Safety Center	MAJ. GEN. FRANCIS C. GIDEON, JR.
Director, Safety Issues	COL. CHARLES BERGMAN
Director of Security Forces	BRIG. GEN. RICHARD A. COLEMAN, JR.
Chairman, Scientific Advisory Board	GENE H. MCCALL
Director, Test and Evaluation	JOHN MANLARK
Air Force Historian	RICHARD P. HALLION
Chief Scientist of the Air Force	EDWARD A. FEIGENBAUM
Chief, Air Force Reserve	MAJ. GEN. ROBERT A. MCINTOSH
Chief, National Guard Bureau	LT. GEN. EDWARD D. BACA, USA
Surgeon General of the Air Force	LT. GEN. CHARLES H. ROADMAN II
Chief of the Chaplain Service	MAJ. GEN. WILLIAM J. DENDINGER
Judge Advocate General	MAJ. GEN. BRYAN G. HAWLEY

Named Activities

Commander, Air Force Office of Colonel Matters	COL. PAUL M. HANKINS
Commander, Air Force General Officer Matters Office	COL. RICHARD S. HASSAN
Director, Air Force Office of Senior Executive Matters	WILLIAM KELLY

The Department of the Air Force is responsible for defending the United States through control and exploitation of air and space.

The Department of the Air Force (USAF) was established as part of the National Military Establishment by the National Security Act of 1947 (61 Stat. 502) and came into being on September 18, 1947. The National Security Act Amendments of 1949 redesignated the National Military Establishment as the Department of Defense, established it as an executive department, and made the Department of the Air Force a military department within the Department of Defense (63 Stat. 578). The Department of the Air Force is separately organized under the Secretary of the Air Force. It operates under the authority, direction, and control of the Secretary of Defense (10 U.S.C. 8010). The Department consists of the Office of the Secretary of the Air Force, the Air Staff, and field organizations.

OFFICE OF THE SECRETARY

The Office of the Secretary consists of the offices of the Under Secretary, four Assistant Secretaries, the General Counsel, the Administrative Assistant, Legislative Liaison, Public Affairs, International Affairs, Small and Disadvantaged Business Utilization, the Auditor General, and the Inspector

DEPARTMENT OF THE AIR FORCE

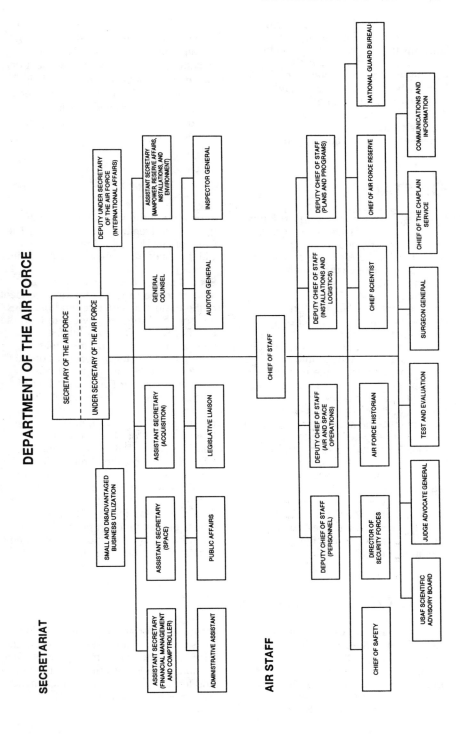

SECRETARIAT

SECRETARY OF THE AIR FORCE

UNDER SECRETARY OF THE AIR FORCE

DEPUTY UNDER SECRETARY OF THE AIR FORCE (INTERNATIONAL AFFAIRS)

ASSISTANT SECRETARY (FINANCIAL MANAGEMENT AND COMPTROLLER)

ASSISTANT SECRETARY (SPACE)

ASSISTANT SECRETARY (ACQUISITION)

ASSISTANT SECRETARY (MANPOWER, RESERVE AFFAIRS, INSTALLATIONS, AND ENVIRONMENT)

SMALL AND DISADVANTAGED BUSINESS UTILIZATION

ADMINISTRATIVE ASSISTANT

PUBLIC AFFAIRS

LEGISLATIVE LIAISON

GENERAL COUNSEL

AUDITOR GENERAL

INSPECTOR GENERAL

AIR STAFF

CHIEF OF STAFF

CHIEF OF SAFETY

DEPUTY CHIEF OF STAFF (PERSONNEL)

DEPUTY CHIEF OF STAFF (AIR AND SPACE OPERATIONS)

DEPUTY CHIEF OF STAFF (INSTALLATIONS AND LOGISTICS)

DEPUTY CHIEF OF STAFF (PLANS AND PROGRAMS)

USAF SCIENTIFIC ADVISORY BOARD

DIRECTOR OF SECURITY FORCES

AIR FORCE HISTORIAN

CHIEF SCIENTIST

JUDGE ADVOCATE GENERAL

TEST AND EVALUATION

SURGEON GENERAL

CHIEF OF THE CHAPLAIN SERVICE

CHIEF OF AIR FORCE RESERVE

COMMUNICATIONS AND INFORMATION

NATIONAL GUARD BUREAU

General. The heads of these offices are staff advisers to the Secretary for functions the Secretary assigns to them.

The Department of the Air Force is administered by the Secretary of the Air Force, who is responsible for and has the authority to conduct all affairs of the Department. The Secretary's responsibilities include matters pertaining to organization, training, logistical support, maintenance, welfare of personnel, administrative, recruiting, research and development, and other activities prescribed by the President or the Secretary of Defense. The principal assistant to the Secretary is the Under Secretary, who acts with the full authority of the Secretary on all affairs of the Department.

AIR STAFF

The mission of the Air Staff is to furnish professional assistance to the Secretary, Under Secretary, and Assistant Secretaries of the Air Force and to the Chief of Staff in executing their responsibilities.

Structure   The Air Staff is a management headquarters functional organization under the Chief of Staff, United States Air Force.

Functions and Activities   Air Staff functions are specialized into well-defined areas to effect the management principles of functionality, integration, flexibility, simplicity, and decentralization. The Air Staff retains those management functions that legally cannot be delegated or decentralized, are needed by the Secretary and Chief of Staff, are essential to respond promptly to the Secretary of Defense, or are required to determine the design and structure of the Air Force in the future.

Chief of Staff   The Chief of Staff is directly responsible to the Secretary of the Air Force for the efficiency and operational readiness of the USAF. He is a member of the Joint Chiefs of Staff (JCS) of the Department of Defense. The Chief of Staff is assisted by the Vice Chief of Staff in all areas of responsibility except JCS.

Special Staff   The Special Staff is an adjunct to the Chief of Staff, independent of the basic staff structure, and provides advisory and support services to both the Chief of Staff and the Air Staff. The Special Staff consists of: the Chief of Safety; the Director of Security Forces; the Air Force Historian; the Chief Scientist of the Air Force; the Chief of Air Force Reserve; the National Guard Bureau; the Scientific Advisory Board; the Judge Advocate General; the Director, Test and Evaluation; the Surgeon General; the Chief of the Chaplain Service; the Director of Communications and Information; and the Chief Master Sergeant of the Air Force.

Deputy Chiefs of Staff   The Deputy Chiefs of Staff function primarily as a coordinating level on policy matters and represent the corporate structure.

FIELD ORGANIZATIONS

The major commands, field operating agencies, and direct reporting units together represent the field organizations of the Air Force. These are organized primarily on a functional basis in the United States and on an area basis overseas. These commands are responsible for accomplishing certain phases of the worldwide activities of the Air Force. They also are responsible for organizing, administering, equipping, and training their subordinate elements for the accomplishment of assigned missions.

Major Commands

The Continental U.S. Commands

Air Combat Command   This Command operates Air Force bombers and CONUS-based, combat-coded fighter and attack aircraft. It organizes, trains, equips, and maintains combat-ready forces for rapid deployment and employment while ensuring strategic air defense forces are ready to meet the challenges of peacetime air sovereignty and wartime air defense.

Air Force Materiel Command   This Command advances, integrates, and uses technology to develop, test, acquire, and sustain weapons systems. It also performs single-manager continuous product and process improvement throughout a product's life cycle. The Command contributes to combat superiority, readiness, and sustainability.

Air Mobility Command   This Command provides airlift, air refueling, special air mission, and aeromedical evacuation for U.S. forces. It also supplies forces to theater commands to support wartime tasking.

Air Force Reserve Command   This Command supports the Air Force mission of defending the United States through control and exploitation of air and space. It plays an integral role in the day-to-day Air Force mission and is not a force held in reserve for possible war or contingency operations.

Air Force Space Command   This Command operates space and ballistic missile systems, including ballistic missile warning, space control, spacelift, and satellite operations.

Air Force Special Operations Command   This Command provides the air component of U.S. Special Operations Command, deploying specialized air power and delivering special operations combat power.

Air Education and Training Command   This Command recruits, accesses, commissions, educates, and trains Air Force enlisted and officer personnel. It provides basic military training, initial and advanced technical training, flying training, and professional military and degree-granting professional education. The Command also conducts joint, medical service, readiness, and Air Force security assistance training.

Major Commands

Command	Address	Commander
Air Combat Command	Langley AFB, VA 23665–2788	Gen. Richard E. Hawley
Air Force Materiel Command	Wright-Patterson AFB, OH 45433–5001	Gen. George T. Babbitt, Jr.
Air Mobility Command	Scott AFB, IL 62225–5310	Gen. Walter Kross
Air Force Reserve Command	Robins AFB, GA 31098–1635	Maj. Gen. Robert A. McIntosh
Air Force Space Command	Peterson AFB, CO 80914–4020	Gen. Howell M. Estes III
Air Force Special Operations Command	Hurlburt Field, FL 32544–5273	Maj. Gen. Charles R. Holland
Air Education and Training Command	Randolph AFB, TX 78150–4324	Gen. Lloyd W. Newton

Overseas Commands

Pacific Air Forces   The Command is responsible for planning, conducting, and coordinating offensive and defensive air operations in the Pacific and Asian theaters.

United States Air Forces in Europe   The Command plans, conducts, controls, coordinates, and supports air and space operations to achieve United States national and NATO objectives.

Overseas Commands

Command	Address	Commander
Pacific Air Forces	Hickam AFB, HI 96853–5420	Gen. Richard B. Myers
U.S. Air Forces in Europe	APO AE 09094–0501	(Vacancy)

Field Operating Agencies

Air Force Agency for Modeling and Simulation The Agency implements policies and standards and supports field operations in the areas of modeling and simulation.

Air Force Audit Agency The Agency provides all levels of Air Force management with independent internal audit and appraisal of financial, operational, management, and support activities. Reports of audits evaluate the effectiveness, efficiency, and economy of program management.

Air Force Base Conversion Agency The Agency serves as the Federal real property disposal agent and provides integrated executive management for Air Force bases in the United States as they are closed under the delegated authorities of the Base Closure and Realignment Act of 1988 and the Defense Base Closure and Realignment Act of 1990.

Air Force Center for Environmental Excellence The Center provides the Air Force with services in environmental remediation, compliance, planning, and pollution prevention, as well as construction management and facilities design.

Air Force Center for Quality and Management Innovation The Center provides support to the Air Force corporate structure on a wide range of resource issues, improves Air Force-wide functional processes, advises on opportunities for outsourcing and privatization, and defines manpower requirements for organizations and processes.

Air Force Civil Engineer Support Agency The Agency maximizes Air Force civil engineers' capabilities in base and contingency operations by providing tools, practices, and professional support for readiness, training, technical support, management practices, automation support, vehicles and equipment, and research, development, and acquisition consultation.

Air Force Communications Agency The Agency ensures that command, control, communications, and computer systems used by USAF warfighters are integrated and interoperable. It develops and validates C^4 architectures, technical standards, technical reference codes, policies, processes and procedures, and technical solutions, supporting information superiority through technical excellence.

Air Force Cost Analysis Agency The Agency provides independent cost analysis support and develops Air Force component cost analyses for weapons systems acquisition programs and automated information systems as required by DOD directives. It conducts a full research program in cost models and data bases and maintains a cost library.

Air Force Flight Standards Agency The Agency performs worldwide inspection of airfields, navigation systems, and instrument approaches. It provides flight standards to develop Air Force instrument requirements, and certifies procedures and directives for cockpit display and navigation systems. It also provides air traffic control and airlift procedures and evaluates air traffic control systems and airspace management procedures.

Air Force Frequency Management Agency The Agency develops USAF policy and procedures for radio frequency spectrum management in support of air and space combat operations. It also represents Air Force requirements to regulatory agencies. The Agency analyzes and processes allocations and assignments for all Air Force spectrum-dependent equipment.

Air Force Historical Research Agency The Agency serves as a repository for Air Force historical records and provides research facilities for scholars and the general public.

Air Force History Support Office The Office researches, writes, and publishes books and other studies on Air Force history and provides historical support to Air Force headquarters.

Air Force Inspection Agency The Agency provides the the Air Force Inspector General with an independent assessment of leadership, fighting capability, and resource management. It assesses operational readiness and management effectiveness and efficiency; recommends improvements to existing methods for fulfilling missions; and conducts inquiries and investigations of allegations regarding personnel and activities.

Air Force Legal Services Agency The Agency provides legal services in the functional areas of military justice, patents, claims and tort litigation, general litigation, labor law, preventive law, and legal aid.

Air Force Logistics Management Agency The Agency conducts studies and develops, analyzes, tests, evaluates, and recommends new or improved concepts, methods, systems, or procedures to improve logistics efficiency and effectiveness.

Air Force Management Engineering Agency The Agency ensures the best possible use of Air Force resources through the development and application of process improvement tools and techniques in partnership with customers.

Air Force Medical Operations Agency The Agency assists the USAF Surgeon General in developing plans, programs, and policies for the medical service, aerospace medicine, clinical investigations, quality assurance, health promotion, family advocacy, bioenvironmental engineering, military public health, and radioactive material management.

Air Force Medical Support Agency The Agency assists the USAF Surgeon General in developing programs, policies, and practices relating to health care in peace and war.

Air Force National Security Emergency Preparedness Office The Office is responsible for Air Force-related national security emergency preparedness functions, including military support to civil authorities, civil defense, and law enforcement agencies and planning for continuity of operations during emergencies.

Air Force News Agency The Agency gathers information and packages and disseminates electronic and printed news and information products. It manages and operationally controls Air Force Internal Information, the Army and Air Force Hometown News Service, the Air Force Broadcasting Service, and the Air Force Armed Forces Radio and Television outlets worldwide; operates the Air Force hotline; and provides electronic information through the Air Force bulletin board and the Internet.

Air Force Office of Special Investigations The Office provides criminal investigative and counterintelligence information and services to commanders worldwide in order to identify and prevent criminal activity that may threaten Air Force resources.

Air Force Operations Group The Group is responsible for the Headquarters Air Force Operations Center, Air Force Emergency Operations Center, the President's Operational Weather Forecaster, the Chief of Staff Current Operations Briefing Team, and the Status of Resources and Training System. It develops policy, funding, and support for Air Force participation in Joint Chiefs of Staff exercises and all Air Force readiness programs. It also organizes, manages, and trains the Air Force Crisis Action Team.

Air Force Pentagon Communications Agency The Agency provides 24-hour communications and computer support to high-level customers in the Secretary of Defense's office, the Joint Chiefs of Staff, the Air Force Secretary, and the Air Staff.

Air Force Personnel Center The Center manages personnel programs and policies affecting Air Force personnel and ensures the availability of appropriate personnel to perform the missions of unit commanders worldwide.

Air Force Personnel Operations Agency The Agency establishes and manages procedures and practices governing relations between Air Force management and its civilian work force.

Air Force Program Executive Office The Office manages and is directly accountable for the cost, schedule, and performance of major and selected acquisition programs.

Air Force Real Estate Agency   The Agency acquires, manages, and disposes of land for the Air Force worldwide and maintains a complete land and facilities inventory.

Air Force Review Boards Agency   The Agency directs the activities of the Air Force Personnel Council, the Air Force Board for Correction of Military Records, and the Air Force Civilian Appellate Review Office.

Air Force Safety Center   The Center implements and executes Air Force safety and nuclear surety policies, plans, and programs.

Air Force Services Agency   The Agency provides technical assistance to programs contributing to readiness and improved productivity, including programs promoting fitness, *esprit de corps,* and increased quality of life. It also operates central systems for field support.

Air Force Studies and Analyses Agency   The Agency performs studies to assist and support the Air Force decision-making process. It performs independent studies and evaluations of Air Force requirements, proposals, plans, and programs, while providing comparisons and trade-off analyses. The Agency also evaluates critical technical and operational issues and monitors applicable tests and evaluations that address such issues.

Air Force Technical Applications Center   The Center monitors compliance with various nuclear treaties. It provides real-time reporting of nuclear weapons tests and operates a global network of sensors

and analytical laboratories to monitor foreign nuclear activity. It conducts research and development of proliferation detection technologies for all weapons of mass destruction.

Air Intelligence Agency   The Agency provides intelligence services to support Air Force operations through flexible collection, tailored air and space intelligence, weapons monitoring, and information warfare products and services.

Air National Guard Readiness Center   The Center performs the operational and technical tasks associated with manning, equipping, and training Air National Guard units to required readiness levels.

Air Reserve Personnel Center   The Center provides personnel support and administration for the men and women of the reserve components. It maintains the master personnel records for members of the Air National Guard and Air Force Reserve not on extended active duty.

Air Weather Service   The Service provides centralized weather services to the Air Force, Army joint staff, designated unified commands, and other agencies, ensuring standardization of procedures and interoperability within the USAF weather system and assessing its technical performance and effectiveness.

Joint Services Survival, Evasion, Resistance, and Escape Agency   The Agency serves as DOD's executive agent for the Joint Chiefs of Staff operational evasion and escape matters; code of conduct, survival, evasion, resistance, and escape training; and DOD's POW/MIA program.

Field Operating Agencies

Agency	Address	Commander/Director
Air Force Agency for Modeling and Simulation	Orlando, FL 32826–3276	Col. Jimmy H. Wilson
Air Force Audit Agency	Washington, DC 20330–1125	Jackie Crawford
Air Force Base Conversion Agency	Arlington, VA 22209–2808	(Vacancy)
Air Force Center for Environmental Excellence	Brooks AFB, TX 78235–5318	Gary M. Erickson
Air Force Center for Quality and Management Innovation	Randolph AFB, TX 78150–4451	Brig. Gen. Hugh C. Cameron
Air Force Civil Engineer Support Agency	Tyndall AFB, FL 32403–5319	Col. Donald J. Thomas
Air Force Communications Agency	Scott AFB, IL 62225–5233	Col. M. Ryan Patrick
Air Force Cost Analysis Agency	Arlington, VA 22202–4306	Robert F. Hale
Air Force Flight Standards Agency	Washington, DC 20330–1480	(Vacancy)
Air Force Frequency Management Agency	Arlington, VA 22203–1613	Col. Michael D. Acres
Air Force Historical Research Agency	Maxwell AFB, AL 36112–6424	Col. Richard Rauschkolb

Field Operating Agencies—Continued

Agency	Address	Commander/Director
Air Force History Support Office	Bolling AFB, Washington, DC 20332–4113	Jacob Neufeld
Air Force Inspection Agency	Kirtland AFB, NM 87117–5670	(Vacancy)
Air Force Legal Services Agency	Bolling AFB, Washington, DC 20332	Col. Richard F. Rohenberg
Air Force Logistics Management Agency	Maxwell AFB, AL 36114–3236	Col. Russell G. Stafford
Air Force Management Engineering Agency	Randolph AFB, TX 78150–4451	Col. Charles F. Dibrell
Air Force Medical Operations Agency	Bolling AFB, Washington, DC 20332–7050	Maj. Gen. Earl W. Mabry II
Air Force Medical Support Agency	Brooks AFB, TX 78235–5121	Col. Richard Rushmore
Air Force National Security Emergency Preparedness Office	Washington, DC 20330–1480	Col. Bob Manning
Air Force News Agency	Kelly AFB, TX 78241–5601	Col. Teddy G. Tilma
Air Force Office of Special Investigations	Bolling AFB, Washington, DC 20332–6000	Brig. Gen. Francis X. Taylor
Air Force Operations Group	Washington, DC 20330–1480	Col. James S. Sheehan
Air Force Pentagon Communications Agency	Washington, DC 20330–1600	Col. Richard Hange
Air Force Personnel Center	Randolph AFB, TX 78150–4703	Maj. Gen. Susan L. Pamerleau
Air Force Personnel Operations Agency	Washington, DC 20330–1040	Susan O'Neal
Air Force Program Executive Office	Washington, DC 20330–1060	(Vacancy)
Air Force Real Estate Agency	Bolling AFB, Washington, DC 20332–5107	William E. Edwards
Air Force Review Boards Agency	Washington, DC 20330–1661	Joe G. Lineberger
Air Force Safety Center	Kirtland AFB, NM 87117	Col. John R. Clapper
Air Force Services Agency	Randolph AFB, TX 78150–4755	Col. David F. Honeycutt
Air Force Studies and Analyses Agency	Washington, DC 20330–1570	Col. Thomas A. Cardwell III
Air Force Technical Applications Center	Patrick AFB, FL 32925–3002	(Vacancy)
Air Intelligence Agency	San Antonio, TX 78243–7009	Brig. Gen. James E. Miller, Jr.
Air National Guard Readiness Center	Andrews AFB, MD 20331–5157	(Vacancy)
Air Reserve Personnel Center	Denver, CO 80280–5400	Col. Margie L. Humphrey
Air Weather Service	Scott AFB, IL 62225–5206	Col. Frank Misciasci
Joint Services Survival, Evasion, Resistance, and Escape Agency	Fort Belvoir, VA 22060–5788	Col. Robert C. Bonn, Jr.

Direct Reporting Units

11th Wing   The Wing provides support for Headquarters Air Force and other Air Force units in the National Capital Region, including day-to-day operations of Bolling Air Force Base. The Wing plans and directs the Air Force Band and the Air Force Honor Guard support to ceremony activities of the Air Force Chief of Staff, the Air Force Secretary, the White House, and Arlington National Cemetery.

Air Force Communication and Information Center   The Center applies information technology to improve operations processes and manages all Air Force information technology systems.

Air Force Doctrine Center   The Center develops and publishes basic and operational level doctrine for the USAF. It provides USAF input into joint and multinational doctrine development, ensures that Air Force doctrine is consistent with policy and joint doctrine, and serves as the Air Force's primary source of expertise for military operations other than war doctrine and strategy development as well as training, education, exercises, and simulations.

Air Force Operational Test and Evaluation Center   The Center plans and conducts test and evaluation procedures to determine operational effectiveness and suitability of new or modified USAF systems and their capacity to meet mission needs.

Air Force Security Forces Center   The Center ensures quick and effective security responses to protect U.S. personnel around the globe.

U.S. Air Force Academy   The Academy provides academic and military instruction and experience to prepare future USAF career officers. Graduates receive Bachelor of Science degrees in one of 26 academic majors and commissions as second lieutenants.

Direct Reporting Units

Unit	Address	Commander
11th Wing	Bolling AFB, Washington, DC 20332–0101	Col. Duane W. Deal
Air Force Communications and Information Center	Washington, DC 20330–1250	Lt. Gen. William J. Donahue
Air Force Doctrine Center	Maxwell AFB, AL 36112–6335	Maj. Gen. Ronald E. Keys

Direct Reporting Units—Continued

Unit	Address	Commander
Air Force Operational Test and Evaluation Center	Kirtland AFB, NM 87117–5558	Maj. Gen. Jeffrey G. Cliver
Air Force Security Forces Center	Lackland AFB, TX 78236–5226	Brig. Gen. Richard A. Coleman, Jr.
U.S. Air Force Academy	CO 80840–5001	Lt. Gen. Tad J. Oelstrom

For further information concerning the Department of the Air Force, contact the Office of the Director of Public Affairs, Department of the Air Force, 1670 Air Force Pentagon, Washington, DC 20330–1670. Phone, 703–697–6061.

DEPARTMENT OF THE ARMY

The Pentagon, Washington, DC 20310
Phone, 703–545–6700. Internet, http://www.army.mil/.

SECRETARY OF THE ARMY	ROBERT M. WALKER, *Acting*
Senior Military Assistant	COL. MICHAEL FREEMAN
Military Assistants	COL. CHARLES CARTWRIGHT, LT. COL. ROSE WALKER
Aide-de-Camp	CAPT. KATHRYN BURBA
Under Secretary of the Army	ROBERT M. WALKER
Executive Officer	LT. COL. DOUGLAS WATSON
Military Assistant	LT. COL. HENRY TURNER, JR.
Aide-de-Camp	CAPT. STEVE E. LAMBERT
Assistant Secretary of the Army (Civil Works)	JOHN H. ZIRSCHKY, *Acting*
Principal Deputy Assistant Secretary	JOHN H. ZIRSCHKY
Executive Officer	COL. ROBERT J. SPERBERG
Deputy Assistant Secretary, Policy, and Legislation	MICHAEL L. DAVIS
Assistant Secretary of the Army (Financial Management and Comptroller)	HELEN T. MCCOY
Principal Deputy Assistant Secretary	NEIL R. GINNETTI
Executive Officer	COL. ERVIN PEARSON
Deputy Assistant Secretary, Army Budget	MAJ. GEN. CLAIR F. GILL
Deputy Assistant Secretary, Financial Operations	ERNEST J. GREGORY
Deputy Assistant Secretary, Resource Analysis and Business Practices	ROBERT RAYNSFORD
Deputy for Cost Analysis	ROBERT W. YOUNG
Assistant Secretary of the Army (Installations, Logistics, and Environment)	ALMA B. MOORE, *Acting*
Principal Deputy Assistant Secretary	ALMA B. MOORE
Executive Officer	COL. DAVID R. POWERS
Deputy Assistant Secretary, Environment, Safety, and Occupational Health	RAYMOND J. FATZ
Deputy Assistant Secretary, Installations and Housing	PAUL W. JOHNSON
Deputy Assistant Secretary, Logistics	ERIC A. ORSINI
Assistant Secretary of the Army (Manpower and Reserve Affairs)	JAYSON L. SPIEGEL, *Acting*
Principal Deputy Assistant Secretary	TODD WEILER, *Acting*
Executive Officer	COL. WILLIAM A. BROWN III
Deputy Assistant Secretary, Civilian Personnel Policy	CAROL A. SMITH
Deputy Assistant Secretary, Force Management, Manpower, and Resources	JAYSON L. SPIEGEL
Deputy Assistant Secretary, Military Personnel Management and Equal Opportunity Policy	JOHN P. MCLAURIN III

Deputy Assistant Secretary, Reserve Affairs, Mobilization Readiness, and Training	TODD A. WEILER
Deputy Assistant Secretary, Review Boards and Equal Employment Opportunity Compliance and Complaints Review	KARL SCHNEIDER
Assistant Secretary of the Army (Research, Development, and Acquisition)	KENNETH J. OSCAR
Military Deputy to the Assistant Secretary	LT. GEN. PAUL J. KERN
Executive Officer	COL. EDWARD M. HARRINGTON
Deputy Assistant Secretary, Plans, Programs, and Policy	KEITH CHARLES
Deputy Assistant Secretary, Procurement	EDWARD E. ELGART, *Acting*
Deputy Assistant Secretary, Research and Technology	A. FENNER MILTON
General Counsel	WILLIAM T. COLEMAN III
Principal Deputy General Counsel	LAWRENCE M. BASKIR
Executive Officer	COL. JOHN GREENBAUGH
Deputy General Counsel, Acquisition	LEVATOR NORSWORTHY
Deputy General Counsel, Civil Works and Environment	EARL H. STOCKDALE, JR.
Deputy General Counsel, Ethics and Fiscal	MATT RERES
Deputy General Counsel, Operations and Personnel	THOMAS W. TAYLOR
Administrative Assistant to the Secretary of the Army	JOEL B. HUDSON
Deputy Administrative Assistant	SANDRA R. RILEY
Director of Policy and Plans	FRITZ W. KIRKLIGHTER
Headquarters Services—Washington:	
Executive Director	SANDRA R. RILEY
Director of Equal Employment Opportunity	DEBRA A. MUSE
Director of Information Management Support Center	MICHAEL SELVES
Commander of Defense Supply Service (Washington)	COL. KIMBERLY SMITH
Director of Defense Telecommunications Service (Washington)	MICHAEL A. NEWTON
Director of Personnel and Employment Services (Washington)	SHERRI V. WARD
Director of Safety, Security, and Support Services (Washington)	LACY SAUNDERS, *Acting*
Director of Space and Building Management Service (Washington)	R. WES BLAINE
Director, Single Agency Manager	FRED BUDD
Director, Information Systems for Command, Control, Communications, and Computers	LT. GEN. WILLIAM H. CAMPBELL
Vice Director	DAVID BORLAND
Deputy Director	BRIG. GEN. JAMES D. BRYAN
Executive Officer	COL. JOHN C. DEAL
The Inspector General	LT. GEN. LARRY R. JORDAN
Deputy Commander (Investigations and Oversight)	(VACANCY)
Auditor General	FRANCIS E. REARDON
Deputy Auditor General, Acquisition and Force Management Audits	THOMAS W. BROWN
Deputy Auditor General, Financial Audits	THOMAS DRUZGAL

Deputy Auditor General, Logistical Audits	C.A. ARIGO
Deputy Auditor General, Policy and Operations Management	STEPHEN E. KEEFER
Deputy Under Secretary of the Army (International Affairs)	LT. GEN. CLAUDE M. KICKLIGHTER, USA (RET.)
Deputy Under Secretary of the Army (Operations Research)	WALTER W. HOLLIS
Chief of Legislative Liaison	BRIG. GEN. BRUCE SCOTT
Deputy Chief	SHEILA MCCREADY
Chief of Public Affairs	BRIG. GEN. JOHN G. MEYER, JR.
Deputy Chief	COL. ROBERT E. GAYLORD
Chairman, Army Reserve Forces Policy Committee	MAJ. GEN. JOHN T. CROWE
Deputy Chairman	MAJ. GEN. JAMES RUEGER
Director of Small and Disadvantaged Business Utilization	TRACEY L. PINSON
Deputy Director	SARAH A. CROSS

Office of the Chief of Staff:

Chief of Staff, United States Army	GEN. DENNIS J. REIMER
Vice Chief of Staff	GEN. WILLIAM W. CROUCH
Assistant Vice Chief of Staff	LT. GEN. DAVID K. HEEBNER
Director of the Army Staff	LT. GEN. JOHN A. DUBIA

Army Staff:

Deputy Chief of Staff for Intelligence	LT. GEN. CLAUDIA J. KENNEDY
Deputy Chief of Staff for Logistics	LT. GEN. JOHN G. COBURN
Deputy Chief of Staff for Operations and Plans	LT. GEN. THOMAS N. BURNETTE
Deputy Chief of Staff for Personnel	LT. GEN. FREDERICK E. VOLLRATH
Assistant Chief of Staff for Installation Management	MAJ. GEN. DAVID WHALEY
The Judge Advocate General	MAJ. GEN. WALTER HUFFMAN
The Surgeon General	LT. GEN. RONALD R. BLANCK
Chief, Army Reserve	MAJ. GEN. MAX BARATZ
Chief of Chaplains	MAJ. GEN. DONALD W. SHEA
Chief of Engineers	LT. GEN. JOE N. BALLARD
Chief, National Guard Bureau	LT. GEN. EDWARD D. BACA

Major Army Commands:

Commanding General, U.S. Army Material Command	GEN. JOHNNIE E. WILSON
Commanding General, U.S. Army Corps of Engineers	LT. GEN. JOE N. BALLARD
Commanding General, U.S. Army Criminal Investigation Command	BRIG. GEN. DANIEL A. DOHERTY
Commanding General, U.S. Army Forces Command	GEN. DAVID A. BRAMLETT
Commanding General, U.S. Army Intelligence and Security Command	MAJ. GEN. JOHN D. THOMAS, JR.
Commanding General, U.S. Army Medical Command	LT. GEN. RONALD R. BLANCK
Commanding General, U.S. Army Military District of Washington	MAJ. GEN. ROBERT F. FOLEY
Commanding General, U.S. Army Military Traffic Management Command	MAJ. GEN. MARIO F. MONTERO, JR.
Commanding General, U.S. Army Special Operations Command	MAJ. GEN. WILLIAM P. TANGNEY

Commanding General, U.S. Army Training and Doctrine Command	GEN. WILLIAM W. HARTZOG
Commanding General, U.S. Army South	MAJ. GEN. PHILIP R. KENSINGER, JR.
Commanding General, 8th U.S. Army	LT. GEN. RANDOLPH W. HOUSE
Commanding General, U.S. Army Pacific	LT. GEN. WILLIAM M. STEELE
Commanding General, U.S. Army Europe and 7th Army	GEN. ERIC K. SHINSEKI

The mission of the Department of the Army is to organize, train, and equip active duty and reserve forces for the preservation of peace, security, and the defense of our Nation. As part of our national military team, the Army focuses on land operations; its soldiers must be trained with modern arms and equipment and be ready to respond quickly. The Army also administers programs aimed at protecting the environment, improving waterway navigation, flood and beach erosion control, and water resource development. It provides military assistance to Federal, State, and local government agencies, including natural disaster relief assistance.

The American Continental Army, now called the United States Army, was established by the Continental Congress on June 14, 1775, more than a year before the Declaration of Independence.

The Department of War was established as an executive department at the seat of government by act approved August 7, 1789 (1 Stat. 49). The Secretary of War was established as its head.

The National Security Act of 1947 (50 U.S.C. 401) created the National Military Establishment, and the Department of War was designated the Department of the Army. The title of its Secretary became Secretary of the Army (5 U.S.C. 171).

The National Security Act Amendments of 1949 (63 Stat. 578) provided that the Department of the Army be a military department within the Department of Defense.

The Army Organization Act of 1950 (64 Stat. 263) provided the statutory basis for the internal organization of the Army and the Department of the Army. The act consolidated and revised the numerous earlier laws, incorporated various adjustments made necessary by the National Security Act of 1947 and other postwar enactments, and provided for the organization of the Department of the Army in a single comprehensive statute, with certain minor exceptions. In general, the act followed the policy of vesting broad organizational powers in the Secretary of the Army, subject to delegation by the Secretary, rather than specifying duties of subordinate officers (10 U.S.C. 3012, 3062).

Army Secretariat

Secretary The Secretary of the Army is the head of the Department of the Army. Subject to the direction, authority, and control of the President as Commander in Chief and of the Secretary of Defense, the Secretary of the Army is responsible for and has the authority to conduct all affairs of the Department of the Army, including its organization, administration, operation, efficiency, and such other activities as may be prescribed by the President or the Secretary of Defense as authorized by law.

Certain civilian functions, such as comptroller, acquisition, inspector general, auditing and information management, are also under the authority of the Army Secretariat. Additionally, the Secretary is responsible for civil functions, such as oversight of the Panama Canal Commission and execution of the Panama Canal Treaty; the civil works program of the Corps of

DEPARTMENT OF THE ARMY

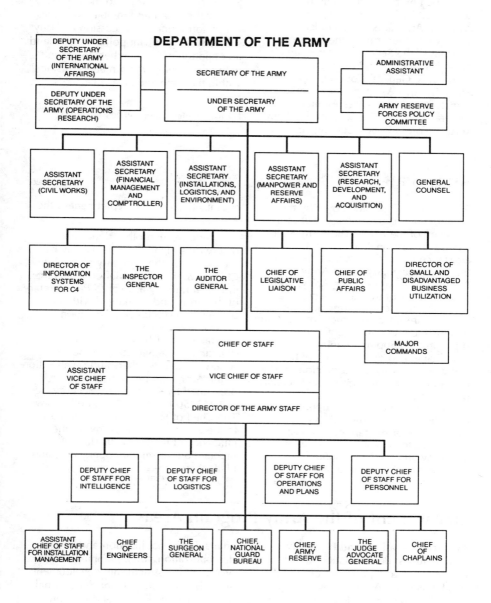

Engineers; Arlington and Soldiers' Home National Cemeteries; and such other activities of a civil nature as may be prescribed by higher authority or authorized by law.

Principal Assistants   The Under Secretary of the Army is the primary assistant to the Secretary. Other principal assistants include: the Assistant Secretaries, General Counsel, Administrative Assistant, the several Directors and Chiefs, the Auditor General, and the Chairman of the Army Reserve Forces Policy Committee.

Army Policy Council   The Council is the senior policy advisory council of the Department of the Army. It provides the Secretary of the Army and the Secretary's principal civilian and military assistants with a forum for the discussion of Army subjects of significant policy interest and an opportunity for members to consult with other members on matters arising within their specific areas of responsibility.

For further information, call 703–695–7922.

Army Staff

The Army Staff, presided over by the Chief of Staff, is the military staff of the Secretary of the Army. The Army Staff renders professional advice and assistance to the Secretary of the Army, the Under Secretary of the Army, the Assistant Secretaries of the Army, and other officials of the Army Secretariat.

It is the duty of the Army Staff to:

—prepare for employment of the Army and for such recruiting, organizing, supplying, equipping, training, mobilizing, and demobilizing of the Army as will assist the execution of any power, duty, or function of the Secretary or the Chief of Staff;

—investigate and report upon the efficiency of the Army and its preparation for military operations;

—act as the agent of the Secretary of the Army and the Chief of Staff in coordinating the action of all

organizations of the Department of the Army; and

—perform such other duties not otherwise assigned by law as may be prescribed by the Secretary of the Army.

Chief of Staff   The Chief of Staff is the principal military adviser to the Secretary of the Army and is charged with the planning, development, execution, review, and analysis of the Army programs. The Chief of Staff, under the direction of the Secretary of the Army, supervises the members and organization of the Army and performs the duties prescribed by the National Security Act of 1947 (50 U.S.C. 401) and other laws. The Chief of Staff is directly responsible to the Secretary of the Army for the efficiency of the Army, its state of preparation for military operations, and plans therefor.

Department of the Army Program Areas

Military Operations and Plans   This area includes: determination of requirements and priorities for, and the employment of, Army forces strategy formation; mid-range, long-range, and regional strategy application; arms control, negotiation, and disarmament; national security affairs; joint service matters; net assessment; politico-military

affairs; force mobilization and demobilization; force planning, programming structuring, development, analysis and management; operational readiness; overall roles and missions; collective security; individual and unit training; psychological operations; unconventional warfare; counterterrorism; operations security;

signal security; military aspects of space and sea; special plans; table of equipment development and approval; electronic warfare; nuclear and chemical matters; civil affairs; military support of civil defense; civil disturbance; domestic actions; audiovisual activities; command and control; automation and communications programs and activities; management of the program for law enforcement, correction and crime prevention for military members of the Army; and physical security.

Personnel This area includes: management of military and civilian personnel for overall integrated support of the Army, including policies and programs for manpower utilization standards, allocation and documentation, career development, equal opportunity, leadership, alcohol and drug abuse control, welfare and morale, promotion, retention, and separation; military compensation, transportation, and travel entitlements; repatriation plans and operations; the personnel aspects of military construction and housing management; and research and development related to training personnel, manpower systems, and human factors.

Reserve Components This area includes: management of individual and unit readiness and mobilization for Reserve Components, comprised of the Army National Guard and the U.S. Army Reserve.

Intelligence This area includes: management of Army intelligence and counterintelligence activities, personnel, equipment, systems, and organizations; Army cryptology, topography, and meteorology; coordination of Army requirements for mapping, charting, and geodesy; and Army industrial security.

Management-Comptrollership This area includes: review and analysis of Army programs and major Army commands; management information systems in the financial area, progress and statistical reporting, and reports control; financial management, budgeting, finance and accounting, cost analysis, economic analysis, military pay and allowances, resource management,

and productivity and value improvement; regulatory policies and programs pertaining to the overall management of the Army; and legislative policies and programs pertaining to appropriation acts affecting the Army.

Research, Development, and Materiel Acquisition This area includes: management of Army research, development and materiel acquisition; planning, programming, budgeting and execution for the acquisition of materiel obtained by the procurement appropriations for the Army; materiel life cycle management from concept phase through acquisition; and international acquisition programs.

Information Management This area includes: automation, communications, audiovisual, records management, publications, and information management.

Logistics This area includes: management of Department of the Army logistical activities for the movement and maintenance of forces; logistical planning and support of Army and joint service operations; materiel and supply management and maintenance; transportation; and Army interservice supply operations.

Engineering This area includes: management of Army engineering, construction, installations, family housing, real estate, facilities requirements and stationing, and real property maintenance activities; environmental preservation and improvement activities; applicable research and development activities for engineer missions to include environmental sciences; Army topographic and military geographic information activities; and engineer aspects of Army strategic and operational plans.

Civil Functions Civil functions of the Department of the Army include the Civil Works Program, the administration of Arlington and Soldiers' Home National Cemeteries, and other related matters. The Army's Civil Works Program, a responsibility of the Corps of Engineers under the direction and supervision of the Secretary of the Army, dates back to 1824 and is the Nation's major Federal water resources development activity and involves engineering works such as major dams, reservoirs, levees, harbors, waterways, locks, and many other types of structures. These works provide flood protection for cities and major river valleys, reduce the cost of transportation, supply water for municipal and industrial use, generate hydroelectric power, provide recreational opportunities for vast numbers of people, regulate the rivers for many purposes including the improvement of water quality, protect the shores of oceans and lakes, and provide other types of benefits. Planning assistance is also provided to States and other non-Federal entities for the comprehensive management of water resources, including pollution abatement works. In addition, through the Civil Works Program the Federal Government protects the navigable waters and wetlands of the United States under legislation empowering the Secretary of the Army to prohibit activities that would reduce their value to the Nation.

Medical   This area includes: management of health services for the Army and, as directed for other services, agencies, and organizations; health standards for Army personnel; health professional education and training; career management authority over commissioned and warrant officer personnel of the Army Medical Department; medical research, materiel development, testing and evaluation; policies concerning health aspects of Army environmental programs and prevention of disease; and planning, programming, and budgeting for Army-wide health services.

Inspection   This area includes: management of inquiries, inspections, and reports on matters affecting the performance of mission and the state of discipline, efficiency, economy, and morale of the Department of the Army.

Religious   This area includes: management of religious and moral leadership and chaplain support activities Armywide; religious ministrations, religious education, pastoral care, and counseling for Army military personnel; liaison with the ecclesiastical agencies; chapel construction requirements and design approval; and career management of clergymen serving in the Chaplains Branch.

Legal   This area includes: legal advisory services provided for all military personnel and agencies of the Army; review and final action as designee of the Secretary of the Army on complaints of wrongs by service personnel submitted under the Uniform Code of Military Justice; administration of military justice and civil law matters pertaining to the Army; administration of Army claims and legal assistance services; operation of the legal system for appellate review of court-martial records as provided by the Uniform Code of Military Justice; general court-martial records custodianship; records administration for proceedings of inquiry and military commissions; liaison service with the Department of Justice and other Federal and State agencies on matters connected with litigation and legal proceedings concerning the Army; and career management of Judge Advocate General's Corps officers.

Public Affairs   This area includes media relations, command information, and community relations services, as well as preparation of information plans and programs in support of Army basic plans and programs.

History   This area includes: advisory and coordination service provided on historical matters, including historical properties; formulation and execution of the Army Historical Program; and preparation and publication of histories required by the Army.

Major Army Commands

United States Army Materiel Command
The U.S. Army Materiel Command
(AMC) is the Army's principal materiel
developer. AMC's missions include the
development of weapon systems,
advanced research on future
technologies, and maintenance and
distribution of spare parts and
equipment. AMC works closely with
industry, academe, the other military
services, and other Government agencies
to develop, test, and acquire every piece
of equipment that soldiers and units
need to accomplish their missions.

For further information, call 703–617–9625.
Internet, http://www.amc.army.mil/.

**United States Army Criminal
Investigation Command**   The U.S. Army
Criminal Investigation Command (CID)
investigates felony violations of the
Uniform Code of Military Justice and
other criminal provisions of the United
States Code in which the Army has an
interest. CID also provides protective
services for senior Defense Department
and Army leaders and supports field
commanders and communities to solve
major and violent crimes.

For further information, call 703–756–1232.
Internet, http://www.belvoir.army.mil/cidc/
index.htm/.

Eighth U.S. Army   The 8th U.S. Army
provides forces to the commander in
chief of United Nations Command;
United States Forces, Korea; and
Republic of Korea/U.S. Combined Forces
Command.

For further information, call 703–694–3475.
Internet, http://www.korea.army.mil/usfk/eusa/
eusa.htm/.

United States Army Forces Command
The U.S. Army Forces Command
(FORSCOM) trains, mobilizes, deploys,
and sustains combat-ready forces
capable of responding rapidly to crises
worldwide. FORSCOM is the Army
component of U.S. Atlantic Command.
Consequently, the FORSCOM
commander functions as commander of
the Army forces of this unified command
and plans for and provides military

support to civil authorities, including
response to natural disasters and civil
emergencies.

For further information, call 404–464–5607.
Internet, http://www.forscom.army.mil/.

**United States Army Intelligence and
Security Command**   The U.S. Army
Intelligence and Security Command
plans and conducts intelligence, security,
and information operations for military
commanders and national
decisionmakers.

For further information, call 703–706–1232.
Internet, http://www.vulcan.belvoir.army.mil/.

**United States Army Military District of
Washington**   The U.S. Army Military
District of Washington conducts security
and disaster-relief operations in the
National Capital Region (NCR), provides
base operations support to Army and
other Defense Department organizations
in the NCR, and conducts official and
public events on behalf of the Nation's
civilian and military leadership.

For further information, call 202–685–3217.
Internet, http://www.mdw.army.mil/.

United States Army Medical Command
The U.S. Army Medical Command
(MEDCOM) provides direction and
planning for the Army Medical
Department in conjunction with the
Office of the Surgeon General. It
develops and integrates doctrine,
training, leader development,
organization, and materiel for Army
health services. MEDCOM also allocates
resources and evaluates delivery of
services.

For further information, call 210–221–6313.

Military Traffic Management Command
The U.S. Army Military Traffic
Management Command (MTMC)
manages, for the Department of Defense,
the worldwide transportation of troops,
equipment, and personal property during
peace and war. This entails single-port
management, transportation, and traffic-
management services, deployment
planning and engineering, and

development of new technologies. MTMC is also the link between DOD shippers and the commercial surface transportation industry, and maintains a presence in 25 ports worldwide as DOD's port manager.

For further information, call 703–681–6242. Internet, http://mtmc.army.mil/.

U.S. Army South   The U.S. Army South (USARSO) acts as the primary land component for United States Southern Command and provides support to U.S. Embassies and military groups throughout Central and South America and the Caribbean. USARSO is a major hub for deploying U.S. Army Reserve and National Guard forces to participate in humanitarian and civic assistance exercises in underdeveloped portions of countries in Latin America. It frequently supports missions to conduct search and rescue and disaster assistance requested by host governments through the U.S. Embassy.

For further information, call 011–507–288–3003. Internet, http://www.army.mil/USARSO/ default.htm/.

United States Army Training and Doctrine Command   The U.S. Army Training and Doctrine Command (TRADOC) serves as the architect for the 21st century Army, while ensuring that the Army is prepared to fight and win wars today. It does this through training—TRADOC develops and maintains the Army's institutional training base. Leaders and soldiers are trained at combined arms schools and combined arms support schools; through doctrine—TRADOC sustains a shared vision of how the Army operates as a member of joint service, combined arms, and multinational teams; and through combat developments—TRADOC identifies requirements for America's Army with a spirit of innovation that will enhance the broader Army process that translates concepts and requirements to production and acquisition. To assist in these efforts, TRADOC integrates the activities of battlefield laboratories that develop and experiment with concepts in battlefield dynamics.

For further information, call 804–727–4465. Internet, http://www.tradoc.army.mil/.

United States Army Corps of Engineers The U.S. Army Corps of Engineers (USACE) provides engineering, construction management, and environmental services in peace and war. The civil works program includes navigation, flood damage reduction, recreation, hydropower, environmental regulation, and other missions. The military program includes construction of Army and Air Force facilities, base realignment and closure activities, installation support, military contingency support, environmental restoration, strategic mobility, and international activities. USACE provides real estate acquisition, management, and disposal for the Army and Air Force, and researches and develops advanced technology for mobility/countermobility, force protection, and sustainment engineering. It also supports several Federal agencies and responds to natural disasters and other emergencies as the Nation's primary engineering agency.

For further information, call 202–761–0660. Internet, http://www.usace.army.mil/.

U.S. Army Europe   As U.S. European Command's primary land component, U.S. Army Europe (USAREUR) monitors armed conflicts and potential flashpoints throughout an 80-nation area. The U.S. Army's largest forward-deployed command, USAREUR supports NATO and U.S. bilateral, multinational, and unilateral objectives. It supports U.S. Army forces in the European Command area; receives and assists in the reception, staging, and onward movement and integration of U.S. forces; establishes, operates, and expands operational lines of communication; and supports U.S. combat commanders with forces and joint task forces headquarters.

For further information, call 011–49–6221–57– 8831. Internet, http://www.hqusareur.army.mil/.

U.S. Army Pacific   The U.S. Army Pacific (USARPAC) provides Army forces worldwide in support of military operations and peacetime engagements to contribute to victory and promote regional stability. USARPAC carries out a cooperative engagement strategy known as the Expanded Relations Program with the 43 Asian and Pacific nations within or bordering its area of responsibility. These countries include The Philippines, Thailand, Vietnam, Japan, Mongolia, Russia, China, South Korea, India, Bangladesh, Australia, New Zealand, Marshall Islands, and Papua New Guinea.

For further information, call 808–438–2206. Internet, http://www.usarpac.army.mil/.

U.S. Army Special Operations Command The U.S. Army Special Operations Command (USASOC) trains, equips, deploys, and sustains Army special operations forces for worldwide special operations supporting regional combatant commanders and country ambassadors. USASOC soldiers deploy to numerous countries conducting missions such as peacekeeping, humanitarian demining, and foreign internal defense. USASOC includes special forces, rangers, civil affairs, psychological operations, special operations aviation, and signal and support.

For further information, call 919–432–7587. Internet, http://www.usasoc.soc.mil/.

U.S. Space and Missile Defense Command The U.S. Space and Missile Defense Command (SMDC) is the proponent for space and national missile defense, a materiel developer, and the Army's integrator for theater missile defense. SMDC ensures missile defense to protect the Nation and deployed forces, and facilitates Army access to space assets and products.

For further information, call 703–607–1873. Internet, http://www.smdc.army.mil/.

United States Military Academy

West Point, NY 10996

Superintendent	LT. GEN. DANIEL W. CHRISTMAN
Commandant of Cadets	BRIG. GEN. JOHN P. ABIZAID
Dean of the Academic Board	BRIG. GEN. FLETCHER M. LAMKIN

The United States Military Academy is located at West Point, NY. The course is of 4 years' duration, during which the cadets receive, besides a general education, theoretical and practical training as junior officers. Cadets who complete the course satisfactorily receive the degree of Bachelor of Science and a commission as second lieutenant in the Army.

For further general information concerning the United States Military Academy, contact the Public Affairs Office, United States Military Academy, West Point, NY 10996. Phone, 914–938–4261. For information about Military Academy admission criteria and policies, contact the Office of the Registrar, United States Military Academy, West Point, NY 10996.

Sources of Information

Arlington and Soldiers' Home National Cemeteries For information write to the Superintendent, Arlington National Cemetery, Arlington, VA 22211–5003. Phone, 703–695–3175.

Army Historical Program For information concerning the Army Historical Program, write to the U.S. Army Center of Military History, HQDA (DAMH), Franklin Court Building, 1099

14th Street NW., Washington, DC 20005–3402. Phone, 202–761–5400. Information on Army historical publications, archival and artifact resources, unit history, and other areas of public interest is available electronically through the Internet, at http://www.army.mil/cmh-pg/.

Civilian Employment Employment inquiries and applications should be directed to the following: (1) For employment in the Washington, DC, metropolitan area—Personnel and Employment Service—Washington, Room 1A909, The Pentagon, Washington, DC 20310–6800 (phone, 703–693–3881); (2) For employment outside the Washington, DC, metropolitan area—address or apply directly to the Army installation where employment is desired, Attn: Civilian Personnel Office; (3) For employment overseas—U.S. Army Civilian Personnel Center, Attn: PECC–CSS, Hoffman II Building, 200 Stovall Street, Alexandria, VA 22332–0300 (phone, 703–325–8712).

Contracts Contract procurement policies and procedures are the responsibility of the Deputy for Procurement, Office of the Assistant Secretary of the Army (Research, Development and Acquisition), Room 2E661, The Pentagon, Washington, DC 20310–0103. Phone, 703–695–4101.

Environment Contact the Public Affairs Office, Office of the Chief of Engineers, Washington, DC 20314–1000, phone, 202–761–0010; or the nearest Corps of Engineers Division or District Office located in most major cities throughout the United States.

Films, Videotapes, and Videodiscs Requests for loan of Army-produced films, videotapes, and videodiscs should be addressed to the Visual Information Support Centers of Army installations. Army productions are available for sale from the National Audiovisual Center (NAC), Washington, DC 20409–3701. Department of the Army pamphlet 25–90, *Visual Information Products Catalog,* lists the products that have been cleared for public release.

Freedom of Information and Privacy Act Requests Requests should be addressed to the Information Management Officer of the Army installation or activity responsible for the requested information.

Military Traffic Management Command Information concerning military transportation news and issues is available electronically through the Internet, at http://mtmc.army.mil/.

Public Affairs and Community Relations For official Army information and community relations, contact the Office of the Chief of Public Affairs, Department of the Army, Washington, DC 20310–1508. Phone, 703–697–5081. During nonoffice hours, call 703–697–4200.

Publications Requests should be addressed to the Information Management Officer of the Army activity that publishes the requested publication. Official publications published by Headquarters, Department of the Army, are available from the National Technical Information Service, Department of Commerce, Attn: Order Preprocessing Section, 5285 Port Royal Road, Springfield, VA 22161–2171. Phone, 703–487–4600. If it is uncertain which Army activity published the publication, requests should be addressed to the Publishing Division, U.S. Army Publications and Printing Command, Room 1050, 2461 Eisenhower Avenue, Alexandria, VA 22331–0301. Phone, 202–325–6292.

Research Industry may obtain information on long-range research and development plans concerning future materiel requirements and objectives from the Commander, U.S. Army Materiel Command, Attn: AMCPA, 5001 Eisenhower Ave., Alexandria, VA 22333–0001.

Small Business Activities Aids to assist small businesses in obtaining defense procurement contracts are available through the Office of Small and Disadvantaged Business Utilization, Office of the Secretary of the Army, Room 2A712, The Pentagon, Washington, DC 20310–0106. Phone, 703–697–2868.

Speakers Civilian organizations desiring an Army speaker may contact a nearby Army installation or write or call the Community Relations Division, Office of the Chief of Public Affairs, Department of the Army, Washington, DC 20310–1508. Phone, 703–697–5081. Requests for Army Reserve speakers may be addressed to HQDA (DAAR–PA), Washington, DC 20310–2423, or the local Army Reserve Center. Organizations in the Washington, DC, area desiring chaplain speakers may contact the Chief of Chaplains, Department of the Army, Washington, DC 20310–2700. Phone, 703–601–1140. Information on speakers may be obtained by contacting the Public Affairs Office, Office of the Chief of Engineers, Washington, DC 20314, or the nearest Corps of Engineer Division or District Office.

Military Career and Training Opportunities

Information on all phases of Army enlistments and specialized training are available by writing the United States Army Recruiting Command, Fort Sheridan, IL 60037. Phone, 312–926–3322.

Army Health Professions For information concerning career opportunities in Army Health Professions, write to HQDA (SGPS–PD), Skyline No. 5, 5100 Leesburg Pike, Falls Church, VA 22041–3258. Phone, 703–681–8022.

Army ROTC The Army Reserve Officers' Training Corps is an educational program designed to develop college-educated officers for the Active Army, the Army National Guard, and the Army Reserve. For information, write or contact the Professor of Military Science at the nearest college or university offering the program, or the Army ROTC Regional Headquarters in your area.

Army National Guard For information concerning individual training opportunities in the National Guard, contact the Army National Guard, ARO–OAC–ME, Edgewood, MD 21010–5420. Phone, 301–671–4789.

Chaplains Corps For information concerning career opportunities as a chaplain, write to the Office, Chief of Chaplains, HQDA (DACH–PER), Washington, DC 20310–2700. Phone, 703–601–1172.

Commissioning Opportunities for Women All commissioning sources available to men are available to women.

Judge Advocate General's Corps For information concerning career opportunities as a lawyer, military and civilian, write to the Personnel, Plans, and Training Office, Office of the Judge Advocate General, Department of the Army, HQDA (DAJA–PT), Washington, DC 20310–2200. Phone, 703–695–1353.

Officer Candidate Schools Members of the Active Army and Reserve Components may attend the 14-week course at Fort Benning, GA.

United States Military Academy For information write to the Director of Admissions, United States Military Academy, West Point, NY 10996. Phone, 914–938–4041.

For further information concerning the Department of the Army, contact the Office of the Chief of Public Affairs, Headquarters, Department of the Army, Washington, DC 20310–1508. Phone, 703–697–5081. Internet, http://www.army.mil/.

DEPARTMENT OF THE NAVY

The Pentagon, Washington, DC 20350
Phone, 703–545–6700

SECRETARY OF THE NAVY	JOHN H. DALTON
Executive Assistant and Naval Aide	CAPT. L.W. CRENSHAW, USN
Military Assistant and Marine Corps Aide	COL. J.R. BATTAGLINI, USMC
Administrative Aide	COMDR. K.S. LIPPOLD, USN
Special Assistant for Public Affairs	CAPT. C.D. CONNOR, USN
Special Assistant for Legislation	COMDR. J.D. MCCARTHY, USN
Director, Office of Program Appraisal	VICE ADM. C.C. LAUTENBACHER, JR., USN
Deputy Director	(VACANCY)
Under Secretary of the Navy	JERRY M. HULTIN
Executive Assistant and Naval Aide	CAPT. KEVIN J. COSGRIFF, USN
Special Assistant and Marine Corps Aide	COL. J.J. PAXTON, USMC
Assistant for Administration	ROY L. CARTER
Director, Small and Disadvantaged Business Utilization	D.L. HATHAWAY
Director, Total Quality Leadership Office	LINDA DOHERTY
Auditor General of the Navy	RICHARD L. SHAFFER
Director, Naval Criminal Investigative Service	(VACANCY)
Chief of Information	REAR ADM. K. PEASE, USN
Deputy Chief of Information	CAPT. JAMES P. MITCHELL, USN
Chief of Legislative Affairs	REAR ADM. NORBERT R. RYAN, JR., USN
Deputy Chief of Legislative Affairs	CAPT. JAY M. COHEN, USN
General Counsel	STEVEN S. HONIGMAN
Executive Assistant and Special Counsel	BRYAN H. WOOD
Principal Deputy General Counsel	LEIGH A. BRADLEY
Deputy General Counsel	EUGENE P. ANGRIST
Associate General Counsel (Management)	FRED A. PHELPS
Associate General Counsel (Litigation)	ARTHUR H. HILDEBRANDT
Assistant General Counsel (Research, Development, and Acquisition)	SOPHIE A. KRASIK
Assistant General Counsel (Manpower and Reserve Affairs)	JOSEPH G. LYNCH
Assistant General Counsel (Installation and Environment)	C. JOHN TURNQUIST
Assistant General Counsel (Financial Management and Comptroller)	MARGARET A. OLSEN
Counsel, Commandant of the Marine Corps	PETER M. MURPHY
Counsel, Naval Air Systems Command	CHARLES J. MCMANUS
Counsel, Space and Naval Warfare Systems Command	TIMOTHY K. DOWD
Counsel, Naval Facilities Engineering Command	CHRISTINE C. MUTH
Counsel, Naval Sea Systems Command	WILLIAM P. MOLZAHN

Counsel, Naval Supply Systems Command	DIANE K. TOWNSEND
Counsel, Military Sealift Command	RICHARD S. HAYNES
Counsel, Office of the Chief of Naval Research	ELWARD L. SAUL
Naval Inspector General	(VACANCY)
Deputy Naval Inspector General	JILL VINES LOFTUS
Judge Advocate General of the Navy	REAR ADM. JOHN D. HUTSON, JAGC, USN
Deputy Judge Advocate General	REAR ADM. D.J. GUTER, JAGC, USN
Assistant Secretary of the Navy (Financial Management and Comptroller)	DEBORAH P. CHRISTIE
Principal Deputy	GLADYS J. COMMONS
Executive Assistant and Naval Aide	CAPT. MARK E. EASTON, USN
Special Assistant and Marine Corps Aide	MAJ. BEVERLY J. RUNOLFSON, USMC
Director, Office of Budget	REAR ADM. JAMES F. AMERAULT, USN
Director, Office of Financial Operations	A. ANTHONY TISONE
Assistant Secretary of the Navy (Manpower and Reserve Affairs)	BERNARD S. ROSTKER
Executive Assistant and Naval Aide	CAPT. STEWART BARNETT, USN
Military Assistant and Marine Corps Aide	COL. MARY LOWERY, USMC
Deputy Assistant Secretary (Manpower)	KAREN S. HEATH
Deputy Assistant Secretary (Reserve Affairs)	WADE R. SANDERS
Deputy Assistant Secretary (Personnel Programs)	CHARLES L. TOMPKINS
Deputy Assistant Secretary (Civilian Personnel/Equal Employment Opportunity)	BETTY S. WELCH
Director, Naval Council of Personnel Boards	CAPT. JACOB JOHNSON, USN
Deputy Director	(VACANCY)
Executive Director, Board for Correction of Naval Records	W. DEAN PFEIFFER
Deputy Executive Director	ROBERT D. ZSALMAN
Assistant Secretary of the Navy (Installations and Environment)	ROBERT B. PIRIE, JR.
Executive Assistant and Naval Aide	CAPT. DOROTHY E. SHOTT
Special Assistant and Marine Corps Aide	LT. COL. DONALD W. SAPP, USMC
Principal Deputy	DIANA H. JOSEPHSON
Deputy Assistant Secretary (Environment and Safety)	ELSIE L. MUNSELL
Deputy Assistant Secretary (Installation and Facilities)	DUNCAN HOLADAY
Deputy Assistant Secretary (Shore Resources)	RICHARD O. THOMAS
Deputy Assistant Secretary (Conversion and Redevelopment)	WILLIAM J. CASSIDY, JR.
Assistant Secretary of the Navy (Research, Development, and Acquisition)	JOHN W. DOUGLASS
Executive Assistant and Naval Aide	CAPT. JOSEPH CARNEVALE, USN
Special Assistant and Marine Corps Aide	COL. DAVID SADDLER, USMC
Principal Deputy	REAR ADM. M.P. SULLIVAN, USN
Deputy Assistant Secretary (Air Programs)	WILLIAM A. STUSSIE

Deputy Assistant Secretary (Command, Control, Communications, Computers, and Intelligence)	MARVIN LANGSTON
Deputy Assistant Secretary (Expeditionary Forces Programs)	BRIG. GEN. MICHAEL A. HOUGH, USMC
Deputy Assistant Secretary (Mines and Undersea Warfare Programs)	(VACANCY)
Deputy Assistant Secretary (Planning, Programming, and Resources)	WILLIAM J. SCHAEFER, JR.
Deputy Assistant Secretary (Ships)	MICHAEL C. HAMMES
Deputy for Acquisition and Business Management/Competition Advocate General	CAPT. RICHARD GINMAN, USN
Director, Acquisition Career Management	W.H. HAUENSTEIN
Acquisition Reform Executive	DANIEL E. PORTER
Chief of Naval Research	REAR ADM. PAUL G. GAFFNEY II, USN
Executive Assistant	COMDR. MARK TOMB, USN
Program Executive Officers/Direct Reporting Program Managers	REAR ADM. J.A. COOK, USN; J. DESALME, JR.; TIM DOUGLASS; COL. J.M. FEIGLEY, USMC; REAR ADM. R.E. FRICK, USN; CAPT. JOSEPH HADDOCK, USN; REAR ADM. G.A. HUCHTING, USN; REAR ADM. HERBERT C. KALER, USN; REAR ADM. G.P. NANOS, JR., USN; REAR ADM. R.P. REMPT, USN; REAR ADM. DAVID P. SARGENT, JR., USN; REAR ADM. C.E. STEIDLE, USN; REAR ADM. B.D. STRONG, USN

U.S. Navy

Chief of Naval Operations	ADM. J.L. JOHNSON, USN
Vice Chief of Naval Operations	ADM. D.L. TILLING, USN
Deputy Chief, Manpower and Personnel	VICE ADM. D.T. OLIVER, USN
Director of Naval Intelligence	REAR ADM. L.E. JACOBY, USN
Deputy Chief, Logistics	VICE ADM. W.J. HANCOCK, USN
Deputy Chief, Plans, Policy and Operations	REAR ADM. W.F. DORAN, USN
Director of Space and Information Warfare	VICE ADM. T.B. FARGO, USN
Director of Naval Training	VICE ADM. P.A. TRACEY, USN
Deputy Chief, Resources, Warfare Requirements and Assessments	VICE ADM. C.C. LAUTENBACHER, USN
Director of Navy Staff	REAR ADM. A.N. LANGSTON III, USN
Director of Naval Nuclear Propulsion Program	ADM. F.L. BOWMAN, USN
Director of Test and Evaluation and Technology Requirements	REAR ADM. R.A. RIDDELL, USN
Surgeon General of the Navy	VICE ADM. H.M. KOENIG, MC, USN
Director of Naval Reserve	REAR ADM. G.D. VAUGHAN, USN
Oceanographer of the Navy	REAR ADM. P.E. TOBIN, JR., USN
Chief of Chaplains of the Navy/Director of Religious Ministries	REAR ADM. A.B. HOLDERBY, JR., CHC, USN

Special Assistant for Public Affairs Support	REAR ADM. K. PEASE, USN
Special Assistant for Safety Matters	REAR ADM. R.E. BESAL, USN
Special Assistant for Inspection Support	VICE ADM. J.R. FITZGERALD, USN
Special Assistant for Legal Services	REAR ADM. J.D. HUTSON, JAGC, USN
Special Assistant for Legislative Support	REAR ADM. N.R. RYAN, USN
Special Assistant for Naval Investigative Matters and Security	R.O. NEDROW
Special Assistant for Material Inspections and Surveys	REAR ADM. H.F. HERRERA, USN

Major Shore Commands:

Director, Strategic Systems Program	REAR ADM. G.P. NANOS, JR., USN
Commander, Naval Air Systems Command	VICE ADM. J.A. LOCKARD, USN
Commander, Space and Naval Warfare Systems Command	REAR ADM. G.F.A. WAGNER, USN
Commander, Naval Facilities Engineering Command	REAR ADM. D.J. NASH, CEC, USN
Commander, Naval Sea Systems Command	VICE ADM. G.R. STERNER, USN
Commander, Naval Supply Systems Command	REAR ADM. D.E. HICKMAN, SC, USN
Chief, Bureau of Medicine and Surgery	VICE ADM. H.M. KOENIG, MC, USN
Chief of Naval Personnel	VICE ADM. D.T. OLIVER, USN
Commander, Naval Meteorology and Oceanography Command	REAR ADM. K.E. BARBOR, USN
Commander, Naval Computer and Telecommunications Command	CAPT. M.P. FINN, USN
Director, Office of Naval Intelligence	REAR ADM. L.E. JACOBY, USN
Commander, Naval Security Group Command	REAR ADM. T.F. STEVENS, USN
Chief of Naval Education and Training	VICE ADM. P.A. TRACEY, USN
Commander, Naval Legal Service Command	REAR ADM. D.J. GUTER, JAGC, USN
Commander, Naval Doctrine Command	REAR ADM. M.L. BOWMAN, USN
Commander, Naval Space Command	REAR ADM. P.D. MONEYMAKER, USN

Major Fleet Commands:

Commander in Chief, U.S. Atlantic Fleet	ADM. J.P. REASON, USN
Commander in Chief, U.S. Pacific Fleet	ADM. A.R. CLEMINS, USN
Commander in Chief, U.S. Naval Forces Europe	ADM. T.J. LOPEZ, USN
Commander, Military Sealift Command	VICE ADM. J.B. PERKINS III, USN
Commander, U.S. Naval Forces Central Command	VICE ADM. T.B. FARGO, USN
Commander, Naval Special Warfare Command	REAR ADM. T.R. RICHARDS, USN
Commander, Naval Reserve Force	REAR ADM. G.D. VAUGHN, USN
Commander, Operational Test and Evaluation Force	REAR ADM. S.H. BAKER, USN

U.S. Marine Corps

Commandant of the Marine Corps	GEN. C.C. KRULAK, USMC
Military Secretary to the Commandant	COL. R.E. APPLETON, USMC
Aide-de-Camp	MAJ. K. FOSS, USMC
Assistant Commandant of the Marine Corps	GEN. R.I. NEAL, USMC
Aide-de-Camp	MAJ. J. HOFFMAN, USMC
Sergeant Major of the Marine Corps	SGT. MAJ. L.G. LEE, USMC

Director, Marine Corps Staff	MAJ. GEN. L.M. PALM, USMC
Secretary of the General Staff	COL. P.F. SHUTLER, USMC
Director, Special Projects Directorate	COL. R.M. BACHILLER, USMC
Counsel for the Commandant	PETER M. MURPHY
Deputy Chief of Staff for Plans, Policies, and Operations	LT. GEN. M.R. STEELE, USMC
Director, Operations Division	BRIG. GEN. M.E. BRODERICK, USMC
Director, Plans Division	BRIG. GEN. W.C. GREGSON, JR., USMC
Deputy Chief of Staff for Aviation	LT. GEN. T.R. DAKE, USMC
Assistant Deputy Chief of Staff for Aviation and Director, Aviation Plans, Policy, and Requirements Division	BRIG. GEN. B. BYRUM, USMC
Deputy Chief of Staff for Manpower and Reserve Affairs	LT. GEN. C.A. MUTTER, USMC
Assistant Deputy Chief of Staff for Manpower and Reserve Affairs	D.S. HOWELL
Director, Reserve Affairs Division	BRIG. GEN. D.M. MIZE, USMC
Director, Personnel Management Division	BRIG. GEN. R.M. FLANAGAN, USMC
Director, Manpower Plans and Policy Division	BRIG. GEN. G.S. NEWBOLD, USMC
Director, Morale, Welfare, and Recreation Support Activity	(VACANCY)
Director, Human Resources Division	COL. K.W. HILLMAN, USMC
Deputy Chief of Staff for Installations and Logistics	MAJ. GEN. J.D. STEWART, USMC
Director, Facilities and Services Division	(VACANCY)
Director, Contracts Division	P.E. ZANFAGNA
Director, Logistics Plans, Policies, and Strategic Mobility Division	BRIG. GEN. P.M. LEE, USMC
Director, Programs and Financial Management Division	SUSAN E. FOX
Deputy Chief of Staff for Programs and Resources	LT. GEN. J.W. OSTER, USMC
Director, Programs Division	MAJ. GEN. T.A. BRAATEN, USMC
Director, Fiscal Division	H.L. DIXSON
Assistant Chief of Staff for Command, Control, Communications, Computers, and Intelligence	MAJ. GEN. J.T. ANDERSON, USMC
Deputy Assistant Chief of Staff	M.H. DECKER
Director of Intelligence	COL. B.A. HARDER, USMC
Legislative Assistant to the Commandant	BRIG. GEN. R.L. WEST, USMC
Director of Public Affairs	BRIG. GEN. C.L. STANLEY, USMC
Staff Judge Advocate to the Commandant of the Marine Corps	BRIG. GEN. T.G. HESS, USMC
Director of Administration and Resource Management	L.J. KELLY
Director of Marine Corps History and Museums	COL. M.F. MONIGAN, USMC
President, Permanent Marine Corps Uniform Board	BRIG. GEN. R.R. BLACKMON, JR., USMC
The Medical Officer, U.S. Marine Corps	CAPT. A. DIAZ, JR., USN
The Dental Officer, U.S. Marine Corps	CAPT. L.G. HERMAN, USN
The Chaplain, U.S. Marine Corps	CAPT. G.W. PUCCIARELLI, USN

Commanding General, Marine Corps Recruiting Command	MAJ. GEN. J.W. KLIMP, USMC
Commanding General, Marine Corps Combat Development Command	LT. GEN. J.E. RHODES, USMC
Commander, Marine Corps Systems Command	MAJ. GEN. M.J. WILLIAMS, USMC
Commanding General, Marine Corps Base, Quantico	BRIG. GEN. F.C. WILSON, USMC

[For the Department of the Navy statement of organization, see the *Code of Federal Regulations,* Title 32, Part 700]

The primary mission of the Department of the Navy is to protect the United States, as directed by the President or the Secretary of Defense, by the effective prosecution of war at sea including, with its Marine Corps component, the seizure or defense of advanced naval bases; to support, as required, the forces of all military departments of the United States; and to maintain freedom of the seas.

The United States Navy was founded on October 13, 1775, when Congress enacted the first legislation creating the Continental Navy of the American Revolution. The Department of the Navy and the Office of Secretary of the Navy were established by act of April 30, 1798 (10 U.S.C. 5011, 5031). For 9 years prior to that date, by act of August 7, 1789 (1 Stat. 49), the conduct of naval affairs was under the Secretary of War.

The National Security Act Amendments of 1949 provided that the Department of the Navy be a military department within the Department of Defense (63 Stat. 578).

The Secretary of the Navy is appointed by the President as the head of the Department of the Navy and is responsible to the Secretary of Defense for the operation and efficiency of the Navy (10 U.S.C. 5031).

The organization of the Department of the Navy is reflected in the organization chart and personnel listing. The Department of the Navy includes the U.S. Coast Guard when it is operating as a Service in the Navy.

Office of the Secretary of the Navy

Secretary of the Navy

The Secretary of the Navy is the head of the Department of the Navy, responsible for the policies and control of the Department of the Navy, including its organization, administration, functioning, and efficiency. The members of the Secretary's executive administration assist in the discharge of the responsibilities of the Secretary of the Navy.

During the temporary absence of the Secretary of the Navy, the Under Secretary of the Navy is next in succession to act as the Secretary of the Navy. The Under Secretary functions as deputy and principal assistant to the Secretary, and acts with full authority of the Secretary in the general management of the Department.

Civilian Executive Assistants

The Civilian Executive Assistants to the Secretary of the Navy are the Under Secretary of the Navy, the Assistant Secretaries of the Navy, and the General Counsel of the Navy. It is the policy of the Secretary to assign departmentwide responsibilities essential to the efficient administration of the Department of the Navy to the Civilian Executive Assistants.

Each Civilian Executive Assistant, within an assigned area of responsibility, is the principal adviser and assistant to the Secretary on the administration of the affairs of the Department of the Navy. The Civilian Executive Assistants

DEPARTMENT OF THE NAVY

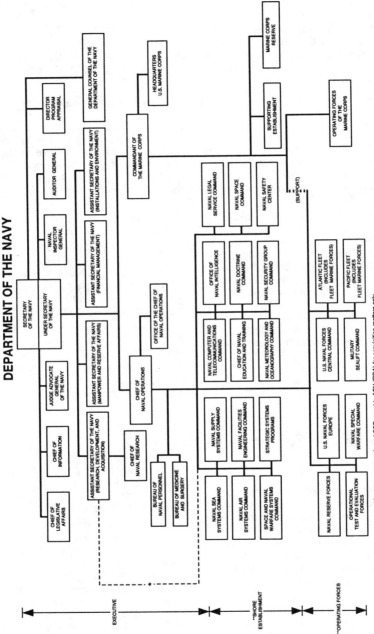

*Systems commands and SSP report to ASN (RDA) for acquisition matters only.
**Also includes other Echelon 2 commands and subordinate activities under the command or supervision of the designated organizations.

carry out their duties in harmony with the statutory positions of the Chief of Naval Operations, who is the principal military adviser and executive to the Secretary regarding naval matters, and the Commandant of the Marine Corps, who is the principal military adviser and executive regarding Marine Corps matters. Each Civilian Executive Assistant is authorized and directed to act for the Secretary within his or her assigned area of responsibility.

The Staff Assistants

The Staff Assistants to the Secretary of the Navy are the Judge Advocate General of the Navy, the Chief of Naval Research, the Chief of Legislative Affairs, the Director, Office of Program Appraisal, the Naval Inspector General, the Auditor General of the Navy, the Chief of Information, and the heads of such other offices and boards established by law or by the Secretary for the purpose of assisting the Secretary or one or more of the Civilian Executive Assistants in the administration of the Department of the Navy.

Judge Advocate General The Judge Advocate General is the senior officer and head of the Judge Advocate General's Corps, and the Office of the Judge Advocate General. The Judge Advocate General provides or supervises the provision of all legal advice and related services throughout the Department of the Navy, except for the advice and services provided by the General Counsel. He also performs functions required or authorized by law; provides legal and policy advice to the Secretary of the Navy on military justice, ethics, administrative law, claims, environmental law, operational and international law and treaty interpretation, and litigation involving these issues; and acts on other matters as directed by the Secretary.

The Judge Advocate General also supervises the administration of military justice throughout the Department of the Navy, performs functions required or authorized by the Uniform Code of Military Justice, and provides technical supervision for the Naval Justice School at Newport, RI.

The Judge Advocate General maintains a close working relationship with the General Counsel on all matters of common interest.

For further information, contact the Public Affairs Officer, Office of the Judge Advocate General, Department of the Navy, 200 Stovall Street, Alexandria, VA 22332–2400. Phone, 703–614–7420.

Chief of Naval Research The Chief of Naval Research commands the Office of the Chief of Naval Research, the Office of Naval Research, the Office of Naval Technology, and assigned shore activities. The Office of Naval Research performs such duties as the Secretary of the Navy prescribes relating to the encouragement, promotion, planning, initiation, and coordination of naval research; the conduct of naval research in augmentation of and in conjunction with the research and development conducted by other agencies and offices of the Department of the Navy; and the supervision, administration, and control of activities within or for the Department of the Navy relating to patents, inventions, trademarks, copyrights and royalty payments, and matters connected therewith.

For further information, contact the Public Affairs Office, Office of Naval Research, Ballston Tower One, 800 North Quincy Street, Arlington, VA 22217–5660. Phone, 703–696–5031. Fax, 703–696–5940.

Chief of Legislative Affairs The Chief of Legislative Affairs plans, develops, and coordinates relationships between the Department of the Navy and members of congressional committees and their staffs which are necessary in the transaction of official Government business (except appropriations matters) affecting the Department of the Navy; and furnishes staff support, advice, and assistance to the Secretary of the Navy, the Chief of Naval Operations, the Commandant of the Marine Corps, and all other principal civilian and military officials of the Department of the Navy concerning congressional aspects of the

Department's policies, plans, and programs.

For further information, contact the Public Affairs Office, Office of Legislative Affairs, Department of the Navy, Pentagon, Washington, DC 20350–1300. Phone, 703–695–0395. Fax, 703–697–0353.

Office of Program Appraisal The Director, Office of Program Appraisal, directs the Office of Program Appraisal which assists the Secretary of the Navy in assuring that existing and proposed Navy and Marine Corps programs provide the optimum means of achieving the objectives of the Department of the Navy.

For further information, contact the Office of Program Appraisal, Department of the Navy, Pentagon, Washington, DC 20350–1400. Phone, 703–697–9396.

Naval Inspector General The Naval Inspector General inspects, investigates, or inquires into any and all matters of importance to the Department of the Navy, with particular emphasis on readiness, including but not limited to effectiveness, efficiency, economy, and integrity; exercises broad supervision, general guidance, and coordination for all Department of the Navy inspection, evaluation, and appraisal organizations; identifies areas of weakness in the Department relating to matters of integrity and efficiency and provides appropriate recommendations for improvement; receives allegations of inefficiency, misconduct, impropriety, mismanagement, or violations of law and investigates or refers for investigation, as appropriate; and serves as principal adviser to the Secretary of the Navy, the Chief of Naval Operations, and the Commandant of the Marine Corps on all inspection and investigation matters.

In addition, the Naval Inspector General provides an alternative to the normal chain of command for receipt of complaints of personnel; serves as the official to whom employees may complain without fear of reprisal; provides oversight of intelligence and special activities; cooperates with the Inspector General, Department of Defense; serves as the Department of the Navy coordinator for fraud, waste, and

efficiency matters; serves as program management and focal point for the Department of the Navy Hotline programs; and investigates fraud or corruption relating to procurement activities affecting the Department of the Navy.

For further information, contact the Office of the Navy Inspector General, Building 200, Washington Navy Yard, Washington, DC 20375. Phone, 202–433–2000.

Auditor General of the Navy The Auditor General of the Navy serves as Director of the Naval Audit Service and develops and implements Navy internal audit policies, programs, and procedures. The Auditor General can provide information and may provide assistance and support to the Chief of Naval Operations and the Commandant of the Marine Corps to enable them to discharge their duties and responsibilities.

For further information, contact the Office of the Auditor General, 5611 Columbia Pike, Falls Church, VA 22041–5080. Phone, 703–681–9120.

Chief of Information The Chief of Information is the direct representative of the Secretary of the Navy in all public affairs and internal relations matters. The Chief of Information is authorized to implement Navy public affairs and internal relations policies and to coordinate those Navy and Marine Corps activities of mutual interest.

For further information, contact the Office of the Chief of Naval Information, 1200 Navy Pentagon, Room 2D332, Washington, DC 20350–1200. Phone, 703–695–0965.

Naval Criminal Investigative Service The Director, Naval Criminal Investigative Service, commands a worldwide organization with representation in more than 160 geographic locations to provide criminal investigative, counterintelligence, law enforcement and physical security, and information and personnel security support to the Navy and Marine Corps, both ashore and afloat. The Naval Criminal Investigative Service is comprised of law enforcement professionals who are investigators, crime laboratory technicians, technical investigative specialists, security specialists, and administrative support personnel.

For further information, contact the Director, Naval Criminal Investigative Service, Department of the Navy, Washington, DC 20388–5000. Phone, 202–433–8800; or contact the Operations Control Center/Headquarters Duty Officer at 202–433–9323.

Personnel Boards   The Naval Council of Personnel Boards, comprised of the Naval Discharge Review Board, Naval Complaints Review Board, Naval Clemency and Parole Board, and the Physical Evaluation Board administers, under the Assistant Secretary of the Navy (Manpower and Reserve Affairs), personnel services and support as indicated by each component board's title.

The Naval Discharge Review Board reviews, pursuant to 10 U.S.C. 1553, upon its own motion or upon request by or on behalf of former Navy and Marine Corps members, the type and reason for discharge or dismissal received by that former member, except a discharge or dismissal by reason of the sentence of general court-martial. It determines whether, under reasonable standards of naval law and discipline, a discharge or dismissal should be changed and, if so, what change should be made.

The Naval Complaints Review Board reviews, upon request, decisional documents and/or index entries created by the Naval Discharge Review Board after April 1, 1977. The Naval Complaints Review Board determines whether decisional documents conform to those applicable regulations of the Department of Defense and the Department of the Navy.

The Naval Clemency and Parole Board reviews, pursuant to 10 U.S.C. 953–954, Navy and Marine Corps court-martial cases referred to it and grants or denies clemency; and, pursuant to 10 U.S.C. 952, reviews and directs that parole be granted or denied in cases referred to it for review.

The Physical Evaluation Board organizes and administers disability evaluations within the Department of the Navy, pursuant to 10 U.S.C., chapter 61, and other applicable provisions of law and regulation. It is comprised of the Record Review Panel, regional hearing panels at Bethesda, MD, and San Diego, CA, and disability evaluation system counselors located at major medical centers. The system considers evidence concerning disabilities of personnel and determines the appropriate disposition in each case.

For further information, contact the Naval Council of Personnel Boards, Department of the Navy, Room 905, 801 North Randolph Street, Arlington, VA 22203. Phone, 703–696–4356.

Naval Records   The Board for Correction of Naval Records is a statutory civilian board established, pursuant to the provisions of 10 U.S.C. 1552, to relieve the Congress of the burden and necessity of considering private relief legislation for the correction of errors and injustices suffered by members and former members of the Navy and Marine Corps. The Secretary of the Navy, acting through this board of civilians of the executive part of the Department, is authorized to take action consistent with law and regulation to correct naval or military records of the Department of the Navy where such action is necessary or appropriate to correct an error or to remove an injustice. The Board represents the highest echelon of review of administrative errors and injustices. The Board reviews, on application, actions taken by various boards and officials in the Department.

For further information, contact the Board for Correction of Naval Records, Department of the Navy, Room 2432, Navy Annex, Washington, DC 20370–5100. Phone, 703–614–1402.

United States Navy

Chief of Naval Operations

In the performance of his duties within the Department of the Navy, the Chief of Naval Operations (CNO) takes precedence above all other officers of the naval service. He is the Navy member of the Joint Chiefs of Staff.

The Chief of Naval Operations, under the Secretary of the Navy, exercises command over certain central executive organizations, assigned shore activities, and the Operating Forces of the Navy.

The Chief of Naval Operations plans for and provides the manpower, material, weapons, facilities, and services to support the needs of the Navy, with the exception of the Fleet Marine Forces; maintains water transportation services, including sea transportation services for the Department of Defense; directs the Naval Reserve; and exercises authority for matters of naval administration, including matters related to customs and traditions of the naval service, security, intelligence, discipline, naval communications, and naval operations.

The Chief of Naval Operations exercises area coordination authority over all shore activities of the Department of the Navy to ensure that total efforts afford adequate support to the combatant forces and are coordinated among themselves to assure economy and efficiency of operation.

Operating Forces of the Navy

The Operating Forces of the Navy are responsible for naval operations necessary to carry out the Department of the Navy's role in upholding and advancing the national policies and interests of the United States. The Operating Forces of the Navy include the several fleets, seagoing forces, Fleet Marine Forces and other assigned Marine Corps forces, the Military Sealift Command, Naval Reserve forces, and other forces and activities as may be assigned by the President or the Secretary of the Navy. The Chief of Naval Operations is responsible for the command and administration of the Operating Forces of the Navy.

The Pacific Fleet is composed of ships, submarines, and aircraft operating throughout the Pacific and Indian Oceans.

The Atlantic Fleet is composed of ships, submarines, and aircraft that operate throughout the Atlantic Ocean and Mediterranean Sea.

The Naval Forces, Europe, includes forces assigned by the Chief of Naval Operations or made available from either the Pacific or Atlantic Fleet to operate in the European theater.

The Military Sealift Command provides ocean transportation (by Government-owned or commercial vessels) for personnel and cargo of all components of the Department of Defense and as authorized for other Federal agencies; operates and maintains underway replenishment ships and other vessels providing mobile logistic support to elements of the combatant fleets; and operates ships in support of scientific projects and other programs for Federal agencies.

Other major commands of the Operating Forces of the Navy are the Commander, U.S. Naval Forces Central Command; Commander, Operational Test and Evaluation Force; Commander, Naval Special Warfare Command; and Commander, Naval Reserve Force.

Navy Command Structure

The Chief of Naval Operations manages and supports the Operating Forces of the Navy through the following executive and functional organization structure.

Chief of Naval Operations   The Office of the Chief of Naval Operations is the headquarters of the Navy which advises and assists the Secretary, the Under Secretary, the Assistant Secretaries, and the Chief of Naval Operations in the discharge of their responsibilities. The Office of the Chief of Naval Operations was established basically in its present structure by Executive Order 9635 of September 29, 1945, and later by act of March 5, 1948 (10 U.S.C. 141, 171,

5036(b), 5081–5088); and by act of October 1, 1986 (10 U.S.C. 111 note).

Sea Systems The Commander, Naval Sea Systems Command, provides material support to the Navy and Marine Corps, and for mobilization purposes to the Department of Defense and Department of Transportation, for ships, submarines, and other sea platforms, shipboard combat systems and components, other surface and undersea warfare and weapons systems, and ordnance expendables not specifically assigned to other system commands.

For further information, contact the Commander, Naval Sea Systems Command, Washington, DC 20362–5101. Phone, 703–602–3328.

Air Systems The Commander, Naval Air Systems Command, provides for the material support to the Navy and Marine Corps for aircraft, airborne weapon systems, avionics, related photographic and support equipment, ranges, and targets.

For further information, contact the Commander, Naval Air Systems Command, Naval Air Warfare Center, Patuxent River, MD 20570. Phone, 301–342–3282.

Space and Naval Warfare Systems The Commander, Space and Naval Warfare Systems Command, provides technical and material support to the Department of the Navy for space systems; command, control, communications, and intelligence systems; and electronic warfare and undersea surveillance.

For further information, contact the Commander, Space and Naval Warfare Systems Command, 4301 Pacific Highway, San Diego, CA 92110. Phone, 619–524–7059.

Supply Systems The Commander, Naval Supply Systems Command, provides for the material support to the Navy and Marine Corps for materials, supplies, and supporting services by providing supply management policies and methods and administering related support service systems.

For further information, contact the Commander, Naval Supply Systems Command, 5450 Carlisle Pike, Mechanicsburg, PA 17055–0791. Phone, 717–790–6906.

Naval Facilities The Commander, Naval Facilities Engineering Command, provides for material and technical support to the Navy and Marine Corps for shore facilities, real property and utilities, fixed ocean systems and structures, transportation and construction equipment, energy, environmental and natural resources management, and support of the Naval Construction Forces.

For further information, contact the Commander, Naval Facilities Engineering Command, 200 Stovall Street, Alexandria, VA 22332–2300. Phone, 703–325–0589.

Strategic Systems The Director, Strategic Systems Programs, provides for the development, production, and material support to the Navy for fleet ballistic missile and strategic weapon systems, including the missiles, platforms, and associated equipment; security, training of personnel, and the installation and direction of necessary supporting facilities.

For further information, contact the Director, Strategic Systems Programs, Department of the Navy, 1931 Jefferson Davis Highway, Arlington, VA 22202–3518. Phone, 703–607–2715.

Naval Personnel The Chief of Naval Personnel directs the procurement, distribution, administration, and career motivation of the military personnel of the regular and reserve components of the United States Navy to meet the quantitative and qualitative manpower requirements determined by the Chief of Naval Operations. He also directs the management and administration of the Navy Civilian Personnel/Equal Employment Opportunity Programs and develops servicewide programs for improved human resources management.

For further information, contact the Bureau of Naval Personnel, Department of the Navy, Federal Office Building No. 2, Washington, DC 20370–5000. Phone, 703–614–1271.

Naval Medicine The Chief, Bureau of Medicine and Surgery:

—directs the provision of medical and dental services for Navy and Marine Corps personnel and other persons authorized by law;

—ensures that health care program policies are optimally executed through the acquisition and effective utilization of financial and manpower resources;

—maintains all assigned activities in a proper state of material and personnel readiness to fulfill assigned peacetime and contingency mission taskings;

—administers the execution and implementation of contingency support plans and programs that provide for an effective medical and dental readiness capability;

—acquires, trains, and maintains a force of professional and technical personnel;

—provides professional and technical medical and dental service to the Fleet, Fleet Marine Force, and shore activities of the Navy;

—ensures that assigned activities are able to achieve successful accreditation and recognition by appropriate governmental and civilian agencies and commissions; and

—ensures cooperation with civil authorities in matters pertaining to public health disasters and other emergencies, in conjunction with maintaining and safeguarding the health of Navy and Marine Corps personnel.

For further information, contact the Bureau of Medicine and Surgery, Department of the Navy, Twenty-third and E Streets NW., Washington, DC 20372–5120. Phone, 202–762–3701.

Oceanography The Commander, Naval Meteorology and Oceanography Command, and the Superintendent, U.S. Naval Observatory, are responsible for the science, technology, engineering, operations, and those personnel and facilities associated with each, which are essential to explore the ocean and the atmosphere and to provide astronomical data and time for naval and related national objectives. Oceanography examines how naval operations are influenced by the physical environment and applies its findings to the development of technology and methods for improving naval operations.

The Naval Oceanographic Program embraces five major disciplines of physical science to investigate the nature and behavior of the ocean environment in which the Navy operates. They are:

Hydrography—to collect data for the charting of the oceans and to establish geodetic references for navigation;

Oceanography—to define the characteristics of the water volume for use in ocean reporting and prediction, and studies of underwater acoustics, water dynamics, corrosion, and other factors influencing the performance of naval systems;

Meteorology—to define the characteristics of the atmosphere for use in weather reporting and prediction, and studies of upper atmosphere winds and currents, refractive indices for radar performance, and similar factors;

Astrometry—to determine the position and motions of celestial bodies required for accurate navigation, operational support, and use in calculating precise geodetic positions and azimuth references on Earth; and

Precise Time—to determine, provide, and manage the distribution of precise time and time interval (frequency), both atomic and astronomical, for use in electronic navigation and command, control, and communications.

For further information, contact the following offices: Oceanographer of the Navy, U.S. Naval Observatory, Washington, DC 20392–1800. Phone, 202–762–1026. Commander, Naval Meteorology and Oceanography Command, Stennis Space Center, MS 39529–5005. Phone, 601–688–4726. Superintendent, Naval Observatory, Washington, DC 20392–5100. Phone, 202–653–1541.

Computers and Telecommunications The Commander, Naval Computer and Telecommunications Command, performs functions to provide, operate, and maintain all Navy ashore communications resources and all non-tactical information and resources for command, control, and administration of the Navy and those elements of the Defense Communications System assigned to the Navy.

For further information, contact the Commander, Naval Computer and Telecommunications Command, 4401 Massachusetts Avenue NW., Washington, DC 20390–5290. Phone, 202–685–1085.

Cryptology The Commander, Naval Security Group Command, performs cryptologic functions; provides, operates, and maintains an adequate Naval

Security Group; approves requirements for the use of existing Naval Security Group capabilities and resources; and coordinates the execution of approved cryptologic programs.

For further information, contact the Commander, Naval Security Group Command, 3801 Nebraska Avenue NW., Washington, DC 20393–5210. Phone, 301–617–3650.

Intelligence   The Director, Office of Naval Intelligence, ensures the fulfillment of the intelligence requirements and responsibilities of the Department of the Navy.

For further information, contact the Director, Office of Naval Intelligence, Department of the Navy, 4600 Silver Hill Road, Washington, DC 20389–5000. Phone, 202–763–3552; or 301–763–3557 (hotline).

Education and Training   The mission of the Chief of Naval Education and Training is to:
—provide assigned shore-based education and training for Navy, certain Marine Corps, and other personnel in support of the Fleet, Naval Shore Establishment, Naval Reserve, Interservice Training Program, and Security Assistance Program;
—develop specifically designated education and training afloat programs for the Fleet;
—execute the Navy's responsibility for voluntary education and dependents education;

—participate with research and development activities in the development and implementation of the most effective teaching and training systems and devices for optimal education and training; and
—perform such other functions as directed.

For further information, contact the Chief of Naval Education and Training, Naval Air Station, Department of the Navy, Pensacola, FL 32508–5100. Phone, 904–452–4858.

Naval Doctrine Command   The Commander, Naval Doctrine Command, is the primary authority for the development of naval concepts and integrated naval doctrine and is charged to:
—serve as coordinating authority for the development and evaluation of Navy service-specific doctrine;
—provide a coordinated Navy/Marine Corps naval voice in joint and combined doctrine development; and
—ensure that Navy, naval, and joint doctrine are addressed in training and education curricula and in operations, exercises, and wargames.

For further information, contact the Commander, Naval Doctrine Command, Suite 200, 8952 First Street, Norfolk, VA 23511–3790. Phone, 804–445–0555.

United States Marine Corps

Commandant of the Marine Corps,
Headquarters, U.S. Marine Corps, Washington, DC 20380–0001
Phone, 703–614–2344. Internet, http://www.usmc.mil/.

The United States Marine Corps was established on November 10, 1775, by resolution of the Continental Congress. Marine Corps composition and functions are detailed in 10 U.S.C. 5063.
The Marine Corps, which is part of the Department of the Navy, is the smallest of the Nation's combat forces and is the only service specifically tasked by Congress to be able to fight in the air, on land, and at sea. Although marines fight in each of these dimensions, they are

primarily a maritime force, inextricably linked with the Navy to move from the sea to fight on land.
For most of the country's history, integrated Navy-Marine Corps expeditionary forces have been routinely forward deployed around the world. The Marine Corps is tasked by law to be "the most ready when the Nation is least ready." All marines, regardless of speciality, are fundamentally the same, forged from a common experience in

boot camp or officer training, sharing a common set of values, and trained as a cohesive air-ground team from the moment they join the Marine Corps.

The Marine Corps conducts entry-level training for its enlisted marines at two bases, Marine Corps Recruit Depot, Parris Island, SC, and Marine Corps Recruit Depot, San Diego, CA. Officer candidates are evaluated at Officer Candidate School at Marine Corps Combat Development Command, Quantico, VA.

The Marine Corps has a global perspective which is not focused on any particular threat. While the primary responsibility for winning wars lies with the Army, Navy, and Air Force, the Marine Corps wins battles, ever ready to respond to international "brush fires." Marines train to be first on the scene to respond to attacks on the United States or its interests, acts of political violence against Americans abroad, disaster relief, humanitarian assistance, or evacuation of Americans from foreign countries. Operating from Navy ships afloat, the Navy-Marine team provides a unique range of options for the country's leadership. At sea, these units can operate from a protected sea base, unencumbered by political constraints often encountered by U.S. forces based in foreign countries.

At the very basic level, the Marine Corps uses a system of ranks similar to that of the U.S. Army. Ground units are organized into squads, platoons, battalions, regiments, divisions, etc., also similar to the Army. Marine aviation units are organized into squadrons, groups, and wings, similar to the Air Force and Navy. However, the size, number, and composition of Marine Corps ground and aviation units differ from the other services. Expanding on this basic organizational framework, the Marine Corps employs a versatile and flexible organizational approach by task organizing its units for deployments and contingencies. These are called Marine Air Ground Task Forces (MAGTF's), which can emphasize whatever capability is required to accomplish the mission. Regardless of size, all MAGTF's share four common elements, which vary in size and composition according to the mission: Command Element, Ground Combat Element, Aviation Combat Element, and Combat Service Support Element. MAGTF's are organized, trained, and equipped to conduct operations across three dimensions: air, land, and sea. Through a combination of strategic basing and prepositioning of equipment, global forward operations, and an ability to rapidly deploy by air and sea, MAGTF's provide a building block approach to deploying Marine Corps combat power.

The Marine Corps also has other marines and units that provide specialized support and capabilities. Marine Security Guards provide security at each U.S. Embassy around the world. The Marine Corps Security Force Battalion, headquartered in Norfolk, VA, provides mobile training teams to support antiterrorism training at naval installations and maintains Fleet Antiterrorist Security Teams for deployment as directed by the Chief of Naval Operations. With the advent of the chemical and biological weapons threat, the Marine Corps has created the Chemical Biological Incident Response Force, based at Camp Lejeune, NC, to respond on short notice to chemical or biological incidents worldwide.

Marine Corps Districts

District	Address
1st	605 Stewart Ave., Garden City, NY 11530–4761
4th	Bldg. 54, Suite 3, New Cumberland, PA 17072–0806
6th	Marine Corps Recruit Depot, P.O. Box 19201, Parris Island, SC 29905–9201
8th	Bldg. 10, Naval Support Activity, New Orleans, LA 70142
9th	3805 E. 155th St., Kansas City, MO 64147–1309
12th	3704 Hochmuth Ave., San Diego, CA 92140–5191

For further information, contact the Division of Public Affairs, Headquarters, U.S. Marine Corps, 2 Navy Annex, Washington, DC 20380–1775. Phone, 703–614–1034. Internet, http://www.usmc.mil/.

United States Naval Academy

Annapolis, MD 21402–5018
Phone, 800–638–9156 (Office of the Dean of Admissions—Candidate Guidance)

The United States Naval Academy is the undergraduate college of the naval service. Through its comprehensive 4-year program, which stresses excellence in academics, physical education, professional training, conduct, and honor, the Academy prepares young men and women morally, mentally, and physically to be professional officers in the Navy and Marine Corps. All graduates receive a bachelor of science degree in 1 of 18 majors.

For further information concerning the United States Naval Academy, contact the Superintendent, United States Naval Academy, Annapolis, MD 21402–5018.

Sources of Information

Astronomy   The United States Naval Observatory provides the astronomical data and precise time required by the Navy and other components of the Department of Defense for navigation, precise positioning, and command, control, and communications. These data also are made available to other Government agencies and to the general public. To broaden the understanding of the mission, functions, and programs of the Naval Observatory, regular night tours and special group day tours are conducted. The night tours are open to the general public and are given every Monday night, except on Federal holidays. Information concerning activities of the observatory and public tours may be obtained by writing to the Superintendent, Naval Observatory, Washington, DC 20392–5100. Phone, 202–762–1538.

Civilian Employment   Information about civilian employment opportunities within the Department of the Navy in the Washington, DC, metropolitan area can be obtained from the Office of Civilian Personnel Management, Northeast Region, Washington Detachment, 801 North Randolph Street, Arlington, VA 22203–1927 (phone, 703–696–4567); or the Commandant of the Marine Corps (ARCA), Headquarters, U.S. Marine Corps, Washington, DC 20380 (phone, 703–697–7474).

Consumer Activities   Research programs of the Office of the Chief of Naval Research cover a broad spectrum of scientific fields, primarily for the needs of the Navy, but much information is of interest to the public. Inquiries on specific research programs should be directed to the Office of Naval Research, ONR (Code 10), 800 North Quincy Street, Arlington, VA 22217–5660. Phone, 703–696–5031. Inquiries on specific technology programs should be directed to the Director, Office of Naval Technology, ONT (Code 20), 800 North Quincy Street, Arlington, VA 22217–5000. Phone, 202–696–5115.

Contracts and Small Business Activities   Information in these areas can be obtained from the Assistant Secretary of the Navy (Research, Engineering, and Systems), Department of the Navy, 2211 Jefferson Davis Highway, Arlington, VA 22244–5120 (phone, 703–602–2700). Information pertaining specifically to the Marine Corps in the areas of small businesses, minority-owned businesses, and labor surplus activities can be obtained from the Marine Corps Small Business Specialist (LS), Installations and Logistics Department, Headquarters, U.S. Marine Corps, Washington, DC 20380. Phone, 703–696–1022.

Environment   For information on environmental protection and natural resources management programs of the Navy and Marine Corps, contact the Assistant Secretary of the Navy (Installations and Environment), Environment and Safety, 1000 Navy

Pentagon, Room 4A686, Washington, DC, 20350–1000. Phone, 703–614–1304.

General Inquiries Navy and Marine Corps recruiting offices, installation commanders, and Commanding Officers of Marine Corps Districts (see listing in the preceding text) can answer general inquiries concerning the Navy and Marine Corps and their community and public information programs.

Also, the Chief of Information makes accurate and timely information about the Navy available so that the general public, the press, and Congress may understand and assess the Navy's programs, operations, and needs; coordinates Navy participation in community events; and supervises the Navy's internal information programs. Phone, 703–697–5342.

Speakers and Films Information can be obtained on the following: speakers (phone, 703–697–8711); films (phone, 703–697–5342); and the Naval Recruiting Exhibit Center (phone, 904–452–5348). For information concerning the Navy, contact the Office of Information, Department of the Navy, Washington, DC 20350. Phone, 202–695–0965. For information on Marine Corps speakers, contact the Director of Public Affairs, Headquarters, U.S. Marine Corps, Washington, DC 20380–0001; or contact the Director of any Marine Corps District (see listing in the preceding text).

Military Career and Training Opportunities

Marine Corps The Marine Corps conducts enlisted and officer training programs requiring various lengths of service and provides the assurance of specialized skill training and other benefits.

The Marine Corps provides opportunities for training in a variety of technical skills that are necessary in support of ground and aviation combat operations. Radar operation and repair, meteorology, engineer equipment and automotive mechanics, artillery and armor repair, data processing, communications-electronics, jet aircraft repair, avionics, and air control are but a few specialized fields available.

The Marine Corps participates in the Naval Reserve Officers Training Corps Program for commissioning officers in the Marine Corps.

Platoon Leaders Class is a Marine Corps program for commissioning officers in the Marine Corps Reserve. Freshmen, sophomores, or juniors in an accredited college may apply. The Program provides financial assistance to undergraduates.

The Officer Candidate Class is another program for commissioning officers in the Marine Corps Reserve. Applicants must be college graduates or in their senior year.

Information on the above programs is available at most civilian educational institutions and Navy and Marine Corps recruiting stations. Local telephone directories list the address and telephone number of the Recruiting Station and Officer Selection Officer under U.S. Government. Interested persons also may write directly to the Commandant of the Marine Corps (M&RA), Washington, DC 20380–0001. Phone, 703–614–2914.

Information concerning Marine Corps Reserve opportunities can be obtained from local Marine Corps recruiting stations or Marine Corps Reserve Drill Centers. Interested persons may also write directly to the Commandant of the Marine Corps (M&RA, RA), Washington, DC 20380–0001.

For further information concerning the Navy and Marine Corps, contact the Office of Information, Department of the Navy, Washington, DC 20350 (phone, 703–697–7391); or the Legislative Assistant to the Commandant and Director of Public Affairs, Headquarters, U.S. Marine Corps, Washington, DC 20380 (phone, 703–614–1492).

DEFENSE AGENCIES

Ballistic Missile Defense Organization

The Pentagon, Washington, DC 20301–7100
Phone, 703–697–4040

Director	LT. GEN. LESTER LYLES, USAF
Deputy Director	REAR ADM. RICHARD WEST, USN
Chief of Staff	COL. WILLIAM SMITH, USAF

[For the Ballistic Missile Defense Organization statement of organization, see the *Code of Federal Regulations*, Title 32, Part 388]

The Ballistic Missile Defense Organization (formerly the Strategic Defense Initiative Organization) was established as a separate agency of the Department of Defense and is Presidentially chartered and mandated by Congress to develop ballistic and cruise missile defense systems that are capable of providing highly effective defense of the United States and a flexible, interoperable family of theater missile defense systems that may be forward deployed to protect elements of the U.S. Armed Forces and allies of the United States.

The agency's mission is to manage and direct DOD's Ballistic Missile Defense acquisition programs, which include theater missile defense, and to develop a national missile defense program for the United States. The agency also is responsible for the continuing research and development of follow-on technologies that are relevant for long-term ballistic missile defense. These programs will build a technical foundation for evolutionary growth in future ballistic missile defenses. In developing these programs, the agency utilizes the services of the Military Departments, the Department of Energy, the National Aeronautics and Space Administration, private industries, and educational and research institutions.

For further information, contact Management Operations, Ballistic Missile Defense Organization, Washington, DC 20301–7100. Phone, 703–693–1532.

Defense Advanced Research Projects Agency

3701 North Fairfax Drive, Arlington, VA 22203–1714
Phone, 703–696–2444

Director	F.L. FERNANDEZ
Deputy Director	H. LEE BUCHANAN III

The Defense Advanced Research Projects Agency is a separately organized agency within the Department of Defense under a Director appointed by the Secretary of Defense. The Agency, under the authority, direction, and control of the Director of Defense Research and Engineering (DDR&E), engages in advanced basic and applied research and development projects essential to the Department of Defense, and conducts prototype projects that embody technology that may be incorporated into joint programs, programs in support of deployed U.S. forces, selected Military Department programs, or dual-use programs and, on request, assists the Military Departments in their research and development efforts.

In this regard, the Agency arranges, manages, and directs the performance of work connected with assigned advanced projects by the Military Departments, other government agencies, individuals, private business entities, and educational or research institutions, as appropriate; recommends through the DDR&E to the Secretary of Defense assignment of advanced projects to the Agency; keeps the DDR&E, the Chairman of the Joint Chiefs of Staff, the Military Departments, and other Department of Defense agencies informed on significant new developments and technological advances within assigned projects; and performs other such functions as the Secretary of Defense or the DDR&E may assign.

For further information, contact the Defense Advanced Research Projects Agency, 3701 North Fairfax Drive, Arlington, VA 22203–1714. Phone, 703–696–2444 or 703–526–4170.

Defense Commissary Agency

1300 "E" Avenue, Fort Lee, VA 23801–1800
Phone, 804–734–8721. Internet, http://www.deca.mil/.

Director	MAJ. GEN. RICHARD E. BEALE, JR., USA (RET.)
Executive Director for Operations	CROSBY H. JOHNSON
Executive Director for Support	JOHN F. MCGOWAN

The Defense Commissary Agency was established by direction of the Secretary of Defense on November 9, 1990, and operates under DOD Directive 5105.55.

The Agency is responsible for providing an efficient and effective worldwide system of commissaries for reselling groceries and household supplies at low, practical prices (consistent with quality) to members of the Military Services, their families, and other authorized patrons, while maintaining high standards of quality, facilities, products, and service. Commissary savings are a valued part of military pay and benefits. They are also important in recruitment and reenlistment of the all-volunteer force.

Sources of Information

Employment   General employment inquiries should be addressed to Defense Supply Center Richmond, Attn: DSCR–HS, 8000 Jefferson Davis Highway, Richmond, VA 23297–5100. Phone, 804–279–6393.

Procurement and Small Business Activities   For information, contact the Director, Small and Disadvantaged Business Utilization, Headquarters, Defense Commissary Agency, 1300 "E" Avenue, Fort Lee, VA 23801–1800. Phone, 804–734–8740.

Publication   *How To Do Business with DeCA* is available free of charge from the Director, Small and Disadvantaged

Business Utilization, at the address above.

For further information, contact the Chief, Safety, Security, and Administration, 1300 "E" Avenue, Fort Lee, VA 23801–1800. Phone, 804–734–8808. Internet, http://www.deca.mil/.

Defense Contract Audit Agency

Suite 2135, 8725 John J. Kingman Road, Fort Belvoir, VA 22060–6219
Phone, 703–767–3200

Director	WILLIAM H. REED
Deputy Director	MICHAEL J. THIBAULT

The Defense Contract Audit Agency was established in 1965 and operates under Department of Defense Directive 5105.36.

The Agency performs all necessary contract audit functions for the Department of Defense and provides accounting and financial advisory services to all Defense components responsible for procurement and contract administration. These services are provided in connection with the negotiation, administration, and settlement of contracts and subcontracts.

They include evaluating the acceptability of costs claimed or proposed by contractors and reviewing the efficiency and economy of contractor operations. Other Government agencies may request the Agency's services under appropriate arrangements.

The Agency manages its operations through 5 regional offices responsible for approximately 108 field audit offices throughout the United States and overseas. Each region is responsible for the contract auditing function in its assigned area.

Regional Offices—Defense Contract Audit Agency

Region	Address	Director	Telephone
CENTRAL	Suite 300, 106 Decker Ct., Irving, TX 75062–2795	C.T. Cherry	214–650–4831
EASTERN	Suite 300, 2400 Lake Park Dr., Smyrna, GA 30080–7644	Richard R. Buhre	770–319–4400
MID–ATLANTIC	Suite 1000, 615 Chestnut St., Philadelphia, PA 19106–4498.	Barbara C. Reilly	215–597–7451
NORTHEASTERN	83 Hartwell Ave., Lexington, MA 02173–3163	Francis Summers, Jr.	617–377–9710
WESTERN	Suite 300, 16700 Valley View Ave., La Mirada, CA 90638–5830.	Robert W. Matter	714–228–7001

For further information, contact the Executive Officer, Defense Contract Audit Agency, Suite 2135, 8725 John J. Kingman Road, Fort Belvoir, VA 22060–6219. Phone, 703–767–3265. Information regarding employment may be obtained from the regional offices.

Defense Finance and Accounting Service

Room 425, Crystal Mall 3, Arlington, VA 22240–5291
Phone, 703–607–2616

Director	GARY W. AMLIN

Deputy Director	BRIG. GEN. ROGER W. SCEARCE, USA

The Defense Finance and Accounting Service was established by direction of the Secretary of Defense on November 26, 1990, and operates under DOD Directive 5118.5.

The Service is responsible for making all payments, including payroll and contracts, and for maintaining all finance and accounting records for the Department of Defense. The Service is responsible for preparing annual financial statements for DOD in accordance with the Chief Financial Officers Act of 1990. The Service is also responsible for the consolidation, standardization, upgrading, and integration of finance and accounting requirements, functions, processes, operations, and systems in the Department.

For further information, contact the Public Affairs Office, Room 416, Crystal Mall 3, Arlington, VA 22240–5291. Phone, 703–607–2821.

Defense Information Systems Agency

701 South Courthouse Road, Arlington, VA 22204–2199
Phone, 703–607–6900

Director	LT. GEN. DAVID J. KELLEY, USA
Vice Director	MAJ. GEN. JOHN W. MEINCKE, USAF
Chief of Staff	COL. A. FRANK WHITEHEAD, USA

The Defense Information Systems Agency (DISA), originally established as the Defense Communications Agency, is a combat support agency of the Department of Defense.

The Agency is organized into a headquarters and field activities acting for the Director in assigned areas of responsibility. The field organizations include the White House Communications Agency, Joint Interoperability and Engineering Organization, DISA Western Hemisphere, Joint Interoperability Test Command, Defense Information Technology Contracting Organization, Defense Technical Information Center, and the Joint Spectrum Center.

The Agency is responsible for planning, developing, and supporting command, control, communications, and information systems that serve the needs of the National Command Authorities under all conditions of peace and war. It manages the Defense Information Infrastructure (DII) and is responsible for the DOD telecommunications and information processing facilities. It provides guidance and support on technical and operational C^3 and information systems issues affecting the Office of the Secretary of Defense, the Military Departments, the Chairman of the Joint Chiefs of Staff, the combatant commands, and the defense agencies. It ensures the interoperability of DII, theater and tactical command and control systems, North Atlantic Treaty Organization and/or allied C^3 systems, and those national and/or international commercial systems that affect the DISA mission. It supports national security emergency preparedness telecommunications functions of the National Communications System (NCS),

as prescribed by Executive Order 12472
of April 3, 1984.

For further information, contact the Public Affairs Office, Defense Information Systems Agency, 701 South Courthouse Road, Arlington, VA 22204–2199. Phone, 703–607–6900.

Defense Intelligence Agency

The Pentagon, Washington, DC 20340–7400
Phone, 703–695–0071. Internet, http://www.dia.mil/.

Director	LT. GEN. PATRICK M. HUGHES, USA
Deputy Director	JEREMY C. CLARK
Chief of Staff	BARBARA A. DUCKWORTH

The Defense Intelligence Agency (DIA) was established by DOD Directive 5105.21, effective October 1, 1961, under provisions of the National Security Act of 1947, as amended (50 U.S.C. 401 et seq.).

The Defense Intelligence Agency is a combat support agency committed to the provision of timely, objective, and cogent military intelligence to the warfighters—soldiers, sailors, airmen, and marines—and to the decisionmakers and policymakers of DOD and the Federal Government. To accomplish its assigned mission, DIA produces military intelligence for national foreign intelligence and counterintelligence products; coordinates all DOD intelligence collection requirements; operates the Central Measurement and Signals Intelligence (MASINT) Office; manages the Defense Human Intelligence (HUMINT) Service and the Defense Attache System; and provides foreign intelligence and counterintelligence support to the Secretary of Defense and the Chairman of the Joint Chiefs of Staff.

The Director of DIA coordinates the Defense General Intelligence and Applications Program, an element of the DOD Joint Military Intelligence Program, and manages the General Defense Intelligence Program within the National Foreign Intelligence Program.

For further information, contact the Public Affairs Office, Defense Intelligence Agency, Washington, DC 20340. Phone, 703–695–0071. Internet, http://www.dia.mil/.

Defense Legal Services Agency

The Pentagon, Washington, DC 20301–1600
Phone, 703–695–3341

Director (General Counsel, Department of Defense)	JUDITH A. MILLER
Principal Deputy Director (Principal Deputy General Counsel)	DOUGLAS A. DWORKIN

The Defense Legal Services Agency was established August 12, 1981. It is currently chartered under DOD Directive 5145.4. The Agency is under the authority, direction, and control of the General Counsel of the Department of Defense, who also serves as its Director.

The Agency provides legal advice and services for Defense agencies and DOD field activities. It also provides technical support and assistance for development of the Department's legislative program; coordinates positions on legislation and Presidential Executive orders; provides a centralized legislative and congressional document reference and distribution point for the Department; and maintains the Department's historical legislative files. In addition, the Agency includes the Defense Office of Hearings and Appeals program and the DOD Standards of Conduct Office.

For further information, contact the Administrative Officer, Defense Legal Services Agency, The Pentagon, Washington, DC 20301–1600. Phone, 703–697–8343.

Defense Logistics Agency

Suite 2533, 8725 John J. Kingman Road, Fort Belvoir, VA 22060–6221
Phone, 703–767–6666

Director	LT. GEN. H.T. GLISSON, USA
Principal Deputy Director	REAR ADM. E.R. CHAMBERLIN, USN

The Defense Logistics Agency (DLA) was established by the Secretary of Defense and operates under Department of Defense Directive 5105.22. It supports both the logistics requirement of the Military Services and their acquisition of weapons and other materiel. Support begins with joint planning with the Services for parts for a new weapons system, extends through production, and concludes with the disposal of material which is obsolete, worn out, or no longer needed. The Agency provides logistics support, contract administration services, and technical services to all branches of the military and to a number of Federal agencies.

Within the Agency's Defense Logistics Support Command (DLSC), professional logisticians buy and manage a vast number and variety of items used by all of the Military Services and some civilian agencies. The Military Services determine their requirements for supplies and materiel and establish their priorities. Agency supply centers consolidate the Services' requirements and procure the supplies in sufficient quantities to meet the Services' projected needs, critical to maintaining the readiness of our forces. The Agency manages supplies in eight commodity areas: fuel, food, clothing, construction material, electronic supplies, general supplies, industrial supplies, and medical supplies. The DLSC also manages the distribution function for the Agency through the Defense Distribution Center. Distribution is defined as all actions involving the receipt of new procurements, redistributions, and field returns; storage of materiel, including care of materiel and supplies in storage; the issuance of materiel; consolidation and containerization of materiel; preservation, packaging, packing, and marking; physical inventory; quality control; traffic management; other transportation services, unit materiel fielding, and set assembly/disassembly; and transshipment and minor repair.

The Agency's Defense Contract Management Command (DCMC) administers contracts awarded to industry by the Military Services, DLA, the National Aeronautics and Space

Administration, other Federal agencies, and foreign governments. The DCMC is responsible for ensuring that procured materiel is of satisfactory quality and is delivered when and where needed. Services of the DCMC include but are not limited to establishing overhead rates, approving progress payments, negotiations, property management, quality assurance, manufacturing, engineering, law, safety, small business assistance, and contractor employment compliance. These duties are performed at or near contractor plants through a complex of offices which vary in size, depending on workload and the concentration of Government contractors in the area.

Other Logistics Support Services The Defense Logistics Information Service is the Department of Defense's consolidated site for managing all supply cataloging functions. As such, it manages the Federal Supply Catalog System, which lists a National Stock Number and description of over 6 million items. This catalog system is used throughout the Federal Government. The Center also maintains a data bank of information used to design, purchase, transport, store, transfer, and dispose of Government supplies.

The Defense National Stockpile of strategic and critical materials is maintained to reduce the Nation's dependence upon foreign sources of supply for such materials in times of national emergency. The Defense National Stockpile Center is authorized to procure and dispose of materials as needed.

The Defense Reutilization and Marketing Service provides for the redistribution and disposal of DOD equipment and supplies no longer needed by the original user. Assets are matched against requirements of the Military Services and Federal agencies and transferred as needed. When equipment becomes surplus, it is offered to the General Services Administration and State agencies, after which it is offered for sale to the public. The Service is a worldwide organization with offices on many major military installations.

Primary Level Field Activities—Defense Logistics Agency

Activity	Commander
DEFENSE SUPPLY CENTERS:	
Defense Supply Center, Columbus	Brig. Gen. P.L. Bielowicz, USAF
Defense Supply Center, Richmond	Rear Adm. D.H. Stone, USN
Defense Industrial Supply Center	N. Ranalli
Defense Supply Center, Philadelphia	Brig. Gen. H.L. Proctor, USA
Defense Energy Support Center	Col. J.T. Thomas, USA, *Acting*
DEFENSE DISTRIBUTION CENTER:	
Defense Distribution Center	Brig. Gen. K.L. Privratsky, USA
DEFENSE SERVICE CENTERS:	
Defense Logistics Information Service	Col. R. Haglund, USMC
Defense Reutilization and Marketing Service	Col. R.E. Mansfield, USAF
Defense National Stockpile Center	R.H. Connelly
DEFENSE CONTRACT MANAGEMENT DISTRICTS:	
East	Col. W.A. MacKinlay, USA
West	Col. L.S. Johnson, USAF
International	Capt. D.L. Wright, SC, USN

Sources of Information

DOD Surplus Sales Program Questions concerning this program or placement on the Department of Defense bidders list should be addressed to DOD Surplus Sales, International Sales Office, 74 Washington Avenue North, Battle Creek, MI 49017–3092. Phone, 800–468–8289.

Employment For the Washington, DC, metropolitan area, inquiries and applications should be addressed to Defense Logistics Agency, Attn: DASC–R, Suite 2533, 8725 John J. Kingman Road, Fort Belvoir, VA 22060–6221. Phone, 703–767–7100.

Schools interested in participating in the Agency's job recruitment program should direct inquiries to the Defense Logistics Agency, Attn: CAHS, Suite 2533, 8725 John J. Kingman Road, Fort Belvoir, VA 22060–6221.

Environment   For information concerning the Agency's program, contact the Defense Logistics Agency, Attn: CAAE, Suite 2533, 8725 John J. Kingman Road, Fort Belvoir, VA 22060– 6221. Phone, 703–767–6303.

Procurement and Small Business Activities   For information, contact the Director, Small and Disadvantaged Business Utilization, Defense Logistics Agency, Attn: DDAS, Suite 2533, 8725 John J. Kingman Road, Fort Belvoir, VA 22060–6221. Phone, 703–767–1650.

For further information, contact the Defense Logistics Agency, Suite 2533, 8725 John J. Kingman Road, Fort Belvoir, VA 22060–6221. Phone, 703–767–6666.

Defense Security Assistance Agency

The Pentagon, Washington, DC 22202
Phone, 703–604–6513

Director	LT. GEN. MICHAEL S. DAVISON, USA
Deputy Director	H. DIEHL MCKALIP

The Defense Security Assistance Agency was established on September 1, 1971. It is currently chartered under DOD Directive 5105.38.

The Agency directs, administers, and supervises the execution of approved security assistance plans and programs, such as military assistance, international military education and training, and foreign military sales. In so doing, it works closely with the U.S. Security Assistance offices worldwide.

For further information, contact the Defense Security Assistance Agency, The Pentagon, Washington, DC 22202. Phone, 703–604–6513.

Defense Security Service

1340 Braddock Place, Alexandria, VA 22314–1651
Phone, 703–325–9471

Director	STEVEN T. SCHANZER
Deputy Director for Policy	RENE DAVIS-HARDING
Chief Operating Officer	JUDITH M. HUGHES
Comptroller	DELORES I. MOELLER

The Defense Security Service (formerly the Defense Investigative Service) was established by the Secretary of Defense in the Defense Reform Initiative dated November 1997. The Service is chartered by Department of Defense Directive 5105.42.

The Service provides a full range of security support services for the Department of Defense, other Federal Government agencies, defense contractors, and other authorized recipients. It is responsible for all personnel security investigations for

Department components and, when authorized, investigations for other U.S. Government activities. These include investigation of allegations of subversive affiliations, adverse suitability information, or any other situation that requires resolution to complete the personnel security investigation. The Service is also responsible for industrial security management; automated systems security; polygraph research, education,

training, and examinations; and security research, education, and training.

Regional Offices—Defense Investigative Service

City	Director
Alexandria, VA 22331–1000	Raphael G. Syah, *Acting*
Cherry Hill, NJ 08034–1908	Joseph T. Cashin, *Acting*
Irving, TX 75062	James S. Rogner
Long Beach, CA 90807–4013	William H. Williams
Smyrna, GA 30080–7606	Patricia F. Dodson, *Acting*

For further information, contact the Office of Congressional and Public Affairs, Defense Security Service, 1340 Braddock Place, Alexandria, VA 22314–1651. Phone, 703–325–6059.

Defense Special Weapons Agency
Alexandria, VA 22310–3398
Phone, 703–325–7095

Director	MAJ. GEN. GARY L. CURTIN, USAF
Deputy Director	GEORGE W. ULLRICH
Chief of Staff	COL. ARTHUR T. HOPKINS, USAF

The Defense Special Weapons Agency (DSWA) is the oldest defense agency, having evolved from the Manhattan Project of World War II. Known variously over the years as the Armed Forces Special Weapons Project, the Defense Atomic Support Agency, and the Defense Nuclear Agency, DSWA is currently chartered under DOD Directive 5105.31. The Agency is designated to be the DOD center of expertise for nuclear and special weapons effects, and operates under the authority, direction, and control of the Assistant to the Secretary of Defense for Nuclear and Chemical and Biological Defense Programs (ATSD(NCB)).

The Agency supports the ATSD(NCB) in all nuclear weapons stockpile stewardship matters, including the annual nuclear weapons stockpile certification and the nuclear weapons dual revalidation program with the Department of Energy. As part of its stockpile stewardship mission, DSWA tracks the location and status of all U.S. nuclear weapons. Agency personnel also

conduct weapons effects research, training, and operational unit inspections to ensure the safety, security, and reliability of the nuclear weapons stockpile. Furthermore, DSWA provides planning assistance to combatant commanders and support in case of a nuclear weapons accident or incident.

Through the use of simulators, computer models, and non-nuclear field tests, the Agency supports the military services and combatant commanders by verifying that essential military systems can operate in hostile nuclear environments. It also supports the targeting community through the development of automated analysis and planning tools to ensure the effective employment of both nuclear and conventional weapons across the spectrum of potential targets. One area of specific interest has been the effectiveness of conventional weapons against hardened and deeply buried targets and facilities that may be used to produce or store weapons of mass destruction.

For the Secretary of Defense, the Agency conducts the Cooperative Threat Reduction Program, which provides support to the states of the former Soviet Union as they comply with a variety of recent arms control treaties. The Agency also carries out the arms control treaty verification technology and counterproliferation technology programs for the Department of Defense. For the Chairman of the Joint Chiefs of Staff, DSWA provides field support in the form of vulnerability assessments for the force protection program. Other unique responsibilities include operating the Defense Nuclear Weapons School, supporting the Nuclear Test Personnel Review and the Radiation Experimentation Center, and providing base support at Johnston Atoll, one of the U.S. Army's chemical weapons storage and destruction sites.

Sources of Information

Employment Inquiries should be directed as follows:

Headquarters—Defense Special Weapons Agency, Attn: MPCH, 6801 Telegraph Road, Alexandria, VA 22310–2298. Phone, 703–325–7593.

Field Command—Attn: FCRIC, 1680 Texas Street SE., Kirtland Air Force Base, NM 87117–5669. Phone, 505–846–8671.

Procurement and Small Business Activities Contact the Defense Special Weapons Agency, Attn: AM, 6801 Telegraph Road, Alexandria, VA 22310–3398. Phone, 703–325–5021.

For further information, contact the Public Affairs Office, Defense Special Weapons Agency, 6801 Telegraph Road, Alexandria, VA 22310–3398. Phone, 703–325–7095.

National Imagery and Mapping Agency

4600 Sangamore Road, Bethesda, MD 20816–5003
Phone, 301–227–7400. Internet, http://www.nima.mil/.

Director	MAJ. GEN. JAMES C. KING, USA, *Acting*
Deputy Director	LEO HAZLEWOOD
Deputy Director, Operations	ROBERTA E. LENCZOWSKI
Deputy Director, Systems and Technology	WILLIAM M. MULARIE
Deputy Director, Corporate Affairs	W. DOUGLAS SMITH
Chief of Staff	LT. COL. JOHN BIGGS, USA

The National Imagery and Mapping Agency (NIMA) was established as a separate agency of the Department of Defense on October 1, 1996, by DOD Directive 5105.60 pursuant to the National Imagery and Mapping Agency Act of 1996 (10 U.S.C. 441 *et seq.*). The successor agency of both the Defense Mapping Agency and the Central Imagery Office, NIMA also incorporates imagery exploitation and dissemination functions transferred from other DOD offices and from the Central Intelligence Agency. It serves under the authority, direction, and control of the Secretary of Defense, with the advice of the Chairman of the Joint Chiefs of Staff, and in accordance with policies and priorities established by the Director of Central Intelligence. The Assistant Secretary of Defense for Command, Control, Communications, and Intelligence exercises overall supervision over NIMA, which is designated as a combat support agency and as an element of the intelligence community.

The Agency is responsible for providing timely, relevant, and accurate imagery, imagery intelligence, and geospatial information in support of the national security objectives of the United States. Its creation represents a fundamental step toward achieving the Department of Defense vision of dominant battlespace awareness. By exploiting the tremendous potential of enhanced collection systems, digital processing technology, and the prospective expansion in commercial imagery, NIMA works to guarantee customers the information edge.

Headquartered in Bethesda, MD, NIMA operates major facilities in northern Virginia, Washington, DC, Bethesda, MD, and St. Louis, MO, as well as support and liaison offices worldwide.

For further information, contact the National Imagery and Mapping Agency, 4600 Sangamore Road, Bethesda, MD 20816–5003. Phone, 800–826–0342 (Customer Help Line), or 301–227–3105 (Public Liaison Office). Internet, http://www.nima.mil/.

National Security Agency/Central Security Service

Fort George G. Meade, MD 20755–6000
Phone, 301–688–6524. Internet, http://www.nsa.gov/.

Director	LT. GEN. KENNETH A. MINIHAN, USAF
Deputy Director	BARBARA A. MCNAMARA

The National Security Agency was established by Presidential directive in 1952 as a separately organized agency within the Department of Defense. In this directive, the President designated the Secretary of Defense as Executive Agent for the signals intelligence and communications security activities of the Government. In 1972, the Central Security Service was established, also in accordance with a Presidential memorandum, to provide a more unified cryptologic organization within the Department of Defense, with control over the signals intelligence activities of the military services.

As the U.S. cryptologic organization, NSA/CSS employs the Nation's premier codemakers and codebreakers. It ensures an informed, alert, and secure environment for U.S. warfighters and American policymakers. The cryptologic resources of NSA/CSS, foreign signals intelligence (SIGINT) and information systems security (INFOSEC), unite to provide U.S. policymakers with intelligence information derived from America's adversaries while protecting U.S. signals and information systems from exploitation by those same adversaries.

Executive Order 12333 of December 4, 1981, describes in more detail the responsibilities of the National Security Agency.

For further information, contact the Public Affairs Office, National Security Agency/Central Security Service, Fort Meade, MD 20755–6000. Phone, 301–688–6524. Internet, http://www.nsa.gov/.

On-Site Inspection Agency

Washington, DC 20041–0498
Phone, 703–810–4326

Director	BRIG. GEN. JOHN C. REPPERT, USA
Principal Deputy Director	JOERG H. MENZEL

The On-Site Inspection Agency (OSIA) was established as a separate Department of Defense agency on January 26, 1988, to implement the 13-year inspection regime of the Intermediate-Range Nuclear Forces (INF) Treaty. The Agency's mission has since expanded to include implementation of on-site inspection and escort requirements of the nuclear testing treaties, including the Threshold Test Ban Treaty (TTBT) and the Peaceful Nuclear Explosions Treaty (PNET); the Conventional Armed Forces in Europe (CFE) Treaty; the Strategic Arms Reduction Treaty (START); the Vienna Document of 1994; the Open Skies (OS) Treaty; the Chemical Weapons (CW) Agreements; and the Dayton peace accords for multilateral inspection activities in Bosnia and Herzegovina.

The Agency acts as the Defense Department's executive agent to the United Nations Special Commission on Iraq. OSIA also serves as the executive agent for the Defense Treaty Inspection Readiness Program (DTIRP) and provides support to the Cooperative Threat Reduction (CTR) Program for their denuclearization and dismantlement programs.

The Agency is manned by military personnel from all of the armed services, as well as civilian technical experts and support personnel. It maintains liaison with various Government agencies interested in arms control and draws its three civilian deputy directors from the U.S. Arms Control and Disarmament Agency, State Department, and Federal Bureau of Investigation.

For further information, contact the Public Affairs Office, On-Site Inspection Agency, P.O. Box 17498, Washington, DC 20041–0498. Phone, 703–810–4326.

JOINT SERVICE SCHOOLS

Defense Acquisition University

2001 North Beauregard Street, Alexandria, VA 22311–1772
Phone, 703–845–6772

President	THOMAS M. CREAN

The Defense Acquisition University (DAU), established pursuant to the Defense Acquisition Workforce Improvement Act of 1990 (10 U.S.C. 1701 note), serves as the DOD center for acquisition education, training, research, and publication. The University is structured as an educational consortium, with centralized planning and management of the acquisition education and training activities of Army, Navy, Air Force, and DOD component schools.

The University's mission is to educate and train military and civilian professionals for effective service in defense acquisition, to centrally manage resources for course development delivery, research, and publications.

For further information, contact the Director for University Operations, Defense Acquisition University, 2001 North Beauregard Street, Alexandria, VA 22311–1772. Phone, 703–845–6763.

Defense Systems Management College

Fort Belvoir, VA 22060–5565
Phone, 703–805–3363; 800–845–7606 (toll-free)

Commandant	REAR ADM. LEONARD VINCENT, USN
Provost	RICHARD H. REED

The Defense Systems Management College (DSMC), established July 1, 1971, is a joint service educational institution, and is the largest school in the Defense Acquisition University. The mission of the College is to promote and support the adoption and practice of sound systems management principles by the acquisition workforce through education, research, consulting, and information dissemination.

In addition to a 14-week Advanced Program Management Course, DSMC's academic program consists of 29 other courses of 3 days to 4 weeks in duration, all with the purpose of educating DOD acquisition professionals, military and civilian, in a broad spectrum of management activities through formal studies, simulation exercises, and case studies. Many of these courses are mandatory for certification in various career fields within Service acquisition corps. Individuals from Defense industry and other Federal agencies may attend DSMC courses on a space-available basis. In addition to the main campus located at Fort Belvoir, VA, courses are taught at the four regions of Boston, MA; Huntsville, AL; Los Angeles, CA; and Fort Monmouth, NJ; and at selected on-site locations on an as-requested basis.

For further information, contact the Office of the Registrar, Defense Systems Management College, Fort Belvoir, VA 22060. Phone, 703–805–2227; 888–284–4906 (toll-free).

Joint Military Intelligence College

Defense Intelligence Analysis Center, Washington, DC 20340–5100
Phone, 202–231–3299

President	A. DENIS CLIFT
Deputy to the President	COL. LEWIS S. WALLACE, JR., USAF
Provost	RONALD D. GARST

The Joint Military Intelligence College (previously the Defense Intelligence College) was established by a Department of Defense directive in 1962. It is a joint service educational institution serving the entire intelligence community and operates under the authority of the Director, Defense Intelligence Agency. Its mission is to educate military and civilian intelligence professionals and conduct and disseminate relevant intelligence research.

The College is authorized by Congress to award the Bachelor of Science in Intelligence (BSI) and Master of Science of Strategic Intelligence (MSSI) degrees and also offers two diploma programs: Undergraduate Intelligence Program (UGIP), and Post Graduate Intelligence Program (PGIP). Qualified students may enroll for full- or part-time study at the main campus located at the Defense Intelligence Analysis Center, Bolling Air Force Base. Part-time study is also available at the National Security Agency. Two weekend programs are available as well; one is specifically for military reservists and is taught by reserve faculty.

The College is accredited by the Middle States Association of Colleges and Schools.

For further information, contact the Admissions Office, MCA–2, Joint Military Intelligence College, Defense Intelligence Analysis Center, Washington, DC 20340–5100. Phone, 202–231–3299.

National Defense University

Building 62, 300 Fifth Avenue, Fort McNair, Washington, DC 20319–5066
Phone, 202–685–3922

President	LT. GEN. RICHARD A. CHILCOAT, USA
Vice President	THOMAS M.T. NILES
Chief of Staff	COL. JOHN M. BROWN III, USA

The National Defense University was established by the Department of Defense on January 16, 1976, thereby merging the Industrial College of the Armed Forces and the National War College to form a university. Because the two senior service colleges are located at Fort McNair, Washington, DC, their close affiliation reduces administrative costs, provides for the sharing of faculty expertise and educational resources, and promotes a constructive dialog, which benefits both colleges. On August 16, 1981, the Armed Forces Staff College in Norfolk, VA, an institution educating mid-career officers, was incorporated into the National Defense University.

The Institute for National Strategic Studies was created in 1984 as an interdisciplinary research institute staffed by senior civilian and military analysts from all four military services. In 1990, the Information Resources Management College was established to provide graduate-level courses in information resources management. The two most recent additions to the University's structure are the Center for Hemispheric Defense Studies (1997) and the Defense Leadership and Management Program (1998).

The mission of the National Defense University is to ensure excellence in joint professional military education and research in the essential elements of national security.

For further information, contact the Administrative Office, National Defense University, Building 62, 300 Fifth Avenue, Fort McNair, Washington, DC 20319–5066. Phone, 202–685–3958.

The National War College

Building 61, 300 D Street, Fort McNair, Washington, DC 20319–5078
Phone, 202–685–3715. Fax, 202–685–6461

Commandant	REAR ADM. THOMAS F. MARFIAK, USN
Dean of Students/Executive Officer	CAPT. CHARLES A. MILETICH, USN
Dean of Faculty and Academic Programs	COL. DAVID A. TRETLER, USAF

The National War College provides education in national security policy to selected military officers and career civil service employees of Federal departments and agencies concerned with national security. It is the only senior service college with the primary mission of offering a course of study that emphasizes national security policy formulation and the planning and implementation of national strategy.

Its 10-month academic program is an issue-centered study in U.S. national security. The elective program is designed to permit each student to tailor his academic experience to meet individual professional development needs.

For further information, contact the Department of Administration, The National War College, Building 61, 300 D Street, Fort McNair, Washington, DC 20319–5078. Phone, 202–685–3715.

Industrial College of the Armed Forces

Building 59, 408 Fourth Avenue, Fort McNair, Washington, DC 20319–5062
Phone, 202–685–4337

Commandant	MAJ. GEN. JOHN S. COWINGS, USA

The Industrial College of the Armed Forces is the Nation's leading educational institution for the study of the resources component of national power and its integration into national security strategy. The College prepares selected military and civilians for senior leadership positions by conducting postgraduate executive-level courses of study and associated research. Its 10-month academic program is organized into two semesters: focusing on national security strategy and management of natural resources, respectively.

For further information, contact the Director of Administration, Industrial College of the Armed Forces, Building 59, 408 Fourth Avenue, Fort McNair, Washington, DC 20319–5062. Phone, 202–685–4333.

Armed Forces Staff College

Norfolk, VA 23511–1702
Phone, 757–444–5302

Commandant	BRIG. GEN. WILLIAM R. LOONEY III, USAF

The Armed Forces Staff College (AFSC), a major component of the National Defense University, is an intermediate- and senior-level joint college in the professional military education system dedicated to the study of the principles, perspectives, and techniques of joint operational planning and warfare.

The mission of AFSC is to educate staff officers and other leaders in joint operational planning and warfighting in order to instill a primary commitment of joint and combined teamwork, attitudes, and perspectives. The College accomplishes this mission through three schools: the Joint and Combined Warfighting School (JCWS), the Joint and Combined Staff Officer School (JCSOS), and the Joint Command, Control, and Information Warfare School (JCIWS).

For further information, contact the Department of Academic Affairs, Armed Forces Staff College, 7800 Hampton Boulevard, Norfolk, VA 23511–1702. Phone, 757–444–5074. Fax, 757–444–5422.

Information Resources Management College

Building 62, 300 Fifth Avenue, Fort McNair, Washington, DC 20319–5066
Phone, 202–685–3892

Dean   JEROME F. SMITH, JR.

The Information Resources Management College (IRMC) was established on March 1, 1990, as a full college of the National Defense University. It provides graduate-level courses in information resources management. The College prepares senior DOD officials for joint management of the information resources component of national power and its integration with, and support to, national strategy.

The College's curriculum is designed to provide a forum where senior Defense professionals—interacting with the faculty—not only gain knowledge, qualifications, and competencies for Defense IRM leadership, but contribute to the growth and excellence of the field itself. The premier offering of the college is the 14-week Advanced Management Program (AMP), which is supplemented by a number of advanced studies courses available to students in all colleges of the National Defense University. Additionally, the College offers a series of intensive courses related to specific problematic areas and emerging concepts of IRM, and special symposia, seminars, and workshops focusing on critical IRM issues and directions.

For further information, contact the Registrar, Information Resources Management College, Building 62, 300 Fifth Avenue, Fort McNair, Washington, DC 20319–5066. Phone, 202–685–3892.

Uniformed Services University of the Health Sciences

4301 Jones Bridge Road, Bethesda, MD 20814–4799
Phone, 301–295–3030

President   JAMES A. ZIMBLE
Dean, School of Medicine   VAL G. HEMMING
Dean, Graduate School of Nursing   FAYE G. ABDELLAH

Authorized by act of September 21, 1972 (10 U.S.C. 2112), the Uniformed Services University of the Health Sciences was established to educate career-oriented medical officers for the Military Departments and the Public Health Service.

The University currently incorporates the F. Edward Hebert School of Medicine (including graduate and continuing education programs) and the Graduate School of Nursing. It is located on the National Naval Medical Center (NNMC) reservation in Bethesda, MD.

Students are selected by procedures recommended by the Board of Regents and prescribed by the Secretary of Defense. The actual selection is carried out by a faculty committee on admissions and is based upon motivation and dedication to a career in the uniformed services and an overall appraisal of the personal and intellectual characteristics of the candidates without regard to sex, race, religion, or national origin. Applicants must be U.S. citizens.

Medical school matriculants will be commissioned officers in one of the uniformed services. They must meet the physical and personal qualifications for such a commission and must give evidence of a strong commitment to serving as a uniformed medical officer. The graduating medical student is required to serve a period of obligation of not less than 7 years, excluding graduate medical education.

Students of the Graduate School of Nursing must be commissioned officers of the Army, Navy, Air Force, or Public Health Service prior to application. Graduate nursing students must serve a commitment determined by their respective service.

For further information, contact the President, Uniformed Services University of the Health Sciences, 4301 Jones Bridge Road, Bethesda, MD 20814–4799. Phone, 301–295–3030.

DEPARTMENT OF EDUCATION

600 Independence Avenue SW., Washington, DC 20202
Phone, 800–USA–LEARN (toll-free). Internet, http://www.ed.gov/.

SECRETARY OF EDUCATION	RICHARD W. RILEY
Chief of Staff	LESLIE THORNTON
Director, Office of Public Affairs	DAVID FRANK
Deputy Secretary	MARSHALL S. SMITH, *Acting*
Chief of Staff	(VACANCY)
Director, Office of Educational Technology	LINDA ROBERTS
Director, Office of Small and Disadvantaged Business Utilization	VIOLA J. SANCHEZ
Assistant Secretary for Civil Rights	NORMA V. CANTÚ
Deputy Assistant Secretaries	ARTHUR COLEMAN, RAYMOND C. PIERCE
Director, Enforcement, East	SUSAN BOWERS
Director, Enforcement, West	CATHY LEWIS, *Acting*
Director, Resource Management Group	PAUL FAIRLEY
Director, Program Legal Group	JEANETTE LIM
Under Secretary	MARSHALL S. SMITH
Director, Management Operations Staff	DOUGLAS M. FLAMM
Director, Planning and Evaluation Service	ALAN L. GINSBURG
Director, Budget Service	THOMAS P. SKELLY
Inspector General	STEVEN MCNAMARA, *Acting*
Deputy Inspector General	JOHN P. HIGGINS, JR.
Assistant Inspector General for Audit Services	STEVEN MCNAMARA
Assistant Inspector General for Investigation Services	DIANNE VAN RIPER
Executive Officer, Planning, Analysis, and Management Services	ROBERT K. NAGLE
General Counsel	JAMIENNE S. STUDLEY, *Acting*
Deputy General Counsel for Program Service	STEVEN Y. WINNICK
Deputy General Counsel for Postsecondary and Departmental Service	(VACANCY)
Deputy General Counsel for Regulations and Legislation Service	JAMIENNE S. STUDLEY
Assistant Secretary for Special Education and Rehabilitative Services	JUDITH E. HEUMANN
Deputy Assistant Secretary	HOWARD R. MOSES
Director, Special Education Programs	THOMAS HEHIR
Director, National Institute on Disability and Rehabilitation Research	KATHERINE D. SEELMAN
Commissioner, Rehabilitation Services Administration	FREDRIC K. SCHROEDER
Associate Commissioner, Program Operations	MARK SHOOB, *Acting*
Associate Commissioner, Developmental Programs	(VACANCY)

Assistant Secretary for Legislation and Congressional Affairs	SCOTT FLEMING, *Acting*
Deputy Assistant Secretary	SCOTT FLEMING
Director, Legislation Staff	CHARLOTTE FRASS
Director, Congressional Affairs Staff	SCOTT FLEMING, *Acting*
Assistant Secretary for Intergovernmental and Interagency Affairs	GILBERTO MARIO MORENO
Deputy Assistant Secretary for Intergovernmental and Constituent Relations	JENNIFER DAVIS
Director, Intergovernmental and Interagency Affairs Coordination	PEGGY KERNS
Director, Constituent Relations	FRITZ EDELSTEIN
Director, Office of Non-Public Education	MICHELLE DOYLE
Deputy Assistant Secretary for Regional and Community Services	WILSON GOODE
Director, Community Services	JOHN MCGRATH
Chief Financial and Chief Information Officer	DONALD RAPPAPORT
Deputy Chief Financial Officer	(VACANCY)
Director, Contracts and Purchasing Operations	GLENN PERRY
Director, Financial Improvement, Receivables, and Post Audit Operations	HAZEL FIERS
Director, Grants Policy and Oversight Staff	BLANCA RODRIGUEZ
Deputy Chief Information Officer	GLORIA PARKER
Director, Financial Payments and Cash Management Operations	CHARLIE COLEMAN
Director, Financial Reporting and Systems Operations	MAUREEN SMITH
Director for Management	JOHN P. HIGGINS, JR., *Acting*
Deputy Director	MARY ELLEN DIX
Director, Equal Employment Opportunity Group	JAMES R. WHITE
Director, Family Policy Compliance Group	LEROY ROOKER
Director, Human Resources Group	VERONICA D. TRIETSCH
Director, Management Systems Improvement Group	ANN MANHEIMER, *Acting*
Director, Office of Hearings and Appeals	FRANK J. FUREY
Director, Labor Relations Group	JAMES KEENAN
Director, Real Property Group	DAVID HAKOLA
Director, Quality Workplace Group	TONY CONQUES
Director, Health and Environmental Safety Group	DIANE SCHMITZ
Director, Training and Development Group	INGRID KOLB
Assistant Secretary for Postsecondary Education	DAVID A. LONGANECKER
Deputy Assistant Secretary for Policy, Planning, and Innovation	MAUREEN MCLAUGHLIN
Deputy Assistant Secretary for Higher Education Programs	CLAUDIO R. PRIETO
Deputy Assistant Secretary for Student Financial Assistance Programs	DIANE E. ROGERS
Director, Policy, Training, and Analysis Service	NINA C. WINKLER
Director, Accounting and Financial Management Service	LINDA L. PAULSEN

Director, Guarantor and Lender Oversight Service	LARRY OXENDINE
Director, Program Systems Service	GERARD A. RUSSOMANO
Director, Institutional Participation and Oversight Service	JEANNE VAN VLANDREN
Director, Debt Collection Service	THOMAS J. PESTKA
Assistant Secretary for Educational Research and Improvement	RICKY TAKAI, *Acting*
Director, National Institute on Student Achievement, Curriculum, and Assessment	JOSEPH CONATY
Director, National Institute on the Education of At-Risk Students	EDWARD FUENTES
Director, National Institute on Early Childhood Development and Education	NAOMI KARP
Director, National Institute on Educational Governance, Finance, Policymaking, and Management	DEBORAH IMAN
Director, National Institute on Postsecondary Education, Libraries, and Lifelong Learning	CAROLE B. LACAMPAGNE
Director, Office of Reform Assistance and Dissemination	PEIRCE HAMMOND III
Director, National Library of Education	BLANE K. DESSY
Director, Media and Information Services	CYNTHIA DORFMAN
Commissioner, National Center for Education Statistics	PASCAL D. FORGIONE, JR.
Assistant Secretary for Elementary and Secondary Education	GERALD N. TIROZZI
Deputy Assistant Secretaries	JUDITH JOHNSON, JAMES KOHLMOOS
Director, Impact Aid Programs	CATHERINE SCHAGH
Director, School Improvement Programs	ARTHUR COLE
Director, Compensatory Education Programs	MARY JEAN LETENDRE
Director, Goals 2000 Program	THOMAS FAGAN
Director, Office of Migrant Education	FRANCISCO GARCIA, *Acting*
Director, Safe and Drug-Free Schools Program	WILLIAM MODZELESKI
Director, Office of Indian Education	DAVID BEAULIEU
Director, Office of Bilingual Education and Minority Languages Affairs	DELIA POMPA
Deputy Directors	PHYLLIS BARAJAS, DANG PHAM
Assistant Secretary for Vocational and Adult Education	PATRICIA W. MCNEIL
Deputy Assistant Secretary	GARY J. RASMUSSEN
Director, Adult Education and Literacy Division	RONALD S. PUGSLEY
Director, Vocational-Technical Education Division	RONALD CASTALDI, *Acting*
Director, National Programs Division	DENNIS BERRY

The Department of Education establishes policy for, administers, and coordinates most Federal assistance to education. Its mission is to ensure equal access to education and to promote educational excellence throughout the Nation.

DEPARTMENT OF EDUCATION

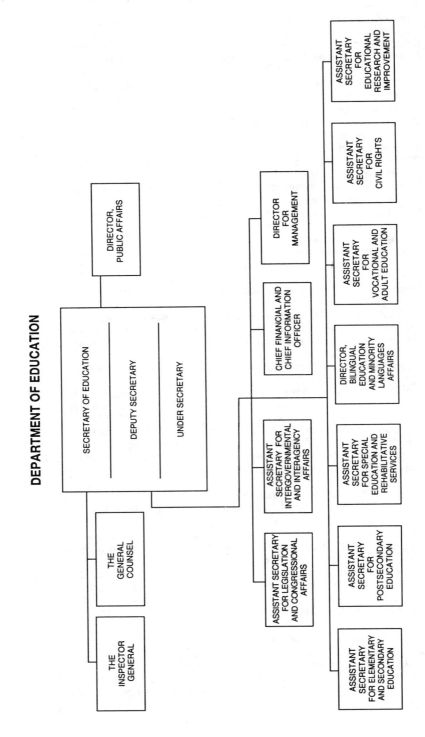

The Department of Education was created by the Department of Education Organization Act (20 U.S.C. 3411). The Department is administered under the supervision and direction of the Secretary of Education.

Office of the Secretary

Secretary The Secretary of Education advises the President on education plans, policies, and programs of the Federal Government. The Secretary also serves as the Chief Executive Officer of the Department, coordinating and overseeing all Department activities, providing support and encouragement to States and localities on matters related to education, and focusing the resources of the Department and the attention of the country on ensuring equal access to education and promoting educational excellence throughout the Nation. The Deputy Secretary, the Under Secretary, the Assistant Secretaries, the Inspector General, the General Counsel, the Chief Financial Officer, and the Chief Information Officer are the principal officers who assist the Secretary in the overall management of the Department.

Activities

Bilingual Education The Office of Bilingual Education and Minority Languages Affairs administers programs designed to fund activities that assist students with limited English proficiency. The Office administers the discretionary grant competition for 12 grant programs established by law and 1 formula grant program under the Immigrant Education Program. The Office also administers contracts for research and evaluation, technical assistance, and clearinghouse activities to meet the special educational needs of populations with limited English proficiency.

Civil Rights The Assistant Secretary for Civil Rights is responsible for ensuring that institutional recipients of Federal financial assistance do not discriminate against American students, faculty, or other individuals on the basis of race, color, national origin, sex, disability, or age.

Educational Research and Improvement The Assistant Secretary for Educational Research and Improvement provides national leadership in expanding fundamental knowledge and improving the quality of education. This Office is responsible for conducting and supporting education-related research activities; monitoring the state of education through the collection and analysis of statistical data; promoting the use and application of research and development to improve instructional practices in the classroom; and disseminating these findings and providing technical assistance for specific problems at school sites.

Elementary and Secondary Education The Assistant Secretary for Elementary and Secondary Education formulates policy for, directs, and coordinates the Department's activities relating to preschool, elementary, and secondary education. Included are grants and contracts to State educational agencies and local school districts, postsecondary schools, and nonprofit organizations for State and local reform, compensatory, migrant, and Indian education; drug-free schools; other school improvement programs; and impact aid.

Postsecondary Education The Assistant Secretary for Postsecondary Education formulates policy and directs and coordinates programs for assistance to postsecondary educational institutions and students pursuing a postsecondary education. Programs include assistance for the improvement and expansion of American educational resources for international studies and services, grants to improve instruction in crucial academic subjects, and construction assistance for academic facilities. Also included are programs of student financial assistance, including Pell Grants, Supplemental Educational Opportunity Grants, Grants to States for State Student Incentives, Work-Study, Federal Direct Student Loans, Stafford Loans, Parent Loans for Undergraduate Students (PLUS), Supplemental Loans for Students (SLS), Consolidation Loans, and Perkins Loans.

Special Education and Rehabilitative Services The Office of Special Education and Rehabilitative Services (OSERS) provides leadership to ensure that people with disabilities have services, resources, and equal opportunities to learn, work, and live as fully integrated, contributing members of society. OSERS supports programs that serve millions of disabled children, youth, and adults and that impact on the lives of the Nation's 49 million citizens with disabilities. It coordinates the activities of the Office of Special Education Programs, which works to help States provide quality educational opportunities and early-intervention services to help students with disabilities achieve their goals. OSERS' Rehabilitation Services Administration, among other efforts, supports State vocational rehabilitation programs that give disabled people the education, job training, and job placement services they need to gain meaningful employment. OSERS' National Institute on Disability and Rehabilitation Research supports research and technological programs that are crafting blueprints for a barrier-free, inclusive society.

Vocational and Adult Education The Assistant Secretary for Vocational and Adult Education administers grant, contract, and technical assistance programs for vocational-technical education and for adult education and literacy. The Office is also responsible for coordinating these programs with other Education Department and Federal programs supporting services and research for adult education, literacy, and occupational training.

Regional Offices Each regional office serves as a center for the dissemination of information and provides technical assistance to State and local educational agencies and other institutions and individuals interested in Federal education activities. Offices are located in Atlanta, GA; Boston, MA; Chicago, IL; Dallas, TX; Denver, CO; Kansas City, MO; New York, NY; Philadelphia, PA; San Francisco, CA; and Seattle, WA.

Federally Aided Corporations

[These Corporations are supported in part by Federal funds appropriated in the budget of the Department of Education.]

American Printing House for the Blind

P.O. Box 6085, Louisville, KY 40206
Phone, 502–895–2405

President	TUCK TINSLEY
Chairman of the Board	JOHN BARR III

The American Printing House for the Blind was incorporated by the Kentucky Legislature in 1858 to assist in the education of the blind by distributing Braille books, talking books, and educational aids without cost to educational institutions educating blind children pursuant to the act "To Promote the Education of the Blind," as amended (20 Stat. 467), adopted by Congress in 1879.

Gallaudet University

800 Florida Avenue NE., Washington, DC 20002
Phone, 202–651–5000. Internet, http://www.gallaudet.edu/.

Chairman, Board of Trustees	GLENN B. ANDERSON
President, Gallaudet University	I. KING JORDAN
Vice President, Academic Affairs	ROSLYN ROSEN
Vice President, Administration and Business	PAUL KELLY
Vice President, Institutional Advancement	MARGARETE HALL
Vice President, Precollege National Mission Programs	JANE K. FERNANDES

The Columbia Institution for the Instruction of the Deaf and Dumb, and the Blind was incorporated by act of February 16, 1857 (11 Stat. 161). An amendatory act of February 23, 1865 (13 Stat. 436), changed the name to the Columbia Institution for the Instruction of the Deaf and Dumb. The name was subsequently changed to Columbia Institution for the Deaf by act of March 4, 1911 (36 Stat. 1422). The act of June 18, 1954 (20 U.S.C. 691 *et seq.*), changed its name to Gallaudet College. The Education of the Deaf Act of 1986 (20 U.S.C. 4301) changed the name to Gallaudet University.

Gallaudet University was established to provide a liberal higher education for deaf persons who need special facilities to compensate for their loss of hearing. The primary purpose of the university is to afford its students the intellectual and spiritual development that can be acquired through a study of the liberal arts and sciences.

In addition to its undergraduate program, the University operates a graduate program at the master's level to prepare teachers and other professional personnel to work with persons who are deaf, a research program focusing on problems related to deafness, and continuing education for deaf adults.

Accreditation   Gallaudet University is accredited by the Middle States Association of Colleges and Secondary Schools, the National Council for Accreditation of Teacher Education, and the Council on Social Work Education.

Model Secondary School for the Deaf   The school was established by act of October 15, 1966 (20 U.S.C. 693), when the Department of Health, Education, and Welfare entered into an agreement with Gallaudet College for the establishment and operation, including construction, of such a facility. It was established as an exemplary educational facility for deaf students of high school age from the District of Columbia, Maryland, Virginia, West Virginia, Pennsylvania, Delaware, and the rest of the Nation on a space-available basis. The school's mission is to provide maximum flexibility in curricula and to encourage the originality, imagination, and innovation needed to satisfy deaf students' high aspirations.

The objectives of the school are to provide day and residential facilities for deaf youth of high school age, in order to prepare them for college or for postsecondary opportunities other than college; to prepare all students to the maximum extent possible to be independent, contributing members of society; and to stimulate the development of similar programs throughout the Nation.

Kendall Demonstration Elementary School   The School became the Nation's first demonstration elementary school for the deaf by act of December 24, 1970 (20 U.S.C. 695), which authorized Gallaudet College to operate and maintain it as a model that will experiment in techniques and materials, and to disseminate information from these and future projects to educational facilities for deaf children throughout the country. The School is located on the campus of Gallaudet University and is

equipped to serve approximately 200
students.

**For further information, contact the Public
Relations Office, Gallaudet University, 800 Florida
Avenue NE., Washington, DC 20002. Phone, 202–
651–5505. Internet, http://www.gallaudet.edu/.**

Howard University

*2400 Sixth Street NW., Washington, DC 20059
Phone, 202–806–6100. Internet, http://www.howard.edu/.*

President   H. Patrick Swygert

Howard University was established by
act of March 2, 1867 (14 Stat. 438). It is
governed by a 29-member self-
perpetuating board of trustees. The
University maintains a special
relationship with the Federal
Government through the Department of
Education.

Howard University, jointly supported
by congressional appropriations and
private funds, is a comprehensive
university organization offering
instruction in 16 schools and colleges as
follows: the college of arts and sciences,
the school of engineering, the school of
architecture and planning, the school of
business, the college of fine arts, the
college of medicine, the college of
dentistry, the college of pharmacy, the
school of law, the school of divinity, the
graduate school of arts and sciences, the
school of social work, the school of

communications, the school of
education, the college of nursing, the
college of allied health sciences, and a
summer school. In addition, Howard
University has research institutes in the
following areas: the arts and the
humanities, urban affairs and research,
drug abuse and addiction, science,
space, and technology, small business
education, and the study of educational
policy.

The University is coeducational and
admits students of every race, creed,
color, and national origin, but it accepts
and discharges a special responsibility
for the admission and training of black
students.

**For further information, contact the Office of
University Communications, Howard University,
2400 Sixth Street NW., Washington, DC 20059.
Phone, 202–806–0970. Internet, http://
www.howard.edu/.**

National Institute for Literacy

*Suite 200, 800 Connecticut Avenue NW., Washington, DC 20006
Phone, 202–632–1500*

Director   Andrew Hartman

The National Institute for Literacy is an
independent Federal organization that
leads the national effort towards a fully
literate America. By building and
strengthening national, regional, and
State literacy infrastructures, the Institute

fosters collaboration and innovation. Its
goal is to ensure that all Americans with
literacy needs receive the high-quality
education and basic skills services
necessary to achieve success in the
workplace, family, and community.

National Technical Institute for the Deaf

Rochester Institute of Technology
52 Lomb Memorial Drive, Rochester, NY 14623
Phone, 716–475–6853 (voice/TDD)

President, Rochester Institute of Technology   ALBERT J. SIMONE
Vice President, National Technical Institute for   ROBERT R. DAVILA
   the Deaf

The National Technical Institute for the Deaf (NTID) was established by act of June 8, 1965 (20 U.S.C. 681), and after several years of planning, programs began in 1968. Funded primarily through the Department of Education, it is an integral part of a larger institution known as the Rochester Institute of Technology (RIT).

The presence of NTID at RIT is the first effort to educate large numbers of deaf students within a college campus planned primarily for hearing students. Unique in the world, NTID is a vital part of RIT's main 1,300-acre campus in suburban Rochester, NY. It provides educational opportunities for qualified students from every State in the Nation and, through educational outreach, publications, and related service, serves deaf persons throughout the world. In addition, NTID conducts research to better understand the role of deafness in education and employment, and to develop innovative teaching techniques. It develops training activities for its faculty and staff, as well as for other professionals working with deaf persons across the country.

One of the major reasons for NTID's success in helping deaf students join the mainstream of American life is its close working relationship with other RIT colleges in developing career-oriented programs of study. One of RIT's main strengths over the years has been its ability to adapt its educational programs to technological and social change, and NTID helps keep that tradition alive. It has served more than 7,000 deaf students since 1968.

Deaf graduates from RIT have found employment throughout the Nation or have moved on to advanced academic studies. In academic year 1996–1997, of those who pursued employment, more than 96 percent have been placed in jobs. Of those employed, 71 percent work in business and industry, more than 5 percent in government, and the remaining 24 percent in education and human services.

The Institutes accept applications from U.S. residents, as well as a limited number of international students. An overall eighth grade achievement level or above is required, and, except under special circumstances, an applicant must have completed a secondary program. An applicant also must show evidence of need for special services because of hearing loss and have an unaided better ear average of 70dB ISO. International applicants generally are required to take the Test of English as a Foreign Language (TOEFL) and must provide documentation of availability of financial resources to meet the full cost of attending RIT. References are requested.

Both Institutes are accredited by the Middle States Association of Colleges and Secondary Schools. Rochester Institute of Technology also has been accredited by the Engineers' Council for Professional Development, National Association of Schools of Art, Committee on Professional Training of American Chemical Society, Council on Social Work Education, and the National Accrediting Agency for Clinical Laboratory Sciences.

For further information, contact the Rochester Institute of Technology, National Technical Institute for the Deaf, Department of Recruitment and Admissions, Lyndon Baines Johnson Building, 52 Lomb Memorial Drive, Rochester, NY 14623–5604. Phone, 716–475–6700.

Sources of Information

Inquiries on the following information may be directed to the specified office, Department of Education, 600 Independence Avenue SW., Washington, DC 20202.

Contracts and Small Business Activities Call or write the Office of Small and Disadvantaged Business Utilization. Phone, 202–708–9820.

Employment Inquiries and applications for employment, and inquiries regarding the college recruitment program, should be directed to the Human Resources Group. Phone, 202–401–0553.

Organization Contact the Executive Office, Office of Management. Phone, 202–401–0690. TDD, 202–260–8956.

For further information, contact the Information Resources Center, Department of Education, Room 2434 (FB10B), 600 Independence Avenue SW., Washington, DC 20202. Phone, 800–USA–LEARN. Internet, http://www.ed.gov/.

DEPARTMENT OF ENERGY

1000 Independence Avenue SW., Washington, DC 20585
Phone, 202–586–5000. Internet, http://www.doe.gov/.

SECRETARY OF ENERGY	FEDERICO PEÑA
Deputy Secretary	ELIZABETH A. MOLER
Under Secretary	ERNEST MONIZ
General Counsel	ERIC J. FYGI, *Acting*
Inspector General	GREGORY H. FRIEDMAN, *Acting*
Assistant Secretary, Congressional and Intergovernmental Affairs	JOHN C. ANGELL
Assistant Secretary, Policy and International Affairs	ROBERT W. GEE
Assistant Secretary, Environment, Safety, and Health	PETER N. BRUSH, *Acting*
Assistant Secretary, Human Resources and Administration	THOMAS T. TAMURA, *Acting*
Assistant Secretary, Fossil Energy	PATRICIA FRY GODLEY
Assistant Secretary, Defense Programs	VICTOR H. REIS
Assistant Secretary, Energy Efficiency and Renewable Energy	DAN W. REICHER
Assistant Secretary, Environmental Management	JAMES M. OWENDOFF, *Acting*
Administrator, Energy Information Administration	JAY E. HAKES
Director, Field Management	G. THOMAS TODD
Director, Fissile Materials Disposition	HOWARD R. CANTER, *Acting*
Director, Public Affairs	BROOKE D. ANDERSON
Director, Worker and Community Transition	ROBERT W. DeGRASSE, JR.
Director of Energy Research	MARTHA A. KREBS
Director of Civilian Radioactive Waste Management	LAKE H. BARRETT, *Acting*
Director of Hearings and Appeals	GEORGE B. BREZNAY
Director of Nonproliferation and National Security	ROSE E. GOTTEMOELLER
Director of Intelligence	NOTRA TRULOCK, *Acting*
Director of Counterintelligence	EDWARD CURRAN
Chief Financial Officer	MICHAEL L. TELSON
Chief Information Officer	HOWARD E. LEWIS, JR., *Acting*
Director of Nuclear Energy, Science, and Technology	WILLIAM D. MAGWOOD IV, *Acting*
Director of Economic Impact and Diversity	CORLISS S. MOODY
Director, Contract Reform and Privatization Project Office	(VACANCY)
Executive Director of Secretary of Energy Advisory Board	SKILA S. HARRIS
Departmental Representative, Defense Nuclear Facilities Safety Board	MARK B. WHITTAKER
Chair, Federal Energy Regulatory Commission	JAMES J. HOECKER

The Department of Energy, in partnership with its customers, is entrusted to contribute to the welfare of the Nation by providing the technical information and the scientific and educational foundation for the technology, policy, and institutional leadership necessary to achieve efficiency in energy use, diversity in energy sources, a more productive and competitive economy, improved environmental quality, and a secure national defense.

The Department of Energy (DOE) was established by the Department of Energy Organization Act (42 U.S.C. 7131), effective October 1, 1977, pursuant to Executive Order 12009 of September 13, 1977. The act consolidated the major Federal energy functions into one Cabinet-level Department.

Offices managing programs which require large budget outlays or provide technical direction and support are structured to reflect the principal programmatic missions of the Department: energy programs, national security programs, environmental management programs, and science and technology programs. The energy programs area includes the Assistant Secretary for Energy Efficiency and Renewable Energy, the Assistant Secretary for Fossil Energy, the Office of Nuclear Energy, Science, and Technology, the Power Marketing Administrations, and the Energy Information Administration. The national security programs area includes the Assistant Secretary for Defense Programs, the Office of Nonproliferation and National Security, the Office of Intelligence, the Office of Counterintelligence, and the Office of Fissile Materials Disposition. The environmental management programs area includes the Assistant Secretary for Environment, Safety, and Health, the Assistant Secretary for Environmental Management, and the Office of Civilian Radioactive Waste Management. The science and technology programs area includes the Office of Energy Research and the Laboratory Operations Board and the Research and Development Council, which have been established under the Secretary of Energy Advisory Board to provide advice regarding the strategic direction for the Department's laboratories, and to coordinate and

integrate research and development across the Department, respectively.

The Department's organization also includes the Federal Energy Regulatory Commission, which is an independent regulatory organization within the Department.

Office of the Secretary

Secretary   The Secretary provides the overall vision, programmatic leadership, management and direction, and administration of the Department; decides major energy policy and planning issues; acts as the principal spokesperson for the Department; and ensures that effective communication and working relationships with State, local, and tribal governments, the President, the Congress, other Federal agencies and departments, the private sector, and the public are achieved. The Secretary is the principal adviser to the President on energy policies, plans, and programs.

Deputy Secretary   The Deputy Secretary acts for the Secretary in the Secretary's absence and assists the Secretary in deciding major energy policy and planning issues and in representing the Department before Congress and the public. The Deputy Secretary, assisted by the Under Secretary, provides daily management guidance and decisionmaking and coordinates the efforts of the energy, weapons/waste cleanup, and science and technology programs to achieve the Department's goals by delivering quality services to the public. The Deputy Secretary has primary oversight responsibility for the Department's environmental management and crosscutting programs and shares responsibility with the Under Secretary for energy and national security programs.

DEPARTMENT OF ENERGY

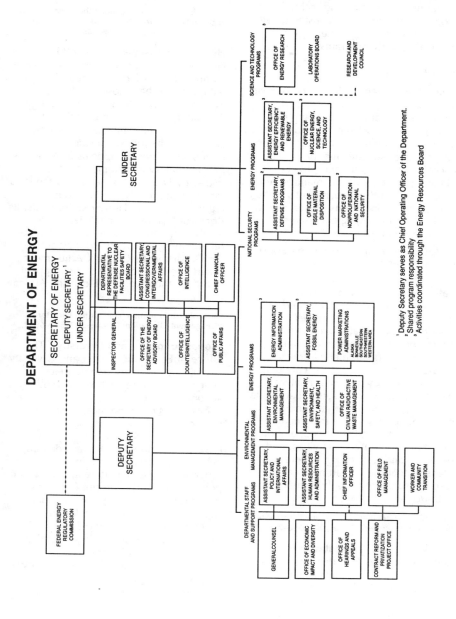

[1] Deputy Secretary serves as Chief Operating Officer of the Department.
[2] Shared program responsibility
[3] Activities coordinated through the Energy Resources Board

Under Secretary   The Under Secretary has primary responsibility for the Department's science and technology programs and shares responsibility with the Deputy Secretary for energy and national security programs.

Staff Offices

Field Management   The Office of Field Management provides centralized responsibility for strategic planning, management coordination, and oversight of the Department's field operations in general; and, specifically, for coordinating program and project planning, execution, and management assignments of the Department's eight multipurpose operations offices and two field offices managing environmental restoration efforts.

For further information, contact the Director of Resource Management and Services. Phone, 202–586–7438.

Policy and International Affairs   The Assistant Secretary for Policy and International Affairs formulates and develops national and international energy policy, strategic plans, and integration of departmental policy, program, and budget goals; conducts integrated policy analyses; analyzes, develops, and coordinates departmental technology, environmental, and economic policy; leads the Department's bilateral and multilateral cooperation, investment, and trade activities; and develops and tests energy emergency plans so that the Department can respond to energy supply disruptions and catastrophic disasters.

For further information, contact the Director of Resource Management. Phone, 202–586–2555.

Departmental Representative to the Defense Nuclear Facilities Safety Board   The Office of the Departmental Representative to the Defense Nuclear Facilities Safety Board (DNFSB) manages the Department's interaction with DNFSB as mandated by law, including achievement of the mutual goal of ensuring protection of public and employee health and safety and the environment by appropriate and timely resolution of DNFSB recommendations and concerns.

For further information, contact the Departmental Representative to the Defense Nuclear Facilities Safety Board. Phone, 202–586–3887.

Hearings and Appeals   The Office of Hearings and Appeals reviews and issues all final DOE orders of an adjudicatory nature, other than those involving matters over which the Federal Energy Regulatory Commission exercises final jurisdiction. The Office is responsible for conducting hearings, considering, and issuing decisions on appeals from orders of a regulatory or adjudicative nature issued by DOE components and requests for exception or exemption from any regulatory or mandatory requirements. Its Board of Contract Appeals hears and resolves appeals pertaining to contract-related matters. The Board may act as the Department's Contract Adjustment Board, the Financial Assistance Appeal Board, or the Invention Licensing Appeal Board.

For further information, contact the Director of Management Operations. Phone, 202–586–6622.

Economic Impact and Diversity   The Office of Economic Impact and Diversity advises the Secretary on the effects of energy policies, regulations, and other actions of the Department and its components on minorities, minority business enterprises, and minority educational institutions, and on ways to ensure that minorities are afforded an opportunity to participate in energy programs of the Department; carries out policy, plan, and oversight functions under sections 8 and 15 of the Small Business Act relating to preferred programs for small businesses, disadvantaged business, labor surplus area concerns, and women-owned businesses; and administers the policy, procedures, plans, and systems of the Department's equal opportunity and civil rights activities.

For further information, contact the Office of Economic Impact and Diversity. Phone, 202–586–8383.

Worker and Community Transition   The Office of Worker and Community

Transition develops policies and programs necessary to plan for and mitigate the impacts of changing conditions on the workers and communities affected by the Department's mission changes; ensures that those policies and programs are carried out in a way that guarantees fair treatment of all concerned, while at the same time recognizing the unique conditions at each site and in each contract; assists those communities most affected by the changing missions at Department sites by using the Department's resources to stimulate economic development; and manages a program for disposition of departmental assets.

For further information, contact the Office of Worker and Community Transition. Phone, 202–586–7550.

Secretary of Energy Advisory Board
The Office of the Secretary of Energy Advisory Board provides executive management to the Board, which advises the Secretary of Energy on issues related to the Department of Energy and the Nation's future energy and national security needs, as well as analysis of scientific, technical, and research and development responsibilities, activities, and operations of the Department.

For further information, contact the Office of the Secretary of Energy Advisory Board. Phone, 202–586–8979.

Contract Reform and Privatization   The Contract Reform and Privatization Project Office guides and coordinates the implementation of the Department of Energy's privatization and contract reform initiatives. Privatization includes the divestiture and transfer of assets and functions of the Department and its contractors to the private sector.

For further information, contact the Contract Reform and Privatization Project Office. Phone, 202–586–0800.

Energy Programs

Energy Efficiency and Renewable Energy
The Assistant Secretary for Energy Efficiency and Renewable Energy is responsible for formulating and directing programs designed to increase the production and utilization of renewable energy (solar, biomass, wind, geothermal, alcohol fuels, etc.) and improving the energy efficiency of the transportation, buildings, industrial, and utility sectors through support of long-term, high-risk research and development and technology transfer activities. The Assistant Secretary manages the program and facilities of the National Renewable Energy Laboratory through its Golden, CO, field office. The Assistant Secretary also has responsibility for administering, through a network of regional support offices, programs that provide financial assistance for State energy planning; weatherization of housing owned by the poor and disadvantaged; the implementation of energy conservation measures by schools and hospitals, local units of government, and public care institutions; and the promotion of energy efficient construction and renovation of Federal facilities.

For further information, contact the Director of Management and Resources. Phone, 202–586–6768.

Fossil Energy   The Assistant Secretary for Fossil Energy is responsible for research and development programs involving fossil fuels—coal, petroleum, and gas. The fossil energy program involves applied research, exploratory development, and limited proof-of-concept testing targeted to high-risk and high-payoff endeavors. The objective of the program is to provide the general technology and knowledge base that the private sector can use to complete development and initiate commercialization of advanced processes and energy systems. The program is principally executed through the Federal Energy Technology Center located in the field.

The Assistant Secretary also manages the Clean Coal Technology Program, the Strategic Petroleum Reserve, and the Naval Petroleum and Oil Shale Reserves.

For further information, contact the Deputy Assistant Secretary for Management. Phone, 301–903–2617.

Nuclear Energy, Science, and Technology The Office of Nuclear Energy, Science, and Technology manages the Department's research and development programs associated with fission and fusion energy. This includes programs relating to nuclear reactor development, both civilian and naval, nuclear fuel cycle, and space nuclear applications. The Office manages a program to provide radioactive and stable isotope products to various domestic and international markets for medical research, health care, and industrial research. In addition, the Office conducts technical analyses and provides advice concerning nonproliferation, assesses alternative nuclear systems and new reactor and fuel cycle concepts, and evaluates proposed advanced nuclear fission energy concepts and technical improvements for possible application to nuclear powerplant systems.

For further information, contact the Director of Policy and Analysis. Phone, 202–586–6630.

Energy Information Administration The Energy Information Administration is responsible for the timely and accurate collection, processing, publication, and distribution of data in the areas of energy resource reserves, energy production, demand, consumption, distribution, and technology.

The Administration performs analyses of energy data to assist government and nongovernment users in understanding energy trends. Analyses are prepared on complex, long-term energy trends and the impacts of energy trends on regional and industrial sectors. Special purpose analyses are prepared involving competition within the energy industries, the capital/financial structure of energy companies, and interfuel substitution.

For further information, contact the Director, National Energy Information Center. Phone, 202–586–1185. TDD, 202–586–1181.

National Security Programs

Defense Programs The Assistant Secretary for Defense Programs directs the Nation's nuclear weapons research, development, testing, production, and surveillance program, as well as the production of the special nuclear materials used by the weapons program within the Department, and management of defense nuclear waste and byproducts. The Office ensures the technology base for the surety, reliability, military effectiveness, and credibility of the nuclear weapon stockpile. The Office also manages research in inertial confinement fusion.

For further information, contact the Deputy Assistant Secretary for Program Support. Phone, 301–903–4016.

Nonproliferation and National Security The Office of Nonproliferation and National Security directs the development of the Department's policy, plans, procedures, and research and development activities relating to arms control, nonproliferation, export controls, and international nuclear safety and safeguard activities; safeguards and secures classified information and protects departmental and DOE contractor facilities and installations; manages the Department's Emergency Management System, which responds to and mitigates the consequences resulting from operational, energy, and continuity–of–Government emergencies; manages a personnel security program for sensitive positions within the Department; and provides threat assessments and support to headquarters and field offices.

For further information, contact the Director of Resource Management. Phone, 202–586–4544.

Intelligence The Office of Intelligence ensures that intelligence information requirements of the Secretary and senior departmental policymakers are met and that the Department's technical, analytical, and research expertise is made available to support U.S. intelligence efforts. The Office ensures effective use of the U.S. Government's intelligence apparatus in support of the Department of Energy's needs for information on global nuclear weapons development, nonproliferation, and foreign hydrocarbon, nuclear, and other energy production and consumption.

For further information, contact the Office of Intelligence. Phone, 202–586–2610.

Counterintelligence   The Office of Counterintelligence develops and implements an effective counterintelligence program to identify, neutralize, and deter foreign government or industrial intelligence activities directed at or involving DOE programs, personnel, facilities, technologies, classified information, and unclassified sensitive information. The Office approves, conducts, and coordinates all policy and investigative matters with the Federal Bureau of Investigation in headquarters and the field.

For further information, contact the Office of Counterintelligence. Phone, 202–586–5901.

Fissile Materials Disposition   The Office of Fissile Materials Disposition is responsible for all activities of the Department relating to the management, storage, and disposition of fissile materials from weapons and weapon systems that are excess to national security needs of the United States. The Office coordinates the development of Department of Energy policy regarding these fissile materials and oversees the development of technical and economic analyses and related research and development for this effort.

For further information, contact the Office of Fissile Materials Disposition. Phone, 202–586–2695.

Environmental Management Programs

Environment, Safety, and Health   The Assistant Secretary for Environment, Safety, and Health provides independent oversight of departmental execution of environmental, occupational safety and health, and nuclear/nonnuclear safety and security laws, regulations, and policies; ensures that departmental programs are in compliance with environmental, health, and nuclear/nonnuclear safety protection plans, regulations, and procedures; exercises independent review and approval of environmental impact statements

prepared within the Department; and carries out the legal functions of the nuclear safety civil penalty and criminal referral activities.

For further information, contact the Deputy Assistant Secretary for Planning and Administration. Phone, 202–586–4704.

Environmental Management   The Assistant Secretary for Environmental Management provides program policy guidance and manages the assessment and cleanup of inactive waste sites and facilities, directs a program in safe and effective waste management operations, and develops and implements an aggressive applied waste research and development program to provide innovative environmental technologies that yield permanent disposal solutions at reduced costs. The Office provides centralized management for the Department for waste management operations, and applied research and development programs and activities, including environmental restoration and waste management program policy and guidance to DOE field offices in these areas, and develops plans for the handling, storage, treatment, or disposal of DOE waste material.

For further information, contact the Director of Administrative Services. Phone, 202–586–2661.

Civilian Radioactive Waste Management   The Office of Civilian Radioactive Waste Management has responsibility for the Nuclear Waste Fund and for the management of Federal programs for recommending, constructing, and operating repositories for disposal of high-level radioactive waste and spent nuclear fuel; interim storage of spent nuclear fuel; monitored retrievable storage; and research, development, and demonstration regarding disposal of high-level radioactive waste and spent nuclear fuel.

For further information, contact the Director for Human Resources and Administration. Phone, 202–586–9173.

Science and Technology Programs

Energy Research   The Office of Energy Research manages the Department's program of basic and applied physical and energy research and development, as well as financial assistance and budgetary priorities for these activities.

The Office manages the basic energy sciences, high energy physics, and fusion energy research programs; administers DOE programs supporting university researchers; funds research in mathematical and computational sciences critical to the use and development of supercomputers; and administers a financial support program for research and development projects not funded elsewhere in the Department. The Office also manages a research program directed at determining the generic environmental, health, and safety aspects of energy technologies and programs.

The Office monitors DOE research and development programs for deficiencies or duplications and, in conjunction with the Assistant Secretary for Congressional, Public, and Intergovernmental Affairs, monitors the international exchange of scientific and technical personnel.

For further information, contact the Associate Director of Resource Management. Phone, 301–903–4944.

Independent Commission

Federal Energy Regulatory Commission

An independent, five-member commission within the Department of Energy, the Federal Energy Regulatory Commission sets rates and charges for the transportation and sale for resale of natural gas, and for the transmission and sale at wholesale of electricity. It also licenses hydroelectric power projects. In addition, the Commission establishes rates or charges for the transportation of oil by pipeline, as well as the valuation of such pipelines.

For further information, contact the Office of External Affairs. Phone, 202–208–0055.

Field Structure

DOE Operations Offices and Contractor-Operated Field Installations

The vast majority of the Department's energy and physical research and development, nuclear weapons research and development, testing and production, environmental restoration, and waste management activities are carried out by contractors who operate Government-owned facilities. Management and administration of Government-owned, contractor-operated facility contracts are the major responsibility of the Department's eight operations offices and two special purpose field offices.

Department operations offices provide a formal link between Department headquarters and the field laboratories and other operating facilities. They also manage programs and projects as assigned from headquarters. Routine management guidance, coordination, and oversight of the operations and field offices is provided by the Office of Field Management. Daily specific program direction for the operations offices is provided by the cognizant Assistant Secretary, Office Director, or program officer.

Operations and Field Offices—Department of Energy

Office/Address	Telephone
Operations Offices	
Albuquerque, NM (P.O. Box 5400, 87185)	505–845–6049
Chicago, IL (9800 S. Cass Ave., Argonne, IL 60439)	708–252–2110
Idaho Falls, ID (785 Doe Pl., 83401)	208–526–1322
Las Vegas, NV (P.O. Box 98518, 89193–8518)	702–295–3211
Oak Ridge, TN (P.O. Box 2001, 37831)	423–576–4444
Oakland, CA (1301 Clay St., 94612–5208)	510–637–1801
Richland, WA (P.O. Box 550, 825 Jadwin Ave., 99352)	509–376–7395

Operations and Field Offices—Department of Energy—Continued

Office/Address	Telephone
Savannah River, SC (P.O. Box A, Aiken, SC 29802)	803–725–2277
Field Offices	
Miamisburg, OH (P.O. Box 3020, 45342–3020)	513–865–3977
Rocky Flats, CO (P.O. Box 928, Golden, CO 80402–0928)	303–966–2025

Power Administrations

The marketing and transmission of electric power produced at Federal hydroelectric projects and reservoirs is carried out by the Department's five Power Administrations. Management oversight of the Power Administrations is the responsibility of the Deputy Secretary.

Bonneville Power Administration   The Administration markets power produced by the Federal Columbia River Power System at the lowest rates, consistent with sound business practices, and gives preference to public entities.

In addition, the Administration is responsible for energy conservation, renewable resource development, and fish and wildlife enhancement under the provisions of the Pacific Northwest Electric Power Planning and Conservation Act of 1980 (16 U.S.C. 839 note).

For further information, contact the Bonneville Power Administration, P.O. Box 3621, 1002 NE. Holladay Street, Portland, OR 97208. Phone, 503–230–5101.

Southeastern Power Administration

The Administration is responsible for the transmission and disposition of surplus electric power and energy generated at reservoir projects in the States of West Virginia, Virginia, North Carolina, South Carolina, Georgia, Florida, Alabama, Mississippi, Tennessee, and Kentucky.

The Administration sets the lowest possible rates to consumers, consistent with sound business principles, and gives preference in the sale of such power and energy to public bodies and cooperatives.

For further information, contact the Southeastern Power Administration, Elberton, GA 30635. Phone, 706–283–9911.

Alaska Power Administration   The Administration is responsible for operating and marketing power for the Eklutna and Snettisham Hydroelectric Projects in Alaska, including transmission systems serving the Anchorage and Juneau areas.

For further information, contact the Alaska Power Administration, Suite 2B, 2770 Sherwood Lane, Juneau, AK 99801. Phone, 907–586–7405.

Southwestern Power Administration

The Administration is responsible for the sale and disposition of electric power and energy in the States of Arkansas, Kansas, Louisiana, Missouri, Oklahoma, and Texas.

The Southwestern Power Administration transmits and disposes of the electric power and energy generated at Federal reservoir projects, supplemented by power purchased from public and private utilities, in such a manner as to encourage the most widespread and economical use. The Administration sets the lowest possible rates to consumers, consistent with sound business principles, and gives preference in the sale of power and energy to public bodies and cooperatives.

The Administration also conducts and participates in the comprehensive planning of water resource development in the Southwest.

For further information, contact the Southwestern Power Administration, P.O. Box 1619, Tulsa, OK 74101. Phone, 918–581–7474.

Western Area Power Administration

The Administration is responsible for the Federal electric power-marketing and transmission functions in 15 central and western States, encompassing a geographic area of 1.3 million square miles. The Administration sells power to cooperatives, municipalities, public utility districts, private utilities, Federal and State agencies, and irrigation districts. The wholesale power customers, in turn, provide service to millions of retail consumers in the States of Arizona, California, Colorado, Iowa, Kansas, Minnesota, Montana, Nebraska, Nevada, New Mexico, North Dakota, South Dakota, Texas, Utah, and Wyoming.

The Administration is responsible for the operation and maintenance of transmission lines, substations, and various auxiliary power facilities in the aforementioned geographic area and also for planning, construction, and operation and maintenance of additional Federal transmission facilities that may be authorized in the future.

For further information, contact the Western Area Power Administration, P.O. Box 3402, Golden, CO 80401. Phone, 303–231–1513.

Sources of Information

Contracts and Small and Disadvantaged Business Utilization Activities Information on business opportunities with the Department and its contractors is available electronically through the Internet, at http://www.pr.doe.gov/ prbus.html. For assistance, call 202–634–4511. For information on existing DOE awards, call 202–586–9051.

Electronic Access Information concerning the Department is available through the Internet, at http:// www.doe.gov/.

Employment Most jobs in the Department are in the competitive service. Positions are filled through hiring individuals with Federal civil service status, but may also be filled using lists of competitive eligibles from the Office of Personnel Management or the Department's special examining units. Contact the Office of Personnel. Phone, 202–586–8676.

Freedom of Information Act To obtain administrative and technical support in matters involving the Freedom of Information, Privacy, and Computer Matching Acts, call 202–586–6025.

Inspector General Hotline Persons who wish to raise issues of concern regarding departmental operations, processes, or practices or who may be aware of or suspect illegal acts or noncriminal violations should contact the hotline. Phone, 202–586–4073.

Office of Scientific and Technical Information The Office manages a system for the centralized collection, announcement, and dissemination of and historical reference to the Department's scientific and technical information and worldwide energy information. Contact the Office of Scientific and Technical Information, P.O. Box 62, Oak Ridge, TN 37831. Phone, 423–576–1323.

Public Information Issuances, Press Releases, and Publications For media contacts, call 202–586–5575.

Public Reading Room For information materials on DOE and public access to DOE records, call 202–586–3142.

Whistleblower Assistance Federal or DOE contractor employees wishing to make complaints of alleged wrongdoing against the Department or its contractors should call 202–586–8289.

For further information concerning the Department of Energy, contact the Office of Public Affairs, Department of Energy, 1000 Independence Avenue SW., Washington, DC 20585. Phone, 202–586–4940. Internet, http://www.doe.gov/.

DEPARTMENT OF HEALTH AND HUMAN SERVICES

200 Independence Avenue SW., Washington, DC 20201
Phone, 202–619–0257. Internet, http://www.dhhs.gov/.

SECRETARY OF HEALTH AND HUMAN SERVICES	DONNA E. SHALALA
Confidential Assistant to the Secretary	JOLINDA GAITHER
Counselor to the Secretary	ANN ROSEWATER
Deputy Secretary	KEVIN THURM
Executive Secretary	LAVARNE BURTON
Chief of Staff	MARY BETH DONAHUE
Director, Intergovernmental Affairs	LANCE SIMMENS
Chair, Departmental Appeals Board	CECILIA SPARKS FORD, *Acting*
Assistant Secretary for Health and Surgeon General	DAVID SATCHER
Principal Deputy Assistant Secretary	(VACANCY)
Executive Officer	HAROLD P. THOMPSON
Deputy Assistant Secretary for Health	JAMES O'HARA
Deputy Assistant Secretary, Disease Prevention and Health Promotion	SUSANNE STOIBER, *Acting*
Deputy Assistant Secretary, Minority Health	CLAY E. SIMPSON
Deputy Assistant Secretary, Population Affairs	THOMAS KRING, *Acting*
Deputy Assistant Secretary, Women's Health	WANDA JONES
Director, Office of Emergency Preparedness	ROBERT KNOUSS
Director, Office of HIV/AIDS Policy	ERIC GOOSBY
Director, Office of International and Refugee Health	LINDA A. VOGEL
Director, Office of Research Integrity	CHRISTOPHER PASCAL, *Acting*
Executive Director, President's Council on Physical Fitness and Sports	SANDRA PERLMUTTER
Assistant Secretary for Legislation	RICHARD J. TARPLIN
Principal Deputy Assistant Secretary	(VACANCY)
Deputy Assistant Secretary (Congressional Liaison)	IRENE B. BUENO
Deputy Assistant Secretary (Health)	JANE C. HORVATH
Deputy Assistant Secretary (Human Services)	MARY M. BOURDETTE
Assistant Secretary for Management and Budget	JOHN J. CALLAHAN
Principal Deputy Assistant Secretary	(VACANCY)
Deputy Assistant Secretary, Policy Initiatives	ELIZABETH D'JAMOOS
Deputy Assistant Secretary, Budget	DENNIS P. WILLIAMS
Deputy Assistant Secretary, Finance	GEORGE H. STRADER
Deputy Assistant Secretary, Grants and Acquisition Management	TERRANCE J. TYCHAN
Deputy Assistant Secretary, Human Resources	EVELYN WHITE
Deputy Assistant Secretary, Information Resources Management	NEIL J. STILLMAN

Director, Office of Facilities Services	PEGGY J. DODD
Assistant Secretary for Planning and Evaluation	MARGARET A. HAMBURG
Principal Deputy Assistant Secretary	(VACANCY)
Executive Assistant	JEFFREY MERKOWITZ
Deputy Assistant Secretary, Disability, Aging, and Long-Term Care Policy	ROBERT WILLIAMS
Deputy Assistant Secretary, Health Policy	GARY CLAXTON
Deputy Assistant Secretary, Human Services Policy	PATRICIA RUGGLES
Deputy Assistant Secretary, Program Systems	SUSANNE A. STOIBER
Deputy Assistant Secretary, Science Policy	WILLIAM RAUB
Assistant Secretary for Public Affairs	MELISSA SKOLFIELD
Deputy Assistant Secretary, Policy and Communications	LAURIE BOEDER
Deputy Assistant Secretary, Media	VICTOR ZONANA
Director, Freedom of Information/Privacy Act Office	ROSS CIRRINCIONE
Director, News Division	P. CAMPBELL GARDETT
Director, Office for Civil Rights	DAVID GARRISON, *Acting*
Deputy Director	OMAR V. GUERRERO
Associate Deputy Director, Management Planning and Evaluation	OMAR V. GUERRERO, *Acting*
Associate Deputy Director, Program Operations	RONALD COPELAND
General Counsel	HARRIET S. RABB
Executive Officer	DONALD E. WATTS
Deputy General Counsel	BEVERLY DENNIS III
Deputy General Counsel, Legal Counsel	(VACANCY)
Deputy General Counsel, Program Review	ANNA L. DURAND
Deputy General Counsel, Regulation	RENEE LANDERS
Associate General Counsel, Business and Administrative Law Division	LESLIE L. CLUNE
Associate General Counsel, Children, Families, and Aging	ROBERT KEITH, *Acting*
Associate General Counsel, Civil Rights	GEORGE LYON
Associate General Counsel, Ethics and Special Counsel for Ethics	JACK M. KRESS
Associate General Counsel, Food and Drug	MARGARET J. PORTER
Associate General Counsel, Health Care Financing	ROBERT JAYE, *Acting*
Associate General Counsel, Legislation	SONDRA S. WALLACE
Associate General Counsel, Public Health	RICHARD RISEBERG
Inspector General	JUNE GIBBS BROWN
Principal Deputy Inspector General	MICHAEL F. MANGANO
Chief Counsel to the Inspector General	D. MCCARTY THORNTON
Deputy Inspector General, Audit Services	THOMAS D. ROSLEWICZ
Deputy Inspector General, Evaluation and Inspections	GEORGE F. GROB
Deputy Inspector General, Investigations	JOHN E. HARTWIG
Deputy Inspector General, Management and Policy	DENNIS J. DUQUETTE

ADMINISTRATION ON AGING

330 Independence Avenue SW., Washington, DC 20201
Phone, 202–401–4541. Internet, http://www.aoa.dhhs.gov/.

Assistant Secretary	JEANETTE C. TAKAMURA
Deputy Assistant Secretary	(VACANCY)
Deputy Assistant Secretary for Governmental Affairs and Elder Rights	(VACANCY)
Special Assistant for Legislation, Public Affairs, and White House Liaison	MOYA BENOIT THOMPSON
Director, Office of Management	JOHN F. MCCARTHY
Director, Office of Program Operations and Development	EDWIN L. WALKER
Director, Office of American Indian, Alaskan Native, and Native Hawaiian Programs	M. YVONNE JACKSON
Director, Office of Program Development	ALFRED DUNCKER

ADMINISTRATION FOR CHILDREN AND FAMILIES

370 L'Enfant Promenade SW., Washington, DC 20447
Phone, 202–401–9200

Assistant Secretary	OLIVIA A. GOLDEN
Principal Deputy Assistant Secretary	JOHN MONAHAN
Deputy Assistant Secretary, Administration	ELIZABETH M. JAMES
Deputy Assistant Secretary, Policy and External Affairs	JOAN LOMBARDI
Commissioner, Children, Youth, and Families	JAMES A. HARRELL, *Acting*
Associate Commissioner, Child Care Bureau	CARMEN NAZARIO
Associate Commissioner, Children's Bureau	CAROL W. WILLIAMS
Associate Commissioner, Family and Youth Services Bureau	TERRY LEWIS
Associate Commissioner, Head Start Bureau	HELEN TAYLOR
Commissioner, Developmental Disabilities	BOB WILLIAMS
Commissioner, Native Americans	GARY N. KIMBLE
Director, Child Support Enforcement	OLIVIA A. GOLDEN
Deputy Director, Child Support Enforcement	DAVID G. ROSS
Director, Community Services	DONALD SYKES
Director, Family Assistance	DIANN DAWSON, *Acting*
Director, Legislative Affairs and Budget	MADELINE MOCKO
Director, Planning, Research, and Evaluation	HOWARD ROLSTON
Director, Public Affairs	MICHAEL KHARFEN
Director, Refugee Resettlement	LAVINIA LIMON
Director, Regional Operations	DIANN DAWSON

AGENCY FOR HEALTH CARE POLICY AND RESEARCH

2101 East Jefferson Street, Rockville, MD 20852
Phone, 301–594–6662. Internet, http://www.ahcpr.gov/. E-mail, info@ahcpr.gov.

Administrator	JOHN M. EISENBERG
Deputy Administrator	LISA SIMPSON
Director, Practice and Technology Assessment	DOUGLAS B. KAMEROW
Director, Management	WILLIARD B. EVANS

Director, Policy Analysis	LARRY T. PATTON
Director, Extramural Policy, Training, and Review	LINDA DEMLO
Director, Center for Cost and Financing Studies	ROSS H. ARNETT III
Director, Health Care Information	CHRISTINE G. WILLIAMS
Director, Organization and Delivery Studies	IRENE FRASER
Director, Outcomes and Effectiveness Research	CAROLYN M. CLANCY
Director, Primary Care Research	CAROLYN M. CLANCY, *Acting*
Director, Quality Measurement and Improvement	SANDRA ROBINSON, *Acting*

AGENCY FOR TOXIC SUBSTANCES AND DISEASE REGISTRY

1600 Clifton Road NE., Atlanta, GA 30333
Phone, 404–639–0700. Internet, http://atsdr1.atsdr.cdc.gov:8080/.

Administrator	CLAIRE V. BROOME, *Acting*
Deputy Administrator	STEPHEN B. THACKER, *Acting*
Assistant Administrator	BARRY L. JOHNSON
Deputy Assistant Administrator	PETER J. MCCUMISKEY

CENTERS FOR DISEASE CONTROL AND PREVENTION

1600 Clifton Road NE., Atlanta, GA 30333
Phone, 404–639–3311. Internet, http://www.cdc.gov/.

Director	CLAIRE V. BROOME, *Acting*
Deputy Director	STEPHEN B. THACKER, *Acting*
Associate Director, Communications	VICKI FREIMUTH
Associate Director, Global Health	STEVE BLOUNT
Associate Director, Management and Operations	ARTHUR C. JACKSON
Associate Director, Minority Health	WALTER W. WILLIAMS
Associate Director, Policy, Planning, and Evaluation	KATHY CAHILL
Associate Director, Science	DIXIE SNIDER
Associate Director, Washington Office	DONALD E. SHRIBER
Director, Equal Employment Opportunity	SUE PORTER-ANDERSON
Director, Office of Health Communication	VICKI FREIMUTH
Director, Office of Health and Safety	JONATHAN Y. RICHMOND
Director, Office of Program Planning and Evaluation	KATHY CAHILL
Director, Office of Program Support	ARTHUR C. JACKSON
Director, Office of Women's Health	KAREN STEINBERGER, *Acting*
Director, Epidemiology Program Office	BARBARA HOLLOWAY, *Acting*
Director, International Health Program Office	STEVE BLOUNT
Director, National Immunization Program Office	WALTER A. ORENSTEIN
Director, National Vaccine Program Office	ROBERT F. BREIMAN
Director, Public Health Practice Program Office	EDWARD L. BAKER

Director, National Center for Chronic Disease Prevention and Health Promotion	JAMES S. MARKS
Director, National Center for Environmental Health	RICHARD J. JACKSON
Director, National Center for Health Statistics	EDWARD J. SONDIK
Director, National Center for HIV, STD, and TB Prevention	HELENE GAYLE
Director, National Center for Infectious Diseases	JAMES M. HUGHES
Director, National Center for Injury Prevention/Control	MARK L. ROSENBERG
Director, National Institute for Occupational Safety and Health	LINDA ROSENSTOCK

FOOD AND DRUG ADMINISTRATION

5600 Fishers Lane, Rockville, MD 20857
Phone, 301–443–1544. Internet, http://www.fda.gov/.

Commissioner	(VACANCY)
Deputy Commissioner/Senior Adviser	(VACANCY)
Executive Assistant to the Commissioner	JEROLD R. MANDE
Chief Mediator and Ombudsman	AMANDA BRYCE NORTON
Administrative Law Judge	DANIEL J. DAVIDSON
Chief Counsel	MARGARET J. PORTER
Special Assistant for Investigations	JOHN H. MITCHELL
Special Agent in Charge, Internal Affairs	LOUIS CAPUTO
Lead Deputy Commissioner for Operations	MICHAEL A. FRIEDMAN
Associate Commissioner, Consumer Affairs	CHARLES A. GAYLORD, *Acting*
Associate Commissioner, Health Affairs	STUART L. NIGHTINGALE
Associate Commissioner, Information Resources Management and Chief Information Officer	WILLIAM M. BRISTOW II
Associate Commissioner, Legislative Affairs	DIANE V. THOMPSON
Associate Commissioner, Planning and Evaluation	PAUL COPPINGER
Associate Commissioner, Public Affairs	LORRIE MCHUGH-WYTKIND
Associate Commissioner, Regulatory Affairs	RONALD G. CHESEMORE
Associate Commissioner, Science	BERNARD A. SCHWETZ
Deputy Commissioner, External Affairs	SHARON SMITH HOLSTON
Deputy Commissioner, Management and Systems	ROBERT J. BYRD
Deputy Commissioner, Policy	WILLIAM B. SCHULTZ
Director, Center for Biologics Evaluation and Research	KATHRYN C. ZOON
Director, Center for Devices and Radiological Health	D. BRUCE BURLINGTON
Director, Center for Drug Evaluation and Research	JANET WOODCOCK
Director, Center for Food Safety and Applied Nutrition	JOE LEVITT
Director, Center for Toxicological Research	BERNARD A. SCHWETZ
Director, Center for Veterinary Medicine	STEPHEN F. SUNDLOF

Director, Office of Facilities, Acquisitions and Central Services	JAMES L. TIDMORE
Director, Office of Financial Management	JAMES DONAHUE
Director, Office of Human Resources and Management Services	MARY L. BABCOCK
Director, Office of International Affairs	WALTER BATTS
Director, Office of Special Health Issues	THERESA A. TOIGA
Director, Office of Women's Health	AUDREY SHEPPARD, *Acting*
Director, Orphan Products Development	MARLENE E. HAFFNER
Team Leader, Industry and Small Business Liaison	BEVERLY COREY, *Acting*

HEALTH CARE FINANCING ADMINISTRATION

200 Independence Avenue SW., Washington, DC 20201
Phone, 202–690–6726. Internet, http://www.hcfa.gov/.

Administrator	NANCY-ANN MIN DEPARLE
Deputy Administrator	MICHAEL HASH
Executive Associate Administrator	KATHLEEN KING
Director, Press Office	CHRIS PEACOCK
Director, Office of Legislation	DEBBIE CHANG
Director, Office of Equal Opportunity and Civil Rights	JOANNE HITCHCOCK
Director, Office of Strategic Planning	BARBARA COOPER
Chief Actuary, Office of the Actuary	RICHARD FOSTER
Director, Office of Communications and Operations Support	PAMELA GENTRY
Director, Office of Clinical Standards and Quality	PETER BOUXSEIN, *Acting*
Director, Center for Beneficiary Relations	CAROL CRONIN
Director, Center for Health Plans and Providers	ROBERT BERENSON
Director, Center for Medicaid and State Operations	SALLY RICHARDSON
Chief of Operations	STEVEN PELOVITZ
Director, Office of Internal Customer Support	MICHAEL ODACHOWSKI
Director, Office of Financial Management	ELIZABETH CUSICK
Director, Office of Information Services	GARY G. CHRISTOPH
Administrator, Northeastern Consortium	JUDY BEREK, *Acting*
Administrator, Southern Consortium	ROSE CRUM-JOHNSON
Administrator, Midwestern Consortium	JOE TILGHMAN
Administrator, Western Consortium	MARY KAY SMITH, *Acting*

HEALTH RESOURCES AND SERVICES ADMINISTRATION

5600 Fishers Lane, Rockville, MD 20857
Phone, 301–443–2086. Internet, http://www.dhhs.gov/hrsa/.

Administrator	CLAUDE E. FOX, *Acting*
Deputy Administrator	THOMAS MORFORD, *Acting*
Chief Medical Officer	WILLIAM A. ROBINSON
Associate Administrator for AIDS	JOSEPH O'NEILL
Associate Administrator for Operations, Management and Program Support	JAMES CORRIGAN, *Acting*

Director, Bureau of Health Professions	NEIL SAMPSON, *Acting*
Director, Bureau of Health Resources Development	JOSEPH F. O'NEILL
Director, Bureau of Maternal and Child Health	AUDREY H. NORA
Director, Bureau of Primary Health Care	MARILYN H. GASTON
Director, Office of Equal Opportunity and Civil Rights	J. CALVIN ADAMS
Director, Office of Information Resources Management	NANCY PAQUIN
Director, Office of Minority Health	ILEANA C. HERRELL
Director, Office of Planning, Evaluation, and Legislation	RONALD H. CARLSON
Director, Office of Policy and Information Coordination	HENRY MONTES
Director, Office of Rural Health Policy	DENA PUSKIN

INDIAN HEALTH SERVICE

5600 Fishers Lane, Rockville, MD 20857
Phone, 301–443–1083. Internet, http://www.tucson.ihs.gov/.

Director	MICHAEL H. TRUJILLO
Senior Adviser to the Director	CAROLE ANNE HEART
Chief Medical Officer	KERMIT C. SMITH
Deputy Director	MICHEL E. LINCOLN
Director, Field Operations	DON J. DAVIS, *Acting*
Director, Headquarters Operations	LUANA L. REYES
Director, Congressional and Legislative Affairs	MICHAEL MAHSETKY
Director, Equal Employment Opportunity and Civil Rights Staff	CECELIA HEFTEL
Director, Public Affairs	TONY KENDRICKS
Director, Tribal Self-Governance	PAULA WILLIAMS
Director, Tribal Programs	DOUGLAS P. BLACK
Director, Urban Indian Health	JAMES CUSSEN

NATIONAL INSTITUTES OF HEALTH

9000 Rockville Pike, Bethesda, MD 20892
Phone, 301–496–4000. Internet, http://www.nih.gov/.

Director	HAROLD E. VARMUS
Deputy Director	RUTH L. KIRSCHSTEIN
Deputy Director, Extramural Research	WENDY BALDWIN
Deputy Director, Intramural Research	MICHAEL M. GOTTESMAN
Deputy Director, Management	ANTHONY L. ITTEILAG
Associate Director, Administration	LEAMON M. LEE
Associate Director, AIDS Research	JACK WHITESCARVER, *Acting*
Associate Director, Behavioral and Social Sciences Research	NORMAN B. ANDERSON
Associate Director, Clinical Research	JOHN I. GALLIN
Associate Director, Communications	R. ANNE THOMAS
Associate Director, Disease Prevention	WILLIAM R. HARLAN
Associate Director, Legislative Policy and Analysis	DIANE SHARTSIS WAX

Associate Director, Research on Minority Health	JOHN RUFFIN
Associate Director, Research on Women's Health	VIVIAN W. PINN
Associate Director, Research Services	STEPHEN A. FICCA
Associate Director, Science Policy	LANA R. SKIRBOLL
Assistant Director, Office of Program Coordination	VIDA BEAVEN
Director, Office of Community Liaison	JANYCE HEDETNIEMI
Director, Office of Equal Opportunity	NAOMI CHURCHILL
Director, Office of Financial Management	FRANCINE LITTLE
Director, Office of Human Resource Management	STEPHEN C. BENOWITZ
Director, Fogarty International Center	PHILIP E. SCHAMBRA
Director, National Center for Research Resources	JUDITH L. VAITUKAITIS
Director, National Library of Medicine	DONALD A.B. LINDBERG
Director, Warren G. Magnuson Clinical Center	JOHN I. GALLIN
Director, Center for Information Technology	ALAN GRAEFF
Director, Center for Scientific Review	ELLIE EHRENFELD
Director, National Institute on Aging	RICHARD J. HODES
Director, National Institute of Alcohol Abuse and Alcoholism	ENOCH GORDIS
Director, National Institute of Allergy and Infectious Diseases	ANTHONY S. FAUCI
Director, National Institute of Arthritis and Musculoskeletal and Skin Diseases	STEVEN I. KATZ
Director, National Cancer Institute	RICHARD KLAUSNER
Director, National Institute of Child Health and Human Development	DUANE F. ALEXANDER
Director, National Institute on Deafness and Other Communication Disorders	JAMES F. BATTEY, JR.
Director, National Institute of Dental Research	HAROLD C. SLAVKIN
Director, National Institute of Diabetes, Digestive, and Kidney Diseases	PHILLIP GORDEN
Director, National Institute on Drug Abuse	ALAN I. LESHNER
Director, National Institute of Environmental Health Sciences	KENNETH OLDEN
Director, National Eye Institute	CARL KUPFER
Director, National Institute of General Medical Sciences	MARVIN CASSMAN
Director, National Heart, Lung, and Blood Institute	CLAUDE J.M. LENFANT
Director, National Human Genome Research Institute	FRANCIS S. COLLINS
Director, National Institute of Mental Health	STEVEN E. HYMAN
Director, National Institute of Neurological Disorders and Stroke	AUDREY S. PENN, *Acting*
Director, National Institute of Nursing Research	PATRICIA A. GRADY

PROGRAM SUPPORT CENTER

5600 Fishers Lane, Rockville, MD 20857
Phone, 301–443–3921. Internet, http://www.dhhs.gov/psc/.

Director	LYNNDA M. REGAN
Staff Director	NORMAN E. PRINCE, JR.
Chief Financial Officer	JOHN C. WEST
Director, Office of Budget and Finance	JERRILYN ANDERSON
Director, Office of Management Operations	DOUGLAS F. MORTL
Director, Office of Marketing	MARSHA E. ALVAREZ
Director, Administrative Operations Service	RICHARD W. HARRIS
Director, Financial Management Service	JOHN C. WEST
Director, Human Resources Service	(VACANCY)

SUBSTANCE ABUSE AND MENTAL HEALTH SERVICES ADMINISTRATION

5600 Fishers Lane, Rockville, MD 20857
Phone, 301–443–4797. Internet, http://www.samhsa.gov/.

Administrator	NELBA CHAVEZ
Deputy Administrator	PAUL M. SCHWAB
Special Assistant	LORINDA DANIEL
Associate Administrator, Communications	MARK WEBER
Associate Administrator, Managed Care	ERIC GOPLERUD
Associate Administrator, Minority Health	DELORIS L-JAMES HUNTER
Associate Administrator, Policy and Program Coordination	MARY C. KNIPMEYER, *Acting*
Director, Center for Mental Health Services	BERNARD S. ARONS
Director, Center for Substance Abuse Prevention	KAROL L. KUMPFER
Director, Center for Substance Abuse Treatment	CAMILLE BARRY, *Acting*
Director, Office of Program Services and Executive Officer	RICHARD KOPANDA
Director, Office of Applied Studies	DONALD GOLDSTONE

The Department of Health and Human Services is the Cabinet-level department of the Federal executive branch most concerned with people and most involved with the Nation's human concerns. In one way or another, it touches the lives of more Americans than any other Federal agency. It is literally a department of people serving people, from newborn infants to persons requiring health services to our most elderly citizens.

The Department of Health and Human Services (HHS) was created as the Department of Health, Education, and Welfare on April 11, 1953 (5 U.S.C. app.), and redesignated, effective May 4, 1980, by the Department of Education Organization Act (20 U.S.C. 3508).

Office of the Secretary

The Secretary of Health and Human Services advises the President on health, welfare, and income security plans, policies, and programs of the Federal Government. The Secretary directs Department staff in carrying out the approved programs and activities of the Department and promotes general public understanding of the Department's goals, programs, and objectives. The Secretary administers these functions through the Office of the Secretary and the Department's 12 operating divisions.

The Office of the Secretary includes the offices of Deputy Secretary, the

DEPARTMENT OF HEALTH AND HUMAN SERVICES

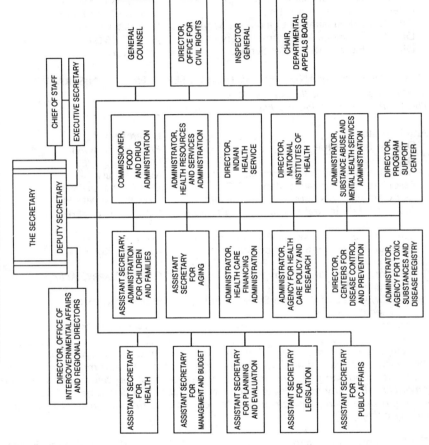

Assistant Secretaries, Inspector General, and General Counsel. Some offices whose public purposes are broadly applied are detailed further.

Civil Rights The Office is responsible for the administration and enforcement of the following laws that prohibit discrimination in federally assisted health and human services programs:

—title VI of the Civil Rights Act of 1964;

—section 504 of the Rehabilitation Act of 1973, as amended;

—the Age Discrimination Act of 1975;

—title IX of the Education Amendments of 1972;

—section 407 of the Drug Abuse Offense and Treatment Act of 1972;

—section 321 of the Comprehensive Alcohol Abuse and Alcoholism Prevention, Treatment and Rehabilitation Act of 1970;

—the Equal Employment Opportunity provisions of the Communications Finance Act of 1934, as amended;

—titles VI and XVI of the Public Health Service Act;

—the nondiscrimination provisions of the Omnibus Budget Reconciliation Act of 1981;

—section 307(a) of the Family Violence Prevention and Services Act;

—titles VII and VIII of the Public Health Service Act; and

—subtitle A, title II, of the Americans with Disabilities Act of 1990.

Public Health and Science The Office provides leadership and serves as the focal point for coordination across the Department in public health and science by:

—ensuring that the Department conducts broad-based public health assessments designed to anticipate future public health issues and problems and that it devises and implements appropriate interventions and evaluations to maintain, sustain, and improve the health of the Nation;

—providing assistance in managing the implementation and coordination of Secretarial decisions for Public Health Service (PHS) operating divisions and coordination of population-based health, clinical preventive services, and science initiatives that cut across operating divisions;

—providing management of the following offices: Office of Women's Health, Office of Minority Health, Office of Emergency Preparedness, Office of Population Affairs, Office of International and Refugee Health, Office of Disease Prevention and Health Promotion, President's Council on Physical Fitness and Sports, Office of Research Integrity, Office of HIV/AIDS, and the Office of the Surgeon General;

—providing presentations to foreign governments and multilateral agencies on international health issues; and

—providing direction and policy oversight through the Surgeon General for the Public Health Service Commissioned Corps.

Regional Offices The 10 HHS Regional Directors are the Secretary's representatives in direct, official dealings with State and local government organizations. They provide a central focus in each region for departmental relations with Congress and promote general understanding of Department programs, policies, and objectives. They also advise the Secretary on the potential effects of decisions.

Regional Offices—Department of Health and Human Services

Address (Areas Served)	Director	Telephone
Atlanta, GA, Rm. 1515, 101 Marietta Twr., 30323 (AL, FL, GA, KY, MS, NC, SC, TN).	Patricia Ford-Roegner	404–562–7888
Boston, MA, Rm. 2100, Government Ctr., 02203 (CT, MA, ME, NH, RI, VT)	Judith Kurland	617–565–1500
Chicago, IL, 23d Fl., 105 W. Adams St., 60603 (IL, IN, MI, OH, WI)	Hannah Rosenthal	312–353–5160
Dallas, TX, Suite 1124–ORD, 1301 Young St., 75202–4348 (AR, LA, NM, OK, TX).	Patricia Montoya	214–767–3301
Denver, CO, Rm. 1076, 1961 Stout St., 80294–3538 (CO, MT, ND, SD, UT, WY).	Margaret Cary	303–844–3372
Kansas City, MO, Rm. 210, 601 E. 12th St., 64106 (IA, KS, MO, NE)	Kathleen Steele	816–426–2821
New York, NY, Rm. 3835, 26 Federal Plz., 10278 (NJ, NY, PR, VI)	Allison E. Greene	212–264–4600
Philadelphia, PA, Rm. 11480, 3535 Market St., 19104 (DC, DE, MD, PA, VA, WV).	Lynn Yeakel	215–596–6492

Regional Offices—Department of Health and Human Services—Continued

Address (Areas Served)	Director	Telephone
San Francisco, CA, Rm. 431, 50 United Nations Plz., 94102 (AS, AZ, CA, GU, HI, NV).	Grantland Johnson	415–437–8500
Seattle, WA, Rm. 911F, 2201 6th Ave., 98121 (AK, ID, OR, WA)	Jay Inslee	206–615–2010

Administration on Aging

The Administration on Aging (AOA) is the principal agency designated to carry out the provisions of the Older Americans Act of 1965, as amended (42 U.S.C. 3001 *et seq.*). It serves as the lead agency within HHS on all issues involving the elderly population. The Administration:
—advises the Secretary, Department components, and other Federal departments and agencies on the characteristics, circumstances, and needs of older persons;
—develops policies, plans, and programs designed to promote their welfare and advocates for their needs in HHS program planning and policy development;
—administers a program of formula grants to States to establish State and community programs for older persons under the title III of the Act (45 CFR 1321);

—administers a program of grants to American Indians, Alaskan Natives, and Native Hawaiians to establish programs for older Native Americans under title VI of the Act (45 CFR 1328);
—provides policy, procedural direction, and technical assistance to States and Native American grantees to promote the development of community-based systems of comprehensive social, nutrition, and support services for older persons;
—administers programs of training, research, and demonstration under title IV of the Act; and
—administers ombudsman, legal services oversight, and protective services for older people under title VII of the Act.

For further information, contact the Assistant Secretary for Aging. Phone, 202–401–4634.

Administration for Children and Families

The Administration for Children and Families (ACF) was created on April 15, 1991, under authority of section 6 of Reorganization Plan No. 1 of 1953 and pursuant to the authority vested in the Secretary of Health and Human Services.

The Administration, led by the Assistant Secretary for Children and Families, reports to the Secretary. The Assistant Secretary also serves as the Director of Child Support Enforcement. The Administration advises the Secretary on issues pertaining to children and families, including Native Americans, people with developmental disabilities, refugees, and legalized aliens.

The Administration for Children and Families provides national leadership and direction to plan, manage, and coordinate the nationwide administration of comprehensive and supportive programs for vulnerable children and families. The Administration oversees and finances a broad range of programs for children and families including Native Americans, persons with developmental disabilities, refugees, and legalized aliens to help them develop and grow toward a more independent, self-reliant life. These programs, carried out by State, county, city, and tribal governments and public and private local agencies, are designed to promote stability, economic security, responsibility, and self-sufficiency. The Administration coordinates development and implementation of family-centered strategies, policies, and linkages among its programs and with other Federal and State programs serving children and families.

Administration on Children, Youth, and Families (ACYF) The Administration, through the Assistant Secretary for Children and Families, advises the Secretary on matters relating to the sound development of children, youth, and families.

ACYF administers State grant programs under titles IV–B and IV–E of the Social Security Act to assist States in providing child welfare services, foster care, adoption assistance, and independent living; child care programs authorized under title IV–A of the Social Security Act and the Child Care and Development Block Grant which provide support to working families and families moving from welfare to work; the State grant programs to improve and increase child abuse prevention and treatment activities and develop family preservation and family support services; the Head Start Program; programs which provide services for runaway and homeless youth and their families; child welfare training programs; and child abuse and neglect research and demonstration programs. ACYF also supports and encourages initiatives to involve the private and voluntary sectors in the areas of children, youth, and families.

In concert with other components of ACF, ACYF develops and implements research, demonstration, and evaluation strategies for the discretionary funding of activities designed to improve and enrich the lives of children and youth and to strengthen families.

For further information, contact the Commissioner, Administration on Children, Youth, and Families, Administration for Children and Families, Department of Health and Human Services, 370 L'Enfant Promenade SW., Washington, DC 20447. Phone, 202–205–8347 or 202–401–2337.

Administration on Developmental Disabilities (ADD) The Administration, through the Assistant Secretary for

Children and Families, advises the Secretary on matters relating to persons with developmental disabilities and their families. ADD serves as the focal point in the Department for supporting and encouraging the provision of quality services to persons with developmental disabilities; assists States, through the design and implementation of a comprehensive and continuing State plan, in increasing independence, productivity, and community inclusion of persons with developmental disabilities; administers the State Developmental Disabilities Councils, the Protection and Advocacy Grant Program, and the discretionary grant programs; and serves as a resource in developing policies and programs to reduce or eliminate barriers experienced by persons with developmental disabilities.

In concert with other components of ACF, ADD develops and implements research, demonstration, and evaluation strategies for discretionary funding of activities to improve lives of persons with developmental disabilities.

For further information, contact the Commissioner, Administration on Developmental Disabilities, Administration for Children and Families, Department of Health and Human Services, 370 L'Enfant Promenade SW., Washington, DC 20447. Phone, 202–690–6590.

Administration for Native Americans (ANA) The Administration promotes the goal of social and economic self-sufficiency of American Indians, Alaskan Natives, Native Hawaiians, and other Native American Pacific Islanders, including natives of Samoa, Guam, Palau, and the Northern Marianas. Self-sufficiency is that level of development at which a Native American community can control and internally generate resources to provide for the needs of its members and meet its own economic and social goals. Social and economic underdevelopment is the paramount obstacle to the self-sufficiency of Native American communities and families.

ANA promotes lasting self-sufficiency and seeks to enhance self-government and strengthen community social and economic infrastructures through competitive financial assistance grants in support of locally determined and designed projects addressing community needs and goals. Competitive grants are offered in the areas of social and economic development, Native American languages preservation and enhancement, environmental regulatory enhancement, and mitigation of environmental damage on Indian lands.

ANA represents the concerns of all Native Americans and serves as the focal point in the Department on the full range of developmental, social, and economic strategies that support Native American self-determination and self-sufficiency.

The Commissioner of ANA is the Chair of the Intra-Departmental Council on Native American Affairs (IDCNAA), composed of 25 heads of the Department's major agencies, and advises the Secretary on all matters affecting Native Americans that involve the Department.

For further information, contact the Commissioner, Administration for Native Americans, Administration for Children and Families, Department of Health and Human Services, 370 L'Enfant Promenade SW., Washington, DC 20447. Phone, 202–690–7776.

Child Support Enforcement (CSE)   The Office of Child Support Enforcement advises the Secretary on matters relating to child support enforcement. It provides direction, guidance, and oversight to State CSE program offices and on activities authorized and directed by section D, part IV of the Social Security Act, and other pertinent legislation requiring States to develop programs locating absent parents, establishing paternity when necessary, obtaining child support orders, and enforcing those orders.

The Office assists States in establishing adequate reporting procedures and in maintaining records. It operates the Federal Parent Locator Service, including the National New Hire Directory; certifies to the Secretary of the Treasury amounts of overdue child support that require collection in specific instances; works with States to automate their child support enforcement programs; and

reviews State applications for use of U.S. courts to enforce child support orders.

For further information, contact the Public Inquiries and Information Branch, Office of Child Support Enforcement, Administration for Children and Families, Department of Health and Human Services, 370 L'Enfant Promenade SW., Washington, DC 20447. Phone, 202–401–9373.

Community Services   The Office, through the Assistant Secretary for Children and Families, advises the Secretary on matters relating to community programs that promote economic self-sufficiency. It is responsible for administering programs that serve low-income and needy individuals and addresses the overall goal of personal responsibility in achieving and maintaining self-sufficiency.

The Office administers the Community Services Block Grant, Social Services Block Grant, and the Low-Income Home Energy Assistance programs, as well as a variety of discretionary grant programs that foster family stability, economic security, responsibility, and self-support. It also promotes and provides services to homeless and low-income individuals and develops new and innovative approaches to reduce welfare dependency.

For further information, contact the Director, Office of Community Services, Administration for Children and Families, Department of Health and Human Services, 370 L'Enfant Promenade SW., Washington, DC 20447. Phone, 202–401–9333.

Refugee Resettlement   The Office of Refugee Resettlement (ORR) advises the Secretary, through the Assistant Secretary for Children and Families, on policies and programs regarding refugee resettlement, immigration, and repatriation matters. It plans, develops, and directs implementation of a comprehensive program for domestic refugee and entrant resettlement assistance.

The Office provides direction and technical guidance to the nationwide administration of programs including

Refugee and Entrant Resettlement, and the U.S. Repatriate Program.

For further information, contact the Director, Office of Refugee Resettlement, Administration for Children and Families, Department of Health and Human Services, 370 L'Enfant Promenade SW., Washington, DC 20447. Phone, 202–401–9246.

Family Assistance   The Office of Family Assistance (OFA), through the Assistant Secretary for Children and Families, advises the Secretary on matters relating to public assistance and economic self-sufficiency programs. It provides leadership, direction, and technical guidance in administering the Temporary Assistance for Needy Families Program and the Aid to the Aged, Blind, and Disabled Program in Guam, Puerto Rico, and the Virgin Islands.

The Office provides technical assistance to States and territories, and assesses their performance in administering these programs; reviews State plans and amendments for

completeness; and shares information and suggests actions to improve effectiveness. It directs reviews, provides consultation, and conducts necessary negotiations to achieve effective public assistance programs.

For further information, contact the Director, Office of Family Assistance, Administration for Children and Families, Department of Health and Human Services, 370 L'Enfant Promenade SW., Washington, DC 20447. Phone, 202–401–9275.

Office of Regional Operations   The Office makes recommendations to and advises the Assistant Secretary for Children and Families on all strategic and operations activities related to implementation of the agency's programs at the regional level.

For further information, contact the Director, Office of Regional Operations, Administration for Children and Families, Department of Health and Human Services, 370 L'Enfant Promenade SW., Washington, DC 20447. Phone, 202–401–4802.

Regional Offices—Administration for Children and Families
(RHD: Regional Hub Director; RA: Regional Administrator)

Address (Areas Served)	Director	Telephone
Atlanta, GA, Suite 4M60, 61 Forsyth St. SW., 30323–8909 (AL, FL, GA, KY, MS, NC, SC, TN).	Steven J. Golightly (RHD).	404–562–2922
Boston, MA, Rm. 2000, Government Ctr., 02203–0131 (CT, MA, ME, NH, RI, VT).	Hugh Galligan (RA)	617–565–1020
Chicago, IL, 20th Fl., 105 W. Adams St., 60603–6201 (IL, IN, MI, OH, WI)	Linda Carson (RHD)	312–353–4237
Dallas, TX, Rm. 914, 1301 Young St., 75202 (AR, LA, NM, OK, TX)	Leon McCowan (RHD) ...	214–767–9648
Denver, CO, Rm. 924, 1961 Stout St., 80294–1185 (CO, MT, ND, SD, UT, WY).	Beverly Turnbo (RA)	303–844–2622 (Ext. 301)
Kansas City, MO, Rm. 384, 601 E. 12th St., 64106–2898 (IA, KS, MO, NE)	Linda Lewis (RA)	816–426–3981
New York, NY, Rm. 4049, 26 Federal Plz., 10278–0022 (NJ, NY, PR, VI)	Mary Ann Higgins (RA) ..	212–264–2890
Philadelphia, PA, Rm. 5450, 3535 Market St., 19104–3309 (DC, DE, MD, PA, VA, WV).	David Lett (RA)	215–596–0352
San Francisco, CA, Rm. 450, 50 United Nations Plz., 94102–4988 (AS, AZ, CA, GU, HI, NV).	Sharon Fujii (RA)	415–437–8400
Seattle, WA, Suite 600, 2201 6th Ave., 98121–1827 (AK, ID, OR, WA)	Stephen Henigson (RA) ..	206–615–2547 (Ext. 2249)

Agency for Health Care Policy and Research

A reorganization order, signed by the Secretary on October 31, 1995, established the Agency for Health Care Policy and Research (AHCPR) as an operating division within Public Health Service of the U.S. Department of Health and Human Services.

As the health services research arm of the Public Health Service, AHCPR's goals are to work with the private sector

and other public organizations to help consumers make better informed choices; determine what works best in clinical practice; measure and improve quality of care; monitor and evaluate health care delivery; improve the cost-effective use of health care resources; assist health care policymakers; and build and sustain the health services research infrastructure.

AHCPR supports and conducts research which creates the science base to guide improvements in both clinical care and the organization and financing of health care; promotes the incorporation of science into practice through the development of tools for public and private decisionmakers at all levels of the health care system; and develops the data and information infrastructure to study and track the performance of the health care system and the needs of stakeholders.

Currently, AHCPR supports and conducts research and evaluation projects in the areas of consumer choice; clinical improvement; health care cost, financing, and access; health information technology; outcomes and effectiveness of health care; health care organization and delivery; quality measurement and improvement; and technology assessment.

For further information, contact the Agency for Health Care Policy and Research. Phone, 301–594–1364. Internet, http://www.ahcpr.gov/. E-mail, info@ahcpr.gov.

Agency for Toxic Substances and Disease Registry

A reorganization order, signed by the Secretary on October 31, 1995, established the Agency for Toxic Substances and Disease Registry (ATSDR) as an operating division within the Public Health Service of the U.S. Department of Health and Human Services. Statutory authority for the Agency is derived from the Comprehensive Environmental Response, Compensation, and Liability Act of 1980 (42 U.S.C. 9601 et seq.), as amended by the Superfund Amendments and Reauthorization Act of 1986, the Resource Conservation and Recovery Act (42 U.S.C. 6901 et seq.), and provisions of the Solid Waste Disposal Act relating to sites and substances found at those sites and other forms of uncontrolled releases of toxic substances into the environment.

The Agency's mission is to prevent exposure and adverse human health effects and diminished quality of life associated with exposure to hazardous substances from waste sites, unplanned releases, and other sources of pollution present in the environment. To carry out this mission, ATSDR, in cooperation with States and other Federal and local agencies:

—evaluates information on the release of hazardous substances into the environment to assess any current or future impact on public health;

—through epidemiologic, surveillance, and other studies of toxic substances and their effects, increases understanding of the relationship between exposure to hazardous substances and adverse human health effects;

—establishes and maintains registries of persons exposed to specific substances for long-term followup of scientific studies;

—establishes and maintains a complete listing of areas closed to the public or otherwise restricted in use because of toxic substance contamination;

—summarizes and makes available to the public, researchers, and physicians and other health care providers data on the health effects of hazardous substances;

—conducts or sponsors research to increase scientific knowledge about the effects on human health of hazardous substances released from waste sites or during transportation accidents; and

—provides health-related support, including health consultations and training for first responders to ensure adequate response to public health emergencies.

For further information, contact the Office of Policy and External Affairs, Agency for Toxic Substances and Disease Registry, 1600 Clifton Road NE., MS E–60, Atlanta, GA 30333. Phone, 404–639–0501. Internet, http://www.atsdr1.atsdr.cdc.gov:8080/.

Centers for Disease Control and Prevention

A reorganization order, signed by the Secretary on October 31, 1995, established the Centers for Disease Control and Prevention (CDC) as an operating division within the Public Health Service of the U.S. Department of Health and Human Services.

CDC is the Federal agency charged with protecting the public health of the Nation by providing leadership and direction in the prevention and control of diseases and other preventable conditions and responding to public health emergencies. It is composed of 11 major operating components: Epidemiology Program Office, International Health Program Office, National Immunization Program Office, Public Health Practice Program Office, National Center for HIV, STD, and TB Prevention, National Center for Environmental Health, National Center for Injury Prevention and Control, National Institute for Occupational Safety and Health, National Center for Chronic Disease Prevention and Health Promotion, National Center for Infectious Diseases, and National Center for Health Statistics.

CDC administers national programs for the prevention and control of communicable and vector-borne diseases, injury, and other preventable conditions. It develops and implements programs in chronic disease prevention and control, including consultation with State and local health departments. It develops and implements programs to deal with environmental health problems, including responding to environmental, chemical, and radiation emergencies.

CDC directs and enforces foreign quarantine activities and regulations; provides consultation and assistance in upgrading the performance of public health and clinical laboratories; and organizes and implements a National Health Promotion Program, including a nationwide program of research, information, and education in the field of smoking and health. It also collects, maintains, analyzes, and disseminates national data on health status and health services.

Through the National Institute for Occupational Safety and Health, CDC develops occupational safety and health standards and carries out research and other activities to ensure safe and healthful working conditions for all working people.

CDC also provides consultation to other nations in the control of preventable diseases and participates with national and international agencies in the eradication or control of communicable diseases and other preventable conditions.

For further information, contact the Centers for Disease Control and Prevention, 1600 Clifton Road NE., Atlanta, GA, 30333. Phone, 404–639–3286. Internet, http://www.cdc.gov/.

Food and Drug Administration

A reorganization order, signed by the Secretary on October 31, 1995, established the Food and Drug Administration (FDA) as an operating division of the Public Health Service within the U.S. Department of Health and Human Services. The name Food and Drug Administration was first provided by the Agriculture Appropriation Act of 1931 (46 Stat. 392), although similar law enforcement functions had been in existence under different organizational titles when the Food and Drug Act of 1906 (21 U.S.C. 1–15) became effective January 1, 1907.

Food and Drug Administration programs are designed to achieve the single, overall objective of consumer protection. FDA's mission is to ensure that food is safe, pure, and wholesome; human and animal drugs, biological products, and medical devices are safe and effective; and electronic products that emit radiation are safe.

FDA is headed by a Commissioner. The Office of Policy directs and coordinates agency rulemaking and regulations development activities. The Office of Operations develops and administers agency programs and field operations, through the Office of Regulatory Affairs, the regional field offices, the Center for Drug Evaluation and Research, the Center for Biologics Evaluation and Research, the Center for Food Safety and Applied Nutrition, the Center for Veterinary Medicine, the Center for Devices and Radiological Health, the National Center for Toxicological Research, and the Office of Orphan Products Development. Selected FDA activities are detailed below.

For further information, call 301–443–1544.

Center for Drug Evaluation and Research   The Center develops administration policy with regard to the safety, effectiveness, and labeling of all drug products for human use; reviews and evaluates new drug applications and investigational new drug applications; develops and implements standards for the safety and effectiveness of all over-the-counter drugs; and monitors the quality of marketed drug products through product testing, surveillance, and compliance programs.

The Center coordinates with the Center for Biologics Evaluation and Research regarding activities for biological drug products, including research, compliance, and product review and approval, and develops and promulgates guidelines on current good manufacturing practices for use by the drug industry. It develops and disseminates information and educational material dealing with drug products to the medical community and the public in coordination with the Office of the Commissioner.

The Center conducts research and develops scientific standards on the composition, quality, safety, and effectiveness of human drugs; collects and evaluates information on the effects and use trends of marketed drug

products; monitors prescription drug advertising and promotional labeling to ensure their accuracy and integrity; and analyzes data on accidental poisonings and disseminates toxicity and treatment information on household products and medicines. In carrying out these functions, the Center cooperates with other FDA and Department components, governmental and international agencies, volunteer health organizations, universities, individual scientists, nongovernmental laboratories, and manufacturers of drug products.

For further information, call 301–827–4573.

Center for Biologics Evaluation and Research   The Center administers regulation of biological products under the biological product control provisions of the Public Health Service Act and applicable provisions of the Federal Food, Drug, and Cosmetic Act. It provides dominant focus in the Administration for coordination of the AIDS program, works to develop an AIDS vaccine and AIDS diagnostic tests, and conducts other AIDS-related activities. It inspects manufacturers' facilities for compliance with standards, tests products submitted for release, establishes written and physical standards, and approves licensing of manufacturers to produce biological products.

The Center plans and conducts research related to the development, manufacture, testing, and use of both new and old biological products to develop a scientific base for establishing standards designed to ensure the continued safety, purity, potency, and efficacy of biological products and coordinates with the Center for Drug Evaluation and Research regarding activities for biological drug products, including research, compliance, and product review and approval.

The Center plans and conducts research on the preparation, preservation, and safety of blood and blood products, the methods of testing safety, purity, potency, and efficacy of such products for therapeutic use, and the immunological problems concerned with products, testing, and use of diagnostic reagents employed in grouping and typing blood.

In carrying out these functions, the Center cooperates with other FDA and Department components, governmental and international agencies, volunteer health organizations, universities, individual scientists, nongovernmental laboratories, and manufacturers of biological products.

For further information, call 301–827–2000.

Center for Food Safety and Applied Nutrition   The Center conducts research and develops standards on the composition, quality, nutrition, and safety of food, food additives, colors, and cosmetics. It conducts research designed to improve the detection, prevention, and control of contamination that may be responsible for illness or injury conveyed by foods, colors, and cosmetics. It also coordinates and evaluates the FDA's surveillance and compliance programs relating to foods, colors, and cosmetics.

The Center reviews industry petitions and develops regulations for food standards to permit the safe use of color additives and food additives; collects and interprets data on nutrition, food additives, and environmental factors affecting the total chemical result posed by food additives; and maintains a nutritional data bank.

For further information, call 800–332–4010.

Center for Veterinary Medicine   The Center develops and conducts programs with respect to the safety and efficacy of veterinary preparations and devices, evaluates proposed use of veterinary preparations for animal safety and efficacy, and evaluates the FDA's surveillance and compliance programs relating to veterinary drugs and other veterinary medical matters.

For further information, call 301–594–1755.

Center for Devices and Radiological Health   The Center develops and carries out a national program designed to control unnecessary exposure of humans to, and ensure the safe and efficacious use of, potentially hazardous ionizing and non-ionizing radiation. It develops policy and priorities regarding FDA programs relating to the safety, effectiveness, and labeling of medical devices for human use, and conducts an electronic product radiation control program, including the development and administration of performance standards.

The Center plans, conducts, and supports research and testing relating to medical devices and to the health effects of radiation exposure, and reviews and evaluates medical devices premarket approval applications, product development protocols, and exemption requests for investigational devices. It develops, promulgates, and enforces performance standards for appropriate categories of medical devices and good manufacturing practice regulations for manufacturers, and provides technical and other non-financial assistance to small manufacturers of medical devices.

The Center develops regulations, standards, and criteria and recommends changes in FDA legislative authority necessary to protect the public health; provides scientific and technical support to other components within FDA and other agencies on matters relating to radiological health and medical devices; and maintains appropriate liaison with other Federal, State, and international agencies, industry, and consumer and professional organizations.

For further information, call 800–638–2041.

National Center for Toxicological Research   The Center conducts research programs to study the biological effects of potentially toxic chemical substances found in the environment, emphasizing the determination of the health effects resulting from long-term, low-level exposure to chemical toxicants and the basic biological processes for chemical toxicants in animal organisms; develops improved methodologies and test protocols for evaluating the safety of chemical toxicants and the data that will facilitate the extrapolation of toxicological data from laboratory animals to man; and develops Center programs as a natural resource under the National Toxicology Program.

For further information, call 501–543–7000.

Regional Offices   Regional operations for the enforcement of the laws under the jurisdiction of the FDA are carried out by 6 Regional Field Offices located in the cities of the Department's regional offices, through 21 district offices and 135 resident inspection posts located throughout the United States and Puerto Rico.

For further information, call 301–827–3101.

Health Care Financing Administration

[For the Health Care Financing Administration statement of organization, see the *Federal Register* of May 2, 1997, 62 FR 24120]

The Health Care Financing Administration (HCFA) was created as a principal operating component of HHS by the Secretary on March 8, 1977, to combine under one administration the oversight of the Medicare program, the Federal portion of the Medicaid program, and related quality assurance activities. Today, HCFA serves millions of elderly, disabled, and poor Americans through Medicare and Medicaid— approximately one-quarter of the United States population.

Medicare   The program provides health insurance coverage for people age 65 and over, younger people who are receiving social security disability benefits, and persons who need dialysis or kidney transplants for treatment of end-stage renal disease. As a Medicare beneficiary, one can choose how to receive hospital, doctor, and other health care services covered by Medicare. Beneficiaries can receive care either through the traditional fee-for-service delivery system or through coordinated care plans, such as health maintenance organizations and competitive medical plans, which have contracts with Medicare.

Medicaid   Medicaid is a medical assistance program jointly financed by State and Federal governments for eligible low-income individuals. Medicaid covers health care expenses for all recipients of Aid to Families with Dependent Children, and most States also cover the needy elderly, blind, and disabled who receive cash assistance under the Supplemental Security Income Program. Coverage also is extended to certain infants and low-income pregnant women and, at the option of the State, other low-income individuals with medical bills that qualify them as categorically or medically needy.

Quality Assurance   The Medicare/ Medicaid programs include a quality assurance focal point to carry out the quality assurance provisions of the Medicare and Medicaid programs; the development and implementation of health and safety standards of care providers in Federal health programs; and the implementation of the end-stage renal disease and the peer review provisions.

For further information, contact the Administrator, Health Care Financing Administration, Department of Health and Human Services, 200 Independence Avenue SW., Washington, DC 20201. Phone, 410– 786–3151.

Health Resources and Services Administration

A reorganization order, signed by the Secretary on October 31, 1995, established the Health Resources and Services Administration (HRSA) as an operating division within the Public Health Service of the U.S. Department of Health and Human Services. The Administration is the principal primary health care service agency of the Federal Government. Its mission is to make essential primary care services accessible to the poor, uninsured, and geographically isolated—populations severely underserved by the private health care system. Although the HRSA portfolio of programs is unusually diverse, most can be categorized as pertaining to the primary care workforce, direct service to the underserved, or primary care for special populations.

HRSA works integrally with State and local governments to improve and expand primary health care services through a broad array of categorical and block grants. Among them are HRSA programs to bolster training for primary care physicians, physician assistants, and advanced practice nurses; place qualified primary care providers in communities certified to be health professional shortage areas through the National Health Service Corps; assist health providers that serve the underserved in keeping pace with changes in health care, including managed care; track the adequacy of the supply and preparation of primary care providers and record the malpractice and disciplinary actions taken against physicians and dentists through the National Practitioner Databank; provide primary care services to the working poor and uninsured through community and migrant health centers; reinforce the health care system serving pregnant women and their infants through the Maternal and Child Health Block Grant; reduce infant mortality with formula grants to communities with extraordinarily high numbers of infant deaths; address the multiple health care needs of people and communities affected by HIV/AIDS through the Ryan White Comprehensive AIDS Resources Emergency Act; encourage the donation of organs and tissue for transplantation and ensure their equitable distribution; compensate the families of children harmed by the administration of routine immunizations through the Vaccine Injury Compensation Program; provide health care to people with Hansen's disease; and attend to the special health care needs of people with chronic health

needs, minorities, and those living along the U.S. border with Mexico.

For further information, contact the Office of Communications. Phone, 301–443–2086.

Bureau of Primary Health Care BPHC serves as a national focus for efforts to ensure the availability and delivery of health care services in health professional shortage areas, to medically underserved populations, and to those with special needs. Its mission is to increase access to comprehensive primary and preventive health care and to improve the health status of underserved and vulnerable populations. This mission is achieved through the development and support of systems and providers of high quality, community-based, culturally competent services.

To accomplish this goal, the Bureau provides funds to meet the health needs of populations in medically underserved areas by supporting the development of primary health care delivery capacity where the community can benefit from high quality health care and improved health status outcomes through project grants to community-based organizations; provides funds to help them meet the health needs of special populations such as migrants, Alzheimer's disease patients, the homeless, AIDS victims, Pacific Basin inhabitants, Native Hawaiians, residents of public housing projects, and victims of black lung disease through project grants to State, local, voluntary, public, and private entities; administers the National Health Service Corps Program, which recruits and places highly trained primary care clinicians to serve in health professional shortage areas; designates health professional shortage and medically underserved areas and populations; administers the National Health Service Corps Scholarship and Loan Repayment programs; provides leadership and direction for the Bureau of Prisons Medical Program and the National Hansen's Disease Program; provides comprehensive occupational health consultation and assistance to Federal agencies to enhance productivity and limit employment-related liability through the Federal Employee

Occupational Health Program on a reimbursable basis; and administers the Veterans Health Care Act of 1992 (38 U.S.C. 101 note), which provides that participating manufacturers sell Medicaid-covered outpatient drugs to eligible entities at discount prices.

Division of Immigration Health Services The Division serves as the primary focal point for planning, management, policy formulation, program coordination, direction, and liaison for all health matters pertaining to aliens detained by the Immigration and Naturalization Service.

For further information, contact the Public Affairs Officer. Phone, 301–594–4148.

Bureau of Health Professions (BHP) The Bureau provides national leadership in coordinating, evaluating, and supporting the development and utilization of the Nation's health personnel. To accomplish this goal, the Bureau provides for financial aid to health professions students and support for health professions data analysis and research; supports multidisciplinary training networks and certain discipline-specific educational activities to improve health workforce distribution and quality; supports increasing representation in the health professions of underserved minorities and other disadvantaged groups; trains primary care medical providers and public health workers in short medical supply in the United States; focuses on specific aspects of nursing workforce development; and conducts AIDS programs designed to increase the number of health care providers who are effectively educated and motivated to counsel, diagnose, treat, and manage persons with HIV infections.

BHP also serves as a focus for health care quality assurance activities, issues related to malpractice, and operation of the National Practitioner Data Bank and the Vaccine Injury Compensation Program; supports health professions and nurse training institutions, targeting resources to areas of high national priority such as disease prevention, health promotion, bedside nursing, care of the elderly, and HIV/AIDS through

grants; funds regional centers that provide educational services and multidisciplinary training for health professions faculty and practitioners in geriatric health care; administers several loan programs supporting students training for careers in the health professions and nursing; supports programs to increase the supply of primary care practitioners and to improve the distribution of health professionals; collects and analyzes data and disseminates information on the characteristics and capacities of U.S. health training systems; assesses the Nation's health personnel force and forecasts supply and requirements; develops, tests, and demonstrates new and improved approaches to the development and utilization of health personnel within various patterns of health care delivery and financing systems; provides leadership for promoting equity in access to health services and health careers for the disadvantaged; funds regional centers to train faculty and practicing health professionals in the counseling, diagnosis, and management of HIV/ AIDS-infected individuals; and serves as a focus for technical assistance activities in the international projects relevant to domestic health personnel problems in coordination with the Office of the Administrator, HRSA.

For further information, contact the Information Officer. Phone, 301–443–1590.

HIV/AIDS Bureau The Bureau funds, develops, coordinates, administers, and monitors programs supporting increased access to health care and support services for people living with HIV/AIDS. The Bureau also houses a national network of activities associated with organ and bone marrow donation, procurement, and transplants. It evaluates and monitors insured loans for hospital construction and oversight activities of historically awarded Hill Burton hospital construction projects, under an interdepartmental agreement.

The Bureau provides national leadership in the administration of the Ryan White Comprehensive AIDS Resources Emergency Act grant program to improve the quality and the availability of care for low-income, uninsured, and underinsured people living with HIV/AIDS; manages contracts to provide Federal oversight of the Organ Procurement and Transplantation Network, the Scientific Registry of Transplant Recipients, and the National Marrow Donor Program and works to increase the availability of donor organs and unrelated bone marrow donors by working with Organ Procurement Organizations (OPO's) and donor centers; provides technical assistance to States, cities, nonprofit organizations, OPO's, and health care delivery systems and facilities in a wide variety of specific technical and technological systems; administers the HUD–242 hospital mortgage insurance program which insures private sector loans to hospitals for construction, renovations, or the purchase of major movable equipment; develops long- and short-range program goals and objectives for health facilities and specific health promotions, organ transplantation, and AIDS activities; advises and coordinates activities with private and public organizations, other Federal organizations inside and outside the Department, State and local governments, and professional and scientific organizations; develops, promotes, and directs efforts to improve the management, operational effectiveness, and efficiency of health care systems, organizations, and facilities; collects and analyzes data and disseminates information on the scope and impact of program operations; maintains liaison and coordinates with non-Federal public and private entities to accomplish the Bureau's mission and objectives; and designs and implements special epidemiological and evaluation studies regarding the impact of Bureau programs and initiatives.

For further information, contact the Communications Office, Phone, 301–443–6652. Fax, 301–443–0791.

Maternal and Child Health Bureau The Bureau develops, administers, directs, coordinates, monitors, and supports Federal policy and programs pertaining to health and related-care systems for the Nation's mothers and children. Programs administered by the Bureau address the full spectrum of primary, secondary, and tertiary care services and related activities conducted in the public and private sector which impact upon maternal and child health.

To accomplish this goal, the Bureau: provides national leadership in supporting, identifying, and interpreting national trends and issues relating to the health needs of mothers, infants, and children (both normal and with special health care needs), and administers State block and discretionary grants, contracts, and funding arrangements designed to address these issues; administers grants, contracts, and other funding arrangements and programs under title V of the Social Security Act, as amended, relating to the implementation of State maternal and child health (MCH) service programs; research, training, and education programs located in institutions of higher learning; and State and local health agencies and organizations involved in the care of mothers and children; administers grants, contracts, and other funding arrangements under section 2671 of the Public Health Service Act for research and services pertaining to the health status of and services for pediatric AIDS patients; administers grants, contracts, and other funding arrangements under title V of the Social Security Act, as amended, relating to the care of persons affected by hemophilia (regardless of age); administers grants and contracts under title XIX of the Public Health Service Act relating to pediatric emergency medical systems development and care improvement; develops, promotes, and directs efforts to improve the management, financing, and operational effectiveness and efficiency of health care systems, the Healthy Start Initiative to reduce infant mortality, organizations, and providers of maternal and child health and related care; serves as the principal adviser to and coordinates activities with other Administration organizational elements, other Federal organizations within and outside the Department, and with State and local agencies and professional and scientific organizations; provides technical assistance and consultation to the full spectrum of primary, secondary, and tertiary MCH agencies and organizations in both the public and private sector; and maintains liaison and coordinates with non-Federal public and private entities to accomplish the Bureau's mission and objectives.

For further information, contact the Communications Office. Phone, 301–443–0205.

Indian Health Service

A reorganization order, signed by the Secretary on October 31, 1995, established the Indian Health Service (IHS) as an operating division within the Public Health Service of the U.S. Department of Health and Human Services. The goal of the Indian Health Service is to raise the health status of American Indians and Alaska Natives to the highest possible level.

The Service provides a comprehensive health services delivery system for American Indians and Alaska Natives, with opportunity for maximum tribal involvement in developing and managing programs to meet their health needs. To carry out its mission and attain its goal, the Service assists Indian tribes in developing their health programs through activities such as health management training, technical assistance, and human resource development; facilitates and assists Indian tribes in coordinating health planning, in obtaining and utilizing health resources available through Federal, State, and local programs, in operating comprehensive health programs, and in health program evaluation; provides comprehensive health care services, including hospital and ambulatory medical care, preventive and rehabilitative services, and development of community sanitation facilities; and serves as the principal Federal advocate in the health care field for Indians to ensure comprehensive health services for American Indian and Alaska Native people.

For further information, contact the Indian Health Service Communications Office. Phone, 301–443–3593.

National Institutes of Health

A reorganization order, signed by the Secretary on October 31, 1995, established the National Institutes of Health (NIH) as an operating division within the Public Health Service of the U.S. Department of Health and Human Services. The NIH is the principal biomedical research agency of the Federal Government. Its mission is to employ science in the pursuit of knowledge to improve human health conditions.

NIH seeks to expand fundamental knowledge about the nature and behavior of living systems, to apply that knowledge to extend the health of human lives, and to reduce the burdens resulting from disease and disability. It supports biomedical and behavioral research domestically and abroad, conducts research in its own laboratories and clinics, trains promising young researchers, and promotes acquiring and distributing medical knowledge.

Focal points have been established to assist in developing NIH-wide goals for health research and research training programs related to women and minorities, coordinating program direction, and ensuring that research pertaining to women's and minority health is identified and addressed through research activities conducted and supported by NIH. Research activities conducted by or supported by NIH will determine the scope and direction of medical treatment and disease prevention in the future.

National Cancer Institute Research on cancer is a high priority program as a result of the National Cancer Act, which made the conquest of cancer a national goal. The Institute developed a National Cancer Program to expand existing scientific knowledge on cancer cause and prevention as well as on the diagnosis, treatment, and rehabilitation of cancer patients.

Research activities conducted in the Institute's laboratories or supported through grants or contracts include many investigative approaches to cancer, including chemistry, biochemistry, biology, molecular biology, immunology, radiation physics, experimental chemotherapy, epidemiology, biometry, radiotherapy, and pharmacology. Cancer research facilities are constructed with Institute support, and training is provided under university-based programs. The Institute, through its cancer control element, applies research findings in preventing and controlling human cancer as rapidly as possible.

The Institute sponsors extensive programs to disseminate cancer information and supports the Cancer Information Service, which responds to 600,000 callers a year. Phone, 800–422–6237.

For further information, call 301–496–5585. Internet, http://www.nci.nih.gov/.

National Heart, Lung, and Blood Institute The Institute provides leadership for a national program in diseases of the heart, blood vessels, lung, and blood; sleep disorders; and blood resources. It plans, conducts, fosters, and supports an integrated and coordinated program of basic research, clinical investigations and trials, and observational studies. It conducts research on clinical use of blood and all aspects of the management of blood resources.

The Institute plans and directs research in the development, trials, and evaluation of interventions (including emergency medical treatment) and devices related to prevention, treatment, and rehabilitation of patients suffering from such diseases and disorders. It conducts research in its own laboratories and supports scientific institutions and individuals by research grants and contracts.

The Institute also supports and conducts research training and coordinates with other research institutes and all Federal health programs relevant to activities in the areas of heart, blood vessel, lung, and blood, sleep disorders, and blood resources. It maintains continuing relationships with institutions and professional associations, and with international, national, State, and local officials, as well as voluntary organizations working in the above areas.

For further information, call 301–496–2411. Internet, http://www.nhlbi.nih.gov/nhlbi/nhlbi.htm/.

National Library of Medicine The Library serves as the Nation's chief medical information source and is authorized to provide medical library services and on-line bibliographic searching capabilities, such as MEDLINE, TOXLINE, and others, to public and private agencies and organizations, institutions, and individuals. It sponsors and conducts research and development in biomedical communications, in such areas as telemedicine, expert systems, and advanced medical imaging projects.

The Library operates a computer-based toxicology information system for the scientific community, industry, and Federal agencies. Through its National Center for Biotechnology Information, the Library has a leadership role in developing new information technologies to aid in the understanding of the molecular processes that control health and disease.

Through grants and contracts, the Library administers programs of assistance to the Nation's medical libraries that include support of a National Network of Libraries of Medicine, research in the field of medical library science, establishment and improvement of the basic library resources, and supporting biomedical scientific publications of a nonprofit nature.

For further information, call 301–496–6308. Internet, http://www.nlm.nih.gov/.

National Institute of Diabetes, Digestive, and Kidney Diseases The Institute conducts, fosters, and supports basic and clinical research into the causes, prevention, diagnosis, and treatment of diabetes, endocrine, and metabolic diseases; digestive diseases and nutrition; kidney and urologic diseases; and blood diseases. The Institute fulfills its mission through research performed in its own laboratories and clinics, research grants, individual and institutional research training awards, epidemiologic and clinical studies on selected populations in the United States, and collection and dissemination of information on Institute programs.

For further information, call 301–496–3583. Internet, http://www.niddk.nih.gov/.

National Institute of Allergy and Infectious Diseases The Institute conducts and supports broadly based research, research training, and clinical evaluations on the cause, treatment, and prevention of a wide variety of infectious, allergic, and immunologic diseases. The goal of this research is to develop new or improved diagnostics, drugs, and vaccines. Areas of special emphasis include AIDS; asthma and allergic diseases; immunologic diseases; transplantation; sexually transmitted diseases; enteric diseases such as hepatitis; influenza and other viral respiratory infections; tropical diseases; tuberculosis; and vaccine development.

For further information, call 301–496–5717. Internet, http://www.niaid.nih.gov/.

National Institute of Child Health and Human Development The Institute conducts and supports biomedical and behavioral research on child and maternal health; on problems of human development; on family structure, the dynamics of human population, and the reproductive process; and on medical rehabilitation.

Specific areas of research include mental retardation; pediatric and maternal AIDS; birth defects and genetic diseases; endocrine and growth disorders; nutrition; infertility; women's health; learning disabilities such as dyslexia; behavioral development; rehabilitation of people with physical disabilities; and the causes of infant morbidity and mortality, including low birth weight, premature birth, and sudden infant death syndrome. Research-related findings are disseminated to other researchers, medical practitioners, and the general public to improve the health of children and families.

For further information, call 301–496–5133. Internet, http://www.nih.gov/nichd/.

National Institute on Deafness and Other Communication Disorders The Institute conducts and supports biomedical and behavioral research and research training on normal mechanisms as well as diseases and disorders of hearing, balance, smell, taste, voice, speech, and language through a diversity of research performed in its own laboratories, and a program of research grants, individual and institutional research training awards, career development awards, center grants, and contracts to public and private research institutions and organizations.

For further information, call 301–496–7243. Internet, http://www.nih.gov/nidcd/.

National Institute of Dental Research The Institute conducts and supports research and research training into the causes, prevention, diagnosis, and treatment of craniofacial, oral, and dental diseases and disorders. Areas of special emphasis include inherited diseases and disorders; infectious diseases and immunity; oral, pharyngeal, and esophageal cancers; chronic and disabling diseases, including pain research; biomaterials, biomimetics, and tissue engineering; and behavior, health promotion, and environment.

For further information, call 301–496–6621. Internet, http://www.nidr.nih.gov/.

National Institute of Environmental Health Sciences The Institute, located in Research Triangle Park, NC, conducts and supports basic and applied research on how the environment interacts with genetic factors to cause disease and dysfunction. The primary emphasis is on disease prevention through identification and assessment of risks.

For further information, call 919–541–3211. Internet, http://www.niehs.nih.gov/.

National Institute of General Medical Sciences The Institute's programs for support of research and research training emphasize basic biomedical science, with activities ranging from cell biology, chemistry, and biophysics to genetics, pharmacology, and systemic response to trauma.

For further information, call 301–496–7301. Internet, http://www.nih.gov/nigms/.

National Institute of Neurological Disorders and Stroke The Institute conducts and supports fundamental and applied research on human neurological disorders such as Parkinson's disease, epilepsy, multiple sclerosis, muscular dystrophy, head and spinal cord injuries, and stroke. The Institute also conducts and supports research on the development and function of the normal brain and nervous system in order to better understand normal processes relating to disease states.

For further information, call 301–496–5751. Internet, http://www.ninds.nih.gov/.

National Eye Institute The Institute conducts, fosters, and supports research on the causes, natural history, prevention, diagnosis, and treatment of disorders of the eye and visual system and in related fields.

For further information, call 301–496–4583. Internet, http://www.nei.nih.gov/.

National Institute on Aging The Institute conducts and supports biomedical and behavioral research to increase knowledge of the aging process and the physical, psychological, and social factors associated with aging. Alzheimer's disease, health and

retirement, menopause, and frailty are among the areas of special concern.

For further information, call 301–496–1752. Internet, http://www.nih.gov/nia/.

National Institute of Alcohol Abuse and Alcoholism The Institute conducts and supports biomedical and behavioral research, health services research, research training, and health information dissemination with respect to the prevention and treatment of alcohol abuse and alcoholism. It provides a national focus for the Federal effort to increase knowledge and promote effective strategies to deal with health problems and issues associated with alcohol abuse and alcoholism.

For further information, call 301–443–3885. Internet, http://www.niaaa.nih.gov/.

National Institute of Arthritis and Musculoskeletal and Skin Diseases The Institute conducts and supports fundamental research in the major disease categories of arthritis and musculoskeletal and skin diseases through research performed in its own laboratories and clinics, epidemiologic studies, research contracts and grants, and cooperative agreements to scientific institutions and to individuals. It supports training of personnel in fundamental sciences and clinical disciplines, conducts educational activities, including the collection and dissemination of health educational materials on these diseases, and coordinates with the other research institutes and all Federal health programs relevant activities in the categorical diseases.

For further information, call 301–496–4353. Internet, http://www.nih.gov/niams/.

National Institute on Drug Abuse The Institute's mission is to lead the Nation in bringing the power of science to bear on drug abuse and addiction, through the strategic support and conduct of research across a broad range of disciplines, and the rapid and effective dissemination and use of the results of that research to significantly improve drug abuse and addiction prevention, treatment, and policy.

For further information, call 301–443–6480. Internet, http://www.nida.nih.gov/.

National Institute of Mental Health (NIMH)   The Institute supports and conducts fundamental research in neuroscience, genetics, molecular biology, and behavior as the foundation of an extensive clinical research portfolio which seeks to expand and refine treatments available for illnesses such as schizophrenia, depressive disorders, severe anxiety, childhood mental disorders including autism and attention-deficit/hyperactivity disorder, and other mental disorders which occur across the life span. In addition, NIMH supports research on treatment outcomes in actual practice settings, including primary care settings; seeks to establish a sound scientific basis for the prevention of mental illness; and distributes educational and informational materials about mental disorders and related science to public and scientific audiences.

For further information, call 301–443–3673. Internet, http://www.nimh.nih.gov/.

Clinical Center   The Center is designed to bring scientists working in the Center's laboratories into proximity with clinicians caring for patients, so that they may collaborate on problems of mutual concern. The research institutes select patients, referred to NIH by physicians throughout the United States and overseas, for clinical studies of specific diseases and disorders. A certain percentage of the patients are normal volunteers, healthy persons who provide an index of normal body functions against which to measure the abnormal. Normal volunteers come under varied sponsorship, such as colleges, civic groups, and religious organizations.

For further information, call 301–496–3227. Internet, http://www.cc.nih.gov/.

Fogarty International Center   The Center is dedicated to advancing the health of the people of the United States and other nations through international scientific cooperation. In pursuit of its

mission, the Center fosters biomedical research partnership between U.S. scientists and foreign counterparts through grants, fellowships, and international agreements, and provides leadership in international science policy and research strategies.

For further information, call 301–496–2075. Internet, http://www.nih.gov/fic/.

National Human Genome Research Institute   The Institute provides leadership for and formulates research goals and long-range plans to accomplish the mission of the Human Genome Project, including the study of ethical, legal, and social implications of human genome research. Through grants, contracts, cooperative agreements, and individual and institutional research training awards, the Institute supports and administers research and research training programs in human genome research including chromosome mapping, DNA sequencing, database development, and technology development for genome research. It provides coordination of genome research, both nationally and internationally, serves as a focal point within NIH and the Department for Federal interagency coordination and collaboration with industry and academia, and sponsors scientific meetings and symposia to promote progress through information sharing.

For further information, call 301–496–0844. Internet, http://www.nhgri.nih.gov/.

National Institute of Nursing Research   The Institute provides leadership for nursing research, supports and conducts research and training, and disseminates information to build a scientific base for nursing practice and patient care and to promote health and ameliorate the effects of illness on the American people.

For further information, call 301–496–0207. Internet, http://www.nih.gov.ninr/.

Division of Computer Research and Technology   The Division conducts an integrated research, development, and service program in computer-related physical and life sciences in support of Institute biomedical research programs.

For further information, call 301–496–5206.

National Center for Research Resources The National Center for Research Resources (NCRR) creates, develops, and provides a comprehensive range of human, animal, technological, and other cost-effective, shared resources. NCRR also funds a variety of investigator-initiated research projects and training and career enhancement programs. NCRR's intramural component provides NIH scientists with state-of-the-art bioengineering and instrumentation, veterinary resources, and services such as the NIH Library and the Medical Arts and Photography Branch.

For further information, call 301–435–0888. Internet, http://www.ncrr.nih.gov/.

Division of Research Grants The Division's mission is to provide excellence in the scientific and technical merit review of Public Health Service (PHS) grant applications for research and research training support and to provide state-of-the-art automated information systems for the NIH intramural and extramural grant programs. The Division supports this mission by serving as the central receipt point for all PHS competing grant applications, assigning all PHS applications to an appropriate initial review group for scientific and technical merit review and to the awarding component for potential funding, providing the initial review of grant applications to the NIH through its study sections consisting of experts in scientific disciplines or current research areas, and providing staff support to the Office of the Director, NIH, in the formulation of grant and award policies and procedures.

For further information, call 301–435–1111.

Program Support Center

[For the Program Support Center statement of organization, see the *Federal Register* of November 15, 1995, 60 FR 57452]

The Program Support Center is a self-supported operating division within the Department with a unique mission to provide administrative support services to HHS components and other Federal agencies. The Center was created as a business enterprise to provide services on a competitive fee-for-service basis to customers who wish to purchase the services.

The Center is comprised of the Administrative Operations Service, Financial Management Service, Human Resources Service, and Information Technology Service. Information may be obtained from the following offices:

Administrative Operations Service. Phone, 301–443–2516.
Financial Management Service. Phone, 301–443–1478.
Human Resources Service. Phone, 301–443–1200.
Information Technology Service. Phone, 301–443–9343.

For further information, contact the Director of Marketing, Program Support Center, Department of Health and Human Services, 5600 Fishers Lane, Rockville, MD 20857. Phone, 301–443–1494.

Substance Abuse and Mental Health Services Administration

A reorganization order, signed by the Secretary on October 31, 1995, established the Substance Abuse and Mental Health Services Administration (SAMHSA) as an operating division within the Public Health Service of the Department.

The Administration provides national leadership to ensure that knowledge, based on science and state-of-the-art practice, is effectively used for the prevention and treatment of addictive and mental disorders. It strives to improve access and reduce barriers to high-quality, effective programs and services for individuals who suffer from or are at risk for these disorders, as well as for their families and communities.

For further information, call 301–443–4795.

Center for Substance Abuse Prevention The Center provides a national focus for the Federal effort to prevent alcohol and other drug abuse. In carrying out its responsibility, the Center provides a national focus for the Federal effort to demonstrate and promote effective strategies to prevent the abuse of alcohol and other drugs; develops, implements, and reviews prevention and health promotion policy related to alcohol and other drug abuse, analyzing the impact of Federal activities on State and local governments and private program activities; administers grants, contracts, and cooperative agreements which support the development and application of new knowledge in the substance abuse prevention field; participates in the application and dissemination of research demonstration findings on the prevention of substance abuse; fosters interagency and State prevention networks; develops and implements workplace prevention programs with business and industry; and supports training for substance abuse practitioners and other health professionals involved in alcohol and drug abuse education, prevention, and early intervention.

The Center also provides technical assistance to States and local authorities and other national organizations and groups in the planning, establishment, and maintenance of substance abuse prevention efforts; reviews and approves and/or disapproves the State prevention plans developed under the Substance Abuse Prevention and Treatment Block Grant Program authority; implements the tobacco regulations and other

regulations as appropriate, and as they relate to Center programs; collects and compiles substance abuse prevention literature and other materials, and supports a clearinghouse to disseminate such materials among States, political subdivisions, educations agencies and institutions, health and drug treatment/ rehabilitation networks, and the general public; and serves as a national authority and resource for the development and analysis of information relating to the prevention of substance abuse.

In addition, the Center collaborates with, and encourages other Federal agencies, national foreign, international, State, and local organizations to promote substance abuse prevention activities; provides and promotes the evaluation of individual projects as well as overall programs; collaborates with the alcohol, drug abuse, mental health, and child development institutes of NIH on services research issues as well as on other programmatic issues; conducts managed care activities and coordinates these activities within SAMHSA and other HHS components; and provides a focus for addressing the substance abuse prevention needs of individuals with multiple, co-occurring drug, alcohol, mental, and physical problems.

For further information, call 301–443–0365.

Center for Substance Abuse Treatment The principal function of the Center is to provide national leadership for the Federal effort to enhance approaches and provide resources to ensure provision of services programs focusing on the treatment of substance abuse and co-occurring physical and/or psychiatric conditions. In carrying out this responsibility, the Center collaborates with States, communities, health care providers, and national organizations to upgrade the quality of addiction treatment, to improve the effectiveness of substance treatment programs, and to provide resources to ensure provision of services; provides a focus for addressing the treatment of needs of individuals with multiple, co-occurring drug, alcohol, mental, and physical and co-morbidity problems; administers grants, contracts, and cooperative agreements which support the development and application of new knowledge in the substance abuse treatment field; coordinates the evaluation of Center programs; collaborates with the National Institute on Drug Abuse and the States to promote development, dissemination, and application of treatment outcome standards; collaborates with the office of the Administrator and other SAMHSA components in treatment data collection; administers programs for training of health and allied health care providers; administers the Substance Abuse Prevention and Treatment Block Grant Program including compliance reviews, technical assistance to States, Territories, and Indian Tribes, and application and reporting requirements related to the block grants programs; conducts managed care activities and coordinates these activities within SAMHSA and other HHS components; and collaborates with the alcohol, drug abuse and mental health institutes of NIH on services research issues as well as on other programmatic issues.

For further information, call 301–443–5700.

Center for Mental Health Services The Center provides national leadership to ensure the application of scientifically established findings and practice-based knowledge in the prevention and treatment of mental disorders; to improve access, reduce barriers, and promote high-quality effective programs and services for people with or at risk for these disorders, as well as for their families and communities; and to promote an improved state of mental health within the Nation and the rehabilitation of people with mental disorders.

To accomplish this, the Center supports service and demonstration programs designed to improve access to care and improve the quality of treatment, rehabilitation, prevention, and related services, especially for those traditionally unserved, underserved, or inappropriately serviced; identifies national mental goals and develops strategies to meet them; administers grants, contracts, and cooperative

agreements which support the development and application of new knowledge in the mental health field; supports activities to improve the administration, availability, organization, and financing of mental health care, including managed care activities; supports technical assistance activities to educate professionals, consumers, family members, and communities and promotes training efforts to enhance the human resource necessary to support mental health services; and collects data on the various forms of mental illness, including data on treatment programs, types of care provided, characteristics of those treated, national incidence and prevalence, and such other data as may be appropriate.

The Center administers the Block Grants for Community Mental Health Services and other programs providing direct assistance to States; collects, synthesizes, and disseminates mental health information and research findings to the States, other governmental and mental health-related organizations, and the general public; coordinates and plans administrative and budget functions within the Center; collaborates with other Federal agencies, State and local government, and the private sector to improve the system of treatment and social welfare supports for seriously mentally ill adults and severely emotionally disturbed children and adolescents; conducts activities to promote advocacy, self-help, and mutual support and to ensure the legal rights of mentally ill persons, including those in jails and prisons; cooperates with other Federal components to coordinate disaster assistance, community response, and other mental health emergency services as a consequence of national disasters; collaborates with the alcohol, drug abuse, and mental heath institutes of NIH on services research issues as well as other programmatic issues; promotes the development, dissemination, and application of standards and best practices; and provides a focus for addressing the mental health needs of individuals with multiple, co-occurring drug, alcohol, mental, and physical problems.

For further information, call 301–443–0001.

Sources of Information

Office of the Secretary

Unless otherwise indicated, inquiries on the following subjects may be directed to the specified office, Department of Health and Human Services, Humphrey Building, 200 Independence Avenue SW., Washington, DC 20201.

Civil Rights For information on enforcement of civil rights laws, contact the Office for Civil Rights, Room 502E. Phone, 202–619–0671.

Contracts and Small Business Activities For information concerning programs, contact the Director, Office of Small and Disadvantaged Business Utilization. Phone, 202–690–7300.

Electronic Access Information concerning the Department is available electronically through the Internet, at http://www.dhhs.gov/.

Employment Inquiries regarding applications for employment and the college recruitment program should be directed to: Director, Human Resources Service, Program Support Center, 5600 Fishers Lane, Rockville, MD 20857. Phone, 301–443–1200.

Inspector General General inquiries may be directed to the Office of Inspector General, Wilbur J. Cohen Building, 330 Independence Avenue SW., Washington, DC 20201. Single copies of most Office of Inspector General publications are available free of charge by calling the Office. Phone, 202–619–1142. Internet, http://www.dhhs.gov/progorg/oig/.

Inspector General Hotline Individuals wishing to report fraud, waste, or abuse against Department programs should write to: Office of Inspector General, HHS–TIPS Hotline, P.O. Box 23489, L'Enfant Plaza Station, Washington, DC 20026–3489. Phone (toll-free), 800–HHS–TIPS (800–447–8477). TTY, 800–377–4950. Fax, 800–223–8164. E-mail, htips@os.dhhs.gov.

Locator Inquiries about the location and telephone numbers of HHS offices should be directed to: Information Technology Service, HHS Locator, Room G–644, Wilbur J. Cohen Building, 330 Independence Avenue SW., Washington, DC 20201. Phone, 202–619–0257.

Public Health and Science Inquiries should be directed to the Assistant Secretary for Health, Room 716G. Phone, 202–690–7694.

Administration on Aging

Inquiries on the following subjects may be directed to the specified office, Department of Health and Human Services, Wilbur J. Cohen Building, 330 Independence Avenue SW., Washington, DC 20201.

Elder Care Locator For information concerning services available to elderly persons in any given community in the Nation, contact the Elder Care Locator. Phone, 800–677–1116.

Employment Applications for employment and college recruitment programs should be directed to the Director, Office of Management, Room 4644. Phone, 202–619–1557.

Locator For information about the location and telephone numbers of Administration offices and programs, call 202–619–4541.

National Aging Information Center Individuals seeking biographic data; practical material for planners/practitioners; reports on demographic; health, social, and economic status of older Americans; specialized technical reports on current aging issues; and analytical reports on aging statistics should contact the National Aging Information Center, Room 4656. Phone, 202–619–7501. Fax, 202–401–7620.

TDD, 202–401–7575. E-mail, naic@ageinfo.org.

Public Inquiries/Publications Copies of publications are available free of charge by contacting the Office of the Executive Secretariat. Phone, 202–619–0724. Fax, 202–260–1012. TDD, 202–401–7575. E-mail, aoa_esec@ban-gate.aoa.dhhs.gov. Internet, http://www.aoa.dhhs.gov/.

Administration for Children and Families

General inquiries may be directed to the Administration for Children and Families, Department of Health and Human Services, 370 L'Enfant Promenade SW., Washington, DC 20447. Phone, 202–401–9200. Inquiries on the following subjects may be directed to the specified office.

Contracts Contact the Division of Acquisition Management, Office of Program Support. Phone, 202–401–5149.

Employment Contact the Office of Human Resource Management, Fourth Floor West, 370 L'Enfant Promenade SW., Washington, DC 20447. Phone, 202–401–9260.

Information Center Contact the Office of Public Affairs, Seventh Floor, 370 L'Enfant Promenade SW., Washington, DC 20744. Phone, 202–401–9215.

Mental Retardation For information on mental retardation programs, contact the President's Committee on Mental Retardation, Administration for Children and Families. Phone, 202–619–0634.

Agency for Health Care Policy and Research

Inquiries on the following subjects may be directed to the appropriate office at the Agency for Health Care Policy and Research, Department of Health and Human Services, 2101 East Jefferson Street, Rockville, MD 20852.

Contracts Contact the Chief, Contracts Management Branch. Phone, 301–594–1445.

Employment Inquiries should be addressed to the Chief, Human Resources Management Staff. Phone, 301–594–2408.

Grants Contact the Chief, Grants Management Branch. Phone, 301–594–1447.

Publications Single copies of most publications produced by the Agency are available free of charge from the AHCPR Publications Clearinghouse, P.O. Box 8547, Silver Spring, MD 20907. Phone, 800–358–9295 (toll-free).

Agency for Toxic Substances and Disease Registry

Information regarding programs and activities is available electronically through the Internet, at http://atsdr1.atsdr.cdc.gov:8080/.

Centers for Disease Control and Prevention

Inquiries on the following subjects may be directed to the office indicated at the Centers for Disease Control and Prevention, Department of Health and Human Services, 1600 Clifton Road NE., Atlanta, GA 30333.

Electronic Access Information regarding programs and activities is available electronically through the Internet, at http://www.cdc.gov/.

Employment The majority of scientific and technical positions are filled through the Commissioned Corps of the U.S. Government. Inquiries may be addressed to the Human Resources Management Office (phone, 770–488–1725), or the Division of Commissioned Personnel, Room 4A–15, 5600 Fishers Lane, Rockville, MD 20857.

Films Information concerning availability of audiovisual materials related to program activities may be obtained from the Office of Communications. Phone, 404–639–7290.

Publications Single copies of most publications are available free of charge from the Management Analysis and Services Office. Phone, 404–639–3534. Bulk quantities of publications may be purchased from the Superintendent of Documents, Government Printing Office, Washington, DC 20402.

Food and Drug Administration

Inquiries on the following subjects may be directed to the specified office, Food and Drug Administration, Department of Health and Human Services, 5600 Fishers Lane, Rockville, MD 20857.

Consumer Activities Public Affairs Offices are located in a number of cities across the country, as listed in the table which follows. Consumer phones in these same cities provide recorded messages of interest to the consumer. The general FDA consumer phone number is 301–443–5006.

Contracts Contact the Director, Office of Facilities, Acquisition, and Central Services (HFA–500). Phone, 301–443–6890.

Electronic Access Information on FDA is available electronically through the Internet, at http://www.fda.gov/.

Employment FDA uses various civil service examinations and registers in its recruitment for positions such as consumer safety officers, pharmacologists, microbiologists, physiologists, chemists, mathematical statisticians, physicians, dentists, animal caretakers, etc. Inquiries for positions in the Washington, DC, metropolitan area

should be directed to the Personnel Officer (HFA–400) (phone, 301–827–4120); inquiries for positions outside the Washington, DC, area should be directed to the appropriate local FDA office. Schools interested in the college recruitment program should contact the Personnel Officer (HFA–400) (phone, 301–827–4120).

Publications *FDA Consumer*, FDA's official magazine, is available from the Superintendent of Documents, Government Printing Office, Washington, DC 20402. Phone, 202–512–1800.

Reading Rooms Freedom of Information, Room 12A–30 (phone, 301–443–1813); Hearing Clerk, Room 123, 12420 Parklawn Drive, Rockville, MD 20852 (phone, 301–443–1751); Press Office, Room 15A–07 or Room 3807, FB–8, 200 C Street SW.., Washington, DC 20204 (phone, 301–443–3285).

Speakers Speakers are available for presentations to private organizations and community groups. Requests should be directed to the local FDA office.

Public Affairs Offices—Food and Drug Administration

Office	Address	Telephone
Alameda, CA	1431 Harbor Bay Pkwy., 94502	510–337–6888
Atlanta, GA	60 8th St NE., 30309	404–347–7355
Baltimore, MD	900 Madison Ave., 21201	410–962–3731
Boston, MA	One Montvale Ave., Stoneham, MA 02180	617–279–1675
Brooklyn, NY	850 3d Ave., 11232	718–965–5300
Buffalo, NY	599 Delaware Ave., 14202	716–551–4461
Chicago, IL	Suite 550, 300 S. Riverside Plz., 60606	312–353–5863
Cincinnati, OH	1141 Central Pkwy., 45202–1097	513–684–3501
Cleveland, OH	P.O. Box 838, Brunswick, 44212	216–273–1038
Dallas, TX	3210 Live Oak St., 75204	214–655–5315
Denver, CO	P.O. Box 25087, 80225–0087	303–236–3000
Detroit, MI	1560 E. Jefferson Ave., 48207	313–226–6158
Houston, TX	Suite 420, 1445 N. Loop W., 77008	713–802–9095
Indianapolis, IN	Rm. 300, 101 N. Ohio St., 46204	317–226–6500
Irvine, CA	Suite 300, 19900 MacArthur Blvd., 92612	714–798–7607
Lenexa, KS	W. 11650 80th St., 66214	913–752–2141
Minneapolis, MN	240 Hennepin Ave., 55401	612–334–4100
Nashville, TN	297 Plus Park Blvd., 37217	615–781–5372
New Orleans, LA	4298 Elysian Fields Ave., 70122	504–589–2420
Omaha, NE	200 S. 16th St., 68102	402–331–8536
Orlando, FL	Suite 120, 7200 Lake Ellenor Dr., 32809	407–648–6922
Parsippany, NJ	3d Fl., 10 Waterview Blvd., 07054	201–331–2926
Philadelphia, PA	Rm. 900, 2d and Chestnut Sts., 19106	215–597–4390
San Antonio, TX	Rm. 119, 10127 Morocco, 78216	210–229–4381
San Juan, PR	466 Fernandez Juncos Ave., 00901–3223	809–729–6852
Seattle, WA	22201 23d Dr. SE., Bothell, WA 98021–4421	206–483–4953
St. Louis, MO	808 N. Collins Alley, 63143	314–645–1167

Health Care Financing Administration

Inquiries on the following subjects may be directed to the Health Care Financing Administration, Department of Health

and Human Services, 7500 Security Boulevard, Baltimore, MD 21244–1850.

Contracts and Small Business Activities Contact the Director, Research Contracts and Grants Division. Phone, 410–786–5157.

Electronic Access Information on HCFA is available electronically through the Internet, at http://www.hcfa.gov/.

Employment Inquiries should be addressed to the Human Resources Management Group. Phone, 410–786–2032.

Publications Contact the Distribution Management Branch, Division of Printing and Distribution Services. Phone, 410–786–7892.

Health Resources and Services Administration

Inquiries on the following subjects should be directed to the specified office, Health Resources and Services Administration, Department of Health and Human Services, 5600 Fishers Lane, Rockville, MD 20857.

Electronic Access Information on HRSA is available electronically through the Internet, at http://www.dhhs.gov/hrsa/.

Employment The majority of positions are in the Federal civil service. For positions in the Washington, DC, metropolitan area and field locations throughout the Nation, inquiries may be addressed to the Division of Personnel, Room 14A46. Phone, 301–443–5460. TDD, 301–443–5278. For information on vacant positions, call 301–443–1230. Some health professional positions are filled through the Commissioned Corps of the Public Health Service, a uniformed service of the U.S. Government. Inquiries may be addressed to Division of Commissioned Personnel, Room 4A–15, 5600 Fishers Lane, Rockville, MD 20857.

Films Information concerning the availability of audiovisual materials related to program activities, including films for recruiting minorities into health professions and women into dentistry, is available from the Office of Communications.

Publications Single copies of most publications are available free of charge from the Office of Communications, Room 14–45; the National Maternal and Child Health Clearinghouse (phone, 703–821–8955, Ext. 254); or the

National Clearinghouse for Primary Care Information (phone, 703–821–8955, Ext. 248. Fax, 703–821–2098). Bulk quantities of publications may be purchased from the Superintendent of Documents, Government Printing Office, Washington, DC 20402.

Indian Health Service

Inquiries on the following subjects should be directed to the specified office, Indian Health Service, Department of Health and Human Services, 5600 Fishers Lane, Rockville, MD 20857.

Electronic Access Information on IHS is available electronically through the Internet, at http://www.tucson.ihs.gov/.

Employment The majority of positions are in the Federal civil service. For positions in the Washington, DC, metropolitan area, employment inquiries may be addressed to the Division of Personnel Management, Office of Human Resources, Room 4B–44. Phone, 301–443–6520. Hiring in other parts of the country is decentralized to the 12 area offices. For specific area office addresses, see the U.S. Government listings in the commercial telephone directories for Aberdeen, SD; Albuquerque, NM; Anchorage, AK; Bemidji, MN; Billings, MT; Nashville, TN; Oklahoma City, OK; Phoenix, AZ; Portland, OR; Sacramento, CA; Tucson, AZ; and Window Rock, AZ. Some health professional positions are filled through the Commissioned Corps of the Public Health Service, a uniformed service of the U.S. Government. Inquiries may be addressed to the Division of Commissioned Personnel, Room 4A–15, 5600 Fishers Lane, Rockville, MD 20857. Phone, 301–443–3464.

Publications Single copies of publications describing the Indian Health Service and the health status of American Indians and Alaska Natives are available free of charge from the Communications Office, Room 6–35. Phone, 301–443–3593.

National Institutes of Health

Inquiries on the following subjects may be directed to the office indicated at the

National Institutes of Health, Bethesda, MD 20892, or at the address given.

Contracts   For information on research and development contracts, contact the Office of Contracts Management. Phone, 301–496–4422. For all other contracts, contact the Office of Procurement Management. Phone, 301–496–2501.

Employment   A wide range of civil service examinations and registers are used. Staff fellowships are available to recent doctorates in biomedical sciences. College recruitment is conducted as necessary to meet requirements. Contact the Office of Human Resource Management. Phone, 301–496–2404.

Environment   Research on the biological effects of chemical, physical, and biological substances present in the environment are conducted and supported by the National Institute of Environmental Health Sciences, Research Triangle Park, NC 22709. Phone, 919–541–2605.

Films   Research and health–related films are available for loan from the National Library of Medicine, Collection Access Section, Bethesda, MD 20984. Films are available for purchase from the National Audiovisual Center, General Services . Administration, Washington, DC 20409.

Public Health Service Commissioned Officer Program   For information on the Commissioned Officer programs at NIH and the program for early commissioning of senior medical students in the Reserve Corps of the Public Health Service, contact the Division of Senior Systems. Phone, 301–496–1443.

Publications   Publications, brochures, and reports on health and disease problems, medical research, and biomedical communications, as well as single copies of the *Journal of National Cancer Institute; Environmental Health Perspectives; Scientific Directory and Annual Bibliography;* and *NLM— Medline* (brochure) are available through the Division of Public Information, Office of Communications, National Institutes of Health, Bethesda, MD 20892. Phone, 301–496–4461.

NIH Publications List, Index Medicus, Cumulated Index Medicus Annual, and *Research Grants Index* may be ordered

from the Government Printing Office, Washington, DC 20402. Internet, http://www.nih.gov/.

Program Support Center

General inquiries may be directed to the Program Support Center, Department of Health and Human Services, 5600 Fishers Lane, Rockville, MD 20857.

Electronic Access   Information is available electronically through the Internet, at http://www.dhhs.gov/psc/.

Employment   Inquiries may be directed to the following offices:

Personnel Operations Division, Suite 700, 8455 Colesville Road, Silver Spring, MD 20910. Phone, 301–504–3304.

Public Health Service Commissioned Corps, Room 4A–15, 5600 Fishers Lane, Rockville, MD 20857. Phone, 301–594–3360.

Administrative Operations Service, Program Support Center, 5600 Fishers Lane, Rockville, MD 20857. Phone, 301–443–2516.

Financial Management Service, Program Support Center, 5600 Fishers Lane, Rockville, MD 20857. Phone, 301–443–1478.

Human Resources Service, Program Support Center, 5600 Fishers Lane, Rockville, MD 20857. Phone, 301–443–1200.

Information Technology Service, Program Support Center, Rockville, MD 20857. Phone, 301–443–9343.

Substance Abuse and Mental Health Services Administration

Inquiries on the following subjects may be directed to the specified office, Substance Abuse and Mental Health Services Administration, Department of Health and Human Services, 5600 Fishers Lane, Rockville, MD 20857.

Contracts   Contact the Director, Division of Contracts Management. Phone, 301–443–4980.

Electronic Access   Information is available electronically through the Internet, at http://www.samhsa.gov/.

Employment   Inquiries should be addressed to the Director, Division of Human Resources Management. Phone, 301–443–3408.

Grants   Contact the Director, Division of Grants Management. Phone, 301–443–8926.

Publications   The Office of Communications collects and compiles alcohol and drug abuse prevention literature and other materials, and supports the Center for Substance Abuse Prevention national clearinghouse for alcohol and drug information and the Regional Alcohol and Drug Awareness Resource Network to disseminate such materials among States, political subdivisions, educational agencies and institutions, health and drug treatment and rehabilitation networks, and the general public. It also supports a clearinghouse to serve as a focal point for information dissemination to meet the mental health service needs of professionals. Contact the Associate Administrator for Communications. Phone, 301–443–8956.

For further information concerning the Department of Health and Human Services, contact the Information Center, Department of Health and Human Services, 200 Independence Avenue SW., Washington, DC 20201. Phone, 202–619–0257. Internet, http://www.dhhs.gov/.

DEPARTMENT OF HOUSING AND URBAN DEVELOPMENT

451 Seventh Street SW., Washington, DC 20410
Phone, 202–708–1422

SECRETARY OF HOUSING AND URBAN DEVELOPMENT	ANDREW M. CUOMO
Chief of Staff	JONATHAN COWAN
Senior Adviser to the Secretary for Community Policy	(VACANCY)
Special Adviser to the Secretary for Equal Employment Opportunity and Labor Management	(VACANCY)
Assistant to the Secretary for Labor Relations	(VACANCY)
Director, Office of Executive Scheduling	(VACANCY)
Director, Office of Special Actions	ALVIN BROWN
Director, Executive Secretariat	TERRY NICOLOSKI
Deputy Secretary	SAUL RAMIREZ, JR., Acting
Assistant Deputy Secretary for Field Policy and Management	MAXINE GRIFFITH
Assistant to the Deputy Secretary for Field Management	(VACANCY)
Director, Office of Small and Disadvantaged Business Utilization	CASIMIR BONKOWSKI
Chair, HUD Board of Contract Appeals and Chief Administrative Judge	DAVID T. ANDERSON
Chief Administrative Law Judge	ALAN W. HEIFETZ
Assistant Secretary for Administration	(VACANCY)
Assistant Secretary for Community Planning and Development	SAUL RAMIREZ, JR.
General Deputy Assistant Secretary for Office of General Counsel	HOWARD B. GLASER, Acting
Assistant Secretary for Congressional and Intergovernmental Relations	HAL C. DECELL III
Assistant Secretary for Fair Housing and Equal Opportunity	EVA M. PLAZA
Assistant Secretary for Housing—Federal Housing Commissioner	(VACANCY)
General Deputy Assistant Secretary	(VACANCY)
Associate General Deputy Assistant Secretary	JAMES E. SCHOENBERGER
Assistant Secretary for Policy Development and Research	(VACANCY)
General Deputy Assistant Secretary	LAWRENCE L. THOMPSON
Assistant Secretary for Public Affairs	(VACANCY)
Assistant Secretary for Public and Indian Housing	KEVIN MARCHMAN
General Deputy Assistant Secretary	MICHAEL B. JANIS
Director, Office of Departmental Equal Employment Opportunity	(VACANCY)

300

Deputy Director	WILLIAM O. ANDERSON
Director, Office of Departmental Operations and Coordination	FRANK L. DAVIS
Director, Office of Federal Housing Enterprise Oversight	MARK A. KINSEY, *Acting*
Director, Office of Lead Hazard Control	DAVID E. JACOBS
Chief Financial Officer	RICHARD KEEVEY
Inspector General	SUSAN M. GAFFNEY
President, Government National Mortgage Association	KEVIN G. CHAVERS
Executive Vice President	GEORGE S. ANDERSON

The Department of Housing and Urban Development is the principal Federal agency responsible for programs concerned with the Nation's housing needs, fair housing opportunities, and improvement and development of the Nation's communities.

The Department of Housing and Urban Development (HUD) was established by the Department of Housing and Urban Development Act (42 U.S.C. 3532–3537), effective November 9, 1965. It was created to:

—administer the principal programs that provide assistance for housing and for the development of the Nation's communities;

—encourage the solution of housing and community development problems through States and localities; and

—encourage the maximum contributions that may be made by vigorous private homebuilding and mortgage lending industries, both primary and secondary, to housing, community development, and the national economy.

Although HUD administers many programs, its major functions may be grouped into six categories:

—insuring mortgages for single-family and multi-family dwellings, and extending loans for home improvement and for purchasing mobile homes;

—channeling funds from investors into the mortgage industry through the Government National Mortgage Association;

—making direct loans for construction or rehabilitation of housing projects for the elderly and the handicapped;

—providing Federal housing subsidies for low- and moderate-income families;

—providing grants to States and communities for community development activities; and

—promoting and enforcing fair housing and equal housing opportunity.

Office of the Secretary

Secretary   The Department is administered under the supervision and direction of a Cabinet-level Secretary who:

—formulates recommendations for basic policies in the fields of housing and community development;

—works with the Executive Office of the President and other Federal agencies to ensure that economic and fiscal policies in housing and community development are consistent with other economic and fiscal policies of the Government;

—encourages private enterprise to serve as large a part of the Nation's total housing and community development needs as possible;

—promotes the growth of cities and States and the efficient and effective use of housing and community and economic development resources by stimulating private sector initiatives, public/private sector partnerships, and public entrepreneurship;

—ensures equal access to housing and affirmatively prevents discrimination in housing; and

—provides general oversight, as required by law, of the Federal National Mortgage Association.

Staff Offices

Administrative Law Judges   The Office of Administrative Law Judges hears and

DEPARTMENT OF HOUSING AND URBAN DEVELOPMENT

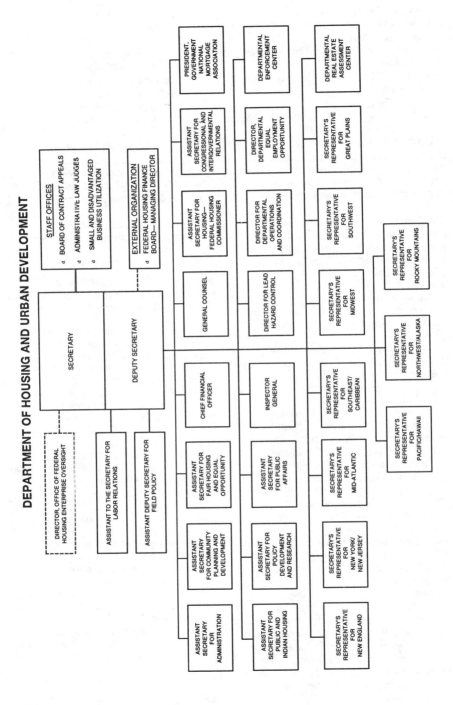

decides Federal housing discrimination cases under the Administrative Procedure Act, as well as those arising under departmental regulations.

HUD Board of Contract Appeals The Board issues binding decisions on all appeals of HUD actions in contracting, awarding grants, disciplining mortgagees, and offsetting tax refunds of people indebted to HUD.

Small and Disadvantaged Business Utilization The Office of Small and Disadvantaged Business Utilization oversees HUD's small and disadvantaged set-aside contracting activities and the minority business enterprise programs.

External Organization

Federal Housing Finance Board An independent agency in the executive branch, the Board oversees the Federal Home Loan Banks to ensure that they carry out their housing finance mission, remain adequately capitalized, and operate in a safe and sound manner.

Program Areas

Community Planning and Development The Office administers grant programs to help communities plan and finance their growth and development, increase their capacity to govern, and provide shelter and services for homeless people. The Office is responsible for implementing:

—Community Development Block Grant (CDBG) programs for entitlement communities; State- and HUD-administered small cities programs; Section 108 community development loan guarantees; special purpose grants for insular areas, historically black colleges and universities, and technical assistance; and Appalachian Regional Commission grants;

—Home Investment in Affordable Housing (HOME), which provides Federal assistance for use by participating jurisdictions or Indian tribes for housing rehabilitation, tenant-based assistance, assistance to first-time homebuyers, and new construction when a jurisdiction is determined to need new rental housing;

—the Department's programs to address homelessness, including the supportive housing program (transitional housing and permanent housing components), supplemental assistance for facilities to assist the homeless (SAFAH), shelter plus care, surplus property for use to assist the homeless, Section 8 moderate rehabilitation single room occupancy (SRO) program, housing opportunities for persons with AIDS, emergency shelter grants, and safe havens;

—the John Heinz Neighborhood Development Program;

—community outreach partnerships;

—the Joint Community Development Plan, assisting institutions of higher education working in concert with State and local governments to undertake activities under the CDBG program;

—community adjustment and economic diversification planning grants;

—the Uniform Relocation Assistance and Real Property Acquisition Policies Act of 1970;

—the YouthBuild Program, which provides opportunities and assistance to very low income high school dropouts, ages 16–24;

—the Consolidated Plan;

—empowerment zones and enterprise communities;

—efforts to improve the environment, pursuant to the National Environmental Policy Act of 1969 and related statutes and Executive orders; and

—community planning and development efforts with other departments and agencies, public and private organizations, private industry, financial markets, and international organizations.

For further information, contact the Office of Community Planning and Development. Phone, 202–708–2690.

Fair Housing and Equal Opportunity The Office administers:

—fair housing laws and regulations prohibiting discrimination in public and private housing on the basis of race, color, religion, sex, national origin, handicap, or familial status;

—equal opportunity laws and regulations prohibiting discrimination in HUD-assisted housing and community development programs on the basis of race, handicap, sex, age, or national origin;

—the Fair Housing Assistance grants program to provide financial and technical assistance to State and local government agencies to implement local fair housing laws and ordinances; and

—the Community Housing Resources Boards (CHRB's) program to provide grants for fair housing activities such as outreach and education, identification of institutional barriers to fair housing, and complaint telephone hotlines.

For further information, contact the Office of Fair Housing and Equal Opportunity. Phone, 202–708–4252.

Federal Housing Enterprise Oversight
The Office oversees the financial safety and soundness of the Federal National Mortgage Association (Fannie Mae) and the Federal Home Loan Mortgage Corporation (Freddie Mac) to ensure that they are adequately capitalized and operating safely.

For further information, contact the Office of Federal Housing Enterprise Oversight. Phone, 202–414–3800.

Government National Mortgage Association (GNMA)   The mission of this Government corporation, also known as Ginnie Mae, is to support expanded affordable housing by providing an efficient Government-guaranteed secondary market vehicle to link the capital markets with Federal housing markets. Ginnie Mae guarantees mortgage-backed securities composed of FHA-insured or VA-guaranteed mortgage loans that are issued by private lenders and guaranteed by GNMA with the full faith and credit of the United States. Through these programs, Ginnie Mae increases the overall supply of credit available for housing by providing a vehicle for channeling funds from the securities market into the mortgage market.

For further information, contact the Government National Mortgage Association. Phone, 202–708–0926.

Housing   The Office of Housing is responsible for the Department's housing functions and oversees aid for construction and financing of new and rehabilitated housing and for preservation of existing housing. The Office:

— underwrites single-family, multi-family, property improvement, and manufactured home loans;

—administers special purpose programs designed specifically for the elderly, the handicapped, and the chronically mentally ill;

—administers assisted housing programs for low-income families who are experiencing difficulties affording standard housing;

—administers grants to fund resident ownership of multifamily house properties; and

—protects consumers against fraudulent practices of land developers and promoters.

For further information, contact the Office of Housing. Phone, 202–708–3600.

Lead Hazard Control   The Office is responsible for lead hazard control policy development, abatement, training, regulations, and research. Activities of the Office include:

—increasing public and building industry awareness of the dangers of lead-based paint poisoning and the options for detection, risk reduction, and abatement;

—encouraging the development of safer, more effective, and less costly methods for detection, risk reduction, and abatement; and

—encouraging State and local governments to develop lead-based paint programs covering primary prevention, including public education; contractor certification; hazard reduction; financing; and enforcement.

For further information, contact the Office of Lead Hazard Control. Phone, 202–755–1785.

Policy Development and Research The Office supervises the Department's research activities and the development of its policies and is responsible for experimental housing and technical studies. The Office:

—develops a research agenda to reflect the overall policy needs of the Department;

—performs background analyses, studies, and priority assessments concerning housing and community development issues;

—provides economic analyses and recommendations, performs housing and financial market research, and designs and monitors housing-related data series;

—evaluates existing and proposed HUD programs;

—analyzes the adequacy of existing and proposed program information systems to provide timely and relevant information;

—provides technical and analytical assistance to program Assistant Secretaries;

—evaluates new housing and construction materials and techniques and encourages use of new technologies;

—supports the Secretary in carrying out responsibilities for Federal National Mortgage Association and Federal Home Loan Mortgage Corporation regulations;

—manages research contracts, cooperative agreements, and grants; and

—administers the Office of University Partnerships and oversees grants awarded for the community development work study, joint community development, and community outreach programs.

For further information, contact the Office of Policy Development and Research. Phone, 202–708–1600.

Public and Indian Housing The Office:

—administers public and Indian housing programs, including rental and homeownership programs, and provides technical and financial assistance in planning, developing, and managing low-income projects;

—provides operating subsidies for public housing agencies (PHA's) and Indian housing authorities (IHA's), including procedures for reviewing the management of public housing agencies;

—administers the comprehensive improvement assistance and comprehensive grant programs for modernization of low-income housing projects to upgrade living conditions, correct physical deficiencies, and achieve operating efficiency and economy;

—administers the Resident Initiatives Program for resident participation, resident management, homeownership, economic development and supportive services, and drug-free neighborhood programs;

—protects tenants from the hazards of lead-based paint poisoning by requiring PHA's and IHA's to comply with HUD regulations for the testing and removal of lead-based paint from low-income housing units;

—implements and monitors program requirements related to program eligibility and admission of families to public and assisted housing, and tenant income and rent requirements pertaining to continued occupancy;

—administers the HOPE VI and vacancy reduction programs;

—administers the Section 8 voucher and certificate programs and the Moderate Rehabilitation program;

—coordinates all departmental housing and community development programs for Indian and Alaskan Natives; and

—awards grants to PHA's and IHA's for the construction, acquisition, and operation of public and Indian housing projects, giving priority to projects for larger families (3 or more bedrooms) and acquisition of existing units (as opposed to new construction).

For further information, contact the Office of Public and Indian Housing. Phone, 202–708–0950.

Field Structure

The field offices of the Department have boundaries prescribed by the Secretary. Each field office is headed by a Secretary's Representative, who is responsible to the Secretary for the management of the offices within the prescribed area.

For information concerning the detailed jurisdiction of an office, contact the nearest area office.

Regional Offices—Department of Housing and Urban Development

Region	Address	Secretary's Representative	Telephone
New England	Rm. 375, 10 Causeway St., Boston, MA 02222–1092	Mary Lou K. Crane	617–565–5234
New York/New Jersey	26 Federal Plz., New York, NY 10278–0068	Warren DeBlasio-Wilhelm	212–264–6500
Mid-Atlantic	100 Penn Sq. E., Philadelphia, PA 19107–3380	Karen A. Miller	215–656–0500
Southeast/Caribbean	75 Spring St. SW., Atlanta, GA 30303–3388	Davey L. Gibson	404–331–5136
Midwest	77 W. Jackson Blvd., Chicago, IL 60604–3507	(Vacancy)	312–353–5680
Southwest	P.O. Box 2905, Fort Worth, TX 76113–2905	Elizabeth Julian	817–885–5401
Great Plains	Rm. 200, 400 State Ave., Kansas City, KS 66106–2406	Michael L. Tramontina	913–551–5462
Rocky Mountains	1st Interstate Twr. N., 633 17th St., Denver, CO 80202–3607	Anthony J. Hernandez	303–672–5440
Pacific/Hawaii	P.O. Box 36003, 450 Golden Gate Ave., San Francisco, CA 94102–3448	Arthur C. Agnos	415–436–6532
Northwest/Alaska	Suite 200, 909 1st Ave., Seattle, WA 98104–1000	Robert N. Santos	206–220–5101

Sources of Information

Inquiries on the following subjects should be directed to the nearest regional office or to the specified headquarters office, U.S. Department of Housing and Urban Development, 451 Seventh Street SW., Washington, DC 20410. Phone, 202–708–1112. TDD, 202–708–1455.

Contracts   Contact the Contracting Division. Phone, 202–708–1290.

Directory Locator   Phone, 202–708–1112. TDD, 202–708–1455.

Employment   Inquiries and applications should be directed to the headquarters Office of Personnel (phone, 202–708–0408); or the Personnel Division at the nearest HUD regional office.

Freedom of Information Act (FOIA) Requests   Persons interested in inspecting documents or records under the Freedom of Information Act should contact the Freedom of Information Officer. Phone, 202–708–3054. Written requests should be directed to the Director, Executive Secretariat, U.S. Department of Housing and Urban Development, Room 10139, 451 Seventh Street SW., Washington, DC 20410.

HUD Hotline   The Hotline is maintained by the Office of the Inspector General as a means for individuals to report activities involving fraud, waste, or mismanagement. Phone, 202–708–4200, or 800–347–3735 (toll-free). TDD, 202–708–2451.

Program Information Center   The Center provides viewing facilities for information regarding departmental activities and functions and publications and other literature to headquarters visitors. Phone, 202–708–1420.

Property Disposition   For single family properties, contact the Property Disposition Division (phone, 202–708–0740); or the Chief Property Officer at the nearest HUD regional office. For multifamily properties, contact the Property Disposition Division (phone, 202–708–3343); or the Regional Housing Director at the nearest HUD regional office.

For further information, contact the Office of Public Affairs, U.S. Department of Housing and Urban Development, 451 Seventh Street SW., Washington, DC 20410. Phone, 202–708–0980.

DEPARTMENT OF THE INTERIOR

1849 C Street NW., Washington, DC 20240
Phone, 202–208–3171. Internet, http://www.doi.gov/.

SECRETARY OF THE INTERIOR	BRUCE BABBITT
Deputy Secretary	(VACANCY)
Chief of Staff	ANNE H. SHIELDS
Deputy Chief of Staff	(VACANCY)
Special Trustee for American Indians	PAUL N. HOMAN
Chief Information Officer	DARYL W. WHITE
Director of Congressional and Legislative Affairs	(VACANCY)
Counselors to the Secretary	ROBERT T. ANDERSON, DAVID J. HAYES, MOLLIE S. MCUSIC
	ROBERT K. HATTOY
Special Assistant to the Secretary and White House Liaison	WILLIAM BROWN
Science Adviser to the Secretary	MICHAEL GAULDIN
Director, Office of Communications	PADDY MCGUIRE
Director of Intergovernmental Affairs	JULIETTE A. FALKNER
Special Assistant to the Secretary and Director, Executive Secretariat and Office of Regulatory Affairs	
Special Assistant to the Secretary for Alaska	DEBORAH L. WILLIAMS
Solicitor	JOHN D. LESHY
Deputy Solicitor	EDWARD B. COHEN
Associate Solicitor (Administration)	ROBERT S. MORE
Associate Solicitor (Conservation and Wildlife)	BARRY E. HILL
Associate Solicitor (Land and Water Resources)	RENEE STONE
Associate Solicitor (General Law)	KAREN M. SPRECHER
Associate Solicitor (Indian Affairs)	DERRIL B. JORDAN
Associate Solicitor (Mineral Resources)	KATHRINE HENRY
Inspector General	(VACANCY)
Deputy Inspector General	(VACANCY)
Assistant Inspector General (Administration)	SHARON D. ELLER
Assistant Inspector General (Audits)	ROBERT J. WILLIAMS
Assistant Inspector General (Investigations)	JOHN R. SINCLAIR
General Counsel	RICHARD N. REBACK
Assistant Secretary—Water and Science	PATRICIA J. BENEKE
Deputy Assistant Secretary	MARK SCHAEFER
Director, U.S. Geological Survey	(VACANCY)
Commissioner, Bureau of Reclamation	ELUID L. MARTINEZ
Assistant Secretary—Fish and Wildlife and Parks	(VACANCY)
Deputy Assistant Secretary	DONALD J. BARRY
Director, U.S. Fish and Wildlife Service	JAMIE R. CLARK
Director, National Park Service	ROBERT G. STANTON
Assistant Secretary—Indian Affairs	KEVIN GOVER

Deputy Assistant Secretary	MICHAEL J. ANDERSON
Commissioner of Indian Affairs	(VACANCY)
Deputy Commissioner of Indian Affairs	HILDA MANUEL
Assistant Secretary—Land and Minerals Management	ROBERT L. ARMSTRONG
Deputy Assistant Secretary	SYLVIA V. BACA
Director, Minerals Management Service	CYNTHIA L. QUARTERMAN
Director, Bureau of Land Management	PATRICK A. SHEA
Director, Office of Surface Mining Reclamation and Enforcement	KATHLEEN M. KARPAN
Assistant Secretary—Policy, Management, and Budget	JOHN BERRY
Director, Office of Hearings and Appeals	ROBERT L. BAUM
Director, Office of Small and Disadvantaged Business Utilization	RALPH RAUSCH
Director, Office of Information Resources Management	DARYL W. WHITE
Deputy Assistant Secretary—Human Resources	MARI R. BARR
Director, Office of Educational Partnerships	DOLORES L. CHACON
Director, Office of Personnel Policy	CAROLYN COHEN
Director, Ethics Staff	GABRIELE J. PAONE
Deputy Assistant Secretary—Workforce Diversity	DAVID F. MONTOYA
Director, Office for Equal Opportunity	E. MELODEE STITH
Deputy Assistant Secretary—Policy and International Affairs	BROOKS B. YEAGER
Director, Office of Environmental Policy and Compliance	WILLIE R. TAYLOR
Director, Office of Policy Analysis	JAMES H. PIPKIN
Director, Office of Insular Affairs	ALLEN P. STAYMAN
Director, Office of Managing Risk and Public Safety	L. MICHAEL KAAS
Deputy Assistant Secretary—Budget and Finance	ROBERT J. LAMB
Director of Planning and Performance Management	JODY Z. KUSEK
Director, Office of Budget	MARY ANN LAWLER
Director, Office of Financial Management	R. SCHUYLER LESHER
Director of Administration/Senior Procurement Executive	PAUL A. DENETT
Director, Interior Service Center	TIMOTHY G. VIGOTSKY
Director, Office of Aircraft Services	ELMER J. HURD
Director, Office of Acquisition and Property Management	DEBRA SONDERMAN

The mission of the Department of the Interior is to protect and provide access to our Nation's natural and cultural heritage and honor our trust responsibilities to tribes. The Department manages the Nation's public lands and minerals, national parks, national wildlife refuges, and western water resources and upholds Federal trust responsibilities to Indian tribes. It is responsible for migratory wildlife conservation; historic preservation; endangered species; surface-mined lands protection and restoration; mapping; and geological, hydrological, and biological science.

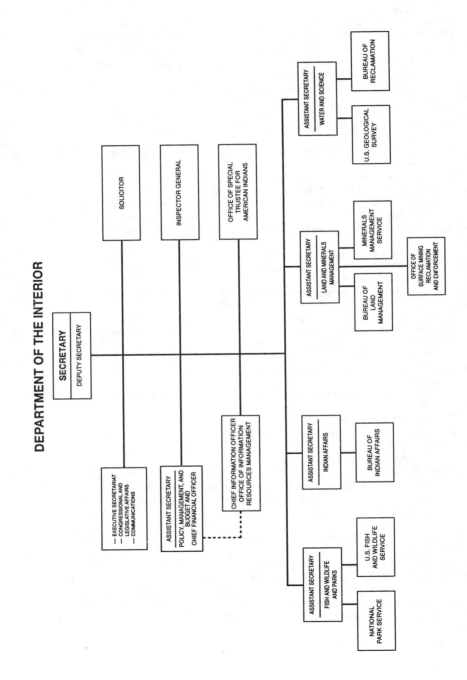

DEPARTMENT OF THE INTERIOR

The Department of the Interior was created by act of March 3, 1849 (43 U.S.C. 1451), which transferred to it the General Land Office, the Office of Indian Affairs, the Pension Office, and the Patent Office. It was reorganized by Reorganization Plan No. 3 of 1950, as amended (5 U.S.C. app.).

Over the years, other functions have been added and removed, so that its role has changed from that of general housekeeper for the Federal Government to that of custodian of the Nation's natural resources.

Office of the Secretary

Secretary   The Secretary of the Interior reports directly to the President and is responsible for the direction and supervision of all operations and activities of the Department. The Office of the Secretary includes the offices of Deputy Secretary, the Assistant Secretaries, the Special Trustee for American Indians, the Solicitor, and the Inspector General. Some areas where public purposes are broadly applied include:

Fish and Wildlife and Parks   The Office of the Assistant Secretary (Fish and Wildlife and Parks) has responsibility for programs associated with conservation in the use of natural and cultural resources, and the enhancement and protection of fish, wildlife, vegetation, and habitat. The Office represents the Department in the coordination of marine environmental quality and biological resources programs with other Federal agencies. It also exercises Secretarial direction and supervision over the United States Fish and Wildlife Service and the National Park Service.

Water and Science   The Office of the Assistant Secretary (Water and Science) carries out the statutory mandate to manage and direct programs that support the development and implementation of water, mineral, and science policies and assist the development of economically

and environmentally sound resource activities. It oversees the programs of the Bureau of Reclamation and the United States Geological Survey. It also provides advice on Earth science matters to the Secretary and represents the Department in interagency efforts on a range of scientific issues.

Land and Minerals Management   The Office of the Assistant Secretary (Land and Minerals Management) has responsibility for programs associated with public land management; operations management and leasing for minerals on public lands, including the Outer Continental Shelf to the outer limits of the United States economic jurisdiction; minerals operations management on Indian lands; surface mining reclamation and enforcement functions; and management of revenues from Federal and Indian mineral leases. The Office exercises Secretarial direction and supervision over the Bureau of Land Management, the Minerals Management Service, and the Office of Surface Mining Reclamation and Enforcement.

Indian Affairs   The Office of the Assistant Secretary (Indian Affairs) has responsibility for activities pertaining to Indians and Indian affairs, including:

—providing the Secretary with detailed and objective advice on matters involving Indians and Indian affairs;

—identifying and acting on issues affecting Indian policy and programs;

—establishing policy on Indian affairs;

—maintaining liaison and coordination between the Department and other Federal agencies that provide services or funding to Indians;

—representing the Department in transactions with Congress;

—monitoring and evaluating ongoing activities related to Indian affairs; and

—providing leadership in special assignments and projects for the Secretary.

Policy, Management, and Budget   The Office of the Assistant Secretary (Policy, Management, and Budget) has responsibility for all phases of management, budget, and other administrative activities. The Assistant Secretary serves as the principal policy adviser to the Secretary and is the Department's Chief Financial Officer.

For further information, contact the Office of the Assistant Secretary (Policy, Management, and Budget). Internet, http://www.usgs.gov/doi/policy-management-budget.html.

Office of the Solicitor

The Office of the Solicitor performs all of the legal work of the Department with the exception of that performed by the Office of Hearings and Appeals, the Office of Congressional and Legislative Affairs, and the Office of Inspector General. The Solicitor is the principal legal adviser to the Secretary and the chief law officer of the Department.

The headquarters office, located in Washington, DC, consists of six divisions:

The Division of Conservation and Wildlife is responsible for legal matters involving the programs of the Assistant Secretary for Fish and Wildlife and Parks, the Assistant Secretary for Water and Science, the Fish and Wildlife Service, the National Park Service, and the Biological Research Division of the Geological Survey.

The Division of General Law is responsible for general administrative law and legal matters involving programs of the Office of the Secretary, the Assistant Secretary for Policy, Management, and Budget, and the Office for Equal Opportunity.

The Division of Indian Affairs is responsible for legal matters involving programs of the Assistant Secretary for Indian Affairs and the Bureau of Indian Affairs.

The Division of Land and Water Resources is responsible for legal matters involving programs (other than minerals programs) of the Assistant Secretary for Land and Minerals Management, the Assistant Secretary for Water and Science, the Bureau of Reclamation, and the Bureau of Land Management.

The Division of Mineral Resources is responsible for legal matters involving minerals-related programs of the Assistant Secretary for Land and Minerals Management, the Bureau of Land Management, the Geological Survey, the Minerals Management Service, and the Office of Surface Mining Reclamation and Enforcement.

The Division of Administration is responsible for administrative and information support services for the Office of the Solicitor.

The field organization of the Office consists of seven regions, each headed by a Regional Solicitor.

For further information, contact the Associate Solicitor for Administration, Office of the Solicitor, Department of the Interior, Washington, DC 20240. Phone, 202–208–6115.

Regional Offices—Office of the Solicitor

Region	Address	Telephone
ALASKA—AK	Suite 300, 4230 University Dr., Anchorage, AK 99508–4626	907–271–4131
NORTHEAST—CT, DE, IL, IN, ME, MD, MA, MI, MN, NH, NJ, NY, ND, OH, PA, RI, SD, VT, VA, WV, WI	Suite 612, 1 Gateway Ctr., Newton Corner, MA 02158–2802	617–527–3400
PACIFIC NORTHWEST—ID, MT, OR, WA	Suite 607, 500 NE. Multnomah St., Portland, OR 97232	503–231–2125
PACIFIC SOUTHWEST—AZ, CA, HI, NV, Pacific islands, UT	Rm. E–1712, 2800 Cottage Way, Sacramento, CA 95825–1890	916–978–5670
ROCKY MOUNTAIN—CO, IA, KS, MO, NE, WY	Rm. 151, 755 Parfet St., Lakewood, CO 80215	303–231–5353
SOUTHEAST—AL, AR, FL, GA, KY, LA, MS, NC, PR, SC, TN, VI	Suite 304, 75 Spring St. SW., Atlanta, GA 30303	404–331–5504
SOUTHWEST—Navajo Reservation, NM, OK, TX	Suite 200, 2400 Louisiana Blvd. NE., Albuquerque, NM 87110–4316	505–883–6700

Office of Special Trustee for American Indians

The Office of Special Trustee for American Indians oversees Indian trust asset reform efforts departmentwide to ensure the establishment of policies, procedures, systems, and practices to allow the Secretary to effectively discharge his trust responsibilities. The Special Trustee has authority over and responsibility for trust monies of Indian tribes and individual Indians.

For further information, contact the Office of the Special Trustee, Department of the Interior, Washington, DC 20240. Phone, 202–208–4866.

Office of Inspector General

The Office of Inspector General provides policy direction for and conducts, supervises, and coordinates audits, investigations, and other activities in the Department of the Interior (DOI) to promote economy, efficiency, and effectiveness and to prevent and detect fraud, waste, abuse, and mismanagement. The Inspector General is DOI's focal point for independent and objective reviews of the integrity of DOI operations and is the central authority concerned with the quality, coverage, and coordination of the audit and investigative services between DOI and other Federal, State, and local governmental agencies.

In the insular areas of Guam, American Samoa, the U.S. Virgin Islands, and the Commonwealth of the Northern Mariana Islands, OIG is responsible for "establishing an organization which will maintain a satisfactory level of independent audit oversight" for these areas, in accordance with the Insular Areas Act of 1982 (48 U.S.C. 1422). OIG has additional audit responsibilities in the Federal States of Micronesia, the Republic of the Marshall Islands, and the Republic of Palau pursuant to the Compact of Free Association Act of 1985 (Public Law 99–239).

Regional Offices—Office of Inspector General
(A: Audits; I: Investigations)

Region/Headquarters	Address	Telephone
EASTERN:		
Arlington, VA (A)	Suite 425, 1550 Wilson Blvd., 22209	703–235–9231
Arlington, VA (I)	Suite 402, 1550 Wilson Blvd., 22209	703–235–9221
CENTRAL:		
Lakewood, CO (A)	Suite 510, 134 Union Blvd., 80228	303–236–9243
WESTERN:		
Sacramento, CA (A)	Rm. W2400, 2800 Cottage Way, 95825	916–978–5650
Lakewood, CO (I)	Suite 540, 134 Union Blvd., 80228	303–236–8296
CARIBBEAN:		
St. Thomas, VI (A)	Rm. 207, Federal Bldg., Veterans Dr., 00802	340–774–8300
NORTH PACIFIC:		
Agana, GU (A)	Suite 807, 238 Archbishop F.C. Flores St., 96910	700–550–7279

For further information, contact the Office of Inspector General, Department of the Interior, Washington, DC 20240. Phone, 202–208–4599. Internet, http://www.access.gpo.gov/doi/.

Office of Hearings and Appeals

The Office of Hearings and Appeals is responsible for departmental quasi-judicial and related functions. Administrative law judges and three formal boards of appeal render decisions in cases pertaining to contract disputes; Indian probate and administrative appeals; public and acquired lands and their resources; submerged offshore lands of the Outer Continental Shelf; surface coal mining control and reclamation; claims under the Alaska Native Claims Settlement Act; and enforcement of the importation and transportation of rare and endangered species. The Director of the Office of Hearings and Appeals may assign administrative law judges or other officials from the Office of Hearings and Appeals for the purpose of holding rulemaking hearings and may also assign administrative law judges or establish ad hoc boards of appeal to meet special requirements of disputes not falling under one of the previously listed categories. Board decisions are final for the Department.

The Office includes the headquarters organization and five field offices for administrative law judges.

For further information, contact the Office of Hearings and Appeals, Department of the Interior, 4015 Wilson Boulevard, Arlington, VA 22203. Phone, 703–235–3810.

Office of Insular Affairs

The Office of Insular Affairs carries out the Department's responsibility to help coordinate Federal policy for the territories of American Samoa, Guam, the U.S. Virgin Islands, and the Commonwealth of the Northern Mariana Islands, and oversee Federal programs and funds in the freely associated states of the Federal States of Micronesia, the Republic of the Marshall Islands, and the Republic of Palau. The insular areas now have popularly elected executive and legislative branches of government and administer their own affairs

The Office of the Insular Affairs mission is to assist the islands in developing more efficient and effective government by providing financial and technical assistance, and to help manage Federal-island relations by promoting appropriate Federal policies. The mission is derived from Organic Acts, Executive orders, negotiated agreements ratified in law, and other legislation enacted to authorize programs and funding. These acts and orders also enunciate the fundamental relationship between the Federal Government and each of the insular areas.

For further information, contact the Office of Insular Affairs, Department of the Interior, Washington, DC 20240. Phone, 202-208-6816. Internet, http://www.usgs.gov/doi/oia/oia.html.

Bureaus

United States Fish and Wildlife Service

[For the United States Fish and Wildlife Service statement of organization, see the *Code of Federal Regulations,* Title 50, Subchapter A, Part 2]

The United States Fish and Wildlife Service's national responsibility in the service of fish, wildlife, and people spans more than 120 years to the establishment in 1871 of a predecessor agency, the Bureau of Fisheries. First created as an independent agency, the Bureau of Fisheries was later placed in the Department of Commerce. A second predecessor agency, the Bureau of Biological Survey, was established in 1885 in the Department of Agriculture. In 1939 the two Bureaus and their functions were transferred to the Department of the Interior. They were consolidated into one agency and redesignated the Fish and Wildlife Service in 1940 by Reorganization Plan III (5 U.S.C. app.).

Further reorganization came in 1956 when the Fish and Wildlife Act (16 U.S.C. 742a) created the United States Fish and Wildlife Service and provided for it to replace and succeed the former Fish and Wildlife Service. The Act established two Bureaus within the new Service: the Bureau of Commercial Fisheries and the Bureau of Sport Fisheries and Wildlife.

In 1970, under Reorganization Plans 3 and 4 (5 U.S.C. app.), the Bureau of Commercial Fisheries was transferred to the Department of Commerce. The Bureau of Sport Fisheries and Wildlife, which remained in Interior, was renamed by an act of Congress in April 1974 (16 U.S.C. 742b) as the United States Fish and Wildlife Service.

The Service is composed of a headquarters office in Washington, DC, seven regional offices, a variety of field units and installations, and a nationwide network of law enforcement agents. The Service manages more than 94 million acres of land and water consisting of more than 500 national wildlife refuges, 65 national fish hatcheries, 38 wetland management districts with waterfowl production areas, and 50 wildlife coordination areas.

The United States Fish and Wildlife Service is responsible for migratory birds, endangered species, certain marine mammals, and inland sport fisheries. Its mission is to conserve, protect, and enhance fish and wildlife and their habitats for the continuing benefit of the American people. Within this framework, the Service strives to foster an environmental stewardship ethic based on ecological principles and scientific knowledge of wildlife; works with the States to improve the conservation and management of the Nation's fish and wildlife resources; and administers a national program providing opportunities to the American public to understand, appreciate, and wisely use these resources.

In the area of resource management, the Service provides leadership for the protection and improvement of land and water environments (habitat preservation), which directly benefits the living natural resources and adds quality to human life. Activities include:

—surveillance of pesticides, heavy metals, and other contaminants;

—studies of fish and wildlife populations;

—ecological studies;

—environmental impact assessment, including hydroelectric dams, nuclear power sites, stream channelization, and dredge-and-fill permits; and

—environmental impact statement review.

The Service is responsible for improving and maintaining fish and wildlife resources by proper management of wildlife and habitat. It also helps fulfill the public demand for recreational fishing while maintaining the Nation's fisheries at a level and in a condition that will ensure their continued survival. Specific wildlife and fishery resources programs include:

—migratory birds: wildlife refuge management for production, migration,

and wintering; law enforcement; game; and bird population, production, and harvest surveys;

—mammals and nonmigratory birds: refuge management of resident species, law enforcement, protection of certain marine mammals, and technical assistance;

—coastal anadromous fish: hatchery production and stocking;

—Great Lakes fisheries: hatchery production of lake trout and fishery management in cooperation with Canada and the States; and

—other inland fisheries: hatchery production and stocking of Indian lands, and technical assistance.

The Service provides national and international leadership in identifying, protecting, and restoring endangered species of fish, wildlife, and plants. This program includes:

—developing the Federal Endangered and Threatened Species List, conducting status surveys, preparing recovery plans, and coordinating efforts nationally and internationally;

—operating national wildlife refuges;

—law enforcement;

—foreign importation enforcement; and

—consultation with foreign countries.

Public use and information programs include preparing leaflets and brochures; operating environmental study areas on Service lands; operating visitor centers, self-guided nature trails, observation towers, and display ponds; and providing recreational activities such as hunting, fishing, and wildlife photography.

The Service's Federal aid programs apportion funds generated by excise taxes on sporting arms and fishing equipment to the States and territories for projects designed to conserve and enhance the Nation's fish and wildlife resources.

Regional Offices—United States Fish and Wildlife Service

Region	Address	Telephone
ALBUQUERQUE—AZ, NM, OK, TX	P.O. Box 1306, Albuquerque, NM 87103	505–248–6900
ANCHORAGE—AK	1011 E. Tudor Rd., Anchorage, AK 99503	907–786–3542
ATLANTA—AL, AR, FL, GA, KY, LA, MS, NC, PR, SC, TN, VI	1875 Century Blvd., Atlanta, GA 30345	404–679–4000

Regional Offices—United States Fish and Wildlife Service—Continued

Region	Address	Telephone
HADLEY—CT, DE, ME, MA, MD, NH, NJ, NY, PA, RI, VT, VA, WV	300 Westgate Ctr. Dr., Hadley, MA 01035–9589	413–253–8200
DENVER—CO, KS, MT, NE, ND, SD, UT, WY	P.O. Box 25486, Denver, CO 80225	303–236–7920
PORTLAND—CA, HI, ID, NV, OR, WA, Pacific Islands	911 NE. 11th Ave., Portland, OR 97232–4181	503–231–6118
TWIN CITIES—IL, IN, IA, MI, MN, MO, OH, WI	Federal Bldg., Fort Snelling, Twin Cities, MN 55111	612–713–5302

For further information, contact the Office of Public Affairs, Fish and Wildlife Service, Department of the Interior, Washington, DC 20240. Phone, 202–208–5634. Internet, http://www.fws.gov/.

National Park Service

The National Park Service was established in the Department of the Interior on August 25, 1916 (16 U.S.C. 1).

The National Park Service is dedicated to conserving unimpaired the natural and cultural resources and values of the National Park System for the enjoyment, education, and inspiration of this and future generations. There are more than 370 units in the National Park System, including national parks and monuments; scenic parkways, preserves, trails, riverways, seashores, lakeshores, and recreation areas; and historic sites associated with important movements, events, and personalities of the American past.

The National Park Service has a Service Center in Denver that provides planning, architectural, engineering, and other professional services. The Service is also responsible for managing a great variety of national and international programs designed to help extend the benefits of natural and cultural resource conservation and outdoor recreation throughout this country and the world.

Activities The National Park Service develops and implements park management plans and staffs the areas under its administration. It relates the natural values and historical significance of these areas to the public through talks, tours, films, exhibits, publications, and other interpretive media. It operates campgrounds and other visitor facilities and provides—usually through concessions—lodging, food, and transportation services in many areas.

The National Park Service also administers the following programs: the State portion of the Land and Water Conservation Fund, Nationwide Outdoor Recreation coordination and information and State comprehensive outdoor recreation planning, planning and technical assistance for the National Wild and Scenic Rivers System, and the National Trails System, natural area programs, the National Register of Historic Places, national historic landmarks, historic preservation, technical preservation services, Historic American Buildings Survey, Historic American Engineering Record, and interagency archaeological services.

Field Area Offices—National Park Service

Field Area	Address	Telephone
ALASKA—AK	Rm. 107, 2525 Gambell St., Anchorage, AK 99503–2892	907–257–2690
INTERMOUNTAIN—AZ, CO, MT, NM, OK, TX, UT, WY	P.O. Box 25287, 12795 W. Alameda Pkwy., Denver, CO 80225–0287	303–969–2504
MIDWEST—AR, IL, IN, IA, KS, MI, MN, MO, ND, NE, OH, SD, WI	1709 Jackson St., Omaha, NE 68102	402–221–3431
NATIONAL CAPITAL—Washington, DC, and nearby MD, VA, and WV	1100 Ohio Dr. SW., Washington, DC 20242	202–619–7222
NORTHEAST—CT, DE, ME, MA, MD, NH, NJ, NY, PA, RI, VT, VA, WV	Rm. 306, 200 Chestnut St., Philadelphia, PA 19106	215–597–7013
PACIFIC WEST—CA, HI, ID, NV, OR, WA	Suite 600, 600 Harrison St., San Francisco, CA 94107–1372	415–744–3876

Field Area Offices—National Park Service—Continued

Field Area	Address	Telephone
SOUTHEAST—AL, FL, GA, KY, LA, MS, NC, SC, TN	100 Alabama St. SW., Atlanta, GA 30303	404–562–3100

For further information, contact the Chief, Office of Public Affairs, National Park Service, Department of the Interior, P.O. Box 37127, Washington, DC 20013-7127. Phone, 202-208-6843. Internet, http://www.nps.gov/.

United States Geological Survey

The United States Geological Survey (USGS) was established by the Organic Act of March 3, 1879 (43 U.S.C. 31), which provided that the USGS is directed to classify the public lands and examine the geological structure, mineral resources, and products within and outside the national domain. This section also established the Office of the Director of the Geological Survey, under the Department of the Interior. Public Law 102–285, section 10(a) established the United States Geological Survey as its official name. In 1894, provision was made for gauging the streams and determining the water supply of the United States.

The September 5, 1962, amendment to the Organic Act (43 U.S.C. 31 *et seq.*) expanded this authorization to include such examinations outside the public domain. Specific provision was made for topographic mapping and chemical and physical research through subsequent legislation. Authorizations for publication, sale, and distribution of material prepared by USGS are contained in several statutes (43 U.S.C. 41–45; 44 U.S.C. 1318–1320). The Balanced Budget Downpayment Act, I (110 Stat. 26) incorporated into the USGS the responsibility to provide the management and conservation of the Nation's biological resources and mineral information.

The USGS provides relevant, objective scientific studies and information used to help address issues and solve problems dealing with natural resources, natural hazards, and the environmental effects on human and wildlife health. The major responsibilities of the USGS are:

—investigating and assessing the Nation's land, water, energy, biological, and mineral resources;

—conducting research on global change;

—providing information to resource managers in the Department in a form that helps them to assess and manage the biological consequences of management practices;

—investigating natural hazards such as earthquakes, volcanoes, landslides, floods, and droughts;

—maintaining an archive of land-remote sensing data for historical, scientific, and technical purposes, including long-term global environmental monitoring;

—maintaining a national geochemical, geophysical, mineral deposit, mineral commodity, and mine geology data bases;

—collecting, interpreting, and disseminating a variety of information on world mineral commodities;

—establishing a National Geologic Mapping Program;

—supporting the Federal Geographic Data Committee, which is chaired by the Secretary of the Interior; and

—serving as the designated lead agency for the Federal Water Information Coordination Program.

To attain these objectives, USGS prepares maps and digital and cartographic data; collects and interprets data on energy and mineral resources; conducts nationwide assessments of the quality, quantity, and use of the Nation's water resources; performs fundamental and applied research in the sciences and techniques involved; and publishes the results of its investigations through new maps, technical reports and publications, and fact sheets.

As the Nation's largest water, earth, and biological science and civilian mapping agency, the USGS works in cooperation with more than 2,000 organizations across the country to provide reliable, impartial scientific information to resource managers, planners, and other customers. This information is gathered in every State by USGS scientists to minimize the loss of life and property from natural disasters, to contribute to the conservation and the sound economic and physical development of the Nation's natural resources, and to enhance the quality of life by monitoring water, biological, energy, and mineral resources.

For further information, contact the U.S. Geological Survey, Department of the Interior, 12201 Sunrise Valley Drive, Reston, VA 20192. Phone, 703–648–4000. Fax-on-demand, 703–648–4888. Internet, http://www.usgs.gov/.

Office of Surface Mining Reclamation and Enforcement

The Office of Surface Mining Reclamation and Enforcement (OSM) was established in the Department of the Interior by the Surface Mining Control and Reclamation Act of 1977 (30 U.S.C. 1211).

The Office's primary goal is to assist States in operating a nationwide program that protects society and the environment from the adverse effects of coal mining, while ensuring that surface coal mining can be done without permanent damage to land and water resources. With most coal-mining States responsible for regulating coal mining and reclamation activities within their borders, OSM's main objectives are to oversee State mining regulatory and abandoned mine reclamation programs, assist States in meeting the objectives of the surface mining law, and regulate mining and reclamation activities on Federal and Indian lands, and in those States choosing not to assume primary responsibility.

The Office's headquarters are in Washington, DC. In addition, regional coordinating centers (located in Pittsburgh, PA; Alton, IL; and Denver, CO) provide technical support to the States and to OSM's 10 field offices and 6 area offices. The field offices interact with State, tribal and Federal agencies, assisting the States in implementing their regulatory and reclamation programs. The regional coordinating centers also review mine plans and permit applications on Federal lands.

Activities The Office establishes national policy for the surface mining control and reclamation program provided for in the surface mining law, reviews and approves amendments to previously approved State programs, and reviews and recommends approval of new State program submissions. Other activities include:

—managing the collection, disbursement, and accounting for abandoned mine land reclamation fees;

—administering civil penalties programs;

—establishing technical standards and regulatory policy for reclamation and enforcement efforts;

—providing guidance for environmental considerations, research, training, and technology transfer for State, tribal, and Federal regulatory and abandoned mine land reclamation programs;

—monitoring and evaluating State and tribal regulatory programs, cooperative agreements, and abandoned mine land reclamation programs; and

—coordinating the Appalachian clean streams initiative, a public-private joint effort, at the Federal, State, and local levels, to clean up streams and rivers polluted by acid mine drainage.

For further information, contact the Office of Communications, Office of Surface Mining Reclamation and Enforcement, Department of the Interior, Washington, DC 20240. Phone, 202–208–2719. TDD, 202–208–2737. Internet, http://www.osmre.gov/. Frequently requested documents are available 24 hours a day by fax-on-demand, 202–219–1703.

Bureau of Indian Affairs

The Bureau of Indian Affairs (BIA) was created as part of the War Department in 1824 and transferred to the Department of the Interior when the latter was established in 1849. The Snyder Act of 1921 (25 U.S.C. 13) provided substantive law for appropriations covering the conduct of activities by the Bureau of Indian Affairs. The scope and character of the authorizations contained in this act were broadened by the Indian Reorganization Act of 1934 (25 U.S.C.

461 *et seq.*), the Indian Self-Determination and Education Assistance Act of 1975, as amended (25 U.S.C. 450), title XI of the Education Amendments of 1978 (20 U.S.C. 2701 note), and the Hawkins-Stafford Elementary and Secondary School Improvement Amendments of 1988 (20 U.S.C. 2701).

The principal objectives of the Bureau are to encourage and assist Indian and Alaska Native people to manage their own affairs under the trust relationship to the Federal Government; to facilitate, with maximum involvement of Indian and Alaska Native people, full development of their human and natural resource potential; to mobilize all public and private aids to the advancement of Indian and Alaska Native people for use by them; and to promote self-determination by utilizing the skill and capabilities of Indian and Alaska Native people in the direction and management of programs for their benefit.

In carrying out these objectives, the Bureau works with Indian and Alaska Native people, tribal governments, Native American organizations, other Federal agencies, State and local governments, and other interested groups in the development and implementation of effective programs for their advancement.

Area Offices—Bureau of Indian Affairs

Area	Address	Telephone
Aberdeen, SD	115 4th Ave. SE., 57401–4382	605–226–7343
Albuquerque, NM	P.O. Box 26567, 615 1st St. NW., 87125–6567	505–766–3170
Anadarko, OK	P.O. Box 368, Hwy. 8, 75003	405–247–6673
Arlington, VA	Suite 260, 3701 N. Fairfax Dr., 22203	703–235–2571
Billings, MT	316 N. 26th St., 59101–1397	406–247–7943
Gallup, NM	P.O. Box 1060, 87305	505–863–8314
Juneau, AK	Suite 5, 9109 Mendenhall Rd., 99802–5520	907–586–7177
Minneapolis, MN	331 S. 2d Ave., 55401–2241	612–373–1000
Muskogee, OK	Old Federal Bldg., 5th and W. Okmulgee, 74401–4898	918–687–2296
Phoenix, AZ	P.O. Box 10, 1 N. 1st St., 85001–0010	602–379–6600
Portland, OR	911 NE. 11th Ave., 97232–4169	503–231–6702
Sacramento, CA	2800 Cottage Way, 95825–1884	916–484–4682
Window Rock, AZ	P.O. Box M, WR–1, Window Rock Blvd., 86515–0714	602–871–5151

For further information, contact the Public Affairs Office, Bureau of Indian Affairs, Department of the Interior, Washington, DC 20240. Phone, 202–208–3710. Internet, http://www.usgs.gov/doi/bureau-indian-affairs.html.

Minerals Management Service

The Minerals Management Service was established on January 19, 1982, by Secretarial Order 3071, under the authority provided by section 2 of Reorganization Plan No. 3 of 1950 (5 U.S.C. app.), and further amended on May 10 and May 26, 1982.

Secretarial Order 3087, dated December 3, 1982, and amendment 1, dated February 7, 1983, provided for the transfer of royalty and mineral revenue management functions, including collection and distribution, to the Minerals Management Service and transferred all onshore minerals management functions on Federal and Indian lands to the Bureau of Land Management.

The Service assesses the nature, extent, recoverability, and value of leasable minerals on the Outer Continental Shelf. It ensures the orderly and timely inventory and development, as well as the efficient recovery, of mineral resources; encourages utilization of the best available and safest technology; provides for fair, full, and accurate returns to the Federal Treasury for produced commodities; and safeguards against fraud, waste, and abuse.

Offshore Minerals Management The Service is responsible for resource evaluation, environmental review, leasing activities (including public liaison and planning functions), lease management, and inspection and enforcement programs for Outer Continental Shelf lands.

Five-year oil and gas leasing programs are developed for leasing on the Outer

Continental Shelf in consultation with the Congress, the 23 coastal States, local governments, environmental groups, industry, and the public.

The Service conducts extensive environmental studies and consultations with State officials prior to issuing leases. Once leases have been issued, inspectors conduct frequent inspections of offshore operations, and environmental studies personnel collect more data to ensure that marine environments are kept free of pollutants.

Royalty Management The Service is responsible for the collection and distribution of all royalty payments, rentals, bonus payments, fines, penalties, assessments, and other revenues due the Federal Government and Indian lessors as monies or royalties-in-kind from the

extraction of mineral resources from Federal and Indian lands onshore and from the leasing and extraction of mineral resources on the Outer Continental Shelf.

The revenues generated by minerals leasing are one of the largest nontax sources of income to the Federal Government. As specified by law, these revenues are distributed to the States, to the general fund of the Treasury, and to Indian tribes and allottees.

The basic organization of the Service consists of a headquarters in Washington, DC, with program components located in Herndon, VA, and Lakewood, CO; three Outer Continental Shelf regional offices; and two administrative service centers.

Field Offices—Minerals Management Service

Office	Address	Telephone
ROYALTY MANAGEMENT PROGRAM	P.O. Box 25165, Denver, CO 80225–0165	303–231–3386
OCS Regional Offices		
ALASKA REGION	Rm. 308, 949 E. 36th Ave., Anchorage, AK 99508–4302	907–271–6010
GULF OF MEXICO REGION	1201 Elmwood Park Blvd., New Orleans, LA 70123–2394	504–736–2589
PACIFIC REGION	770 Paseo Camarillo, Camarillo, CA 93010–6064	805–389–7502
Administrative Service Centers		
WESTERN SERVICE CENTER	P.O. Box 25165, Denver, CO 80225–0165	303–275–7300
SOUTHERN SERVICE CENTER	1201 Elmwood Park Blvd., New Orleans, LA 70123–2394	504–736–2616

For further information, contact the Office of Communications, Minerals Management Service, Department of the Interior, Room 4260, (MS 4230), 1849 C Street NW., Washington, DC 20240–7000. Phone, 202–208–3985. Internet, http://www.mms.gov/.

Bureau of Land Management

The Bureau of Land Management (BLM) was established July 16, 1946, by the consolidation of the General Land Office (created in 1812) and the Grazing Service (formed in 1934).

The Federal Land Policy and Management Act of 1976 (90 Stat. 2743) repealed and replaced many obsolete or overlapping statutes. It provides a basic mission statement for the Bureau and establishes policy guidelines and criteria for the management of public lands and resources administered by the Bureau.

The Bureau's basic organization consists of a headquarters in Washington, DC; five national level support and service centers (National Interagency Fire Center, Boise, ID; National Training Center, Phoenix, AZ;

National Applied Resource Sciences Center, National Human Resources Management Center, and National Business Center, Denver, CO); and a field organization of State, and field offices. The Bureau also uses a system of advisory councils to assist in the development of management plans and policies.

The Bureau is responsible for the total management of about 270 million acres of public lands. These lands are located primarily in the West and Alaska; however, small scattered parcels are located in other States. In addition to minerals management responsibilities on the public lands, BLM is also responsible for subsurface resource management of an additional 300 million acres where mineral rights are owned by the Federal Government.

Resources managed by the Bureau include timber, solid minerals, oil and gas, geothermal energy, wildlife habitat, endangered plant and animal species, rangeland vegetation, recreation and cultural values, wild and scenic rivers, designated conservation and wilderness areas, and open space. Bureau programs provide for the protection (including fire suppression), orderly development, and use of the public lands and resources under principles of multiple use and sustained yield. Land use plans are developed with public involvement to provide orderly use and development while maintaining and enhancing the quality of the environment. The Bureau also manages watersheds to protect soil and enhance water quality; develops recreational opportunities on public lands; administers programs to protect and manage wild horses and burros; and, under certain conditions, makes land available for sale to individuals, organizations, local governments, and other Federal agencies when such transfer is in the public interest. Lands may be leased to State and local government agencies and to nonprofit organizations for certain purposes.

The Bureau oversees and manages the development of energy and mineral leases and ensures compliance with applicable regulations governing the extraction of these resources. It has responsibility to issue rights-of-way, leases, and permits.

The Bureau is also responsible for the survey of Federal lands and establishes and maintains public land records and records of mining claims. It administers a program of payments in lieu of taxes based on the amount of federally owned lands in counties and other units of local government.

Field Offices—Bureau of Land Management

State Office	Address	Telephone
ALASKA—AK	No. 13, 222 W. 7th Ave., Anchorage, 99513–7599	907–271–5076
ARIZONA—AZ	222 N. Central Ave., Phoenix, 85004–2203	602–417–9206
CALIFORNIA—CA	2135 Butano Dr., Sacramento, 95825	916–979–2845
COLORADO—CO	2850 Youngfield St., Lakewood, 80215–7076	303–239–3700
EASTERN STATES—All States bordering on and east of the Mississippi River.	7450 Boston Blvd., Springfield, VA 22153	703–440–1700
IDAHO—ID	1387 S. Vinnell Way, Boise, 83709	208–373–4001
MONTANA—MT, ND, SD	P.O. Box 36800, 222 N. 32d St., Billings, MT 59107–6800	406–255–2904
NEVADA—NV	P.O. Box 12000, 850 Harvard Way, Reno, 89520–0006	702–785–6590
NEW MEXICO—KS, NM, OK, TX	P.O. Box 27115, 1474 Rodeo Rd., Santa Fe, NM 87502–0115.	505–438–7501
OREGON—OR, WA	P.O. Box 2965, 1515 SW. 5th Ave, Portland, OR 97208–2965.	503–952–6024
UTAH—UT	P.O. Box 45155, 324 S. State St., Salt Lake City, 84145–1550.	801–539–4010
WYOMING—NE, WY	P.O. Box 1828, 5353 Yellowstone Rd., Cheyenne, WY 82003.	307–775–6001
Service and Support Offices		
NATIONAL INTERAGENCY FIRE CENTER	3833 South Development Ave., Boise, ID 83705–5354	208–387–5446
NATIONAL TRAINING CENTER	9828 N. 31st Ave., Phoenix, AZ 85051–2517	602–906–5500
NATIONAL BUSINESS CENTER	Bldg. 50, BC–600, P.O. Box 25047, Denver, CO 80225–0047.	303–236–6455
NATIONAL HUMAN RESOURCES MANAGEMENT CENTER.	Bldg. 50, HR–200, P.O. Box 25047, Denver, CO 80225–0047.	303–236–6503
NATIONAL APPLIED RESOURCE SCIENCES CENTER.	Bldg. 50, RS–100, P.O. Box 25047, Denver, CO 80225–0047.	303–236–1142

For further information, contact the Office of Public Affairs, Bureau of Land Management, Department of the Interior, LS–406, 1849 C St. NW., Washington, DC 20240. Phone, 202–452–5125. Internet, http://www.blm.gov/.

Bureau of Reclamation

The mission of the Bureau of Reclamation is to manage, develop, and protect, for the public welfare, water and related resources in an environmentally and economically sound manner.

The Reclamation Act of 1902 (43 U.S.C. 371 *et seq.*) authorized the Secretary of the Interior to administer a reclamation program that would provide the arid and semiarid lands of the 17 contiguous Western States a secure, year-round water supply for irrigation. To perform the mission, the Reclamation Service was created within the United States Geological Survey. In 1907 the Reclamation Service was separated from the Survey, and in 1923 was renamed the Bureau of Reclamation.

The Reclamation program has helped to settle and develop the West by providing for sustained economic growth, an improved environment, and an enhanced quality of life through the development of a water storage and delivery infrastructure, which provides safe and dependable water supplies and hydroelectric power for agricultural, municipal, and industrial users; protects and improves water quality; provides recreational and fish and wildlife benefits; enhances river regulations; and helps control damaging floods.

With this infrastructure largely in place, the Reclamation program is now focusing greater emphasis on resource management and protection than on development. Following a balanced approach to the stewardship of the West's water and related land and energy resources, the Bureau:

—works in partnership with others to develop water conservation plans, provide for the efficient and effective use of water and related resources, and improve the management of existing water resources;

—designs and constructs water resources projects, as authorized by the Congress;

—helps to develop and supports or enhances recreational uses at Reclamation projects;

—conducts research and encourages technology transfer to improve resource management, development, and protection;

—ensures that the lands it manages are free from hazardous and toxic waste and assists other Federal and State agencies in protecting and restoring surface water and ground water resources from hazardous waste contamination;

—operates and maintains its facilities to ensure reliability, safety, and economic operation to protect the public, property, and the Nation's investment in the facilities, and to preserve and enhance environmental resources; and

—provides engineering and technical support to Federal and State agencies, to Native American tribes, and to other nations to help accomplish national, regional, and international resource management, development, and protection objectives.

Through contracts with project beneficiaries, the Bureau arranges repayment to the Federal Treasury for construction, operation, and maintenance costs. Approximately 80 percent of all direct project costs are repaid to the Government.

Reclamation project facilities in operation include 355 storage reservoirs, 69,400 miles of canals and other water conveyances and distribution facilities, and 52 hydroelectric powerplants.

Major Offices—Bureau of Reclamation

Office/Region	Address	Telephone
COMMISSIONER	Rm. 7654, Dept. of Interior, Washington, DC 20240–0001 ..	202–208–4157
RECLAMATION SERVICE CENTER	Bldg. 67, Box 25007, Denver, CO 80225	303–236–7000
GREAT PLAINS REGION	Box 36900, 316 N. 26th St., Billings, MT 59107	406–247–7610
LOWER COLORADO REGION	Box 61470, Nevada Hwy. & Park St., Boulder City, NV 89005.	702–293–8420
MID–PACIFIC REGION	2800 Cottage Way, Sacramento, CA 95825	916–978–5101
PACIFIC NORTHWEST REGION	1150 N. Curtis Rd., Boise, ID 83706	208–378–5020
UPPER COLORADO REGION	Box 11568, 125 S. State St., Salt Lake City, UT 84147	801–524–3774

For further information, contact the Public Affairs Division, Bureau of Reclamation, Department of the Interior, Washington, DC 20240–0001. Phone, 202–208–4662. Internet, http://www.usbr.gov/.

Sources of Information

Inquiries on the following subjects should be directed to the specified office, Department of the Interior, Washington, DC 20240.

Contracts Contact the Office of Acquisition and Property Management, Room 5512. Phone, 202–208–3668.

Departmental Museum The Museum has exhibits on topics pertaining to the bureaus and a changing exhibits gallery with new displays every 3–4 months. It presents public programs related to departmental themes and provides tours to school and adult groups on the building's New Deal murals, the Museum, and American Indians. Contact the staff office, Room 1024, Main Interior Building. Phone, 202–208–4743.

Electronic Access Information is available electronically from the Department of the Interior. Internet, http://www.doi.gov/ (or see listings for specific Department components). Access the Interior Museum's home page through "Index," "Select a Subject," "Museums," and "Department of the Interior Museum."

Employment Direct general inquiries to the Personnel Liaison Staff, 202–208–6702, the personnel office of a specific bureau or office, or visit any of the field personnel offices.

Publications Most departmental publications are available from the Superintendent of Documents, Government Printing Office, Washington, DC 20402. All other inquiries regarding publications should be directed to the individual bureau or office's publications or public affairs office.

Information regarding bibliographies on select subjects is available from the Natural Resources Library. Phone, 202–208–5815.

Reading Room Visit the Natural Resources Library, Main Interior Building. Phone, 202–208–5815.

Telephone Directory The Department of the Interior telephone directory is available for sale by the Superintendent of Documents, Government Printing Office, Washington, DC 20402.

Telephone Locator Phone, 202–208–3100.

United States Fish and Wildlife Service

Inquiries on the following subjects should be directed to the specified office, U.S. Fish and Wildlife Service, Department of the Interior, Washington, DC 20240.

Congressional/Legislative Services Congressional staffers and persons seeking information about specific legislation should call the Congressional/Legislative Services office. Phone, 202–208–5403.

Contracts Contact the Washington, DC, headquarters Division of Contracting and General Services (phone, 703–358–1728); or any of the regional offices.

Electronic Access The Fish and Wildlife Service offers a range of information through the Internet, at http://www.fws.gov/.

Employment For information regarding employment opportunities with the U.S. Fish and Wildlife Service, contact the Headquarters Personnel Office (phone, 703–358–1743); or the regional office within the area you are seeking employment.

Import/Export Permits To obtain CITES permits for importing and exporting wildlife, contact the Office of Management Authority. Phone, 800–358–2104 or 703–358–2104.

Law Enforcement To obtain information about the enforcement of wildlife laws or to report an infraction of those laws, contact the Division of Law Enforcement (phone, 703–358–1949); or the nearest regional law enforcement office.

National Wildlife Refuges For general information about the National Wildlife Refuge System, as well as information about specific refuges, contact the Division of Refuges (phone, 800–344–WILD or 703–358–2029); or the nearest national wildlife refuge or regional refuge office.

News Media Inquiries Specific information about the U.S. Fish and

Wildlife Service and its activities is available from the Office of Media Services (phone, 202–208–5634); or the public affairs officer in each of the Service's regional offices.

Publications The U.S. Fish and Wildlife Service has publications available on subjects ranging from the National Wildlife Refuge System to endangered species. Some publications are only available as sales items from the Superintendent of Documents, Government Printing Office, Washington, DC 20402. Further information is available from the Publications Unit, U.S. Fish and Wildlife Service, Mail Stop NCTC Washington, DC 20240. Phone, 304–876–7203.

National Park Service

Contracts Contact the nearest regional office; Administrative Services Division, National Park Service, P.O. Box 37127, Washington, DC 20013–7127 (phone, 202–523–5133); or the Denver Service Center, P.O. Box 25287, 12795 West Alameda Parkway, Denver, CO 80225 (phone, 303–969–2110).

Employment Employment inquiries and applications may be sent to the Personnel Office, National Park Service, Department of the Interior, Washington, DC, and to the field area offices and individual parks. Applications for seasonal employment (which must be received between September 1 and January 15) should be sent to the Division of Personnel Management, National Park Service, P.O. Box 37127, Washington, DC 20013–7127. Phone, 202–208–5074. Schools interested in the recruitment program should write to: Chief Personnel Officer, National Park Service, P.O. Box 37127, Department of the Interior, Washington, DC 20013–7127. Phone, 202–208–5093.

Films The National Park Service has many films on environmental and historical themes. For a list of these films and sales and for information on how to obtain them, write: National Technical Information Service, U.S. Department of Commerce, 5285 Port Royal Rd., Springfield, VA 22161. Phone, 703–487–4650.

Grants-in-Aid For information on grants authorized under the Land and Water Conservation Fund, the Urban Park and Recreation Recovery Program, and the Historic Preservation Fund, write the National Park Service, P.O. Box 37127, Washington, DC 20013–7127. Phone, 202–343–3700 or 202–343–9564.

Publications Items related to the National Park Service are available from the Superintendent of Documents, Government Printing Office, Washington, DC 20402. Phone, 202–512–1800. Items available for sale include the *National Park System Map & Guide* (stock no. 024–005–01135–8); *The National Parks: Index 1995* (stock no. 024–005–01160–4); and *National Parks: Lesser Known Areas* (stock no. 024–005–01152–8). Contact the Consumer Information Center, Pueblo, CO 81009, for other publications about the National Park Service available for sale. For general park and camping information, write to the National Park Service, Office of Public Inquiries, P.O.Box 37127, Room 1013, Washington, DC 20013–7127.

United States Geological Survey

Contracts, Grants, and Cooperative Agreements Write to the Office of Program Support, Office of Acquisition and Federal Assistance, 205 National Center, 12201 Sunrise Valley Drive, Reston, VA 20192. Phone, 703–648–7373.

Employment Inquiries should be directed to one of the following Personnel Offices:

Recruitment and Placement, 601 National Center, 12201 Sunrise Valley Dr., Reston, VA 20192. Phone, 703–648–6131.

Personnel Office, United States Geological Survey, Suite 160, 3850 Holcomb Bridge Rd., Norcross, GA 30092. Phone, 770–409–7750.

Personnel Office, United States Geological Survey, Box 25046, MS 603, Bldg. 53, Denver, CO 80225. Phone, 303–236–5900 ext. 361.

Personnel Office, United States Geological Survey, 345 Middlefield Rd., MS 613, Menlo Park, CA 94025. Phone, 650–329–4104.

General Inquiries A network of nine Earth Science Information Centers (ESIC's) responds to requests for Earth science information that are made in person, by mail, or by telephone and assists in the selection and ordering of all U.S. Geological Survey products:

Rm. 101, 4230 University Dr., Anchorage, AK 99508–4664. Phone, 907–786–7011.

345 Middlefield Rd., Menlo Park, CA 94025. Phone, 650–329–4309.

Box 25286, Bldg. 810, Denver, CO 80225. Phone, 303–202–4200.

Rm. 2650, 1849 C St. NW., Washington, DC 20240. Phone, 202–208–4047.

MS 231, 1400 Independence Rd., Rolla, MO 65401. Phone, 573–308–3500.

2d Fl., 2222 W. 2300 S., Salt Lake City, UT 84119. Phone, 801–975–3742.

Rm. 1C402, 12201 Sunrise Valley Dr., Reston, VA 20192. Phone, 703–648–6045.

Rm. 135, 904 W. Riverside Ave., Spokane, WA 99201. Phone, 509–353–2524.

EROS Data Center, Sioux Falls, SD 57198. Phone, 605–594–6151.

Maps Maps are sold by the Information Services Branch, United States Geological Survey, Box 25286, Denver Federal Center, Denver, CO 80225 (phone, 303–202–4700); and the Earth Science Information Centers (*see* General Inquiries). Information about the status of U.S. Geological Survey mapping in any State and availability of maps by other Federal and State agencies can be obtained from the Earth Science Information Center, 507 National Center, 12201 Sunrise Valley Drive, Reston, VA 20192. Phone, 800–USA–MAPS; or in Virginia, 703–648–6045.

Outreach/External and Media Affairs The Outreach Office of the U.S. Geological Survey coordinates external contacts and special events, responds to news media inquiries, arranges interviews, and prepares news releases and other informational products pertaining to Survey programs and activities. The headquarters office is located at 119 National Center, 12201 Sunrise Valley Drive, Reston, VA 20192. Phone, 703–648–4460. Outreach and media affairs are also conducted on a regional basis at Menlo Park/San Francisco (phone, 650–329–4000); Denver (phone, 303–236–5900); and Reston, VA (phone, 703–648–4582).

Publications The U.S. Geological Survey publishes technical and scientific reports and maps, described in the quarterly periodical *New Publications of the U.S. Geological Survey,* with yearly supplements; *Publications of the U.S. Geological Survey, 1879–1961; Publications of the Geological Survey, 1962–1970;* and a variety of nontechnical publications described in *General Interest Publications of the United States Geological Survey.*

Book, map, fact sheet, and Digital Data Series (CD–ROM) publications are sold by the Information Services Branch, Denver Federal Center, Box 25286, Denver, CO 80225 (phone, 303–202–4200), and by the U.S. Geological Survey's Earth Science Information Centers (*see* General Inquiries).

Open-file reports, in the form of microfiche and/or black and white paper copies, diskettes, and CD–ROM's are sold by the United States Geological Survey, Open File Reports—ESIC, Denver Federal Center, Box 25286, Denver, CO 80225. Phone, 303–202–4200.

Single copies of a variety of nontechnical leaflets, technical reports, books, and special interest publications on Earth science subjects and U.S. Geological Survey activities are available to the public at the Earth Science Information Centers or upon request from the U.S. Geological Survey, Information Services Branch, Denver Federal Center, Box 25286, Denver, CO 80225. Phone, 303–202–4200. Bulk quantities may be purchased from the Superintendent of Documents, Government Printing Office, Washington, DC 20402.

Reading Rooms Facilities for examination of reports, maps, publications of the U.S. Geological Survey, and a wide selection of general Earth science information resources and historical documents are located at the U.S. Geological Survey's libraries at the National Center, 12201 Sunrise Valley Drive, Reston, VA 20192; Denver Federal Center, Building 20, Box 25046, Denver, CO 80225; 345 Middlefield Road, Menlo Park, CA 94025; and 2255 North Gemini Drive, Flagstaff, AZ 86001; and Earth Science Information Centers (*see* General Inquiries). Maps, aerial photographs, geodetic control data or index material, and cartographic data in digital form may be examined at the following Earth Science Information Centers:

Rm. 1C402, 12201 Sunrise Valley Dr., Reston, VA 20192.

1400 Independence Rd., Rolla, MO 65401.

Bldg. 810, Box 25286, MS 504, Denver Federal Ctr., Denver, CO 80225.

345 Middlefield Rd., Menlo Park, CA 94025.

4230 University Dr., Anchorage, AK 99508–4664.

Spacecraft and aircraft remote sensor data may be examined at the EROS Data Center, Sioux Falls, SD 57198. Phone, 605–594–6151.

Water Data   Information on the availability of and access to water data acquired by the U.S. Geological Survey and other local, State, and Federal agencies may be obtained from the National Water Data Exchange, 421 National Center, 12201 Sunrise Valley Drive, Reston, VA 20192. Phone, 703–648–5676.

Office of Surface Mining Reclamation and Enforcement

Contracts   Contact the Procurement Branch, Office of Surface Mining, Department of the Interior, 1951 Constitution Avenue NW., Washington, DC 20240. Phone, 202–208–2839. TDD, 202–208–2737.

Employment   For information on employment opportunities throughout the United States, contact the Chief, Division of Personnel, Office of Surface Mining, Department of the Interior, 1951 Constitution Avenue NW., Washington, DC 20240. Phone, 202–208–2965. TDD, 202–208–2737.

Bureau of Indian Affairs

Inquiries regarding the Bureau of Indian Affairs may be obtained by calling the Office of Public Affairs at 202–208–3710, or writing to the Chief, Office of Public Affairs, 1849 C Street, NW., MS 4542 MIB, Washington, DC 20240.

Minerals Management Service

Inquiries on specific subjects should be directed to the appropriate headquarters office at 1849 C Street NW., Washington, DC 20240, or to the appropriate Minerals Management Service field office (see listing in the preceding text).

Public and News Media Inquiries   Specific information about the Minerals Management Service and its activities is available from the Chief, Office of Communications, Room 4260, MS 4230, 1849 C Street NW., Washington, DC 20240.

Bureau of Land Management

Contracts   Contracts in excess of $100,000 for public land projects are awarded by the contracting teams of the National Business Center. Contracts for construction and nonprofessional services are awarded by the Construction and Nonprofessional Services Team (phone, 303–236–9433). Environmental and professional services contracts are awarded by the Environmental and Professional Services Team (phone, 303–236–9439). Contracts for information technology are awarded by the Federal Information Processing Automated Land and Minerals Record System Team (phone, 303–236–6498). Contracts for public land projects in the States of Oregon and Washington are awarded by the Contracting Office in Portland, OR (phone, 503–952–6216). Bureau of Land Management helium operation contracts are awarded by the Contracting Office in Amarillo, TX (phone, 806–324–2618).

Employment   Initial appointments to the Bureau are made from registers established by the Office of Personnel Management as a result of examination announcements issued by area offices of the Office of Personnel Management throughout the country. The following Office of Personnel Management announcements are applicable to most professional positions within the Bureau. Announcement No. 421, Biological and Agricultural Sciences; Announcement No. 424, Engineering, Physical Sciences and Related Professions. The Mid-Level and Senior-Level registers are also used in a limited number of cases for social sciences professionals and other positions.

Inquiries should be directed to the National Human Resource Management

Center, any Bureau of Land Management State Office, or the Personnel Officer, Bureau of Land Management, Eastern States Office, Department of the Interior, Springfield, VA, from whom the booklet *Career Opportunities in the BLM* is available.

General Inquiries The Bureau's mandate under the Federal Land Policy and Management Act of 1976 is generally to retain public lands in long-term public ownership. The Bureau occasionally sells parcels of land that, as a result of land-use planning, are either uneconomical to manage or would serve an important public objective. These lands are sold at fair market value. Land exchanges can be used to acquire non-BLM lands to protect important natural resources. The Bureau acts as the leasing agent for mineral rights on public and other federally administered lands. Information may be obtained from any of the State offices or from the Bureau of Land Management, Office of Public Affairs, Department of the Interior, Washington, DC 20240. Phone, 202–452–5125. Fax, 202–452–5124.

Publications The annual publication *Public Land Statistics,* which relates to public lands, is available from the Superintendent of Documents, Government Printing Office, Washington, DC 20402.

Reading Rooms All State offices provide facilities for individuals who wish to examine status records, tract books, or other records relating to the public lands and their resources.

Small Business Activities The Bureau has four major buying offices that provide contacts for small business activities: the Headquarters Office in Washington, DC (phone, 202–452–5196); the National Business Center in Lakewood, CO (phone, 303–236–9447); the Oregon State Office (phone, 503–952–6216); and the BLM Office of Helium Operations (phone, 806–324–2618). In addition, there are 12 BLM State offices that acquire goods and services less than $100,000 using simplified acquisition procedures. The Headquarters Office provides procurement support for the Washington, DC, area. The National Business Center provides major contracting services for goods and services more than $100,000 for the western operations of the Bureau, except for the Oregon State Office and the BLM Office of Helium Operations. The Bureau's acquisition plan and procurement office contacts are available through the Internet, at http://www.blm.gov/natacq/.

Speakers Local Bureau offices will arrange for speakers to explain Bureau programs upon request from organizations within their areas of jurisdiction.

Bureau of Reclamation

Contracts Information is available to contractors, manufacturers, and suppliers from Acquisition and Assistance Management Services, Building 67, Denver Federal Center, Denver, CO 80225. Phone, 303–236–3750.

Employment Information on engineering and other positions is available from the Personnel Office, Denver, CO (phone, 303–236–3834); or from the nearest regional office (see listing in the preceding text).

Publications Publications for sale are available through the National Technical Information Service. Phone, 1–800–553–6847.

Speakers and Films A volunteer speaker service provides engineers and scientists for schools and civic groups in the Denver area. Films are available on free loan. For speakers or films, contact the Reclamation Service Center in Denver, CO. Phone, 303–236–7000.

For further information, contact the U.S. Department of the Interior, 1849 C Street NW., Washington, DC 20240. Phone, 202–208–3171. Internet, http://www.doi.gov/.

DEPARTMENT OF JUSTICE

Tenth Street and Constitution Avenue NW., Washington, DC 20530
Phone, 202–514–2000. Internet, http://www.usdoj.gov/.

THE ATTORNEY GENERAL	JANET RENO
Chief of Staff	JOHN M. HOGAN
Deputy Chief of Staff	KENT MARKUS
Confidential Assistant to the Attorney General	BESSIE L. MEADOWS
Assistants to the Attorney General	SIDNEY ESPINOSA, WILFREDO A. FERRER, DAVID JONES, CHERYL L. MONTGOMERY, THOMAS J. PERRELLI, E. KINNEY ZALESNE
Deputy Attorney General	ERIC H. HOLDER, JR.
Confidential Assistant	ANNIE BRADLEY
Principal Associate Deputy Attorney General	ROBERT S. LITT
Chief of Staff	KEVIN A. OHLSON
Associate Deputy Attorneys General	PAUL J. FISHMAN, MARSHALL JARRETT, DAVID MARGOLIS, EILEEN MAYER, ROSLYN A. MAZER, JONATHAN SCHWARTZ, ROBERT M. WILKINSON
Counsels to the Deputy Attorney General	JOHN BENTIVOGLIO, CRAIG ISCOE
Special Assistants to the Deputy Attorney General	BERNARD DELIA, LISA WINSTON
Director, Executive Office for National Security	DANIEL S. SEIKALY
Deputy Director/Associate Deputy Attorney General	MICHAEL A. VATIS
Counsel for National Affairs	JAMES A. MCATAMNEY
Associate Attorney General	RAYMOND C. FISHER
Confidential Assistant	JAYNE SCHREIBER
Deputy Associate Attorneys General	FRANCIS M. ALLEGRA, JOHN DWYER, RICHARD JEROME, REGINALD ROBINSON, LEWIS ANTHONY SUTIN, MICHAEL SMALL
Assistant Associate Attorney General	KENNETH CHERNOF
Senior Counsel, Office of Alternative Dispute Resolution	PETER R. STEENLAND, JR.
Solicitor General	SETH P. WAXMAN, *Acting*
Inspector General	MICHAEL BROMWICH
Assistant Attorney General, Office of Legal Counsel	DAWN JOHNSEN, *Acting*
Assistant Attorney General, Office of Legislative Affairs	ANDREW FOIS
Assistant Attorney General, Office of Policy Development	ELEANOR D. ACHESON
Assistant Attorney General for Administration	STEPHEN R. COLGATE
Assistant Attorney General, Antitrust Division	JOEL I. KLEIN

328

Assistant Attorney General, Civil Division	FRANK W. HUNGER
Assistant Attorney General, Civil Rights Division	BILL LANN LEE, *Acting*
Assistant Attorney General, Criminal Division	JOHN C. KEENEY, *Acting*
Assistant Attorney General, Environment and Natural Resources Division	LOIS J. SCHIFFER
Assistant Attorney General, Tax Division	LORETTA C. ARGRETT
Assistant Attorney General, Office of Justice Programs	LAURIE ROBINSON
Director, Office of Public Affairs	BERT BRANDENBURG
Directors, Office of Information and Privacy	RICHARD L. HUFF, DANIEL J. METCALFE
Director, Office of Intergovernmental Affairs	NICHOLAS M. GESS
Director, Executive Office for U.S. Attorneys	CAROL DIBATTISTE
Director, Bureau of Prisons	KATHLEEN M. HAWK
Director, Federal Bureau of Investigation	LOUIS J. FREEH
Director, United States Marshals Service	EDUARDO GONZALEZ
Director, Executive Office for Immigration Review	ANTHONY C. MOSCATO
Director, Executive Office for United States Trustees	JOSEPH PATCHAN
Director, Community Relations Service	ROSE OCHI
Director, Community Oriented Policing Services	JOSEPH BRANN
Administrator, Drug Enforcement Administration	THOMAS A. CONSTANTINE
Commissioner, Immigration and Naturalization Service	DORIS MEISSNER
Chairman, United States Parole Commission	MICHAEL GAINES
Chairman, Foreign Claims Settlement Commission	DELISSA A. RIDGWAY
Chief, INTERPOL–U.S. National Central Bureau	JAMES CHRISTENSEN, *Acting*
Counsel, Office of Intelligence Policy and Review	GERALD E. SCHROEDER, *Acting*
Counsel, Office of Professional Responsibility	MICHAEL E. SHAHEEN, JR.
Pardon Attorney	ROGER C. ADAMS, *Acting*

[For the Department of Justice statement of organization, see the *Code of Federal Regulations,* Title 28, Chapter I, Part 0]

As the largest law firm in the Nation, the Department of Justice serves as counsel for its citizens. It represents them in enforcing the law in the public interest. Through its thousands of lawyers, investigators, and agents, the Department plays the key role in protection against criminals and subversion, in ensuring healthy competition of business in our free enterprise system, in safeguarding the consumer, and in enforcing drug, immigration, and naturalization laws. The Department also plays a significant role in protecting citizens through its efforts for effective law enforcement, crime prevention, crime detection, and prosecution and rehabilitation of offenders.

Moreover, the Department conducts all suits in the Supreme Court in which the United States is concerned. It represents the Government in legal matters generally, rendering legal advice and opinions, upon request, to the President and to the heads of the executive departments. The Attorney General supervises and directs these activities, as well as those of the U.S. attorneys and U.S. marshals in the various judicial districts around the country.

DEPARTMENT OF JUSTICE

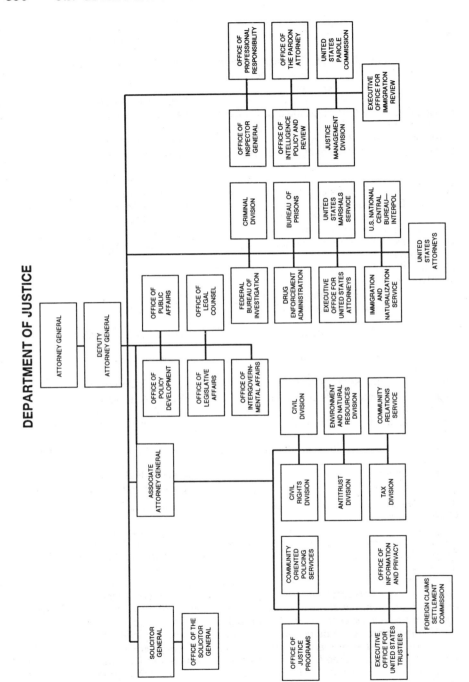

The Department of Justice was established by act of June 22, 1870, as amended (28 U.S.C. 501, 503, 509 note), with the Attorney General as its head. Prior to 1870 the Attorney General was a member of the President's Cabinet, but not the head of a department, the office having been created under authority of act of September 24, 1789, as amended (28 U.S.C. 503).

The affairs and activities of the Department of Justice are generally directed by the Attorney General. The offices, divisions, bureaus, and boards of the Department follow.

Offices

Attorney General   The Attorney General, as head of the Department of Justice and chief law enforcement officer of the Federal Government, represents the United States in legal matters generally and gives advice and opinions to the President and to the heads of the executive departments of the Government when so requested. The Attorney General appears in person to represent the Government before the U.S. Supreme Court in cases of exceptional gravity or importance. The Office of the Attorney General oversees the Offices of Deputy Attorney General, Associate Attorneys General, Legal Counsel, and Inspector General, as well as the following offices whose public purposes are widely applied.

Solicitor General   The Solicitor General represents the U.S. Government in cases before the Supreme Court. He decides what cases the Government should ask the Supreme Court to review and what position the Government should take in cases before the Court. Also, he supervises the preparation of the Government's Supreme Court briefs and other legal documents and the conduct of the oral arguments in the Court. He or his staff argue most of the Government's cases in the Supreme Court. The Solicitor General's duties also include deciding whether the United States should appeal in all cases it loses before the lower courts.

Legal Counsel   The Assistant Attorney General in charge of the Office of Legal Counsel assists the Attorney General in fulfilling the Attorney General's function as legal adviser to the President and all the executive branch agencies. The Office drafts legal opinions of the Attorney General rendered in response to requests from the President and heads of the executive departments. It also provides its own written opinions and informal advice in response to requests from the various agencies of the Government, as well as offices within the Department and from Presidential staff and advisers, typically dealing with legal issues involving agency disagreements or with pending legislation. The Office also is responsible for providing legal advice to the executive branch on all constitutional questions.

All Executive orders and proclamations proposed to be issued by the President are reviewed by the Office of Legal Counsel for form and legality, as are various other matters that require the President's formal approval. In addition, the Office of Legal Counsel functions as general counsel for the Department. It reviews all proposed orders of the Attorney General and all regulations requiring the Attorney General's approval.

The Office coordinates the work of the Department with respect to treaties, executive agreements, and international organizations. It performs a variety of special assignments referred by the Attorney General or the Deputy Attorney General. However, it is not authorized to give legal advice to private persons.

Information and Privacy   The Office of Information and Privacy (OIP) operates under the supervision of a Director, who manages the Department's responsibilities related to the Freedom of Information Act (FOIA) and the Privacy

Act. These responsibilities include coordinating policy development and compliance Governmentwide for FOIA, and by the Department for the Privacy Act; and adjudicating all appeals from denials by any Department component of access to information under those acts. OIP also processes all initial requests under those acts for access to the records of the Offices of the Attorney General, Deputy Attorney General, Associate Attorney General, and other senior management offices of the Department.

Pardon Attorney The Office of the Pardon Attorney, in consultation with the Attorney General or the Attorney General's designee, assists the President in the exercise of his pardon power under Article II, section 2, of the Constitution. Generally, all requests for pardon or other forms of executive clemency, including commutation of sentence, are directed to the Pardon Attorney for investigation and review. The Pardon Attorney prepares the Department's recommendation to the President for final disposition of each application.

Community Relations Service The Service was created by title X of the Civil Rights Act of 1964 (42 U.S.C. 2000g et seq.). The Community Relations Service is under the general authority of the Attorney General and is headed by a Director, appointed by the President with the advice and consent of the Senate.

The mission of the Service is to prevent and resolve community conflicts and reduce community tensions arising from actions, policies, and practices perceived to be discriminatory on the basis of race, color, or national origin. The Service offers assistance to communities in resolving disputes relating to race, color, or national origin and facilitates the development of viable agreements as alternatives to coercion, violence, or litigation. It also assists and supports communities in developing local mechanisms as proactive measures to prevent or reduce racial/ethnic tensions.

The services provided include conciliation, mediation, technical assistance, and training, and involve specialized procedures for preventing and resolving racial and ethnic conflicts. The Service provides assistance directly to people and their communities. It shows no partiality among disputing parties and, in promoting the principles and ideals of nondiscrimination, applies skills that allow parties to mediate their own disputes. The Service's conciliators, who are located in 10 regional offices and 4 field offices around the country, assist people of diverse racial and cultural backgrounds.

The Service offers its assistance either on its own motion, when in its judgment peaceful relations among the citizens of a community are threatened, or upon request of State or local officials or other interested persons. The Service seeks the cooperation of appropriate State and local, and public and private agencies in carrying out the agency's mission.

Regional Offices—Community Relations Service

Address	Director	Phone/FTS
Boston, MA (99 Summer St., 02110)	Martin A. Walsh	617–424–5715
New York, NY (26 Federal Plz., 10278)	Patricia Glenn	212–264–0700
Philadelphia, PA (2d and Chestnut Sts., 19106)	Jonathan Chace	215–597–2344
Atlanta, GA (75 Piedmont Ave. NE., 30303)	Ozell Sutton	404–331–6883
Chicago, IL (55 W. Monroe St., 60603)	Jesse Taylor	312–353–4391
Dallas, TX (1420 W. Mockingbird Ln., 75247)	Gilbert J. Chavez	214–655–8175
Kansas City, MO (323 W. 8th St., 64105)	Atkins Warren	816–426–7434
Denver, CO (1244 Speer Blvd., 80204–3584)	Silke Hansen, *Acting*	303–844–2973
San Francisco, CA (33 New Montgomery St., 94105–4511)	Booker Neal, *Acting*	415–744–6565
Seattle, WA (915 2d Ave., 98101)	Robert Lamb, Jr.	206–220–6700

For further information, contact any regional office or the Director, Community Relations Service, Department of Justice, Suite 2000, 600 E Street NW., Washington, DC 20530. Phone, 202–305–2935.

Justice Management Division   Under the direction of the Assistant Attorney General for Administration, the Division provides assistance to senior management officials relating to basic Department policy for evaluation, budget and financial management, asset forfeiture management, personnel management and training, equal opportunity programs, automatic data processing and telecommunications, security, records management, procurement, real property and materiel management, and for all other matters pertaining to organization, management, and administration.

The Division provides direct administrative support services, such as personnel, accounting, payroll, procurement, budget, and facilities and property management to the offices, boards, and divisions of the Department; and operates several central services, such as automated data processing.

The Division develops and promulgates Departmentwide policies, standards, and procedures for the management of automated information processing resources and for the directive system and reviews their implementation. The Division collects, organizes, and disseminates recorded information that is necessary for the Department to carry out its statutory mandate and provides general research and reference assistance regarding information to Department staff, other Government attorneys, and members of the public.

Professional Responsibility   The Office of Professional Responsibility, which reports directly to the Attorney General, is responsible for investigating allegations of criminal or ethical misconduct by employees of the Justice Department. The Counsel on Professional Responsibility heads the Office, the role of which is to ensure that departmental employees continue to perform their duties in accordance with the high professional standards expected of the Nation's principal law enforcement agency.

All allegations of misconduct against Department attorneys that relate to the exercise of their discretion to investigate, litigate, or provide legal advice are reported to the Office of Professional Responsibility. The Office also has jurisdiction to investigate allegations of misconduct by law enforcement personnel when they are related to allegation of misconduct by attorneys within the Office's jurisdiction. The Office usually conducts its own investigations into allegations.

The Office may also participate in or direct an investigation conducted by another component of the Department, or may simply monitor an investigation conducted by an appropriate agency having jurisdiction over the matter. In addition, the Office oversees the internal inspection operations of the Federal Bureau of Investigation and Drug Enforcement Administration.

The Counsel submits an annual report to the Attorney General that reviews and evaluates the Department's internal inspection units. The Counsel makes recommendations to the Attorney General on the need for changes in policies or procedures that become evident during the course of internal inquiries reviewed or initiated by the Office.

Intelligence Policy and Review   The Office of Intelligence Policy and Review, under the direction of the Counsel to the Attorney General for Intelligence Policy, is responsible for advising the Attorney General on all matters relating to the national security activities of the United States. The Office also serves as adviser to the Attorney General and various client agencies, including the Central Intelligence Agency, the Federal Bureau of Investigation, the National Security Agency, and the Defense and State Departments, concerning questions of law, regulation, and guidelines as well as the legality of domestic and overseas intelligence operations.

The Office prepares and files all applications for surveillances and searches under the Foreign Intelligence Surveillance Act of 1978, assists Government agencies by providing legal advice on matters of national security law and policy and represents the Department of Justice on a variety of interagency committees. The Office also comments on and coordinates other agencies' views regarding proposed legislation affecting national security and intelligence matters.

The Office maintains an Intelligence Analytic Unit (IAU) to keep the Attorney General, Deputy Attorney General, and other senior Department officials currently informed on matters pertaining to their responsibilities.

Executive Office for United States Attorneys (EOUSA)   The Office was created on April 6, 1953, by Attorney General Order No. 8–53, to meet a need for a closer liaison between the Department of Justice in Washington, DC, and the U.S. attorneys. The Office is under the supervision of the Deputy Attorney General.

The mission of EOUSA is to provide general executive assistance to the 94 Offices of the U.S. attorneys and to coordinate the relationship between the U.S. attorneys and the organization components of the Department of Justice and other Federal agencies.

U.S. Trustee Program   The U.S. Trustee Program acts in the public interest to promote the efficiency and to protect and preserve the integrity of the bankruptcy system. It works to secure the just, speedy, and economical resolution of bankruptcy cases; monitors the conduct of parties, takes action to ensure compliance with applicable laws and procedures, and identifies and investigates bankruptcy fraud and abuse; and oversees administrative functions in bankruptcy cases. The Program is funded by the U.S. Trustee System Fund, which consists mainly of filing fees paid by debtors invoking the protections of the bankruptcy laws.

The U.S. Trustees supervise the administration of four of the five types of bankruptcy proceedings defined under the Bankruptcy Code. These are:

—proceedings under chapter 7 in which the assets of the debtor are liquidated;

—reorganization proceedings under chapter 11 for rehabilitation of the business debtor;

—adjustments of debts of a family farmer with regular income under chapter 12; and

—adjustment of debts of an individual with regular income under chapter 13, pursuant to which an individual can discharge debts by arranging for payments over a period of time. The U.S. Trustee does not have a significant role in proceedings under chapter 9, which relates to the adjustment of debts of a municipality.

Specific responsibilities of the U.S. Trustees include:

—appointing and supervising the performance of private trustees in individual cases;

—appointing and convening creditors' committees in chapter 11 corporate reorganization cases;

—reviewing applications for the retention of professionals and the payment of fees;

—reviewing disclosure statements and submitting statements to the court regarding their adequacy;

—appointing trustees or examiners in such cases as needed;

—ensuring that the assets involved in bankruptcy cases are protected during the administration of cases;

—serving as trustees in chapters 7, 12, and 13 cases where private trustees are unwilling to serve; and

—presenting matters relating to the Bankruptcy Code in court.

Executive Office for U.S. Trustees   The Attorney General is charged with the appointment, supervision, and coordination of the U.S. Trustees and Assistant U.S. Trustees. Day-to-day policy and legal direction, coordination, and control are provided by the Director of the Executive Office for U.S. Trustees who is appointed by the Attorney General. The Executive Office also provides administrative and management support to individual U.S. Trustee Offices.

For further information, contact the Executive Office for U.S. Trustees, Department of Justice, Suite 700, 901 E Street NW., Washington, DC 20530. Phone, 202–307–1391.

Divisions

Antitrust Division

The Assistant Attorney General in charge of the Antitrust Division is responsible for promoting and maintaining competitive markets by enforcing the Federal antitrust laws. Such enforcement, which is the principal function of the Division, involves investigating possible antitrust violations, conducting grand jury proceedings, preparing and trying antitrust cases, prosecuting appeals, and negotiating and enforcing final judgments. The antitrust laws affect virtually all industries and apply to every phase of business, including manufacturing, transportation, distribution, and marketing. They prohibit a variety of practices that restrain trade, such as price-fixing conspiracies, corporate mergers likely to reduce the competitive vigor of particular markets, and predatory acts designed to achieve or maintain monopoly power. The Division prosecutes serious and willful violations of the antitrust laws by filing criminal suits that can lead to large fines and jail sentences. Where criminal prosecution is not appropriate, the Division seeks a court order forbidding future violations of the law and requiring steps by the defendant to remedy the anticompetitive effects of past violations.

The Division also is responsible for acting as an advocate of competition within the Federal Government. This involves formal appearances in Federal administrative agency proceedings, development of legislative initiatives to promote deregulation and eliminate unjustifiable exemptions from the antitrust laws, participation on executive branch policy task forces, and publication of reports on regulated industry performance. The Division provides formal advice to other agencies on the competitive implications of proposed transactions requiring Federal approval, such as construction of nuclear powerplants and mergers of financial institutions. It also consults with Federal agencies on a variety of other matters, including the issuance of Federal coal and oil drilling leases and the disposition of surplus Government property.

In addition, the Antitrust Division represents the United States in judicial proceedings to review certain orders of regulatory agencies and provides direct court representation for the Secretary of the Treasury in certain Bureau of Alcohol, Tobacco and Firearms cases. It also participates in Federal Trade Commission cases before the Supreme Court.

In the international law area, the Division represents the United States on the Committee on Competition Law and Policy of the Organization for Economic Cooperation and Development; participates in the United Nations Conference on Trade and Development and in the World Trade Organization's trade and competition working group; and, in conjunction with the Department of State, maintains liaison with foreign governments on antimonopoly laws and policies.

For further information, contact the FOIA Unit, Antitrust Division, Department of Justice, 325 Seventh Street NW., Washington, DC 20530. Phone, 202–514–2692.

Civil Division

The Civil Division represents the United States, its departments and agencies, Members of Congress, Cabinet officers, and other Federal employees. Its litigation reflects the diversity of Government activities, involving, for example, the defense of challenges to Presidential actions; national security issues; benefit programs; energy policies; commercial issues such as contract disputes, banking, insurance, patents, fraud, and debt collection; all manner of accident and liability claims; and violations of the immigration and consumer protection laws. Each year, Division attorneys handle thousands of cases that collectively involve billions of dollars in claims and recoveries. The Division confronts significant policy issues, which often rise to constitutional dimensions, in defending and enforcing various Federal programs and actions.

The Civil Division litigates cases in all Federal district courts, the U.S. Courts of Appeals, the U.S. Court of Federal Claims, other Federal and State courts, and the courts of foreign nations. Division attorneys either conduct this litigation personally or they supervise or assist the U.S. attorneys and foreign counsel to whom the Division refers the cases. The Division is composed of seven major groups: the Torts Branch, the Commercial Litigation Branch, the Federal Programs Branch, the Appellate Staff, the Office of Consumer Litigation, the Office of Immigration Litigation, and an Office of Management Programs.

Torts The Torts Branch is responsible for suits under the Federal Tort Claims Act, including medical malpractice, aviation disasters, environmental and occupational disease, and radiation and toxic substance exposure. It also handles maritime litigation and suits that seek personal monetary judgments against individual officers or employees.

Tort litigation more specifically includes the defense of all Federal Tort Claims Act suits against the United States, and the prosecution of suits in tort on behalf of the United States. Suits and administrative claims for death, personal injury, and property damage brought under the Tort Claims Act allege negligence on the part of Government employees acting within the scope of their employment and involve matters such as the operation of Government vehicles, the maintenance of Government premises, and the performance of Federal services and regulatory functions such as medical treatment, hospital care, and the control of civilian, military, and commercial air traffic. In addition, the Torts Branch defends petitions filed pursuant to the Vaccine Injury Compensation Program and is responsible for administering the Radiation Exposure Compensation Act.

Tort litigation also includes all legal proceedings involving the United States related to ships, shipping, navigable waters, and workmen's compensation. The Division's admiralty litigation includes suits for personal injury and property damage involving vessels, shore installations, and maritime personnel, equipment, and cargoes; suits arising out of contracts involving shipping, chartering of vessels, and the construction, repair, and salvaging of vessels; proceedings to enforce navigation and shipping laws; and litigation based on international maritime agreements.

Commercial Litigation The Commercial Litigation Branch is responsible for litigation associated with the Government's diverse financial involvements.

This litigation includes all monetary suits involving contracts, express or implied; actions to foreclose on Government mortgages and liens; bankruptcy and insolvency proceedings; and suits against guarantors and sureties.

Branch attorneys bring suit under the False Claims Act (31 U.S.C. 3729) for the recovery of treble damages and civil penalties and alternative remedies, in connection with fraud in the award or performance of Government contracts, false claims presented in connection with Federal programs such as Medicare, the submission of false statements and vouchers to Government agencies, and the use of other fraudulent devices in transactions with the Government. These suits include those filed pursuant to the *qui tam* provisions of the False Claims Act, in which private citizens with knowledge of fraud against the Government may file a lawsuit against the perpetrators on behalf of the United States and share in a percentage of any monetary recovery. Branch attorneys also bring suits to recover sums paid to bribe Government officials and kickbacks in Government procurement.

The Branch is responsible for all cases in the U.S. Court of International Trade, including suits brought by importers of merchandise to challenge the appraisement or classification of imported goods or other decisions of the

U.S. Customs Service in its administration of the tariff laws and schedules.

The Branch has responsibility for all litigation in the U.S. Court of Federal Claims except for those cases assigned to the Environment and Natural Resources Division and the Tax Division. Included are:

—patent cases and suits arising out of construction, procurement, service contracts, and claims associated with contract terminations;

—claims involving freight rate disputes arising out of the transportation of Government property;

—claims for just compensation under the fifth amendment;

—claims for salary or retirement by civilian and military personnel; and

—cases assigned by congressional reference or special legislation.

Likewise, Branch attorneys handle the majority of cases before the Court of Appeals for the Federal Circuit. This litigation involves appeals of decisions made by the U.S. Court of Federal Claims, the U.S. Court of Veterans Appeals, Boards of Contract Appeals, the Merit Systems Protection Board, and Federal district courts.

The Branch handles all litigation involving the rights, liabilities, and administrative functions of the Government with respect to patent, copyright, and trademark matters. This includes:

—defense of patent infringement suits based on the liability of the United States for infringements in connection with the performance of Government contracts;

—legal proceedings to establish Government priority of invention;

—suits for specific performance to require transfer of rights and title and payment of royalties;

—suits to cancel patents acquired by fraud upon the Patent Office;

—defense of administrative acts of the Register of Copyrights; and

—actions on behalf of the Government involving the use of trademarks.

The Branch is also responsible for the supervision of litigation in foreign courts involving the United States as a party and suits against U.S. employees stationed abroad who are being sued in the course of their Government service. Additionally, the Branch renders international judicial assistance to foreign and international tribunals.

Federal Programs   The Federal Programs Branch defends the programs, policies, and decisions of virtually all Federal departments and agencies, the President, Cabinet officers, Members of Congress, and other Government officials. It defends against constitutional challenges to statutes, suits to overturn Government policies and programs, and challenges to the legality of Government decisions. These suits typically seek injunctive and declaratory relief and range from objections to the way that the Government deals with its employees to allegations that the President has violated the Constitution or Federal law. The Branch also initiates suits to enforce regulatory statutes and to remedy or prevent statutory or regulatory violations.

The areas of litigation include:

—defense of suits against the heads of Federal departments and agencies and other government officials to enjoin official actions, as well as suits for judicial review of administrative decisions, orders, and regulations;

—defense and prosecution of suits involving national security, including suits to protect sensitive intelligence sources and materials;

—prosecution of suits to prevent interference with Government operations;

—litigation concerning the constitutionality of Federal laws;

—defense of suits raising employment discrimination claims and Government personnel issues; and

—defense of suits involving specialized statutes, such as the Freedom of Information Act, the Federal Advisory Committee Act, and the Privacy Act.

Appellate Staff   The Appellate Staff has primary responsibility for the litigation of Civil Division cases in the appellate courts. The Staff prepares Government briefs and presents oral argument for the cases. Additionally, the Appellate Staff participates in drafting all documents filed for these cases in the United States Supreme Court, including briefs on the merits, petitions for certiorari, and jurisdictional statements.

Consumer Litigation The Office of Consumer Litigation is responsible for civil and criminal litigation and related matters arising under various consumer protection and public health statutes, including the Federal Food, Drug, and Cosmetic Act, the Federal Trade Commission Act, the Consumer Product Safety Act, the Hazardous Substances Act, and the Truth in Lending Act. The Office also serves as a liaison with other Federal agencies and with local enforcement agencies for the referral of consumer complaints outside the jurisdiction of the Department of Justice.

Immigration Litigation The Office of Immigration Litigation is responsible for conducting civil litigation under the Immigration and Nationality Act (8 U.S.C. 1101) and related laws and for representing the United States in civil litigation brought against employees of the Immigration and Naturalization Service. In addition, this Office handles district court litigation, removal order review proceedings, habeas corpus review and general advice, and immigration-related appellate matters. The Office is also responsible for cases pertaining to the issuance of visas and passports, and for litigation arising under the amnesty and employer sanctions provisions of the Immigration Reform and Control Act of 1986 (8 U.S.C. 1255a, 1324a), the criminal and terrorist alien reforms of 1990 and 1996, and the immigration enforcement reforms of the Illegal Immigration Reform and Immigrant Responsibility Act of 1996.

Management Programs The Office of Management Programs provides management and administrative services to the Division, including policy analysis and planning, administrative management, budget formulation and execution, management information systems, office automation, and automated litigation support.

For further information, contact the Office of the Assistant Attorney General, Civil Division, Department of Justice, Tenth Street and Pennsylvania Avenue NW., Washington, DC 20530. Phone, 202–514–3301.

Civil Rights Division

The Civil Rights Division, headed by an Assistant Attorney General, was established in 1957 to secure effective Federal enforcement of civil rights. The Division is the primary institution within the Federal Government responsible for enforcing Federal statutes prohibiting discrimination on the basis of race, sex, disability, religion, and national origin. The Division is composed of the following Sections:

Appellate Section The Appellate Section handles civil rights cases in the courts of appeals and, in cooperation with the Solicitor General, in the Supreme Court. The Section frequently participates in *amicus curiae* cases that affect the Division, and provides counsel to the Department on civil rights and appellate litigation. It handles all appeals from both favorable and adverse judgments in which the Government participates.

Coordination and Review Section This Section coordinates the enforcement by Federal agencies of various civil rights statutes that prohibit discrimination on the basis of race, color, national origin, sex, and religion in programs and activities that receive Federal financial assistance. The Section also conducts compliance reviews and investigates complaints of discrimination on the basis of race, color, national origin, sex, age, and religion in the services and activities of recipients of Federal financial assistance from the Department of Justice. The Section is taking the lead role in implementing the President's initiative, announced in June 1997, to reinvigorate the enforcement of title IX of the Education Amendments of 1972 (20 U.S.C. 1681 *et seq.*).

Criminal Section Under the Federal criminal civil rights statutes, the Criminal Section prosecutes conduct involving conspiracies to interfere with federally protected rights, deprivation of rights under color of law, the use of force or threat of force to injure or intimidate someone in their enjoyment of specific rights (such as voting, housing, employment, education, public facilities, and accommodations), interference with the free exercise of religious beliefs or damage to religious property, and the holding of a worker in a condition of slavery or involuntary servitude. More recently, the Section began enforcing the criminal aspects of the new Freedom of Access to Clinic Entrances Act (FACE). This statute prohibits conduct intended to injure, intimidate, or interfere with persons seeking to obtain or provide reproductive services. Also, a task force staffed by attorneys from both the Criminal and Civil Rights Divisions was created by the Attorney General to determine if there is any organized criminal effort to commit violence upon abortion providers. The National Church Arson Task Force created in June 1996 is a joint effort of Federal, State, and local law enforcement in investigating incidents of arson at houses of worship and apprehending and prosecuting those responsible.

Disability Rights Section   This Section (previously the Public Access Section) enforces titles I, II, and III of the Americans with Disabilities Act of 1990 (ADA) and Department of Justice regulations implementing these provisions, provides technical assistance to entities covered by the ADA and to persons protected by the ADA, and coordinates the technical assistance efforts of all Federal agencies with technical assistance responsibilities under the ADA. The Section also certifies that State or local building codes meet or exceed the requirements of the ADA. In addition, the Section is responsible for carrying out the Department's responsibilities under section 504 of the Rehabilitation Act of 1973. For the ADA Information Line, phone 800–514–0301 (voice) or 800–514–0383 (TDD). ADA information is also available through the Internet, at http://www.usdoj.gov/crt/ada/adahom1.htm/.

Educational Opportunities Section   The Educational Opportunities Section enforces title IV of the Civil Rights Act of 1964 and the Equal Educational Opportunities Act of 1974. In addition, it represents the Department of Education in certain suits filed against and on behalf of the Secretary of Education. The Section closely monitors approximately 400 school districts operating under desegregation court orders.

Employment Litigation Section   The Employment Litigation Section enforces the provisions of title VII of the Civil Rights Act of 1964, as amended, and other Federal laws prohibiting employment practices that discriminate on the grounds of race, sex, religion, and national origin, as they apply to State and local government employers.

Housing and Civil Enforcement Section   The Housing and Civil Enforcement Section has principal responsibility for enforcing the Fair Housing Act of 1968, as amended, which prohibits discrimination in housing on the basis of race, color, religion, sex, national origin, disability, and familial status. The act allows the Section to bring cases on behalf of individuals where a complaint is filed with the Department of Housing and Urban Development (HUD). Additionally, the Section enforces the Equal Credit Opportunity Act, which prohibits discrimination in credit transactions; and title II of the Civil Rights Act of 1964, which prohibits discrimination in places of public accommodations, such as hotels, restaurants, and places of entertainment.

Office of Special Counsel for Immigration Related Unfair Employment Practices   The Office of Special Counsel for Immigration Related Unfair Employment Practices was established pursuant to section 102 of the Immigration Reform and Control Act of 1986 (8 U.S.C. 1324b). The Special Counsel is responsible for investigating and prosecuting charges of national origin and citizenship status discrimination in hiring, firing, or recruitment. Jurisdiction over national origin charges is limited to those not covered by the Equal Employment

Opportunity Commission. Jurisdiction over citizenship status is exclusive.

The Special Counsel files complaints before an administrative law judge based on charges filed with this Office or on its own independent investigations. Appeals of administrative decisions are to the U.S. Courts of Appeals.

In addition, the Special Counsel coordinates with the Immigration and Naturalization Service, the Equal Employment Opportunity Commission, and other Federal agencies in promoting public awareness of the antidiscrimination provisions of the act, through employer and public interest conferences, public service announcements, and nationwide distribution of enforcement information.

Special Litigation Section The Special Litigation Section is responsible for protecting the constitutional and statutory rights of persons confined in certain institutions owned or operated by State or local governments, including facilities for individuals with mental and developmental disabilities, nursing homes, prisons, jails, and juvenile detention facilities where a pattern or practice of violations exist. This authority is granted by the Civil Rights of Institutionalized Persons Act. The Section is also responsible for civil enforcement provisions of the Freedom of Access to Clinic Entrances Act (FACE) which prohibits force or the threat of force for the purpose of interfering with the provision of reproductive services; and the police misconduct provision of the Violent Crime Control and Law Enforcement Act of 1994, which gives the Attorney General authority to remedy patterns and practices of misconduct by certain law enforcement authorities.

Voting Section The Voting Section is responsible for the enforcement of the Voting Rights Act of 1965, the Voting Accessibility for the Elderly and Handicapped Act, the Uniformed and Overseas Citizens Absentee Voting Act, the National Voter Registration Act of 1993, and other statutory provisions designed to safeguard the right to vote of racial and language minorities, illiterate persons, individuals with disabilities, overseas citizens, persons who change their residence shortly before a Presidential election, and persons 18 to 20 years of age.

Under section 2 of the Voting Rights Act, the Section brings lawsuits to remedy discriminatory election practices. Under section 5 of the Voting Rights Act, the Section reviews voting changes submitted to the Attorney General and defends section 5 litigation in court to assure that redistricting plans and other changes in voting practices and procedures do not abridge the right to vote of racial or language minorities. Under section 8 of the Voting Rights Act, the Attorney General requests the assignment of Federal observers—who generally are employees of the Office of Personnel Management—to monitor polling place activities on election day to document and deter discriminatory practices.

Administrative Management Section This Section supports the Division by providing a diverse array of management and technical services, including personnel administration, budget formulation and execution, facilities services, mail and file operations, litigation support, office automation, databases, and geographic information system support. This Section also contains the Freedom of Information/Privacy Act Branch, which ensures that the Division complies with all aspects of the Freedom of Information and Privacy Acts.

Another component of the Administrative Management Section is the Office of Redress Administration (ORA), which implements the responsibilities given to the Attorney General under section 105 of the Civil Liberties Act of 1988. The Act provides for redress to American citizens and permanent resident aliens of Japanese ancestry who were evacuated, relocated, and interned by the United States during World War II. ORA's functions will end August 10, 1998. For further information about ORA, phone 888–219–6900 (toll-free).

For further information, contact the Executive Officer, Civil Rights Division, Department of Justice, P.O. Box 65310, Washington, DC 20035–5310. Phone, 202–514–4224. Internet, http://www.usdoj.gov/crt.

Criminal Division

The Criminal Division develops, enforces, and supervises the application of all Federal criminal laws, except those specifically assigned to other divisions. The Division and the 93 U.S. attorneys are responsible for overseeing criminal matters under more than 900 statutes, as well as certain civil litigation. In addition to its direct litigation responsibilities, the Division formulates and implements criminal enforcement policy and provides advice and assistance. The Division approves or monitors sensitive areas of law enforcement such as participation in the Witness Security Program and the use of electronic surveillance; advises the Attorney General, Congress, the Office of Management and Budget, and the White House of matters of criminal law; provides legal advice and assistance to Federal prosecutors and investigative agencies; and provides leadership for coordinating international as well as Federal, State, and local law enforcement matters.

Office of Administration The Office of Administration performs a wide range of administrative and managerial functions for the components of the Criminal Division, including budget preparation and execution, personnel actions, computer support services, mail and records services, procurement, and security.

Appellate Section The Appellate Section prepares draft briefs and certiorari petitions for the Solicitor General to be filed in the U.S. Supreme Court; makes recommendations to the Solicitor General as to whether further review on adverse decisions in the district courts and courts of appeals is necessary; and prepares briefs and argues cases in the courts of appeals.

The Section assists U.S. attorneys and Division prosecutors in preparing briefs for the courts of appeals and provides advice on Speedy Trial Act [of 1974] problems and a variety of other legal issues.

Asset Forfeiture/Money Laundering Section The Section provides centralized management for the Department's asset forfeiture program to ensure its integrity and maximize its law enforcement potential, while also providing managerial direction to the Department's components concerned with money laundering. The Section initiates, coordinates, and reviews legislative and policy proposals impacting on the asset forfeiture program and money laundering enforcement and serves as the Department's contact for Congress, other executive branch agencies, and State and local law enforcement agencies.

The Section works with the entire spectrum of law enforcement and regulatory agencies using an interagency, interdisciplinary, and international approach. The Section is mandated to coordinate multidistrict investigations and prosecutions; develop regulatory and legislative initiatives; ensure the uniform application of forfeiture and money laundering statutes; litigate complex, sensitive, and multidistrict cases; and provide litigation assistance to the U.S. attorneys' offices and Criminal Division components.

The Section oversees asset forfeiture and money laundering training and conducts seminars for Federal prosecutors, investigating agents, and law enforcement personnel. It also produces legal publications and training materials to enhance its legal support functions.

The Section also adjudicates all petitions for remission or mitigation of forfeited assets in judicial forfeiture cases, administers the Weed and Seed Program and the Equitable Sharing Program, and oversees the approval of the placement of forfeited property into official use by Federal agencies.

Child Exploitation and Obscenity The Child Exploitation and Obscenity Section (CEOS) is responsible for overseeing the Federal response to child sexual abuse and exploitation. In carrying out these duties, CEOS attorneys work with U.S. attorneys' offices and participate in the prosecution of violations of Federal law involving child sexual exploitation, child sexual abuse on Federal lands (Indian country, U.S. military installations, and U.S. parks, prisons, and buildings), child pornography, activities under the Mann Act, and interstate and foreign commerce and mailing of obscene materials. CEOS attorneys also work with Federal law enforcement officers to identify major offenders of the applicable statutes and coordinate national investigative efforts. In addition to the case litigation by Section attorneys, CEOS provides training to assistant U.S. attorneys and Federal law enforcement agents as well as substantial assistance to U.S. attorneys' offices in the prosecution and appeals of such cases.

Since CEOS's formation in 1987, it has directed a substantial amount of its resources to the prosecution of child pornography. Working with the U.S. Postal Inspection Service and U.S. Customs Service, CEOS has coordinated and helped with several successful undercover efforts to identify and prosecute child pornography users. Programs have also targeted the illegal importation, distribution, sale, and possession of child pornography by computer.

CEOS participates in the development of legislative proposals and policy to address issues such as child pornography and child molestation through computers; child prostitution; technical corrections to existing Federal laws on child pornography and sexual abuse; and changes to sentencing guidelines for these crimes.

Further, CEOS is responsible for protection of the rights of children under the child victim-witness provisions of the Federal criminal code and under the Child Support Recovery Act. It has also been designated as the legal advisor to the Morgan P. Hardiman Missing and Exploited Children Task Force.

Fraud The Fraud Section, the largest component of the Criminal Division, directs and coordinates the Federal effort against fraud and white-collar crime, focusing primarily on complex frauds that involve: multidistrict and international activities; financial institutions; the insurance industry; Government programs and procurement procedures, including health care providers, defense procurement fraud, and Housing and Urban Development fraud; the securities and commodities exchanges; and multidistrict schemes that involve consumer victimization, such as telemarketing. The Section conducts investigations and prosecutes on its own about 100 fraud cases of national significance or great complexity annually. It also assists U.S. attorneys with cases, where requested. The Section maintains a regional Bank Fraud Task Force field office in Boston, MA. The Section also trains Federal agents and prosecutors through its conferences and participation in other Federal conferences.

Computer Crime and Intellectual Property The Computer Crime and Intellectual Property Section (CCIP) is responsible for implementing the Department's Computer Crime Initiative, a comprehensive program designed to address the growing global computer crime problem and ensure the appropriate protection of intellectual property rights (copyrights, trademarks, and trade secrets). Section attorneys are actively working with other Government agencies, the private sector (including hardware and software vendors and telecommunications companies), academic institutions, and foreign officials to develop a global response to cyber attacks and protect intellectual property. These attorneys litigate cases, provide litigation support to other prosecutors, train Federal law enforcement personnel, comment upon and propose legislation, and coordinate international efforts to combat computer crime and thefts of intellectual property. They also provide assistance in resolving the unique issues raised by emerging computer and telecommunications technologies.

Internal Security The Internal Security Section supervises the investigation and prosecution of cases affecting national security, foreign relations, and the export of military and strategic commodities and technology. The Section has exclusive responsibility for authorizing the prosecution of cases under criminal statutes relating to espionage, sabotage, neutrality, and atomic energy. It provides legal advice to U.S. attorneys' offices and investigative agencies on all matters within its area of responsibility, which includes 88 Federal statutes affecting national security. It also coordinates criminal cases involving the application of the Classified Information Procedures Act. The Section also administers and enforces the Foreign Agents Registration Act of 1938 and related disclosure statutes.

Narcotics and Dangerous Drugs The Narcotic and Dangerous Drug Section (NDDS) has supervisory jurisdiction of those statutes pertaining to controlled substances. Section attorneys participate in the development and implementation of domestic and international narcotics law enforcement programs and policies, and provide direct litigation support to the Organized Crime Drug Enforcement Task Force (OCDETF) and High Intensity Drug Trafficking Area (HIDTA) programs, to the Southwest Border and other multi-agency initiatives, and to U.S. attorneys in recusal matters or in cases where the Section's expertise is requested. NDDS attorneys represent the Department in developing and administering other cooperative drug enforcement strategies, initiatives, and projects conducted by the law enforcement and intelligence communities.

The Section Chief serves as the Department's designated representative on several senior level committees of the intelligence and law enforcement communities that plan and coordinate joint international counternarcotics initiatives. Additionally, the Chief acts as the designated representative of the Federal Government in the implementation of the joint U.S.-Colombia evidence sharing initiative, intended to facilitate the successful investigation and prosecution of major Colombian narcotics traffickers in Colombia.

The Section plays a central coordinating role in a number of multi-district, multi-agency initiatives and prosecutions, including the Southwest Border Initiative (SWBI), the Department's priority narcotics enforcement program targeting major Mexican trafficking organizations. The Litigation Unit provides direct trial and appellate litigation support to U.S. attorneys nationwide, with emphasis on prosecutions that support the OCDETF, HIDTA, and SWBI programs. These attorneys also litigate appeals arising from cases prosecuted by NDDS attorneys and denials or revocations of controlled substance registrations by the Drug Enforcement Administrator.

Enforcement Operations The Office of Enforcement Operations oversees the use of the most sophisticated investigative tools at the Department's disposal. It reviews all Federal electronic surveillance requests and requests to apply for court orders permitting the use of video surveillance; provides legal advice to Federal, State, and local law enforcement agencies on the use of Federal electronic surveillance statutes; and assists in developing Department policy on emerging technologies and telecommunications issues. It authorizes or denies the entry of all applicants into the Federal Witness Security Program (WSP), coordinates and administers matters relating to all aspects of the WSP among all program components, and approves or denies requests by Federal agencies to utilize Federal prisoners for investigative purposes. The Office approves or reviews matters such as witness immunity requests, transfer of prisoners to and from foreign countries to serve the remainder of their prison sentences, attorney and press subpoenas, applications for S-visa status, and disclosure of grand jury information. It provides legal advice and assistance in a wide variety of matters, such as crimes affecting government operations, mental competency and insanity, interstate property crimes, and crimes in Indian country. The Office processes all requests for Criminal Division records made pursuant to the Freedom of

Information Act and the Privacy Act, and assists U.S. attorneys' offices in advocating the Division's position in civil litigation filed under these statutes. It registers entities as required by the Gambling Devices Act of 1962.

International Affairs The Office of International Affairs supports the Department's legal divisions, the U.S. attorneys, and State and local prosecutors regarding questions of foreign and international law, including issues related to extradition and mutual legal assistance treaties. The Office also coordinates all international evidence gathering. In conjunction with the State Department, the Office engages in the negotiation of new extradition and mutual legal assistance treaties and executive agreements throughout the world. Office attorneys also participate on a number of committees established under the auspices of the United Nations and other international organizations that are directed at resolving a variety of international law enforcement problems, such as narcotics trafficking and money laundering. The Office maintains a permanent field office in Rome.

Policy and Legislation The legislative component of the Office of Policy and Legislation (OPL) develops legislative proposals, legal memoranda, and congressional testimony. It also prepares comments on pending legislation affecting the Federal criminal justice system, works closely with the U.S. Sentencing Commission on a variety of sentencing-related issues, and provides legal support to the Advisory Committee on Criminal Rules and Evidence of the Judicial Conference regarding the Federal rules of criminal procedure and the Federal rules of evidence.

The policy component of OPL analyzes policy and management issues related to criminal law enforcement and the criminal justice system. It identifies problems and emerging trends; develops options and recommendations; and provides research, technical, and management support to the Assistant Attorney General and other Division and Department policy makers. The policy staff also analyzes crime data, Federal caseload statistics, and other criminal justice system information for various decisionmakers within the Department.

Office of Overseas Prosecutorial Development, Assistance, and Training The mission of the Office of Overseas Prosecutorial Development, Assistance, and Training (OPDAT) is to assist prosecutors and judicial personnel in other countries to develop and sustain democratic criminal justice institutions. To further the Department's interest in fostering the fair and efficient administration of justice abroad, OPDAT promotes the rule of law and regard for human rights; assists nations, especially emerging democracies, to build and maintain viable criminal justice institutions; and focuses on transnational criminal matters. Currently, OPDAT provides long-term rule-of-law assistance, using resident legal advisers, in Colombia, Haiti, Latvia, Poland, and Russia. OPDAT also serves as the Justice Department's liaison between various private and public agencies that sponsor visits to the United States by foreign officials and other visitors who study aspects of the U.S. legal system. This opportunity for comparative law dialog with foreign experts aids the Department in its efforts to promote mutual legal assistance.

Organized Crime and Racketeering The Organized Crime and Racketeering Section coordinated the Department's program to combat organized crime. The principal enforcement efforts are currently directed against traditional groups, such as La Cosa Nostra families, and emerging groups from Asia and Europe, such as Chinese Triads, the Sicilian Mafia, and Russian organized crime. The Section supervises the investigation and prosecution of these cases by Strike Force Units within U.S. attorneys' offices in 21 Federal districts having a significant organized crime presence. These cases involve a broad spectrum of criminal statutes, including extortion, murder, bribery, fraud, narcotics, and labor racketeering.

The Section is involved in setting national priorities for the organized crime program by coordinating with investigative agencies such as the Federal Bureau of Investigation, the Drug Enforcement Administration, and others; and by working with the Attorney General's Organized Crime Council, which is ultimately responsible for the Federal Government's policy in this area.

In addition to its close supervision of all Federal organized crime cases, the Section maintains close control over all Government uses of the Racketeer Influenced and Corrupt Organizations (RICO) statute, and provides extensive advice to prosecutors about the use of this powerful tool for cases involving patterns of serious criminal conduct.

In a more specialized context, the Section provides support for criminal prosecutions involving labor-management disputes, the internal affairs of labor unions in the private sector, and the operation of employee pension and welfare benefit plans. The Section maintains a cadre of experienced prosecutors in its Litigation Unit who travel as needed to prosecute or assist in the prosecution of organized crime cases in the various U.S. attorneys' offices, particularly in multi-defendant RICO cases, especially in the field of labor racketeering.

Public Integrity   The Public Integrity Section oversees the Federal effort to combat corruption through the prosecution of elected and appointed public officials at all levels of Government. The Section has exclusive jurisdiction over allegations of criminal misconduct by Federal judges, and also monitors the investigation and prosecution of election and conflict of interest crimes. Section attorneys prosecute selected cases against Federal, State, and local officials, and are available as a source of advice and expertise to other prosecutors and to investigators. Since 1978, the Section has supervised the administration of the Independent Counsel provisions of the Ethics in Government Act.

Terrorism and Violent Crime   The Terrorism and Violent Crime Section is responsible for the design, implementation, and support of law enforcement efforts, legislative initiatives, policies, and strategies relating to international and domestic terrorism. This includes the investigation and prosecution of acts of terrorism occurring anywhere in the world which impact significant U.S. interests. The Section coordinates the systematic collection and analysis of data related to the investigation and prosecution of domestic terrorism cases, thereby facilitating prevention of terrorist activity through early detection. The Section coordinates interagency efforts to designate international terrorist organizations and their agents and to investigate and prosecute support of such organizations. The Section also oversees the prosecution of domestic violent crime offenses for which Federal jurisdiction exists, as well as the prosecution of firearms and explosives violations. In appropriate instances, Section attorneys assume direct responsibility for the prosecution of violent crime cases. The Section assists in the implementation of an initiative designed to deter criminals from possessing firearms by using Federal firearms laws which generally provide longer, and often mandatory, sentences for gun offenses. Additionally, the Section administers the national anti-violent-crime strategy, which focuses particular attention on the investigation and prosecution of gang-related crimes. Section attorneys provide legal advice to Federal prosecutors concerning Federal statutes relating to murder, assault, kidnapping, threats, robbery, weapons and explosives control, malicious destruction of property, and aircraft and sea piracy. The Section also formulates legislative initiatives and Department policies relating to terrorism and violent crime, and coordinates such initiatives and strategies with other Government agencies.

Executive Office for the Organized Crime Drug Enforcement Task Force
The Organized Crime Drug Enforcement Task Force (OCDETF) is a Federal drug enforcement program that focuses attention and resources on the disruption and dismantling of major drug trafficking organizations. The Task Force provides a framework for Federal, State, and local

law enforcement agencies to work together to target well-established and complex organizations that direct, finance, or engage in illegal narcotics trafficking and related crimes, including money laundering and tax violations, public corruption, illegal immigration, weapons violations, and violent crimes. The program has been in existence since 1982 and operates under the guidance and oversight of the Attorney General. Utilizing the resources and expertise of its 11 member Federal agencies, along with support from its State and local law enforcement partners, OCDETF has contributed to the successful prosecution and conviction of more than 44,000 members of criminal organizations and resulted in the seizure of cash and property assets totaling more than $3 billion.

The Executive Office for OCDETF supports the work of over 2,500 Federal agents and prosecutors and approximately 6,000 State and local law enforcement officers who participate in OCDETF cases. The Executive Office, in conjunction with a council of Washington agency representatives, provides policy guidance and coordination, administrative management and support, collection and reporting of statistical information, and budgetary planning, coordination, and disbursement.

International Criminal Investigative Training Assistance Program   Activities of the International Criminal Investigative Training Assistance Program (ICITAP) encompass two principal types of assistance projects: the development of police forces and the reform of existing police forces in the context of international peacekeeping operations, and the enhancement of capabilities of existing police forces in emerging democracies. Assistance is based on internationally recognized principles of human rights, the rule of law, and modern police practices.

ICITAP programs are instituted at the request of the National Security Council and the Department of State in agreement with governments which have requested assistance. The programs'

goals and objectives are determined by U.S. interests in promoting democracy and respect for human rights. Project activities are determined by administration priorities, an ever-changing world situation, and budgeting limitations. ICITAP is unique among Federal law enforcement assistance programs in that its budget is totally based on project-specific funding provided to the Justice Department by the State Department and the Agency for International Development.

For further information, contact the Office of the Assistant Attorney General, Criminal Division, Department of Justice, Tenth Street and Pennsylvania Avenue NW., Washington, DC 20530. Phone, 202–514–2601.

Environment and Natural Resources Division

The Environment and Natural Resources Division, formerly known as the Land and Natural Resources Division, is the Nation's environmental lawyer. It is responsible for litigating cases ranging from protection of endangered species, to global climate change, to cleaning up the Nation's hazardous waste sites. A key Division responsibility is enforcing civil and criminal environmental laws in order to protect its citizens' health and environment. The Division defends environmental challenges to Government activities and programs and ensures that environmental laws are implemented in a fair and consistent manner nationwide. It also represents the United States in all matters concerning the protection, use, and development of the Nation's natural resources and public lands, wildlife protection, Indian rights and claims, and the acquisition of Federal property. To carry out this broad mission, the Division is organized into nine sections described below.

Environmental Crimes   The Environmental Crimes Section prosecutes individuals and corporate entities which have violated laws designed to protect the environment. The Section works closely with the Federal Bureau of Investigation and criminal investigators from the Environmental Protection Agency (EPA) to enforce statutes such as the Clean Air Act, the Comprehensive

Environmental Response, Compensation, and Liability Act (Superfund), and the Resource Conservation and Recovery Act, among others.

Environmental Enforcement   The Environmental Enforcement Section is responsible for most of the affirmative civil litigation brought on behalf of EPA; claims for damages to our natural resources filed on behalf of the Departments of Interior, Commerce, and Agriculture; claims for contribution against private parties for contamination of public land; and recoupment of money spent to clean up certain oil spills on behalf of the United States Coast Guard. The Section supports the regulatory programs of its client agencies through litigation to obtain compliance with environmental statutes, establishes a credible deterrent against violation of those laws, recoups Federal funds spent to abate environmental contamination, and obtains funds to restore or replace natural resources damaged through oil spills or the release of hazardous substances into the environment. The primary statutes within the Section's scope of responsibility are: the Comprehensive Environmental Response, Compensation, and Liability Act (Superfund); the Clean Air Act; the Clean Water Act; the Resource Conservation and Recovery Act; the Safe Drinking Water Act; and the Oil Pollution Act of 1990.

Environmental Defense   The Environmental Defense Section represents the United States, principally EPA, in suits challenging the Government's administration of Federal environmental laws. The lawsuits, which arise in Federal district and appellate courts, include claims by industries that regulations are too strict, claims by environmental groups that Federal standards are too lax, and claims by States and citizens alleging that Federal agencies are out of compliance with environmental standards. The Section also handles both defensive and enforcement litigation involving the wetlands program under section 404 of the Clean Water Act. This requires persons wishing to fill or discharge waste into wetlands to first obtain a permit from the U.S. Army Corps of Engineers. If this requirement is not met, the Section files a civil action seeking civil penalties and injunctive relief against the violator.

Wildlife and Marine Resources   The Wildlife and Marine Resources Section tries both civil and criminal cases under Federal wildlife laws and other laws protecting marine fish and mammals. Prosecutions focus on smugglers and black-market dealers in protected wildlife. Civil litigation, particularly under the Endangered Species Act, often sets the needs of protected species against the economic interests of both the Federal Government and private enterprise.

General Litigation   The General Litigation Section is primarily responsible for litigation involving the use and protection of federally owned public lands and natural resources. Its varied docket comprises cases arising under more than 80 different land management and natural resource statutes including the National Environmental Policy Act, the Federal Land Policy Management Act, and the National Historic Preservation Act. Cases address such issues as water rights, land use plans, timber and mineral production, landowner compensation, and trust obligations to Indian tribes.

Indian Resources   The Indian Resources Section represents the United States in its trust capacity for Indian tribes. These suits include establishing water rights, establishing and protecting hunting and fishing rights, collecting damages for trespass on Indian lands, and establishing reservation boundaries and rights to land.

Land Acquisition   The Land Acquisition Section is responsible for acquiring land, either by direct purchase or through condemnation proceedings, for use by the Federal Government for purposes ranging from establishing public parks to creating missile sites. The Section attorneys seek to implement the protection of the fifth amendment in a way which is fair to both property owners and taxpayers. The legal and factual issues in such cases can include the power of the Federal Government to condemn property under specific acts of Congress; ascertainment of the fair market value of property sought by the Federal Government; applicability of local zoning regulations and problems related to subdivisions; capitalization of income; and the admissibility of evidence.

Policy, Legislation, and Special Litigation The Policy, Legislation, and Special Litigation Section advises and assists the Assistant Attorney General on policy issues including coordination of the Division's international and environmental justice activities. The Section directs the Division's legislative program, including testimony of Division managers before congressional committees, and representation of the Department in meetings with congressional staff and on interagency groups that develop the administration's position on legislation proposed or passed by Congress. The Section also litigates *amicus* cases, undertakes specially assigned litigation projects at the trial and appellate levels, serves as the Division's ethics office, and responds to citizen requests under the Freedom of Information Act.

Appeals The Appellate Section is responsible for handling all appeals in cases initially tried in lower courts by any of the sections within the Division. In addition, the Section drafts the briefs for all Division cases which reach the Supreme Court and formulates recommendations to the Solicitor General that seek authority to appeal unfavorable decisions.

Executive Office The Executive Office serves as administrator to the Division, providing financial management, personnel, planning, procurement, office automation, and automated litigation support services.

For further information, contact the Office of the Assistant Attorney General, Environment and Natural Resources Division, Department of Justice, Tenth Street and Pennsylvania Avenue NW., Washington, DC 20530. Phone, 202–514–2701.

Tax Division

The primary mission of the Tax Division is to enforce the Nation's tax laws in Federal and State courts and thereby generate revenue for the Federal Government. The Division conducts enforcement activities to deter specific taxpayers, as well as the taxpaying public at large, from conduct that deprives the Federal Government of its tax-related revenue.

The Tax Division was established under Executive Order 6166 of June 10, 1933, which called for the consolidated control of all tax litigation in the Department of Justice. In November 1933, the Attorney General issued Circular No. 2494 creating the Division and charging it with the duty of representing the Government in internal revenue cases.

The Division represents the United States and its officers in all civil and criminal litigation arising under the internal revenue laws, other than proceedings in the United States Tax Court. While the Division's primary client is the Internal Revenue Service, it also represents Federal officials and employees in actions arising out of the performance of their official duties, as well as representing other Federal departments and agencies in their dealings with State and local tax authorities. In civil tax litigation the Division's responsibility involves cases in the United States District Courts, the United States Court of Federal Claims, the United States Courts of Appeals, and the U. S. Supreme Court, as well as cases in the State courts.

The Division represents the United States in many different types of disputes, both civil and criminal, dealing with the interpretation of Federal tax laws. For example, when the Internal Revenue Service challenges a tax return and determines a deficiency, the taxpayer may pay the full amount of tax assessed and then bring a suit against the Government for refund. The Division defends the Government in these refund actions.

Other areas of civil litigation in which the Division is involved on behalf of the Federal Government include:

—suits brought by individuals to foreclose mortgages or to quiet title to property in which the United States is named as a party defendant because of the existence of a Federal tax lien on the property;

—suits brought by the United States to collect unpaid assessments, to foreclose Federal tax liens or determine the priority of such liens, to obtain judgments against delinquent taxpayers, to enforce summonses, and to establish tax claims in bankruptcy, receivership, or probate proceedings;

—proceedings involving mandamus, injunctions, and other specific writs arising in connection with internal revenue matters;

—suits against Internal Revenue Service employees for damages claimed because of alleged injuries caused in the performance of their official duties;

—suits against the Secretary of the Treasury, the Commissioner of Internal Revenue, or similar officials to test the validity of regulations or rulings not in the context of a specific refund action;

—suits brought by the United States to enjoin the promotion of abusive tax shelters and to enjoin activities relating to aiding and abetting the understatement of tax liabilities of others;

—suits brought by taxpayers for a judicial determination of the reasonableness of a jeopardy or termination assessment and the appropriateness of the amount;

—proceedings brought against the Tax Division and the Internal Revenue Service for disclosure of information under the Freedom of Information Act; and

—intergovernmental immunity suits in which the United States resists attempts to apply a State or local tax to some activity or property of the United States.

The Division also collects judgments in tax cases. To this end, the Division directs collection efforts and coordinates with, monitors the efforts of, and provides assistance to the various United States attorneys' offices in collecting outstanding judgments in tax cases.

With respect to criminal tax litigation, the Division prosecutes or supervises the prosecution of all criminal offenses committed under the internal revenue laws, including attempts to evade and defeat taxes, willful failures to file returns and to pay taxes, filing false returns and other deceptive documents, making false statements to revenue officials, and other miscellaneous offenses involving internal revenue matters. These duties include the institution of criminal proceedings and collaboration with U.S. attorneys in the conduct of litigation in the trial and appellate courts. Further, Division attorneys frequently conduct grand jury investigations and actual trials of criminal tax cases, often as a result of requests for assistance by the appropriate U.S. attorney. In its efforts to deter willful deception through prosecution of criminal offenders, the Division also plays a significant role in curbing organized crime, public corruption, narcotics trafficking, and financial institution fraud.

The primary functions of the Division are to aid the Internal Revenue Service in collecting the Federal revenue and to establish principles of law that will serve as guidelines to taxpayers and their representatives, as well as to the Internal Revenue Service, in the administration of the Internal Revenue Code. As a result, coordination with the Internal Revenue Service's administrative policies and the Treasury Department's legislative tax concerns in developing litigating postures is essential.

The Division also provides input into the preparation of reports to the Congress, the Office of Management and Budget, and the Office of Legislative Affairs on pending or proposed legislation and monitors congressional activities with respect to matters of interest to the Division.

In accordance with the Attorney General's program to enhance the litigating skills of Department attorneys, the Division conducts training programs for its attorneys, with special emphasis on matters unique to tax litigation and the development of advocacy skills.

For further information, contact the Office of the Assistant Attorney General, Tax Division, Department of Justice, Tenth Street and Pennsylvania Avenue NW., Washington, DC 20530. Phone, 202–514–2901. Internet, http://www.usdoj.gov/tax/.

Bureaus

Federal Bureau of Investigation

935 Pennsylvania Avenue NW., Washington, DC 20535. Phone, 202–324–3000

The Federal Bureau of Investigation (FBI) is the principal investigative arm of the United States Department of Justice. It is charged with gathering and reporting facts, locating witnesses, and compiling evidence in cases involving Federal jurisdiction.

The Federal Bureau of Investigation was established in 1908 by the Attorney General, who directed that Department of Justice investigations be handled by its own staff. The Bureau is charged with investigating all violations of Federal law except those that have been assigned by legislative enactment or otherwise to another Federal agency. Its jurisdiction includes a wide range of responsibilities in the criminal, civil, and security fields. Priority has been assigned to the five areas that affect society the most: organized crime/drugs, counterterrorism, white-collar crime, foreign counterintelligence, and violent crime.

On January 28, 1982, the Attorney General assigned concurrent jurisdiction for the enforcement of the Controlled Substances Act (21 U.S.C. 801) to the Bureau and the Drug Enforcement Administration (DEA). The DEA Administrator reports to the Attorney General through the FBI Director.

The Bureau also offers cooperative services such as fingerprint identification, laboratory examination, police training, and the National Crime Information Center to duly authorized law enforcement agencies.

The Bureau headquarters in Washington, DC, consists of nine separate divisions, a Deputy Director, an Office of the General Counsel, an Office of Public and Congressional Affairs, an Office of Equal Employment Opportunity Affairs, an Office of Professional Responsibility, and a Director's staff.

The Bureau's investigations are conducted through 56 field offices. Most of its investigative personnel are trained at the FBI Academy in Quantico, VA.

For further information, contact the Office of Public and Congressional Affairs, Federal Bureau of Investigation, J. Edgar Hoover F.B.I. Building, 935 Pennsylvania Avenue NW., Washington, DC 20535. Phone, 202–324–2727.

Bureau of Prisons

320 First Street NW., Washington, DC 20534. Phone, 202–307–3198

The mission of the Bureau of Prisons is to protect society by confining offenders in the controlled environments of prisons and community-based facilities that are safe, humane, and appropriately secure, and which provide work and other self-improvement opportunities to assist offenders in becoming law-abiding citizens.

The Executive Office of the Director provides overall direction for agency operations. In addition to typical administrative functions performed by an agency head, the Offices of General Counsel, Program Review, and Internal Affairs are within the Office and report to the Director.

The Administration Division develops plans, programs, and policies concerning the acquisition, construction, and staffing of new facilities, as well as budget development, financial management, procurement, and contracting.

The Community Corrections and Detention Division is responsible for program development and contracts relating to community-based and detention programs, as well as privatization and citizen participation.

The Correctional Programs Division is responsible for managing the correctional services (security) operations in Bureau institutions and case and unit management, as well as religious and psychological services, drug treatment programs, programs for special needs offenders, and inmate systems.

Federal Prison Industries (trade name UNICOR) is a wholly owned Government corporation whose mission is to provide employment and training opportunities for inmates confined in Federal correctional facilities. UNICOR manufactures a wide range of items—from executive and systems furniture to electronics, textiles, and graphics/signage. Services performed by UNICOR's inmates include data entry, printing, and furniture refinishing. The corporation funds selected preindustrial, vocational, and experimental training programs.

The Health Services Division has oversight responsibility for all medical and psychiatric programs; environmental and occupational health services; food and nutrition services; and farm operations.

The Human Resource Management Division provides personnel, training, and labor management within the agency. Its functions also include pay and position management and recruitment.

The Information, Policy, and Public Affairs Division encompasses the Bureau's Information Systems; Research and Evaluation; Security Technology; Office of Public Affairs; and Office of Policy and Information Resource Management.

The National Institute of Corrections provides technical assistance, information services, and training for State and local corrections agencies throughout the country. It also provides technical assistance for selected foreign governments. The Institute's administrative offices, Prison Division, and Community Corrections Division are located in Washington, DC. Its Jails Division, Training Academy, and Information Center are located in Longmont, CO.

The Bureau is subdivided into six geographic regions, each staffed with field-qualified personnel who are responsible for policy development and oversight, providing operational guidance to field locations, and providing support functions in areas such as auditing, technical assistance, budget, and personnel. Each regional office is headed by an experienced career Bureau manager who is a full member of the Bureau's executive staff.

For further information, contact the Public Information Officer, Bureau of Prisons, Department of Justice, Washington, DC 20534. Phone, 202–307–3198.

United States Marshals Service

600 Army Navy Drive, Arlington, VA 22202–4210. Phone, 202–307–9000

The United States Marshals Service is the Nation's oldest Federal law enforcement agency, having served as a vital link between the executive and judicial branches of the Government since 1789. Today, the Presidentially appointed marshals and their support staff of approximately 4,300 deputy marshals and administrative personnel operate from more than 400 office locations in all 94 Federal judicial districts nationwide, from Guam to Puerto Rico, and from Alaska to Florida.

The Marshals Service performs tasks that are essential to the operation of virtually every aspect of the Federal justice system. The Service is responsible for:

—providing support and protection for the Federal courts, including security for 800 judicial facilities and nearly 2,000 judges and magistrates, as well as countless other trial participants such as jurors and attorneys;

—apprehending the majority of all Federal fugitives;

—operating the Federal Witness Security program, ensuring the safety of endangered government witnesses;

—maintaining custody of and transporting thousands of Federal prisoners annually;

—executing court orders and arrest warrants;

—managing and selling seized property forfeited to the Government by drug traffickers and other criminals, and assisting the Justice Department's asset forfeiture program;

—responding to emergency circumstances, including civil disturbances, terrorist incidents, and other crisis situations, through its Special Operations Group, and restoring order in riot and mob-violence situations; and

—operating the U.S. Marshals Service Training Academy.

The Director of the U.S. Marshals Service, who is appointed by the President, supervises the operations of the Service throughout the United States and its territories, assisted by the Deputy Director, nine Assistant Directors, and a General Counsel.

For further information, contact the Office of Congressional and Public Affairs, U.S. Marshals Service, Department of Justice, Suite 1260, 600 Army Navy Drive, Arlington, VA 22202. Phone, 202–307–9065. Internet, http://www.usdoj.gov/ marshals/.

United States National Central Bureau–International Criminal Police Organization

Washington, DC 20530. Phone, 202–616– 9000

The U.S. National Central Bureau (USNCB) represents the United States in INTERPOL, the International Criminal Police Organization. Also known as INTERPOL—Washington, USNCB provides an essential communications link between the U.S. police community and their counterparts in the foreign member countries.

INTERPOL is an association of 177 countries dedicated to promoting mutual assistance among law enforcement authorities in the prevention and suppression of international crime. With no police force of its own, INTERPOL has no powers of arrest or search and seizure. Instead, INTERPOL serves as a channel of communication among the police of the member countries, and provides a forum for discussions, working group meetings, and symposia to enable police to focus on specific areas of criminal activity affecting their countries.

United States participation in INTERPOL began in 1938 by congressional authorization, designating the Attorney General as the official representative to the organization. INTERPOL operations were interrupted during World War II, but resumed in 1947.

The Attorney General officially designated the Secretary of the Treasury as the U.S. representative to INTERPOL in 1958, and the U.S. National Central Bureau was established within the Treasury Department in 1969. In 1977, an arrangement was effected between Justice and Treasury officials establishing dual authority in administering USNCB. This Memorandum of Understanding designates the Attorney General as the permanent representative to INTERPOL and the Secretary of the Treasury as the alternate representative.

The Bureau operates through cooperative efforts with Federal, State, and local law enforcement agencies. Programs and initiatives, such as the State Liaison Program and the Canadian Interface Project, broaden the scope of U.S. investigative resources to include the international community, thus forming an integral part of the United States efforts to confront the problem of international crime.

Federal and State law enforcement agencies represented at the USNCB include the Federal Bureau of Investigation; U.S. Marshals Service; Drug Enforcement Administration; Immigration and Naturalization Service; U.S. Customs Service; U.S. Secret Service; Internal Revenue Service; Bureau of Alcohol, Tobacco and Firearms; Office of the Comptroller of the Currency; Office of the Inspector General, Department of Agriculture; U.S. Postal Inspection Service; Bureau of Diplomatic Security, Department of State; Federal Law Enforcement Training Center; Financial Crimes Enforcement

Network; Environmental Protection Agency; and the Maryland State Police.

Under the State Liaison Program, States establish an office within their own law enforcement community to serve as liaison to USNCB. International leads developed in criminal investigations being conducted by a State or local police entity can be pursued through their Liaison Office, and criminal investigative requests from abroad are funneled through the relevant State liaison office for action by the appropriate State or local agency. All 50 States now participate in the liaison program, which is currently coordinated by a representative from the Maryland State Police.

USNCB has two sub-bureaus which serve to more effectively address the law enforcement needs of U.S. territories. The sub-bureaus are located in San Juan, Puerto Rico; and Pago Pago, American Samoa.

For further information, contact the U.S. National Central Bureau–INTERPOL, Washington, DC 20530. Phone, 202–616–9000.

Immigration and Naturalization Service

425 I Street NW., Washington, DC 20536. Phone, 202–514–4316, 4330, or 4354

[For the Immigration and Naturalization Service statement of organization, see the *Code of Federal Regulations,* Title 8, Aliens and Nationality]

The Immigration and Naturalization Service (INS) was created by act of March 3, 1891 (8 U.S.C. 1551 note), and its purpose and responsibilities were further specified by the Immigration and Nationality Act, as amended (8 U.S.C. 1101 note), which charges the Attorney General with the administration and enforcement of its provisions. The Attorney General has delegated authority to the Commissioner of the Immigration and Naturalization service to carry out these provisions of immigration law.

Overall policy and executive direction flow from the Washington, DC, headquarters office through 3 regional offices to 33 district offices and 21 border patrol sectors throughout the United States. INS also maintains three

district offices in Bangkok, Thailand; Mexico City, Mexico; and Rome, Italy.

The Service carries out its mission through operational programs in adjudications and nationality, inspections, investigations, and detention and deportation, as well as the U.S. Border Patrol. These programs are divided into the following mission responsibilities:

—facilitating entry of those legally admissible as visitors or immigrants to the United States;

—granting benefits under the Immigration and Nationality Act, as amended, including providing assistance to those seeking asylum, temporary or permanent resident status, or naturalization;

—preventing improper entry and the granting of benefits to those not legally entitled to them;

—apprehending and removing those aliens who enter or remain illegally in the United States and/or whose stay is not in the public interest; and

—Enforcing sanctions against those who act or conspire to subvert the requirements for selective and controlled entry, including sanctions against employers who knowingly hire aliens not authorized to work in the United States.

The Service also has a firm commitment to strengthen criminal investigations and seek the most effective deterrents to illegal immigration.

For further information, contact the Office of Information, Immigration and Naturalization Service, Department of Justice, 425 I Street NW., Washington, DC 20536. Phone, 202–514–4316, 4330, or 4354.

Drug Enforcement Administration

600–700 Army Navy Drive, Arlington, VA 22202. Phone, 202–307–1000; FTS, 367–1000

The Drug Enforcement Administration (DEA) is the lead Federal agency in enforcing narcotics and controlled substances laws and regulations. It was created in July 1973, by Reorganization Plan No. 2 of 1973 (5 U.S.C. app.), which merged four separate drug law enforcement agencies.

The Administration enforces the provisions of the controlled substances and chemical diversion and trafficking laws and regulations of the United States, and operates on a worldwide basis. It presents cases to the criminal and civil justice systems of the United States—or any other competent jurisdiction—on those significant organizations and their members involved in cultivation, production, smuggling, distribution, or diversion of controlled substances appearing in or destined for illegal traffic in the United States. DEA immobilizes these organizations by arresting their members, confiscating their drugs, and seizing their assets; and creates, manages, and supports enforcement-related programs—domestically and internationally—aimed at reducing the availability of and demand for controlled substances.

The Administration's responsibilities include:

—investigation of major narcotic violators who operate at interstate and international levels;

—seizure and forfeiture of assets derived from, traceable to, or intended to be used for illicit drug trafficking;

—enforcement of regulations governing the legal manufacture, distribution, and dispensing of controlled substances;

—management of a national narcotics intelligence system;

—coordination with Federal, State, and local law enforcement authorities and cooperation with counterpart agencies abroad; and

—training, scientific research, and information exchange in support of drug traffic prevention and control.

The Administration manages the El Paso Intelligence Center (EPIC), a 24-hour tactical drug intelligence center, which utilizes DEA and Federal personnel from 13 other agencies.

The Administration concentrates its efforts on high-level narcotics smuggling and distribution organizations in the United States and abroad, working closely with such agencies as the Customs Service, the Internal Revenue Service, and the Coast Guard. It also chairs the 11-agency National Narcotics Intelligence Consumers Committee, which develops an annual report on drug production, trafficking, and abuse trends.

Approximately 400 Administration compliance investigators enforce regulation of the legal manufacture and distribution of prescription drugs. The agency also maintains an active training program for narcotics officers in other Federal, State, and local agencies—as well as foreign police.

The Administration maintains liaison with the United Nations, INTERPOL, and other organizations on matters relating to international narcotics control programs. It has offices throughout the United States and in 50 foreign countries.

For further information, contact the Public Affairs Section, Drug Enforcement Administration, Department of Justice, Washington, DC 20537. Phone, 202–307–7977.

Office of Justice Programs

633 Indiana Avenue NW., Washington, DC 20531. Phone, 202–307–0781

The Office of Justice Programs (OJP) was established by the Justice Assistance Act of 1984 and reauthorized in 1994 to provide Federal leadership, coordination, and assistance needed to make the Nation's justice system more efficient and effective in preventing and controlling crime. OJP and its five program bureaus, the Bureau of Justice Assistance, Bureau of Justice Statistics, National Institute of Justice, Office of Juvenile Justice and Delinquency Prevention, and Office for Victims of Crime, are responsible for collecting statistical data and conducting analyses; identifying emerging criminal justice issues; developing and testing promising approaches to address these issues; evaluating program results, and disseminating these findings and other information to State and local governments.

The Office is headed by an Assistant Attorney General who, by statute and delegation of authority from the Attorney General, establishes, guides, promotes, and coordinates policy; focuses efforts on the priorities established by the President and the Attorney General; and promotes coordination among the bureaus and offices within OJP.

Through the programs developed and financed by its bureaus and offices, OJP works to form partnerships among Federal, State, and local government officials to control drug abuse and trafficking, rehabilitate crime-ridden neighborhoods, improve the administration of justice in America, meet the needs of crime victims, and find innovative ways to address problems such as gang violence, prison crowding, juvenile crime, and white-collar crime. The functions of each bureau or office are interrelated. For example, the statistics generated by the Bureau of Justice Statistics may drive the research that is conducted through the National Institute of Justice and the Office of Juvenile Justice and Delinquency Prevention. Research results may generate new programs that receive support from the Bureau of Justice Assistance and the Office of Juvenile Justice and Delinquency Prevention.

Although some research and technical assistance is provided directly by OJP's bureaus and offices, most of the work is accomplished through Federal financial assistance to scholars, practitioners, and State and local governments.

Program bureaus and offices award formula grants to State agencies, which, in turn, subgrant funds to units of State and local government. Formula grant programs—drug control and system improvement, juvenile justice, victims compensation, and victims assistance—are administered by State agencies designated by each State's Governor. Discretionary grant programs usually are announced in the *Federal Register,* and applications are made directly to the sponsoring Office of Justice Programs bureau or office.

Bureau of Justice Assistance (BJA)   The Bureau is the primary funding source for grants to State and local law enforcement agencies. In addition to funding crime prevention and control projects, BJA provides training, technical assistance, evaluation, and comprehensive strategic planning to criminal justice practitioners. The Bureau's mission is to provide leadership and assistance in support of local criminal justice strategies to achieve safe communities. Its goals are to promote effective, innovative crime control and prevention strategies; to demonstrate and promote replication of effective crime control programs which support public/private partnerships, planning, and criminal justice system improvement; and to leverage and efficiently administer available resources.

The Anti-Drug Abuse Act of 1988 (42 U.S.C. 3750) established the Edward Byrne Memorial State and Local Law Enforcement Assistance Program. Under this authorization, Congress appropriates funds to BJA for awards to the States to implement violent crime control and illegal drug reduction strategies. Other BJA discretionary awards are made for innovative programs such as Tribal Strategies Against Violence, Firearms Trafficking, and a Comprehensive Homicide Initiative. Earmarked funds are used for special programs such as National Crime Prevention Council Campaigns (McGruff, The Crime Dog) and Drug Abuse Resistance Education. The Bureau also administers line-item appropriations for national programs such as the Regional Information Sharing System Program and the Public Safety Officers' Benefits Program.

The Bureau expects, measures, and reports results in the following broad areas of award investment: comprehensive programs, crime prevention, law enforcement, adjudication, corrections/options, evaluation, systems improvement, and information dissemination.

Bureau of Justice Statistics (BJS)   The Bureau is responsible for collecting, analyzing, publishing, and disseminating statistical information on crime, criminal offenders, victims of crime, and the operation of justice systems at all levels of government and internationally. The Bureau provides data which is critical to Federal, State, and local policymakers in combating crime and ensuring that justice is both efficient and evenhanded. The Bureau also assists State governments in developing capabilities in criminal justice statistics and improving the quality of criminal justice records and information systems.

The National Crime Victimization Survey (NCVS) is the second largest ongoing household survey undertaken by the Federal Government, and is the only national forum for victims to systematically describe how crime affects them and the characteristics of those who committed the crime against them. During a collection year, a nationally representative sample of more than 100,000 persons residing in about 49,000 households is interviewed by representatives of the Bureau of the Census in order to obtain data on the impact, frequency, and consequences of criminal victimization in the United States.

Other statistical series cover populations under correctional supervision, Federal criminal offenders and case processing, criminal justice expenditures and employment, felony convictions, pretrial release practices, characteristics of correctional populations, prosecutorial practices and policies, profile of civil cases, and the administration of law enforcement agencies and correctional facilities.

The Bureau maintains more than two dozen major data collection series and publishes a wide variety of reports annually which receive nationwide distribution.

The Bureau supports a statistical component in the National Criminal Justice Reference Service. The Bureau of Justice Statistics Clearinghouse provides reference services for people requesting information, maintains a mailing list, and distributes Bureau publications.

The Bureau also manages the Drugs and Crime Clearinghouse, funded by the Office of National Drug Control Policy, which disseminates BJA, ONDCP, and other drug-related crime documents; serves as the sole repository with public access for the BJA State Drug Control Strategies and the individual U.S. attorneys' reports; produces national directories of State and local drug-related agencies, topical fact sheets, bibliographies, and other special reports; maintains a library and database; and

responds to telephone, mail, and electronic requests for information.

For further information, contact the Bureau of Justice Statistics. Phone, 800–732–3277 (toll-free). Internet, http://www.ojp.usdoj.gov/bjs/.

National Institute of Justice (NIJ) The Institute sponsors research and development programs designed to improve and strengthen the criminal justice system and reduce or prevent crime. It also conducts national demonstration projects that employ innovative or promising approaches for improving criminal justice, and develops new technologies to fight crime and improve criminal justice.

The Institute conducts evaluations to determine the effectiveness of criminal justice programs, particularly programs funded by the Bureau of Justice Assistance and Crime Act Program offices within the Office of Justice Programs and the Community Oriented Policing Services (COPS) Office, and identifies programs that promise to be successful if continued or replicated in other jurisdictions. For example, it has evaluated the effectiveness of innovative drug control programs, including community-oriented policing, community antidrug initiatives, Weed and Seed, multijurisdictional task forces, and drug testing programs.

The Institute's evaluations of new approaches for holding offenders accountable for their crimes has provided invaluable information regarding such programs as drug courts, bootcamps, youth challenge camps, intensive community supervision, specialized probation, and prison work-release programs.

In addition, NIJ works to fulfill the information needs of the criminal justice system by publishing and disseminating reports and other materials from its research, demonstration, evaluation, and other programs; provides training and technical assistance to justice officials on innovations developed through its programs; and serves as the national and international clearinghouse of justice information for Federal, State, and local governments.

For further information, contact the National Criminal Justice Reference Service. Phone, 1–800–851–3420.

Office of Juvenile Justice and Delinquency Prevention   The Office was created by the Juvenile Justice and Delinquency Prevention Act of 1974 (42 U.S.C. 5601) in response to national concern about juvenile crime. It is the primary Federal agency for addressing juvenile crime and delinquency and the problem of missing and exploited children. The Office is comprised of five divisions.

The State Relations and Assistance Division oversees the Formula Grants Program. States can receive formula grants and technical assistance to help implement delinquency prevention, control, and system improvement programs, including the core requirements of the Juvenile Justice and Delinquency Prevention Act. The Division also administers the Title V Prevention Incentive Grants Program and the State Challenge Grants Program. Beginning in 1998, the division will also administer the Juvenile Accountability Incentive Block Grant Program and the formula grant component of the Combating Underage Drinking Program.

The Special Emphasis Division provides funds directly to public and private nonprofit agencies and individuals to foster new approaches to delinquency prevention and control and the improvement of the juvenile justice system. The Division focuses on such areas as serious, violent, and chronic juvenile offenders; gangs; at-risk female juvenile offenders; and school dropouts.

The Research and Program Development Division sponsors research and studies about national trends in juvenile delinquency and drug use, serious juvenile crime, the causes of delinquency, prevention strategies, program evaluation, and improvement of the juvenile justice system. It is also responsible for program evaluation, statistics, and demonstration programs.

The Training and Technical Assistance Division funds training for juvenile justice practitioners, policymakers, and organizations and provides technical assistance in planning, funding, establishing, operating, and evaluating juvenile delinquency programs. In addition, the Division administers juvenile court and prosecutor training, court-appointed special advocates, and children's advocacy center programs under the Victims of Child Abuse Act of 1990 (42 U.S.C. 13001).

The Information Dissemination Unit conducts a wide variety of information dissemination activities for the Office in support of its statutory mandate to serve as a clearinghouse and information center for the preparation, publication, and dissemination of information on juvenile delinquency and missing children. The Unit also monitors the operations of the Juvenile Justice Clearinghouse, which collects, stores, and disseminates the Office's and other juvenile justice-related publications. The toll-free telephone number is 1–800–638–8736.

Programs   The Concentration of Federal Efforts Program and the Missing Children's Program are also under the Office's direction. The Concentration of Federal Efforts Program coordinates Federal programs dealing with juvenile delinquency and assists Federal agencies that have responsibility for delinquency prevention and treatment. It also promotes interagency cooperation in eliminating duplicate efforts and provides direction for the use of Federal resources in facilitating a comprehensive, unified Federal juvenile justice policy.

The Missing Children's Program was created in 1984 by the Missing Children's Assistance Act to provide Federal leadership in ensuring that every practical step is taken in recovering missing children, reuniting them with their families, and prosecuting abductors. The Program serves as a central focus for research, data collection, policy development, training professionals in the field, and providing information about missing and exploited children. It also funds the National Center for Missing and Exploited Children, which operates a national toll-free telephone line and serves as a national information clearinghouse.

Office for Victims of Crime (OVC)   The Office serves as the Justice Department's chief advocate for crime victims and their families. This includes carrying out the activities mandated by the Victims of Crime Act of 1984 (VOCA), as amended (42 U.S.C. 10601 note); monitoring compliance with the provisions regarding assistance for Federal crime victims of the Victim and Witness Protection Act of 1982; and implementing the recommendations of the President's Task Force on Victims of Crime, and the Attorney General's Task Force on Family Violence.

A Crime Victims Fund was created by VOCA in the U.S. Treasury to provide Federal financial assistance to State governments to compensate and assist victims of crime. Monies in the fund come from fines and penalties assessed on convicted Federal defendants. The Office awards grants to States to compensate crime victims for expenses, such as medical costs, resulting from their victimization. Grants also are awarded to State governments to support State and local programs that provide direct assistance to crime victims and their families. Priority for victim assistance funds is given to programs providing direct services to victims of sexual assault, spouse abuse, and child abuse. States also must use grant funds to assist previously underserved victim populations, such as victims of drunk drivers or the families of homicide victims.

A small portion of the Crime Victims Fund is available to support services for victims of Federal crimes. Programs under this initiative have focused on developing victim assistance services for Federal crime victims in Indian country, creating a Federal crime victim assistance fund for use by U.S. attorneys offices to pay for emergency services for Federal crime victims, and assisting Native American child abuse victims.

In addition, each year OVC sponsors National Crime Victims' Rights Week to increase public awareness of crime victims' special needs and to honor those who work on behalf of victims.

The OVC Resource Center, which provides information concerning victims issues to victims advocates, criminal justice practitioners, and the public, is funded by OVC. The Center may be reached toll-free on 1–800–627–6872.

Violence Against Women Grants Office   The Violence Against Women Grants Office administers the Department's formula and discretionary grant programs authorized by the Violence Against Women Act of 1994.

These programs assist the Nation's criminal justice system to respond to the needs and concerns of women who have been, or potentially could be, victimized by violence. The programs emphasize enhanced delivery of services to women victimized by violence, and work to strengthen outreach efforts to minorities and disabled women. The Office provides technical assistance to State and tribal government officials in planning innovative and effective criminal justice responses to violent crimes committed against women. The Office provides Indian tribal governments with funds to develop and strengthen the tribal justice system's response to violent crimes committed against Native American women through a discretionary grant program.

Drug Court Program Office   The Drug Court Program Office was established to support the development and implementation of effective Drug Court programming at the State, local, and tribal level. The Office administers the Drug Court Grant Program as authorized by Title V of the Violent Crime Control and Law Enforcement Act of 1994.

This discretionary grant program assists local units of government in the planning, implementation, and improvement of Drug Courts which target non-violent, drug-involved offenders. The Office strives to strengthen existing Drug Courts and develop new Drug Courts, encouraging them to provide continuing judicial supervision, mandatory periodic testing for substance abuse among clients, substance abuse treatment, offender supervision, management and aftercare, combined with appropriate sanctions for failure to comply with program requirements. The Office works closely with agencies and organizations involved in the areas of justice and recovery. The Office also develops and delivers appropriate technical assistance and training to enhance the effectiveness and operation of both existing and new Drug Courts.

Corrections Program Office   The Corrections Program Office provides leadership and assistance to State and local governments related to correctional policy and programs designed to reduce crime, increase public safety, and restore integrity to sentencing practices for violent offenders. The Office administers correctional programs authorized by the Violent Crime Control and Law Enforcement Act of 1994, as amended, including the Violent Offender Incarceration/Truth in Sentencing and Residential Substance Abuse Treatment for State Prisoners Programs.

The Violent Offender Incarceration/ Truth in Sentencing Program provides formula grant funds to the States to build and expand correctional facilities to increase secure space for the confinement of violent offenders and the implementation of truth in sentencing laws. The Residential Substance Abuse Treatment Program is designed to reduce drug and criminal activity among offenders released back into the community by producing formula grant funds to develop and expand substance abuse treatment programs for offenders while incarcerated in State and local correctional facilities.

The Corrections Program Office also provides technical assistance and training to State and local correctional policymakers and practitioners to encourage the adoption of sound correctional policies and "best practices."

Executive Office for Weed and Seed   The Executive Office for Weed and Seed administers the Department's premier community-based public safety program. Operation Weed and Seed is a comprehensive, community-based strategy to "weed out" violent crime, gang activity, drug trafficking, and drug use, and "seed in" neighborhood revitalization. Programs are implemented through the leadership of U.S. attorneys working closely with community officials and residents. By bringing together law enforcement, businesses, schools, and community residents, Weed and Seed neighborhoods have succeeded in achieving long-term, positive change. The Executive Office for Weed and Seed works closely with OJP's other bureaus and offices, which fund model programs in Weed and Seed sites from which other communities can learn promising approaches to solving problems affecting residents and their neighborhoods. The Weed and Seed Program is funded through a congressional earmark from Byrne Discretionary Grant Program.

For further information, contact the Office of Congressional and Public Affairs, Office of Justice Programs, Department of Justice, 810 Seventh Street NW., Washington, DC 20531. Phone, 202–307–0781.

Boards

Executive Office for Immigration Review

Falls Church, VA 22041. Phone, 703–305–0289. Internet, http://www.usdoj.gov/eoir/.

The Attorney General has delegated certain powers and authorities for the administration and interpretation of the Immigration and Nationality Act of 1952 (8 U.S.C. 1101) and other Federal immigration laws to the Executive Office for Immigration Review, which is completely independent of and separate from both the Immigration and Naturalization Service, the agency charged with the enforcement of the immigration laws, and the Office of Special Counsel for Immigration Related Unfair Employment Practices, the agency charged with the enforcement of the anti-discrimination provisions of the Immigration Reform and Control Act. The Executive Office for Immigration Review includes the Board of Immigration Appeals, the Office of the Chief Immigration Judge, and the Office of the Chief Administrative Hearing Officer. It is headed by a Director, who is responsible for the immediate supervision of these components and who reports to the Deputy Attorney General.

Board of Immigration Appeals The Board of Immigration Appeals is a quasi-judicial body composed of 15 members including the Chair and Vice Chair, and a Chief Attorney-Examiner who is also an alternate Board Member.

The Board hears oral arguments at its Falls Church, VA, location. A staff of attorney advisors assists the Board in the preparation of decisions.

The Board has been given nationwide jurisdiction to hear appeals of decisions made by immigration judges and by district and center directors of the Immigration and Naturalization Service. In addition, the Board is responsible for hearing appeals involving the suspension or barring from practice of attorneys and representative before the Service and the Board.

Decisions of the Board are binding on all Service officers and immigration judges unless modified or overruled by judicial review in the Federal courts. The majority of appeals reaching the Board involve orders of removal and application for relief from removal. Other cases before the Board include the removal of aliens applying for admission to the United States, petitions to classify the status of alien relatives for the issuance of preference immigrant visas, fines imposed upon carriers for the violation of the immigration laws, and motions for reopening and reconsideration of decisions previously rendered.

Following a review of the record and research into questions of law raised by the parties, an attorney-adviser drafts a proposed order for consideration of the Board members, frequently conferring with individual Board members concerning the proposed order. Attorney-advisers also assist in various administrative and support functions. In addition to developing expertise in the field of immigration law, they are often called upon to analyze questions of constitutional law, State, Federal, and foreign civil and criminal law.

Office of the Chief Immigration Judge The Office of the Chief Immigration Judge provides overall direction for the 209 immigration judges located in approximately 40 immigration courts throughout the Nation. Immigration judges are responsible for conducting formal administrative proceedings and act independently in their decisionmaking capacity. Their decisions are administratively final, unless appealed or certified to the Board. Through its Criminal Alien Institutional Hearing Program, the Office currently has programs in all 50 States, Puerto Rico, the District of Columbia, and selected municipalities and Bureau of Prison facilities to adjudicate the immigration status of alien inmates incarcerated by Federal, State, and municipal correction authorities as a result of convictions for criminal offense.

In removal proceedings, an immigration judge determines whether an individual from a foreign country should be admitted or allowed to stay in the United States or be removed. Judges are located throughout the United States, and each judge has jurisdiction to consider various forms of relief available under the law, including applications for asylum.

Office of the Chief Administrative Hearing Officer The Office is responsible for the general supervision of administrative law judges in the performance of their duties under 8 U.S.C. 1324a–1324c. Administrative law judge proceedings are mandated by the Immigration and Nationality Act and concern allegations of unlawful employment of aliens, unfair immigration-related employment practices, and immigrations document fraud.

For further information, contact the Office of Public Affairs, Executive Office for Immigration Review, Department of Justice, Falls Church, VA 22041. Phone, 703–305–0289. Internet, http://www.usdoj.gov/eoir/.

United States Parole Commission

5550 Friendship Boulevard, Chevy Chase, MD 20815. Phone, 301–492–5990

The Parole Commission presently consists of three members, appointed by the President with the advice and consent of the Senate. It has sole authority to grant, modify, or revoke paroles of eligible U.S. prisoners serving sentences of more than one year, including military prisoners and D.C. Code prisoners housed in Federal institutions. It is responsible for the supervision of parolees and prisoners released upon the expiration of their sentences with allowances for statutory good time, and the determination of supervisory conditions and terms. Probation officers supervise parolees and mandatory releases under the direction of the Commission.

Under the Labor Management Reporting and Disclosure Act of 1959 (29 U.S.C. 401), the Commission determines whether or not persons convicted of certain crimes may serve as officials in the field of organized labor or in labor-oriented management positions; likewise, under the Employment Retirement Income and Security Act of 1974 (29 U.S.C. 1111), the Commission determines whether or not such persons may provide services to or be employed by employment benefit plans. The Commission has also had jurisdiction since 1977 to set release dates for U.S. citizens who are returned to the United States, pursuant to treaty, to serve foreign criminal sentences. For offenders who committed their crimes after November 1, 1987, the Commission applies the guidelines of the U.S. Sentencing Commission.

The Sentencing Reform Act of 1984 (98 Stat. 2032) abolished parole eligibility for Federal offenders who commit offenses on or after November 1, 1987. It also provided for the abolition of the Commission on November 1, 1992. However, the Judicial Improvements Act of 1990 (104 Stat. 5089) and the Parole Commission Phaseout Act of 1996 (18 U.S.C. 4201 note) extended the Commission in 5-year increments, through November 1, 2002. In the National Capital Revitalization and Self-Government Improvement Act of 1997 (111 Stat. 712), Congress transferred the function of granting or denying parole for all District of Columbia Code offenders, wherever imprisoned, to the Parole Commission from the District of Columbia Board of Parole, effective August 5, 1998. This act also authorized the Commission to expand to five members. In subsequent years, pursuant to this same legislation, the Parole Commission will assume from the D.C. Board the functions of supervising and revoking the paroles granted to D.C. offenders. The Commission will also supervise D.C. Code offenders placed on supervised release and revoke supervised release terms for violation.

For further information, contact the Office of the Chairman, United States Parole Commission, Department of Justice, 5550 Friendship Boulevard, Chevy Chase, MD 20815. Phone, 301–492–5990. Internet, http://www.usdoj.gov/uspc/parole.htm/.

Office of Community Oriented Policing Services

The Office of Community Oriented Policing Services (COPS) was created with the passage of the Violent Crime Control and Law Enforcement Act of 1994 to achieve several goals: to advance the philosophy of community policing as a national law enforcement strategy; to deploy 100,000 new police officers in community policing roles; to reinforce partnerships that will sustain community policing; and to evaluate and demonstrate the effectiveness of community policing to improve the quality of life by reducing the levels of disorder, violence, and crime in our communities.

The primary activity of the COPS Office is the awarding of competitive, discretionary grants directly to law enforcement agencies across the United

States and its territories. Over the life of the COPS Office, approximately $8 billion in grant funding will be made available to achieve these goals.

The COPS Office is headed by a Director, appointed by the Attorney General, and is organized into several divisions. The Grants Administration Division is responsible for developing and designing new programs to provide resources for the hiring of new officers and to further the adoption and implementation of community policing, reviewing grant applications, maintaining liaison with the Office of Justice Programs for financial review of applications, monitoring grant awards, developing and maintaining databases to support policymaking, participating in the evaluation of the grant programs, and coordination of the Office's research agenda. Within the Grants Administration Division are the Police Hiring section and the Program Planning, Research and Evaluation section.

The Training and Technical Assistance Division is responsible for coordinating the provision of training and technical assistance to advance the adoption, implementation and sustaining of community policing in the thousands of communities served by the COPS Office.

The Legal Division is responsible for providing legal advice to the Director and other functional areas of the COPS Office, and for ensuring compliance with the legal requirements applicable to the activities of the COPS Office.

The Congressional Relations Division assists Members of Congress in serving their constituents, thereby facilitating greater dissemination of information about COPS programs and activities, and provides input in program design and development and policy formulation so that programs and policies reflect legislative intent and address congressional needs.

The Communications Division provides ongoing information about community policing and COPS programs through every available channel of communication, including timely and accurate responses to media inquiries, interviews, public events, publications and related materials produced by and for any telecommunication format.

The Intergovernmental and Public Liaison Division maintains channels for communication and feedback regarding COPS programs with representatives of interested local, State, and national organizations and with local elected officials.

Finally, the Administrative Division provides support services to the COPS Office, including resource management to recruit, train, and maintain a professional workforce; fiscal resource management to perform the accounting and budget formulation and execution functions necessary to administer the COPS appropriation; facilities management to acquire and maintain space, provide security, and procure supplies, equipment, telephones, and other services; and information resource management.

Office of Intergovernmental Affairs

The Office of Intergovernmental Affairs is responsible for advising the Attorney General and other leadership and senior Department officials on matters affecting the Department of Justice's relationship with State and local government and the advocacy groups which represent these entities. The Office consists of a Director, principal Deputy Director, three Deputy Directors, and two support staff. All professional staff are attorneys.

For further information, contact the Office of Intergovernmental Affairs, Department of Justice, Room 1521 Main, 950 Pennsylvania Avenue, Washington, DC 20530. Phone, 202–514–3465.

Foreign Claims Settlement Commission of the United States

The Foreign Claims Settlement Commission of the United States is a quasi-judicial, independent agency within the Department of Justice which adjudicates claims of U.S. nationals against foreign governments, either under specific jurisdiction conferred by Congress or pursuant to international claims settlement agreements. The decisions of the Commission are final and are not reviewable under any standard by any court or other authority.

Funds for payment of the Commission's awards are derived from congressional appropriations, international claims settlements, or the liquidation of foreign assets in the United States by the Departments of Justice and the Treasury.

The Commission is currently conducting an Albanian Claims Program, adjudicating claims and making awards compensating U.S. nationals for losses resulting from nationalization, expropriation, intervention and other property-taking by the former Communist regime in Albania which took power at the end of World War II.

The Commission is compiling a registry of the estimated $5 billion in outstanding claims against Iraq held by U.S. nationals, in preparation for future Commission adjudication of such claims. Claims to be registered include those that predate the invasion of Kuwait by Iraq in August 1990, and certain claims of military personnel or their survivors arising out of Desert Shield and Desert Storm or Iraq's attack on the U.S.S. *Stark* in 1987.

The Commission is also conducting a Holocaust Survivors Claims Program, to adjudicate the claims of U.S. nationals who were interned and persecuted by the German Nazi regime before and during World War II. The Commission's decisions will be used by the Department of State as the basis for negotiation of a final settlement of such claims with Germany.

In addition, the Commission will play a role in the implementation of the Cuban Liberty and Democratic Solidarity (LIBERTAD) Act of 1996. Under Title III of the act, Commission determinations on the ownership and value of expropriated property in Cuba which were rendered in its Cuban Claims Program (conducted from 1965–72) will serve as the basis for lawsuits that may be filed by U.S. nationals in the U.S.

district court against foreigners who have invested in or otherwise benefited from property formerly owned by the U.S. nationals. The act further designates the Commission as a "Special Master" available to the courts beginning in 1998 to determine the ownership and value of expropriated property that was not the subject of claims filed in the Commission's Cuban Claims Program.

The Commission also has authority under the War Claims Act of 1948, as amended, to receive, determine the validity and amount, and provide for the payment of claims by members of the U.S. armed services and civilians held as prisoners of war or interned by a hostile force in Southeast Asia during the Vietnam conflict, or by the survivors of such service members and civilians.

Finally, the Commission is responsible for maintaining records and responding to inquiries related to the various claims programs it has conducted against the Governments of Yugoslavia, Panama, Poland, Bulgaria, Hungary, Romania, Italy, the Soviet Union, Czechoslovakia, Cuba, the German Democratic Republic, the People's Republic of China, Vietnam, Ethiopia, Egypt, and Iran, as well as those authorized under the War Claims Act of 1948, and other statutes.

The Commission's organization and functions are defined in the International Claims Settlement Act of 1949, as amended (22 U.S.C. 1621 *et seq.*), the War Claims Act of 1948, as amended (50 U.S.C. app. 2001 *et seq.*), the Balanced Budget Downpayment Act, I (Public Law 104–99), and the Cuban Liberty and Democratic Solidarity (LIBERTAD) Act of 1996 (Public Law 104–114).

For further information, contact the Office of the Chair, Foreign Claims Settlement Commission of the United States, Department of Justice, Suite 6002, 600 E Street NW., Washington, DC 20579. Phone, 202–616–6975; or fax, 202–616–6993.

Sources of Information

Controlled Substances Act Registration Information about registration under the

Controlled Substances Act may be obtained from the Registration Section of the Drug Enforcement Administration, P.O. Box 28083, Central Station, Washington, DC 20038. Phone, 202–307–7255.

Disability-Related Matters Contact the Civil Rights Division's ADA Hotline. Phone, 800–514–0301. TDD, 800–514–0383. Internet, http://www.usdoj.gov/crt/ada/adahom1.htm/.

Drugs and Crime Clearinghouse Phone, 800–666–3332 (toll-free).

Electronic Access Information concerning Department of Justice programs and activities is available electronically through the Internet, at http://www.usdoj.gov/.

Employment The Department maintains an agencywide job line. Phone, 202–514–3397.

Attorneys' applications: Director, Office of Attorney Personnel Management, Department of Justice, Room 6150, Tenth Street and Constitution Avenue NW., Washington, DC 20530. Phone, 202–514–1432. Assistant U.S. attorney applicants should apply to individual U.S. attorneys.

United States Marshals Service: Field Staffing Branch, United States Marshals Service, Department of Justice, 600 Army Navy Drive, Arlington, VA 22202–4210.

Federal Bureau of Investigation: Director, Washington, DC 20535, or any of the field offices or resident agencies whose addresses are listed in the front of most local telephone directories.

Immigration and Naturalization Service: Central Office, 425 I Street NW., Washington, DC 20536 (phone, 202–514–2530); or any regional or district office.

Drug Enforcement Administration: regional offices, laboratories, or Washington Headquarters Office of Personnel.

Bureau of Prisons: Central Office, 320 First Street NW., Washington, DC 20534 (phone, 202–307–3082); or any regional or field office.

Office of Justice Programs, 633 Indiana Avenue NW., Washington, DC 20531. Phone, 202–307–0730.

United States Trustee Program, Room 770, 901 E Street NW., Washington, DC 20530. Phone, 202–616–1000.

Foreign Claims Settlement Commission: Attorneys: Office of the Chief Counsel, Suite 6002, 600 E Street NW., Washington, DC 20579 (phone, 202–616–6975); Other: Administrative Officer, same address and phone.

Housing Discrimination Matters Contact the Civil Rights Division's Housing and Civil Enforcement Section. Phone, 800–896–7743.

Immigration-Related Employment Matters The Civil Rights Division maintains a Worker Hotline. Phone, 800–255–7688. TDD, 800–237–2515. It also offers information for employers. Phone, 800–255–8155. TDD, 800–362–2735.

Publications and Films The *FBI Law Enforcement Bulletin* and *Uniform Crime Reports—Crime in the United States* are available from the Superintendent of Documents, Government Printing Office, Washington, DC 20402.

The Annual Report of the Attorney General of the United States is published each year by the Department of Justice, Washington, DC 20530.

Approximately nine textbooks on citizenship, consisting of teachers manuals and student textbooks at various reading levels, are distributed free to public schools for applicants for citizenship and are on sale to all others from the Superintendent of Documents, Government Printing Office, Washington, DC 20402. Public schools or organizations under the supervision of public schools which are entitled to free textbooks should make their requests to the appropriate Immigration and Naturalization Service Regional Office (See appropriate section of this manual for mailing addresses.). For general information, call 202–514–3946.

The Freedom of Information Act Guide and Privacy Act Overview and the *Freedom of Information Case List,* both published annually, are available from the Superintendent of Documents, Government Printing Office, Washington, DC 20530; and in electronic format through INTERNET–Library of Congress. ISBN 0–16–042921–8.

FOIA Update (Stock No. 727–002–00000–6), published quarterly, is available free of charge to FOIA offices and other interested offices Governmentwide. This publication is also available from the Superintendent of Documents, Government Printing Office, Washington, DC 20402; and in electronic format through INTERNET– Library of Congress.

Guidelines for Effective Human Relations Commissions, Annual Report of the Community Relations Service, Community Relations Service Brochure, CRS Hotline Brochure, Police Use of Deadly Force: A Conciliation Handbook for Citizens and Police, Principles of Good Policing: Avoiding Violence Between Police and Citizens, Resolving Racial Conflict: A Guide for Municipalities, and *Viewpoints and Guidelines on Court-Appointed Citizens Monitoring Commissions in School Desegregation* are available upon request from the Public Information Office, Community Relations Service, Department of Justice, Washington, DC 20530.

A limited number of drug educational films are available, free of charge, to civic, educational, private, and religious groups.

A limited selection of pamphlets and brochures is available. The most widely requested publication is *Drugs of Abuse,* an identification manual intended for professional use. Single copies are free.

Copies of the Foreign Claims Settlement Commission's semiannual (through December 1966) and annual (from January 1967) reports to the Congress concerning its activities are available at the Commission in limited quantities.

Reading Rooms Located in Washington, DC, at: U.S. Department of Justice, Room 6505, Tenth Street and Constitution Avenue NW., Washington, DC 20530 (phone, 202–514–3775). Bureau of Prisons, 320 First Street NW., 20534 (phone, 202–307–3029); Immigration and Naturalization Service, 425 I Street NW., 20536 (phone, 202–514–2837); Foreign Claims Settlement Commission, 600 E Street NW., 20579 (phone, 202–616–6975). Also at the U.S. Parole Commission, 5550 Friendship Boulevard, Chevy Chase, MD 20815

(phone, 301–492–5959); Board of Immigration Appeals, Suite 2400, 5107 Leesburg Pike, Falls Church, VA 22041 (phone, 703–305–0168); some of the Immigration and Naturalization Service district offices; and the National Institute of Justice, 9th Floor, 633 Indiana Avenue NW., Washington, DC 20531 (phone, 202–307–5883).

Redress for Wartime Relocation/ Internment Contact the Civil Rights Division's Office of Redress Administration. Helpline phone, 202–219–6900. TDD, 202–219–4710. Internet, http://www.usdoj.gov/.

Reference Service In 1972, the National Institute of Justice established the National Criminal Justice Reference Service (NCJRS). All five OJP bureaus now support NCJRS, a clearinghouse of information and publications concerning OJP programs and other information of interest to the criminal justice community. The Office's National Institute of Justice, which has supported the clearinghouse for almost 20 years, provides most of the funding for the National Criminal Justice Reference Service. Police, corrections agencies, courts, criminal justice planners, juvenile justice practitioners, community crime prevention groups, and others needing information for planning and problem solving in criminal justice can refer to this international information service specially designed to assist the justice community.

The National Criminal Justice Reference Service provides information from its computerized data base system free or at a minimal cost to users through a variety of products and services including the bimonthly *NIJ Catalog,* which contains abstracts of significant additions to the data base and pertinent information and a Calendar of Events announcing upcoming training courses and conferences; selected hardcopy documents upon request; three types of data base search packages; various microfiche products; and referrals to other information sources. Under contracts with OJP bureaus, the National Criminal Justice Reference Service also operates the Drugs and

Crime Data Center and Clearinghouse, the Bureau of Justice Assistance Clearinghouse, the Justice Statistics Clearinghouse, the Juvenile Justice Clearinghouse, the National Victims Resource Center, and the Construction Information Exchange. All the Service's clearinghouses may be contacted on 800–851–3420 (toll-free); or in the Washington, DC, metropolitan area on 301–251–5500.

The NCJRS Electronic Bulletin Board, with 3,000 registered users, makes NCJRS' services available online. The Bulletin Board may be accessed by modem on 301–738–8895.

Organizations and individuals may register to receive information from the National Criminal Justice Reference Service by writing NCJRS, Box 6000, 1600 Research Boulevard, Rockville, MD 20850.

Small Business Activities Contract information for small businesses can be obtained from the Office of Small and Disadvantaged Business Utilization, Department of Justice, Tenth Street and Pennsylvania Avenue NW., Washington, DC 20530. Phone, 202–616–0521.

For further information concerning the Department of Justice, contact the Office of Public Affairs, Department of Justice, Tenth Street and Constitution Avenue NW., Washington, DC 20530. Phone, 202–514–2007 (voice); 202–786–5731 (TDD). Internet, http://www.usdoj.gov/.

DEPARTMENT OF LABOR

200 Constitution Avenue NW., Washington, DC 20210
Phone, 202–219–5000. Internet, http://www.dol.gov/.

SECRETARY OF LABOR	ALEXIS M. HERMAN
Chief of Staff	LEE SATTERFIELD
Executive Assistant to the Secretary	LEAH DAUGHTRY
Counselor to the Secretary	(VACANCY)
Executive Secretary	MICHAEL GRANT
Deputy Secretary	KATHRYN O. HIGGINS
Associate Deputy Secretary	WILLIAM SAMUEL
Chief Economist	EDWARD B. MONTGOMERY
Director, Office of Small Business Programs	JUNE M. ROBINSON
Director, Administrative Review Board	DAVID A. O'BRIAN, *Acting*
Chief Administrative Law Judge	JOHN VITTONE, *Acting*
Chief Administrative Appeals Judge, Benefits Review Board	BETTY J. HALL
Chairman, Employees Compensation Appeals Board	MICHAEL J. WALSH
Chairman, Wage Appeals Board	DAVID A. O'BRIAN
Director, Women's Bureau	IDA CASTRO, *Acting*
Deputy Director	(VACANCY)
Inspector General	CHARLES C. MASTEN
Deputy Inspector General	PATRICIA DALTON
Assistant Inspector General for Audit	JOSEPH E. FISCH
Assistant Inspector General for Investigation	F.M. BROADWAY
Assistant Inspector General for Management and Counsel	SYLVIA HOROWITZ
Assistant Secretary for Public Affairs	SUSAN R. KING
Deputy Assistant Secretaries	PEGGY LEWIS, HOWARD WADDELL
Solicitor of Labor	(VACANCY)
Deputy Solicitor, National Operations	MARVIN KRISLOV
Deputy Solicitor, Regional Operations	RONALD G. WHITING
Deputy Solicitor, Planning and Coordination	JUDITH E. KRAMER
Director, Office of Management	WESLEY CURL, *Acting*
Associate Solicitor, Employment and Training Legal Services	CHARLES D. RAYMOND
Associate Solicitor, Fair Labor Standards	STEVEN MANDEL
Associate Solicitor, Legislation and Legal Counsel	ROBERT A. SHAPIRO
Associate Solicitor, Labor-Management Laws	JOHN F. DEPENBROCK
Associate Solicitor, Black Lung Benefits	DONALD S. SHIRE
Associate Solicitor, Employee Benefits	CAROL DEDEO
Associate Solicitor, Occupational Safety and Health	JOSEPH M. WOODWARD
Associate Solicitor, Civil Rights	JAMES D. HENRY
Associate Solicitor, Plan Benefits Security	MARC I. MACHIZ
Associate Solicitor, Mine Safety and Health	EDWARD P. CLAIR

Associate Solicitor, Special Appellate and Supreme Court Litigation	ALLEN H. FELDMAN
Assistant Secretary for Congressional and Intergovernmental Affairs	GERI D. PALAST
Deputy Assistant Secretaries	DARLA J. LETOURNEAU, (VACANCY)
Deputy Under Secretary for International Affairs	ANDREW J. SAMET
Associate Deputy Under Secretary for Policy	(VACANCY)
Director, Office of Management, Administration and Planning	RONALD VAN HELDEN, *Acting*
Assistant Secretary for Policy	RICHARD MCGAHEY
Deputy Assistant Secretaries	ROLAND G. DROITSCH, SETH HARRIS
Assistant Secretary for Administration and Management	PATRICIA W. LATTIMORE
Deputy Assistant Secretary	JAMES MCMULLEN
Chief Financial Officer	KEN BRESNAHAN, *Acting*
Director, Business Operations Center	FELIX CONTREAS
Director, Information Technology Center	SHIRLEY MALIA
Director, Civil Rights Center	ANNABELLE T. LOCKHART
Director, Human Resources Center	(VACANCY)
Director, Safety and Health	(VACANCY)
Assistant Secretary for Veterans' Employment and Training	ESPIRIDION A. BORREGO
Deputy Assistant Secretary	TOM KEEFE
Assistant Secretary for Employment and Training	RAYMOND J. UHALDE, *Acting*
Deputy Assistant Secretaries	JOHN ROBINSON, RAYMOND J. UHALDE
Administrator, Office of Financial and Administrative Management	BRYAN T. KEILTY
Administrator, Office of Job Training Programs	SHIRLEY M. SMITH
Administrator, Office of Policy and Research	GERRI FIALA
Administrator, Office of Regional Management	ROBERT KENYON, *Acting*
Administrator, Office of Work-Based Learning	BARBARA ANN FARMER
Director, Unemployment Insurance Service	GRACE KILBANE
Director, United States Employment Service	JOHN BEVERLY
Director, Intergovernmental Communications and Publications Information	STEPHANIE POWERS
Deputy Assistant Secretary for Workplace Programs	(VACANCY)
Deputy Assistant Secretary for Labor-Management Programs	CHARLES RICHARDS
Deputy Assistant Secretary for Labor-Management Standards	JOHN KOTCH, *Acting*
Director, Public Affairs Team	MEG INGOLD
Director, Administrative Management and Technology Team	JOAN RIND
Assistant Secretary, Pension and Welfare Benefits Administration	OLENA BERG
Deputy Assistant Secretaries	ALAN D. LEBOWITZ, MEREDITH MILLER

Director, Office of Enforcement	CHARLES LERNER
Director, Office of Regulations and Interpretations	ROBERT DOYLE
Chief Accountant	IAN DINGWALD
Director, Program Services	SHARON WATSON
Director, Exemption Determinations	IVAN STRASFELD
Director, Information Management	MERVYN SCHWEDT
Director, Program Planning and Evaluation	BRIAN MCDONNELL
Director, Office of Policy and Legislative Analysis	GERALD LINDREW
Director, Office of Research and Economic Analysis	RICHARD HINZ
Assistant Secretary, Employment Standards Administration	BERNARD E. ANDERSON
Deputy Assistant Secretary	GENE KARP
Director, Equal Employment Opportunity Unit	CARVIN COOK
Deputy Assistant Secretary, Wage and Hour Division	JOHN R. FRASER, *Acting*
Deputy Administrator	JOHN R. FRASER
Deputy Assistant Secretary for Federal Contract Compliance Programs	SHIRLEY J. WILCHER
Deputy Director	JOE N. KENNEDY
Director, Division of Policy, Planning and Program Development	JAMES MELVIN
Director, Division of Program Operation	ROBERT B. GREAUX
Deputy Assistant Secretary for Office of Workers' Compensation Programs	T. MICHAEL KERR
Deputy Director	SHELBY HALLMARK
Director, Office of Management, Administration and Planning	DONNA G. COPSON
Deputy Director	ELEANOR H. SMITH
Director, Office of Public Affairs	MATT LOSAK
Chief, Branch of Legislative and Regulatory Analysis	PATRICK J. MOWRY
Assistant Secretary for Occupational Safety and Health	CHARLES JEFFRESS
Deputy Assistant Secretaries	E.B. BLANTON, EMILY SHEKETOFF, GREGORY WATCHMAN
	ANN CYR, *Acting*
Director, Office of Information and Consumer Affairs	
Director, Office of Construction and Engineering	RUSSELL SWANSON
Director, Office of Statistics	STEPHEN NEWELL
Director, Policy	JOHN MORAN
Director, Administrative Programs	DAVID C. ZEIGLER
Director, Federal/State Operations	PAULA WHITE
Director, Technical Support	STEVEN F. WITT
Director, Compliance Programs	JOHN MILES
Director, Health Standards Programs	ADAM FINKEL
Director, Safety Standards Programs	THOMAS SEYMOUR
Commissioner of Labor Statistics	KATHARINE G. ABRAHAM
Deputy Commissioner	WILLIAM G. BARRON, JR.
Associate Commissioner for Technology and Survey Processing	CARL J. LOWE

Director for Survey Processing	JOHN D. SINKS
Director for Technology and Computing Services	ARNOLD BRESNICK
Associate Commissioner for Administration	DANIEL J. LACEY
Director, Quality and Information Management	(VACANCY)
Associate Commissioner for Employment and Unemployment Statistics	(VACANCY)
Deputy Associate Commissioner for Employment and Unemployment Statistics	(VACANCY)
Director, Office of Employment Research and Program Development	MARILYN E. MANSER
Assistant Commissioner for Federal/State Programs	GEORGE S. WERKING, JR.
Assistant Commissioner for Current Employment Analysis	PHILLIP L. RONES
Associate Commissioner for Prices and Living Conditions	KENNETH V. DALTON
Deputy Associate Commissioner for Prices and Living Conditions	(VACANCY)
Assistant Commissioner for Consumer Prices and Price Indexes	JOHN S. GREENLEES
Assistant Commissioner for Industrial Prices and Price Indexes	JOHN M. GALVIN
Assistant Commissioner for International Prices	KATRINA W. REUT
Associate Commissioner for Compensation and Working Conditions	KIMBERLY D. ZIESCHANG
Deputy Associate Commissioner for Compensation and Working Conditions	(VACANCY)
Assistant Commissioner for Safety, Health, and Working Conditions	(VACANCY)
Assistant Commissioner for Compensation Levels and Trends	KATHLEEN M. MACDONALD
Associate Commissioner for Productivity and Technology	EDWIN R. DEAN
Associate Commissioner for Employment Projections	NEALE H. ROSENTHAL, *Acting*
Associate Commissioner for Publications and Special Studies	DEBORAH P. KLEIN
Associate Commissioner for Field Operations	LOIS ORR
Associate Commissioner for Research and Evaluation	(VACANCY)
Assistant Commissioner for Survey Methods Research	CATHRYN S. DIPPO
Assistant Secretary for Mine Safety and Health	J. DAVITT MCATEER
Deputy Assistant Secretary for Policy	(VACANCY)
Deputy Assistant Secretary for Operations	EDWARD C. HUGLER
Administrator for Coal Mine Safety and Health	MARVIN W. NICHOLS, JR.
Administrator for Metal and Nonmetal Mine Safety and Health	VERNON R. GOMEZ
Director of Technical Support	KENNETH T. HOWARD

Director of Educational Policy and Development	FRANK SCHWAMBERGER, *Acting*
Director, Office of Standards, Regulations and Variances	PATRICIA W. SILVEY
Director, Office of Assessments	RICHARD G. HIGH, JR.
Director of Administration and Management	RICHARD L. BRECHBIEL
Director of Program Policy Evaluation	GEORGE M. FESAK, JR.
Director, Office of Information and Public Affairs	WAYNE E. VENEMAN
Chief, Office of Congressional and Legislative Affairs	(VACANCY)
Legislative Affairs Specialist	SYLVIA MILANESE

The purpose of the Department of Labor is to foster, promote, and develop the welfare of the wage earners of the United States, to improve their working conditions, and to advance their opportunities for profitable employment. In carrying out this mission, the Department administers a variety of Federal labor laws guaranteeing workers' rights to safe and healthful working conditions, a minimum hourly wage and overtime pay, freedom from employment discrimination, unemployment insurance, and workers' compensation. The Department also protects workers' pension rights; provides for job training programs; helps workers find jobs; works to strengthen free collective bargaining; and keeps track of changes in employment, prices, and other national economic measurements. As the Department seeks to assist all Americans who need and want to work, special efforts are made to meet the unique job market problems of older workers, youths, minority group members, women, the handicapped, and other groups.

The Department of Labor (DOL), the ninth executive department, was created by act of March 4, 1913 (29 U.S.C. 551). A Bureau of Labor was first created by Congress in 1884 under the Interior Department. The Bureau of Labor later became independent as a Department of Labor without executive rank. It again returned to bureau status in the Department of Commerce and Labor, which was created by act of February 14, 1903 (15 U.S.C. 1501).

Office of the Secretary of Labor

Secretary   The Secretary is the head of the Department of Labor and the principal adviser to the President on the development and execution of policies and the administration and enforcement of laws relating to wage earners, their working conditions, and their employment opportunities. The Office of the Secretary includes the Offices of Deputy Secretary, Inspector General, the Assistant Secretaries, and the Solicitor of Labor. Other offices whose public

purposes are widely applied are detailed below and on the following pages.

Office of the Deputy Secretary of Labor

Deputy Secretary   The Deputy Secretary of Labor is the principal adviser to the Secretary and serves as Acting Secretary in the Secretary's absence.

Employees' Compensation Appeals Board   The Employees' Compensation Appeals Board consists of three members and three alternate members appointed by the Secretary of Labor, one of whom is designated as Chairman. The function of the Board is to consider and decide appeals from final decisions in cases arising under the Federal Employees' Compensation Act (5 U.S.C. 8101). The decisions of the Board are final and not subject to court review.

For further information, call 202–208–1900.

Administrative Review Board   The Administrative Review Board issues final agency decisions on cases arising in

DEPARTMENT OF LABOR

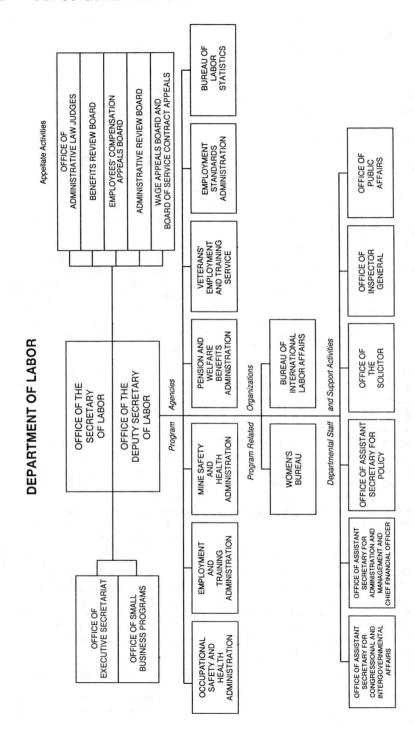

Appellate Activities

OFFICE OF ADMINISTRATIVE LAW JUDGES

BENEFITS REVIEW BOARD

EMPLOYEES' COMPENSATION APPEALS BOARD

ADMINISTRATIVE REVIEW BOARD

WAGE APPEALS BOARD AND BOARD OF SERVICE CONTRACT APPEALS

BUREAU OF LABOR STATISTICS

EMPLOYMENT STANDARDS ADMINISTRATION

VETERANS' EMPLOYMENT AND TRAINING SERVICE

OFFICE OF THE SECRETARY OF LABOR

OFFICE OF THE DEPUTY SECRETARY OF LABOR

OFFICE OF EXECUTIVE SECRETARIAT

OFFICE OF SMALL BUSINESS PROGRAMS

Program   Agencies

PENSION AND WELFARE BENEFITS ADMINISTRATION

MINE SAFETY AND HEALTH ADMINISTRATION

EMPLOYMENT AND TRAINING ADMINISTRATION

OCCUPATIONAL SAFETY AND HEALTH ADMINISTRATION

Program Related   Organizations

BUREAU OF INTERNATIONAL LABOR AFFAIRS

WOMEN'S BUREAU

Departmental Staff   and Support Activities

OFFICE OF THE SOLICITOR

OFFICE OF ASSISTANT SECRETARY FOR POLICY

OFFICE OF ASSISTANT SECRETARY FOR ADMINISTRATION AND MANAGEMENT AND CHIEF FINANCIAL OFFICER

OFFICE OF ASSISTANT SECRETARY FOR CONGRESSIONAL AND INTERGOVERNMENTAL AFFAIRS

OFFICE OF INSPECTOR GENERAL

OFFICE OF PUBLIC AFFAIRS

review or appeal of decisions or recommended decisions of the Administrator for the Wage and Hour Division, the Employment Standards Administration, or the Office of Administrative Law Judges under a broad range of Federal labor laws.

For further information, contact the Executive Director, Administrative Review Board. Phone, 202–219–4728. Fax, 202–219–9315.

Women's Bureau The Women's Bureau is responsible for formulating standards and policies that promote the welfare of wage earning women, improve their working conditions, increase their efficiency, and advance their opportunities for profitable employment.

For further information, call 202–219–6611.

Regional Offices—Women's Bureau

Address (Areas Served)	Administrator
Atlanta, GA (Suite 7T95, 61 Forsyth St. SW., 30303) (AL, FL, GA, KY, MS, NC, SC, TN) ...	Delores L. Crockett
Boston, MA (Rm. E–270, JFK Federal Bldg., 02203) (CT, MA, ME, NH, RI, VT)	Jacqueline Cooke
Chicago, IL (230 S. Dearborn St., 60604) (IL, IN, MI, OH, WI)	Nancy Chen
Dallas, TX (525 Griffin St., 75202) (AR, LA, NM, OK, TX)	Delores L. Crockett, *Acting*
Denver, CO (Suite 905, 1801 California St., 80202–2614) (CO, MT, ND, SD, UT, WY)	Oleta Crain
Kansas City, MO (Suite 1230, 1100 Main St., 64105) (IA, KS, MO, NE)	Rose A. Kemp
New York, NY (201 Varick St., 10014) (NJ, NY, PR, VI)	Mary Murphree
Philadelphia, PA (3535 Market St., 19104) (DC, DE, MD, PA, VA, WV)	Cornelia Moore
San Francisco, CA (71 Stevenson St., 94105) (AZ, CA, GU, HI, NV)	Barbara Sanford, *Acting*
Seattle, WA (1111 3d Ave., 98101) (AK, ID, OR, WA)	Karen Furia

Office of Small Business Programs This office, reporting to the Deputy Secretary of Labor, administers the Department's responsibility to ensure procurement opportunities for small, small disadvantaged, and women-owned small businesses; serves as the Department's central referral point for small-business regulatory compliance information and questions; manages the Department's minority colleges and universities program; and provides management oversight and guidance for the Department's advisory committees and other similar committees and agreements to assure compliance with applicable statutes and related requirements.

For further information, call 202–219–9148. Fax, 202–219–9167.

Office of Administrative Law Judges Administrative law judges preside over formal hearings to determine violations of minimum wage requirements, overtime payments, compensation benefits, employee discrimination, grant performance, alien certification, employee protection, and health and safety regulations set forth under numerous statutes, Executive orders, and regulations. With few exceptions, hearings are required to be conducted in accordance with the Administrative Procedure Act (5 U.S.C. note prec. 551).

For further information, contact the Office of the Chief Administrative Law Judge. Phone, 202–565–5330.

Benefits Review The Benefits Review Board is a five-member quasi-judicial body with exclusive jurisdiction to consider and decide appeals raising substantial questions of law or fact from decisions of Administrative Law Judges with respect to cases arising under the Longshoremen's and Harbor Workers' Compensation Act (33 U.S.C. 901) and its extensions and the Black Lung Benefits Act of 1972 (30 U.S.C. 801). The Board exercises the same review authority that the United States District Courts formerly held in these areas of the law prior to the 1972 amendments to both acts.

For further information, contact the Administrative Officer. Phone, 202–565–7500.

The Solicitor of Labor

The Office of the Solicitor (SOL) provides the Secretary of Labor and departmental officials with the legal services required to accomplish the mission of the Department of Labor and the priority goals established by the

Secretary. Through attorney staff in Washington and 15 field offices, the Solicitor directs a broad-scale litigation effort in the Federal courts pertaining to the statutes administered by the Department, including institution and prosecution of Civil Court actions under the Fair Labor Standards Act, the Employment Retirement Income Security Act of 1971, and the Migrant Seasonal Agricultural Worker Protection Act. The attorney staff also represents the Department in hearings under various laws including the Occupational Safety and Health Act of 1970, the Black Lung Benefits Reform Act, Federal Mine Safety and Health Act of 1977, and various Government contract labor standards laws. Appellate litigation is conducted by attorneys in the national headquarters, and trial litigation is carried out by attorneys under the direction of regional solicitors.

The Solicitor of Labor also coordinates the Department's legislative program; prepares testimony and reports on proposed legislation; provides legal advice to interagency groups responsible for U.S. trade matters; participates in international organizations including the International Labor Organization; and reviews rules, orders, and regulations.

For further information, contact the Office of Administration, Management and Litigation Support, Office of the Solicitor, Department of Labor, 200 Constitution Avenue NW., Washington, DC 20210. Phone, 202–219–6863.

Regional Offices—Office of the Solicitor
(RS: Regional Solicitor; ARS: Associate Regional Solicitor)

Region	Address	Solicitor
Atlanta, GA (AL, FL, GA, KY, MS, NC, SC, TN).	Rm. 7T10, 61 Forsyth St. SW., 30303	Jaylynn K. Fortney (RS)
Branch Offices	Suite 150, 100 Centerview Dr., Birmingham, AL 35216	Cynthia W. Brown (ARS)
....	2002 Richard Jones Rd., Nashville, TN 37215	Theresa Ball (ARS)
Boston, MA (CT, ME, MA, NH, RI, VT) ...	One Congress St., 02114	Frank V. McDermott (RS)
Chicago, IL (IL, IN, MI, MN, OH, WI)	230 S. Dearborn St., 60604	Richard J. Fiore (RS)
Branch Office	1240 E. 9th St., Cleveland, OH 44199	Benjamin Chinni (ARS)
Dallas, TX (AR, LA, NM, OK, TX)	525 S. Griffin St., 75202	James E. White (RS)
Kansas City, MO (CO, IA, KS, MO, MT, NE, ND, SD, UT, WY).	Suite 1210, 1100 Main St., 64105	Michael A. Stable, *Acting* (RS)
Branch Office	Suite 1600, 1999 Broadway, Denver, CO 80202-5716	Ann M. Noble (ARS)
New York, NY (NJ, NY, PR, VI)	201 Varick St., 10014	Patricia M. Rodenhausen (RS)
Philadelphia, PA (DE, DC, MD, PA, VA, WV).	Rm. 14480, 3535 Market St., 19104	Deborah Pierce (RS)
Branch Office	Rm. 516, 4015 Wilson Blvd., Arlington, VA 22203	Douglas N. White (ARS)
San Francisco, CA (AK, AZ, CA, HI, ID, NV, OR, WA).	Suite 1110, 71 Stevenson St., 94105	Daniel W. Teehan (RS)
Branch Offices	300 N. Los Angeles St., Los Angeles, CA 90012	John C. Nangle (ARS)
....	1111 3d Ave., Seattle, WA 98101	Rochelle Kleinberg (ARS)

International Affairs

The Bureau of International Labor Affairs (ILAB) carries out the Department's international responsibilities under the direction of the Deputy Under Secretary for International Affairs; assists in formulating international economic, social, trade, and immigration policies affecting American workers, with a view to maximizing higher wage and higher value U.S. jobs derived from global economic integration; gathers and disseminates information on child labor practices worldwide; promotes respect for international labor standards to protect the economic and physical well-being of workers in the United States and around the world; gathers and disseminates information on foreign labor markets and programs so that U.S. employment policy formulation might benefit from international experiences; disseminates information on the implementation of the North American Agreement on Labor Cooperation, the labor side agreement to the North American Free Trade Agreement; carries out overseas technical assistance projects; assists in the administration of U.S. labor attache programs at embassies abroad; participates in the development of the Department's immigration policy; and conducts research on the labor market consequences of immigration proposals and legislation.

The Bureau represents the United States on delegations to multilateral and bilateral trade negotiations and on such international bodies as the General Agreement on Tariffs and Trade, the International Labor Organization, the Organization for Economic Cooperation and Development, and other United Nations organizations. In addition, it provides counsel and support for the President's Committee on the International Labor Organization, a Federal advisory committee established to promote continued reform and progress in that organization.

Employment and Training Administration

The Employment and Training Administration, through a variety of programs, fulfills responsibilities assigned to the Secretary of Labor that relate to employment services, job training, and unemployment insurance. Component offices and services of the Administration administer a Federal-State employment security system; fund and oversee programs to provide work experience and training for groups having difficulty entering or returning to the work force; formulate and promote apprenticeship standards and programs; and conduct continuing programs of research, development, and evaluation.

The Assistant Secretary for Employment and Training directs the administration of agency programs and is responsible for ensuring that programs funded through the agency are free from unlawful discrimination, fraud, and abuse, and that they comply with constitutional, statutory, and regulatory provisions. It is the policy of the Administration to promote equal opportunity, affirmative action, and integrity in programs to which the Administration extends financial assistance.

The Administration has five major components that cover employment security, job training, planning and policy development, financial and administrative management, and regional management.

Federal Unemployment Insurance Service The Federal-State Unemployment Compensation Program, under provisions of the Social Security Act of 1935 (42 U.S.C. 1305), is the basic program of income support for the Nation's unemployed workers. With limited Federal intervention, unemployment insurance benefits are payable under laws of individual States. The Federal Unemployment Insurance Service provides leadership and policy guidance to State employment security agencies for the development, improvement, and operation of the Federal-State unemployment insurance system and of related wage-loss, worker dislocation, and adjustment assistance compensation programs, including to ex-service personnel and Federal civilian workers, and supplemental or extended benefits programs.

The Service reviews State unemployment insurance laws and their administration by the States to determine whether they are in conformity with Federal requirements; supervises the development of programs and methods for benefit, adjudication, appeals, tax collection, and trust fund management activities implemented by the State agencies; oversees the actuarial soundness of the level and relationship of State expenditures, revenues, and reserves, and of Federal appropriations for payment of benefits; and is implementing a comprehensive system to help ensure continuous improvement in the performance of unemployment insurance operations.

The Service also provides national leadership and direction in implementing its responsibilities under trade adjustment assistance, airline deregulation, and disaster unemployment assistance legislation.

For further information, call 202–219–7831.

United States Employment Service   The Service, under the provisions of the Wagner-Peyser Act (29 U.S.C. 49 *et seq.*), provides assistance to States in establishing and maintaining a system of local public employment offices in the States and territories and interstate clearance of Labor. The State public employment service is responsible for providing unemployed individuals and other jobseekers with job placement, and other employment services and for providing employers with recruitment services and referrals of job-seeking applicants.

The Service, through the State public employment service system, also provides subsidiary services which include:

—certifying aliens who seek to enter the United States for permanent employment as immigrants or as temporary workers;

—providing specialized recruitment assistance to employers;

—determining classifications of labor surplus area annually and for exceptional circumstance petitions;

—providing labor surplus area information to the general public and to other Federal or State agencies to meet various program responsibilities;

—disseminating labor market information;

—providing individuals with guidance, counseling, testing referral, and job opportunities;

—reviewing rural industrialization loan and grant certification applications under the Rural Development Act of 1972 (7 U.S.C. 1921);

—distributing airline job opening information for rehiring under the Airline Deregulation Act (49 U.S.C. app. 1301);

—providing supportive services to employers and applicants through the Federal bonding program; and

—providing reemployment services to dislocated workers.

For further information, call 202–219–5257.

Office of Work-Based Learning   The Office administers activities under several Federal laws regarding worker training and retraining. These include the dislocated worker program under the Economic Dislocation and Worker Adjustment Assistance Act (EDWAA) (Title III of the Job Training Partnership Act (JTPA); Federal activities under the Worker Adjustment and Retraining Notification Act (WARN); and the Trade Adjustment Assistance Program under the Trade Act. In addition, the Office carries out research and demonstration programs.

For further information, call 202–219–6236.

Office of Worker Retraining and Adjustment Programs   The Office performs dislocated worker programs functions under the Economic Dislocation and Worker Adjustment Assistance Act (Title III of JTPA), and Federal activities under the Worker Adjustment and Retraining Notification Act.

For further information, call 202–219–5339.

Office of Trade Adjustment Assistance   The Office administers the Trade Adjustment Assistance (TAA) program provisions of the Trade Act of 1974, as amended (19 U.S.C. 2101 *et seq.*), through agreements with the States. The program provides reemployment services such as training, job search and relocation allowances, and weekly cash payments to U.S. workers who are separated from employment because of foreign imports.

The Office receives petitions for adjustment assistance from either adversely affected workers, a duly recognized union, or an authorized representative of the workers and conducts factfinding investigations to develop necessary data on which certification determinations can be based. Determinations may involve approval, denial, or termination of worker groups' eligibility for trade adjustment assistance benefits.

The Office administers the North American Free Trade Agreement— Transitional Adjustment Assistance

(NAFTA–TAA) program to help workers who become dislocated as a result of increased trade with Mexico or Canada after January 1, 1994, when NAFTA went into effect. The program emphasizes a comprehensive, timely array of retraining and reemployment services, including both rapid response and basic readjustment services. Similar to TAA, the NAFTA–TAA program provides training, job search and relocation allowances, and income support while in training.

The Office develops policies and prepares program directives to regional offices and State agencies on the administration and funding of reemployment services, and develops and maintains a system for allocating funds to those offices and agencies for reemployment services. It also directs and conducts industry studies of the number of workers in a domestic industry likely to be certified as eligible for adjustment assistance and of the extent to which existing training and employment programs may facilitate the workers' adjustment to import competition when an industry petitions the Federal Government that it is being injured because of import competition.

For further information, call 202–219–5555.

Office of One-Stop/Labor Market Information (LMI)   The Department's multi-year investments in the One-Stop Career Centers System, including America's Labor Market Information System, are designed to transform a fragmented array of employment and training programs into an integrated service delivery system. One-Stop Career Centers offer a number of service or business lines to adult customers of the employment and training system, including labor exchange services, income maintenance, job search assistance, individual intensive services, training, and labor market information.

Fifty-four States and jurisdictions have received one-stop planning or implementation grants. With these funds, the States and their local partners make strategic investments in infrastructure (including technology, movement to client-server systems, addition of Internet connections, cross-training of staff, creation of public access resource rooms and other media-assisted self-service mechanisms) while integrating employment and training programs into an effective and flexible system for the provision of customer services.

One-stop also supports the development of products, services, and hardware, software, and communications infrastructure associated with an improved labor market information program. Resources are devoted to the development and delivery of a set of core products and services in each State; ongoing research and development to improve the quality of labor market information available to job seekers and employers, including consumer reports; and maintenance and expansion of a nationwide electronic exchange system which includes job openings and resumes.

For further information, call 202–219–6540.

Bureau of Apprenticeship and Training
The National Apprenticeship Act (29 U.S.C. 50) was passed in 1937 to enable the Department of Labor to formulate and promote the furtherance of labor standards necessary to safeguard the welfare of apprentices and cooperate with the States in the promotion of such standards, and to bring together employers and labor for the formulation of programs of apprenticeship.

Sponsors and potential sponsors are encouraged and assisted in the development, expansion, and improvement of apprenticeship and other forms of allied industrial training. Technical information on training methods, public training facilities, and successfully executed systems are made available to industry. Through field representatives in States, the Bureau works closely with employers, labor unions, vocational schools, community planning groups, and others concerned with apprenticeship.

Programs must meet standards established by the Bureau or a recognized State Apprenticeship Council to be registered. Field compliance reviews are conducted to determine conformity with Federal equal employment opportunity and other standards for apprenticeship and training.

For further information, call 202–219–5921.

Job Training Partnership Act

The Office of Job Training Programs is responsible for the development and issuance of Federal procedures and policies pertaining to the operation of the Job Training Partnership Act (JTPA) programs.

Under the act, the Secretary of Labor makes block grants to the States, insular areas, and the District of Columbia to establish programs to prepare youth and adults facing serious barriers to employment for participation in the labor force. Program services include assessment of unemployed individuals' needs and abilities; classroom training; on-the-job training; job search assistance; work experience; counseling; basic skills training; and support services. In addition to the block grants, JTPA provides for national programs for special target groups such as Native Americans and migrant and seasonal farmworkers. It also provides authority for the Job Corps, a residential training program for disadvantaged youth.

For further information, call 202–219–6236.

Office of Job Corps Programs   Job Corps is a national residential training and employment program administered by the Department to address the multiple barriers to employment faced by disadvantaged youth throughout the United States. Job Corps is currently authorized under title IV–B of the Job Training Partnership Act.

Job Corps assists young people 16 to 24 years of age who need and can benefit from an unusually intensive program, operated primarily in the residential setting of a Job Corps center, to become more responsible, employable, and productive citizens. The program is highly targeted to the most severely disadvantaged youth and provides a comprehensive mix of services which address multiple barriers to employment in an integrated and coordinated manner in one facility. The

array of services includes diagnostic testing of reading and math levels; occupational exploration programs; world of work training; basic education programs; competency-based vocational education programs; counseling and related support services; work experience programs; social skills training; intergroup relations; recreational programs; meals, lodging, and clothing; health care; and child care.

The program operates through a successful partnership of government, labor, and the private sector, with the Federal Government providing the facilities and equipment for Job Corps centers. Because the residential nature of the program dictates unique space and facility requirements, Job Corps center sites are fixed.

For further information, call 202–219–8550.

Senior Community Service Employment Program   Authorized by title V of the Older Americans Act (42 U.S.C. 3056), the program makes subsidized, part-time job opportunities in community service activities available to low-income persons aged 55 and above. Project grants are made to national-level public and private nonprofit agencies and to units of State governments. The distribution of funds among the States is governed by a statutory apportionment formula.

For further information, call 202–219–5500.

Regional Management

The Office of Regional Management provides leadership to the Employment and Training Administration's regional offices that are located in 10 areas throughout the United States. The Office executes direct-line authority over Administration field activities (except the Bureau of Apprenticeship and Training and Job Corps) and provides a central point of contact at the headquarters level in connection with national office component dealings with regional staff.

Within its area of jurisdiction, each regional office is responsible for the oversight and grant administration of employment and training programs operated by State governments. Other public interest responsibilities include the coordination of Administration activities with Federal assistance programs of other agencies within the region; the implementation of employment training administrative

policies on equal employment opportunity; and assistance to the States in carrying out operational responsibilities for employment and training programs at the State and local levels.

For further information, call 202–219–5585.

Regional Offices—Employment and Training Administration

Address (Areas Served)	Administrator	Telephone	Fax
Atlanta, GA (Rm. 6M12, 61 Forsyth St. SW., 30303) (AL, FL, GA, KY, MS, NC, SC, TN).	Toussaint L. Hayes ...	404–562–2092	404–562–2149
Boston, MA (Rm. E–350, JFK Federal Bldg., 02203) (CT, MA, ME, NH, RI, VT).	Robert J. Semler	617–565–3630	617–565–2229
Chicago, IL (Rm. 628, 230 S. Dearborn St., 60604) (IL, IN, MI, OH, WI).	Byron Zuidema	312–353–0313	312–353–4474
Dallas, TX (Rm. 317, 525 Griffin St., 75202) (AR, LA, NM, OK, TX).	Joseph Juarez	214–767–8263	214–767–5113
Denver, CO (Suite 1780, 1999 Broadway St., 80202–5716) (CO, MT, ND, SD, UT, WY).	John Sweeney, Act- ing.	303–844–1650	303–844–1685
Kansas City, MO (Suite 1050, 1100 Main St., 64105) (IA, KS, MO, NE).	Raymond Moritz, Act- ing.	816–426–3796	816–426–2729
New York, NY (Rm. 755, 201 Varick St., 10014) (NJ, NY, PR, VI)	Marilyn K. Shea	212–337–2139	212–337–2144
Philadelphia, PA (Rm. 13300, 3535 Market St., 19104) (DC, DE, MD, PA, VA, WV).	Edwin G. Strong	215–596–6336	215–596–0329
San Francisco, CA (Rm. 830, 71 Stevenson St., 94119–3767) (AZ, CA, HI, NV).	Armando Quiroz	415–975–4610	415–975–4612
Seattle, WA (Suite 900, 1111 3d Ave., 98101–3212) (AK, ID, OR, WA).	Michael Brauser	206–553–7700	206–553–0098

For further information concerning the Employment and Training Administration, call 202–219–6050.

Pension and Welfare Benefits Administration

The Pension and Welfare Benefits Administration (PWBA) is responsible for the administration of title I of the Employee Retirement Income Security Act of 1974, as amended (ERISA). The primary mission of PWBA is to promote and protect the pension, health, and other benefits of the over 150 million participants and beneficiaries in over 6 million private sector employee benefit plans which hold more than $3.5 trillion in assets. Private sector employee benefit plans provide income and benefits on which the majority of Americans rely to maintain an acceptable quality of life. The economic security of an individual or family may be jeopardized if pension, health, or other benefits are not paid as promised.

In administering its responsibilities, PWBA assists workers in understanding their rights and protecting their benefits; facilitates compliance by plan sponsors, plan officials, service providers, and other members of the regulated community; encourages the growth of employment-based benefits; and deters and corrects violations of the relevant statutes. ERISA is enforced through 15 PWBA field offices nationwide and the national office in Washington, DC.

Vesting, participation, and funding standards are primarily administered by the Internal Revenue Service.

For further information, call 202–219–8921.
Brochure request line, 800–998–7542 (toll-free).
Internet, http://www.dol.gov/dol/pwba/.

Field Offices—Pension and Welfare Benefits Administration

Area/Address	Director
Atlanta, GA (Suite 7B54, 61 Forsyth St. SW., 30303)	Howard Marsh
Boston, MA (Rm. 575, John F. Kennedy Bldg., 02203)	James Benages

Field Offices—Pension and Welfare Benefits Administration—Continued

Area/Address	Director
Chicago, IL (Suite 1600, 200 W. Adams St., 60606)	Kenneth Bazar
Cincinnati, OH (Suite 210, 1885 Dixie Hwy., Fort Wright, KY 41011)	Joseph Menez
Detroit, MI (Suite 1310, 211 W. Fort St., 48226–3211)	Robert Jogan
Dallas, TX (Rm. 707, 525 Griffin St., 75202)	Bruce Ruud
Kansas City, MO (Suite 1200, 1100 Main St., 64105–2112)	Gregory Egan
Los Angeles, CA (Suite 514, 790 E. Colorado Blvd., 91101)	David Ganz
New York, NY (Rm. 226, 1633 Broadway, 10019)	John Wehrum, Jr.
Philadelphia, PA (Rm. M300, 3535 Market St., 19104)	Mabel Capolongo
Plantation, FL (Suite 104, Bldg. H, 8040 Peters Rd., 33324)	Jesse Day
St. Louis, MO (Rm. 338, 815 Olive St., 63101–1559)	Gary Newman
San Francisco, CA (Suite 915, 71 Stevenson St., 94119–0250)	Bette Briggs, *Acting*
Seattle, WA (Rm. 860, 1111 3d Ave., 98101–3212)	John Scanlon
Washington, DC (Suite 556, 1730 K St. NW., 20006)	Caroline Sullivan

Employment Standards Administration

The Office of the Assistant Secretary for Employment Standards is responsible for administering and directing employment standards programs dealing with minimum wage and overtime standards; registration of farm labor contractors; determining prevailing wage rates to be paid on Government contracts and subcontracts; nondiscrimination and affirmative action for minorities, women, veterans, and handicapped Government contract and subcontract workers; workers' compensation programs for Federal and certain private employers and employees; safeguarding the financial integrity and internal democracy of labor unions; and administering statutory programs to certify employee protection provisions for various federally sponsored transportation programs.

For further information, call 202–219–6535. Information is also available electronically through the Internet, at http://www.dol.gov/dol/esa/.

Office of Federal Contract Compliance Programs

The Office of Federal Contract Compliance Programs (OFCCP) ensures that companies that do business with the Government promote affirmative action and equal employment opportunity on behalf of minorities, women, the disabled, and Vietnam Veterans. Through its 10 regional offices, as well as district and area offices in major

metropolitan centers, OFCCP enforces the following laws and orders:

—Executive Order 11246, as amended, which prohibits discrimination in hiring or employment opportunities on the basis of race, color, gender, religion, and national origin. It applies to all contractors and subcontractors holding any Federal or federally assisted contracts worth more than $10,000 annually. In addition, it requires contractors and subcontractors with a Federal contract of $50,000 or more, and 50 or more employees, to develop a written affirmative action program that sets forth specific and result-oriented procedures to which the contractor is committed to apply every good faith effort.

—Section 503 of the Rehabilitation Act of 1973, as amended, which prohibits discrimination and requires affirmative action in all personnel practices for persons with disabilities. It applies to firms with Federal contracts of $10,000 or more annually;

—the Vietnam Era Veterans' Readjustment Assistance Act of 1974 (38 USC 4212), which prohibits discrimination and requires affirmative action in all personnel practices for special disabled veterans and Vietnam Era veterans. It applies to firms with Federal contracts of $10,000 or more annually;

—the Immigration Reform and Control Act of 1986, which requires employers to maintain certain records pertaining to the citizenship status of new employees. These records are examined during the course of compliance reviews and complaint investigations, and results are reported to the Immigration and Naturalization Service; and

—the Americans with Disabilities Act of 1990, which became effective in July 1992 and provides disabled employees protection against discrimination.

In carrying out its responsibilities, the Office conducts compliance reviews and complaint investigations of Federal contractors' personnel policies and procedures; obtains letters of commitment and conciliation agreements from contractors who are in violation of regulatory requirements;

monitors contractors' progress in fulfilling the terms of their agreements through periodic compliance reports; forms linkage agreements between contractors and Department job training programs to help employers identify and recruit qualified workers; offers technical assistance to contractors to help them understand the regulatory requirements and review process; and recommends enforcement actions to the Solicitor of Labor.

The ultimate sanction for violations is debarment—the loss of a company's Federal contracts. Other forms of relief to victims of discrimination may also be available, including back pay for lost wages.

Regional Directors—Office of Federal Contract Compliance Programs

Address (Areas Served)	Director
Atlanta, GA (61 Forsyth St. SW., 30303) (AL, FL, GA, KY, MS, NC, SC, TN)	Carol A. Gaudin
Boston, MA (Rm. E–235, JFK Federal Bldg., 02203) (CT, MA, ME, NH, RI, VT)	James R. Turner, *Acting*
Chicago, IL (230 S. Dearborn St., 60604) (IA, IL, IN, KS, MI, MN, MO, NE, OH, WI)	Halcolm Holliman
Dallas, TX (525 Griffin St., 75202) (AR, CO, LA, MT, ND, NM, OK, SD, TX, UT, WY)	Albert Padilla
New York, NY (201 Varick St., 10014) (NJ, NY, PR, VI)	James R. Turner
Philadelphia, PA (3535 Market St., 19104) (DC, DE, MD, PA, VA, WV)	Joseph J. Dubray, Jr.
San Francisco, CA (71 Stevenson St., 94105) (AZ, CA, HI, NV)	Helene Haase
Seattle, WA (1111 3d Ave., 98101) (AK, ID, OR, WA)	Helene Haase, *Acting*

For further information, contact the Office of Federal Contract Compliance Programs Ombudsperson. Phone, 888–37–OFCCP (toll-free).

Wage and Hour Division

The Wage and Hour Administrator is responsible for planning, directing, and administering programs dealing with a variety of Federal labor legislation. These programs are designed to:

—protect low-wage incomes as provided by the minimum wage provisions of the Fair Labor Standards Act (29 U.S.C. 201);

—safeguard the health and welfare of workers by discouraging excessively long hours of work through enforcement of the overtime provisions of the Fair Labor Standards Act;

—safeguard the health and well-being of minors;

—prevent curtailment of employment and earnings for students, trainees, and handicapped workers;

—minimize losses of income and job rights caused by indebtedness; and

—direct a program of farm labor contractor registration designed to

protect the health, safety, and welfare of migrant and seasonal agricultural workers; and

—administer and enforce a number of immigration-related programs (with INS) designed to safeguard the rights of both American and foreign workers and to prevent American workers similarly employed from being adversely affected by employment of alien workers.

The Wage and Hour Division is also responsible for predetermination of prevailing wage rates for Federal construction contracts and federally assisted programs for construction, alteration and repair of public works subject to the Davis-Bacon (40 U.S.C. 276a) and related acts, and a continuing program for determining wage rates under the Service Contract Act (41 U.S.C. 351). The Division also has enforcement responsibility in ensuring that prevailing wages and overtime standards are paid in accordance with the provisions of the Davis-Bacon and related acts: Service Contract Act, Public Contracts Act, and Contract Work Hours and Safety Standards Act.

Regional Administrators—Wage and Hour Division

Address (Areas Served)	Regional Administrator
Atlanta, GA (100 Alabama St. SW., 30303) (AL, GA, KY, MS, NC, SC, TN)	Alfred H. Perry
Boston, MA (Rm. E234, JFK Bldg., 02203) (CT, MA, ME, NH, RI, VT)	James E. Sykes, *Acting*
Chicago, IL (230 S. Dearborn St., 60604) (IL, IN, MI, OH, WI)	Everett P. Jennings, *Acting*
Dallas, TX (Rm. 800, 525 Griffin St., 75202) (AR, CO, LA, MT, ND, NM, OK, SD, TX, UT, WY).	Manuel J. Villareal
Kansas City, MO (1100 Main St., 64105) (IA, KS, MO, NE)	Everett P. Jennings
New York, NY (201 Varick St., 10014) (NJ, NY)	James E. Sykes, *Acting*
Philadelphia, PA (3535 Market St., 19104) (DC, DE, MD, PA, PR, VA, VI, WV)	James E. Sykes, *Acting*
San Francisco, CA (71 Stevenson St., 94119) (AK, AZ, CA, HI, ID, NV, OR, WA)	William C. Buhl

For further information, contact the Office of the Administrator, Wage and Hour Division, Department of Labor, Room S–3502, 200 Constitution Avenue NW., Washington, DC 20210. Phone, 202–219–8305.

Office of Labor-Management Standards

This office administers provisions of the Labor-Management Reporting and Disclosure Act of 1959 (29 U.S.C. 401) and section 1209 of the Postal Reorganization Act (39 U.S.C. 1209), which establish standards of conduct for labor organizations in the private sector and labor organizations composed of Postal Service employees; as well as section 701 of the Civil Service Reform Act (5 U.S.C. 7120) and section 1017 of the Foreign Service Act (22 U.S.C. 4117), which affect labor organizations composed of employees of most agencies of the executive branch of the Federal Government. These provisions regulate certain internal union procedures, protect the rights of members in approximately 36,000 unions; govern the handling of union funds; provide for reporting and public disclosure of certain financial transactions and administrative practices of unions, union officers and employees, surety companies, employers, and labor relations consultants; establish

requirements for the election of union officers; and establish requirements for the imposition and administration of trusteeships.

This office conducts criminal and civil investigations to safeguard the financial integrity of unions and to ensure union democracy; and conducts investigative audits of labor unions to uncover and remedy criminal and civil violations of the Labor-Management Reporting and Disclosure Act and related statutes. However, the standards of conduct are enforced only by administrative action with a final decision by the Assistant Secretary.

The Office also administers a public disclosure program for financial and other reports filed by unions and others and provides compliance assistance to help unions and others comply with the statutes. In administering responsibilities of the Department under Federal transit law, the office ensures that fair and equitable arrangements protecting mass transit employees are in place before the referral of Federal transit grant funds.

Regional Offices—Office of Labor-Management Standards

Region	Address	Director
Atlanta, GA	Suite 8B85, 61 Forsyth St. SW., 30303	Ronald Lehman
Kansas City, MO	Suite 950, 1100 Main St., 64105	Kamil Bishara
Philadelphia, PA	Suite 4151, 801 Arch St., 19107	Eric Feldman
San Francisco, CA	Suite 725, 71 Stevenson St., 94105	C. Russell Rock
Washington, DC	Suite 558, 1730 K St. NW., 20006	Robert L. Merriner

For further information on union elections and reporting, call 202–219–7353. For general information, call 202–219–7373.

Office of Workers' Compensation Programs

The Office of Workers' Compensation Programs is responsible for the administration of the three basic Federal workers' compensation laws: the Federal Employees Compensation Act, which provides workers' compensation for Federal employees and others; the Longshore and Harbor Workers' Compensation Act and its various extensions (the Defense Base Act, Outer Continental Shelf Lands Act, Nonappropriated Fund Instrumentalities Act, the District of Columbia Compensation Act, the War Hazards Compensation Act, and the War Claims Act), which provide benefits to employees in private enterprise while engaged in maritime employment on navigable waters in the United States, as well as employees of certain government contractors and to private employers in the District of Columbia for injuries that occurred prior to July 27, 1982; and the Black Lung Benefits Act, as amended, which extends benefits to coal miners who are totally disabled due to pneumoconiosis, a respiratory disease contracted after prolonged inhalation of coal mine dust, and to their survivors when the miner's death is due to pneumoconiosis.

Regional/District Offices—Office of Workers' Compensation Programs

Address (Areas Served)	Director
Regional Offices	
Boston, MA, One Congress St., 02203 (CT, MA, ME, NH, RI, VT)	Charity Benz
Chicago, IL, 230 S. Dearborn St., 60604 (IL, IN, MI, OH, WI)	Deborah Sanford
Dallas, TX, 525 Griffin St., 75202 (AR, LA, NM, OK, TX)	Thomas Bouis
Denver, CO, 1801 California St., 80294 (CO, MT, ND, SD, UT, WY)	Robert J. Mansanares
Jacksonville, FL, 214 N. Hogan St., 32202 (FL)	Nancy L. Ricker
Kansas City, MO, 1100 Main St., 64105 (IA, KS, MO, NE)	Charles O. Ketcham, Jr.
New York, NY, 201 Varick St., 10014 (NJ, NY)	Kenneth Hamlett
Philadelphia, PA, 3535 Market St., 19104 (DC, DE, MD, PA, PR, VA, VI, WV)	Robert D. Lotz
San Francisco, CA, 71 Stevenson St., 94119 (AZ, CA, HI, NV)	Donna Onodera
Seattle, WA, 1111 3d Ave., 98101 (AK, ID, OR, WA)	Thomas K. Morgan
District Offices	
Federal Employee Compliance Act	
Boston, MA (One Congress St., 02114)	Michael Harvil
Chicago, IL (230 S. Dearborn St., 60604)	Richard Kadus
Cleveland, OH (1240 E. 9th St., 44199)	Robert M. Sullivan
Dallas, TX (525 Griffin St., 75202)	E. Martin Walker
Denver, CO (1801 California St., 80202–2614)	Robert Mitchell
Jacksonville, FL (214 N. Hogan St., 32202)	William C. Franson
Kansas City, MO (Suite 750, 1100 Main St., 64105)	Charles O. Ketcham, Jr.
New York, NY (201 Varick St., 10014)	Jonathan A. Lawrence
Philadelphia, PA (3535 Market St., 19104)	William Staarman
San Francisco, CA (71 Stevenson St., 94119)	Ed Bounds
Seattle, WA (1111 3d Ave., 98101–3212)	William Howard
Washington, DC (800 N. Capitol St. NW., 20211)	Ora T. Wright
Division of Longshore and Harbor Workers' Compensation	
Baltimore, MD (31 Hopkins Plz., 21201)	Bruno DiSimone
Boston, MA (One Congress St., 02114)	Randolph L. Regula
Chicago, IL (230 S. Dearborn St., 60604)	Thomas C. Hunter
Honolulu, HI (300 Ala Moana Blvd., 96850)	Joyce Terry
Houston, TX (Suite 140, 8866 Gulf Freeway, 77014)	Chris John Gleasman
Jacksonville, FL (214 N. Hogan St., 32202)	Jeana Jackson
Long Beach, CA (401 E. Ocean Blvd., 90802)	Joyce Terry
New Orleans, LA (701 Loyola St., 70113)	Marilyn Felkner
New York, NY (201 Varick St., 10014)	Richard V. Robilotti
Norfolk, VA (200 Granby Mall, 23510)	Basil E. Voultsides
Philadelphia, PA (3535 Market St., 19104)	John McTaggart
San Francisco, CA (71 Stevenson St., 94119)	Joyce Terry
Seattle, WA (1111 3d Ave., 98101–3212)	Karen Staats
Division of Coal Mine Workers' Compensation	
Charleston, WV (2 Hale St., 25301)	Robert Hardesty
Columbus, OH (274 Marconi Blvd., 43215)	Don Dopps
Denver, CO (1801 California St., 80202–2614)	John Martin
Greensburg, PA (1225 S. Main St., 15601	John Ciszek
Johnstown, PA (Rm. 201, 319 Washington St., 15901)	Stuart Glassman
Pikeville, KY (334 Main St., 41501)	Harry Skidmore
Wilkes-Barre, PA (Suite 100, 105 N. Main St., 18701)	Jack Geller

For further information, contact the Office of the Director, Office of Workers' Compensation Programs, Department of Labor, Room S–3524, 200 Constitution Avenue NW., Washington, DC 20210. Phone, 202–219–7503.

Occupational Safety and Health Administration

The Assistant Secretary for Occupational Safety and Health has responsibility for occupational safety and health activities.

The Occupational Safety and Health Administration, established pursuant to the Occupational Safety and Health Act of 1970 (29 U.S.C. 651 *et seq.*), develops and promulgates occupational safety and health standards; develops and issues regulations; conducts investigations and inspections to determine the status of compliance with safety and health standards and regulations; and issues citations and proposes penalties for noncompliance with safety and health standards and regulations.

Regional Offices—Occupational Safety and Health Administration

Address	Administrator	Telephone
Atlanta, GA (61 Forsyth St. SW., 30303) (AL, FL, GA, KY, MS, NC, SC, TN)	R. Davis Layne	404–562–2300
Boston, MA (Rm. E–340, JFK Federal Bldg., 02203) (CT, MA, ME, NH, RI, VT)	Cindy Coe, *Acting*	617–565–9860
Chicago, IL (230 S. Dearborn St., 60604) (IL, IN, MI, OH, WI)	Michael Connors	312–353–2220
Dallas, TX (525 Griffin St., 75202) (AR, LA, NM, OK, TX)	Joe Reina, *Acting*	214–767–4731
Denver, CO (1999 Broadway, 80202) (CO, MT, ND, SD, UT, WY)	Gregory Baxter, *Acting.*	303–844–1600
Kansas City, MO (1100 Main St., 64105) (IA, KS, MO, NE)	Charles Adkins	816–426–5861
New York, NY (201 Varick St., 10014) (NJ, NY)	Patricia Clark	212–337–2378
Philadelphia, PA (3535 Market St., 19104) (DC, DE, MD, PA, PR, VA, VI, WV)	Linda R. Anku	215–596–1201
San Francisco, CA (71 Stevenson St., 94105) (AZ, CA, HI, NV)	Frank Strasheim	415–975–4310
Seattle, WA (1111 3d Ave., 98101) (AK, ID, OR, WA)	Richard Terrill, *Acting*	206–553–5930

For further information, contact the Occupational Safety and Health Administration, Department of Labor, 200 Constitution Avenue NW., Washington, DC 20210. Phone, 202–219–8151.

Mine Safety and Health Administration

The Assistant Secretary of Labor for Mine Safety and Health has responsibility for safety and health in the Nation's mines.

The Federal Coal Mine Health and Safety Act of 1969 (30 U.S.C. 801 *et seq.*) gave the Administration strong enforcement provisions to protect the Nation's coal miners and, in 1977, the Congress passed amendments which strengthened the act, expanding its protections and extending its provisions to the noncoal mining industry.

The Administration develops and promulgates mandatory safety and health standards, ensures compliance with such standards, assesses civil penalties for violations, and investigates accidents. It cooperates with and provides assistance to the States in the development of effective State mine safety and health programs; improves and expands training programs in cooperation with the States and the mining industry; and, in coordination with the Department of Health and Human Services, contributes to the improvement and expansion of mine safety and health research and development. All of these activities are aimed at preventing and reducing mine accidents and occupational diseases in the mining industry.

The statutory responsibilities of the Administration are administered by a headquarters staff located at Arlington, VA, reporting to the Assistant Secretary for Mine Safety and Health and by a field network of district, subdistrict, and field offices, technology centers, and the Approval and Certification Center.

District Offices—Mine Safety and Health Administration

District/Address	Telephone
Coal Mine Safety and Health	
Barbourville, KY (HC 66, Box 1762, 40906)	606–546–5123
Birmingham, AL (Suite 213, 135 Gemini Cir., 35209–4896)	205–290–7300
Denver, CO (P.O. Box 25367, 80225–0367)	303–231–5458
Hunker, PA (R 1, Box 736, 15639)	412–925–5150
Madisonville, KY (100 YMCA Dr., 42431–9019)	502–821–4180
Morgantown, WV (5012 Mountaineer Mall, 26505)	304–291–4277
Mount Hope, WV (100 Bluestone Rd., 25880)	304–877–3900
Norton, VA (P.O. Box 560, 24273)	540–679–0230
Pikeville, KY (100 Ratliff Creek Rd., 41501)	606–432–0943
Vincennes, IN (P.O. Box 418, 47591)	812–882–7617
Wilkes-Barre, PA (Suite 034, 7 N. Wilkes-Barre Blvd., 18702)	717–826–6321
Metal/Nonmetal Mine Safety and Health	
Northeastern District (230 Executive Dr., Cranberry Township, PA 16066–6415)	412–772–2333
Southeastern District (Suite 212, 135 Gemini Cir., Birmingham, AL 35209–4896)	205–290–7294
North Central District (515 W. 1st St., Duluth, MN 55802–1302)	218–720–5448
South Central District (Rm. 4C50, 1100 Commerce St., Dallas, TX 75242–0499)	214–767–8401
Rocky Mountain District (P.O. Box 25367, Denver, CO 80225–0367)	303–231–5465
Western District (Suite 610, 2060 Peabody Rd., Vacaville, CA 95687)	707–447–9844

For further information, contact the Office of Information and Public Affairs, Mine Safety and Health Administration, Department of Labor, Room 601, 4015 Wilson Boulevard, Arlington, VA 22203. Phone, 703–235–1452.

Labor Statistics

The Bureau of Labor Statistics (BLS) is the principal fact-finding agency of the Federal Government in the broad field of labor economics and statistics. The Bureau is an independent national statistical agency that collects, processes, analyzes, and disseminates essential statistical data to the American public, Congress, other Federal agencies, State and local governments, businesses, and labor relating to employment, unemployment, and other characteristics of the labor force; consumer and producer prices, consumer expenditures, and import and export prices; wages and employee benefits; productivity and technological change; employment projections; occupational illness and injuries; and international comparisons of labor statistics. Most of the data are collected in surveys conducted by the Bureau, the Bureau of the Census (on a contract basis), or on a cooperative basis with State agencies.

The Bureau strives to have its data satisfy a number of criteria, including: relevance to current social and economic issues, timeliness in reflecting today's rapidly changing economic conditions, accuracy and consistently high statistical quality, and impartiality in both subject matter and presentation.

The basic data—practically all supplied voluntarily by business establishments and members of private households—are issued in monthly, quarterly, and annual news releases; bulletins, reports, and special publications; and periodicals. Data are also made available through an electronic news service, magnetic tape, diskettes, and microfiche, as well as on Internet. Regional offices issue additional reports and releases usually presenting locality or regional detail.

Regional Offices—Bureau of Labor Statistics

Region	Address	Commissioner
Atlanta, GA (AL, FL, GA, KY, MS, NC, SC, TN)	61 Forsyth St. SW., 30303	Janet S. Rankin
Boston, MA (CT, ME, MA, NH, RI, VT)	JFK Federal Bldg., 02203	Anthony J. Ferrara
Chicago, IL (IL, IN, MI, MN, OH, WI)	230 S. Dearborn St., 60604	(Vacancy)
Dallas, TX (AR, LA, NM, OK, TX)	525 Griffin Sq. Bldg., 75202	Robert A. Goddie

Regional Offices—Bureau of Labor Statistics—Continued

Region	Address	Commissioner
Kansas City, MO (CO, IA, KS, MO, MT, NE, ND, SD, UT, WY).	Suite 600, 1100 Main St., 64105).	Gunnan Engen
New York, NY (CZ, NJ, NY, PR, VI)	201 Varick St., 10014	John Wieting
Philadelphia, PA (DE, DC, MD, PA, VA, WV)	3535 Market St., 19104	Alan M. Paisner
San Francisco, CA (AK, American Samoa, AZ, CA, GU, HI, ID, NV, OR, Pacific Islands, WA).	71 Stevenson St., 94119–3766	Stanley P. Stephenson

For further information, contact the Associate Commissioner, Office of Publications, Bureau of Labor Statistics, Department of Labor, Room 4110, 2 Massachusetts Ave. NW., Washington, DC 20212. Phone, 202–606–5900.

Veterans' Employment and Training Service

The Veterans' Employment and Training Service is the component of the Department of Labor administered by the Assistant Secretary for Veterans' Employment and Training. The Assistant Secretary is the principal adviser to the Secretary of Labor in the formulation and implementation of all departmental policies, procedures, and regulations affecting veterans and is responsible for administering veterans' employment and training programs and activities through the Service to ensure that legislative and regulatory mandates are accomplished.

The Service carries out its responsibilities for directing the Department's veterans' employment and training programs through a nationwide network that includes Regional Administrators, Directors (in each State) and Assistant Directors (one for each 250,000 veterans in each State) for Veterans' Employment and Training, Assistant Regional Administrators, Veterans' Program Specialists, and program support staff.

The Service field staff works closely with and provides technical assistance to State Employment Security Agencies and Job Training Partnership Act grant recipients to ensure that veterans are provided the priority services required by law. They also coordinate with employers, labor unions, veterans service organizations, and community organizations through planned public information and outreach activities. Federal contractors are provided management assistance in complying with their veterans affirmative action and reporting obligations.

Also administered by the Assistant Secretary through the Service is the Job Training Partnership Act, title IV, part C grant program designed to meet the employment and training needs of service-connected disabled veterans, Vietnam-era veterans, and veterans recently separated from military service. IV–C grants are awarded and monitored through the Service's national office and field staff.

Certain other Service staff also administer the veterans reemployment rights program. They provide assistance to help restore job, seniority, and pension rights to veterans following absences from work for active military service and to protect employment and retention rights of members of the Reserve or National Guard.

Regional Administrators/State Directors—Veterans' Employment and Training Service

(RA: Regional Administrator; D: Director)

Region/Address	Director	Telephone
Aberdeen, SD (420 S. Roosevelt St., 57402–4730)	Earl R. Schultz (D)	605–626–2325
Albany, NY (Rm. 518, Bldg. 12, Harriman State Campus, 12240)	James H. Hartman (D)	518–457–7465
Albuquerque, NM (401 Broadway NE., 87102)	Jacob Castillo (D)	505–766–2113
Atlanta, GA (Rm. 6–T85, 61 Forsyth St. SW., 30303)	William Bolls (RA)	404–562–2305
Atlanta, GA (Suite 504, 148 International Blvd. NE., 30303)	Hartwell H. Morris (D)	404–331–3893
Austin, TX (Suite 516–T, 1117 Trinity St., 78701)	John McKinny (D)	512–463–2207

Regional Administrators/State Directors—Veterans' Employment and Training Service—Continued

(RA: Regional Administrator; D: Director)

Region/Address	Director	Telephone
Baltimore, MD (Rm. 210, 1100 N. Eutaw St., 21201)	Stanley Seidel (D)	410–767–2110
Baton Rouge, LA (Rm. 184,, Admin. Bldg. 1001 N. 23d St., 70802)	Lester Parmenter (D)	504–389–0440
Bismarck, ND (1000 E. Divide Ave., 58502–1632)	Richard Ryan (D)	701–250–4337
Boise, ID (Rm. 303, 317 Main St., 83735)	(Vacancy) (D)	208–334–6163
Boston, MA (2d Fl., 19 Staniford St., 02114–2502)	Paul Desmond (D)	617–626–6690
Boston, MA (Rm. E–315, JFK Federal Bldg., 02203)	David Houle (RA)	617–565–2080
Carson City, NV (Rm. 205, 1923 N. Carson St., 89702)	(Vacancy) (D)	702–687–4632
Casper, WY (100 W. Midwest Ave., 82602–2760)	David McNulty (D)	307–261–5454
Charleston, WV (Rm. 205, 112 California Ave., 25305–0112)	David L. Bush (D)	304–558–4001
Chicago, IL (Rm. 1064, 230 S. Dearborn St., 60604)	Ronald G. Bachman (RA)	312–353–0970
Chicago, IL (2 N., 401 S. State St., 60605)	Samuel Parks (D)	312–793–3433
Columbia, SC (Suite 140, 631 Hampton St., 29201)	William C. Plowden, Jr. (D)	803–765–5195
Columbus, OH (Rm. 523, 145 S. Front St., 43215)	Carl Price (D)	614–466–2768
Concord, NH (Rm. 208, 143 N. Main St., 03301)	Richard Ducey (D)	603–225–1424
Dallas, TX (Rm. 858, 525 Griffin St., 75202)	Lester L. Williams, Jr. (RA)	214–767–4987
Denver, CO (Suite 956, 1801 California St., 80202–2614)	Ronald G. Bachman (RA)	303–844–1175
Denver, CO (Suite 400, 1515 Arapahoe St., 80202–2117)	Mark A. McGinty (D)	303–844–2151
Des Moines, IA (150 Des Moines St., 50309–5563)	Leonard E. Shaw, Jr. (D)	515–281–9061
Detroit, MI (6th Fl., 7310 Woodward Ave., 48202)	Kim Fulton (D)	313–876–5613
Frankfort, KY (2d. Fl. W., 275 E. Main St., 40621–2339)	Charles R. Netherton (D)	502–564–7062
Harrisburg, PA (Rm. 1108, 7th and Forster Sts., 17121)	Larry Babbitts (D)	717–787–5834
Hato Rey, PR (No. 198, Calle Guayama, 00917)	Angel Mojica (D)	787–754–5391
Helena, MT (1215 8th Ave., 59601)	H. Polly LaTray-Holmes (D)	406–449–5431
Honolulu, HI (Rm. 315, 830 Punch Bowl St., 96813)	Gilbert Hough (D)	808–522–8216
Indianapolis, IN (Rm. SE–103, 10 N. Senate Ave., 46204)	Bruce Redman (D)	317–232–6804
Jackson, MS (1520 W. Capitol St., 39215–1699)	(Vacancy) (D)	601–965–4204
Jefferson City, MO (421 E. Dunklin St., 65104–3138)	Mickey J. Jones (D)	573–751–3921
Juneau, AK (1111 W. 8th St., 99802–5509)	Daniel Travis (D)	907–465–2723
Kansas City, MO (Suite 850, 1100 Main St., 64105–2112)	Lester Williams (RA)	816–426–7151
Lewiston, ME (522 Lisbon St., 04243)	Jon Guay (D)	207–783–5352
Lincoln, NE (550 S. 16th St., 68508)	Richard Nelson (D)	402–437–5289
Little Rock, AR (Rm. G–12, State Capitol Mall, 72201)	Billy R. Threlkeld (D)	501–682–3786
Madison, WI (Rm. 250, 201 E. Washington Ave., 53702)	James R. Gutowski (D)	608–266–3110
Montgomery, AL (Rm. 543, 649 Monroe St., 36131–6300)	Thomas M. Karrh (D)	334–223–7677
Montpelier, VT (Rm. 303, 87 State St., 05601)	Richard Gray (D)	802–828–4441
Nashville, TN (915 8th Ave. N., 37208)	Richard E. Ritchie (D)	615–736–7680
New York, NY (Rm. 766, 201 Varick St., 10014)	H. Miles Sisson (RA)	212–337–2211
Oklahoma City, OK (400 Will Rogers Memorial Office Bldg., 73105)	Darrell H. Hill (D)	405–557–7189
Olympia, WA (3d Fl., 605 Woodview Sq. Loop SE., 98503–1040)	Donald J. Hutt (D)	360–438–4600
Philadelphia, PA (Rm. 802, 2d & Chestnut Sts., 19106)	Joseph W. Hortiz, Jr. (RA)	215–597–1664
Phoenix, AZ (1400 W. Washington St., 85005)	Marco A. Valenzuela (D)	602–379–4961
Raleigh, NC (Bldg. M, 700 Wade Ave., 27605)	Steven Guess (D)	919–856–4792
Richmond, VA (Rm. 118, 703 E. Main St., 23219)	Roberto Pineda (D)	804–786–6599
Sacramento, CA (Rm. W1142, 800 Capitol Mall, 94280–0001)	Rosendo A. (Alex) Cuevas (D) ..	916–654–8178
St. Paul, MN (610 Piper Jaffray Plz., 444 Cedar St., 55101)	Michael D. Graham (D)	612–290–3028
Salem, OR (Rm. 108, 875 Union St. NE., 97311–0100)	Rex A. Newell (D)	503–947–1490
Salt Lake City, UT (Suite 209, 140 E. 300 South St., 84111–2333)	Dale Brockbank (D)	801–524–5703
San Francisco, CA (Suite 705, 71 Stevenson St., 94105)	Charles Martinez (RA)	415–975–4702
Seattle, WA (Suite 800, 1111 3d Ave., 98101–3212)	Charles Martinez (RA)	206–553–4831
Tallahassee, FL (Suite 205, 2574 Seagate Dr., 32399–0676)	LaMont P. Davis (D)	904–877–4164
Topeka, KS (401 Topeka Blvd., 66603–3182)	Gayle A. Gibson (D)	913–296–5032
Trenton, NJ (11th Fl., Labor Bldg., CN–058, 08625)	Alan E. Grohs (D)	609–292–2930
Washington, DC (Rm. 108, 500 C St. NW., 20001)	Stanley Williams (D)	202–724–7004
Westerly, RI (57 Spruce St., 02891–1921)	John Dunn (D)	401–528–5134
Wethersfield, CT (200 Follybrook Blvd., 06109)	(Vacancy) (D)	860–566–3326
Wilmington, DE (Rm. 420, 4425 N. Market St., 19809–0828)	(Vacancy) (D)	302–761–8138

For further information, contact the Assistant Secretary for Veterans' Employment and Training, Department of Labor, 200 Constitution Avenue NW., Washington, DC 20210. Phone, 202–219–9116.

Sources of Information

Contracts General inquiries may be directed to the Office of the Acquisition Advocate, OASAM, Room N–5425, 200 Constitution Avenue NW., Washington, DC 20210. Phone, 202–219–8904.

Inquiries on doing business with the Job Corps should be directed to the Job

Corps Regional Director in the appropriate Employment and Training Administration regional office listed in the preceding text.

Electronic Access   Information concerning Department of Labor agencies, programs, and activities is available electronically through the Internet, at http://www.dol.gov/.

Employment   Personnel offices use lists of eligibles from the clerical, scientific, technical, and general examinations of the Office of Personnel Management.

Inquiries and applications may be directed to any of the eight personnel offices at: Department of Labor, 200 Constitution Avenue NW., Washington, DC 20210, or the nearest regional office. Information on specific vacancies may be obtained by calling the Department's Job Opportunity Bank System. Phone, 800–366–2753.

Publications   The Office of Public Affairs distributes a brochure entitled *Department of Labor,* which describes the activities of the major agencies within the Department, and *Publications of the Department of Labor,* a subject listing of publications available from the Department.

The Employment and Training Administration issues periodicals such as *Area Trends in Employment and Unemployment* available by subscription through the Superintendent of Documents, Government Printing Office, Washington, DC 20402. Information about publications may be obtained from the Administration's Information Office. Phone, 202–219–6871.

The Office of Labor-Management Standards publishes the text of the Labor-Management Reporting and Disclosure Act (29 U.S.C. 401) and pamphlets that explain the reporting, election, bonding, and trusteeship provisions of the act. The pamphlets and reporting forms used by persons covered by the act are available free in limited quantities from the OLMS National Office at Room N–5616, 200 Constitution Avenue NW., Washington, DC 20210, and from OLMS field offices listed in the telephone directory under United States Government, Department of Labor.

The Pension and Welfare Benefits Administration distributes fact sheets, pamphlets, and booklets on employer obligations and employee rights under ERISA. A list of publications is available by writing: PWBA, Division of Public Information, Room N–5666, 200 Constitution Avenue NW., Washington, DC 20210. Phone, 202–219–8921.

The Bureau of Labor Statistics has an Information Office at 2 Massachusetts Avenue NE., Room 2850, Washington, DC 20212. Phone, 202–606–5886. Periodicals include the *Monthly Labor Review, Consumer Price Index, Producer Prices and Price Indexes, Employment and Earnings, Current Wage Developments, Occupational Outlook Handbook,* and *Occupational Outlook Quarterly.* Publications are both free and for sale, but for-sale items must be obtained from the Superintendent of Documents, Government Printing Office. Inquiries may be directed to the Washington Information Office or to the Bureau's regional offices.

Publications of the Employment Standards Administration, such as *Handy Reference Guide to the Fair Labor Standards Act,* and *OFCCP, Making Affirmative Action Work,* are available from the nearest area office. Single copies are free.

Reading Rooms   Department of Labor Library, Room N2439, Frances Perkins Building, 200 Constitution Avenue NW., Washington, DC 20210. Phone, 202–219–6992.

The Office of Labor-Management Standards maintains a Public Disclosure Room at Room N–5616, 200 Constitution Avenue NW., Washington, DC 20210. Reports filed under the Labor-Management Reporting and Disclosure Act may be examined there and purchased for 15 cents per page. Reports also may be obtained by calling the Public Disclosure Room at 202–219–7393, or by contacting an Office field office listed in the telephone directory under United States Government, Department of Labor.

The Pension and Welfare Benefits Administration maintains a Public Disclosure Room at Room N–5507, 200 Constitution Avenue NW., Washington,

DC 20210. Reports filed under the Employee Retirement Income Security Act may be examined there and purchased for 10 cents per page or by calling the Public Disclosure Room at 202–219–8771.

For further information concerning the Department of Labor, contact the Office of Public Affairs, Department of Labor, Room S–1032, 200 Constitution Avenue NW., Washington, DC 20210. Phone, 202–219–7316. Internet, http://www.dol.gov/.

DEPARTMENT OF STATE

2201 C Street NW., Washington, DC 20520
Phone, 202–647–4000. Internet, http://www.state.gov/.

SECRETARY OF STATE	MADELEINE K. ALBRIGHT
Chief of Staff	ELAINE K. SHOCAS
Executive Assistant	DAVID M. HALE
Special Assistant to the Secretary and Executive Secretary of the Department	KRISTIE A. KENNEY
Deputy Assistant Secretary for Equal Employment Opportunity and Civil Rights	DEIDRE A. DAVIS
Chief of Protocol	MARY MEL FRENCH
Chairman, Foreign Service Grievance Board	THOMAS J. DiLAURO
Civil Service Ombudsman	TED A. BOREK
Deputy Secretary of State	STROBE TALBOTT
Under Secretary for Political Affairs	THOMAS R. PICKERING
Under Secretary for Economic, Business, and Agricultural Affairs	STUART E. EIZENSTAT
Under Secretary for Arms Control and International Security Affairs	JOHN HOLUM, *Acting*
Under Secretary for Management	BONNIE R. COHEN
Under Secretary for Global Affairs	WENDY SHERMAN, *Acting*
Counselor of the Department of State	WENDY SHERMAN
Assistant Secretary for Administration	PATRICK R. HAYES, *Acting*
Assistant Secretary for Consular Affairs	MARY A. RYAN
Assistant Secretary for Diplomatic Security	PATRICK F. KENNEDY, *Acting*
Chief Financial Officer	RICHARD L. GREENE
Director General of the Foreign Service and Director of Personnel	EDWARD W. GNEHM, *Acting*
Medical Director, Department of State and the Foreign Service	CEDRIC E. DUMONT
Executive Secretary, Board of the Foreign Service	JONATHAN MUDGE
Director of the Foreign Service Institute	RUTH A. DAVIS
Director, Office of Foreign Missions	PATRICK F. KENNEDY, *Acting*
Assistant Secretary for Population, Refugee, and Migration Affairs	JULIA V. TAFT
Inspector General	JACQUELINE L. WILLIAMS-BRIDGER
Director, Policy Planning Staff	GREGORY P. CRAIG
Assistant Secretary for Legislative Affairs	BARBARA LARKIN
Assistant Secretary for Democracy, Human Rights, and Labor	JOHN SHATTUCK
Legal Advisor	DAVID R. ANDREWS
Assistant Secretary for African Affairs	SUSAN E. RICE
Assistant Secretary for East Asian and Pacific Affairs	STANLEY O. ROTH
Assistant Secretary for European and Canadian Affairs	MARC GROSSMAN

Assistant Secretary for Inter-American Affairs	JEFFREY DAVIDOW
Permanent Representative of the United States of America to the Organization of American States	VICTOR MARRERO
Assistant Secretary for Near East Affairs	MARTIN S. INDYK
Assistant Secretary for South Asian Affairs	KARL F. INDERFURTH
Assistant Secretary for Economics and Business Affairs	ALAN LARSON
Assistant Secretary for Intelligence and Research	PHYLLIS E. OAKLEY
Assistant Secretary for International Organization Affairs	PRINCETON LYMAN
Assistant Secretary for Oceans and International Environmental and Scientific Affairs	MELINDA L. KIMBLE, *Acting*
Assistant Secretary for Public Affairs and Spokesman for the Department of State	JAMES RUBIN
Assistant Secretary for Politico-Military Affairs	ERIC NEWSOM, *Acting*
Assistant Secretary for International Narcotics and Law Enforcement Affairs	RAND BEERS, *Acting*
U.S. Coordinator, International Communications and Information Policy	VONYA B. MCCANN

United States Mission to the United Nations [1]

799 United Nations Plaza, New York, NY 10017

United States Representative to the United Nations and Representative in the Security Council	BILL RICHARDSON
Deputy United States Representative to the United Nations	A. PETER BURLEIGH
United States Representative for Special Political Affairs in the United Nations	NANCY SODERBERG
United States Representative on the Economic and Social Council	BETTY E. KING
United States Representative for U.N. Management and Reform	RICHARD SKLAR

[For the Department of State statement of organization, see the *Code of Federal Regulations*, Title 22, Part 5]

The Department of State advises the President in the formulation and execution of foreign policy. As Chief Executive, the President has overall responsibility for the foreign policy of the United States. The Department of State's primary objective in the conduct of foreign relations is to promote the long-range security and well-being of the United States. The Department determines and analyzes the facts relating to American overseas interests, makes recommendations on policy and future action, and takes the necessary steps to carry out established policy. In so doing, the Department engages in continuous consultations with the American public, the Congress, other U.S. departments and agencies, and foreign governments; negotiates treaties and agreements with foreign nations; speaks for the United States in the United Nations and in more than 50 major international organizations in which the

[1] A description of the organization and functions of the United Nations can be found under *Selected Multilateral Organizations* in this book.

United States participates; and represents the United States at more than 800 international conferences annually.

The Department of State, the senior executive department of the U.S. Government, was established by act of July 27, 1789, as the Department of Foreign Affairs and was renamed Department of State by act of September 15, 1789 (22 U.S.C. 2651 note).

Office of the Secretary

Secretary of State The Secretary of State, the principal foreign policy adviser to the President, is responsible for the overall direction, coordination, and supervision of U.S. foreign relations and for the interdepartmental activities of the U.S. Government abroad. The Secretary is the first-ranking member of the Cabinet, is a member of the National Security Council, and is in charge of the operations of the Department, including the Foreign Service. The Office of the Secretary includes the offices of the Deputy Secretary, Under Secretaries, Assistant Secretaries, Counselor, Legal Adviser, and Inspector General. Some areas where public purposes are widely applied are detailed below and on the following pages.

Economic, Business, and Agricultural Affairs The Under Secretary for Economic, Business, and Agricultural Affairs is principal adviser to the Secretary and Deputy Secretary in the formulation and conduct of foreign economic policy. Specific areas for which the Under Secretary is responsible include international trade, agriculture, energy, finance, transportation, and relations with developing countries.

Bureau for Arms Control and International Security Affairs The Under Secretary for Arms Control and International Security Affairs is responsible for integrating and prioritizing the full range of international security, nonproliferation, and arms control issues into the Department's conduct of foreign policy. This includes directing and coordinating arms control policy; nonproliferation policy (including nuclear, chemical, biological, missile, and conventional weapons proliferation); export control policy; and certain foreign assistance programs. The Under Secretary coordinates diplomatic efforts to obtain the agreement of all appropriate countries to the Missile Technology Control Regime and exercises various authorities relating to the imposition of proliferation sanctions as required by U.S. law.

Regional Bureaus

Six Assistant Secretaries direct the activities of the geographic bureaus, which are responsible for our foreign affairs activities throughout the world. These are the Bureaus of African Affairs, European and Canadian Affairs, East Asian and Pacific Affairs, Inter-American Affairs, and Near Eastern Affairs, and South Asian Affairs.

The regional Assistant Secretaries also serve as Chairmen of Interdepartmental Groups in the National Security Council system. These groups discuss and decide issues that can be settled at the Assistant Secretary level, including those arising out of the implementation of National Security Council decisions. They prepare policy papers for consideration by the Council and contingency papers on potential crisis areas for Council review.

DEPARTMENT OF STATE

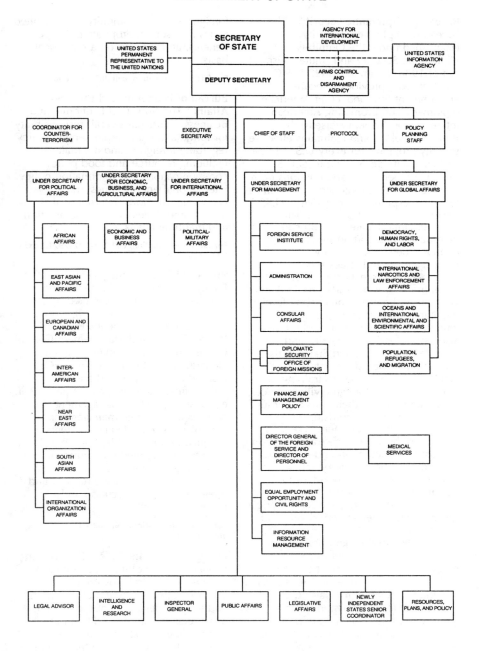

Functional Areas

Bureau of Diplomatic Security   The Bureau of Diplomatic Security, established under the Omnibus Diplomatic Security and Antiterrorism Act of 1986, as amended (22 U.S.C. 4803 et seq.), provides a secure environment for conducting American diplomacy and promoting American interests worldwide. Overseas, the Bureau develops and maintains effective security programs for every U.S. Embassy and consulate abroad; protects U.S. diplomatic personnel and missions from physical and electronic attack as well as technical espionage; and advises U.S. Ambassadors on all security matters.

In the United States, the Bureau investigates passport and visa fraud, conducts personnel security investigations, and issues security clearances. It protects the Secretary of State, the U.S. Ambassador to the United Nations, and many cabinet-level foreign dignitaries and other foreign officials who visit the United States. The Bureau also assists foreign embassies and consulates in the United States in the protection of their diplomats and facilities, and arranges for training in the United States for foreign civilian police who then return to their own countries better able to fight terrorism.

The Diplomatic Courier Service supervises the worldwide transportation of classified documents and equipment contained in diplomatic pouches.

The Overseas Security Advisory Council promotes cooperation on security-related issues between American private sector interests worldwide and the Department of State.

The Office of Foreign Missions, through the employment of reciprocity, ensures equitable treatment for U.S. diplomatic and consular missions abroad and their personnel; regulates the activities of foreign missions in this country to protect foreign policy and national security interests of the United States; protects the American public from abuses of privileges and immunities by members of foreign missions; and provides service and assistance to the foreign mission community in the United States to assure appropriate privileges, benefits, and services on a reciprocal basis.

For further information, call 202–663–0067.

Bureau of Economic and Business Affairs   The Bureau of Economic and Business Affairs has overall responsibility for formulating and implementing policy regarding foreign economic matters, including resource and food policy, communications and information policy, international energy issues, trade, economic sanctions, international finance and development, and aviation and maritime affairs.

For further information, call 202–647–7971. Fax, 202–647–5713.

Bureau of Finance and Management Policy   The Bureau of Finance and Management Policy is directed by the Chief Financial Officer (CFO), who serves as the Department's Principal Budget Officer and Management Control Officer and assists in managing the Department and its posts. The CFO, assisted by well-qualified and well-trained financial management personnel, establishes effective management policies and internal management controls; ensures adequate systems to produce useful, reliable, and timely financial and related programmatic information; develops useful financial analysis and performance reports; and integrates budget execution and accounting functions.

For further information, call 202–647–6778. Fax, 202–736–7010.

Foreign Service Institute   The Foreign Service Institute of the Department of State is the Federal Government's primary training institution for officers and support personnel of the foreign affairs community. In addition to the Department of State, the Institute provides training for more than 40 other governmental agencies. The Institute's more than 300 courses, including 60 language courses, range in length from one day to 2 years. The courses are designed to promote successful performance in each professional assignment, to ease the adjustment to other countries and cultures, and to enhance the leadership and management capabilities of the foreign affairs community.

For further information, call 703–302–6729. Fax, 703–302–7227.

Intelligence and Research The Bureau of Intelligence and Research coordinates programs of intelligence, analysis, and research for the Department and produces current intelligence analyses essential to foreign policy determination and execution. Through its Office of Research, the Bureau maintains liaison with cultural and educational institutions and oversees contract research and organizes conferences on foreign affairs subjects of high interest to policymakers.

For further information, call 202–647–1080.

International Narcotics and Law Enforcement Affairs The Bureau of International Narcotics and Law Enforcement Affairs is responsible for developing, coordinating, and implementing international narcotics control and anticrime assistance activities of the Department of State as authorized under sections 481 and 482 of the Foreign Assistance Act of 1961, as amended (22 U.S.C. 2291, 2292). It is the principal point of contact and provides advice on international narcotics control matters for the Office of Management and Budget, the National Security Council, and the White House Office of National Drug Control Policy in ensuring implementation of U.S. policy in international narcotics matters.

The Bureau provides guidance on narcotics control and anticrime matters to chiefs of missions and directs narcotics control coordinators at posts abroad; communicates or authorizes communication, as appropriate with foreign governments, on drug control and anticrime matters including negotiating, concluding, and terminating agreements relating to international narcotics control and anticrime programs

as authorized by section 1(g)(3) of State Department Delegation of Authority No. 145 of February 4, 1980.

For further information, call 202–776–8750. Fax, 202–776–8775.

International Organization Affairs The Bureau of International Organization Affairs provides guidance and support for United States participation in international organizations and conferences. It leads in the development, coordination, and implementation of United States multilateral policy. The Bureau formulates and implements United States policy toward international organizations, with particular emphasis on those organizations which make up the United Nations system.

For further information, call 202–647–6400.

Legal Advisor The Office of the Legal Advisor furnishes advice on all legal issues, domestic and international, arising in the course of the Department's work. This includes assisting Department principals and policy officers in formulating and implementing the foreign affairs policies of the United States, promoting the development of international law and its institutions as a fundamental element of those policies, and managing the Department and the Foreign Service.

For further information, call 202–647–8323. Fax, 202–736–7508.

Medical Services The Office of Medical Services develops, manages, and staffs a worldwide primary health care system for U.S. citizen employees, and their eligible dependents, residing overseas. Agencies which participate in this medical program include the Department of State, the U.S. Information Agency, the U.S. Agency for International Development, and over 48 other foreign affairs agencies and offices. In support of its overseas operations, the Office approves and monitors the medical evacuation of patients, conducts pre-employment and in-service physical examinations, and provides clinical referral and advisory services. Domestically, the Office offers occupational health care, as well as numerous health education and health maintenance programs.

For further information, call 202–647–3617.

Consular Affairs The Bureau of Consular Affairs, under the direction of the Assistant Secretary, is responsible for the administration and enforcement of the provisions of the immigration and nationality laws, insofar as they concern the Department and the Foreign Service, for the issuance of passports and visas and related services, and for the protection and welfare of American citizens and interests abroad. Approximately 6 million passports a year are issued by the Passport Office of the Bureau, which has agencies in Boston, Chicago, Honolulu, Houston, Los Angeles, Miami, New Orleans, New York, Philadelphia, San Francisco, Seattle, Stamford, and Washington, DC.

For further information, see Sources of Information.

Political-Military Affairs The Bureau of Political-Military Affairs provides guidance and coordinates policy formulation on national security issues, including: nonproliferation of weapons of mass destruction and missile technology; nuclear and conventional arms control; defense relations and security assistance; complex contingency operations and consequence management of weapons of mass destruction incidents; and export controls. It acts as the Department's primary liaison with the Department of Defense. The Bureau also participates in all major arms control, nonproliferation, and other security-related negotiations.

The Bureau's major activities are designed to further U.S. national security objectives by: stabilizing regional military balances through negotiations and security assistance; negotiating reductions in global inventories of weapons of mass destruction and curbing their proliferation; maintaining global access for U.S. military forces; managing humanitarian assistance and demining programs; inhibiting adversaries' access to militarily

significant technologies; and promoting responsible U.S. defense trade.

For further information, call 202–647–6968.

Protocol The Chief of Protocol is the principal adviser to the U.S. Government, the President, the Vice President, and the Secretary of State on matters of diplomatic procedure governed by law or international custom and practice. The Office is responsible for:

—visits of foreign chiefs of state, heads of government, and other high officials to the United States;

—organizing credential presentations of newly arrived Ambassadors to the President and to the Secretary of State.

—operation of the President's guest house, Blair House;

—delegations representing the President at official ceremonies abroad;

—conduct of official ceremonial functions and public events;

—official interpretation of the Order of Precedence;

—conducting an outreach program of cultural enrichment and substantive briefings of the Diplomatic Corps;

—accreditation of over 100,000 embassy, consular, international organization, and other foreign government personnel, members of their families, and domestics throughout the United States;

—determining entitlement to diplomatic or consular immunity;

—publication of diplomatic and consular lists;

—resolution of problems arising out of diplomatic or consular immunity such as legal and police matters; and

—approving the opening of embassy and consular offices in conjunction with the Office of Foreign Missions.

For further information, call 202–647–2663. Fax, 202–647–1560.

Oceans, Environment, and Science The Bureau of Oceans, Environment, and Science (OES) serves as the foreign policy focal point for international oceans, environmental, and scientific efforts. OES projects, protects, and promotes U.S. global interests in these areas by articulating U.S. foreign policy, encouraging international cooperation, and negotiating treaties and other instruments of international law. The Bureau serves as the principal adviser to the Secretary of State on international environment, science, and technology matters and takes the lead in coordinating and brokering diverse interests in the interagency process, where the development of international policies or the negotiation and implementation of relevant international agreements are concerned. The Bureau seeks to promote the peaceful exploitation of outer space, protect public health from reemerging infectious diseases, encourage government to government scientific cooperation, and prevent the destruction and degradation of the planet's natural resources and the global environment.

For further information, call 202–647–0978. Fax, 202–647–0217.

Population, Refugees, and Migration The Bureau of Population, Refugees, and Migration (PRM) has primary responsibility for formulating U.S. policies on population, refugees, and migration and for administering U.S. refugee assistance and admissions programs. PRM administers and monitors U.S. contributions to multilateral organizations and nongovernmental organizations to provide assistance and protection to refugees abroad. The Bureau oversees the annual admissions of refugees to the United States for permanent resettlement, working closely with the Immigration and Naturalization Service, the Department of Health and Human Services, and various State and private voluntary agencies. PRM coordinates U.S. international population policy and promotes its goals through bilateral and multilateral cooperation. It works closely with the U.S. Agency for International Development, which administers U.S. international population programs. The Bureau also coordinates U.S. international migration policy within the U.S. Government and through bilateral and multilateral diplomacy.

For further information, call 202–663–1071. Internet, http://www.state.gov/www/global/prm/ index.html/.

Public Affairs The Bureau of Public Affairs directs public affairs activities in the Department and provides information about the goals, developments, and implementation of U.S. foreign policy to the American people. The Assistant Secretary for Public Affairs serves as the principal adviser to the Secretary, other senior Department officials, and other U.S. Government agencies on all public affairs, media relations, and information aspects of the Department's responsibilities to the U.S. public. The Bureau also serves as a liaison between the Department and State and local government officials.

For further information, call 202–647–6575.

Foreign Service

To a great extent the future of our country depends on the relations we have with other countries, and those relations are conducted principally by the United States Foreign Service. Presently, representatives at 164 Embassies, 12 missions, 1 U.S. liaison office, 1 U.S. interests section, 66 consulates general, 14 consulates, 3 branch offices, and 45 consular agencies throughout the world report to the State Department on the multitude of foreign developments that have a bearing on the welfare and security of the American people. These trained representatives provide the President and the Secretary of State with much of the raw material from which foreign policy is made and with the recommendations that help shape it.

The Ambassador is the personal representative of the President and reports to the President through the Secretary of State. Ambassadors have full responsibility for implementation of U.S. foreign policy by any and all U.S. Government personnel within their country of assignment, except those under military commands. Their responsibilities include negotiating agreements between the United States and the host country, explaining and disseminating official U.S. policy, and maintaining cordial relations with that country's government and people.

A listing of Foreign Service posts, together with addresses and telephone numbers and key personnel, appears in *Key Officers of Foreign Service Posts— Guide for Business Representatives,* which is for sale by the Superintendent of Documents, Government Printing Office, Washington, DC 20402.

United States Diplomatic Offices— Foreign Service

(C: Consular Office; N: No Embassy or Consular Office)

Country/Embassy	Ambassador
Albania/Tirana	Marisa R. Lino
Algeria/Algiers	Cameron R. Hume
Angola/Luanda	Donald K. Steinberg
Antigua and Barbuda/St. John's (N).	Jeanette W. Hyde
Argentina/Buenos Aires	(Vacancy)
Armenia/Yerevan	Peter Tomsen
Australia/Canberra	Genta Hawkins Holmes
Austria/Vienna	Kathryn W. Hall
Azerbaijan/Baku	Stanley T. Escudero
Bahamas/Nassau	Sidney Williams
Bahrain/Manama	Johnny Young
Bangladesh/Dhaka	John C. Holzman
Barbados/Bridgetown	Jeanette W. Hyde
Belarus/Minsk	Daniel W. Speckhard
Belgium/Brussels	Alan J. Blinken
Belize/Belize City	Carolyn Curiel
Benin/Cotonou	John M. Yates
Bolivia/La Paz	Donna J. Hrinak
Bosnia and Herzegovina/Sarajevo.	Richard D. Kauzlarich
Botswana/Gaborone	Robert Krueger
Brazil/Brasilia	Melvyn Levitsky
Brunei Darussalam/Bandar Seri Begawan.	Glen R. Rase
Bulgaria/Sofia	Avis T. Bohlen
Burkina Faso/Ouagadougou	Sharon P. Wilkinson
Burundi/Bujumbura	Morris N. Hughes, Jr.
Cambodia/Phnom Penh	Kenneth M. Quinn
Cameroon/Yaounde	Charles H. Twining
Canada/Ottawa	Gordon Giffen
Cape Verde/Praia	Lawrence N. Benedict
Central African Republic/Bangui	Mosina H. Jordan
Chad/N'Djamena	David C. Halsted
Chile/Santiago	Gabriel Guerra-Mondragon
China, People's Republic of/Beijing.	Jim Sasser
Colombia/Bogota	Myles R.R. Frechette
Comoros/Moroni (N)	Harold W. Geisel
Congo, Democratic Republic of the (formerly Zaire)/Kinshasa.	Daniel H. Simpson
Congo, Republic of/Brazzaville	Aubrey Hooks
Costa Rica/San Jose	Thomas J. Dodd

United States Diplomatic Offices— Foreign Service—Continued

(C: Consular Office; N: No Embassy or Consular Office)

Country/Embassy	Ambassador
Cote d'Ivoire/Abidjan	Lannon Walker
Croatia/Zagreb	William D. Montgomery
Cuba/Havana (U.S. Interests Section).	Michael G. Kozak
Cyprus/Nicosia	Kenneth C. Brill
Czech Republic/Prague	Jenonne R. Walker
Denmark/Copenhagen	Edward E. Elson
Djibouti, Republic of/Djibouti	Lange Schermerhorn
Dominica/Roseau (N)	Jeanette W. Hyde
Dominican Republic/Santo Domingo.	(Vacancy)
Ecuador/Quito	Leslie M. Alexander
Egypt/Cairo	Daniel C. Kurtzer
El Salvador/San Salvador	Anne W. Patterson
Equatorial Guinea/Malabo	Charles H. Twining
Eritrea/Asmara	(Vacancy)
Estonia/Tallinn	(Vacancy)
Ethiopia/Addis Ababa	David H. Shinn
Fiji/Suva	(Vacancy)
Finland/Helsinki	(Vacancy)
France/Paris	Felix Rohatyn
Gabonese Republic/Libreville	Elizabeth Raspolic
Gambia/Banjul	Gerald W. Scott
Georgia/Tbilisi	William H. Courtney
Germany/Bonn	John C. Kornblum
Ghana/Accra	Edward Brynn
Greece/Athens	R. Nicholas Burns
Grenada/St. George (N)	Jeanette W. Hyde
Guatemala/Guatemala	Donald J. Planty
Guinea/Conakry	Tibor P. Nagy, Jr.
Guinea-Bissau/Bissau	Peggy Blackford
Guyana/Georgetown	James F. Mack
Haiti/Port-au-Prince	Timothy M. Carney
Holy See/Vatican City	Corinne Claiborne Boggs
Honduras/Tegucigalpa	James F. Creagan
Hong Kong/Hong Kong (C)	Richard Boucher
Hungary/Budapest	Peter F. Tufo
Iceland/Reykjavik	Day Mount
India/New Delhi	Richard F. Celeste
Indonesia/Jakarta	J. Stapleton Roy
Ireland/Dublin	Jean K. Smith
Israel/Tel Aviv	Edward S. Walker, Jr.
Italy/Rome	Thomas M. Foglietta
Jamaica/Kingston	Jerome G. Cooper
Japan/Tokyo	Thomas S. Foley
Jerusalem	John E. Herbst
Jordan/Amman	Wesley W. Egan
Kazakstan/Almaty	A. Elizabeth Jones
Kenya/Nairobi	Prudence Bushnell
Kiribati/Tarawa (N)	Joan M. Plaisted
Korea/Seoul	Steven W. Bosworth
Kuwait/Kuwait	James A. Larocco
Kyrgyz Republic/Bishkek	Anne Marie Sigmund
Laos/Vientiane	Wendy Chamberlin
Latvia/Riga	Larry C. Napper
Lebanon/Beirut	Richard H. Jones
Lesotho/Maseru	Bismarck Myrick
Liberia/Monrovia	William B. Milam
Lithuania/Vilnius	Keith C. Smith
Luxembourg/Luxembourg	Clay Constantinou
Madagascar/Antananarivo	(Vacancy)
Malawi/Lilongwe	Amelia E. Shippy
Malaysia/Kuala Lumpur	John L. Malott
Maldives/Male (N)	Shaun E. Donnelly
Mali/Bamako	David P. Rawson
Malta/Valletta	Kathryn L. Haycock-Proffitt
Marshall Islands/Majuro	Joan M. Plaisted
Mauritania/Nouakchott	Timberlake Foster
Mauritius/Port Louis	Harold W. Geisel
Mexico/Mexico City	(Vacancy)

United States Diplomatic Offices—Foreign Service—Continued

(C: Consular Office; N: No Embassy or Consular Office)

Country/Embassy	Ambassador
Micronesia/Kolonia	(Vacancy)
Moldova/Chisinau	John T. Stewart
Mongolia/Ulaanbaatar	Alphonse F. La Porta
Morocco/Rabat	Edward M. Gabriel
Mozambique/Maputo	Brian D. Curran
Namibia/Windhoek	George F. Ward, Jr.
Nauru/Yaren (N)	(Vacancy)
Nepal/Kathmandu	Ralph Frank
Netherlands/The Hague	K. Terry Dornbush
New Zealand/Wellington	Josiah H. Beeman
Nicaragua/Managua	Lino Gutierrez
Niger/Niamey	Charles O. Cecil
Nigeria/Abuja	William H. Twaddell
Norway/Oslo	David B. Hermelin
Oman/Muscat	Frances D. Cook
Pakistan/Islamabad	Thomas W. Simons, Jr.
Panama/Panama	William J. Hughes
Papua New Guinea/Port Moresby.	Arma Jane Karaer
Paraguay/Asuncion	Maura Harty
Peru/Lima	Dennis C. Jett
Philippines/Manila	Thomas Hubbard
Poland/Warsaw	Daniel Fried
Portugal/Lisbon	Gerald S. McGowan
Qatar/Doha	Patrick N. Theros
Romania/Bucharest	James C. Rosapepe
Russian Federation/Moscow	James F. Collins
Rwanda/Kigali	Robert E. Gribbin III
St. Kitts and Nevis (N)	Jeanette W. Hyde
St. Lucia/Castries (N)	Jeanette W. Hyde
St. Vincent and the Grenadines (N).	Jeanette W. Hyde
Sao Tome and Principe/Sao Tome (N).	Elizabeth Raspolic
Saudi Arabia/Riyadh	Wyche Fowler, Jr.
Senegal/Dakar	Dane Farnsworth Smith, Jr.
Seychelles/Victoria	Harold W. Geisel
Sierra Leone/Freetown	John L. Hirsch
Singapore/Singapore	Steven J. Green
Slovak Republic/Bratislava	Ralph R. Johnson
Slovenia/Ljubljana	Victor Jackovich
Solomon Islands/Honiara	Arma Jane Karaer
South Africa/Pretoria	James A. Joseph
Spain/Madrid	(Vacancy)
Sri Lanka/Colombo	Shaun E. Donnelly
Sudan/Khartoum	(Vacancy)

United States Diplomatic Offices—Foreign Service—Continued

(C: Consular Office; N: No Embassy or Consular Office)

Country/Embassy	Ambassador
Suriname/Paramaribo	Dennis K. Hays
Swaziland/Mbabane	Alan R. McKee
Sweden/Stockholm	Lyndon L. Olson, Jr.
Switzerland/Bern	Madeleine M. Kunin
Syrian Arab Republic/Damascus	Christopher W.S. Ross
Tajikistan/Dushanbe	R. Grant Smith
Tanzania/Dar es Salaam	(Vacancy)
Thailand/Bangkok	William H. Itoh
Togo/Lome	Brenda Schoonover
Tonga/Nuku'alofa (N)	(Vacancy)
Trinidad and Tobago/Port-of-Spain.	Edward E. Shumaker III
Tunisia/Tunis	Robin L. Raphel
Turkey/Ankara	Mark R. Barris
Turkmenistan/Ashgabat	Michael W. Cotter
Tuvalu/Funafuti (N)	(Vacancy)
Uganda/Kampala	Nancy Jo Powell
Ukraine/Kiev	Steven K. Pifer
United Arab Emirates/Abu Dhabi	David C. Litt
United Kingdom/London	Philip Lader
Uruguay/Montevideo	Christopher C. Ashby
Uzbekistan/Tashkent	Joseph A. Presel
Vanuatu/Port Vila (N)	Arma Jane Karaer
Venezuela/Caracas	John F. Maisto
Western Samoa/Apia	Josiah H. Beeman
Yemen/Sanaa	Barbara K. Bodine
Zambia/Lusaka	Arlene Render
Zimbabwe/Harare	Tom McDonald

United States Permanent Diplomatic Missions to International Organizations

Organization	Ambassador
European Union/Brussels	A. Vernon Weaver
North Atlantic Treaty Organization/Brussels.	Alexander R. Vershbow
Organization of American States/Washington, DC.	Victor Marrero
Organization for Economic Co-operation and Development/Paris.	Amy L. Bondurant
United Nations/Geneva	George E. Moose
United Nations/New York	Bill Richardson
United Nations/Vienna	John B. Ritch III

Sources of Information

Audiovisual Materials The Bureau of Consular Affairs has a 12-minute videotape on the safety of international travel. "Traveling Abroad More Safely" provides general practical advice to U.S. citizen travelers on avoiding the hazards of foreign travel. It includes steps to take prior to departure, ways to protect against theft and legal problems, and ways U.S. embassies and consulates can assist U.S. citizens who encounter difficulty abroad. The tape is available for $9 in VHS and $12.50 in 3/4-inch format, plus a $3 mailing and handling fee from Video Transfer, Inc., 5710 Arundel Avenue, Rockville, MD 20852. Phone, 301–881–0270. Fax, 301–770–9131.

Contracts General inquiries may be directed to the Office of Acquisitions (A/OPR/ACQ), Department of State, Washington, DC 20520. Phone, 703–875–6060. Fax, 703–875–6085.

Diplomatic and Official Passports Department employees may use diplomatic and official passports only as long as they are retained in the position or status for which originally issued. Section 51.4 of title 22 of the *Code of Federal Regulations* states that such passports must be returned upon termination of the bearer's diplomatic or official status.

In accordance with the Department's *Foreign Affairs Manual* (3 FAM 784), it is the responsibility of administrative officers to ensure that Form DS–8A includes a record of the disposition of passports issued to separating or retiring employees and their dependents. This includes all diplomatic and official passports, as well as any tourist passports for which the employee has been reimbursed by the Department.

Because of the possibility of misuse of these documents, it is important that all offices establish and maintain effective control over passport use. These passports are normally destroyed by Passport Services; however, they may be canceled and returned as mementos if requested.

Diplomatic passports may not be used by employees for strictly personal travel. Regulations permit their use for incidental personal travel related to an official assignment if the host government does not object. However, if employees or their dependents prefer to travel on a regular tourist passport in connection with official travel, they may apply by paying the regular passport fees and claiming reimbursement on their travel voucher.

Inquiries on these matters should be directed to Passport Services, Special Issuance Agency. Phone, 202–955–0200.

Electronic Access The Department's Bureau of Public Affairs, Office of Public Communication, coordinates the dissemination of public electronic information for the Department. The main Web site at http://www.state.gov/ and the Secretary's Web site at http://secretary.state.gov/ provide comprehensive, up-to-date information on foreign policy, travel and consular information, support for U.S. businesses,

careers, the counterterrorism rewards program, and much more.

The State Department Electronic Reading Room at http://foia.state.gov/ uses new information technologies to enable access to unique historical records of international significance which have been made available to the public under the Freedom of Information Act or as a special collection.

Employment Inquiries about employment in the Foreign Service should be directed to: PER/REE/REC, P.O. Box 9317, Arlington, VA 22210. Phone, 703–875–7490. Inquiries about civil service positions in the Department of State should be directed to: PER/CSP/POD, P.O. Box 18657, Washington, DC 20036–8657. The Department's Civil Service Employment Information Office is located inside the D Street north lobby entrance of the Department of State building, Washington, DC. The Civil Service Personnel Office provides a 24-hour job information line. Phone, 202–647–7284.

Freedom of Information Act and Privacy Act Requests Requests from the public for Department of State records should be addressed to the Director, Office of IRM Programs and Service, Department of State, Room 1512, 2201 C Street NW., Washington, DC 20520–1512. Phone, 202–647–8300. Individuals are requested to indicate on the outside of the envelope the statute under which they are requesting access: FOIA REQUEST or PRIVACY REQUEST.

Any identifiable Department of State document can be requested under the Freedom of Information Act (5 U.S.C. 552). Requesters should provide as much identifying information as possible about the document, such as subject matter, timeframe, originator of the information, or any other helpful data, to assist the Department in locating it. Please include your daytime telephone number.

Only persons who are U.S. citizens or aliens who are lawfully admitted to the United States for permanent residence can request information under the Privacy Act (5 U.S.C. 552a). Under this act, individuals may request access to records that are maintained under the individual's name or some other personally identifiable symbol. Descriptions of record systems from which documents can be retrieved by the individual's name are published in the *Federal Register*, copies of which are available from the Director, Office of IRM Programs and Services. To expedite processing of requests, individuals should specify the system of records they wish to have searched and should provide the following identifying information: full name; aliases (if any); date and place of birth; and circumstances, including approximate time period, which would have led to the creation of the record.

A public reading room, where unclassified and declassified documents may be inspected, is located in the Department of State, 2201 C Street NW., Washington, DC. Phone, 202–647–8300. Directions to the reading room may be obtained from receptionists at public entrances to the Department.

Additional information about the Department's FOIA program can be found on the FOIA Electronic Reading Room Web site at http://foia.state.gov/.

Missing Persons, Emergencies, Deaths of Americans Abroad For information concerning missing persons, emergencies, travel warnings, overseas voting, judicial assistance, and arrests or deaths of Americans abroad, contact the Office of American Citizens Services and Crisis Management, Department of State. Phone, 202–647–5225. Fax, 202–647–3732. Fax-on-demand, 202–647–3000.

Internet, http://travel.state.gov/. Correspondence should be directed to: Overseas Citizens Services, Bureau of Consular Affairs, Department of State, Washington, DC 20520.

Inquiries regarding international parental child abduction or adoption of foreign children by private U.S. citizens should be directed to the Office of Children's Issues, CA/OCS/CI, Room 4811, Department of State, Washington, DC 20520. Phone, 202–647–2688. Fax, 202–647–2835. Internet, http://travel.state.gov/.

Passports Passport information is available through the Internet, at http://travel.state.gov/. For recorded general passport information, contact any of the Regional Passport Agencies at the telephone numbers listed in the following table. For passport assistance and information, you may call the National Passport Information Center (phone, 900–225–5674; TDD, 900–225–7778) and you will be charged 35 cents per minute to listen to automated messages and $1.05 per minute to speak with an operator. You may also call the National Passport Information Center using a major credit card at a flat rate of $4.95 (phone, 888–362–8668; TDD, 888–498–3648). These rates are subject to change. Correspondence should be directed to the appropriate Regional Agency or the Correspondence Branch, Passport Services, Room 510, 1111 Nineteenth Street NW., Washington, DC 20524.

Regional Passport Agencies

City	Address	Telephone
Boston, MA	Thomas P. O'Neill Federal Bldg., 02222	617–565–6990
Chicago, IL	Federal Bldg., 60604	312–341–6020
Honolulu, HI	Federal Bldg., 96850	808–522–8283
Houston, TX	1919 Smith St., 77002	713–209–3153
Los Angeles, CA	11000 Wilshire Blvd., 90024–3615	310–575–5700
Miami, FL	Federal Office Bldg., 33130	305–539–3600
National Passport Center	31 Rochester Ave., Portsmouth, NH 03801–2900	603–334–0500
New Orleans, LA	701 Loyola Ave., 70113	504–589–6161
New York, NY	376 Hudson St., 10014	212–206–3500
Philadelphia, PA	Federal Bldg., 19106	215–597–7480
San Francisco, CA	95 Hawthorne St., 94105–3901	415–538–2700
Seattle, WA	Federal Bldg., 98174	206–808–5700
Stamford, CT	1 Landmark Sq., 06901	203–325–4401
Washington, DC	1111 19th St. NW., 20524	202–647–0518

Publications The Department's Bureau of Public Affairs produces a variety of

publications on the Department and foreign policy, including the official U.S.

documentary series, *Foreign Relations of the United States,* and two publications on U.S. foreign policy, *Dispatch* and *Background Notes.*

The series *Foreign Relations of the United States,* published since 1861 in over 300 volumes, constitutes the official documentary record of U.S. foreign policy. It is the most extensive and most near-current publication of diplomatic papers in the world. The Office of the Historian has completed the 75 print volumes and microfiche supplements documenting the foreign policy of the Eisenhower administration (1953–1960). Publication of 32 print volumes and supplements on the foreign policy of the Kennedy administration (1961–1963) is nearing completion. Of 34 volumes documenting the Johnson administration (1964–1968), 8 were published by 1997.

U.S. Foreign Affairs on CD–ROM provides a wealth of foreign policy information such as *Dispatch* magazine (the monthly foreign policy magazine issued by the Department of State), *Background Notes,* speeches and testimonies by senior State Department officials, reports to Congress, miscellaneous policy publications, and daily press briefings in a searchable format. Single copies are available from the Superintendent of Documents, U.S. Government Printing Office, P.O. Box 371954, Pittsburgh, PA 15250–7954. Phone, 202–512–1800. Fax, 202–512–2233. Payments can be made by check (payable to the Superintendent of Documents), GPO Deposit Account, VISA, or MasterCard.

Reading Room To review declassified Department documents, contact the receptionists at the public entrance to the Department of State, 2201 C Street NW., Washington, DC, for the specific location. Phone, 202–647–8484.

Telephone Directory The Department's telephone directory is available for sale by the Superintendent of Documents, Government Printing Office, Washington, DC 20402.

Tips for U.S. Travelers Abroad The following pamphlets from the Bureau of Consular Affairs are posted on the Internet at http://travel.state.gov/ and are for sale for $1 (except where noted) by the Superintendent of Documents, U.S. Government Printing Office, Washington, DC 20402:

Travel Warning on Drugs Abroad contains important facts on the potential dangers of being arrested for illegal drugs abroad and the type of assistance that U.S. consular officers can and cannot provide. This booklet is free from the Department of State, Consular Affairs/Public Affairs Staff, Room 6831, Washington, DC 20520.

Travel Tips for Older Americans contains basic information on passports, currency, health, aid for serious problems, and other useful travel tips for senior citizens.

Your Trip Abroad ($1.25) contains basic information on passports, vaccinations, unusual travel requirements, dual nationality, drugs, modes of travel, customs, legal requirements, and many other topics for the American tourist, business representative, or student traveling overseas.

A Safe Trip Abroad contains helpful precautions to minimize one's chances of becoming a victim of terrorism and also provides other safety tips.

Tips for Americans Residing Abroad contains advice for more than 2 million Americans living in foreign countries.

Regional *Tips for Travelers* cover customs, currency regulations, dual nationality, and other local conditions. Currently available are: *Tips for Travelers to Canada; Tips for Travelers to the Caribbean; Tips for Travelers to Mexico; Tips for Travelers to the Middle East and North Africa* ($1.50); *Tips for Travelers to the People's Republic of China; Tips for Travelers to Russia and the Newly Independent States; Tips for Travelers to South Asia; Tips for Travelers to Central and South America;* and *Tips for Travelers to Sub-Saharan Africa* ($1.50).

Foreign Entry Requirements contains visa and other entry requirements of foreign countries. *Passports: Applying for Them the Easy Way* contains information on where, how, and when to apply for passports. Order these from the Consumer Information Center, Pueblo, CO 81009.

Visas To obtain information on visas for foreigners wishing to enter the United States, call 202–663–1225. Internet, http://travel.state.gov/.

For further information concerning the Department of State, contact the Office of Public Communication, Public Information Service, Bureau of Public Affairs, Department of State, Washington, DC 20520. Phone, 202–647–6575. Fax, 202–647–7120. Internet, http://www.state.gov/.

DEPARTMENT OF TRANSPORTATION

400 Seventh Street SW., Washington, DC 20590
Phone, 202–366–4000. Internet, http://www.dot.gov/.

SECRETARY OF TRANSPORTATION	RODNEY E. SLATER
Chief of Staff	MICHAEL P. HUERTA
Deputy Chiefs of Staff	JERRY MALONE, SUZANNE SULLIVAN
White House Liaison	(VACANCY)
Special Assistant to the Secretary	(VACANCY)
Deputy Secretary	MORTIMER L. DOWNEY
Director of Drug and Alcohol Policy and Compliance	MARY BERNSTEIN
Associate Deputy Secretary and Director, Office of Intermodalism	JOHN C. HORSLEY
Deputy Director	RICHARD M. BITER
Director, Executive Secretariat	JAMIE SHELL WILLIAMS
Chairman, Board of Contract Appeals	THADDEUS V. WARE
Director of Civil Rights	RONALD A. STROMAN
Director of Small and Disadvantaged Business Utilization	LUZ A. HOPEWELL
Director of Intelligence and Security	REAR ADM. PAUL J. PLUTA, USCG
Chief Information Officer	MICHAEL P. HUERTA, *Acting*
Director, Information Resource Management	EUGENE K. TAYLOR, JR.
Inspector General	KENNETH M. MEAD
Deputy Inspector General	RAYMOND J. DECARLI
Senior Counsel to the Inspector General	ROGER P. WILLIAMS
Assistant Inspector General for Auditing	LAWRENCE H. WEINTROB
Deputy Assistant Inspector General for Auditing	(VACANCY)
Assistant Inspector General for Investigations	TODD J. ZINSER
Deputy Assistant Inspector General for Investigations	DONALD L. WISEMAN
General Counsel	NANCY E. MCFADDEN
Deputy General Counsel	ROSALIND A. KNAPP
Special Counsel	STEVEN R. OKUN
Assistant General Counsel for Environmental, Civil Rights, and General Law	ROBERTA D. GABEL
Deputy Assistants	JAMES R. DANN, DAVID K. TOCHEN
Patent Counsel	OTTO M. WILDENSTEINER
Chief, Freedom of Information Act Division	(VACANCY)
Assistant General Counsel for International Law	DONALD H. HORN
Deputy Assistant	JOSEPH A. BROOKS
Assistant General Counsel for Litigation	PAUL M. GEIER
Deputy Assistant	DALE C. ANDREWS
Assistant General Counsel for Legislation	THOMAS W. HERLIHY
Deputy Assistant	JANE B. DECELL
Assistant General Counsel for Regulation and Enforcement	NEIL R. EISNER

404

Deputy Assistant	ROBERT C. ASHBY
Chairman, Board for Correction of Military Records	ROBERT H. JOOST
Deputy Chairman	DOROTHY J. ULMER
Assistant General Counsel for Aviation Enforcement and Proceedings	SAMUEL PODBERESKY
Deputy Assistant	DAYTON LEHMAN, JR.
Assistant Director for Aviation Consumer Protection	HOYTE B. DECKER, JR.
Assistant Secretary for Transportation Policy	(VACANCY)
Deputy Assistant Secretaries	JOSEPH F. CANNY, JOHN N. LIEBER
Director of Environment, Energy, and Safety	DONALD R. TRILLING
Director of Economics	(VACANCY)
Assistant Secretary for Aviation and International Affairs	CHARLES A. HUNNICUTT
Deputy Assistant Secretaries	PATRICK V. MURPHY, JR., (VACANCY)
Director of International Transportation and Trade	BERNARD GAILLARD
Director of International Aviation	PAUL GRETCH
Director of Aviation Analysis	JOHN COLEMAN
Director of Aviation and International Economics	JAMES CRAUN
Assistant Secretary for Budget and Programs and Chief Financial Officer	(VACANCY)
Deputy Assistant Secretary	PETER J. BASSO
Deputy Chief Financial Officer	DAVID K. KLEINBERG
Director of Budget and Program Performance	BEVERLY PHETO
Director of Financial Management	EILEEN T. POWELL
Assistant Secretary for Administration	MELISSA J. SPILLENKOTHEN
Director of Human Resource Management	GLENDA M. TATE
Director of Security and Administrative Management	LEE A. PRIVETT, *Acting*
Director of Acquisition and Grant Management	DAVID J. LITMAN
Director of Hearings	ROY J. MAURER
Assistant Secretary for Governmental Affairs	STEVEN O. PALMER
Deputy Assistant Secretary	JOHN C. HORSLEY
Director of Congressional Affairs	NADINE HAMILTON, *Acting*
Director of Intergovernmental Affairs	HAROLD GIST, *Acting*
Assistant to the Secretary and Director of Public Affairs	STEVEN J. AKEY
Deputy Director of Public Affairs	WILLIAM H. SCHULZ
Director, Transportation Administrative Service Center	GEORGE C. FIELDS
Principal, Customer Service	PATRICIA PARRISH
Principal, Business Support	ED HANSEN
Principal, Worklife Wellness	LINDA RHOADS
Principal, Facilities Service Center	JANET KRAUS
Principal, Learning and Development	FREDERICA BURNETT
Principal, Space Management	EUGENE SPRUILL
Principal, Security Operations	JEFF JOHNS
Principal, Information Services	PATRICIA PROSPERI
Principal, Information Systems Management Consulting	DAVID CHAO

Principal, Information Technology
  Operations   HOLLY TWINING
Principal, Acquisition Services   RICHARD LIEBER
Principal, Human Resource Services   TERRY SMITH

UNITED STATES COAST GUARD

2100 Second Street SE., Washington, DC 20593–0001
Phone, 202–267–2229. Internet, http://www.uscg.mil/.

Commandant   ADM. JAMES M. LOY, USCG
Vice Commandant   VICE ADM. JAMES C. CARD, USCG
  Chaplain   CAPT. LEROY GILBERT, USCG
  International Affairs Director/Foreign Policy   GERARD P. YOEST
    Adviser
  Chief Administrative Law Judge   JOSEPH N. INGOLIA
  Chairman, Marine Safety Council   REAR ADM. JOHN E. SHKOR, USCG
  Chief, Congressional Affairs Staff   CAPT. JEFFREY J. HATHAWAY, USCG
  Chief, Public Affairs Staff   CAPT. ERIC FAGERHOLM, USCG
Chief of Staff   VICE ADM. TIMOTHY W. JOSIAH,
                                                       USCG
  Deputy Chief of Staff   CAPT. TIMOTHY L. TERRIBERRY,
                                                       USCG
Director of Resources   REAR ADM. THAD W. ALLEN, USCG
Director of Finance and Procurement   WILLIAM H. CAMPBELL
Assistant Commandant for Acquisition   REAR ADM. ROY J. CASTO, USCG
Assistant Commandant for Systems   REAR ADM. JOHN T. TOZZI, USCG
Chief, Office of Civil Rights   WALTER R. SOMERVILLE
Medical Adviser to the Commandant and   REAR ADM. JOYCE M. JOHNSON,
  Director of Health and Safety   USPHS
Chief Counsel   REAR ADM. JOHN E. SHKOR, USCG
Assistant Commandant for Marine Safety   REAR ADM. ROBERT C. NORTH,
                                                       USCG
Assistant Commandant for Operations   REAR ADM. ERNEST R. RIUTTA,
                                                       USCG
Assistant Commandant for Human Resources   REAR ADM. FRED L. AMES, USCG
Director of Personnel Management   (VACANCY)
Director of Reserve and Training   REAR ADM. THOMAS J. BARRETT,
                                                       USCG
Director of Information and Technology   REAR ADM. GEORGE N. NACCARA,
                                                       USCG

FEDERAL AVIATION ADMINISTRATION

800 Independence Avenue SW., Washington, DC 20591
Phone, 202–366–4000

Administrator   JANE F. GARVEY
Deputy Administrator   MONTE R. BELGER, *Acting*
Associate Administrator for Airports   SUSAN L. KURLAND
  Deputy Associate Administrator for Airports   QUENTIN S. TAYLOR
  Director of Airport Planning and   PAUL L. GALIS
    Programming
  Director of Airport Safety and Standards   DAVID L. BENNETT
Chief Counsel   NICHOLAS GARAUFIS
Associate Administrator for Civil Aviation   CATHAL L. FLYNN
  Security

Director of Civil Aviation Security Intelligence	PATRICK T. MCDONNELL
Director of Civil Aviation Security Operations	BRUCE R. BUTTERWORTH
Director of Civil Aviation Security Policy and Planning	ANTHONY FAINBERG
Assistant Administrator for Civil Rights	FANNY RIVERA
Associate Administrator for Commercial Space Transportation	PATRICIA GRACE SMITH, *Acting*
Assistant Administrator for Government and Industry Affairs	A. BRADLEY MIMS
Assistant Administrator for Policy, Planning, and International Aviation	LOUISE E. MAILLETT, *Acting*
Deputy Assistant Administrator for Policy, Planning, and International Aviation	LOUISE E. MAILLETT
Director of Aviation Policy and Plans	JOHN M. RODGERS
Director of Environment and Energy	JAMES D. ERICKSON
Director of International Aviation	JOAN W. BAUERLEIN
Assistant Administrator for Public Affairs	ELIOT BRENNER
Assistant Administrator for System Safety	CHRISTOPHER A. HART
Associate Administrator for Administration	WOODIE WOODWARD, *Acting*
Deputy Associate Administrator for Administration	RICHARD L. RODINE, *Acting*
Director of Financial Services	JOEL C. TAUB, *Acting*
Director of Flight Program Oversight	EDGAR C. FELL
Director of Business Information and Consultation	LAWRENCE COVINGTON
Director of Human Resource Management	CINDY MEDLOCK, *Acting*
Associate Administrator for Regulation and Certification	GUY S. GARDNER
Deputy Associate Administrator for Regulation and Certification	PEGGY M. GILLIGAN
Federal Air Surgeon	JON L. JORDAN
Director of Accident Investigation	DAVID F. THOMAS
Director, Aircraft Certification Service	THOMAS E. MCSWEENEY
Director, Flight Standards Service	THOMAS E. STUCKEY, *Acting*
Director of Rulemaking	JOSEPH A. HAWKINS
Associate Administrator for Air Traffic Services	RONALD E. MORGAN, *Acting*
Deputy Associate Administrator for Air Traffic Services	CARL B. SCHELLENBERG, *Acting*
Director, Air Traffic Service	JAMES H. WASHINGTON, *Acting*
Director, Air Traffic System Requirements Service	NEIL R. PLANZER
Director, Airway Facilities Service	STANLEY RIVERS
Director of System Capacity	CARL SCHELLENBERG
Director of Independent Operational Test and Evaluation	A. MARTIN PHILLIPS
Associate Administrator for Research and Acquisitions	DENNIS N. DEGAETANO, *Acting*
Deputy Associate Administrator for Research and Acquisitions	DENNIS N. DEGAETANO
Director of Acquisitions	GILBERT B. DEVEY
Director of Air Traffic Systems Development	EDWARD E. SEYMOUR
Director of Aviation Research	JAN BRECHT-CLARK, *Acting*

Director of Communication, Navigation, and Surveillance Systems	DANIEL P. SALVANO, *Acting*
Director of System Architecture and Investment Analysis	STEVEN ZAIDMAN
Director of Information Technology	THERON A. GRAY

FEDERAL HIGHWAY ADMINISTRATION
400 Seventh Street SW., Washington, DC 20590
Phone, 202–366–0660

Administrator	KENNETH R. WYKLE
Deputy Administrator	GLORIA J. JEFF
Executive Director	ANTHONY R. KANE
Chief Counsel	(VACANCY)
Deputy Chief Counsel	EDWARD V.A. KUSSY
Director of External Communications	(VACANCY)
Director of Civil Rights	EDWARD W. MORRIS, JR.
Director of Program Quality Coordination	FRED J. HEMPEL
Director of Intelligent Transportation Systems Joint Program Office	CHRISTINE M. JOHNSON
Associate Administrator for Policy	(VACANCY)
Director of Policy Development	MADELEINE S. BLOOM
Director of Highway Information Management	GARY E. MARING
Director of International Programs	KING W. GEE
Associate Administrator for Research and Development	ROBERT J. BETSOLD
Director of Engineering, Research, and Development	CHARLES J. NEMMERS
Director of Safety and Traffic Operations Research and Development	A. GEORGE OSTENSEN
Director of Research and Development Operations and Support	ROBERT J. KREKLAU
Associate Administrator for Program Development	THOMAS J. PTAK
Director of Engineering	HENRY H. RENTZ
Director of Environment and Planning	KEVIN E. HEANUE
Director of Real Estate Services	CYNTHIA BURBANK
Associate Administrator for Safety and System Applications	DENNIS C. JUDYCKI
Director of Highway Safety	MICHAEL F. TRENTACOSTE
Director of Traffic Management and Intelligent Transportation Systems Applications	SUSAN B. LAUFFER
Director of Technology Applications	JOSEPH S. TOOLE
Director of the National Highway Institute	MOGES AYELE
Associate Administrator for Motor Carriers	GEORGE L. REAGLE
Director of Motor Carrier Research and Standards	PAUL L. BRENNAN
Director of Motor Carrier Information Analysis	JOHN F. GRIMM
Director of Motor Carrier Planning and Customer Liaison	JILL L. HOCHMAN
Director of Motor Carrier Field Operations	CLINTON O. MAGBY

Director of Motor Carrier Safety and Technology	ROSE MCMURRAY
Associate Administrator for Administration	GEORGE S. MOORE, JR.
Deputy Associate Administrator for Administration	(VACANCY)
Director of Personnel and Training	JERRY A. HAWKINS
Director of Information and Management Services	MICHAEL J. VECCHIETTI
Director of Budget and Finance	FREDERICK G. WRIGHT
Director of Acquisition Management	(VACANCY)
Federal Lands Highway Program Administrator	(VACANCY)

FEDERAL RAILROAD ADMINISTRATION

400 Seventh Street SW., Washington, DC 20590
Phone, 202–366–4000. Internet, http://www.fra.dot.gov/.

Administrator	JOLENE M. MOLITORIS
Deputy Administrator	DONALD M. ITZKOFF
Chief of Staff	NORMA M. KRAYEM
Director, Office of Civil Rights	BERTHA L. JACKSON, *Acting*
Director, Office of Public Affairs	DAVID BOLGER
Chief Counsel	S. MARK LINDSEY
Deputy Chief Counsel	MICHAEL T. HALEY
Assistant Chief Counsel, General Law Division	ROBERT S. VERMUT
Assistant Chief Counsel, Safety Law Division	DANIEL C. SMITH
Associate Administrator for Administration and Finance	RAY ROGERS
Director, Office of Human Resources	MARGARET B. REID
Director, Office of Information Technology and Support Systems	MARIE S. SAVOY
Director, Office of Acquisition and Grants Services	ELAINE C. DUKE
Director, Office of Financial Services	GERALD SCHOENAUER
Director, Office of Budget	KATHRYN B. MURPHY
Associate Administrator for Policy and Program Development	(VACANCY)
Deputy Associate Administrator for Industry and Intermodal Policy	JANE H. BACHNER
Deputy Associate Administrator for Policy Systems	RAPHAEL KEDAR
Associate Administrator for Safety	GEORGE GAVALLA, *Acting*
Deputy Associate Administrators for Safety, Standards and Program Development	GRADY C. COTHEN
Deputy Associate Administrator for Safety Compliance and Program Implementation	MICHAEL J. LOGUE, *Acting*
Director, Office of Safety Assurance and Compliance	EDWARD R. ENGLISH
Director, Office of Safety Analysis	JOHN G. LEEDS
Associate Administrator for Railroad Development	JAMES T. MCQUEEN
Deputy Associate Administrator for Railroad Development	ARRIGO MONGINI

Director, Office of Passenger and Freight Services	ARRIGO MONGINI, *Acting*
Director, Northeast Corridor Program	MICHAEL SAUNDERS
Director, Office of Research and Development	STEVEN R. DITMEYER
DOT Contact, Transportation Test Center, Pueblo, CO	GUNARS SPONS

NATIONAL HIGHWAY TRAFFIC SAFETY ADMINISTRATION

400 Seventh Street SW., Washington, DC 20590
Phone, 202–366–9550

Administrator	RICARDO MARTINEZ
Deputy Administrator	PHILIP R. RECHT
Executive Director	DONALD C. BISCHOFF
Director, Executive Correspondence	LINDA DIVELBISS
Chief Counsel	JOHN WOMACK, *Acting*
Director, Office of Civil Rights	GEORGE B. QUICK
Director, Office of Public and Consumer Affairs	MICHAEL RUSSELL
Director, Office of International Harmonization	(VACANCY)
Director, Office of Intergovernmental Affairs	CHARLOTTE HRNCIR
Associate Administrator for Plans and Policy	WILLIAM H. WALSH, JR.
Director, Office of Strategic and Program Planning	(VACANCY)
Director, Office of Regulatory Analysis and Evaluation	JAMES F. SIMONS
Director, Office of Fiscal Services	(VACANCY)
Associate Administrator for Safety Performance Standards	L. ROBERT SHELTON
Director, Office of Crashworthiness Standards	JAMES HACKNEY
Director, Office of Crash Avoidance Standards	STEPHEN R. KRATZKE
Director, Office of Planning and Consumer Programs	NOBLE N. BOWIE
Associate Administrator for Research and Development	RAYMOND P. OWINGS
Director, Office of Crash Avoidance Research	JOSEPH N. KANIANTHRA
Director, Office of Crashworthiness Research	JOSEPH N. KANIANTHRA, *Acting*
Director, Vehicle Research and Test Center	MICHAEL MONK
Director, National Center for Statistics and Analysis	PATRICIA P. BRESLIN
Associate Administrator for Safety Assurance	KENNETH WEINSTEIN
Director, Office of Defects Investigation	KATHLEEN DeMETER
Director, Office of Vehicle Safety Compliance	MARILYNNE E. JACOBS
Associate Administrator for Traffic Safety Programs	JAMES NICHOLS, *Acting*
Director, Office of Communications and Outreach	SUSAN G. McLAUGHLIN
Director, Office of Research and Traffic Records	JAMES FELL, *Acting*

Director, Office of Traffic Injury Controls Program — MARILENA AMONI

Associate Administrator for State and Community Services — ADELE DERBY

Chief, Program Implementation Staff — JOHN OATES
Chief, Program Support Staff — MARLENE MARKINSON
Associate Administrator for Administration — HERMAN L. SIMMS
Director, Office of Human Resources — PAMELA K. WISE
Director, Office of Contracts and Procurement — LINDA BOOR
Director, Office of Information Resource Management — JOSEPH CASSELL

FEDERAL TRANSIT ADMINISTRATION

400 Seventh Street SW., Washington, DC 20590
Phone, 202–366–4043. Internet, http://www.fta.dot.gov/.

Administrator — GORDON J. LINTON
Deputy Administrator — NURIA FERNANDEZ
Chief Counsel — PATRICK W. REILLY
Director, Office of Civil Rights — ARTHUR A. LOPEZ
Director, Office of Public Affairs — BRUCE C. FRAME
Associate Administrator for Budget and Policy — MICHAEL A. WINTER
Associate Administrator for Program Management — HIRAM J. WALKER
Associate Administrator for Planning — CHARLOTTE M. ADAMS
Associate Administrator for Research, Demonstration, and Innovation — EDWARD L. THOMAS
Associate Administrator for Administration — DORRIE Y. ALDRICH

MARITIME ADMINISTRATION

400 Seventh Street SW., Washington, DC 20590
Phone, 202–366–5807. Internet, http://www.marad.dot.gov/.

Administrator — JOHN E. GRAYKOWSKI, *Acting*
Deputy Administrator — JOAN M. BONDAREFF, *Acting*
Deputy Administrator for Inland Waterways and Great Lakes — JOHN E. GRAYKOWSKI
Director of Congressional and Public Affairs — (VACANCY)
Chief Counsel — JOAN M. BONDAREFF
Deputy Chief Counsel — ROBERT J. PATTON, JR.
Secretary, Maritime Administration/Maritime Subsidy Board — JOEL C. RICHARD
Coordinator of Research and Development — PAUL B. MENTZ
Director, Office of Maritime Labor, Training, and Safety — TAYLOR E. JONES II
Associate Administrator for Administration — JOHN L. MANN, JR.
Director, Office of Management and Information Services — RALPH W. FERGUSON
Director, Office of Budget — THOMAS R. BRUNEEL
Director, Office of Accounting — JOHN G. HOBAN
Director, Office of Personnel — SHERRY D. GILSON
Director, Office of Acquisition — TIMOTHY P. ROARK

Associate Administrator for Policy and International Trade	BRUCE J. CARLTON
Director, Office of Policy and Plans	ELLEN L. HEUP
Director, Office of International Activities	JAMES A. TREICHEL
Director, Office of Statistical and Economic Analysis	WILLIAM B. EBERSOLD
Associate Administrator for Ship Financial Assistance and Cargo Preference	JAMES J. ZOK
Director, Office of Ship Financing	MITCHELL D. LAX
Director, Office of Costs and Rates	MICHAEL P. FERRIS
Director, Office of Subsidy and Insurance	EDMOND J. FITZGERALD
Director, Office of Financial Approvals	RICHARD J. MCDONNELL
Director, Office of Cargo Preference	THOMAS W. HARRELSON
Associate Administrator for National Security	JAMES E. CAPONITI
Director, Office of Ship Operations	MICHAEL DELPERCIO, JR.
Director, Office of National Security Plans	THOMAS M.P. CHRISTENSEN
Director, Office of Sealift Support	RAYMOND R. BARBERESI
Associate Administrator for Shipbuilding and Technology Development	(VACANCY)
Director, Office of Ship Construction	EDWIN B. SCHIMLER
Director, Office of Shipyard Revitalization	JOSEPH A. BYRNE
Associate Administrator for Port, Intermodal, and Environmental Activities	MARGARET D. BLUM
Deputy Associate Administrator for Port, Intermodal, and Environmental Activities	CARMINE P. GERACE
Director, Office of Intermodal Development	RICHARD L. WALKER
Director, Office of Environmental Activities	MICHAEL C. CARTER
Director, Office of Ports and Domestic Shipping	JOHN M. PISANI
Director, North Atlantic Region	ROBERT MCKEON
Director, Great Lakes Region	ALPHA H. AMES, JR.
Director, Central Region	JOHN W. CARNES
Director, South Atlantic Region	MAYANK JAIN
Director, Western Region	FRANCIS X. JOHNSTON
Superintendent, United States Merchant Marine Academy	THOMAS T. MATTESON

SAINT LAWRENCE SEAWAY DEVELOPMENT CORPORATION

Washington Office: 400 Seventh Street SW., Washington, DC 20590
Phone, 202–366–0091; 800–785–2779 (toll-free). Internet, http://www.dot.gov/slsdc/.

Administrator	(VACANCY)
Deputy Administrator	DAVID G. SANDERS
Director of Congressional and Public Affairs	GINGER VUICH
Director of Development and Logistics	ROBERT J. LEWIS
Chief Counsel	MARC OWEN

Massena Office: 180 Andrews Street, Massena, NY 13662
Phone, 315–764–3200

Associate Administrator	ERMAN J. COCCI
Director of Finance	EDWARD MARGOSIAN
Director of Engineering and Strategic Planning	STEPHEN C. HUNG

Director of Lock Operations	CAROL A. FENTON
Director of Maintenance and Marine Services	PETER A. BASHAW
Director of Administration	MARY ANN HAZEL

RESEARCH AND SPECIAL PROGRAMS ADMINISTRATION

400 Seventh Street SW., Washington, DC 20590
Phone, 202–366–4433

Administrator	(VACANCY)
Deputy Administrator	KELLEY S. COYNER
Director, Special Projects	PATRICIA CARROLL
Chief Counsel	JUDITH S. KALETA
Director, Office of Civil Rights	HELEN HAGIN
Director, Office of Policy and Program Support	WILLIAM E. VINCENT
Director, Office of Emergency Transportation	WILLIAM M. MEDIGOVICH
Director, Volpe National Transportation Systems Center	RICHARD R. JOHN
Associate Administrator for Management and Administration	JERRY FRANKLIN
Associate Administrator for Pipeline Safety	RICHARD B. FELDER
Associate Administrator for Hazardous Materials Safety	ALAN I. ROBERTS
Associate Administrator for Research, Technology, and Analysis	FENTON CAREY
Director, Transportation Safety Institute	(VACANCY)

BUREAU OF TRANSPORTATION STATISTICS

400 Seventh Street SW., Washington, DC 20590
Phone, 202–366–DATA. Internet, http://www.bts.gov/.

Director	(VACANCY)
Deputy Director	ROBERT A. KNISELY
Associate Director, Transportation Studies	ROLF R. SCHMITT
Associate Director, Statistical Programs and Services	PHILIP N. FULTON
Assistant Director, Geographic Information Services	BRUCE D. SPEAR
Assistant Director, Information Technology Center	ROBERT C. ZARNETSKE, *Acting*
Assistant Director, Transportation Analysis	WENDELL FLETCHER
Administrative Officer	LORELEI S. EVANS
Director, Office of Airline Information	TIMOTHY E. CARMODY
Chief, Regulations Division	M. CLAY MORITZ
Chief, Data Administration Division	DONALD W. BRIGHT
Chief, Automated Data Processing Services Division	CHARLES K. BRADFORD

SURFACE TRANSPORTATION BOARD

1925 K Street NW., Washington, DC 20423–0001
Phone, 202–565–1674

Chairman	LINDA J. MORGAN
Vice Chairman	GUS A. OWEN

Board Member   (VACANCY)

Staff Offices:

Director, Office of Economics, Environmental   LELAND L. GARDNER
   Analysis, and Administration
General Counsel   HENRI F. RUSH
Secretary   VERNON A. WILLIAMS
Director, Office of Compliance and   MELVIN F. CLEMENS, JR.
   Enforcement
Director, Office of Congressional and Public   DAN G. KING
   Services
Director, Office of Proceedings   DAVID M. KONSCHNIK

[For the Department of Transportation statement of organization, see the *Code of Federal Regulations,* Title 49, Part 1, Subpart A]

The U.S. Department of Transportation establishes the Nation's overall transportation policy. Under its umbrella there are 10 administrations whose jurisdictions include highway planning, development, and construction; urban mass transit; railroads; aviation; and the safety of waterways, ports, highways, and oil and gas pipelines. Decisions made by the Department in conjunction with the appropriate State and local officials strongly affect other programs such as land planning, energy conservation, scarce resource utilization, and technological change.

The Department of Transportation (DOT) was established by act of October 15, 1966, as amended (49 U.S.C. 102 and 102 note), "to assure the coordinated, effective administration of the transportation programs of the Federal Government" and to develop "national transportation policies and programs conducive to the provision of fast, safe, efficient, and convenient transportation at the lowest cost consistent therewith." It became operational in April 1967 and was comprised of elements transferred from eight other major departments and agencies. It presently consists of the Office of the Secretary and 10 operating administrations whose heads report directly to the Secretary and who have highly decentralized authority.

Office of the Secretary of Transportation

[For the Office of the Secretary of Transportation statement of organization, see the *Code of Federal Regulations,* Title 49, Part 1, Subpart B]

The Department of Transportation is administered by the Secretary of Transportation, who is the principal adviser to the President in all matters relating to Federal transportation programs. The Secretary is assisted in the administration of the Department by a Deputy Secretary of Transportation, an Associate Deputy Secretary, the Assistant Secretaries, a General Counsel, the Inspector General, and several Directors and Chairmen. Areas where public purposes are widely served are detailed in the following text.

Aviation and International Affairs   The Office of the Assistant Secretary for Aviation and International Affairs has principal responsibility for the development, review, and coordination of policy for international transportation, and for development, coordination, and implementation of policy relating to economic regulation of the airline industry. The Office:

—licenses U.S. and foreign carriers to serve in international air transportation and conducts carrier fitness determinations;

—develops policies to support the Department in aviation and maritime multilateral and bilateral negotiations with foreign governments and participates on the U.S. negotiating delegations;

—develops policies on a wide range of international transportation and trade matters;

U.S. DEPARTMENT OF TRANSPORTATION

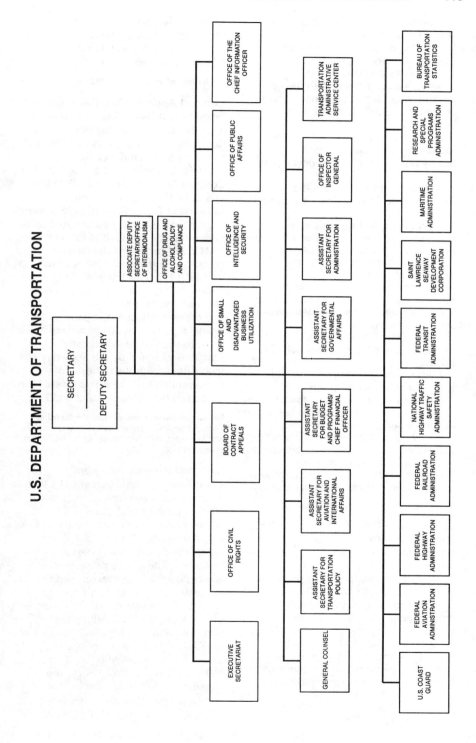

—furnishes guidance to the United States Trade Representative's Trade Policy Committee in efforts to improve the U.S. balance of payments;

—arranges and coordinates cooperative agreements with foreign governments for the exchange of state-of-the-art scientific and technical information;

—provides assistance to the Agency for International Development's transportation programs in developing countries;

—participates on the U.S.-Saudi Arabian Joint Commission for Economic Cooperation;

—processes and resolves complaints concerning unfair competitive practices in international fares and rates;

—establishes international and intra-Alaska mail rates; and

—determines the disposition of requests for approval and immunization from the antitrust laws of international aviation agreements.

The Office also administers the essential air service program, which involves:

—establishing appropriate subsidy levels for subsidized carriers;

—processing applications to terminate, suspend, or reduce air service below the defined essential level;

—determining which carrier among various applicants should be selected to provide subsidized service; and

—continuously reviewing essential air service definitions for each community.

For further information, call 202–366–4551.

Civil Rights The Office of Civil Rights advises the Secretary on civil rights and equal opportunity matters. It assures full and affirmative implementation of civil rights and equal opportunity precepts within the Department in all official actions, including departmental employment practices, services rendered to the public, operation of federally assisted activities, and other programs and efforts involving departmental assistance, participation, or endorsement. It is also responsible for adjudicating appeals and other dispositions relating to denials of disadvantaged business enterprise certification by a

transportation financial assistance recipient, including investigating third-party challenges and issuing final administrative decisions.

For further information, call 202–366–4648.

Contract Appeals The Board conducts hearings and issues final decisions in appeals from contracting officer decisions under contracts awarded by the Department and its constituent administrations in accordance with the Contract Disputes Act of 1978 (41 U.S.C. 601); sits as the Contract Adjustment Board with plenary authority to grant extraordinary contractual relief under Public Law 85–804 (50 U.S.C. 1431); and hears and decides all contractor debarment cases pursuant to 41 CFR 12–1.604–1 (1984). Judges are designated as hearing officers to hear cases arising as a result of suspensions and debarments of participants in DOT financial assistance programs and perform such other adjudicatory functions assigned by the Secretary not inconsistent with the duties and responsibilities of the Board as set forth in the Contract Disputes Act of 1978.

For further information, contact the Board of Contract Appeals, Department of Transportation, 400 Seventh Street SW., Washington, DC 20590. Phone, 202–366–4305.

Drug and Alcohol Policy and Compliance The Office ensures that the national and international drug and alcohol policies and goals of the Secretary are developed and carried out in a consistent, efficient, and effective manner within the transportation industries. The Office provides expert advice, counsel, and recommendations to the Secretary regarding drugs and alcohol as it pertains to the Department of Transportation and testing within the transportation industry. The Director of the Office serves as the principal Department liaison with the Office of National Drug Control Policy, the Department of Health and Human Services, and other executive branch agencies concerning demand reduction activities and workplace substance abuse programs.

For further information, contact the Office of Drug and Alcohol Policy and Compliance. Phone, 202–366–3784.

Intelligence and Security   The Office advises the Secretary on domestic and international intelligence and security matters; coordinates the development and implementation of long-term strategic plans, information management systems, and integrated research and development programs affecting the security of traveling public and of cargo; serves as the focal point in the Department for intelligence and security policy; and provides oversight of transportation security and intelligence programs.

For further information, contact the Office of Intelligence and Security. Phone, 202–366–6525.

Intermodalism   The mission of the Office is to help the transportation community achieve the connections and choices they would like to see in their transportation systems by providing departmental leadership and coordination in developing intermodal transportation solutions that move people and goods in an energy-efficient manner, provide the foundation for improved productivity growth, strengthen the Nation's ability to compete in the global economy, and obtain the optimum yield from the Nation's transportation resources. The Office:

—serves as the Department's principal adviser and advocate for intermodal transportation;

—coordinates Federal intermodal transportation policy and initiates policies to promote efficient intermodal transportation;

—provides technical assistance to States and metropolitan planning organizations in large metropolitan areas that facilitates their collection of intermodal data and assists in intermodal planning;

—coordinates Federal research on intermodal transportation in accordance with section 6009(b) of the Intermodal Surface Transportation Efficiency Act of 1991 (ISTEA), including additional research needs identified by the Director;

—reviews State-generated intermodal management systems to ensure continued progress towards improving and integrating modal transportation systems, where appropriate; and

—coordinates miscellaneous DOT intermodal issues as required by ISTEA and/or as raised by the Secretary and the modal agencies.

Small and Disadvantaged Business Utilization   The Office provides policy direction and Department goals for small, minority, women-owned, and small disadvantaged business participation in the Department's procurement and Federal financial assistance activities. It also monitors and evaluates accomplishment of these goals.

The Minority Business Resource Center offers a Short Term Lending Program, under which lines of credit up to $500,000 are available at prime interest rates to finance accounts receivable, and a Bonding Assistance Program which enables firms to obtain bid, performance, and payment bonds of up to $1,000,000 per contract in support of transportation-related contracts. Other program initiatives provide technical and educational assistance, outreach, and information dissemination involving partnerships with chambers of commerce and trade associations, historically black colleges and universities, and Hispanic-serving institutions. The Center also operates a National Information Clearinghouse.

For further information, call 202–366–1930 or 800–532–1169 (toll-free). Internet, http://osdbuweb.dot.gov/.

Transportation Policy   The Office of the Assistant Secretary for Transportation Policy has principal responsibility for analysis, development, articulation, and review of policies and plans for all modes of transportation. The Office:

—develops, coordinates, and evaluates public policy related to the transportation industries, and maintains policy and economic oversight of regulatory programs and legislative initiatives of the Department;

—reviews transportation matters involving the public and private sectors, analyzes current and emerging transportation policy issues, and assesses their economic and institutional implications;

—leads the Department in the development of transportation policies and ensures that departmental actions and programs comprise a coherent and coordinated strategy leading to an effectively functioning integrated national transportation system;

—provides departmental policy leadership and coordination on safety, energy, and environmental initiatives which affect air, surface, marine, and pipeline transportation; and

—provides leadership on questions involving the financing of transportation infrastructure projects, and provides economic analyses of new transportation technologies.

The Assistant Secretary chairs the DOT Position/Navigation Executive Committee and serves on the Global Positioning System Executive Board with DOD. In addition, he represents the Department on the President's Advisory Council on Historic Preservation.

United States Coast Guard

The Coast Guard, established by act of January 28, 1915 (14 U.S.C. 1), became a component of the Department of Transportation on April 1, 1967, pursuant to the Department of Transportation Act of October 15, 1966 (49 U.S.C. app. 1651 note). The Coast Guard is a branch of the Armed Forces of the United States at all times and is a service within the Department of Transportation except when operating as part of the Navy in time of war or when the President directs.

The predecessor of the Coast Guard, the Revenue Marine, was established in 1790 as a Federal maritime law enforcement agency. Many other major responsibilities have since been added.

Activities

Aids to Navigation The Coast Guard establishes and maintains the U.S. aids to navigation system that includes lights, buoys, daybeacons, fog signals, marine radiobeacons, racons, and long-range radionavigation aids. Long-range radionavigation aids include loran-C and the Global Positioning System (GPS) and its augmentations such as Differential GPS. Aids are established in or adjacent to waters subject to the jurisdiction of the United States. These aids are intended to assist a navigator to determine a position or plot a safe course or to warn the navigator of dangers or obstructions to navigation. Other functions related to navigation aids include broadcasting marine information and publishing Local Notice to Mariners and Light Lists.

Information regarding navigational aids is available electronically. Phone (modem), 703–313–5900. Internet, http://www.navcen.uscg.mil/.

For further information, call 202–267–0980.

Boating Safety The Coast Guard develops and directs a national boating safety program aimed at making the operation of small craft in U.S. waters both pleasurable and safe. This is accomplished by establishing uniform safety standards for recreational boats and associated equipment; encouraging State efforts through a grant-in-aid and liaison program; coordinating public education and information programs; administering the Coast Guard Auxiliary; and enforcing compliance with Federal laws and regulations relative to safe use and safety equipment requirements for small boats.

For further information, call 202–267–1077.

Bridge Administration The Coast Guard administers the statutes regulating the construction, maintenance, and operation of bridges and causeways across the navigable waters of the

United States to provide for safe navigation through and under bridges.

For further information, call 202–267–0368.

Coast Guard Auxiliary The Auxiliary is a nonmilitary volunteer organization of private citizens who own small boats, aircraft, or radio stations. Auxiliary members assist the Coast Guard by conducting boating education programs, patrolling marine regattas, participating in search and rescue operations, and conducting courtesy marine examinations.

For further information, call 202–267–0982.

Deepwater Ports Under the provisions of the Deepwater Port Act of 1974 (33 U.S.C. 1501), the Coast Guard administers a licensing and regulatory program governing the construction, ownership (international aspects), and operation of deepwater ports on the high seas to transfer oil from tankers to shore.

For further information, call 202–267–0495.

Ice Operations The Coast Guard operates the Nation's icebreaking vessels (icebreakers and ice-capable cutters), supported by aircraft, for ice reconnaissance, to facilitate maritime transportation and aid in prevention of flooding in domestic waters. Additionally, icebreakers support logistics to U.S. polar installations and also support scientific research in Arctic and Antarctic waters.

For further information, call 202–267–1456.

Marine Environmental Response The Coast Guard is responsible for enforcing the Federal Water Pollution Control Act (33 U.S.C. 1251) and various other laws relating to the protection of the marine environment. Program objectives are to ensure that public health and welfare and the environment are protected when spills occur. Under these laws, U.S. and foreign vessels are prohibited from using U.S. waters unless they have insurance or other guarantees that potential pollution liability for cleanup and damages will be met.

Other functions include providing a National Response Center to receive reports of oil and hazardous substance spills, investigating spills, initiating subsequent civil penalty actions when warranted, encouraging and monitoring responsible party cleanups, and when necessary, coordinating federally funded spill response operations. The program also provides a National Strike Force to assist Federal On-Scene Coordinators in responding to pollution incidents.

For further information, call 202–267–0518.

Marine Inspection The Coast Guard is charged with formulating, administering, and enforcing various safety standards for the design, construction, equipment, and maintenance of commercial vessels of the United States and offshore structures on the Outer Continental Shelf. The program includes enforcement of safety standards on foreign vessels subject to U.S. jurisdiction.

Investigations are conducted of reported marine accidents, casualties, violations of law and regulations, misconduct, negligence, and incompetence occurring on commercial vessels subject to U.S. jurisdiction. Surveillance operations and boardings are conducted to detect violations of law and regulations. The program also functions to facilitate marine transportation by admeasuring and administering the vessel documentation laws.

For further information, call 202–267–1464.

Marine Licensing The Coast Guard administers a system for evaluating and licensing of U.S. Merchant Marine personnel. This program develops safe manning standards for commercial vessels. The Coast Guard also maintains oversight and approval authority for the numerous mariner training programs.

For further information, call 703–235–1951.

Marine Safety Council The Marine Safety Council acts as a deliberative body to consider proposed Coast Guard regulations and to provide a forum for the consideration of related problems.

For further information, call 202–267–1477.

Maritime Law Enforcement The Coast Guard is the primary maritime law enforcement agency for the United States. It enforces or assists in the enforcement of applicable Federal laws and treaties and other international agreements to which the United States is party, on, over, and under the high seas and waters subject to the jurisdiction of the United States, and may conduct investigations into suspected violations of such laws and international agreements. The Coast Guard works with other Federal agencies in the enforcement of such laws as they pertain to the protection of living and nonliving resources and in the suppression of smuggling and illicit drug trafficking.

For further information, call 202–267–1890.

Military Readiness   As required by law, the Coast Guard maintains a state of readiness to function as a specialized service in the Navy in time of war, or as directed by the President. Coastal and harbor defense, including port security, are the most important military tasks assigned to the Coast Guard in times of national crisis.

For further information, call 202–267–2025.

Port Safety and Security   This program is administered by the Coast Guard Captains of the Port. The Coast Guard is authorized to enforce rules and regulations governing the safety and security of ports and anchorages, and the movement of vessels and prevention of pollution in U.S. waters. Port safety and security functions include supervising cargo transfer operations, both storage and stowage, conducting harbor patrols and waterfront facility inspections,

establishing security zones as required, and the control of vessel movement.

For further information, call 202–267–0495.

Reserve Training   The Coast Guard Reserve provides qualified individuals and trained units for active duty in time of war or national emergency and at such other times as the national security requires. In addition to its role in national defense, the Reserve augments the active service in the performance of peacetime missions during domestic emergencies and during routine and peak operations.

For further information, call 202–267–1240.

Search and Rescue   The Coast Guard maintains a system of rescue vessels, aircraft, and communications facilities to carry out its function of saving life and property in and over the high seas and the navigable waters of the United States. This function includes flood relief and removing hazards to navigation.

For further information, call 202–267–1943.

Waterways Management   The Coast Guard has a significant role in the safe and orderly passage of cargo, people, and vessels on our nation's waterways. It has established Vessel Traffic Services in six major ports to provide for the safe movement of vessels at all times, but particularly during hazardous conditions, restricted visibility, or bad weather. The program's goal is to ensure the safe, efficient flow of commerce. The Coast Guard also regulates the installation of equipment necessary for vessel safety.

For further information, call 202–267–0407.

District and Field Organizations—United States Coast Guard

Organization	Address	Commander	Telephone
Atlantic Area	431 Crawford St., Portsmouth, VA 23704–5004	Vice Adm. Roger T. Rufe, USCG	757–398–6287
Maintenance and Logistics Command–Atlantic	300 Main St. Twr., Norfolk, VA 23510	Rear Adm. Erroll M. Brown, USCG	757–628–4275
1st District	408 Atlantic Ave., Boston, MA 02110–3350	Rear Adm. Richard M. Larrabee III, USCG	617–223–8480
7th District	Rm. 944, 909 SE. 1st Ave., Miami, FL 33131–3050	Rear Adm. Norman T. Saunders, USCG	305–536–5654
8th District	501 Magazine St., New Orleans, LA 70130–3396	Rear Adm. Paul J. Pluta, USCG	504–589–6298
9th District	1240 E. 9th St., Cleveland, OH 44199–2060	Rear Adm. John F. McGowan, USCG	216–902–6001

District and Field Organizations—United States Coast Guard—Continued

Organization	Address	Commander	Telephone
Pacific Area	Coast Guard Island, Alameda, CA 94501–5100	Vice Adm. Thomas H. Collins, USCG	510–437–3196
Maintenance and Logistics Command-Pacific	Coast Guard Island, Alameda, CA 94501–5100	Rear Adm. John L. Parker, USCG	510–437–3939
13th District	915 2d Ave., Seattle, WA 98174–1067	Rear Adm. Paul M. Blayney, USCG	206–220–7090
14th District	9th Fl., 300 Ala Moana Blvd., Honolulu, HI 96850–4982	Rear Adm. Joseph J. McClelland, USCG	808–541–2051
17th District	P.O. Box 25517, Juneau, AK 99802–1217	Rear Adm. Terry M. Cross, USCG	907–463–2025
U.S. Coast Guard Academy	New London, CT 06320–4195	Rear Adm. Douglas H. Teeson, USCG	203–444–8285
National Pollution Funds Center	Suite 1000, 4200 Wilson Blvd., Arlington, VA 22203–1804	Daniel F. Sheehan	703–235–4700
Coast Guard Personnel Command	2100 2d St. SW., Washington, DC 20593–0001	Capt. Thomas B. Taylor, USCG	202–267–2321

For further information, contact the Information Office, United States Coast Guard, Department of Transportation, 2100 Second Street SW., Washington, DC 20593. Phone, 202–267–2229. Internet, http://www.uscg.mil/.

Federal Aviation Administration

The Federal Aviation Administration (FAA), formerly the Federal Aviation Agency, was established by the Federal Aviation Act of 1958 and now operates under the authority of Subtitle VII, Aviation Programs, of title 49, United States Code. The agency became a component of the Department of Transportation in 1967 pursuant to the Department of Transportation Act (49 U.S.C. app. 1651 note).

The mission of the Federal Aviation Administration involves safety considerations in the public interest. The Administrator of the Federal Aviation Administration considers the following matters, among others, as being in the public interest:

—assigning, maintaining, and enhancing safety and security as the highest priorities in air commerce;

—regulating air commerce in a way that best promotes safety and fulfills national defense requirements;

—encouraging and developing civil aeronautics, including new aviation technology;

—controlling the use of the navigable airspace and regulating civil and military operations in that airspace in the interest

of safety and efficiency of both of those operations;

—consolidating research and development for air navigation facilities and the installation and operation of those facilities;

—developing and operating a common system of air traffic control and navigation for military and civil aircraft; and

—providing assistance to law enforcement agencies in the enforcement of laws related to regulation of controlled substances, to the extent consistent with aviation safety.

FAA's activities also include:

—developing and implementing programs and regulations to control aircraft noise, sonic boom, and other environmental effects of civil aviation; and

—regulating U.S. commercial space transportation.

Activities

Air Navigation Facilities The agency is responsible for the location, construction or installation, maintenance, operation, and quality assurance of Federal visual and electronic aids to air navigation. The agency operates and maintains voice/

data communications equipment, radar facilities, computer systems, and visual display equipment at flight service stations, airport traffic control towers, and air route traffic control centers.

Airport Programs The agency maintains a national plan of airport requirements, administers a grant program for development of public use airports to assure and improve safety and to meet current and future airport capacity needs, evaluates the environmental impacts of airport development, and administers an airport noise compatibility program with the goal of reducing noncompatible uses around airports. It also develops standards and technical guidance on airport planning, design, safety, and operations and provides grants to assist public agencies in airport system and master planning and airport development and improvement.

Airspace and Air Traffic Management The safe and efficient utilization of the navigable airspace is a primary objective of the agency. To meet this objective, it operates a network of airport traffic control towers, air route traffic control centers, and flight service stations. It develops air traffic rules and regulations and allocates the use of the airspace. It also provides for the security control of air traffic to meet national defense requirements.

Civil Aviation Abroad Under the Federal Aviation Act of 1958 and the International Aviation Facilities Act (49 U.S.C. app. 1151), the agency promotes aviation safety and civil aviation abroad by exchanging aeronautical information with foreign aviation authorities; certifying foreign repair stations, airmen, and mechanics; negotiating bilateral airworthiness agreements to facilitate the import and export of aircraft and components; and providing technical assistance and training in all areas of the agency's expertise. It provides technical representation at international conferences, including participation in the International Civil Aviation Organization and other international organizations.

Commercial Space Transportation The agency regulates and promotes the U.S. commercial space transportation industry. It licenses the private sector launching of space payloads on expendable launch vehicles and commercial space launch facilities. It also sets insurance requirements for the protection of persons and property and ensures that space transportation activities comply with U.S. domestic and foreign policy.

Registration and Recordation The agency provides a system for the registration of aircraft and recording of documents affecting title or interest in the aircraft, aircraft engines, propellers, appliances, and spare parts.

Research, Engineering, and Development The research, engineering, and development activities of the agency are directed toward providing the systems, procedures, facilities, and devices needed for a safe and efficient system of air navigation and air traffic control to meet the needs of civil aviation and the air defense system. The agency also performs an aeromedical research function to apply knowledge gained from its research program and the work of others to the safety and promotion of civil aviation and the health, safety, and efficiency of agency employees. The agency also supports development and testing of improved aircraft, engines, propellers, and appliances.

Safety Regulation The Administration issues and enforces rules, regulations, and minimum standards relating to the manufacture, operation, and maintenance of aircraft, as well as the rating and certification (including medical) of airmen and the certification of airports serving air carriers.

The agency performs flight inspection of air navigation facilities in the U.S. and, as required, abroad. It also enforces regulations under the Hazardous Materials Transportation Act (49 U.S.C. app. 1801 note) applicable to shipments by air.

Test and Evaluation The agency conducts tests and evaluations of specified items such as aviation systems, subsystems, equipment, devices, materials, concepts, or procedures at any phase in the cycle of their development from conception to acceptance and implementation, as well as assigned independent testing at key decision points.

Other Programs   The agency administers the aviation insurance and aircraft loan guarantee programs. It is an allotting agency under the Defense Materials System with respect to priorities and allocation for civil aircraft and civil aviation operations. The agency develops specifications for the preparation of aeronautical charts. It publishes current information on airways and airport service and issues technical publications for the improvement of safety in flight, airport planning and design, and other aeronautical activities. It serves as the executive administration for the operation and maintenance of the Department of Transportation automated payroll and personnel systems.

Major Field Organizations—Federal Aviation Administration

Region/Field Office	Address	Administrator/Director
Alaskan—AK	P.O. Box 14, 701 C St., Anchorage, AK 99513	Andrew S. Billick
Central—IA, KS, MO, NE	601 E. 12th St., Kansas City, MO 64106	John E. Turner
Eastern—DE, MD, MA, NJ, NY, PA, VA, WV	Federal Bldg., JFK International Airport, Jamaica, NY 11430	Arlene B. Feldman
Great Lakes—IL, IN, MI, MN, ND, OH, SD, WI	2300 E. Devon Ave., Des Plaines, IL 60018	Cecilia Hunziker
New England—CT, MA, ME, NH, RI, VT	12 New England Executive Park, Burlington, MA 01803	Robert Bartanowicz
Northwest Mountain—CO, ID, MT, OR, UT, WA, WY	1601 Lind Ave. SW., Renton, WA 98055	Larry Andriesen
Southern—AL, FL, GA, KY, MS, NC, PR, SC, TN	P.O. Box 20636, Atlanta, GA 30320	Carolyn C. Blum
Southwest—AR, LA, NM, OK, TX	Fort Worth, TX 76193–0001	Clyde M. DeHart
Western-Pacific—AZ, CA, HI, NV	P.O. Box 92007, Los Angeles, CA 90009	William C. Withycombe
Europe, Africa, and Middle East	15, Rue de la Loi B–1040, Brussels, Belgium	Patrick N. Poe
Asia-Pacific	U.S. Embassy, FAA, Singapore	Eugene Ross Hamory
Latin America-Caribbean	Miami International Airport, Miami FL	Joaquin Archilla
William J. Hughes Technical Center	Atlantic City, NJ 08405	Anne Harlan
Mike Monroney Aeronautical Center	P.O. Box 25082, Oklahoma City, OK 73125	Lindy Ritz

For further information, contact the Office of Public Affairs, Federal Aviation Administration, Department of Transportation, 800 Independence Avenue SW., Washington, DC 20591. Phone, 202–267–8521. Fax, 202–267–5039.

Federal Highway Administration

The Federal Highway Administration became a component of the Department of Transportation in 1967 pursuant to the Department of Transportation Act (49 U.S.C. app. 1651 note). It administers the highway transportation programs of the Department of Transportation under Title 23 U.S.C., other pertinent legislation, and the provisions of law cited in section 6(a) of the act (49 U.S.C. 104).

The Administration encompasses highway transportation in its broadest scope, seeking to coordinate highways with other modes of transportation to achieve the most effective balance of transportation systems and facilities under cohesive Federal transportation policies pursuant to the act.

Activities

Federal-Aid Highway Program   The Administration manages the Federal-aid highway program of financial assistance to the States for planning, constructing, and improving highways and their operation. This program provides for the improvement of approximately 159,000 miles of the National Highway System (NHS), which includes the approximately 45,000-mile Dwight D. Eisenhower System of Interstate and Defense Highways and other public roads (except those classified as local or rural minor collectors). The Interstate System's construction and preservation is financed generally on a 90-percent Federal, 10-percent State basis. However, projects not on the Interstate System and most projects on other roads are funded on an 80-percent Federal, 20-percent State basis.

The Surface Transportation Program (STP) may be used by the States and local authorities for any roads (including NHS) that are not functionally classified as local or rural minor collectors. Fifty percent of STP funds must be used in metropolitan areas containing an urbanized population over 200,000. Ten percent of STP funds are set aside for transportation enhancement activities, which include bicycle and pedestrian facilities, scenic enhancements, historic preservation, and mitigation of water pollution due to highway runoff. Another 10 percent of STP funds are set aside for safety-related activities.

The Administration is also responsible for the Highway Bridge Replacement and Rehabilitation Program to assist in the inspection, analysis, and rehabilitation or replacement of bridges on public roads. In addition, it administers an emergency relief program to assist in the repair or reconstruction of Federal-aid highways and certain Federal roads that have suffered serious damage by natural disasters over a wide area or catastrophic failures.

The Congestion Mitigation and Air Quality Improvement (CMAQ) program provides funding to assist nonattainment and maintenance areas, as defined under the Clean Air Act, to help achieve healthful levels of air quality. Transportation improvement projects and programs which reduce transportation-related emissions are eligible for funding under the major categories of transit, shared-ride, traffic flow improvements, demand management, pedestrian/bicycle, inspection/maintenance, and experimental pilot projects.

A metropolitan and statewide planning program is administered jointly with the Federal Transit Administration for the purpose of strengthening the transportation decisionmaking process and ensuring that transportation investments address other key issues in metropolitan and State areas, including development, land use, social, economic, and environmental impacts. Metropolitan planning organizations are supported by a one percent share of the funds authorized for the NHS, STP, CMAQ, and Interstate Maintenance and Bridge programs. Statewide planning, conducted by State departments of transportation, is supported by 2 percent of the major highway programs.

Funds are also available to State revenue agencies for enforcement of highway use taxes, and to State and local governments and public authorities for projects involving market-based approaches to congestion management.

Highway Safety Programs   The Administration is responsible for several highway-related safety programs, including a State and community safety program jointly administered with NHTSA and a highway safety construction program to eliminate road hazards and improve rail/highway crossing safety. These safety construction programs fund activities that remove, relocate, or shield roadside obstacles, identify and correct hazardous locations, eliminate or reduce hazards at railroad grade crossings, and improve signing, pavement markings, and signalization.

Motor Carrier Programs   The Administration works cooperatively with States and private industry to achieve uniform motor carrier requirements in safety regulations, inspections and fines, licensing, registration and taxation requirements, and crash data. It provides grants to States for roadside inspections, compliance reviews, traffic enforcement, technical assistance, training, and equipment.

Under the authority of the motor carrier safety provisions of title 49 of the United States Code, the agency exercises Federal regulatory jurisdiction over the safety performance of all commercial motor carriers engaged in interstate or foreign commerce. It deals with more than 430,000 carriers, approximately 12,000 passenger carriers, and 36,000 shippers of hazardous materials. Reviews are conducted at the carrier's facilities to determine the safety performance of the carrier's over-the-road operations. These reviews may lead to prosecution or other sanctions against violators of the Federal motor carrier safety regulations or the hazardous materials transportation regulations.

Federal Lands Highway Program The Administration, through cooperative agreements with Federal land managing agencies, administers a coordinated Federal lands program relating to forest highways, public lands highways, national park roads and parkways, and Indian reservation roads. This program provides for the funding of more than 80,000 miles of federally owned roads or public authority-owned roads that are open for public travel and serve Federal lands. In addition, the agency's Federal Lands Highway Office administers the Defense Access Road Program, funded by the Department of Defense, for State and local roads providing access to military installations. The Office and three field divisions provide for program coordination and administration, and conduct transportation planning, engineering studies, design, construction engineering assistance, and construction contract administration.

Research and Technology The Administration coordinates varied research, development, and technology transfer activities consisting of six principal programs: Intelligent Transportation Systems, Highway Research and Development, Long-Term Pavement Performance, Technology Applications, Local Technical Assistance, and the National Highway Institute.

Through its National Highway Institute (NHI), the Administration develops and administers, in cooperation with State highway agencies, instructional training programs designed for public sector employees, private citizens, and foreign nationals engaged in highway work of interest to the United States. NHI acts as one of the 86 technology transfer centers of the Pan American Institute of Highways which provides training and technology transfer to Latin American countries. NHI works closely with universities through the Dwight David

Eisenhower Transportation Fellowship Program and the University Transportation Centers Program.

International Programs The Administration supports and participates in efforts to find innovative research and technology abroad which can be applied in the United States to provide a better quality, more cost-effective highway system. It manages technology transfer and training centers in developing countries and participates in international technical organizations, committees, deliberations, and studies. Other efforts are aimed at facilitating the exports of highway related goods and services and providing technical assistance to foreign governments, specifically on institutional efforts financed by the World Bank group. FHWA also supports efforts aimed at improving the efficiency of international trade flows at the border in the context of the North American Free Trade Agreement and other regional trade agreements.

Additional Programs The Administration manages the highway construction phase of the Appalachian Regional Development Program and the Territorial Highway Program and provides highway program support and technical assistance on an allocation/transfer basis for other Federal agencies, as well as program and technical support on a wide range of policy and information programs and issues. It also administers civil rights programs pursuant to a variety of statutes, with the aims of preventing discrimination (based on race, color, sex, national origin, religion/creed, age, disability, or low income) in the impacts of all programs and activities of recipients and subrecipients; providing equal employment opportunities and promoting diversity in public employment (Federal and State transportation agencies, motor carrier safety, and commercial driver's license program recipients and subrecipients) and private employment (contractors, subcontractors, material suppliers, vendors, and consultants) related to agency-funded projects; providing training opportunities for minorities, women, and the disadvantaged in highway construction crafts; ensuring contracting opportunities for socially and economically disadvantaged business enterprises; and increasing opportunities for historically black colleges and universities, members of the Hispanic Association of Colleges and Universities, and tribal colleges and universities.

Major Field Organizations—Federal Highway Administration

Areas Served	Address	Administrator	Telephone
CT, MA, ME, NH, NJ, NY, PR, RI, VT	Rm. 719, Leo W. O'Brien Federal Bldg., Albany, NY 12207	Nelson Castellanos, *Acting*	518–431–4236
DC, DE, MA, PA, VA, WV	Suite 4000, 10 S. Howard St., Baltimore, MD 21201	David S. Gendell	410–962–0093
AL, FL, GA, KY, MS, NC, SC, TN	Suite 17T26, 61 Forsyth St. SW., Atlanta, GA 30303–3104	Leon N. Larson	404–562–3570
IL, IN, MI, MN, OH, WI	Suite 301, 19900 Governors Hwy., Olympia Fields, IL 60461–1021	Dale E. Wilken	708–283–3510
AR, LA, NM, OK, TX	Rm. 8A00, 819 Taylor St., Fort Worth, TX 76102	Edward A. Wueste	817–978–4393
IA, KS, MO, NE	6301 Rockhill Rd., Kansas City, MO 64141–6715	Arthur E. Hamilton	816–276–2700
CO, MT, ND, SD, UT, WY	Rm. 400, 555 Zang St., Lakewood, CO 80228	Vincent F. Schimmoller	303–969–6722
AZ, CA, HI, NV	Suite 2100, 201 Mission St., San Francisco, CA 94105	Julie A. Cirillo	415–744–2639
AK, ID, OR, WA	Suite 600, 222 SW. Columbia St., Portland, OR 97201	Leon J. Whitman, Jr.	503–326–2048

For further information, contact the Office of Information and Management Services, Federal Highway Administration, Department of Transportation, 400 Seventh Street SW., Washington, DC 20590. Phone, 202–366–0534.

Federal Railroad Administration

The purpose of the Federal Railroad Administration is to promulgate and enforce rail safety regulations, administer railroad financial assistance programs, conduct research and development in support of improved railroad safety and national rail transportation policy, provide for the rehabilitation of Northeast Corridor rail passenger service, and consolidate government support of rail transportation activities.

The Federal Railroad Administration was created pursuant to section 3(e)(1) of the Department of Transportation Act of 1966 (49 U.S.C. app. 1652).

Activities

Railroad Safety The Administration administers and enforces the Federal laws and related regulations designed to promote safety on railroads; exercises jurisdiction over all areas of rail safety under the Rail Safety Act of 1970, such as track maintenance, inspection standards, equipment standards, and operating practices. It also administers and enforces regulations resulting from railroad safety legislation for locomotives, signals, safety appliances, power brakes, hours of service, transportation of explosives and other dangerous articles, and reporting and investigation of railroad accidents. Railroad and related industry equipment, facilities, and records are inspected and required reports reviewed. In addition, the administration educates the public about safety at highway-rail grade crossings and the danger of trespassing on rail property.

Research and Development The Administration's ground transportation research and development program seeks to advance all aspects of intercity ground transportation and railroad safety pertaining to the physical sciences and engineering, in order to improve railroad safety and ensure that railroads continue to be a viable national transportation resource.

Transportation Test Center This 50-square-mile facility, located near Pueblo, CO, provides testing for advanced and conventional systems and techniques designed to improve ground transportation. The facility has been managed and staffed for the Administration by the Association of American Railroads since October 1, 1982. The United States and Canadian Governments and private industry use this facility to explore, under controlled conditions, the operation of both conventional and advanced systems. It is used by the Federal Transit Administration for testing of urban rapid transit vehicles.

For further information, contact the Transportation Test Center, Pueblo, CO 81001. Phone, 719–584–0507.

Policy The Administration provides program management for new and revised policies, plans, and projects related to railroad transportation economics, finance, system planning, and operations; performs appropriate studies and analyses; conducts relevant tests, demonstrations, and evaluations; and evaluates labor/management programs. It also carries out analyses of issues before regulatory agencies and makes recommendations to the Secretary as to the positions to be taken by DOT.

Passenger and Freight Services The Administration administers various programs of Federal assistance in the following areas: development, implementation, and administration of rail system policies, plans, and programs for the Northeast corridor, in support of applicable provisions of legislation; rail freight service assistance; rail service continuation and State rail planning; and rail passenger service on a national, regional, and local basis.

Major Field Organizations—Federal Railroad Administration

Region	Address/Telephone	Regional Administrator of Railroad Safety
Northeastern—CT, MA, ME, NH, NJ, NY, RI, VT	Rm. 1077, 55 Broadway, Cambridge, MA 02142. Phone, 617–494–2302	Mark H. McKeon
Eastern—DC, DE, MA, OH, PA, VA, WV	Suite 550, Scott Plz. II, Philadelphia, PA 19113. Phone, 610–521–8200	David R. Myers
Southern—AL, FL, GA, KY, MS, NC, SC, TN	Suite 16T20, 61 Forsyth St. SW., Atlanta, GA 30303–3104. Phone, 404–562–3800	L.F. Dennin II
Central—IL, IN, MI, MN, WI	Suite 655, 111 N. Canal St., Chicago, IL 60606. Phone, 312–353–6203	Laurence A. Hasvold
Southwestern—AR, LA, NM, OK, TX	Suite 425, 8701 Bedford Euless Rd., Hurst, TX 76053. Phone, 817–284–8142	John F. Megary
Midwestern—CO, IA, KS, MO, NE	Suite 1130, 1100 Main St., Kansas City, MO 64105. Phone, 816–426–2497	Darrell J. Tisor
Western—AZ, CA, NV, UT	Suite 466, 801 I St., Sacramento, CA 95814. Phone, 916–498–6540	Alvin Settje
Northwestern—AK, ID, MT, ND, OR, SD, WA, WY	Suite 650, 703 Broadway, Vancouver, WA 98660. Phone, 360–696–7536	Dick L. Clairmont

For further information, contact the Public Affairs Officer, Federal Railroad Administration, Department of Transportation, 400 Seventh Street SW., Washington, DC 20590. Phone, 202–632–3124. Internet, http://www.fra.dot.gov/.

National Highway Traffic Safety Administration

[For the National Highway Traffic Safety Administration statement of organization, see the *Code of Federal Regulations,* Title 49, Part 501]

The National Highway Traffic Safety Administration (NHTSA) was established by the Highway Safety Act of 1970 (23 U.S.C. 401 note) to carry out a congressional mandate to reduce the mounting number of deaths, injuries, and economic losses resulting from motor vehicle crashes on the Nation's highway.

Under the authority of title 49 of the United States Code, chapter 301, the

Administration carries out programs relating to the safety performance of motor vehicles and related equipment. Under the authority of the Highway Safety Act of 1966, as amended (23 U.S.C. 401 *et seq.*), the Administration carries out the Nation's State and community highway safety program (jointly administered with the Federal Highway Administration), known by its U.S. Code provision as the section 402 program. The major goal of the section 402 program is to provide Federal leadership, encouragement, and technical assistance to States and communities in their efforts to develop and implement the most effective highway safety programs to reduce traffic crashes and resulting deaths, injuries, and property damage. Section 402 enhances State and local programs by providing seed money to start new, more effective projects. Section 402 funds are provided to all States, territories, the District of Columbia, and the Secretary of the Interior on behalf of Indian Nations. At least 40 percent of these funds are used for local and community projects.

Under the authority of title 49 of the United States Code, chapters 321, 323, 325, 327, 329, and 331, the Administration carries out programs and studies aimed at reducing economic losses in motor vehicle crashes and repairs through general motor vehicle programs; administers the Federal odometer law; and issues theft prevention standards for passenger and nonpassenger motor vehicles.

Under the authority of title 49 of the United States Code, chapter 303, the Administration carries out the National Driver Register (NDR) Program to facilitate the interstate exchange of State records on problem drivers.

Activities

Research and Development The Administration's broad-scale program of research, development, testing, demonstration, and evaluation of motor vehicles, motor vehicle equipment, advanced technologies, and crash data collection and analysis provides a foundation for the development of motor vehicle and highway safety program standards.

The research program covers numerous areas affecting safety problems and includes provision for appropriate laboratory testing facilities to obtain necessary basic data. In this connection, research in both light and heavy vehicle crashworthiness and crash avoidance is being pursued. The objectives are to encourage industry to adopt advanced motor vehicle safety designs, stimulate public awareness of safety potentials, and provide a base for vehicle safety information.

The Administration maintains a collection of scientific and technical information related to motor vehicle safety, and operates the National Center for Statistics and Analysis, whose activities include the development and maintenance of highway crash data collection systems and related analysis efforts. These comprehensive motor vehicle safety information resources serve as documentary reference points for Federal, State, and local agencies, as well as industry, universities, and the public.

Safety Assurance The Office of Safety Assurance identifies and investigates problems with motor vehicles and motor vehicle equipment. If the Office determines that the vehicle or item of equipment contains a defect which is safety related or that it does not meet all applicable Federal motor vehicle safety standards, the Office will seek a recall in which owners are notified and the vehicles or equipment are remedied free of charge. The Office monitors recalls to ensure that owners are being notified, that the notifications are done in a timely manner, and that the scope of the recall and the remedy are adequate to correct the problem.

The Office operates the toll-free Auto Safety Hotline to identify safety problems in motor vehicles and motor vehicle equipment. Consumers can call the hotline at 800–424–9393 to report safety-related problems. These calls form the basis for investigations and ultimately recalls if safety-related defects are identified. The hotline also provides information and literature to consumers about vehicle and child-seat recalls, New Car Assessment Program test results, and a variety of other highway safety information.

To reduce odometer fraud, the Office investigates odometer tampering and supports prosecutions by the U.S. Department of Justice and the States.

Safety Performance Standards The Administration manages motor vehicle safety programs to:

—reduce the occurrence of highway crashes and the severity of resulting injuries;

—reduce the economic losses in crashes; and

—provide consumer information in the areas of crash test results, proper usage of vehicle safety features, and tire grading for treadwear, temperature resistance, and traction.

The Administration issues Federal Motor Vehicle Safety Standards that prescribe safety features and levels of safety-related performance for vehicles and items of motor vehicle equipment.

The Administration conducts the New Car Assessment Program, under which high-speed crash tests are conducted on passenger cars, light trucks, and vans to assess their frontal and side impact safety performance. Results from these tests are provided to the public to assist them in selecting and purchasing safer motor vehicles. The Administration also informs consumers on how to properly use vehicle safety features.

The Administration administers a Fuel Economy Program that is mandated by the Energy Policy and Conservation Act of 1975. The Administration establishes and revises, as appropriate, fleet average fuel economy standards for passenger car and light truck manufacturers to ensure that maximum feasible fuel economy is attained.

The Administration also carries out a Theft Program, issuing rules requiring the designation of likely high-theft vehicles that must comply with parts-marking requirements, and calculating and publishing annual motor vehicle theft rates.

State and Community Services The State and Community Highway Safety Grant Program provides funds to the States, Indian nations, and the Territories each year to support planning to identify and quantify highway safety problems, provide startup money for new programs, and give new direction to existing safety programs, particularly in the following national priority program areas: occupant protection, alcohol and other drug countermeasures, police traffic services, emergency medical services, traffic records, motorcycle safety, pedestrian and bicycle safety, speed control, and roadway safety. Incentive funds encourage States to implement effective impaired-driving programs.

Traffic Safety Programs The Administration leads the national traffic safety and emergency services efforts in order to save lives, reduce injuries, and lessen medical and other costs. In accomplishing these tasks, it utilizes behavioral research, demonstration, and evaluation, in addition to developing safety programs and strategies, for use by a variety of public and private agencies and organizations.

The Administration maintains a national register of information on individuals whose licenses to operate a motor vehicle have been revoked, suspended, canceled, or denied; or who have been convicted of certain traffic-related violations such as driving while impaired by alcohol or other drugs. The information obtained from the register assists State driver licensing officials in determining whether or not to issue a license.

For information concerning the National Highway Traffic Safety Administration, contact the Office of Public and Consumer Affairs, National Highway Traffic Safety Administration, Department of Transportation, 400 Seventh Street SW., Washington, DC 20590. Phone, 202–366–9550. Additional information may be obtained from the Technical Reference Division, Office of Administrative Operations. Phone, 202–366–2768.

Regional Offices—National Highway Traffic Safety Administration

Region/Address	Administrator
Atlanta, GA (Suite 17T30, 61 Forsyth St. SW., 30303)	Troy Ayers
Baltimore, MD (Suite 4000, 10 S. Howard St., 21201)	(Vacancy)
Cambridge, MA (Kendall Sq., Code 903, 02142)	George A. Luciano
Denver, CO (4th Fl., 555 Zang St., 80228)	Louis R. De Carolis
Fort Worth, TX (819 Taylor St., 76102–6177)	Georgia Chakiris
Kansas City, MO (P.O. Box 412515, 64141)	Romell Cooks
Olympia Fields, IL (Suite 201, 19900 Governors Dr., 60461)	Donald J. McNamara
San Francisco, CA (201 Mission St., 94105)	Joseph M. Cindrich
Seattle, WA 98174 (915 2d Ave.)	Curtis A. Winston
White Plains, NY (222 Mamaroneck Ave., 10605)	Tom Louizou

For further information, contact the Office of Public and Consumer Affairs, National Highway Traffic Safety Administration, Department of Transportation, 400 Seventh Street SW., Washington, DC 20590. Phone, 202–366–9550.

Federal Transit Administration

[For the Federal Transit Administration statement of organization, see the *Code of Federal Regulations*, Title 49, Part 601]

The Federal Transit Administration was established as a component of the Department of Transportation by section 1 of Reorganization Plan No. 2 of 1968 (5 U.S.C. app. 1), effective July 1, 1968. The Administration (formerly the Urban Mass Transportation Administration) administers the mass transportation programs of the Department of Transportation authorized by 49 U.S.C. 5301 *et seq.*, mass transportation and other applicable provisions of title 23 of the United States Code, and other pertinent legislation.

The missions of the Administration are:

—to assist in developing improved mass transportation equipment, facilities, techniques, and methods with the cooperation of public and private mass transportation companies;

—to encourage the planning and establishment of areawide mass transportation systems needed for economical and desirable development with the cooperation of public and private mass transportation companies;

—to assist States and local governments and their authorities in financing areawide mass transportation systems that are to be operated by public or private mass transportation companies as decided by local needs;

—to provide financial assistance to State and local governments and their authorities to help carry out national goals related to mobility for elderly individuals, individuals with disabilities, and economically disadvantaged individuals; and

—to establish a partnership that allows a community, with financial assistance from the Government, to satisfy its mass transportation requirements.

Programs

Capital Program The section 5309 grants are authorized to assist in financing the acquisition, construction, reconstruction, and improvement of facilities and equipment for use—by operation, lease, or otherwise—in mass transportation service in urban areas. Only public agencies are eligible as applicants. Private transit operators may be assisted under the program through arrangements with an eligible public body.

The Federal grant is 80 percent of the net project cost. If the project is in an urbanized area, it must be part of a program for a unified or officially coordinated urban transportation system as a part of the comprehensive planned development of the area.

Annual funding is allocated in three categories: 40-percent funding for fixed guideway modernization in which funds are apportioned by a statutory formula;

40-percent funding for construction of new, fixed guideway systems and their extensions; and 20-percent funding for replacement, rehabilitation, and purchase of buses and related equipment and the construction of bus-related facilities.

For further information, call 202–366–2053.

Elderly and Persons With Disabilities Program The section 5310 program provides financial assistance in meeting the transportation needs of elderly persons and persons with disabilities where services provided by public operators are unavailable, insufficient, or inappropriate; to public bodies approved by the State to coordinate services for elderly persons or persons with disabilities; or to public bodies which certify to the Governor that no nonprofit corporation or association is readily available in an area to provide the service. Funds are allocated by formula to the States; local organizations apply for funding through a designated State agency.

For further information, call 202–366–2053.

National Transit Institute The National Transit Institute (NTI) was established by Congress in section 29 of the Federal Transit Act (49 U.S.C. 5315) and funded for 6 years at $3 million a year. The NTI develops and conducts training and technical assistance activities in cooperation with the FTA and the transit industry. In addition, the NTI provides technical support relating to training, a clearinghouse function which includes cataloging of curriculum offered at the NTI and elsewhere, and referral services relating to the training and development needs of the transit industry.

For further information, call 202–366–0245.

Planning Programs The section 5303 program provides financial assistance in meeting the transportation planning needs of Metropolitan Planning Organizations (MPO's). Funds are allocated by formula to the States, and the States in turn allocate these funds by formula to MPO's representing urbanized areas, or parts thereof, within the States. Funding is provided on an 80 percent/20 percent funding match basis. The section 5313(b) program provides financial assistance to States for transportation planning, technical assistance studies and assistance, demonstrations, management training, and cooperative research. Funds are allocated to the States by formula on an 80 percent/20 percent funding match basis.

For further information, call 202–366–1626.

Nonurbanized Area Formula Program The section 5311 program provides capital and operating assistance for public transportation in nonurbanized areas (under 50,000 population). Funds are allocated by formula to the Governor and the program is administered at the State level by the designated transportation agency. Eligible activities are operating assistance, planning, administrative and program development activities, coordination of public transportation programs, vehicle acquisition, and other capital investments in support of general or special transit services, including services provided for the elderly and handicapped and other transit-dependent persons. A fixed percentage of a State's annual apportionment must be spent to carry out a program for the development and support of rural and intercity transportation, unless the State Governor certifies that such needs are adequately met. A Rural Transit Assistance Program authorized under section 18(h) provides funding for training and technical assistance for transit operators in nonurbanized areas. Capital assistance is funded up to an 80-percent Federal share and operating assistance is funded with up to a 50-percent Federal share.

Rural The Rural Transportation Assistance Program provides assistance for transit research, technical assistance, training, and related support activities in non-urbanized areas (less than 50,000 population). A portion of this is used at the national level for development of training materials, development and maintenance of a national clearing house on rural activities, and technical assistance through peer practitioners to promote exemplary techniques and practices.

For further information, call 202–366–4052.

Safety   The Federal Transit Administration Safety Program supports State and local agencies in fulfilling their responsibility for the safety and security of urban mass transportation facilities and services, through the encouragement and sponsorship of safety and security planning, training, information collection and analysis, drug control programs, system/safety assurance reviews, generic research, and other cooperative government/industry activities.

For further information, call 202–366–2896.

Technical Assistance   The Administration provides funds for research, development, and demonstration projects in urban transportation for the purpose of increasing productivity and efficiency in urban and nonurban area transportation systems, improving mass transportation service and equipment, and assisting State and local governments in providing total urban transportation services in a cost-effective, safe manner, and expanding private-sector participation in all facets of urban transportation.

The Administration conducts a program of research, development, and demonstration addressing the following principal areas: advanced public transportation systems, clean air, finance, information, human resources and productivity, regional mobility, rural transportation, safety and security, technology development, and transit accessibility.

Major project areas include developing and demonstrating new approaches to involve employers, developers, local governments, and transportation providers in finding solutions to the problems of regional mobility, with special emphasis on the following:

—promoting institutional changes required to improve mobility in suburban areas and between suburbs and central city locations;

—encouraging management and organized labor to jointly seek opportunities for improving performance through upgrading of skills for nonmanagerial personnel;

—identifying, evaluating, and documenting significant cost-effective approaches to modernizing existing rail transit systems;

—encouraging participation by the private sector in the provision of transportation services and encouragement of joint public/private financing of transit capital investments;

—providing guidance and training concerning long-term financial planning and leasing of capital assets;

—implementing a program of new model bus testing and test facility improvements;

—promoting the delivery of safe and effective public transportation in nonurbanized areas;

—assisting new safety and security initiatives, including safety training; and

—compiling information on costs, benefits, financial feasibility, and performance of new energy sources including nonpolluting fuels.

Projects are conducted under grants and cooperative agreements with public bodies, including State and local governments, or contracts with private organizations, both profit and nonprofit.

For further information, contact the Regional Office for the area concerned.

Urbanized Area Formula Program   Section 5307 is a formula-apportioned resource for capital, operating, and planning assistance. Recipients of funds in urbanized areas of over 200,000 population are jointly designated by the Governors of the respective States, local officials, and public transit operators. The Governor acts as recipient for urbanized areas with populations from 50,000 up to 200,000. Recipients must be State, regional, or local governmental bodies or public agencies. Private transit operators may be assisted under the program through arrangements with an eligible public entity.

Grants may be made for 80 percent of the project cost for capital and planning activities. Operating assistance is subject to changes in the 1998 budget. Each year, potential grantees submit a proposed program of projects for funding based on the State Transportation Improvement Program. This program contains all of the highway and transit projects endorsed at the metropolitan and State levels for Federal funding, resulting from the State and local transportation planning process.

For further information, contact the Regional Office for the area concerned.

For information concerning the Federal Transit Administration, contact the regional office for the area concerned or contact the Office of Public Affairs, Federal Transit Administration, Department of Transportation, 400 Seventh Street SW., Washington, DC 20590. Phone, 202–366–4043. Technical information may be obtained by contacting the Transit Research Information Center. Phone, 202–366–9157. Information is also available electronically through the Internet, at http://www.fta.dot.gov/.

Field Organization—Federal Transit Administration

Region/Address	Telephone
Arlington, TX (Suite 175, 524 E. Lamar Blvd., 76011–3900)	817–860–9663
Atlanta, GA (Suite 17T50, 61 Forsyth St. SW., 30303)	404–562–3500
Cambridge, MA (Suite 920, 55 Broadway, 02142)	617–494–2055
Chicago, IL (Suite 2410, 200 W. Adams St., 60606)	312–353–2789
Denver, CO (Suite 650, 216 16th St., 80202)	303–844–3242
Kansas City, MO (Suite 303, 6301 Rockhill Rd., 64131)	816–523–0204
New York, NY (Suite 2940, 26 Federal Plz., 10278)	212–264–8162
Philadelphia, PA (Suite 500, 1760 Market St., 19103)	215–656–7100
San Francisco, CA (Suite 2210, 201 Mission St., San Francisco, CA 94105)	415–744–3133
Seattle, WA (Suite 3142, 915 2d Ave., 98174)	206–220–7954

Metropolitan Offices—Federal Transit Administration

Office/Address	Telephone
Chicago, IL (24th Fl., 200 W. Adams St., 60606–5232)	312–886–1616
Los Angeles, CA (Suite 1460, 210 Figueroa, 90012)	213–202–3950
New York, NY (1 Bowling Green, 10274)	212–264–8162
Philadelphia, PA (Suite 500, 1760 Market St., 19103–4142)	215–656–7070

For further information, contact the Office of Public Affairs, Federal Transit Administration, Department of Transportation, 400 Seventh Street SW., Washington, DC 20590. Phone, 202–366–4043. Internet, http://www.fta.dot.gov/.

Maritime Administration

The Maritime Administration was established by Reorganization Plan No. 21 of 1950 (5 U.S.C. app.), effective May 24, 1950. The Maritime Act of 1981 (46 U.S.C. 1601) transferred the Maritime Administration to the Department of Transportation, effective August 6, 1981.

The Maritime Administration administers programs to aid in the development, promotion, and operation of the U.S. merchant marine. It is also charged with organizing and directing emergency merchant ship operations.

The Maritime Administration administers subsidy programs, through the Maritime Subsidy Board, under which the Federal Government, subject to statutory limitations, pays the difference between certain costs of operating ships under the U.S. flag and foreign competitive flags on essential services, and the difference between the costs of constructing ships in U.S. and foreign shipyards. It provides financing guarantees for the construction, reconstruction, and reconditioning of ships; and enters into capital construction fund agreements that grant tax deferrals on moneys to be used for the acquisition, construction, or reconstruction of ships.

The Administration constructs or supervises the construction of merchant type ships for the Federal Government. It helps industry generate increased business for U.S. ships and conducts programs to develop ports, facilities, and intermodal transport, and to promote domestic shipping.

The Administration conducts program and technical studies and administers a War Risk Insurance Program that insures operators and seamen against losses caused by hostile action if domestic commercial insurance is not available.

Under emergency conditions the Maritime Administration charters Government-owned ships to U.S. operators, requisitions or procures ships owned by U.S. citizens, and allocates them to meet defense needs.

It maintains a National Defense Reserve Fleet of Government-owned ships that it operates through ship managers and general agents when required in national defense interests. An element of this activity is the Ready Reserve Force consisting of a number of ships available for quick-response activation.

It regulates sales to aliens and transfers to foreign registry of ships that are fully or partially owned by U.S. citizens. It also disposes of Government-owned ships found nonessential for national defense.

The Administration operates the U.S. Merchant Marine Academy, Kings Point, NY, where young people are trained to become merchant marine officers, and conducts training in shipboard firefighting at Earle, NJ, and Toledo, OH. It also administers a Federal assistance program for the maritime academies operated by California, Maine, Massachusetts, Michigan, New York, and Texas.

Field Organization—Maritime Administration

Region	Address	Telephone
Central	Rm. 1223, 501 Magazine St., New Orleans, LA 70130–3394	504–589–2000
Great Lakes	Suite 185, 2860 South River Rd., Des Plaines, IL 60018–2413	847–298–4535
North Atlantic	Rm. 3737, 26 Federal Plz., New York, NY 10278	212–264–1300
South Atlantic	Rm. 211, 7737 Hampton Blvd., Norfolk, VA 23505	757–441–6393
U.S. Merchant Marine Academy	Kings Point, NY 11024–1699	516–773–5000
Western	Suite 2200, 201 Mission St., San Francisco, CA 94105–1905	415–744–3125

For further information, contact the Office of Congressional and Public Affairs, Maritime Administration, Department of Transportation, 400 Seventh Street SW., Washington, DC 20590. Phone, 202–366–5807; or 800–996–2723 (toll-free). Internet, http://www.marad.dot.gov/.

Saint Lawrence Seaway Development Corporation

The Saint Lawrence Seaway Development Corporation was established by the Saint Lawrence Seaway Act of May 13, 1954 (33 U.S.C. 981–990) and became an operating administration of the Department of Transportation in 1966.

The Corporation, working cooperatively with the Saint Lawrence Seaway Authority (SLSA) of Canada, is dedicated to operating and maintaining a safe, reliable, and efficient deep draft waterway between the Great Lakes and the Atlantic Ocean. It regulates U.S.

pilotage on the Great Lakes and the Saint Lawrence River, and ensures the safe transit of commercial and noncommercial vessels through the two U.S. locks and the navigation channels of the Saint Lawrence Seaway System. The Corporation works jointly with SLSA on all matters related to rules and regulations, overall operations, vessel inspections, traffic control, navigation aids, safety, operating dates, and trade development programs.

The Great Lakes/Saint Lawrence Seaway System extends from the Atlantic

Ocean to the Lake Superior ports of Duluth/Superior, a distance of 2,342 miles. The Corporation's main customers are vessel owners and operators, Midwest States and Canadian provinces, Great Lakes port communities, shippers and receivers of domestic and international cargo, and the Lakes/Seaway maritime and related services industries. International and domestic commerce through the Seaway contributes to the economic prosperity of the entire Great Lakes region.

For further information, contact the Director of Congressional and Public Affairs, Saint Lawrence Seaway Development Corporation, Department of Transportation, P.O. Box 44090, Washington, DC 20026–4090. Phone, 202–366–0091. Fax, 202–366–7147. Internet, http://www.dot.gov/slsdc/.

Research and Special Programs Administration

The Research and Special Programs Administration (RSPA) was established formally on September 23, 1977. It is responsible for hazardous materials transportation and pipeline safety, transportation emergency preparedness, safety training, and multimodal transportation research and development activities.

Office of Hazardous Materials Safety

400 Seventh Street SW., Washington, DC 20590. Phone, 202–366–0656

The Office of Hazardous Materials Safety develops and issues regulations for the safe transportation of hazardous materials by all modes, excluding bulk transportation by water. The regulations cover shipper and carrier operations, packaging and container specifications, and hazardous materials definitions. The Office is also responsible for the enforcement of regulations other than those applicable to a single mode of transportation. The Office manages a user-fee funded grant program to assist States in planning for hazardous materials emergencies and to assist States and Indian tribes with training for hazardous materials emergencies. Additionally, the Office executes a national safety program to safeguard food and certain other products from contamination during motor or rail transportation. A computer bulletin board, in conjunction with the Federal Emergency Management Agency, offers nationwide access to topics related to hazardous materials transportation safety and can be accessed by dialing 1–800–PLANFOR (752–6367). The Office is the national focal point for coordination and control of the Department's multimodal hazardous materials regulatory program, ensuring uniformity of approach and action by all modal administrations.

Regional Offices—Office of Hazardous Materials Safety

Region	Address	Chief
Central—IA, IL, IN, KY, MI, MN, MO, ND, NE, OH, SD, WI	Suite 136, 2350 E. Devon Ave., Des Plaines, IL 60018	Kevin Boehne
Eastern—CT, DC, DE, MA, MD, ME, NH, NJ, NY, PA, RI, VA, VT, WV	Suite 306, 820 Bear Tavern Rd., W. Trenton, NJ 08628	Colleen Abbenhaus
Southern—AL, FL, GA, MS, NC, PR, SC, TN	Suite 520, 1701 Columbia Ave., College Park, GA 30337	John Heneghan
Southwest—AR, CO, KS, LA, NM, OK, TX	Suite 2118, 2320 LaBranch St., Houston, TX 77002	Jesse Hughes
Western—AK, AZ, CA, HI, ID, MT, NV, OR, UT, WA, WY	Suite 230, 3200 Inland Empire Blvd., Ontario, CA 91764	Anthony Smialek

Office of Pipeline Safety

400 Seventh Street SW., Washington, DC 20590. Phone, 202–366–4595

The Office of Pipeline Safety establishes and provides for compliance with standards that assure public safety and environmental protection in the transportation of gas and hazardous liquids by pipeline. The Office administers a program whereby a State agency can voluntarily assert safety regulatory jurisdiction over all or some intrastate pipeline facilities. The Federal Government is authorized to pay a State agency grant-in-aid funds of up to 50 percent of the actual cost for carrying out its pipeline safety program. The Office under the Oil Pollution Act of 1990 established regulations requiring petroleum pipeline operators to prepare and submit plans to respond to oil spills for Federal review and approval.

Regional Offices—Office of Pipeline Safety

Region	Address	Chief
Central—IA, IL, IN, KS, MI, MN, MO, ND, NE, OH, SD, WI	Rm. 1120, 1100 Main St., Kansas City, MO 64105	Ivan Huntoon
Eastern—CT, DC, DE, MA, MD, ME, NH, NJ, NY, PA, RI, VA, VT, WV	Rm. 2108, 400 7th St. SW., Washington, DC 20590	William Gute
Southern—AL, AR, FL, GA, KY, MS, NC, PR, SC, TN	Suite 6T15, 61 Forsyth St., Atlanta, GA 30303	Frederick Joyner
Southwest—AZ, LA, NM, OK, TX	Rm. 2116, 2320 LaBranch St., Houston, TX 77004	Rodrick M. Seeley
Western—AK, CA, CO, HI, ID, MT, NV, OR, UT, WA, WY	Suite A250, 12600 W. Colfax Ave., Lakewood, CO 80215	Edward Ondak

Office of Research, Technology, and Analysis

400 Seventh Street SW., Washington, DC 20590. Phone, 202–366–4434

The Office of Research, Technology, and Analysis shapes and advances the United States transportation research and development (R&D) agenda by leading departmental and national strategic planning efforts; conducting system-level assessments; facilitating national and international partnerships; stimulating university research and safety training; disseminating information on departmental, national, and international transportation R&D; and managing Department-wide strategic (intermodal/multimodal) transportation research, technology, education, and training activities.

Strategic Planning and System Assessment   In addition to publishing the Surface Transportation R&D Plan, the Office plays a leading role in developing the National Transportation Science and Technology Strategy and the Transportation Technology and Intermodal/Multimodal Transportation Research Plans, producing the National Transportation System Assessment, International Transportation S&T Assessment, and Transportation Energy and Environmental Assessments in support of national economic goals.

Coordination and Facilitation   The Office supports White House and departmental transportation science and technology coordination activities. It creates international transportation R&D partnerships and establishes innovative government-university-industry R&D partnership processes. The Office created and maintains the national Transportation Science and Technology web site (Internet, http://scitech.dot.gov).

Intermodal and Multimodal Research and Education   The Office serves as principal adviser to RSPA and the Department on university research and education activities; provides a point of contact with the academic community; stimulates broad-based university involvement with international transportation issues and research; and manages a national grant program to establish and operate university-based centers of excellence in transportation education, research, and technology transfer (Internet, http://educ.dot.gov). The Office manages intermodal/multimodal strategic transportation R&D programs, leveraging Government transportation R&D investments.

Transportation Safety Institute

Department of Transportation, 6500 South McArthur Boulevard, Oklahoma City, OK 73125. Phone, 405–954–3153

The Institute was established in 1971 by the Secretary of Transportation to support the Department's efforts to reduce the number and cost of transportation accidents by promoting safety and security management through education. The Institute is a primary source of transportation safety and security training and technical assistance on domestic and international levels for Department of Transportation elements, as well as other Federal, State, and local government agencies.

Office of Emergency Transportation

400 Seventh Street SW., Washington, DC 20590. Phone, 202–366–5270

The Office of Emergency Transportation provides the staff to administer and execute the Secretary of Transportation's statutory and administrative responsibilities in the area of transportation civil emergency preparedness. It is the primary element of the Department engaged in the development, coordination, and review of policies, plans, and programs for attaining and maintaining a high state of Federal transportation emergency preparedness. This Office oversees the effective discharge of the Secretary's responsibilities in all emergencies affecting the national defense and in national or regional emergencies, including those caused by natural disasters and other crisis situations.

Volpe National Transportation Systems Center

Kendall Square, Cambridge, MA 02142. Phone, 617–494–2224

The Volpe National Transportation Systems Center (Volpe Center), as part of RSPA, provides research, analysis, and systems capability to the Department of Transportation (DOT) and other agencies requiring expertise in national transportation and logistics programs.

Integrated systems approaches are developed by Volpe Center to address Federal transportation issues of national importance. It does not appear as a line item in the Federal budget, but is funded directly by its sponsors. Volpe Center projects are therefore responsive to customer needs. The Center has come to be increasingly recognized by government, industry, and academia as a focal point for the assimilation, generation, and interchange of knowledge and understanding concerning national and international transportation and logistics systems. The Volpe Center is widely valued as a vital national resource for solving complex transportation and logistics problems.

Based on shifting national priorities and availability of its resources, Volpe Center programmatic activities for DOT and other agencies vary from year to year.

Volpe Center programs emphasize policy support and analysis, cost-effective Government procurement, environmental protection and remediation, transportation safety and security, and infrastructure modernization.

For further information, contact the Office of Program and Policy Support, Research and Special Programs Administration, Department of Transportation, 400 Seventh Street SW., Washington, DC 20590. Phone, 202–366–4831.

Bureau of Transportation Statistics

The Bureau of Transportation Statistics (BTS) was organized pursuant to section 6006 of the Intermodal Surface Transportation Efficiency Act of 1991 (ISTEA) (49 U.S.C. 111), and was formally established by the Secretary of

Transportation on December 16, 1992. The Bureau has an intermodal transportation focus whose missions are to compile, analyze, and make accessible information on the Nation's transportation systems; to collect information on intermodal transportation and other areas; and to enhance the quality and effectiveness of DOT statistical programs through research, the development of guidelines, and the promotion of improvements in data acquisition and use.

The Bureau is mandated by ISTEA to:

—compile, analyze, and publish statistics;

—develop a long-term data collection program;

—develop guidelines to improve the credibility and effectiveness of the Department's statistics;

—represent transportation interests in the statistical community;

—make statistics accessible and understandable; and

—identify data needs.

The Bureau acquired the Office of Airline Information (OAI) pursuant to DOT 1100.70 Chg. 1 and 60 FR 30195, in June of 1995. The Office collects air carrier financial and traffic data (passenger and freight) pursuant to 49 U.S.C. 329 and 41708. This information provides uniform and comprehensive economic and market data on individual airline operations.

The Bureau is also responsible for collecting motor carrier financial data pursuant to 49 U.S.C. 14123 (Public Law 104–88). This function was transferred to BTS, effective January 1, 1996, after the termination of the Interstate Commerce Commission.

For further information, call 202–366–DATA. Fax, 202–366–3640. Fax-on-demand, 800–671–8012. Internet, http://www.bts.gov/. E-mail, info@bts.gov. Gopher, gopher.bts.gov. Phone (modem), 800–363–4BTS.

Surface Transportation Board

The Surface Transportation Board was established in 1996 by the ICC Termination Act of 1995 (49 U.S.C. 10101 et seq.) as a decisionally independent, bipartisan, adjudicatory body organizationally housed within the Department of Transportation, with jurisdiction over certain surface transportation economic regulatory matters formerly under ICC jurisdiction.

The Board consists of three members, appointed by the President with the advice and consent of the Senate for 5-year terms. The Board's Chairman is designated by the President from among the members.

The Board adjudicates disputes and regulates interstate surface transportation through various laws pertaining to the different modes of surface transportation. The Board's general responsibilities include the oversight of firms engaged in transportation in interstate and foreign commerce to the extent that it takes place within the United States, or

between or among points in the contiguous United States and points in Alaska, Hawaii, or U.S. territories or possessions. Surface transportation matters under the Board's jurisdiction in general include railroad rate and service issues, rail restructuring transactions (mergers, line sales, line construction, and line abandonments), and labor matters related thereto; certain trucking company, moving van, and noncontiguous ocean shipping company rate matters; certain intercity passenger bus company structure, financial, and operational matters; and certain pipeline matters not regulated by the Federal Energy Regulatory Commission.

In the performance of its functions, the Board is charged with promoting, where appropriate, substantive and procedural regulatory reform and providing an efficient and effective forum for the resolution of disputes. Through the granting of exemptions from regulations where warranted, the streamlining of its decisionmaking process and the regulations applicable thereto, and the consistent and fair application of legal and equitable principles, the Board seeks to provide an effective forum for efficient dispute resolution and facilitation of appropriate market-based business transactions. Through rulemakings and case disposition, it strives to develop new and better ways to analyze unique and complex problems, to reach fully justified decisions more quickly, to reduce the costs associated with regulatory oversight, and to encourage private sector negotiations and resolutions to problems, where appropriate.

For further information, contact the Office of Congressional and External Affairs, Surface Transportation Board, Room 843, 1925 K Street NW., Washington, DC 20423–0001. Phone, 202–565–1594.

Sources of Information

Inquiries for information on the following subjects should be directed to the specified office, Department of Transportation, Washington, DC 20590, or to the address indicated.

Coast Guard Career and Training Opportunities For information on the U.S. Coast Guard Academy, contact the Director of Admissions, U.S. Coast Guard Academy, New London, CT 06320. Phone, 860–444–8444. Internet, http://www.uscg.mil/.

Information on the enlistment program and the Officer Candidate School may be obtained from the local recruiting offices or the U.S. Coast Guard Personnel Command (CGPC) Recruiting Center. Phone, 703–235–1169.

Persons interested in joining the Coast Guard Auxiliary may obtain information from the Commandant (G–OCX), U.S. Coast Guard, Washington, DC 20593. Phone, 202–267–0982.

Consumer Activities For information about air travelers' rights or for assistance in resolving consumer problems with providers of commercial air transportation services, contact the Consumer Affairs Division (phone, 202–366–2220); for consumer assistance, to report possible boat safety defects, and to obtain information on boats and associated equipment involved in safety defect (recall) campaigns, call the U.S. Coast Guard's Boating Safety Hotline. Residents of Washington, DC, call 267–0780. Other residents nationwide, call 800–368–5647 (toll-free).

To report vehicle safety problems, obtain information on motor vehicle and highway safety, or to request consumer information publications, call the National Highway Traffic Safety Administration's 24-hour auto safety hotline. Phone, 202–366–0123 (Washington, DC, area) or 800–424–9393 (toll-free except Alaska and Hawaii).

Contracts Contact the Office of Acquisition and Grant Management. Phone, 202–366–4285.

Employment The principal occupations in the Department are air traffic controller, aviation safety specialist, electronics maintenance technician, engineer (civil, aeronautical, automotive, electronic, highway, and general), administrative/management, and clerical. For further information, contact the Transportation Administrative Service Center (TASC) DOT Connection, Room PL–402, 400 Seventh Street SW., Washington, DC 20590. Phone, 202–366–9391 or 800–525–2878 (toll-free).

Environment Inquiries on environmental activities and programs should be directed to the Assistant Secretary for Transportation Policy, Office of Environment, Energy, and Safety, Washington, DC 20590. Phone, 202–366–4366.

Films Many films on transportation subjects are available for use by educational institutions, community groups, private organizations, etc. Requests for specific films relating to a particular mode of transportation may be directed to the appropriate operating administration.

Fraud, Waste, and Abuse　To report, contact the Office of Inspector General hotline, P.O. Box 23178, Washington, DC 20026–0178. Phone, 202–366–1461 or 800–424–9071 (toll-free).

Publications　The Department and its operating agencies issue publications on a wide variety of subjects. Many of these publications are available from the issuing agency or for sale from the Government Printing Office and the National Technical Information Service, 5285 Port Royal Road, Springfield, VA 22151. Contact the Department or the specific agency at the addresses indicated in the text.

Reading Rooms　Contact the Department of Transportation TASC Dockets, PL–401, 400 Seventh Street SW., Washington, DC 20590. Phone, 800–647–5527. Administrations and their regional offices maintain reading rooms for public use. Contact the specific administration at the address indicated in the text.

Other reading rooms include: TASC Department of Transportation Library, Room 2200, 400 Seventh Street SW., Washington, DC 20590 (phone, 202–366–0745); Department of Transportation/TASC Law Library, Room 2215, 400 Seventh Street SW., Washington, DC 20590 (phone, 202–366–0749); Department of

Transportation/TASC Library, FB–10A Branch, Room 930, 800 Independence Avenue SW., Washington, DC 20591 (phone, 202–267–3115); and Department of Transportation/TASC Library, Transpoint Branch, B–726, 2100 Second Street SW., Washington, DC 20593 (phone, 202–267–2536).

Speakers　The Department of Transportation and its operating administrations and regional offices make speakers available for civic, labor, and community groups. Contact the specific agency or the nearest regional office at the address indicated in the text.

Surface Transportation Board Proceedings and Public Records
Requests for public assistance with pending or potential proceedings of the Board should be addressed to the Office of Public Services, Surface Transportation Board, Room 848, 1925 K Street NW., Washington, DC 20423–0001. Phone, 202–565–1592.

Requests for access to the Board's public records should be made to the Office of the Secretary, Surface Transportation Board, Room 700, 1925 K Street NW., Washington, DC 20423–0001. Phone, 202–565–1674.

Telephone Directory　The Department of Transportation telephone directory is available for sale by the Superintendent of Documents, Government Printing Office, Washington, DC 20402.

For further information concerning the Department of Transportation, contact the Office of the Assistant Secretary for Public Affairs, Department of Transportation, 400 Seventh Street SW., Washington, DC 20590. Phone, 202–366–5580. Internet, http://www.dot.gov/.

DEPARTMENT OF THE TREASURY

1500 Pennsylvania Avenue NW., Washington, DC 20220
Phone, 202–622–2000. Internet, http://www.treas.gov/.

SECRETARY OF THE TREASURY	ROBERT E. RUBIN
Deputy Secretary	LAWRENCE H. SUMMERS
Chief of Staff	MICHAEL FROMAN
Executive Secretary	NEAL COMSTOCK
Under Secretary (Domestic Finance)	JOHN D. HAWKE, JR.
Senior Adviser for Domestic Finance	GERALD MURPHY
Principal Deputy Assistant Secretary for Government Finance Policy Analysis	(VACANCY)
Director, Office of Corporate Finance	(VACANCY)
Director, Office of Government Financing	CHARLES D. HAWORTH
Director, Office of Synthetic Fuels	(VACANCY)
Deputy Assistant Secretary (Community Development Policy)	MICHAEL BARR
Director, Community Development Financial Institutions Fund	ELLEN LAZAR
Assistant Secretary (Financial Institutions)	RICHARD S. CARNELL
Deputy Assistant Secretary for Financial Institutions Policy	GREGORY A. BAER
Director, Office of Financial Institutions Policy	JOAN AFFLECK-SMITH
Director, Office of Government Sponsored Enterprise Policy	EDWARD J. DEMARCO
Assistant Secretary (Financial Markets)	GARY GENSLER
Senior Advisor, New Currency	MALCOLM CARTER
Deputy Assistant Secretary for Federal Finance	ROGER L. ANDERSON
Director, Office of Market Finance	JILL K. OUSELEY
Director, Office of Federal Finance Policy Analysis	NORMAN K. CARLETON
Fiscal Assistant Secretary	DONALD V. HAMMOND, *Acting*
Deputy Fiscal Assistant Secretary	DONALD V. HAMMOND
Assistant Fiscal Assistant Secretary	DAVID LEBRYK
Director, Office of Cash and Debt Management	DONALD A. CHIODO
Senior Adviser for Fiscal Management	ROGER A. BEZDEK
Senior Policy Adviser	DIANE DOGAN HILLIARD
Under Secretary (Enforcement)	RAYMOND W. KELLY
Director, Office of Finance and Administration	ANNA FAY DICKEY
Assistant Secretary (Enforcement)	JAMES E. JOHNSON
Senior Adviser	CLAIRE S. WELLINGTON
Deputy Assistant Secretary (Law Enforcement)	ELISABETH BRESEE
Director, Project Outreach	HERBERT JONES

441

Director, Executive Office of Asset Forfeiture	JAN BLANTON
Deputy Assistant Secretary (Enforcement Policy)	DAVID MEDINA
Director, Office of Financial Crimes Enforcement Network (FinCEN)	WILLIAM BAITY, *Acting*
Deputy Assistant Secretary (Regulatory, Tariff, and Trade Enforcement)	JOHN P. SIMPSON
Director, Office of Trade and Tariff Affairs	DENNIS M. O'CONNELL
Director, Office of Foreign Assets Control	R. RICHARD NEWCOMB
Assistant Secretary (Economic Policy)	DAVID WILCOX
Deputy Assistant Secretary (Economic Policy)	(VACANCY)
Director, Office of Financial Analysis	JOHN H. AUTEN
Deputy Assistant Secretary for Policy Coordination	ROBERT F. GILLINGHAM
Director, Office of Economic Analysis	(VACANCY)
Director, Office of Policy Analysis	JOHN C. HAMBOR
Director, Office of International Financial Analysis	THOMAS A. MCCOWN, JR.
Director, Office of Foreign Portfolio Investment Survey	WILLIAM L. GRIEVER
Deputy Assistant Secretary (Policy Analysis)	JONATHAN GRUBER
Inspector General	(VACANCY)
Deputy Inspector General	RICHARD B. CALAHAN
Special Assistant to the Inspector General	DONALD KASSEL
Director, Inspectors General Auditor Training Institute	ANDREW J. PASDEN
Counsel to the Inspector General	LORI Y. VASSAR
Deputy Counsel to the Inspector General	RICHARD DOERY
Director of Evaluations	EMILIE M. BAEBEL
Director of Information Technology	(VACANCY)
Assistant Inspector General for Investigations and Oversight	RAISA OTERO-CESARIO
Deputy Assistant Inspector General for Investigations and Oversight	(VACANCY)
Assistant Inspector General for Audit	DENNIS S. SCHINDEL
Deputy Assistant Inspector General for Audit (Financial Management)	WILLIAM H. PUGH
Assistant Inspector General for Resources/ Chief Financial Officer	GARY L. WHITTINGTON
Deputy Assistant Inspector General for Resources/Deputy Chief Financial Officer	CLIFFORD H. JENNINGS
General Counsel	EDWARD S. KNIGHT
Deputy General Counsel	NEAL S. WOLIN
Associate General Counsel (Legislation, Litigation, and Regulation)	RICHARD S. CARRO
Assistant General Counsel (Banking and Finance)	ROBERT MCINERNEY
Assistant General Counsel (Enforcement)	(VACANCY)
Assistant General Counsel (General Law and Ethics)	KENNETH R. SCHMALZBACH
Assistant General Counsel (International Affairs)	RUSSELL L. MUNK
Chief Counsel, Foreign Assets Control	WILLIAM B. HOFFMAN

Tax Legislative Counsel	(VACANCY)
International Tax Counsel	PHILLIP WEST
Benefits Tax Counsel	J. MARK IWRY
Under Secretary (International Affairs)	DAVID A. LIPTON
Assistant Secretary (International Affairs)	TIMOTHY GEITHNER
Director of Program Services	DANIEL A. O'BRIEN, *Acting*
Deputy Assistant Secretary for International Monetary and Financial Policy	CAROLINE ATKINSON
Director, International Banking and Securities Markets	WILLIAM C. MURDEN
Director, Office of International Monetary Policy	JAMES M. LISTER
Director, Office of Foreign Exchange Operations	TIMOTHY DULANEY
Director, Office of Industrial Nations and Global Analysis	JOSEPH GAGNON
Deputy Assistant Secretary for Asia, the Americas, and Africa	DANIEL M. ZELIKOW
Director, Office of East Asian Nations	TODD CRAWFORD
Director, Office of African Affairs	EDWIN L. BARBER
Director, Office of Latin American and Caribbean Nations	WESLEY MCGREW
Deputy Assistant Secretary for International Development, Debt, and Environmental Policy	WILLIAM SCHUERCH
Director, Office of Multilateral Development Banks	JOSEPH EICHENBERGER
Director, Office of International Debt Policy	MARY E. CHAVES
Deputy Assistant Secretary for Trade and Investment Policy	MARGRETHE LUNDSAGER
Director, Office of International Trade	T. WHITTIER WARTHIN
Director, Office of International Investment	GAY S. HOAR
Director, Office of Trade Finance	STEPHEN TVARDEK
Director, Office of Financial Services	MATTHEW HENNESEY
Deputy Assistant Secretary for Eurasia and Middle East	MARK MEDISH
Director, Bosnia Task Force	MICHAEL MONDERER
Director, Office of Central and Eastern European Nations	NANCY LEE
Director, Office of Middle Eastern and Central Asian Nations	KAREN MATHIASEN, *Acting*
Deputy Assistant Secretary for Technical Assistance Policy	JAMES H. FALL III
Director, Office of Technical Assistance	ROBERT T. BANQUE
Director, U.S.-Saudi Arabian Joint Commission Program Office	JAN M. GASSERUD
Assistant Secretary (Legislative Affairs and Public Liaison)	LINDA L. ROBERTSON
Director, Office of Legislative Affairs	GAIL E. PETERSON
Congressional Inquiries	ORA STARKS
Deputy Assistant Secretary (Banking and Finance)	VICTORIA ROSTOW
Deputy Assistant Secretary (Tax and Budget)	RUTH M. THOMAS

Deputy Assistant Secretary (Appropriation and Management)	ROBERT BEAN
Deputy Assistant Secretary for Public Liaison	JOYCE H. CARRIER
Directors, Office of Business and Public Liaison	LISA ANDREWS, SARAH FORDNEY
Assistant Secretary for Management/Chief Financial Officer	NANCY KILLEFER
Deputy Chief Financial Officer	STEVEN O. APP
Director, Office of Accounting and Internal Control	JAMES LINGEBACH
Director, Office of Financial and Budget Execution	BARRY K. HUDSON
Director, Office of Financial Systems and Reports	DENNIS MITCHELL
Deputy Assistant Secretary for Strategy and Finance	LISA ROSS
Director, Office of Strategic Planning	JOHN MURPHY
Director, Office of Budget	CARL MORAVITZ
Director, Office of Organizational Improvement	NANCY PROVENZANO, *Acting*
Executive Director (IRS Management Board)	ROBERT MILLER
Deputy Assistant Secretary for Management Operations	THEODORE CARTER
Director, Office of Security	RICHARD P. RILEY
Director, Office of Real and Personal Property Management	ROBERT T. HARPER
Director, Office of Procurement	ANNELIE KUHN, *Acting*
Director, Office of Small and Disadvantaged Business Utilization	T.J. GARCIA
Director, Office of Treasury Reinvention	ANTHONY A. FLEMING
Deputy Assistant Secretary for Administration	ALEX RODRIGUEZ
Director, Administrative Operations Division	IDA HERNANDEZ
Director, Automated Systems Division	G. DALE SEWARD
Director, Office of the Curator	PAULA A. MOHR
Director, Facilities Management Division	JAMES R. HAULSEY
Director, Financial Management Division	LINDA RIPETTA, *Acting*
Director, Printing and Graphics Division	KIRK B. MARKLAND
Director, Procurement Services Division	WESLEY L. HAWLEY
Deputy Assistant Secretary for Information Systems/Chief Information Officer	JAMES J. FLYZIK
Director, Office of Information Technology Policy and Management	JANE L. SULLIVAN
Director, Office of Corporate Systems Management	BRIAN P. CARMAN, *Acting*
Director, Office of CIO Liaison and Business Services	CANDACE HARDESTY
Deputy Assistant Secretary for Human Resources	KAY FRANCES DOLAN
Director, Office of Personnel Policy	RONALD A. GLASER, *Acting*
Director, Office of Equal Opportunity Program	MARIAM G. HARVEY, *Acting*
Director, Treasury Integrated Management Information Systems	EDWARD B. POWELL III

Director, Treasury Executive Institute	HARRIET BOBO
Director, Personnel Resources Division	(VACANCY)
Assistant Secretary (Public Affairs)	HOWARD M. SCHLOSS
Deputy Assistant Secretary for Public Affairs	SUSAN LEWIS SALLET
Director, Public Affairs	MICHELLE SMITH
Assistant Secretary (Tax Policy)	DONALD C. LUBICK
Deputy Assistant Secretary (Tax Policy)	JONATHAN TALISMAN
Tax Legislative Counsel	(VACANCY)
International Tax Counsel	PHILLIP WEST
Benefits Tax Counsel	J. MARK IWRY
Deputy Assistant Secretary (International Tax Policy)	JOSEPH GUTTENTAG
Deputy Assistant Secretary (Tax Analysis)	JOHN KARL SCHOLZ
Director, Office of Tax Analysis	LOWELL DWORIN
Treasurer of the United States	MARY ELLEN WITHROW

BUREAU OF ALCOHOL, TOBACCO, AND FIREARMS

650 Massachusetts Avenue NW., Washington, DC 20226
Phone, 202–927–8500. Fax, 202–927–8868. Internet, http://www.atf.treas.gov/.

Director	JOHN W. MAGAW
Deputy Director	BRADLEY A. BUCKLES
Ombudsman	STANLEY ZIMMERMAN
Executive Assistant (Legislative Affairs)	STEVE J. PIROTTE
Executive Assistant (Equal Opportunity)	MARJORIE R. KORNEGAY
Chief, Strategic Planning Office	WAYNE MILLER
Assistant Director (Liaison and Public Information)	DAVID BENTON
Chief Counsel	STEPHEN J. MCHALE
Assistant Director (Inspection)	RICHARD J. HANKINSON
Assistant Director (Management)/Chief Financial Officer	WILLIAM T. EARLE
Assistant Director (Field Operations)	ANDY L. VITA
Assistant Director (Firearms, Explosives, and Arson)	JIMMY WOOTEN
Assistant Director (Alcohol and Tobacco)	ARTHUR J. LIBERTUCCI
Assistant Director (Science and Information Technology)/Chief Information Officer	PATRICK R. SCHAMBACH
Assistant Director (Training and Professional Development)	GALE D. ROSSIDES

OFFICE OF THE COMPTROLLER OF THE CURRENCY

250 E Street SW., Washington, DC 20219
Phone, 202–874–5000

Comptroller	JULIE WILLIAMS, *Acting*
Senior Adviser to the Comptroller	MARK P. JACOBSEN
Deputy Comptroller for Risk Evaluation and Market Risks	MICHAEL L. BROSNAN, *Acting*
Deputy Comptroller for Information Technology Services	STEVEN M. YOHAI
Deputy to the FDIC Director (Comptroller of the Currency)	THOMAS E. ZEMKE
Senior Deputy Comptroller for Public Affairs	LEONORA CROSS, *Acting*

Director, Banking Relations	WILLIAM F. GRANT III
Director, Community Relations	BUD KANITZ
Director, Congressional Liaison	CAROLYN S. MCFARLANE
Special Adviser for External Relations	J. CHRISTOPHER LEWIS, JR.
Deputy Comptroller for Public Affairs	LEONORA CROSS
Director, Communications	THOMAS BAUCOM, *Acting*
Director, Press Relations	ROBERT M. GARSSON, JR.
Senior Deputy Comptroller for Bank Supervision Operations	LEANN G. BRITTON
Deputy Comptrollers for Large Banks	DELORA NG JEE, TIMOTHY W. LONG, DOUGLAS W. ROEDER
Deputy Comptroller for Continuing Education	MARK A. NISHAN
Deputy Comptroller for Supervisory Support	ANN F. JAEDICKE
Senior Deputy Comptroller for Bank Supervision Policy	E. WAYNE RUSHTON
Senior Adviser	RALPH E. SHARPE
Deputy Comptroller for Community and Consumer Policy	STEPHEN M. CROSS
Deputy Comptroller for Core Policy	KEVIN J. BAILEY
Deputy Comptroller for Credit Risk	DAVID D. GIBBONS
Senior Deputy Comptroller for Economic and Policy Analysis	JAMES D. KAMIHACHI
Senior Adviser	EMILY MARWELL
Deputy Comptroller for Economics	DAVID H. NEBHUT
Senior Deputy Comptroller for International Affairs	SUSAN F. KRAUSE
Deputy Comptroller for International Banking and Finance	JOHN M. ABBOTT
Ombudsman	SAMUEL P. GOLDEN
Senior Deputy Comptroller for Administration	EDWARD J. HANLEY
Deputy Comptroller for Resource Management	GARY W. NORTON
Chief Financial Officer	RONALD P. PASSERO
Chief Counsel	JULIE L. WILLIAMS
Deputy Chief Counsels	ROBERT B. SERINO
	RAYMOND NATTER
Deputy Comptroller for Bank Organization and Structure	STEVEN J. WEISS

UNITED STATES CUSTOMS SERVICE

1300 Pennsylvania Avenue NW., Washington, DC 20229
Phone, 202–927–6724

Commissioner of Customs	SAMUEL BANKS, *Acting*
Confidential Assistant	DAWN RENEAU
Chief of Staff	HOLM J. KAPPLER
Deputy Commissioner	SAMUEL BANKS
Special Assistant to the Deputy Commissioner	ROBERT MITCHELL
Assistant Commissioner (Regulations and Rulings)	STUART SEIDEL
Assistant Commissioner (Investigations)	BONNI TISCHLER
Assistant Commissioner (International Affairs)	DOUGLAS BROWNING

Assistant Commissioner (Congressional and Public Affairs)	SETH STATLER
Assistant Commissioner (Field Operations)	ROBERT TROTTER
Assistant Commissioner (Finance)	VINCETTE GOERL
Assistant Commissioner (Information and Technology)	ROBERT MCNAMARA
Assistant Commissioner (Human Resources Management)	DEBORAH SPERO
Assistant Commissioner (Strategic Trade)	CHARLES WINWOOD
Assistant Commissioner (Internal Affairs)	HOMER WILLIAMS
Chief Counsel	ELIZABETH ANDERSON
Director, Planning and Evaluation	WILLIAM F. RILEY
Ombudsman	WALTER CORLEY
Special Assistant to the Commissioner and Director, Equal Employment Opportunity	LINDA BATTS

BUREAU OF ENGRAVING AND PRINTING
Fourteenth and C Streets SW., Washington, DC 20228
Phone, 202–874–3019

Director	(VACANCY)
Deputy Director	THOMAS A. FERGUSON
Associate Director (Chief Financial Officer)	GREGORY D. CARPER
Associate Director (Chief Operating Officer)	(VACANCY)
Associate Director (Management)	(VACANCY)
Associate Director (Technology)	CARLA F. KIDWELL
Chief Counsel	CARROL H. KINSEY

FEDERAL LAW ENFORCEMENT TRAINING CENTER
Glynco, GA 31524. Phone, 912–267–2100. Fax, 912–267–2495
Washington, DC. Phone, 202–927–8940. Fax, 202–927–8782
Artesia, NM, Operations. Phone, 505–748–8000. Fax, 505–748–8100

Director	W. RALPH BASHAM
Deputy Director	R.J. MILLER
Associate Director	JOHN C. DOOHER
Director (Administration)	KENNETH A. HALL
Director (General Training)	CONNIE L. PATRICK
Director (Special Training)	RAY M. RICE
Director (State and Local Training)	HOBART M. HENSON
Director (Artesia, NM, Operations)	JEFFERY HESSER
Director (Washington, DC, Office)	JOHN C. DOOHER

FINANCIAL MANAGEMENT SERVICE
401 Fourteenth Street SW., Washington, DC 20227
Phone, 202–874–6740. Internet, http://www.fms.treas.gov/.

Commissioner	RICHARD L. GREGG
Deputy Commissioner	KENNETH R. PAPAJ, *Acting*
Director, Legislative and Public Affairs	JIM L. HAGEDORN
Director, Office of Quality and Diversity Management	SONDRA HUTCHINSON
Chief Counsel	DAVID A. INGOLD

Assistant Commissioner, Agency Services — MICHAEL T. SMOKOVICH
Assistant Deputy Commissioner for Debt Management Services — NANCY C. FLEETWOOD
Assistant Commissioner, Federal Finance — LARRY D. STOUT
Assistant Commissioner, Financial Information — MITCHELL A. LEVINE
Assistant Commissioner, Information Resources — CONSTANCE E. CRAIG
Assistant Commissioner, Management (CFO) — DIANE E. CLARK
Assistant Commissioner, Regional Operations — JOHN D. NEWELL

INTERNAL REVENUE SERVICE

1111 Constitution Avenue NW., Washington, DC 20224
Phone, 202–622–5000

Commissioner of Internal Revenue — CHARLES O. ROSSOTTI
  Special Assistant to the Commissioner — ADRIENNE GRIFFEN
  Chief of Staff — JOANN BUCK
  Assistant to the Commissioner — KIRSTEN WIELOBOB
Deputy Commissioner — MICHAEL P. DOLAN
  Assistant to the Deputy Commissioner — JUDY TOMASO
  National Director, Equal Employment Opportunity and Diversity — CHARLES D. FOWLER
  National Director of Quality — THOMAS J. CARROLL
Taxpayer Advocate — LEE MONKS
National Director of Appeals — VINCE CANCIELLO
Chief Counsel — STUART BROWN
  Deputy Chief Counsel — MARLENE GROSS
    Associate Chief Counsel (Domestic) — JUDY DUNN
    Associate Chief Counsel (Employee Benefits/Exempt Organizations) — SARAH HALL INGRAM
    Associate Chief Counsel (Enforcement Litigation) — ELIOT FIELDING
    Associate Chief Counsel (Finance/ Management) — RICHARD MIHELCIC
    Associate Chief Counsel (International) — MICHAEL DANILACK
Chief Compliance Officer — JOHN DALRYMPLE, *Acting*
  Technical Adviser — DIANNE GRANT
  Assistant Commissioner (Collection) — DEBORAH S. REILLY
  Assistant Commissioner (Criminal Investigation) — TED F. BROWN
  Assistant Commissioner (Examination) — TOM SMITH
  Assistant Commissioner (Employee Plans/ Exempt Organizations) — EVELYN PETSCHEK
  Assistant Commissioner (International) — JOHN T. LYONS
Chief Financial Officer — TONY MUSICK
  Controller/National Director for Financial Management — LISA FIELY
  National Director for Budget — RICH MORGANTE
  National Director for Systems and Accounting Standards — PAT HEALY
  National Director for Financial Analysis — TOM ANDRETTA
Associate Commissioner for Modernization/ Chief Information Officer — ARTHUR A. GROSS

Chief Inspector	GARY BELL
Deputy Chief Inspector	DOUG CROUCH
Assistant Chief Inspector (Internal Audit)	BILLY MORRISON
Assistant Chief Inspector (Internal Security)	SEBASTIAN LORIGO
Chief, Management and Administration	DAVID A. MADER
Assistant Commissioner (Procurement)	GREG ROTHWELL
Assistant Commissioner (Support Services)	MARY LU BURCHARD, *Acting*
National Director, Strategic Planning Division	CHARLOTTE PERDUE
Chief, Communications and Liaison	DAVID R. WILLIAMS
National Director, Communications Division	FRANK KEITH, *Acting*
Director, Small Business Affairs	SUSANNE M. SOTTILE, *Acting*
Director, Office of Public Liaison	SUSANNE M. SOTTILE
National Director, Legislative Affairs Division	FLOYD L. WILLIAMS III
Chief, Taxpayer Service	JOHN DALRYMPLE
Assistant Commissioner (Forms and Submission Processing)	BRIAN T. DOWNING
National Director, Tax Forms and Publications Division	SHELDON SCHWARTZ
Executive Officer for Service Center Operations	JOHN A. RESSLER
Executive Officer for Customer Service	RON WATSON
Assistant Commissioner (Electronic Tax Administration)	ROBERT E. BARR
Chief, Headquarters Operations	DAVID W. JUNKINS

UNITED STATES MINT

633 Third Street NW., Washington, DC 20220
Phone, 202–874–6000

Director of the Mint	PHILIP N. DIEHL
Deputy Director	JOHN P. MITCHELL
Special Assistant to the Director	SUSAN SCATES
Chief Counsel	KENNETH B. GUBIN
Chief, Security/Mint Police	WILLIAM F. DADDIO
Associate Director for Policy and Management/ Chief Financial Officer	JAY WEINSTEIN
Deputy Associate Director for Finance/Deputy Chief Financial Officer	TERRY BOWIE
Associate Director/Chief Operating Officer	ANDREW COSGAREA, JR.
Associate Director for Marketing	DAVID PICKENS
Deputy Associate Director for Marketing	BRADFORD E. COOPER

BUREAU OF THE PUBLIC DEBT

999 E Street NW., Washington, DC 20239–0001
Phone, 202–219–3300. Internet, http://www.publicdebt.treas.gov/.

Commissioner	VAN ZECK
Deputy Commissioner	ANNE MEISTER, *Acting*
Director, Government Securities Regulation Staff	KERRY LANHAM, *Acting*
Chief Counsel	WALTER T. ECCARD
Assistant Commissioner (Administration)	THOMAS W. HARRISON

Assistant Commissioner (Automated Information Systems)	NOEL E. KEESOR
Assistant Commissioner (Financing)	CARL M. LOCKEN, JR.
Assistant Commissioner (Public Debt Accounting)	DEBRA HINES
Assistant Commissioner (Savings Bond Operations)	ARTHUR A. KLASS
Assistant Commissioner (Securities and Accounting Services)	JANE O'BRIEN
Executive Director (Savings Bonds Marketing Office)	DINO DECONCINI

UNITED STATES SECRET SERVICE

1800 G Street NW., Washington, DC 20223
Phone, 202–435–5708

Director	LEWIS C. MERLETTI
Deputy Director	BRUCE J. BOWEN
Assistant Director (Administration)	JANE E. VEZERIS
Assistant Director (Government Liaison and Public Affairs)	H. TERRENCE SAMWAY
Assistant Director (Inspection)	GORDON S. HEDDELL
Assistant Director (Investigations)	KEVIN T. FOLEY
Assistant Director (Protective Operations)	BRIAN L. STAFFORD
Assistant Director (Protective Research)	STEPHEN M. SERGEK
Assistant Director (Training)	CHARLES N. DEVITA
Chief Counsel	JOHN J. KELLEHER

OFFICE OF THRIFT SUPERVISION

1700 G Street NW., Washington, DC 20552
Phone, 202–906–6000. Internet, http://www.ots.treas.gov/.

Director	ELLEN SEIDMAN
Chief Counsel	CAROLYN J. BUCK
Executive Director, Administration	CORA PRIFOLD BEEBE
Executive Director, External Affairs	(VACANCY)
Executive Director, Research and Analysis	KENNETH F. RYDER
Executive Director, Supervision	JOHN E. RYAN, *Acting*
Associate Director for FDIC	WALTER B. MASON
Director, Congressional Affairs	KEVIN PETRASIC
Director, Minority Affairs	BARBARA DAVIS, *Acting*
Director, Press Relations	WILLIAM E. FULWIDER

The Department of the Treasury performs four basic functions: formulating and recommending economic, financial, tax, and fiscal policies; serving as financial agent for the U.S. Government; enforcing the law; and manufacturing coins and currency.

The Treasury Department was created by act of September 2, 1789 (31 U.S.C. 301 and 301 note). Many subsequent acts have figured in the development of the Department, delegating new duties to its charge and establishing the numerous bureaus and divisions that now comprise the Treasury.

DEPARTMENT OF THE TREASURY

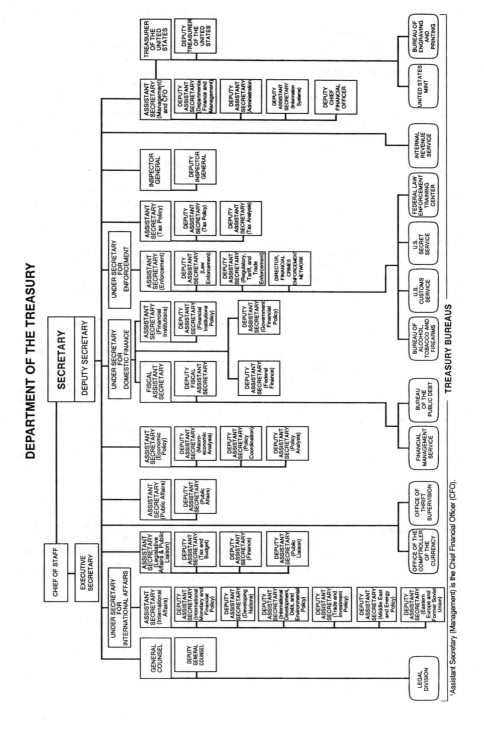

¹Assistant Secretary (Management) is the Chief Financial Officer (CFO).

Secretary

As a major policy adviser to the President, the Secretary has primary responsibility for formulating and recommending domestic and international financial, economic, and tax policy; participating in the formulation of broad fiscal policies that have general significance for the economy; and managing the public debt. The Secretary also oversees the activities of the Department in carrying out its major law enforcement responsibility; in serving as the financial agent for the U.S. Government; and in manufacturing coins, currency, and other products for customer agencies.

In addition, the Secretary has many responsibilities as chief financial officer of the Government. The Secretary serves as a member of the National Economic Council and as U.S. Governor of the International Monetary Fund, the International Bank for Reconstruction and Development, the Inter-American Development Bank, and the African Development Bank. The Office of the Secretary includes the offices of Deputy Secretary, General Counsel, Inspector General, the Under Secretaries, the Assistant Secretaries, and Treasurer. Some offices whose public purposes are broadly applied are detailed further.

Deputy Secretary

The position of Deputy Secretary was established by act of May 18, 1972 (31 U.S.C. 1004–1005). The Deputy Secretary is appointed by the President, by and with the advice and consent of the Senate. The Deputy Secretary is the principal adviser to the Secretary on all matters of policy and administration within the jurisdiction of the Department and acts for the Secretary in his absence. The Deputy Secretary frequently represents the Secretary in public events and meetings with Members of Congress, foreign officials, government officials, and representatives from the private sector. All Bureau heads, Under Secretaries, and Assistant Secretaries report to the Secretary through the Deputy Secretary.

Under Secretary for International Affairs

The Office of the Under Secretary for International Affairs advises and assists the Secretary and Deputy Secretary of the Treasury in the formulation and execution of U.S. international policy, including the development of policies and guidance of Department activities in the areas of international, financial, economic, and monetary affairs; trade and investment policy; international debt, environmental, and energy policy; and U.S. participation in international financial institutions. The Office assists in coordinating U.S. economic policy with finance ministries of the other G–7 industrial nations and in preparing the President for the annual economic summits.

Under Secretary for Domestic Finance

Office of the the Under Secretary for Domestic Finance advises and assists the Secretary and Deputy Secretary of the Treasury in the areas of domestic finance, banking, and other related economic matters. These responsibilities include the development of policies and guidance for Treasury Department activities in the areas of financial institutions, Federal debt finance, financial regulation, and capital markets.

Under Secretary for Enforcement

The Office of the Under Secretary for Enforcement was established in fiscal year 1994 to promote and protect the Treasury Department's enforcement interest, to effect an equalization across other departmental secretariats as they deal on enforcement issues.

Assistant Secretaries

Economic Policy   The Office of the Assistant Secretary for Economic Policy informs the Secretary and other senior Treasury officials of current and prospective economic developments and assists in the determination of appropriate economic policies. The Office:

—reviews and analyzes both domestic and international economic issues, as well as developments in the financial markets;

—participates with the Secretary in the Economic Policy Council and the Troika Forecasting Group, which develops official economic projections and advises the President on choices among alternative courses of economic policy; and

—works closely with officials of the Office of Management and Budget, the Council of Economic Advisers, and other Government agencies on the economic forecasts underlying the yearly budget process, and advises the Secretary on the economic effects of tax and budget policy.

Within the Office of Economic Policy, staff support is provided by the Office of Financial Analysis, the Office of Special Studies, the Office of Monetary Policy Analysis, and the Applied Econometric Staff.

Enforcement   The Office of the Assistant Secretary for Enforcement coordinates Treasury law enforcement matters, including the formulation of policies for Treasury enforcement activities, and cooperates on law enforcement matters with other Federal agencies. It oversees the U.S. Secret Service; U.S. Customs Service; Federal Law Enforcement Training Center; Bureau of Alcohol, Tobacco, and Firearms; Office of Financial Enforcement; and Office of Foreign Assets Control.

The important missions of protecting the President and other high Government officials and preventing counterfeiting of U.S. currency and theft and forgery of Government securities and checks are entrusted to the U.S. Secret Service.

The U.S. Customs Service collects revenue from imports and enforces the customs laws. In addition, it interdicts contraband, including narcotics, along the land and sea borders of the United States.

The Federal Law Enforcement Training Center provides law enforcement training for personnel of Federal agencies.

The Bureau of Alcohol, Tobacco, and Firearms is charged with collecting excise taxes on alcoholic beverages and tobacco products; suppressing traffic in illicit distilled spirits and illegal use of explosives; and controlling the sale and registration of firearms.

The Office of Financial Enforcement assists in implementing the Bank Secrecy Act and administering related Treasury regulations.

The Office of Foreign Assets Control assists U.S. foreign policy aims by controlling assets in the United States of "blocked" countries and the flow of funds and trade to them.

Financial Institutions   The Office of the Assistant Secretary for Financial Institutions advises and assists the Secretary, the Deputy Secretary, and the Under Secretary for Domestic Finance on all matters relating to financial institutions. It exercises policy direction and control over Department activities relating to the substance of proposed legislation pertaining to the general activities and regulation of private financial intermediaries, and Department activities relating to other Federal regulatory agencies.

Fiscal Affairs   The Office of the Fiscal Assistant Secretary supervises the administration of the Government's fiscal affairs. This includes the administration of Treasury financing operations; management of Treasury's cash balances in tax and loan investment accounts in commercial financial institutions and operating balances with Federal Reserve Banks; and the Department's participation in the Joint Financial Management Improvement Program for improvement of accounting in the Federal Government. Supervision and oversight over the functions and activities of the Financial Management Service and the Bureau of the Public Debt are also provided.

The Office is responsible for improved cash management, debt collection, and credit administration on a Governmentwide basis under the umbrella of the Administration's Reform '88 initiative.

The Office:

—acts as liaison between the Secretary and other Government agencies with respect to their financial operations;

—manages the cash position of the Treasury and projects and monitors "debt subject-to-limit;"

—directs the performance of the fiscal agency functions of the Federal Reserve Banks;

—conducts governmentwide accounting and cash management activities;

—exercises supervision over depositories of the United States; and

—provides management overview of investment practices for Government trust and other accounts.

General Counsel   The General Counsel is the chief law officer of the Department and serves as the senior legal advisor to the Secretary, Deputy Secretary, and other senior Department officials. Responsibilities of the Office of General Counsel include consideration of legal issues relating to broad policy aspects of management of the public debt; administration of internal revenue and tariff laws; international cooperation in the monetary and financial fields; implementation of economic sanctions; development and review of legislation and regulations; management issues such as personnel, procurement, and ethics; and law enforcement affairs. All legal counsels of Department bureaus report to the General Counsel.

International Affairs   The Office of the Assistant Secretary for International Affairs advises and assists the Secretary, Deputy Secretary, and Under Secretary for International Affairs in the formulation and execution of policies dealing with international financial, economic, monetary, trade, investment, environmental, and energy policies and programs. The work of the Office is organized into groups responsible for monetary and financial policy; international development, debt, and environmental policy; trade and investment policy; economic and financial technical assistance; and geographical areas (Asia, the Americas, Africa, Eurasia, and the Middle East).

These functions are performed by supporting staff offices, which:

—conduct financial diplomacy with industrial and developing nations and regions;

—work toward improving the structure and operations of the international monetary system;

—monitor developments in foreign exchange and other markets and official operations affecting those markets;

—facilitate structural monetary cooperation through the International Monetary Fund and other channels;

—oversee U.S. participation in the multilateral development banks and coordinate U.S. policies and operations relating to bilateral and multilateral development lending programs and institutions;

—formulate policy concerning financing of trade;

—coordinate policies toward foreign investments in the United States and U.S. investments abroad; and

—analyze balance of payments and other basic financial and economic data, including energy data, affecting world payment patterns and the world economic outlook.

As part of those functions, the Office supports the Secretary in his role as co-Chairman of the U.S.-Saudi Arabian Joint Commission on Economic Cooperation, co-Chairman of the U.S.-China Joint Economic Committee, and Chairman of the National Advisory Council on International Monetary and Financial Policies.

Tax Policy   The Office of the Assistant Secretary for Tax Policy advises and assists the Secretary and the Deputy Secretary in the formulation and execution of domestic and international tax policies and programs.

These functions, carried out by supporting staff offices, include:

—analysis of proposed tax legislation and tax programs;

—projections of economic trends affecting tax bases;

—studies of effects of alternative tax measures;

—preparation of official estimates of Government receipts for the President's annual budget messages;

—legal advice and analysis on domestic and international tax matters;

—assistance in the development and review of tax legislation and domestic and international tax regulations and rulings; and

—participation in international tax treaty negotiations and in maintenance of relations with international organizations on tax matters.

Treasurer of the United States The Office of the Treasurer of the United States was established on September 6, 1777. The Treasurer was originally charged with the receipt and custody of Government funds, but many of these functions have been assumed by different bureaus of the Department of the Treasury. In 1981, the Treasurer was assigned responsibility for oversight of the Bureau of Engraving and Printing and the United States Mint. The Treasurer reports to the Secretary through the Assistant Secretary for Management/Chief Financial Officer.

For further information concerning the Departmental Offices, contact the Public Affairs Office, Department of the Treasury, 1500 Pennsylvania Avenue NW., Washington, DC 20220. Phone, 202–622–2960.

Bureau of Alcohol, Tobacco, and Firearms

The mission of the Bureau of Alcohol, Tobacco, and Firearms (ATF) is to reduce violent crime, collect revenue, and protect the public through criminal law enforcement, regulatory enforcement, and tax collection.

The Bureau was established by Department of Treasury Order No. 221, effective July 1, 1972, which transferred the functions, powers, and duties arising under laws relating to alcohol, tobacco, firearms, and explosives from the Internal Revenue Service to the Bureau. On December 5, 1978, Department of Treasury Order No. 120–1 assigned to ATF the responsibility of enforcing chapter 114 of title 18 of the United States Code (18 U.S.C. 2341 *et seq.*) relating to interstate trafficking in contraband cigarettes. With passage of the Anti-Arson Act of 1982, ATF was given the additional responsibility of addressing commercial arson nationwide. ATF is also responsible for enforcing the provisions of the "Brady law" concerning the transfer of handguns (107 Stat. 1536), which was enacted in 1993.

The Bureau Headquarters is located in Washington, DC, but since the Bureau is decentralized, most of its personnel are stationed throughout the country where many of its operational functions are performed.

ATF is responsible for enforcing and administering firearms and explosives laws, as well as those covering the production, taxation, and distribution of alcohol and tobacco products. The Bureau's objectives are to maximize compliance with and investigate violations of these laws.

In collaborative partnerships with government agencies, industry, academia, and others, ATF works to reduce crime and violence by safeguarding the public from arson and explosives incidents, denying criminals access to firearms, removing violent offenders from communities, and preventing violence through community outreach; and to maintain a sound revenue management and regulatory system which reduces the burden on industry, collects revenues which are rightfully due, and uses electronic commerce. ATF also works to protect the public and prevent consumer deception by assuring the integrity of the products, people, and companies in the marketplace; ensuring compliance with laws and regulations through education, inspection, and investigations; and informing the public about ATF regulations and product safety using various media.

District Offices—Regulatory Enforcement

District	Address/Telephone	Director
MIDWEST—IL, IN, KY, MI, MN, ND, OH, SD, WV, WI	Suite 310, 300 S. Riverside Plz., Chicago, IL 60606–6616. Phone, 312–353–1967	Candace E. Moberly
NORTH ATLANTIC—CT, DC, DE, MA, MD, ME, NH, NJ, NY, PA, RI, VT	Rm. 620, 6 World Trade Ctr., New York, NY 10048. Phone, 212–264–2328	(Vacancy)
SOUTHEAST—AL, FL, GA, MS, NC, PR, SC, TN, VA, VI	Suite 300, 2600 Century Pkwy., Atlanta, GA 30345. Phone, 404–679–5000	(Vacancy)
SOUTHWEST—AR, AZ, CO, IA, KS, LA, MO, NE, NM, OK, TX	Room 707, 1114 Commerce St., Dallas, TX 75242. Phone, 214–767–2280	(Vacancy)
WESTERN—AK, AS, CA, GU, HI, ID, MT, NV, OR, Pacific Islands, UT, WA, WY	Room 1130, 221 Main St., San Francisco, CA 94105. Phone, 415–744–7013	Victoria J. Renneckar

Field Division Offices—Office of Enforcement

Field Division	Address	Special Agent in Charge	Telephone
Atlanta, GA	Suite 406, 101 Marietta St. NW., 30303	John C. Killorin	404–331–6526
Baltimore, MD	6th Fl., 22 S. Howard St., 21201	Larry D. Stewart	410–962–0897
Boston, MA	Rm. 253, 10 Causeway St., 02222–1047	Charles Thomson	617–565–7042
Charlotte, NC	Suite 400, 4530 Park Rd., 28209	Richard Fox	704–344–6125
Chicago, IL	Suite 350 S., 300 S. Riverdale Plz., 60606	Kathleen Kiernan	312–353–6935
Dallas, TX	Suite 2550, 1200 Main Twr. Bldg., 75250	Karl Stankovic	214–767–2250
Detroit, MI	Suite 300, 1155 Brewery Park Blvd., 48207–2602	(Vacancy)	313–393–6000
Houston, TX	Suite 210, 15355 Vantage Pkwy. W., 77032	George Hopgood	281–449–2073
Kansas City, MO	Suite 200, 2600 Grand Ave., 64108	James R. Switzer	816–421–3440
Los Angeles, CA	Suite 800, 350 S. Figueroa St., 90071	Richard A. Curd	213–894–4812
Louisville, KY	Suite 322, 600 Dr. Martin Luther King Jr. Pl., 40202	James L. Brown	502–582–5211
Miami, FL	Suite 120, 8420 NW. 52d St., 33166	Patricia L. Galupo	305–597–4800
Middleburg Heights, OH.	Suite 200, 6745 Engle Rd., 44130	James L. Brown	216–522–7210
Nashville, TN	Suite 215, 215 Centerview Dr., Brentwood, 37027	James Cavanaugh	615–781–5364
New Orleans, LA	Suite 1050, 111 Veterans Blvd., Metairie, 70005	Guy K. Hummel	504–589–2048
New York, NY	Suite 600, 6 World Trade Center, 10048–0206	Pete Gagliardi	212–466–5145
Philadelphia, PA	Rm. 504, U.S. Customs House, 2d & Chestnut Sts., 19106.	Larry Duchnowski	215–597–7266
Phoenix, AZ	Suite 1010, 3003 N. Central Ave., 85012	Christopher P. Sadowski	602–640–2840
San Francisco, CA	Suite 1250, 221 Main St., 94105	Paul M. Snabel	415–744–7001
Seattle, WA	Rm. 806, 915 2d Ave., 98174	John Ross	206–220–6440
Washington, DC	Suite 620, 607 14th St. NW., 20005	Patrick D. Hynes	202–219–7751

For further information, contact the Office of Liaison and Public Information, Bureau of Alcohol, Tobacco, and Firearms. Phone, 202–927–8500. Internet, http://www.atf.treas.gov/.

Office of the Comptroller of the Currency

[For the Office of the Comptroller of the Currency statement of organization, see the *Code of Federal Regulations,* Title 12, Part 4]

The Office of the Comptroller of the Currency (OCC) was created February 25, 1863 (12 Stat. 665), as a bureau of the Department of the Treasury. Its primary mission is to regulate national banks. The Office is headed by the Comptroller, who is appointed for a 5-year term by the President with the advice and consent of the Senate. By statute, the Comptroller also serves a concurrent term as Director of the Federal Deposit Insurance Corporation (FDIC).

The Office regulates national banks by its power to examine banks; approve or deny applications for new bank charters, branches, or mergers; take enforcement action—such as bank closures—against banks that are not in compliance with laws and regulations; and issue rules, regulations, and interpretations on banking practices.

The Office supervises approximately 2,700 national banks, including their trust activities and overseas operations.

Each bank is examined annually through a nationwide staff of approximately 1,800 bank examiners supervised in 6 district offices. The Office is independently funded through assessments of the assets of national banks.

For further information, contact the Communications Division, Office of the Comptroller of the Currency, Department of the Treasury, 250 E Street SW., Washington, DC 20219. Phone, 202–874–4700.

United States Customs Service

The fifth act of the first Congress, passed on July 31, 1789 (1 Stat. 29), established customs districts and authorized customs officers to collect duties on goods, wares, and merchandise imposed by the second act of the first Congress, dated July 4, 1789 (1 Stat. 24). The Bureau of Customs was established as a separate agency under the Treasury Department on March 3, 1927 (19 U.S.C. 2071) and, effective August 1, 1973, was redesignated the United States Customs Service by Treasury Department Order 165–23 of April 4, 1973.

The Customs Service enforces customs and related laws and collects the revenue from imports. Customs also administers the Tariff Act of 1930, as amended (19 U.S.C. 1654), and other customs laws. Some of the responsibilities that Customs is specifically charged with are:

—interdicting and seizing contraband, including narcotics and illegal drugs;

—assessing and collecting customs duties, excise taxes, fees, and penalties due on imported merchandise;

—processing persons, carriers, cargo, and mail into and out of the United States;

—administering certain navigation laws; and

—detecting and apprehending persons engaged in fraudulent practices designed to circumvent customs and related laws; copyright, patent, and trademark provisions; quotas; and marking requirements for imported merchandise.

As the principal border enforcement agency, Customs' mission has been extended over the years to assisting in the administration and enforcement of some 400 provisions of law on behalf of more than 40 Government agencies. Today, in addition to enforcing the Tariff Act of 1930 and other customs statutes, the Customs Service:

—cooperates with other Federal agencies and foreign governments in suppressing the traffic of illegal narcotics and pornography;

—enforces export control laws and intercepts illegal high-technology and weapons exports;

—enforces reporting requirements of the Bank Secrecy Act; and

—collects international trade statistics.

Also, Customs enforces a wide range of requirements to protect the public, such as auto safety and emission control standards; radiation and radioactive material standards; counterfeit monetary instruments; flammable fabric restrictions; animal and plant quarantine requirements; and food, drug, and hazardous substance prohibitions.

Customs is extensively involved with outside commercial and policy organizations and trade associations, and with international organizations and foreign customs services. Customs is a member of the multinational World Customs Organization, the Cabinet Committee to Combat Terrorism, and the International Narcotics Control Program. In addition, Customs participates in and supports the activities and programs of various international organizations and agreements, including the World Trade Organization, the International Civil Aviation Organization, and the Organization of American States (OAS).

Headquarters of the U.S. Customs Service is located in Washington, DC, under the supervision of the Commissioner of Customs, who is appointed by the President and confirmed by the Senate.

The 50 States, plus the Virgin Islands and Puerto Rico, are divided into 20 customs management center areas, under which there are approximately 300 ports of entry.

The foreign field offices of the Customs Service are located in Bangkok, Beijing, Bonn, Brussels, Caracas, Hermosillo, Hong Kong, London, Merida, Mexico City, Milan, Monterrey, Montevideo, Ottawa, Panama City, Paris, Rome, Seoul, Singapore, Tokyo, Vienna, and The Hague. An attaché represents U.S. Customs in the U.S. Mission to the European Communities in Brussels.

The Customs Service also operates a Canine Enforcement Training Center at Front Royal, VA.

Customs Management Centers—U.S. Customs Service

District Offices	Address	Director	Telephone
Mid America/Chicago	Suite 900, 610 S. Canal St., Chicago, IL 60607.	Garnet Fee	312–353–4733
East Texas/Houston	Suite 1200, 2323 S. Shepard St., Houston, TX 77019.	Robert Trotter	713–313–2841
Southern California/San Diego	Suite 1200, 610 W. Ash St., San Diego, CA 92101.	Rudy Camacho	619–557–5455
North Pacific/Portland	Rm. 592, 511 NW. Broadway, Portland, OR 97209.	Lois Fields	503–326–7625
Mid Pacific/San Francisco	Suite 1501, 33 New Montgomery St., San Francisco, CA 94105.	Paul Andrews	415–744–7700
Puerto Rico & Virgin Islands	Rm. 203, 1 La Puntilla St., Old San Juan, PR 00901.	Alfonso Robles	787–729–6950
West Great Lakes/Detroit	Suite 310, 613 Abbott St., Detroit, MI 48226	William Morandini	313–226–2955
South Texas/Laredo	P.O. Box 3130, Laredo, TX 78044–3130	Maria Reba	210–718–4161
Arizona/Tucson	Suite 310, 4740 N. Oracle Rd., Tucson, AZ 85705.	Donna De La Torre	520–670–5900
South Atlantic/Atlanta	Suite 270, 1691 Phoenix Blvd., College Park, GA 30349.	Mamie Pollock	770–994–2306
Northwest Great Plains/Seattle	Rm. 2200, 1000 2d Ave., Seattle, WA 98104	Thomas Hardy	206–553–6944
West Texas/El Paso	Suite 104, 9400 Viscount Blvd., El Paso, TX 79925.	Gundit Dhillon	915–540–5800
North Florida/Tampa	Suite 301, 1624 E. 7th Avenue, Tampa, FL 33605.	Jeffrey Baldwin	813–228–2381
Mid Atlantic/Baltimore	Suite 208, 103 S. Gay St., Baltimore, MD 21202.	Steven Knox	410–962–6200
New York/New York	Rm. 716, 6 World Trade Ctr., New York, NY 10048.	Anthony Liberta	212–466–4444
Gulf/New Orleans	Rm. 337, 423 Canal St., New Orleans, LA 70130–2341.	J. Robert Grimes	504–589–6324
North Atlantic/Boston	Rm. 801, 10 Causeway St., Boston, MA 02222–1056.	Philip Spayd	617–565–6210
East Great Lakes/Buffalo	4455 Genessa St., Buffalo, NY 14225	Richard McMullen	716–626–0400
South Florida/Miami	Suite 980, 909 SE. 1st Ave., Miami, FL 33131	D. Lynn Gordon	305–536–6600
South Pacific/Los Angeles	Rm. 705, 1 World Trade Ctr., Long Beach, CA 90831.	John Heinrich	310–980–3100

For further information, contact the U.S. Customs Service, Department of the Treasury, 1300 Pennsylvania Avenue NW., Washington, DC 20229. Phone, 202–927–6724.

Bureau of Engraving and Printing

The Bureau of Engraving and Printing operates on basic authorities conferred by act of July 11, 1862 (31 U.S.C. 303) and additional authorities contained in past appropriations made to the Bureau that are still in force. A working capital fund was established in accordance with the provisions of section 2 of the act of August 4, 1950, as amended (31 U.S.C. 5142), which placed the Bureau on a completely reimbursable basis. The Bureau is headed by a Director, who is appointed by the Secretary of the Treasury and reports to the Treasurer of the United States.

At the Bureau of Engraving and Printing, the timeless artistry of the engraver is combined with the most technologically advanced printing equipment to produce United States securities. The Bureau designs, prints, and finishes all of the Nation's paper currency (Federal Reserve notes), as well as U.S. postage stamps, Treasury securities, certificates, and other security products, including White House invitations and military identification cards. It also is responsible for advising and assisting Federal agencies in the design and production of other Government documents that, because of their innate value or for other reasons, require security or counterfeit-deterrence characteristics.

The Bureau operates two facilities: the headquarters in Washington, DC, and a second currency manufacturing plant in Fort Worth, TX.

For further information, contact the Office of Communications, Bureau of Engraving and Printing, Department of the Treasury, Room 533M, Fourteenth and C Streets SW., Washington, DC 20228. Phone, 202–874–3019.

Federal Law Enforcement Training Center

The Federal Law Enforcement Training Center was established by Treasury Department Order No. 217, effective March 2, 1970; and reaffirmed by Treasury Department Order No. 140–01 of September 20, 1994.

The Federal Law Enforcement Training Center is headed by a Director, who is appointed by the Secretary of the Treasury. The Center conducts operations at its training facility located at Glynco, GA. The Center also maintains a Washington, DC, office at 650 Massachusetts Avenue NW., Washington, DC 20226 (phone, 202–927–8940). In addition, the Center has a satellite operation located at Artesia, NM 88210 (phone, 505–748–8000).

The Center is an interagency training facility serving over 70 Federal law enforcement organizations. The major training effort is in the area of basic programs to teach common areas of law enforcement skills to police and investigative personnel. The Center also conducts advanced programs in areas of common need, such as white-collar crime, the use of microcomputers as an investigative tool, advanced law enforcement photography, international banking/money laundering, marine law enforcement, and several instructor training courses. In addition to the basic and common advanced programs, the Center provides the facilities and support services for participating organizations to conduct advanced training for their own law enforcement personnel. The Center offers selective, highly specialized training programs to State and local officers as well as international law enforcement officers as an aid in deterring crime. These programs include a variety of areas such as fraud and financial investigations, marine law enforcement, arson for profit, international banking/money laundering, and criminal intelligence analyst training.

The Center develops the curriculum content and training techniques for recruit training, and advises and assists the participating organizations in producing, formulating, and operating specialized training materials and equipment.

Administrative and financial activities are supervised by the Department of the Treasury. However, training policy, programs, criteria, and standards are governed by the interagency Board of Directors, comprised of senior officials from eight departments and independent agencies.

For further information, contact the Public Affairs Office, Federal Law Enforcement Training Center, Department of the Treasury, Glynco, GA 31524. Phone, 912–267–2447.

Financial Management Service

The mission of the Financial Management Service (FMS) is to develop and manage Federal financial systems to move the Government's cash flows efficiently, effectively, and securely. It supports other Federal agencies by serving as the Government's primary disbursing agent; collections agent; accountant and reporter of financial information; and collector of delinquent Federal debt.

Working Capital Management The Service is responsible for programs to improve cash management, credit management, debt collection, and financial management systems Governmentwide. For cash management, the Service issues guidelines and regulations and assists other agencies in managing financial transactions to maximize investment earnings and reduce the interest costs of borrowed funds. For credit management, the Service issues guidelines and regulations and assists program agencies with management of credit activities, including loan programs, to improve all parts of the credit cycle, such as credit extension, loan servicing, debt collection, and write-off procedures. The Service is presently working with other agencies to improve financial management systems and the way Government handles its payments, collections, and receivables, and to take advantage of new automation technology.

Payments The Service issues approximately 370 million Treasury checks and close to 500 million electronic fund transfer payments annually for Federal salaries and wages, payments to suppliers of goods and services to the Federal Government, income tax refunds, and payments under major Government programs such as social security and veterans' benefits. The Service pays all Treasury checks and reconciles them against the accounts of Government disbursing officers, receives and examines claims for checks that are cashed under forged endorsements or that are lost, stolen, or destroyed; and issues new checks on approved claims. The Service uses two electronic funds-transfer methods: the automated clearinghouses—for recurring payments such as Government benefits and salaries—and wire transfers through the Fedline System. The latter is a computer-to-computer link with the Federal Reserve System that allows for the electronic transfer of funds to virtually any financial institution in the United States.

Collections FMS is responsible for administering the world's largest collections system, gathering approximately $1.5 trillion annually. The Service is working with all Federal agencies to improve the availability of collected funds and the reporting of collection information to Treasury. Current collection systems include the Electronic Federal Tax Payment System, the Treasury General Account System, the Treasury Tax and Loan System for withholding and other Federal tax deposits, and the Treasury National Automated Lockbox System for accelerating the processing of agency receipts. FMS also retains the services of private debt collection agencies and utilizes standard private sector techniques to collect delinquent debts on behalf of agencies.

Central Accounting and Reporting The Service maintains a central system that accounts for the monetary assets and liabilities of the Treasury and tracks Government collection and payment operations. Periodic reports are prepared to show budget results, the Government's overall financial status, and other financial operations. These reports include the *Daily Treasury Statement,* the *Monthly Treasury*

Statement, the *Quarterly Treasury Bulletin,* the annual *Treasury Report,* and the annual *Treasury Consolidated Financial Statement.*

Disbursing Centers—Financial Management Service

Center/Address	Director
Austin, TX (1619 Woodward St., 78741)	Gordon Hickam
Birmingham, AL (190 Vulcan Rd., 35209)	Andy Wilson
Chicago, IL (536 S. Clark St., 60605)	Ollice C. Holden
Kansas City, MO (4241 NE. 34th St., 64117)	John H. Adams
Philadelphia, PA (13000 Townsend Rd., 19154)	Michael Colarusso
San Francisco, CA (390 Main St., 94105)	Philip Belisle

For further information, contact the Office of Legislative and Public Affairs, Financial Management Service, Department of the Treasury, Room 555, 401 Fourteenth Street SW., Washington, DC 20227. Phone, 202–874–6740. Internet, http://www.fms.treas.gov/.

Internal Revenue Service

The Office of the Commissioner of Internal Revenue was established by act of July 1, 1862 (26 U.S.C. 7802).

The Internal Revenue Service (IRS) is responsible for administering and enforcing the internal revenue laws and related statutes, except those relating to alcohol, tobacco, firearms, and explosives. Its mission is to collect the proper amount of tax revenue at the least cost to the public, and in a manner that warrants the highest degree of public confidence in the Service's integrity, efficiency, and fairness. To achieve that purpose, the Service:

—strives to achieve the highest possible degree of voluntary compliance in accordance with the tax laws and regulations;

—advises the public of their rights and responsibilities;

—determines the extent of compliance and the causes of noncompliance;

—properly administers and enforces the tax laws; and

—continually searches for and implements new, more efficient ways of accomplishing its mission.

Basic activities include:

—ensuring satisfactory resolution of taxpayer complaints, providing taxpayer service and education;

—determining, assessing, and collecting internal revenue taxes;

—determining pension plan qualifications and exempt organization status; and

—preparing and issuing rulings and regulations to supplement the provisions of the Internal Revenue Code.

The source of most revenues collected is the individual income tax and the social insurance and retirement taxes, with other major sources being the corporation income, excise, estate, and gift taxes. Congress first received authority to levy taxes on the income of individuals and corporations in 1913, pursuant to the 16th amendment of the Constitution.

Organization

Service organization is designed for maximum decentralization, consistent with the need for uniform interpretation of the tax laws and efficient utilization of resources. There are three organizational levels: the National Office; the Regional Offices; and the District Offices and Service Centers. Districts may have local offices, the number and location of which are determined by taxpayer and agency needs.

Headquarters Organization The National Office, located in Washington, DC, develops nationwide policies and programs for the administration of the internal revenue laws and provides overall direction to the field organization. Also assigned to the National Office are the Martinsburg Computing Center in Martinsburg, WV; the Detroit Computing Center in Detroit,

MI; and the 10 Service Centers (located in various States across the country).

Field Organization

As IRS is a decentralized organization, most agency personnel and activities are assigned to field installations.

Regional Offices There are four Regional Offices, each headed by a Regional Commissioner, which supervise and evaluate the operations of District Offices.

Regional Offices—Internal Revenue Service

Region	Address	Commissioner
MIDSTATES—AR, IA, IL, KS, MN, MO, NE, ND, OK, SD, TX, WI	4050 Alpha Rd., Dallas, TX 75244–4203	Ladd Ellis, Jr.
NORTHEAST—CT, MA, ME, MI, NH, NJ, NY, OH, PA, RI, VT	90 Church St., New York, NY 10007	Herma Hightower
SOUTHEAST—AL, DE, FL, GA, IN, KY, LA, MD, MS, NC, SC, TN, VA, WV	401 W. Peachtree St. NE., Atlanta, GA 30365	Robert T. Johnson
WESTERN—AK, AZ, CA, CO, HI, ID, MT, NV, NM, OR, UT, WA, WY	1650 Mission St., San Francisco, CA 94103	Marilyn W. Day

District Offices There are 33 Internal Revenue districts, each administered by a District Director. Districts may encompass several States, an entire State, or a certain number of counties within a State, depending on population. Programs of the District include taxpayer service, examination, collection, criminal investigation, and, in some districts, pension plans and exempt organizations. Functions performed are: assistance and service to taxpayers, determination of tax liability by examination of tax returns, determination of pension plan qualification, collection of delinquent returns and taxes, and investigation of criminal and civil violations of internal revenue laws (except those relating to alcohol, tobacco, firearms, and explosives). Directors are responsible for the deposit of taxes collected by the District and for initial processing of original applications for admission to practice before the Internal Revenue Service and renewal issuances for those practitioners already enrolled. Local offices are established to meet taxpayer needs and agency workload requirements.

District Offices—Internal Revenue Service

District	Address	Director
ALABAMA	600 S. Maestri Pl., New Orleans, LA 70130	Richard F. Moran
ALASKA	915 2d Ave., Seattle, WA 98174	J. Paul Beene
ARIZONA	210 E. Earll Dr., Phoenix, 85012	Jack B. Cheskaty
ARKANSAS	55 N. Robinson St., Oklahoma City, OK 73102	Richard Auby
CALIFORNIA:		
Laguna Niguel	24000 Avila Rd., 92677	Marilyn A. Soulsburg
Los Angeles	300 N. Los Angeles St., 90012	Steven A. Jensen
Sacramento/San Francisco	Suite 1600 S, 1301 Clay St., Oakland, 94612	Robert D. AhNee
San Jose	55 S. Market St., 95103	Billy J. Brown
COLORADO	600 17th St., Denver, 80202–2490	Wally Hutton
CONNECTICUT	135 High St., Hartford, 06103	Deborah Nolan
DELAWARE	31 Hopkins Plz., Baltimore, MD 21201	Paul M. Harrington
DISTRICT OF COLUMBIA	31 Hopkins Plz., Baltimore, MD 21201	Paul M. Harrington
FLORIDA:		
Fort Lauderdale	1 N. University Dr., Bldg. B, 33318	Bruce R. Thomas
Jacksonville	400 W. Bay St., 32202	Henry O. Lamar, Jr.
GEORGIA	401 W. Peachtree St. NW., Atlanta, 30385	James E. Donelson
HAWAII	915 2d Ave., Seattle, WA 98174	J. Paul Beene
IDAHO	600 17th St., Denver, CO 80202–2490	Wally Hutton
ILLINOIS	Suite 2890, 230 S. Dearborn St., Chicago, 60604	Robert W. Brock
INDIANA	575 N. Pennsylvania St., Indianapolis, 46204	James E. Rogers, Jr.
IOWA	310 W. Wisconsin Ave., Milwaukee, WI 53203–2221	Robert E. Brazzil
KANSAS	Suite 2300, 1222 Spruce St., St. Louis, MO 63103	David Palmer
KENTUCKY	801 Broadway, Nashville, TN 37202	John C. Stocker
LOUISIANA	600 S. Maestri Pl., New Orleans, 70130	Richard F. Moran
MAINE	JFK Federal Bldg., Boston, MA 02203	Stephen L. Daige
MARYLAND	31 Hopkins Plz., Baltimore, 21201	Paul M. Harrington

District Offices—Internal Revenue Service—Continued

District	Address	Director
MASSACHUSETTS	JFK Federal Bldg., Boston, 02203	Stephen L. Daige
MICHIGAN	Suite 2483, 477 Michigan Ave., Detroit, 48226	Arlene G. Kay
MINNESOTA	316 N. Robert St., St. Paul, 55101	Thomas E. Palmer
MISSISSIPPI	600 S. Maestri Pl., New Orleans, LA 70130	Richard F. Moran
MISSOURI	Suite 2300, 1222 Spruce St., St. Louis, MO 63103	David Palmer
MONTANA	600 17th St., Denver, CO 80202–2490	Wally Hutton
NEBRASKA	310 W. Wisconsin Ave., Milwaukee, WI 53203–2221	Robert E. Brazzil
NEVADA	210 E. Earll Dr., Phoenix, AZ 85012	Jack B. Cheskaty
NEW HAMPSHIRE	JFK Federal Bldg., Boston, MA 02203	Stephen L. Daige
NEW JERSEY	970 Broad St., Newark, 07102	Frank P. Nixon
NEW MEXICO	210 E. Earll Dr., Phoenix, AZ 85012	Jack B. Cheskaty
NEW YORK:		
Albany/Buffalo	111 W. Huron St., Buffalo, 14202	Charles W. Peterson
Brooklyn	Suite 10, 625 Fulton St., 11201	Herbert J. Huff
Manhattan	290 Broadway, New York, 10007	Charles R. Baugh
NORTH CAROLINA	320 Federal Pl., Greensboro, 27401	J.R. (Bob) Starkey
NORTH DAKOTA	316 N. Robert St., St. Paul, MN 55101	Thomas E. Palmer
OHIO	Suite 5106, 550 Main St., Cincinnati, 45202	C. Ashley Bullard
OKLAHOMA	55 N. Robinson St., Oklahoma City, 73102	Richard Auby
OREGON	915 2d Ave., Seattle, WA 98174	J. Paul Beene
PENNSYLVANIA	600 Arch St., Philadelphia, 19106	Darlene R. Berthod
PUERTO RICO	Stop 27½, Ponce de Leon Ave., Hato Rey, 00917	Robert Keller
RHODE ISLAND	135 High St., Hartford, CT 06103	Deborah Nolan
SOUTH CAROLINA	320 Federal Pl., Greensboro, NC, 27401	J.R. (Bob) Starkey
SOUTH DAKOTA	316 N. Robert St., St. Paul, MN 55101	Thomas E. Palmer
TENNESSEE	801 Broadway, Nashville, 37203	John C. Stocker
TEXAS:		
Austin	300 E. 8th St., 78701	Pamela Bigelow
Dallas	1100 Commerce St., 75242	Glenn Henderson
Houston	1919 Smith St., 77002	James J. Walsh
UTAH	600 17th St., Denver, CO 80202–2490	Wally Hutton
VERMONT	JFK Federal Bldg., Boston, MA 02203	Stephen L. Daige
VIRGINIA	400 N. 8th St., Richmond, 23240	Roger Burgess
WASHINGTON	915 2d Ave., Seattle, 98174	J. Paul Beene
WEST VIRGINIA	400 N. 8th St., Richmond, VA 23240	Roger Burgess
WISCONSIN	310 W. Wisconsin Ave., Milwaukee, 53203–2221	Robert E. Brazzil
WYOMING	600 17th St., Denver, CO 80202–2490	Wally Hutton

Overseas Taxpayers

Office	Address
Office of Taxpayer Service and Compliance	950 L'Enfant Plz. SW. (CP:IN), Washington, DC 20024

Service Centers Under the supervision of the Executive Officer for Service Center Operations having jurisdiction over the area of their location are 10 service centers, located at Andover, MA; Austin, TX; Holtsville, NY; Chamblee, GA; Covington, KY; Fresno, CA; Kansas City, MO; Memphis, TN; Ogden, UT; and Philadelphia, PA. Each service center processes tax returns and related documents and maintains accountability records for taxes collected. Programs include the processing, verification, and accounting control of tax returns; the assessment and certification of refunds of taxes; and administering assigned examination, criminal investigation, and collection functions.

For further information, contact any District Office or the Internal Revenue Service Headquarters, Department of the Treasury, 1111 Constitution Avenue NW., Washington, DC 20224. Phone, 202–622–5000.

United States Mint

The establishment of a mint was authorized by act of April 2, 1792 (1 Stat. 246). The Bureau of the Mint was established by act of February 12, 1873

(17 Stat. 424) and recodified on September 13, 1982 (31 U.S.C. 304, 5131). The name was changed to United States Mint by Secretarial order dated January 9, 1984.

The primary mission of the Mint is to produce an adequate volume of circulating coinage for the Nation to conduct its trade and commerce. The Mint also produces and sells numismatic coins, American Eagle gold and silver bullion coins, and national medals. In addition, the Fort Knox Bullion Depository is the primary storage facility for the Nation's gold bullion.

The U.S. Mint maintains sales centers at the Philadelphia and Denver Mints, and at Union Station in Washington, DC. Public tours are conducted, with free admission, at the Philadelphia and Denver Mints.

Field Facilities
(S: Superintendent; O: Officer in Charge)

Facility/Address	Facility Head
United States Mint, Philadelphia, PA 19106	Augustine A. Albino (S)
United States Mint, Denver, CO 80204	Raymond J. DeBroekert (S)
United States Mint, San Francisco, CA 94102	Dale DeVries (S)
United States Mint, West Point, NY 10996	(Vacancy)
United States Bullion Depository, Fort Knox, KY 40121	James M. Curtis (O)

For further information, contact the United States Mint, Department of the Treasury, Judiciary Square Building, 633 Third Street NW., Washington, DC 20220. Phone, 202–874–9696.

Bureau of the Public Debt

The Bureau of the Public Debt was established on June 30, 1940, pursuant to the Reorganization Act of 1939 (31 U.S.C. 306).

Its mission is to borrow the money needed to operate the Federal Government; account for the resulting public debt; and to issue Treasury securities to refund maturing debt and raise new money.

The Bureau fulfills its mission through six programs: commercial book-entry securities, direct access securities, savings securities, Government securities, market regulation, and public debt accounting.

The Bureau auctions and issues Treasury bills, notes, and bonds and manages the U.S. Savings Bond Program. It issues, services, and redeems bonds through a nationwide network of issuing and paying agents. The Bureau also promotes the sale and retention of savings bonds through payroll savings plans and financial institutions and is supported by a network of volunteers. It provides daily and other periodic reports to account for the composition and size of the debt. In addition, the Bureau implements the regulations for the Government securities market. These regulations provide for investor protection while maintaining a fair and liquid market for Government securities.

The Bureau of the Public Debt was established on June 30, 1940, pursuant to the Reorganization Act of 1939 (31 U.S.C. 306). Principal offices of the Bureau are located in Washington, DC, and Parkersburg, WV.

For more information, contact the Public Affairs Officer, Office of the Commissioner, Bureau of the Public Debt, Washington, DC 20239–0001. Phone, 202–219–3302. Internet, http://www.publicdebt.treas.gov/.

United States Secret Service

Pursuant to certain sections of titles 3 and 18 of the United States Code, the mission of the Secret Service includes the authority and responsibility:

—to protect the President, the Vice President, the President-elect, the Vice-President-elect, and members of their immediate families; major Presidential and Vice Presidential candidates; former Presidents and their spouses, except that protection of a spouse shall terminate in the event of remarriage; minor children of a former President until the age of 16; visiting heads of foreign states or governments; other distinguished foreign visitors to the United States; and official representatives of the United States performing special missions abroad, as directed by the President;

—to provide security at the White House complex and other Presidential offices, the temporary official residence of the Vice President in the District of Columbia, and foreign diplomatic missions in the Washington, DC, metropolitan area and throughout the United States, its territories and possessions, as prescribed by statute;

—to detect and arrest any person committing any offense against the laws of the United States relating to currency, coins, obligations, and securities of the United States or of foreign governments;

—to suppress the forgery and fraudulent negotiation or redemption of Federal Government checks, bonds, and other obligations or securities of the United States;

—to conduct investigations relating to certain criminal violations of the Federal Deposit Insurance Act, the Federal Land Bank Act, and the Government Losses in Shipment Act; and

—to detect and arrest offenders of laws pertaining to electronic funds transfer frauds, credit and debit card frauds, false identification documents or devices, computer access fraud, and U.S. Department of Agriculture food coupons, including authority-to-participate cards.

District Offices—United States Secret Service

District	Address	Telephone
Akron, OH	Suite 403, 441 Wolf Ledges Pkwy., 44311–1054	330–761–0544
Albany GA	Suite 221, 235 Roosevelt Ave., 31701–2374	912–430–8442
Albany, NY	Rm. 244, 445 Broadway, 12207	518–431–0205
Albuquerque, NM	Suite 1700, 505 Marquette St. NW., 87102	505–248–5290
Anchorage, AK	Rm. 526, 222 W. 7th Ave., 99513–7592	907–271–5148
Atlanta, GA	Suite 2906, 401 W. Peachtree St., 30308–3516	404–331–6111
Atlantic City, NJ	Suite 501, 6601 Ventnor Ave., Ventnor City, 08406	609–487–1300
Austin, TX	Suite 972, 300 E. 8th St., 78701	512–916–5103
Bakersfield, CA	Suite 190, 5701 Truxton Ave., 93309	805–861–4112
Baltimore, MD	Suite 1124, 100 S. Charles St., 21201	410–962–2200
Baton Rouge, LA	Rm. 1502, 1 American Pl., 70825	504–389–0763
Birmingham, AL	Suite 1125, 15 S. 20th St., 35233	205–731–1144
Bismarck, ND	Rm. 432, Federal Bldg., 58501	701–255–3294
Boise, ID	Rm. 730, 550 W. Fort St., 83724–0001	208–334–1403
Boston, MA	Suite 791, 10 Causeway St., 02222–1080	617–565–5640
Buffalo, NY	Suite 300, 610 Main St., 14202	716–551–4401
Canton, OH	Rm. 211, 201 Cleveland Ave. SW., 44702	330–489–4400
Charleston, SC	Suite 630, 334 Meeting St., 29403	803–727–4691
Charleston, WV	Suite 910, 1 Valley Sq., 25301	304–347–5188
Charlotte, NC	Suite 400, 6302 Fairview Rd., 28210	704–442–8370
Chattanooga, TN	Rm. 204, Martin Luther King Blvd. & Georgia Ave., 37401	615–752–5125
Cheyenne, WY	Suite 3026, 2120 Capitol Ave., 82001	307–772–2380
Chicago, IL	Suite 1200 N., 300 S. Riverside Plz., 60606	312–353–5431
Cincinnati, OH	Rm. 6118, 550 Main St., 45202	513–684–3585
Cleveland, OH	Rm. 440, 6100 Rockside Woods Blvd., 44131–2334	216–522–4365
Colorado Springs, CO	P.O. Box 666, 80901	719–632–3325
Columbia, SC	Suite 1425, 1835 Assembly St., 29201	803–765–5446
Columbus, OH	Suite 800, 500 S. Front St., 43215	614–469–7370
Concord, NH	Suite 250, 197 Loudon Rd., 03301	603–228–3428
Dallas, TX	Suite 300, 125 E. John W. Carpenter Fwy., Irving, 75062–2752	972–868–3200
Dayton, OH	P.O. Box 743, 200 W. 2d St., 45402	937–222–2013
Denver, CO	Suite 1430, 1660 Lincoln St., 80264	303–866–1010
Des Moines, IA	637 Federal Bldg., 210 Walnut St., 50309–2107	515–284–4565
Detroit, MI	Suite 1000, 477 Michigan Ave., 48226–2518	313–226–6400
El Paso, TX	Suite 210, 4849 N. Mesa, 79912	915–533–6950

District Offices—United States Secret Service—Continued

District	Address	Telephone
Fresno, CA	Suite 207, 5200 N. Palm Ave., 93704	209–487–5204
Fort Myers, FL	Suite 804, 2000 Main St., 33901	941–334–0660
Grand Rapids, MI	Suite 302, 330 Ionia Ave. NW., 49503–2350	616–454–4671
Great Falls, MT	No. 11, 3d St. N., 59401	406–452–8515
Greenville, SC	P.O. Box 29603	864–233–1490
Harrisburg, PA	P.O. Box 1244, 17108	717–782–4811
Honolulu, HI	P.O. Box 50046, Rm. 6309, 300 Ala Moana Blvd., 96850	808–541–1912
Houston, TX	Suite 500, 602 Sawyer St., 77007	713–868–2299
Indianapolis, IN	Suite 211, 575 N. Pennsylvania St., 46204	317–226–6444
Jackson, MS	Suite 840, 100 W. Capitol St., 39269	601–965–4436
Jacksonville, FL	Suite 500, 7820 Arlington Expy., 32211	904–232–2777
Jamaica, NY	Rm. 246, Bldg. 75, John F. Kennedy International Airport, 11430	718–553–0911
Kansas City, MO	Suite 510, 1150 Grand Ave., 64106	816–374–6102
Knoxville, TN	Rm. 517, 710 Locust St., 37902	423–545–4627
Las Vegas, NV	P.O. Box 16027, 89101	702–388–6446
Lexington, KY	P.O. Box 13310, 40583	606–233–2453
Little Rock, AR	Suite 1700, 111 Center St., 72201–4419	501–324–6241
Los Angeles, CA	17th Fl., 255 E. Temple St., 90012	213–894–4830
Louisville, KY	Rm. 377, 600 Dr. Martin Luther King, Jr. Pl., 40202	502–582–5171
Lubbock, TX	P.O. Box 2975, 79048	806–472–7347
Madison, WI	P.O. Box 2154, 53701	608–264–5191
McAllen, TX	Suite 1107, 200 S. 10th St., 78501	210–630–5811
Melville, NY	Suite 216E, 35 Pinelawn Rd., 11747–3154	516–249–0984
Memphis, TN	Suite 204, 5350 Poplar Ave., 38119	901–544–0333
Miami, FL	Suite 100, 8375 NW. 53d St., 33166	305–591–3660
Milwaukee, WI	572 Federal Courthouse, 517 E. Wisconsin Ave., 53202	414–297–3587
Minneapolis, MN	Rm. 218, 110 S. 4th St., 55401	612–348–1800
Mobile, AL	Suite 200, 182 St. Francis St., 36602–3501	334–441–5851
Montgomery, AL	Suite 605, 1 Commerce St., 36104	334–223–7601
Morristown, NJ	34 Headquarters Plz., 07960–3990	201–984–5760
Nashville, TN	658 U.S. Courthouse, 801 Broadway St., 37203	615–736–5841
New Haven, CT	P.O. Box 45, 06501	203–865–2449
New Orleans, LA	Rm. 807, 501 Magazine St., 70130	504–589–4041
New York, NY	9th Fl., 7 World Trade Ctr., 10048–1901	212–637–4500
Newark, NJ	34 Headquarters Plaza, Morristown, 07960–3990	973–984–5760
Norfolk, VA	Suite 640, 200 Granby St., 23510	757–441–3200
Oklahoma City, OK	Suite 650, 4013 NW. Expressway, 73102–9229	405–810–3000
Omaha, NE	Rm. 905, 106 S. 15th St., 68102	402–221–4671
Orlando, FL	Suite 670, 135 W. Central Blvd., 32801	407–648–6333
Philadelphia, PA	7236 Federal Bldg., 600 Arch St., 19106–1676	215–597–0600
Phoenix, AZ	Suite 2180, 3200 N. Central Ave., 85012	602–640–5580
Pittsburgh, PA	Rm. 835, 1000 Liberty Ave., 15222	412–644–3384
Portland, ME	2d Fl., Tower B, 100 Middle St., 04104	207–780–3493
Portland, OR	Suite 1330, 121 SW. Salmon St., 97204	503–326–2162
Providence, RI	Suite 343, 380 Westminster St., 02903	401–331–6456
Raleigh, NC	Suite 210, 4407 Bland Rd., 27609–6296	919–790–2834
Reno, NV	Suite 850, 100 W. Liberty St., 89501	702–784–5354
Richmond, VA	Suite 1910, 600 E. Main St., 23219	804–771–2274
Riverside, CA	P.O. Box 1525, 92502	909–276–6781
Roanoke, VA	Suite 2, 105 Franklin Rd. SW., 24011	540–857–2208
Rochester, NY	Rm. 606, 100 State St., 14614	716–263–6830
Sacramento, CA	Suite 530, 501 J St., 95814	916–498–5141
Saginaw, MI	Suite 200, 301 E. Genesee Ave., 48607–1242	517–752–8076
St. Louis, MO	Rm. 924, 1114 Market St., 63101	314–539–2238
Salt Lake City, UT	Suite 450, 57 W. 200 St., 84101–1610	801–524–5910
San Antonio, TX	Rm. B410, 727 E. Durango Blvd., 78206–1265	210–472–6175
San Diego, CA	Suite 660, 550 W. C St., 92101–3531	619–557–5640
San Francisco, CA	Suite 530, 345 Spear St., 94105	415–744–9026
San Jose, CA	Suite 2050, 280 S. 1st St., 95113	408–535–5288
San Juan, PR	Suite 3–B, 1510 F.D. Roosevelt Ave., Guaynabo, 00968	787–277–1515
Santa Ana, CA	Suite 500, 200 W. Santa Ana Blvd., 92701–4164	714–246–8257
Savannah, GA	Suite 570, 33 Bull St., 31401–3334	912–652–4401
Scranton, PA	Rm. 304, Washington & Linden Sts., 18501	717–346–5781
Seattle, WA	Rm. 890, 915 2d Ave., 98174	206–220–6800
Shreveport, LA	Suite 525, 401 Edwards St., 71101	318–676–3500
Sioux Falls, SD	Suite 405, 230 S. Phillips Ave., 57104–6321	605–330–4565
Spokane, WA	Suite 1340, 601 W. Riverside Ave., 99201–0611	509–353–2532
Springfield, IL	Suite 301, 400 W. Monroe St., 62704	217–492–4033
Springfield, MO	Suite 306, 901 E. St. Louis St., 65806	417–864–8340
Syracuse, NY	Post Box 7006, Federal Station, 13261	315–448–0304
Tallahassee, FL	Suite 120, Bldg. F, 325 John Knox Rd., 32303	850–942–9523
Tampa, FL	Rm. 1101, 501 E. Polk St., 33602	813–228–2636
Toledo, OH	Rm. 305, 234 Summit St., 43604	419–259–6434
Trenton, NJ	Suite 202, 101 Carnegie Ctr., Princeton, 08540–6231	609–989–2008
Tucson, AZ	Box FB–56, 300 W. Congress St., 85701	520–670–4730

District Offices—United States Secret Service—Continued

District	Address	Telephone
Tulsa, OK	Suite 400, 125 W. 15 St., 74119–3824	918–581–7272
Tyler, TX	Suite 395, 6101 S. Broadway, 75703	903–534–2933
Ventura, CA	Suite 161, 5500 Telegraph Rd., 93003	805–339–9180
Washington, DC	Suite 1000, 1050 Connecticut Ave. NW., 20036–5305	202–435–5100
West Palm Beach, FL	Suite 800, 505 S. Flagler Dr., 33401	561–659–0184
White Plains, NY	Suite 300, 140 Grand St., 10601	914–682–6300
Wichita, KS	Suite 275, 301 N. Main, 67202	316–267–1452
Wilmington, DE	Rm. 414, 920 King St., 19801	302–573–6188
Wilmington, NC	P.O. Box 120, 28402	910–815–4511

District Offices Overseas—United States Secret Service

District	Address	Telephone
Bangkok, Thailand	American Embassy, Box 64/Bangkok, APO AP 96546	011–662–205–4000
Bogota, Colombia	U.S. Embassy, Unit 5116, APO AA 34038	011–57–1–315–0811
Bonn, West Germany	American Embassy/Bonn, Unit 21701, Box 300, APO New York, NY 09080.	011–49–228–339–2587
Hong Kong	11th Fl., St. John's Bldg., 33 Garden Rd., Central Hong Kong	011–852–2841–2524
London, England	American Embassy/USSS, PSC 801, Box 64, FPO AE, 09498–4064	011–44–171–499–9000
Manila, Philippines	American Embassy/Manila APO AP 96515	011–63–2–523–1167
Milan, Italy	Consulate General of the USA, Via Principe Amedeo 2/10 20121	011–39–2–2903–5447
Nicosia, Cyprus	U.S. Secret Service, American Embassy Nicosia, PSC 815, FPO AE 09836.	011–357–2–476–100
Paris, France	Paris Embassy/USSS, Unit 21551, Box D306, APO AE, 09777	011–33–1–4312–7100
Quebec, Canada	U.S. Consulate, 455 Rene Levesque Blvd., West Montreal, Quebec, Canada H2Z 1Z2.	1–514–398–9695
Rome, Italy	American Embassy/Rome, PSC 59, Box 100, USSS, APO AE, 09624	011–39–6–4674–1
Vancouver, Canada	P.O. Box 5002, Point Roberts, WA 98281–5002	604–689–3179

For further information, contact any District Office or the Office of Government Liaison and Public Affairs, United States Secret Service, Department of the Treasury, 1800 G Street NW., Washington, DC 20223. Phone, 202–435–5708.

Office of Thrift Supervision

The Office of Thrift Supervision (OTS) regulates Federal and State-chartered savings institutions. Created by the Financial Institutions Reform, Recovery, and Enforcement Act of 1989 (FIRREA), its mission is to effectively and efficiently supervise thrift institutions to maintain the safety and soundness of institutions and to ensure the viability of the industry. It also supports the industry's efforts to meet housing and other community credit and financial services needs. The Office works to:
—maintain and enhance its risk-focused, differential, and proactive approach to the supervision of institutions;
—improve credit availability by encouraging safe and sound housing and other lending in those areas of greatest need; and
—enhance competitiveness of the thrift industry.

The Office is headed by a Director appointed by the President, with the advice and consent of the Senate, for a 5-year term. The Director is responsible for the overall direction and policy of the agency. To carry out its mission, OTS is organized in five main program areas: Supervision, Research and Analysis, External Affairs, Chief Counsel, and Administration.

Activities of OTS include:
—examining and supervising thrift institutions in the five OTS regions to ensure the safety and soundness of the industry;
—ensuring that thrifts comply with consumer protection laws and regulations;
—conducting a regional quality assurance program to ensure consistent applications of policies and procedures;
—developing national policy guidelines to enhance statutes and

regulations and to establish programs to implement new policy and law;

—issuing various financial reports, including the quarterly report on the financial condition of the thrift industry;

—preparing regulations, bulletins, other policy documents, congressional testimony, and official correspondence on matters relating to the condition of the thrift industry, interest rate risk,

financial derivatives, and economic issues;

—and prosecuting enforcement actions relating to thrift institutions.

The Office of Thrift Supervision is a nonappropriated agency and thus uses no tax money to fund its operations. Its expenses are met by fees and assessments on the thrift institutions it regulates.

For further information, contact the Dissemination Branch, Office of Thrift Supervision, 1700 G Street NW., Washington, DC 20552. Phone, 202–906–6000. Fax, 202–906–7755. Internet, http:// www.ots.treas.gov/.

Sources of Information

Departmental Offices

Contracts   Write to the Director, Office of Procurement, Suite 400–W, 1310 G Street NW., Washington, DC 20220. Phone, 202–622–0203.

Environment   Environmental statements prepared by the Department are available for review in the Departmental Library. Information on Treasury environmental matters may be obtained from the Office of the Assistant Secretary of the Treasury for Management and Chief Financial Officer, Treasury Department, Washington, DC 20220. Phone, 202–622–0043.

General Inquiries   For general information about the Treasury Department, including copies of news releases and texts of speeches by high Treasury officials, write to the Office of the Assistant Secretary (Public Affairs and Public Liaison), Room 3430, Departmental Offices, Treasury Department, Washington, DC 20220. Phone, 202–622–2920.

Reading Room   The Reading Room is located in the Treasury Library, Room 5030, Main Treasury Building, 1500 Pennsylvania Avenue NW., Washington, DC 20220. Phone, 202–622–0990.

Small and Disadvantaged Business Activities   Write to the Director, Office of Small and Disadvantaged Business Utilization, Suite 400–W, 1310 G Street NW., Washington, DC 20220. Phone, 202–622–0530.

Tax Legislation   Information on tax legislation may be obtained from the Assistant Secretary (Tax Policy), Departmental Offices, Treasury Department, Washington, DC 20220. Phone, 202–622–0050.

Telephone Directory   The Treasury Department telephone directory is available for sale by the Superintendent of Documents, Government Printing Office, Washington, DC 20402.

Office of Inspector General

Employment   Contact the Human Resources Division, Office of Inspector General, Suite 510, 740 15th Street NW., Washington, DC 20220. Phone, 202–927–5230.

Freedom of Information Act/Privacy Act Requests   Inquiries should be directed to Freedom of Information Act Request, Department of the Treasury, Room 1054, 1500 Pennsylvania Avenue NW., Washington, DC 20220.

General Inquiries   Write to the Office of Inspector General, Room 2418, 1500 Pennsylvania Avenue NW., Washington, DC 20220.

Publications   Semiannual reports to the Congress on the Office of Inspector General are available from the Office of Inspector General, Room 2418, 1500 Pennsylvania Avenue NW., Washington, DC 20220.

Office of the Comptroller of the Currency

Contracts Contact the procurement officer at 250 E Street SW., Washington, DC 20219. Phone, 202–874–5040. Fax, 202–874–5625.

Employment The primary occupation is national bank examiner. Examiners are hired generally at the entry level through a college recruitment program. Descriptive literature and information are available from the Director for Human Resources, 250 E Street SW., Washington, DC 20219. Phone, 202–874–4490. Fax, 202–874–5447.

Freedom of Information Act Requests Write or call the disclosure officer, Communications Division, 250 E Street SW., Washington, DC 20219. Phone, 202–874–4700. Fax, 202–874–5263.

Publications Write or call the Communications Division, 250 E Street SW., Washington, DC 20219. Phone, 202–874–4700. Fax, 202–874–5263.

United States Customs Service

Address inquiries on the following subjects to the specified office, U.S. Customs Service, 1300 Pennsylvania Avenue NW., Washington, DC 20229. Phone, 202–927–6724.

Contracts Write to the Regional Procurement Center, 6026 Lakeside Boulevard, Indianapolis, IN 46278.

Employment The U.S. Customs Service recruits from the Treasury Enforcement Agent examination. Employment inquiries may be addressed to the Personnel Director, Office of Human Resources Management in Washington, DC.

Forms Forms are available from any district director's office. There is a nominal charge for large quantities of certain forms.

General Inquiries Contact the nearest port director's office for information regarding customs regulations and procedures for all persons entering the United States and the entry and clearance of imported merchandise.

Publications The U.S. Customs Service issues publications of interest to the general, importing, and traveling public

that can be obtained from any of the port directors' offices or by writing to the Office of Communications in Washington, DC. Single copies of many of these publications are available at no charge to the public.

Reading Rooms Reading rooms are located at the headquarters library and in some field offices.

Speakers Speakers are available for private organizations or community groups throughout the country. Contact any local customs officer or the Office of Communications in Washington, DC.

Bureau of Engraving and Printing

Address inquiries on the following subjects to the specified office, Bureau of Engraving and Printing, Fourteenth and C Streets SW., Washington, DC 20228.

Contracts and Small Business Activities Information relating to contracts and small business activity may be obtained by contacting the Office of Procurement. Phone, 202–874–2534.

Employment The Bureau, as the world's largest security printer, employs personnel in a multitude of different craft, administrative, and professional fields. Competitive job opportunities may be available in the printing crafts, maintenance trades/crafts, engineering, electromachinists, research, chemistry, data processing/computers, quality assurance, personnel, procurement, financial management, and other administrative fields. Due to the high level of security required, the Bureau also employs its own police force and a range of security specialists.

The Bureau participates in the student educational employment program that enables students to gain work experience while pursuing their education. Periodically, apprenticeship programs may be announced in selected crafts.

Information regarding employment opportunities and required qualifications is available from the Staffing and Classification Division, Office of Human Resources. Phone, 202–874–3747.

Freedom of Information Act Requests Inquiries should be directed to the Bureau Disclosure Officer, Room 112M. Phone, 202–874–2769.

General Inquiries   Requests for information about the Bureau, its products, or numismatic and philatelic interests should be addressed to the Office of External Relations and Customer Service, Room 533M, Fourteenth and C Streets SW., Washington, DC 20228. Phone, 202–874–3019.

Product Sales   Uncut sheets of currency, engraved Presidential portraits, historical engravings of national landmarks, and other souvenirs and mementos are available for purchase in the Visitors Center or through the mail. The Visitors Center gift shop, located in the Fifteenth Street (Raoul Wallenberg Place) lobby of the main building, is open from 8:30 a.m. to 3:30 p.m. Monday through Friday, excluding Federal holidays and Christmas week. In June, July, and August, the gift shop will reopen at 4:30 p.m. and close at 8:30 p.m. Information and order forms for sales items by mail may be obtained by writing to the Office of External Relations and Customer Service, Fourteenth and C Streets SW., Room 533M, Washington, DC 20228, or by calling 202–874–3019.

Tours   Tours of the Bureau's facility in Washington, DC are provided throughout the year according to the following schedule:

Peak season, April through September, 9 a.m. until 1:50 p.m. Tours begin every 10 minutes, with the last tour beginning at 1:50 p.m. The ticket booth is located on Raoul Wallenberg Place (formerly Fifteenth Street) and is open from 8 a.m. until 2 p.m. Tour tickets are free. Lines queue up on Raoul Wallenberg Place.

Evening tours, June through August, 5 p.m. until 7:30 p.m. Tours are offered every 10 minutes. The ticket booth for evening tour tickets is open from 3:30 until 7:30 p.m. Tour tickets are free. Lines queue up on Raoul Wallenberg Place.

Non-peak season, October through March, 9 a.m. until 2 p.m. No tickets are necessary for tours during this time. Lines queue up on Fourteenth Street.

No tours are given on weekends, Federal holidays, or between Christmas and New Year's Day.

Financial Management Service

Inquiries on the following subjects should be directed to the specified office, Financial Management Service, 401 Fourteenth Street SW., Washington, DC 20227.

Contracts   Write to the Director, Acquisition Management Division, Room 427 LCB. Phone, 202–874–6910.

Employment   Inquiries may be directed to the Personnel Management Division, Room 120 LCB. Phone, 202–874–7080.

Fax   Facsimile transmittal services are available by dialing 202–874–7016.

Internal Revenue Service

Audiovisual Materials   Films, some of which are available in Spanish, provide information on the American tax system, examination and appeal rights, and the tax responsibilities of running a small business. The films can be obtained by contacting any District Office.

Also available are audio and video cassette tapes that provide step-by-step instructions for preparing basic individual income tax forms. These tapes are available in many local libraries.

Contracts   Write to the Internal Revenue Service, 1111 Constitution Avenue NW. (M:P:C), Washington, DC 20224 (phone, 202–283–1710); or the Director of Support Services, at any of the Internal Revenue regional offices.

Educational Programs   The Service provides, free of charge, general tax information publications and booklets on specific tax topics. Taxpayer information materials also are distributed to major television networks and many radio and television stations, daily and weekly newspapers, magazines, and specialized publications. Special educational materials and films are provided for use in high schools and colleges. Individuals starting a new business are given specialized materials and information at small business workshops, and community colleges provide classes based on material provided by the Service. The Community Outreach Tax Assistance program provides agency employees to assist community groups at mutually convenient times and locations.

Through the Volunteer Income Tax Assistance program and the Tax Counseling for the Elderly program, the Service recruits, trains, and supports volunteers who offer free tax assistance to low-income, elderly, military, and non-English-speaking taxpayers.

Materials, films, and information on the educational programs can be obtained by contacting any District Office.

Employment Almost every major field of study has some application to the work of the Service. A substantial number of positions are filled by persons whose major educational preparation was accounting, business administration, finance, economics, criminology, and law. There are, however, a great number of positions that are filled by persons whose college major was political science, public administration, education, liberal arts, or other fields not directly related to business or law. Extensive use is made of competitive registers and examinations in selecting employees. Schools interested in participating in the extensive recruitment program, or anyone considering employment with the Service, may direct inquiries to the Recruitment Coordinator at any of the Regional or District Offices.

Publications The *Annual Report— Commissioner of Internal Revenue* (Pub. 55) and *Internal Revenue Service Data Book* (Pub. 55B), as well as periodic reports of statistics of income, which present statistical tabulations concerning various tax returns filed, are available from the Superintendent of Documents, Government Printing Office, Washington, DC 20402. *Audit of Returns, Appeal Rights, and Claims for Refund* (Pub. 556), *Your Federal Income Tax* (Pub. 17), *Farmers Tax Guide* (Pub. 225), *Tax Guide for Small Business* (Pub. 334), and other publications are available at Internal Revenue Service offices free of charge.

Reading Rooms Public reading rooms are located in the National Office and in each Regional Office or, in some cases, a District Office located in a Regional Office building.

Speakers Speakers on provisions of the tax law and operations of the Internal Revenue Service for professional and community groups may be obtained by writing to the District Directors or, for national organizations only, to the Communications Division at the IRS National Headquarters in Washington, DC.

Taxpayer Advocate Each District has a problem resolution staff which attempts to resolve taxpayer complaints not satisfied through regular channels.

Taxpayer Service The Internal Revenue Service provides year-round tax information and assistance to taxpayers, primarily through its toll-free telephone system. Taxpayers requesting information about the tax system, their rights and obligations under it, and the tax benefits available to them can call the number listed in their local telephone directory and in the tax form packages mailed to them annually. This service allows taxpayers anywhere in the United States to call the service without paying a long-distance charge. Special toll-free telephone assistance also is available to deaf and hearing-impaired taxpayers who have access to a teletypewriter or television/phone. These special numbers are included in the annual tax form packages and also are available from any agency office.

Taxpayers may also visit agency offices for help with their tax problems. The Service provides return preparation assistance to taxpayers by guiding groups of individuals line by line on the preparation of their returns. Individual preparation is available for handicapped or other individuals unable to use the group preparation method.

Foreign language tax assistance also is available at many locations.

United States Mint

Contracts and Employment Inquiries should be directed to the facility head of the appropriate field office or to the Director of the Mint.

Numismatic Services The United States Mint maintains public exhibit and sales areas at the Philadelphia and Denver Mints, and at Union Station in

Washington, DC. Brochures and order forms for official coins, medals, and other numismatic items may also be obtained by writing to the United States Mint, 10003 Derekwood Lane, Lanham, MD 20706. Phone, 202–283–COIN.

Publications The *CFO Annual Financial Report* is available from the United States Mint, Department of the Treasury, Judiciary Square Building, 633 Third Street NW., Washington, DC 20220. Phone, 202–874–9696.

Bureau of the Public Debt

Electronic Access Information about the public debt, U.S. Savings Bonds, Treasury bills, notes, and bonds, and other Treasury securities is available through the Internet, at http:// www.publicdebt.treas.gov/. Forms and publications may be ordered electronically at the same address.

Employment General employment inquiries should be addressed to the Bureau of the Public Debt, Division of Personnel Management, Employment and Classification Branch, Parkersburg, WV 26106–1328. Phone, 304–480–6144.

Savings Bonds Savings bonds are continuously on sale at more than 40,000 financial institutions and their branches in virtually every locality in the United States. Information about bonds is provided by such issuing agents.

Current rate information is available toll-free by calling 1–800–4US–BOND.

Requests for information about all series of savings bonds, savings notes, and retirement plans or individual retirement bonds should be addressed to the Bureau of the Public Debt, Department of the Treasury, 200 Third Street, Parkersburg, WV 26106–1328. Phone, 304–480–6112.

Treasury Securities Information inquiries regarding the purchase of Treasury bills, bonds, and notes should be addressed to your local Federal Reserve Bank or branch, or to the Bureau of the Public Debt, Department F, Washington, DC 20239–1200. Phone, 202–874–4060.

United States Secret Service

Information about employment opportunities and publications and general public information may be obtained by contacting the nearest Secret Service field office or the Office of Government Liaison and Public Affairs, 1800 G Street NW., Washington, DC 20223. Phone, 202–435–5708.

Office of Thrift Supervision

Electronic Access Information about OTS and institutions regulated by OTS is available through the Internet, at http:// www.ots.treas.gov/.

Employment Inquiries about employment opportunities with the Office of Thrift Supervision should be directed to the Human Resources Office. Phone, 202–906–6061.

Fax-on-Demand Documents are available through the OTS PubliFax Line, which employs a series of voice prompts to determine requested documents. Phone/fax, 202–906–5660.

Freedom of Information Act/Privacy Act Requests For information not readily available from the Public Reference Room, the OTS PubliFax, or the OTS order department, a written request may be submitted to the Office of Thrift Supervision, Dissemination Branch, 1700 G Street NW., Washington, DC 20552. Requests may also be submitted by facsimile (fax, 202–906–7755). Requests should clearly describe the information sought, include a firm agreement to pay fees, and state how the documents will be used.

General Information General information about the Office of Thrift Supervision may be obtained by calling 202–906–6000. Information about the OTS public disclosure program may be obtained by contacting the Manager, Dissemination Branch (phone, 202–906–5900) or the Director, Records Management and Information Policy Division (phone, 202–906–7571).

Public Reference Room The Public Reference Room makes available a wide variety of OTS records and information about federally insured savings associations. It is open Monday through

Friday from 9 a.m. to 4 p.m. and is located at 1700 G Street NW., Washington, DC 20552.

Publications Publications that provide information and guidance regarding the thrift industry are available for purchase. A complete publications list is available from the Public Reference Room, the PubliFax, and the Internet. Publications can be purchased by check or credit card through the OTS Order Department, P.O. Box 753, Waldorf, MD 20604. Phone, 301–645–6264.

For further information concerning the Department of the Treasury, contact the Public Affairs Office, Department of the Treasury, 1500 Pennsylvania Avenue NW., Washington, DC 20220. Phone, 202–622–2960. Internet, http://www.treas.gov/.

DEPARTMENT OF VETERANS AFFAIRS

810 Vermont Avenue NW., Washington, DC 20420
Phone, 202–273–4900. Internet, http://www.va.gov/.

SECRETARY OF VETERANS AFFAIRS	TOGO D. WEST, JR.
Executive Assistant to the Secretary and Deputy Chief of Staff	JANICE F. JOYNER
Special Assistants to the Secretary	JANESE M. BECHTOL, LISA S. WETZL
Deputy Secretary	HERSHEL W. GOBER
Executive Assistant to the Deputy Secretary	DINA WOOD
Chief of Staff	HAROLD F. GRACEY, JR.
Veterans' Service Organizations Liaison	ALLEN (GUNNER) KENT
Director, Executive Secretariat	LINDA KAUFMANN
Inspector General	RICHARD J. GRIFFIN
Chairman, Board of Contract Appeals	GUY H. MCMICHAEL III
Director, Office of Small and Disadvantaged Business Utilization	SCOTT F. DENNISTON
Director, Office of Employment Discrimination Complaint Adjudication	CHARLES R. DELOBE
Director, Center for Women Veterans	JOAN A. FUREY
General Counsel	MARY LOU KEENER
Special Assistant to the General Counsel	(VACANCY)
Deputy General Counsel	ROBERT E. COY
Assistant General Counsels	PHILLIPA L. ANDERSON, E. DOUGLAS BRADSHAW, RONALD H. GARVIN, WALTER A. HALL, NEAL C. LAWSON, HOWARD C. LEM, JOHN H. THOMPSON
Chairman, Board of Veterans' Appeals	RICHARD B. STANDEFER, *Acting*
Executive Assistant to the Chairman	MARJORIE A. AUER
Director, Management and Administration	RONALD R. AUMENT
Chief Counsel	STEVEN L. KELLER
Deputy Chief Counsel, Litigation Support	RICHARD C. THRASHER
Deputy Chief Counsel, Legal Affairs	THOMAS D. ROBERTS
Vice Chairman	RICHARD B. STANDEFER
Senior Deputy Vice Chairman	STEVEN L. KELLER, *Acting*
Deputy Vice Chairman, Decision Team I	CHARLES E. HOGEBOOM
Deputy Vice Chairman, Decision Team II	JOAQUIN AQUAYO-PERELES
Deputy Vice Chairman, Decision Team III	NANCY R. ROBIN
Deputy Vice Chairman, Decision Team IV	MARY M. SABULSKY
Director, Administrative Service	NANCY D. STACKHOUSE
Under Secretary for Health, Veterans Health Administration	KENNETH W. KIZER
Chief of Staff	ROBYN Y. NISHIMI
Director, Executive Correspondence	PAMELA E. GALYEAN
Deputy Under Secretary for Health	THOMAS GARTHWAITE
Chief Network Officer	KENNETH J. CLARK
Director, Network Program Support	WILLIAM W. GRAHAM, ACTING

Veterans Integrated Service Network (VISN)
    Directors:

Director, VISN No. 1	DENIS J. FITZGERALD
Director, VISN No. 2	FREDERICK L. MALPHURS
Director, VISN No. 3	JAMES J. FARSETTA
Director, VISN No. 4	JUDITH FELDMAN, *Acting*
Director, VISN No. 5	JAMES J. NOCKS
Director, VISN No. 6	LEROY P. GROSS
Director, VISN No. 7	LARRY R. DEAL
Director, VISN No. 8	ROBERT H. ROSWELL
Director, VISN No. 9	KENNETH MULHOLLAND, *Acting*
Director, VISN No. 10	LAURA J. MILLER
Director, VISN No. 11	LINDA W. BELTON
Director, VISN No. 12	JOAN E. CUMMINGS
Director, VISN No. 13	ROBERT A. PETZEL
Director, VISN No. 14	SHELIA C. GELMAN, *Acting*
Director, VISN No. 15	PATRICIA A. CROSETTI
Director, VISN No. 16	JOHN R. HIGGINS
Director, VISN No. 17	VERNON CHONG
Director, VISN No. 18	THOMAS A. TRUJILLO
Director, VISN No. 19	TERRENCE S. BATLINER
Director, VISN No. 20	TED GALEY, *Acting*
Director, VISN No. 21	ROBERT L. WIEBE
Director, VISN No. 22	SMITH JENKINS, JR.
Medical Inspector	JAMES E. MCMANUS
Chief, Office of Employee Education	ROBERT P. MEANS
Veterans Canteen Service Officer	JERRY KELLY
Director, Emergency Medical Preparedness	JOE GRAY
Chief, Policy, Planning, and Performance Office	GREGG PANE
Director, Performance Equality Service	NANCY J. WILSON
Director, Delivery System Planning Office	BRUCE PLECINSKI
Director, Policy and Forecasting Office	MAUREEN S. BALTAY
Director, Reports Review and Analysis	PAUL C. GIBERT, JR.
Cheif, Legislative Programs	BILL RAMSEY
Chief Patient Care Services Officer	THOMAS HOLOHAN
Director, Nutrition and Food Service	BRENDA L. JENKINS, *Acting*
Director, Social Work Service	DONALD G. MOSES, *Acting*
Director, Chaplain Service (VAMC, Hampton, VA)	MATTHEW A. ZIMMERMAN
Chief Consultant, Acute Care Strategic Healthcare Group	TONI A. MITCHELL
Deputy Associate Deputy Chief Medical Director for Ambulatory Care	RONALD J. GEBHART
Director, National Center for Health Promotion and Disease Prevention	ROBERT SULLIVAN
Director, Spinal Cord Injury Service	MARGARET HAMMOND
Director, Optometry Service	SHARON ATKIN
Director, Podiatry Service	JOHN RAINIERI
Assistant Chief Medical Director for Dentistry	ROBERT T. FRME, *Acting*
Chief Consultant, Prosthetic and Sensory Aids Service Strategic Healthcare Group	JOHN CLEMENTS, *Acting*
Chief Consultant, Geriatrics and Extended Care Strategic Healthcare Group	JUDITH A. SALERNO

Chief Consultant, Diagnostic Services Strategic Healthcare Group	THEODORE F. BEALS
Director, Mental Health and Behavioral Sciences Services	THOMAS B. HORVATH
Chief Consultant, Rehabilitation Strategic Healthcare Group	LEIGH C. ANDERSON, *Acting*
Chief Consultant, Nursing Strategic Healthcare Group	NANCY M. VALENTINE
Chief Consultant, Pharmacy Benefits Management Strategic Healthcare Group	JOHN E. OGDEN
Chief Research and Development Officer	JOHN R. FEUSSNER
Director, Medical Research Program	PAUL HOFFMAN
Director, Rehabilitation Research and Development Program	(VACANCY)
Director, Health Services Research and Development Service	JOHN DEMAKIS, *Acting*
Chief Public Health and Environmental Hazards Officer	SUSAN H. MATHER
Director, Environmental Agents Service	FRAN M. MURPHY
Director, AIDS Service	LAWRENCE R. DEYTON
Chief Academic Affiliations Officer	DAVID P. STEVENS
Director, Graduate Medical Education Office	ELIZA M. WOLFF, *Acting*
Director, Associated Health Education Office	LINDA JOHNSON, *Acting*
Director, Administrative Operations Office	EVERT MELANDER
Director, Readjustment Counseling Service	ALFONSO R. BATRES
Director, Volunteer Service Office	JIM W. DELGADO
Director, Management and Administrative Support Office	THOMAS J. HOGAN
Director, Health Care Staff Development and Retention Office	H. BERNARD PALMER
Director, Acquisition and Materiel Management Liaison	JUDITH MABRY
Director, Medical Sharing and Purchasing Office	ARTHUR S. HAMERSCHLAG
Chief Financial Officer	W. TODD GRAMS
Director, Resource Formulation	(VACANCY)
Director, Resource Allocation and Execution	JIMMY A. NORRIS
Director, Financial Management Office	JAMES P. BRAKEFIELD
Director, Accounting/Reports and Systems Service	ED ROBBINS
Director, Medical Care Cost Recovery Office	WALTER J. BESECKER
Chief Facilities Management Officer	C.V. YARBROUGH
Director, Program Management and Planning Office	PAM DIX
Director, Claims and Risk Management Office	ROBERT L. CLONTZ
Director, Real Property Management Office	LAWRENCE J. HILL
Director, Environmental Management Service	WAYNE WARREN
Director, Construction Management Office	JAMES W. LAWSON
Director, Facilities Quality Office	LLOYD H. SIEGEL
Director, Consulting Support Office	HAROLD M. GOODE
Director, Asset and Enterprise Development Office	ANATOLIJ KUSHNIR

Chief Information Officer	R. DAVID ALBINSON
Director, IRM Policy and Planning Service	LEONARD R. BOURGET
Associate Chief Information Officer, Business Enterprise Solutions and Technology Services	ROBERT KOLODNER
Associate Chief Information Officer, Technical Services	ROY SWATZELL
Associate Chief Information Officer, Customer Service	GAIL BELLES
Director, Library and Audiovisual Communication Programs	WENDY CARTER
Director, Office of Information Management	MICHAEL WILLIAMS
Associate Chief Information Officer, Implementation and Training Services	DANIEL MARSH
Director, Telecommunications Support Service	ROBERT BRUCE, *Acting*
Under Secretary for Benefits, Veterans Benefits Administration	JOSEPH THOMPSON
Deputy Under Secretary for Benefits for Operations	PATRICK NAPPI
Deputy Under Secretary for Benefits for Management	NORA EGAN
Chief Financial Officer	ROBERT W. GARDNER
Chief Information Officer	NEWELL QUINTON
Director, Office of Executive Management and Communications	DOROTHY MACKAY, *Acting*
Director, Office of Human Resources	JAMES A. COYNE, *Acting*
Director, Eastern Area	DAVID A. BRIGHAM
Director, Central Area	(VACANCY)
Director, Southern Area	LEO C. WURSCHMIDT
Director, Western Area	DAVID WALLS, *Acting*
Director, Compensation and Pension Service	KRISTINE A. MOFFITT
Director, Education Service	CELIA DOLLARHIDE
Director, Insurance Service	THOMAS LASTOWKA
Director, Loan Guaranty Service	KEITH PEDIGO
Director, Vocational Rehabilitation Service	JULIUS WILLIAMS
Director, National Cemetery System	(VACANCY)
Consultant	LOUISE WARE
Director, Office of Field Operations	ROGER R. RAPP
Director, Field Programs Service	FRED L. WATSON
Director, Technical Support Service	ROBERT B. HOLBROOK
Director, State Cemetery Grants Service	WILLIAM JAYNE
Director, Office of Operations Support	VINCENT L. BARILE
Director, Administration Service	MICHAEL HERWAY
Director, Budget and Planning Service	DANIEL TUCKER
Director, Executive Communications and Public Affairs Service	(VACANCY)
Director, Information Systems Service	MARK P. DUROCHER
Director, Memorial Program Service	(VACANCY)
Directors, National Cemetery System Area Offices:	
Philadelphia, PA	PATRICK J. GARTLAND
Atlanta, GA	ROBERT WILK
Denver, CO	THOMAS G. BALSANEK
Assistant Secretary for Management	D. MARK CATLETT, *Acting*

Deputy to the Assistant Secretary	STANLEY R. SINCLAIR
Deputy Assistant Secretary for Budget	D. MARK CATLETT
Deputy Assistant Secretary for Financial Management	FRANK W. SULLIVAN
Deputy Assistant Secretary for Information Resources Management	NADA D. HARRIS
Deputy Assistant Secretary for Acquisition and Materiel Management	GARY J. KRUMP
Assistant Secretary for Policy and Planning	DENNIS DUFFY
Executive Assistant	NANCY TACKETT
Special Assistant	PATRICIA J. O'NEIL
Deputy Assistant Secretary for Policy	EDWARD CHOW, JR.
Deputy Assistant Secretary for Planning	(VACANCY)
Director, National Center for Veterans Analysis and Statistics	H. DAVID BURGE
Assistant Secretary for Human Resources and Administration	EUGENE A. BRICKHOUSE
Deputy Assistant Secretary for Human Resources Management	RONALD E. COWLES
Deputy Assistant Secretary for Equal Opportunity	GERALD K. HINCH
Deputy Assistant Secretary for Administration	ROBERT W. SCHULTZ
Deputy Assistant Secretary for Security and Law Enforcement	JOHN H. BAFFA
Assistant Secretary for Public and Intergovernmental Affairs	JOHN T. HANSON, *Acting*
Deputy Assistant Secretary for Public Affairs	JAMES H. HOLLEY
Deputy Assistant Secretary for Intergovernmental Affairs	JOHN T. HANSON
Assistant Secretary for Congressional Affairs	(VACANCY)
Deputy Assistant Secretary for Congressional Affairs	PHILIP RIGGIN

The Department of Veterans Affairs operates programs to benefit veterans and members of their families. Benefits include compensation payments for disabilities or death related to military service; pensions; education and rehabilitation; home loan guaranty; burial; and a medical care program incorporating nursing homes, clinics, and medical centers.

The Department of Veterans Affairs (VA) was established as an executive department by the Department of Veterans Affairs Act (38 U.S.C. 201 note). The Department's predecessor, the Veterans Administration, had been established as an independent agency under the President by Executive Order 5398 of July 21, 1930, in accordance with the act of July 3, 1930 (46 Stat. 1016). This act authorized the President to consolidate and coordinate the U.S. Veterans Bureau, the Bureau of Pensions, and the National Home for Volunteer Soldiers.

The Department of Veterans Affairs comprises three organizations that administer veterans programs: the Veterans Health Administration, the Veterans Benefits Administration, and the National Cemetery System. Each organization has field facilities and a Central Office component. The Central Office also includes separate offices that provide support to the top organizations' operations as well as to top VA executives. Top Central Office managers, including the Inspector General and General Counsel, report to the highest level of Department management, which

DEPARTMENT OF VETERANS AFFAIRS

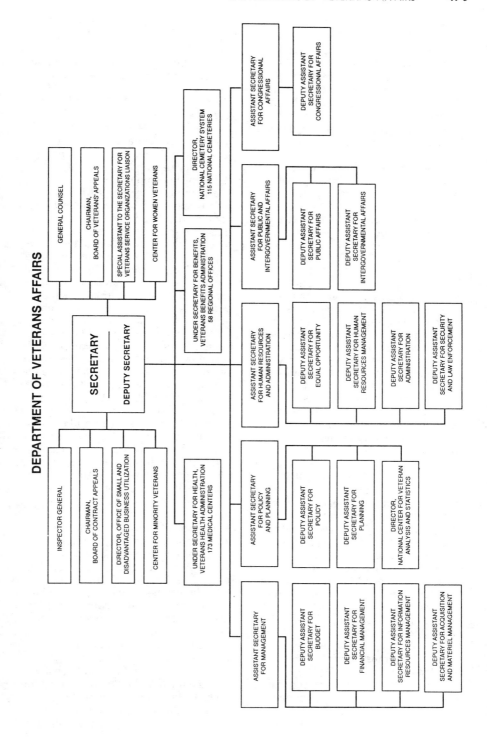

consists of the Secretary of Veterans Affairs and the Deputy Secretary.

Assistant Secretaries   Five Assistant Secretaries provide policy guidance, operational support, and managerial oversight to the Secretary and Deputy Secretary, the administrations, and other top offices. They include the Assistant Secretaries for Management, Policy and Planning, Human Resources and Administration, Public and Intergovernmental Affairs, and Congressional Affairs. Other central management offices are detailed as follows.

Center for Minority Veterans   The Center for Minority Veterans was established under Public Law 103–446 (108 Stat. 4645). The Center is responsible for promoting the use of VA benefits, programs, and services by minority veterans and assessing the needs of minority group members. Under the law, the Center's work focuses on the unique and special needs of five distinct groups of veterans: African-Americans, Hispanics, Asian-Americans, Pacific Islanders, and Native Americans, which include American Indians, Native Hawaiians, and Alaskan Natives. The Center also oversees the administrative functions of the VA's Federal Advisory Committee on Minority Veterans.

The primary mission of the Center for Minority Veterans is to ensure that the Department of Veterans Affairs addresses the unique and special needs of minority veterans. The Center also focuses on circumstances, policies, and practices that impede the use of programs and services by minority veterans.

Center for Women Veterans   The Center for Women Veterans acts as the Secretary's primary adviser on women veterans issues and evaluates VA programs, policies, and practices to ensure they are responsive and accessible to eligible women veterans.

Board of Veterans' Appeals   The Board of Veterans' Appeals (BVA) is responsible, on behalf of the Secretary of Veterans Affairs, for entering the final appellate decisions in claims of entitlement to veterans' benefits. The Board is also responsible for deciding matters concerning fees charged by attorneys and agents for representation of veterans before VA, as well as requests for revision of prior BVA decisions on the basis of clear and unmistakable error. The mission of the Board, set forth in title 38 of the United States Code, sections 7101–7109, is to conduct hearings, consider and dispose of appeals properly before the Board in a timely manner, and issue quality decisions in compliance with the law. The Board is headed by a Chairman, who is appointed by the President and confirmed by the Senate, and who is directly responsible to the Secretary of Veterans Affairs. Members of the Board are appointed by the Secretary with the approval of the President and are under the administrative control and supervision of the Chairman. Each BVA decision is signed by a Board member acting as an agent of the Secretary. Final BVA decisions are appealable to the United States Court of Veterans Appeals.

Board of Contract Appeals   The Board of Contract Appeals was established on March 1, 1979, pursuant to the Contract Disputes Act of 1978 (41 U.S.C. 601–613). The Board is a statutory, quasi-judicial tribunal that hears and decides appeals from decisions of Contracting Officers on claims relating to contracts awarded by VA, or by any other agency when such agency or the Administrator for Federal Procurement Policy has designated the Board to decide the appeal.

The Board's jurisdiction includes applications for attorney fees and expenses under the Equal Access to Justice Act, as amended (5 U.S.C. 504 note). Board decisions are final within VA, but may be appealed, either by the Government or by the contractor, to the United States Court of Appeals for the Federal Circuit.

The Board also acts as a trier of disputed material facts in debarment/suspension proceedings. Additionally, the Chairman of the Board is the senior official within the Department to promote alternate dispute resolution pursuant to the Administrative Dispute

Resolution Act (5 U.S.C. 581 note). Finally, the Board is charged with resolving any disputes between drug manufacturers and the Secretary with regard to pharmaceutical pricing agreements provisions of the Veterans Health Care Act of 1992 (38 U.S.C. 101 note).

Health Services

The Veterans Health Administration, formerly the Veterans Health Services and Research Administration, provides hospital, nursing home, and domiciliary care, and outpatient medical and dental care to eligible veterans of military service in the Armed Forces. It operates 173 medical centers, 39 domiciliaries, 376 outpatient clinics, 131 nursing home care units, and 205 Vietnam Veteran Outreach Centers in the United States, the Commonwealth of Puerto Rico, and the Republic of the Philippines, and provides for similar care under VA auspices in non-VA hospitals and community nursing homes and for visits by veterans to non-VA physicians and dentists for outpatient treatment. It also supports veterans under care in hospitals, nursing homes, and domiciliaries operated by 35 States. Under the Civilian Health and Medical Program, dependents of certain veterans are provided with medical care supplied by non-VA institutions and physicians.

The Administration conducts both individual medical and health-care delivery research projects and multihospital research programs. It assists in the education of physicians and dentists, and with training of many other health care professionals through affiliations with educational institutions and organizations. These programs are all conducted as prescribed by the Secretary of Veterans Affairs pursuant to sections 4101–4115 of title 38 of the United States Code and other statutory authority and regulations.

Veterans Benefits

The Veterans Benefits Administration (VBA), formerly the Department of Veterans Benefits, conducts an integrated program of veterans benefits. It provides information, advice, and assistance to veterans, their dependents, beneficiaries, representatives, and others applying for VA benefits. It also cooperates with the Department of Labor and other Federal, State, and local agencies in developing employment opportunities for veterans and referral for assistance in resolving socioeconomic, housing, and other related problems. In addition, VBA provides information regarding veterans benefits to various branches of the Armed Forces.

Programs are provided through VA regional offices, medical centers, visits to communities, and a special toll-free telephone service (800–827–1000) and are available in all 50 States, the District of Columbia, and Puerto Rico.

Compensation and Pension   The Compensation and Pension Service has responsibility for:

—claims for disability compensation and pension;

—automobile allowances and special adaptive equipment;

—claims for specially adapted housing;

—special clothing allowances;

—emergency officers' retirement pay;

—eligibility determinations based on military service for other VA benefits and services or those of other Government agencies;

—survivors' claims for death compensation, dependency and indemnity compensation, death pension, burial and plot allowance claims;

—claims for accrued benefits;

—forfeiture determinations;

—claims for adjusted compensation in death cases;

—claims for reimbursement for headstone or marker; and

—a benefits protection program (fiduciary activities) for minors and incompetent adult beneficiaries.

The Service also provides field investigative services for other VA components.

Education   The Education Service has responsibility for: the Montgomery GI Bill—Active Duty and Selected Reserve (chapters 30 and 1606); the Post Vietnam Era Veterans' Educational Assistance Program (chapter 32); the

Survivors' and Dependents' Educational Assistance Program (chapter 35); the Section 901 Test Program; and school approvals, compliance surveys, and work study.

Vocational Rehabilitation The Vocational Rehabilitation Service has responsibility for: outreach, motivation, evaluation, counseling, training, employment, and other rehabilitation services to disabled veterans (chapters 31 and 15); evaluation, counseling, and miscellaneous services to veterans and service persons (chapter 30) and other VA education programs; evaluation, counseling, education, and miscellaneous services to sons, daughters, and spouses of totally and permanently disabled veterans and to surviving orphans, widows, or widowers of certain deceased veterans, including rehabilitation services to certain handicapped dependents (chapter 35); and affirmative action activities. Effective October 1, 1997, the Service has responsibility to provide vocational training and rehabilitation to children with spina bifida who are children of Vietnam veterans (chapter 18).

Loan Guaranty Loan guaranty operations include: appraising properties to establish their values; approving grants for specially adapted housing; supervising the construction of new residential properties; establishing the eligibility of veterans for the program; evaluating the ability of a veteran to repay a loan and the credit risk; servicing and liquidating defaulted loans; and disposing of real estate acquired as the consequence of defaulted loans.

Insurance Life insurance operations are for the benefit of service members, veterans, and their beneficiaries. The day-to-day processing of all matters related to individual insurance accounts is handled by the Regional Office and Insurance Centers in Philadelphia, PA, and St. Paul, MN. These two centers provide the full range of functional activities necessary for a national life insurance program. Activities include the complete maintenance of individual accounts, underwriting functions, and life and death insurance claims awards,

as well as any other insurance-related transactions. For information, call toll-free, 800–669–8477

The agency is also responsible for the administration of the Veterans Mortgage Life Insurance program for those disabled veterans who receive a VA grant for specially adapted housing. Accounts are maintained at the Regional Office and Insurance Center in St. Paul, MN.

In addition, the agency is responsible for supervising the Servicemen's Group Life Insurance (SGLI) and Veterans Group Life Insurance (VGLI) programs. Both programs are handled through the Office of Servicemen's Group Life Insurance, 213 Washington Street, Newark, NJ 07102. For information, call toll-free, 800–419–1473.

National Cemetery System

The National Cemetery System (NCS) provides services to veterans, active duty personnel, reservists, and National Guard members with 20 years' qualifying service and their families by operating national cemeteries; furnishing headstones and markers for the graves of U.S. veterans worldwide, service members, and reservists and National Guard members with 20 years' qualifying service; awarding grants to aid States in establishing, improving, and expanding veterans cemeteries; and serving as the operations element for the Presidential Memorial Certificate Program.

The mission of the National Cemetery System is:

—to provide, upon request, the interment of eligible service members, veterans, reservists and National Guard members with 20 years' qualifying service, their spouses, and certain children in VA national cemeteries and to maintain their graves;

—to mark, upon application, the graves of eligible veterans worldwide, and reservists and National Guard members with 20 years' qualifying service who are buried in national, State, or private cemeteries;

—to administer the State Cemetery Grants Program, which provides financial assistance to States for establishing, improving, and expanding State veterans cemeteries; and

—to provide Presidential Memorial Certificates to the loved ones of honorably discharged, deceased service members or veterans.

The National Cemetery area offices (located in Atlanta, GA; Philadelphia, PA; and Denver, CO) provide direct support to the 115 national cemeteries located throughout the United States and Puerto Rico.

Field Facilities

Insurance Centers   Two field sites house all individual insurance records covering service members and veterans under the Government–administered programs: WW I United States Government Life Insurance; WW II National Service Life Insurance; Post-Korean Conflict; Veterans Reopened Insurance for the disabled of WW II and Korea; and Service-Disabled Veterans Insurance, the only Government–administered program open for new issues to disabled veterans only.

The two field locations are the VA Regional Office and Insurance Centers in Philadelphia, PA, and St. Paul, MN. All World War I insurance accounts, accounts for which the premium is paid by allotment from military service pay, and those paid by deduction from VA compensation or preauthorized debit are located at Philadelphia. All remaining insurance accounts are geographically distributed between the two VA Centers—with the Mississippi River serving as the approximate line of division. The Philadelphia Veterans Affairs Center is also responsible for formulating policy for the veterans insurance programs.

The insurance functions performed by the two field stations include the total range of insurance operations to provide individual policy, underwriting, and life and death insurance claims service for service members, veterans, and their beneficiaries.

Regional Offices   Department of Veterans Affairs regional offices:

—grant benefits and services provided by law for veterans, their dependents, and beneficiaries within an assigned territory;

—furnish information regarding VA benefits and services;

—adjudicate claims and make awards for disability compensation and pension;

—supervise the payment of VA benefits to incompetent beneficiaries;

—aid, guide, and prescribe vocational rehabilitation training and administer educational benefits;

—guarantee loans for purchase of manufactured homes and lots and condominium units, purchase or construction or alteration of homes and farm residences, and under certain conditions, guarantee refinancing loans;

—process grants for specially adapted housing;

—process death claims;

—assist the veteran in exercising rights to benefits and services; and

—supervise VA offices under their jurisdiction.

The offices are also responsible for veterans assistance activities, including coordination of efforts of participating agencies in an outreach program to assist returning service members.

Services to U.S. veterans in most foreign countries normally are provided by the VA Regional Office, District of Columbia. The Honolulu Regional Office serves the Islands of American Samoa, the Commonwealth of the Northern Mariana Islands, Guam, Wake, and Midway and the Trust Territory of the Pacific Islands. U.S. veterans in the Virgin Islands and Mexico are served by the San Juan and Houston offices, respectively. Service is provided in cooperation with embassy staffs of the Department of State.

Department of Veterans Affairs Regional Office, District of Columbia   The Department of Veterans Affairs Regional Office, District of Columbia, is a typical regional office with additional functions. It has global jurisdiction and grants benefits and services provided by law for veterans and their beneficiaries and dependents residing outside the territorial limits of the United States, and it adjudicates certain unusual claims and actions not common to all regional offices, such as WW I adjusted compensation death cases, forfeiture cases, and benefits under special enactments provided by the Congress. It also maintains liaison with the Treasury Department on types and methods of payments to recipients in foreign countries.

VA Offices   The VA office provides veterans assistance and such other services as cannot be conveniently provided to veterans, their dependents and beneficiaries, and others in a given locality by a regional office or center.

Medical Centers   Veterans Affairs Medical Centers provide eligible beneficiaries with medical and other health care services equivalent to those provided by private-sector institutions, augmented in many instances by services to meet the special requirements of veterans. One hundred and twenty-six VA medical facilities are affiliated with 107 medical facilities for residency training; 72 VA medical facilities are affiliated with 59 dental schools; and all centers cooperate with one or more educational institutions in programs of nursing, associated health professions and occupations, and administrative training and related research, both in individual projects and in association with other VA medical centers in broad cooperative studies. There are 131 nursing home care units associated with VA medical centers to provide skilled nursing care and related medical services to patients who are no longer in need of hospital care.

VA Regional Office and Insurance Centers   Veterans Affairs Regional Office and Insurance Centers combine a regional office and an insurance center under the jurisdiction of one director.

VA Medical and Regional Office Centers   Veterans Affairs Medical and Regional Office Centers combine a regional office and a medical center or a regional office, medical center, and domiciliary under the jurisdiction of one director.

Domiciliaries   Veterans Affairs Domiciliaries provide the least intensive level of inpatient medical care. This includes necessary ambulatory medical treatment, rehabilitation, and support services in a structured environment to veterans who are unable because of their disabilities to provide adequately for themselves in the community.

Outpatient Clinics   Veterans Affairs Outpatient Clinics provide eligible beneficiaries with ambulatory care.

VA National Cemeteries   Veterans Affairs national cemeteries are the final resting places for burial of the remains of veterans, active duty personnel, reservists, and National Guard members with 20 years' qualifying service, their spouses, and certain eligible dependents. Memorial markers for veterans, service members, and reservists and National Guard members with 20 years' qualifying service, whose remains are not available for burial, may also be placed in a national cemetery. These cemeteries are designated as national shrines created in tribute to the sacrifices of all Americans who have served in the U.S. Armed Forces.

National Facilities—Department of Veterans Affairs

Address	Type of facility	Director
National Facilities Under the Veterans Health Administration, Veterans Benefits Administration, and National Cemetery System—Centers, Domiciliaries, Medical Centers, Medical and Regional Office Centers, Outpatient Clinics, Insurance Centers, Regional Offices, Supply Activities, and National Cemeteries		
ALABAMA:		
Birmingham, 35233 (700 S. 19th St.)	Medical Center	Y.C. Parris
Mobile, 36604 (1202 Virginia St.) (Mail: Barrancas National Cemetery, FL).	National Cemetery	Sandra Beckley
Montgomery, 36109–3798 (215 Perry Hill Rd.)	Medical Center	(Vacancy)
Montgomery, 36109 (345 Perry Hill Rd.)	Regional Office	Patrick K. Courtney
Seale, 36875 (553 Hwy. 165) (Fort Mitchell National Cemetery).	National Cemetery	William Trower
Tuscaloosa, 35404	Medical Center	W. Kenneth Ruyle
Tuskegee, 36083	Medical Center	Jimmie L. Clay
ALASKA:		
Anchorage, 99508 (2925 Debarr Rd.)	Outpatient Clinic and Regional Office.	Alex Spector

National Facilities—Department of Veterans Affairs—Continued

Address	Type of facility	Director
Fort Richardson, 99505 (P.O. Box 5–498)	National Cemetery	Yvonne Payne, Program Specialist
Sitka, 99835 (P.O. Box 1065) (Mail: Fort Richardson National Cemetery, AK).	National Cemetery	Yvonne Payne, Program Specialist
ARIZONA:		
Phoenix, 85012 (7th St. and Indian School Rd.)	Medical Center	John R. Fears
Phoenix, 85012 (3225 N. Central Ave.)	Regional Office	David W. Walls
Phoenix, 85024 (23029 N. Cave Creek Rd.) (National Memorial Cemetery of Arizona).	National Cemetery	Mary Dill
Prescott, 86313	Medical Center (medical and domiciliary).	Patricia A. McKlem
Prescott, 86301 (VA Medical Center) (500 Highway 89 N.) (Mail: National Memorial Cemetery of Arizona).	National Cemetery	Mary Dill
Tucson, 85723	Medical Center	Jonathan H. Gardner
ARKANSAS:		
Fayetteville, 72703	Medical Center	Richard F. Robinson
Fayetteville, 72701 (700 Government Ave.)	National Cemetery	Darrell W. Lindsey, *Trainee*
Fort Smith, 72901 (522 Garland Ave.)	National Cemetery	John Bacon
Little Rock, 72206 (2523 Confederate Blvd.)	National Cemetery	Mary Ann Fisher
Little Rock, 72205 (300 Roosevelt Rd.) (John L. McClellan Memorial Veterans Hospital). Little Rock Division North Little Rock Division (Mail: Little Rock)	Medical Center	George Gray, Jr.
North Little Rock, 72115, (P.O. Box 1280, Bldg. 65, Fort Roots).	Regional Office	Fred King
CALIFORNIA:		
Fresno, 93703 (2615 Clinton Ave.)	Medical Center	(Vacancy)
Gustine, 95322 (32053 W. McCabe Rd.) (San Joaquin Valley National Cemetery).	National Cemetery	Carla Williams
Loma Linda, 92357 (11201 Benton St.) (Jerry L. Pettis Memorial Veterans Hospital).	Medical Center	Dean R. Stordahl
Long Beach, 90822 (5901 E. 7th St.)	Medical Center	Lawrence Stewart
Los Angeles, 90013 (425 S. Hill St.)	Outpatient Clinic	Lee Nackman
Los Angeles, 90024 (11000 Wilshire Blvd.)	Regional Office	Stewart F. Liff
Los Angeles, 90049 (950 S. Sepulveda Blvd.)	National Cemetery	Lucy Devenney
Northern California Health Care System, 94523 (150 Muir Rd., Benicia).	Medical Center	Sheila M. Cullen
Oakland, 94612–5209 (Oakland Federal Bldg., 1301 Clay St.).	Regional Office	Donald E. Stout
Palo Alto Health Care System, 94304 (3801 Miranda Ave.).	Medical Center	James A. Goff
Riverside, 92518 (22495 Van Buren Blvd.)	National Cemetery	Steve Jorgensen
San Bruno, 94066 (1300 Sneath Lane) (Golden Gate National Cemetery).	National Cemetery	Gloria Gomez
San Diego, 92161 (3350 La Jolla Village Dr.)	Medical Center	Gary Rossio
San Diego, 92108 (2022 Camino Del Rio N.)	Regional Office	Ray W. Hall
San Diego, 92166 (Point Loma, P.O. Box 6237) (Fort Rosecrans National Cemetery).	National Cemetery	Cynthia Nunez
San Francisco, 94121 (4150 Clement St.)	Medical Center	Sheila Cullen, *Acting*
San Francisco, 94129 (P.O. Box 29012, Presidio of San Francisco) (Mail: Golden Gate National Cemetery, CA).	National Cemetery	Gloria Gomez
Sepulveda, 91343	Medical Center	Jule Moravce
West Los Angeles, 90073	Medical Center (medical and domiciliary).	(Vacancy)
COLORADO:		
Denver, 80220 (1055 Clermont St.)	Medical Center	Edgar Thorsland, Jr.
Denver, 80225	Denver Distribution Center	Robert Shields
Denver, 80235 (3698 S. Sheridan Blvd.) (Fort Logan National Cemetery).	National Cemetery	Art Smith
Fort Lyon, 81038	Denver Distribution Center	Robert E. Lee
Fort Lyon, 81038 (VA Medical Center)	National Cemetery	Maintained by VAMC Engineering Service
Fort Lyon, 81038	Medical Center	W. David Smith
Grand Junction, 81501	Medical Center	Kurt Schlegelmilch
Lakewood, 80228 (P.O. Box 25126, 155 Van Gordon St.).	Regional Office	Catherine L. Smith
CONNECTICUT:		
Connecticut Health Care System, 06111 (555 Willard Ave., Newington).	Medical Center	Vincent Ng
Hartford, 06103 (450 Main St.)	Regional Office	Jeffrey Alger

National Facilities—Department of Veterans Affairs—Continued

Address	Type of facility	Director
DELAWARE:		
Wilmington, 19805 (1601 Kirkwood Hwy.)	Medical and Regional Office Center	Dexter Dix
DISTRICT OF COLUMBIA:		
Washington, 20422 (50 Irving St. NW.)	Medical Center	Sanford M. Garfunkel
Washington, 20421 (1120 Vermont Ave. NW.)	Regional Office	C. Fay Norred
FLORIDA:		
Bay Pines, 33504 (1000 Bay Pines Blvd. N.)	Medical Center (medical and domi-ciliary).	Thomas Weaver
Bay Pines, 33504 (P.O. Box 477)	National Cemetery	Jorge Baltar, *Trainee*
Bushnell, 33513 (Florida National Cemetery) (6502 SW. 102d Ave.).	National Cemetery	Ronald R. Pemberton
Gainesville, 32608–1197 (1601 SW. Archer Rd.)	Medical Center	J. Malcom Randall
Lake City, 32055–5898 (801 S. Marion St.)	Medical Center	(Vacancy)
Miami, 33125 (1201 NW. 16th St.)	Medical Center	Thomas C. Doherty
Pensacola, 32508–1099 (Naval Air Station) (Barrancas National Cemetery).	National Cemetery	Sandra Beckley
St. Augustine, 32084 (104 Marine St.) (Mail: Florida National Cemetery, FL).	National Cemetery	Ronald R. Pemberton
St. Petersburg, 33731 (P.O. Box 1437)	Regional Office	William D. Stinger
Tampa, 33612 (13000 Bruce B. Downs Blvd.) (James A. Haley Veterans Hospital).	Medical Center	Richard A. Silver
GEORGIA:		
Atlanta, 30033 (1670 Clairmont Rd.)	Medical Center	Robert Perreault
Atlanta, 30365 (730 Peachtree St. NE.)	Regional Office	Robert Perreault
Augusta, 30904–6285 (2460 Wrightsboro Rd. (10)) Forest Hills Division Lenwood Division	Medical Center	(Vacancy)
Dublin, 31021	Medical Center (medical and domi-ciliary).	James Trusley
Marietta, 30060 (500 Washington Ave.)	National Cemetery	James Wallace
HAWAII:		
Honolulu, 96850 (P.O. Box 50188)	Medical and Regional Office Center	(Vacancy)
Honolulu, 96813–1729 (2177 Puowaina Dr.) (National Memorial Cemetery of the Pacific).	National Cemetery	Gene E. Castagnetti
IDAHO:		
Boise, 83702 (805 W. Franklin St.)	Regional Office	Barry M. Barker
Boise, 83702–4598 (5th & Fort Sts.)	Medical Center	Wayne Tippets
ILLINOIS:		
Alton, 62003 (600 Pearl St.) (Mail: Jefferson Barracks National Cemetery, MO).	National Cemetery	Ralph E. Church
Chicago Health Care System, 60611 (333 E. Huron St.).	Medical Center	Joseph L. Moore
Chicago, 60680 (P.O. Box 8136)	Regional Office	(Vacancy)
Danville, 61832	Medical Center	James S. Jones
Danville, 61832 (1900 E. Main St.)	National Cemetery	Richard J. Pless
Hines, 60666–0303 (Lock Box 66303, AMF O'Hare, IL).	Finance Center	James Burkett
Hines, 60141 (Edward Hines, Jr. Hospital)	Medical Center	John J. DeNardo
Hines, 60141 (P.O. Box 76)	VA National Acquisition Center	George T. Patterson
Hines, 60141 (P.O. Box 27)	Service and Distribution Center	David Garcia
Marion, 62959 (2401 W. Main St.)	Medical Center	Linda Kurz
Moline, 61265 (P.O. Box 737, Rock Island Arsenal) (Rock Island National Cemetery).	National Cemetery	Larry Williams
Mound City, 62963 (P.O. Box 128, Hwys. 37 & 51) (Mail: Jefferson Barracks National Cemetery, MO).	National Cemetery	Ralph E. Church
North Chicago, 60064	Medical Center	Alfred S. Pete
Quincy, 62301 (36th & Maine Sts.) (Mail: Rock Island National Cemetery, Rock Island, IL).	National Cemetery	Larry Williams
Springfield, 62707 (5063 Camp Butler Rd., R #1) (Camp Butler National Cemetery).	National Cemetery	Leon Murphy
INDIANA:		
Indianapolis, 46202 (1481 W. 10th St.) .... Cold Spring Road Division Tenth Street Division (Mail: 1481 W. 10th St., Indianapolis)	Medical Center	Alice L. Wood
Indianapolis, 46204 (575 N. Pennsylvania St.)	Regional Office	Dennis R. Wyant
Indianapolis, 46208 (700 W. 38th St.) (Crown Hill National Cemetery) (Mail: Marion National Cemetery, IN).	National Cemetery	Bobby A. Motan
Marion, 46952 (1700 E. 38th St.)	National Cemetery	Bobby A. Motan
New Albany, 47150 (1943 Elkin Ave.) (Mail: Zachary Taylor National Cemetery, KY).	National Cemetery	Gary D. Peak
Northern Indiana Health Care System, 46805 (1600 Randalia Dr., Fort Wayne).	Medical Center	Michael W. Murphy

National Facilities—Department of Veterans Affairs—Continued

Address	Type of facility	Director
IOWA:		
Central Iowa Health Care System, 50310–5774 (30th and Euclid Ave.. Des Moines).	Medical Center	Ellen DeGeorge-Smith
Des Moines, 50309 (210 Walnut St.)	Regional Office	Norman W. Bauer
Iowa City, 52246–5774 (Highway 6 W.)	Medical Center	Gary L. Wilkinson
Keokuk, 52632 (1701 J St.) (Mail: Rock Island National Cemetery, IL).	National Cemetery	Larry Williams
KANSAS:		
Eastern Kansas Health Care System, 66048 (Leavenworth).	Medical Center (medical and domiciliary).	Edgar L. Tucker
Fort Leavenworth (Mail: Leavenworth National Cemetery, KS).	National Cemetery	Jeffrey S. Barnes
Fort Scott, 66701 (P.O. Box 917)	National Cemetery	Jeffrey S. Barnes
Leavenworth, 66048 (P.O. Box 1694)	National Cemetery	Jeffrey S. Barnes
Wichita, 67218 (5500 E. Kellogg)	Medical Center	Kent Hill
Wichita, 67218 (5500 E. Kellogg)	Regional Office	Robert Morrell, *Acting*
KENTUCKY:		
Danville, 40442 (277 N. 1st St.) (Mail: Camp Nelson National Cemetery, KY).	National Cemetery	Jeffrey Teas
Lebanon, 40033 (20 Hwy. 208E) (Mail: Zachary Taylor National Cemetery, KY).	National Cemetery	Gary D. Peak
Lexington, 40511	Medical Center	Helen K. Cornish
Cooper Drive Division		
Leestown Division		
Lexington, 40508 (833 W. Main St.) (Mail: Camp Nelson National Cemetery, KY).	National Cemetery	Jeffrey Teas
Louisville, 40202 (545 S. 3d St.)	Regional Office	Henry W. Gresham
Louisville, 40202 (800 Zorn Ave.)	Medical Center	Larry J. Sander
Louisville, 40204 (701 Baxter Ave.) (Cave Hill National Cemetery) (Mail: Zachary Taylor National Cemetery, KY).	National Cemetery	Gary D. Peak
Louisville, 40207 (4701 Brownsboro Rd.) (Zachary Taylor National Cemetery).	National Cemetery	Gary D. Peak
Nancy, 42544 (Mill Springs National Cemetery) (Mail: Camp Nelson National Cemetery, KY).	National Cemetery	Jeffrey Teas
Nicholasville, 40356 (6980 Danville Rd.) (Camp Nelson National Cemetery).	National Cemetery	Jeffrey Teas
LOUISIANA:		
Alexandria, 71301	Medical Center	Allen S. Goss
Baton Rouge, 70806 (220 N. 19th St.) (Mail: Port Hudson National Cemetery, LA).	National Cemetery	Virgil M. Wertenberger
New Orleans, 70146 (1601 Peridido St.)	Medical Center	John D. Church, Jr.
New Orleans, 70113 (701 Loyola Ave.)	Regional Office	Gary Cole
Pineville, 71360 (209 E. Shamrock Ave.) (Alexandria National Cemetery) (Mail: Natchez, NC).	National Cemetery	Sharon Bell-Goodrich, *Trainee*
Shreveport, 71130 (510 E. Stoner Ave.)	Medical Center	Billy Valentine
Zachary, 70791 (20978 Port Hickey Rd.) (Port Hudson National Cemetery).	National Cemetery	Virgil M. Wertenberger
MAINE:		
Togus, 04330	Medical and Regional Office Center	John H. Sims, Jr.
Togus, 04330 (VA Medical and Regional Office Center) (Mail: Massachusetts National Cemetery, MA).	National Cemetery	Kurt Rotar
MARYLAND:		
Annapolis, 21401 (800 West St.) (Mail: Baltimore National Cemetery, MD).	National Cemetery	Robin Pohlman
Baltimore, 21201 (31 Hopkins Plz.)	Regional Office	John W. Smith
Baltimore, 21228 (5501 Frederick Ave.)	National Cemetery	Robin Pohlman
Baltimore, 21228 (3445 Frederick Ave.) (Loudon Park National Cemetery) (Mail: Baltimore National Cemetery, MD).	National Cemetery	Robin Pohlman
Maryland Health Care System, 21218 (3900 Loch Raven Blvd., Baltimore).	Medical Center	Dennis Smith
MASSACHUSETTS:		
Bedford, 01730 (200 Springs Rd.) (Edith Nourse Rogers Memorial Veterans Hospital).	Medical Center	William A. Conte
Boston, 02130 (150 S. Huntington Ave.)	Medical Center	Elwood Headley
Boston, 02203 (John F. Kennedy Federal Bldg.)	Regional Office	Michael D. Olson
Boston, 02108 (17 Court St.)	Outpatient Clinic	combined VA Boston
Bourne, 02532 (Connary Ave.) (Massachusetts National Cemetery).	National Cemetery	Kurt Rotar
Brockton/West Roxbury, 02132 (1400 Veterans of Foreign Wars Pkwy., West Roxbury).	Medical Center	Michael Lawson
Northampton, 01060	Medical Center	Bruce A. Gordon

National Facilities—Department of Veterans Affairs—Continued

Address	Type of facility	Director
MICHIGAN:		
Ann Arbor, 48105 (2215 Fuller Rd.)	Medical Center	James Roseborough
Augusta, 49012 (15501 Dickman Rd.) (Fort Custer National Cemetery).	National Cemetery	Robert Poe
Battle Creek, 49106	Medical Center	Michael K. Wheeler
Detroit, 48101	Medical Center	James Roseborough
Detroit, 48226 (477 Michigan Ave.)	Regional Office	Carlos B. Lott, Jr.
Iron Mountain, 49801	Medical Center	Thomas Arnold
Saginaw, 48602 (1500 Weiss St.)	Medical Center	Robert H. Sabin
MINNESOTA:		
Minneapolis, 55417 (1 Veterans Dr.)	Medical Center	Charles A. Milbrandt
Minneapolis, 55450 (7601 34th Ave., S.) (Fort Snelling National Cemetery).	National Cemetery	Steve Muro
St. Cloud, 56301 (4801 8th St. N.)	Medical Center	Barry T. Bahl, *Acting*
St. Paul, 55111 (Bishop Henry Whipple Federal Bldg., Fort Snelling). Remittances: P.O. Box 1820.	Regional Office and Insurance Center.	Ronald J. Henke
MISSISSIPPI:		
Biloxi, 39531	Medical Center (medical and domiciliary).	Julie Catellies
Biloxi Hospital and Domiciliary Division Gulfport Hospital Division (Mail: Biloxi, MS)		
Biloxi, 39535–4968 (P.O. Box 4968)	National Cemetery	Douglas W. Smith, Sr.
Corinth, 38834 (1551 Horton St.) (Mail: Memphis National Cemetery, TN).	Medical Center (medical and domiciliary).	Mark E. Maynard
Jackson, 39216 (1500 E. Woodrow Wilson Ave.)	Medical Center	Richard P. Miller
Jackson, 39269 (1660 E. Woodrow Wilson Ave.)	Regional Office	Mary F. Leyland
Natchez, 39120 (41 Cemetery Rd.)	National Cemetery	Sharon Bell-Goodrich, Trainee
MISSOURI:		
Columbia, 65201 (800 Hospital Dr.) (Harry S. Truman Memorial Veterans Hospital).	Medical Center	Gary Campbell
Jefferson City, 65101 (1024 E. McCarthy) (Mail: Jefferson Barracks National Cemetery, MO).	National Cemetery	Ralph E. Church
Kansas City, 64128 (4801 Linwood Blvd.)	Medical Center	Hugh F. Doran
Poplar Bluff, 63901	Medical Center	(Vacancy)
Springfield, 65804 (1702 E. Seminole St.)	National Cemetery	Dane Freeman
St. Louis, 63125	Medical Center	Donald L. Ziegenhorn
John J. Cochran Division Jefferson Barracks Division		
St. Louis, 63115 (P.O. Box 5020)	Records Management Center	Michael C. Baker
St. Louis, 63103-2271 (400 S. 18th St.)	Regional Office	Robert J. Epley
St. Louis, 63125 (2900 Sheridan Dr.) (Jefferson Barracks National Cemetery).	National Cemetery	Ralph E. Church
MONTANA:		
Fort Harrison, 59636	Medical and Regional Office Center	Joseph M. Underkofler
Miles City, 59301	Medical Center	Richard J. Stanley
NEBRASKA:		
Greater Nebraska Health Care System, 68510 (600 S. 70th St., Lincoln).	Medical Center	David A. Asper
Lincoln, 68516 (5631 S. 48th St.)	Regional Office	Geraldine Johnson
Maxwell, 69151 (HCO 1, Box 67) (Fort McPherson National Cemetery).	National Cemetery	Jim Schwartz
Omaha, 68105 (4101 Woolworth Ave.)	Medical Center	John J. Phillips
NEVADA:		
Las Vegas, 89015 (102 Lake Mead Dr.)	Outpatient Clinic	Ramon J. Reevey
Reno, 89520 (1000 Locust St.)	Medical Center	Gary R. Whitfield
Reno, 89520 (1201 Terminal Way)	Regional Office	Eileen Straub
NEW HAMPSHIRE:		
Manchester, 03104 (718 Smyth Rd.)	Medical Center	Paul J. McCoch
Manchester, 03101 (275 Chestnut St.)	Regional Office	Edward J. Hubbard
NEW JERSEY:		
Beverly, 08010 (R #1, Bridgeboro Rd.)	National Cemetery	Delores T. Blake
Newark, 07102 (20 Washington Pl.)	Regional Office	Robert P. Van Sprang
New Jersey Health Care System, 07019 (East Orange)	Medical Center	Kenneth Mizrach
Salem, 08079 (R.F.D. 3, Fort Mott Rd., Box 542) (Finn's Point National Cemetery) (Mail: Beverly National Cemetery, NJ).	National Cemetery	Delores T. Blake
Somerville, 08876	Asset Management Service	Sharon Dufour
NEW MEXICO:		
Albuquerque, 87108 (2100 Ridgecrest Dr. SE.)	Medical Center	Norman E. Browne
Albuquerque, 87102 (500 Gold Ave. SW.)	Regional Office	Sandra D. Epps
Fort Bayard, 88036 (P.O. Box 189) (Fort Bayard National Cemetery) (Mail: Fort Bliss National Cemetery, TX).	National Cemetery	Gerald T. Vitela

National Facilities—Department of Veterans Affairs—Continued

Address	Type of facility	Director
Santa Fe, 87501 (P.O. Box 88, 501 N. Guadalupe St.).	National Cemetery	Gilbert Gallo
NEW YORK:		
Albany, 12208 (113 Holland Ave.)	Medical Center	Lawrence Flesh
Bath, 14810	Medical Center (medical and domiciliary).	Michael J. Sullivan
Bath, 14810 (VA Medical Center)	National Cemetery	David G. Dimmick
Bronx, 10468 (130 W. Kingsbridge Rd.)	Medical Center	MaryAnn Musumeci
Brooklyn, 11209 (800 Poly Pl.) Brooklyn Division St. Albans Division	Medical Center	John Donnellan, *Acting*
Brooklyn, 11205 (35 Ryerson St.)	Outpatient Clinic	James J. Farsetta
Brooklyn, 11208 (625 Jamaica Ave.) (Cypress Hills National Cemetery) (Mail: Long Island National Cemetery, NY).	National Cemetery	(Vacancy)
Buffalo, 14202 (111 W. Huron St.)	Regional Office	Gregory L. Mason
Calverton, 11933 (210 Princeton Blvd.)	National Cemetery	Patrick Hallinan
Canandaigua, 14424	Medical Center	Stuart Collyer
Elmira, 14901 (1825 Davis St.) (Woodlawn National Cemetery) (Mail: Bath National Cemetery, NY).	National Cemetery	David G. Dimmick
Farmingdale, 11735–1211 (2040 Wellwood Ave.) (Long Island National Cemetery).	National Cemetery	(Vacancy)
Hudson Valley Health Care System, 10548 (Franklin Delano Roosevelt Hospital, Montrose).	Medical Center	Michael Sabo
New York, 10014 (245 W. Houston Street)	Regional Office	(Vacancy)
New York, 10001 (1st Ave. at E. 24th St.)	Medical Center	John Donnellan, Jr.
New York Health Care System, 14215 (3495 Bailey Ave., Buffalo).	Medical Center	Richard S. Droske
Northport, Long Island, 11768	Medical Center	Mary Dowling
Syracuse, 13210 (Irving Ave. and University Pl.)	Medical Center	Phillip Thomas
NORTH CAROLINA:		
Asheville, 28805	Medical Center	James A. Christian
Durham, 27705 (508 Fulton St. and Erwin Rd.)	Medical Center	Michael Phaup
Fayetteville, 28301 (2300 Ramsey St.)	Medical Center	Richard Baltz
New Bern, 28560 (1711 National Ave.)	National Cemetery	(Vacancy)
Raleigh, 27610 (501 Rock Quarry Rd.)	National Cemetery	Abe Stice
Salisbury, 28144 (1601 Brenner Ave.)	Medical Center	(Vacancy)
Salisbury, 28144 (202 Government Rd.)	National Cemetery	Margaret S. Yarborough
Wilmington, 28403 (2011 Market St.) (Mail: New Bern National Cemetery, NC).	National Cemetery	(Vacancy)
Winston-Salem, 27155 (251 N. Main St.)	Regional Office	John Montgomery
NORTH DAKOTA:		
Fargo, 58102 (655 First Ave.)	Medical and Regional Office Center	Douglas M. Kenyon
OHIO:		
Chillicothe, 45601	Medical Center	Michael W. Walton
Cincinnati, 45220 (3200 Vine St.)	Medical Center	Gary N. Nugent
Cleveland, 44106–3800 (10701 East Blvd.) Becksville Division Wade Park Division	Medical Center	William Montague
Cleveland, 44199 (1240 E. 9th St.)	Regional Office	Phillip J. Ross
Columbus, 43221 (2090 Kenny Rd.)	Outpatient Clinic	Lilian T. Thome
Dayton, 45428 (VA Medical Center, 4100 W. 3d St.).	Medical Center (medical and domiciliary).	Steve Cohen
Dayton, 45428 (VA Medical Center, 4100 W. 3d St.).	National Cemetery	Karen J. DuHart
OKLAHOMA:		
Fort Gibson, 74434 (1423 Cemetery Rd.)	National Cemetery	Candice Underwood
Muskogee, 74401 (Memorial Station, Honor Heights Dr.).	Medical Center	(Vacancy)
Muskogee, 74401 (125 S. Main St.)	Regional Office	William D. Fillman, Jr.
Oklahoma City, 73104 (921 NE. 13th St.)	Medical Center	Steve J. Gentling
OREGON:		
Eagle Point, 97524 (2763 Riley Rd.)	National Cemetery	Darryl Ferrell
Portland, 97207 (3710 SW. U.S. Veterans Hospital Rd.).	Medical Center	William Ted Galey
Portland, 97204 (1220 SW. 3d Ave.)	Regional Office	Joseph Williams
Portland, 97266–6937 (11800 SE. Mt. Scott Blvd., P.O. Box 66147) (Willamette National Cemetery).	National Cemetery	Billy D. Murphy
Roseburg, 97470–6513	Medical Center	Alan S. Perry
Roseburg, 97470 (VA Medical Center) (Mail: Willamette National Cemetery, OR).	National Cemetery	Billy D. Murphy
White City, 97503	Domiciliary	George H. Andries, Jr.
PENNSYLVANIA:		
Altoona, 16602–4377	Medical Center	Gerald L. Williams
Annville, 17003–9618 (R 2, Box 484) (Indiantown Gap National Cemetery).	National Cemetery	Charlene R. Lewis

National Facilities—Department of Veterans Affairs—Continued

Address	Type of facility	Director
Aspinwall (see Pittsburgh, 15240)		
Butler, 16001–2480	Medical Center	Michael Moreland
Coatesville, 19320	Medical Center	Gary W. Devansky
Erie, 16501 (135 E. 38th St. Blvd.)	Medical Center	Stephen M. Lucas
Lebanon, 17042	Medical Center	(Vacancy)
Philadelphia, 19101 (5000 Wissahickon Ave.) (Insurance remittances: P.O. Box 7787). (Mail: P.O. Box 42954).	Regional Office and Insurance Center.	Thomas M. Lastowka
Philadelphia, 19104 (University and Woodland Aves.).	Medical Center	Earl F. Falast
Philadelphia, 19138 (Haines St. and Limekiln Pike) (Mail: Beverly National Cemetery, NJ).	National Cemetery	Delores T. Blake
Pittsburgh, 15222 (1000 Liberty Ave.)	Regional Office	Barry S. Jackson
Pittsburgh, 15206 (Highland Dr.)	Medical Center	Thomas A. Cappello
Pittsburgh, 15240 (University Dr. C)	Medical Center	Thomas A. Cappello
Aspinwall Division		
Pittsburgh Division		
(Mail: University Drive, Pittsburgh)		
Wilkes-Barre, 18711 (1111 East End Blvd.)	Medical Center	Reedes Hurt
PHILIPPINE REPUBLIC:		
Manila (1131 Roxas Blvd.) (APO 96440)	Regional Office and Outpatient Clinic.	(Vacancy)
PUERTO RICO:		
Bayamon, 00960 (P.O. Box 1298) (Puerto Rico National Cemetery).	National Cemetery	Jorge Lopez
Hato Rey, 00918 (U.S. Courthouse and Federal Bldg., Carlos E. Chardon St.).		
San Juan, 00927–5800 (Barrio Monacillos G.P.O., Box 364867).	Medical Center	Jamie Palmer
San Juan, 00936 (U.S. Courthouse and Federal Bldg., Carlos E. Chardon St., Hato Rey, G.P.O. Box 364867).	Regional Office	Mary F. Leyland
RHODE ISLAND:		
Providence, 02903 (380 Westminster Mall)	Regional Office	Peter Wells
Providence, 02908 (Davis Park)	Medical Center	Edward H. Seiler
SOUTH CAROLINA:		
Beaufort, 29902 (1601 Boundary St.)	National Cemetery	Walter A. Gray
Charleston, 29401–5799 (109 Bee St.)	Medical Center	R. John Vogel
Columbia, 29201 (William Jennings Bryan Dorn Veterans Hospital).	Medical Center	Robert M. Athey
Columbia, 29201 (1801 Assembly St.)	Regional Office	R. Stedman Sloan, Jr.
Florence, 29501 (803 E. National Cemetery Rd.)	National Cemetery	Kenneth LaFevor
SOUTH DAKOTA:		
Fort Meade, 57741	Medical Center	Peter P. Henry
Hot Springs, 57747 (Fort Meade National Cemetery).	Medical Center (medical and domiciliary).	Daniel Marsh
Hot Springs, 57747 (VA Medical Center) (Mail: Black Hills National Cemetery, SD).	National Cemetery	Douglas D. Miner
Sioux Falls, 57117 (Royal C. Johnson Veterans Memorial Hospital) (Mail: P.O. Box 5046, 25051 W. 22d St.).	Medical Center and Regional Office	R. Vincent Crawford
Sturgis, 57785 (P.O. Box 640) (Mail: Black Hills National Cemetery).		
Sturgis, 57785 (P.O. Box 640) (Black Hills National Cemetery).	National Cemetery	Douglas D. Miner
TENNESSEE:		
Chattanooga, 37404 (1200 Bailey Ave.)	National Cemetery	James Wallace
Knoxville, 37917 (939 Tyson St. NW.) (Mail: Mountain Home).	National Cemetery	Rodney Dunn
Madison, 37115–4619 (1420 Gallatin Rd. S.) (Nashville National Cemetery).	National Cemetery	Joe Nunnally
Memphis, 38104 (1030 Jefferson Ave.)	Medical Center	Kenneth L. Mulholland, Jr.
Memphis, 38122 (3568 Townes Ave.)	National Cemetery	Mark E. Maynard
Mountain Home, 37684 (Johnson City)	Medical Center (medical and domiciliary).	Carl Gerber
Mountain Home, 37684 (P.O. Box 8)	National Cemetery	Rodney Dunn
Murfreesboro, 37129–1236	Medical Center	Brian Heckert
Nashville, 37212–2637 (1310 24th Ave. S.)	Medical Center	William Mountcastle
Nashville, 37203 (110 9th Ave. S.)	Regional Office	Thomas R. Jensen
TEXAS:		
Amarillo, 79106 (6010 Amarillo Blvd. W.)	Medical Center	Wallace M. Hopkins
Austin, 78772 (1615 E. Woodward St.)	Automation Center	Robert Evans
Austin, 78714–9575 (P.O. Box 149975)	Financial Services Center	Harlan R. Hively
Big Spring, 79720	Medical Center	Cary Brown
Bonham, 75418 (Sam Rayburn Memorial Veterans Center).	Medical Center (medical and domiciliary).	George Moore, Jr.

National Facilities—Department of Veterans Affairs—Continued

Address	Type of facility	Director
Central Texas Health Care System, 76504 (Olin E. Teague Veterans Center, Temple).	Medical Center (medical and domiciliary).	Dean Billik
Dallas, 75216 (4500 S. Lancaster Rd.)	Medical Center	Alan Harper
El Paso, 79925 (5919 Brook Hollow Dr.)	Outpatient Clinic	Frank Caldwell
Fort Bliss, 79906 (5200 Fred Wilson Rd., P.O. Box 6342).	National Cemetery	Gerald T. Vitela
Houston, 77030 (2002 Holcombe Blvd.)	Medical Center	David Whately
Houston, 77030 (6900 Almeda Rd.)	Regional Office	Thomas R. Wagner
Houston, 77038 (10410 Veterans Memorial Dr.)	National Cemetery	Jose R. Coronado
Kerrville, 78028 (VA Medical Center, 3600 Memorial Blvd.) (Mail: Fort Sam Houston, TX).	National Cemetery	Joe A. Ramos
San Antonio, 78202 (517 Paso Hondo St.) (Mail: Fort Sam Houston National Cemetery, TX).	National Cemetery	Joe A. Ramos
San Antonio, 78209 (1520 Harry Wurzbach Rd.) (Fort Sam Houston National Cemetery).	National Cemetery	Joe A. Ramos
South Texas Veterans Health Care System, 78285 (7400 Merton Minter Blvd., San Antonio) (Audie L. Murphy Memorial Veterans Hospital).	Medical Center	Jose R. Coronado
Waco, 76711 (4800 Memorial Dr.)	Medical Center	A. Reddy, *Acting*
Waco, 76799 (701 Clay Ave.)	Regional Office	Jerry G. McRae
UTAH:		
Salt Lake City, 84147 (125 S. State St.)	Regional Office	Douglas B. Wadsworth
Salt Lake City, 84148 (500 Foothill Blvd.)	Medical Center	James Floyd
VERMONT:		
White River Junction, 05009	Medical and Regional Office Center	Gary M. DeGasta
VIRGINIA:		
Alexandria, 22314 (1450 Wilkes St.) (Mail: Culpeper National Cemetery, VA).	National Cemetery	Lawrence Bibbs
Culpeper, 22701 (305 U.S. Ave.)	National Cemetery	Lawrence Bibbs
Danville, 24541 (721 Lee St.) (Mail: Salisbury National Cemetery, NC).	National Cemetery	Margaret S. Yarborough
Hampton, 23667	Medical Center (medical and domiciliary).	Bettye Story
Hampton, 23667 (Cemetery Rd. at Marshall Ave., VA).	National Cemetery	Homer D. Hardamon
Hampton, 23667 (VA Medical Center) (Mail: Cemetery Rd. at Marshall Ave., VA).	National Cemetery	Homer D. Hardamon
Hopewell, 23860 (10th Ave. and Davis St.) (City Point National Cemetery) (Mail: Richmond National Cemetery, VA).	National Cemetery	Homer D. Hardamon
Leesburg, 22075 (Route 7) (Balls Bluff National Cemetery) (Mail: Culpeper National Cemetery, VA).	National Cemetery	Lawrence Bibbs
Mechanicsville, 23111 (Route 156 N.) (Cold Harbor National Cemetery) (Mail: Richmond National Cemetery, VA).	National Cemetery	Homer D. Hardamon
Richmond, 23249 (1201 Broad Rock Rd.)	Medical Center	James W. Dudley
Richmond, 23231 (1701 Williamsburg Rd.)	National Cemetery	Homer D. Hardamon
Richmond, 23231 (8620 Varina Rd.) (Fort Harrison National Cemetery) (Mail: Richmond National Cemetery, VA).	National Cemetery	Homer D. Hardamon
Richmond, 23231 (8301 Willis Church Rd.) (Glendale National Cemetery) (Mail: Richmond National Cemetery, VA).	National Cemetery	Homer D. Hardamon
Roanoke, 24011 (210 Franklin Rd. SW.)	Regional Office	James A. Maye
Salem, 24153	Medical Center	John M. Presley
Sandston, 23150 (400 E. Williamsburg Rd.) (Seven Pines National Cemetery) (Mail: Richmond National Cemetery, VA).	National Cemetery	Homer D. Hardamon
Staunton, 24401 (901 Richmond Ave.) (Mail: Culpeper National Cemetery, VA).	National Cemetery	Lawrence Bibbs
Triangle, 22172 (R #619, 18424 Joplin Rd.) (Quantico National Cemetery).	National Cemetery	Patricia K. Novak
Winchester, 22601 (401 National Ave.) (Mail: Culpeper National Cemetery, VA).	National Cemetery	Lawrence Bibbs
WASHINGTON:		
Pugent Sound Health Care System, 98108 (4435 Beacon Ave. S., Seattle).	Medical Center	Timothy Williams
Seattle, 98174 (915 2d Ave.)	Regional Office	Michael Walcoff
Spokane, 99205 (N. 4815 Assembly St.)	Medical Center	Joseph M. Manley
Walla Walla, 99362 (77 Wainwright Dr.)	Medical Center	George Marnell
WEST VIRGINIA:		
Beckley, 25801 (200 Veterans Ave.)	Medical Center	Gerald Husson
Clarksburg, 26301	Medical Center	Michael W. Neusch

National Facilities—Department of Veterans Affairs—Continued

Address	Type of facility	Director
Grafton, 26354 (R #2, Box 127) (West Virginia National Cemetery).	National Cemetery	Patrick Lovett
Grafton, 26354 (431 Walnut St.) (Mail: West Virginia National Cemetery, WV) (Grafton National Cemetery, WV).	National Cemetery	Patrick Lovett
Huntington, 25701 (1540 Spring Valley Dr.)	Medical Center	David Pennington
Huntington, 25701 (640 4th Ave.)	Regional Office	David Allen, *Acting*
Martinsburg, 25401	Medical Center (medical and domiciliary).	Glen Grippen
WISCONSIN:		
Madison, 53705 (2500 Overlook Ter.) (William S. Middleton Memorial Veterans Hospital).	Medical Center	Nathan L. Geraths
Milwaukee, 53295–4000 (5000 W. National Ave.)	Medical Center (medical and domiciliary).	Russell E. Struble
Milwaukee, 53295–4000 (5000 W. National Ave., Bldg. 6).	Regional Office	Jon A. Baker
Milwaukee, 53295–4000 (5000 W. National Ave.) (Wood National Cemetery).	National Cemetery	Richard A. Anderson
Tomah, 54660	Medical Center	Stanley Q. Johnson
WYOMING:		
Cheyenne, 82001 (2360 E. Pershing Blvd.)	Medical Center	Richard Fry
Sheridan, 82801	Medical Center	Maureen Humphrys

Sources of Information

Audiovisuals Persons interested in the availability of VA video productions or exhibits for showing outside VA may write the Chief, Media Services Division (032B), Department of Veterans Affairs, 810 Vermont Avenue NW., Washington, DC 20420. Phone, 202–273–9781 or 9782.

Contracts and Small Business Activities Persons seeking to do business with the Department of Veterans Affairs may contact the Director, Acquisition Resources Service (95), 810 Vermont Avenue NW., Washington, DC 20420. Phone, 202–273–8815. A brochure entitled *Doing Business With the Department of Veterans Affairs,* which describes acquisition opportunities and contact points, is available upon request. The Office of Acquisition and Materiel Management also distributes information regarding VA business opportunities electronically through the Internet, at http://www.va.gov/oa&mm/index.htm.

The *Handbook for Veterans in Business,* prepared with the veteran in mind, which contains information on procurement programs, acquisition regulatory requirements, and general guidance on marketing the Federal Government, and more specifically VA, is also available to veterans upon request. Persons seeking information regarding special contracting and subcontracting programs for small, disadvantaged, 8(a) certified, and women- and veteran-owned small businesses may contact the Director, Office of Small and Disadvantaged Business Utilization (00SB). Phone, 202–565–8124.

The Veterans Benefits Administration enforces laws which prohibit discrimination on the basis of race, color, national origin, disability, and age in federally assisted programs. Information regarding these laws can be obtained from the nearest VA regional office.

Electronic Access Information concerning the Department of Veterans Affairs is available electronically through the Internet, at http://www.va.gov/.

Employment The Department of Veterans Affairs employs physicians, dentists, podiatrists, optometrists, nurses, nurse anesthetists, physician assistants, expanded-function dental auxiliaries, registered respiratory therapists, certified respiratory technicians, licensed physical therapists, occupational therapists, pharmacists, and licensed practical or vocational nurses under VA's excepted merit system. This system does not require civil service eligibility. Other professional, technical, administrative, and clerical occupations exist in VA that do require civil service eligibility. Persons interested in employment should contact the Human Resources Management Office at their nearest VA facility. All qualified applicants will receive consideration for appointments without regard to race, religion, color, national origin, sex, political affiliation, or any nonmerit factor.

Freedom of Information Act Requests Inquiries should be directed to the Assistant Secretary for Management, Information Management Service (045A4), 810 Vermont Avenue NW., Washington, DC 20420. Phone, 202–273–8135.

Inspector General Inquiries and Hotline Publicly available documents and information on the VA Office of Inspector General are available electronically through the Internet, at http://www.va.gov/oig/homepage.htm. Complaints may be sent by mail to the VA Inspector General (53E), P.O. Box 50410, Washington, DC 20091–0410. Hotline phone, 800–488–8244. E-mail, vaoig.hotline@forum.va.gov.

Medical Center (Hospital) Design, Construction, and Related Services VA projects requiring services for design, construction, and other related services are advertised in the *Commerce Business Daily.* Architectural/engineering firms interested in designing VA medical center construction projects may write to the Director, Program Support Service (187B). Phone, 202–565–4181. Construction contractors should address their inquiries to the Chief, Office and Library Support Division (182C). Phone, 202–565–5171. Contact either office at the Department of Veterans Affairs Central Office, 810 Vermont Avenue NW., Washington, DC 20420; or write to the Chief, Acquisition and Materiel Management, at any VA medical center or regional office center (see listing in the preceding text).

News Media Representatives of the media outside Washington, DC, may contact VA through the nearest regional Office of Public Affairs:

Atlanta (404–347–3236)
Chicago (312–353–4076)
Dallas (214–767–9270)
Denver (303–914–5855)
Los Angeles (310–268–4207)
New York (212–807–3429)

National and Washington, DC, media may contact the Office of Public Affairs in the VA Central Office, 810 Vermont Avenue NW., Washington, DC 20420. Phone, 202–273–5700.

Publications *Annual Report of the Secretary of Veterans Affairs* may be obtained (in single copies), without charge, from the Reports and Information Service (008C2), 810 Vermont Avenue NW., Washington, DC 20420.

The 1998 VA pamphlet *Federal Benefits for Veterans and Dependents* (80–98–1) is available for sale by the Superintendent of Documents, Government Printing Office, Washington, DC 20402.

Board of Veterans Appeals Index (I–01–1), an index to appellate decisions, is available on microfiche in annual cumulation from July 1977 through December 1994. The quarterly indexes may be purchased for $7 and annual cumulative indexes for $22.50. Annual indexes and BVA decisions for 1992 and 1993 are also available on CD–ROM for $30. The VADEX/CITATOR of Appellate Research Materials is a complete printed quarterly looseleaf cumulation of research material which may be purchased for $175 with binder and for $160 without binder. The Vadex Infobase, a computer-searchable version of the VADEX, is also available on diskettes for $100 per copy. These publications may be obtained by contacting Promisel and Korn, Inc. Phone, 301–986–0650. Beginning in 1993, archived decisions of the Board of Veterans' Appeals are available on CD–ROM, which may be obtained from the Superintendent of Documents, Government Printing Office, Washington, DC 20402.

VA Pamphlet, *A Summary of Department of Veteran Affairs Benefits* (27–82–2), may be obtained, without charge, from any VA regional office.

Interments in VA National Cemeteries, VA NCS–IS–1, provides a list of national cemeteries and information on procedures and eligibility for burial. Copies may be obtained without charge from the National Cemetery System (402B2), 810 Vermont Avenue NW., Washington, DC 20420.

A construction research report listing may be obtained from the Director, Program Management and Planning Office (O82), Office of Facilities, Department of Veterans Affairs, 811 Vermont Avenue NW., Washington, DC 20420. Phone, 202–565–5781.

For further information, contact the Office of Public Affairs, Department of Veterans Affairs, 810 Vermont Avenue NW., Washington, DC 20420. Phone, 202–273–5700. Internet, http://www.va.gov/.

Independent Establishments and Government Corporations

AFRICAN DEVELOPMENT FOUNDATION

1400 Eye Street NW., Washington, DC 20005
Phone, 202–673–3916. Internet, http://www.adf.gov/.

Board of Directors:

Chairman	ERNEST G. GREEN
Vice Chair	WILLIE GRACE CAMPBELL
Members of the Board	CECIL BANKS, MARION DAWSON-CARR, JOHN HICKS, HENRY McKOY, GEORGE MOOSE

Staff:

President	WILLIAM R. FORD
Vice President	NATHANIEL FIELDS
General Counsel	PAUL MAGID

[For the African Development Foundation statement of organization, see the *Code of Federal Regulations,* Title 22, Part 1501]

The African Development Foundation assists and supports indigenous, community-based self-help organizations in their efforts to solve their own development problems.

The African Development Foundation was established by the African Development Foundation Act (22 U.S.C. 290h) as a nonprofit Government corporation to support the self-help efforts of poor people in African countries. The Foundation became operational in 1984 and is governed by a seven-member Board of Directors, appointed by the President with the advice and consent of the Senate. By law, five Board members are from the private sector and two are from the Government.

The purposes of the Foundation are to:

—strengthen the bonds of friendship and understanding between the people of Africa and the United States;

—support self-help development activities at the local level designed to promote opportunities for community development;

—stimulate and promote effective and expanding participation of Africans in their development process; and

—encourage the establishment and growth of development institutions that are indigenous to particular countries in Africa and that can respond to the requirements of the poor in those countries.

To carry out its purposes, the Foundation makes grants, loans, and loan guarantees to African private groups, associations, or other entities engaged in peaceful activities that

495

enable the people of Africa to develop more fully.

For further information, contact the Public Affairs Officer, African Development Foundation, 10th Floor, 1400 Eye Street NW., Washington, DC 20005. Phone, 202–673–3916. Fax, 202–673–3810. Internet, http://www.adf.gov/.

CENTRAL INTELLIGENCE AGENCY

Washington, DC 20505
Phone, 703–482–1100. Internet, http://www.odci.gov/cia.

Director of Central Intelligence	GEORGE J. TENET
Deputy Director of Central Intelligence	GEN. JOHN A. GORDON, USAF

[For the Central Intelligence Agency statement of organization, see the *Code of Federal Regulations*, Title 32, Part 1900]

The Central Intelligence Agency collects, evaluates, and disseminates vital information on political, military, economic, scientific, and other developments abroad needed to safeguard national security.

The Central Intelligence Agency was established under the National Security Council by the National Security Act of 1947, as amended (50 U.S.C. 401 *et seq.*). It now functions under that statute, Executive Order 12333 of December 4, 1981, and other laws, regulations, and directives.

The Director of Central Intelligence heads both the Intelligence Community and the Central Intelligence Agency and is the President's principal adviser on intelligence matters. The Director and Deputy Director of Central Intelligence are appointed by the President with the advice and consent of the Senate.

The Central Intelligence Agency, under the direction of the President or the National Security Council:

—advises the National Security Council in matters concerning such intelligence activities of the Government departments and agencies as relate to national security;

—makes recommendations to the National Security Council for the coordination of such intelligence activities of the departments and agencies of the Government as relate to the national security;

—correlates and evaluates intelligence relating to the national security and provides for the appropriate dissemination of such intelligence within the Government;

—collects, produces, and disseminates counterintelligence and foreign intelligence, including information not otherwise obtainable. The collection of counterintelligence or foreign intelligence within the United States shall be coordinated with the Federal Bureau of Investigation (FBI) as required by procedures agreed upon by the Director of Central Intelligence and the Attorney General;

—collects, produces, and disseminates intelligence on foreign aspects of narcotics production and trafficking;

—conducts counterintelligence activities outside the United States and, without assuming or performing any internal security functions, conducts counterintelligence activities within the United States in coordination with the FBI as required by procedures agreed upon by the Director of Central Intelligence and the Attorney General;

—coordinates counterintelligence activities and the collection of information not otherwise obtainable when conducted outside the United States by other departments and agencies;

—conducts special activities approved by the President. No agency, except the Central Intelligence Agency (or the Armed Forces of the United States in time of war declared by Congress or during any period covered by a report from the President to the Congress under the War Powers Resolution (50 U.S.C. 1541 *et seq.*)), may conduct any special activity unless the President determines that another agency is more likely to achieve a particular objective;

—carries out or contracts for research, development, and procurement of technical systems and devices relating to authorized functions;

—protects the security of its installations, activities, information, property, and employees by appropriate means, including such investigations of applicants, employees, contractors, and other persons with similar associations with the Agency, as are necessary;

—collects, produces, and disseminates military intelligence to military commands to enhance battlefield awareness;

—conducts such administrative and technical support activities within and outside the United States as are necessary to perform its functions, including procurement and essential cover and proprietary arrangements; and

—performs such other functions and duties relating to intelligence that affect the national security as the National Security Council may from time to time direct.

The Agency has no police, subpoena, or law enforcement powers or internal security functions.

For further information, contact the Central Intelligence Agency, Washington, DC 20505. Phone, 703–482–1100. Internet, http://www.odci.gov/cia.

COMMODITY FUTURES TRADING COMMISSION

1155 21st Street NW., Washington, DC 20581
Phone, 202–418–5000

Chairperson	BROOKSLEY BORN
Commissioners	BARBARA P. HOLUM, DAVID D. SPEARS, JOHN E. TULL, JR., (VACANCY)
General Counsel	DANIEL R. WALDMAN
Executive Director	LINDA FERREN

[For the Commodity Futures Trading Commission statement of organization, see the *Code of Federal Regulations*, Title 17, Part 140]

The Commodity Futures Trading Commission promotes healthy economic growth, protects the rights of customers, and ensures fairness and integrity in the marketplace through regulation of futures trading. To this end, it also engages in the analysis of economic issues affected by or affecting futures trading.

The Commodity Futures Trading Commission (CFTC) , the Federal regulatory agency for futures trading, was established by the Commodity Futures Trading Commission Act of 1974 (7 U.S.C. 4a). The Commission began operation in April 1975, and its authority to regulate futures trading was renewed by Congress in 1978, 1982, 1986, 1992, and 1995.

The Commission consists of five Commissioners who are appointed by the President, with the advice and consent of the Senate. One Commissioner is designated by the President to serve as Chairperson. The

COMMODITY FUTURES TRADING COMMISSION

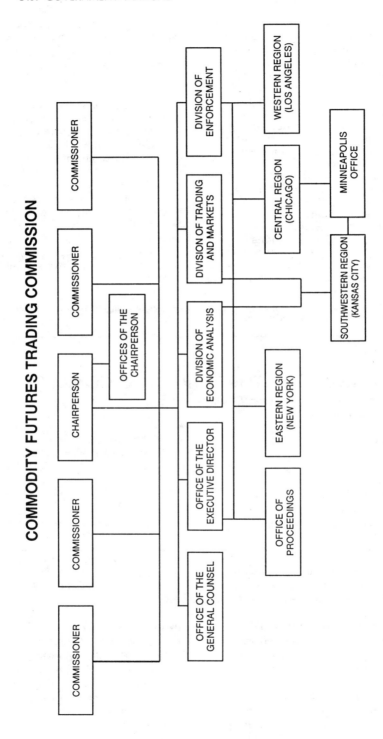

Commissioners serve staggered 5-year terms, and by law no more than three Commissioners can belong to the same political party.

The Commission has five major operating components: the Divisions of Enforcement, Economic Analysis, and Trading and Markets, and the Offices of the Executive Director and the General Counsel.

Activities

The Commission regulates trading on the 11 U.S. futures exchanges, which offer active futures and options contracts. It also regulates the activities of numerous commodity exchange members, public brokerage houses (futures commission merchants), Commission-registered futures industry salespeople (associated persons), commodity trading advisers, and commodity pool operators. Some off-exchange transactions involving instruments similar in nature to futures contracts also fall under Commission jurisdiction.

The Commission's regulatory and enforcement efforts are designed to ensure that the futures trading process is fair and that it protects both the rights of customers and the financial integrity of the marketplace. It approves the rules under which an exchange proposes to operate and monitors exchange enforcement of those rules. It reviews the terms of proposed futures contracts, and registers companies and individuals who handle customer funds or give trading advice. The Commission also protects the public by enforcing rules that require that customer funds be kept in bank accounts separate from accounts maintained by firms for their own use, and that such customer accounts be marked to present market value at the close of trading each day.

Large regional offices are maintained in Chicago, IL, and New York, NY, where many of the Nation's futures exchanges are located. Smaller regional offices are located in Kansas City, MO, and Los Angeles, CA. A suboffice of the Kansas City regional office is located in Minneapolis, MN.

For further information, contact the Office of Public Affairs, Commodity Futures Trading Commission, 1155 21st Street NW., Washington, DC 20581. Phone, 202–418–5080.

CONSUMER PRODUCT SAFETY COMMISSION

East West Towers, 4330 East West Highway, Bethesda, MD 20814
Phone, 301–504–0580. Internet, http://www.cpsc.gov/.

Chairman	ANN BROWN
Commissioners	MARY SHEILA GALL, THOMAS H. MOORE, (2 VACANCIES)
General Counsel	JEFFREY S. BROMME
Director, Office of Congressional Relations	ROBERT J. WAGER
Director, Office of the Secretary	SADYE E. DUNN
Freedom of Information Officer	TODD A. STEVENSON
Director, Office of Equal Employment Opportunity and Minority Enterprise	JOHN W. BARRETT, JR.
Executive Director	PAMELA GILBERT
Deputy Executive Directors	CLARENCE T. BISHOP, THOMAS W. MURR, JR.
Inspector General	THOMAS F. STEIN
Director, Office of Human Resources Management	BEVERLY M. ST.CLAIR

Director, Office of Information Services	DOUGLAS G. NOBLE
Director, Office of Planning and Evaluation	ROBERT E. FRYE
Director, Office of Information and Public Affairs	KATHLEEN P. BEGALA
Director, Office of the Budget	EDWARD E. QUIST
Associate Executive Director for Administration	MAUNA V. KAMMER
Associate Executive Director for Field Operations	THOMAS W. MURR, JR.
Assistant Executive Director for Compliance	ALAN H. SCHOEM
Associate Executive Director for Recalls and Compliance	MARC J. SCHOEM
Assistant Executive Director for Hazard Identification and Reduction	RONALD L. MEDFORD
Associate Executive Director for Engineering Sciences	ANDREW G. STADNIK
Associate Executive Director for Epidemiology and Health Sciences	MARY ANN DANELLO
Associate Executive Director for Laboratory Sciences	ANDREW G. ULSAMER
Associate Executive Director for Economic Analysis	WARREN J. PRUNELLA

[For the Consumer Product Safety Commission statement of organization, see the *Code of Federal Regulations*, Title 16, Part 1000]

The Consumer Product Safety Commission protects the public against unreasonable risks of injury from consumer products; assists consumers in evaluating the comparative safety of consumer products; develops uniform safety standards for consumer products and minimizes conflicting State and local regulations; and promotes research and investigation into the causes and prevention of product-related deaths, illnesses, and injuries.

The Consumer Product Safety Commission is an independent Federal regulatory agency established by the Consumer Product Safety Act (15 U.S.C. 2051 *et seq.*). The Commission consists of five Commissioners, appointed by the President with the advice and consent of the Senate, one of whom is appointed Chairman.

The Commission is responsible for implementing provisions of the Flammable Fabrics Act (15 U.S.C. 1191), the Poison Prevention Packaging Act of 1970 (15 U.S.C. 1471), the Federal Hazardous Substances Act (15 U.S.C. 1261), and the act of August 2, 1956 (15 U.S.C. 1211), which prohibits the transportation of refrigerators without door safety devices.

Activities

To help protect the public from unreasonable risks of injury associated with consumer products, the Commission:

—requires manufacturers to report defects in products that could create substantial hazards;

—requires, where appropriate, corrective action with respect to specific substantially hazardous consumer products already in commerce;

—collects information on consumer product-related injuries and maintains a comprehensive Injury Information Clearinghouse;

—conducts research on consumer product hazards;

—encourages and assists in the development of voluntary standards related to the safety of consumer products;

—establishes, where appropriate, mandatory consumer product standards;

—bans, where appropriate, hazardous consumer products; and

CONSUMER PRODUCT SAFETY COMMISSION

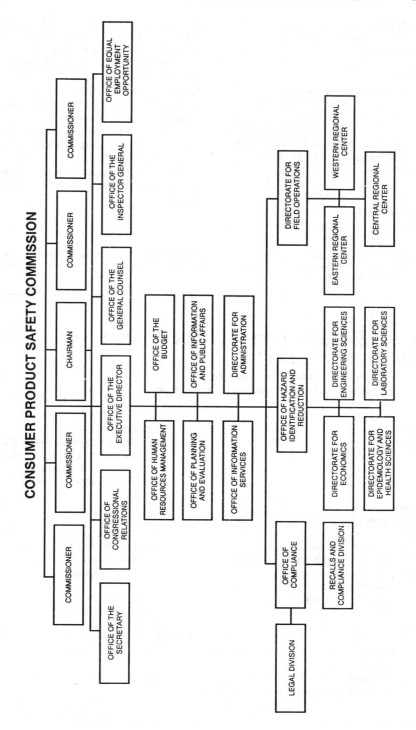

—conducts outreach programs for consumers, industry, and local governments.

Offices

The Commission's headquarters is located at East West Towers, 4330 East West Highway, Bethesda, MD 20814. Regional offices are located in Chicago, IL; New York, NY; and San Francisco, CA. Field offices are maintained in various cities.

Sources of Information

Consumer Information   The Commission operates a toll-free Consumer Product Safety Hotline, 800–638–CPSC (English and Spanish); and a teletypewriter for the hearing-impaired, 800–638–8270 (or in Maryland only, 800–492–8140).

General Inquiries   Information on Commission activities may be obtained from the Office of Information and Public Affairs, Consumer Product Safety Commission, Washington, DC 20207. Phone, 301–504–0580.

Reading Room   A public information room is maintained at the Commission headquarters.

For further information, contact the Office of Information and Public Affairs, Consumer Product Safety Commission, East West Towers, 4330 East West Highway, Bethesda, MD 20814. Phone, 301–504–0580. Internet, http://www.cpsc.gov/.

CORPORATION FOR NATIONAL AND COMMUNITY SERVICE

1201 New York Avenue NW., Washington, DC 20525
Phone, 202–606–5000. Internet, http://www.nationalservice.org/.

Board of Directors:	
Chair	BOB ROGERS
Members	VICTOR ASHE, THOMAS EHRLICH, CHRISTOPHER GALLAGHER, CAROL KINSLEY, LESLIE LENKOWSKY, ARTHUR NAPARSTEK, ELI SEGAL, (7 VACANCIES)
Members (*ex officio*)	
(Secretary of Agriculture)	DAN GLICKMAN
(Secretary of Defense)	WILLIAM S. COHEN
(Secretary of Education)	RICHARD W. RILEY
(Secretary of Health and Human Services)	DONNA E. SHALALA
(Secretary of Housing and Urban Development)	ANDREW M. CUOMO
(Secretary of the Interior)	BRUCE BABBITT
(Secretary of Labor)	ALEXIS M. HERMAN
(Attorney General)	JANET RENO
(Director, Peace Corps)	MARK GEARAN
(Administrator, Environmental Protection Agency)	CAROL M. BROWNER
(Chief Executive Officer, Corporation for National and Community Service)	HARRIS WOFFORD
Staff:	
Chief Executive Officer	HARRIS WOFFORD

Chief Operating Officer	LOUIS CALDERA
Chief of Staff to the CEO	JOHN S. GOMPERTS
Director, AmeriCorps	DEBORAH JOSPIN
Director, National Senior Service Corps	THOMAS ENDRES
Director, Learn and Serve America	MARILYN W. SMITH
Chief Financial Officer	DONNA H. CUNNINGHAME
Director, Planning and Program Integration	GARY KOWALCZYK
Director, Evaluation and Effective Practices	BILL BENTLEY
Inspector General	LUISE S. JORDAN
General Counsel	KENNETH KLOTHEN
Director, Congressional and Intergovernmental Affairs	EUGENE SOFER
Director, Public Affairs	TARA MURPHY
Director, Public Liaison	MELINDA HUDSON
Director, Human Resources	PHYLLIS BEAULIEU

The Corporation for National and Community Service engages Americans of all backgrounds in community-based service that addresses the Nation's educational, public safety, environmental, and other human needs to achieve direct and demonstrable results. In so doing, the Corporation fosters civic responsibility, strengthens the ties that bind us together as a people, and provides educational opportunity for those who make a substantial service contribution.

The Corporation for National and Community Service (Corporation) was established by the National and Community Service Trust Act of 1993 (42 U.S.C. 12651 *et seq.*). The Corporation assumed the programs and authorities of the Commission on National and Community Service and effective April 1, 1994, incorporated programs previously administered by ACTION under authority of the Domestic Volunteer Service Act of 1973, as amended (42 U.S.C. 4950).

The Corporation is a Federal corporation governed by a 15-member bipartisan Board of Directors, appointed by the President with the advice and consent of the Senate. The Secretaries of Agriculture, Defense, Education, Health and Human Services, Housing and Urban Development, Interior, and Labor; the Attorney General, the Environmental Protection Agency Administrator, the Peace Corps Director, and the Chief Executive Officer of the Corporation serve as *ex officio* members of the Board. The Board has responsibility for overall policy direction of the Corporation's activities and has the power to make all final grant decisions, approve the strategic plan and annual budget, and advise and make recommendations to the President and the Congress regarding changes in the national service laws.

Programs and Activities

The Corporation serves its mission through three major program areas:

AmeriCorps

AmeriCorps is the Nation's national service initiative that engages thousands of Americans of all ages and backgrounds in solving the most pressing community and national problems.

AmeriCorps members get things done by providing service to meet educational, public safety, environmental, and other human needs. In exchange for 1 or 2 years of service, members receive service education awards of up to $4,725 per year to help finance their college education or vocational training, or to pay back their student loans. The

CORPORATION FOR NATIONAL AND COMMUNITY SERVICE

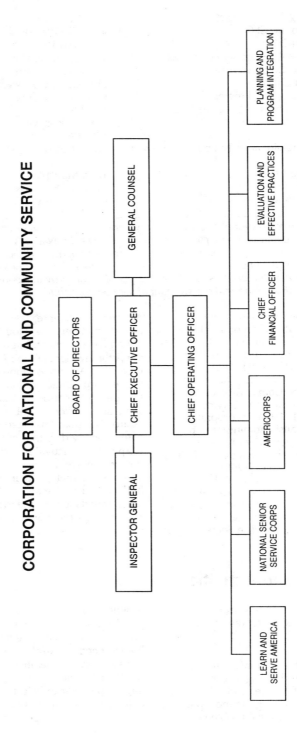

Corporation has established an Education Award Trust Fund to administer the award moneys.

AmeriCorps has three components: AmeriCorps*State and National is administered through grants, while AmeriCorps*VISTA and AmeriCorps*National Civilian Community Corps are run directly by the Corporation. Currently, some 25,000 members are serving in AmeriCorps.

AmeriCorps*State and National AmeriCorps*State and National members accomplish their mission by providing direct service in the four issue areas established by law: education, public safety, the environment, and other human needs. Services include: tutoring school-age children; serving as mentors to teenage parents; developing crime prevention workshops and providing victim assistance; helping the homebound and disabled live independently; coordinating needed services for public housing projects; starting citywide recycling programs; and restoring national parks. Full-time AmeriCorps*State and National members must serve at least 1,700 hours during a period of not less than 9 months and not more than 12 months to be eligible for the education award. Part-time members must serve at least 900 hours during a period of not more than 2 years (unless the part-time member is enrolled in an institution of higher education while performing some or all of the service, in which case the member must provide at least 900 hours of service during a period of not more than 3 years).

The Corporation funds AmeriCorps*State and National through population-based State allocations; funds distributed to programs selected by the States and submitted to the Corporation through competitive consideration; and programs operated by national nonprofit organizations, professional corps, and programs operating in more than one State. The funds granted to the States, on both formula and competitive bases, are administered by State Commissions on National and Community Service, which make subgrants to individual community-based programs. Information regarding annual grants requirements

and schedules is published in the *Federal Register.*

AmeriCorps*National Civilian Community Corps (AmeriCorps*NCCC) AmeriCorps*NCCC's mission is to promote civic pride and responsibility through community service. Members work in collaboration with community representatives to complete service-learning projects in the issue areas of education, public safety, the environment, and other human needs— with the primary focus on environmental needs. Corps members, ages 18–24, are recruited nationally and participate in innovative training programs that uniquely combine the best in military training techniques, Civilian Conservation Corps values, and service-learning models. AmeriCorps*NCCC is a residential program, with members living at campuses located at closed or downsized military facilities at Charleston, SC; Denver, CO; San Diego, CA; and Washington, DC; and at the Veterans Hospital at Perry Point, MD. AmeriCorps*NCCC is directly administered by the Corporation.

AmeriCorps*VISTA AmeriCorps*VISTA (Volunteers in Service to America) is a full-time service program established in 1965 and required by law to address poverty and poverty-related problems. AmeriCorps*VISTA members are supported directly by the Corporation, but serve with community-based public and private nonprofit organizations through memoranda of agreement between the Corporation and community-based groups. AmeriCorps*VISTA members must be assigned to antipoverty activities and are expected to serve in capacity-building assignments, whereas the AmeriCorps*State and National and AmeriCorps*NCCC programs emphasize direct service. Full-time AmeriCorps*VISTA service is 12 months, with members receiving a living allowance and health and child care; or they may elect to take a $1,200 cash stipend at the close of service rather than an education award.

Learn and Serve America

Learn and Serve America supports service-learning by students from kindergarten through graduate school. Service-learning is an innovative concept through which students participate in organized service experiences that meet community needs and are supported by a curriculum that allows research, reflection, and discussion of their experiences. The focus of Learn and Serve America is to build a solid foundation for service-learning in the curriculum of every school in America. The Corporation awards competitive grants to support Learn and Serve America on an annual basis. Notices of funds availability published in the *Federal Register* provide information concerning application deadlines and program requirements.

School-Based and Community-Based Programs   The goal of Learn and Serve America's School-Based and Community-Based Programs is to increase opportunities for school-age youth to learn and develop through service to their communities. The Corporation supports these initiatives through distribution of funds to State education agencies according to a population-based allotment. Grants to State commissions on national service, nonprofit grantmaking entities, Indian tribes, and U.S. territories are competitive.

School-based programs are administered by State education agencies, local education agencies in States not applying for funding, Indian tribes, and U.S. territories. Participants are elementary and secondary school students and out-of-school youth ages 5–17. Schools use Learn and Serve America grants for adult volunteer programs and teacher training in service-learning, along with planning, implementing, and expanding service-learning programs. Community-based programs are administered by State commissions on national and community service and nonprofit organizations.

Higher Education Programs   Service-learning at the postsecondary level is supported by grants to institutions of higher learning, consortia of institutions of higher learning, and public and private nonprofit organizations in partnership with institutions of higher education. These grants enable creation or expansion of community service opportunities for students and explore new ways to integrate service into the college curriculum and support model community service programs on campus. The programs are located in 38 States, the District of Columbia, and Puerto Rico.

National Senior Service Corps (Senior Corps)

The three Senior Corps programs—the Retired and Senior Volunteers Program (RSVP), the Foster Grandparent Program, and the Senior Companion Program—support community service by senior adults. These programs demonstrate the continued resource of seniors, provide valuable community service, and engage the experience, expertise, and commitment of seniors in the community. Each of these programs is funded through renewable project grants to public and private nonprofit organizations, who enter into memoranda of agreement with local institutions, including schools, hospitals, senior centers, and other organizations, who directly assign and supervise participants. Most Corporation funding supports continuation projects; new projects are awarded competitively when funds are available.

Retired and Senior Volunteer Program   The Retired and Senior Volunteer Program provides part-time, uncompensated service opportunities for persons age 55 or older. Participants serve a wide range of national and community needs, working with persons of all ages in community-based projects across America.

Foster Grandparent Program   The Foster Grandparent Program provides service to children with special needs. Participants must be 60 years of age or older, and must be considered low-income by published Corporation criteria. Participants serve 20-hour weeks, typically 4 hours a day, and provide personal love, attention, and support to children. Children served include those with physical and developmental disabilities, living in conditions of poverty, or involved in the juvenile justice system; teen-age mothers and their children; and Head Start participants. Foster Grandparents receive a stipend of $2.45 per hour and are provided meals, transportation, and physical examinations. They serve in all 50 States, the District of Columbia, Puerto Rico, and the Virgin Islands.

Senior Companion Program The Senior Companion Program engages low-income seniors age 60 and older in service to adults with special needs, with a focus on service to the frail elderly. Eligibility criteria and program benefits for Senior Companions are the same as those provided to Foster Grandparents. Senior Companions provide support, assistance, and companionship to those whom they serve in both in-home and institutional settings. They also provide respite care to caregivers, especially family members of the frail elderly.

Other Corporation Initiatives The Corporation's mission to develop and support an ethic of service in America involves initiatives, special demonstration projects, and other activities, in addition to the three major program areas. These include the National Service Scholarship Program, the AmeriCorps Leaders Program (and similar leaders programs in AmeriCorps*VISTA and AmeriCorps*NCCC), a disaster response initiative, and short-term summer service initiatives. The Corporation also carries

out an extensive training and technical assistance effort to support and assist State Commissions and service programs. Through partnerships with the private sector, other Federal agencies, and the Points of Light Foundation, the Corporation further advocates and advances service in America. The Corporation provides timely information about grants and financial assistance through notices of funds availability in the *Federal Register.*

Sources of Information

Electronic Access Information regarding the Corporation's programs and activities is available in electronic form through the Internet, at http://www.nationalservice.org/.

General Information To obtain additional information regarding AmeriCorps, call 800–942–2677 (toll-free), or for Senior Corps programs, 800–424–8867 (toll-free).

Grants Notices of funds availability are published in the *Federal Register* for most Corporation programs. Corporation State Program Offices and State Commissions on National and Community Service are located in most States and are the best source of information on programs in specific States or communities.

National Service Recruitment Persons interested in joining AmeriCorps should call 800–942–2677 (toll-free). To participate in other national service programs, contact Corporation State Offices or State Commissions on National and Community Service.

For further information, contact the Corporation for National and Community Service, 1201 New York Avenue NW., Washington, DC 20525. Phone, 202–606–5000. Internet, http://www.nationalservice.org/.

DEFENSE NUCLEAR FACILITIES SAFETY BOARD

Suite 700, 625 Indiana Avenue NW., Washington, DC 20004
Phone, 202–208–6400. Fax, 202–208–6518. Internet, http://www.dnfsb.gov/.

Chairman	JOHN T. CONWAY
Vice Chairman	A.J. EGGENBERGER

DEFENSE NUCLEAR FACILITIES SAFETY BOARD

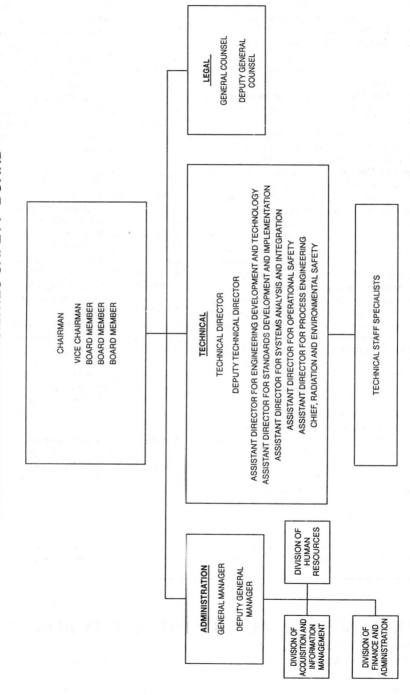

Members	JOSEPH J. DiNUNNO, HERBERT J.C. KOUTS, JOHN E. MANSFIELD
General Counsel	ROBERT M. ANDERSEN
General Manager	KENNETH M. PUSATERI
Technical Director	GEORGE W. CUNNINGHAM

The Defense Nuclear Facilities Safety Board reviews and evaluates the content and implementation of standards relating to the design, construction, operation, and decommissioning of defense nuclear facilities of the Department of Energy (DOE).

The Defense Nuclear Facilities Safety Board was established as an independent agency on September 29, 1988, by the Atomic Energy Act of 1954, as amended (42 U.S.C. 2286–2286i).

The Board is composed of five members appointed by the President with the advice and consent of the Senate. Members of the Board are appointed from among United States citizens who are respected experts in the field of nuclear safety.

Activities

The Defense Nuclear Facilities Safety Board reviews and evaluates the content and implementation of standards for defense nuclear facilities of DOE; investigates any event or practice at these facilities which may adversely affect public health and safety; and reviews and monitors the design, construction, and operation of facilities. The Board makes recommendations to the Secretary of Energy concerning DOE defense nuclear facilities to ensure adequate protection of public health and safety. In the event that any aspect of operations, practices, or occurrences reviewed by the Board is determined to present an imminent or severe threat to public health and safety, the Board transmits its recommendations directly to the President.

For further information, contact the Defense Nuclear Facilities Safety Board, Suite 700, 625 Indiana Avenue NW., Washington, DC 20004. Phone, 202–208–6400. Internet, http://www.dnfsb.gov/.

ENVIRONMENTAL PROTECTION AGENCY

401 M Street SW., Washington, DC 20460
Phone, 202–260–2090. Internet, http://www.epa.gov/.

Administrator	CAROL M. BROWNER
Deputy Administrator	FRED J. HANSEN
Office of the Administrator:	
Associate Administrator for Communications, Education, and Media Relations	LORETTA UCELLI
Associate Administrator for Congressional and Intergovernmental Relations	JOSEPH CRAPA
Associate Administrator for Reinvention	J. CHARLES FOX
Director, Executive Support Office	DIANE N. BAZZLE
Director, Executive Secretariat	SANDRA HUDNALL
Chief Judge, Office of Administrative Law Judges	SUSAN L. BIRO
Director, Office of Civil Rights	ANNE E. GOODE
Director, Office of Small and Disadvantaged Business Utilization	JEANETTE L. BROWN

Director, Science Advisory Board	DONALD G. BARNES
Senior Adviser, Office of Children's Health Protection	E. RAMONA TROVATO
Lead Environmental Appeals Judge, Environmental Appeals Board	RONALD L. MCCALLUM
Director, Regional Operations Staff	FRANCES GREENBERG, *Acting*
Director, Cooperative Environmental Management	CLARENCE HARDY
Other Offices:	
Assistant Administrator for Administration and Resources Management	ALVIN PESACHOWITZ, *Acting*
Deputy Assistant Administrator for Administration and Resources Management	(VACANCY)
Director, Office of Human Resources Management	DAVID J. O'CONNOR
Director, Office of Administration	JOHN C. CHAMBERLIN
Director, Office of Grants and Debarment	ELIZABETH CRAIG, *Acting*
Director, Office of Acquisition Management	BETTY L. BAILEY
Director, Office of Information Resources Management	MARK DAY, *Acting*
Director, Office of Policy and Resources Management	JOHN J. SANDY
Director, Office of Administration and Resources Management—Research Triangle Park, NC	WILLIAM G. LAXTON
Director, Office of Administration and Resources Management—Cincinnati, OH	WILLIAM M. HENDERSON
Chief Financial Officer	SALLYANNE HARPER, *Acting*
Deputy Chief Financial Officer	SALLYANNE HARPER
Director, Program Management Operations	BRIGID RAPP
Director, Office of the Comptroller	MICHAEL W.S. RYAN
Director, Office of Planning, Analysis, and Accountability	DAVID ZIEGELE
Assistant Administrator for Enforcement and Compliance Assurance	STEVEN A. HERMAN
Deputy Assistant Administrators for Enforcement and Compliance Assurance	SYLVIA LOWRANCE, MICHAEL M. STAHL
Director, Enforcement Capacity and Outreach Office	PETER D. ROSENBERG, *Acting*
Director, Federal Facilities Enforcement Office	CRAIG HOOKS, *Acting*
Director, Criminal Enforcement, Forensics, and Training	EARL E. DEVANEY
Director, Office of Environmental Justice	ROBERT J. KNOX, *Acting*
Director, Office of Planning and Policy Analysis	NANCY STONER
Director, Administration and Resource Management Support Staff	LAURIE R.G. FORD, *Acting*
Director, Office of Compliance	ELAINE G. STANLEY
Director, Office of Regulatory Enforcement	ERIC V. SCHAEFFER
Director, Office of Site Remediation Enforcement	BARRY N. BREEN
Director, Office of Federal Activities	RICHARD E. SANDERSON

General Counsel	JONATHAN Z. CANNON
Principal Deputy General Counsel	SCOTT FULTON
Director, Resource Management Office	DEBORAH S. INGRAM
Associate General Counsel, Air and Radiation Law Office	ALAN W. ECKERT
Associate General Counsel, Cross-Cutting Issues Law Office	JAMES C. NELSON, *Acting*
Associate General Counsel, Finance and Operations Law Office	RAY E. SPEARS
Associate General Counsel, Inspector General Law Office	MARLA E. DIAMOND
Director, International Environmental Law Office	DANIEL B. MAGRAW, JR.
Associate General Counsels, Pesticides and Toxic Substances Law Office	KEVIN M. LEE, *Acting*, PATRICIA A. ROBERTSON, *Acting*
Associate General Counsel, Solid Waste and Emergency Response Law Office	LISA K. FRIEDMAN
Associate General Counsel, Water Law Office	SUSAN G. LEPOW
Assistant Administrator for Policy, Planning, and Evaluation	DAVID GARDINER
Deputy Assistant Administrator for Policy, Planning, and Evaluation	ROBERT M. WOLCOTT, *Acting*
Director, Office of Strategic Planning and Environmental Data	FREDERICK W. ALLEN
Director, Office of Policy Development	MARYANN B. FROECHLICH
Director, Office of Regulatory Management and Information	THOMAS E. KELLEY
Director, Office of Economy and Environment	ALBERT M. MCGARLAND
Director, Office of Programmatic Support and Resources Management	PAMELA P. STIRLING
Director, Office of Sustainable Ecosystems and Communities	WENDY CLELAND-HAMNETT
Inspector General	NIKKI L. TINSLEY, *Acting*
Deputy Inspector General	NIKKI L. TINSLEY
Assistant Inspector General, Office of Audit	KENNETH A. KONZ
Assistant Inspector General, Office of Investigations	ALLEN P. FALLIN
Assistant Inspector General, Office of Management	JOHN C. JONES
Assistant Administrator for International Activities	WILLIAM A. NITZE
Principal Deputy Assistant Administrator for International Activities	ALAN D. HECHT
Director, Office of International Environmental Policy	PAUL F. COUGH
Director, Office of Management Operations	JOAN FIDLER
Director, Office of Technology Cooperation and Assistance	JAMISON KOEHLER
Director, Office of Western Hemisphere and Bilateral Affairs	PATRICIA KOSHEL
Assistant Administrator for Water	ROBERT PERCIASEPE
Deputy Assistant Administrator for Water	DANA D. MINERVA

Director, Policy and Resources Management Office	DIANE E. REGAS
Director, Office of Ground Water and Drinking Water	ROBERT J. BLANCO
Director, Office of Wastewater Management	MICHAEL B. COOK
Director, Office of Science and Technology	TUDOR T. DAVIES
Director, American Indian Environmental Office	KATHY GOROSPE
Director, Office of Wetlands, Oceans, and Watersheds	ROBERT H. WAYLAND III
Assistant Administrator for Solid Waste and Emergency Response	TIMOTHY FIELDS, JR., *Acting*
Deputy Assistant Administrator for Solid Waste and Emergency Response	MICHAEL SHAPIRO, *Acting*
Director, Office of Program Management	DEVEREAUX BARNES
Director, Federal Facilities Restoration and Reuse Office	JAMES E. WOOLFORD
Director, Outreach and Special Projects Staff	LINDA GARCZYNSKI
Director, Chemical Emergency Preparedness and Prevention Office	JAMES L. MAKRIS
Director, Technology Innovation Office	WALTER W. KOVALICK, JR.
Director, Office of Solid Waste	ELIZABETH COTSWORTH, *Acting*
Director, Office of Emergency and Remedial Response (Superfund)	STEPHEN D. LUFTIG
Director, Office of Underground Storage Tanks	ANNA VIRBICK
Assistant Administrator for Air and Radiation	RICHARD D. WILSON, *Acting*
Deputy Assistant Administrator for Air and Radiation	ROBERT D. BRENNER, *Acting*
Director, Office of Air Quality Planning and Standards	JOHN S. SEITZ
Director, Office of Program Management Operations	JERRY A. KURTZWEG
Director, Office of Policy Analysis and Review	ROBERT D. BRENNER
Director, Office of Atmospheric Programs	PAUL STOLPMAN
Director, Office of Radiation and Indoor Air	LAWRENCE G. WEINSTOCK, *Acting*
Director, Office of Mobile Sources	MARGO T. OGE
Assistant Administrator for Prevention, Pesticides, and Toxic Substances	LYNN R. GOLDMAN
Deputy Assistant Administrator for Pesticides and Toxic Substances	SUSAN H. WAYLAND
Director, Office of Program Management Operations	MARYLOUISE M. UHLIG
Director, Office of Pesticide Programs	MARCIA E. MULKEY
Director, Office of Pollution Prevention and Toxics	WILLIAM H. SANDERS III
Assistant Administrator for Research and Development	HENRY L. LONGEST II
Deputy Assistant Administrator for Management	STEPHEN A. LINGLE, *Acting*
Deputy Assistant Administrator for Science	JOSEPH K. ALEXANDER
Director, Office of Resources Management and Administration	PETER M. DURANT, *Acting*
Director, Office of Science Policy	DOROTHY E. PATTON

Director, National Exposure Research Laboratory	GARY J. FOLEY
Director, National Risk Management Research Laboratory	E. TIMOTHY OPPELT
Director, National Health and Environmental Effects Research Laboratory	LAWRENCE W. REITER
Director, National Center for Environmental Assessment	WILLIAM H. FARLAND
Director, National Center for Environmental Research and Quality Assurance	PETER W. PREUSS

[For the Environmental Protection Agency statement of organization, see the *Code of Federal Regulations*, Title 40, Part 1]

The mission of the Environmental Protection Agency is to protect human health and to safeguard the natural environment—air, water, and land—upon which life depends to the fullest extent possible under the laws enacted by Congress.

The Environmental Protection Agency was established in the executive branch as an independent agency pursuant to Reorganization Plan No. 3 of 1970 (5 U.S.C. app.), effective December 2, 1970. It was created to permit coordinated and effective governmental action on behalf of the environment. The Agency is designed to serve as the public's advocate for a livable environment.

Activities

Air and Radiation   The air activities of the Agency include:

—development of national programs, technical policies, and regulations for air pollution control;

—enforcement of standards;

—development of national standards for air quality, emission standards for new stationary and mobile sources, and emission standards for hazardous pollutants;

—conducting research and providing information on indoor air pollutants to the public;

—technical direction, support, and evaluation of regional air activities; and

—training in the field of air pollution control.

Related activities include technical assistance to States and agencies having radiation protection programs, including radon mitigation programs and a national surveillance and inspection program for measuring radiation levels in the environment.

For further information, call 202–260–7400.

Water   The Agency's water quality activities represent a coordinated effort to restore the Nation's waters, including:

—development of national programs, technical policies, and regulations for water pollution control and water supply;

—ground water protection;

—marine and estuarine protection;

—enforcement of standards;

—water quality standards and effluent guidelines development;

—technical direction, support, and evaluation of regional water activities;

—development of programs for technical assistance and technology transfer; and

—training in the field of water quality.

For further information, call 202–260–5700.

Solid Waste and Emergency Response
The Office of Solid Waste and Emergency Response provides policy, guidance, and direction for the Agency's hazardous waste and emergency response programs, including:

—development of policies, standards, and regulations for hazardous waste treatment, storage, and disposal;

—national management of the Superfund toxic waste cleanup program;

—development of guidelines for the emergency preparedness and "Community Right To Know" programs;

ENVIRONMENTAL PROTECTION AGENCY

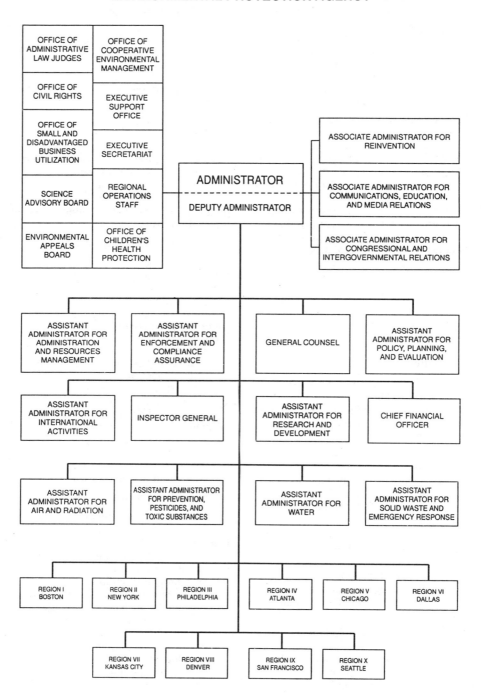

—implementation of special initiatives such as the Brownfields National Partnership and the Environmental Teachers Institute;

—management of environmental justice/public participation programs related to waste siting issues;

—development of guidelines and standards for the land disposal of hazardous wastes and for underground storage tanks;

—analysis of technologies and methods for the recovery of useful energy from solid waste;

—economic impact assessment of RCRA and CERCLA regulations;

—coordination with the Department of Defense on base closure environmental issues; and

—technical assistance in the development, management, and operation of waste management activities, including technical assistance to Federal facilities.

For further information, call 202–260–4610.

Prevention, Pesticides, and Toxic Substances The Office of Prevention, Pesticides, and Toxic Substances is responsible for:

—promoting pollution prevention and the public's right to know about chemical risk;

—developing and implementing strategies to promote pollution prevention through source reduction;

—evaluating and regulating pesticides and chemicals to safeguard all Americans;

—establishing safe levels for pesticide residues on food;

—developing national strategies for control of toxic substances;

—developing criteria for assessing chemical substances, standards for test protocols for chemicals, rules and procedures for industry reporting, and regulations for the control of substances that may be hazardous to people or the environment; and

—evaluating and assessing the impact of existing chemicals, new chemicals, and chemicals with new uses to

determine the hazard and develop appropriate restrictions.

The Office also coordinates activities under its statutory responsibilities with other agencies for the assessment and control of toxic substances and pesticides.

For further information, call 202–260–2902.

Research and Development The Office of Research and Development (ORD) provides the scientific foundation for the Agency's environmental protection mission. ORD's chief role is to conduct and support high quality research targeted to understanding and resolving the Nation's most serious environmental threats. In addition, ORD develops methods and technologies to reduce exposures to pollution and prevent its creation, and shares information on technological innovations to protect people and the environment. ORD prepares health and ecological risk assessments and makes recommendations for sound risk management strategies in order to assure that highest risk pollution problems receive optimum remediation. The Office manages a vital extramural grants program entitled Science To Achieve Results, which awards research grants to scientists in universities and not-for-profit institutions, and supports fellowships to promising young graduate students in environmental science.

For further information, call 202–564–6620.

Regional Offices

The Agency's 10 regional offices represent its commitment to the development of strong local programs for pollution abatement. The Regional Administrators are responsible for accomplishing, within their regions, the national program objectives established by the Agency. They develop, propose, and implement an approved regional program for comprehensive and integrated environmental protection activities.

Regional Offices—Environmental Protection Agency

Region/Address/Areas Served	Administrator
Region I (John F. Kennedy Federal Bldg., Boston, MA 02203) (CT, MA, ME, NH, RI, VT)	John P. DeVillars
Region II (290 Broadway, New York, NY 10007) (NJ, NY, PR, VI)	Jeanne M. Fox
Region III (841 Chestnut St., Philadelphia, PA 19107) (DC, DE, MD, PA, VA, WV)	W. Michael McCabe
Region IV (61 Forsyth St., Atlanta GA 30303) (AL, FL, GA, KY, MS, NC, SC, TN)	John H. Hankinson, Jr.
Region V (77 W. Jackson Blvd., Chicago, IL 60604) (IL, IN, MI, MN, OH, WI)	David A. Ullrich, *Acting*
Region VI (1445 Ross Ave., Dallas, TX 75202) (AR, LA, NM, OK, TX)	Gerald (Jerry) Clifford, *Acting*
Region VII (726 Minnesota Ave., Kansas City, KS 66101) (IA, KS, MO, NE)	Dennis D. Grams
Region VIII (999 18th St., Denver, CO 80202) (CO, MT, ND, SD, UT, WY)	William P. Yellowtail
Region IX (75 Hawthorne St., San Francisco, CA 94105) (AS, AZ, CA, GU, HI, NV)	Felicia Markus
Region X (1200 6th Ave., Seattle, WA 98101) (AK, ID, OR, WA)	Charles C. Clarke

Sources of Information

Inquiries for information on the following subjects should be directed to the specified office of the Environmental Protection Agency, 401 M Street SW., Washington, DC 20460.
Contracts and Procurement   Office of Acquisition Management. Phone, 202–260–5020.
Employment   Office of Human Resources and Organizational Services. Phone, 202–260–4467.

Freedom of Information Act Requests

Freedom of Information Officer. Phone, 202–260–4048.
Reading Room   EPA Headquarters Information Resources Center, Room 2904 Mall. Phone, 202–260–5922.
Telephone Directory   Available for sale by the Superintendent of Documents, Government Printing Office, Washington, DC 20402.

For further information, contact the Office of Communications, Education, and Media Relations, Environmental Protection Agency, 401 M Street SW., Washington, DC 20460 (phone, 202–260–7963); or write to the Public Information Office of the nearest regional office. Internet, http://www.epa.gov/.

EQUAL EMPLOYMENT OPPORTUNITY COMMISSION

1801 L Street NW., Washington, DC 20507
Phone, 202–663–4900. TTY, 202–663–4494. Internet, http://www.eeoc.gov/.

Chairman	PAUL M. IGASAKI
Executive Assistant	J. KENNETH L. MORSE
Attorney Advisor	JASON S. HEGY
Special Assistant	MARK W. WONG
Executive Director	MARIA BORRERO
Special Assistant	(VACANCY)
Vice Chairman	PAUL M. IGASAKI
Executive Assistant	J. KENNETH L. MORSE
Attorney Advisor	JASON S. HEGY
Special Assistant	MARK W. WONG
Commissioner	PAUL STEVEN MILLER
Senior Adviser	R. PAUL RICHARD
Special Assistants	LISA S. COTTLE, ANTOINETTE M. EATES, JUSTIN S. LISSER
Commissioner	REGINALD E. JONES
Special Assistants	NAOMI LEVIN, WALLACE LEW, CASSANDRA MENOKEN

Commissioner	(VACANCY)
Executive Officer	FRANCES M. HART
Attorney Advisor	STEPHEN LLEWELLYN
General Counsel	C. GREGORY STEWART
Inspector General	ALETHA L. BROWN
Director, Office of Communications and Legislative Affairs	WILLIAM J. WHITE, JR., *Acting*
Director, Office of Equal Opportunity	CYNTHIA C. MATTHEWS
Director, Office of Federal Operations	RONNIE BLUMENTHAL
Legal Counsel	ELLEN J. VARGYAS
Director, Office of Field Programs	ELIZABETH M. THORNTON
Director, Office of Financial and Resource Management	KASSIE A. BILLINGSLEY
Director, Office of Information Resources Management	SALLIE T. HSIEH
Director, Office of Human Resources	PATRICIA CORNWELL JOHNSON
Director, Office of Research, Information, and Planning	DEIDRE FLIPPEN

The Equal Employment Opportunity Commission enforces laws which prohibit discrimination based on race, color, religion, sex, national origin, disability, or age in hiring, promoting, firing, setting wages, testing, training, apprenticeship, and all other terms and conditions of employment. The Commission conducts investigations of alleged discrimination; makes determinations based on gathered evidence; attempts conciliation when discrimination has taken place; files lawsuits; and conducts voluntary assistance programs for employers, unions, and community organizations. The Commission also has adjudicatory and oversight responsibility for all compliance and enforcement activities relating to equal employment opportunity among Federal employees and applicants, including discrimination against individuals with disabilities.

The Equal Employment Opportunity Commission (EEOC) was created by title VII of the Civil Rights Act of 1964 (42 U.S.C. 2000e–4), and became operational July 2, 1965. Title VII was amended by the Equal Employment Opportunity Act of 1972, the Pregnancy Discrimination Act of 1978, and the Civil Rights Act of 1991.

Executive Order 12067 of June 30, 1978, abolished the Equal Employment Opportunity Coordinating Council and transferred its duties to the Commission with responsibility for providing coherence and direction to the Government's equal employment opportunity efforts.

Reorganization Plan No. 1 of 1978 (5 U.S.C. app.) effective January 1, 1979, transferred Federal equal employment functions from the Civil Service Commission to the EEOC. Authorities for transferred functions include:

—section 717 of title VII of the Civil Rights Act of 1964 (42 U.S.C. 2000e–16), which prohibits discrimination in employment in the Federal Government on the basis of race, color, religion, sex, or national origin;

—Executive Order 11478 of August 8, 1969, which sets forth the U.S. policy of providing for equal employment opportunity in the Federal Government through affirmative action programs in Federal departments and agencies;

—the Equal Pay Act of 1963 (29 U.S.C. 206) in the Federal sector;

—section 15 of the Age Discrimination in Employment Act of 1967, as amended (29 U.S.C. 633a) in the Federal sector; and

—section 501 of the Rehabilitation Act of 1973 (29 U.S.C. 791), which pertains to employment discrimination against individuals with disabilities in the Federal Government.

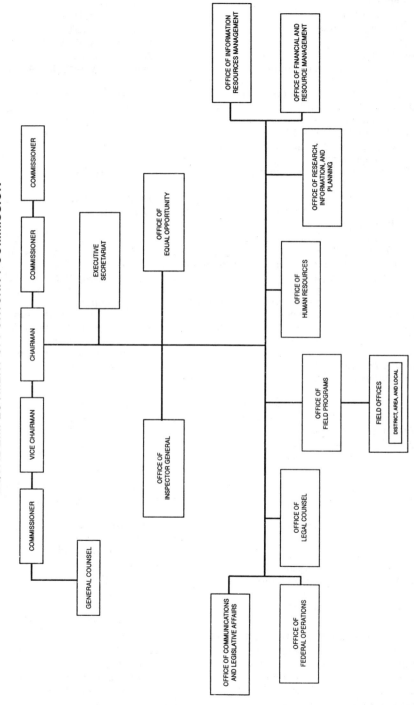

EQUAL EMPLOYMENT OPPORTUNITY COMMISSION

On July 1, 1979, responsibility for enforcement—in private industry as well as in State and local governments—of the Equal Pay Act of 1963 (EPA) and the Age Discrimination in Employment Act of 1967 (ADEA) was transferred from the Department of Labor to the Commission. The EPA prohibits sex-based pay differences where substantially equal work is performed in the same establishment under similar working conditions and requires equal skill, effort, and responsibility; and the ADEA prohibits employment discrimination against workers or applicants 40 years of age or older. In addition to employers, the ADEA covers activities of employment agencies, and both acts cover activities of labor organizations.

The Americans with Disabilities Act of 1990 (ADA) (42 U.S.C. 12101 *et seq.*) was approved on July 26, 1990. Title I of the act has been enforced by EEOC since July 26, 1992, for employers with 25 or more employees, and since July 26, 1994, for employers with 15 or more employees. Title I governs private employers, State and local governments, employment agencies, labor organizations, and joint labor-management committees. The ADA prohibits employment discrimination against qualified individuals with disabilities and requires that employers make reasonable accommodations for such qualified individuals if it would not create undue hardship.

The Civil Rights Act of 1991 reversed parts of several U.S. Supreme Court rulings and provided for compensatory and punitive damages for intentional discrimination under title VII, the Rehabilitation Act of 1973, and the ADA.

The Commission is comprised of five Commissioners appointed by the President, with the advice and consent of the Senate, for 5-year staggered terms. The President designates a Chairman and a Vice Chairman.

The Commission operates through 50 field offices, each of which processes charges.

Activities

Enforcement   The Commission's field offices receive charges of job discrimination under title VII, the ADA, the EPA, and the ADEA. Field offices may initiate investigations to find violations of the acts. Members of the Commission also may initiate charges alleging that a violation of title VII or the ADA has occurred. Section 501 of the Rehabilitation Act of 1973 covers Federal employees and applicants only.

Charges Under Title VII   Title VII prohibits employment discrimination based on race, color, religion, sex, or national origin by private employers, State and local governments, and educational institutions with 15 or more employees, or by the Federal Government, private and public employment agencies, labor organizations, and joint labor-management committees for apprenticeship and training.

Charges of title VII violations in the private sector must be filed with the Commission within 180 days of the alleged violation (or up to 300 days in a State or locality in which a fair employment practices agency is located), and the Commission is responsible for notifying persons so charged within 10 days of the receipt of a new charge. Before investigation, charges must be deferred for 60 days to a State or local fair employment practices agency in States and municipalities where there is a fair employment practices law covering the alleged discrimination. The deferral period is 120 days if the agency has been operating less than 1 year. Under worksharing agreements executed between the Commission and State and local fair employment practices agencies, the Commission routinely will assume jurisdiction over certain charges of discrimination and proceed with its investigation rather than wait for the expiration of the deferral period.

If there is reasonable cause to believe the charge is true, the district, area, or local office attempts to remedy the alleged unlawful practices through informal methods of conciliation, conference, and persuasion. If an acceptable conciliation agreement is not secured, the case is considered for possible litigation. If litigation is approved, the Commission will bring suit in an appropriate Federal district court.

Under title VII, the Attorney General brings suit when a State or local government, or political subdivision is involved. If the Commission or the Attorney General does not approve litigation or if a finding of no reasonable cause is made, at the conclusion of the administrative procedures (or earlier at the request of the charging party) a Notice of Right-to-Sue is issued that allows the charging party to proceed within 90 days in a Federal district court. In appropriate cases, the Commission may intervene in such civil action if the case is of general public interest. The investigation and conciliation of charges having an industrywide or national impact are coordinated or conducted by Systemic Investigations and Individual Compliance Programs, Office of Program Operations.

Under the provisions of title VII, section 706(f)(2), as amended by section 4 of the Equal Employment Opportunity Act of 1972 (42 U.S.C. 2000e–5), if it is concluded after a preliminary investigation that prompt judicial action is necessary to carry out the purposes of the act, the Commission or the Attorney General, in a case involving a State or local government, governmental agency or political subdivision, may bring an action for appropriate temporary or preliminary relief pending final disposition of a charge.

Americans with Disabilities Act Charges The ADA specifically incorporates the powers, remedies, and procedures contained in title VII of the Civil Rights Act of 1964, as amended. Employment discrimination charges based on disability may be filed at any of the Commission's field offices. The Commission will investigate and attempt to conciliate the charges using the same procedures it uses to investigate and conciliate charges filed under title VII. The litigation procedures under this title apply to charges filed under the act.

Age Discrimination in Employment or Equal Pay Act Charges and Complaints

The ADEA and the EPA cover most employees and job applicants in private industry and Federal, State, and local governments.

An age discrimination charge must be filed with the Commission within 180 days of the alleged violation or, in a case where the alleged discriminatory action took place in a State which has its own age discrimination law and authority administering that law, within 300 days of the alleged violation or 30 days after the receipt of a notice of termination of State proceedings, whichever is earlier. The Commission will attempt to eliminate the unlawful practice through informal methods of conciliation, conference, and persuasion. A lawsuit may be brought by the Commission if conciliation fails, or individuals may file suit on their own behalf 90 days after filing a charge with the Commission and the appropriate State agency, but no later than 90 days after receipt of notice of final action by the Commission. Should the Commission take legal action, an individual covered by such action may not file a private suit. If an individual files a complaint of age discrimination, instead of a charge, his or her name will be kept confidential, but the individual filing the complaint may not bring a private suit unless he or she elects to file a charge first in accordance with the above requirements.

A lawsuit under the EPA may be filed by the Commission or by the complainant. There are no administrative prerequisites to individual actions under this law. Wages may be recovered for a period of up to 2 years prior to the filing of a suit, except in the case of willful violation, where 3 years' backpay may be recovered. The name of the individual filing the complaint may be kept confidential at the administrative level.

Complaints Against the Federal Government The Commission's Federal sector processing regulations, codified in 29 CFR 1614, effective October 1, 1992, guide Federal employees or job applicants who want to file complaints of job discrimination based on race, color, national origin, sex, religion, age, or physical or mental disability. Complainants must first consult an equal employment opportunity counselor within their agency within 45 calendar days of the alleged discriminatory event or the effective date of the alleged discriminatory personnel action. If the matter cannot be resolved informally, the person may file a formal complaint within 15 calendar days after the date of receipt of the notice of the right to file a complaint. An accepted complaint is investigated by the respondent agency, and there is a right to a hearing before an EEOC administrative judge before the agency issues its final decision.

An individual who wishes to file a complaint under the EPA must also follow these procedures. However, an individual may also elect to file suit under the EPA without prior resort to the agency or to the Commission.

Federal-sector age discrimination complainants may bypass the administrative complaint process and file a civil action directly in a U.S. district court by first notifying the Commission within 180 calendar days of the alleged discriminatory act and thereafter waiting 30 calendar days before filing suit.

Federal employees may file appeals of final agency decisions or decisions of an arbitrator or the Federal Labor Relations Authority with the Commission's Office of Federal Operations at any time up to 30 calendar days after receipt of the agency notice of final decision. A petition for review of a Merit Systems Protection Board decision may be filed within 30 days of the date that the Board decision becomes final. A request for reopening and reconsideration of any decision of the Commission should be made in writing within 30 days of receipt of such decision. Commission decisions are issued in writing to the complainant and the agency. The Office of Federal Operations monitors and ensures compliance by Federal agencies with Commission orders and appellate decisions, and provides technical assistance and training to other Federal agencies.

Other Activities   The Commission actively promotes voluntary compliance with equal employment opportunity statutes through a variety of educational and technical assistance activities. A distinct activity of the Commission is the Voluntary Assistance Program. This outreach program is designed to provide educational and technical assistance to small and midsize employers and unions—through 1-day seminars on equal employment opportunity laws—about their rights and obligations under all the statutes that the Commission enforces.

Another activity initiated by the Commission is the Expanded Presence Program, which is designed to make the Commission accessible in areas identified as underserved by Commission offices.

Through its Educational Technical Assistance and Training Revolving Fund, the Commission is also able to provide its constituency with advanced and specialized technical assistance offerings. Fees charged for Revolving Fund products are not to exceed the cost of producing the materials or services provided, are to bear a direct relationship to the cost of providing such outreach, and are to be imposed on a uniform basis.

The Commission participates in the development of employment discrimination law through the issuance of guidelines, publication of significant Commission decisions, and involvement in litigation brought under title VII, the Equal Pay Act of 1963, the Age Discrimination in Employment Act of 1967, the Rehabilitation Act of 1973, and the Americans with Disabilities Act of 1990.

The Commission has direct liaison with Federal, State, and local governments, employers and union organizations, trade associations, civil rights organizations, and other agencies and organizations concerned with employment of minority group members and women.

The Commission develops and implements affirmative employment policies designed to enhance the occupational status of minorities, women, and persons with disabilities in the Federal Government.

The Commission also publishes data on the employment status of minorities and women. Through 6 employment surveys covering private employers, apprenticeship programs, labor unions, State and local governments, elementary and secondary schools, and colleges and universities, the Commission tabulates and stores data on the ethnic, racial, and sex composition of employees at all job levels within the reported groups.

Research information thus collected is shared with selected Federal agencies, and is made available, in appropriate form, for public use.

Field Offices—Equal Employment Opportunity Commission

(DO: District Office; AO: Area Office; LO: Local Office; FO: Field Office)

Office	Address/Telephone	Director
Albuquerque, NM (DO)	Suite 900, 505 Marquette NW., 87102. Ph., 505–248–5201. Fax, 505–248–5233. TTY, 505–248–5240.	(Vacancy)
Atlanta, GA (DO)	Suite 4R30, 100 Alabama St. NW., 30303. Ph., 404–562–6930. Fax, 404–562–6909. TTY, 404–562–6801.	Bernice Williams-Kimbrough
Baltimore, MD (DO)	3d Fl., 10 S. Howard St., 21201. Ph., 410–962–3932. Fax, 410–962–2817. TTY, 410–962–6065.	Issie L. Jenkins
Birmingham, AL (DO)	Suite 101, 1900 3d Ave. N., 35203–2397. Ph., 205–731–0082. Fax, 205–731–2101. TTY, 205–731–0175.	Donald Burris
Boston, MA (AO)	Rm. 475, John F. Kennedy Fed. Bldg., 02203. Ph., 617–565–3190. Fax, 617–565–3196. TTY, 617–565–3204.	Robert L. Sanders
Buffalo, NY (LO)	Suite 350, 6 Fountain Plz., 14202. Ph., 716–551–4441. Fax, 716–551–4387. TTY, 716–551–5923.	Elizabeth Cadle
Charlotte, NC (DO)	Suite 400, 129 W. Trade St., 28202. Ph., 704–344–6682. Fax, 704–344–6734. TTY, 704–334–6684.	Marsha J. Drane
Chicago, IL (DO)	Suite 2800, 500 W. Madison St., 60661. Ph., 312–353–2713. Fax, 312–353–4041. TTY, 312–353–2421.	John P. Rowe
Cincinnati, OH (AO)	Suite 810, 525 Vine St., 45202–3122. Ph., 513–684–2851. Fax, 513–684–2361. TTY, 513–684–6698.	(Vacancy)
Cleveland, OH (DO)	Suite 850, 1660 W. 2d St., 44113–1454. Ph., 216–522–2001. Fax, 216–522–7395. TTY, 216–522–8441.	Dorothy J. Porter
Dallas, TX (DO)	3d Fl., 207 S. Houston St., 75202–4726. Ph., 214–655–3355. Fax, 214–655–3443. TTY, 214–655–3363.	Jacqueline R. Bradley
Denver, CO (DO)	Suite 510, 303 E. 17th Ave., 80203. Ph., 303–866–1300. Fax, 303–866–1386. TTY, 303–866–1950.	Francisco J. Flores
Detroit, MI (DO)	Rm. 865, 477 Michigan Ave., 48226–9704. Ph., 313–226–4600. Fax, 313–226–2778. TTY, 313–226–7599.	James R. Neely, Jr.
El Paso, TX (AO)	Suite 100, Bldg. C, 4171 N. Mesa St., 79902. Ph., 915–534–6550. Fax, 915–534–6552. TTY, 915–534–6545.	Robert Calderon
Fresno, CA (LO)	Suite 103, 1265 W. Shaw Ave., 93711. Ph., 209–487–5793. Fax, 209–487–5053. TTY, 209–487–5837.	David Rodriguez
Greensboro, NC (LO)	801 Summit Ave., 27405–7813. Ph., 336–333–5174. Fax, 336–333–5051. TTY, 336–333–5542.	Patricia B. Fuller
Greenville, SC (LO)	Suite 530, 15 S. Main St., 29601. Ph., 864–241–4400. Fax, 864–241–4416. TTY, 864–241–4403.	Denise Anderson
Honolulu, HI (LO)	Rm. 7–127, 300 Ala Moana Blvd., 96850–0051. Ph., 808–541–3120. Fax, 808–541–3390. TTY, 808–541–3131.	Timothy A. Riera
Houston, TX (DO)	7th Fl., 1919 Smith St., 77002. Ph., 713–209–3320. Fax, 713–209–3381. TTY, 713–209–3439.	Harriet J. Ehrlich
Indianapolis, IN (DO)	Suite 1900, 101 W. Ohio St., 46204–4203. Ph., 317–226–7212. Fax, 317–226–7953. TTY, 317–226–5162.	Thomas P. Hadfield
Jackson, MS (AO)	207 W. Amite St., 39201. Ph., 601–965–4537. Fax, 601–965–5272. TTY, 601–965–4915.	Benjamin Bradley
Kansas City, KS (AO)	Suite 905, 400 State Ave., 66101. Ph., 913–551–5655. Fax, 913–551–6956. TTY, 913–551–5657.	George Dixon
Little Rock, AR (AO)	Suite 625, 425 W. Capitol Ave., 72201. Ph., 501–324–5060. Fax, 501–324–5991. TTY, 501–324–5481.	Kay Klugh
Los Angeles, CA (DO)	4th Fl., 255 E. Temple St., 90012. Ph., 213–894–1000. Fax, 213–894–1118. TTY, 213–894–1121.	Thelma Taylor
Louisville, KY (AO)	Suite 268, 600 Dr. Martin Luther King Jr. Pl., 40202. Ph., 502–582–6082. Fax, 502–582–5895. TTY, 502–582–6285.	Marcia Hall Craig
Memphis, TN (DO)	Suite 621, 1407 Union Ave., 38104. Ph., 901–544–0115. Fax, 901–544–0111. TTY, 901–544–0112.	Walter S. Grabon
Miami, FL (DO)	Suite 2700, 2 S. Biscayne Blvd., 33131. Ph., 305–536–4491. Fax, 305–536–4011. TTY, 305–536–5721.	Federico Costales
Milwaukee, WI (DO)	Suite 800, 310 W. Wisconsin Ave., 53203–2292. Ph., 414–297–1111. Fax, 414–297–4133. TTY, 414–297–1115.	Chester V. Bailey
Minneapolis, MN (AO)	Suite 430, 330 S. 2d Ave., 55401–2224. Ph., 612–335–4040. Fax, 612–335–4044. TTY, 612–335–4045.	Michael J. Bloyer
Nashville, TN (AO)	Suite 202, 50 Vantage Way, 37228–9940. Ph., 615–736–5820. Fax, 615–736–2107. TTY, 615–736–5870.	(Vacancy)
Newark, NJ (AO)	21st Fl., One Newark Ctr., 07102–5233. Ph., 973–645–6383. Fax, 973–645–4524. TTY, 973–645–3004.	Corrado Gigante

Field Offices—Equal Employment Opportunity Commission—Continued
(DO: District Office; AO: Area Office; LO: Local Office; FO: Field Office)

Office	Address/Telephone	Director
New Orleans, LA (DO)	Suite 600, 701 Loyola Ave., 70113–9936. Ph., 504–589–2329. Fax, 504–589–6861. TTY, 504–589–2958.	Patricia T. Bivins
New York, NY (DO)	18th Fl., 7 World Trade Ctr., 10048–1102. Ph., 212–748–8500. Fax, 212–748–8464. TTY, 212–748–8399.	Spencer H. Lewis, Jr.
Norfolk, VA (AO)	Suite 4300, 101 W. Main St., 23510. Ph., 757–441–3470. Fax, 757–441–6720. TTY, 757–441–3578.	Herbert Brown
Oakland, CA (LO)	Suite 1170–N, 1301 Clay St., 94612–5217. Ph., 510–637–3230. Fax, 510–637–3235. TTY, 510–637–3234.	Joyce A. Hendy
Oklahoma City, OK (AO)	Suite 1350, 210 Park Ave., 73102. Ph., 405–231–4911. Fax, 405–231–4140. TTY, 405–231–5745.	Alma Anderson
Philadelphia, PA (DO)	Suite 400, 21 S. 5th St., 19106–2515. Ph., 215–451–5800. Fax, 215–451–5804. TTY, 215–451–5814.	Marie M. Tomasso
Phoenix, AZ (DO)	Suite 690, 3300 N. Central Ave., 85012–2504. Ph., 602–640–5000. Fax, 602–640–5071. TTY, 602–640–5072.	Charles D. Burtner
Pittsburgh, PA (AO)	Suite 300, 1001 Liberty Ave., 15222–4187. Ph., 412–644–3444. Fax, 412–644–2664. TTY, 412–644–2720.	Eugene V. Nelson
Raleigh, NC (AO)	1309 Annapolis Dr., 27608–2129. Ph., 919–856–4064. Fax, 919–856–4151. TTY, 919–856–4296.	Richard E. Walz
Richmond, VA (AO)	Rm. 229, 3600 W. Broad St., 23230. Ph., 804–278–4651. Fax, 804–278–4660. TTY, 804–278–4654.	Gloria L. Underwood
San Antonio, TX (DO)	Suite 200, 5410 Fredericksburg Rd., 78229–3555. Ph., 210–229–4810. Fax, 210–229–4381. TTY, 210–229–4858.	Pedro Esquivel
San Diego, CA (AO)	Suite 1550, 401 B St., 92101. Ph., 619–557–7235. Fax, 619–557–7274. TTY, 619–557–7232.	Patrick Matarazzo
San Francisco, CA (DO)	Suite 500, 901 Market St., 94103. Ph., 415–356–5100. Fax, 415–356–5126. TTY, 415–356–5098.	Susan L. McDuffie
San Jose, CA (LO)	Suite 200, 96 N. 3d St., 95112. Ph., 408–291–7352. Fax, 408–291–4539. TTY, 408–291–7374.	(Vacancy)
Savannah, GA (LO)	Suite G, 410 Mall Blvd., 31406–4821. Ph., 912–652–4234. Fax, 912–652–4248. TTY, 912–652–4439.	Marvin C. Frazier
Seattle, WA (DO)	Suite 400, 909 First Ave., 98104–1061. Ph., 206–220–6883. Fax, 206–220–6911. TTY, 206–220–6882.	Jeanette M. Leino
St. Louis, MO (DO)	Rm. 8.100, 1222 Spruce St., 63103. Ph., 314–539–7800. Fax, 314–539–7894. TTY, 314–539–7803.	Lynn Bruner
Tampa, FL (AO)	Rm. 1020, 501 E. Polk St., 33602. Ph., 813–228–2310. Fax, 813–228–2841. TTY, 813–228–2003.	James D. Packwood, Jr.
Washington, DC (FO)	Suite 200, 1400 L St. NW., 20005. Ph., 202–275–7377. Fax, 202–275–6834. TTY, 202–275–7518.	Tulio Diaz, Jr.

Sources of Information

Electronic Access   Information regarding the programs, publications, and activities of the Commission is available through the Internet, at http://www.eeoc.gov/.

Employment   The Commission selects its employees from various examinations and registers, including mid- and senior-level registers, secretarial, typing, and stenographic registers, and the Equal Opportunity Specialist register. Employment inquiries or applications for positions in the headquarters office should be directed to the Office of Human Resources, Equal Employment Opportunity Commission, 1801 L Street NW., Washington, DC 20507 (phone, 202–663–4306), or contact the appropriate district office for district office positions.

General Inquiries   A nationwide toll-free telephone number links callers with the appropriate field office where charges may be filed. Phone, 800–669–4000. TTY, 800–669–6820.

Information About Survey Forms (EEO–1, 2, 3, 4, 5, and 6). Phone, 202–663–4958.

Media Inquiries   Office of Communications and Legislative Affairs, 1801 L Street NW., Washington, DC 20507. Phone, 202–663–4900.

Publications   Phone, 800–669–3362 (toll-free). TTY, 800–800–3302 (toll-free).

Reading Room   EEOC Library, 1801 L Street NW., Washington, DC 20507. Phone, 202-663–4630.

Speakers   Office of Communications and Legislative Affairs, 1801 L Street NW., Washington, DC 20507. Phone, 202–663–4900.

For further information, contact the Equal Employment Opportunity Commission, 1801 L Street NW., Washington, DC 20507. Phone, 202–663–4900. Internet, http:///www.eeoc.gov/.

EXPORT–IMPORT BANK OF THE UNITED STATES

811 Vermont Avenue NW., Washington, DC 20571
Phone, 800–565–EXIM. Internet, http://www.exim.gov/.

President and Chairman	JAMES A. HARMON
First Vice President and Vice Chair	JACKIE M. CLEGG
Director and Chief Operating Officer	JULIE D. BELAGA
Directors	MARIA LUISA HALEY, RITA M. RODRIGUEZ
Chief of Staff	ANDREA B. ADELMAN
Vice President and Counselor to the Chairman	CLYDE ROBINSON
Counselor to the Board	GLORIA B. CABE
Executive Vice President	ALLAN I. MENDELOWITZ
Chief Financial Officer and Chief Information Officer	JAMES K. HESS
General Counsel	KENNETH W. HANSEN
Coordinator Counsel, NIS and Central Europe	STEPHEN G. GLAZER
Group Manager, Structured Export Finance	JEFFREY L. MILLER
Group Manager, New and Small Business	WILLIAM W. REDWAY
Vice President, Aircraft Finance	ROBERT MORIN
Vice President, Americas	KENNETH M. TINSLEY
Deputy Vice President, Asia and Africa	DEBORAH THOMPSON
Vice President, Asset Management	CLEMENT K. MILLER, *Acting*
Vice President, Communications	DAVID W. CARTER
Vice President, Congressional and External Affairs	DAVID W. CARTER, *Acting*
Vice President, Country Risk Analysis	PETER GOSNELL, *Acting*
Vice President, Credit Administration	WALTER B. HILL, JR., *Acting*
Vice President, Engineering and Environment	JAMES A. MAHONEY, JR.
Vice President, NIS/Central Europe	LEROY M. LAROCHE, *Acting*
Vice President, Information Management	CANDELARIO TRUJILLO, JR.
Vice President, Insurance	PIPER STARR, *Acting*
Vice President, Policy, Planning, and Program Development	JAMES C. CRUSE
Vice President, Project Finance	BARBARA O'BOYLE
Vice President, Working Capital	SAM Z. ZYTCER
Director, Broker Relations and Product Development	ROBERT L. CHARAMELLA
Group Vice President, Resource Management	DELORES DE LA TORRE BARTNING
Director, Administrative Services	RALPH KAISER, *Acting*
Director, Equal Opportunity and Diversity Programs and Training	CYNTHIA B. WILSON
Director, Human Resources	DENNIS H. HEINS

The Export-Import Bank of the United States helps the private sector to create and maintain U.S. jobs by financing exports of the Nation's goods and services. To accomplish this mission, the Bank offers a variety of loan, guarantee, and insurance programs to support transactions that would not be awarded to U.S. companies without the Bank's assistance.

The Export-Import Bank (Ex-Im Bank), established in 1934, operates as an independent agency of the U.S. Government under the authority of the Export-Import Bank Act of 1945, as amended (12 U.S.C. 635 *et seq.*). Its Board of Directors consists of a President and Chairman, a First Vice President and Vice Chairman, and three other Directors, all of whom are appointed by the President with the advice and consent of the Senate.

Ex-Im Bank's mission is to help American exporters meet government-supported financing competition from other countries, so that U.S. exports can compete for overseas business on the basis of price, performance, and service. The Bank also fills gaps in the availability of commercial financing for creditworthy export transactions.

Ex-Im Bank is required to find a reasonable assurance of repayment for each transaction it supports. Its legislation requires it to meet the financing terms of competitor export credit agencies, but not to compete with commercial lenders. An export must have a minimum of 50 percent U.S. content in order to be eligible for Ex-Im Bank support. There is no maximum or minimum dollar limit for Ex-Im Bank financing. Legislation restricts the Bank's operation in some countries and its support for military goods and services.

Activities

Ex-Im Bank is authorized to have outstanding at any one time loans, guarantees, and insurance in aggregate amount not in excess of $75 billion. During fiscal year 1997, it authorized a total of $12.1 billion in financing, including a wide range of capital goods exports to developing countries.

Ex-Im Bank supports U.S. exporters through a range of diverse programs, which are offered under four broad categories of export financing:

—working capital guarantees, provided to lenders, so that they can provide creditworthy small- and medium-sized exporters with working capital they need to buy, build, or assemble products for export sale.

—export credit insurance which protects the exporter against both the commercial and political risks of a foreign buyer defaulting on payment. Ex-Im Bank offers a variety of policies: short- and medium-term, single- and multi-buyer, and small business and umbrella policies.

—loan guarantees which encourage sales to creditworthy foreign buyers by providing private sector lenders in medium- and long-term transactions with Ex-Im Bank guarantees against the political and commercial risks of nonpayment. Political-risk-only guarantees are also available.

—direct loans made to provide foreign buyers with competitive, fixed-rate medium- or long-term financing from Ex-Im Bank for their purchases from U.S. exporters. Direct loans carry the minimum interest rate allowed by the Organization for Economic Cooperation and Development.

Ex-Im Bank has initiated several new programs to broaden the range of customers and types of exporters it supports. The Environmental Exports Program provides enhanced financing terms for environmentally beneficial goods and services. Ex-Im Bank has also expanded its capabilities in the area of limited recourse project finance, and has adopted a policy of matching foreign tied-aid credits to ensure that U.S. exporters do not lose sales in critical emerging markets. In order to make its programs more readily available, Ex-Im Bank works closely with many State and local governments in its City/State Program.

Regional Offices

The Export-Import Bank operates five regional offices, listed in the table below.

Regional Offices—Export-Import Bank

Region	Address	Telephone	Fax
New York	Suite 635, 6 World Trade Ctr., New York, NY 10048	212–466–2950	212–466–2959
Miami	Suite 617, 5600 NW. 36th St., Miami, FL 33166	305–526–7425	305–526–7435
Chicago	Suite 2440, 55 W. Monroe St., Chicago, IL 60603	312–353–8081	312–353–8098
Houston	Suite 585, 1880 S. Dairy Ashford II, Houston, TX 77077	281–589–8182	281–589–8184
Los Angeles	Suite 1670, 1 World Trade Ctr., Long Beach, CA 90831	562–980–4580	562–980–4590

For further information, contact the Export-Import Bank, Business Development Office, 811 Vermont Avenue NW., Washington, DC 20571. Phone, 202–565–3900; or 800–565–EXIM (3946) (toll-free). Internet, http://www.exim.gov/.

FARM CREDIT ADMINISTRATION

1501 Farm Credit Drive, McLean, VA 22102–5090
Phone, 703–883–4000. Internet, http://www.fca.gov/.

Farm Credit Administration Board:

Chairman and Chief Executive Officer	MARSHA PYLE MARTIN
Members of the Board	DOYLE L. COOK, ANN JORGENSEN
Secretary to the Board	FLOYD J. FITHIAN

Staff:

Director, Office of Congressional and Public Affairs	EILEEN M. MCMAHON
General Counsel	JEAN NOONAN
Associate General Counsels	KATHLEEN V. BUFFON, VICTOR A. COHEN
Inspector General	ELDON W. STOEHR
Director, Office of Examination and Chief Examiner	ROLAND E. SMITH
Director, Office of Policy and Analysis	THOMAS G. MCKENZIE
Director, Office of Secondary Market Oversight	LARRY W. EDWARDS
Director, Office of Resources Management	DONALD P. CLARK

[For the Farm Credit Administration statement of organization, see the *Code of Federal Regulations,* Title 12, Parts 600 and 611]

The Farm Credit Administration is responsible for ensuring the safe and sound operation of the banks, associations, affiliated service organizations, and other entities that collectively comprise what is known as the Farm Credit System, and for protecting the interests of the public and those who borrow from Farm Credit institutions or invest in Farm Credit securities.

The Farm Credit Administration was established as an independent financial regulatory agency in the executive branch of the Federal Government by Executive Order 6084 of March 27, 1933. The Administration carries out its responsibilities by conducting examinations of the various Farm Credit lending institutions, which are Farm Credit Banks, the Bank for Cooperatives, the Agricultural Credit Bank, Federal Land Bank Associations, Production Credit Associations, Agricultural Credit Associations, and Federal Land Credit Associations. It also examines the service organizations owned by the Farm Credit lending institutions, as well as the National Consumer Cooperative Bank (also known as the National Cooperative Bank (NCB)) and its subsidiaries,

FARM CREDIT ADMINISTRATION

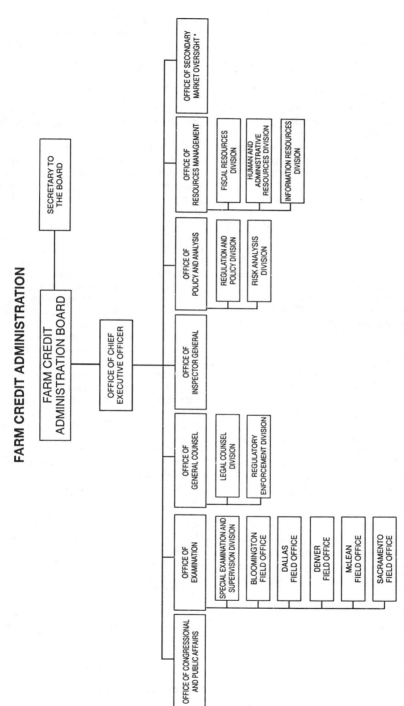

*Reports to the Board for policy and to the CEO for administration.

including the NCB Development Corporation.

FCA policymaking is vested in the Farm Credit Administration Board, whose three full-time members are appointed to 6-year terms by the President, with the advice and consent of the Senate. One member of the Board is designated by the President as Chairman and serves as the Administration's chief executive officer. The Board is responsible for approving rules and regulations, providing for the examination and regulation of and reporting by Farm Credit institutions, and establishing the policies under which the Administration operates. Board meetings are regularly held on the second Thursday of the month and are subject to the Government in the Sunshine Act. Public announcements of these meetings are published in the *Federal Register*.

The lending institutions of the Farm Credit System were established to provide adequate and dependable credit and closely related services to farmers, ranchers, and producers or harvesters of aquatic products; persons engaged in providing on-the-farm services; rural homeowners; and associations of farmers, ranchers, and producers or harvesters of aquatic products, or federations of such associations that operate on a cooperative basis and are engaged in marketing, processing, supply, or business service functions for the benefit of their members. Initially capitalized by the United States Government, the Farm Credit lending institutions are organized as cooperatives and are completely owned by their borrowers. The loan funds provided to borrowers by these institutions are obtained primarily through the sale of securities to investors in the Nation's capital markets.

The Agricultural Credit Act of 1987, as amended (12 U.S.C. 2279aa–1), established the Federal Agricultural Mortgage Corporation (commonly known as "Farmer Mac"). The Corporation, designated as part of the Farm Credit System, is a federally chartered instrumentality of the United States and promotes the development of a secondary market for agricultural real estate and rural housing loans. Farmer Mac also provides guarantees for the timely payment of principal and interest on securities, representing interests in or obligations backed by pools of agricultural real estate loans. The Administration is responsible for the examination and regulation of Farmer Mac to ensure the safety and soundness of its operations.

The Administration manages regulations under which Farm Credit institutions operate. These regulations implement the Farm Credit Act of 1971, as amended, and have the force and effect of law. Similar to other Federal regulators of financial institutions, the Administration's authorities include the power to issue cease-and-desist orders, to levy civil monetary penalties, to remove officers and directors of Farm Credit institutions, and to establish financial and operating reporting requirements. Although it is prohibited from participation in routine management or operations of Farm Credit institutions, the Administration is authorized to become involved in these institutions' management and operations when the Farm Credit Act or its regulations have been violated, when taking an action to correct an unsafe or unsound practice, or when assuming a formal conservatorship over an institution.

The Administration does not operate on funds appropriated by Congress. Its income is derived from assessments collected from the institutions it regulates and examines. In addition to the headquarters office located in McLean, VA, the Administration maintains 4 field offices located in Aurora, CO; Bloomington, MN; Irving, TX; and Sacramento, CA.

Authority for the organization and activities of the institutions comprising the cooperative Farm Credit System and that operate under the regulation of the Farm Credit Administration may be found in the Farm Credit Act of 1971, as amended (12 U.S.C. 2001).

Sources of Information

Inquiries for information on the following subjects may be directed to the specified office, Farm Credit Administration, 1501 Farm Credit Drive, McLean, VA 22102–5090.

Contracts and Procurement   Inquiries regarding the Administration's procurement and contracting activities should be directed in writing to Contracting and Procurement. Phone, 703–883–4145.

Employment   Inquiries regarding employment with the Administration should be directed to the Human

Resources Division. Phone, 703–883–4135.

Freedom of Information Requests Requests for agency records must be submitted in writing, clearly identified with "FOIA Request" and addressed to the Office of the General Counsel. Phone, 703–883–4020.

Publications   Publications and information on the Farm Credit Administration may be obtained by writing the Office of Congressional and Public Affairs. Phone, 703–883–4056.

For further information, contact the Office of Congressional and Public Affairs, Farm Credit Administration, 1501 Farm Credit Drive, McLean, VA 22102–5090. Phone, 703–883–4056. E-mail, info-line@fca.gov. Internet, http://www.fca.gov/.

FEDERAL COMMUNICATIONS COMMISSION

1919 M Street NW., Washington, DC 20554
Phone, 202–418–0200; 888–225–5322 (toll-free). TTY, 202–418–2555; 888–835–5322 (toll-free). Internet, http://www.fcc.gov/.

Chairman	WILLIAM E. KENNARD
Commissioners	HAROLD FURCHTGOTT-ROTH, SUSAN NESS, MICHAEL POWELL, GLORIA TRISTANI
Managing Director	ANDREW S. FISHEL
General Counsel	CHRISTOPHER J. WRIGHT
Inspector General	H. WALKER FEASTER III
Director, Office of Public Affairs	ELIZABETH ROSE
Director, Office of Legislative and Intergovernmental Affairs	SHERYL WILKERSON
Chief, International Bureau	REGINA KEENEY
Chief, Office of Plans and Policy	ROBERT M. PEPPER
Chief, Office of Administrative Law Judges	JOSEPH CHACHKIN, *Acting*
Chief, Mass Media Bureau	ROY J. STEWART
Chief, Common Carrier Bureau	RICHARD METZGER
Chief, Compliance and Information Bureau	RICHARD D. LEE
Chief, Wireless Telecommunications Bureau	DANIEL B. PHYTHYON
Chief, Cable Services Bureau	JOHN E. LOGAN, *Acting*
Director, Office of Communications Business Opportunities	CATHERINE SANDOVAL
Director, Office of Workplace Diversity	JACK W. GRAVELY
Chief, Office of Engineering and Technology	RICHARD M. SMITH

[For the Federal Communications Commission statement of organization, see the *Code of Federal Regulations,* Title 47, Part 0]

The Federal Communications Commission regulates interstate and foreign communications by radio, television, wire, satellite, and cable. It is responsible for the orderly development and operation of broadcast services and the provision of

rapid, efficient nationwide and worldwide telephone and telegraph services at reasonable rates. Its responsibilities also include the use of communications for promoting safety of life and property and for strengthening the national defense.

The Federal Communications Commission (FCC) was created by the Communications Act of 1934 (47 U.S.C. 151 *et seq.*) to regulate interstate and foreign communications by wire and radio in the public interest. The Commission was assigned additional regulatory jurisdiction under the provisions of the Communications Satellite Act of 1962 (47 U.S.C. 701–744), and a major overhaul of the Communications Act of 1934 was enacted with passage of the Telecommunications Act of 1996 (Public Law 104–104, 110 Stat. 56). The scope of FCC regulation includes radio and television broadcasting; telephone, telegraph, and cable television operation; two-way radio and radio operators; and satellite communication.

The Commission is composed of five members, who are appointed by the President with the advice and consent of the Senate. One of the members is designated by the President as Chairman.

The Commission's Office of the General Counsel reviews initial decisions, writes decisions, and assists the Commission and individual Commissioners in the disposition of matters arising in cases of adjudication, as defined in the Administrative Procedure Act (5 U.S.C. note prec. 551), that have been designated for hearings. The Commission's administrative law judges, qualified and appointed pursuant to the requirements of the Administrative Procedure Act, conduct evidentiary adjudicatory hearings and write initial decisions.

Activities

Mass Media   The Mass Media Bureau administers the regulatory program for amplitude modulation (AM), frequency modulation (FM), television, low-power TV, translators, multipoint distribution service (MDS), instructional TV, and auxiliary services. The Bureau issues construction permits, operating licenses, and renewals or transfers of such

broadcast licenses except for broadcast auxiliary services. It also oversees compliance by broadcasters with statutes and Commission policies.

For further information, contact the Mass Media Bureau. Phone, 202–418–2600.

Common Carrier Communications   The Common Carrier Bureau administers the regulatory program for interstate common carrier communications by telephone. Common carriers include companies, organizations, or individuals providing communications services to the public for hire, who must serve all who wish to use them at established rates. In providing interstate communications services, common carriers may employ landline wire or electrical or optical cable facilities.

For further information, contact the Common Carrier Bureau. Phone, 202–418–1500.

Wireless Telecommunications   The Wireless Telecommunications Bureau administers all domestic commercial and private wireless telecommunications programs and rules. The commercial wireless services include cellular, paging, personal communications, specialized mobile radio, air-ground, and basic exchange telecommunications services. The private wireless services generally serve the specialized internal communications needs of eligible users, and include the public safety, microwave, aviation, and marine services. Additionally, the Bureau serves as FCC's principal policy and administrative resource with regard to all spectrum auctions. It also implements the compulsory provisions of laws and treaties covering the use of radio for the safety of life and property at sea and in the air. The commercial and amateur radio operator programs are also administered by the Bureau.

For further information, contact the Wireless Telecommunications Bureau. Phone, 202–418–0600.

FEDERAL COMMUNICATIONS COMMISSION

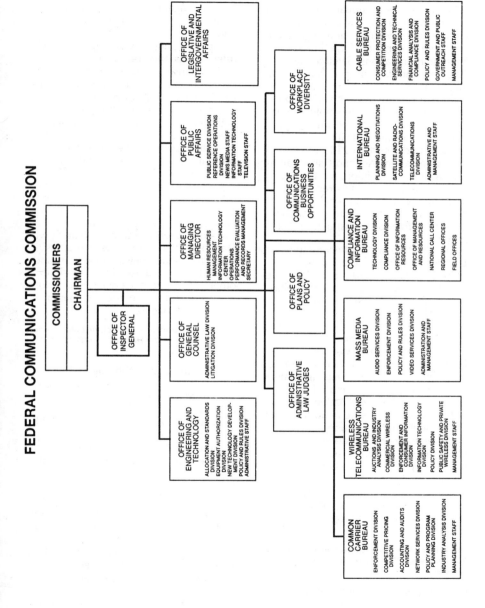

International Bureau The International Bureau manages all FCC international telecommunications and satellite programs and policies, and has the principal representational role on behalf of the Commission at international conferences, meetings, and negotiations. The Bureau consists of three divisions: Telecommunications, Satellite and Radiocommunication, and Planning and Negotiations.

The Telecommunications Division develops and administers policy, rules, and procedures for the regulations of telecommunications facilities and services under section 214 of the Communications Act and Cable Landing License Act. In addition, the Division develops and administers regulatory assistance and training programs in conjunction with the administration's global information infrastructure (GII) initiative.

The Satellite and Radiocommunication Division develops and administers policy, rules, standards, and procedures for licensing and regulation of satellite and earth station facilities, both international and domestic, and oversight of Comsat as the U.S. Signatory to INTELSAT and Inmarsat.

The Planning and Negotiations Division represents the Commission in negotiations of international agreements with Mexico, Canada, and other countries on the coordination and notification of domestic radio frequency assignments and resolution of international radio interference involving U.S. licensees. The Division processes license applications and conducts international coordination for high frequency (HF) international broadcast stations and acts on applications for delivery of broadcast programs to foreign stations.

For further information, contact the International Bureau. Phone, 202–418–0420, or 888–225–5322 (toll-free).

Cable Services Communications The Cable Services Bureau develops, recommends, and administers policies and programs for the regulation of cable television systems. The Bureau advises and recommends to the Commission, or acts for the Commission under delegated authority, in matters pertaining to the regulation and development of cable television. The Bureau is responsible for:

—investigating complaints and answering general inquiries from the public;

—planing and developing proposed rulemakings and conducting comprehensive studies and analyses (legal, social, and economic) of various petitions for policy or rule changes;

—processing applications for authorizations in the cable television relay service;

—participating in hearings before Administrative Law Judges and the Commission;

—conducting studies and compiling data relating to the cable industry for the Commission to develop and maintain an adequate regulatory program;

—collaborating and coordinating with State and local authorities in matters involving cable television systems; and

—advising and assisting the public, other Government agencies, and industry groups on cable television regulation and related matters.

For further information, contact the Cable Services Bureau. Phone, 202–418–7200 or 888–225–5322 (toll-free).

Engineering and Technology The Office of Engineering and Technology administers the Table of Frequency Allocations which specifies the frequency ranges that can be utilized by various radio services. The Office also administers the Experimental Radio Service and the Equipment Authorization Program. The Experimental Radio Service permits the public to experiment with new uses of radio frequencies. This allows development of radio equipment and exploration of new radio techniques prior to licensing under other regulatory programs. The Equipment Authorization Program includes several specific procedures by which the agency approves radio equipment as a prerequisite to importation, marketing, or use. The procedures involve either an FCC review of applications and accompanying test reports submitted by the applicants, or a self-authorization, whereby the manufacturer certifies that the product complies with the standards.

For further information, contact the Office of Engineering and Technology. Phone, 202–418–2470, or 888–225–5322 (toll-free).

Compliance Much of the investigative and enforcement work of the Commission is carried out by its field staff. The Compliance and Information Bureau has 3 regional offices and 16 field offices, as well as resident agents in

9 additional cities. It also operates a nationwide fleet of mobile radio direction-finding vehicles for technical enforcement purposes. The field staff, in effect, are the Commission's "eyes and ears" in detecting problems in the telecommunications environment and enforcing communications legislation and Commission rules.

For further information, contact the Compliance and Information Bureau. Phone, 888–225–5322 (toll-free).

Regional and Field Offices—Federal Communications Commission
Compliance and Information Bureau

Office	Address	Director
Regional Offices		
Kansas City, MO	Rm. 320, 8800 E. 63d St., 64133	Dennis P. Carlton
Park Ridge, IL	Rm. 306, 1550 Northwest Hwy., 60068–1460	Russell D. Monie
San Francisco, CA	Rm. 420, 3777 Depot Rd., Hayward, CA 94545–2756	Serge Marti-Volkoff
Field Offices		
Atlanta, GA	Rm. 320, 3575 Koger Blvd., Duluth 30136–4958	Fred L. Broce
Boston, MA	1 Batterymarch Pk., Quincy 02169–7495	Vincent F. Kajunski
Chicago, IL	Rm. 306, 1550 Northwest Hwy., Park Ridge 60068–1460	George M. Moffitt
Columbia, MD	P.O. Box 250, 21045–9998	Charles C. Magin
Dallas, TX	Rm. 1170, 9330 LBJ Fwy., 75243–3429	James D. Wells
Denver, CO	Rm. 860, 165 S. Union Blvd., 80228–2213	Leo E. Cirbo
Detroit, MI	24897 Hathaway St., Farmington Hills 48335–1552	James A. Bridgewater
Kansas City, MO	Rm. 320, 8800 E. 63d St., 64133–4895	Robert C. McKinney
Los Angeles, CA	Rm. 660, 1800 Studebaker Rd., Cerritos 90701–3684	James R. Zoulek
New Orleans, LA	Rm. 505, 800 W. Commerce Rd., 70123–3333	James C. Hawkins
New York, NY	201 Varick St., 10014–4870	Alexander J. Zimney
Philadelphia, PA	Rm. 404, 2300 E. Lincoln Hwy., Langhorne 19047–1859	John Rahtes
San Francisco, CA	Rm. 420, 3777 Depot Rd., Hayward 94545–2756	Thomas N. Van Stavern
San Diego, CA	Rm. 370, 4542 Ruffner St., 92111–2216	William H. Grisby
Seattle, WA	Rm. 312, 11410 NE. 122d Way, Kirkland 98034–6927	Dennis Anderson
Tampa, FL	Rm. 1215, 2203 N. Lois Ave., 33607–2356	Ralph M. Barlow

Sources of Information

Inquiries for information on the special subjects listed in the following paragraphs and those concerning licensing/grant requirements in the various services may be directed to the person or office specified or to the Chief of the Bureau or Office listed below as having responsibility for the service: Federal Communications Commission, 1919 M Street NW., Washington, DC 20554.

Licensing/Grant Responsibility—Federal Communications Commission

Service	Bureau or Office
All broadcasting (except broadcast auxiliary services) and multipoint distribution services	Mass Media Bureau
Cable television relay radio	Cable Services Bureau
Cable TV rate regulation	
Cable TV relay services (CARS)	
Cable signal leakage	
Cable television questions	
Registration of cable systems	
Common carrier radio	Common Carrier Bureau
Section 214 of FCC Act	
Equipment approval services:	Office of Engineering and Technology
Certification	
Type acceptance	
Type approval	
Notification	
Verification	

Licensing/Grant Responsibility—Federal Communications Commission—Continued

Service	Bureau or Office
Experimental radio	Office of Engineering and Technology
Amateur radio	Wireless Telecommunications Bureau
Auxiliary broadcast services	
Aviation radio	
Commercial radio operators	
Common carrier microwave services	
Interactive video and data services	
Land mobile radio	
Marine radio	
Private microwave radio	
International Section 214	International Bureau
International high frequency broadcast stations	
Satellite Earth stations	
Satellite space stations	
Section 325–C applications	

Advisory Committee Management
Direct inquiries to the Office of
Performance Evaluation and Records
Management. Phone, 202–418–0442.

Consumer Assistance   Inquiries
concerning general information on
Commission operations and public
participation in the decisionmaking
process should be addressed to the
Public Service Division, Room 254,
1919 M Street NW., Washington, DC
20554. Phone, 202–418–0200, or 888–
225–5322 (toll-free).

Contracts and Procurement   Direct
inquiries to the Chief, Acquisitions
Branch. Phone, 202–418–0930.

Electronic Access   Information
regarding the Commission is also
available electronically through the
Internet, at http://www.fcc.gov/.

Employment and Recruitment   The
Commission's programs require
attorneys, electronics engineers,
economists, accountants, administrative
management and computer specialists,
and clerical personnel. Requests for
employment information should be
directed to the Chief, Staffing and
Recruitment Service Center. Phone, 202–
418–0130.

Equal Employment Practices by Industry
Direct inquiries to the Public Service
Division. Phone, 888–225–5322 (toll-
free).

Internal Equal Employment Practices
Direct Inquiries to the Office of
Workplace Diversity. Phone, 202–418–
1799.

Ex-Parte Presentations   Information
concerning ex-parte presentations should
be directed to the Commission's Office
of General Counsel. Phone, 202–418–
1720.

Fees   Inquiries concerning the
Commission's Fee Program should be
addressed to the Public Service Division,
Room 254, 1919 M Street NW.,
Washington, DC 20554. Phone, 888–
225–5322 (toll-free) or 202–418–0200.

Freedom of Information Act Requests
Requests should be directed to the
Managing Director. Phone, 202–418–
1919.

**Information Available for Public
Inspection**   At the Commission's
headquarters office in Washington, DC,
dockets concerning rulemaking and
adjudicatory matters, copies of
applications for licenses and grants, and
reports required to be filed by licensees
and cable system operators are
maintained in the public reference
rooms (some reports are by law held
confidential). The Library has on file
Commission rules and regulations
(phone, 202–418–0450). General
information is also available through the
Commission's fax-on-demand (phone,
202–418–2830).

In addition to the information
available at the Commission, each
broadcasting station makes available for
public reference certain information
pertaining to the operation of the station,
a current copy of the application filed

for license, and nonconfidential reports filed with the Commission.

Publications The Office of Public Affairs distributes publications, public notices, and press releases. Phone, 202–418–0500.

For further information, contact the Public Service Division, Federal Communications Commission, 1919 M Street NW., Washington, DC 20554. Phone, 202–418–0200, or 888–522–5322. TTY, 202–418–2555, or 888–835–5322. Internet, http://www.fcc.gov/.

FEDERAL DEPOSIT INSURANCE CORPORATION

550 Seventeenth Street NW., Washington, DC 20429
Phone, 202–393–8400. Internet, http://www.fdic.gov/.

Board of Directors:

Chairman	(VACANCY)
Vice Chairman	ANDREW C. HOVE, JR., *Acting*
Directors:	
(Comptroller of the Currency)	JULIE WILLIAMS, *Acting*
(Director, Office of Thrift Supervision)	ELLEN S. SEIDMAN
Appointive Director	JOSEPH H. NEELY

Officials:

Deputy to the Chairman and Chief Operating Officer	DENNIS F. GEER
Chief Financial Officer	PAUL L. SACHTLEBEN
Deputy to the Vice Chairman	ROGER A. HOOD
Deputy to the Director (Comptroller of the Currency)	THOMAS E. ZEMKE
Deputy to the Director (Office of Thrift Supervision)	WALTER B. MASON
Deputy to the Director (Appointive)	A. DAVID MEADOWS
Executive Secretary	ROBERT E. FELDMAN
General Counsel	WILLIAM F. KROENER III
Director, Division of Administration	JANE L. SARTORI
Director, Division of Compliance and Consumer Affairs	CARMEN J. SULLIVAN
Director, Division of Finance	PAUL L. SACHTLEBEN
Director, Division of Information Resources Management	DONALD C. DEMITROS
Director, Division of Insurance	ARTHUR J. MURTON
Director, Division of Research and Statistics	WILLIAM R. WATSON
Director, Division of Resolutions and Receiverships	JOHN F. BOVENZI
Director, Division of Supervision	NICHOLAS J. KETCHA, JR.
Director, Office of Corporate Communications	PHIL BATTEY
Director, Office of Diversity and Economic Opportunity	JO-ANN HENRY
Director, Office of Internal Control Management	VIJAY DESHPANDE
Director, Office of Legislative Affairs	ALICE C. GOODMAN
Director, Office of Ombudsman	ARLEAS UPTON KEA

Director, Office of Policy Development	ROBERT W. RUSSELL
Inspector General	GASTON L. GIANNI, JR.

The Federal Deposit Insurance Corporation promotes and preserves public confidence in U.S. financial institutions by insuring bank and thrift deposits up to the legal limit of $100,000; by periodically examining State-chartered banks that are not members of the Federal Reserve System for safety and soundness as well as compliance with consumer protection laws; and by liquidating assets of failed institutions to reimburse the insurance funds for the cost of failures.

The Federal Deposit Insurance Corporation (FDIC) was established under the Banking Act of 1933 in response to numerous bank failures during the Great Depression. The Corporation began insuring banks on January 1, 1934. Congress has increased the limit on deposit insurance five times since 1934, the most current level being $100,000.

The Corporation does not operate on funds appropriated by Congress. Its income is derived from assessments on deposits held by insured banks and from interest on the required investment of its surplus funds in Government securities. It also has authority to borrow from the Treasury up to $30 billion for insurance purposes.

Management of FDIC consists of a Board of Directors that includes the Chairman, Vice Chairman, and Appointive Director. The Comptroller of the Currency, whose office supervises federally chartered or national banks, and the Director of the Office of Thrift Supervision, which supervises federally chartered savings associations, are also members of the Board. All five Board members are appointed by the President and confirmed by the Senate, with no more than three being from the same political party.

Activities

The Federal Deposit Insurance Corporation insures about $3 trillion of U.S. bank and thrift deposits. The insurance funds are composed of insurance premiums paid by banks and savings associations and the interest on the investment of those premiums in U.S. Government securities, as required by law. Banks pay premiums to the Bank Insurance Fund (BIF), while savings associations pay premiums to the Savings Association Insurance Fund (SAIF). Premiums are determined by an institution's level of capitalization and potential risk to its insurance fund.

The Corporation examines about 6,000 commercial and savings banks that are not members of the Federal Reserve System, called State-chartered nonmember banks. The Corporation also has back-up authority to examine other types of FDIC-insured institutions. The two types of examinations conducted are for safety and soundness, and for compliance with applicable consumer laws such as Truth in Lending, the Home Mortgage Disclosure Act, and the Community Reinvestment Act. Examinations are performed on the institution's premises and off-site through computer data analysis.

A failed bank is generally closed by its chartering authority, and FDIC is named receiver. In that capacity, FDIC attempts to locate a healthy institution to acquire the failed entity. If an acquirer cannot be found, FDIC pays depositors the amount of their insured funds, usually by the next business day following the closing. Depositors with funds that exceed the insurance limit often receive an advance dividend, which is a portion of their uninsured funds that is determined by an estimate of the future proceeds from liquidating the failed bank's remaining assets. Depositors with funds in a failed bank that exceed the insurance limit receive a receivership certificate for those funds and partial payments of their uninsured funds as asset liquidation permits.

In addition to its insurance, supervisory, and liquidation responsibilities, FDIC performs other functions relating to State nonmember banks, including:

FEDERAL DEPOSIT INSURANCE CORPORATION

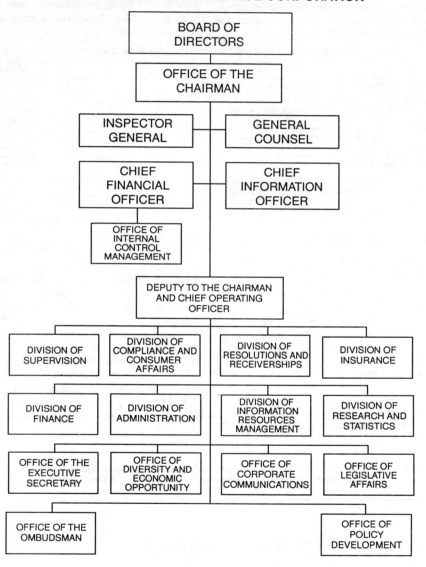

—approval or disapproval of mergers, consolidations, and acquisitions where the resulting bank is an insured State nonmember;

—approval or disapproval of a proposal by a bank to establish and operate a new branch, close an existing branch, or move its main office from one location to another;

—issuance of enforcement actions, including cease-and-desist orders, for specific violations or practices requiring corrective action; and

—reporting changes in ownership or control of a bank, and reporting any loan secured by 25 percent or more of the bank's stock.

Regional Offices—Federal Deposit Insurance Corporation

Region/Address	Telephone
Supervision/Compliance and Consumer Affairs.	
Atlanta, GA (Suite 1600, 1201 W. Peachtree St. NE., 30309)	404–817–1300
Boston, MA (15 Braintree Hill Office Park, Braintree, MA 02184)	781–794–5500
Chicago, IL (Suite 3600, 500 W. Monroe St., 60661)	312–382–7500
Dallas, TX (Suite 1900, 1910 Pacific Ave., 75201)	214–220–3342
Kansas City, MO (Suite 1500, 2345 Grand Ave., 64108)	816–234–8000
Memphis, TN (Suite 1900, 5100 Poplar Ave., 38137)	901–685–1603
New York, NY (19th Fl., 452 5th Ave., 10018)	212–704–1200
San Francisco, CA (Suite 2300, 25 Ecker St., 94105)	415–546–0160
Resolutions and Receiverships.	
NORTHEAST (101 E. River Dr., E. Hartford, CT 06108)	860–291–4000
SOUTHWEST (1910 Pacific Ave., Dallas, TX 75201)	214–754–0098
WESTERN (4 Park Plz., Jamboree Ctr., Irvine, CA 92714)	714–263–7100

Sources of Information

Consumer Information   Information about deposit insurance and other consumer matters is available from the Division of Compliance and Consumer Affairs (DCA) at the same address or any regional office, or DCA's hotline, 800–934–3342. For a copy of a bank's quarterly Report of Condition, call 800–945–2186. E-mail, consumer@fdic.gov.

General Inquiries   Written requests for general information may be directed to the Office of Corporate Communications, Federal Deposit Insurance Corporation, 550 Seventeenth Street NW., Washington, DC 20429.

Public Records   Inquiries about the types of records available to the public, including records available under the Freedom of Information Act, should be directed to the Office of the Executive Secretary (phone, 202–898–3811) or any regional office.

Publications   Publications, press releases, congressional testimony, directives to financial institutions, and other documents are available through the Public Information Center. Phone, 800–276–6003. E-mail, publicinfo@fdic.gov. Internet, http://www.fdic.gov/.

For further information, contact the Corporate Communications Office, Federal Deposit Insurance Corporation, 550 Seventeenth Street NW., Washington, DC 20429. Phone, 202–898–6993.

FEDERAL ELECTION COMMISSION

999 E Street NW., Washington, DC 20463
Phones: 202–694–1100; 800–424–9530 (toll-free)

Chairman	JOAN D. AIKENS
Vice Chairman	SCOTT E. THOMAS

Commissioners	LEE ANN ELLIOTT, DANNY L. MCDONALD, JOHN WARREN MCGARRY, (VACANCY)
Statutory Officers:	
Staff Director	JOHN C. SURINA
General Counsel	LAWRENCE M. NOBLE
Inspector General	LYNNE A. MCFARLAND

The Federal Election Commission has exclusive jurisdiction in the administration and civil enforcement of laws regulating the acquisition and expenditure of campaign funds to ensure compliance by participants in the Federal election campaign process. Its chief mission is to provide public disclosure of campaign finance activities and effect voluntary compliance by providing the public with information on the laws and regulations concerning campaign finance.

The Federal Election Commission is an independent agency established by section 309 of the Federal Election Campaign Act of 1971, as amended (2 U.S.C. 437c). It is composed of six Commissioners appointed by the President with the advice and consent of the Senate. The act also provides for three statutory officers—the Staff Director, the General Counsel, and the Inspector General—who are appointed by the Commission.

Activities

The Commission administers and enforces the Federal Election Campaign Act of 1971, as amended (2 U.S.C. 431 *et seq.*), and the Revenue Act, as amended (26 U.S.C. 1 *et seq.*). These laws provide for the public funding of Presidential elections, public disclosure of the financial activities of political committees involved in Federal elections, and limitations and prohibitions on contributions and expenditures made to influence Federal elections (Presidency, Senate, and House of Representatives).

Public Funding of Presidential Elections The Commission oversees the public financing of Presidential elections by certifying Federal payments to primary candidates, general election nominees, and national nominating conventions. It also audits recipients of Federal funds and may require repayments to the U.S. Treasury if a committee makes nonqualified campaign expenditures.

Disclosure The Commission ensures the public disclosure of the campaign finance activities reported by political committees supporting Federal candidates. Committee reports, filed regularly, disclose where campaign money comes from and how it is spent. The Commission places reports on the public record within 48 hours after they are received and computerizes the data contained in the reports.

Sources of Information

Clearinghouse on Election Administration The Clearinghouse compiles and disseminates election administration information related to Federal elections. It also conducts independent contract studies on the administration of elections. For further information, call 202–694–1095, or 800–424–9530 (toll-free).

Congressional Affairs Office This Office serves as primary liaison with Congress and executive branch agencies. The Office is responsible for keeping Members of Congress informed about Commission decisions and, in turn, for informing the Commission on legislative developments. For further information, call 202–694–1006, or 800–424–9530 (toll-free).

Employment Inquiries regarding employment opportunities should be directed to the Director, Personnel and Labor Management Relations. Phone, 202–694–1080, or 800–424–9530 (toll-free).

General Inquiries   The Information Services Division provides information and assistance to Federal candidates, political committees, and the general public. This division answers questions on campaign finance laws, conducts workshops and seminars on the law, and provides publications and forms. For information or materials, call 202–694–1100, or 800–424–9530 (toll-free).

Media Inquiries   The Press Office answers inquiries from print and broadcast media sources around the country, issues press releases on Commission actions and statistical data, responds to informational requests, and distributes other materials. All persons representing media should direct inquiries to the Press Office. Phone, 202–694–1220, or 800–424–9530 (toll-free).

Public Records   The Office of Public Records, located at 999 E Street NW., Washington, DC, provides space for public inspection of all reports and statements relating to campaign finance since 1972. It is open weekdays from 9 a.m. to 5 p.m. and has extended hours during peak election periods. The public is invited to visit the Office or obtain information by calling 202–694–1120, or 800–424–9530 (toll-free).

Reading Room   The library contains a collection of basic legal research resources, with emphasis on political campaign financing, corporate and labor political activity, and campaign finance reform. It is open to the public on weekdays between 9 a.m. and 5 p.m. For further information, call 202–694–1600, or 800–424–9530 (toll-free).

For further information, contact Information Services, Federal Election Commission, 999 E Street NW., Washington, DC 20463. Phone, 202–694–1100; or 800–424–9530 (toll-free).

FEDERAL EMERGENCY MANAGEMENT AGENCY

500 C Street SW., Washington, DC 20472
Phone, 202–646–4600

Director	JAMES LEE WITT
Deputy Director	(VACANCY)
Chief of Staff	JANE BULLOCK
General Counsel	ERNIE ABBOTT
Chief Financial Officer	GARY JOHNSON
Inspector General	GEORGE OPFER
Director of Strategic Communications	MAURICE F. GOODMAN
Director, Office of Congressional and Legislative Affairs	MARTHA S. BRADDOCK
Director, Office of Emergency Information and Media Affairs	VALLEE BUNTING
Associate Director, Response and Recovery Directorate	LACY E. SUITER
Associate Director, Information Technology Services Directorate	CLAY G. HOLLISTER
Associate Director, Mitigation Directorate	MICHAEL ARMSTRONG
Associate Director, Preparedness, Training and Exercises Directorate	KAY GOSS
Associate Director, Operations Support Directorate	BRUCE CAMPBELL
Administrator, Federal Insurance Administration	JO ANN HOWARD

Administrator, United States Fire   CARRYE BROWN
Administration

[For the Federal Emergency Management Agency statement of organization, see the *Code of Federal Regulations,* Title 44, Part 2]

The Federal Emergency Management Agency is the central agency within the Federal Government for emergency planning, preparedness, mitigation, response, and recovery. Working closely with State and local governments, the Agency funds emergency programs, offers technical guidance and training, and deploys Federal resources in times of catastrophic disaster. These coordinated activities ensure a broad-based program to protect life and property and provide recovery assistance after a disaster.

The Federal Emergency Management Agency (FEMA) was established by Executive Order 12127 of March 31, 1979, consolidating the Nation's emergency-related programs.

The Agency reports directly to the White House and manages the President's Disaster Relief Fund, the source of most Federal funding assistance after major disasters. Agency programs include response to and recovery from major natural disasters and human-caused emergencies, emergency management planning, flood-plain management, hazardous materials planning, dam safety, and multihazard response planning. Other activities include off-site planning for emergencies at commercial nuclear power plants and the Army's chemical stockpile sites, emergency food and shelter funding for the homeless, plans to ensure the continuity of the Federal Government during national security emergencies, and Federal response to the consequences of major terrorist incidents.

The U.S. Fire Administration (USFA) and its National Fire Academy (NFA) are a part of FEMA, providing national leadership in fire safety and prevention. The U.S. Fire Administration has responsibility for all fire and emergency medical service programs and training activities. The Federal Insurance Administration (FIA) is also a part of FEMA and manages the National Flood Insurance Program and crime insurance programs. The Emergency Management Institute (EMI) at Emmitsburg, Maryland, offers centralized professional courses for the Nation's emergency managers.

The Agency is responsible for coordinating Federal efforts to reduce the loss of life and property through a comprehensive risk-based, all-hazards emergency management program of mitigation, preparedness, response, and recovery. The Agency also works to assure the effectiveness and the availability of all-hazard systems and resources in coping with manmade and natural disasters; consolidates the programs aimed at preventing and mitigating the effects of potential disasters with the programs designed to deal with the disasters once they occur; coordinates and plans for the emergency deployment of resources that are used on a routine basis by Federal agencies; and helps to coordinate preparedness programs with State and local governments, private industry, and voluntary organizations. In addition, FEMA provides a Federal focus on fire prevention and public fire safety education.

Activities

The principal activities of FEMA include:
Response and Recovery This activity provides for the development and maintenance of an integrated operational capability to respond to and recover from the consequences of a disaster, regardless of its cause, in partnership with other Federal agencies, State and local governments, volunteer organizations, and the private sector.
Preparedness, Training, and Exercises This activity provides policy guidance, financial and technical assistance, training, and exercise support required to establish or enhance all-hazard, risk-

FEDERAL EMERGENCY MANAGEMENT AGENCY

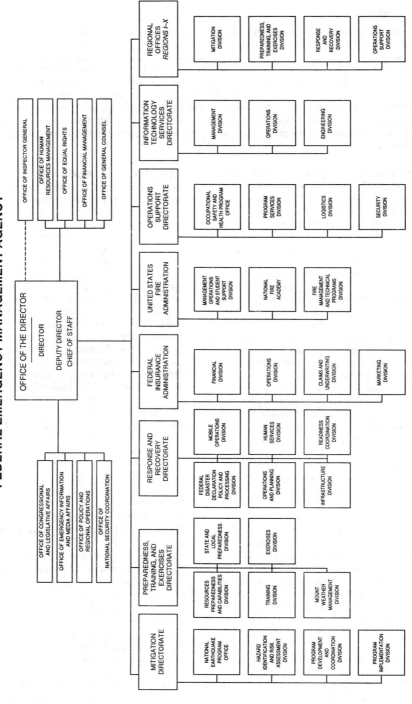

based emergency management capabilities of Federal, State, and local governments. In addition, this activity maintains a family protection program, utilizing private sector and volunteer organizations to encourage and assist families and neighborhoods to take actions to increase their emergency preparedness capabilities.

Fire Prevention and Training This activity prepares Federal, State, and local officials, their staffs, emergency first responders, volunteer groups, and the public to meet the responsibilities of domestic emergencies through planning, mitigation, preparedness, response, and recovery. Educational programs are provided through the National Fire Academy at the National Emergency Training Center and through the field fire training delivery systems.

Operations Support This activity provides direct support and services which address the common needs of all agency programs, such as administration, acquisition, logistics, information systems, security, and specialized capabilities and integration of the FEMA-wide networks.

Mitigation Programs This activity provides for the development, coordination, and implementation of policies, plans, and programs to eliminate or reduce the long-term risk to life and property from natural hazards such as floods, earthquakes, hurricanes, and dam failures. A goal of this activity is to encourage and foster mitigation strategies at the State and local levels.

Information Technology Services This activity provides leadership and direction for management of information resources, ADP, telecommunications, and systems to accomplish the agency's mission. It provides direct support and services to FEMA's all-hazards emergency management program of mitigation, preparedness, and response and recovery.

Executive Direction This activity develops strategies to address public information issues and provides staff and supporting resources for the general management and administration of the Agency in legal affairs, congressional affairs, emergency information and public affairs, policy development, national security, personnel, and financial management.

Regional Offices

Ten regional offices primarily carry out FEMA's programs at the regional, State, and local levels. The regional offices are responsible for accomplishing the national program goals and objectives of the Agency and supporting development of national policy.

Regional Offices—Federal Emergency Management Agency

Region/Address	Telephone
Atlanta, GA (3003 Chamblee-Tucker Rd., 30341)	770–220–5200
Boston, MA (Rm. 442, J.W. McCormack Post Office & Courthouse Bldg., 02109–4595)	617–223–9540
Bothell, WA (Federal Regional Ctr., 130 228th St. SW., 98021–9796)	206–487–4765
Chicago, IL (4th Fl., 175 W. Jackson Blvd., 60604–2698)	312–408–5504
Denton, TX (Federal Regional Ctr., 800 N. Loop 288, 76201–3698)	817–898–5104
Denver, CO (Bldg. 710, Denver Federal Ctr., Box 25267, 80225–0267)	303–235–4812
Kansas City, MO (Suite 900, 2323 Grand Blvd., 64108–2670)	816–283–7061
New York, NY (Rm. 1337, 26 Federal Plz., 10278–0002)	212–225–7209
Philadelphia, PA (2d Fl., Liberty Sq. Bldg., 105 S. 7th St., 19106–3316)	215–931–5608
San Francisco, CA (Bldg. 105, Presidio of San Francisco, 94129–1250)	415–923–7105

Sources of Information

Inquiries on the following subjects should be directed to the appropriate office of the Federal Emergency Management Agency, 500 C Street SW., Washington, DC 20472.

Acquisition Services Office of Acquisition Management. Phone, 202–646–4168.

Employment Office of Human Resources Management. Phone, 202–646–4040.

Freedom of Information Act Requests
Office of General Counsel. Phone, 202–
646–3840.

For further information, contact the Office of Emergency Information and Media Affairs, Federal Emergency Management Agency, 500 C Street SW., Washington, DC 20472. Phone, 202–646–4600.

FEDERAL HOUSING FINANCE BOARD

1777 F Street NW., Washington, DC 20006
Phone, 202–408–2500. Internet, http://www.fhfb.gov/.

Board of Directors:	
Chairman	BRUCE A. MORRISON
Members:	J. TIMOTHY O'NEILL, (2 VACANCIES)
(Secretary of Housing and Urban Development, *ex officio*)	ANDREW M. CUOMO
Housing and Urban Development Secretary's Designee to the Board	ART AGNOS
Special Assistant to the Chairman	STEPHEN P. HUDAK
Executive Assistant to the HUD Secretary	JAMES H. GRAY
Assistant to Board Director	JULIE FALLON STANTON
Officials:	
Managing Director	WILLIAM W. GINSBERG
Inspector General	EDWARD KELLEY
General Counsel	DEBORAH F. SILBERMAN
Director, Office of Supervision	MITCHELL BERNS
Director, Office of Policy	JAMES L. BOTHWELL
Director, Office of Congressional Affairs	RANDALL H. MCFARLANE
Director, Office of Public Affairs	NAOMI P. SALUS
Director, Office of Resource Management	BARBARA L. FISHER
Director, Office of Strategic Planning	KAREN H. CROSBY
Secretary to the Board	ELAINE L. BAKER

[For the Federal Housing Finance Board statement of organization, see the *Code of Federal Regulations*, Title 12, Part 900]

The Federal Housing Finance Board is responsible for the administration and enforcement of the Federal Home Loan Bank Act, as amended.

The Federal Housing Finance Board (Finance Board) was established on August 9, 1989, by the Federal Home Loan Bank Act, as amended by the Financial Institutions Reform, Recovery, and Enforcement Act of 1989 (FIRREA) (12 U.S.C. 1421 *et seq.*), as an independent regulatory agency in the executive branch. The Finance Board succeeded the Federal Home Loan Bank Board for those functions transferred to it by FIRREA.

The Finance Board is governed by a five-member Board of Directors. Four members are appointed by the President with the advice and consent of the Senate for 7-year terms; one of the four is designated as Chairman. The Secretary of the Department of Housing and Urban Development is the fifth member and serves in an *ex officio* capacity.

The Finance Board supervises the 12 Federal Home Loan Banks created in 1932 by the Federal Home Loan Bank

FEDERAL HOUSING FINANCE BOARD

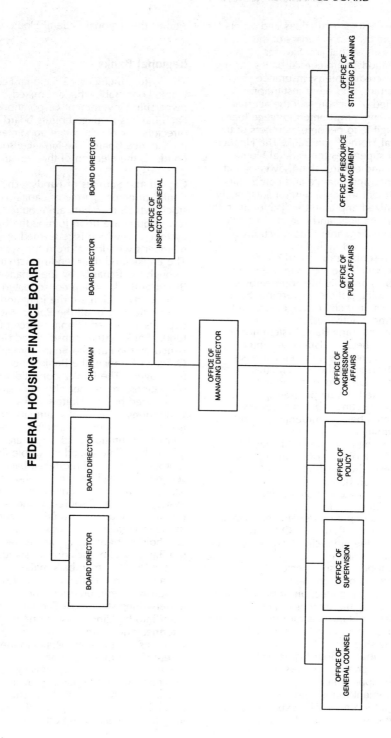

Act and issues regulations and orders for carrying out the purposes of the provisions of that act. Savings associations, commercial banks, savings banks, credit unions, insurance companies, and other institutions specified in section 4 of the act that make long-term home-mortgage loans are eligible to become members of the Federal Home Loan Bank. The Finance Board supervises the Federal Home Loan Banks and ensures that they carry out their housing finance and community investment mission, remain adequately capitalized and able to raise funds in the capital markets, and operate in a safe and sound manner. The functions of the Finance Board include:

—prescribing rules and conditions under which the Banks may lend to members and eligible nonmembers;

—issuing policies governing the Bank System's financial management and investment activities;

—maintaining Bank System financial and membership data bases and preparing reports on a regular basis;

—overseeing the implementation of the community investment and affordable housing programs;

—conducting a biennial review of each member's community support performance;

—issuing consolidated Federal Home Loan Bank obligations which are joint and several obligations of all Federal Home Loan Banks;

—annually examining each Federal Home Loan Bank;

—requiring an independent financial audit of each Bank, the Office of Finance, the Financing Corporation, and the Bank System;

—appointing six directors to the board of directors of each Bank and conducting the election of the remaining directors by the members; and

—setting standards for the review and approval of applications for Bank membership.

The Finance Board is not subject to the appropriation process. Its funds are neither appropriated nor derived from Government funds, and are not subject to apportionment. The expenses of the Finance Board are paid by assessment against the regional Federal Home Loan Banks.

Regional Banks

The System includes 12 regional Federal Home Loan Banks that are mixed-ownership Government corporations. Each Bank is managed by its board of directors, six of whom are appointed by the Finance Board. The Finance Board conducts the election of the remaining directors.

Capital and Sources of Funds The Banks' principal source of capital is stock, which members are required by law to purchase upon joining the Bank System, and which is redeemed upon a member's withdrawal from the System. The Banks fund their lending activity through the issuance by the Finance Board of Bank System consolidated obligations, which are the joint and several liability of all the Banks. Member deposits are an additional source of funds. Bank System consolidated debt is issued by the Finance Board through the Office of Finance, the Bank System's fiscal agent. The Banks' consolidated obligations are neither obligations of, nor guaranteed by, the United States.

Operations The Banks' primary activity is extending secured loans (advances) to member institutions. Advances are generally collateralized by whole first mortgage loans and mortgage-backed securities, as well as other high-quality assets. In making advances, the Bank System serves as a source of short- and long-term funds for institutions operating in the mortgage markets as originators and holders of mortgage assets. Because the Bank System does not set standards for the loans its members make, members have the flexibility to develop responsive credit products and underwriting standards. The Banks also enter into hedging transactions as intermediaries with their members, which assists the members with their asset-liability management.

Under the Affordable Housing Program (AHP), the Banks provide subsidized advances or direct subsidies to Bank members engaged in lending for long-term owner-occupied and affordable rental housing targeted to households with very low, low, or moderate incomes. This competitive program is financed from a specified percentage of each Bank's previous year's net income. The greater of $100 million or 10 percent of the previous year's net income is available for the program.

Under the Community Investment Program (CIP), each Bank provides advances priced at the Bank's cost of consolidated obligations of comparable maturities plus reasonable administrative costs, to members engaged in community-oriented mortgage lending. Advances are used for loans to finance rental and owner-occupied housing for families whose incomes do not exceed 115 percent of area median income and commercial and economic development activities that benefit low- and moderate-income families or that are located in low- and moderate-income neighborhoods.

To maintain access to long-term advances, Bank members must establish reasonable commitments to residential lending and community support activities. Every 2 years, the Finance Board reviews the community support performance of each member by taking into account factors such as each

member's Community Reinvestment Act performance and its lending to first-time homebuyers. The Banks provide technical assistance to their members in meeting the community support standards.

Financing Corporation

The Financing Corporation (FICO) was established by the Competitive Equality Banking Act of 1987 (12 U.S.C. 1441) with the sole purpose of issuing and servicing bonds, the proceeds of which were used to fund thrift resolutions. The principal on the bonds was defeased with capital contributions from the Banks. The Corporation has a three-member directorate, consisting of the Managing Director of the Office of Finance and two Federal Home Loan Bank presidents.

The Financing Corporation operates subject to the regulatory authority of the Federal Housing Finance Board.

Sources of Information

Requests for information relating to human resources and procurement should be sent to the Office of Resource Management, at the address listed below.

For further information, contact the Executive Secretariat, Federal Housing Finance Board, 1777 F Street NW., Washington, DC 20006. Phone, 202–408–2500. Fax, 202–408–2895. Internet, http://www.fhfb.gov/.

FEDERAL LABOR RELATIONS AUTHORITY

607 Fourteenth Street NW., Washington, DC 20424–0001
Phone, 202–482–6560. Internet, http://www.flra.gov/.

Chair	PHYLLIS N. SEGAL
Chief Counsel	SUSAN D. MCCLUSKEY
Director of External Affairs	KIMBERLY A. WEAVER
Member	DALE CABANISS
Chief Counsel	STEVEN H. SVARTZ
Member	DONALD S. WASSERMAN
Chief Counsel	ALICE BODLEY
Chief Administrative Law Judge	SAMUEL A. CHAITOVITZ
Solicitor	DAVID M. SMITH
Executive Director	SOLLY J. THOMAS, JR.

Assistant to the Executive Director	HAROLD D. KESSLER
Inspector General	FRANCINE C. EICHLER
General Counsel	JOSEPH SWERDZEWSKI
Deputy General Counsel	DAVID L. FEDER
Director of Operations and Resources Management	CLYDE B. BLANDFORD, JR.
Deputy Director of Operations, Field Management	NANCY A. SPEIGHT
Director of Appeals and Special Programs	CAROL W. POPE
Director, Collaboration and Alternative Dispute Resolution Program	FERN J. FEIL

Federal Service Impasses Panel

Chair	BETTY BOLDEN
Members	GILBERT CARRILLO, BONNIE P. CASTREY, DOLLY M. GEE, EDWARD F. HARTFIELD, MARY E. JACKSTEIT, STANLEY M. FISHER
Executive Director	H. JOSEPH SCHIMANSKY

Foreign Service Labor Relations Board

Chair	PHYLLIS N. SEGAL
Members	TIA SCHNEIDER DENENBERG, RICHARD I. BLOCH
General Counsel	JOSEPH SWERDZEWSKI

Foreign Service Impasse Disputes Panel

Chair	THOMAS COLOSI
Members	BETTY BOLDEN, DAVID GEISS, GEORGE LANNON, DOROTHY YOUNG

The Federal Labor Relations Authority oversees the Federal service labor-management relations program. It administers the law that protects the right of employees of the Federal Government to organize, bargain collectively, and participate through labor organizations of their own choosing in decisions affecting them. The Authority also ensures compliance with the statutory rights and obligations of Federal employees and the labor organizations that represent them in their dealings with Federal agencies.

The Federal Labor Relations Authority was created as an independent establishment by Reorganization Plan No. 2 of 1978 (5 U.S.C. app.), effective January 1, 1979, pursuant to Executive Order 12107 of December 28, 1978, to consolidate the central policymaking functions in Federal labor-management relations. Its duties and authority are specified in title VII (Federal Service Labor-Management Relations) of the Civil Service Reform Act of 1978 (5 U.S.C. 7101–7135).

Activities

The Authority provides leadership in establishing policies and guidance relating to the Federal service labor-management relations program. In addition, it determines the appropriateness of bargaining units, supervises or conducts representation elections, and prescribes criteria and resolves issues relating to the granting of consultation rights to labor organizations with respect to internal agency policies and governmentwide rules and regulations. It also resolves negotiability disputes, unfair labor practice complaints, and exceptions to arbitration

FEDERAL LABOR RELATIONS AUTHORITY

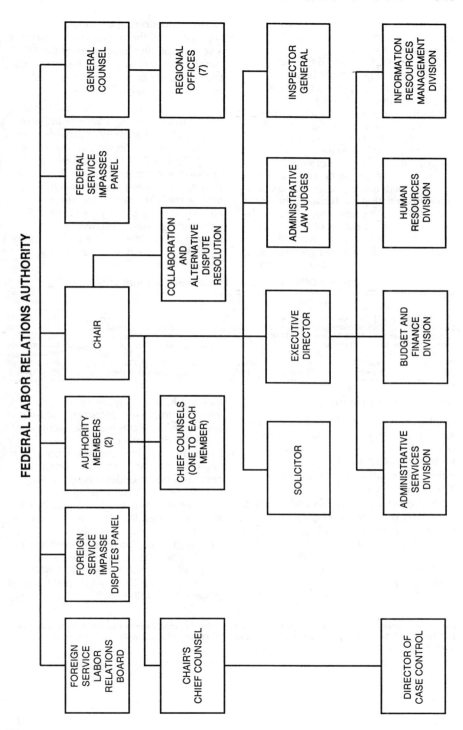

awards. The Chair of the Authority serves as the chief executive and administrative officer.

The General Counsel of the Authority investigates alleged unfair labor practices, files and prosecutes unfair labor practice complaints before the Authority, and exercises such other powers as the Authority may prescribe.

The Federal Service Impasses Panel, an entity within the Authority, is assigned the function of providing assistance in resolving negotiation impasses between agencies and unions. After investigating an impasse, the Panel can either recommend procedures to the parties for the resolution of the impasse or assist the parties in resolving the impasse through whatever methods and procedures, including factfinding and

recommendations, it considers appropriate. If the parties do not arrive at a settlement after assistance by the Panel, the Panel may hold hearings and take whatever action is necessary to resolve the impasse.

The Foreign Service Labor Relations Board and the Foreign Service Impasse Disputes Panel administer provisions of chapter 2 of the Foreign Service Act of 1980 (22 U.S.C. 3921), concerning labor-management relations. This chapter establishes a statutory labor-management relations program for Foreign Service employees of the U.S. Government. Administrative and staff support is provided by the Federal Labor Relations Authority and the Federal Service Impasses Panel.

Regional Offices—Federal Labor Relations Authority

City/Address	Director	Telephone
Atlanta, GA (Suite 701, 285 Peachtree Center Ave., 30303–1270)	Brenda M. Robinson	404–331–5212
Boston, MA (Suite 1500, 99 Summer St., 02110–1200)	Edward S. Davidson	617–424–5730
Chicago, IL (Suite 1150, 55 W. Monroe, 60603–9729)	William E. Washington	312–353–6306
Dallas, TX (Suite 926, 525 Griffin St., 75202–5903)	James Petrucci	214–767–4996
Denver, CO (Suite 100, 1244 Speer Blvd., 80204–3581)	Marjorie K. Thompson	303–844–5224
San Francisco, CA (Suite 220, 901 Market St., 94103–1791)	Gerald M. Cole	415–356–5000
Washington, DC (Suite 400, 1255 22d St. NW., 20037—0001)	Michael W. Doheny	202–653–8500

Sources of Information

Employment   Employment inquiries and applications may be sent to the Director of the Human Resources Division. Phone, 202–482–6660.

Public Information and Publications
The Authority will assist in arranging reproduction of documents and ordering transcripts of hearings. Requests for publications should be submitted to the Assistant to the Executive Director. Phone, 202–482–6560 or 202–482–6690, ext. 440. Internet, http://www.flra.gov/.

Reading Room   Anyone desiring to inspect formal case documents or read agency publications may use facilities of the Authority's offices.

Speakers   To give agencies, labor organizations, and other interested persons a better understanding of the Federal service labor-management relations program and the Authority's role and duties, its personnel participate as speakers or panel members before various groups. Requests for speakers or panelists should be submitted to the Office of the Chair (phone, 202–482–6500); or to the Deputy General Counsel (phone, 202–482–6680).

For further information, contact the Assistant to the Executive Director, Federal Labor Relations Authority, 607 Fourteenth Street NW., Washington, DC 20424–0001. Phone, 202–482–6560. Internet, http://www.flra.gov/.

FEDERAL MARITIME COMMISSION

800 North Capitol Street NW., Washington, DC 20573–0001
Phone, 202–523–5707. Internet, http://www.fmc.gov/.

Chairman	HAROLD J. CREEL, JR.
Commissioners	MING C. HSU, JOE SCROGGINS, JR., DELMOND J.H. WON, (VACANCY)
General Counsel	THOMAS PANEBIANCO
Secretary	JOSEPH C. POLKING
Director, Office of Informal Inquiries, Complaints, and Informal Dockets	JOSEPH T. FARRELL
Chief Administrative Law Judge	NORMAN D. KLINE
Director, Office of Equal Employment Opportunity	ALICE M. BLACKMON
Inspector General	TONY P. KOMINOTH
Managing Director	EDWARD PATRICK WALSH
Deputy Managing Director	BRUCE A. DOMBROWSKI
Director, Bureau of Economics and Agreements Analysis	AUSTIN SCHMITT
Director, Bureau of Tariffs, Certification, and Licensing	BRYANT L. VANBRAKLE
Director, Bureau of Enforcement	VERN W. HILL
Director, Bureau of Administration	SANDRA L. KUSUMOTO

The Federal Maritime Commission regulates the waterborne foreign commerce of the United States, ensures that U.S. international trade is open to all nations on fair and equitable terms, and protects against unauthorized, concerted activity in the waterborne commerce of the United States. This is accomplished through maintaining surveillance over steamship conferences and common carriers by water; ensuring that only the rates on file with the Commission are charged; reviewing agreements between persons subject to the Shipping Act of 1984; guaranteeing equal treatment to shippers, carriers, and other persons subject to the shipping statutes; and ensuring that adequate levels of financial responsibility are maintained for indemnification of passengers.

The Federal Maritime Commission was established by Reorganization Plan No. 7 of 1961 (5 U.S.C. app.), effective August 12, 1961. It is an independent agency that regulates shipping under the following statutes: the Shipping Act of 1984 (46 U.S.C. app. 1701–1720); the Merchant Marine Act, 1920 (46 U.S.C. app. 861 *et seq.*); the Foreign Shipping Practices Act of 1988 (46 U.S.C. app. 1710a); the Merchant Marine Act, 1936 (46 U.S.C. app. 1101 *et seq.*); and certain provisions of the act of November 6, 1966 (46 U.S.C. app. 817(d) and 817(e)).

Activities

Agreements The Commission reviews for legal sufficiency agreements filed under section 5 of the Shipping Act of 1984 (46 U.S.C. app. 1704), including conference, interconference, and cooperative working agreements among common carriers, terminal operators, and other persons subject to the shipping statutes. It also monitors activities under all effective agreements for compliance with the provisions of law and its rules, orders, and regulations.

Tariffs The Commission accepts or rejects tariff filings, including filings dealing with service contracts, of

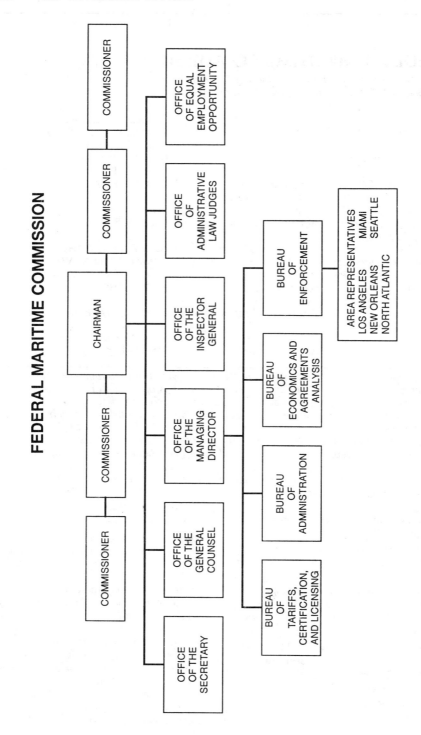

FEDERAL MARITIME COMMISSION

common carriers engaged in the foreign and domestic offshore commerce of the United States, or conferences of such carriers. Special permission applications may be submitted for relief from statutory and/or Commission tariff requirements. The Commission monitors the activities of controlled carriers under section 9 of the Shipping Act of 1984 (46 U.S.C. app. 1708, 1709, 1714).

Licenses The Commission issues licenses to persons, partnerships, corporations, or associations desiring to engage in ocean freight forwarding activities.

Passenger Indemnity The Commission administers the passenger indemnity provisions of the act of November 6, 1966, which require shipowners and operators to obtain certificates of financial responsibility to pay judgments for personal injury or death or to refund fares in the event of nonperformance of voyages.

Informal Complaints The Commission reviews alleged or suspected violations of the shipping statutes and rules and regulations of the Commission and may take administrative action to institute formal proceedings, to refer matters to other governmental agencies, or to bring about voluntary agreement between the parties.

Formal Adjudicatory Procedure The Commission conducts formal investigations and hearings on its own motion and adjudicates formal complaints in accordance with the Administrative Procedure Act (5 U.S.C. note prec. 551).

Rulemaking The Commission promulgates rules and regulations to interpret, enforce, and ensure compliance with shipping and related statutes by common carriers and other persons subject to the statutes.

Investigation, Audit, and Financial and Economic Analyses The Commission prescribes and administers programs to ensure compliance with the provisions of the shipping statutes. These programs include the submission of information; field investigations and audits of activities and practices of common carriers, conferences, terminal operators, freight forwarders, and other persons subject to the shipping statutes; and rate analyses, studies, and economic reviews of current and prospective trade conditions, including the extent and nature of competition in various trade areas.

International Affairs The Commission conducts investigations of foreign governmental and foreign carrier practices that adversely affect the U.S. shipping trade and, in conjunction with the Department of State, conducts activities to effect the elimination of discriminatory practices on the part of foreign governments against United States-flag shipping and to achieve comity between the United States and its trading partners.

Area Representatives—Federal Maritime Commission

District	Address/Phone	Representative
Los Angeles	Rm. 1018, 300 S. Ferry St., San Pedro, CA 90731. Phone, 310–514–4905. Fax, 310–514–3931. E-mail, clarko@cris.com	Oliver E. Clark
Miami	Rm. 736, 909 SE. First Ave., Miami, FL 33131. Phone, 305–536–4316. Fax, 305–536–4317. E-mail, margolis@cris.com	Andrew Margolis
New Orleans	Rm. 303, 423 Canal St., New Orleans, LA 70130. Phone, 504–589–6663. Fax, 504–589–6664. E-mail, kellogga@cris.com	Alvin N. Kellogg
North Atlantic	800 N. Capitol St., Washington, DC 20573–0001. Phone, 202–523–0300. Fax, 202–523–3725. E-mail, michaelc@fmc.gov	Michael F. Carley
Seattle	Suite 100, 7 S. Nevada St., Seattle, WA 98134. Phone, 206–553–0221. Fax, 206–553–0222. E-mail, moneckm@cris.com	Michael A. Moneck

Sources of Information

Electronic Access Information about the Federal Maritime Commission is available in electronic form through the Internet, at http://www.fmc.gov/.

Employment Employment inquiries may be directed to the Office of Personnel, Federal Maritime Commission, 800 North Capitol Street NW., Washington, DC 20573–0001. Phone, 202–523–5773.

Informal Complaints   Phone, 202–523–5807. E-mail, josephf@fmc.gov.

Publications   The *Thirty-sixth Annual Report (1997)* is a recent publication of the Federal Maritime Commission.

For further information, contact the Office of the Secretary, Federal Maritime Commission, 800 North Capitol Street NW., Washington, DC 20573–0001. Phone, 202–523–5725. Fax, 202–523–0014. Internet, http://www.fmc.gov/.

FEDERAL MEDIATION AND CONCILIATION SERVICE

2100 K Street NW., Washington, DC 20427
Phone, 202–606–8100. Internet, http://www.fmcs.gov/.

Director	JOHN CALHOUN WELLS
Deputy Director, Field Operations	C. RICHARD BARNES
Deputy Director, National Office	VELLA M. TRAYNHAM

The Federal Mediation and Conciliation Service assists labor and management in resolving disputes in collective bargaining contract negotiation through voluntary mediation and arbitration services; provides training to unions and management in cooperative processes to improve long-term relationships under the Labor Management Cooperation Act of 1978, including Federal sector partnership training authorized by Executive Order 12871; provides alternative dispute resolution services and training to Government agencies, including the facilitation of regulatory negotiations under the Administrative Dispute Resolution Act and the Negotiated Rulemaking Act of 1996; and awards competitive grants to joint labor-management committees to encourage innovative approaches to cooperative efforts.

The Federal Mediation and Conciliation Service (FMCS) was created by the Labor Management Relations Act, 1947 (29 U.S.C. 172). The Director is appointed by the President with the advice and consent of the Senate.

Activities

The Federal Mediation and Conciliation Service helps prevent disruptions in the flow of interstate commerce caused by labor-management disputes by providing mediators to assist disputing parties in the resolution of their differences. Mediators have no law enforcement authority and rely wholly on persuasive techniques.

The Service offers its facilities in labor-management disputes to any industry affecting interstate commerce with employees represented by a union, either upon its own motion or at the request of one or more of the parties to

the dispute, whenever in its judgment such dispute threatens to cause a substantial interruption of commerce. The Labor Management Relations Act requires that parties to a labor contract must file a dispute notice if agreement is not reached 30 days in advance of a contract termination or reopening date. The notice must be filed with the Service and the appropriate State or local mediation agency. The Service is required to avoid the mediation of disputes that would have only a minor effect on interstate commerce if State or other conciliation services are available to the parties.

For further information, contact one of the regional offices listed below.

Mediation   Efforts of FMCS mediators are directed toward the establishment of sound and stable labor-management relations on a continuing basis, thereby helping to reduce the incidence of work stoppages. The mediator's basic function is to encourage and promote better day-to-day relations between labor and management, so that issues arising in negotiations may be faced as problems to be settled through mutual effort rather than issues in dispute.

For further information, contact the Office of Public Affairs. Phone, 202–606–8080.

Arbitration The Service, on the joint request of employers and unions, will also assist in the selection of arbitrators from a roster of private citizens who are qualified as neutrals to adjudicate matters in dispute.

For further information, contact the Office of Arbitration Services. Phone, 202–606–5111.

Regional Offices—Federal Mediation and Conciliation Service

Region/Address	Director	Telephone
Northeastern (16th Fl., One Newark Center, Newark, NJ 17102)	Kenneth C. Kowalski	973–645–2200
Southern (Suite 472, 401 W. Peachtree St. NW., Atlanta, GA 30308)	C. Richard Barnes	404–331–3995
Midwestern (Suite 120, 6161 Oak Tree Blvd., Independence, OH 44131)	Thomas M. O'Brien	216–522–4800
Upper Midwestern (Suite 3950, 1300 Godward St., Minneapolis, MN 55413)	Scot Beckenbaugh	612–370–3300
Western (Suite 410, 1100 Town and Country Rd., Orange, CA 92668)	Jan Jung-Min Sunoo	714–246–8378

For further information, contact the Public Affairs Office, Federal Mediation and Conciliation Service, 2100 K Street NW., Washington, DC 20427. Phone, 202–606–8100. Internet, http://www.fmcs.gov/.

FEDERAL MINE SAFETY AND HEALTH REVIEW COMMISSION

1730 K Street NW., Washington, DC 20006–3867
Phone, 202–653–5625

Chairman	MARY LU JORDAN
Commissioners	ROBERT H. BEATTY, JR., MARK L. MARKS, JAMES C. RILEY, THEODORE F. VERHEGGEN
Chief Administrative Law Judge	PAUL MERLIN
General Counsel	NORMAN M. GLEICHMAN
Executive Director	RICHARD L. BAKER

The Federal Mine Safety and Health Review Commission is an independent, quasi-judicial agency established by the Federal Mine Safety and Health Act of 1977 (30 U.S.C. 801 *et seq.*). The act, enforced by the Secretary of Labor through the Mine Safety and Health Administration, governs compliance with occupational safety and health standards in the Nation's surface and underground coal, metal, and nonmetal mines.

The Commission consists of five members who are appointed by the President with the advice and consent of the Senate and who serve staggered, 6-year terms. The Chairman is selected from among the Commissioners.

The Commission and its Office of Administrative Law Judges are charged with deciding cases brought pursuant to the act by the Mine Safety and Health Administration, mine operators, and miners or their representatives. These cases generally involve review of the Administration's enforcement actions including citations, mine closure orders, and proposals for civil penalties issued for violations of the act or the mandatory safety and health standards promulgated by the Secretary of Labor. The Commission also has jurisdiction over

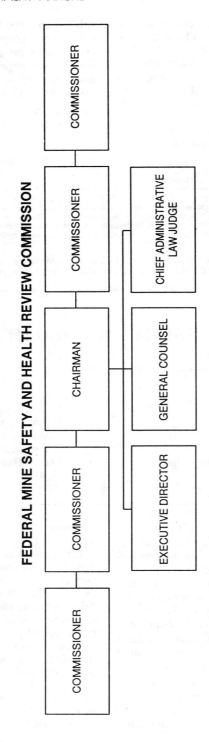

FEDERAL MINE SAFETY AND HEALTH REVIEW COMMISSION

discrimination complaints filed by miners or their representatives in connection with their safety and health rights under the act, and over complaints for compensation filed on behalf of miners idled as a result of mine closure orders issued by the Administration.

Activities

Cases brought before the Commission are assigned to the Office of Administrative Law Judges, and hearings are conducted pursuant to the requirements of the Administrative Procedure Act (5 U.S.C. 554, 556) and the Commission's procedural rules (29 CFR Part 2700).

A judge's decision becomes a final but nonprecedential order of the Commission 40 days after issuance unless the Commission has directed the case for review in response to a petition or on its own motion. If a review is conducted, a decision of the Commission becomes final 30 days after issuance unless a party adversely affected seeks review in the U.S. Circuit Court of Appeals for the District of Columbia or the Circuit within which

the mine subject to the litigation is located.

As far as practicable, hearings are held at locations convenient to the affected mines. The Office of Administrative Law Judges has two offices: the Falls Church Office, 2 Skyline, 5203 Leesburg Pike, Falls Church, VA 22041; and the Denver Office, Colonnade Center, Room 280, 1244 Speer Boulevard, Denver, CO 80204.

Sources of Information

Commission decisions are published monthly and are available through the Superintendent of Documents, U.S. Government Printing Office, Washington, DC 20402. Requests for Commission records should be submitted in accordance with the Commission's Freedom of Information Act regulations. Other information, including Commission rules of procedure and brochures explaining the Commission's functions, is available from the Executive Director, Federal Mine Safety and Health Review Commission, Sixth Floor, 1730 K Street NW., Washington, DC 20006-3867. E-mail, info@fmshrc.gov.

For further information, contact the Executive Director, Federal Mine Safety and Health Review Commission, Sixth Floor, 1730 K Street NW., Washington DC 20006–3867. Phone, 202–653–5625. Fax, 202–653–5030. E-mail, info@fmshrc.gov.

FEDERAL RESERVE SYSTEM

Board of Governors of the Federal Reserve System
Twentieth Street and Constitution Avenue NW., Washington, DC 20551
Phone, 202–452–3000

Board of Governors

Chairman	ALAN GREENSPAN
Vice Chair	ALICE M. RIVLIN
Members	ROGER W. FERGUSON, JR., EDWARD M. GRAMLICH, EDWARD W. KELLEY, JR., LAURENCE H. MEYER, SUSAN M. PHILLIPS
Official Staff:	
Assistants to the Board	JOSEPH R. COYNE, DONALD J. WINN, THEODORE E. ALLISON
General Counsel	J. VIRGIL MATTINGLY, JR.
Secretary	WILLIAM W. WILES

Deputy Secretary	JENNIFER J. JOHNSON
Associate Secretary and Ombudsman	BARBARA R. LOWREY
Director, Division of Consumer and Community Affairs	GRIFFITH L. GARWOOD
Director, Division of Banking Supervision and Regulation	RICHARD SPILLENKOTHEN
Director, Division of Monetary Affairs	DONALD L. KOHN
Deputy Director	DAVID E. LINDSEY
Director, Division of Research and Statistics	MICHAEL J. PRELL
Deputy Directors	EDWARD C. ETTIN, DAVID J. STOCKTON
Staff Director, Division of International Finance	EDWIN M. TRUMAN
Senior Associate Directors	LARRY J. PROMISEL, CHARLES J. SIEGMAN
Staff Director, Office of Staff Director for Management	S. DAVID FROST
Director, Division of Information Resources Management	STEPHEN R. MALPHRUS
Director, Division of Human Resources Management	DAVID L. SHANNON
Associate Director	JOHN R. WEIS
Comptroller	GEORGE E. LIVINGSTON
Director, Division of Support Services	ROBERT E. FRAZIER
Director, Division of Federal Reserve Bank Operations and Payment Systems	CLYDE H. FARNSWORTH, JR.
Deputy Director, Finance and Control	DAVID L. ROBINSON
Inspector General	BRENT L. BOWEN

Officers of the Federal Reserve Banks

Chairmen and Federal Reserve Agents:

Atlanta	DAVID R. JONES
Boston	WILLIAM C. BRAINARD
Chicago	LESTER H. MCKEEVER, JR.
Cleveland	G. WATTS HUMPHREY, JR.
Dallas	ROGER R. HEMMINGHAUS
Kansas City	JO MARIE DANCIK
Minneapolis	DAVID A. KOCH
New York	JOHN C. WHITEHEAD
Philadelphia	JOAN CARTER
Richmond	CLAUDINE B. MALONE
St. Louis	JOHN F. MCDONNELL
San Francisco	GARY G. MICHAEL

Presidents:

Atlanta	JACK GUYNN
Boston	CATHY E. MINEHAN
Chicago	MICHAEL H. MOSKOW
Cleveland	JERRY L. JORDAN
Dallas	ROBERT D. MCTEER, JR.
Kansas City	THOMAS M. HOENIG
Minneapolis	GARY H. STERN
New York	WILLIAM J. MCDONOUGH
Philadelphia	EDWARD G. BOEHNE
Richmond	J. ALFRED BROADDUS, JR.
St. Louis	WILLIAM POOLE
San Francisco	ROBERT T. PARRY

Federal Open Market Committee

Chairman	ALAN GREENSPAN
Vice Chairman	WILLIAM J. MCDONOUGH
Members	ROGER W. FERGUSON, JR., EDWARD M. GRAMLICH, THOMAS M. HOENIG, JERRY L. JORDAN, EDWARD W. KELLEY, JR., LAURENCE H. MEYER, CATHY E. MINEHAN, SUSAN M. PHILLIPS, ALICE M. RIVLIN, (1 VACANCY)

Official Staff:

Secretary and Economist	DONALD L. KOHN
Deputy Secretary	NORMAND R.V. BERNARD
Assistant Secretaries	JOSEPH R. COYNE, GARY P. GILLUM
General Counsel	J. VIRGIL MATTINGLY, JR.
Deputy General Counsel	THOMAS C. BAXTER, JR.
Economists	MICHAEL J. PRELL, EDWIN M. TRUMAN
Manager, System Open Market Account	PETER R. FISHER
Co-Secretaries, Federal Advisory Council	JAMES ANNABLE, WILLIAM J. KORSVIK
Chairman, Consumer Advisory Council	JULIA W. SEWARD
President, Thrift Institutions Advisory Council	DAVID F. HOLLAND

The Federal Reserve System, the central bank of the United States, is charged with administering and formulating the Nation's credit and monetary policy. Through its supervisory and regulatory banking functions, the Federal Reserve maintains the safety and soundness of the Nation's economy, responding to the Nation's domestic and international financial needs and objectives.

The Federal Reserve System was established by the Federal Reserve Act (12 U.S.C. 221), approved December 23, 1913. The System serves as the Nation's central bank. As such, its major responsibility is in the execution of monetary policy. It also performs other functions, such as the transfer of funds, handling Government deposits and debt issues, supervising and regulating banks, and acting as lender of last resort.

It is the responsibility of the Federal Reserve System to contribute to the strength and vitality of the U.S. economy. By influencing the lending and investing activities of depository institutions and the cost and availability of money and credit, the Federal Reserve System helps promote the full use of human and capital resources, the growth of productivity, relatively stable prices, and equilibrium in the Nation's international balance of payments. Through its supervisory and regulatory banking functions, the Federal Reserve System helps maintain a commercial

banking system that is responsive to the Nation's financial needs and objectives.

The System consists of seven parts: the Board of Governors in Washington, DC; the 12 Federal Reserve Banks and their 25 branches and other facilities situated throughout the country; the Federal Open Market Committee; the Federal Advisory Council; the Consumer Advisory Council; the Thrift Institutions Advisory Council; and the Nation's financial institutions, including commercial banks, savings and loan associations, mutual savings banks, and credit unions.

Board of Governors

Broad supervisory powers are vested in the Board of Governors, which has its offices in Washington, DC. The Board is composed of seven members appointed by the President with the advice and consent of the Senate. The Chairman of the Board of Governors is, by Executive Order 11269 of February 14, 1966, a member of the National Advisory

Council on International Monetary and Financial Policies.

The Board determines general monetary, credit, and operating policies for the System as a whole and formulates the rules and regulations necessary to carry out the purposes of the Federal Reserve Act. The Board's principal duties consist of monitoring credit conditions; supervising the Federal Reserve Banks, member banks, and bank holding companies; and regulating the implementation of certain consumer credit protection laws.

Power To Influence Credit Conditions Pursuant to the Depository Institutions Deregulation and Monetary Control Act of 1980, referred to as the Monetary Control Act of 1980 (12 U.S.C. 226 note), the Board is given the power, within statutory limitations, to fix the requirements concerning reserves to be maintained by depository institutions on transaction accounts or nonpersonal time deposits. Another important instrument of credit control is found in open market operations. The members of the Board of Governors also are members of the Federal Open Market Committee, whose work and organization are described in the following text. The Board of Governors reviews and determines the discount rate charged by the Federal Reserve Banks. For the purpose of preventing excessive use of credit for the purchase or carrying of securities, the Board is authorized to regulate the amount of credit that may be initially extended and subsequently maintained on any security (with certain exceptions).

Supervision of Federal Reserve Banks The Board is authorized to make examinations of the Federal Reserve Banks, to require statements and reports from such Banks, to supervise the issue and retirement of Federal Reserve notes, to require the establishment or discontinuance of branches of Reserve Banks, and to exercise supervision over all relationships and transactions of those Banks with foreign branches. The Board of Governors reviews and follows the examination and supervisory activities of the Federal Reserve Banks aimed at

further coordination of policies and practices.

Supervision of Bank Holding Companies The Bank Holding Company Act of 1956 (12 U.S.C. 1841 *et seq.*) gave the Federal Reserve primary responsibility for supervising and regulating the activities of bank holding companies. This act was designed to achieve two basic objectives: to control the expansion of bank holding companies by avoiding the creation of monopoly or restraining trade in banking; and to limit the expansion of bank holding companies to those nonbanking activities that are closely related to banking, thus maintaining a separation between banking and commerce. A company that seeks to become a bank holding company must obtain the prior approval of the Federal Reserve. Any company that qualifies as a bank holding company must register with the Federal Reserve System and file reports with the System.

Supervision of Banking Organizations The Federal Reserve is responsible for the supervision and regulation of domestic and international activities of U.S. banking organizations. It supervises State-chartered banks that are members of the System, all bank holding companies, and Edge Act and agreement corporations (corporations chartered to engage in international banking). In 1991, Congress expanded the Federal Reserve's supervisory authority over the U.S. activities of all foreign banking organizations.

The Board has jurisdiction over the admission of State banks and trust companies to membership in the Federal Reserve System, the termination of membership of such banks, the establishment of branches by such banks, and the approval of bank mergers and consolidations where the resulting institution will be a State member bank. It receives copies of condition reports submitted by them to the Federal Reserve Banks. It has power to examine all member banks and the affiliates of member banks and to require condition reports from them. It has authority to require periodic and other public disclosure of information with respect to an equity security of a State member bank that is held by 500 or more persons. It establishes minimum standards with respect to installation, maintenance, and operation of security devices and procedures by State member banks. Also, it has authority to issue cease-and-desist orders in connection with violations of law or unsafe or unsound banking practices by State member banks and to remove directors or officers of such banks in certain circumstances, and it may, in its discretion, suspend member banks from the use of the credit facilities of the Federal Reserve System for making undue use of bank credit for speculative purposes or for any other purpose inconsistent with the maintenance of sound credit conditions.

The Board may grant authority to member banks to establish branches in foreign countries or dependencies or insular possessions of the United States, to invest in the stocks of banks or corporations engaged in international or foreign banking, or to invest in foreign banks. It also charters, regulates, and supervises certain corporations that engage in foreign or international banking and financial activities.

The Board is authorized to issue general regulations permitting interlocking relationships in certain circumstances between member banks and organizations dealing in securities or between member banks and other banks.

Other Activities   Under the Change in Bank Control Act of 1978 (12 U.S.C. 1817(j)), the Board is required to review other bank stock acquisitions.

Under the Truth in Lending Act (15 U.S.C. 1601), the Board is required to prescribe regulations to ensure a meaningful disclosure by lenders of credit terms so that consumers will be able to compare more readily the various credit terms available and will be informed about rules governing credit cards, including their potential liability for unauthorized use.

Under the International Banking Act of 1978 (12 U.S.C. 3101), the Board has authority to impose reserve requirements and interest rate ceilings on branches and agencies of foreign banks in the United States, to grant loans to them, to provide them access to Federal Reserve services, and to limit their interstate banking activities.

The Board also is the rulemaking authority for the Equal Credit Opportunity Act, the Home Mortgage Disclosure Act, the Fair Credit Billing Act, the Expedited Funds Availability Act, and certain provisions of the Federal Trade Commission Act as they apply to banks.

Expenses   To meet its expenses and pay the salaries of its members and its employees, the Board makes semiannual assessments upon the Reserve Banks in proportion to their capital stock and surplus.

Federal Open Market Committee

The Federal Open Market Committee is comprised of the Board of Governors and five of the presidents of the Reserve Banks. The Chairman of the Board of Governors is traditionally the Chairman of the Committee. The president of the Federal Reserve Bank of New York serves as a permanent member of the Committee. Four of the twelve Reserve Bank presidents rotate annually as members of the Committee.

Open market operations of the Reserve Banks are conducted under regulations adopted by the Committee and pursuant to specific policy directives issued by the Committee, which meets in Washington at frequent intervals. Purchases and sales of securities in the open market are undertaken to supply bank reserves to support the credit and money needed for long-term economic growth, to offset cyclical economic swings, and to accommodate seasonal demands of businesses and consumers for money and credit. These operations are carried out principally in U.S. Government obligations, but they also include purchases and sales of Federal agency obligations. All operations are conducted in New York, where the primary markets for these securities are located; the Federal Reserve Bank of New York executes transactions for the Federal Reserve System Open Market Account in carrying out these operations.

Under the Committee's direction, the Federal Reserve Bank of New York also undertakes transactions in foreign currencies for the Federal Reserve System Open Market Account. The purposes of these operations include helping to safeguard the value of the dollar in international exchange markets and facilitating growth in international liquidity in accordance with the needs of an expanding world economy.

Federal Reserve Banks

The 12 Federal Reserve Banks are located in Atlanta, Boston, Chicago, Cleveland, Dallas, Kansas City, Minneapolis, New York, Philadelphia, Richmond, San Francisco, and St. Louis. Branch banks are located in Baltimore, Birmingham, Buffalo, Charlotte, Cincinnati, Denver, Detroit, El Paso, Helena, Houston, Jacksonville, Little Rock, Los Angeles, Louisville, Memphis, Miami, Nashville, New Orleans, Oklahoma City, Omaha, Pittsburgh, Portland, Salt Lake City, San Antonio, and Seattle.

Directors and Officers of Reserve Banks
The Board of Directors of each Reserve Bank is composed of nine members, equally divided into three designated classes: class A, class B, and class C. Directors of class A are representative of the stockholding member banks. Directors of class B must be actively engaged in their districts in commerce, agriculture, or some other industrial pursuit, and may not be officers, directors, or employees of any bank. Class C directors may not be officers, directors, employees, or stockholders of any bank. The six class A and class B directors are elected by the stockholding member banks, while the three class C directors are appointed by the Board of Governors. The terms of office of the directors are so arranged that the term of one director of each class expires each year.

One of the class C directors appointed by the Board of Governors is designated as Chairman of the Board of Directors of the Reserve Bank and as Federal Reserve agent, and in the latter capacity he is required to maintain a local office of the

Board of Governors on the premises of the Reserve Bank. Another class C director is appointed by the Board of Governors as deputy chairman. Each Reserve Bank has as its chief executive officer a president appointed for a term of 5 years by its Board of Directors with the approval of the Board of Governors.

Reserves on Deposit   In accordance with provisions of the Monetary Control Act of 1980 (12 U.S.C. 226 note), the Reserve Banks receive and hold on deposit the reserve or clearing account deposits of depository institutions. These banks are permitted to count their vault cash as part of their required reserve.

Extensions of Credit   The Monetary Control Act of 1980 (12 U.S.C. 226 note) directs the Federal Reserve to open its discount window to any depository institution that is subject to Federal Reserve reserve requirements on transaction accounts or nonpersonal time deposits.

Discount window credit provides for Federal Reserve lending to eligible depository institutions under two basic programs. One is the adjustment credit program; the other supplies more extended credit for certain limited purposes.

Short-term adjustment credit is the primary type of Federal Reserve credit. It is available to help borrowers meet temporary requirements for funds. Borrowers are not permitted to use adjustment credit to take advantage of any spread between the discount rate and market rates.

Extended credit is provided through three programs designed to assist depository institutions in meeting longer term needs for funds. One provides seasonal credit—for periods running up to 9 months—to smaller depository institutions that lack access to market funds. A second program assists institutions that experience special difficulties arising from exceptional circumstances or practices involving only that institution. Finally, in cases where more general liquidity strains are affecting a broad range of depository institutions—such as those whose portfolios consist primarily of longer term assets—credit may be provided to address the problems of particular institutions being affected by the general situation.

Currency Issue The Reserve Banks issue Federal Reserve notes, which constitute the bulk of money in circulation. These notes are obligations of the United States and are a prior lien upon the assets of the issuing Federal Reserve Bank. They are issued against a pledge by the Reserve Bank with the Federal Reserve agent of collateral security including gold certificates, paper discounted or purchased by the Bank, and direct obligations of the United States.

Other Powers The Reserve Banks are empowered to act as clearinghouses and as collecting agents for depository institutions in the collection of checks and other instruments. They are also authorized to act as depositories and fiscal agents of the United States and to exercise other banking functions specified in the Federal Reserve Act. They perform a number of important functions in connection with the issue and redemption of United States Government securities.

Federal Advisory Council

The Federal Advisory Council acts in an advisory capacity, conferring with the Board of Governors on general business conditions.

The Council is composed of 12 members, one from each Federal Reserve district, being selected annually by the Board of Directors of the Reserve Bank of the district. The Council is required to meet in Washington, DC, at least four times each year, and more often if called by the Board of Governors.

Consumer Advisory Council

The Consumer Advisory Council confers with the Board of Governors several times each year on the Board's responsibilities for many of the consumer credit protection laws. The Council was established by Congress in 1976 at the suggestion of the Board and replaced the Advisory Committee on Truth in Lending

that was established by the 1968 Truth in Lending Act.

The 30 Council members represent the interests of consumers, community groups, and creditors nationwide. They advise the Board on its responsibilities under such laws as Truth in Lending, Equal Credit Opportunity, and Home Mortgage Disclosure.

Thrift Institutions Advisory Council

The Thrift Institutions Advisory Council is an advisory group established by the Board in 1980 made up of representatives from nonbank depository thrift institutions, which includes savings and loans, mutual savings bankers, and credit unions. The Council meets at least four times each year with the Board of Governors to discuss developments relating to thrift institutions, the housing industry and mortgage finance, and certain regulatory issues.

Sources of Information

Employment Written inquiries regarding employment should be addressed to the Director, Division of Personnel, Board of Governors of the Federal Reserve System, Washington, DC 20551.

Procurement Firms seeking business with the Board should address their inquiries to the Director, Division of Support Services, Board of Governors of the Federal Reserve System, Washington, DC 20551.

Publications Among the publications issued by the Board are *The Federal Reserve System—Purposes and Functions*, and a series of pamphlets including *Guide to Business Credit and the Equal Credit Opportunity Act; Consumer Handbook; Making Deposits: When Will Your Money Be Available;* and *When Your Home Is On the Line: What You Should Know About Home Equity Lines of Credit.* Copies of these pamphlets are available free of charge. Information regarding publications may be obtained in Room MP–510 (Martin Building) of the Board's headquarters. Phone, 202–452–3244.

Reading Room A reading room where persons may inspect records that are available to the public is located in Room B–1122 at the Board's headquarters, Twentieth Street and Constitution Avenue NW., Washington, DC. Information regarding the availability of records may be obtained by calling 202–452–3684.

For further information, contact the Office of Public Affairs, Board of Governors, Federal Reserve System, Washington, DC 20551. Phone, 202–452–3204 or 202–452–3215.

FEDERAL RETIREMENT THRIFT INVESTMENT BOARD

1250 H Street NW., Washington, DC 20005
Phone, 202–942–1600. Fax, 202–942–1676. Internet, http://www.tsp.gov/.

Chairman	JAMES H. ATKINS
Members	THOMAS A. FINK, SCOTT B. LUKINS, SHERYL R. MARSHALL, JEROME A. STRICKER

Officials:

Executive Director	ROGER W. MEHLE
General Counsel	JOHN J. O'MEARA
Deputy General Counsel	JAMES B. PETRICK
Associate General Counsel	ELIZABETH S. WOODRUFF
Director of Accounting	DAVID L. BLACK
Director of Administration	STRAT D. VALAKIS
Director of Automated Systems	LAWRENCE E. STIFFLER
Director of Benefits and Program Analysis	ALISONE M. CLARKE
Director of Communications	VEDA R. CHARROW
Director of External Affairs	THOMAS J. TRABUCCO
Director of Investments	PETER B. MACKEY

The Federal Retirement Thrift Investment Board administers the Thrift Savings Plan, which provides Federal employees the opportunity to save for additional retirement security.

The Federal Retirement Thrift Investment Board was established as an independent agency by the Federal Employees' Retirement System Act of 1986 (5 U.S.C. 8472). The act vests responsibility for the agency in six named fiduciaries: the five Board members and the Executive Director. The five members of the Board, one of whom is designated as Chairman, are appointed by the President with the advice and consent of the Senate and serve on the Board on a part-time basis. The members appoint the Executive Director, who is responsible for the management of the agency and the Plan.

Activities

The Thrift Savings Plan is a tax-deferred, defined contribution plan that was established as one of the three parts of the Federal Employees' Retirement System. For employees covered under the System, savings accumulated through the Plan make an important addition to the retirement benefits provided by Social Security and the System's Basic Annuity. Civil Service Retirement System employees may also take advantage of the Plan to supplement their annuities.

The Board operates the Thrift Savings Plan and manages the investments of the Thrift Savings Fund solely for the benefit of participants and their beneficiaries. As part of these responsibilities, the Board maintains an account for each Plan

participant, makes loans, purchases annuity contracts, and provides for the payment of benefits.

For further information, contact the Director of External Affairs, Federal Retirement Thrift Investment Board, 1250 H Street NW., Washington, DC 20005.   Phone, 202–942–1640.   Internet, http:// www.tsp.gov/.

FEDERAL TRADE COMMISSION

Pennsylvania Avenue at Sixth Street NW., Washington, DC 20580
Phone, 202–326–2222. Internet, http://www.ftc.gov/.

Chairman	ROBERT PITOFSKY
Executive Assistant	JAMES C. HAMILL
Commissioners	SHEILA F. ANTHONY, MARY L. AZCUENAGA, ORSON SWINDLE, MOZELLE W. THOMPSON
Executive Director	ROSEMARIE A. STRAIGHT
Counsel to the Executive Director	JUDITH BAILEY
Chief Information Officer	KEITH GOLDEN, *Acting*
Director, Bureau of Competition	WILLIAM J. BAER
Senior Deputy Director	RICHARD PARKER
Deputy Director	WILLARD K. TOM
Director, Bureau of Consumer Protection	JODIE BERNSTEIN
Deputy Directors	LYDIA B. PARNES
	HUGH STEVENSON, *Acting*
Director, Bureau of Economics	JONATHAN B. BAKER
General Counsel	DEBRA A. VALENTINE
Deputy General Counsel	(VACANCY)
Director, Office of Congressional Relations	LORRAINE C. MILLER
Director, Office of Public Affairs	VICTORIA A. STREITFELD
Director, Office of Policy Planning	SUSAN S. DeSANTI
Secretary of the Commission	DONALD S. CLARK
Chief Administrative Law Judge	LEWIS F. PARKER
Inspector General	FREDERICK J. ZIRKEL

[For the Federal Trade Commission statement of organization, see the *Code of Federal Regulations,* Title 16, Part 0]

The objective of the Federal Trade Commission is to maintain competitive enterprise as the keystone of the American economic system, and to prevent the free enterprise system from being fettered by monopoly or restraints on trade or corrupted by unfair or deceptive trade practices. The Commission is charged with keeping competition both free and fair.

The purpose of the Federal Trade Commission is expressed in the Federal Trade Commission Act (15 U.S.C. 41– 58) and the Clayton Act (15 U.S.C. 12), both passed in 1914 and both successively amended in the years since. The Federal Trade Commission Act

prohibits the use in or affecting commerce of "unfair methods of competition" and "unfair or deceptive acts or practices." The Clayton Act outlaws specific practices recognized as instruments of monopoly. As an independent administrative agency,

FEDERAL TRADE COMMISSION

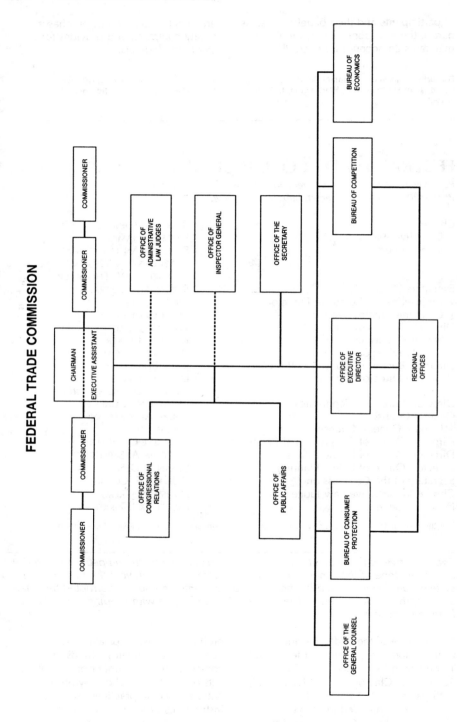

acting quasi-judicially and quasi-legislatively, the Commission was established to deal with trade practices on a continuing and corrective basis. It has no authority to punish; its function is to prevent, through cease-and-desist orders and other means, those practices condemned by Federal trade regulation laws. However, court-ordered civil penalties up to $11,000 may be obtained for each violation of a Commission order or trade regulation rule.

Congress has delegated a variety of duties to the Commission under such statutes as the Wheeler-Lea Act, the Clayton Act, the Consumer Credit Protection Act, the Robinson-Patman Act, the Magnuson-Moss Warranty-Federal Trade Commission Improvement Act, the Federal Trade Commission Improvements Act of 1980, the Smokeless Tobacco Health Education Act of 1986, the Telephone Disclosure and Dispute Resolution Act, the Federal Trade Commission Improvements Act of 1994, the International Antitrust Enforcement Assistance Act of 1994, the Telemarketing and Consumer Fraud and Abuse Prevention Act, and the Federal Trade Commission Act Amendments of 1994.

The Commission is composed of five members. Each member is appointed by the President, with the advice and consent of the Senate, for a term of 7 years. Not more than three of the Commissioners may be members of the same political party. One Commissioner is designated by the President as Chairman of the Commission and is responsible for its administrative management.

Activities

The Commission's principal functions are to:

—promote competition in or affecting commerce through the prevention of general trade restraints such as price-fixing agreements, boycotts, illegal combinations of competitors, and other unfair methods of competition;

—safeguard the public by preventing the dissemination of false or deceptive advertisements of consumer products and services, as well as other unfair or deceptive practices;

—prevent pricing discrimination; exclusive-dealing and tying arrangements; corporate mergers, acquisitions, or joint ventures, when such practices or arrangements may substantially lessen competition or tend to create a monopoly; interlocking directorates or officers' positions that may restrain competition; the payment or receipt of illegal brokerage; and discrimination among competing customers by sellers in the furnishing of or the payment for services or facilities used to promote the resale of a product;

—stop various fraudulent telemarketing schemes and protect consumers from abusive and deceptive telephone sales tactics;

—ensure truthful labeling of textile, wool, and fur products;

—supervise the registration and operation of associations of American exporters engaged in export trade;

—require creditors to disclose in writing certain cost information, such as the annual percentage rate, before consumers enter into credit transactions, as required by the Truth in Lending Act;

—protect consumers against circulation of inaccurate or obsolete credit reports and ensure that credit bureaus, consumer reporting agencies, credit grantors, and bill collectors exercise their responsibilities in a manner that is fair and equitable and in conformity with the Fair Credit Reporting Act, the Fair Credit Billing Act, the Equal Credit Opportunity Act, and the Fair Debt Collection Practices Act;

—educate consumers and businesses about their rights and responsibilities under FTC rules and regulations; and

—gather factual data concerning economic and business conditions and make it available to the Congress, the President, and the public.

Enforcement The Commission's law enforcement work falls into two general categories: actions to foster voluntary compliance with the law, and formal administrative or Federal court litigation leading to mandatory orders against offenders.

For the most part, compliance with the law is obtained through voluntary and cooperative action by private companies in response to nonbinding staff advice, formal advisory opinions by the Commission, and guides and policy statements delineating legal requirements as to particular business practices.

Formal litigation is instituted either by issuing an administrative complaint or by filing a Federal district court complaint charging a person, partnership, or corporation with violating one or more of the statutes administered by the Commission. Cases may be settled by consent orders. If the charges in an administrative matter are not contested, or if the charges are found to be true after an administrative hearing in a contested case, an order may be issued requiring discontinuance of the unlawful practices. Such orders may include other related requirements. Federal district court charges are resolved through either settlements or court-ordered injunctive or other equitable relief.

Investigations Investigations by the Commission may originate through complaint by a consumer or a competitor; the Congress; or from Federal, State, or municipal agencies. Also, the Commission itself may initiate an investigation into possible violations of the laws it administers. No formality is required in submitting a complaint. A letter giving the facts in detail, accompanied by all supporting evidence in possession of the complaining party, is sufficient. It is the general policy of the Commission not to disclose the identity of any complainant, except as permitted by law or Commission rules.

Upon receipt of a complaint, various criteria are applied in determining whether the particular matter should be investigated. Within the limits of available resources, investigations are initiated that are considered to best support the Commission's goals of maintaining competition and protecting consumers.

Under the Federal Trade Commission Act, an order issued after an administrative proceeding that requires the respondent to cease and desist or to take other corrective action—such as affirmative disclosure, divestiture, or restitution—becomes final 60 days after date of service upon the respondent, unless within that period the respondent petitions an appropriate United States court of appeals to review the order, and also petitions the Commission to stay the order pending review. If the Commission does not stay the order, the respondent may seek a stay from the reviewing appeals court. The appeals court has the power to affirm, modify, or set the order aside. If the appeals court upholds the Commission's order, the respondent may seek certiorari to the Supreme Court and ask that the appeals court or the Supreme Court continue to stay the order. Violations of a cease-and-desist order, after it becomes effective, subject the offender to suit by the Government in a United States district court for the recovery of a civil penalty of not more than $11,000 for each violation and, where the violation continues, each day of its continuance is a separate violation.

In addition to, or in lieu of, the administrative proceeding initiated by a formal complaint, the Commission may, in some cases, request that a United States district court issue a preliminary or permanent injunction to halt the use of allegedly unfair or deceptive practices, to prevent an anticompetitive merger from taking place, or to prevent violations of any statute enforced by the Commission.

Compliance Activities Through systematic and continuous review, the Commission obtains and maintains compliance with its cease-and-desist orders. All respondents against whom such orders have been issued are required to file reports with the Commission to substantiate their compliance. In the event compliance is not obtained, or if the order is subsequently violated, civil penalty proceedings may be instituted.

Cooperative Procedures In carrying out the statutory directive to "prevent" the use in or affecting commerce of unfair practices, the Commission makes extensive use of voluntary and cooperative procedures. Through these procedures business and industry may obtain authoritative guidance and a substantial measure of certainty as to what they may do under the laws administered by the Commission.

The Commission issues industry guides, which are administrative interpretations in laymen's language of laws administered by the Commission for the guidance of the public in conforming with legal requirements. Guides provide the basis for voluntary and simultaneous abandonment of unlawful practices by members of a particular industry or by industry in general. Failure to comply with the guides may result in corrective action by the Commission under applicable statutory provisions.

Consumer Protection Consumer protection is one of the two main missions of the Commission. The Commission works to increase the usefulness of advertising by ensuring that it is truthful and not misleading; reduce instances of fraudulent, deceptive, or unfair marketing practices; prevent creditors from using unlawful practices when granting credit, maintaining credit information, collecting debts, and operating credit systems; and educate the public about Commission activities. The Commission initiates investigations in many areas of concern to consumers, including health and nutrition claims in advertising; environmental advertising and labeling; general advertising issues; health care, telemarketing, business opportunity, and franchise and investment fraud; mortgage lending and discrimination; enforcement of Commission orders; and enforcement of credit statutes and trade regulation rules.

The Commission has issued and enforces many trade regulation rules important to consumers. The Telemarketing Sales Rule requires telemarketers to make certain disclosures and prohibits certain misrepresentations. The Mail/Telephone Order Merchandise Rule requires companies to ship merchandise that consumers order by mail or telephone within a certain time, and sets out requirements for notifying consumers about delays and offering them the option of agreeing to the delays or canceling their orders. The Care Labeling Rule requires manufacturers

and importers of textile clothing and fabrics for home sewing to attach care instructions. The Funeral Rule requires that price and other specific information regarding funeral arrangements be made available to consumers to help them make informed choices and pay only for services they select. The Franchise Rule requires the seller to provide each prospective franchisee with a basic disclosure document containing detailed information about the nature of its business and terms of the proposed franchise relationship. The Used Car Rule requires that dealers display a buyers guide containing warranty information on each vehicle offered for sale to consumers. Under the Cooling-Off Rule, consumers can cancel purchases of $25 or more made door-to-door, or at places other than the seller's usual place of business, within 3 business days of purchase.

Maintaining Competition (Antitrust) The second major mission of the Commission is to encourage competitive forces in the American economy. Under the Federal Trade Commission Act, the Commission seeks to prevent unfair practices that may keep one company from competing with others. Under the Federal Trade Commission Act and the Clayton Act, the Commission attempts to prevent mergers of companies if the result may be to lessen competition. Under some circumstances, companies planning to merge must first give notice to the Commission and the Department of Justice's Antitrust Division and provide certain information concerning the operations of the companies involved.

The Commission also enforces the provisions of the Robinson-Patman Act, a part of the Clayton Act prohibiting companies from discriminating among other companies that are its customers in terms of price or other services provided.

Economic Factfinding The Commission makes economic studies of conditions and problems affecting competition in the economy. Such reports may be used to inform legislative proposals, as part of a rulemaking record, in response to requests of the Congress and statutory directions, or for the information and guidance of the Commission and the executive branch of the Government as well as the public. The reports have provided the basis for significant legislation and, by spotlighting poor economic or regulatory performance, they have also led to voluntary changes in the conduct of business, with resulting benefits to the public.

Competition and Consumer Advocacy To promote competition, consumer protection, and the efficient allocation of resources, the Commission has an ongoing program designed to advocate the consumer interest in a competitive marketplace by encouraging courts, legislatures, and government administrative bodies to consider efficiency and consumer welfare as important elements in their deliberations.

The Commission uses these opportunities to support procompetitive means of regulating the Nation's economy, including the elimination of anticompetitive restrictions that reduce the welfare of consumers and the implementation of regulatory programs that protect the public and preserve as much as possible the discipline of competitive markets. The competition and consumer advocacy program relies on persuasion rather than coercion.

Regional Offices—Federal Trade Commission

Region	Address	Director
Atlanta, GA—AL, FL, GA, MS, NC, SC, TN, VA	Suite 5M35, 60 Forsyth St. SW., 30303	Anthony E. DiResta
Boston, MA—CT, ME, MA, NH, RI, VT	Suite 810, 101 Merrimac St., 02114–4719	Andrew D. Caverly, *Acting*
Chicago, IL—IA, IL, IN, KY, MN, MO, WI	Suite 1860, 55 E. Monroe St., 60603–5701	C. Steven Baker
Cleveland, OH—DE, DC, MD, MI, OH, PA, WV	Suite 200, 1111 Superior Ave., 44114	John M. Mendenhall, *Acting*
Dallas, TX—AR, LA, NM, OK, TX	Suite 2150, 1999 Bryan St., 75201	Thomas B. Carter
Denver, CO—CO, KS, MT, ND, NE, SD, UT, WY	Suite 1523, 1961 Stout St., 80294–0101	Janice L. Charter, *Acting*
Los Angeles, CA—AZ, southern CA	Suite 700, 10877 Wilshire Blvd., 90024	Gregory W. Staples, *Acting*
New York—NJ, NY	Suite 1300, 150 William St., 10038	Michael J. Bloom
San Francisco, CA—Northern CA, HI, NV	Suite 570, 901 Market St., 94103	Jeffrey A. Klurfeld
Seattle, WA—AK, ID, OR, WA	Suite 2896, 915 2d Ave., 98174	Charles A. Harwood

Sources of Information

Contracts and Procurement Persons seeking to do business with the Federal Trade Commission should contact the Assistant CFO for Acquisitions, Federal Trade Commission, Washington, DC 20580. Phone, 202–326–2258. Fax, 202–326–3529. Internet, http://www.ftc.gov/ftc/procurement/procure.htm.

Electronic Access Commission consumer and business education publications are available electronically through the Internet, at http://www.ftc.gov/.

Employment Civil service registers are used in filling positions for economists, accountants, investigators, and other professional, administrative, and clerical personnel. The Federal Trade Commission employs a sizable number of attorneys under the excepted appointment procedure. All employment inquiries should be directed to the Director of Human Resource Management, Federal Trade Commission, Washington, DC 20580. Phone, 202–326–2022. Fax, 202–326–2328.

General Inquiries Persons desiring information on consumer protection, or restraint of trade questions, or to register a complaint, should contact the Federal Trade Commission or the nearest regional office.

Publications A copy of *Federal Trade Commission—"Best Sellers,"* which lists publications of interest to the general public, is available free upon request from the Public Reference Section, Federal Trade Commission, Washington, DC 20580. Phone, 202–326–2222. TTY, 202–326–2502.

For further information, contact the Office of Public Affairs, Federal Trade Commission, Pennsylvania Avenue at Sixth Street NW., Washington, DC 20580. Phone, 202–326–2180. Fax, 202–326–3676. Internet, http://www.ftc.gov/.

GENERAL SERVICES ADMINISTRATION

General Services Building, Eighteenth and F Streets NW., Washington, DC 20405
Phone, 202–708–5082. Internet, http://www.gsa.gov/.

Administrator of General Services	DAVID J. BARRAM
Special Assistant to the Administrator	JACKIE ROBINSON
Deputy Administrator	THURMAN M. DAVIS, SR.
Chief of Staff	MARTHA N. JOHNSON
Deputy Chief of Staff	ERIC M. DODDS
Associate Administrator for Equal Employment Opportunity	JAMES M. TAYLOR, *Acting*
Associate Administrator for Enterprise Development	DIETRA L. FORD
Associate Administrator for Communications	BETH NEWBURGER
Associate Administrator for Congressional and Intergovernmental Affairs	WILLIAM R. RATCHFORD
Associate Administrator for Management and Workplace Programs	SUSAN CLAMPITT
Chief of Staff for Management and Workplace Programs	ELAINE P. DADE
Director of Human Resources	GAIL T. LOVELACE
Director of Management Services	JOSEPH R. RODRIGUEZ
Controller	ELISABETH GUSTAFSON
Chief Information Officer	SHEREEN G. REMEZ
Deputy Chief Information Officer	DONALD P. HEFFERNAN, *Acting*
Assistant Chief Information Officer for Information Infrastructure and Support	DONALD P. HEFFERNAN
Assistant Chief Information Officer for Planning and Information Architecture	L. DIANE SAVOY, *Acting*
Director, Corporate Information Network	DIANE L. HERDT
Director, GSA Data Warehousing	JOHN J. LANDERS
Inspector General	WILLIAM R. BARTON
Deputy Inspector General	JOEL S. GALLAY
Executive Assistant to the Inspector General	GARRETT J. DAY
Assistant Inspector General for Administration	JAMES E. LE GETTE
Assistant Inspector General for Auditing	WILLIAM E. WHYTE, JR.
Assistant Inspector General for Investigations	JAMES E. HENDERSON
Counsel to the Inspector General	KATHLEEN S. TIGHE
Director, Internal Evaluation Staff	ANDREW A. RUSSONIELLO
Chairman, GSA Board of Contract Appeals	STEPHEN M. DANIELS
Vice Chairman	ROBERT W. PARKER
Board Counsel	ANNE M. QUIGLEY
Clerk of the Board	BEATRICE JONES
Chief Financial Officer	THOMAS R. BLOOM
Director of Budget	WILLIAM B. EARLY, JR.
Director of Finance	RONALD H. RHODES, *Acting*
Director of Performance Management	CAROLE A. HUTCHINSON

Director of Financial Management Systems	WILLIAM J. TOPOLEWSKI
General Counsel	EMILY CLARK HEWITT
Associate General Counsel for General Law	EUGENIA D. ELLISON, *Acting*
Associate General Counsel for Personal Property	GEORGE N. BARCLAY
Associate General Counsel for Real Property	SAMUEL J. MORRIS III

FEDERAL SUPPLY SERVICE

1941 Jefferson Davis Highway, Arlington, VA; Mailing address: Washington, DC 20406
Phone, 703–305–6667. Fax, 703–305–6577

Commissioner, Federal Supply Service	FRANK P. PUGLIESE, JR.
Deputy Commissioner	DONNA D. BENNETT
Chief of Staff	BARNEY BRASSEUX
Comptroller	JON JORDAN
Director of Transportation Audits	JEFFREY W. THURSTON
FSS Chief Information Officer	RAYMOND J. HANLEIN
Assistant Commissioner for Acquisition	WILLIAM N. GORMLEY
Assistant Commissioner for Business Management and Marketing	GARY FEIT
Assistant Commissioner for Contract Management	PATRICIA MEAD
Assistant Commissioner for Distribution Management	JOHN ROEHMER
Assistant Commissioner for Transportation and Property Management	ALLAN ZAIC
Assistant Commissioner for Vehicle Acquisition and Leasing Services	LESTER GRAY JR.

FEDERAL TECHNOLOGY SERVICE

Suite 210 North, 7799 Leesburg Pike, Falls Church, VA 22043
Phone, 703–285–1020

Commissioner for Federal Technology Service	DENNIS J. FISCHER
Deputy Commissioner	SANDRA N. BATES
Chief Financial Officer	ROBERT E. SUDA
Assistant Commissioner for Acquisition	C. ALLEN OLSON
Assistant Commissioner for Information Security	THOMAS R. BURKE
Assistant Commissioner for Information Technology Integration	CHARLES SELF
Assistant Commissioner for Regional Services	MARGARET BINNS
Assistant Commissioner for Service Delivery	FRANK E. LALLEY
Assistant Commissioner for Service Development	BRUCE BRIGNULL
Assistant Commissioner for Strategic Planning and Business Development	ABBY PIRNIE

PUBLIC BUILDINGS SERVICE

General Services Building, Eighteenth and F Streets NW., Washington, DC 20405
Phone, 202–501–1100

Commissioner, Public Buildings Service	ROBERT A. PECK
Deputy Commissioner	PAUL E. CHISTOLINI

Chief of Staff	ANTHONY E. COSTA
Chief Information Officer	PAUL WOHLLEBEN
Assistant Commissioner for Business Performance	ANTHONY ARTIGLIERE, *Acting*
Assistant Commissioner for External Affairs	JOEL ODUM
Assistant Commissioner for the Federal Protective Service	CLARENCE EDWARDS
Assistant Commissioner for Financial and Information Services	FREDERICK T. ALT
Assistant Commissioner for Portfolio Management	PAMELA WESSLING
Assistant Commissioner for Property Disposal	BRIAN K. POLLY
Assistant Commissioner for Strategic Innovations	SHARON ROACH
Director, PBS Centers of Expertise	JOHN PETKEWICH

OFFICE OF GOVERNMENTWIDE POLICY

General Services Building, Eighteenth and F Streets NW., Washington, DC 20405
Phone, 202–501–8880

Associate Administrator for Governmentwide Policy	G. MARTIN WAGNER
Chief of Staff	JOHN SINDELAR
Executive Officer	STEPHANIE FONTENOT
Director, Committee Management Secretariat Staff	JAMES DEAN
Director of Electronic Commerce	ANTHONY TRENKLE
Director, Information Systems Management Staff	MIKE MCNEILL
Director, Regulatory Information Service Center	MARK SCHOENBERG
Deputy Associate Administrator for Acquisition Policy	IDA M. USTAD
Deputy Associate Administrator for Information Technology	JOAN STEYAERT
Deputy Associate Administrator for Intergovernmental Solutions	FRANCIS A. MCDONOUGH
Deputy Associate Administrator for Real Property	DAVID L. BIBB
Deputy Associate Administrator for Transportation and Personal Property	REBECCA R. RHODES

[For the General Services Administration statement of organization, see the *Code of Federal Regulations*, Title 41, Part 105–53]

The General Services Administration establishes policy for and provides economical and efficient management of Government property and records, including construction and operation of buildings; procurement and distribution of supplies; utilization and disposal of real and personal property; transportation, traffic, and communications management; and management of the governmentwide automatic data processing resources program. Its functions are carried out at three levels of organization: the central office, regional offices, and field activities.

The General Services Administration (GSA) was established by section 101 of the Federal Property and Administrative Services Act of 1949 (40 U.S.C. 751).

GENERAL SERVICES ADMINISTRATION

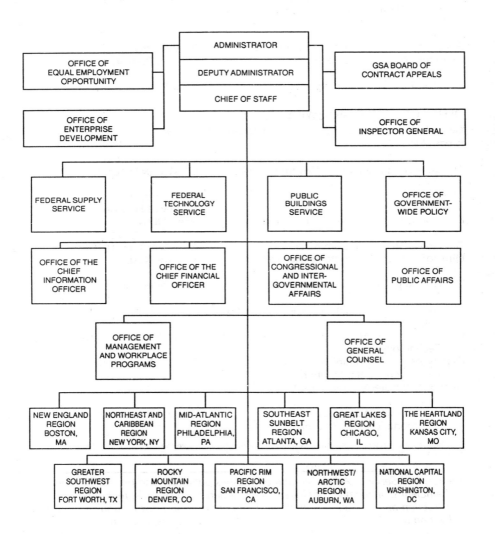

Acquisition Policy The Office of Acquisition Policy within the Office of Governmentwide Policy, plans, directs, and coordinates a comprehensive, agencywide acquisition policy program, including the establishment of major agency acquisition goals and objectives.

The Office of Acquisition Policy has a major role in developing, maintaining, issuing, and administering guiding principles via the Federal Acquisition Regulation (FAR), which is applicable to all Federal agencies. It chairs the Civilian Agency Acquisition Council and provides administrative support through the FAR Secretariat. The Office develops GSA implementing and supplementing principles required by FAR, which is published as the General Services Administration Acquisition Regulation.

The Office manages the agency's internal system for the suspension and debarment of nonresponsive contractors and a governmentwide system for exchanging information on debarred, suspended, and ineligible parties. The Office also is responsible for overseeing the agency's acquisition information system and serves as agency coordinator for the Federal Procurement Data System.

The Office's Federal Acquisition Institute fosters and promotes governmentwide career management and training programs to develop a professional workforce and coordinates

governmentwide studies to improve the procurement process.

For further information, call 202–501–1043.

Domestic Assistance Catalog The Federal Domestic Assistance Catalog Program collects and disseminates information on all federally operated domestic assistance programs such as grants, loans, and insurance. This information is published annually in the Catalog of Federal Domestic Assistance, and is available through the Federal Assistance Programs Retrieval System, a nationally accessible computer system.

For further information, contact the Federal Domestic Assistance Catalog staff. Phone, 202–708–5126.

Office of Enterprise Development The Office of Enterprise Development (OED) focuses on programs, policy, and outreach to assist the small business community nationwide in doing business with GSA. By accessing the Office's home page, small businesses can obtain information on GSA's current and proposed solicitations, on OED's national and regional contacts where small business counseling services are available, and on upcoming GSA outreach workshops and conferences. The Web site address is http://www.gsa.gov/oed.

For further information, call 202–501–1021.

Small Business Centers—General Services Administration

Region	Address	Telephone
National Capital—Washington, DC	Rm. 1050, 7th & D Sts. SW., 20407	202–708–5804
New England—Boston, MA	Rm. 290, 10 Causeway St., 02222	617–565–8100
Northeast and Caribbean—New York, NY	Rm. 18–130, 26 Federal Plz., 10278	212–264–1234
Mid-Atlantic—Philadelphia, PA	Rm. 808, 100 Penn Sq. E., 19107–3396	215–656–5523
Southeast Sunbelt—Atlanta, GA	Rm. 2832, 401 W. Peachtree St. NW., 30303	404–331–5103
Great Lakes—Chicago, IL	Rm. 3714, 230 S. Dearborn St., 60604	312–353–5383
Heartland—Kansas City, MO	Rm. 1160, 1500 E. Bannister Rd., 64131	816–926–7203
Southwest—Fort Worth, TX	Rm. 11A09, 819 Taylor St., 76102	817–978–3284
Rocky Mountain—Denver, CO	Rm. 145, Denver Federal Ctr., 80225–0006	303–326–7408
Pacific Rim—San Francisco, CA	Rm. 405, 450 Golden Gate Ave., 94102	415–522–2700
Satellite office—Los Angeles, CA	Rm. 3259, 300 N. Los Angeles St., 90012	213–894–3210
Northwest/Arctic—Auburn, WA	400 15th St. SW., 98001	206–931–7956

Contract Appeals The General Services Administration Board of Contract Appeals is responsible for resolving disputes arising out of contracts with the

General Services Administration, the Department of the Treasury, the Department of Education, the Department of Commerce, and other

Government agencies. The Board is also empowered to hear and decide requests for review of transportation audit rate determinations; claims by Federal civilian employees regarding travel and relocation expenses; and claims for the proceeds of the sale of property of certain Federal civilian employees. In addition, the Board provides alternative dispute resolution services to executive agencies in both contract disputes which are the subject of a contracting officer's decision and other contract-related disputes. Although the Board is located within the agency, it functions as an independent tribunal.

For further information, contact the Board of Contract Appeals (G), General Services Administration, Washington, DC 20405. Phone, 202–501–0585.

Equal Employment Opportunity   The Office of Equal Employment Opportunity is responsible for the agency's equal employment opportunity program and nondiscrimination in Federal financial assistance compliance and federally conducted programs.

For further information, call 202–501–0767.

Federal Technology Service

The Federal Technology Service (FTS) delivers reimbursable local and long-distance telecommunications, information technology, and information security services to Federal agencies. Its mission is to provide information technology solutions and network services to support its customers' missions worldwide through its two business lines: Network Services and Information Technology Solutions.

The Network Services business line enables the FTS to provide its customers with end-to-end telecommunications services. Also included in this business line are several information technology (IT) applications approved by the Interagency Management Council which ensure that state-of-the-art technologies are deployed throughout the Government in a timely and cost-effective manner.

—The FTS2000 contracts provide long-distance telecommunications

service that offers the Federal Government low-cost, state-of-the-art, integrated voice, data, and video telecommunications. FTS2000 services are provided to more than 1.7 millions users through two multi-billion dollar 10-year contacts that were awarded to AT&T and Sprint in December 1988. In the December 1997 *GSA Report to Congress on the Cost Effectiveness of the FTS2000 Program*, FTS2000 prices were shown to be 14 percent lower in the aggregate for the Government's telecommunications requirements than the lowest commercial equivalent. With the contracts due to expire in December 1998, FTS has worked with industry, Congress, and the Executive branch to develop a post-FTS2000 program strategy, or FTS2001, which outlines a flexible, evolving approach to provide for comprehensive contracts offering all telecommunications services worldwide. As allowed by law, FTS2001 will no longer be mandatory for Federal agencies; thus it will be increasingly important for FTS2001 services to be better, faster, cheaper, and easier to use than commercial services.

—Local Telecommunications Service provides local voice and data telecommunications to Federal agencies nationwide. In the wake of reforms effected by the Telecommunications Act of 1996, FTS is pursuing lower prices for service in the major markets through its Metropolitan Area Acquisition program. The program will take advantage of competition to achieve substantial price reductions for local telecommunications services in metropolitan areas.

The IT Solutions business line helps agencies acquire, manage, integrate, and use technology resources and protect the security of Federal information on-line. The programs under this business line are nonmandatory and fully self-supporting.

—The Federal Information Systems Support Program (FISSP) provides agencies with systems definition and design, business and scientific software services, computer security studies and risk analyses, facilities management, and other related services through contracts with private sector vendors. Its business volume grew 13%, from $276 million in FY 1995 to $312 million in FY 1996.

—The Federal Systems Integration and Management Center (FEDSIM) helps agencies acquire and use information systems and technology, including hardware, software, maintenance, training, and analyst support. FEDSIM, through the Virtual Data Center Services contract, provides data processing outsourcing services to Federal agencies, offering a quick, low-cost alternative for obtaining commercial data processing services.

—The Federal Computer Acquisition Center (FEDCAC) delivers full-service management of computer acquisitions worth more than $100 million. Its achievements include the FBI Fingerprint Identification System, the State Department mainframe upgrades, the Agriculture Department Forest Service Automation System, the National Institutes of Health computer facilities acquisition, and the Department of Energy telecommunications system. FEDCAC is currently working with FTS' Seat Management Program Office to award the Seat Management contract to provide desktop computing as a comprehensive service.

—The Federal Acquisition Support for Technology (FAST) procures commercially available off-the-self information technology software, equipment, and noncomplex integration services.

—The Office of Information Security provides worldwide information technology support services to all Government activities, including United States allies, conducting classified, sensitive but unclassified, diplomatic, or military missions. To meet this responsibility, the program participates in the development of governmentwide information security policies and provides a comprehensive range of information security technical services necessary to manage and support clients' mission critical information systems.

Federal Information Center Program A clearinghouse for information about the Federal Government, the program can eliminate the maze of referrals that people have experienced in contacting the Federal Government. Persons with questions about a Government program, service, or agency, and who are unsure of which agency to contact, should contact the Center. A specialist will either answer the question or locate an expert who can.

The Center's telephones are answered by information specialists between 9 a.m. and 8 p.m., eastern time, Monday through Friday, except Federal holidays. The Center's information recordings that discuss frequently asked questions are available 24 hours a day.

For further information, contact the Federal Information Center toll-free. Phone, 800–688–9889. TDD, 800–326–2996.

Federal Information Relay Service (FIRS) The Service acts as an intermediary for telecommunications between hearing individuals and individuals who are deaf, hard of hearing, and/or have speech disabilities. FIRS is accessible nationwide to all 50 States as well as the District of Columbia, Puerto Rico, the Virgin Islands, and Guam.

FIRS enables Federal employees to conduct official duties and the general public to conduct business with the Federal Government and its agencies. FIRS broadens employment and advances opportunities for individuals who are deaf, hard of hearing, and/or with speech disabilities by ensuring them accessibility to the Federal telecommunications system. There are no restrictions on the length or numbers of calls placed.

For a free copy of the *U.S. Government TDD/TTY Directory*, contact the Consumer Information Center, Department TDD/TTY, Pueblo, CO 81009. The directory is also available electronically through the Internet, at http://www.pueblo.gsa.gov/.

For a free copy of the *Federal Information Relay Service Brochure*, contact the GSA Federal Telecommunications Service. Phone, 703–904–2848. TDD, 202–501–2860 or 703–904–2440. To reach the Federal Information Relay Service, call 800–877–

8339. For FIRS online directory access, call 800–877–8845 (TDD).

For further information, contact the General Services Administration Federal Telecommunications Service. Phone, 703–904–2848. TDD, 202–501–2860.

Federal Supply Service

The Federal Supply Service (FSS) ensures that the Federal Government's requirements for personal property and administrative services are effectively met at the least overall cost to the taxpayer. It operates a worldwide supply system to contract for and distribute personal property and services to Federal agencies; provides governmentwide programs for transportation and travel management, transportation audits, and Federal fleet management; and administers a governmentwide property management program for the utilization of excess personal property and the donation and sale of surplus personal property.

The Service provides over $14 billion annually in commercial goods and services to customers worldwide. The supply and procurement business line focuses on obtaining quality goods and services at the best value using the aggregate purchasing power of the Government to pass savings to customers. It actively seeks participation from small businesses and serves as the distributor for mandatory sources under the Javits-Wagner-O'Day Act and Federal Prison Industries. It is also ready to respond to national or military emergencies.

FSS operates a network of distribution facilities which make available over 18,000 high-demand items for freight shipments to large customers or express shipments to customer desktops. Customer orders are filled through the business line distribution system or direct delivery from contractors.

The business line contracts for over 4 million items and services used by both military and civilian agencies, including computers and software, automobiles, airline travel, office equipment and supplies, scientific and law enforcement equipment, small package delivery, and the governmentwide purchase card. The business line reduces the Federal Government's financial, warehousing, transportation, and other administrative costs by eliminating the need for multiple agencies to make repetitive procurements for similar items. It procures a wide range of environmentally oriented products and services aimed at minimizing waste, conserving natural resources, and preventing pollution, including recycled-content products, alternative fuel vehicles, Energy Star computers and other office equipment, energy efficient appliances, safer paints and cleaning products, and recycling systems and services.

To eliminate unnecessary expenditures and maximize the utilization of federally owned personal property, FSS directs and coordinates, on a worldwide basis, a Government property management program. Under the business line, excess personal property valued at approximately $17.4 billion annually, at original acquisition cost, is available for transfer to other agencies and, when no longer needed by the Federal Government, is allocated to the States for donation to eligible recipients or disposed of through competitive public sales.

To provide Government agencies with economical fleet management services, FSS operates an Interagency Fleet Management System comprised of approximately 150,000 vehicles, ranging from compact sedans to buses and ambulances. GSA acquires the vehicles, ensures that fuel and maintenance/repair services are available, and disposes of the vehicles when due for replacement. In conjunction with the Department of Energy, FSS introduced alternative fuel vehicles into the Federal fleet, and currently has approximately 10,000 in use.

The Service's Fleet Management Program is also responsible for developing regulations and procedures governing the management and oversight of all Federal Government motor vehicles, except those exempted under the Federal Property and Administrative Services Act of 1949, as amended.

As the Government's civilian freight manager, the FSS transportation business line provides rating and routing services to customer agencies at 20–50 percent off commercial rates, as well as small package overnight delivery service at a savings of 70 percent below commercial rates.

In addition, FSS coordinates governmentwide policy development for the management of Government aircraft through the Interagency Committee for Aviation Policy. Through its Federal Aviation Management Information System, FSS stores aircraft and facility inventory, cost and utilization data, and contract, rental, and charter data pertinent to all civilian agency aircraft.

For further information, contact the Federal Supply Service, Washington, DC 20406. Phone, 703–305–5600.

Public Buildings Service

The Public Buildings Service (PBS) provides work environments for over one million Federal employees nationwide. Since 1949, PBS has served as a builder, developer, lessor, and manager of federally owned and leased properties, currently totaling more than 280 million square feet in the 50 States, the District of Columbia, Puerto Rico, and the Virgin Islands. PBS provides a full range of real estate services, property management, construction and repairs, security services, property disposal, and overall portfolio management.

For further information, contact the Office of the Commissioner. Phone, 202–501–1100.

Office of Portfolio Management The Office of Portfolio Management has broad responsibility for the management of GSA's portfolio of Government-owned and leased buildings. Its mission is to enhance the value and performance of the portfolio in four areas: maximizing return on investment; promoting effective building utilization and operation; supporting Federal social and economic programs; and serving GSA customers. Its principal activities include strategic and business planning, capital investment and divestment

decisionmaking, and analysis of portfolio and asset performance.

For further information, contact the Office of Portfolio Management. Phone, 202–501–0638.

Office of Financial and Information Systems The Office of Financial and Information Systems manages PBS' financial management and information technology systems. The Office's chief responsibility is to ensure the financial viability of PBS and the Federal Buildings Fund. The Office's information systems responsibilities include providing customer service, system develop, oversight of the nationwide information technology platform, and project management. The Office provides integration for major information technology projects to ensure data integrity, quality, and a standard environment.

For further information, contact the Office of Financial and Information Systems. Phone, 202–501–0658.

Office of Federal Protective Service The Office of Federal Protective Service (FPS) enforces security rules and regulations governing public buildings, maintains law and order, and protects life and property in GSA-controlled buildings. FPS offers a range of security services to protect employees and visitors in GSA-controlled buildings. The Office develops and administers guidelines and standards for uniformed force operations, investigates criminal offenses, and oversees communications and alarm systems. The Federal Protective Service coordinates with appropriate Federal, State, and local government officials for security and law enforcement requirements. Through Executive Order 12977, FPS plays a critical role in providing security for all Federal facilities through its leadership of the Federal Interagency Security Committee.

For further information, contact the Office of Federal Protective Service. Phone, 202–501–0907.

Office of Business Performance The Office of Business Performance develops and implements the nationwide PBS performance standards for the management of real property programs.

Business Performance provides performance measures, technical expertise and guidance, and program advocacy for a range of real property programs, including building operations, capital improvement, realty services, building environmental management, fire and occupational safety, historic preservation, accessibility, and recycling. Business Performance serves PBS regional offices by disseminating best practices, coordinating management initiatives such as reengineering and activity based costing, and acting as a data/information clearinghouse. The Office also works to improve PBS performance by coordinating benchmarking among regions, other Government agencies, and industry.

For further information, contact the Office of Business Performance. Phone, 202–501–0971.

Office of Strategic Innovations The Office of Strategic Innovations is responsible for nurturing and facilitating the development of innovative products, practices, and strategies that improve PBS' performance, services, and competitive edge. Responsibilities include innovating and evaluating emerging issues affecting PBS through teams or working groups; developing ideas until they are well-framed; working with other parts of PBS to coordinate and shepherd initiatives in alliance with their eventual "owners," either within the National Office, a Center of Expertise, or in the regions; and bringing together resources to review, evaluate, and pursue concepts and ideas.

For further information, contact the Office of Strategic Innovations. Phone, 202–501–0376.

Office of Property Disposal Property Disposal manages the use and disposal of surplus real property governmentwide. Surplus properties are redistributed to other Federal agencies, State and local governments, and eligible nonprofit institutions for various public purposes, or are sold competitively to the general public. As a central broker, PBS is a one-stop agency for property disposal, with an expansive network of market contacts in the private and public sectors. Property Disposal provides assistance

and advice on complex disposal issues to Congress, military departments, other Federal agencies, State and local governments, and the private sector. The majority of this work is performed on a reimbursable basis.

For further information, contact the Office of Property Disposal. Phone, 202–501–0210.

Office of External Affairs The Office of External Affairs focuses on customer relations, strategic marketing, industry outreach, and communications. External Affairs is responsible for pursuing an active strategy of external communications focused on customer agencies, Congress, the Office of Management and Budget, industry, and the public. External Affairs' National Account Executive Program is a special effort to partner with key customers to raise their awareness of current and future services offered by PBS.

For further information, contact the Office of External Affairs. Phone, 202–501–0018.

Centers of Expertise PBS Centers of Expertise are located at both the National Office and in regional offices across the country to deliver state-of-the-art information and hands-on operating assistance quickly and efficiently for a particular project or situation. Centers of Expertise are groups of recognized leaders in a particular area who keep abreast of state-of-the-art techniques, propose new solutions to problems, and provide technical assistance and guidance to PBS regional activities. The missions of the 12 Centers reflect the diversity in PBS operations and include Design Programs, Historic Buildings and Arts, Presidential Libraries, Retail Tenant Services, Energy and Public Utilities, Courthouse Management, Complex Leases, Child Care, Site Selection and Acquisition, Project Management, Border Stations, and Property Disposal.

For further information about the Centers, call 202–501–0887.

Regional Offices Regional offices are located in 11 U.S. cities. Within its area of jurisdiction, each regional office is responsible for executing assigned programs.

Regional Offices—General Services Administration

Region	Address	Administrator
New England	Boston, MA (10 Causeway St., 02222)	Robert J. Dunfey, Jr.
Northeast and Caribbean	New York, NY (26 Federal Plz., 10278)	Robert Martin, *Acting*
Mid-Atlantic	Philadelphia, PA (100 Penn Sq. E., 19107–3396)	Rafael Borras
Southeast Sunbelt	Atlanta, GA (Suite 2800, 401 W. Peachtree St. NW., 30365)	Carol A. Dortch
Great Lakes	Chicago, IL (230 S. Dearborn St., 60604)	William C. Burke
The Heartland	Kansas City, MO (1500 E. Bannister Rd., 64131)	Glen W. Overton
Greater Southwest	Fort Worth, TX (819 Taylor St., 76102)	John Pouland
Rocky Mountain	Denver, CO (Denver Federal Ctr., 80225–0006)	Polly B. Baca
Pacific Rim	San Francisco, CA (5th Fl., 450 Golden Gate Ave., 94102)	Kenn N. Kojima
Northwest/Arctic	Auburn, WA (GSA Ctr., 98002)	L. Jay Pearson
National Capital	Washington, DC (7th and D Sts. SW., 20407)	Nelson B. Alcalde

Sources of Information

Consumer Information Center (CIC)
Organized under the Office of Communications, CIC assists Federal agencies in the release of relevant and useful consumer information and generates increased public awareness of this information. CIC publishes quarterly the *Consumer Information Catalog,* which is free to the public and lists more than 200 free or low-cost Federal consumer interest publications. Topics include health, food, nutrition, money management, employment, Federal benefits, the environment, and education. The *Catalog* is widely distributed through congressional offices, Federal facilities, educators, State and local governmental consumer offices, and private nonprofit organizations. For a free copy of the *Catalog,* write to the Consumer Information Center, Pueblo, CO 81009. Phone, 888–8–PUEBLO (toll-free). Bulk copies are free to nonprofit organizations. Information regarding the Consumer Information Center is also available electronically through the Internet, at http://www.pueblo.gsa.gov/.

Contracts Individuals seeking to do business with the General Services Administration may obtain detailed information from the Business Service Centers listed in the preceding text. Inquiries concerning programs to assist small business should be directed to one of the Business Service Centers.

Electronic Access Information about GSA is available electronically through the Internet, at http://www.gsa.gov/.

Employment Inquiries and applications should be directed to the Human Resources Operations Division (CPS), Office of Human Resources, General Services Administration, Washington, DC 20405. Schools interested in the recruitment program should contact the Human Resources Operations Division (CPS), Office of Human Resources, Washington, DC 20405 (phone, 202–501–0370), and/or the appropriate regional office listed above.

Fraud and Waste Contact the Inspector General's Office at 800–424–5210 (toll-free) or 202–501–1780 (in the Washington, DC, metropolitan area).

Freedom of Information and Privacy Act Requests Inquiries concerning policies pertaining to Freedom of Information Act and Privacy Act matters should be addressed to the General Services Administration (CAI), Attn: GSA FOIA or Privacy Act Officer, Room 7100, Washington, DC 20405. Phone, 202–501–2262 or 501–1659. Fax, 202–501–2727. FOIA or Privacy Act requests concerning GSA regions should be directed to the FOIA or Privacy Act officers for the particular region (see regional office listing in the preceding text).

Public and News Media Inquiries The Office of Communications is responsible for the coordination of responses to inquiries from both the general public and news media, as well as for maintaining an information network with agency employees with regard to items of interest to the Federal worker. The Office issues news releases and is responsible for publishing the *GSA Update,* a daily bulletin of noteworthy items designed to keep agency employees apprised of pertinent issues.

Publications Many publications are available at moderate prices through the bookstores of the Government Printing

Office or from customer supply centers. Others may be obtained free or at production cost from a Small Business Center or the Federal Information Center. (*See* pages 575 and 577, respectively.) The telephone numbers and addresses of the Federal Information Centers and of the Government Printing Office bookstores are listed in local telephone directories. If a publication is not distributed by any of the centers or stores, inquiries should be directed to the originating agency's service or office. The addresses for inquiries are:

Public Buildings Service (P), General Services Administration, Washington, DC 20405

Federal Supply Service (F), General Services Administration, Washington, DC 20406

Office of Finance (BC), General Services Administration, Washington, DC 20405

Federal Technology Service (T), General Services Administration, Falls Church, VA 22043

Those who would like a list of publications or who are not certain of the service or office of origin should write to the Director of Publications (XD), General Services Administration, Washington, DC 20405. Phone, 202–501–1235.

Small Business Activities   Inquiries concerning programs to assist small businesses should be directed to one of the Small Business Centers listed in the preceding text.

Speakers   Inquiries and requests for speakers should be directed to the Office of Communications (X), General Services Administration, Washington, DC 20405 (phone, 202–501–0705); or contact the nearest regional office.

For further information concerning the General Services Administration, contact the Office of Communications (X), General Services Administration, Washington, DC 20405. Phone, 202–501–0705. Internet, http://www.gsa.gov/.

INTER–AMERICAN FOUNDATION

901 North Stuart Street, Arlington, VA 22203
Phone, 703–841–3800

Board of Directors:

Chair	MARIA OTERO
Vice Chair	NEIL H. OFFEN
Directors	HARRIET C. BABBITT, JEFFREY DAVIDOW, NANCY P. DORN, MARK L. SCHNEIDER, PATRICIA HILL WILLIAMS, FRANK D. YTURRIA, (1 VACANCY)

Staff:

President	GEORGE A. EVANS
Senior Vice President and General Counsel	ADOLFO A. FRANCO
Vice President for Financial Management and Systems	WINSOME WELLS
Vice President for Learning and Dissemination	ANNE TERNES
Vice President for Programs	LINDA P. BORST

The Inter-American Foundation is an independent Federal agency that supports social and economic development in Latin America and the Caribbean. It makes grants primarily to private, indigenous organizations that carry out self-help projects benefiting poor people.

The Inter-American Foundation (IAF) was created in 1969 (22 U.S.C. 290f) as an experimental U.S. foreign assistance program. IAF works in Latin America and the Caribbean to promote equitable, participatory, and sustainable self-help development by awarding grants directly to local organizations throughout the region. It also enters into partnerships with public and private sector entities to scale up support and mobilize local, national, and international resources for grassroots development. From all of its innovative funding experiences, the Foundation extracts lessons learned and best practices to share with other donors and development practitioners throughout the hemisphere.

IAF is governed by a nine-person Board of Directors appointed by the President with the advice and consent of the Senate. Six members are drawn from the private sector and three from the Federal Government. The Board of Directors appoints the President of IAF.

Since 1972, IAF has made 3,996 grants totaling $448 million. Its operating budget consists of congressional appropriations and funds derived through the Social Progress Trust Fund of the Inter-American Development Bank.

For further information, contact the Office of the President, Inter-American Foundation, 901 North Stuart Street, Arlington, VA 22203. Phone, 703–841–3810.

MERIT SYSTEMS PROTECTION BOARD

1120 Vermont Avenue NW., Washington, DC 20419
Phone, 202–653–7124. Internet, http://www.mspb.gov/.

Chairman	BENJAMIN L. ERDREICH
Chief Counsel to the Chairman	WILLIAM B. WILEY
Legal Specialist to the Chairman	DENISE L. MILLER
Chief of Staff	ANITA LACY BOLES
Vice Chair	BETH S. SLAVET
Chief Counsel	TERRY VANN
Confidential Assistant	DONNA D. NEEDHAM
Member	SUSANNE T. MARSHALL
Senior Legal Counsel	ROBERT F. CONDON
Executive Assistant	MICHAL SUE PROSSER
Legal Counsel	LYNORE M. CARNES
Office of the Chairman:	
Chief Administrative Law Judge	PAUL G. STREB
Clerk of the Board	ROBERT E. TAYLOR
Director, Financial and Administrative Management	ROBERT W. LAWSHE
Director, Human Resources Management	MARSHA SCIALDO BOYD
Director, Information Resources Management	BARBARA B. WADE
Director, Office of Appeals Counsel	STEPHEN E. ALPERN
Director, Office of Equal Employment Opportunity	JANICE E. FRITTS
Director, Office of Policy and Evaluation	JOHN PALGUTA
Director, Office of Regional Operations	DARRELL L. NETHERTON

General Counsel   MARY L. JENNINGS
Legislative Counsel   SUSAN L. WILLIAMS

[For the Merit Systems Protection Board statement of organization, see the *Code of Federal Regulations*, Title 5, Part 1200]

The Merit Systems Protection Board protects the integrity of Federal merit systems and the rights of Federal employees working in the systems. In overseeing the personnel practices of the Federal Government, the Board conducts special studies of the merit systems, hears and decides charges of wrongdoing and employee appeals of adverse agency actions, and orders corrective and disciplinary actions when appropriate.

The Merit Systems Protection Board is a successor agency to the United States Civil Service Commission, established by act of January 16, 1883 (22 Stat. 403). Reorganization Plan No. 2 of 1978 (5 U.S.C. app.), effective January 1, 1979, pursuant to Executive Order 12107 of December 28, 1978, redesignated part of the Commission as the Merit Systems Protection Board. The Board's duties and authority are specified in 5 U.S.C. 1201–1210.

Activities

The Board has responsibility for hearing and adjudicating appeals by Federal employees of adverse personnel actions, such as removals, suspensions, and demotions. It also resolves cases involving reemployment rights, the denial of periodic step increases in pay, actions against administrative law judges, and charges of prohibited personnel practices, including charges in connection with whistleblowing. The

Board has the authority to enforce its decisions and to order corrective and disciplinary actions. An employee or applicant for employment involved in an appealable action that also involves an allegation of discrimination may ask the Equal Employment Opportunity Commission to review a Board decision. Final decisions and orders of the Board can be appealed to the U.S. Court of Appeals for the Federal Circuit.

The Board reviews regulations issued by the Office of Personnel Management and has the authority to require agencies to cease compliance with any regulation that could constitute a prohibited personnel practice. It also conducts special studies of the civil service and other executive branch merit systems and reports to the President and the Congress on whether the Federal work force is being adequately protected against political abuses and prohibited personnel practices.

Regional Offices—Merit Systems Protection Board

Region	Address	Director	Telephone
Atlanta Regional Office	401 W. Peachtree St. NW., 30308	Thomas J. Lanphear	404–730–2751
Central Regional Office	31st Fl., 230 S. Dearborn St., Chicago, IL 60604	Martin W. Baumgaertner	312–353–2923
Northeastern Regional Office.	Rm. 501, 2d & Chestnut Sts., Philadelphia, PA 19106.	Lonnie L. Crawford, Jr. ..	215–597–9960
Washington Regional Office.	Suite 1109, 5203 Leesburg Pike, Falls Church, VA 22041.	P.J. Winzer	703–756–6250
Western Regional Office	4th Fl., 250 Montgomery St., San Francisco, CA 94104.	Denis Marachi	415–705–2935

Field Offices—Merit Systems Protection Board

Region	Address	Chief Administrative Judge	Telephone
Boston, MA	Suite 1810, 99 Summer St., 02110	William Carroll	617–424–5700
Dallas, TX	Rm. 6F20, 1100 Commerce St., 75242	Sharon Jackson	214–767–0555
Denver, CO	Suite 100, 12567 W. Cedar Dr., Lakewood, CO 80228.	Joseph H. Hartman	303–969–5101
New York, NY	Rm. 3137A, 26 Federal Plz., 10278	Arthur Joseph	212–264–9372

MERIT SYSTEMS PROTECTION BOARD

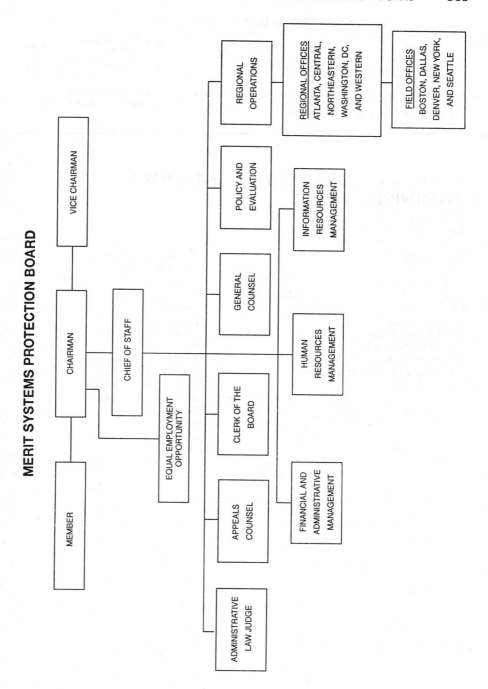

Field Offices—Merit Systems Protection Board

Region	Address	Chief Administrative Judge	Telephone
Seattle, WA	Rm. 1840, 915 2d Ave., 98174	Carl Berkenwald	206–220–7975

For further information, contact the Merit Systems Protection Board, 1120 Vermont Avenue NW., Washington, DC 20419. Phone, 202–653–7200; or 800–209–8960 (toll-free). TDD, 202–653–8896. Fax, 202–653–7130. Internet, http://www.mspb.gov/.

NATIONAL AERONAUTICS AND SPACE ADMINISTRATION

300 E Street SW., Washington, DC 20546
Phone, 202–358–0000

Administrator	DANIEL S. GOLDIN
Deputy Administrator	J.R. DAILEY, *Acting*
Associate Deputy Administrator	J.R. DAILEY
Associate Deputy Administrator (Technical)	MICHAEL I. MOTT
Chief Scientist	(VACANCY)
Chief Engineer	DANIEL R. MULVILLE
Chief Technologist	SAMUEL R. VENNERI
Chief Information Officer	LEE B. HOLCOMB
NASA Chief Financial Officer	ARNOLD G. HOLZ
Deputy Chief Financial Officer	KENNETH J. WINTER
Comptroller	MALCOLM L. PETERSON
Director, Financial Management Division	STEPHEN J. VARHOLY
Director, Resource Analysis Division	RICHARD BROZEN
Chief, Budget Operations Office	(VACANCY)
Associate Administrator for Headquarters Operations	MICHAEL D. CHRISTENSEN
Director, Headquarters Business and Administrative Services Division	TIMOTHY M. SULLIVAN
Director, Headquarters Information Technology and Communications Division	SANDRA DANIELS-GIBSON
Director, Headquarters Human Resources Management Division	ALFRED CASTILLO
Associate Administrator for Policy and Plans	ALAN M. LADWIG
Staff Director, NASA Advisory Council	ANNE L. ACCOLA
Director for Special Studies	SYLVIA K. KRAEMER
Chief Historian	ROGER LAUNIUS
Associate Administrator for Legislative Affairs	EDWARD HEFFERNAN, *Acting*
Deputy Associate Administrator	LYNN W. HENNINGER
Deputy Associate Administrator (Programs)	MARY D. KERWIN
Deputy Associate Administrator (Policy)	PHYLLIS A. LOVE
Director, Congressional Inquiries Division	HELEN ROTHMAN
Director, Congressional Liaison Division	MARY D. KERWIN, *Acting*
Director, Outreach Division	PHYLLIS A. LOVE, *Acting*
Associate Administrator for Life and Microgravity Sciences and Applications	ARNAULD E. NICOGOSSIAN
Deputy Associate Administrator	BETH M. McCORMICK

Director, Aerospace Medicine Division	JAMES D. COLLIER
Director, Flight Systems Office	EDMOND M. REEVES
Director, Life Sciences Division	JOAN VERNIKOS
Director, Microgravity Research Division	ROBERT C. RHOME
Director, Policy and Program Management	BETH M. MCCORMICK, *Acting*
Director, Space Development and Commercial Research Division	EDWARD A. GABRIS
Associate Administrator for Earth Science	GHASSEM R. ASRAR
Deputy Associate Administrator (Programs)	WILLIAM F. TOWNSEND
Deputy Associate Administrator (Management)	MICHAEL B. MANN
Director, Management Integration Division	DOUGLAS R. NORTON
Director, Flight Systems Division	MICHAEL R. LUTHER
Director, Science Division	(VACANCY)
Associate Administrator for Space Science	WESLEY T. HUNTRESS, JR.
Deputy Associate Administrator	EARLE K. HUCKINS
Director, Administration and Resources Management Division	ROY MAIZEL
Director, Advanced Technology and Mission Studies Division	PETER ULRICH
Director, Mission and Payload Development Division	KENNETH LEDBETTER
Director, Research Program Management Division	HENRY BRINTON
General Counsel	EDWARD A. FRANKLE
Deputy General Counsel	ROBERT M. STEPHENS
Associate General Counsel (Commercial)	JUNE W. EDWARDS
Associate General Counsel (Contracts)	DAVID P. FORBES
Associate General Counsel (General Law)	DORIS WOJNAROWSKI
Associate General Counsel (Intellectual Property)	JOHN G. MANNIX
Associate Administrator for Procurement	DEIDRE A. LEE
Deputy Associate Administrator	THOMAS S. LUEDTKE
Director, Analysis Division	ANNE C. GUENTHER
Director, Contract Management Division	R. SCOTT THOMPSON
Director, Program Operations Division	JAMES A. BALINSKAS
Associate Administrator for Small and Disadvantaged Business Utilization	RALPH C. THOMAS III
Associate Administrator for Public Affairs	PEGGY C. WILHIDE
Deputy Associate Administrator	PAULA M. CLEGGETT-HALEIM
Director, Media Services Division	BRIAN D. WELCH, *Acting*
Director, Public Services Division	(VACANCY)
Associate Administrator for Space Flight	JOSEPH H. ROTHENBERG
Deputy Associate Administrator	RICHARD J. WISNIEWSKI
Deputy Associate Administrator (Space Station Program)	GRETCHEN W. MCCLAIN
Deputy Associate Administrator (Business Management)	(VACANCY)
Deputy Associate Administrator (Space Shuttle)	STEPHEN S. OSWALD
Associate Administrator for Management Systems and Facilities	JEFFREY E. SUTTON, *Acting*
Deputy Associate Administrator	(VACANCY)
Director, Environmental Management Division	OLGA DOMINGUEZ, *Acting*

Director, Facilities Engineering Division	WILLIAM W. BRUBAKER
Director, Information Resources Management Division	ALI S. MONTASSER
Director, Management Assessment Division	DANALEE GREEN
Director, Security, Logistics, Aircraft, and Industrial Relations Division	MARK R.J. BORSI, *Acting*
Associate Administrator for Safety and Mission Assurance	FREDERICK D. GREGORY
Deputy Associate Administrator	MICHAEL A. GREENFIELD
Executive Director, Aerospace Safety Advisory Panel	NORMAN B. STARKEY
Director, Enterprise Safety and Mission Assurance Division	PEGGY L. EVANICH
Director, Safety and Risk Management Division	JAMES D. LLOYD
Associate Administrator for Aeronautics and Space Transportation Technology	RICHARD S. CHRISTIANSEN, *Acting*
Deputy Associate Administrator	(VACANCY)
Deputy Associate Administrator (Space Transportation Technology)	GARY E. PAYTON
Director, Research and Technology Division	TERRENCE J. HERTZ, *Acting*
Director, Alliance Development Office	LOUIS J. WILLIAMS
Director, Enterprise Management Office	ANNGIENETTA R. JOHNSON
Director, Resources Management Office	GLENN C. FULLER
Director, Commercial Programs Division	ROBERT L. NORWOOD
Associate Administrator for Human Resources and Education	SPENCE M. ARMSTRONG
Director, Education Division	FRANKLIN C. OWENS
Director, Management Systems Division	STANLEY S. KASK, JR.
Director, Personnel Division	VICKI A. NOVAK
Director, Training and Development Division	JOSEPH MCELWEE, JR.
Associate Administrator for Equal Opportunity Programs	GEORGE E. REESE
Deputy Associate Administrator	OCEOLA S. HALL
Director, Affirmative Employment and Diversity Policy Division	JAMES A. WESTBROOKS
Director, Discrimination Complaints Division	BRENDA MANUEL-ALEXANDER, *Acting*
Director, Minority University Research and Education Division	BETTIE L. WHITE
Inspector General	ROBERTA L. GROSS
Assistant Inspector General for Investigations	RICHARD D. TRIPLETT
Assistant Inspector General for Auditing	RUSSELL A. RAU
Assistant Inspector General for Inspections and Assessments	DAVID M. CUSHING
Assistant Inspector General for Partnerships and Alliances	LEWIS D. RINKER
Advanced Technology Program Manager	THOMAS J. TALLEUR
Director, Resources Management Division	CHARLES E. HEATON, JR.
Associate Administrator for External Relations	JOHN D. SHUMACHER
Deputy Associate Administrator	LYNN F.H. CLINE
Deputy Associate Administrator (Space Flight)	MICHAEL F. O'BRIEN

Director, Assessments and Technology Division	MICHAEL F. O'BRIEN, *Acting*
Director, Resources Management Office	SHIRLEY A. PEREZ
Director, Space Science and Aeronautics Division	JAMES B. HIGGINS, *Acting*
Director, Mission to Planet Earth Division	WILLIAM W. TURNER, *Acting*
Director, Space Flight Division	ANGELA P. DIAZ
Director, Inventions and Contributions Board	ROBERT J. BOBEK

NASA Centers

Director, Ames Research Center	HENRY MCDONALD
Director, George C. Marshall Space Flight Center	(VACANCY)
Director, Goddard Space Flight Center	ALPHONSO V. DIAZ
Manager, NASA Management Office, Jet Propulsion Laboratory	KURT LINDSTROM
Director, John F. Kennedy Space Center	ROY D. BRIDGES
Director, Langley Research Center	JEREMIAH F. CREEDON
Director, Lewis Research Center	DONALD J. CAMPBELL
Director, Lyndon B. Johnson Space Center	GEORGE W.S. ABBEY
Director, John C. Stennis Space Center	ROY S. ESTESS
Director, Dryden Flight Research Center	KENNETH J. SZALAI

[For the National Aeronautics and Space Administration statement of organization, see the *Code of Federal Regulations*, Title 14, Part 1201]

The National Aeronautics and Space Administration conducts research for the solution of problems of flight within and outside the Earth's atmosphere and develops, constructs, tests, and operates aeronautical and space vehicles. It conducts activities required for the exploration of space with manned and unmanned vehicles and arranges for the most effective utilization of the scientific and engineering resources of the United States with other nations engaged in aeronautical and space activities for peaceful purposes.

The National Aeronautics and Space Administration was established by the National Aeronautics and Space Act of 1958, as amended (42 U.S.C. 2451 *et seq.*).

NASA Headquarters

Planning, coordinating, and controlling Administration programs are vested in Headquarters. Directors of NASA centers are responsible for the execution of agency programs, largely through contracts with research, development, and manufacturing enterprises. A broad range of research and development activities are conducted in NASA Centers by Government-employed scientists, engineers, and technicians to evaluate new concepts and phenomena and to maintain the competence required to manage contracts with private enterprises.

Planning, directing, and managing research and development programs are the responsibility of seven program offices, all of which report to and receive overall guidance and direction from the Administrator. The overall planning and direction of institutional operations at NASA Centers and management of agencywide institutional resources are the responsibility of the appropriate Institutional Associate Administrator under the overall guidance and direction of the Administrator.

Aeronautics and Space Transportation Technology The Office of Aeronautics and Space Transportation Technology conducts programs that pioneer the identification, development, verification, transfer, application, and

NATIONAL AERONAUTICS AND SPACE ADMINISTRATION

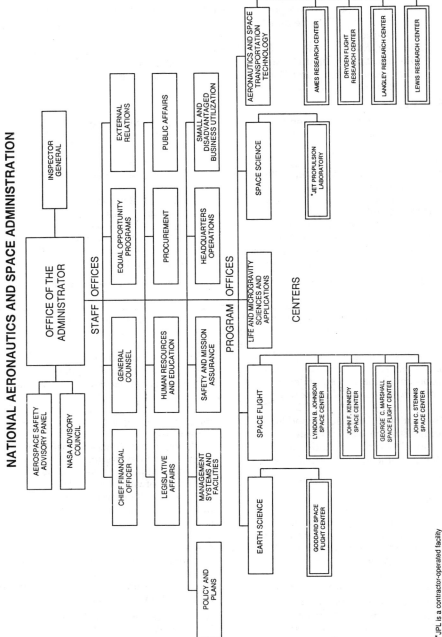

*JPL is a contractor-operated facility

commercialization of high-payoff aeronautics and space transportation technologies. The Office seeks to promote economic growth and security and to enhance U.S. competitiveness through safe, superior, and environmentally compatible U.S. civil and military aircraft, through a safe, efficient national aviation system, and through low-cost access to space. In addition, the Office is responsible for managing the Ames, Dryden Flight, Langley, and Lewis Research Centers.

For further information, call 202–358–2693.

Life and Microgravity Sciences and Applications   The Office of Life and Microgravity Sciences and Applications conducts programs concerned with life sciences, microgravity sciences and applications, aerospace medicine and occupational health programs, and space development and commercialization. The Office directs the planning, development, integration, and operations support for NASA missions which use the space shuttle, free flyers, international space station *Mir*, and other advanced carriers. The Office also establishes all requirements and standards for design, development, and operation of human space flight systems and facilities.

For further information, call 202–358–0123.

Earth Science Enterprise   The Office of Earth Science (OES) manages NASA's Earth Science Enterprise. The goal of the Earth Science Enterprise is to understand the effects of natural and human-induced changes on the global environment. The unique vantage point of space provides information about Earth's land, atmosphere, ice, oceans, and life that could not be gathered in any other way. Data returned by satellites, expanded by data from aircraft, balloons, and ground-based platforms, give public and private resource managers the scientific understanding they need to craft sound environmental policies and make informed economic decisions for the future. The Office also has institutional management responsibility for the Goddard Space Flight Center and

maintains contact with the National Academy of Sciences and other science advisory and coordinating boards and committees.

For further information, call 202–358–2165.

Space Flight   The Office of Space Flight (OSF) is NASA's principal organization for space flight operations and utilization involving human space flight. It consists of the following programmatic missions: flight to and from space for people and cargo, operating habitable space facilities, and managing the utilization of these facilities in support of NASA's space missions, such as space missions from and to Earth. The Office is responsible for the space shuttle, space communications, and spectrum management, and is currently leading development of the international space station. The Office is also responsible for institutional management of the Kennedy Space Center, Marshall Space Flight Center, Johnson Space Flight Center, and the Stennis Space Center.

Through its centers, the Office plans, directs, and executes the development, acquisition, testing, and operation of all elements of the Space Shuttle Program; plans, directs, and manages execution of prelaunch, launch, flight landing, post-flight operations, and payload assignments; maintains and upgrades the design of ground and flight systems throughout the operational period; procures recurring system hardware; develops and implements necessary policy with other government and commercial users of the space shuttle; and coordinates all associated research.

NASA is leading an international effort to build and deploy a permanently manned space station into Earth's orbit. Elements of the space station will be provided by Canada, Japan, Italy, Russia, and 10 European nations represented by the European Space Agency. The space station will be a permanent outpost in space where humans will live and work productively for extended periods of time. It will provide an advanced research laboratory to explore space and employ its resources, as well as the opportunity to learn to build, operate, and maintain systems in space. U.S.

elements of the space station will be launched aboard the space shuttle and assembled in orbit. The first flight is currently scheduled for 1998.

For further information, call 202–358–2015.

Space Science The Office of Space Science conducts programs and research designed to understand the origin, evolution, and structure of the universe and the solar system. The Office also manages NASA's activities at the Jet Propulsion Laboratory and maintains contacts with the Space Studies Board of the National Academy of Sciences and with other science advisory boards and committees.

For further information, call 202–358–1409.

NASA Centers

Ames Research Center The Center, located at Moffett Field, CA, provides leadership for NASA in aviation operations systems, astrobiology, and information systems research and technology development. The Center fulfills this mission through the development and operation of unique national facilities and the conduct and management of leading edge research and technology programs. These activities are vital to the achievement of the Nation's aeronautics and space goals, and to its security and economic prosperity.

Dryden Flight Research Center The Center, which is located in Edwards, CA, conducts safe, timely aerospace flight research and aircraft operations in support of agency and national needs. It assures preeminent flight research capability through effective management and maintenance of unique national expertise and facilities, and provides operational landing support for the national space transportation system.

Goddard Space Flight Center The Center, which is located in Greenbelt, MD, conducts Earth science and applications programs and Earth-orbiting spacecraft and experiment development and flight operations. It develops and operates tracking and data acquisition systems and conducts supporting mission

operations. It also develops and operates *Spacelab* payloads; space physics research programs; life science programs; information systems technology; sounding rockets and sounding rocket payloads; launch vehicles; balloons and balloon experiments; planetary science experiments; sensors for environmental monitoring and ocean dynamics; and manages the development of operational weather satellites for the National Oceanic and Atmospheric Administration.

Lyndon B. Johnson Space Center The Center, which is located in Houston, TX, is the NASA center of excellence for human operations in space. The Center strives to advance the national capability for human exploration and utilization of space by research, development, and operation of the space shuttle, the international space station (ISS), and other space systems and by developing and maintaining excellence in the fields of project management, space systems engineering, medical and life sciences, lunar and planetary geosciences, and crew and mission operations. It is also the lead center for several agencywide programs and initiatives, including the space shuttle and ISS program, space operations, extra-vehicular activity (EVA) projects, astromaterials sciences, biomedical research, advanced human support technology, and space medicine.

John F. Kennedy Space Center The Center, which is located in Florida, is the NASA center of excellence for launch and payload processing operations. The Center is home to the space shuttle fleet, which transports astronaut crews, space station elements, and a wide variety of payloads into Earth orbit and beyond. It also provides Government oversight of NASA expendable vehicle launches and the launch of NASA-sponsored payloads.

Langley Research Center The Center, located in Hampton, VA, provides leadership in airframe systems and atmospheric science and is a center of excellence for structures and materials. It conducts research in the critical disciplines of fundamental

aerodynamics, propulsion/airframe integration, and hypersonic propulsion and operates unique national facilities in support of national research programs.
Lewis Research Center The Center, located in Cleveland, OH, provides leadership in aeropropulsion technology and is a center of excellence for turbomachinery. The Center also conducts research in critical disciplines of materials, structures, internal fluid mechanics instrumentation, and controls and electronics. All of these efforts are supported by unique research and development facilities.
George C. Marshall Space Flight Center The Center, which is located in Huntsville, AL, is the principal NASA center for design, development, integration, and testing of propulsion systems, launch vehicles, and space transportation systems, including propulsive stages for orbital transfer and deep space missions. It develops, integrates, and operates astrophysics, space physics, and microgravity sciences payloads and experiments. It has a supporting role in developing capabilities in the astronomy, astrophysics, and Earth sciences disciplines. It is the prime center for integrated payload utilization across all science disciplines.
John C. Stennis Space Center The Center, which is located in Stennis Space Center, MS, operates, maintains, and manages a world-class propulsion testing facility for the development, certification, and acceptance testing of the space shuttle main engine. It has a supporting role in technology utilization, applications, and commercialization programs in environmental system sciences and observations, remote sensing, and image processing systems.

Government-Owned/Contractor-Operated Facility

Jet Propulsion Laboratory The Laboratory, which is operated under contract by the California Institute of Technology in Pasadena, CA, develops spacecraft and space sensors and conducts mission operations and ground-based research in support of solar system

exploration, Earth science and applications, Earth and ocean dynamics, space physics and astronomy, and life science and information systems technology. It is also responsible for the operation of the Deep Space Network in support of NASA projects.

Sources of Information

Contracts and Small Business Activities Inquiries regarding contracting for small business opportunities with NASA should be directed to the Associate Administrator for Small and Disadvantaged Business Utilization, NASA Headquarters, 300 E Street SW., Washington, DC 20546. Phone, 202–358–2088.
Employment Direct all inquiries to the Personnel Director of the nearest NASA Center or, for the Washington, DC, metropolitan area, to the Chief, Headquarters Personnel Branch, NASA Headquarters, Washington, DC 20546. Phone, 202–358–1562.
Publications, Speakers, Films, and Exhibit Services Several publications concerning these services can be obtained by contacting the Public Affairs Officer of the nearest NASA Center. Publications include *NASA Directory of Services for the Public, NASA Film List,* and *NASA Educational Publications List.* The Headquarters telephone directory and certain publications and picture sets are available for sale from the Superintendent of Documents, Government Printing Office, Washington, DC 20402. Telephone directories for NASA Centers are available only from the Centers. Publications and documents not available for sale from the Superintendent of Documents or the National Technical Information Service (Springfield, VA 22151) may be obtained from the NASA Center's Information Center in accordance with the NASA regulation concerning freedom of information (14 CFR, part 1206).
Reading Room NASA Headquarters Information Center, Room 1H23, 300 E Street SW., Washington, DC 20546. Phone, 202–358–0000.

For further information, contact the Headquarters Information Center, National Aeronautics and Space Administration, Washington, DC 20546. Phone, 202–358–0000.

NATIONAL ARCHIVES AND RECORDS ADMINISTRATION

8601 Adelphi Road, College Park, Maryland 20740–6001
Phone, 301–713–6800. Internet, http://www.nara.gov/.

Archivist of the United States	JOHN W. CARLIN
Deputy Archivist of the United States	LEWIS J. BELLARDO
Executive Director, National Historical Publications and Records Commission	ROGER A. BRUNS, *Acting*
Director of the Federal Register	RAYMOND A. MOSLEY
Assistant Archivist for Regional Records Services	RICHARD L. CLAYPOOLE
Assistant Archivist for Presidential Libraries	DAVID F. PETERSON
Assistant Archivist for Records Services— Washington, DC	MICHAEL J. KURTZ
Assistant Archivist for Human Resources and Information Services	L. REYNOLDS CAHOON
Assistant Archivist for Administrative Services	ADRIENNE C. THOMAS
General Counsel	CHRISTOPHER M. RUNKEL, *Acting*
Inspector General	KELLY A. SISARIO
Director, Information Security Oversight Office	STEVEN GARFINKEL

[For the National Archives and Records Administration statement of organization, see the *Federal Register* of June 25, 1985, 50 FR 26278]

The National Archives and Records Administration (NARA) ensures, for citizens and Federal officials, ready access to essential evidence that documents the rights of American citizens, the actions of Federal officials, and the national experience. It establishes policies and procedures for managing U.S. Government records and assists Federal agencies in documenting their activities, administering records management programs, scheduling records, and retiring noncurrent records. NARA accessions, arranges, describes, preserves, and provides access to the essential documentation of the three branches of Government; manages the Presidential Libraries system; and publishes the laws, regulations, and Presidential and other public documents. It also assists the Information Security Oversight Office, which manages Federal classification and declassification policies, and the National Historical Publications and Records Commission, which makes grants nationwide to help nonprofit organizations identify, preserve, and provide access to materials that document American history.

The National Archives and Records Administration is the successor agency to the National Archives Establishment, which was created in 1934 and subsequently incorporated into the General Services Administration as the National Archives and Records Service in 1949. NARA was established as an independent agency in the executive branch of the Government by act of October 19, 1984 (44 U.S.C. 2101 *et seq.*), effective April 1, 1985.

Activities

Archival Program   The National Archives and Records Administration maintains the historically valuable

NATIONAL ARCHIVES AND RECORDS ADMINISTRATION

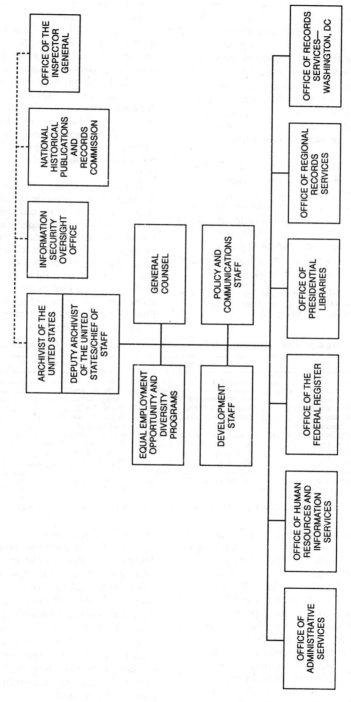

records of the U.S. Government dating from the Revolutionary War era to the recent past; arranges and preserves records and prepares finding aids to facilitate their use; makes records available for use in research rooms in its facilities; answers written and oral requests for information contained in its holdings; and, for a fee, provides copies of records. In addition, many important records are available on microfilm. Historically valuable records created in the Washington, DC, area and in the custody of NARA are maintained in NARA facilities in the Washington, DC, area. Historically valuable records that are primarily of regional or local interest and in the custody of NARA are maintained in the NARA regional records services facilities (see "Regional Records Services" below).

For further information concerning records in the custody of NARA, contact the User Services Branch. Phone, 202–501–5400.

Presidential Libraries Through the Presidential libraries, which are located at sites selected by the Presidents and built with private funds, NARA preserves and makes available the records and personal papers of a particular President's administration. In addition to providing reference services on Presidential documents, each library prepares documentary and descriptive publications and operates a museum to exhibit documents, historic objects, and other memorabilia of interest to the public.

The records of each President since Herbert Hoover are administered by NARA. While such records were once considered personal papers, all Presidential records created on or after January 20, 1981, are declared by law to be owned and controlled by the United States and are required to be transferred to NARA at the end of the administration, pursuant to the Presidential Records Act of 1978 (44 U.S.C. 2201 et seq.).

Presidential Libraries—National Archives and Records Administration

Library	City/Address	Director	Telephone
Herbert Hoover Library	West Branch, IA 52358–0488	Timothy G. Walch	319–643–5301
Franklin D. Roosevelt Library	Hyde Park, NY 12538–1999	Verne W. Newton	914–229–8114
Harry S. Truman Library	Independence, MO 64050–1798	Larry J. Hackman	816–833–1400
Dwight D. Eisenhower Library	Abilene, KS 67410–2900	Daniel D. Holt	785–263–4751
John F. Kennedy Library	Boston, MA 02125–3398	Bradley S. Gerratt	617–929–4500
Lyndon B. Johnson Library	Austin, TX 78705–5702	Harry J. Middleton	512–916–5137
Nixon Presidential Materials Staff	College Park, MD 20740–6001	Karl Weissenbach, Acting	301–713–6950
Gerald R. Ford Library	Ann Arbor, MI 48109–2114	Richard Norton Smith	734–741–2218
Gerald R. Ford Museum	Grand Rapids, MI 49504–5353	Richard Norton Smith	616–451–9263
Jimmy Carter Library	Atlanta, GA 30307–1498	Donald B. Schewe	404–331–3942
Ronald Reagan Library	Simi Valley, CA 93065–0666	Mark A. Hunt	805–522–8444
George Bush Library	College Station, TX 77843	David E. Alsobrook	409–260–9554

For further information, contact the Office of Presidential Libraries. Phone, 301–713–6050.

Regional Records Services Outside the Washington, DC, area, NARA operates a system of nine regions comprised of individual regional records services facilities plus the National Personnel Records Center. Each of the nine regional administrators operates a program encompassing the full life cycle of records, including records management activities with records creators, disposal, archival accessioning, records processing, and access to records by the public. Historically valuable records that are primarily of regional or local interest are maintained in most of these facilities, which arrange and preserve the records and prepare finding aids to facilitate their use; make the records available for use in research rooms; answer written and oral requests for information contained in the holdings; and, for a fee, provide copies of the records. In addition, many important original records held in NARA facilities in the Washington, DC, area, are available in microform in most of these regional facilities.

In addition to the archival holdings, most of these regional records services facilities maintain low-cost storage to which Federal agencies retire certain noncurrent records for specified periods. For such records, the regional records services facilities provide reference services, including loan or return of records to the agency of origin; prepare authenticated reproductions of documents; and furnish information from records. The facilities also dispose of records of transitory value and transfer into archival custody those that have enduring value. In addition, the facilities offer to Federal agencies in the region technical assistance workshops and advice on records creation, maintenance, storage, disposition, and vital records. Reimbursable microfilming services are available from some of the facilities.

Regional Records Services Facilities—National Archives and Records Administration
(A: Facility holding archival records)

City	Address	Director	Telephone
NORTHEAST REGION.			
Headquarters	Waltham, MA	Diane LeBlanc	617–647–8745
Boston (A)	380 Trapelo Rd., Waltham, MA 02154–6399		617–647–8104
Pittsfield	100 Conte Dr., Pittsfield, MA 01201–8230		413–445–6885
New York City (A)	201 Varick St., New York, NY 10014–4811		212–337–1300
Bayonne	Bldg. 22, Military Ocean Terminal, Bayonne, NJ 07002–5388.		201–823–7241
MID ATLANTIC REGION.			
Headquarters	Philadelphia, PA	James W. Mouat	215–671–9027
Center City Philadelphia (A) ..	900 Market St., Philadelphia, PA 19107–4292		215–597–3000
Northeast Philadelphia	14700 Townsend Rd., Philadelphia, PA 19154–1096.		215–671–9027
SOUTHEAST REGION.			
Headquarters (A)	1557 St. Joseph Ave., East Point, GA 30344–2593.	Gayle P. Peters	404–763–7477
GREAT LAKES REGION.			
Headquarters	Chicago, IL	David E. Kuehl	773–581–7816
Chicago (A)	7358 S. Pulaski Rd., Chicago, IL 60629–5898		773–581–7816
Dayton	3150 Springboro Rd., Dayton, OH 45439–1883 ..		513–225–2852
CENTRAL PLAINS REGION.			
Headquarters (A)	2312 E. Bannister Rd., Kansas City, MO 64131–3011.	R. Reed Whitaker	816–926–6920
Lee's Summit	200 Space Center Dr., Lee's Summit, MO 64064–1182.		816–478–7089
SOUTHWEST REGION.			
Headquarters (A)	501 W. Felix St., Fort Worth, TX 76115–3405	Kent C. Carter	817–334–5515
ROCKY MOUNTAIN REGION.			
Headquarters (A)	Bldg. 48, Denver Federal Ctr., Denver, CO 80225–0307.	Robert Svenningsen	303–236–0801
PACIFIC REGION.			
Headquarters	San Bruno, CA	Sharon L. Roadway	415–876–9249
Laguna Niguel (A)	1st Fl. E., 24000 Avila Rd., Laguna Niguel, CA 92607–3497.		714–360–2618
San Francisco (A)	1000 Commodore Dr., San Bruno, CA 94066		415–876–9009
PACIFIC ALASKA REGION.			
Headquarters	Seattle, WA	Steven M. Edwards	206–526–6501
Seattle (A)	6125 Sand Point Way NE., Seattle, WA 98115–7999.		206–526–6501
Anchorage (A)	654 W. 3d Ave., Anchorage, AK 99501–2145		907–271–2443
NATIONAL PERSONNEL RECORDS CENTER.			
Headquarters	9700 Page Ave., St. Louis, MO 63132	David L. Petree	314–538–4201

For further information, contact the Office of Regional Records Services. Phone, 301–713–7200.

Records Management To ensure proper documentation of the organization, policies, and activities of the Government, NARA develops standards and guidelines for the management and disposition of recorded information. It appraises Federal records and approves records disposition schedules. It also inspects agency records and records management practices, develops records management training programs, provides guidance and assistance on proper records management, and provides for storage of inactive records. For agencies headquartered in the Washington, DC, vicinity, these functions are assigned to the Office of Records Services. The Washington National Records Center, part of the Office of Records Services, also provides tailored workshops and reimbursable micrographic services. For records management services outside the Washington, DC, area, see "Regional Records Services" (above).

For further information, contact Modern Records Programs. Phone, 301–713–7100. For records center services in the Washington, DC, area, contact the Washington National Records Center. Phone, 301–457–7000.

Laws, Regulations, and Presidential Documents   The agency prepares and publishes a wide variety of public documents. Upon issuance, acts of Congress are published immediately in slip law (pamphlet) form and then cumulated and published for each session of Congress in the *United States Statutes at Large*.

Each Federal workday, the *Federal Register* publishes (in both paper and electronic format) current Presidential proclamations and Executive orders, Federal agency regulations having general applicability and legal effect, proposed agency rules, and documents required by statute to be published. All Federal regulations in force are codified annually in the *Code of Federal Regulations*.

Presidential speeches, news conferences, messages, and other materials released by the White House Office of the Press Secretary are published each week in the *Weekly Compilation of Presidential Documents* (in both paper and electronic format) and annually in the *Public Papers of the Presidents*.

The *United States Government Manual*, published annually in both paper and electronic format, serves as the official handbook of the Federal Government, providing extensive information on agencies of the legislative, judicial, and executive branches.

For further information, contact Customer Service, Office of the Federal Register. Phone, 202–523–5227. TDD, 202–523–5229. Fax, 202–523–5216. E-mail, info@fedreg.nara.gov/. Internet access to the Federal Register system of publications is available at http://www.nara.gov/fedreg/.

Public Programs   The agency has extensive education, exhibits, and publications programs that serve the general public, researchers, scholars, educators and their students, and Government. The Declaration of Independence, the Constitution, and the Bill of Rights are on permanent display in the Rotunda of the National Archives building in Washington, DC, and numerous other Federal documents on a wide variety of historical themes are exhibited in its other facilities nationwide. Educational programs vary from the elementary to the college and professional teaching levels, stressing the use of primary sources. Free and fee publications based on the holdings of the agency are available in both print and electronic formats, and range from general information leaflets to archival finding aids. Many of the high-interest subject area records are published in microform.

For further information, contact Public Programs. Phone, 202–501–5210. Fax, 202–219–1250.

Other Activities

Development Staff   The Development Staff raises funds from private sources to further public-private National Archives initiatives. The Director of Development is liaison to the Foundation for the National Archives.

For further information, contact the Development Staff. Phone, 301–713–7340. Fax, 301–713–7344.

National Archives Trust Fund Board The National Archives Trust Fund Board receives funds from the sale of reproductions of historic documents and publications about the records, as well as from gifts and bequests. The Board invests these funds and uses income to support archival functions such as the preparation of publications that make information about historic records more widely available. Members of the Board are the Archivist of the United States, the Secretary of the Treasury, and the Chairman of the National Endowment for the Humanities.

For further information, contact the Secretary, National Archives Trust Fund Board. Phone, 301–713–6405.

National Historical Publications and Records Commission   The Commission is the grant-making affiliate of the National Archives and Records Administration. The Archivist of the United States chairs the Commission and makes grants on its recommendation. The Commission's 14 other members represent the President of the United States (2 appointees), the Federal Judiciary, the U.S. Senate and House of Representatives, the Departments of State and Defense, the Librarian of Congress, the American Association for State and Local History, the American Historical Association, the Association for Documentary Editing, the National Association of Government Archives and Records Administrators, the Organization of American Historians, and the Society of American Archivists.

The Commission carries out a statutory mission to ensure understanding of our Nation's past by promoting, nationwide, the identification, preservation, and dissemination of essential historical documentation. Its grants help State and local archives, universities, historical societies, and other nonprofit organizations solve preservation problems, improve training and techniques, strengthen archival programs, preserve and process records collections, and provide access to them through the publication of finding aids and edited texts. The Commission works in partnership with a national network of State Historical Records Advisory Boards.

For further information, contact the National Historical Publications and Records Commission. Phone, 202–501–5600.

Sources of Information

Calendar of Events   The *National Archives Calendar of Events* is published monthly. To be added to the mailing list,

call 301–713–7360. For a recorded announcement of events at the National Archives building and the National Archives at College Park, call 202–501–5000. The hearing impaired should call 202–501–5404 for events at the National Archives building and 301–713–7343 for events at the College Park building.

Congressional Affairs   The Congressional Affairs staff maintains contact with and responds to inquiries from congressional offices. Phone, 301–713–7340. Fax, 301–713–7344.

Contracts   Individuals seeking to do business with NARA may obtain detailed information from the Acquisitions Services Division, National Archives at College Park, 8601 Adelphi Road, College Park, MD 20740–6001. Phone, 301–713–6755. Fax, 301–713–6910.

Educational Opportunities   The agency offers several courses on archival and records management principles and on using NARA resources.

"Going to the Source: An Introduction to Research in Archives," is an annual 4-day course on doing research in primary sources. The course provides experience with documents, microfilm, finding aids, and research methodology to researchers from such varied positions as public policy analysts, museum curators, and historical novelists. For further information, contact the Public Programs Education Staff. Phone, 202–501–6303.

"Introduction to Genealogy" is a half-day course offered several times a year in the Washington, DC, area to introduce genealogists to the records in NARA that can further their research in family history. There are also several half-day workshops each month that focus on specific aspects of genealogical research. For further information, contact the Public Programs Education Staff at 202–501–6694. Most regional records services facilities also offer genealogy workshops. For more information, contact the individual facility or contact the Office of Regional Records Services at 301–713–7200.

The secondary school program annually offers an 8-day workshop in the Washington, DC, area, "Primarily Teaching," to introduce educators to the holdings of NARA and provide strategies for teaching with primary sources. For further information, contact the Public Programs Education Staff. Phone, 202–501–6729.

The "Modern Archives Institute" is a 2-week course for archivists that introduces students to the principles and techniques of archival work. It is offered twice a year, in January and June, in the Washington, DC, area, for a fee. Students are advised to register 3 months in advance. Inquiries should be sent to Staff Development Services, Room 1510, National Archives and Records Administration, 8601 Adelphi Road, College Park, MD 20740–6001. Phone 301–713–7390.

NARA offers 11 records management workshops in the Washington, DC, area, lasting from 1 day to 5 days. Most are designed for any Federal employee who has records management responsibility. Topics range from files maintenance to evaluating and promoting records management programs, and separate workshops are offered on audiovisual and electronic records. For further information, contact the Life Cycle Management Division at 301–713–6677. Similar training is offered by most regional records services facilities for Federal agency field employees. For further information, contact any regional records services facility, or contact the Office of Regional Records Services at 301–713–7200.

A half-day program is offered by the Office of the Federal Register to provide public instruction on researching Federal regulations. The program, "The Federal Register: What It Is and How To Use It," is conducted in Washington, DC, and in major regional cities. For further information, call 202–523–4534.

The National Historical Publications and Records Commission cosponsors an "Institute for the Editing of Historical Documents," a one-week summer training program at the University of Wisconsin, Madison. Admission is competitive.

The Commission also offers an annual fellowship in documentary editing and an annual fellowship in archival administration. The editorial fellow works with a document publication project supported by or endorsed by the Commission. The archival fellow works at a historical records repository in areas such as appraisal, collection development, personnel administration, budget preparation, and external affairs. Fellows receive stipends and fringe benefits for a period of 9–10 months. For application information, contact NHPRC, National Archives and Records Administration, 700 Pennsylvania Avenue NW., Washington, DC 20408–0001. Phone, 202–501–5610.

Electronic Access   Inquiries concerning the holdings and services of NARA can be made electronically. E-mail, inquire@arch2.nara.gov. Information about NARA and its holdings and publications is also available through the Internet, at http://www.nara.gov/.

The National Archives and Records Administration maintains an interactive fax retrieval system that allows users to select and receive by fax a wide variety of agency-related information. To use the fax-on-demand service, call 301–713–6905 from a fax machine handset and follow the voice instructions. One of the options that can be selected is a list of the available documents. There is no charge for using fax-on-demand, other than for the long distance telephone charges users may incur.

Employment   For job opportunities nationwide, contact the nearest NARA facility or the Human Resources Operations Branch, Room 2004, 9700 Page Avenue, St. Louis, MO 63132. Phone, 800–827–4898 (toll free). TDD, 314–538–4799.

Freedom of Information Act/Privacy Act Requests   Requests should be directed as follows:

For administrative records of the National Archives and Records Administration, contact the NARA Freedom of Information Act/Privacy Act Officer, General Counsel Staff, National Archives at College Park, 8601 Adelphi Road, College Park, MD 20740–6001. Phone, 301–713–6035. Fax, 301–713–6040.

For historically valuable records in the custody of the Office of Records Services, contact the Special Access/FOIA Staff, National Archives and

Records Administration, 8601 Adelphi Road, College Park, MD 20740–6001. Phone, 301–713–6620.

For historically valuable records in the custody of a regional records services facility, contact the facility serving the appropriate region (see listing in the preceding text), or contact the Office of Regional Records Services at 301–713–7200.

For historical records in the custody of a Presidential library, contact the library that has custody of the records (see listing in the preceding text).

For records in the physical custody of the Washington National Records Center or the records center operation in a regional records services facility, contact the Federal agency that transferred the records to the facility.

Museum Shops Publications, document facsimiles, and souvenirs are available for sale at the National Archives building, at each Presidential library, and at some regional records services facilities.

Public Affairs The Public Affairs staff maintains contact with and responds to inquiries from the media, issues press releases and other literature, and maintains contact with organizations representing the archival profession, scholarly organizations, and other groups served by NARA. Phone, 301–713–6000.

Publications Agency publications, including facsimiles of certain documents, finding aids to records, and *Prologue*, a scholarly journal published quarterly, are available from the National Archives Shop (NWCPN), NARA, Room G–9, 700 Pennsylvania Avenue, NW, Washington, DC 20408–0001. Phone, 1–800–234–8861 (toll free) or 202–501–5235. Fax, 202–501–7170.

Records management publications are available from the National Archives Shop. Phone, 202–501–5235.

Publication information concerning laws, regulations, and Presidential documents is available from the Office of the Federal Register. Phone, 202–523–5227. Information is also available through the Internet, at http://www.nara.gov/fedreg/.

Reference Services Records are available for research purposes in reading rooms at the National Archives building, 700 Pennsylvania Avenue NW., Washington, DC (phone, 202–501–5400); at the National Archives at College Park, 8601 Adelphi Road, College Park, MD (phone, 301–713–6800); and at each Presidential library and regional records services facility that holds archival records (see listings in the preceding text). Written requests for information may be sent to any of these units. All requests for information and records may be addressed to NARA, Archives II, Research Room Services, Room 2400, 8601 Adelphi Road, College Park, MD 20470–6001. Phone, 301–713–6800. E-mail, inquire@arch2.nara.gov.

The Nixon Presidential Materials Staff is located at the National Archives at College Park, Room 1320. Some Nixon materials are available for public inspection, but researchers are advised to contact the staff in advance to ascertain the availability of materials before visiting the facility. Phone, 301–713–6950.

The Public Inspection Desk of the Office of the Federal Register is open every Federal business day for public inspection of documents filed for publication in the next day's edition of the *Federal Register,* at Suite 700, 800 North Capitol Street NW., Washington, DC. Phone, 202–523–5240.

Speakers and Presentations Community and school outreach programs are presented upon request. Interested groups in the Washington, DC, area should call 202–501–5205. Groups outside the Washington, DC, area should contact the regional records services facility or Presidential library in their areas (see listings in the preceding text).

Education specialists present workshops at regional and national conferences of humanities professionals and as in-service training for teachers. For further information, contact the Public Programs Education Staff. Phone, 202–501–6729.

Teaching Materials Education specialists have developed low-cost documentary teaching materials for classroom use. Each kit deals with an historical event or theme and includes document facsimiles and teaching aids. For further information, contact the Public Programs Education Staff. Phone, 202–501–6729.

Tours Individuals or groups may request general or specialty tours behind the scenes at the National Archives building. Tours are given by reservation only, and individuals are requested to make reservations at least 3 weeks in advance. Tours are given at 10:15 a.m. or 1:15 p.m., Monday through Friday. Tours of the National Archives at College Park, MD, may also be arranged. Contact Visitor and Volunteer Services between 9 a.m. and 4 p.m., Monday through Friday. Phone, 202–501–5205.

Volunteer Service Opportunities A wide variety of opportunities is available for volunteers. At the National Archives building and the National Archives at College Park, MD, volunteers conduct tours, provide information in the Exhibition Hall, work with staff archivists in processing historic documents, and serve as genealogical aides in the genealogical orientation room. For further information, call 202–501–5205. Similar opportunities exist in the Presidential libraries and at the regional records services facilities that house archival records. If outside the Washington, DC, area, contact the facility closest to you for further information on volunteer opportunities.

For further information, write or visit the National Archives and Records Administration, 700 Pennsylvania Avenue NW., Washington, DC 20408–0001. Phone, 202–501–5400. E-mail, inquire@arch2.nara.gov. Internet, http://www.nara.gov/.

NATIONAL CAPITAL PLANNING COMMISSION

Suite 301, 801 Pennsylvania Avenue NW., Washington, DC 20576
Phone, 202–482–7200. Internet, http://www.ncpc.gov/.

Chairman	HARVEY B. GANTT
Vice Chairman	PATRICIA ELWOOD
Members	ARRINGTON DIXON, ROBERT A. GAINES, MARGARET G. VANDERHYE
Ex Officio:	
(Secretary of the Interior)	BRUCE BABBITT
(Secretary of Defense)	WILLIAM S. COHEN
(Administrator of General Services)	DAVID J. BARRAM
(Chairman, Senate Committee on Governmental Affairs)	FRED THOMPSON
(Chairman, House Committee on Government Reform and Oversight)	DAN BURTON
(Mayor of the District of Columbia)	MARION S. BARRY, JR.
(Chairman, Council of the District of Columbia)	LINDA W. CROPP
Staff:	
Executive Director	REGINALD W. GRIFFITH
Assistant Executive Director	(VACANCY)
Executive Assistant	PRISCILLA A. BROWN
Writer-Editor	DENISE H. LIEBOWITZ
Executive Officer	CONNIE M. HARSHAW

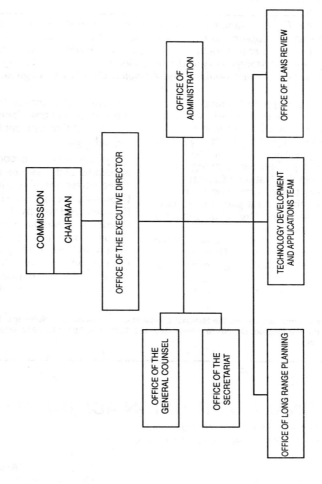

NATIONAL CAPITAL PLANNING COMMISSION

COMMISSION

CHAIRMAN

OFFICE OF THE EXECUTIVE DIRECTOR

OFFICE OF
ADMINISTRATION

OFFICE OF THE
GENERAL COUNSEL

OFFICE OF THE
SECRETARIAT

OFFICE OF LONG RANGE PLANNING

TECHNOLOGY DEVELOPMENT
AND APPLICATIONS TEAM

OFFICE OF PLANS REVIEW

General Counsel	SANDRA H. SHAPIRO
Secretariat	RAE N. ALLEN
Director, Office of Long-Range Planning	JOHN M. DUGAN
Director, Technology Development and Applications Team	DAVID A. NYSTROM
Director, Office of Plans Review	GEORGE V. EVANS, JR.

[For the National Capital Planning Commission statement of organization, see the *Code of Federal Regulations*, Title 1, Part 456.2]

The National Capital Planning Commission is the central agency for conducting planning and development activities for Federal lands and facilities in the National Capital region. The region includes the District of Columbia and all land areas within the boundaries of Montgomery and Prince Georges Counties in Maryland and Fairfax, Loudoun, Prince William, and Arlington Counties in Virginia.

The National Capital Planning Commission was established as a park planning agency by act of June 6, 1924, as amended (40 U.S.C. 71 *et seq.*). Two years later its role was expanded to include comprehensive planning. In 1952, under the National Capital Planning Act, the Commission was designated the central planning agency for the Federal and District of Columbia governments.

In 1973, the National Capital Planning Act was amended by the District of Columbia Home Rule Act, which made the Mayor of the District of Columbia the chief planner for the District; however, the Commission continues to serve as the central planning agency for the Federal Government in the National Capital region.

The Commission is composed of five appointed and seven *ex officio* members. Three citizen members, including the Chairman, are appointed by the President and two by the mayor of the District of Columbia. Presidential appointees include one resident each from Maryland and Virginia and one from anywhere in the United States; however, the two mayoral appointees must be District of Columbia residents.

For further information, contact the National Capital Planning Commission, Suite 301, 801 Pennsylvania Avenue NW., Washington, DC 20576. Phone, 202–482–7200. Fax, 202–482–7272. Internet, http://www.ncpc.gov/.

NATIONAL CREDIT UNION ADMINISTRATION

1775 Duke Street, Alexandria, VA 22314–3428
Phone, 703–518–6300. Internet, http://www.ncua.gov/.

Chairman	NORMAN E. D'AMOURS
Members of the Board	DENNIS DOLLAR, YOLANDA TOWNSEND WHEAT (VACANCY)
Executive Director	BECKY BAKER
Secretary to the Board	W. ROBERT HALL
Executive Assistant to the Chairman	KIRK CUEVES
Executive Assistant to Board Member Dollar	MARGARET BROADAWAY
Executive Assistant to Board Member Wheat	ROBERT FENNER
General Counsel	ROBERT E. LOFTUS
Director, Public and Congressional Affairs	DAVID M. MARQUIS
Director, Office of Examination and Insurance	

Inspector General   H. FRANK THOMAS
Chief Financial Officer   DENNIS WINANS
Director, Office of Community Development   JOYCE JACKSON
    Credit Unions
Director, Office of Investment Services   EDWARD DUPCAK
Director, Office of Technology and Information   DOUG VERNER
    Services
Director, Office of Administration   JAMES L. BAYLEN
Director, Office of Human Resources   (VACANCY)
Director, Office of Training and Development   ROBERT POMPA
Director, Office of Corporate Credit Unions   ROBERT F. SCHAFER

[For the National Credit Union Administration statement of organization, see the *Code of Federal Regulations,* Title 12, Part 720]

The National Credit Union Administration Board is responsible for chartering, insuring, supervising, and examining Federal credit unions and administering the National Credit Union Share Insurance Fund. The Board also administers the Community Development Revolving Loan Fund and manages the Central Liquidity Facility, a mixed-ownership Government corporation whose purpose is to supply emergency loans to member credit unions.

The National Credit Union Administration was established by act of March 10, 1970 (12 U.S.C. 1752), and reorganized by act of November 10, 1978 (12 U.S.C. 226), as an independent agency in the executive branch of the Federal Government. It regulates and insures all Federal credit unions and insures State-chartered credit unions that apply and qualify for share insurance.

Activities

Chartering The Administration's Board grants Federal credit union charters to groups sharing a common bond of occupation or association, or groups within a well-defined neighborhood, community, or rural district. A preliminary investigation is made to determine if certain minimum standards are met before granting a Federal charter.

For further information, contact the appropriate regional office listed in the table below.

Supervision Supervisory activities are carried out through annual examiner contacts and through periodic policy and regulatory releases from the Administration. The Administration also maintains a warning system designed to identify emerging problems as well as to monitor operations between examinations.

Examinations The Administration conducts annual examinations of Federal credit unions to determine their solvency and compliance with laws and regulations and to assist credit union management and operations.

For further information, contact the Director, Office of Examination and Insurance. Phone, 703–518–6360.

Share Insurance The act of October 19, 1970 (12 U.S.C. 1781 *et seq.*), provides for a program of share insurance. The insurance is mandatory for Federal credit unions and for State-chartered credit unions in many States and is optional for other State-chartered credit unions that meet Administration standards. Credit union members' accounts are insured up to $100,000. The National Credit Union Share Insurance Fund requires each insured credit union to place and maintain a 1-percent deposit of its insured savings with the Fund.

For further information, contact the Director, Office of Examination and Insurance. Phone, 703–518–6360.

Regional Offices—National Credit Union Administration

Region	Address	Director	Telephone	Fax
Albany, NY—CT, MA, ME, NH, NY, RI, VT	9 Washington Sq., Washington Ave. Ext., 12205	Layne L. Bumgardner	518–464–4180	518–464–4195
Capital—DC, DE, MD, NJ, PA, VA, WV	Suite 4206, 1775 Duke St., Alexandria, VA 22314	Jane Walters	703–838–0401	703–838–0571
Atlanta, GA—AL, AR, FL, GA, KY, LA, MS, NC, PR, SC, TN, VI	Suite 1600, 7000 Central Pkwy., 30328	H. Allen Carver	770–396–4042	770–698–8211
Chicago, IL—IL, IN, MI, MO, OH, WI	Suite 155, 4225 Naperville Rd., Lisle, 60532–3658	Nicholas Veghts	708–245–1000	708–245–1016
Austin, TX—AZ, CO, IA, KS, MN, ND, NE, NM, OK, SD, TX, UT, WY	Suite 5200, 4807 Spicewood Springs Rd., 78759–8490	Phillip R. Crider	512–349–4500	512–349–4511
Pacific—AK, AS, CA, GU, HI, ID, MT, NV, OR, WA	Suite 1350, 2300 Clayton Rd., Concord, CA 94520	Daniel L. Murphy	510–825–6125	510–486–3729

Sources of Information

Consumer Complaints The Administration investigates the complaints of members who are unable to resolve problems with their Federal credit union when these problems relate to a possible violation of the Federal Credit Union Act or consumer protection regulations. Complaints should be sent directly to the appropriate regional office.

Employment Inquiries and applications for employment should be directed to the Office of Human Resources, National Credit Union Administration, 1775 Duke Street, Alexandria, VA 22314–3428.

Federally Insured Credit Unions A list of federally insured credit union names, addresses, asset levels, and number of members is available for review at NCUA's Alexandria and regional offices. Copies of the listing are available at a nominal fee from NCUA, Publications, 1775 Duke Street, Alexandria, VA 22314–3428. Phone, 703–518–6340.

Publications A listing and copies of NCUA publications are available from NCUA, Publications, 1775 Duke Street, Alexandria, VA 22314–3428. Phone, 703–518–6340. Publications are also available electronically through the Internet, at http://www.ncua.gov/.

Starting a Federal Credit Union Groups interested in forming a Federal credit union may obtain free information by writing to the appropriate regional office.

For further information concerning the National Credit Union Administration, contact the Office of Public and Congressional Affairs, National Credit Union Administration, 1775 Duke Street, Alexandria, VA 22314–3428. Phone, 703–518–6330. Internet, http://www.ncua.gov/.

NATIONAL FOUNDATION ON THE ARTS AND THE HUMANITIES

NATIONAL ENDOWMENT FOR THE ARTS

1100 Pennsylvania Avenue NW., Washington, DC 20506–0001
Phone, 202–682–5400

Chairman	KATHRYN (KITTY) HIGGINS, *Acting*
Chief of Staff	ALEXANDER CRARY
Senior Deputy Chairman	SCOTT SHANKLIN-PETERSON
Congressional Liaison	DICK WOODRUFF
General Counsel	KAREN CHRISTENSEN

Inspector General	ED JOHNS
Deputy Chairman for Grants and Partnership	KAREN CHRISTENSEN, *Acting*
Deputy Chairman for Management and Budget	(VACANCY)
Director, Enterprise Development	(VACANCY)
Director, Office of Communications	CHERIE SIMON
Director, Policy, Research, and Technology	OLIVE MOSIER
Director, Guidelines and Panel Operations	A.B. SPELLMAN
Director of Administration	LARRY BADEN
Budget Officer	RON FINCMAN
Finance Officer	MARVIN MARKS
Contracts and Grants Officer	DONNA DIRICCO
Administrative Services Officer	MURRAY WELSH
Director, Office of Human Resources	MAXINE JEFFERSON
Coordinator, Creation and Presentation Division	JENNIFER DOWLEY
Coordinator, Education and Access Division	PATRICE POWELL
Coordinator, Heritage and Preservation Division	DANIEL SHEEHY
Coordinator, Partnership, Planning, and Stabilization Division	ED DICKEY
Director, Civil Rights	ANGELIA RICHARDSON
Director, Information Management	ANDREA FOWLER
Council Coordinator	YVONNE SABINE

NATIONAL ENDOWMENT FOR THE HUMANITIES

1100 Pennsylvania Avenue NW., Washington, DC 20506
Phone, 202–606–8400. Internet, http://www.neh.gov/.

Chairman	WILLIAM R. FERRIS
Deputy Chairman	JUAN MESTAS
General Counsel	NANCY WEISS, *Acting*
Director of Enterprise and Congressional Liaison	ANN S. YOUNG ORR
Director, Office of Planning and Budget	STEPHEN F. CHERRINGTON
Director, Office of Communications Policy	GARY KRULL
Director, Federal/State Partnership	EDITH MANZA
Director, Division of Research and Education	JAMES HERBERT
Director, Division of Public Programs	NANCY ROGERS
Director, Division of Preservation and Access	GEORGE FARR
Director, Office of Challenge Grants	STEPHEN M. ROSS
Accounting Officer	TONY BANKO
Administrative Services Officer	BARRY MAYNES
IRM Systems Officer	BRETT BOBLEY
Equal Employment Opportunity Officer	WILLIE MCGHEE
Grants Officer	DAVID WALLACE
Director, Office of Human Resources	TIMOTHY G. CONNELLY
Inspector General	SHELDON BERNSTEIN

INSTITUTE OF MUSEUM AND LIBRARY SERVICES

Room 510, 1100 Pennsylvania Avenue NW., Washington, DC 20506
Phone, 202–606–8536. E-mail, lmlsinfo@imls.fed.us. Internet, http://www.imls.fed.us/.

Director	DIANE B. FRANKEL
Deputy Director of IMLS for the Office of Library Services	ELIZABETH SYWETZ
Deputy Director of IMLS for the Office of Museum Services	BEVERLY SHEPPARD
Director, Policy, Planning, and Budget	LINDA BELL
Director, Legislative and Public Affairs	MAMIE BITTNER
Museum Program Director	MARY ESTELLE KENNELLY
Library Program Director	ROBERT KLASSEN
Director, Research and Technology	REBECCA DANVERS

[For the National Foundation on the Arts and the Humanities statement of organization, see the *Code of Federal Regulations*, Title 45, Part 1100]

The National Foundation on the Arts and the Humanities encourages and supports national progress in the humanities and the arts.

The National Foundation on the Arts and the Humanities was created as an independent agency by the National Foundation on the Arts and the Humanities Act of 1965 (20 U.S.C. 951). The Foundation consists of the National Endowment for the Arts, the National Endowment for the Humanities, the Federal Council on the Arts and the Humanities, and the Institute of Museum and Library Services. Each Endowment has its own Council, composed of the Endowment Chairman and 26 other members appointed by the President, which advises the Chairman with respect to policies, programs, and procedures, in addition to reviewing and making recommendations on applications for financial support.

The Federal Council on the Arts and the Humanities consists of 20 members, including the two Endowment Chairmen and the Director of the Institute of Museum and Library Services, and is designed to coordinate the activities of the two Endowments and related programs of other Federal agencies. Four members are excluded from the Federal Council when it is considering matters under the Arts and Artifacts Indemnity Act (20 U.S.C. 971).

National Endowment for the Arts

The National Endowment for the Arts supports the visual, literary, and performing arts to benefit all Americans by fostering artistic excellence, preserving and transmitting our diverse cultural heritage, making the arts more accessible to all Americans, and making the arts intrinsic to education.

The Arts Endowment serves as a catalyst to increase opportunities for artists and resources for arts organizations. It promotes involvement in the arts by citizens, public and private nonprofit organizations, and States and local communities. The Endowment awards grants to nonprofit arts organizations in support of outstanding projects; provides fellowships to exceptionally talented American artists in selected fields; works to expand the Nation's artistic resources and promote preservation of the country's cultural heritage; and funds projects whose goal is to educate, formally or informally, both children and adults in the arts. The Endowment also disburses funds to State arts agencies and local and regional organizations in order to promote broad dissemination of the arts across America. Its grantmaking is conducted through the following divisions: Creation and Presentation, Education and Access, Heritage and Preservation, Planning and Stabilization, and partnerships with State and regional arts agencies.

Sources of Information

Grants Persons interested in applying for a grant in the arts should contact the appropriate program at the National Endowment for the Arts by calling 202–682–5400 for further information.

Publications A report of the National Endowment for the Arts is issued annually and may be obtained from the Superintendent of Documents, Government Printing Office, Washington, DC 20402.

Information for prospective applicants may be obtained by requesting the publication entitled *National Endowment for the Arts: A New Look*. Contact the National Endowment for the Arts, Washington, DC 20506–0001.

For further information, contact the Public Information Office, National Endowment for the Arts, 1100 Pennsylvania Avenue NW., Washington, DC 20506–0001. Phone, 202–682–5400.

National Endowment for the Humanities

The National Endowment for the Humanities is an independent, grantmaking agency established by Congress in 1965 to support research, education, and public programs in the humanities.

According to the agency's authorizing legislation, the term "humanities" includes, but is not limited to, the study of the following: language, both modern and classical; linguistics; literature; history; jurisprudence; philosophy; archaeology; comparative religion; ethics; the history, criticism, and theory of the arts; and those aspects of the social sciences that employ historical or philosophical approaches.

The Endowment makes grants to individuals, groups, or institutions—schools, colleges, universities, museums, public television stations, libraries, public agencies, and nonprofit private groups—to increase understanding and appreciation of the humanities. Its grantmaking is conducted through three operating divisions—Research and Education, Public Programs, and Preservation and Access, and through the Federal/State Partnership and the Office of Challenge Grants.

Research and Education Through grants to educational institutions, fellowships to scholars and teachers, and through the support of significant research, this division is designed to strengthen sustained, thoughtful study of the humanities at all levels of education and promote original research in the humanities.

For further information, call 202–606–8200.

Public Programs This division strives to fulfill the Endowment's mandate "to increase public understanding of the humanities" by supporting those institutions and organizations that develop and present humanities programming for general audiences.

For further information, call 202–606–8269.

Preservation and Access This division supports projects that will create, preserve, and increase the availability of resources important for research, education, and public programming in the humanities.

For further information, call 202–606–8570.

Federal/State Partnership Humanities committees in each of the 50 States, the Virgin Islands, Puerto Rico, the District of Columbia, the Northern Mariana Islands, American Samoa, and Guam receive grants from the Endowment,

NATIONAL ENDOWMENT FOR THE HUMANITIES

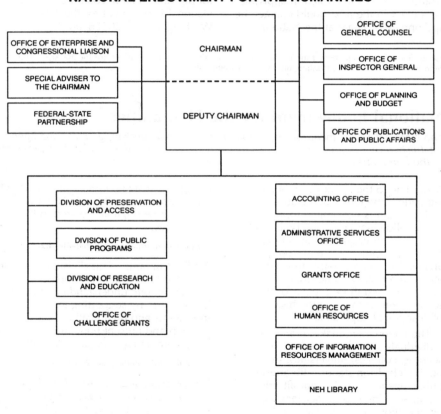

which they then re-grant to support humanities programs at the local level.

For further information, call 202–606–8254.

Challenge Grants Nonprofit institutions interested in developing new sources of long-term support for educational, scholarly, preservation, and public programs in the humanities may be assisted in these efforts by a challenge grant.

For further information, call 202–606–8309.

Sources of Information

Employment For employment information, contact the NEH Job Line. Phone, 202–606–8281.

Grants Those interested in applying for a grant in the humanities should request information, guidelines, and application forms from the Endowment's Public Information Office, Room 401, 1100 Pennsylvania Avenue NW., Washington, DC 20506. Phone, 202–606–8400.

Publications The annual report of the National Endowment for the Humanities may be obtained from the Endowment's Public Information Office, Room 401, 1100 Pennsylvania Avenue NW., Washington, DC 20506. Phone, 202–606–8400.

Overview of Endowment Programs, which contains information for prospective applicants, may be obtained by writing to the Public Information Office, at the address given above.

Humanities, a bimonthly review of issues in the humanities published by the Endowment, is available by subscription ($16 domestic, $20 foreign) through the Superintendent of Documents, P.O. Box 371954, Pittsburgh, PA 15250–7954.

For further information, contact the Public Information Office, National Endowment for the Humanities, Room 401, 1100 Pennsylvania Avenue NW., Washington, DC 20506. Phone, 202–606–8400. E-mail, info@neh.gov. Internet, http://www.neh.gov/.

Institute of Museum and Library Services

The Institute of Museum and Library Services is an independent, grant-making agency which serves the public by strengthening museums and libraries.

The Institute of Museum and Library Services was established within the National Foundation on the Arts and the Humanities by the Museum and Library Services Act of September 30, 1996 (110 Stat. 3009–293), which amended the Museum Services Act (20 U.S.C. 961 *et seq.*). The Institute combines administration of Federal museum programs formerly carried out by the Institute of Museum Services and Federal library programs formerly carried out by the Department of Education. The Institute's Director is appointed by the President with the advice and consent of the Senate and is authorized to make grants to museums and libraries. The Director receives policy advice on museum programs from the National Museum Services Board, which is comprised of 14 Presidentially appointed members and the Director. The Director receives policy advice on library programs from the National Commission on Libraries and Information Sciences, a 16-member independent commission which advises the President and the Congress on library services. The Director is an *ex officio* member of the National Commission on Libraries and Information Sciences.

In addition to providing distinct programs of support for museums and libraries, IMLS encourages collaboration between these community resources. The Institute's library programs help libraries use new technologies to identify, preserve, and share library and information resources across institutional, local, and State boundaries and to reach those for whom library use requires extra effort or special materials. Museum programs strengthen museum operations, improve care of collections, increase professional development opportunities, and enhance the community service role of museums.

IMLS awards grants to all types of museums and libraries. Eligible museums include art, history, general, children's, natural history, science and technology, as well as historic houses, zoos and aquariums, botanical gardens and arboretums, nature centers, and planetariums. Eligible libraries include public, school, academic, research, and special libraries. The Institute makes grants in 11 program categories.

Library Grants to States These grants improve electronic sharing of information and expand public access to an increasing wealth of information and services. Each State provides a 5-year plan to establish goals and identify priorities that address the purposes of the Library Services and Technology Act subtitle of the Museum and Library Services Act. Grants to States may be expended directly or through subgrants or cooperative agreements.

Native American Library Services This program provides small grants for core library operations of tribes and Alaska Native villages, technical assistance for these libraries, and enhancement grants to promote innovative practices in libraries serving Native Americans and Alaskan Native villages.

Native Hawaiian Library Services This program provides a single grant to an organization that primarily serves and represents Native Hawaiians.

National Leadership Grants This program awards grants, contracts, and cooperative agreements to enhance the quality of library services nationwide and to provide coordination between museums and libraries. Activities that may be funded include: education and training in library and information services; research and demonstration projects to improve library services; preservation or digitization of library materials and resources; and model programs of cooperation between libraries and museums.

General Operating Support Program This program awards unrestricted grants to museums for ongoing institutional activities. General operating support, often cited as the most difficult type of money to raise, helps museums enhance their educational services, strengthen collections care, and raise funds from other sources.

Conservation Project Support Program This program awards matching grants to help museums identify conservation needs and priorities and perform activities to ensure the safekeeping of their collections.

Museum Leadership Initiatives Program In 1998, this program offers cooperative agreements to institutions for projects to cultivate interaction between museums and community-based organizations. The program's focus may change annually.

Museum Assessment Program This program offers museums grants of technical assistance in three areas: institutional assessment, collections management assessment, and a public dimension assessment.

Conservation Assessment Program This program provides eligible museums with an alternative source of a general conservation survey, as an adjunct to the IMLS Conservation Project Support Program.

Professional Services Program This program offers cooperative agreements to professional-museum organizations to help their members to better serve the public.

National Award for Museum Service This program recognizes outstanding museums that provide meaningful public service for their communities.

Sources of Information

Electronic Access Information about IMLS programs, application guidelines, and lists of grantees are available electronically through the Internet, at http://www.imls.fed.us/. E-mail, lmlsinfo@imls.fed.us.

Grants, Contracts, and Cooperative Agreements For information about applying for IMLS funding, contact the appropriate program office. Museums should contact the Office of Museum Services, Institute of Museum and Library Services, Room 609, 1100 Pennsylvania Avenue NW., Washington, DC 20506 (phone, 202–606–8539). Libraries should contact the Office of Library Services, Institute of Museum and Library Services, Room 802, 1100 Pennsylvania Avenue NW., Washington, DC 20506 (phone, 202–606–5227).

For further information, contact the Office of Legislative and Public Affairs, Institute of Museum and Library Services, Room 510, 1100 Pennsylvania Avenue NW., Washington, DC 20506. Phone, 202–606–8536. E-mail, lmlsinfo@imls.fed.us. Internet, http://www.imls.fed.us/.

NATIONAL LABOR RELATIONS BOARD

1099 Fourteenth Street NW., Washington, DC 20570
Phone, 202–273–1000. TDD, 202–273–4300. Internet, http://www.nlrb.gov/.

Chairman	WILLIAM B. GOULD IV
Members	J. ROBERT BRAME III, SARAH M. FOX, PETER J. HURTGEN, WILMA B. LIEBMAN
Executive Secretary	JOHN J. TONER
Solicitor	JOHN E. HIGGINS, JR.
Inspector General	ROBERT E. ALLEN
Director, Division of Information	DAVID B. PARKER
Chief Administrative Law Judge	ROBERT A. GIANNASI
General Counsel	FRED L. FEINSTEIN
Deputy General Counsel	MARY JOYCE CARLSON
Associate General Counsel, Division of Advice	BARRY J. KEARNEY
Associate General Counsel, Division of Enforcement Litigation	LINDA R. SHER
Associate General Counsel, Division of Operations-Management	RICHARD SIEGEL
Director, Division of Administration	GLORIA J. JOSEPH
Director, Equal Employment Opportunity	BARBARA T. GAINEY

[For the National Labor Relations Board statement of organization, see the *Federal Register* of June 14, 1979, 44 FR 34215]

The National Labor Relations Board administers the Nation's principal labor law, the National Labor Relations Act. The Board is vested with the power to prevent and remedy unfair labor practices committed by private sector employers and unions and to safeguard employees' rights to organize and determine, through secret ballot elections, whether to have unions as their bargaining representative.

The National Labor Relations Board (NLRB) is an independent agency created by the National Labor Relations Act of 1935 (Wagner Act) (29 U.S.C. 167), as amended by acts of 1947 (Taft-Hartley Act), 1959 (Landrum-Griffin Act), and 1974 (Health Care Amendments).

The act affirms the right of employees to self-organization and collective bargaining through representatives of their own choosing, to engage in other protected, concerted activities, or to refrain from such activities. The act prohibits certain unfair labor practices by employers and labor organizations or their agents. It authorizes the Board to designate appropriate units for collective bargaining and to conduct secret ballot elections to determine whether employees desire representation by a labor organization.

As of July 1, 1971, the Postal Reorganization Act (39 U.S.C. note prec. 101) conferred jurisdiction upon the Board over unfair labor practice charges and representation elections affecting U.S. Postal Service employees. As of August 25, 1974, jurisdiction over all privately operated health care institutions was conferred on the Board by an amendment to the act (29 U.S.C. 152 *et seq.*).

Activities

Under the act, NLRB has two principal functions: preventing and remedying unfair labor practices by employers and labor organizations or their agents; and conducting secret ballot elections among employees in appropriate collective-bargaining units to determine whether or not they desire to be represented by a labor organization in bargaining with employers about their wages, hours, and working conditions. The agency also conducts secret ballot elections among employees who have been covered by a union-security agreement to determine whether or not they wish to revoke their union's authority to make such agreements. In jurisdictional disputes between two or more unions, the Board determines which competing group of workers is entitled to perform the work involved.

Two major, separate components comprise NLRB. The Board itself has five members appointed by the President and primarily acts as a quasi-judicial body in deciding cases on the basis of formal records in administrative proceedings. The General Counsel, also appointed by the President, is independent from the Board.

Under the general supervision of the General Counsel, 33 regional directors and their staffs process representation, unfair labor practice, and jurisdictional dispute cases. (Some regions have subregional or resident offices.) They issue complaints in unfair labor practice

cases; seek settlement of unfair labor practice charges; obtain compliance with Board orders and court judgments; and petition district courts for injunctions to prevent or remedy unfair labor practices. The regional directors direct hearings in representation cases; conduct elections pursuant to the agreement of the parties or the decision-making authority delegated to them by the Board or pursuant to Board directions; and issue certifications of representatives when unions win or certify the results when unions lose employee elections. They process petitions for bargaining unit clarification, for amendment of certification, and for rescission of a labor organization's authority to make a union-shop agreement. They also conduct national emergency employee referendums.

The Board can act only when it is formally requested to do so. Individuals, employers, or unions may initiate cases by filing charges of unfair labor practices or petitions for employee representation elections with the Board field offices serving the area where the case arises.

In the event that a regional director declines to proceed on a representation petition, the party filing the petition may appeal to the Board. When a regional director declines to proceed on an unfair labor practice charge, the charging party may appeal to the General Counsel.

For details concerning filing such appeals with those Washington, DC, offices, parties may contact the field office most convenient to them. Field office addresses and telephone numbers are listed below.

Administrative law judges conduct hearings in unfair labor practice cases, make findings of fact and conclusions of law, and recommend remedies for violations found. Their decisions can be appealed to the Board for a final agency determination. The Board's decisions are subject to review in the U.S. courts of appeals.

Field Offices—National Labor Relations Board
(HQ: Headquarters; RO: Resident office; SR: Subregion)

Office/Address	Director	Telephone	Fax
Region 1, 6th Fl., 10 Causeway St., Boston, MA 02222–1072	Rosemary Pye	617–565–6700	617–565–6725
Region 2, Rm. 3614, 26 Federal Plz., New York, NY 10278–0104.	Daniel Silverman	212–264–0300	212–264–8427
Region 3	Sandra Dunbar		
Rm. 901, 111 W. Huron St., Buffalo, NY 14202–2387 (HQ)		716–551–4931	716–551–4972
Rm. 342, Clinton Ave. at N. Pearl St., Albany, NY 12207–2350 (RO).	James J. Palermo	518–431–4155	518–431–4157
Region 4, 7th Fl., 615 Chestnut St., Philadelphia, PA 19106–4404.	Dorothy L. Moore-Duncan	215–597–7601	215–597–7658
Region 5	Louis J. D'Amico		
8th Fl., 103 S. Gay St., Baltimore, MD 21202–4026 (HQ)		410–962–2822	410–962–2198
Suite 5530, 1099 14th St., Washington, DC 20570–0001 (RO) ...	Gary W. Muffley	202–208–3000	202–208–3013
Region 6, Rm. 1501, 1000 Liberty Ave., Pittsburgh, PA 15222–4173.	Gerald Kobell	412–644–2977	412–644–5986
Region 7	William C. Schaub, Jr.		
Rm. 300, 477 Michigan Ave., Detroit, MI 48226–25€9 (HQ)		313–226–3200	313–226–2090
Rm. 330, 82 Ionia NW., Grand Rapids, MI 49503–3022 (RO)	David L. Basso	616–456–2679	616–456–2596
Region 8, Rm. 1695, 1240 E. 9th St., Cleveland, OH 44199–2086.	Frederick Calatrello	216–522–3715	216–522–2418
Region 9, Rm. 3003, 550 Main St., Cincinnati, OH 45202–3721	Richard L. Ahearn	513–684–3686	513–684–3946
Region 10	Martin M. Arlook		
Suite 1000, Harris Twr., 233 Peachtree St. NE., Atlanta, GA 30303 (HQ).		404–331–2896	404–331–2858
3d Fl., 1900 3d Ave. N., Birmingham, AL 35203–3502 (RO)	C. Douglas Marshall	205–731–1062	205–731–0955
Region 11, Suite 200, 4035 University Pkwy., Wïnston-Salem, NC 27106–3325.	Willie L. Clark, Jr.	910–631–5201	910–631–5210
Region 12	Rochelle Kentov		
Suite 530, 201 E. Kennedy Blvd., Tampa, FL 33602–5824 (HQ)		813–228–2641	813–228–2874
Rm. 214, 400 W. Bay St., Jacksonville, FL 32202–4412 (RO)	James L. McDonald	904–232–3768	904–232–3146
Rm. 1320, 51 SW. 1st Ave., Miami, FL 33130–1608 (RO)	Hector O. Nava	305–536–5391	305–536–5320
Region 13, Suite 800, 200 W. Adams St., Chicago, IL 60606–5208.	Elizabeth Kinney	312–353–7570	312–886–1341
Region 14, Suite 400, 611 N. 10th St., St. Louis, MO 63101–1214.	Ralph R. Tremain	314–425–4167	314–539–7794
Region 15, Rm. 610, 1515 Poydras St., New Orleans, LA 70112–3723.	Curtis A. Wells	504–589–6361	504–589–4069
Region 16	Michael Dunn		
Rm. 8A24, 819 Taylor St., Fort Worth, TX 76102–6˙78 (HQ)		817–978–2921	817–978–2928
P.O. Box 23159, El Paso, TX 79923–3159 (RO)	Chris Lerma	915–565–2470	915–565–0847
Suite 550, 440 Louisiana St., Houston, TX 77002–2549 (RO)	Ruth E. Small	713–718–4622	713–718–4640
Rm. 565, 615 E. Houston St., San Antonio, TX 78206–2040 (RO).	Ruben R. Armendariz	210–229–6140	210–472–6143
Region 17	F. Rozier Sharp		
Suite 100, 8600 Farley St., Overland Park, KS 66212–4677 (HQ)		913–967–3000	913–967–3010
Rm. 318, 224 S. Boulder Ave., Tulsa, OK 74103–4214 (RO)	Francis Molenda	918–581–7951	918–581–7970
Region 18	Ronald M. Sharp		
Rm. 316, 110 S. 4th St., Minneapolis, MN 55401–2291 (HQ)		612–348–1757	612–348–1785
Rm. 909, 210 Walnut St., Des Moines, IA 50309–2116 (RO)	Morris E. Petersen	515–284–4391	515–284–4713
Region 19	Paul Eggert		
Rm. 2948, 915 2d Ave., Seattle, WA 98174–1078 (HQ)		206–220–6300	206–220–6305
No. 21, 222 W. 7th Ave., Anchorage, AK 99513–3546 (RO)	Minoru Hayashi	907–271–5015	907–271–3055
Rm. 401, 222 SW. Columbia St., Portland, OR 97201–6604 (SR 36).	(Vacancy)	503–326–3085	503–326–5387
Region 20	Robert H. Miller		
Suite 400, 901 Market St., San Francisco, CA 94103–1735 (HQ)		415–356–5206	415–356–5156
Rm. 7318, 300 Ala Moana Blvd., Honolulu, HI 96850–4980 (SR 37).	Thomas W. Cestare	808–541–2814	808–541–2818
Region 21	Victoria E. Aguayo		
9th Fl., 888 S. Figueroa St., Los Angeles, CA 90017–5455 (HQ)		213–894–5200	213–894–2778
Suite 302, 555 W. Beech St., San Diego, CA 92101–2939 (RO)	Steven J. Sorensen	619–557–6184	619–557–6358
Region 22, Rm. 1600, 970 Broad St., Newark, NJ 07102–2570 ..	William A. Pascarell	973–645–2100	973–645–3852
Region 24, Suite 1002, 525 F.D. Roosevelt Ave., Hato Rey, PR 00918–1720.	Mary Zelma Asseo	787–766–5347	787–766–5478
Region 25, Rm. 238, 575 N. Pennsylvania St., Indianapolis, IN 46204–1577.	Roberto G. Chavarry	317–269–7430	317–226–5103
Region 26	Gerald P. Fleischut		
Suite 800, 1407 Union Ave., Memphis, TN 38104–3627 (HQ)		901–544–0018	901–544–0008
Suite 375, 425 W. Capitol Ave., Little Rock, AR 72201–3489 (RO).	Thomas H. Smith, Jr.	501–324–6311	501–324–5009
Rm. 716, 801 Broadway, Nashville, TN 37203–3816 (RO)	Joseph H. Artilles	615–736–5921	615–736–7761
Region 27, 3d Fl. S. Twr., 600 17th St., Denver, CO 80202–5433.	B. Allan Benson	303–844–3551	303–844–6249
Region 28	Cornele A. Overstreet		
Suite 440, 234 N. Central Ave., Phoenix, AZ 85004–2212 (HQ) ..		602–379–3361	602–379–4982

Field Offices—National Labor Relations Board—Continued
(HQ: Headquarters; RO: Resident office; SR: Subregion)

Office/Address	Director	Telephone	Fax
Suite 1820, 505 Marquette Ave. NW., Albuquerque, NM 87102–2181 (RO).	(Vacancy)	505–248–5125	505–248–5134
Suite 400, 600 Las Vegas Blvd. S., Las Vegas, NV 89101–6637 (RO).	Stephen E. Wamser	702–388–6416	702–388–6248
Region **29**, 10th Fl., Jay St. and Myrtle Ave., Brooklyn, NY 11201–4201.	Alvin P. Blyer	718–330–7713	718–330–7579
Region **30**, Suite 700, 310 W. Wisconsin Ave., Milwaukee, WI 53203–2211.	Philip E. Bloedorn	414–297–3861	414–297–3880
Region **31**, Suite 700, 11150 W. Olympic Blvd., Los Angeles, CA 90064–1824.	James J. McDermott	310–235–7352	310–235–7420
Region **32**, Rm. 300N, 1301 Clay St., Oakland, CA 94612–5211	James S. Scott	510–637–3300	510–637–3315
Region **33**, Suite 200, 300 Hamilton Blvd., Peoria, IL 61602–1246.	Glenn A. Zipp	309–671–7080	309–671–7095
Region **34**, 21st Fl., One Commercial Plz., Hartford, CT 06103–3599.	Peter B. Hoffman	860–240–3522	860–240–3564

Sources of Information

Contracts Prospective suppliers of goods and services may inquire about agency procurement and contracting practices by writing to the Chief, Procurement and Facilities Branch, National Labor Relations Board, Washington, DC 20570. Phone, 202–273–4040.

Electronic Access Information about the Board's programs and activities is available electronically through the Internet, at http://www.nlrb.gov/.

Employment The Board appoints administrative law judges from a register established by the Office of Personnel Management. The agency hires attorneys, stenographers, and typists for all its offices; field examiners for its field offices; and administrative personnel for its Washington office. Inquiries regarding college and law school recruiting programs should be directed to the nearest regional office. Employment inquiries and applications may be sent to any regional office or the Washington personnel office.

Publications Anyone desiring to inspect formal case documents or read agency publications may use facilities of the Washington or field offices. The agency will assist in arranging reproduction of documents and order transcripts of hearings. The Board's offices offer free informational leaflets in limited quantities: *The National Labor Relations Board and YOU (Unfair Labor Practices), The National Labor Relations Board and YOU (Representation Cases), Your Government Conducts an Election for You on the Job,* and *The National Labor Relations Board—What It Is, What It Does.* The Superintendent of Documents, Government Printing Office, Washington, DC 20402, sells *A Guide to Basic Law and Procedures Under the NLRA,* the *Annual Report,* the *Classified Index of National Labor Relations Board Decisions and Related Court Decisions,* volumes of Board decisions, and a number of subscription services, including the *NLRB Casehandling Manual* (in three parts), the *Weekly Summary of NLRB Cases,* the *NLRB Election Report,* and *An Outline of Law and Procedure in Representation Cases.*

Speakers To give the public and persons appearing before the agency a better understanding of the National Labor Relations Act and the Board's policies, procedures, and services, Washington and regional office personnel participate as speakers or panel members before bar associations, labor, educational, civic, or management organizations, and other groups. Requests for speakers or panelists may be made to Washington officials or to the appropriate regional director.

For further information, contact the Information Division, National Labor Relations Board, 1099 Fourteenth Street NW., Washington, DC 20570. Phone, 202–273–1991. Internet, http://www.nlrb.gov/.

NATIONAL MEDIATION BOARD

Suite 250 East, 1301 K Street NW., Washington, DC 20572
Phone, 202–523–5920

Chairman	ERNEST W. DUBESTER
Members	KENNETH B. HIPP, MAGDALENA G. JACOBSEN
Chief of Staff	STEPHEN E. CRABLE
Senior Mediators	JOHN BAVIS, LARRY GIBBONS, JEFF MACDONALD
General Counsel	RONALD M. ETTERS
Senior Hearing Officers	MARY L. JOHNSON, JOYCE M. KLEIN, ROLAND WATKINS
Director, Development and Technical Services	JAMES ARMSHAW
Senior Research Analyst	DONALD L. WEST
Records Officer	REBA STREAKER
Staff Coordinator/Arbitration	PRISCILLA ZEIGLER
Chief Financial Officer	JUNE KING

National Railroad Adjustment Board

Room 944, 844 North Rush Street, Chicago, IL 60611–2092
Phone, 312–751–4688

The National Mediation Board, in carrying out the provisions of the Railway Labor Act, assists in maintaining a free flow of commerce in the railroad and airline industries by resolving disputes that could disrupt travel or imperil the economy. The Board also handles railroad and airline employee representation disputes, and provides administrative and financial support in adjusting minor grievances in the railroad industry under section 153 of the Railway Labor Act.

The National Mediation Board was created on June 21, 1934, by an act amending the Railway Labor Act, as amended (45 U.S.C. 151–158, 160–162, 1181–1188).

The Board's major responsibilities include the mediation of disputes over wages, hours, and working conditions that arise between rail and air carriers and organizations representing their employees; and the investigation of representation disputes and certification of employee organizations as representatives of crafts or classes of carrier employees.

Disputes arising out of grievances or interpretation or application of agreements concerning rates of pay, rules, or working conditions in the railroad industry are referable to the National Railroad Adjustment Board.

This Board is divided into four divisions and consists of an equal number of representatives of the carriers and of national organizations of employees. In deadlocked cases the National Mediation Board is authorized to appoint a referee to sit with the members of the division for the purpose of making an award.

In the airline industry no national airline adjustment board has been established for settlement of grievances. Over the years the employee organizations and air carriers with established bargaining relationships have agreed to grievance procedures with final jurisdiction resting with a system board of adjustment. The Board is frequently called upon to name a neutral referee to serve on a system board when the parties are deadlocked and cannot agree on such an appointment themselves.

Activities

Mediation Disputes The National Mediation Board is charged with mediating disputes between carriers and labor organizations relating to initial contract negotiations or subsequent changes in rates of pay, rules, and working conditions. When the parties fail to reach accord in direct bargaining, either party may request the Board's services or the Board may on its own motion invoke its services. Thereafter, negotiations continue until the Board determines that its efforts to mediate have been unsuccessful, at which time it seeks to induce the parties to submit the dispute to arbitration. If either party refuses to arbitrate, the Board issues a notice stating that the parties have failed to resolve their dispute through mediation. This notice commences a 30-day cooling-off period after which self-help is normally available to either or both parties.

Employee Representation If a dispute arises among a carrier's employees as to who is to be the representative of such employees, it is the Board's duty to investigate such dispute and to determine by secret-ballot election or other appropriate means whether or not and to whom a representation certification should be issued. In the course of making this determination, the Board must determine the craft or class in which the employees seeking representation properly belong.

Additional Duties Additional duties of the Board include the interpretation of agreements made under its mediatory auspices; the appointment of neutral referees when requested by the National Railroad Adjustment Board; the appointment of neutrals to sit on system boards and special boards of adjustment; and finally, the duty of notifying the President when the parties have failed to reach agreement through the Board's mediation efforts and that the labor dispute, in the judgment of the Board, threatens substantially to interrupt interstate commerce to a degree such as to deprive any section of the country of essential transportation service. In these cases, the President may, at his discretion, appoint an Emergency Board to investigate and report to him on the dispute. Self-help is barred for 60 days after appointment of the Emergency Board.

Section 9A of the Railway Labor Act (45 U.S.C. 159a) provides emergency dispute procedures covering publicly funded and operated commuter railroads and their employees. That section attempts to resolve contract disputes between the parties through a series of emergency board procedures with a maximum 8-month status quo period. Section 9A is invoked only after all other procedures under the act have been exhausted.

Sources of Information

Publications Available for public distribution are the following documents: *Determinations of the National Mediation Board* (23 volumes); *Interpretations Pursuant to Section 5, Second of the Act* (2 volumes); Annual Reports of the National Mediation Board including the Report of the National Railroad Adjustment Board; *The Railway Labor Act at Fifty;* and *The National Mediation Board at Fifty—Its Impact on Railroad and Airline Labor Disputes.*
Reading Room At the Board's headquarters in Washington, DC, copies of collective-bargaining agreements between labor and management of various rail and air carriers are available for public inspection, by appointment, during office hours (1 to 4 p.m., Monday through Friday).

For further information, contact the Chief of Staff, National Mediation Board, Suite 250 East, 1301 K Street NW., Washington, DC 20572. Phone, 202–523–5920. Fax, 202–523–1494.

NATIONAL RAILROAD PASSENGER CORPORATION (AMTRAK)

60 Massachusetts Avenue NE., Washington, DC 20002
Phone, 202–906–3000

Board of Directors:

Chairman	(VACANCY)
Members	GOV. THOMAS R. CARPER, DANIEL W. COLLINS, SYLVIA A. DE LEON, CELESTE P. MCLAIN, ROY M. NEEL, DON J. PEASE, AMY ROSEN
Member *ex officio* (Secretary of Transportation)	RODNEY E. SLATER

Officers:

Chairman, President, and Chief Executive Officer	(VACANCY)
Vice President, Operations	RON SCOLARO
Chief Financial Officer	ALFRED S. ALTSCHUL
Vice President, Reservations, Sales, and Customer Relations	ANNE W. HOEY
Corporate Secretary	BARBARA RICHARDSON, *Acting*
Vice President, Government Affairs	THOMAS J. GILLESPIE, JR.
Vice President, Human Resources	LORRAINE A. GREEN
Vice President, Labor	JOSEPH M. BRESS
Vice President, Marketing and Sales	RICHARD P. DONNELLY
President, Amtrak West	GILBERT O. MALLERY
President, Amtrak Northeast Corridor	GEORGE D. WARRINGTON
President, Amtrak Intercity	LEE BULLOCK
Vice President and General Counsel	SARAH DUGGIN

[For the National Railroad Passenger Corporation statement of organization, see the *Code of Federal Regulations,* Title 49, Part 700]

The National Railroad Passenger Corporation was established to develop the potential of modern rail service in meeting the Nation's intercity passenger transportation needs.

The National Railroad Passenger Corporation (Amtrak) was created by the Rail Passenger Service Act of 1970, as amended (49 U.S.C. 241), and was incorporated under the laws of the District of Columbia to provide a balanced national transportation system by developing, operating, and improving U.S. intercity rail passenger service.

Section 411 of the Amtrak Reform and Accountability Act of 1997 (49 U.S.C. 24302) changed Amtrak's Board of Directors structure from a nine-member panel to a seven-member Reform Board, including the Secretary of Transportation and six others appointed by the President with the advice and consent of the Senate. The Reform Board is to assume the responsibilities of the Board of Directors as soon as at least four members have been appointed and qualified. The Corporation is managed by its President/Chief Executive Officer, along with the chief financial officer, seven vice presidents, and three presidents of strategic business units (SBU's).

The three SBU's, the Northeast Corridor, the Intercity, and the West, were created during Amtrak's restructuring in the fall of 1994 in order to increase profitability. Each SBU has a president who has control over business decisions in his area. The Northeast Corridor has been successful in expanding operations south, through Richmond to Newport News.

Amtrak operates an average of 212 trains per day, serving over 540 station locations in 45 States, over a system of approximately 24,500 route miles. Of this route system, Amtrak now owns a right-of-way of 2,611 track miles in the Northeast Corridor (Washington-New York-Boston; New Haven-Springfield; Philadelphia-Harrisburg), and several small track segments in the East, purchased pursuant to the Regional Rail Reorganization Act of 1973 (45 U.S.C. 701 *et seq.*) and the Railroad Revitalization and Regulatory Reform Act of 1976 (45 U.S.C. 801 *et seq.*).

Amtrak owns or leases its stations and owns its own repair and maintenance facilities. The Corporation employs a total work force of approximately 23,000 and provides all reservation, station, and on-board service staffs, as well as train and engine operating crews. Outside the Northeast Corridor, Amtrak has historically contracted with 21 privately owned railroads for the right to operate over their track and has compensated each railroad for its total package of services. Under contract, these railroads are responsible for the condition of the roadbed and for coordinating the flow of traffic.

In fiscal year 1997, Amtrak transported over 21 million people approximately 5.5 billion passenger miles. In addition, under contracts with several transit agencies, Amtrak carried over 48 million commuters.

Although Amtrak's basic route system was originally designated by the Secretary of Transportation in 1971, modifications have been made to the Amtrak system and to individual routes that have resulted in more efficient and cost-effective operations. Currently, in the face of ongoing budget constraints, new service will only be added if a State agrees to share any losses associated with the new service or if the new service demonstrates satisfactory market support.

Amtrak began operation in 1971 with an antiquated fleet of equipment inherited from private railroads; some cars were nearly 30 years old. Since then, the fleet has been modernized and new state-of-the-art single- and bi-level passenger cars and locomotives have been added.

Systemwide ridership is steadily rising, 2.6 percent in fiscal year 1997, and Amtrak is finding it increasingly difficult to meet the demands of increased travel patterns with its limited passenger fleet. To ease these equipment constraints, the Corporation is working to identify innovative funding sources in order to acquire additional passenger cars and locomotives.

Although no rail passenger system in the world makes a profit, Amtrak has made significant progress in reducing its dependence on Federal support, while at the same time improving the quality of service. Every year Amtrak moves further toward increasing the ratio of its earned revenue to total costs, even though Amtrak's appropriation for the current fiscal year is 45 percent below that for fiscal year 1978 (in constant dollars).

For further information, contact the Public Affairs Department, Amtrak, 60 Massachusetts Avenue NE., Washington, DC 20002. Phone, 202–906–3860.

NATIONAL SCIENCE FOUNDATION

4201 Wilson Boulevard, Arlington, VA 22230
Phone, 703-306-1234. Internet, http://www.nsf.gov/.

National Science Board

Chairman	EAMON M. KELLY
Vice Chairman	DIANA NATALICIO
Members	JOHN A. ARMSTRONG, MARY K. GAILLARD, SANFORD D. GREENBERG, M.R.C. GREENWOOD, STANLEY V. JASKOLSKI, JANE LUBCHENCO, EVE L. MENGER, CLAUDIA I. MITCHELL-KERNAN, VERA C. RUBIN, ROBERT M. SOLOW, BOB H. SUZUKI, RICHARD A. TAPIA, WARREN M. WASHINGTON, JOHN A. WHITE, JR., (8 VACANCIES)
(Ex officio)	RITA R. COLWELL
Executive Officer	MARTA C. CEHELSKY
Inspector General	PHILIP L. SUNSHINE, *Acting*
Deputy Inspector General	EDWARD L. BLANSITT III, *Acting*
Counsel to the Inspector General	MONTGOMERY K. FISHER
Assistant Inspector General for Audit	EDWARD L. BLANSITT III
Assistant Inspector General for Oversight	JAMES J. ZWOLENIK

Officials:

Director	RITA R. COLWELL
Deputy Director	JOSEPH BORDOGNA, *Acting*
Senior Science Adviser	KARL A. ERB
Assistant to the Director for Science Policy and Planning	JUDITH S. SUNLEY
Assistant to the Deputy Director for Human Resource Development	WANDA E. WARD
General Counsel	LAWRENCE RUDOLPH
Deputy General Counsel	THEODORE A. MILES
Director, Office of Legislative and Public Affairs	JULIA A. MOORE
Deputy Director, Office of Legislative and Public Affairs	JOEL M. WIDDER
Director, Office of Integrative Activities	NATHANIEL G. PITTS
Director, Office of Polar Programs	JOHN B. HUNT, *Acting*
Assistant Director for Mathematical and Physical Sciences	ROBERT A. EISENSTEIN
Executive Officer	ADRIAAN M. DE GRAAF
Head, Office of Multidisciplinary Activities	HENRY N. BLOUNT III
Director, Division of Physics	JOHN W. LIGHTBODY, JR., *Acting*
Director, Division of Chemistry	JANET G. OSTERYOUNG
Director, Division of Materials Research	THOMAS A. WEBER
Director, Division of Astronomical Sciences	HUGH M. VAN HORN
Director, Division of Mathematical Sciences	DONALD J. LEWIS
Assistant Director for Geosciences	ROBERT W. CORELL

Deputy Assistant Director	THOMAS J. BAERWALD
Director, Division of Atmospheric Sciences	RICHARD S. GREENFIELD
Director, Division of Earth Sciences	IAN D. MACGREGOR
Director, Division of Ocean Sciences	G. MICHAEL PURDY
Assistant Director for Biological Sciences	MARY E. CLUTTER
Deputy Assistant Director	JAMES L. EDWARDS
Director, Division of Biological Infrastructure	MACHI F. DILWORTH, *Acting*
Director, Division of Molecular and Cellular Biosciences	MARYANNA P. HENKART
Director, Division of Integrative Biology and Neuroscience	BRUCE L. UMMINGER
Director, Division of Environmental Biology	BRUCE P. HAYDEN
Assistant Director for Engineering	EUGENE WONG
Deputy Assistant Director for Engineering	ELBERT L. MARSH
Director, Division of Engineering Education and Centers	MARSHALL M. LIH
Director, Division of Electrical and Communications Systems	ARTHUR C. SANDERSON
Director, Division of Chemical and Transport Systems	GARY W. POEHLEIN
Director, Division of Civil and Mechanical Systems	RONALD L. SACK
Director, Division of Design, Manufacture, and Industrial Innovation	BRUCE M. KRAMER
Director, Division of Bioengineering and Environmental Systems	JANIE M. FOUKE
Director, Office of Small Business Research and Development	DONALD SENICH
Director, Office of Small and Disadvantaged Business Utilization	JOSEPH BORDOGNA
Assistant Director for Computer and Information Science and Engineering	JURIS HARTMANIS
Deputy Assistant Director	MELVYN CIMENT
Director, Division of Experimental and Integrative Activities	JOHN CHERNIAVSKY
Director, Division of Advanced Computational Infrastructure and Research	ROBERT R. BORCHERS
Director, Division of Computer-Communications Research	JOHN R. LEHMANN, *Acting*
Director, Division of Information and Intelligent Systems	MICHAEL E. LESK
Director, Division of Advanced Networking Infrastructure and Research	GEORGE O. STRAWN
Assistant Director for Social, Behavioral, and Economic Sciences	BENNETT I. BERTENTHAL
Executive Officer	JEFF FENSTERMACHER
Director, Division of Social, Behavioral, and Economic Research	WILLIAM P. BUTZ
Director, Division of Science Resources Studies	JEANNE E. GRIFFITH
Director, Division of International Programs	PIERRE M. PERROLLE
Assistant Director for Education and Human Resources	LUTHER S. WILLIAMS
Deputy Assistant Director	JANE T. STUTSMAN

Deputy Assistant Director for Integrative Activities	JOHN B. HUNT
Director, Division of Educational System Reform	LUTHER S. WILLIAMS, *Acting*
Director, Division of Elementary, Secondary, and Informal Education	HYMAN H. FIELD, *Acting*
Director, Division of Graduate Education	SUSAN W. DUBY, *Acting*
Director, Division of Human Resource Development	ROOSEVELT CALBERT
Director, Division of Research, Evaluation, and Communication	DARYL E. CHUBIN
Director, Division of Undergraduate Education	NORMAN L. FORTENBERRY
Head, Office of Experimental Program to Stimulate Competitive Research	RICHARD J. ANDERSON
Chief Financial Officer/Director, Office of Budget, Finance, and Award Management	JOSEPH L. KULL
Deputy Chief Financial Officer/Director, Division of Financial Management	ALBERT A. MUHLBAUER
Executive Officer	THOMAS N. COOLEY
Director, Division of Grants and Agreements	JOANNE E. ROM
Director, Division of Contracts, Policy, and Oversight	ROBERT B. HARDY
Director, Budget Division	MARTHA A. RUBENSTEIN
Director, Office of Information and Resource Management	LINDA P. MASSARO
Deputy Director	GERARD R. GLASER
Director, Division of Human Resource Management	JOHN F. WILKINSON, JR.
Director, Division of Information Systems	FRED WENDLING
Director, Division of Administrative Services	ROBERT E. SCHMITZ

[For the National Science Foundation statement of organization, see the *Federal Register* of February 8, 1993, 58 FR 7587–7595; May 27, 1993, 58 FR 30819; May 2, 1994, 59 FR 22690; and Oct. 6, 1995, 60 FR 52431]

The National Science Foundation promotes the progress of science and engineering through the support of research and education programs. Its major emphasis is on high-quality, merit-selected research—the search for improved understanding of the fundamental laws of nature upon which our future well-being as a nation depends. Its educational programs are aimed at ensuring increased understanding of science and engineering at all educational levels, maintaining an adequate supply of scientists, engineers, and science educators to meet our country's needs.

The National Science Foundation is an independent agency created by the National Science Foundation Act of 1950, as amended (42 U.S.C. 1861–1875).

The purposes of the Foundation are: to increase the Nation's base of scientific and engineering knowledge and strengthen its ability to conduct research in all areas of science and engineering; to develop and help implement science and engineering education programs that can better prepare the Nation for meeting the challenges of the future; and to promote international cooperation through science and engineering. In its role as a leading Federal supporter of science and engineering, the agency also has an important role in national policy planning.

The Foundation consists of a National Science Board and a Director. The National Science Board is composed of 24 members and the Director *ex officio*.

NATIONAL SCIENCE FOUNDATION

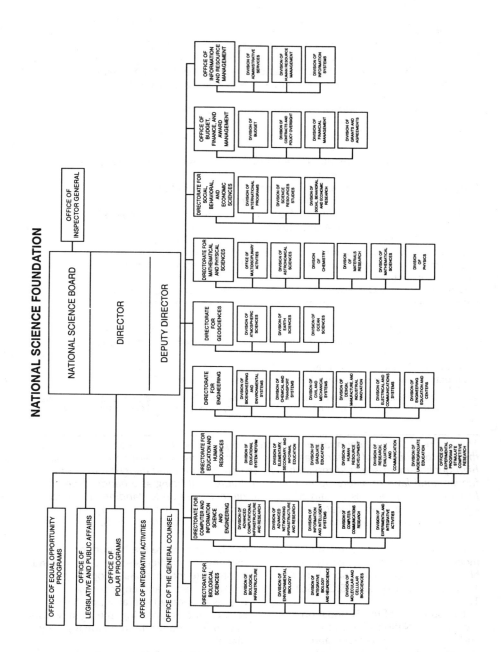

Members are appointed by the President with the advice and consent of the Senate, for 6-year terms, with one-third appointed every 2 years. They are selected because of their records of distinguished service in science, engineering, education, research management, or public affairs to be broadly representative of the views of national science and engineering leadership.

Both the Director and the Deputy Director are appointed by the President with the advice and consent of the Senate, to a 6-year term and an unspecified term, respectively.

The National Science Foundation Act assigns policymaking functions for the Foundation to the National Science Board, within the framework of applicable policies set forth by the President and the Congress, and assigns the administration of the Foundation to the Director. By statute the Director of the Foundation is an *ex officio* member of the Board and Chairman of the Executive Committee of the Board.

The Board also has a broad national policy responsibility to monitor and make recommendations to promote the health of U.S. science and engineering research and education.

The Foundation's Office of Inspector General is responsible for conducting and supervising audits, inspections, and investigations relating to the programs and operations of the Foundation, including allegations of misconduct in science.

Activities

The National Science Foundation initiates and supports fundamental, long-term, merit-selected research in all the scientific and engineering disciplines. This support is made through grants, contracts, and other agreements awarded to universities, colleges, academic consortia, and nonprofit and small business institutions. Most of this research is directed toward the resolution of scientific and engineering questions concerning fundamental life processes, natural laws and phenomena, fundamental processes influencing the

human environment, and the forces affecting people as members of society as well as the behavior of society as a whole.

The Foundation encourages cooperative efforts by universities, industries, and government. It also promotes the application of research and development for better products and services that improve the quality of life and stimulate economic growth.

The Foundation promotes the development of research talent through support of undergraduate and graduate students, as well as postdoctoral researchers. It administers special programs to identify and encourage participation by groups underrepresented in science and technology and to strengthen research capability at smaller institutions, small businesses, undergraduate colleges, and universities.

The Foundation supports major national and international science and engineering activities, including the U.S. Antarctic Program, the Ocean Drilling Program, global geoscience studies, and others. Cooperative scientific and engineering research activities support exchange programs for American and foreign scientists and engineers, execution of jointly designed research projects, participation in the activities of international science and engineering organizations, and travel to international conferences.

Support is provided through contracts and cooperative agreements with national centers where large facilities are made available for use by qualified scientists and engineers. Among the types of centers supported by the Foundation are astronomy and atmospheric sciences, biological and engineering research, science and technology, supercomputers, and long-term ecological research sites.

The Foundation provides competitively awarded grants for repair, renovation, or, in exceptional cases, replacement of facilities used for research and research training at academic and nonprofit institutions.

The Foundation's science and engineering education activities include grants for research and development activities directed to model instructional materials for students and teachers and the application of advanced technologies to education. Grants also are available for teacher preparation and enhancement and informal science education activities. Funding is also provided for college science instrumentation, course and curriculum improvement, faculty and student activities, and minority resource centers. In addition, studies of the status of math, science, and engineering education are supported.

The National Science Board annually presents the Vannevar Bush Award to a person who, through public service activities in science and technology, has made an outstanding contribution toward the welfare of mankind and the Nation. It also presents the Public Service Award to an individual and to a company, corporation, or organization who, through contributions to public service in areas other than research, have increased the public understanding of science or engineering. The National Science Foundation annually presents the Alan T. Waterman Award to an outstanding young scientist or engineer for support of research and study. The Foundation also provides administrative support for the President's Committee on the National Medal of Science.

Information on these awards is available through the Internet, at http://www.nsf.gov/home/nsb/start.htm.

Sources of Information

Board and Committee Minutes Summary minutes of the open meetings of the Board may be obtained from the National Science Board Office. Phone, 703–306–2000. Information on NSB meetings, minutes, and reports is available through the Internet at http://www.nsf.gov/home/nsb/start.htm. Summary minutes of the Foundation's advisory groups may be obtained from the contacts listed in the notice of meetings published in the *Federal Register*. General information about the Foundation's advisory groups may be obtained from the Division of Human Resource Management, Room 315,

Arlington, VA 22230. Phone, 703–306–1181.

Contracts The Foundation publicizes contracting and subcontracting opportunities in the *Commerce Business Daily* and other appropriate publications. Organizations seeking to undertake contract work for the Foundation should contact either the Division of Contracts, Policy, and Oversight (phone, 703–306–1242) or the Division of Administrative Services (phone, 703–306–1122), National Science Foundation, Arlington, VA 22230.

Electronic Access Information regarding NSF programs and services is available through the Internet, at http://www.nsf.gov/.

Employment Inquiries may be directed to the Division of Human Resource Management, National Science Foundation, Room 315, Arlington, VA 22230. Phone, 703–306–1182, or, for the hearing impaired (TDD), 703–306–0189. The Foundation's vacancy hotline numbers are 703–306–0080 or 1–800–628–1487. Internet, http://www.nsf.gov/.

Fellowships Consult the *NSF Guide to Programs* and appropriate announcements and brochures for postdoctoral fellowship opportunities that may be available through some Foundation divisions. Beginning graduate and minority graduate students wishing to apply for fellowships should contact the Directorate for Education and Human Resources. Phone, 703–306–1694.

Freedom of Information Act Requests Requests for agency records should be submitted in accordance with the Foundation FOIA regulation at 45 CFR part 612. Such requests should be clearly identified with "FOIA REQUEST" and be addressed to the FOIA Officer, Office of General Counsel, National Science Foundation, Room 1265, Arlington, VA 22230. Phone, 703–306–1060. Fax, 703–306–0149. E-mail, foia@nsf.gov.

Grants Individuals or organizations who plan to submit grant proposals should refer to the *NSF Guide to Programs, Grant Proposal Guide* (NSF 98–2), and appropriate program brochures and announcements that may be obtained as indicated in the Publications section. Grant information is also available electronically through the Internet, at http://www.nsf.gov/.

Office of Inspector General   General inquiries may be directed to the Office of Inspector General, National Science Foundation, Room 1135, Arlington, VA 22230. Phone, 703–306–2100.

Privacy Act Requests   Requests for personal records should be submitted in accordance with the Foundation Privacy Act regulation at 45 CFR, part 613. Such requests should be clearly identified with "PRIVACY ACT REQUEST" and be addressed to the Privacy Act Officer, National Science Foundation, Room 1265, Arlington, VA 22230. Phone, 703–306–1060.

Publications   The National Science Board assesses the status and health of science and its various disciplines, including such matters as human and material resources, in reports submitted to the President for submission to the Congress. The most recent report is *Science and Engineering Indicators, 1996* (NSB–96–21).

The National Science Foundation issues publications that announce and describe new programs, critical dates, and application procedures for competitions. Single copies of these publications can be ordered in a variety of ways: phone, 301–947–2722; E-mail, pubinfo@nsf.gov; or by writing to: NSF Clearinghouse, P.O. Box 218, Jessup, MD 20794–0218. These publications are also available electronically through the Internet, at http://www.nsf.gov/.

Other Foundation publications include: the *Grant Policy Manual* (NSF–95–26), which contains comprehensive statements of Foundation grant administration policy, procedures, and guidance; *Guide to Programs,* which summarizes information about support programs; the quarterly *Antarctic Journal of the United States* and its annual review issue; and the *NSF Annual Report.* These publications are available from the Superintendent of Documents, Government Printing Office, Washington, DC 20402; or electronically through the Internet, at http://www.nsf.gov/.

Reading Room   A collection of Foundation policy documents and staff instructions, as well as current indexes, are available to the public for inspection and copying during regular business hours, 8:30 a.m. to 5 p.m., Monday through Friday, in the National Science Foundation Library, Room 225, Arlington, VA 22230. Phone, 703–306–0658.

Small Business Activities   The Office of Small Business Research and Development provides information on opportunities for Foundation support to small businesses with strong research capabilities in science and technology. Phone, 703–306–1330. The Office of Small and Disadvantaged Business Utilization oversees agency compliance with the provisions of the Small Business Act and the Small Business Investment Act of 1958, as amended (15 U.S.C. 631, 661, 683). Phone, 703–306–1330.

For further information, contact the National Science Foundation Information Center, 4201 Wilson Boulevard, Second Floor, Arlington, VA 22230. Phone, 703–306–1234. TDD, 703–306–0900. E-mail, info@nsf.gov. Internet, http://www.nsf.gov/.

NATIONAL TRANSPORTATION SAFETY BOARD

490 L'Enfant Plaza SW., Washington, DC 20594
Phone, 202–314–6000. Internet, http://www.ntsb.gov/.

Chairman	JAMES E. HALL
Vice Chairman	ROBERT T. FRANCIS II

Members	GEORGE W. BLACK, JR., JOHN J. GOGLIA, JOHN A. HAMMERSCHMIDT
Managing Director	PETER GOELZ
Deputy Managing Director	RONALD S. BATTOCCHI
Director, Office of Government, Public and Family Affairs	JAMIE FINCH
Deputy Director for Public Affairs	TED LOPATKIEWICZ
Deputy Director for Family Affairs	GARY ABE
General Counsel	DANIEL D. CAMPBELL
Deputy General Counsel	DAVID BASS
Director, Office of Research and Engineering	VERNON ELLINGSTAD
Deputy Director	(VACANCY)
Director, Office of Safety Recommendations and Accomplishments	BARRY M. SWEEDLER
Deputy Director	RICHARD VAN WOERKOM
Director, Office of Aviation Safety	BERNARD S. LOEB
Deputy Director for International Aviation Safety Affairs	RONALD SCHLEEDE
Deputy Director for Technical/Investigative Operations	JOHN CLARK
Deputy Director for Regional Technical/ Investigative Operations	GENE SUNDEEN
Director, Office of Railroad Safety	ROBERT C. LAUBY
Director, Office of Highway Safety	JOSEPH E. OSTERMAN
Deputy Directory	CLAUDE HARRIS
Director, Office of Marine Safety	MARJORIE M. MURTAGH
Director, Office of Pipeline and Hazardous Materials Safety	ROBERT J. CHIPKEVICH
Chief Financial Officer	CRAIG E. KELLER, SR.
Chief Administrative Law Judge	WILLIAM E. FOWLER, JR.

[For the National Transportation Safety Board statement of organization, see the *Code of Federal Regulations*, Title 49, Part 800]

The National Transportation Safety Board seeks to ensure that all types of transportation in the United States are conducted safely. The Board investigates accidents, conducts studies, and makes recommendations to Government agencies, the transportation industry, and others on safety measures and practices.

The National Transportation Safety Board (NTSB) was established in 1967 and made totally independent on April 1, 1975, by the Independent Safety Board Act of 1974 (49 U.S.C. app. 1901).

The Safety Board consists of five members appointed by the President with the advice and consent of the Senate for 5-year terms. The President designates two of these members as Chairman and Vice Chairman of the Board for 2-year terms. The designation of the Chairman is made with the advice and consent of the Senate.

Activities

Accident Investigation   The Board is responsible for investigating, determining probable cause, making safety recommendations, and reporting the facts and circumstances of:

—U.S. civil aviation and certain public-use aircraft accidents;

—railroad accidents in which there is a fatality or substantial property damage, or that involve a passenger train;

—pipeline accidents in which there is a fatality, substantial property damage, or significant injury to the environment;

NATIONAL TRANSPORTATION SAFETY BOARD

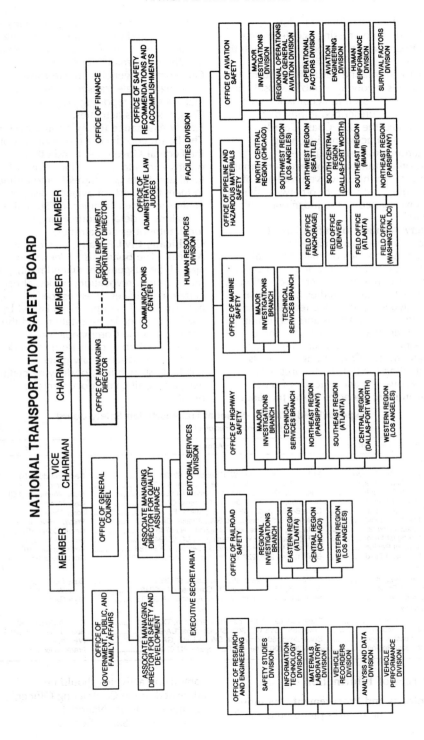

—highway accidents, including railroad grade-crossing accidents, that the Board selects in cooperation with the States;

—major marine casualties, and marine accidents involving a public vessel and a nonpublic vessel, in accordance with regulations prescribed jointly by the Board and the U.S. Coast Guard;

—certain accidents involving hazardous materials; and

—other transportation accidents that are catastrophic, involve problems of a recurring character, or otherwise should be investigated in the judgment of the Board.

Safety Problem Identification In addition, the Board makes recommendations on matters pertaining to transportation safety and is a catalyst for transportation accident prevention by conducting safety studies and special investigations, assessing techniques of accident investigation and publishing recommended procedures for these investigations, establishing regulatory requirements for reporting accidents, evaluating the transportation safety consciousness and efficacy of other Government agencies in the prevention of accidents, evaluating the adequacy of safeguards and procedures concerning the transportation of hazardous materials and the performance of other Government agencies charged with ensuring the safe transportation of such materials, and reporting annually to the Congress on its activities.

Family Assistance for Aviation Disasters The Board coordinates the resources of the Federal Government and other organizations to support the efforts of local and State governments and airlines to meet the needs of aviation disaster victims and their families. NTSB assists in making Federal resources available to local authorities and airlines.

Certificate, Civil Penalty, or License Appeal The Board also reviews on appeal the suspension, amendment, modification, revocation, or denial of certain certificates, licenses, or assessments of civil penalties issued by the Secretary of Transportation and the decisions of the Commandant of the Coast Guard on appeals from the orders of any administrative law judge, revoking, suspending, or denying certain licenses, certificates, documents, or registers.

Regional/Field Offices—National Transportation Safety Board
(R: Regional Director; FC: Field Chief)

Region/Field Office	Address	Officer
AVIATION:		
North Central Region	31 W. 775 North Ave., W. Chicago, IL 60185	Carl Dinwiddie (R)
South Central Region	Suite 150, 624 Six Flags Drive, Arlington, TX 76011	Tim Borson (R)
South Central Field	Suite 500, 4760 Oakland St., Denver, CO 80239	Norm Wiemeyer (FC)
Southwest Region	Suite 555, 1515 W. 190th St., Gardena, CA 90248	Gary Mucho (R)
Southeast Region	Suite B–103, 8405 NW. 53d St., Miami, FL 33166	Jorge Prellezo (R)
Southeast Field	Suite 3M25, 60 Forsyth St. SW., Atlanta, GA 30303	Preston Hicks (FC)
Northeast Region	Suite 203, 2001 Rte. 46, Parsippany, NJ 07054	Dennis Jones (R)
Northeast Field	490 L'Enfant Plz. SW., Washington, DC 20594	(Vacancy) (FC)
Northwest Region	Rm. 201, 19518 Pacific Hwy. S., Seattle, WA 98188	Keith McGuire (R)
Northwest Field	Box 11, Rm. 216, 222 W. 7th Ave., Anchorage, AK 99513	Jim LaBelle (FC)
RAILROAD:		
Central Region	31 W. 775 North Ave., W. Chicago, IL 60185	Russ Seipler (R)
Western Region	Suite 555, 1515 W. 190th St., Gardena, CA 90248	Dave Watson (R)
Eastern Region	Suite 3M25, 60 Forsyth St. SW., Atlanta, GA 30303	Mark Garcia (R)
HIGHWAY:		
Central Region	Suite 150, 624 Six Flags Drive, Arlington, TX 76011	Kennith Rogers (R)
Western Region	Suite 555, 1515 W. 190th St., Gardena, CA 90248	Ronald Robinson (R)
Southeast Region	Suite 3M25, 60 Forsyth St. SW., Atlanta, GA 30303	(Vacancy) (R)
Northeast Region	Suite 203, 2001 Rte. 46, Parsippany, NJ 07054	Frank Ghiorsi (R)

Sources of Information

Contracts and Procurement Inquiries regarding the Board's procurement and contracting activities should be addressed to the Contracting Officer, Facilities Division, National Transportation Safety Board,

Washington, DC 20594. Phone, 202–314–6220.

Electronic Access Agency information, including aircraft accident data, synopses of aircraft accidents, speeches and congressional testimony given by Board members and staff, press releases, job vacancy announcements, and notices of Board meetings, public hearings, and other agency events, is available in electronic form through the Internet, at http://www.ntsb.gov/.

Employment Send applications for employment to the Human Resources Division, National Transportation Safety Board, Washington, DC 20594. Phone, 202–314–6239.

Publications Publications are provided free of charge to the following categories of subscribers: Federal, State, or local transportation agencies; international transportation organizations or foreign governments; educational institutions or public libraries; nonprofit public safety organizations; and the news media. Persons in these categories who are

interested in receiving copies of Board publications should contact the Public Inquiries Branch, National Transportation Safety Board, Washington, DC 20594. Phone, 202–314–6551.

All other persons interested in receiving publications must purchase them from the National Technical Information Service, 5285 Port Royal Road, Springfield, VA 22161. Orders may be placed by telephone to the Subscription Unit at 703–487–4630, or the sales desk at 703–487–4768.

Reading Room The Board's Public Reference Room is available for record inspection or photocopying. It is located in Room 6500 at the Board's Washington, DC, headquarters and is open from 9 a.m. to 4 p.m. every business day. Requests for access to public records should be made in person at Room 6500, or by writing the Public Inquiries Branch, National Transportation Safety Board, Washington, DC 20594. Phone, 202–314–6551.

For further information, contact the Office of Public Affairs, National Transportation Safety Board, 490 L'Enfant Plaza SW., Washington, DC 20594. Phone, 202–314–6100. Fax, 202–314–6110. Internet, http://www.ntsb.gov/.

NUCLEAR REGULATORY COMMISSION

Washington, DC 20555
Phone, 301–415–7000. Internet, http://www.nrc.gov/.

Chairman	SHIRLEY ANN JACKSON
Executive Assistant and Director, Office of the Chairman	MARTIN VIRGILIO
Deputy Director for Policy Development and Technical Support	(VACANCY)
Deputy Director for Corporate Planning and Management	JACQUELINE E. SILBER
Special Assistant for Legal Affairs	KARLA D. SMITH
Special Assistant for Nuclear Material, Waste, and Fuel Cycle	REGIS R. BOYLE
Special Assistant for Regulatory Effectiveness and Oversight	JAMES W. JOHNSON
Special Assistant for Reactor Programs	BRIAN F. HOLIAN
Special Assistant for Internal Affairs	JANICE DUNN LEE
Special Assistant for External Communication	LABAN L. COBLENTZ

Special Assistant for Financial and Information Management	CLARE V. DEFINO
Special Assistant for Nuclear Materials and Waste	JAMES A. SMITH, JR.
Commissioner	GRETA JOY DICUS
Executive/Legal Assistant	BRADLEY W. JONES
Commissioner	NILS J. DIAZ
Executive Assistant	MARIA LOPEZ-OTIN
Legal Assistant	ROGER K. DAVIS
Commissioner	EDWARD McGAFFIGAN, JR.
Executive/Legal Assistant	STEVEN F. CROCKETT
Commissioner	(VACANCY)
Legal Assistant	(VACANCY)
Secretary of the Commission	JOHN C. HOYLE
Director, Office of Commission Appellate Adjudication	JOHN F. CORDES, *Acting*
Director, Office of Congressional Affairs	DENNIS K. RATHBUN
General Counsel	KAREN D. CYR
Director, Office of International Programs	CARLTON R. STOIBER
Director, Office of Public Affairs	WILLIAM M. BEECHER
Chairman, Advisory Committee on Nuclear Waste	B. JOHN GARRICK
Chairman, Advisory Committee on Reactor Safeguards	ROBERT L. SEALE
Chairman, Advisory Committee on Medical Uses of Isotopes	JUDITH A. STITT
Chief Administrative Judge, Atomic Safety and Licensing Board Panel	B. PAUL COTTER, JR.
Inspector General	HUBERT T. BELL, JR.
Chief Information Officer	ANTHONY J. GALANTE
Chief Financial Officer	JESSIE L. FUNCHES
Deputy Chief Financial Officer	PETER J. RABIDEAU
Executive Director for Operations	L. JOSEPH CALLAN
Assistant for Operations	JAMES L. BLAHA
Deputy Executive Director for Regulatory Effectiveness	ASHOK C. THANDANI, *Acting*
Director, Office of Nuclear Regulatory Research	MALCOLM R. KNAPP, *Acting*
Director, Division of Engineering	LAWRENCE C. SHAO
Director, Division of Systems Technology	M. WAYNE HODGES
Director, Division of Regulatory Application	JOSEPH A. MURPHY, *Acting*
Director, Office of Analysis and Evaluation of Operational Data	THOMAS T. MARTIN
Director, Office of Enforcement	JAMES LIEBERMAN
Director, Office of Investigations	GUY P. CAPUTO
Deputy Executive Director for Regulatory Programs	HUGH L. THOMPSON, JR.
Director, Office of State Programs	RICHARD L. BANGART
Director, Office of Nuclear Material Safety and Safeguards	CARL J. PAPERIELLO
Deputy Director, Office of Nuclear Material Safety and Safeguards	WILLIAM F. KANE, *Acting*
Director, Division of Industrial and Medical Nuclear Safety	DONALD A. COOL

Director, Division of Fuel Cycle Safety and Safeguards	ELIZABETH Q. TEN EYCK
Director, Division of Waste Management	JOHN T. GREEVES
Director, Spent Fuel Project Office	CHARLES HAUGHNEY, *Acting*
Director, Office of Nuclear Reactor Regulation	SAMUEL J. COLLINS
Deputy Director, Office of Nuclear Reactor Regulation	FRANK J. MIRAGLIA, JR.
Reactor Regulation	
Associate Director for Projects	BRUCE A. BOGER, *Acting*
Director, Division of Reactor Projects—I/II	JOHN A. ZWOLINSKI, *Acting*
Director, Division of Reactor Projects—III/IV	JACK W. ROE
Director, Division of Reactor Program Management	JACK W. ROE, *Acting*
Associate Director for Technical Reviews	BRIAN W. SHERON
Director, Division of Engineering	GUS C. LAINAS
Director, Division of Systems Safety and Analysis	GARY M. HOLAHAN
Director, Division of Reactor Controls and Human Factors	RICHARD L. SPESSARD
Director, Division of Inspection and Support Program	FRANCIS P. GILLESPIE
Deputy Executive Director for Management Services	PATRICIA G. NORRY
Director, Office of Administration	EDWARD L. HALMAN
Director, Office of Human Resources	PAUL E. BIRD
Director, Office of Small Business and Civil Rights	IRENE P. LITTLE

[For the Nuclear Regulatory Commission statement of organization, see the *Code of Federal Regulations,* Title 10, Part I]

The Nuclear Regulatory Commission licenses and regulates civilian use of nuclear energy to protect public health and safety and the environment. This is achieved by licensing persons and companies to build and operate nuclear reactors and other facilities and to own and use nuclear materials. The Commission makes rules and sets standards for these types of licenses. It also carefully inspects the activities of the persons and companies licensed to ensure that they do not violate the safety rules of the Commission.

The Nuclear Regulatory Commission (NRC) was established as an independent regulatory agency under the provisions of the Energy Reorganization Act of 1974 (42 U.S.C. 5801 *et seq.*) and Executive Order 11834 of January 15, 1975, effective January 19, 1975. Transferred to the Commission were all licensing and related regulatory functions formerly assigned to the Atomic Energy Commission, which was established by the Atomic Energy Act of 1946 (60 Stat. 755), as amended by the Atomic Energy Act of 1954, as amended (42 U.S.C. 2011 *et seq.*).

The Commission's major program components are the Office of Nuclear Reactor Regulation, the Office of Nuclear Material Safety and Safeguards, and the Office of Nuclear Regulatory Research, which were created by the Energy Reorganization Act of 1974. Headquarters offices are located in suburban Maryland, and there are four regional offices.

The Commission ensures that the civilian uses of nuclear materials and facilities are conducted in a manner consistent with the public health and safety, environmental quality, national

NUCLEAR REGULATORY COMMISSION

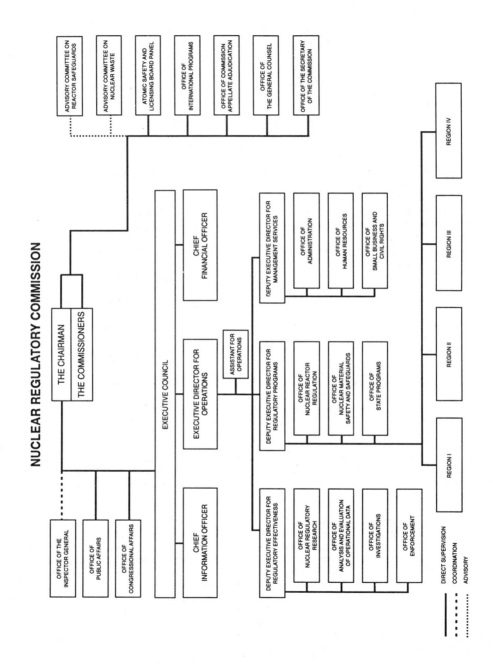

security, and the antitrust laws. The major share of the Commission's effort is focused on regulating the use of nuclear energy to generate electric power.

Activities

The Nuclear Regulatory Commission fulfills its responsibilities through a system of licensing and regulatory activities that include:

—licensing the construction and operation of nuclear reactors and other nuclear facilities, such as nuclear fuel cycle facilities and nonpower test and research reactors, and overseeing their decommissioning;

—licensing the possession, use, processing, handling, and export of nuclear material;

—licensing the siting, design, construction, operation, and closure of low-level radioactive waste disposal sites under NRC jurisdiction and the construction, operation, and closure of the geologic repository for high-level radioactive waste;

—licensing the operators of nuclear power and nonpower test and research reactors;

—inspecting licensed facilities and activities;

—conducting the principal U.S. Government research program on light-water reactor safety;

—conducting research to provide independent expertise and information for making timely regulatory judgments and for anticipating problems of potential safety significance;

—developing and implementing rules and regulations that govern licensed nuclear activities;

—investigating nuclear incidents and allegations concerning any matter regulated by the NRC;

—enforcing NRC regulations and the conditions of NRC licenses;

—conducting public hearings on matters of nuclear and radiological safety, environmental concern, common defense and security, and antitrust matters;

—maintaining the NRC Incident Response Program, including the NRC Operations Center;

—collecting, analyzing, and disseminating information about the operational safety of commercial nuclear power reactors and certain nonreactor activities; and

—developing effective working relationships with the States regarding reactor operations and the regulation of nuclear material, including assurance that adequate regulatory programs are maintained by those States that exercise, by agreement with the Commission, regulatory control over certain nuclear materials in the State.

Sources of Information

Contracts and Procurement   Detailed information on how to do business with the Commission may be obtained by calling the Director, Division of Contracts and Property Management, at 301–415–7305. Information on programs to assist small business is available from the Director, Office of Small Business and Civil Rights, Mail Stop T2F18, Nuclear Regulatory Commission, Washington, DC 20555–0001. Phone, 301–415–7380.

Employment   The Commission's employment activities are exempt from civil service requirements and are conducted under an independent merit system. However, employees receive Federal employee benefits (retirement, group life insurance, and health benefits) on the same basis as other Federal employees. Applicants with veterans preference are accorded the preference granted to them by the Veterans' Preference Act of 1944 (58 Stat. 387).

Recruitment is continual, and applications from individuals qualified for Commission needs are accepted whenever they are received. In addition to receiving applications from candidates at all grade levels throughout the year, the agency recruits annually from colleges as appropriate to fill needs for interns and entry-level professionals.

Employment inquiries, applications, and requests from schools for participation in the recruitment program may be directed to the Director, Office of Human Resources, Mail Stop T3A2, Nuclear Regulatory Commission, Washington, DC 20555–0001. Phone, 301–415–7516.

Freedom of Information Act Requests
Requests for copies of records should be directed to the Chief, FOIA/Privacy Act Section, Mail Stop T6D8, Nuclear Regulatory Commission, Washington, DC 20555–0001. Phone, 301–415–7169.

Publications The NRC publishes several annual reports: the *NRC Annual Report* (NUREG–1145), a summary of major agency activities for the year; a *Report to Congress on Abnormal Occurrences* (NUREG–0090); and analyses of operational data for plants and materials (NUREG–1272, Vols. 1 and 2). Published semiannually are the *Telephone Directory* (NUREG/BR–0046) and the *Regulatory Agenda* (NUREG–0936); published quarterly are the *Regulatory and Technical Reports Abstract Journal* (NUREG–0304) and the *Licensee, Contractor, and Vendor Inspection Status Report* (NUREG–0040); published monthly are the *Title List of Documents Made Publicly Available* (NUREG–0540); and published weekly is the *Weekly Information Report*. The *Nuclear Regulatory Commission Issuances* (NUREG–0750) contain adjudications and other issuances for the Commission, including those for the Atomic Safety and Licensing Boards. Semiannual compilations for the monthly editions are published along with four indices for these issuances.

In addition to these periodic publications, the NRC publishes in its NUREG Series scientific, technical, and administrative information dealing with licensing and regulation of civilian nuclear facilities and materials. The title list (NUREG–0540) identifies these publications and lists docketed and nondocketed material received and produced by the NRC pertinent to its role as a regulatory agency. Some publications and documents are available through the Internet, at http://www.nrc.gov/.

The Government Printing Office sells single copies of or subscriptions to NRC publications, as does the National Technical Information Service. To obtain prices and order NRC publications, contact the Superintendent of Documents, Government Printing Office, P.O. Box 37082, Washington, DC 20013–7082. Phone, 202–512–1800. Internet, http://www.gpo.gov/. Or contact the National Technical Information Service, Springfield, VA 22161–0002. Phone, 703–487–4650. Internet, http://www.ntis.gov/ordernow/.

Active *Regulatory Guides* may be obtained without charge by faxed request to 301–415–5272 or by written request to the Nuclear Regulatory Commission, Washington, DC 20555, Attention: Publishing Services Branch. Active *Regulatory Guides* may also be purchased, as they are issued, on standing orders from the National Technical Information Service. These *Regulatory Guides* are published in 10 subject areas: Power Reactors, Research and Test Reactors, Fuels and Materials Facilities, Environmental and Siting, Materials and Plant Protection, Products, Transportation, Occupational Health, Antitrust and Financial Review, and General.

Draft Regulatory Guides are issued for public comment. These drafts may be downloaded from or commented on through the Internet, at http://www.nrc.gov/. *Draft Regulatory Guides* may also be obtained, to the extent of supply, by faxed request to 301–415–5272 or by written request to the Nuclear Regulatory Commission, Washington, DC 20555, Attention: Publishing Services Branch.

Reading Rooms The Headquarters Public Document Room maintains an extensive collection of documents related to NRC licensing proceedings and other significant decisions and actions, and documents from the regulatory activities of the former Atomic Energy Commission. Persons interested in detailed, technical information about nuclear facilities and other licensees find this specialized research center to be a major resource. (Books, journals, trade publications, or documents on industry standards are not stocked in the Reading Room.) Located at 2120 L Street NW., Washington, DC, the Public Document Room is open Monday through Friday from 7:45 a.m. to 4:15 p.m., except on Federal holidays.

Documents from the collection may be reproduced, with some exceptions, on paper, microfiche, or diskette for a nominal fee. The Public Document Room also offers an order subscription service for selected serially published documents and reports. Certain items of immediate interest, such as press releases and meeting notices, are posted in the Reading Room.

Reference librarians are available to assist users with information requests. The computerized online Bibliographic Retrieval System includes extensive indices to the collection and an online ordering module for the placement of orders for the reproduction and delivery of specific documents. Off-site access to the Bibliographic Retrieval System (at 1200, 2400, and 9600 baud) or via telnet is available for searches 24 hours a day, including weekends and holidays. Access to the system may be arranged by calling the number listed below.

For additional information regarding the Public Document Room, contact the Nuclear Regulatory Commission, Public Document Room, Washington, DC 20555. Phone, 202–634–3273

(Washington, DC, area), or 800–397–4209 (toll-free). E-mail, pdr@nrc.gov. Fax, 202–634–3343.

In addition, the Commission maintains approximately 85 local public document rooms around the country. The document rooms are located in libraries in cities and towns near commercially operated nuclear power reactors and certain nonpower reactor facilities. They contain detailed information specific to the nearby facilities, which are either licensed or under regulatory review. Power reactor and high-level radioactive waste local public document rooms also contain a microfiche file of all publicly available NRC documents issued since January 1981. A list of local public document rooms and information about the availability of documents at local public document rooms is available at the NRC Public Document Room at the address and telephone numbers above.

For further information, contact the Office of Public Affairs, Nuclear Regulatory Commission, Washington, DC 20555–0001. Phone, 301–415–8200. Internet, http://www.nrc.gov/.

OCCUPATIONAL SAFETY AND HEALTH REVIEW COMMISSION

1120 Twentieth Street NW., Washington, DC 20036–3419
Phone, 202–606–5100. Internet, http://www.oshrc.gov/.

Chairman	STUART E. WEISBERG
Commissioners	(2 VACANCIES)
Executive Director	WILLIAM J. GAINER
Chief Administrative Law Judge	IRVING SOMMER
General Counsel	EARL R. OHMAN, JR.
Executive Secretary	RAY H. DARLING, JR.
Public Affairs Specialist	LINDA A. WHITSETT

The Occupational Safety and Health Review Commission works to ensure the timely and fair resolution of cases involving the alleged exposure of American workers to unsafe or unhealthy working conditions.

The Occupational Safety and Health Review Commission is an independent, quasi-judicial agency established by the Occupational Safety and Health Act of 1970 (29 U.S.C. 651–678).

The Commission is charged with ruling on cases forwarded to it by the Department of Labor when disagreements arise over the results of safety and health inspections performed by the Department's Occupational Safety

OCCUPATIONAL SAFETY AND HEALTH REVIEW COMMISSION

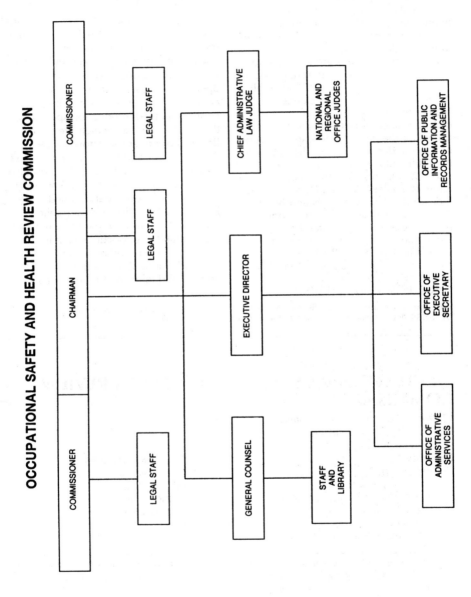

and Health Administration. Employers have the right to dispute any alleged job safety or health violation found during the inspection by the Administration, the penalties it proposed, and the time given by the agency to correct any hazardous situation. Employees and representatives of employees may initiate a case by challenging the propriety of the time the Administration has allowed for correction of any violative condition.

The Occupational Safety and Health Act covers virtually every employer in the country. Enforced by the Secretary of Labor, the act is an effort to reduce the incidence of personal injuries, illness, and deaths among working men and women in the United States that result from their employment. It requires employers to furnish to each of their employees a working environment free from recognized hazards that are causing or likely to cause death or serious physical harm to the employees and to comply with occupational safety and health standards promulgated under the act.

Activities

The Commission was created to adjudicate enforcement actions initiated under the act when they are contested by employers, employees, or representatives of employees. A case arises when a citation is issued against an employer as the result of an Occupational Safety and Health Administration inspection and it is contested within 15 working days.

The Commission is more of a court system than a simple tribunal, for within the Commission there are two levels of adjudication. All cases that require a hearing are assigned to an administrative law judge, who decides the case. Ordinarily the hearing is held in the community where the alleged violation occurred or as close as possible. At the hearing, the Secretary of Labor will generally have the burden of proving the case. After the hearing, the judge must issue a decision, based on findings of fact and conclusions of law.

A substantial number of the decisions of the judges become final orders of the Commission. However, each decision is subject to discretionary review by the three members of the Commission upon the direction of any one of the three, if done within 30 days of the filing of the decision. When that occurs, the Commission issues its own decision.

Once a case is decided, any person adversely affected or aggrieved thereby may obtain a review of the decision in the United States Courts of Appeals.

The principal office of the Commission is in Washington, DC. There are also three regional offices where Commission judges are stationed.

Review Commission Judges—Occupational Safety and Health Review Commission

City/Address	Telephone
Atlanta, GA (Rm. 2R90, Bldg. 1924, 100 Alabama St. SW., 30303–3104)	404–562–1640
Boston, MA (John W. McCormack Post Office and Courthouse, 02110)	617–223–9746
Denver, CO (1050 17th St., 80265)	303–844–2281

Sources of Information

Publications Copies of the Commission's *Rules of Procedure, Guide to the Rules of Procedure, Guide to E–Z Trial Procedures*, decisions, *Annual Report to the President*, and pamphlets explaining the functions of the Commission are available from the Public Affairs Specialist at the Commission's Washington office.

For further information, contact the Public Affairs Specialist, Occupational Safety and Health Review Commission, 1120 Twentieth Street NW., Washington, DC 20036–3419. Phone, 202–606–5398. Fax, 202–606–5050. Internet, http://www.oshrc.gov/.

OFFICE OF GOVERNMENT ETHICS

Suite 500, 1201 New York Avenue NW., Washington, DC 20005–3917
Phone, 202–208–8000. Internet, http://www.usoge.gov/.

Director	STEPHEN D. POTTS
Special Assistant to the Director	STUART C. GILMAN
Deputy Director	F. GARY DAVIS
Deputy Director for Government Relations and Special Projects	JANE S. LEY
General Counsel	MARILYN L. GLYNN
Deputy General Counsel	STUART D. RICK
Senior Associate Director for Agency Programs	JACK COVALESKI
Associate Director for Education	BARBARA A. MULLEN-ROTH
Associate Director for Administration	ROBERT E. LAMMON
Chief Information Officer	JAMES V. PARLE

[For the Office of Government Ethics statement of organization, see the *Code of Federal Regulations*, Title 5, Part 2600]

The Office of Government Ethics provides overall direction of executive branch policies in preventing conflicts of interest on the part of officers and employees of all executive agencies. The Office is the principal agency for administering the Ethics in Government Act for the executive branch.

The Office of Government Ethics is a separate executive agency established under the Ethics in Government Act of 1978, as amended (5 U.S.C. app. 401).

The Director of the Office is appointed by the President with the advice and consent of the Senate for a 5-year term, and is required to submit to Congress a biennial report concerning the implementation of the Director's functions and responsibilities.

Activities

The chief responsibilities of the Office are:

—developing, in consultation with the Attorney General and the Office of Personnel Management, rules and regulations to be promulgated by the President or the Director of the Office of Government Ethics pertaining to standards of ethical conduct of executive branch officials, public and confidential financial disclosure of executive branch officials, executive agency ethics training programs, and the identification and resolution of conflicts of interest;

—monitoring and investigating compliance with the executive branch financial disclosure requirements of the Ethics in Government Act of 1978, as amended;

—providing ethics program assistance and information to executive branch agencies through a desk officer system;

—conducting periodic reviews of the ethics programs of executive agencies;

—ordering corrective action on the part of agencies and employees that the Director of the Office deems necessary, including orders to establish or modify an agency's ethics program;

—providing guidance on and promoting understanding of ethical standards in executive agencies through an extensive program of Government ethics advice, education, and training;

—evaluating the effectiveness of the Ethics Act, the conflict of interest laws, and other related statutes; and

—recommending appropriate new legislation or amendments.

Sources of Information

Electronic Access Information
regarding Office of Government Ethics
services and programs is available in
electronic format on the Internet, at
http://www.usoge.gov/.
Publications The Office of Government
Ethics periodically updates its
publication, *The Informal Advisory
Letters and Memoranda and Formal
Opinions of the United States Office of*

Government Ethics, available from the
Government Printing Office. In addition,
the Office publishes a periodic
newsletter on Government ethics and
has available ethics publications,
instructional videotapes, and a CD–
ROM. Upon request, the Office also
provides copies of executive branch
public financial disclosure reports (SF
278's) in accordance with the Ethics Act
and the Office's regulations.

**For further information, contact the Office of Government Ethics, Suite 500, 1201 New York Avenue NW.,
Washington, DC 20005–3917. Phone, 202–208–8000. TDD, 202–208–8025. Fax, 202–208–8037. Internet,
http://www.usoge.gov/.**

OFFICE OF PERSONNEL MANAGEMENT

1900 E Street NW., Washington, DC 20415–0001
Phone, 202–606–1800

Director	JANICE R. LACHANCE
Deputy Director	(VACANCY)
Inspector General	PATRICK E. MCFARLAND
General Counsel	LORRAINE LEWIS
Director, Office of Congressional Relations	CYNTHIA BROCK-SMITH
Director, Office of Communications	DOUGLAS K. WALKER
Chief Financial Officer	J. GILBERT SEAUX
Chairman, Federal Prevailing Rate Advisory Committee	PHYLLIS G. HEUERMAN, *Acting*
Associate Director for Investigations Service	RICHARD FERRIS
Associate Director for Employment Service	MARY LOU LINDHOLM
Associate Director, Office of Merit Systems Oversight and Effectiveness	CAROL J. OKIN
Associate Director for Retirement and Insurance Service	WILLIAM E. FLYNN III
Associate Director, Workforce Compensation and Performance Service	HENRY ROMERO
Director, Office of Human Resources and Equal Employment Opportunity	DONNA D. BEECHER
Director, Office of Executive Resources	CURTIS J. SMITH
Director, Office of Contracting and Administrative Services	KIRKE HARPER
Director, Office of Workforce Relations	STEVEN R. COHEN
Chief Information Technology Officer	JANET L. BARNES

[For the Office of Personnel Management statement of organization, see the *Federal Register* of Jan. 5, 1979,
44 FR 1501]

*The Office of Personnel Management (OPM) administers a merit system to ensure
compliance with personnel laws and regulations and assists agencies in recruiting,
examining, and promoting people on the basis of their knowledge and skills,
regardless of their race, religion, sex, political influence, or other nonmerit factors.*

The Office's role is to provide guidance to agencies in operating human resources programs which effectively support their missions and to provide an array of personnel services to applicants and employees. The Office supports Government program managers in their human resources management responsibilities and provide benefits to employees, retired employees, and their survivors.

The Office of Personnel Management was created as an independent establishment by Reorganization Plan No. 2 of 1978 (5 U.S.C. app.), effective January 1, 1979, pursuant to Executive Order 12107 of December 28, 1978. Transferred to OPM were many of the functions of the former United States Civil Service Commission. The Office's duties and authority are specified in the Civil Service Reform Act of 1978 (5 U.S.C. 1101).

Office of the Inspector General The Office of the Inspector General conducts comprehensive and independent audits, investigations, and evaluations relating to OPM programs and operations. It is responsible for administrative actions against health care providers who commit sanctionable offenses with respect to the Federal Employees' Health Benefits Program or other Federal programs. The Office keeps the Director and Congress fully informed about problems and deficiencies in the administration of agency programs and operations, and the necessity for corrective action.

For further information, contact the Office of the Inspector General. Phone, 202–606–1200.

Activities

Examining and Staffing The Office of Personnel Management is responsible for providing departments and agencies with technical assistance and guidance in examining competitive positions in the Federal civil service for General Schedule grades 1 through 15 and Federal Wage system positions. In addition, the Office is responsible for:

—providing examination services, at the request of an agency, on a reimbursable basis;

—establishing basic qualification standards for all occupations;

—certifying agency delegated examining units to conduct examining;

—providing employment information for competitive service positions; and

—providing policy direction and guidance on promotions, reassignments, appointments in the excepted and competitive services, reinstatements, temporary and term employment, veterans preference, workforce restructuring, career transition, and other staffing provisions.

Workforce Diversity The Office provides leadership, direction, and policy for governmentwide affirmative recruiting programs for minorities and veterans. It also provides leadership, guidance, and technical assistance to promote merit and equality in systemic workforce recruitment, employment, training, and retention. In addition, OPM gathers, analyzes, and maintains statistical data on the diversity of the Federal workforce, and prepares evaluation reports for Congress and others on individual agency and governmentwide progress toward full workforce representation for all Americans in the Federal sector.

Executive Resources The Office leads in the selection, management, and development of Federal executives. It administers the Senior Executive Service program and other merit-based executive personnel systems that promote the development of a corporate perspective. The Office provides policy guidance, consulting services, and technical support in such areas as recruitment, selection, succession planning, mobility performance, awards, and removals. It reviews agency nominations for SES career appointments and administers the Qualifications Review Boards that certify candidates' executive qualifications. It manages SES, senior-level, and scientific and professional space allocations to agencies, administers the Presidential Rank Awards program, and conducts orientation sessions for newly appointed executives. In addition, the Office

OFFICE OF PERSONNEL MANAGEMENT

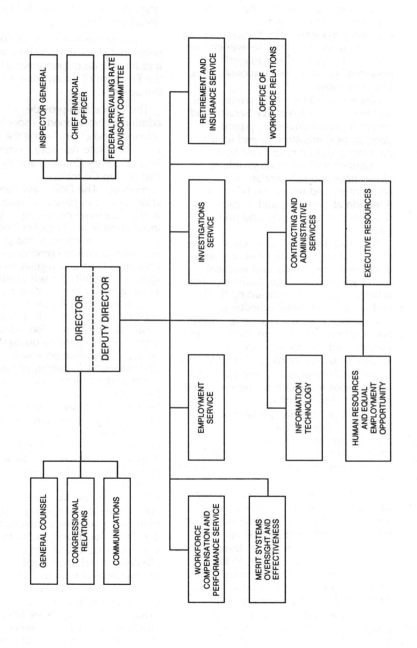

manages three interagency residential development and training centers for executives and managers.

Personnel Systems   The Office provides leadership and guidance to agencies on systems to support the manager's personnel management responsibilities. These include:

—white and blue collar pay systems, including Senior Executive Service and special occupational pay systems; geographical adjustments and locality payments; special rates to address recruitment and retention problems; allowances and differentials, including recruitment and relocation bonuses, retention allowances, and hazardous duty/environmental pay; and premium pay;

—annual and sick leave, court leave, military leave, leave transfer and leave bank programs, family and medical leave, excused absence, holidays, and scheduling of work—including flexible and compressed work schedules;

—performance management, covering appraisal systems, performance pay and awards, and incentive awards for suggestions, inventions, and special acts;

—classification policy and standards for agencies to determine the series and grades for Federal jobs;

—labor-management relations, including labor-management partnerships and consulting with unions on governmentwide issues;

—systems and techniques for resolving disputes with employees;

—quality of worklife initiatives, such as employee health and fitness, work and family, AIDS in the workplace, and employee assistance programs;

—training and employee development, including providing support to the Human Resources Development Council and the Government Performance and Results Act (GPRA) interest group;

—the Training Management Assistance program, to help agencies design and produce training systems and products, performance management systems, workforce productivity systems, business process reengineering, compensation, and employee relations systems;

—information systems to support and improve Federal personnel management decisionmaking; and

—governmentwide instructions for personnel processing and recordkeeping, and for release of personnel data under the Freedom of Information Act and the Privacy Act.

The Office also provides administrative support to special advisory bodies, including the Federal Prevailing Rate Advisory Committee, the Federal Salary Council, and the National Partnership Council.

Oversight   The Office assesses agencies' effectiveness in personnel management at the governmentwide, agency, and installation levels to gather information for policy development and program refinement, ensure compliance with personnel laws and regulations, enhance agency capability for self-evaluation, and assist agencies in operating personnel programs which effectively support accomplishment of their primary missions. The Office also works with other Federal agencies on demonstration projects to explore potential improvements in personnel systems and better and simpler ways to manage Federal personnel.

Employee Benefits   The Office also manages numerous activities that directly affect the well-being of the Federal employee and indirectly enhance employee effectiveness. These include health benefits, life insurance, and retirement benefits.

Other Personnel Programs   The Office coordinates the temporary assignment of employees between Federal agencies and State, local, and Indian tribal governments; institutions of higher education; and other eligible organizations for up to 2 years, for work of mutual benefit to the participating organizations. It administers the Presidential Management Intern Program, which provides 2-year, excepted appointments with Federal agencies to recipients of graduate degrees in appropriate disciplines. In addition, the Office of Personnel Management administers the Federal Merit System

Standards, which apply to certain grant-aided State and local programs.

Federal Executive Boards Federal Executive Boards (FEB's) were established by Presidential directive (a memorandum for heads of Federal departments and agencies dated November 13, 1961) to improve internal Federal management practices and to provide a central focus for Federal participation in civic affairs in major metropolitan centers of Federal activity. They carry out their functions under OPM supervision and control.

Federal Executive Boards serve as a means for disseminating information within the Federal Government and for promoting discussion of Federal policies and activities of importance to all Federal executives in the field. Each Board is composed of heads of Federal field offices in the metropolitan area. A Chairman is elected annually from among the membership to provide overall leadership to the Board's operations. Committees and task forces carry out interagency projects consistent with the Board's missions.

Federal Executive Boards are located in 28 metropolitan areas that are important centers of Federal activity. These areas are: Albuquerque-Santa Fe, Atlanta, Baltimore, Boston, Buffalo, Chicago, Cincinnati, Cleveland, Dallas-Fort Worth, Denver, Detroit, Honolulu-Pacific, Houston, Kansas City, Los Angeles, Miami, New Orleans, New York, Newark, Oklahoma City, Philadelphia, Pittsburgh, Portland, St. Louis, San Antonio, San Francisco, Seattle, and the Twin Cities (Minneapolis-St. Paul).

Federal Executive Associations, Councils, or Committees have been locally organized in over 100 other metropolitan areas to perform functions similar to the Federal Executive Boards but on a lesser scale of organization and activity.

For further information, contact the Assistant for Regional Operations, Office of Personnel Management, Room 5H22L, 1900 E Street NW., Washington, DC 20415–0001. Phone, 202–606–1001.

Sources of Information

Contracts Contact the Chief, Contracting Division, Office of Personnel Management, Washington, DC 20415–0001. Phone, 202–606–2240.

Employment Federal Job Information Centers, located in major metropolitan areas, provide Federal employment information. To obtain the appropriate telephone number, check the blue pages under U.S. Government, Office of Personnel Management. Information about Federal employment and current job openings is also available electronically through the Internet, at http://www.usajobs.opm.gov/. For information about employment opportunities within the Office of Personnel Management, contact the Director for Human Resources. Phone, 202–606–2400.

Publications The Chief, Publications Services Division, can provide information about Federal personnel management publications. Phone, 202–606–1822.

For further information, contact the Office of Communications, Office of Personnel Management, 1900 E Street NW., Washington, DC 20415–0001. Phone, 202–606–1800.

OFFICE OF SPECIAL COUNSEL

Suite 300, 1730 M Street NW., Washington, DC 20036–4505
Phones: Locator, 202–653–7188; Toll-free, 1–800–872–9855

Special Counsel (VACANCY)

OFFICE OF SPECIAL COUNSEL

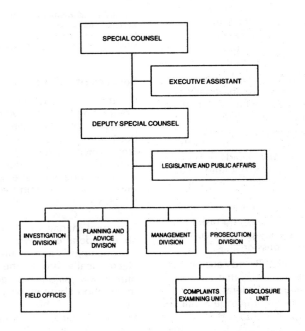

Executive Assistant	(VACANCY)
Deputy Special Counsel	(VACANCY)
Associate Special Counsel for Prosecution	WILLIAM E. REUKAUF
Associate Special Counsel for Investigation	RUTH ROBINSON ERTEL
Associate Special Counsel for Planning and Advice	ERIN MCDONNELL
Director for Management	JOHN KELLEY
Director, Legislative and Public Affairs	(VACANCY)

The Office of Special Counsel investigates allegations of certain activities prohibited by civil service laws, rules, or regulations and litigates before the Merit Systems Protection Board.

Activities

The Office of Special Counsel (OSC) was established on January 1, 1979, by Reorganization Plan No. 2 of 1978 (5 U.S.C. app.). The Civil Service Reform Act of 1978 (5 U.S.C. 1101 note), which became effective on January 11, 1979, enlarged its functions and powers. Pursuant to provisions of the Whistleblower Protection Act of 1989 (5 U.S.C. 1211 et seq.), OSC functions as an independent investigative and prosecutorial agency within the executive branch which litigates before the Merit Systems Protection Board.

The primary role of OSC is to protect employees, former employees, and applicants for employment from prohibited personnel practices, especially reprisal for whistleblowing. Its basic areas of statutory responsibility are:

—receiving and investigating allegations of prohibited personnel practices and other activities prohibited by civil service law, rule, or regulation and, if warranted, initiating corrective or disciplinary action;

—providing a secure channel through which information evidencing a violation of any law, rule, or regulation, gross mismanagement, gross waste of funds, abuse of authority, or substantial and specific danger to public health or safety may be disclosed without fear of retaliation and without disclosure of identity, except with the employee's consent; and

—enforcing the provisions of the Hatch Act.

Sources of Information

Field offices are located in Dallas, TX (Room 7C30, 1100 Commerce Street, 75242; phone, 214–767–8871) and Oakland, CA (Suite 365S, 1301 Clay Street, 94612–5217; phone, 510–637–3460).

For further information, contact the Office of Special Counsel, Suite 300, 1730 M Street NW., Washington, DC 20036–4505. Phone, 202–653–7188 or 800–872–9855 (toll-free).

PANAMA CANAL COMMISSION

Suite 1050, 1825 Eye Street NW., Washington, DC 20006–5402
Phone, 202–634–6441

Official in Washington:

Secretary	JOHN A. MILLS

Officials in the Republic of Panama:

Administrator	ALBERTO ALEMAN ZUBIETA

PANAMA CANAL COMMISSION

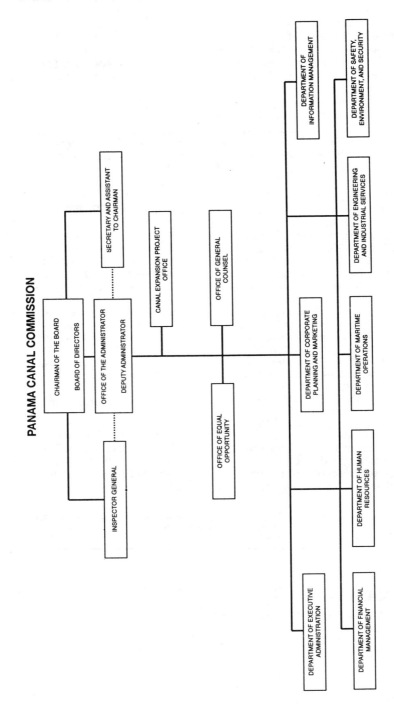

Deputy Administrator   JOSEPH W. CORNELISON

[For the Panama Canal Commission statement of organization, see the *Code of Federal Regulations,* Title 35, Part 9]

The Panama Canal Commission operates, maintains, and improves the Panama Canal to provide efficient, safe, and economical transit service for the benefit of world commerce.

The Panama Canal Commission was established as a wholly owned Government corporation within the executive branch of the Government by the Panama Canal Act of 1979, as amended (22 U.S.C. 3611).

The Commission is supervised by a nine-member Board of which not fewer than five members are nationals of the United States, with the remaining members being nationals of the Republic of Panama. All members of the Board are appointed by the President. The members who are United States nationals are appointed with the advice and consent of the Senate.

Activities

The Commission was established by Congress on October 1, 1979, to carry out the responsibilities of the United States with respect to the Panama Canal under the Panama Canal Treaty of 1977. In fulfilling these obligations, the Commission manages, operates, and maintains the Canal, its complementary works, installations, and equipment, and provides for the orderly transit of vessels through the Canal. This U.S. agency will perform these functions until the treaty terminates on December 31, 1999, at which time the Republic of Panama will assume full responsibility for the Canal.

Sources of Information

Maritime Operations   Director, Maritime Operations. Phone, 011–507–272–4500.
Economic and Marketing Information   Director, Corporate Planning and Marketing. Phone, 011–507–272–7961.
Procurement   Manager, Contracting Division. Phone, 011–507–272–4650. Internet, http://www.cais.net/pancanal/.
Panama Canal Commission   Unit 2300, APO AA 34011–2300. Internet, http://www.pancanal.com/. Fax, 011–507–272–2111.

For further information, contact the Office of the Secretary, Panama Canal Commission, Suite 1050, 1825 Eye Street NW., Washington, DC 20006–5402. Phone, 202–634–6441. Fax, 202–634–6439. E-mail, pancanalwo@aol.com.

PEACE CORPS

1111 20th Street, NW., Washington, DC 20526
Phone, 202–692–2000

Director   MARK D. GEARAN
  Deputy Director   CHARLES R. BAQUET III
  Chief of Staff   THOMAS TIGHE
  General Counsel   NANCY HENDRY
  American Diversity Program Manager   MABEL VALDIVIA
  Inspector General   CHARLES SMITH, *Acting*
  Director of Communications   MICHAEL CHAPMAN
  Director of Congressional Relations   GLORIA JOHNSON

Director of Private Sector Cooperation and International Voluntarism	PATRICIA GARAMENDI
Director of the Crisis Corps	JOAN M. TIMONEY
Regional Director/Africa Operations	MAUREEN CARROLL, *Acting*
Regional Director/Europe, Mediterranean, and Asia Operations	ELLEN PAQUETTE, *Acting*
Regional Director/Inter-American and the Pacific Operations	PATRICK FN'PIERE, *Acting*
Director, Center for Field Assistance and Applied Research	LANI HAVENS
Chief Financial Officer	LANA HURDLE
Associate Director for Management	WILLIAM PIATT
Associate Director for Volunteer Support	MIKE WARD
Associate Director for Volunteer Recruitment and Selection	JUDY HARRINGTON

[For the Peace Corps statement of organization, see the *Code of Federal Regulations,* Title 22, Part 302]

The Peace Corps' purpose is to promote world peace and friendship, to help other countries in meeting their needs for trained men and women, and to promote understanding between the American people and other peoples served by the Peace Corps. The Peace Corps Act emphasizes the Peace Corps commitment toward programming to meet the basic needs of those living in the countries where volunteers work.

The Peace Corps was established by the Peace Corps Act of 1961, as amended (22 U.S.C. 2501), and was made an independent agency by title VI of the International Security and Development Cooperation Act of 1981 (22 U.S.C. 2501–1).

The Peace Corps consists of a Washington, DC, headquarters; 11 area offices; and overseas operations in more than 80 countries. Its presence in foreign countries fluctuates as programs are added or withdrawn.

Activities

To fulfill the Peace Corps mandate, men and women are trained for a 9- to 14-week period in the appropriate local language, the technical skills necessary for their particular job, and the cross-cultural skills needed to adjust to a society with traditions and attitudes different from their own. Volunteers serve for a period of 2 years, living among the people with whom they work. Volunteers are expected to become a part of the community through their voluntary service.

Thousands of volunteers serve throughout Central and South America,

the Caribbean, Africa, Asia, the Pacific, Central and Eastern Europe, Russia, Ukraine, the Baltics, and Central Asia. They work in six program areas, including: education, agriculture, health, small business development, urban development, and the environment. Community-level projects are designed to incorporate the skills of volunteers with the resources of host-country agencies and other international assistance organizations to help solve specific development problems, often in conjunction with private volunteer organizations.

In the United States, the Peace Corps is working to promote an understanding of people in other countries. Through its World Wise Schools Program, volunteers are matched with elementary and junior high schools in the United States to encourage an exchange of letters, pictures, music, and artifacts. Participating students increase their knowledge of geography, languages, and different cultures, while gaining an appreciation for voluntarism.

The Peace Corps offers other domestic programs involving former volunteers, universities, local public school systems, and private businesses and foundations

PEACE CORPS

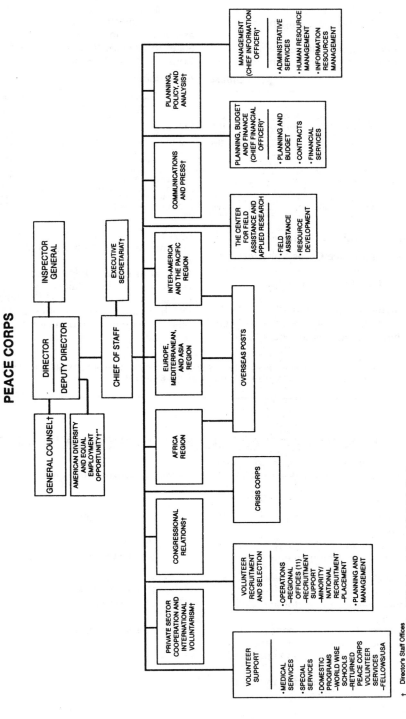

† Director's Staff Offices
* In their function as CIO and CFO, the incumbents report directly to the Director.
** In his/her function as Manager for the American Diversity and EEO Program, the incumbent reports directly to the Deputy Director.

in a partnership to help solve some of the United States most pressing domestic problems.

The Peace Corps Office of Private Sector Cooperation and International Voluntarism works with schools, civic groups, businesses, and neighborhood and youth organizations in the United States to facilitate their support of Peace Corps initiatives here and abroad.

Area Offices—Peace Corps

Office	Address	Telephone
Arlington, VA (DC, DE, MD, NC, VA, WV)	Suite 400, 1400 Wilson Blvd., 22209	703–235–9191
Atlanta, GA (AL, FL, GA, MS, SC, TN)	Rm. 2324, 101 Marietta St. NW., 30323	404–562–3471
Boston, MA (MA, ME, NH, RI, VT)	Rm. 450, 10 Causeway St., 02222	617–565–5555
Chicago, IL (IL, IN, KY, MI, MO, OH)	Suite 450, 55 W. Monroe St., 60603	312–353–4990
Dallas, TX (AR, LA, NM, OK, TX)	Rm. 230, 400 N. Ervay St., P.O. Box 638, 75221	214–767–5435
Denver, CO (CO, KS, NE, UT, WY)	Rm. 550, 140 E. 19th Ave., 80203	303–844–7020
Los Angeles, CA (AZ, southern CA)	Suite 8104, 11000 Wilshire Blvd., 90024	310–235–7444
Minneapolis, MS (IA, MN, ND, SD, WI)	Suite 420, 330 2d Ave. S., 55401	612–348–1480
New York, NY (CT, NJ, NY, PA, PR)	Rm. 611, 6 World Trade Ctr., 10048	212–466–2477
San Francisco, CA (northern CA, HI, NV)	Suite 600, 333 Market St., 94105	415–977–8800
Seattle, WA (AK, ID, MT, OR, WA)	Rm. 1776, 2001 6th Ave., 98121	206–553–5490

Sources of Information

Becoming a Peace Corps Volunteer Contact the nearest area office. Phone, 800–424–8580, extension 2293 (toll-free).

Employment Contact the Peace Corps, Office of Human Resource Management, Washington, DC 20526. Phone, 202– 692–1200. For recorded employment opportunities, call 1–800–818–9579 (toll-free).

General Inquiries Information or assistance may be obtained by contacting the Peace Corps' Washington, DC, headquarters or any of its area offices. Frequently, information is available from local post offices.

For further information, contact the Press Office, Peace Corps, 1990 K Street NW., Washington, DC 20526. Phone, 202–692–2230; or 800–424–8580 (toll-free). Fax, 202–692–2231.

PENSION BENEFIT GUARANTY CORPORATION

1200 K Street NW., Washington, DC 20005
Phone, 202–326–4000; 800–400–4272 (toll-free). Internet, http://www.pbgc.gov/.

Board of Directors:
Chairman (Secretary of Labor)   ALEXIS M. HERMAN
Members:
    (Secretary of the Treasury)   ROBERT E. RUBIN
    (Secretary of Commerce)   WILLIAM M. DALEY

Officials:
Executive Director   DAVID M. STRAUSS
Deputy Executive Director and Chief   NELL HENNESSY
    Negotiator
    Director, Corporate Finance and   ANDREA E. SCHNEIDER
        Negotiations Department
    Director, Participant and Employer Appeals   HARRIET D. VERBURG
        Department
Deputy Executive Director and Chief   JOSEPH H. GRANT
    Operating Officer
    General Counsel   JAMES J. KEIGHTLEY

Director, Corporate Policy and Research Department	STUART A. SIRKIN
Director, Insurance Operations Department	BENNIE L. HAGANS
Deputy Executive Director and Chief Financial Officer	N. ANTHONY CALHOUN
Director, Contracts and Controls Review Department	DALE WILLIAMS
Director, Financial Operations Department	EDWARD KNAPP
Director, Information Resources Management Department	CRIS BIRCH
Deputy Executive Director and Chief Management Officer	JOHN SEAL
Director, Budget Department	HENRY R. THOMPSON
Director, Facilities and Services Department	JANET A. SMITH
Director, Human Resources Department	SHARON BARBEE-FLETCHER
Director, Procurement Department	ROBERT W. HERTING
Assistant Executive Director for Legislative and Congressional Affairs	JUDY SCHUB
Director, Communications and Public Affairs Department	JUDITH WELLES
Inspector General	WAYNE ROBERT POLL

The Pension Benefit Guaranty Corporation guarantees payment of nonforfeitable pension benefits in covered private-sector defined benefit pension plans.

The Pension Benefit Guaranty Corporation is a self-financing, wholly owned Government corporation subject to the Government Corporation Control Act (31 U.S.C. 9101–9109). The Corporation, established by Title IV of the Employee Retirement Income Security Act of 1974 (29 U.S.C. 1301–1461), is governed by a Board of Directors consisting of the Secretaries of Labor, Commerce, and the Treasury. The Secretary of Labor is Chairman of the Board. A seven-member Advisory Committee, composed of two labor, two business, and three public members appointed by the President, advises the agency on various matters.

Activities

Coverage The Corporation insures most private-sector defined benefit pension plans that provide a pension benefit based on factors such as age, years of service, and salary.

The Corporation administers two insurance programs separately covering single-employer and multiemployer plans. More than 42 million workers participate in approximately 50,000 covered plans.

Single-Employer Insurance Under the single-employer program, the Corporation guarantees payment of certain pension benefits if an insured plan terminates without sufficient assets to pay those benefits. However, the law limits the total monthly benefit that the agency may guarantee for one individual to $2,880.68 per month, at age 65, for a plan terminating during 1998, and sets other restrictions on PBGC's guarantee. The Corporation may also pay some benefits above the guaranteed amount depending on amounts recovered from employers.

A plan administrator may terminate a single-employer plan in a "standard" or "distress" termination if certain procedural and legal requirements are met. In either termination, the plan administrator must inform participants in writing at least 60 days prior to the date the administrator proposes to terminate the plan. Only a plan that has sufficient assets to pay all benefit liabilities may terminate in a standard termination. The Corporation also may institute termination proceedings in certain specified circumstances.

PENSION BENEFIT GUARANTY CORPORATION

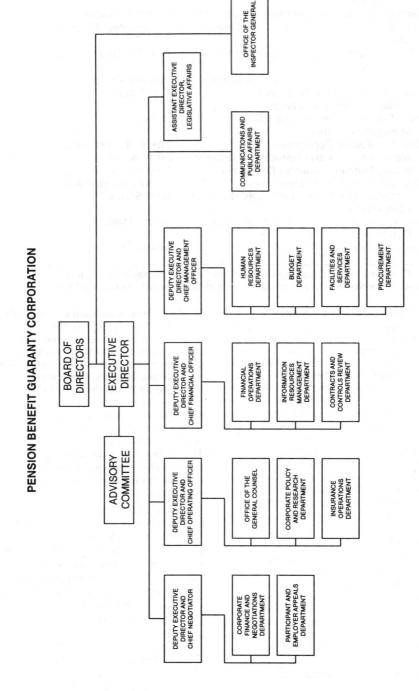

Multiemployer Insurance Under title IV, as originally enacted, the Corporation guaranteed nonforfeitable benefits for multiemployer plans in a similar fashion as for single-employer plans. However, the multiemployer program was revised in 1980 by the Multiemployer Pension Plan Amendments Act (29 U.S.C. 1001 note) which changed the insurable event from plan termination to plan insolvency. The Corporation now provides financial assistance to plans that are unable to pay nonforfeitable benefits. The plans are obligated to repay such assistance. The act also made employers withdrawing from a plan liable to the plan for a portion of its unfunded vested benefits.
Premium Collections All defined benefit pension plans insured by PBGC are required to pay premiums to the Corporation according to rates set by Congress. The annual premium per plan participant for multiemployer pension plans is $2.60 for plan years beginning after September 26, 1988. The basic premium for all single-employer plans is $19 per participant per year. Underfunded single-employer plans must also pay an additional premium equal to $9 per $1,000 of unfunded vested benefits.

Sources of Information

The Pension Benefit Guaranty Corporation provides information electronically through the Internet, at http://www.pbgc.gov/.

For further information, contact the Pension Benefit Guaranty Corporation, 1200 K Street NW., Washington, DC 20005–4026. Phone, 202–326–4000; or 800–400–4272 (toll-free). TTY/TDD users, call the Federal Relay Service toll-free at 800–877–8339 and ask to be connected to 202–326–4000.

POSTAL RATE COMMISSION

1333 H Street NW., Washington, DC 20268–0001
Phone, 202–789–6800. Fax, 202–789–6886. Internet, http://www.prc.gov/.

Chairman	EDWARD J. GLEIMAN
Special Counsel	STEVEN L. KATZ
Vice Chairman	GEORGE W. HALEY
Special Assistant	HENRY W. McCOY
Commissioner	W.H. LeBLANC III
Special Assistant	(VACANCY)
Commissioner	GEORGE A. OMAS
Special Assistant	STEVEN W. WILLIAMS
Commissioner	(VACANCY)
Special Assistant	(VACANCY)
Special Assistant to the Commission	ROBERT W. MITCHELL
Chief Administrative Officer and Secretary	MARGARET P. CRENSHAW
General Counsel	STEPHEN L. SHARFMAN
Director, Office of Rates, Analysis and Planning	ROBERT COHEN
Assistant Director, Office of Rates, Analysis and Planning	WILLIAM FERGUSON
Director, Office of the Consumer Advocate	W. GAIL WILLETTE

Assistant Director, Office of the Consumer Advocate	E. RAND COSTICH
Personnel Officer	CYRIL J. PITTACK

[For the Postal Rate Commission statement of organization, see the *Code of Federal Regulations,* Title 39, Part 3002]

The major responsibility of the Postal Rate Commission is to submit recommended decisions to the United States Postal Service Governors on postage rates, fees, and mail classifications.

The Postal Rate Commission is an independent agency created by the Postal Reorganization Act, as amended (39 U.S.C. 3601–3604). It is composed of five Commissioners, appointed by the President with the advice and consent of the Senate, one of whom is designated as Chairman.

The Commission promulgates rules and regulations, establishes procedures, and takes other actions necessary to carry out its obligations. Acting upon requests from the U.S. Postal Service or on its own initiative, the Commission recommends and issues advisory opinions to the Board of Governors of the U.S. Postal Service on changes in rates or fees in each class of mail or type of service. It studies and submits recommended decisions on establishing or changing the mail classification schedule and holds on-the-record hearings that are lawfully required to attain sound and fair recommendations. It initiates studies on postal matters, such as cost theory and operations.

The Commission also receives, studies, conducts hearings, and issues recommended decisions and reports to the Postal Service on complaints received from interested persons relating to postage rates, postal classifications, and problems of national scope regarding postal services. Additionally, the Commission has appellate jurisdiction to review Postal Service determinations to close or consolidate small post offices.

Sources of Information

Employment The Commission's programs require attorneys, economists, statisticians, accountants, industrial engineers, marketing specialists, and administrative and clerical personnel. Requests for employment information should be directed to the Personnel Officer.

Electronic Access Electronic access to current docketed case materials is available through the Internet, at http://www.prc.gov/. Electronic mail can be sent to the Commission at prc-admin@prc.gov and prc-dockets@prc.gov.

Reading Room Facilities for inspection and copying of records, viewing automated daily lists of docketed materials, and accessing the Commission's Internet site are located at Suite 300, 1333 H Street, Washington, DC. The room is open from 8 a.m. to 5 p.m., Monday through Friday, except legal holidays.

Rules of Practice and Procedure The Postal Rate Commission's Rules of Practice and Procedure governing the conduct of proceedings before the Commission may be found in part 3001 of title 39 of the *Code of Federal Regulations.*

For further information, contact the Secretary, Postal Rate Commission, 1333 H Street NW., Washington, DC 20268–0001. Phone, 202–789–6840. Internet, http://www.prc.gov/.

RAILROAD RETIREMENT BOARD

844 North Rush Street, Chicago, IL 60611–2092
Phone, 312–751–4776. Fax, 312–751–7154. Internet, http://www.rrb.gov/.
Office of Legislative Affairs: Suite 500, 1310 G Street NW., Washington, DC 20005–3004
Phone, 202–272–7742. Fax, 202–272–7728

Chair	CHERRYL T. THOMAS
Labor Member	V.M. SPEAKMAN, JR.
Management Member	JEROME F. KEVER
Inspector General	MARTIN J. DICKMAN
General Counsel	CATHERINE C. COOK
Deputy General Counsel	STEVEN A. BARTHOLOW
Director, Hearings and Appeals	DALE G. ZIMMERMAN
Director, Legislative Affairs	MARIAN P. GIBSON
Director, Programs	BOBBY V. FERGUSON
Director, Assessment and Training	CATHERINE A. LEYSER
Director, Field Service	BOBBY V. FERGUSON, *Acting*
Director, Operations	ROBERT J. DUDA
Director, Policy and Systems	JOHN L. THORESDALE
Director, Resource Management Center	MARTHA M. BARRINGER
Director, Administration	KENNETH P. BOEHNE
Chief Actuary	FRANK J. BUZZI
Chief Financial Officer	PETER A. LARSON
Chief Information Officer	ROBERT T. ROSE
Director of Equal Opportunity	LEO FRANKLIN
Director, Personnel	CHARLENE T. KUKLA
Director, Public Affairs	WILLIAM G. POULOS
Director, Quality Assurance	(VACANCY)
Director, Supply and Service	HENRY M. VALIULIS
Secretary to the Board	BEATRICE E. EZERSKI

[For the Railroad Retirement Board statement of organization, see the *Code of Federal Regulations,* Title 20, Part 200]

The Railroad Retirement Board administers comprehensive retirement-survivor and unemployment-sickness benefit programs for the Nation's railroad workers and their families.

The Railroad Retirement Board was established by the Railroad Retirement Act of 1934, as amended (45 U.S.C. 201—228z–1).

The Board derives statutory authority from the Railroad Retirement Act of 1974 (45 U.S.C. 231–231u) and the Railroad Unemployment Insurance Act (45 U.S.C. 351–369). It administers these acts and participates in the administration of the Social Security Act and the Health Insurance for the Aged Act insofar as they affect railroad retirement beneficiaries.

The Board is composed of three members appointed by the President with the advice and consent of the Senate—one upon recommendations of representatives of employees; one upon recommendations of carriers; and one, the Chairman, as a public member.

Activities

The Railroad Retirement Act provides for the payment of annuities to individuals who have completed at least 10 years of creditable service and have ceased

RAILROAD RETIREMENT BOARD

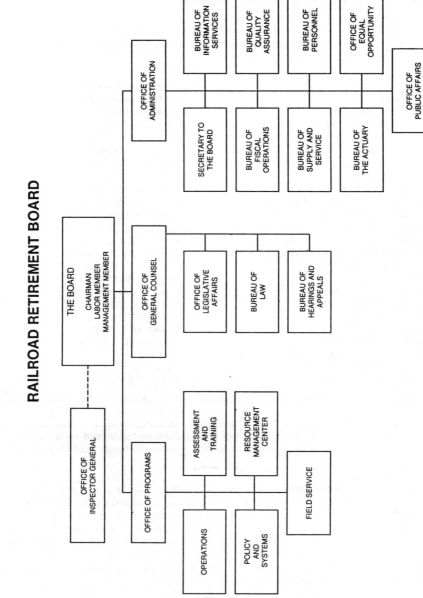

compensated service upon their attainment of specified ages, or at any age if permanently disabled for all employment. In some circumstances occupational disability annuities or supplemental annuities are provided for career employees.

A spouse's annuity is provided, under certain conditions, for the wife or husband of an employee annuitant. Divorced spouses may also qualify.

Survivor annuities are awarded to the qualified spouses, children, and parents of deceased career employees, and various lump-sum benefits are also available under certain conditions.

Benefits based upon qualifying railroad earnings in a preceding one-year period are provided under the Railroad Unemployment Insurance Act to individuals who are unemployed in a benefit year, but who are ready and willing to work, and to individuals who are unable to work because of sickness or injury.

The Board maintains, through its field offices, a placement service for unemployed railroad personnel.

Sources of Information

Benefit Inquiries   The Board maintains direct contact with railroad employees and railroad retirement beneficiaries through its field offices located across the country. Field personnel explain benefit rights and responsibilities on an individual basis, assist employees applying for benefits, and answer questions related to the benefit programs.

To locate the nearest field office, individuals should check with their rail employer, local union official, local post office, or one of the regional offices listed below. Most offices are open to the public from 9 a.m. to 3:30 p.m., Monday through Friday. The Board also relies on railroad labor groups and employers for assistance in keeping railroad personnel informed about its benefit programs.

Regional Offices—Railroad Retirement Board

City	Address	Director	Telephone
Atlanta, GA	Rm. 1703, 401 W. Peachtree St., 30365–2550 ..	Patricia Lawson	404–331–2691
Denver, CO	Suite 3300, 1999 Broadway, 80202–5737	Louis E. Austin	303–844–0800
Philadelphia, PA	Suite 304, 9th and Market Sts., 19107–4228	Richard D. Baird	215–597–2646

Employment   Inquiries and applications for employment should be directed to the Bureau of Personnel, Railroad Retirement Board, 844 North Rush Street, Chicago, IL 60611–2092. Phone, 312–751–4570.

Congressional Assistance   Congressional offices making inquiries regarding constituents' claims should contact the Office of Public Affairs, Congressional Inquiry Section. Phone, 312–751–4974. Information regarding legislative matters may be obtained through the Office of Legislative Affairs. Phone, 202–272–7742.

Publications   General information pamphlets on benefit programs may be obtained from the Board's field offices or Chicago headquarters. Requests for annual reports or statistical data should be directed to the Office of Public Affairs at the Chicago headquarters. Phone, 312–751–4776.

Electronic Access   Railroad Retirement Board information is available electronically through the Internet, at http://www.rrb.gov/.

Telecommunications Devices for the Deaf (TDD)   The Board provides TDD services from 9 a.m. to 3:30 p.m. (CST/CDT) daily. Phone, 312–751–4701 for beneficiary inquiries.

For further information, contact the Office of Public Affairs, Railroad Retirement Board, 844 North Rush Street, Chicago, IL 60611–2092. Phone, 312–751–4776. Internet, http://www.rrb.gov/.

SECURITIES AND EXCHANGE COMMISSION

450 Fifth Street NW., Washington, DC 20549
Phone, 202–942–4150. Internet, http://www.sec.gov/.

Chairman	ARTHUR LEVITT
Commissioners	PAUL R. CAREY, ISAAC C. HUNT, JR., NORMAN S. JOHNSON, LAURA S. UNGER
Secretary	JONATHAN G. KATZ
Executive Director	JAMES M. MCCONNELL
Chief of Staff	JENNIFER SCARDINO
General Counsel	RICHARD H. WALKER
Director, Division of Corporation Finance	BRIAN J. LANE
Director, Division of Enforcement	WILLIAM R. MCLUCAS
Director, Division of Investment Management	BARRY P. BARBASH
Director, Division of Market Regulation	RICHARD R. LINDSEY
Director, Office of Compliance Inspections and Examinations	LORI A. RICHARDS
Chief Accountant	(VACANCY)
Chief Administrative Law Judge	BRENDA P. MURRAY
Chief Economist	ERIK R. SIRRI
Director, Office of International Affairs	MARISA LAGO
Director, Office of Municipal Securities	PAUL S. MACO
Director, Office of Public Affairs, Policy Evaluation, and Research	CHRISTOPHER ULLMAN
Director, Office of Legislative Affairs	KAYE F. WILLIAMS
Inspector General	WALTER STACHNIK
Director, Office of Equal Employment Opportunity	DEBORAH K. BALDUCCHI
Director, Office of Investor Education and Assistance	NANCY M. SMITH
Associate Executive Director, Office of Administrative and Personnel Management	JAYNE L. SEIDMAN
Associate Executive Director, Office of the Comptroller	MARGARET J. CARPENTER
Associate Executive Director, Office of Filings and Information Services	WILSON A. BUTLER
Associate Executive Director, Office of Information Technology	MICHAEL E. BARTELL

[For the Securities and Exchange Commission statement of organization, see the *Code of Federal Regulations,* Title 17, Part 200]

The Securities and Exchange Commission administers Federal securities laws that seek to provide protection for investors; to ensure that securities markets are fair and honest; and, when necessary, to provide the means to enforce securities laws through sanctions.

The Securities and Exchange Commission was created under authority of the Securities Exchange Act of 1934 (15 U.S.C. 78a–78jj) and was organized on July 2, 1934. The Commission serves as adviser to United States district courts in connection with reorganization proceedings for debtor corporations in

SECURITIES AND EXCHANGE COMMISSION

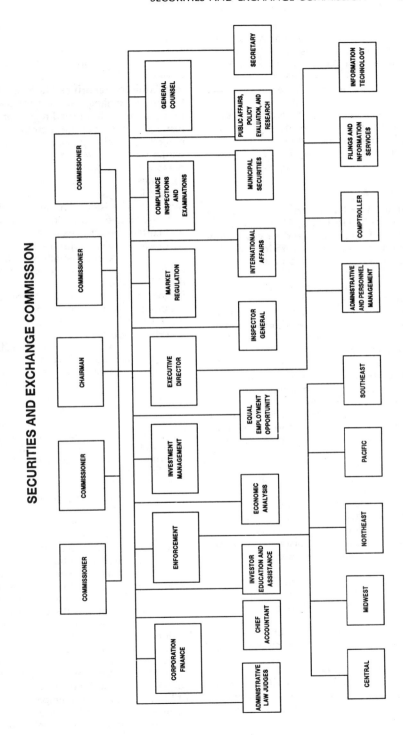

which there is a substantial public interest. The Commission also has certain responsibilities under section 15 of the Bretton Woods Agreements Act of 1945 (22 U.S.C. 286k–1) and section 851(e) of the Internal Revenue Code of 1954 (26 U.S.C. 851(e)).

The Commission is vested with quasi-judicial functions. Persons aggrieved by its decisions in the exercise of those functions have a right of review by the United States courts of appeals.

Activities

Full and Fair Disclosure   The Securities Act of 1933 (15 U.S.C. 77a) requires issuers of securities and their controlling persons making public offerings of securities in interstate commerce or through the mails, directly or by others on their behalf, to file with the Commission registration statements containing financial and other pertinent data about the issuer and the securities being offered. It is unlawful to sell such securities unless a registration statement is in effect. There are limited exemptions, such as government securities, nonpublic offerings, and intrastate offerings, as well as certain offerings not exceeding $1.5 million. The effectiveness of a registration statement may be refused or suspended after a public hearing if the statement contains material misstatements or omissions, thus barring sale of the securities until it is appropriately amended.

Registration of securities does not imply approval of the issue by the Commission or that the Commission has found the registration disclosures to be accurate. It does not insure investors against loss in their purchase, but serves rather to provide information upon which investors may make an informed and realistic evaluation of the worth of the securities.

Persons responsible for filing false information with the Commission subject themselves to the risk of fine or imprisonment or both. Similarly, persons connected with the public offering may be liable for damages to purchasers of the securities if the disclosures in the registration statement and prospectus are

materially defective. Also, the above act contains antifraud provisions that apply generally to the sale of securities, whether or not registered (15 U.S.C. 77a et seq.).

Regulation of Securities Markets   The Securities Exchange Act of 1934 assigns to the Commission broad regulatory responsibilities over the securities markets, the self-regulatory organizations within the securities industry, and persons conducting a business in securities. Persons who execute transactions in securities generally are required to register with the Commission as broker-dealers. Securities exchanges and certain clearing agencies are required to register with the Commission, and associations of brokers or dealers are permitted to register with the Commission. The act also provides for the establishment of the Municipal Securities Rulemaking Board to formulate rules for the municipal securities industry.

The Commission oversees the self-regulatory activities of the national securities exchanges and associations, registered clearing agencies, and the Municipal Securities Rulemaking Board. In addition, the Commission regulates industry professionals, such as securities brokers and dealers, certain municipal securities professionals, government securities brokers and dealers, and transfer agents.

The act authorizes national securities exchanges, national securities associations, clearing agencies, and the Municipal Securities Rulemaking Board to adopt rules that are designed, among other things, to promote just and equitable principles of trade and to protect investors. The Commission is required to approve or disapprove most proposed rules of these self-regulatory organizations and has the power to abrogate or amend existing rules of the national securities exchanges, national securities associations, and the Municipal Securities Rulemaking Board.

In addition, the Commission has broad rulemaking authority over the activities of brokers, dealers, municipal securities dealers, securities information processors, and transfer agents. The

Commission may regulate such securities trading practices as short sales and stabilizing transactions. It may regulate the trading of options on national securities exchanges and the activities of members of exchanges who trade on the trading floors. The Commission may adopt rules governing broker-dealer sales practices in dealing with investors. The Commission also is authorized to adopt rules concerning the financial responsibility of brokers and dealers and reports made by them.

The act also requires the filing of registration statements and annual and other reports with national securities exchanges and the Commission by companies whose securities are listed upon the exchanges, and by companies that have assets of $5 million or more and 500 or more shareholders of record. In addition, companies that distributed securities pursuant to a registration statement declared effective by the Commission under the Securities Act of 1933 must also file annual and other reports with the Commission. Such applications and reports must contain financial and other data prescribed by the Commission as necessary or appropriate for the protection of investors and to ensure fair dealing. In addition, the solicitation of proxies, authorizations, or consents from holders of such registered securities must be made in accordance with rules and regulations prescribed by the Commission. These rules provide for disclosures to securities holders of information relevant to the subject matter of the solicitation.

Disclosure of the holdings and transactions by officers, directors, and large (10-percent) holders of equity securities of companies also is required, and any and all persons who acquire more than 5 percent of certain equity securities are required to file detailed information with the Commission and any exchange upon which such securities may be traded. Moreover, any person making a tender offer for certain classes of equity securities is required to file reports with the Commission if, as a result of the tender offer, such person would own more than 5 percent of the outstanding shares of the particular class of equity security involved. The Commission also is authorized to promulgate rules governing the repurchase by a corporate issuer of its own securities.

Regulation of Mutual Funds and Other Investment Companies   The Investment Company Act of 1940 (15 U.S.C. 80a–1—80a–64) requires investment companies to register with the Commission and regulates their activities to protect investors. The regulation covers sales load, management contracts, composition of boards of directors, and capital structure.

The act prohibits investment companies from engaging in various transactions, including transactions with affiliated persons, unless the Commission first determines that such transactions are fair. In addition, the act provides a somewhat parallel but less stringent regulation of business development companies.

Under the act, the Commission may institute court action to enjoin the consummation of mergers and other plans of reorganization of investment companies if such plans are unfair to securities holders. It also may impose sanctions by administrative proceedings against investment company management for violations of the act and other Federal securities laws and file court actions to enjoin acts and practices of management officials involving breaches of fiduciary duty and personal misconduct and to disqualify such officials from office.

Regulation of Companies Controlling Utilities   The Public Utility Holding Company Act of 1935 (15 U.S.C. 79a—79z–6) provides for regulation by the Commission of the purchase and sale of securities and assets by companies in electric and gas utility holding company systems, their intrasystem transactions and service, and management arrangements. It limits holding companies to a single coordinated utility system and requires simplification of complex corporate and capital structures and elimination of unfair distribution of voting power among holders of system securities.

The issuance and sale of securities by holding companies and their subsidiaries, unless exempt (subject to conditions and terms that the Commission is empowered to impose) as an issue expressly authorized by the State commission in the State in which the issuer is incorporated, must be found by the Commission to meet certain statutory standards.

The purchase and sale of utility properties and other assets may not be made in contravention of rules, regulations, or orders of the Commission regarding the consideration to be received, maintenance of competitive conditions, fees and commissions, accounts, disclosure of interest, and similar matters. In passing upon proposals for reorganization, merger, or consolidation, the Commission must be satisfied that the objectives of the act generally are complied with and that the terms of the proposal are fair and equitable to all classes of securities holders affected.

Regulation of Investment Advisers The Investment Advisers Act of 1940 (15 U.S.C. 80b–1—80b–21) provides that persons who, for compensation, engage in the business of advising others with respect to securities must register with the Commission. The act prohibits certain fee arrangements, makes fraudulent or deceptive practices on the part of investment advisers unlawful, and requires, among other things, disclosure of any adverse personal interests the advisers may have in transactions that they effect for clients. The act authorizes the Commission, by rule, to define fraudulent and deceptive practices and prescribe means to prevent those practices.

Rehabilitation of Failing Corporations Chapter 11, section 1109(a), of the Bankruptcy Code (11 U.S.C. 1109) provides for Commission participation as a statutory party in corporate reorganization proceedings administered in Federal courts. The principal functions of the Commission are to protect the interests of public investors involved in such cases through efforts to ensure their adequate representation, and to participate in legal and policy issues that are of concern to public investors generally.

Representation of Debt Securities Holders The interests of purchasers of publicly offered debt securities issued pursuant to trust indentures are safeguarded under the provisions of the Trust Indenture Act of 1939 (15 U.S.C. 77aaa–77bbbb). This act, among other things, requires the exclusion from such indentures of certain types of exculpatory clauses and the inclusion of certain protective provisions. The independence of the indenture trustee, who is a representative of the debt holder, is assured by proscribing certain relationships that might conflict with the proper exercise of his duties.

Enforcement Activities The Commission's enforcement activities are designed to secure compliance with the Federal securities laws administered by the Commission and the rules and regulations adopted thereunder. These activities include measures to:

—compel compliance with the disclosure requirements of the registration and other provisions of the acts;

—prevent fraud and deception in the purchase and sale of securities;

—obtain court orders enjoining acts and practices that operate as a fraud upon investors or otherwise violate the laws;

—suspend or revoke the registrations of brokers, dealers, investment companies, and investment advisers who willfully engage in such acts and practices;

—suspend or bar from association persons associated with brokers, dealers, investment companies, and investment advisers who have violated any provision of the Federal securities laws; and

—prosecute persons who have engaged in fraudulent activities or other willful violations of those laws.

In addition, attorneys, accountants, and other professionals who violate the securities laws face possible loss of their privilege to practice before the Commission.

To this end, private investigations are conducted into complaints or other indications of securities violations. Evidence thus established of law violations is used in appropriate administrative proceedings to revoke registration or in actions instituted in Federal courts to restrain or enjoin such activities. Where the evidence tends to establish criminal fraud or other willful violation of the securities laws, the facts are referred to the Attorney General for criminal prosecution of the offenders. The Commission may assist in such prosecutions.

Regional/District Offices—Securities and Exchange Commission
(R: Regional Director; D: District Administrator)

Region/District	Address	Official	Telephone
Northeast			
New York, NY	Suite 1300, 7 World Trade Ctr., 10048	Carmen J. Lawrence (R)	212–748–8000
Boston, MA	Suite 600, 73 Tremont St., 02108–3912	Juan Marcel Marcelino (D)	617–424–5900
Philadelphia, PA	Suite 1005 E., 601 Walnut St., 19106–3322	Ronald C. Long (D)	215–597–3100
Southeast			
Miami, FL	Suite 200, 1401 Brickell Ave., 33131	Randall J. Fons (R)	305–536–4700
Atlanta, GA	Suite 1000, 3475 Lenox Rd. NE., 30326–1232	Richard P. Wessel (D)	404–842–7600
Midwest			
Chicago, IL	Suite 1400. 500 W. Madison St., 60661–2511	Mary Keefe (R)	312–353–7390
Central			
Denver, CO	Suite 4800, 1801 California St., 80202–2648	Daniel F. Shea (R)	303–844–1000
Fort Worth, TX	Suite 1900, 801 Cherry St., 76102	Harold F. Degenhardt (D)	817–978–3821
Salt Lake City, UT	Suite 500, 50 S. Main St., 84144–0402	Kenneth D. Israel, Jr. (D)	801–524–5796
Pacific			
Los Angeles, CA	Suite 1100, 5670 Wilshire Blvd., 90036–3648	Elaine M. Cacheris (R)	213–965–3998
San Francisco, CA	Suite 1100, 44 Montgomery St., 94104	David B. Bayless (D)	415–705–2500

Sources of Information

Inquiries regarding the following matters should be directed to the appropriate office, Securities and Exchange Commission, 450 Fifth Street NW., Washington, DC 20549.

Contracts Inquires regarding SEC procurement and contracting activities should be directed to the Office of Administrative and Personnel Management. Phone, 202–942–4990.

Electronic Access Information on the Commission is available through the Internet, at http://www.sec.gov/.

Employment With the exception of the attorney category, positions are in the competitive civil service, which means applicants must apply for consideration for a particular vacancy and go through competitive selection procedures. The Commission operates a college and law school recruitment program, including on-campus visitations for interview purposes. Inquiries should be directed to the Office of Administrative and Personnel Management. Phone, 202–942–4070. Fax, 703–942–4150.

Investor Assistance and Complaints Publications detailing the Commission's activities, which include material of assistance to the potential investor, are available from the Publications Unit. Phone, 202–942–4040. In addition, the Office of Investor Education and Assistance answers questions from investors, assists investors with specific problems regarding their relations with broker-dealers and companies, and advises the Commission and other offices and divisions regarding problems frequently encountered by investors and possible regulatory solutions to such problems. Phone, 202–942–7040. Consumer information line, 800–SEC–0330 (toll-free). Fax, 202–942–9634.

Complaints and inquiries may be directed to headquarters or to any regional or district office. Registration statements and other public documents filed with the Commission are available for public inspection in the public reference room (phone, 202–942–8090) in Washington, DC, and much of the information also is available at the Northeast and Midwest regional offices. Copies of the public material may be purchased from the Commission's contract copying service at prescribed rates.

Publications   Blank copies of SEC forms and other publications are available in the Publications Unit. Phone, 202–942–4040. *Official Summary*—A monthly summary of securities transactions and holdings of officers, directors, and principal stockholders ($36 per issue) is available through the Superintendent of Documents, Government Printing Office, Washington, DC 20402. Phone, 202–512–1800.

Reading Rooms   The Commission maintains a public reference room

(phone, 202–942–8090) in Washington, DC, where registration statements and other public documents filed with the Commission are available for public inspection. Much of this information is also available at the Northeast and Midwest regional offices. Copies of public material may be purchased from the Commission's contract copying service at prescribed rates. The Commission also maintains a library (phone, 202–942–7090; fax, 202–942–9626) where additional information may be obtained.

Small Business Activities   Information on securities laws that pertain to small businesses in relation to securities offerings may be obtained from the Commission. Phone, 202–942–2950.

For further information, contact the Office of Public Affairs, Securities and Exchange Commission, 450 Fifth Street NW., Washington, DC 20549. Phone, 202–942–0020. Fax, 202–942–9654. Internet, http://www.sec.gov/.

SELECTIVE SERVICE SYSTEM

National Headquarters, Arlington, VA 22209–2425
Phone, 703–605–4000

Director	GIL CORONADO
Deputy Director	(VACANCY)
Executive Director	WILLIE L. BLANDING, JR.
Chief of Staff	LT. COL. ROGELIO RODRIGUEZ, USAF
Special Assistant	ARCHIBALD J. KIELLY
Inspector General	ALFRED RASCON
Financial Manager	CARLO VERDINO
Counselor and General Counsel	HENRY N. WILLIAMS
Director for Information Management	NORMAN W. MILLER
Director for Operations	COL. JUSTO GONZALEZ, USA
Director for Resource Management	D. FREIDA BROCKINGTON
Director for Public and Congressional Affairs	LEWIS C. BRODSKY

[For the Selective Service System statement of organization, see the *Code of Federal Regulations*, Title 32, Part 1605]

The purpose of the Selective Service System is to be prepared to supply to the Armed Forces human resources adequate to ensure the security of the United States, with concomitant regard for the maintenance of an effective national economy.

SELECTIVE SERVICE SYSTEM

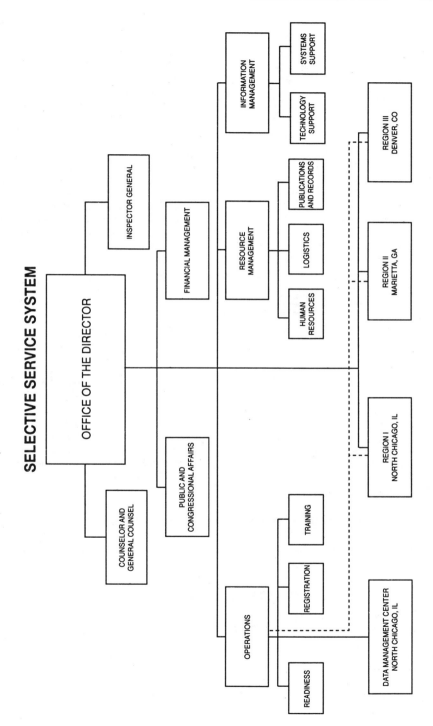

The Selective Service System was established by the Military Selective Service Act (50 U.S.C. app. 451–471a). The act authorizes the registration of male citizens of the United States and all other male persons who are in the United States and who are between the ages of 18½ and 26. The act exempts members of the active Armed Forces and foreign diplomatic and consular personnel from registration and liability for training and service. Likewise exempted are nonimmigrant aliens. Proclamation 4771 of July 2, 1980, requires male persons born after January 1, 1960, and who have attained age 18 to register. Registration is conducted at post offices within the United States and at U.S. Embassies and consulates outside the United States.

The act imposes liability for training and service in the Armed Forces upon registrants who are between the ages of 18½ and 26, except those who are exempted or deferred. Persons who have been deferred remain liable for training and service until age 35. Aliens are not liable for training and service until they have remained in the United States for more than one year. Conscientious objectors who are found to be opposed to any service in the Armed Forces are required to perform civilian work in lieu of induction into the Armed Forces.

The authority to induct registrants, including doctors and allied medical specialists, expired July 1, 1973.

Regional Offices—Selective Service System

Region/Address	Director	Telephone
North Chicago, IL (Suite 276, 2500 Green Bay Rd., 60064–3038)	Col. Ronald V. Meilstrup, USAFR.	847–688–4540
Marietta, GA (Suite 4, 805 Walker St., 30060–2731)	Col. Keith A. Scragg, USAFR	770–590–6602
Denver, CO (Suite 1, 7245 E. Irvington Pl., 80220–6920)	Col. Wayne McDonald, USAFR	303–676–7809

Sources of Information

Employment   Inquiries and applications should be directed to the Director, Selective Service System, Attn: RMH, Arlington, VA 22209–2425. Phone, 703–605–4056.

Procurement   Inquiries should be directed to the Director, Selective Service System, Attn: RML, Arlington, VA 22209–2425. Phone, 703–605–4040.

Publications   Selective Service Regulations appear in chapter XVI of title 32 of the *Code of Federal Regulations.*

Requirements of Law   Persons desiring information concerning the requirements of the Military Selective Service Act should contact the National Headquarters of the Selective Service System. Phone, 703–605–4000.

For further information, contact the Office of Public and Congressional Affairs, Selective Service System, Arlington, VA 22209–2425. Phone, 703–605–4100.

SMALL BUSINESS ADMINISTRATION

409 Third Street SW., Washington, DC 20416
Phone, 202–205–6600. Fax, 202–205–7064. Internet, http://www.sba.gov/.

Administrator	AIDA ALVAREZ
Deputy Administrator	(VACANCY)
Chief Operating Officer	CHRIS SALE
Counselors to the Administrator	DARRYL DENNIS, JEANNE SADDLER
Chief of Staff	PAUL WEECH
Director, Executive Secretariat	SUSAN WALTHALL

General Counsel	JOHN T. SPOTILA
Chief Counsel for Advocacy	JERE W. GLOVER
Inspector General	KAREN S. LEE, *Acting*
Chief Financial Officer	LARRY WILSON
Director, National Advisory Council	MICHAEL NOVELLI
Associate Administrator for Disaster Assistance	BERNARD KULIK
Project Director for Field Operations	BRAD DOUGLAS
Associate Administrator for Communications and Public Liaison	EDWARD EUGENE CARLSON
Assistant Administrator for Congressional and Legislative Affairs	M. KRIS SWEDIN
Assistant Administrator for Equal Employment Opportunity and Civil Rights Compliance	ERLINE PATRICK
Assistant Administrator for Hearings and Appeals	MONA MITNICK
Associate Deputy Administrator for Management and Administration	LAWRENCE BARRETT, *Acting*
Assistant Administrator for Administration	THOMAS DUMARESQ
Assistant Administrator for Human Resources	CAROLYN J. SMITH
Chief Information Officer	LAWRENCE BARRETT
Associate Deputy Administrator for Entrepreneurial Development	BETSY MYERS
Associate Administrator for Business Initiatives	MONIKA HARRISON
Associate Administrator for Small Business Development Centers	JOHNNIE ALBERTSON
Assistant Administrator for International Trade	EILEEN CASSIDY, *Acting*
Assistant Administrator for Native American Affairs	(VACANCY)
Assistant Administrator for Veterans Affairs	CLIFTON TOULSON, JR.
Assistant Administrator for Women's Business Ownership	SHERRYE HENRY
Associate Deputy Administrator for Capital Access	JOHN GRAY
Associate Administrator for Financial Assistance	JANE BUTLER, *Acting*
Associate Administrator for Investment	DON CHRISTENSEN
Associate Administrator for Surety Guarantees	ROBERT J. MOFFITT
Associate Deputy Administrator for Government Contracting and Minority Enterprise Development	RICHARD HAYES
Associate Administrator for Government Contracting	JUDITH A. ROUSSEL
Associate Administrator for Minority Enterprise Development	WILLIAM FISHER, *Acting*
Assistant Administrator for Size Standards	GARY M. JACKSON
Assistant Administrator for Technology	DANIEL O. HILL

[For the Small Business Administration statement of organization, see the *Code of Federal Regulations*, Title 13, Part 101]

The fundamental purposes of the Small Business Administration are to aid, counsel, assist, and protect the interests of small business; ensure that small business concerns receive a fair portion of Government purchases, contracts, and subcontracts, as well as of the sales of Government property; make loans to small business concerns, State and local development companies, and the victims of floods or other catastrophes, or of certain types of economic injury; and license, regulate, and make loans to small business investment companies.

The Small Business Administration (SBA) was created by the Small Business Act of 1953 and derives its present existence and authority from the Small Business Act (15 U.S.C. 631 *et seq.*). It also derives its authority from the Small Business Investment Act of 1958 (15 U.S.C. 661). The Secretary of Commerce has delegated to the Administration certain responsibilities and functions under section 202 of the Public Works and Economic Development Act of 1965 (42 U.S.C. 3142) and is further authorized to delegate to the Administrator certain responsibilities and functions under chapter 3 of the Trade Act of 1974 (19 U.S.C. 2101).

Activities

Disaster Assistance   The Administration serves as the Federal disaster bank for nonfarm, private sector losses. It lends money to help the victims of floods, riots, or other catastrophes repair or replace most disaster-damaged property. Direct loans with subsidized interest rates are made to assist individuals, homeowners, businesses of all sizes and nonprofit organizations. In addition, low interest long-term loans are available to small businesses and small agricultural cooperatives without credit elsewhere that have sustained substantial economic injury resulting from natural disasters.

For further information, contact the Office of Disaster Assistance. Phone, 202–205–6734.

Capital Access   The Office of the Associate Deputy Administrator for Capital Access provides overall direction for the Small Business Administration's finance programs, which include the Office of Financial Assistance, the Investment Division, the Office of Surety Guarantees, and the Office of International Trade. These programs provide a comprehensive array of financial assistance programs for the smallest start-up businesses to those which have been in operation for a number of years and need new capital to expand. The programs range from those needing only a "microloan" to those ready for an infusion of private venture capital or long-term financing for the purchase of new equipment or facilities. In addition to lending to businesses which sell their products and services within the United States, the Office of Capital Access also provides direction for the SBA's business development and financial assistance programs for small business exporters.

For further information, contact the Office of Capital Access. Phone, 202–205–6657.

Financial Assistance   The Administration provides its guaranty to lending institutions which make loans to small businesses to help them finance plant construction, conversion, or expansion and acquire equipment, facilities, machinery, supplies, or materials. It also provides them with working capital. Since enactment of the act of June 4, 1976 (90 Stat. 663), farms are included within the term "small business concerns."

The Administration may provide loan guarantees to finance residential or commercial construction or rehabilitation for sale as well as revolving lines of credit, including those for export purposes, to qualified employee trusts. The Administration may finance small firms that manufacture, sell, install, service, or develop specific energy measures including engineering, architectural, consulting, or other professional services connected with eligible energy measures.

The Administration also provides small-scale financial and technical assistance to very small businesses, through loans and grants to nonprofit organizations that act as intermediaries.

Under the provisions of sections 501–506 of the Small Business Investment Act (15 U.S.C. 695, 696), loans are made to State and local development companies who likewise assist small businesses by

SMALL BUSINESS ADMINISTRATION

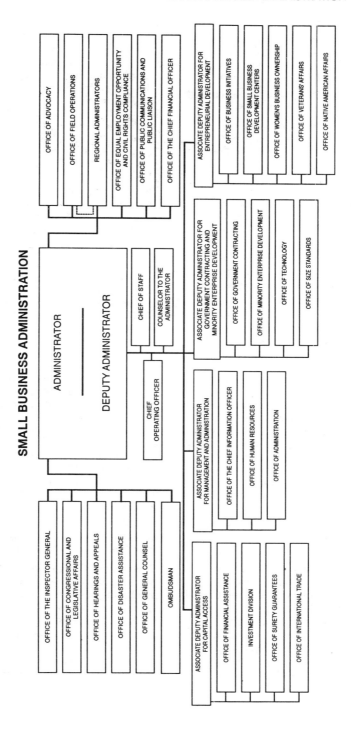

ADMINISTRATOR

DEPUTY ADMINISTRATOR

OFFICE OF THE INSPECTOR GENERAL

OFFICE OF CONGRESSIONAL AND LEGISLATIVE AFFAIRS

OFFICE OF HEARINGS AND APPEALS

OFFICE OF DISASTER ASSISTANCE

OFFICE OF GENERAL COUNSEL

OMBUDSMAN

ASSOCIATE DEPUTY ADMINISTRATOR FOR CAPITAL ACCESS

OFFICE OF FINANCIAL ASSISTANCE

INVESTMENT DIVISION

OFFICE OF SURETY GUARANTEES

OFFICE OF INTERNATIONAL TRADE

CHIEF OF STAFF

COUNSELOR TO THE ADMINISTRATOR

CHIEF OPERATING OFFICER

ASSOCIATE DEPUTY ADMINISTRATOR FOR MANAGEMENT AND ADMINISTRATION

OFFICE OF THE CHIEF INFORMATION OFFICER

OFFICE OF HUMAN RESOURCES

OFFICE OF ADMINISTRATION

ASSOCIATE DEPUTY ADMINISTRATOR FOR GOVERNMENT CONTRACTING AND MINORITY ENTERPRISE DEVELOPMENT

OFFICE OF GOVERNMENT CONTRACTING

OFFICE OF MINORITY ENTERPRISE DEVELOPMENT

OFFICE OF TECHNOLOGY

OFFICE OF SIZE STANDARDS

OFFICE OF ADVOCACY

OFFICE OF FIELD OPERATIONS

REGIONAL ADMINISTRATORS

OFFICE OF EQUAL EMPLOYMENT OPPORTUNITY AND CIVIL RIGHTS COMPLIANCE

OFFICE OF PUBLIC COMMUNICATIONS AND PUBLIC LIAISON

OFFICE OF THE CHIEF FINANCIAL OFFICER

ASSOCIATE DEPUTY ADMINISTRATOR FOR ENTREPRENEURIAL DEVELOPMENT

OFFICE OF BUSINESS INITIATIVES

OFFICE OF SMALL BUSINESS DEVELOPMENT CENTERS

OFFICE OF WOMEN'S BUSINESS OWNERSHIP

OFFICE OF VETERANS AFFAIRS

OFFICE OF NATIVE AMERICAN AFFAIRS

providing long-term loans for the acquisition of land and buildings, construction, conversion, or expansion of facilities, and the purchase of machinery and equipment.

For further information, contact the nearest Small Business Administration district office.

Investment   The Administration licenses, regulates, and provides financial assistance to small business investment companies and section 301(d) licensees (formerly minority enterprise small business investment companies). The sole function of these investment companies is to provide venture capital in the form of equity financing, long-term loan funds, and management services to small business concerns.

For further information, contact the Investment Division. Phone, 202–205–6510.

Surety Bonds   Through its Surety Bond Guarantee Program, the Administration helps to make the contract bonding process accessible to small and emerging contractors who find bonding unavailable. It will guarantee to reimburse a qualified surety up to 90 percent of losses incurred under bid, payment, or performance bonds issued to small contractors on contracts valued up to $1.25 million. The contracts may be for construction, supplies, manufacturing, or services provided by either a prime contractor or subcontractor for governmental or nongovernmental work.

For further information, contact the Office of Surety Guarantees. Phone, 202–205–6540.

International Trade   The Office of International Trade provides export financing to small businesses. It administers the Export Working Capital program, which provides short-term, transaction-specific financing for exporting, including pre-export financing of labor and materials, financing receivables generated from these sales, and standby letters of credit used as performance bonds or payment guarantees to foreign buyers.

The Office is a major participant in the U.S. Export Assistance Center

(USEAC) initiative, authorized by section 202 of the Export Enhancement Act of 1992. The Centers provide a single point of contact for all Federal export promotion and finance programs in the following cities: Atlanta, GA; Baltimore, MD; Boston, MA; Charlotte, NC; Chicago, IL; Cleveland, OH; Dallas, TX; Denver, CO; Detroit, MI; Long Beach, CA; Miami, FL; Minneapolis, MN; New Orleans, LA; New York, NY; Philadelphia, PA; Portland, OR; San Jose, CA; Seattle, WA; and St. Louis, MO. They integrate representatives of the Department of Commerce, the Small Business Administration, the Export-Import Bank of the United States, and the Agency for International Development to deliver services directly and refer clients to appropriate public and private sector partners.

The Office develops and recommends agency policy and procedures to effectively deliver the International Trade program, provides tools for SBA's resource partners, and coordinates activities with agency resource partners and USEAC's to improve accessibility to its programs. The Office also coordinates with other Federal agencies under the auspices of the Trade Promotion Coordinating Committee (TPCC) to ensure that trade promotion information and trade events are communicated to the small business community. The Office also works with agencies of the TPCC in coordinating and facilitating trade between the U.S. small business community and businesses and governments of other countries.

For further information, contact the Office of International Trade. Phone, 202–205–6720.

Government Contracting   The Administration works closely with purchasing agencies of the Federal Government and with the Nation's leading contractors in developing policies and procedures that will maximize the number and dollar value of contracts going to small business.

The Administration provides a wide range of services to small firms to help them obtain and fulfill Government contracts and subcontracts. It sets aside suitable Government purchases for competitive award to small business concerns and provides an appeal procedure for a low-bidding small firm whose ability to perform a contract is questioned by the contracting officer. The Administration develops subcontract opportunities for small businesses by maintaining close contact with prime contractors and referring qualified small firms to them. It cooperates with Federal agencies in setting procurement goals for small businesses, small disadvantaged businesses, and small women-owned businesses for prime contracts and subcontracts.

The Administration maintains a computerized small business source referral system that provides qualified sources for Federal Government and large business procurements. It cooperates with Government agencies in ensuring that small firms have an opportunity to procure a fair share of Government property, such as timber, royalty oil, strategic materials, and mineral leases, that is sold to the private sector. The Administration also works with Federal agencies to ensure that small firms have a fair opportunity to acquire surplus Government property.

For further information, contact the Office of Government Contracting. Phone, 202–205–6460.

Business Initiatives The Administration develops and cosponsors counseling, education, and training for small businesses. The Administration has forged ongoing partnerships with resource partners to deliver most of the business education and training programs offered annually at low cost. One-on-one counseling is provided free of charge by the Service Corps of Retired Executives.

The Business Information Center (BIC) program is among the most innovative methods of providing small business owners with a one-stop approach to information, education, and training. The Centers combine the latest computer technology, hardware, and software, an extensive small business reference library of hard copy books and publications, and current management videotapes to help clients venture into new business areas. The use of software for a variety of business applications offers clients of all types a means of addressing their diverse needs. Although most BIC's are stand-alone centers, in empowerment zones BIC's will form the core element of one-stop capital shops.

In addition to education and training events, SBA cosponsors fact sheets and other materials, ranging from short, single-topic flyers to detailed publications, on a variety of business management and growth topics.

Among the most visible public/private sector cosponsorships undertaken by SBA are those involving major corporations and the national Business Information Center network.

For further information, contact the Office of Business Initiatives. Phone, 202–205–6665.

Minority Enterprise Development Sections 7(j) and 8(a) of the Small Business Act provide the authority for the Minority Enterprise Development Program, designed to promote business ownership by socially and economically disadvantaged persons. Its components include the 8(a) program and the 7(j) management and technical assistance program.

Participation in the 8(a) program may be made available to small businesses that are at least 51 percent unconditionally owned, controlled, and managed by one or more individuals determined by SBA to be socially and economically disadvantaged. In order to gain approval for participation in the 8(a) program, the firms must sell goods and/ or services that the Federal Government purchases, and demonstrate the potential for successful business development.

Program participants receive a wide variety of services from SBA including management and technical assistance, loans, and Federal contracts. Under 8(a) program authority, SBA contracts with Federal Government entities to provide goods and services and, in turn, subcontracts the performance of these contracts to 8(a) program participants.

Information regarding the program and 8(a) program applications are provided by SBA's district offices. The Division of Program Certification and Eligibility addresses issues related to 8(a) program eligibility. The Division of Business Development handles matters related to 8(a) contract awards and the business development of 8(a) participant firms.

Under section 7(j) program authority, SBA provides management and technical assistance to section 8(a) program participants, other socially and economically disadvantaged persons, and those businesses operating in low-income or high-unemployment areas. The Administration enters into cooperative agreements and contracts with qualified organizations and individuals, including businesses, State and local governments, educational institutions, Indian tribes, and nonprofit organizations to provide this assistance. At the local level, services are provided on a one-to-one basis in the areas of bookkeeping and accounting services, production, engineering and technical advice, feasibility studies, marketing analysis and advertising expertise, legal services, and specialized management training. The Administration also funds innovative programs to provide for services in such areas as transition management for 8(a) firms, competitive marketing strategies, financing, comprehensive business plans, and financial management services.

For further information, contact the Office of Minority Enterprise Development. Phone, 202–205–6412.

Advocacy The Office of Advocacy is mandated by Congress to serve as an independent spokesperson within public policy councils for the more than 22.5 million small businesses throughout the country. The Office is headed by the Chief Counsel for Advocacy, appointed by the President with the advice and consent of the Senate, who advances the views, concerns, and interests of small business before the Congress, the White House, and Federal and State regulatory agencies. The Chief Counsel has specific responsibilities for monitoring the compliance of Federal agencies with the Regulatory Flexibility Act (5 U.S.C. 601), which requires that Federal agencies analyze the impact of their regulations on small entities and consider less burdensome alternatives. The Chief

Counsel is also empowered to file *amicus curiae* briefs in appellate court proceedings involving compliance with the act.

The Office of Advocacy is one of the leading national sources for information on the state of small business and the issues that affect small business success and growth. It conducts economic and statistical research into matters affecting the competitive strength of small business and analyzes the impact of Federal laws, regulations, and programs on small businesses, making recommendations to policymakers for appropriate adjustments to meet the special needs of small business.

Additionally, regional advocates enhance communication between the small business community and the Chief Counsel. As the Chief Counsel's direct link to local business owners, State and local government agencies, State legislatures, and small business organizations, they help identify new issues and problems of small business by monitoring the effect of Federal and State regulations and policies on the local business communities within their regions.

For further information, contact the Office of Advocacy. Phone, 202–205–6533.

Women's Business Ownership The Office of Women's Business Ownership (OWBO) is authorized in section 412 of the Small Business Act to provide assistance to the increasing number of current and potential woman business owners, and to act as their advocate in the public and private sector. It is the only office in the Federal Government specifically targeted to the Nation's women business owners, assisting them in becoming full partners in economic development through technical, financial, and management information and training, business skills counseling, and research.

Through a network of local SBA offices, OWBO offers a wide range of education and training services and resources. The Women's Business Ownership Act of 1988 and the Women's Business Development Act of 1991 authorized SBA to establish demonstration projects to provide long-term training and counseling for women at every stage of their entrepreneurial career. There are currently 63 Women's Business Centers in 36 States, the District of Columbia, and Puerto Rico, which provide community-based training and assistance on financial, management, marketing, and procurement matters through a 5-year grant which must be matched by nonfederal funds. The centers offer assistance to current and potential women business owners, tailored to the particular needs of the community.

With the combined expertise of its Women's Business Centers, OWBO has built a new, state-of-the-art Internet site to help women start or expand their businesses. This interactive site, the Online Women's Business Center (http://www.onlinewbc.org), offers business principles and practices, management techniques, networking, a resource data base, industry news, information about SBA services, market research, and technology training.

The Women's Network for Entrepreneurial Training (WNET) is a year-long mentoring program linking seasoned entrepreneurs with women whose businesses are poised for growth. Featuring the group mentoring format of the WNET Roundtable, the program aims to help entrepreneurs avoid the common mistakes of new business owners.

The Office of Government Contracting and OWBO have initiated a women's procurement pilot program with 14 major Federal procurement agencies, with the goal of expanding the pool of women-owned businesses receiving Federal contracts. These efforts include trade fairs, marketing activities, publications on Federal contracting, and utilization of SBA's PRO–Net Internet site, http://www.pro-net.sba.gov/.

In addition, the Women's Prequalification Pilot Loan program, offered through district offices nationwide, enables women to prequalify for an SBA loan guaranty before going to a lender. The program focuses on the character, credit, experience, and repayment ability of the applicant.

For further information, contact the Office of Women's Business Ownership. Phone, 202–205–6673. Internet, http://www.sba.gov/ womeninbusiness/ or http://www.onlinewbc.org/.

Veterans Affairs The Office of Veterans' Affairs (OVA) carries out the Veterans Affairs program to ensure that SBA gives special consideration in all its programs to veterans, their dependents, and survivors. The program helps those who have dedicated significant portions of their lives to the defense of the ideals which make entrepreneurship possible in our Nation. The Office works with the Nation's 27 million veterans and the nearly 500,000 military personnel affected by downsizing. It is the only Federal Government office dedicated exclusively to helping veterans who want to go into business.

Besides ensuring special consideration, OVA designs procurement and management training programs specifically for veterans, and coordinates veteran training and counseling with other departments of SBA. It also measures veteran participation by monitoring loan, surety bond, procurement, and training activity within SBA. The Office maintains liaison with other veteran and veteran-related organizations to accomplish its goals.

For further information, contact the Office of Veterans Affairs. Phone, 202–205–6773.

Technology The Office of Technology has authority and responsibility for directing and monitoring the governmentwide activities of the Small Business Innovation Research Program (SBIR). In accordance with the Small Business Research and Development Enhancement Act of 1992, as amended (15 U.S.C. 631 note), the Office develops and issues policy directives for the general conduct of the programs within the Federal Government and maintains a source file and information program to provide each interested and qualified small business concern with information on opportunities to compete for SBIR program awards. The Office also coordinates with each participating

Federal agency in developing a master release schedule of all program solicitations; publishes the *Presolicitation Announcement* quarterly, which contains pertinent facts on upcoming solicitations; and surveys and monitors program operations within the Federal Government and reports on the progress of the program each year to Congress.

The Office has four main objectives: to expand and improve SBIR; to increase private sector commercialization of technology developed through Federal research and development; to increase small business participation in Federal research and development; and to improve the dissemination of information concerning SBIR, particularly with regard to participation by women-owned small business concerns and by socially and economically disadvantaged small business concerns.

For further information, contact the Office of Technology. Phone, 202–205–6450.

Small Business Development Centers Small Business Development Centers provide counseling and training to existing and prospective small business owners at approximately 1,000 locations around the country, operating in every State, Puerto Rico, the U.S. Virgin Islands, and Guam. The Small Business Development Center Program is a cooperative effort of the private sector, the educational community, and Federal, State, and local governments. It enhances economic development by providing small businesses with management and technical assistance. The Office of Small Business Development Centers develops national policies and goals in accordance with the Small Business Act of 1958, as amended. It establishes standards for the selection and performance of Centers; monitors compliance with applicable Office of Management and Budget circulars and laws; and implements new approaches to improve operations of existing centers.

The Office is responsible for coordinating program efforts with other internal activities of the Administration, as well as with the activities of other Federal agencies, and maintains liaison with other Federal, State, and local agencies and private organizations whose activities relate to Small Business Development Centers. It also assesses how the program is affected by substantive developments and policies in other areas of the agency, in other government agencies, and in the private sector.

For further information, contact the Office of Small Business Development Centers. Phone, 202–205–6766.

National Ombudsman Under the Small Business Regulatory Enforcement Fairness Act of 1996, SBA created the Regulatory Fairness Program (RegFair) to provide small businesses a meaningful process to comment on enforcement and compliance by Federal agencies. The process enables agencies to be evaluated and held accountable for establishing an approach to enforcement that is more friendly to small businesses, and also provides recommendations for improving specific enforcement efforts affecting distinct business sectors.

For further information, contact the Office of the National Ombudsman. Phone, 312–353–0880; or 800–REG–FAIR (734–3247) (toll-free). Internet, http://www.sba.gov/regfair/.

Field Operations The Office of Field Operations provides direction to SBA's 69 district and 10 regional offices, acting as the liaison between the district offices, the agency's program delivery system, and the headquarters' administrative and program offices.

For further information, contact the Office of Field Operations. Phone, 202–205–6808.

Field Offices—Small Business Administration

(RO: Regional Office; DO: District Office; BO: Branch Office; POD: Post of Duty)

Office	Address	Officer in Charge	Telephone
BOSTON, MA (RO)	Suite 812, 10 Causeway St., 02110	Patrick McGowan	617–565–8415
Augusta, ME (DO)	Rm. 512, 40 Western Ave., 04330	Leroy G. Perry	207–622–8378
Boston, MA (DO)	Rm. 265, 10 Causeway St., 02222–1093	Mary McAleney	617–565–5561

Field Offices—Small Business Administration—Continued

(RO: Regional Office; DO: District Office; BO: Branch Office; POD: Post of Duty)

Office	Address	Officer in Charge	Telephone
Concord, NH (DO)	Suite 202, 143 N. Main St., 03302–1258	William K. Phillips	603–225–1400
Hartford, CT (DO)	2d Fl., 330 Main St., 06106	JoAnn VanVechten	860–240–4670
Montpelier, VT (DO)	Rm. 205, 87 State St., 05602	Kenneth Silvia	802–828–4422
Providence, RI (DO)	5th Fl., 380 Westminster Mall, 02903	Joseph Loddo	401–528–4580
Springfield, MA (BO)	Rm. 212, 1550 Main St., 01103	Harold Webb	413–785–0484
NEW YORK, NY (RO)	Rm. 31–08, 26 Federal Plz., 10278	Thomas M. Bettridge	212–264–1450
Buffalo, NY (DO)	Rm. 1311, 111 W. Huron St., 14202	Franklin J. Sciortino	716–551–4301
Elmira, NY (BO)	4th Fl., 333 E. Water St., 14901	James J. Cristofaro	607–734–8130
Hato Rey, PR (DO)	Suite 201, 252 Ponce de Leon Ave., 00918	Ivan Irizarry	787–766–5002
Melville, NY (BO)	Suite 207W, 35 Pinelawn Rd., 11747	Burt Haggerty	516–454–0750
New York, NY (DO)	Rm. 3100, 26 Federal Plz., 10278	Aubrey A. Rogers	212–264–1318
Newark, NJ (DO)	4th Fl., 2 Gateway Ctr., 07102	Francisco Marrero	973–645–2434
Rochester, NY (BO)	Rm. 410, 100 State St., 14614	Peter Flihan	716–263–6700
St. Croix, VI (POD)	Suite 165, 3013 Golden Rock, 00820	Carl Christensen	809–778–5380
St. Thomas, VI (POD)	3800 Crown Bay, 00802	(Vacancy)	809–774–8530
Syracuse, NY (DO)	Rm. 1071, 100 S. Clinton St., 13260	B.J. Paprocki	315–471–9393
PHILADELPHIA, PA (RO)	5th Fl., 900 Market St., 19107	Susan M. McCann	215–580–2807
Baltimore, MD (DO)	Suite 6220, 10 S. Howard St., 21201–2525	Allan Stephenson	410–962–4392
Charleston, WV (BO)	Rm. 309, 550 Egan St., 25301	(Vacancy)	304–347–5220
Clarksburg, WV (DO)	5th Fl., 168 W. Main St., 26301	Jayne Armstrong	304–623–5631
Harrisburg, PA (BO)	Suite 108, 100 Chestnut St., 17101	(Vacancy)	717–782–3840
King of Prussia, PA (DO).	Suite 201, 475 Allendale Rd., 19406	Tom Tolan, *Acting*	215–962–3804
Pittsburgh, PA (DO)	1000 Liberty Ave., 15222	Al Jones	412–395–6560
Richmond, VA (DO)	Suite 200, 1504 Santa Rosa Rd., 23229	Charles J. Gaston	804–771–2400
Washington, DC (DO)	Suite 900, 1110 Vermont Ave. NW., 20036	Darryl Harriston	202–606–4000
Wilkes-Barre, PA (BO)	Rm. 2327, 20 N. Pennsylvania Ave., 18701–3589.	(Vacancy)	717–826–6497
Wilmington, DE (BO)	Suite 610, 824 N. Market St., 19801–3011	Joe Kopp	302–573–6381
ATLANTA, GA (RO)	Suite 496, 1720 Peachtree Rd. NW., S. Twr., 30309–2482.	Billy M. Paul	404–347–4999
Atlanta, GA (DO)	6th Fl., 1720 Peachtree Rd. NW., 30309	Laura Brown	404–347–4147
Birmingham, AL (DO)	Suite 200, 2121 8th Ave. N., 35203–2398	James C. Barksdale	205–731–1344
Charlotte, NC (DO)	Suite A2015, 200 N. College St., 28202–2173	Gary Cook	704–344–6561
Columbia, SC (DO)	Rm. 358, 1835 Assembly St., 29201	Elliott Cooper	803–765–5339
Gulfport, MS (BO)	Suite 203, 2909 13th St., 39501	Charles Gillis	601–863–4449
Jackson, MS (DO)	Suite 400, 101 W. Capitol St., 39201	Janita Stewart	601–965–5371
Jacksonville, FL (DO)	Suite 100–B, 7825 Baymeadows Way, 32256–7504.	Willie Gonzalez	904–443–1970
Louisville, KY (DO)	Rm. 188, 600 Dr. M.L. King, Jr. Pl., 40202	William Federhofer	502–582–5971
Miami, FL (DO)	3rd Fl., 1320 S. Dixie Hwy., Coral Gables 33146–2911.	Charles Anderson	305–536–5521
Nashville, TN (DO)	Suite 201, 50 Vantage Way, 37228–1500	W. Clint Smith, *Acting*	615–736–5881
CHICAGO, IL (RO)	Suite 1240, 500 W. Madison, 60661–2511	Peter Barca	312–353–0357
Chicago, IL (DO)	Rm. 1250, 500 W. Madison St., 60661–2511	John L. Smith	312–353–4508
Cincinnati, OH (BO)	Suite 870, 525 Vine St., 45202	Ronald Carlson	513–684–2814
Cleveland, OH (DO)	Suite 630, 1111 Superior Ave., 44194–2507	Gilbert Goldberg	216–522–4180
Columbus, OH (DO)	Suite 1400, 2 Nationwide Plz., 43215–2592	Frank D. Ray	614–469–6860
Detroit, MI (DO)	Rm. 515, 477 Michigan Ave., 48226	Dwight Reynolds	313–226–6075
Indianapolis, IN (DO)	Suite 100, 429 N. Pennsylvania, 46204–1873	Janice Wolfe	317–226–7275
Madison, WI (DO)	Rm. 213, 212 E. Washington Ave., 53703	Michael Kiser	608–264–5268
Marquette, MI (BO)	501 S. Front St., 49885	Paul Jacobson, *Acting*	906–225–1108
Milwaukee, WI (BO)	Suite 400, 310 W. Wisconsin Ave., 53203	Paul Roppuld, *Acting*	414–297–1178
Minneapolis, MN (DO)	Suite 610, 100 N. 6th St., 55403–1563	Edward A. Daum	612–370–2306
Springfield, IL (BO)	Suite 302, 511 W. Capitol Ave., 62704	Curtis Charter	217–492–4232
FORT WORTH, TX (RO)	Suite 108, 4300 Amon Carter Blvd., 76155	G. Till Phillips	817–885–6581
Albuquerque, NM (DO)	Suite 320, 625 Silver Ave. SW., 87102	Bob Blaney	505–766–1870
Corpus Christi, TX (BO)	Suite 1200, 606 N. Carancahus, 78476	Jesse Sendejo	512–888–3331
El Paso, TX (DO)	Suite 320, 10737 Gateway W., 79935	Carlos Mendoza	915–540–5676
Fort Worth, TX (DO)	Suite 114, 4300 Amon Carter Blvd., 76155	Lavan Alexander	817–885–6500
Harlingen, TX (DO)	Rm. 500, 222 E. Van Buren St., 78550–6855	Sylvia Zamponi	956–427–8533
Houston, TX (DO)	Suite 550, 9301 Southwest Fwy., 77074–1591	Milton Wilson	713–773–6500
Little Rock, AR (DO)	Suite 100, 2120 Riverfront Dr., 72202	Joseph Foglia	501–324–5277
Lubbock, TX (DO)	Suite 200, 1611 10th St., 79401–2693	Tommy Dowell	806–472–7462
New Orleans, LA (DO)	Suite 2250, 1 Canal Pl., 70130	Ron Coulounge	504–589–6685
Oklahoma City, OK (DO)	Suite 670, 200 NW. 5th St., 73102	Raymond Harshman	405–231–5237
San Antonio, TX (DO)	5th Fl., 727 E. Durango Blvd., 78206	Rodney Martin	210–472–5900
KANSAS CITY, MO (RO)	Suite 307, 323 W. 8th St., 64105–1500	Bruce W. Kent	816–374–6380
Cedar Rapids, IA (DO)	Suite 200, 215 4th Ave. SE., 52401–1806	James Thomson	319–362–6405
Des Moines, IA (DO)	Rm. 749, 210 Walnut St., 50309–2186	Cheryl Eftink	515–284–4657
Kansas City, MO (DO)	Suite 501, 323 W. 8th St., 64105	Dorothy Kleeschulte	816–374–6708
Omaha, NE (DO)	11145 Mill Valley Rd., 68154	Glenn Davis	402–221–3620
Springfield, MO (BO)	Suite 110, 620 S. Glenstone St., 65802–3200	James R. Combs	417–864–7670

Field Offices—Small Business Administration—Continued
(RO: Regional Office; DO: District Office; BO: Branch Office; POD: Post of Duty)

Office	Address	Officer in Charge	Telephone
St. Louis, MO (DO)	Rm. 242, 815 Olive St., 63101	Robert L. Andrews	314–539–6600
Wichita, KS (DO)	Suite 510, 100 E. English St., 67202	Elizabeth Auer	316–269–6566
DENVER, CO (RO)	Suite 400, 721 19th St., 80202–2599	Joan Coplan	303–844–0500
Casper, WY (DO)	Rm. 4001, 100 E. B St., 82602–2839	Steve Despain	307–261–6501
Denver, CO (DO)	Suite 426, 721 19th St., 80202–2599	Patricia Rivera-Barel	303–844–4028
Fargo, ND (DO)	Rm. 219, 657 2d Ave. N., 58108–3086	James L. Stai	701–239–5656
Helena, MT (DO)	Rm. 334, 301 S. Park, 59626	Jo Alice Mospan	406–441–1081
Salt Lake City, UT (DO)	Rm. 2237, 125 S. State St., 84138–1195	Stan Nakano	801–524–5804
Sioux Falls, SD (DO)	110 S. Phillips Ave., 57102–1109	Gene Van Arsdale	605–330–4231
SAN FRANCISCO, CA (RO).	Suite 2200, 455 Market St., 94105	Viola Canales	415–744–1958
Agana, GU (BO)	Suite 302, 400 Rt. 8, Mongmong, 96927	Kenneth Lujan	671–472–7277
Fresno, CA (DO)	Suite 200, 2719 N. Air Fresno Dr., 93727–1547	Tony Valdez	209–487–5189
Glendale, CA (DO)	Suite 1200, 330 N. Brand Blvd., 91203–2304	Alberto Alvarado	818–552–3289
Honolulu, HI (DO)	Rm. 2314, 300 Ala Moana Blvd., 96850–4981	Andrew PoePoe	808–541–2965
Las Vegas, NV (DO)	Rm. 301, 301 E. Stewart St., 89125–2527	John Scott	702–388–6611
Phoenix, AZ (DO)	Suite 800, 2828 N. Central Ave., 85004–1025	Phil Mahoney	602–640–2400
Sacramento, CA (DO)	Rm. 215, 660 J St., 95814–2413	Teresa Bellmore	916–498–6432
San Diego, CA (DO)	Suite 550, 550 W. C St., 92101	George P. Chandler, Jr.	619–557–7252
San Francisco, CA (DO)	6th Fl., 455 Market St., 94105	Mark Quinn	415–744–8474
Santa Ana, CA (DO)	Suite 700, 200 W. Santa Ana Blvd., 92701	Sandra Sutton	714–550–7420
SEATTLE, WA (RO)	Suite 1805, 1200 6th Ave., 98101–1128	Gretchen Sorensen	206–553–5676
Anchorage, AK (DO)	222 W. 8th Ave., 99513–7559	Frank Cox	907–271–4022
Boise, ID (DO)	Suite 290, 1020 Main St., 83702–5745	Thomas Bergdoll	208–334–1696
Portland, OR (DO)	Suite 1050, 1515 SW. 5th Ave., 97201–6695	John L. Gilman	503–326–2682
Seattle, WA (DO)	Suite 1700, 1200 6th Ave., 98101–1128	Robert P. Meredith	206–553–7310
Spokane, WA (DO)	601 W. 1st Ave., 99201–3826	Robert Wiebe	509–353–2800

Disaster Area Offices

Office	Address	Telephone
Atlanta, GA	Suite 300, 1 Baltimore Pl., 30308	404–347–3771
Fort Worth, TX	Suite 102, 4400 Amon Carter Blvd., 76155	817–885–7600
Niagara Falls, NY	3d Fl., 360 Rainbow Blvd. S., 14303	716–282–4612
Sacramento, CA	Suite 208, 1825 Bell St., 95825	916–566–7246

Regional Administrators

Region/Address	Administrator	Telephone
Boston, MA (Suite 812, 10 Causeway St., 02110)	Patrick K. McGowan	617–565–8415
New York, NY (Rm. 31–08, 26 Federal Plz., 10278)	Thomas M. Bettridge	212–264–1450
Philadelphia, PA (Suite 201, 475 Allendale Rd., King of Prussia, 19406	Susan M. McCann	610–962–3710
Atlanta, GA (Suite 496, 1720 Peachtree Rd. NW., 30309)	Billy M. Paul	404–347–4999
Chicago, IL (Rm. 1975, 300 S. Riverside Plz., 60606–6611)	Peter Barca	312–353–0357
Fort Worth, TX (Suite 108, 4300 Amon Carter Blvd., 76155)	James W. Breedlove	817–885–6581
Kansas City, MO (13th Fl., 911 Walnut St., 64106)	Bruce W. Kent	816–374–6380
Denver, CO (Suite 400, 721 19th St., 80202–2599)	Thomas J. Redder	303–844–0500
San Francisco, CA (20th Fl., 71 Stevenson St., 94105–2939)	Viola Canales	415–975–4804
Seattle, WA (S–1805, 1200 6th Ave., 98101–1128)	Gretchen Sorensen	206–553–0291

Sources of Information

Electronic Access Information on the Small Business Administration is available electronically by various means. Internet, http://www.sba.gov/. Gopher, gopher:// gopher.sbaonline.sba.gov. FTP, ftp:// ftp.sbaonline.sba.gov. Telnet, sbaonline.sba.gov.

Access the U.S. Business Adviser through the Internet, at http:// www.business.gov/.

Access the Administration's electronic bulletin board by modem at 800–697–4636 (limited access), 900–463–4636 (full access), or 202–401–9600 (Washington, DC, metropolitan area).

General Information   Contact the nearest Small Business Administration field office listed above, or call the SBA answer desk. Phone, 800–8–ASK–SBA. Fax, 202–205–7064. TDD, 704–344–6640.

Publications   A free copy of *The Resource Directory for Small Business Management,* a listing of for-sale publications and videotapes, is available from any local SBA office or the SBA answer desk.

For further information, contact the Office of Public Communications and Public Liaison, Small Business Administration, 409 Third Street SW., Washington, DC 20416. Phone, 202–205–6740. Internet, http://www.sba.gov/.

SOCIAL SECURITY ADMINISTRATION

6401 Security Boulevard, Baltimore, MD 21235
Phone, 410–965–1234. Internet, http://www.ssa.gov/.

Commissioner of Social Security	KENNETH S. APFEL
Principal Deputy Commissioner	JOHN R. DYER, *Acting*
Chief of Staff	BRIAN D. COYNE
Chief Actuary	HARRY C. BALLANTYNE
General Counsel	ARTHUR J. FRIED
Inspector General	DAVID C. WILLIAMS
Deputy Commissioner for Communications	JOAN E. WAINWRIGHT
Deputy Commissioner for Finance, Assessment, and Management/Chief Financial Officer	DALE W. SOPPER, *Acting*
Deputy Commissioner for Human Resources	PAUL D. BARNES
Deputy Commissioner for Legislation and Congressional Affairs	JUDY L. CHESSER
Deputy Commissioner for Operations	JANICE L. WARDEN
Deputy Commissioner for Programs and Policy	CAROLYN W. COLVIN
Deputy Commissioner for Systems	D. DEAN MESTERHARM

[For the Social Security Administration statement of organization, see the Code of Federal Regulations, Title 20, Part 422]

The Social Security Administration manages the Nation's social insurance program, consisting of retirement, survivors, and disability insurance programs, commonly known as Social Security. It also administers the Supplemental Security Income program for the aged, blind, and disabled. The Administration is responsible for studying the problems of poverty and economic insecurity among Americans and making recommendations on effective methods for solving these problems through social insurance. The Administration also assigns Social Security numbers to U.S. citizens and maintains earnings records for workers under their Social Security numbers.

The Social Security Administration (SSA) was established by Reorganization Plan No. 2 of 1946 (5 U.S.C. app.), effective July 16, 1946. It became an independent agency in the executive branch by the Social Security Independence and Program Improvements Act of 1994 (42 U.S.C. 901), effective March 31, 1995.

The Administration is headed by a Commissioner, appointed by the President with the advice and consent of the Senate.

In administering the programs necessary to carry out the agency's mission, by law the Commissioner is assisted by a Deputy Commissioner, who

SOCIAL SECURITY ADMINISTRATION

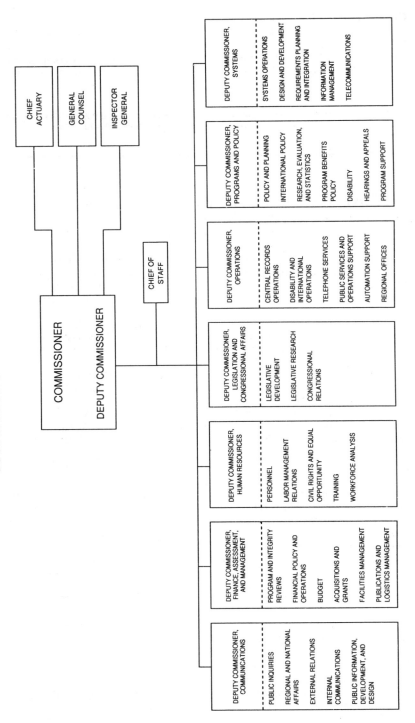

performs duties assigned or delegated by the Commissioner; a Chief Financial Officer; a General Counsel; a Chief Actuary; and an Inspector General.

Programs and Activities

Old-Age, Survivors, and Disability Insurance The agency administers these social insurance programs, which provide monthly benefits to retired and disabled workers, their spouses and children, and to survivors of insured workers. Financing is under a system of contributory social insurance, whereby employees, employers, and the self-employed pay contributions that are pooled in special trust funds. When earnings stop or are reduced because the worker retires, dies, or becomes disabled, monthly cash benefits are paid to partially replace the earnings the family has lost.

Supplemental Security Income The agency administers this needs-based program for the aged, blind, and disabled. A basic Federal monthly payment is financed out of general revenue, rather than a special trust fund. Some States, choosing to provide payments to supplement the benefits, have agreements with the Administration under which it administers the supplemental payments for those States.

Medicare While the administration of Medicare is the responsibility of the Health Care Financing Administration, Department of Health and Human Services, the Social Security Administration provides Medicare assistance to the public through SSA field offices and processing centers, and adjudicates requests for hearings and appeals of Medicare claims.

Black Lung By agreement with the Department of Labor, SSA is involved in certain aspects of the administration of the black lung benefits provisions of the Federal Coal Mine Health and Safety Act of 1969, as amended (30 U.S.C. 901).

Regional Offices Social Security Administration operations are decentralized to provide services at the local level. Each of the SSA 10 regions, under the overall direction of its Regional Commissioner, contains a network of field offices and teleservice centers, which serve as the contact between SSA and the public. The Administration operates 1,292 field offices, 38 teleservice centers, and 6 program service centers. These installations are responsible for:

—informing the public of the purposes and provisions of Social Security programs and their rights and responsibilities;

—assisting with claims filed for retirement, survivors, disability, or health insurance benefits, black lung benefits, or Supplemental Security Income;

—developing and adjudicating claims;

—assisting certain beneficiaries in claiming reimbursement for medical expenses;

—developing cases involving earnings records, coverage, and fraud-related questions;

—making rehabilitation service referrals; and

—assisting claimants in filing appeals on SSA determinations of benefit entitlement or amount.

For further information, contact the Social Security Administration. Phone, 800–772–1213 (toll-free).

Sources of Information

Inquiries on the following subjects may be directed to the appropriate office, Social Security Administration, 6401 Security Boulevard, Baltimore, MD 21235.

Contracts and Small Business Activities Contact the Office of Acquisitions and Grants. Phone, 410–965–9457.

Electronic Access Information regarding the Social Security

Administration may be obtained through the Internet, at http://www.ssa.gov/.

Employment A variety of civil service registers and examinations are used in hiring new employees. Specific employment information may be obtained from the Office of Personnel. Phone, 410–965–4506.

General Information The Office of the Deputy Commissioner for Operations manages SSA's toll-free public service telephone. Phone, 800–772–1213 (toll-free).

Inspector General The Office of the Inspector General maintains a 24-hour toll-free hotline to receive allegations and complaints relative to SSA operations nationwide. Phone, 800–269–0271 (toll-free). Fax, 410–965–3011.

Publications The Office of the Deputy Commissioner for Communications publishes numerous pamphlets concerning SSA programs. Single copies may be obtained at any local office or by calling 800–772–1213. The Administration also collects a substantial volume of economic, demographic, and other data in furtherance of its program

mission. Basic data on employment and earnings, beneficiaries and benefit payments, and other items of program interest are published regularly in the *Social Security Bulletin*, its *Annual Statistical Supplement*, and in special releases and reports that appear periodically on selected topics of interest to the public. Additional information may be obtained from the Publications Staff, Office of Research, Evaluation, and Statistics, 500 E Street SW., Washington, DC 20254. Phone, 202–282–7138.

Reading Rooms Requests for information, for copies of records, or to inspect records may be made at any local office or the Headquarters Contact Unit, Room G–44, Altmeyer Building. Phone, 800–772–1213 (toll-free).

Speakers and Films The Administration makes speakers, films, and exhibits available to public or private organizations, community groups, schools, etc., throughout the Nation. Requests for this service should be directed to the local Social Security Office.

For further information, contact the Office of Public Inquiries, Social Security Administration, 6401 Security Boulevard, Baltimore, MD 21235. Phone, 410–965–7700. Internet, http://www.ssa.gov/.

TENNESSEE VALLEY AUTHORITY

400 West Summit Hill Drive, Knoxville, TN 37902
Phone, 615–632–2101

One Massachusetts Avenue NW., Washington, DC 20444–0001
Phone, 202–898–2999

Chairman	CRAVEN CROWELL
Directors	JOHNNY H. HAYES
	WILLIAM H. KENNOY
Senior Vice President, Communications	ALAN CARMICHAEL
Chief Operating Officer	J.W. DICKEY
Chief Nuclear Officer	OSWALD J. (IKE) ZERINGUE
Chief Financial Officer	DAVID N. SMITH
Chief Administrative Officer	NORMAN A. ZIGROSSI

The Tennessee Valley Authority conducts a unified program of resource development for the advancement of economic growth in the Tennessee Valley region. The Authority's program of activities includes flood control, navigation development, electric power production, recreation improvement, and forestry and wildlife development.

The Tennessee Valley Authority (TVA) is a wholly owned Government corporation created by act of May 18, 1933 (16 U.S.C. 831–831dd). All functions of the Authority are vested in its three-member Board of Directors, the members of which are appointed by the President with the advice and consent of the Senate. The President designates one member as Chairman.

While TVA's electric power program is required to be financially self-supporting, other programs are financed primarily by appropriations.

A system of dams built by TVA on the Tennessee River and its larger tributaries provides flood regulation on the Tennessee and contributes to regulation of the lower Ohio and Mississippi Rivers. The system maintains a continuous 9-foot-draft channel for navigation for the length of the 650-mile Tennessee River main stream, from Paducah, KY, to Knoxville, TN. The dams harness the power of the rivers to produce electricity. They also provide other benefits, including a major asset for outdoor recreation.

The Authority operates the river control system and provides assistance to State and local governments in reducing local flood problems. It also works with cooperating agencies to encourage full and effective use of the navigable waterway by industry and commerce.

The Authority is the wholesale power supplier for many local municipal and cooperative electric systems serving customers in parts of seven States. It supplies power to several Federal installations and industries whose power requirements are large or unusual. Power to meet these demands is supplied from dams, coal-fired powerplants, nuclear powerplants, combustion turbine installations, and a pumped-storage hydroelectric project operated by TVA; U.S. Corps of Engineers dams in the Cumberland Valley; and Aluminum Company of America dams, whose operation is coordinated with TVA's system.

In economic and community development programs, TVA provides technical assistance in areas including industrial development, regional waste management, tourism promotion, community preparedness, and vanpool organization. It works with local communities and groups to develop maximum use of available area resources. Working with regional learning centers, businesses, and industries, the Authority has identified skills that are needed in the high-technology job market and has set up training centers.

At Muscle Shoals, AL, TVA operates a national laboratory for environmental research, focusing on the cleanup and protection of the Nation's land, air, and water resources. Projects include development of methods for reducing nonpoint source pollution from groundwater runoff, contaminated site remediation, bioenergy research, and industrial waste reduction. The work is centered on preventing and correcting environmental problems that are barriers to economic growth.

In cooperation with other agencies, TVA conducts research and development programs in forestry, fish and game, watershed protection, health services related to its operations, and economic development of Tennessee Valley communities.

In the western parts of Kentucky and Tennessee, TVA operates Land Between the Lakes, a demonstration project in outdoor recreation, environmental education, and natural resource management.

Sources of Information

Citizen Participation TVA Communications, ET 12A, 400 West Summit Hill Drive, Knoxville, TN 37902–1499. Phone, 423–632–2101.
Contracts Purchasing, WT 4D, 400 West Summit Hill Drive, Knoxville, TN 37902–1499. Phone, 423–632–4796. This office will direct inquiries to the appropriate procurement officer.

Economic Development WT 11D, 400 West Summit Hill Drive, Knoxville, TN 37902–1499. Phone, 423–632–4312.

Electric Power Supply and Rates ET 12A, 400 West Summit Hill Drive, Knoxville, TN 37902–1499. Phone 423–632–3108.

Employment Human Resources, ET 12A, 400 West Summit Hill Drive, Knoxville, TN 37902–1499. Phone, 423–632–3222. (Other personnel offices may be contacted at other major locations.)

Environmental and Energy Education BR 4F, 1101 Market Street, Chattanooga, TN 37402–2801. Phone, 423–751–4624.

Environmental Research Center TVA Reservation, P.O. Box 1010, Muscle Shoals, AL 35661–1010. Phone, 205–386–2026.

Environmental Quality Environmental Services, LP 5D, 1101 Market Street, Chattanooga, TN 37402–2801. Phone, 423–751–2293.

Land Management/Shoreline Permitting Land Management, FOR 3A, Forestry Building, Ridgeway Road, Norris, TN 37828. Phone, 423–632–1440.

Library Services Corporate Library, ET PC, 400 West Summit Hill Drive, Knoxville, TN 37902–1499. Phone, 423–632–3464. Chattanooga Office Complex, SP 1A, 1101 Market Street, Chattanooga, TN 37402–2801. Phone, 423–751–4913. Muscle Shoals, CTR 1A, P.O. Box 1010, Muscle Shoals, AL 35661–1010. Phone, 205–386–2417.

Maps Maps Information & Sales, HB 1A, 311 Broad Street, Chattanooga, TN 37402–2801. Phone, 423–751–6277.

Medical Services Health Services, EB 8A, 20 East Eleventh Street, Chattanooga, TN 37402–2801. Phone, 423–751–2091.

Publications TVA Communications, ET 6E, 400 West Summit Hill Drive, Knoxville, TN 37902–1499. Phone, 423–632–8039.

For further information, contact TVA Communications, 400 West Summit Hill Drive, Knoxville, TN 37902–1499. Phone, 423–632–2101. Or TVA Washington Office, 1 Massachusetts Avenue NW., Washington, DC 20044. Phone, 202–898–2999.

TRADE AND DEVELOPMENT AGENCY

Suite 300, 1621 North Kent Street, Arlington, VA 22209–2131
Phone, 703–875–4357. E-mail, info@tda.gov. Internet, http://www.tda.gov/.

Director	J. JOSEPH GRANDMAISON
Deputy Director	NANCY D. FRAME
General Counsel	KENNETH FRIES
Assistant Director for Management Operations	LARRY BEVIN
Director of Public Affairs and Marketing	DONALD DUNN
Congressional Liaison Officer	EDWARD CABOT
Regional Directors:	
Africa and Middle East	JOHN RICHTER
Central, Eastern, and Southern Europe	ROD AZAMA
New Independent States, Mongolia, and India	DANIEL D. STEIN
Asia and Pacific	GEOFFREY JACKSON
Latin America and Caribbean	ALBERT W. ANGULO
Special Projects	BARBARA R. BRADFORD
Economist/Evaluation Officer	DAVID DENNY
Financial Manager	NOREEN ST. LOUIS
Contracting Officer	DELLA GLENN
Administrative Officer	CAROLYN HUM
Grants Administrator	PATRICIA SMITH

The Trade and Development Agency's mission is to promote economic development in, and simultaneously export U.S. goods and services to, developing and middle-income nations in the following regions of the world: Africa/Middle East, Asia/ Pacific, Central and Eastern Europe, Latin America and the Caribbean, and the New Independent States.

The Trade and Development Agency (TDA) was established on July 1, 1980, as a component organization of the International Development Cooperation Agency. Section 2204 of the Omnibus Trade and Competitiveness Act of 1988 (22 U.S.C. 2421) made it a separate component agency. The organization was renamed and made an independent agency within the executive branch of the Federal Government on October 28, 1992, by the Jobs Through Exports Act of 1992 (22 U.S.C. 2421).

The Trade and Development Agency assists in the creation of jobs for Americans by helping U.S. companies pursue exports and other overseas business opportunities. It funds feasibility studies, orientation visits, training grants, business briefings, and various forms of technical assistance in support of specific projects, enabling American businesses to become involved in the planning of infrastructure and industrial projects in emerging markets. Working closely with a foreign nation sponsor, TDA makes its funds available on the condition that the foreign entity contracts with a U.S. firm to perform the actual work on the project. This affords American firms market entry, exposure, and information, thus helping them to establish a position in markets that are otherwise difficult to penetrate.

The Agency's focus is the planning and design engineering phase of major infrastructure and industrial projects. It is involved in several sectors, including: agriculture, aviation, energy, environment, health care, manufacturing, mining and minerals development, telecommunications, transportation, and water resources.

Activities

The Agency funds feasibility studies (or project plans) which evaluate the technical, economic, and financial aspects of a development project. These studies advise the host nation about the availability of U.S. goods and services and are required by financial institutions in assessing the creditworthiness of the undertaking. Funding activities are based upon an official request for assistance made by the sponsoring government or private sector organization of a developing or middle-income nation, and costs for a study typically are shared between TDA and the U.S. firm developing the project.

The Agency makes decisions on funding requests for feasibility studies based on the recommendations contained in the definitional mission or desk study report, the advice of the U.S. Embassy, and its internal analysis.

Sources of Information

Requests for proposals (RFP's) to conduct feasibility studies funded by TDA are listed in the *Commerce Business Daily*. Information on definitional mission opportunities can be obtained by calling TDA's "DM Hotline" at 703–875–7447. Small and minority U.S. firms that wish to be included in TDA's consultant database and considered for future solicitations should contact TDA's Contracts Office at 703–875–4357.

In an effort to provide timely information on Agency-supported projects, TDA publishes the *Pipeline* and a calendar of events which are available together on a paid subscription basis by calling 703–875–4246. They are also available through the Internet, at http:// www.tda.gov/. A quarterly publication, *TDA Update*, contains current items of interest on a variety of program activities. Region- or sector-specific fact sheets and case studies also are available. An annual report summarizes the Agency's activities.

Agency news, reports, and lists of upcoming orientation visits and business

TRADE AND DEVELOPMENT AGENCY

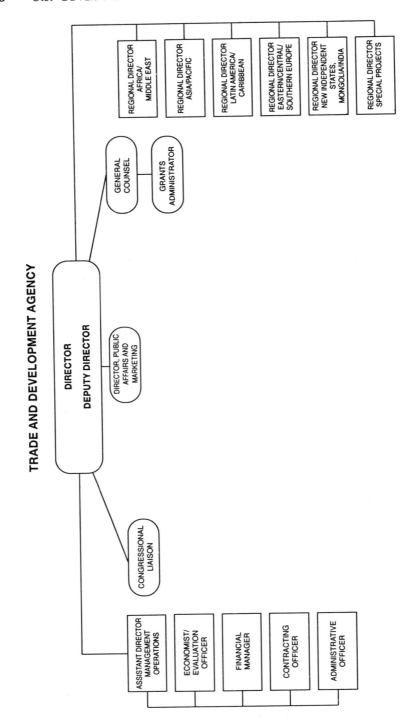

briefings are available through the Internet, at http://www.tda.gov/.

Regional program inquiries should be directed to the assigned Country Manager. Phone, 703–875–4357. Fax, 703–875–4009. E-mail, info@tda.gov.

TDA's library maintains final reports on all TDA activities. These are available for public review Monday through Friday from 8:30 a.m. to 5:30 p.m. Copies of completed feasibility studies must be purchased through the Department of Commerce's National Technical Information Service (NTIS).

For further information, contact the Trade and Development Agency, Suite 300, 1621 North Kent Street, Arlington, VA. 22209–2131. Phone, 703-875–4357. E-mail, info@tda.gov. Internet, http://www.tda.gov/.

UNITED STATES ARMS CONTROL AND DISARMAMENT AGENCY

320 Twenty-first Street NW., Washington, DC 20451
Phone, 202–647–2034

Director	JOHN D. HOLUM
Deputy Director	RALPH EARLE II
Special Assistant	CARLENE ACKERMAN
Counselor	DONALD GROSS
Executive Secretary	BARBARA STARR
Senior Military Adviser	LT. COL. RAYMOND LYNN
Principal Deputy Director, On-Site Inspection Agency	JOERG H. MENZEL
Assistant Director, Nonproliferation and Regional Arms Control Bureau	NORMAN WULF, *Acting*
Assistant Director, Multilateral Affairs Bureau	DONALD MAHLEY, *Acting*
Assistant Director, Strategic and Eurasian Affairs Bureau	R. LUCAS FISCHER, *Acting*
Assistant Director, Intelligence, Verification, and Information Management Bureau	O.J. SHEAKS, *Acting*
General Counsel	MARY ELIZABETH HOINKES
Director of Congressional Affairs	IVO SPALATIN
Director of Public Affairs	MARY DILLON
Director of Administration	CATHLEEN LAWRENCE
U.S. Commissioner, Standing Consultative Commission	STANLEY RIVELES
U.S. Representative to the Conference on Disarmament	ROBERT GREY
U.S. Representative to the Special Verification Commission and the Joint Compliance and Inspection Commission	STEVEN STEINER
Director, Advanced Projects and Director's Advisory Committee	ROBERT SHERMAN

[For the United States Arms Control and Disarmament Agency statement of organization, see the *Code of Federal Regulations*, Title 22, Part 601]

The United States Arms Control and Disarmament Agency formulates and implements arms control nonproliferation and disarmament policies that promote the national security of the United States and its relations with other countries. To

UNITED STATES ARMS CONTROL AND DISARMAMENT AGENCY

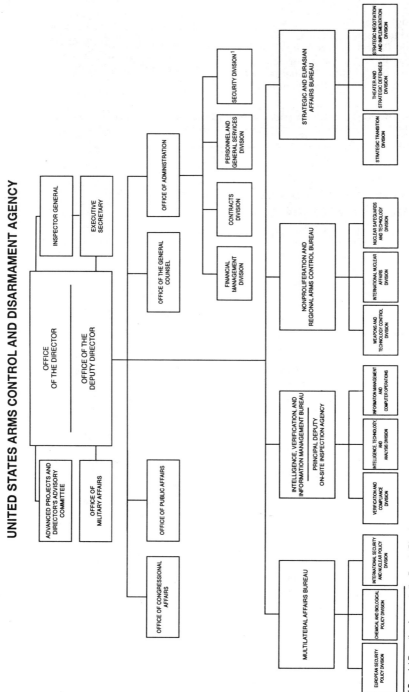

¹ Special Reporting Access to the Deputy Director

effectively carry out its responsibilities, the Agency prepares and participates in discussions and negotiations with foreign countries on such issues as strategic arms limitations, conventional force reductions in Europe, prevention of the spread of nuclear weapons to countries that do not now possess them, prohibitions on chemical weapons, and the international arms trade.

The United States Arms Control and Disarmament Agency was established by act of September 26, 1961 (22 U.S.C. 2561), in response to congressional feeling that the Nation's national security efforts could be most effectively executed by lawfully centralizing arms control and disarmament responsibilities.

Activities

The Agency conducts studies and provides advice relating to arms control, nonproliferation, and disarmament policy formulation; prepares for and manages United States participation in international negotiations in the arms control, nonproliferation, and disarmament field; disseminates and coordinates public information about arms control, nonproliferation, and disarmament; and prepares for, operates, or directs, as needed, U.S. participation in international control systems that may result from United States arms control or disarmament activities.

In addition to directing the activities described above, the Director functions as the principal adviser to the President, the National Security Adviser, and the Secretary of State in arms control, nonproliferation, and disarmament matters. Under the direction of the Secretary of State, the Director also has primary responsibility within the Government for such matters.

In support of its activities, the Agency conducts research and studies or, through contracts and agreements, arranges for involvement by private or public institutions or persons. It also coordinates such efforts by or for other Government agencies, and analyzes selected defense programs for their arms control pursuits.

Sources of Information

Contracts   Individuals seeking to do business with the Agency or to obtain information on research contracts may contact the Contracting Office (phone, 703–235–3288) at the address shown below.

Publications   Copies of publications such as *World Military Expenditures* (annual series), *Documents on Disarmament* (annual series), *Arms Control and Disarmament Agreements,* the Agency's newsletter *ACDA Update,* and the Agency's Annual Report may be ordered from the Superintendent of Documents, Government Printing Office, Washington, DC 20402 (phone, 202–512–1800); or from the Office of Public Affairs (phone, 202–647–8677) at the address shown below.

Speakers   Officers of the Agency will address audiences in all parts of the country, workload permitting. Phone, 202–647–4800.

For further information, contact the United States Arms Control and Disarmament Agency, 320 Twenty-first Street NW., Washington, DC 20451. Phone, 202–647–8677.

UNITED STATES COMMISSION ON CIVIL RIGHTS

624 Ninth Street NW., Washington, DC 20425
Phone, 202–376–8177

Chairperson   MARY FRANCES BERRY
Vice Chairman   CRUZ REYNOSO

Commissioners	CARL A. ANDERSON, ROBERT P. GEORGE, A. LEON HIGGINBOTHAM, JR., CONSTANCE HORNER, YVONNE Y. LEE, RUSSELL G. REDENBAUGH
Staff Director	RUBY G. MOY
Deputy Staff Director	(VACANCY)
General Counsel	STEPHANIE Y. MOORE
Solicitor	STEPHANIE Y. MOORE, *Acting*
Assistant Staff Director for Civil Rights Evaluation	FREDERICK ISLER
Chief, Civil Rights Evaluation	(VACANCY)
Assistant Staff Director for Management	(VACANCY)
Chief, Public Affairs Unit	CHARLES RIVERA
Assistant Staff Director for Congressional Affairs	JAMES S. CUNNINGHAM
Chief, Regional Programs Coordination	CAROL-LEE HURLEY
Director, Eastern Regional Division	KI-TAEK CHUN
Director, Central Regional Division	MELVIN L. JENKINS
Director, Midwestern Regional Division	CONSTANCE D. DAVIS
Director, Rocky Mountain Regional Division	JOHN FOSTER DULLES
Director, Southern Regional Division	BOBBY DOCTOR
Director, Western Regional Division	PHILIP MONTEZ

[For the Commission on Civil Rights statement of organization, see the *Code of Federal Regulations*, Title 45, Part 701]

The Commission on Civil Rights collects and studies information on discrimination or denials of equal protection of the laws because of race, color, religion, sex, age, handicap, national origin, or in the administration of justice in such areas as voting rights, enforcement of Federal civil rights laws, and equal opportunity in education, employment, and housing.

The Commission on Civil Rights was first created by the Civil Rights Act of 1957, as amended, and reestablished by the United States Commission on Civil Rights Act of 1983, as amended (42 U.S.C. 1975).

Activities

The Commission makes findings of fact but has no enforcement authority. Findings and recommendations are submitted to the President and Congress, and many of the Commission's recommendations have been enacted, either by statute, Executive order, or regulation. The Commission evaluates Federal laws and the effectiveness of Government equal opportunity programs. It also serves as a national clearinghouse for civil rights information.
Regional Programs   The Commission maintains six regional divisions.

Regional Divisions—Commission on Civil Rights

Region/Address	Telephone
CENTRAL—Suite 908, 400 State Ave., Kansas City, KS 66101–2406	913–551–1400
EASTERN—Rm. 500, 624 9th St, NW., Washington, DC 20425	202–376–7533
MIDWESTERN—Suite 410, 55 W. Monroe St., Chicago, IL 60603	312–353–8311
ROCKY MOUNTAIN—Suite 710, 1700 Broadway, Denver, CO 80290	303–866–1040
SOUTHERN—Suite 1840T, 100 Alabama St., Atlanta, GA 30303	404–562–7000
WESTERN—Rm. 810, 3660 Wilshire Blvd., Los Angeles, CA 90010	213–894–3437

UNITED STATES COMMISSION ON CIVIL RIGHTS

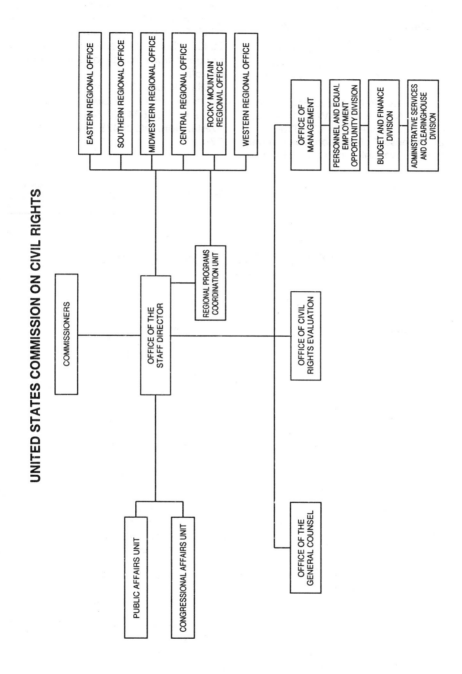

Sources of Information

Complaints Complaints alleging denials of civil rights may be reported to Complaints Referral, 624 Ninth Street NW., Washington, DC 20425. Phone, 202–376–8513 or 800–552–6843 (toll-free).

Employment Personnel Office, Room 510, 624 Ninth Street NW., Washington, DC 20425. Phone, 202–376–8364.

Publications Commission publications are made available upon request from the Administrative Services and Clearinghouse Division, Room 550, 624 Ninth Street NW., Washington, DC 20425. Phone, 202–376–8105. A catalog of publications may be obtained from this office.

Reading Room The National Civil Rights Clearinghouse Library is located in Room 602, 624 Ninth Street NW., Washington, DC 20425. Phone, 202–376–8110.

For further information, contact the Public Affairs Unit, United States Commission on Civil Rights, Room 730, 624 Ninth Street NW., Washington, DC 20425. Phone, 202–376–8312. TTY, 202–376–8116.

UNITED STATES INFORMATION AGENCY

301 Fourth Street SW., Washington, DC 20547
Phone, 202–619–4700. Internet, http://www.usia.gov/.

Director	JOSEPH D. DUFFEY
Chief of Staff	JOYCE KRAVITZ
Deputy Director	PENN KEMBLE
Counselor	HARRIET L. ELAM
Chairman, U.S. Advisory Commission on Public Diplomacy	LEWIS MANILOW
Vice Chairman, U.S. Advisory Commission on Public Diplomacy	WILLIAM HYBL
Director, Office of Civil Rights	HATTIE P. BALDWIN
General Counsel	LES JIN
Director, Office of Congressional and Intergovernmental Affairs	RONNA A. FREIBERG
Director, Office of Public Liaison	MARTHENA COWART
Director, Office of Research and Media Reaction	ANN T. PINCUS
Deputy Director	STEPHEN M. SHAFFER
Associate Director for Broadcasting	KEVIN KLOSE
Director, Voice of America	EVELYN S. LIEBERMAN
Director, Office of Public Affairs	SIDNEY DAVIS
Director, Office of Budget and Planning	(VACANCY)
Director, Office of Affiliate Relations and International Media Training	MYRNA WHITWORTH
Director, Office of Personnel and Administration	EVA JANE FRITZMAN
Director, Office of Policy	STEVE MUNSON
Director, Office of Program Review	FRANK CUMMINS
Director, Office of Engineering and Technical Operations	ROBERT E. KAMOSA
Director, Office of WORLDNET Television and Film Service	JOHN LENNON, *Acting*
Director, Office of Cuba Broadcasting	HERMINIO SAN ROMAN

Director, Radio Marti	ROLANDO BONACHEA
Director, TV Marti	ANTONIO DIEGUEZ
President, Radio Free Europe/Radio Liberty, Inc. (RFE/RL)	(VACANCY)

Broadcasting Board of Governors:

Chairman	DAVID W. BURKE
Members	JOSEPH D. DUFFEY, CHERYL HALPERN, EDWARD E. KAUFMAN, TOM C. KOROLOGOS, BETTE BAO LORD, ALBERTO J. MORA, MARC B. NATHANSON, CARL SPIELVOGEL
Chief of Staff	KATHLEEN HARRINGTON
Director of Evaluation and Analysis	BRIAN T. CONNIFF
Legal Counsel	JOHN A. LINDBURG
Budget Officer	MIKE RINGLER
Program Review Officer	BRUCE SHERMAN
Confidential Assistant	BRENDA THOMAS
Associate Director for Information	(VACANCY)
Deputy Associate Director	MYRON L. HOFFMANN
Director, Geographic Liaison	J. DAVIS HAMELL
Director, Thematic Programs	JUDITH S. SIEGEL
Director, Foreign Press Centers	MARJORIE RANSOM
Director, Support Services	C. ANTHONY JACKSON
Executive Officer	STEPHEN SINCLAIR
Associate Director for Educational and Cultural Affairs	JOHN P. LOIELLO
Deputy Associate Director	ROBERT L. EARLE
Executive Director, Cultural Property Staff	MARIE PAPAGEORGE KOUROUPAS
Staff Director, J. William Fulbright Foreign Scholarship Board	RALPH H. VOGEL
Director, Office of Citizen Exchanges	BRIAN SEXTON
Director, Office of International Visitors	LESLIE A. WILEY
Director, Office of Academic Programs	KEITH GIEGER
Director, Office of Policy and Evaluation	VAN S. WUNDER
Executive Officer	J. DAVID WHITTEN
Associate Director for Management	HENRY HOWARD, JR.
Deputy Associate Director	JOHN BAKER
Director, Office of Administration	EILEEN KEANE BINNS
Director, Office of Technology	DANIEL S. CAMPBELL
Director, Office of Human Resources	JAN BRAMBILLA
Comptroller, Office of the Comptroller	STANLEY M. SILVERMAN
Director, Office of Security	LARRY CARNAHAN, *Acting*
Director, Office of Contracts	EDWARD G. MULLER, *Acting*
Executive Officer	DANIEL D. DUNNING
Director, Office of African Affairs	MARILYN HULBERT
Deputy Director	PATRICK J. CORCORAN
Director, Office of Inter-American Affairs	LINDA JEWELL
Deputy Director	BARBARA MOORE
Director, Office of East Asian and Pacific Affairs	WILLIAM MAURER
Deputy Director	NICHOLAS MELE
Director, Office of West European and Canadian Affairs	C. MILLER CROUCH
Deputy Director	SUSAN ANN CLYDE

Director, Office of East European and NIS Affairs	ROBERT E. MCCARTHY
Deputy Director	PAUL R. SMITH
Director, Office of North African, Near Eastern, and South Asian Affairs	DAVID P. GOOD
Deputy Director	JONATHAN OWEN

[For the United States Information Agency statement of organization, see the *Code of Federal Regulations*, Title 22, Part 504]

The mission of the United States Information Agency is to understand, inform, and influence foreign communities in promotion of the national interest; and to broaden the dialog between Americans, their institutions, and counterparts abroad. In support of that mission, the Agency conducts academic and cultural exchanges, international broadcasting, and a wide variety of informational programs. The Agency is known as the U.S. Information Service overseas.

The legislative mandates of the United States Information Agency (USIA) derive from the United States Information and Educational Exchange Act of 1948 (22 U.S.C. 1431) and the Mutual Educational and Cultural Exchange Act of 1961 (22 U.S.C. 2451). The U.S. Information and Educational Exchange Act's purpose is to increase mutual understanding between the people of the United States and the people of other countries. It prohibits, with certain exceptions approved by Congress, dissemination within the United States of materials produced by the Agency for distribution overseas. It also requires the Agency to make its overseas program materials available for public inspection at its Washington, DC, headquarters. The Mutual Educational and Cultural Exchange Act authorizes educational and cultural exchanges between the United States and other countries, as well as United States participation in international fairs and expositions abroad.

The executive level offices of the Agency are the Office of Public Liaison, Office of the General Counsel, Office of Congressional and Intergovernmental Affairs, Office of Civil Rights, and the Office of Research and Media Reaction.

Activities

The activities of the U.S. Information Agency are based on the premise that government-to-government relations depend on public diplomacy strategies, because they affect individuals and institutions who influence their governments. Increasingly, foreign relations are not simply the prerogative of foreign ministries conducting communications along narrowly defined bureaucratic channels. On this basis, USIA has three established goals:

—increased understanding and acceptance of U.S. policies and U.S. society by foreign audiences;

—broadened dialog between American and U.S. institutions and their counterparts overseas; and

—increased U.S. Government knowledge and understanding of foreign attitudes and their implications for U.S. foreign policy.

To accomplish its goals, the Agency conducts a variety of activities overseas, including educational exchanges, international radio and television broadcasting, distribution of transcripts and official texts of significant U.S. Government policy statements, maintaining information resource centers overseas with online reference capabilities, assisting the mass media in bringing information about U.S. foreign policy to audiences around the world, and facilitating linkages between American and foreign nongovernmental institutions.

Functional Elements

The four major functional elements of the Agency are the International Broadcasting Bureau, the Bureau of Educational and Cultural Affairs, the Bureau of Information, and the Bureau of Management.

UNITED STATES INFORMATION AGENCY

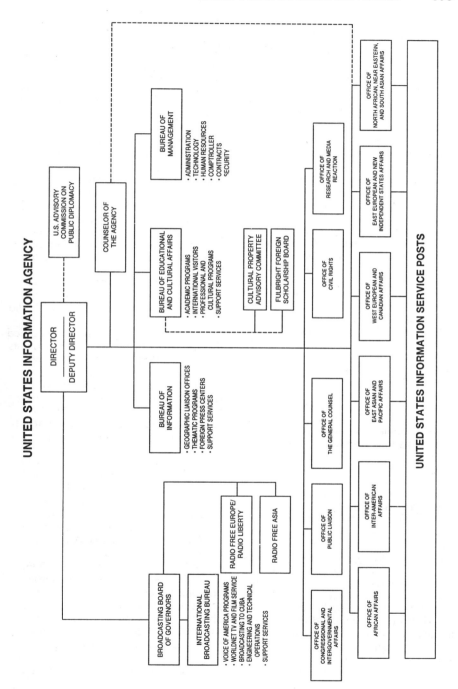

UNITED STATES INFORMATION SERVICE POSTS

International Broadcasting Bureau   The International Broadcasting Bureau (IBB) was established by the United States International Broadcasting Act of 1994. While a part of USIA, IBB receives decisionmaking and operational guidance from the Broadcasting Board of Governors. The Bureau consists of the Voice of America, the Office of Cuba Broadcasting, and WORLDNET Television and Film Service. Two other U.S. Government entities, Radio Free Europe/Radio Liberty and Radio Free Asia, are grantee organizations that receive annual grants of congressionally appropriated funds from the Broadcasting Board of Governors.

The Voice of America (VOA) is the International Broadcasting Bureau's functional element for worldwide radio broadcasting. VOA operates in accordance with the act of January 27, 1948, as amended (22 U.S.C. 1463), which requires that it serve as a consistently reliable, authoritative, accurate, objective, and comprehensive news source. It must present a balanced and comprehensive projection of significant American thought and institutions. VOA produces and broadcasts radio programs in 52 languages, including English, for overseas audiences, and to over 1,100 affiliate stations worldwide. Its programming includes world and regional news, reports from correspondents on the scene, analyses of worldwide events, feature programs, music, and editorials.

The Office of Cuba Broadcasting oversees all programming broadcast for Cuba on Radio Marti and TV Marti programs. In keeping with the principles of the VOA charter, both services offer their audiences accurate and objective news reports and features on American culture and opinion. Radio Marti broadcasts on medium and shortwave frequencies. TV Marti is available on VHF (very high frequency) and international satellite.

The WORLDNET Television and Film Service is responsible for organizing and directing the International Broadcasting Bureau's worldwide television and film activities. The areas of responsibility

encompass: producing programs and interactive press conferences for the WORLDNET satellite delivery system; newsfiles in English, Spanish, French, Arabic, Mandarin, Polish, Serbian, Ukrainian, and Russian; producing and acquiring films and videotapes for direct projection or placement overseas; providing facilitative assistance to visiting foreign television and film producers; operating television news bureaus at foreign press centers; providing assistance to foreign broadcasters in the production and telecast of cooperative television programs; serving as the Bureau's primary point of contact with American motion picture and television industries; and coordinating with other U.S. and foreign government agencies on the dissemination of information overseas through motion pictures and television.

Radio Free Europe/Radio Liberty   Radio Free Europe/Radio Liberty, Inc. (RFE/RL) is a private, nonprofit corporation funded by U.S. Government grants. It broadcasts more than 700 hours weekly of news, analysis, and current affairs in 23 languages to more than 25 million regular listeners in Central Europe and the former Soviet Union. RFE/RL also reaches listeners from U.S. Government-funded shortwave stations in Spain, Portugal, Germany, Thailand, and the Philippines and via satellite to local AM/FM stations including national networks in Ukraine, the Baltic States, Bulgaria, the Czech and Slovak Republics, and Kyrgyzstan. Major AM/FM stations in Russia, the former Yugoslavia, Romania, the Caucasus, and Central Asia also carry RFE/RL programs.

Radio Free Asia   Established in 1996, Radio Free Asia is a private, nonprofit corporation funded by U.S. Government grants. It provides news and commentary about regional events, broadcasting in Mandarin Chinese, Tibetan, Burmese, Korean, Lao, Khmer, and Vietnamese.

Bureau of Information   The Bureau of Information is USIA's primary source of information products for its posts and publics abroad. It is moving into new electronic communications media as fast as technology permits, while maintaining an extensive line of print products, operating a specialized wire service, facilitating the activities of foreign media in the United States, and operating a worldwide speakers bureau on significant issues in foreign affairs.

The Bureau has created an interactive CD–ROM on student counseling and a weekly series of Internet-based electronic journals covering major issues to complement its wide range of electronic media. These products focus on representing enduring American values, particularly individual freedom and equality under the law, and on promoting democratization, market economics, human rights, the rule of law, and the peaceful resolution of disputes.

The Bureau's offices and teams are organized around major themes in public diplomacy, regional concerns and interests, and media specialties. Its products and services are produced in response to requirements set by USIA field posts and U.S. foreign affairs priorities.

The Office of Geographic Liaison serves as the primary point of contact with the field. In addition, it provides comprehensive research and bibliographic assistance and editing and distribution for time-sensitive texts. The Office functions as a regional news service, providing operational support and advice to more than 100 USIS documentation and information resource centers and libraries overseas, and managing regional operations of the Bureau's international wire service, the Washington File. The Office responds to the special needs of each of the Agency's overseas posts.

The Office of Thematic Programs creates information products keyed to themes in American foreign policy that have been identified as vital: Economic Security, Political Security, Democracy and Human Rights, U.S. Society and Values, and Global Issues and Communication. Equally important is the Office's active speakers program, in which physical travel by the Nation's leading experts on identified issues is supplemented by video and audio

conferencing with their counterparts abroad.

Foreign Press Centers have been established in Washington, DC, New York City, and Los Angeles to give foreign journalists visiting or residing in the United States information about U.S. policies and access to policymakers. The Centers are affiliated with a network of locally initiated and funded International Press Centers in Atlanta, Chicago, Houston, Miami, and Seattle.

Bureau of Educational and Cultural Affairs   The Bureau of Educational and Cultural Affairs administers programs authorized by the Mutual Educational and Cultural Exchange Act of 1961 (the Fulbright-Hays Act), including academic exchanges, short-term professional exchanges, youth exchanges, cooperative projects with private organizations, and English-teaching programs. It also provides staff support for the Presidentially appointed J. William Fulbright Foreign Scholarship Board and for the Cultural Property Advisory Committee. The Bureau consists of the following offices:

The Office of Academic Programs develops and coordinates a wide variety of academic educational exchange and English language-teaching programs. It oversees the administration of more than 7,000 grants each year to U.S. citizens to study, teach, and conduct research abroad, and for foreign nationals to conduct similar activities in the United States. The best known of the exchanges supported by this office is the Fulbright Program which operates in more than 120 countries. The Office of Academic Programs maintains a worldwide information network about educational opportunities in the United States, and supports programs which enhance the experiences of foreign students enrolled in U.S. colleges and universities. The Office also encourages and supports U.S.-based studies at foreign universities and other institutions of higher learning. Worldwide support for English language training is provided through overseas-based language consultants, development of English language teaching materials, and a variety of teacher training seminars and fellowships.

The Office of International Visitors arranges informative visits to the United States for almost 5,000 influential foreign leaders each year in such fields as government, economics, labor, journalism, the arts, and education. Selected individuals, who are nominated by United States Information Service posts, travel throughout the country meeting counterparts in their fields of interest. They also meet with Americans in their homes or other informal settings. The Office also manages the Agency's New York reception center; serves as the Agency's liaison with the large network of public and private organizations involved in the international visitor program; and arranges programs in the United States for United Nations fellows and foreign government trainees.

The Office of Citizen Exchanges provides funding to American nonprofit institutions for international exchange and training programs which support agency goals and objectives. Nonprofit institutions may submit proposals only in response to requests for proposals (RFP's) published by the Office, and these proposals are judged among others in the competition. Programs usually involve professional, nonacademic exchanges—often with study tours, workshops, and internships as key components, and taking place in multiple phases overseas and in the United States. Emphasis is usually on nontechnical themes such as democracy-building, journalism, the role of government, or conflict resolution. The Office also administers all high school exchange programs sponsored by USIA, including major special initiatives in East Europe and the former Soviet Union, and the Congress-Bundestag program with Germany.

In addition, the Office identifies and recruits specialists in the fields of literature, film, and the visual and performing arts to speak at or work with host country institutions in their fields of expertise. The Office awards grants to American nonprofit institutions involved in the international exchange of performing and visual artists and encourages linkages between U.S. and foreign cultural institutions. The Office also represents the Agency in the Fund for U.S. Artists at International Festivals and Exhibitions.

The Office of Policy and Evaluation provides policy analysis, coordination, and evaluation of the activities and programs of the Bureau of Educational and Cultural Affairs. The Office also analyzes U.S. Government-funded international exchanges and training programs with the objective of promoting better coordination among government agencies. The Office is responsible for advising the Associate Director on conceptual approaches to the Bureau's activities and on the development and implementation of its policies. It coordinates activities with the Bureau to ensure consistency of approach; evaluates the success, strengths, and weaknesses of programs; and provides staff support to the Cultural Property Advisory Committee, which advises the Director on U.S. efforts to curb illicit trade in artifacts.

Under Executive Order 13055, the Associate Director for Educational and Cultural Affairs chairs a senior-level Interagency Working Group on United States Government-Sponsored International Exchanges and Training. The Bureau provides staff support for the working group, which is responsible for ensuring that the U.S. Government's international exchanges and training activities are consistent with U.S. foreign policy and avoid duplication of effort.

Overseas Posts

Principally an overseas agency, USIA's work is carried out by its foreign service officers and staff assigned to American missions abroad. Overseas posts engage in political advocacy of American foreign policy objectives and conduct cultural and educational exchanges and informational activities in support of those objectives. The Agency maintains 192 posts in 141 countries.

Sources of Information

Administrative Regulations   Inquiries regarding administrative staff manuals and instructions to staff affecting members of the public that were issued, adopted, or promulgated on or after July 5, 1967, should be directed to the Directives, Management Staff, United States Information Agency, Washington, DC 20547. Phone, 202–619–5680.
Contracts   Contact the Office of Contracts, United States Information Agency, Washington, DC 20547. Phone, 202–205–5498.

Employment   For information concerning employment opportunities, contact the Office of Human Resources, Civil Service Division, United States Information Agency, Washington, DC 20547. Phone, 202–619–4659. For Voice of America and WORLDNET Television and Film Service employment information, contact the Office of Personnel, International Broadcasting Bureau, United States Information Agency, Washington, DC 20547. Phone, 202–619–3117. For Office of Cuba Broadcasting employment information, contact the Office of Personnel, Office of Cuba Broadcasting, United States Information Agency, Washington, DC 20547. Phone, 202–401–7114.
International Audiovisual Programs   For information concerning a certification program under international agreement to facilitate the export and import of qualified visual and auditory materials of an educational, scientific, and cultural character, contact the Chief Attestation Officer of the United States, United States Information Agency, Washington, DC 20547. Phone, 202–401–9810.

For further information, contact the Office of Public Liaison, United States Information Agency, Washington, DC 20547. Phone, 202–619–4355. Internet, http://www.usia.gov/.

UNITED STATES INTERNATIONAL DEVELOPMENT COOPERATION AGENCY

1300 Pennsylvania Avenue NW., Washington, DC 20523–0001
Phone, 202–712–0000

Director, U.S. International Development Cooperation Agency	J. BRIAN ATWOOD, *Acting*
Deputy Director	(VACANCY)

AGENCY FOR INTERNATIONAL DEVELOPMENT

1300 Pennsylvania Avenue NW., Washington, DC 20523–0001
Phone, 202–712–0000. Internet, http://www.info.usaid.gov/.

Administrator	J. BRIAN ATWOOD
Deputy Administrator	HARRIET C. BABBITT
Counselor	KELLY C. KAMMERER
Chief of Staff	RICHARD L. MCCALL, JR.
Executive Secretary	RYAN CONROY

Assistant to the Administrator, Bureau for Policy and Program Coordination	THOMAS H. FOX
Assistant Administrator for Management	TERRENCE J. BROWN
Assistant Administrator for Africa	CAROL PEASLEY, *Acting*
Assistant Administrator for Asia and the Near East	KELLY C. KAMMERER, *Acting*
Assistant Administrator for Europe and the New Independent States	DONALD L. PRESSLEY, *Acting*
Assistant Administrator for Latin America and the Caribbean	MARK SCHNEIDER
Assistant Administrator for Humanitarian Response	LEONARD M. ROGERS, *Acting*
Assistant Administrator for Global Programs, Field Support, and Research	SALLY SHELTON
Assistant Administrator for Legislative and Public Affairs	JILL BUCKLEY
Director, Office of Small and Disadvantaged Business Utilization/Minority Resource Center	IVAN R. ASHLEY
Director, Office of Equal Opportunity Programs	JESSALYN L. PENDARVIS
General Counsel	SINGLETON B. MCALLISTER
Inspector General	JEFFREY RUSH, JR.

[For the Agency for International Development statement of organization, see the *Federal Register* of Aug. 26, 1987, 52 FR 32174]

OVERSEAS PRIVATE INVESTMENT CORPORATION

1100 New York Avenue NW., Washington, DC 20527
Phone, 202–336–8400. Fax, 202–408–9859. Internet, http://www.opic.gov/.

President and Chief Executive Officer	GEORGE MUÑOZ
Executive Vice President	KIRK ROBERTSON
Vice President, Investment Development	ROBERT L. SCHIFFER
Vice President and General Counsel	CHARLES D. TOY
Vice President and Treasurer	MILDRED O. CALLEAR
Vice President, Finance	FRANK L. LANGHAMMER
Vice President, Insurance	JULIE A. MARTIN
Vice President, Investment Funds	ROBERT D. STILLMAN
Managing Director for Administration	MICHAEL C. CUSHING
Chairman of the Board	J. BRIAN ATWOOD

[For the Overseas Private Investment Corporation statement of organization, see the *Code of Federal Regulations*, Title 22, Chapter VII]

The United States International Development Cooperation Agency (IDCA) was established by Reorganization Plan No. 2 of 1979 (5 U.S.C. app., effective October 1, 1979) to be a focal point within the U.S. Government for economic matters affecting U.S. relations with developing countries. The Agency's functions are policy planning, policymaking, and policy coordination on international economic issues affecting developing countries. The Director of the Agency serves as the principal international development adviser to the President and the Secretary of State, receiving foreign policy guidance from the Secretary of State. The U.S. Agency for International Development and the Overseas Private Investment Corporation are component agencies of the U.S. International Development Cooperation Agency.

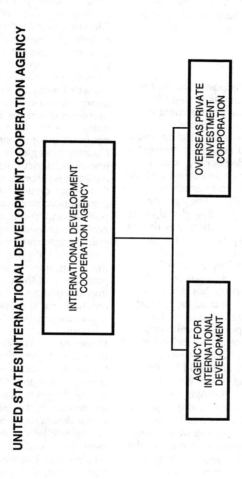

UNITED STATES INTERNATIONAL DEVELOPMENT COOPERATION AGENCY

INTERNATIONAL DEVELOPMENT COOPERATION AGENCY

AGENCY FOR INTERNATIONAL DEVELOPMENT

OVERSEAS PRIVATE INVESTMENT CORPORATION

Agency for International Development

The U.S. Agency for International Development (USAID) administers U.S. foreign economic and humanitarian assistance programs worldwide in the developing world, Central and Eastern Europe, and the New Independent States of the former Soviet Union. The Agency functions under an Administrator, who concurrently serves as the Acting Director of IDCA.

Programs

The Agency meets its post-Cold War era challenges by utilizing its strategy for achieving sustainable development in developing countries. It supports programs in four areas: population and health, broad-based economic growth, environment, and democracy. It also provides humanitarian assistance and aid to countries in crisis and transition.

Population and Health The Agency contributes to a cooperative global effort to stabilize world population growth and support women's reproductive rights. The types of population and health programs supported vary with the particular needs of individual countries and the kinds of approaches that local communities initiate and support. Most USAID resources are directed to the following areas: support for voluntary family planning systems, reproductive health care, needs of adolescents and young adults, infant and child health, and education for girls and women.

Economic Growth The Agency promotes broad-based economic growth by addressing the factors that enhance the capacity for growth and by working to remove the obstacles that stand in the way of individual opportunity. In this context, programs concentrate on strengthening market economies, expanding economic opportunities for the less advantaged in developing countries, and building human skills and capacities to facilitate broad-based participation.

Environment The Agency's environmental programs support two strategic goals: reducing long-term threats to the global environment, particularly loss of biodiversity and climate change; and promoting sustainable economic growth locally, nationally, and regionally by addressing environmental, economic, and developmental practices that impede development and are unsustainable. Globally, Agency programs focus on reducing sources and enhancing sinks of greenhouse gas emissions and on promoting innovative approaches to the conservation and sustainable use of the planet's biological diversity. The approach to national environmental problems differs on a country-by-country basis, depending on a particular country's environmental priorities. Country strategies may include improving agricultural, industrial, and natural resource management practices that play a central role in environmental degradation; strengthening public policies and institutions to protect the environment; holding dialogs with country governments on environmental issues and with international agencies on the environmental impact of lending practices and the design and implementation of innovative mechanisms to support environmental work; and environmental research and education.

Democracy The Agency's strategic objective in the democracy area is the transition to and consolidation of democratic regimes throughout the world. Programs focus on such problems as: human rights abuses; misperceptions about democracy and free-market capitalism; lack of experience with democratic institutions; the absence or weakness of intermediary organizations; nonexistent, ineffectual, or undemocratic political parties; disenfranchisement of women, indigenous peoples, and minorities; failure to implement national charter documents; powerless or poorly defined democratic institutions; tainted elections; and the inability to resolve conflicts peacefully.

Humanitarian Assistance and Post-Crisis Transitions The Agency provides

AGENCY FOR INTERNATIONAL DEVELOPMENT

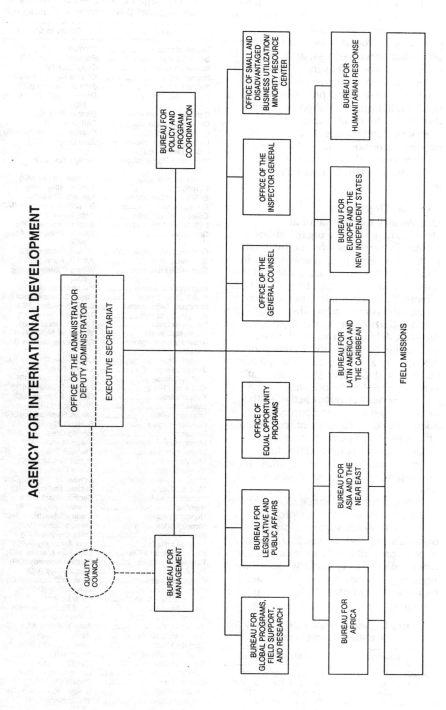

humanitarian assistance that saves lives, reduces suffering, helps victims return to self-sufficiency, and reinforces democracy. Programs focus on disaster prevention, preparedness, and mitigation; timely delivery of disaster relief and short-term rehabilitation supplies and services; preservation of basic institutions of civil governance during disaster crisis; support for democratic institutions during periods of national transition; and building and reinforcement of local capacity to anticipate and handle disasters and their aftermath.

Overseas Organizations

U.S. Agency for International Development country organizations are located in countries where a bilateral program is being implemented. The in-country organizations are subject to the direction and guidance of the chief U.S. diplomatic representative in the country, usually the Ambassador. The organizations report to the Agency's Assistant Administrators for the four geographic bureaus—the Bureaus for Africa, Asia and Near East, Europe and the New Independent States, and Latin America and the Caribbean.

The overseas program activities that involve more than one country are administered by regional offices. These offices may also perform country organizational responsibilities for assigned countries. Generally, the offices are headed by a regional development officer.

Development Assistance Coordination and Representative Offices provide liaison with various international organizations and represent U.S. interests in development assistance matters. Such offices may be only partially staffed by Agency personnel and may be headed by employees of other U.S. Government agencies.

Country Organizations—U.S. Agency for International Development

Country	Officer in Charge[1]
Albania/Tirana	Dianne M. Blane (OR)
Angola/Luanda	James M. Anderson (CO)
Armenia/Yerevan	Geraldine Donnelly (OR)
Bangladesh/Dhaka	Richard Brown (MD)

Country Organizations—U.S. Agency for International Development—Continued

Country	Officer in Charge[1]
Benin/Cotonou	Thomas E. Park (OR)
Bolivia/La Paz	Frank Almaguer (MD)
Bosnia/Sarajevo	Craig Buck (MD)
Brazil/Brasilia	Edward Kadunc (OR)
Bulgaria/Sofia	John A. Tennant (OR)
Burundi/Bujumbura	Donald MacKenzie, *Acting* (MD)
Cambodia/Phnom Penh	Gordon West (OR)
Colombia/Bogota	Carl Cira (OR)
Croatia/Zagreb	Charles R. Aaneson (OR)
Democratic Republic of the Congo/Kinshasa.	John Grayzel (MD)
Dominican Republic/Santo Domingo.	Marilyn Zak (MD)
Ecuador/Quito	Thomas Geiger (MD)
Egypt/Cairo	John Westley (MD)
El Salvador/San Salvador	Kenneth Ellis (MD)
Eritrea/Asmara	G. William Anderson (MD)
Ethiopia/Addis Ababa	Keith Brown (MD)
FYR Macedonia/Skopje	Stephen Haynes (OR)
Ghana/Accra	Thomas Hobgood, *Acting* (MD)
Guatemala/Guatemala City	William Rhodes (MD)
Guinea/Conakry	John B. Flynn (MD)
Guinea-Bissau/Bissau	Willard Pearson, *Acting* (OR)
Guyana/Georgetown	Pat McDuffie (MD)
Haiti/Port-au-Prince	Phyllis Dichter-Forbes (MD)
Honduras/Tegucigalpa	Elena Brineman (MD)
Hungary/Budapest	Thomas Cornell (OR)
India/New Delhi	Linda E. Morse (MD)
Indonesia/Jakarta	Vivikka M. Molldrem (MD)
Israel/Jerusalem (West Bank).	Christopher Crowley (MD)
Israel/Tel Aviv (Gaza)	Christopher Crowley (MD)
Jamaica/Kingston	Carole Tyson (MD)
Jordan/Amman	Lewis W. Lucke (MD)
Kazakstan/Almaty	Patricia Buckles (MD)
Kenya/Nairobi	George E. Jones (MD)
Latvia/Riga	(Vacancy) (OR)
Lebanon/Beirut	James Stephenson (OR)
Liberia/Monrovia	Rudolph Thomas (OR)
Lithuania/Vilnius	Ronald Greenberg (OR)
Madagascar/Antananarivo	Karen M. Poe (MD)
Malawi/Lilongwe	Kiertisak Toh (MD)
Mali/Bamako	James Hradsky (MD)
Mexico/Mexico City	Arthur Danart (OR)
Mongolia/Ulaanbaatar	Edward W. Birgells (OR)
Morocco/Rabat	Michael Farbman (MD)
Mozambique/Maputo	Cynthia Rozell (MD)
Namibia/Windhoeck	Edward Spriggs (OR)
Nepal/Kathmandu	Frederick Machmer (MD)
Nicaragua/Managua	George Carner (MD)
Niger/Niamey	Linda Gregory (MD)
Nigeria/Lagos	Felix Awantang (AAO)
Panama/Panama City	Lawrence Klassen (MD)
Paraguay/Asuncion	Barbara Kennedy (OR)
Peru/Lima	Donald Boyd (MD)
Philippines/Manila	Kenneth Schofield (MD)
Poland/Warsaw	William Frej (OR)
Romania/Bucharest	Peter Lapera (OR)
Russia/Moscow	Janet Ballantyne (MD)
Rwanda/Kigali	George Lewis (MD)
Senegal/Dakar	Anne Williams (MD)
Slovakia/Bratislava	Paula Goddard (OR)
Somalia/Mogadishu	John H. Bierke (MD)
South Africa/Pretoria	Aaron Williams (MD)
Sri Lanka/Colombo	Lisa Chiles (MD)
Tanzania/Dar es Salaam	Lucretia Taylor (MD)
Uganda/Kampala	Donald Clark (MD)
Ukraine/Kiev	Gregory F. Huger (MD)
Zambia/Lusaka	Walter North (MD)

Country Organizations—U.S. Agency for International Development—Continued

Country	Officer in Charge[1]
Zimbabwe/Harare	Rose Marie Depp (MD)

[1] MD: Mission Director; D: Director; OR: Office of the AID Representative; DO: Development Officer; RD: Regional Director; AAO: AID Affairs Officer for Section of Embassy; CO: Coordinator in Washington

International Organizations—Agency for International Development
(Selected Regional Organizations)
(A: Adviser; C: Counselor; D: Director; ED: Executive Director; MD: Mission Director; AID R: AID Representative; RD: Regional Director)

Office	Officer in Charge
Regional Offices	
Regional Center for Southern Africa—Gaborone, Botswana	Valerie Dickson-Horton (RD)
Regional Economic Development Services Offices.	
Office for East and Southern Africa—Nairobi, Kenya	Donald R. MacKenzie (RD)
Office for West and Central Africa—Cote d'Ivoire, Abidjan	Williard Pearson (RD)
Regional Support Center—Budapest, Hungary	Patricia Lerner (RD)
Development Assistance Coordination and Representation Offices	
U.S. Mission to the United Nations Agencies for Food and Agriculture—Rome, Italy	William Baucom (ED)
Office for Humanitarian Assistance, World Food Program Affairs—Rome, Italy	Douglas Sheldon (D)
Office of the U.S. Representative to the Development Assistance Committee of the Organization for Economic Cooperation and Development—Paris, France.	James H. Michel (AID R)
U.S. Mission to the European Office of the United Nations and Other International Organizations—Geneva, Switzerland.	Nance Kyloh (AID R)
AID Office for Development Cooperation—Tokyo, Japan	Paul White (C)
Office of AID Coordination Representative—Brussels, Belgium	Laurier Mailloux (C)

Overseas Private Investment Corporation

The Overseas Private Investment Corporation (OPIC) is a self-sustaining Federal agency whose purpose is to promote economic growth in developing countries by encouraging U.S. private investment in those nations. The Corporation assists American investors in four principal ways: financing of businesses through loans and loan guaranties; supporting private investment funds which provide equity for U.S. companies investing in projects overseas; insuring investments against a broad range of political risks; and engaging in outreach activities. All of these programs are designed to reduce the perceived stumbling blocks and risks associated with overseas investment.

Organized as a corporation and structured to be responsive to private business, OPIC is mandated to mobilize and facilitate the participation of U.S. private capital and skills in the economic and social development of developing

countries and emerging economies. Currently, OPIC programs are available for new business enterprises or expansion in some 140 countries worldwide. The Corporation encourages American overseas private investment in sound business projects, thereby improving U.S. global competitiveness, creating American jobs, and increasing U.S. exports. The Corporation does not support projects that will result in the loss of domestic jobs or have a negative impact on the host country's environment or workers' rights.

The Corporation is governed by a 15-member Board of Directors, of whom 8 are appointed from the private sector and 7 from the Federal Government.

Activities

By reducing or eliminating certain perceived political risks for investors and providing financing and assistance not otherwise available, the Corporation helps to reduce the unusual risks and problems that can make investment opportunities in the developing areas less attractive than in advanced countries. At the same time, it reduces the need for government-to-government lending programs by involving the U.S. private sector in establishing capital-generation and strengthening private-sector economies in developing countries.

The Corporation insures U.S. investors against the political risks of expropriation, inconvertibility of local currency holdings, and damage from war, revolution, insurrection, or civil strife. It also offers a special insurance policy to U.S. contractors and exporters against arbitrary drawings of letters of credit posted as bid, performance, or advance payment guaranties. Other special programs are offered for minerals exploration, oil and gas exploration, and development and leasing operations.

The Corporation offers U.S. lenders protection against both commercial and political risks by guaranteeing payment of principal and interest on loans (up to $200 million) made to eligible private enterprises.

Its Direct Investment loans, offered to small and medium-sized businesses, generally cover terms of from 5 to 15 years and usually range from $2 million to $30 million with varying interest rates, depending on assessment of the commercial risks of the project financed.

Additionally, OPIC supports a family of privately managed direct investment funds in various regions and business sectors. Such funds currently operate in most countries in East Asia, sub-Saharan African, South America, Russia and other New Independent States, Poland and other countries in Central Europe, India, and Israel.

Programs are available only for a new facility, expansion or modernization of an existing plant, or technological or service products designed to generate investment which will produce significant new benefits for host countries.

Sources of Information

U.S. International Development Cooperation Agency

General Inquiries Inquiries may be directed to the Bureau for Legislative and Public Affairs, U.S. International Development Cooperation Agency, Washington, DC 20523–0001. Phone, 202–712–4810. Fax, 202–216–3524.

Agency for International Development

Congressional Affairs Congressional inquiries may be directed to the Bureau for Legislative and Public Affairs, Agency for International Development, Washington, DC 20523–0001. Phone, 202–712–4810.

Contracting and Small Business Inquiries For information regarding contracting opportunities, contact the Office of Small and Disadvantaged Business Utilization, Agency for International Development,

Washington, DC 20523–0001. Phone, 202–712–1500. Fax, 202–216–3056.

Employment For information regarding employment opportunities, contact the Workforce Planning, Recruitment and Personnel Systems Division, Office of Human Resources, Agency for International Development, Washington, DC 20523–0001. Internet, http://www.info.usaid.gov/.

General Inquiries General inquiries may be directed to the Bureau for Legislative and Public Affairs, Agency for International Development, Washington, DC 20523–0001. Phone, 202–712–4810. Fax, 202–216–3524.

News Media Inquiries from the media only should be directed to the Press Relations Division, Bureau for Legislative and Public Affairs, Agency for International Development, Washington,

DC 20523–0001. Phone, 202–712–4320.

Overseas Private Investment Corporation

General Inquiries Inquiries should be directed to the Information Office, Overseas Private Investment Corporation, 1100 New York Avenue NW.,

Washington, DC 20527. Phone, 202–336–8799. Fax, 202–336–8700. E-mail, OPIC@opic.gov. Internet, http://www.opic.gov/.

Publications OPIC programs are further detailed in the *Annual Report* and the *Program Summary*. These publications are available free of charge.

For further information, contact the United States International Development Cooperation Agency, 1300 Pennsylvania Avenue NW., Washington, DC 20523–0001. Phone, 202–712–0000. Internet, http://www.info.usaid.gov/.

UNITED STATES INTERNATIONAL TRADE COMMISSION

500 E Street SW., Washington, DC 20436
Phone, 202–205–2000. Internet, http://www.usitc.gov/.

Chairman	MARCIA E. MILLER
Vice Chairman	LYNN M. BRAGG
Commissioners	CAROL T. CRAWFORD,
	(3 VACANCIES)
General Counsel	LYN M. SCHLITT
Director, Office of External Relations	DANIEL F. LEAHY
Congressional Relations Officer	NANCY M. CARMAN
Public Affairs Officer	MARGARET M. O'LAUGHLIN
Trade Remedy Assistance Officer	ELIZABETH SELTZER
Administrative Law Judges	SIDNEY HARRIS, PAUL J. LUCKERN
Secretary	DONNA R. KOEHNKE
Inspector General	JANE ALTENHOFEN
Director, Office of Operations	ROBERT ROGOWSKY
Director, Office of Investigations	LYNN FEATHERSTONE
Director, Office of Economics	ROBERT ROGOWSKY, *Acting*
Director, Office of Industries	M. VERN SIMPSON, JR.
Division Chief, Agriculture and Forest Products	CATHY L. JABARA
Division Chief, Minerals, Metals, Machinery, and Miscellaneous Manufactures	LARRY L. BROOKHART
Division Chief, Energy, Chemicals, and Textiles	JOHN J. GERSIC
Division Chief, Electronics and Transportation	NORMAN MCLENNAN
Division Chief, Services and Investment	RICHARD BROWN
Director, Office of Tariff Affairs and Trade Agreements	EUGENE A. ROSENGARDEN
Director, Office of Unfair Import Investigations	LYNN LEVINE
Director, Office of Information Services	MARTIN SMITH
Director, Office of Equal Employment Opportunity	JACQUELINE A. WATERS
Director, Office of Administration	STEPHEN MCLAUGHLIN

The United States International Trade Commission furnishes studies, reports, and recommendations involving international trade and tariffs to the President, the U.S. Trade Representative, and congressional committees. The Commission also conducts a variety of investigations pertaining to international trade relief.

The United States International Trade Commission is an independent agency created by act of September 8, 1916 (39 Stat. 795), and originally named the United States Tariff Commission. The name was changed to the United States International Trade Commission by section 171 of the Trade Act of 1974 (19 U.S.C. 2231). The Commission's present powers and duties are provided for largely by the Tariff Act of 1930; the Agricultural Adjustment Act; the Trade Expansion Act of 1962; the Trade Act of 1974; the Trade Agreements Act of 1979; the Omnibus Trade and Competitiveness Act of 1988; the North American Free Trade Agreement Implementation Act; and the Uruguay Round Agreements Act.

Six Commissioners are appointed by the President with the advice and consent of the Senate for 9-year terms, unless appointed to fill an unexpired term. The Chairman and Vice Chairman are designated by the President for 2-year terms, and succeeding Chairmen may not be of the same political party. The Chairman generally is responsible for the administration of the Commission. Not more than three Commissioners may be members of the same political party (19 U.S.C. 1330).

Activities

The Commission performs a number of functions pursuant to the statutes referred to above. Under the Tariff Act of 1930, the Commission is given broad powers of investigation relating to the customs laws of the United States and foreign countries; the volume of importation in comparison with domestic production and consumption; the conditions, causes, and effects relating to competition of foreign industries with those of the United States; and all other factors affecting competition between articles of the United States and imported articles. The Commission is required to make available to the President and to the Committee on Ways and Means of the House of Representatives and to the Committee on Finance of the Senate, whenever requested, all information at its command and is directed to make such investigations and reports as may be requested by the President or by either of said committees or by either branch of the Congress. The Omnibus Trade and Competitiveness Act of 1988 amended several of the statutes administered by the Commission and, in addition, required the Commission to conduct several industry competitiveness investigations.

In order to carry out these responsibilities, the Commission is required to engage in extensive research, conduct specialized studies, and maintain a high degree of expertise in all matters relating to the commercial and international trade policies of the United States.

Imported Articles Subsidized or Sold at Less Than Fair Value   The Commission conducts preliminary-phase investigations under the Tariff Act of 1930 to determine whether there is reasonable indication of material injury to, threat of material injury to, or material retardation of the establishment of an industry in the United States by reason of imports of foreign merchandise allegedly being subsidized or sold at less than fair value (19 U.S.C. 1671, 1673, 1675). If the Commission's determination is affirmative, and the Secretary of Commerce further determines that the foreign merchandise is being subsidized or is being, or is likely to be, sold at less than its fair value, or there is reason to believe or suspect such unfair practices are occurring, then the Commission conducts final-phase investigations to determine whether a U.S. industry is materially injured or threatened with material injury, or its establishment is

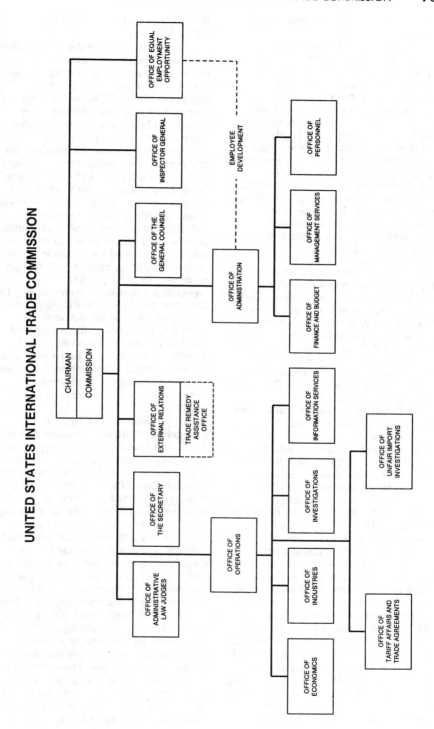

UNITED STATES INTERNATIONAL TRADE COMMISSION

materially retarded by reason of such imports.

If the Secretary of Commerce determines to suspend an investigation upon acceptance of an agreement to eliminate the injurious effect of subsidized imports or imports sold at less than fair value, the Commission may conduct an investigation to determine whether the injurious effect of imports of the merchandise that was the subject of the suspended investigation is eliminated completely by the agreement. The Commission also conducts investigations to determine whether in light of changed circumstances such a suspension agreement continues to eliminate completely the injurious effect of imports of the merchandise.

The Commission conducts investigations to determine whether changed circumstances exist that indicate that an industry in the United States would not be threatened with material injury, or the establishment of such an industry would not be materially retarded, if the countervailing duty order or antidumping order resulting from affirmative final determinations by the Commission and Secretary of Commerce were modified or revoked.

Unfair Practices in Import Trade   The Commission applies U.S. statutory and common law of unfair competition to the importation of products into the United States and their sale (19 U.S.C. 1337). The statute declares unlawful unfair methods of competition and unfair acts in the importation or sale of products in the United States, the threat or effect of which is to destroy or substantially injure a domestic industry, prevent the establishment of such an industry, or restrain or monopolize trade and commerce in the United States. The statute also declares as unlawful per se infringement of a valid and enforceable U.S. patent, copyright, registered trademark, or maskwork; no resulting injury need be found. If the Commission determines that there is a violation of the statute, it is to direct that the articles involved be excluded from entry into the United States, or it may issue cease-and-desist orders directing the person engaged in such violation to cease and desist from engaging in such unfair methods or acts.

Provision is made for the Commission to make certain public interest determinations that could result in the withholding of an exclusion or cease-and-desist order. ITC remedial orders in section 337 cases are effective when issued and become final 60 days after issuance unless disapproved for policy reasons by the President within that 60-day period. Commission determinations of violation are subject to court review.

Trade Negotiations   The Commission advises the President as to the probable economic effect on the domestic industry and consumers of modification of duties and other barriers to trade that may be considered for inclusion in any proposed trade agreement with foreign countries (19 U.S.C. 2151).

Generalized System of Preferences   The Commission advises the President with respect to every article that may be considered for preferential removal of the duty on imports from designated developing countries as to the probable economic effect the preferential removal of duty will have on the domestic industry and on consumers (19 U.S.C. 2151, 2163).

Industry Adjustment to Import Competition (Global Safeguard Actions)   The Commission conducts investigations upon petition on behalf of an industry, a firm, a group of workers, or other entity representative of an industry to determine whether an article is being imported in such increased quantities as to be a substantial cause of serious injury or threat thereof to the domestic industry producing an article like or directly competitive with the imported article (19 U.S.C. 2251–2254). If the Commission's finding is affirmative, it recommends to the President the action that would address such injury and be most effective in facilitating positive adjustment by the industry to import competition. The President has discretion to take action that could be in the form of an increase in duties, imposition of a quota, negotiation of orderly marketing agreements, or provision of adjustment assistance to groups of workers, firms, or communities. If the President does not provide relief or does not provide relief in the form recommended by the Commission, Congress may, by means of a joint resolution disapproving the action of the President, direct the President to provide the relief recommended by the Commission (19 U.S.C. 2251–2254).

The Commission reports with respect to developments within an industry that has been granted import relief and advises the President of the probable economic effect of the reduction or elimination of the tariff increase that has been granted. The President may continue, modify, or terminate the import relief previously granted.

Imports From NAFTA Countries (Bilateral Safeguard Actions) The Commission conducts investigations to determine whether, as a result of the reduction or elimination of a duty provided for under the North American Free Trade Agreement (NAFTA), a Canadian article or a Mexican article, as the case may be, is being imported into the United States in such increased quantities and under such conditions so that imports of the article constitute a substantial cause of serious injury or (except in the case of a Canadian article) a threat of serious injury to the domestic industry producing an article that is like or directly competitive with the imported article (19 U.S.C. 3351–3356). If the Commission's determination is in the affirmative, the Commission recommends to the President the relief which is necessary to prevent or remedy serious injury. Such relief generally would take the form of the suspension of any further reduction in the rate of duty for such article from the subject country provided for in NAFTA, or an increase in the rate of duty on such article from such country to the lesser of the general column 1 rate of duty on such article or the column 1 rate of duty in effect immediately prior to the entry into force of NAFTA. Commission investigations under these provisions are similar procedurally to those conducted under the global safeguard action provisions.

Market Disruption From Communist Countries The Commission conducts investigations to determine whether increased imports of an article produced in a Communist country are causing market disruption in the United States (19 U.S.C. 2436). If the Commission's determination is in the affirmative, the President may take the same action as in the case of serious injury to an industry, except that the action would apply only to imports of the article from the Communist country. Commission investigations conducted under this provision are similar procedurally to those conducted under the global safeguard action provisions.

Import Interference With Agricultural Programs The Commission conducts investigations at the direction of the President to determine whether any articles are being or are practically certain to be imported into the United States under such conditions and in such quantities as to render or tend to render ineffective, or to materially interfere with, programs of the Department of Agriculture for agricultural commodities or products thereof, or to reduce substantially the amount of any product processed in the United States from such commodities or products, and makes findings and recommendations (7 U.S.C. 624). The President may restrict the imports in question by imposition of either import fees or quotas. Such fees or quotas may be applied only against countries that are not members of the World Trade Organization.

Uniform Statistical Data The Commission, in cooperation with the Secretary of the Treasury and the Secretary of Commerce, establishes for statistical purposes an enumeration of articles imported into the United States and exported from the United States, and seeks to establish comparability of such statistics with statistical programs for domestic production (19 U.S.C. 1484).

In conjunction with such activities, the three agencies are to develop concepts for an international commodity code for reporting transactions in international trade and to report thereon to the Congress (19 U.S.C. 1484).

Harmonized Tariff Schedule of the United States, Annotated The

Commission issues a publication containing the U.S. tariff schedules and related matters and considers questions concerning the arrangement of such schedules and the classification of articles (19 U.S.C. note prec. 1202, 1484).

International Trade Studies The Commission conducts studies, investigations, and research projects on a broad range of topics relating to international trade, pursuant to requests of the President, the House Ways and Means Committee, the Senate Finance Committee, either branch of the Congress, or on its own motion (19 U.S.C. 1332). Public reports of these studies, investigations, and research projects are issued in most cases.

The Commission also keeps informed of the operation and effect of provisions relating to duties or other import restrictions of the United States contained in various trade agreements (19 U.S.C. 2482). Occasionally the Commission is required by statute to perform specific trade-related studies.

Industry and Trade Summaries The Commission prepares and publishes, from time to time, a series of summaries of trade and tariff information (19 U.S.C. 1332). These summaries contain descriptions (in terms of the Harmonized Tariff Schedule of the United States) of the thousands of products imported into the United States, methods of production, and the extent and relative importance of U.S. consumption, production, and trade, together with certain basic factors affecting the competitive position and economic health of domestic industries.

Sources of Information

Inquiries should be directed to the specific organizational unit or to the Secretary, United States International Trade Commission, 500 E Street SW., Washington, DC 20436. Phone, 202–205–2000.

Contracts The Chief, Planning and Procurement Division, has responsibility for contract matters. Phone, 202–205–2730.

Electronic Access Commission publications, news releases, *Federal Register* notices, scheduling information, and general information about ITC are available for electronic access. Internet, http://www.usitc.gov/. File transfer protocol, ftp://ftp.usitc.gov/.

Employment Information on employment can be obtained from the Director, Office of Personnel. The agency employs international economists, attorneys, accountants, commodity and industry specialists and analysts, and clerical and other support personnel. Phone, 202–205–2651.

Publications The Commission publishes results of investigations concerning various commodities and subjects. Other publications include *Industry and Trade Summaries,* an annual report to the Congress on the operation of the trade agreements program; and an annual report to the Congress of Commission activities. Specific information regarding these publications can be obtained from the Office of the Secretary.

Reading Rooms Reading rooms are open to the public in the Office of the Secretary and in the ITC National Library of International Trade and the ITC law library.

For further information, contact the Secretary, United States International Trade Commission, 500 E Street SW., Washington, DC 20436. Phone, 202–205–2000. Internet, http://www.usitc.gov/.

UNITED STATES POSTAL SERVICE

475 L'Enfant Plaza SW., Washington, DC 20260–0010
Phone, 202–268–2000. Internet, http://www.usps.gov/.

Board of Governors:
Chairman of the Board   SAM WINTERS

Vice Chairman of the Board	EINAR V. DYHRKOPP
Secretary of the Board	THOMAS J. KOERBER
Inspector General	KARLA WOLFE CORCORAN
Governors	ERNESTA BALLARD, LEGREE S. DANIELS, TIRSO DEL JUNCO, S. DAVID FINEMAN, BERT H. MACKIE, NED R. MCWHERTER, ROBERT F. RIDER
Postmaster General and Chief Executive Officer	WILLIAM J. HENDERSON
Deputy Postmaster General	MICHAEL S. COUGHLIN

Management:

Postmaster General and Chief Executive Officer	WILLIAM J. HENDERSON
Deputy Postmaster General	MICHAEL S. COUGHLIN
Chief Operating Officer and Executive Vice President	CLARENCE E. LEWIS, JR.
Chief Financial Officer and Senior Vice President	M. RICHARD PORRAS
Chief Marketing Officer and Senior Vice President	ALLEN R. KANE
Senior Vice President and General Counsel	MARY S. ELCANO
Senior Vice President, Government Relations	DEBORAH K. WILLHITE
Senior Vice President, Labor Relations	JOHN E. POTTER
Vice President and Consumer Advocate	MICHAEL J. SHINAY
Vice President, Controller	(VACANCY)
Vice President, Core Business Marketing	ROBERT KRAUSE
Vice President, Corporate Relations	FRANK P. BRENNAN, JR.
Vice President, Customer Relations	JOHN R. WARGO
Vice President, Diversity Development	SUZANNE MEDVIDOVICH
Vice President, Engineering	WILLIAM J. DOWLING
Vice President, Expedited/Package Services	JOHN F. KELLY
Vice President, Facilities	RUDOLPH K. UMSCHEID
Vice President, Human Resources	YVONNE D. MAGUIRE
Vice President, Information Systems	RICHARD D. WEIRICH
Vice President, International Business	JAMES F. GRUBIAK
Vice President, Marketing Systems	JOHN H. WARD
Vice President, Operations Redesign	(VACANCY)
Vice President, Operations Support	NICHOLAS F. BARRANCA
Vice President, Purchasing and Materials	A. KEITH STRANGE
Vice President, Quality	NORMAN E. LORENTZ
Vice President, Retail	PATRICIA M. GIBERT
Vice President, Strategic Initiatives	DARRAH PORTER
Vice President, Strategic Planning	ROBERT A.F. REISNER
Vice President, Tactical Marketing and Sales Development	GAIL G. SONNENBERG
Vice President, Workforce Planning and Service Management	(VACANCY)
Judicial Officer	JAMES A. COHEN
Chief Postal Inspector	KENNETH J. HUNTER
Deputy Chief Inspector, Administration	JAMES K. BELZ
Deputy Chief Inspector, Audit	ALAN B. KIEL
Deputy Chief Inspector, Criminal Investigations	MICHAEL BOSWELL

Area Operations:

Vice President, Allegheny Area	(VACANCY)
Vice President, Great Lakes Area	J.T. WEEKER
Vice President, Mid-Atlantic Area	HENRY A. PANKEY
Vice President, Midwest Area	(VACANCY)
Vice President, New York Metro Area	DAVID SOLOMON
Vice President, Northeast Area	JON STEELE
Vice President, Pacific Area	JESSE DURAZO
Vice President, Southeast Area	(VACANCY)
Vice President, Southwest Area	CHARLES K. KERNAN
Vice President, Western Area	CRAIG G. WADE

[For the United States Postal Service statement of organization, see the *Code of Federal Regulations*, Title 39, Parts 221–226]

The United States Postal Service provides mail processing and delivery services to individuals and businesses within the United States. The Service is committed to serving customers through the development of efficient mail-handling systems and operates its own planning and engineering programs. It is also the responsibility of the Postal Service to protect the mails from loss or theft and to apprehend those who violate postal laws.

The Postal Service was created as an independent establishment of the executive branch by the Postal Reorganization Act (39 U.S.C. 101 *et seq.*), approved August 12, 1970. The United States Postal Service commenced operations on July 1, 1971.

The Postal Service has approximately 765,000 employees and handles about 185 billion pieces of mail annually. The chief executive officer of the Postal Service, the Postmaster General, is appointed by the nine Governors of the Postal Service, who are appointed by the President with the advice and consent of the Senate for overlapping 9-year terms. The Governors and the Postmaster General appoint the Deputy Postmaster General, and these 11 people constitute the Board of Governors.

In addition to the national headquarters, there are area and district offices supervising approximately 38,000 post offices, branches, stations, and community post offices throughout the United States.

Activities

In order to expand and improve service to the public, the Postal Service is engaged in customer cooperation activities, including the development of programs for both the general public and major customers. The Consumer Advocate, a postal ombudsman, represents the interest of the individual mail customer in matters involving the Postal Service by bringing complaints and suggestions to the attention of top postal management and solving the problems of individual customers. To provide postal services responsive to public needs, the Postal Service operates its own planning, research, engineering, real estate, and procurement programs specially adapted to postal requirements, and maintains close ties with international postal organizations.

The Postal Service is the only Federal agency whose employment policies are governed by a process of collective bargaining under the National Labor Relations Act. Labor contract negotiations, affecting all bargaining unit personnel, as well as personnel matters involving employees not covered by collective bargaining agreements, are administered by Labor Relations or Human Resources.

The United States Postal Inspection Service is the Federal law enforcement agency which has jurisdiction in criminal matters affecting the integrity and security of the mail. Postal Inspectors enforce more than 100 Federal statutes involving mail fraud, mail bombs, child pornography, illegal

UNITED STATES POSTAL SERVICE

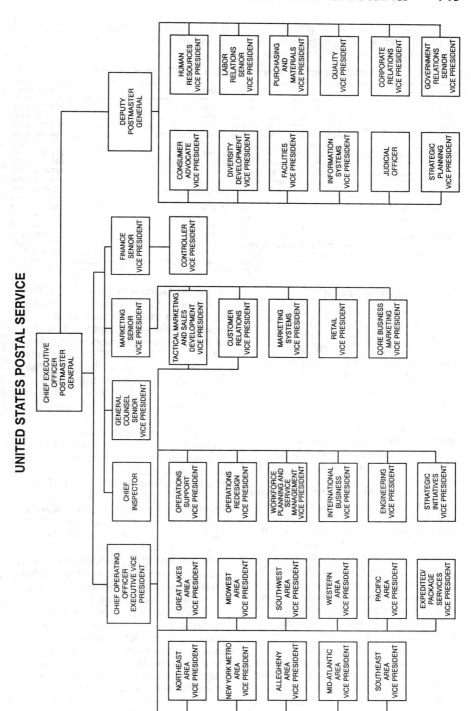

drugs, mail theft, and other postal crimes, as well as being responsible for the protection of all postal employees.

Inspectors also audit postal contracts and financial accounts.

Postal Inspection Service—United States Postal Service

Division	Address	Telephone
Florida	6th Fl., 3400 Lakeside Dr., Miramar, FL 33027–3242	954–436–7200
Gulf Coast	P.O. Box 1276, Houston, TX 77251–1276	713–238–4400
Michiana	P.O. Box 330119, Detroit, MI 48232–6119	313–226–8184
Mid-Atlantic	2901 S. I–85 Service Road, Charlotte, NC 28228–3000	704–329–9120
Midwest	1106 Walnut St., St. Louis, MO 63199–2201	314–539–9300
New York Metro	P.O. Box 555, New York, NY 10116–0555	212–330–3844
North Jersey/Caribbean	P.O. Box 509, Newark, NJ 07101–0509	201–693–5400
Northeast	7th Fl., 425 Summer St., Boston, MA 02210–1736	617–464–8000
Northern California	P.O. Box 882528, San Francisco, CA 94188–2528	415–778–5800
Northern Illinois	Rm. 50190, 433 W. Harrison St., Chicago, IL 60669–2201	312–983–7900
Northwest	P.O. Box 400, Seattle, WA 98111–4000	206–442–6300
Philadelphia Metro	P.O. Box 7500, Philadelphia, PA 19101–9000	215–895–8450
Rocky Mountain	Suite 900, 1745 Stout St., Denver, CO 80202–3034	303–313–5320
Southeast	P.O. Box 16489, Atlanta, GA 30321–0489	404–608–4500
Southern California	P.O. Box 2000, Pasadena, CA 91102–2000	818–405–1200
Southwest	P.O. Box 162929, Fort Worth, TX 76161–2929	817–317–3400
Washington Metro	P.O. Box 96096, Washington, DC 20066–6096	202–636–2300
Western Allegheny	Rm. 2101, 1001 California Ave., Pittsburgh, PA 15290–9000	412–359–7900

Sources of Information

Inquiries on the following information should be directed to the specified office, U.S. Postal Service, 475 L'Enfant Plaza SW., Washington, DC 20260.

Consumer Information   Contact the Consumer Affairs Help Line, 24 hours a day. Phone, 202–268–2284. TDD, 202–268–2310. Express Mail Hotline, 800–222–1811. Fax, 202–268–2304. Information on past and present schemes used to defraud the public is available through Congressional and Public Affairs, Postal Inspection Service. Phone, 202–268–5400.

Contracts and Small Business Activities   Contact Supplier Diversity. Phone, 202–268–4633.

Employment   General information about jobs such as clerk, letter carrier, etc., including information about programs for veterans, may be obtained by contacting the nearest post office.

Individuals interested in working at the Postal Headquarters in Washington, DC, may obtain information by calling 800–562–8777 (800–JOB–USPS).

Information about Postal Inspector employment may be obtained from the Office of Recruitment. Phone, 301–983–7400.

Films   Contact Corporate Relations for films available for loan to the public. Phone, 202–268–2199.

Inspector General Hotline   The Office of Inspector General maintains a toll-free hotline as a means for individuals to report activities involving fraud, waste, or mismanagement. Phone, 888–USPS–OIG. Fax, 703–248–2259. Complaints may be sent by mail to the United States Postal Service, Office of Inspector General Hotline, 7th Floor, 1735 North Lynn Street, Arlington, VA 22209–2020. Publicly available documents and information on the Office of Inspector General are available electronically through the Internet, at http://www.uspsoig.gov/.

Philatelic Information   Contact Stamp Services. Phone, 202–268–2562.

Philatelic Sales   Contact the Philatelic Fulfillment Service Center, Kansas City, MO 64179–1009. Phone, 800–782–6724 (800–STAMP–24).

Publications   Pamphlets on mailability, postage rates and fees, and many other topics may be obtained free of charge from the nearest post office.

Most postal regulations are contained in Postal Service manuals covering domestic mail, international mail, postal operations, administrative support, employee and labor relations, financial management, and procurement. These manuals and other publications including the *National Five-Digit ZIP Code and Post Office Directory* (Publication 65) may be purchased from the Superintendent of Documents, Government Printing Office, Washington, DC 20402–0001. The *National Five-Digit ZIP Code and Post* *Office Directory* is also available through local post offices.

Reading Rooms   Located on 11th Floor North, Library. Phone, 202–268–2900.

For further information, contact the U.S. Postal Service, 475 L'Enfant Plaza SW., Washington, DC 20260. Phone, 202–268–2000. Internet, http://www.usps.gov/.

Boards, Commissions, and Committees

Note: This is a listing of Federal boards, centers, commissions, councils, panels, study groups, task forces, etc., not listed elsewhere in the *Manual*, which were established by congressional or Presidential action, whose functions are not strictly limited to the internal operations of a parent department or agency, and which are authorized to publish documents in the *Federal Register*. While the editors have attempted to compile a complete and accurate listing, suggestions for improving coverage of this guide are welcome. Please address your comments to the Office of the Federal Register, National Archives and Records Administration, Washington, DC 20408. Phone, 202–523–5230.

Federal advisory committees, as defined by the Federal Advisory Committee Act, as amended (5 U.S.C. app.), have not been included here. A complete listing of these committees can be found in the *Annual Report of the President on Federal Advisory Committees*. For further information on Federal advisory committees and this report, contact the Committee Management Secretariat, General Services Administration, General Services Building (MC), Room 5228, Washington, DC 20405. Phone, 202–273–3556.

Administrative Committee of the Federal Register

National Archives and Records Administration, Washington, DC 20408. Phone, 202–523–4534.

Advisory Council on Historic Preservation

Room 809, 1100 Pennsylvania Avenue NW., Washington, DC 20004. Phone, 202–606–8503.

American Battle Monuments Commission

Suite 500, 2300 Clarendon Boulevard, Arlington, VA 22201–3367. Phone, 703–696–6900.

Appalachian Regional Commission

1666 Connecticut Avenue NW., Washington, DC 20235. Phone, 202–884–7799.

Architectural and Transportation Barriers Compliance Board [1]

Suite 1000, 1331 F Street NW., Washington, DC 20004–1111. Phone, 202–272–5434.

Arctic Research Commission

Suite 630, 4350 North Fairfax Drive, Arlington, VA 22203. Phone, 703–525–0111.

Arthritis and Musculoskeletal Interagency Coordinating Committee

National Institutes of Health/NIAMS, Building 31, Room 4C23, Bethesda, MD 20892. Phone, 301–496–8271.

---

[1] Also known as the Access Board.

Barry M. Goldwater Scholarship and Excellence in Education Foundation

Suite 315, 6225 Brandon Avenue, Springfield, VA 22150–2519. Phone, 703–756–6012.

Citizens' Stamp Advisory Committee

United States Postal Service, Room 4474–E, 475 L'Enfant Plaza SW., Washington, DC 20260–2437. Phone, 202–268–6338.

Commission of Fine Arts

Suite 312, 441 F Street NW., Washington, DC 20001. Phone, 202–504–2200.

Committee on Foreign Investment in the United States

Room 1136, Main Treasury Building, 1500 Pennsylvania Avenue NW., Washington, DC 20220. Phone, 202–622–1860.

Committee for the Implementation of Textile Agreements

Department of Commerce, Room 3001A, Fourteenth Street and Constitution Avenue NW., Washington, DC 20230. Phone, 202–482–3737.

Committee for Purchase From People Who Are Blind or Severely Disabled

Suite 310, 1215 Jefferson Davis Highway, Arlington, VA 22202–4302. Phone, 703–603–7740.

Coordinating Council on Juvenile Justice and Delinquency Prevention

Department of Justice, Office of Juvenile Justice and Delinquency Prevention, Eighth Floor, 810 Building, Seventh Street NW., Washington, DC 20531. Phone, 202–307–5911.

Delaware River Basin Commission

P.O. Box 7360, West Trenton, NJ 08628. Phone, 609–883–9500.

Endangered Species Committee [1]

Department of the Interior, Room 4426, 1849 C Street NW., Washington, DC 20240. Phone, 202–208–4077.

Export Administration Review Board

Room 2639, Herbert C. Hoover Building, Fourteenth Street and Constitution Avenue NW., Washington, DC 20230. Phone, 202–482–5863.

Federal Financial Institutions Examination Council

Suite 200, 2100 Pennsylvania Avenue NW., Washington, DC 20037. Phone, 202–634–6526.

Federal Financing Bank

Room 3054, Main Treasury Building, 1500 Pennsylvania Avenue NW., Washington, DC 20220. Phone, 202–622–2470.

Federal Interagency Committee on Education

Department of Education, Federal Office Building 10, Room 3236, 600 Independence Avenue SW., Washington, DC 20202–3500. Phone, 202–401–3679.

Federal Laboratory Consortium for Technology Transfer

Suite 800, 1850 M Street NW., Washington, DC 20036. Phone, 202–331–4220.

Federal Library and Information Center Committee

Suite 725, 701 Pennsylvania Avenue NW., Washington, DC 20540–4930. Phone, 202–707–4800.

Harry S. Truman Scholarship Foundation

712 Jackson Place NW., Washington, DC 20006. Phone, 202–395–4831.

Illinois and Michigan Canal National Heritage Corridor Commission

15701 South Independence Boulevard, Lockport, IL 60441. Phone, 815–740–2047.

---

[1] The Committee accepts applications for Endangered Species Act exemptions.

Indian Arts and Crafts Board

Department of the Interior, Room 4004–MIB, 1849 C Street NW., Washington, DC 20240. Phone, 202–208–3773.

Interagency Committee on Employment of People with Disabilities

Equal Employment Opportunity Commission, Federal Sector Programs, Room 5238, 1801 L Street NW., Washington, DC 20507. Phone, 202–663–4560. TDD, 202–663–4593.

Interagency Savings Bonds Committee

Office of the Committee Chair, Savings Bond Marketing Office, Washington, DC 20226. Phone, 202–219–3914.

J. William Fulbright Foreign Scholarship Board

United States Information Agency, Room 247, 301 Fourth Street SW., Washington, DC 20547. Phone, 202–619–4290.

James Madison Memorial Fellowship Foundation

Suite 303, 2000 K Street NW., Washington, DC 20006–1809. Phone, 202–653–8700.

Japan–United States Friendship Commission

Room 925, 1120 Vermont Avenue NW., Washington, DC 20005. Phone, 202–275–7712.

Joint Board for the Enrollment of Actuaries

Department of the Treasury, Internal Revenue Service, Washington, DC 20224. Phone, 202–401–4091.

Marine Mammal Commission

Room 905, 4340 East-West Highway, Bethesda, MD 20814. Phone, 301–504–0087.

Medicare Payments Advisory Commission

Suite 800, 1730 K Street NW., Washington, DC 20006. Phone, 202–653–7220.

Migratory Bird Conservation Commission

1849 C Street NW., 622 ARLSQ, Washington, DC 20240. Phone, 703–358–1716.

Mississippi River Commission

United States Army Corps of Engineers, Mississippi Valley Division, 1400 Walnut Street, P.O. Box 80, Vicksburg, MS 39180. Phone, 601–634–5757.

Morris K. Udall Scholarship and Excellence in National Environmental Policy Foundation

803/811 East First Street, Tucson, AZ 85719. Phone, 520–670–5523.

National Commission on Libraries and Information Science

Suite 820, 1110 Vermont Avenue NW., Washington, DC 20005. Phone, 202–606–9200.

National Council on Disability

Suite 1050, 1331 F Street NW., Washington, DC 20004. Phone, 202–272–2004. TDD, 202–272–2074.

National Occupational Information Coordinating Committee

Suite 156, 2100 M Street NW., Washington, DC 20037. Phone, 202–653–5665.

National Park Foundation

Suite 1102, 1101 Seventeenth Street NW., Washington, DC 20036–4704. Phone, 202–785–4500.

Navajo and Hopi Relocation Commission

Office of Navajo and Hopi Indian Relocation, P.O. Box KK, Flagstaff, AZ 86002. Phone, 520–779–2721.

Northwest Power Planning Council

Suite 1100, 851 Southwest Sixth Avenue, Portland, OR 97204. Phone, 503–222–5161.

Permanent Committee for the Oliver Wendell Holmes Devise

Library of Congress, Manuscript Division, Washington, DC 20540. Phone, 202–707–5383.

President's Committee on Employment of People With Disabilities
Suite 300, 1331 F Street NW., Washington, DC 20004–1107. Phone, 202–376–6200. TDD, 202–376–6205.

President's Council on Integrity and Efficiency
Office of Management and Budget, New Executive Office Building, Room 6025, Washington, DC 20503. Phone, 202–395–6911.

President's Foreign Intelligence Advisory Board
Room 340, Old Executive Office Building, Washington, DC 20502. Phone, 202–456–2352.

Presidio Trust
34 Graham Street, P.O. Box 29052, San Francisco, CA, 94129–0052. Phone, 415–561–5300.

Susquehanna River Basin Commission
1721 North Front Street, Harrisburg, PA 17102–2391. Phone, 717–238–0422.

Textile Trade Policy Group
Room 309, 600 Seventeenth Street NW., Washington, DC 20506. Phone, 202–395–3026.

Thrift Depositor Protection Oversight Board
Department of the Treasury, Room 3025, Fifteenth and Pennsylvania Avenue NW.,

Washington, DC 20220. Phone, 202–622–2740.

Trade Policy Committee
Office of Policy Coordination, Room 501, 600 Seventeenth Street NW., Washington, DC 20508. Phone, 202–395–3475.

United States Holocaust Memorial Museum
100 Raoul Wallenberg Place SW., Washington, DC 20024. Phone, 202–488–0400.

United States Nuclear Waste Technical Review Board
Suite 1300, 2300 Clarendon Boulevard, Arlington, VA 22201. Phone, 703–235–4473.

Veterans Day National Committee
Department of Veterans Affairs (80D), 810 Vermont Avenue NW., Washington, DC 20420. Phone, 202–273–5735.

White House Commission on Presidential Scholars
Department of Education, Room 3267, 600 Independence Avenue SW., Washington, DC 20202–3500. Phone, 202–401–0961.

QUASI–OFFICIAL AGENCIES

Note: This section contains organizations that are not Executive agencies under the definition in 5 U.S.C. 105 but that are required by statute to publish certain information on their programs and activities in the *Federal Register*.

LEGAL SERVICES CORPORATION

750 First Street NE., Washington, DC 20002–4250
Phone, 202–336–8800. Fax, 202-336-8959. Internet, http://www.lsc.gov/.

President	JOHN MCKAY
General Counsel and Corporate Secretary	VICTOR M. FORTUNO
Vice President for Administration	JAMES HOGAN
Comptroller/Treasurer	DAVID RICHARDSON
Vice President for Programs	JOHN TULL
Inspector General	EDOUARD QUATREVAUX
Director, Government Relations and Public Affairs	MAURICIO VIVERO

[For the Legal Services Corporation statement of organization, see the *Code of Federal Regulations*, Title 45, Part 1601]

The Legal Services Corporation provides quality legal assistance for noncriminal proceedings to those who would otherwise be unable to afford such assistance.

The Legal Services Corporation is a private, nonprofit organization established by the Legal Services Corporation Act of 1974, as amended (42 U.S.C. 2996), to provide financial support for legal assistance in noncriminal proceedings to persons financially unable to afford legal services.

The Corporation is governed by an 11-member Board of Directors, appointed by the President with the advice and consent of the Senate. Each member serves for a term of 3 years, except that five of the members first appointed—as designated by the President at the time of appointment—serve 2-year terms. The President of the Corporation, appointed by the Board of Directors, is the chief executive officer and serves as an *ex officio* Board member.

The Corporation provides financial assistance to qualified programs furnishing legal assistance to eligible clients and makes grants to and contracts with individuals, firms, corporations, and organizations for the purpose of providing legal assistance to these clients.

The Corporation establishes maximum income levels for clients based on family size, urban and rural differences, and

723

LEGAL SERVICES CORPORATION

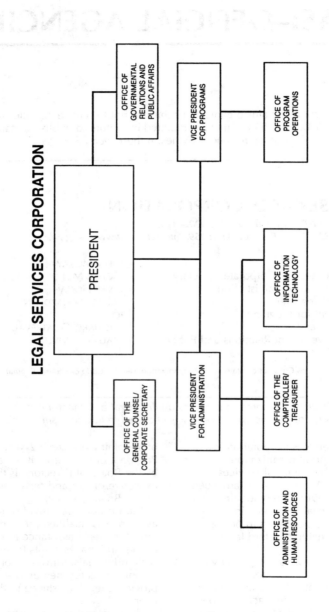

cost-of-living variations. Using these maximum income levels and other financial factors, the Corporation's recipient programs establish criteria to determine the eligibility of clients and priorities of service based on an appraisal of the legal needs of the eligible client community.

For further information, contact the Office of Communications, Legal Services Corporation, 750 First Street NE., Washington, DC 20002–4250. Phone, 202–336–8800. Fax, 202-336-8959. Internet, http://www.lsc.gov/.

SMITHSONIAN INSTITUTION

1000 Jefferson Drive SW., Washington, DC 20560
Phone, 202–357–1300; or 202–357–2700 (Smithsonian Information Center). Internet, http://www.si.edu/.

Board of Regents:

The Chief Justice of the United States (*Chancellor*)	WILLIAM H. REHNQUIST
The Vice President of the United States	AL GORE
Members of the Senate	THAD COCHRAN, WILLIAM FRIST, DANIEL PATRICK MOYNIHAN
Members of the House of Representatives	SAMUEL JOHNSON, ROBERT LIVINGSTON, (1 VACANCY)
Citizen Members	HOWARD H. BAKER, JR., BARBER B. CONABLE, ANNE D'HARNONCOURT, LOUIS V. GERSTNER, JR., HANNA HOLBORN GRAY, MANUEL L. IBAÑEZ, HOMER A. NEAL, FRANK A. SHRONTZ, WESLEY SAMUEL WILLIAMS, JR.

Officials:

The Secretary	I. MICHAEL HEYMAN
The Inspector General	THOMAS D. BLAIR
Director, Office of Planning, Management and Budget	L. CAROLE WHARTON
Counselor to the Secretary for Biodiversity and Environmental Affairs	THOMAS E. LOVEJOY
Counselor to the Secretary for Electronic Communications and Special Projects	MARC PACHTER
Counselor to the Secretary for Community Affairs and Special Projects	MIGUEL BRETOS
Executive Assistant to the Secretary	JAMES M. HOBBINS
Executive Secretary to the Secretary	BARBARA CEDERBORG
Under Secretary	CONSTANCE NEWMAN
General Counsel	JOHN E. HUERTA
Director, Office of Government Relations	DONALD L. HARDY
Director, Office of Communications	DAVID J. UMANSKY
Director, Office of Information Technology	VINCENT MARCALUS
Senior Information Officer	JIM CONKLIN, *Acting*
Senior Business Officer	ROLAND BANSCHER, *Acting*

Ombudsman	CHANDRA HEILMAN
Executive Director, Office of Membership and Development	ROBERT V. HANLE
Director, Office of Special Events and Conference Services	NICOLE L. KRAKORA
Chief Financial Officer	RICK JOHNSON
Director, Office of Sponsored Projects	ARDELLE FOSS
Director, Office of Equal Employment and Minority Affairs	ERA MARSHALL
Director, Office of Human Resources	CAROLYN JONES
Director, Office of Imaging, Printing, and Photographic Services	JAMES H. WALLACE, JR.
Director, Office of Contracting	JOHN W. COBERT
Director, Office of Physical Plant	MICHAEL SOFIELD
Director, Office of Protection Services	DAVID F. MORRELL
Director, Office of Environmental Management and Safety	WILLIAM F. BILLINGSLEY
Treasurer	SUDEEP ANAND
Comptroller	M. LESLIE CASSON
Provost	J. DENNIS O'CONNOR
Director, Anacostia Museum and Center for African American History and Culture	STEVEN NEWSOME
Director, Archives of American Art	RICHARD WATTENMAKER
Building Director, Arts and Industries Building	JAMES HOBBINS
Director, Cooper-Hewitt, National Design Museum	DIANNE PILGRIM
Director, Freer Gallery of Art and Arthur M. Sackler Gallery	MILO C. BEACH
Director, Hirshhorn Museum and Sculpture Garden	JAMES T. DEMETRION
Director, National Air and Space Museum	DONALD D. ENGEN
Director, National Museum of African Art	ROSLYN A. WALKER
Director, National Museum of American Art	ELIZABETH BROUN
Curator in Charge, Renwick Gallery	KENNETH R. TRAPP
Director, National Museum of American History	SPENCER CREW
Director, National Museum of the American Indian	W. RICHARD WEST, JR.
Director, National Campaign for NMAI	JOHN L. COLONGHI
Director, National Museum of Natural History	ROBERT W. FRI
Director, National Portrait Gallery	ALAN M. FERN
Director, National Postal Museum	JAMES BRUNS
Director, National Zoological Park	MICHAEL ROBINSON
Director, Office of Exhibits Central	MICHAEL HEADLEY
Director, Center for Museum Studies	REX ELLIS
Director, Smithsonian Institution Traveling Exhibition Service	ANNA R. COHN
Director, Institutional Studies Office	ZAHAVA DOERING
Editor, Joseph Henry Papers Project	MARC ROTHENBERG
Director, Office of Fellowships and Grants	ROBERTA RUBINOFF
Senior Scientist, Smithsonian Environmental Research Center	DAVID L. CORRELL

Director, Smithsonian Marine Research Station	MARY RICE
Director, Smithsonian Astrophysical Observatory	IRWIN I. SHAPIRO
Director, Smithsonian Tropical Research Institute	IRA RUBINOFF
Director, Smithsonian Center for Materials Research and Education	LAMBERTUS VAN ZELST
Director, Smithsonian Institution Libraries	NANCY E. GWINN
Director, Museum Support Center	CATHERINE J. KERBY
Director, Smithsonian Institution Archives	ETHEL W. HÉDLIN
Director, Smithsonian Office of Education	ANN BAY
Director, Center for Folklife Programs and Cultural Studies	RICHARD KURIN
Director, National Science Resources Center	DOUGLAS LAPP
Director, Wider Audience Development Program	MARSHALL WONG
Director, Office of International Relations	FRANCINE BERKOWITZ
Director, Smithsonian's Affiliates Program	MICHAEL CARRIGAN
Director, Smithsonian Center for Latino Initiatives	(VACANCY)
Director, Institute of Conservation Biology	RUTH STOLK
Counselor to the Provost (Asian-Pacific-American Activities)	FRANKLIN ODO
Director, Smithsonian Press/Smithsonian Productions	DANIEL GOODWIN
Editor, Smithsonian Magazine	DON MOSER
Publisher, Smithsonian Magazine	RONALD WALKER
Director, The Smithsonian Associates	MARA MAYOR

The John F. Kennedy Center for the Performing Arts [1]

Chairman	JAMES A. JOHNSON
President	LAWRENCE J. WILKER

National Gallery of Art [1]

President	ROBERT H. SMITH
Director	EARL A. POWELL III

Woodrow Wilson International Center for Scholars [1]

Director	(VACANCY)
Deputy Director	SAMUEL WELLS
Deputy Director for Planning and Management	DEAN W. ANDERSON
Chairman, Board of Trustees	JOSEPH H. FLOM

More than 150 years old, the Smithsonian Institution is an independent trust instrumentality of the United States that fosters the increase and diffusion of knowledge. The world's largest museum complex, the Smithsonian includes 16 museums and galleries, the National Zoo, and research facilities in several States and the Republic of Panama. The Smithsonian holds more than 140 million artifacts and specimens in its trust for the American people. The Institution, a respected center

---

[1] Administered under a separate Board of Trustees.

for research, is dedicated to public education, national service, and scholarship in the arts, sciences, and history.

The Smithsonian Institution was created by act of August 10, 1846 (20 U.S.C. 41 *et seq.*), to carry out the terms of the will of British scientist James Smithson (1765–1829), who in 1826 had bequeathed his entire estate to the United States "to found at Washington, under the name of the Smithsonian Institution, an establishment for the increase and diffusion of knowledge among men." On July 1, 1836, Congress accepted the legacy and pledged the faith of the United States to the charitable trust.

In September 1838, Smithson's legacy, which amounted to more than 100,000 gold sovereigns, was delivered to the mint at Philadelphia. Congress vested responsibility for administering the trust in the Smithsonian Board of Regents, composed of the Chief Justice, the Vice President, three Members of the Senate, three Members of the House of Representatives, and nine citizen members appointed by joint resolution of Congress.

To carry out Smithson's mandate, the Institution:

—performs basic research;

—publishes the results of studies, explorations, and investigations;

—preserves for study and reference more than 140 million artifacts, works of art, and scientific specimens;

—organizes exhibits representative of the arts, the sciences, and American history and culture; and

—engages in educational programming and national and international cooperative research.

Smithsonian activities are supported by its trust endowments; gifts, grants, and contracts; and funds appropriated to it by Congress.

Activities

Anacostia Museum and Center for African American History and Culture The Museum, located in the historic Fort Stanton neighborhood of southeast Washington, serves as a national resource for exhibitions, historical

documentation, and interpretive and educational programs relating to African-American history and culture. The African-American church, the Harlem Renaissance, and jazz have been the subjects of recent exhibitions produced by the Museum.

The Center mounts exhibitions such as "Jazz Age in Paris," a SITES exhibition that premiered at the Center; sponsors public programs; and collects material (approximately 7,000 objects) representative of the black experience in performing arts and art and culture.

For further information, contact the Anacostia Museum, 1901 Fort Place SE., Washington, DC 20020. Phone, 202–357–2700.

Archives of American Art The Archives contains the Nation's largest collection of documentary materials reflecting the history of visual arts in the United States. On the subject of art in America, it is the largest archives in the world, holding more than 12 million documents. The Archives gathers, preserves, and microfilms the papers of artists, craftsmen, collectors, dealers, critics, and art societies. These papers consist of manuscripts, letters, diaries, notebooks, sketchbooks, business records, clippings, exhibition catalogs, transcripts of tape-recorded interviews, and photographs of artists and their work.

The Archives' chief processing and reference center is in the historic Old Patent Office Building in Washington, DC. The Archives has regional centers in California, Massachusetts, Michigan, and New York.

For further information, contact the Archives of American Art, Smithsonian Institution, Washington, DC 20560. Phone, 202–357–2781.

Cooper-Hewitt, National Design Museum The Museum, located in New York City, is the only museum in the country devoted exclusively to historical and contemporary design. Collections include nearly 250,000 objects in such areas as applied arts and industrial design, drawings and prints, glass, metalwork, wallcoverings, and textiles. A

SMITHSONIAN INSTITUTION

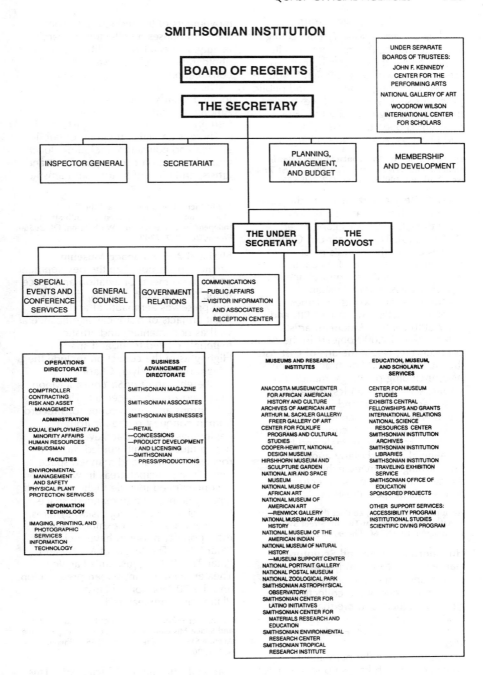

BOARD OF REGENTS

UNDER SEPARATE
BOARDS OF TRUSTEES:
JOHN F. KENNEDY
CENTER FOR THE
PERFORMING ARTS
NATIONAL GALLERY OF ART
WOODROW WILSON
INTERNATIONAL CENTER
FOR SCHOLARS

THE SECRETARY

INSPECTOR GENERAL

SECRETARIAT

PLANNING,
MANAGEMENT,
AND BUDGET

MEMBERSHIP
AND DEVELOPMENT

**THE UNDER
SECRETARY**

**THE
PROVOST**

SPECIAL
EVENTS AND
CONFERENCE
SERVICES

GENERAL
COUNSEL

GOVERNMENT
RELATIONS

COMMUNICATIONS
—PUBLIC AFFAIRS
—VISITOR INFORMATION
AND ASSOCIATES
RECEPTION CENTER

**OPERATIONS
DIRECTORATE**

FINANCE

COMPTROLLER
CONTRACTING
RISK AND ASSET
MANAGEMENT

ADMINISTRATION

EQUAL EMPLOYMENT AND
MINORITY AFFAIRS
HUMAN RESOURCES
OMBUDSMAN

FACILITIES

ENVIRONMENTAL
MANAGEMENT
AND SAFETY
PHYSICAL PLANT
PROTECTION SERVICES

INFORMATION
TECHNOLOGY

IMAGING, PRINTING, AND
PHOTOGRAPHIC
SERVICES
INFORMATION
TECHNOLOGY

**BUSINESS
ADVANCEMENT
DIRECTORATE**

SMITHSONIAN MAGAZINE

SMITHSONIAN ASSOCIATES

SMITHSONIAN BUSINESSES

—RETAIL
—CONCESSIONS
—PRODUCT DEVELOPMENT
AND LICENSING
—SMITHSONIAN
PRESS/PRODUCTIONS

**MUSEUMS AND RESEARCH
INSTITUTES**

ANACOSTIA MUSEUM/CENTER
FOR AFRICAN AMERICAN
HISTORY AND CULTURE
ARCHIVES OF AMERICAN ART
ARTHUR M. SACKLER GALLERY/
FREER GALLERY OF ART
CENTER FOR FOLKLIFE
PROGRAMS AND CULTURAL
STUDIES
COOPER-HEWITT, NATIONAL
DESIGN MUSEUM
HIRSHHORN MUSEUM AND
SCULPTURE GARDEN
NATIONAL AIR AND SPACE
MUSEUM
NATIONAL MUSEUM OF
AFRICAN ART
NATIONAL MUSEUM OF
AMERICAN ART
—RENWICK GALLERY
NATIONAL MUSEUM OF AMERICAN
HISTORY
NATIONAL MUSEUM OF THE
AMERICAN INDIAN
NATIONAL MUSEUM OF NATURAL
HISTORY
—MUSEUM SUPPORT CENTER
NATIONAL PORTRAIT GALLERY
NATIONAL POSTAL MUSEUM
NATIONAL ZOOLOGICAL PARK
SMITHSONIAN ASTROPHYSICAL
OBSERVATORY
SMITHSONIAN CENTER FOR
LATINO INITIATIVES
SMITHSONIAN CENTER FOR
MATERIALS RESEARCH AND
EDUCATION
SMITHSONIAN ENVIRONMENTAL
RESEARCH CENTER
SMITHSONIAN TROPICAL
RESEARCH INSTITUTE

**EDUCATION, MUSEUM,
AND SCHOLARLY
SERVICES**

CENTER FOR MUSEUM
STUDIES
EXHIBITS CENTRAL
FELLOWSHIPS AND GRANTS
INTERNATIONAL RELATIONS
NATIONAL SCIENCE
RESOURCES CENTER
SMITHSONIAN INSTITUTION
ARCHIVES
SMITHSONIAN INSTITUTION
LIBRARIES
SMITHSONIAN INSTITUTION
TRAVELING EXHIBITION
SERVICE
SMITHSONIAN OFFICE OF
EDUCATION
SPONSORED PROJECTS

OTHER SUPPORT SERVICES:
ACCESSIBILITY PROGRAM
INSTITUTIONAL STUDIES
SCIENTIFIC DIVING PROGRAM

major renovation in 1997–1998 has produced a new two-story connecting structure linking the museum with its garden and with two townhouses currently known as the Design Resource Center. Changing exhibitions and public programs seek to educate by exploring the role of design in daily life. The Museum is open daily except Mondays and holidays. Admission is charged.

For further information, contact Cooper-Hewitt, National Design Museum, 2 East Ninety-First Street, New York, NY 10028. Phone, 212–860–6868.

Freer Gallery of Art   The building, the original collection, and an endowment were the gift of Charles Lang Freer (1854–1919). The 75-year-old Gallery houses one of the world's most renowned collections of Asian art as well as an important group of ancient Egyptian glass, early Christian manuscripts, and works by James McNeill Whistler and other 19th and early 20th century American artists.

More than 27,000 objects in the Asian collection represent the arts of East Asia, the Near East, and South and Southeast Asia, including paintings, manuscripts, scrolls, screens, ceramics, metalwork, glass, jade, lacquer, and sculpture. Members of the staff conduct research on objects in the collection and publish results in scholarly journals and books for general and scholarly audiences. They arrange thematic exhibitions from the collection and present lectures in their fields of specialization.

For further information, contact the Freer Gallery of Art, Jefferson Drive at Twelfth Street SW., Washington, DC 20560. Phone, 202–357–2700.

Hirshhorn Museum and Sculpture Garden   The Museum houses major collections of modern and contemporary art. The nucleus of the collection is the gift and bequest of more than 13,000 works of art for the people of the United States from Joseph H. Hirshhorn (1899–1981).

Supplementing the permanent collection, which keeps up with current developments through an active acquisitions program, are loan exhibitions focusing on emerging contemporary artists as well as on art

movements of the modern era. The Museum houses a collection research facility, a specialized art library, and a photographic archive, available for consultation by prior appointment.

The outdoor sculpture garden is located nearby on the National Mall. Among its works is the famous "Burghers of Calais" by Auguste Rodin.

There is an active program of public service and education, including docent tours, lectures on contemporary art and artists, and films of historic and artistic interest.

For further information, contact the Hirshhorn Museum and Sculpture Garden, Seventh Street and Independence Avenue SW., Washington, DC 20560. Phone, 202–357–2700.

National Air and Space Museum Created to memorialize the development and achievements of aviation and space flight, the Museum collects, displays, and preserves aeronautical and space flight artifacts of historical significance as well as documentary and artistic materials related to air and space. Highlights of the collection include the Wright brothers' flyer, Charles Lindbergh's *Spirit of St. Louis*, a Moon rock, and Apollo spacecraft. The exhibitions and study collections record human conquest of the air from its beginnings to recent achievements by high altitude aircraft, guided missiles, rockets, satellites, and manned space flight. The principal areas in which work is concentrated include flight craft of all types, manned and unmanned; space flight vehicles; and propulsion systems.

Recent blockbuster exhibitions at this most popular museum have included "Star Wars: The Magic of Myth" and "Star Trek." The Museum's Langley Theater, with a giant screen presentation, and the 70-foot domed Einstein Planetarium are featured.

For further information, contact the National Air and Space Museum, Sixth Street and Independence Avenue SW., Washington, DC 20560. Phone, 202–357–2700.

National Museum of African Art This is the only art museum in the United States dedicated exclusively to portraying the rich, creative visual traditions of Africa.

Established in 1964 and incorporated as a bureau of the Smithsonian in 1979, the Museum opened at its new location on the National Mall in September 1987. Its research components, collection, exhibitions, and public programs establish the Museum as a primary source for the examination and discovery of the arts and culture of Africa. In recent years, works of outstanding aesthetic quality have been added to a collection numbering about 7,000 works in wood, metal, fired clay, ivory, and fiber. Examples of traditional art include a wooden figure of a Zairian Yombe carver; a Lower Niger Bronze Industry vessel, with chameleons; and a memorial figure from the Cameroon grassfields.

The Eliot Elisofon Photographic Archives includes some 100,000 slides, photos, and film segments on Africa. There is also a specialized library of more than 18,000 volumes and periodicals.

For further information, contact the National Museum of African Art, 950 Independence Avenue SW., Washington, DC 20560. Phone, 202–357–2700.

National Museum of American Art The Museum's art collection spans centuries of American painting, sculpture, folk art, photography, and graphic art. A Puerto Rican religious image (17th century) is now the oldest object in the Museum's collection. The permanent collection of more than 37,500 works of art is drawn upon for special groupings based on subjects, media, and other considerations. Special exhibitions are presented each year on various aspects of American art.

A major center for research in American art, the Museum has contributed to such resources as the Inventory of American Paintings Executed Before 1914, with data on nearly 260,000 works; the Slide and Photographic Archives; the Smithsonian Art Index; and the Inventory of American Sculpture, with information on more than 50,000 indoor and outdoor works. The library, shared with the National Portrait Gallery, contains volumes on art, history, and biography, with special

emphasis on the United States. The building also houses the Archives of American Art, with its vast holdings of documentary material on American art and artists.

The Museum makes hundreds of images from the collection and extensive information on its collections, publications, and activities available electronically to personal computer users (Internet, http://www.nmaa.si.edu/) and commercial online services. There is a research program for visiting scholars, and university interns are welcomed in many museum departments.

Renwick Gallery The Gallery, located at 17th Street and Pennsylvania Avenue NW., Washington, DC, is dedicated to exhibiting crafts of all periods and to collecting 20th century American crafts. It offers changing exhibitions of American crafts and decorative arts, both historical and contemporary, and a rotating selection from its permanent collection. The Gallery's Grand Salon is elegantly furnished in the Victorian style of the 1860's and 1870's.

For further information, contact the National Museum of American Art, Eighth and G Streets NW., Washington, DC 20560. Phone, 202–357–2700.

National Museum of American History In pursuit of its fundamental mission to inspire a broader understanding of the United States and its people, the Museum provides learning opportunities, stimulates the imagination of visitors, and presents challenging ideas about the Nation's past. The Museum's exhibits provide a unique view of the American experience and are developed from a "nation of nations" collections base. Emphasis is placed upon innovative individuals—representing a wide range of cultures—who have shaped our heritage, and upon science and the remaking of our world through technology.

Exhibits draw upon strong collections (around 3 million artifacts) in the sciences and engineering, agriculture, manufacturing, transportation, political memorabilia, costumes, musical instruments, coins, photography, ceramics, and glass. Classic cars, First

Ladies' gowns, musical instruments, the Star-Spangled Banner flag, Whitney's cotton gin, Morse's telegraph, the John Bull locomotive, and other American icons are highlights of the collection. Political, social, military, and cultural history are well represented. Major installations treat everyday life in America just after the Revolutionary War, the U.S. centennial, the Industrial Revolution, the Information Age, the White House, science in American life, and the diverse origins of the American people. Hands-on activities, demonstrations, films, and performances highlight many aspects of the Museum. The Smithsonian Jazz Masterworks Orchestra is located at the Museum.

Scholars may be aided in the use of the Museum's research collections and specialized library facilities by appointment.

For further information, contact the National Museum of American History, Fourteenth Street and Constitution Avenue NW., Washington, DC 20560. Phone, 202–357–2700.

National Museum of the American Indian

The Museum was established by act of November 28, 1989 (20 U.S.C. 80q *et seq.*). It will be located in three facilities:

—the George Gustav Heye Center, located at One Bowling Green, New York City, which is currently open;

—the Cultural Resources Center in Suitland, MD, which will open in 1998 and eventually house a major portion of the Museum's priceless million-object collection; and

—the Mall museum, which will open in 2001 east of the National Air and Space Museum on the National Mall's last available site.

The Museum, whose collections were transferred to the Smithsonian from the former Museum of the American Indian, Heye Foundation, in New York City, is an institution of living cultures dedicated to the collection, preservation, study, and exhibition of the life, languages, literature, history, and arts of the Native peoples of the Americas.

Highlights include Northwest Coast carvings; dance masks; pottery and weaving from the Southwest; painted hides and garments from the North American Plains; goldwork of the Aztecs, Incas, and Maya; and Amazonian featherwork.

Heye Center admission is free. For information on hours, phone 212–825–6700 (New York City) or 202–357–2700 (Washington, DC).

For further information, contact the National Museum of the American Indian, Suite 7102, 470 L'Enfant Plaza SW., Washington, DC 20560. Phone, 202–287–2523 or 202–357–2700.

National Museum of Natural History

This museum, dedicated to understanding the natural world and the place of humans in it, is a popular field trip destination for school groups as well as naturalists and the scholarly. The Museum's permanent exhibits focus on Earth sciences, biology, and anthropology, with the most popular displays featuring gemstones such as the Hope diamond, dinosaurs, marine ecosystems, birds, and mammals. Notable attractions include the O. Orkin Insect Zoo, where a variety of arthropods live in realistic habitats; and the Discovery Room, where visitors can handle specimens and artifacts. The Museum also hosts a variety of special exhibitions, such as "Amber: Window to the Past" and "Ocean Planet."

The public displays represent only a small portion of the national collections housed and maintained by the Museum. These encyclopedic collections comprise more than 122 million specimens, making the Museum one of the world's foremost facilities for natural history research. Museum departments include anthropology, botany, paleobiology, entomology, vertebrate and invertebrate zoology, and mineral sciences. Doctorate-level staff researchers ensure the continued growth and value of the collection by conducting studies in the field and laboratory. The Museum maintains permanent research facilities in Alaska, Florida, Belize, and Africa, among other sites.

For further information, contact the National Museum of Natural History, Tenth Street and Constitution Avenue NW., Washington, DC 20560. Phone, 202–357–2700.

National Portrait Gallery   The Gallery was established by act of April 27, 1962 (20 U.S.C. 75a), as a museum of the Smithsonian Institution "for the exhibition and study of portraiture depicting men and women who have made significant contributions to the history, development, and culture of the people of the United States." It is housed in one of the oldest Government structures in Washington, the former U.S. Patent Office Building.

The first floor of the Gallery is devoted to changing exhibitions from the Gallery's collection of paintings, sculpture, prints, photographs, and drawings as well as to special portrait collections. On the second floor are featured the permanent collection of portraits of eminent Americans and the Hall of Presidents containing portraits of our Chief Executives. The two-story Victorian Renaissance Great Hall on the third floor of the gallery houses a Civil War exhibition (on the mezzanine), and is used for special events and public programs.

A large library is shared with the National Museum of American Art and the Archives of American Art. The education department offers public programs; outreach programs for schools, senior adults, hospitals, and nursing homes; and walk-in and group tours.

For further information, contact the National Portrait Gallery, Eighth and F Streets NW., Washington, DC 20560. Phone, 202–357–2700.

National Postal Museum   The Museum houses the Nation's postal history and philatelic collection, the largest of its kind in the world, with more than 13 million objects. The 75,000 square-foot Museum is devoted to the history of America's mail service. The major galleries include exhibits on mail service in colonial times and during the Civil War, the Pony Express, modern mail service, automation, mail transportation, and the art of letters, as well as displays of the Museum's priceless stamp collection.

Highlights include three mail planes, a replica of a railway mail car, displays of historic letters, handcrafted mail boxes, and rare U.S. and foreign issue stamps and covers.

Located on Capitol Hill next to Union Station, the Postal Museum is geared for a family audience. A state-of-the-art museum setting offers more than 40 videos and interactive displays, as well as a museum shop, a stamp retail store, and a discovery center for educational programs, lectures, and performances.

For further information, contact the National Postal Museum, 2 Massachusetts Avenue NE., Washington, DC 20560. Phone, 202–357–2700.

National Zoological Park   The National Zoo encompasses 163 acres along Rock Creek Park in Northwest Washington, DC. Established in 1889, the Zoo is one of the oldest branches of the Smithsonian Institution. The collection today encompasses 5,000 animals and 500 species, ranging in size and diversity from leaf-cutter ants to giraffes, giant pandas, elephants, and rhinos. Recent exhibits include "Amazonia," a simulated tropical rain forest; "Think Tank," an exhibit focusing on animal thinking; the "Vertebrate" and "Pollinarium" exhibits; and the Reptile Discovery Center, featuring the world's largest lizards, Komodo dragons. The Zoo's exhibits are supported by scientific investigations conducted at the Zoo's Department of Zoological Research. Work focusing on genetics, animal behavior, and reproductive studies has given the National Zoo a leadership role among the Nation's conservation institutions.

In addition to the animals living at its Washington facilities, the Zoo's Conservation and Research Center located on 3,150 acres near Front Royal, VA, houses additional rare and endangered species. Research at the Center explores animal behavior, ecology, nutrition, reproductive physiology, pathology, and clinical medicine. The Center also conducts research into the long-term maintenance of wild animal populations and captive-breeding. It operates a training program for wildlife professionals from other countries, including those with endangered and rare wildlife.

For further information, contact the National Zoo, 3000 Connecticut Avenue NW., Washington, DC 20008. Phone, 202–673–4717. E-mail, listserv@sivm.si.edu. Internet, http://www.si.edu/ natzoo/.

Office of Fellowships and Grants   This office develops and administers the numerous Smithsonian programs designed to assist scholars and students from the United States and throughout the world in utilizing the Institution's unique resources. These academic programs, which include long- and short-term appointments, are an important complement to those offered by universities and support participants' research in art, history, and science.

Predoctoral, postdoctoral, and graduate student fellowship programs provide scholars and students the opportunity to conduct research on independently conceived projects at Smithsonian facilities in conjunction with the Institution's research staff.

The Office of Fellowships and Grants offers internships aimed at increasing minority participation in ongoing Smithsonian research activities and fields of interest. In addition, it administers all internships funded by stipends. The Office also administers other research opportunity programs for many of the Smithsonian bureaus.

For further information, contact the Office of Fellowships and Grants, Suite 7000, 902 L'Enfant Plaza SW., Washington, DC 20560. Phone, 202–287–3271. E-mail, siofg@sivm.si.edu.

Center for Folklife Programs and Cultural Studies   The Center is responsible for research, documentation, and presentation of grassroots cultural traditions. It maintains a documentary collection and produces Smithsonian Folkways Recordings, educational materials, documentary films, publications, and traveling exhibits, as well as the annual Smithsonian Folklife Festival on the National Mall. Recent Folklife Festivals have featured a range of American music styles, a number of State tributes, and performers from around the world. Admission to the

festival is free. The 2-week program includes Fourth of July activities.

For further information, contact the Center for Folklife Programs and Cultural Studies, Suite 2600, 914 L'Enfant Plaza SW., Washington, DC 20560. Phone, 202–287–3424 or 202–357–2700. To purchase recordings, call 800–410–9815.

International Center   The International Center supports Smithsonian activities abroad and coordinates the Smithsonian's international interests, particularly those that do not fall within the scope of a single Smithsonian unit or museum. The International Center provides a meeting place and an organizational channel to bring together the world's scholars, museum professionals, and the general public, to attend and participate in conferences, public forums, lectures, performances, exhibitions, films, and workshops. Through the International Center, the Smithsonian seeks to encourage a broadening of public understanding of the histories, cultures, and natural environments of regions throughout the world.

For further information, contact the Office of International Relations, MRC 705, 1100 Jefferson Drive SW., Washington, DC 20560. Phone, 202–357–1539.

Center for Museum Studies   The Center is an outreach office of the Smithsonian that helps museums in the United States fulfill their public service mission. It conducts training programs for museum professionals on museum operational methods, management of collections, exhibitions techniques, and educational activities.

The Center is also the central intern office for the Institution, registering all interns and administering a central intern application referral service.

Located in the Center is the Smithsonian Institution Libraries Museum Reference Center, the Nation's largest museological library.

For further information, contact the Center for Museum Studies, 900 Jefferson Drive SW., Room 2235, MRC 427, Smithsonian Institution, Washington, DC 20560. Phone, 202–357–3101. Fax, 202–357–3346.

Arthur M. Sackler Gallery   This Asian art museum opened to the public

September 1987 on the National Mall. Changing exhibitions drawn from major collections in the United States and abroad, as well as from the permanent holdings of the Sackler Gallery, are displayed in the distinctive below-ground museum. The Gallery's growing permanent collection is founded on a group of art objects from China, South and Southeast Asia, and the ancient Near East that was given to the Smithsonian by Arthur M. Sackler (1913–1987), a medical researcher, publisher, and art collector. The collection has expanded to include Persian manuscripts; Japanese paintings; ceramics, prints, and textiles; sculptures from India; and paintings and metalware from China, Korea, Japan, and Southeast Asia.

Programs at the Gallery include loan exhibitions and major international shows offering both surveys of distinctive Asian traditions and comparative exhibitions showing the art of different centuries, geographic areas, and types of patronage. Many exhibitions are accompanied by public programs and scholarly symposia.

For further information, contact the Arthur M. Sackler Gallery, 1050 Independence Avenue SW., Washington, DC 20560. Phone, 202–357–2700.

Office of the Smithsonian Institution Archives
The Smithsonian Institution Archives acquires, preserves, and makes available for research the official records of the Smithsonian Institution and the papers of individuals and organizations associated with the Institution or with its work. These holdings document the growth of the Smithsonian and the development of American science, history, and art.

The Institutional History Division explores the history of the Smithsonian by drawing upon the holdings of the Archives and by creating new historical records such as audio and videotaped interviews. Within the Division, the Joseph Henry Papers publishes the correspondence and papers of the Smithsonian's first Secretary, a renowned 19th century scientist.

The National Collections Program assists in and monitors the development of effective collections management policy throughout the Institution and the museum community at large.

For further information, contact the Office of the Smithsonian Institution Archives, 900 Jefferson Drive SW., MRC 414, Washington, DC 20560. Phone, 202–357–1420. Fax, 202–357–2395.

Smithsonian Astrophysical Observatory
The Observatory is located in Cambridge, MA, on the grounds of the Harvard College Observatory. Since 1973, the observatories have coordinated research activities under a single director in a cooperative venture known as the Harvard-Smithsonian Center for Astrophysics.

The Center's research activities are organized in seven divisions, as follows: atomic and molecular physics, radio and geoastronomy, high-energy astrophysics, optical and infrared astronomy, planetary sciences, solar and stellar physics, and theoretical astrophysics.

Data-gathering facilities include a major observatory in Arizona, optical and radio astronomy facilities in Massachusetts, and a submillimeter-wave facility in Hawaii (now under construction). The Smithsonian Astrophysical Observatory's observational capabilities are complemented by library, computation, and laboratory facilities in Cambridge.

Research results are published in the *Center Preprint Series* and other technical and nontechnical bulletins, and distributed to scientific and educational institutions around the world. As a further service to international science, the Smithsonian Astrophysical Observatory serves as the headquarters for Astronomical Telegrams and the Minor Planet Center. Astronomical Telegrams provide rapid international dissemination of news about the discovery of comets, novae, and other astronomical phenomena. The Minor Planet Center is the principal source for all positional observations of asteroids as well as for establishing their orbits and ephemerides.

The Observatory offers an extensive public education program, including a variety of "open nights" held in Cambridge and at other facilities.

Information about these activities and other general materials for students and teachers may be obtained from the Smithsonian Astrophysical Observatory, 60 Garden Street, Cambridge, MA 02138. Phone, 617–495–7461.

Smithsonian Center for Materials Research and Education   The Center is a Smithsonian research institute with a focus on the preservation, conservation, and technical study and analysis of collection materials, with a special emphasis on materials in the national collections. Its researchers investigate the chemical and physical processes that are involved in the deterioration of museum objects and specimens, and attempt to formulate conditions and procedures for storage, exhibit, and stabilization that optimize the preservation of these materials. In interdisciplinary collaborations with archaeologists, anthropologists, and art historians, natural and physical scientists study and analyze objects from the collections and related materials to expand knowledge and understanding of their historical and scientific context. Many of the research projects involve close collaboration with outside scholars and other Government and academic laboratories. The Center also provides active analytical and technical support to conservation and curation efforts in the various museums within and occasionally outside the Smithsonian.

The Center's education program offers a wide range of training opportunities, within the areas of its specialty, to professionals in conservation and related museum disciplines.

For further information, contact the Smithsonian Center for Materials Research and Education, Museum Support Center, 4210 Silver Hill Road, Suitland, MD 20560. Phone, 301–238–3700.

Smithsonian Environmental Research Center   The Center measures physical, chemical, and biological interactions in the environment and determines how these interactions control biological responses. This research is carried out in a 2,600-acre facility in Edgewater, MD, where the ecology of land/water interactions is studied for the estuary and adjacent watersheds of the Chesapeake Bay.

For further information, contact the Smithsonian Environmental Research Center, P.O. Box 28, Edgewater, MD 21037. Phone, 301–261–4190.

Smithsonian Institution Libraries   The libraries of the Smithsonian Institution include more than one million volumes with strengths in natural history, art, science, humanities, and museology. The systems' administrative services and Central Reference and Loan are located in the National Museum of Natural History with 18 branch libraries located in most of the major Smithsonian museums and research units including the Smithsonian Astrophysical Observatory in Cambridge, MA; the Smithsonian Tropical Research Institute in the Republic of Panama; and the National Air and Space Museum. Address inquiries to the appropriate branch library or to Central Reference and Loan.

For further information, contact the Smithsonian Institution Libraries, Tenth Street and Constitution Avenue NW., Washington, DC 20560. Phone, 202–357–2139. E-mail, libhelp@sil.si.edu.

Smithsonian Institution Traveling Exhibition Service (SITES)   Since 1952, SITES has been committed to making Smithsonian exhibitions available to millions of people who cannot view them firsthand at the Smithsonian museums in Washington, DC, and New York City. Each year, audiences across North America experience the treasures and opportunities of the Smithsonian by visiting SITES exhibitions that come to local museums, libraries, science centers, historical societies, zoos, aquariums, community centers, and schools. More than 65 exhibitions on art, history, and science circulate every year. SITES also offers exhibits in its International Gallery on the National Mall, in the S. Dillon Ripley Center, 1100 Jefferson Drive SW.

For further information, to book a SITES exhibition, or to receive a copy of *Update*, the annual catalog of current exhibitions, contact the Smithsonian Institution Traveling Exhibition Service, MRC 706, Smithsonian Institution, Washington, DC 20560. Phone, 202–357–3168.

Smithsonian Marine Research Station
The research institute opens in a new location on South Causeway Island in Fort Pierce, FL, in a state-of-the-art laboratory by the end of 1998. Scientists at the Station catalog species and study marine plants and animals. Among the most important projects being pursued at the site is the search for possible causes of fish kills such as *pfiesteria* and other organisms. National Museum of Natural History scientists also conduct research at the Station, such as documenting the giant squids and conducting biodiversity studies. More than 100 visiting scientists will be accommodated at the new facility, which will include an aquarium, a wet lab, electron microscopes, and conference rooms.

For further information, contact the Smithsonian Marine Research Station, 5612 Old Dixie Highway, Fort Pierce, FL 34946. Phone, 561–465–6632.

Smithsonian Tropical Research Institute (STRI) The Institute is a research organization for advanced studies of tropical ecosystems. Headquartered in the Republic of Panama, STRI maintains extensive facilities in the Western Hemisphere tropics. It is the permanent base of a corps of tropical researchers, who in turn provide an intellectual environment that attracts many visiting scientists and research fellows. The Institute's researchers study the evolution, behavior, ecology, and history of tropical species of systems ranging from coral reefs to tropical rain forests. Growing strengths in molecular biology, plant physiology, and paleoecology complement established excellence in evolutionary biology and ecology.

The Institute operates the Barro Colorado Nature Monument, a 12,000-acre forest reserve, including Barro Colorado Island (protected since 1923) and adjacent peninsulas in Gatun Lake, part of the Panama Canal. It also maintains a research and conference center in Panama City, including one of the world's finest libraries on rain forests and related topics. In addition, STRI has two marine laboratories, one at Naos Island on the Pacific entrance to the Panama Canal and another at Galeta Island on the Atlantic. It administers marine stations in the Caribbean in the San Blas Islands, and at Cayos Cochinos, Honduras, and maintains a research vessel for off-shore studies. The Institute's scientific staff conducts research in these areas as well as in other parts of Central and South America, the Pacific, Asia, and Africa, where comparative studies are clarifying the distinctive role of the tropics.

For a brochure describing the Institute's activities and illustrating some of the facilities and habitats available, contact the Visitor Services Office, Smithsonian Tropical Research Institute, Unit 0948 APO AA.

For further information, contact the Smithsonian Tropical Research Institute, 900 Jefferson Drive SW., MRC 555, Washington, DC 20560. Phone, 202–786–2817. Fax, 202–786–2819. Phone (Panama), 011–507–62–6022. E-mail, siwp01.stridc.bcasana@ic.si.edu.

The John F. Kennedy Center for the Performing Arts The Center, the sole official memorial in Washington to President Kennedy, is an independent bureau of the Smithsonian Institution, administered by a 49-member Board of Trustees.

In a public/private partnership, the Federal Government provides appropriated fund support for the maintenance and operation of the physical facilities of the Presidential monument, while the Board of Trustees is responsible for raising private funds for all of the artistic initiatives. Additional funds for programming and education are derived through box office sales and other earned income, and other government grants. The Center's Board is responsible for administration of the building and for performing arts programming and education.

Since its opening in 1971, the Center has presented a year-round program of the finest in music, dance, and drama from the United States and abroad. Facilities include the Opera House, the Eisenhower Theater, the American Film Institute Theater, the Terrace Theater, the Theater Lab, and the Concert Hall, home of the Center's affiliate, the National Symphony Orchestra.

The Center's Education Department includes the nationwide Performing Arts

Centers and Schools: Partners in Education, American College Theater Festival, Youth and Family Programs, the National Symphony Orchestra Education Program, and the Kennedy Center Alliance for Arts Education Network, designed to increase participation by students throughout the country in Center activities and to establish the Center as a focal point for strengthening the arts in education at all levels.

The Kennedy Center box offices are open daily, and general information and tickets may be obtained by calling 202–467–4600 or 202–416–8524 (TDD). Full-time students, senior citizens over the age of 65, enlisted personnel of grade E–4 and below, fixed low-income groups, and the disabled may purchase tickets for most performances at a 50-percent discount through the Specially Priced Ticket Program. This program is designed to make the Center accessible to all, regardless of economic circumstance.

Visitor services are provided by the Friends of the Kennedy Center volunteers. Tours are available free of charge between 10 a.m. and 1 p.m. daily. Free performances are given every day at 6 p.m. on the Millennium Stage in the Grand Foyer.

For further information, contact the Kennedy Center. Phone, 202–467–4600. Internet, http://www.kennedy-center.org/.

National Gallery of Art   The National Gallery of Art is governed by a Board of Trustees composed of five Trustees and the Secretary of State, the Secretary of the Treasury, the Chief Justice of the United States, and the Secretary of the Smithsonian Institution. It houses one of the finest collections in the world, illustrating Western man's achievements in painting, sculpture, and the graphic arts. The collections, beginning with the 13th century, are rich in European old master paintings and French, Spanish, Italian, American, and British 18th- and 19th-century paintings; sculpture from the late Middle Ages to the present; Renaissance medals and bronzes; Chinese porcelains; and about 75,000 works of graphic art from the 12th to the 20th centuries. The collections are

acquired by private donation rather than by Government funds, which serve solely to operate and maintain the building and its collections.

The National Gallery's West Building, designed by John Russell Pope in neoclassical style, was a gift to the Nation from Andrew W. Mellon, who also bequeathed his collection to the gallery in 1937. On March 17, 1941, President Franklin D. Roosevelt accepted the completed building and works of art on behalf of the people of the United States of America.

The National Gallery's East Building, designed by I.M. Pei, was accepted by President Jimmy Carter in June of 1978 as a gift of Paul Mellon and the late Ailsa Mellon Bruce, son and daughter of the gallery's founder, and the Andrew W. Mellon Foundation. The East Building provides space for temporary exhibitions, the gallery's growing collections, the Center for Advanced Study in the Visual Arts, including greatly expanded library and photographic archives, and administrative and curatorial offices.

A professor-in-residence position is filled annually by a distinguished scholar in the field of art history; graduate and postgraduate research is conducted under a fellowship program; programs for schoolchildren and the general public are conducted daily; and an Extension Service distributes loans of audiovisual materials, including films, slide lectures, and slide sets throughout the world. Publications, slides, and reproductions may be obtained through the Publications Service.

The Micro Gallery, located in the West Building, is the most comprehensive interactive multimedia computer system in any American art museum. Thirteen computers, installed in the redesigned art information room near the Mall entrance, enable visitors to see in magnified detail nearly every work of art on display in the permanent collection, as well as access to information about artists, geographic areas, time periods, pronunciations (with sound), and more. Visitors can design a personal tour of the collection and print it out to use as a guide in the galleries.

For information, call 202–842–6188 or 202–842–6653.

For general information on the National Gallery of Art and its activities, call 202–737–4215. Internet, http://www.nga.gov/.

Woodrow Wilson International Center for Scholars The Center, located in Washington, DC, is the Nation's official memorial to its 28th President. The Center's mandate is to integrate the world of learning with the world of public affairs. Through meetings and conferences, the Center brings scholars together with Members of Congress, Government officials, business leaders, and other policymakers. Through publication of books and the *Wilson Quarterly* and a nationally broadcast radio program, the results of the Center's research and meetings are made publicly available.

The Center awards approximately 20 residential fellowships annually to individuals with project proposals representing the entire range of superior scholarship, with a strong emphasis on the humanities and social sciences.

Applications from any country are welcome. Persons with outstanding capabilities and experience from a wide variety of backgrounds (including government, the corporate world, academia, and other professions) are eligible for appointment. For academic participants, eligibility is limited to the postdoctoral level.

The Center prefers its fellows to be in residence for the academic year— September to May or June—although a few fellowships are available for shorter periods of not less than 4 months.

The Center holds one round of competitive selection per year. The deadline for the receipt of applications is October 1, and decisions on appointments are announced in March of the following year.

For further information, contact the Fellowship Office, Woodrow Wilson Center, Washington, DC 20560. Phone, 202–357–2841. Fax, 202–357–4439. Internet, http://wwics.si.edu/.

Sources of Information

Contracts and Small Business Activities Information may be obtained from the Director, Office of Contracting, Smithsonian Institution, Washington, DC 20560, regarding procurement of supplies; contracts for construction, services, etc.; and property management and utilization services for Smithsonian Institution organizations.

The following independent organizations should be contacted directly: John F. Kennedy Center for the Performing Arts, Washington, DC 20566; and Supply Officer, National Gallery of Art, Sixth Street and Constitution Avenue NW., Washington, DC 20565. Phone, 202–287–3343.

Education and Research Refer to preceding statements on the Office of Fellowships and Grants, the Center for Folklife Programs and Cultural Studies, the National Science Resources Center, the Smithsonian Education Office, and other offices. For information, write to the Directors of these offices at the Smithsonian Institution, Washington, DC 20560.

For information regarding Kennedy Center Education Programs, both in Washington, DC, and in nationwide touring productions and training, contact the John F. Kennedy Center for the Performing Arts, Washington, DC 20566 (phone, 202–416–8000).

The National Gallery of Art's Center for Advanced Study in the Visual Arts was founded in 1979 to promote study of the history, theory, and criticism of art, architecture, and urbanism through the formation of a community of scholars. The activities of the Center for Advanced Study, which include the fellowship program, meetings, research, and publications, are privately funded. For further information, contact the Center for Advanced Study in the Visual Arts, National Gallery of Art, Washington, DC 20565. Phone, 202–842–6480; or fax, 202–842–6733.

Electronic Access Information about the Smithsonian Institution is available electronically through the Internet, at http://www.si.edu/.

Information about programs, activities, and performances at the John F. Kennedy Center for the Performing Arts is available through the Internet, at http://www.kennedy-center.org/.

Information about the National Gallery of Art is available through the Internet, at http://www.nga.gov/.

Information about the programs and activities of the Woodrow Wilson Center for International Scholars is available through the Internet, at http://wwics.si.edu/.

Employment Employment information for the Smithsonian is available from the Office of Human Resources, Smithsonian Institution, Suite 2100, 955 L'Enfant Plaza SW., Washington, DC 20560. Phone, 202–287–3100. Recorded message, 202–287–3102.

Employment information for the following locations may be obtained by contacting the organizations directly as follows: Personnel Office, National Gallery of Art, Fourth Street and Constitution Avenue NW., Washington, DC 20565 (phone, 202–842–6298; or for the hearing impaired (TDD), 202–789–3021); and the John F. Kennedy Center for the Performing Arts, Human Resources Department, Washington, DC 20566 (phone, 202–416–8610).

Films The National Gallery of Art circulates films, slide programs, videos, teaching packets, and videodiscs to schools and civic organizations throughout the country. Contact the Department of Education Resources, National Gallery of Art, Washington, DC 20565. Phone, 202–842–6273. Please write to request a free catalog of programs.

Memberships For information about Smithsonian membership (Resident Program), write to The Smithsonian Associates, MRC 701, 1100 Jefferson Drive SW., Washington, DC 20560. Phone, 202–357–3030. The Resident Program offers a wide variety of performing arts events, courses, lectures, seminars, symposia, films, and guided tours with specialists, authors, celebrities, and other notables. Additional activities include a lecture series for senior adults; classes, workshops, films, and summer camp sessions for young people; and family and adult/child activities. Membership benefits include discounts and admissions priority; a subscription to

Smithsonian magazine; monthly copies of the *Associate,* the award-winning guide to Resident Associate activities; and dining privileges. Additionally, all members receive discounts on museum shop purchases; *Smithsonian Catalog* items; Smithsonian Press/Smithsonian Productions publications and recordings; and discounts on subscriptions to *Air and Space/Smithsonian* magazine. The Smithsonian Associates also offer volunteer opportunities and special services for individuals with disabilities.

For information about Smithsonian membership (National Program), contact The Smithsonian Associates, 1100 Jefferson Drive SW., Washington, DC 20560. Phone, 202–357–4800. National membership benefits include a subscription to *Smithsonian* magazine; information services from the Associates' Reception Center; eligibility to travel on international and U.S. study tours and seminars guided by expert study leaders; discounted tickets for Smithsonian educational events nationwide; and shopping and dining privileges.

The Contributing Membership offers additional opportunities to support the Smithsonian Institution. Contributing members, at various levels, receive an array of benefits—from receiving quarterly issues of *Smithsonian Institution Research Reports* to being invited to the annual James Smithson weekend and other special events. For information about the Contributing Membership, call 202–357–1699.

The Young Benefactors offers individuals between the ages of 25 and 45 the opportunity to increase their understanding of the Institution and to participate in unique fundraising events that assist the Institution in achieving its goals. For additional information about the Young Benefactors, write to The Smithsonian Associates, 1100 Jefferson Drive SW., Washington, DC 20560. Phone, 202–357–1351.

The Circle of the National Gallery of Art is a membership program which provides support for special projects for which Federal funds are not available. Since its inception in 1986, the Circle has provided support for scholarly exhibitions, acquisitions of works of art, publications, films, and symposia at the Gallery's Center for Advanced Study in the Visual Arts. For more information about membership in the Circle of the National Gallery of Art, please write to The Circle, National Gallery of Art, Washington, DC 20565; or call 202–842–6450.

Information about activities of the Friends of the National Zoo and their magazine, *The Zoogoer,* is available by writing to FONZ at the National Zoological Park, Washington, DC 20008. Phone, 202–673–4950.

Information about the national and local activities of Friends of the Kennedy Center (including the bimonthly *Kennedy Center News* for members) is available at the information desks within the Center or by writing to Friends of the Kennedy Center, Washington, DC 20566.

Photographs Color and black-and-white photographs and slides are available to Government agencies, research and educational institutions, publishers, and the general public from the Smithsonian photographic archives. Subjects include photographs of the Smithsonian's scientific, technological, historical, and art collections. Some images date to photography's earliest days. Information, order forms, and price lists may be obtained from the Office of Imaging, Printing, and Photographic Services, Smithsonian Institution, Washington, DC 20560. Phone, 202–357–1933.

Publications Smithsonian Press/ Smithsonian Productions and the Office of Public Affairs publish *Smithsonian Year,* the Institution's annual report. Press/Productions also publishes a range of books and studies related to the sciences, technology, history, air and space, and the arts. A book catalog and a list of studies are available from Publications Sales, Smithsonian Books or Smithsonian Institution University Press, 1111 North Capitol Street, Washington, DC 20002. Phone, 202–287–3738. To purchase a Smithsonian Institution University Press volume, call 800–782–4612. To purchase a recording of the *Smithsonian Collection of Recordings,*

contact Press/Productions. Phone, 800–863–9943.

An events highlight advertisement including opening exhibits is published in the *Washington Post* by the Smithsonian Office of Public Affairs. The advertisement appears the next-to-last Friday of the month.

A free *Welcome* brochure providing a brief guide to the Smithsonian Institution is published in English and several foreign languages. For a copy, call Visitor Information, 202–357–2700. A visitor's guide for individuals with disabilities is also available.

Smithsonian Institution Research Reports, containing news of current research projects in the arts, sciences, and history that are being conducted by Smithsonian staff, is produced by the Smithsonian Office of Public Affairs, 900 Jefferson Drive SW., MRC 421, Washington, DC 20560. Phone, 202–357–2627.

To request a copy of *Smithsonian Runner,* a newsletter about Native American-related activities at the Smithsonian, contact the National Museum of the American Indian, Smithsonian Institution, Washington, DC 20560.

For the newsletter *Art to Zoo* for teachers of fourth through eighth graders, write to the Smithsonian Office of Education, Room 1163, MRC 402, Arts and Industries Building, Washington, DC 20560. Phone, 202–357–2425.

The Gallery Shops, National Gallery of Art (phone, 202–842–6466), makes available quality reproductions and publications about the Gallery's collections. The Information Office provides a monthly Calendar of Events and several brochures including *Brief Guide to the National Gallery of Art* and *An Invitation to the National Gallery of Art* (the latter in several foreign languages).

Radio and Telephone *Radio Smithsonian* produces award-winning radio series and specials about the arts, sciences, and human culture for national broadcast on public radio.

Dial-A-Museum, 202–357–2020 provides a taped message with daily announcements on new exhibits and special events.

Smithsonian Skywatchers Report, 202–357–2000 is a taped message with weekly announcements on stars, planets, and worldwide occurrences of short-lived natural phenomena.

For a *Spanish Listing of Smithsonian Events,* call 202–633–9126.

Concerts From the National Gallery is broadcast 4 weeks after the performance on Washington, DC, area radio station WGTS, 91.9 FM, Sundays at 7 p.m., November through July.

Speakers   The Education Office, National Gallery of Art, Fourth Street and Constitution Avenue NW., Washington, DC 20565, provides gallery talks and lectures. Phone, 202–842–6246.

Special Functions   Inquiries regarding the use of Kennedy Center facilities for special functions may be directed to the Office of Special Events, John F. Kennedy Center for the Performing Arts, Washington, DC 20566. Phone, 202–416–8000.

Theater Operations   Inquiries regarding the use of the Kennedy Center's theaters may be addressed to the Booking Coordinator, John F. Kennedy Center for the Performing Arts, Washington, DC 20566. Phone, 202–416–8000.

Tours   For information about museum and gallery tours, contact the Smithsonian Information Center, 1000 Jefferson Drive, SW., Washington, DC 20560. Phone, 202–357–2700. School groups are welcome.

Special member tours are provided through Friends of the National Zoo, National Zoological Park, 3000 Connecticut Avenue NW., Washington, DC 20008. Phone, 202–673–4821.

Visitor Information   The Smithsonian Information Center, located in the original Smithsonian building, commonly known as "The Castle," provides general orientation, through films, computer interactive programs, and visitor information specialists, to help members and the public learn about the national collections, museum events, exhibitions, and special programs. Write to the Smithsonian Information Center, 1000 Jefferson Drive SW., Washington, DC 20560. Phone, 202–357–2700. TTY, 202–357–1729.

The Visitor Services Office of the National Gallery of Art provides individual assistance to those with special needs, responds to written and telephone requests, supplies crowd control for ticketed exhibitions and programs, and provides information to those planning to visit the Washington, DC, area. For more information, write to the National Gallery of Art, Office of Visitor Services, Washington, DC 20565. Phone, 202–842–6680; or for the hearing impaired (TDD), 202–842–6176.

Volunteer Service Opportunities   The Smithsonian Institution welcomes volunteers and offers a variety of interesting service opportunities. Individuals may serve as tour docents or information volunteers, or may participate in an independent program in which their educational and professional backgrounds are matched with curatorial or research requests from within the Smithsonian. For information, write to the Visitor Information and Associates' Reception Center, 1000 Jefferson Drive SW., Washington, DC 20560. Phone, 202–357–2700. TTY, 202–357–1729.

Volunteers at the National Gallery of Art may select from providing such services as giving tours of the permanent Gallery collection for children and adults in English or foreign languages; serving as art information specialists at the art information desks throughout the West and East buildings; and assisting the library staff on assorted projects. For further details, write the Education Division, National Gallery of Art, Washington, DC 20565. Phone, 202–842–6246; or for the hearing impaired (TDD), 202–842–6176. For library volunteering inquiries, phone 202–842–6510.

For information about volunteer opportunities at the Kennedy Center, write to Friends of the Kennedy Center, Washington, DC 20566. Phone, 202–416–8000.

STATE JUSTICE INSTITUTE

Suite 600, 1650 King Street, Alexandria, VA 22314
Phone, 703–684–6100. Internet, http://www.clark.net/pub/sji/.

Board of Directors:

Cochairmen	JOHN F. DAFFRON, JR., ROBERT A. MILLER
Secretary	SANDRA A. O'CONNOR
Executive Committee Member	TERRENCE B. ADAMSON
Members	JOSEPH F. BACA, ROBERT N. BALDWIN, CARLOS R. GARZA, TOMMY JEWELL, KEITH MCNAMARA, FLORENCE R. MURRAY, JANIE L. SHORES

Officers:

Executive Director	DAVID I. TEVELIN
Deputy Director	RICHARD VAN DUIZEND

The State Justice Institute was established to award grants to improve judicial administration in the State courts of the United States.

The State Justice Institute was created by the State Justice Institute Act of 1984 (42 U.S.C. 10701) as a private, nonprofit corporation to further the development and improvement of judicial administration in the State courts.

The Institute is supervised by a Board of Directors consisting of 11 members appointed by the President with the advice and consent of the Senate. The Board is statutorily composed of six judges, a State court administrator, and four members of the public, of whom no more than two can be of the same political party.

The goals of the Institute are to:

—direct a national program of assistance to ensure that all U.S. citizens have ready access to a fair and effective judicial system;

—foster coordination and cooperation with the Federal Judiciary;

—serve as a clearinghouse and information center for the dissemination of information regarding State judicial systems; and

—encourage education for judges and support personnel of State court systems.

To accomplish these broad objectives, the Institute is authorized to provide funds, through grants, cooperative agreements, and contracts, to State courts and organizations that can assist in the achievement of improving judicial administration of the State courts.

Sources of Information

Inquiries concerning the following programs and activities should be directed to the specified office of the State Justice Institute, Suite 600, 1650 King Street, Alexandria, VA 22314. Phone, 703–684–6100.

Grants—Chief, Program Division.

Publications, consumer information, speakers, Privacy Act/Freedom of Information Act requests—Executive Assistant, Office of the Executive Director.

Employment/personnel—Personnel Specialist.

Information regarding the programs and services of the State Justice Institute is also available through the Internet, at http://www.clark.net/pub/sji/.

For further information, contact the State Justice Institute, Suite 600, 1650 King Street, Alexandria, VA 22314. Phone, 703–684–6100. Internet, http://www.clark.net/pub/sji/.

UNITED STATES INSTITUTE OF PEACE

1550 M Street NW., Washington, DC 20005–1708
Phone, 202–457–1700. Fax, 202–429–6063. Internet, http://www.usip.org/.

Board of Directors:
Public Members:

Chairman	CHESTER A. CROCKER
Vice Chairman	MAX M. KAMPELMAN
Members	DENNIS L. BARK, THEODORE M. HESBURGH, SEYMOUR MARTIN LIPSET, W. SCOTT THOMPSON, ALLEN WEINSTEIN, HARRIET ZIMMERMAN, (3 VACANCIES)

Ex officio:

Deputy Director, U.S. Arms Control and Disarmament Agency	RALPH EARLE II
Assistant Secretary of State for Intelligence and Research	PHYLLIS OAKLEY
President, National Defense University	LT. GEN. RICHARD A. CHILCOAT, USA
Under Secretary of Defense for Policy	WALTER B. SLOCOMBE

Officials:

President	RICHARD H. SOLOMON
Executive Vice President	HARRIET HENTGES
Vice President	CHARLES E. NELSON
Director, Education and Training	PAMELA AALL, *Acting*
Director, Research and Studies	PATRICK CRONIN
Director, Grants Program	DAVID R. SMOCK
Director, Jennings Randolph Fellowship Program for International Peace	JOSEPH L. KLAITS
Director, Jeannette Rankin Library Program	MARGARITA STUDEMEISTER
Director, Administration	BERNICE J. CARNEY
Director, Office of Communications	SHERYL BROWN
Director, Rule of Law Initiative	NEIL J. KRITZ
Senior Scholar for Religion, Ethics, and Human Rights	DAVID LITTLE

The United States Institute of Peace was established to promote research, policy analysis, education, and training on international peace and conflict resolution.

The United States Institute of Peace is an independent Federal institution created and funded by Congress to develop and disseminate knowledge about international peace and conflict resolution. The Institute addresses this mandate in three principal ways:

—by expanding basic and applied knowledge about the origins, nature, and processes of peace and war, encompassing the widest spectrum of approaches and insights;

—by disseminating this knowledge to officials, policymakers, diplomats, and others engaged in efforts to promote international peace; and

—by supporting education and training programs and providing information for secondary and university-level teachers and students and the general public.

The Institute's primary activities are grantmaking, fellowships, in-house research projects, public education and outreach activities, publications, and library services.

The Grants Program provides financial support for research, information services, education, and training. Eligible grantees include nonprofit organizations; official public institutions, such as public schools, colleges, universities, libraries, and State and local agencies; and individuals.

The Jennings Randolph Program for International Peace provides fellowships to scholars, doctoral candidates, practitioners, and other professionals to undertake research and other appropriate forms of work on issues of international peace and the management of

international conflicts. The Research and Studies Program conducts conferences, seminars, and study groups on issues of short- and long-term significance.

The Jeannette Rankin Library Program has four main components: a specialized research library; a network with and support for other libraries, both private and public; an oral history resource; and bibliographic as well as other data bases.

The Office of Communications fulfills requests for speakers and media services, answers general inquiries, and conducts outreach programs in Washington, DC, and elsewhere. Institute-directed activities under the Education and Training Program include educational video programs, teacher training projects, and a National Peace Essay Contest for high school students. Institute publications include the *Biennial Report to Congress and the President;* a newsletter, *Peace Watch;* periodic papers on selected topics, *Peaceworks;* and monographs, books, and *Special Reports* generated from Institute-sponsored projects.

Sources of Information

Electronic access to the Institute is available through the Internet, at http://www.usip.org/.

For further information, contact the Office of Communications, United States Institute of Peace, Suite 700, 1550 M Street NW., Washington, DC 20005–1708.   Phone, 202–457–1700.   Internet, http://www.usip.org/.

SELECTED MULTILATERAL ORGANIZATIONS

MULTILATERAL INTERNATIONAL ORGANIZATIONS IN WHICH THE UNITED STATES PARTICIPATES

Explanatory note: The United States participates in the organizations named below in accordance with the provisions of treaties, other international agreements, congressional legislation, or executive arrangements. In some cases, no financial contribution is involved.

Various commissions, councils, or committees subsidiary to the organizations listed here are not named separately on this list. These include the international bodies for narcotics control, which are subsidiary to the United Nations.

I. United Nations, Specialized Agencies, and International Atomic Energy Agency

Food and Agricultural Organization
International Atomic Energy Agency
International Civil Aviation Organization
International Labor Organization
International Maritime Organization
International Telecommunication Union
United Nations
Universal Postal Union
World Health Organization
World Intellectual Property Organization
World Meteorological Organization

II. Peacekeeping

United Nations Angola Verification Mission III
United Nations Disengagement Observer Force (Golan Heights)
United Nations Force in Cyprus
United Nations Interim Force in Lebanon
United Nations Iraq-Kuwait Observer Mission
United Nations Military Observer Group in India and Pakistan
United Nations Mission in Bosnia-Herzegovina
United Nations Mission in Haiti
United Nations Mission to Prevlaka

United Nations Mission of Observers in Tajikistan
United Nations Mission for the Referendum in Western Sahara
United Nations Observer Mission in Georgia
United Nations Observer Mission in Liberia
United Nations Preventive Deployment Force (Macedonia)
United Nations Transitional Authority in Eastern Slavonia
United Nations Truce Supervision Organization (Middle East)

III. Inter-American Organizations

Inter-American Indian Institute
Inter-American Institute for Cooperation on Agriculture
Inter-American Tropical Tuna Commission
Organization of American States
Pan American Health Organization (PAHO)
Pan American Institute of Geography and History
Postal Union of the Americas and Spain and Portugal

747

IV. Regional Organizations

Asia-Pacific Economic Cooperation
Colombo Plan for Cooperative Economic and Social Development in Asia and the Pacific
North Atlantic Assembly
North Atlantic Treaty Organization
Organization for Economic Cooperation and Development (OECD)
South Pacific Commission

V. Other International Organizations

Bureau of International Expositions
Commission for the Conservation of Antarctic Marine Living Resources
Customs Cooperation Council (CCC)
Fund for the Protection of the World Cultural and Natural Heritage
Hague Conference on Private International Law
International Agency for Research on Cancer
International Bureau of the Permanent Court of Arbitration
International Bureau for the Publication of Customs Tariffs
International Bureau of Weights and Measures
International Center for the Study of the Preservation and the Restoration of Cultural Property (ICCROM)
International Commission for the Conservation of Atlantic Tunas
International Copper Study Group
International Cotton Advisory Committee
International Council for the Exploration of the Seas (ICES)
International Council of Scientific Unions and Its Associated Unions (20)
International Criminal Police Organization (INTERPOL)
International Hydrographic Organization
International Institute for Cotton
International Institute for the Unification of Private Law
International Lead and Zinc Study Group
International Natural Rubber Organization
International North Pacific Fisheries Commission
International Office of Epizootics
International Office of Vine and Wine
International Organization for Legal Metrology
International Rubber Study Group

International Seed Testing Association
International Tropical Timber Organization
International Union for the Conservation of Nature and Natural Resources (IUNC)
International Union for the Protection of New Varieties of Plants (UPOV)
International Whaling Commission
International Wheat Council
Interparliamentary Union
North Atlantic Ice Patrol
North Atlantic Salmon Conservation Organization
Organization for the Prevention of Chemical Weapons
Permanent International Association of Navigation Congresses
Permanent International Association of Road Congresses
United Nations Compensation Commission
World Trade Organization (WTO)/ General Agreement on Tariffs and Trade (GATT)

VI. Special Voluntary Programs

Colombo Plan Drug Advisory Program
Consultative Group on International Agricultural Research
Convention on International Trade in Endangered Species of Wild Fauna and Flora (CITES)
International Atomic Energy Agency Technical Assistance and Cooperation Fund
International Atomic Energy Agency Voluntary Programs
International Civil Aviation Organization (ICAO) Aviation Security Fund
International Contributions for Scientific, Educational, and Cultural Activities
International Fund for Agricultural Development (IFAD)
International Organization for Migration (IOM)
Korean Peninsula Energy Development Organization
Montreal Protocol Multilateral Fund
Organization of American States Fund for Strengthening Democracy
Organization of American States Special Cultural Fund
Organization of American States Special Development Assistance Fund

Organization of American States Special Multilateral Fund (Education and Science)

Organization of American States Special Projects Fund (Mar del Plata)

Pan American Health Organization Special Health Promotion Funds

United Nations Afghanistan Emergency Trust Fund

United Nations Center for Human Settlements (Habitat) (UNCHS)

United Nations Children's Fund (UNICEF)

United Nations Development Fund for Women (UNIFEM)

United Nations Development Program (UNDP)

United Nations Environment Program (UNEP)

United Nations/Food and Agricultural Organization World Food Program (WFP)

United Nations Fund for Drug Abuse Control (UNFDAC)

United Nations High Commissioner for Refugees Program (UNHCR)

United Nations Population Fund

United Nations Relief and Works Agency (UNRWA)

United Nations Volunteers (UNV)

World Health Organization Special Programs

World Meteorological Organization Special Fund for Climate Activities

World Meteorological Organization Voluntary Cooperation Program

African Development Bank

Headquarters: 01 B.P. 1387, Abidjan 01, Côte d'Ivoire

President: Omar Kabbaj

The African Development Bank (AFDB) was established in 1963 and, by charter amendment, opened its membership to non-African countries in 1982. Its mandate is to contribute to the economic development and social progress of its regional members. Bank members total 77, including 53 African countries and 24 nonregional countries. Ownership of the Bank, by charter, is two-thirds African and one-third nonregional.

The African Development Fund (AFDF), the concessional lending affiliate, was established in 1973 to complement AFDB operations by providing concessional financing for high-priority development projects in the poorest African countries. The Fund's membership consists of 25 nonregional member countries and AFDB, which represents its African members and is allocated half of the votes.

Asian Development Bank

Headquarters: 6 ADB Avenue, Mandaluyong City, 0401 Metro Manila, Philippines. Phone, 632-632-4444. Fax, 632-636-2444

President: Mitsuo Sato

The Asian Development Bank commenced operations on December 19, 1966. It now has 56 member countries—40 from Asia and 16 from outside the region.

The purpose of the Bank is to foster sustainable economic development, poverty alleviation, and cooperation among its developing member countries in the Asia/Pacific region.

For further information, contact the Asian Development Bank, P.O. Box 789, 0980 Manila, Philippines. E-mail, adbhq@mail.asiandevbank.org. Internet, http://www.asiandevbank.org/.

Inter-American Defense Board

2600 Sixteenth Street NW., Washington, DC 20441. Phone, 202-939-6600

Chairman: Maj. Gen. John C. Thompson, USA

The Inter-American Defense Board is the oldest permanently constituted, international military organization in the world. It was founded by Resolution XXXIX of the Meeting of Foreign Ministers at Rio de Janeiro in January 1942. Senior army, navy, and air force officers from 25 member nations staff the various agencies of the Board. Its four major agencies are: the Council of Delegates, the decisionmaking body; the International Staff; the Inter-American Defense College; and the Secretariat, which provides administrative and logistical support.

The Board studies and recommends to member governments measures necessary for close military collaboration in preparation for the collective self-defense of the American Continents. It also acts as a technical military adviser for the Organization of American States, and is involved in projects such as disaster relief planning and demining programs in Central America.

The College prepares senior military officers and civilian functionaries for positions in their respective governments.

Inter-American Development Bank

Headquarters: 1300 New York Avenue NW., Washington, DC 20577. Phone, 202–623–1000

President: Enrique V. Iglesias

The Inter-American Development Bank (IDB) was established in 1959 to help accelerate economic and social development in Latin America and the Caribbean. It is based in Washington, DC.

The Bank has 28 member countries in the Western Hemisphere and 18 outside of the region.

Inter-American Investment Corporation

Headquarters: 1300 New York Avenue NW., Washington, DC 20577. Phone, 202–623–3900

Chairman of Board of Directors: Enrique Iglesias
General Manager: John Rahming, *Acting*

The Inter-American Investment Corporation (IIC), an affiliate of the Inter-American Development Bank, was established in 1984 to promote the economic development of its Latin American and Caribbean members by financing small and medium-size private enterprises. IIC makes direct loans and equity investments and grants lines of credit to local financial intermediaries. It is based in Washington, DC.

IIC has 35 member countries, of which 25 are in the Western Hemisphere, including the United States, and 10 are outside the region.

International Bank for Reconstruction and Development

Headquarters: 1818 H Street NW., Washington, DC 20433. Phone, 202–477–1234

President: James D. Wolfensohn

The International Bank for Reconstruction and Development (IBRD), also known as the World Bank, officially came into existence on December 27, 1945.

The Bank's purpose is to promote economic, social, and environmental progress in developing nations by reducing poverty so that their people may live better and fuller lives. The Bank lends funds at market-determined interest rates, provides advice, and serves as a catalyst to stimulate outside investments. Its resources come primarily from funds raised in the world capital markets, its retained earnings, and repayments on its loans.

International Development Association

The International Development Association (IDA) came into existence on September 24, 1960, as an affiliate of IBRD. The Association's resources consist of subscriptions and supplementary resources in the form of general replenishments, mostly from its more industrialized and developed members; special contributions by its richer members; repayments on earlier credits; and transfers from IBRD's net earnings.

The Association promotes economic development, reduces poverty, and raises the standard of living in the least developed areas of the world. It does this by financing their developmental requirements on concessionary terms, which are more flexible and bear less heavily on the balance of payments than those of conventional loans, thereby furthering the objectives of IBRD and supplementing its activities.

International Finance Corporation

Headquarters: 1850 "I" Street NW., Washington, DC 20433. Phone, 202–477–1234

President: James D. Wolfensohn

Executive Vice President: Jannik Lindbaek

The International Finance Corporation (IFC), an affiliate of the World Bank, was established in July 1956, to promote productive private enterprise in developing member countries.

The Corporation pursues its objective principally through direct debt and equity investments in projects that establish new businesses or expand, modify, or diversify existing businesses. It also encourages cofinancing by other investors and lenders. For every dollar of financing approved by IFC for its own account, other investors and lenders provide almost six dollars.

Additionally, advisory services and technical assistance are provided by IFC to developing member countries in areas such as capital market development, privatization, corporate restructuring, and foreign investment.

International Monetary Fund

700 Nineteenth Street NW., Washington, DC 20431. Phone, 202–623–7000. Internet, http:/ /www.imf.org/.

Managing Director and Chairman of the Executive Board: Michel Camdessus

The Final Act of the United Nations Monetary and Financial Conference, signed at Bretton Woods, NH, on July 22, 1944, set forth the original Articles of Agreement of the International Monetary Fund (IMF). The Agreement became effective on December 27, 1945, when the President, authorized by the Bretton Woods Agreements Act (22 U.S.C. 286) accepted membership for the United States in IMF, the Agreement having thus been accepted by countries whose combined financial commitments (quotas) equaled approximately 80 percent of IMF's total commitments. The inaugural meeting of the Board of Governors was held in March 1946, and the first meeting of the Executive Directors was held May 6, 1946.

On May 31, 1968, the Board of Governors approved an amendment to the Articles of Agreement for the establishment of a facility based on Special Drawing Rights (SDR) in IMF and for modification of certain IMF rules and practices. The amendment became effective on July 28, 1969, and the Special Drawing Account became operative on August 6, 1969. United States acceptance of the amendment and participation in the Special Drawing Account were authorized by the Special Drawing Rights Act (22 U.S.C. 286 *et seq.*).

On April 30, 1976, the Board of Governors approved a second amendment to the Articles of Agreement, which entered into force on April 1, 1978. This amendment gave members the right to adopt exchange arrangements of their choice while placing certain obligations on them regarding their exchange rate policies, over which IMF was to exercise firm surveillance. The official price of gold was abolished and the SDR account was promoted as the principal reserve asset of the international monetary system. United States acceptance of this amendment was authorized by the Bretton Woods Agreements Act Amendments (22 U.S.C. 286e–5).

On June 28, 1990, the Board of Governors approved a third amendment to the Articles of Agreement, which became effective on November 11, 1992. Under this amendment, a member's voting rights and certain related rights may be suspended by a 70-percent majority of the executive board if the member, having been declared ineligible to use the general resources of the Fund, persists in its failure to fulfill any of its obligations under the Articles.

As of December 31, 1997, IMF had 182 member countries. Total quotas were SDR 145 billion (equivalent to approximately $200 billion).

The purposes of IMF are to promote international monetary cooperation through a permanent forum for consultation and collaboration on international monetary problems; to facilitate the expansion and balanced growth of international trade; to promote exchange rate stability; to assist in the establishment of an open multilateral system of payments for current transactions between members; and to give confidence to members by making

IMF resources temporarily available to them under adequate safeguards.

In accordance with these purposes, IMF seeks to help its members correct the imbalances in their international balances of payments. It provides financial assistance to aid its members in handling balance-of-payment difficulties through a variety of facilities that are designed to address specific problems. These lending mechanisms include stand-by and extended arrangements, as well as separate facilities to provide compensatory and contingency financing to countries suffering temporary declines in their export earnings, to support structural adjustment programs in the poorest countries, and to provide emergency financial assistance to countries experiencing financial crises. IMF also provides periodic policy advice and technical assistance and training to its members.

For further information, contact the Chief, Editorial Division, External Relations Department, International Monetary Fund, 700 Nineteenth Street NW., Washington, DC 20431. Phone, 202–623–7364. Internet, http://www.imf.org/.

International Organization for Migration

Headquarters: 17 Route des Morillons, Grand-Saconnex, Geneva. Mailing address, P.O. Box 71, CH–1211, Geneva 19, Switzerland. Phone, 011–41–22–717–9111. Fax, 011–41–22–798–6150.

Director General: James N. Purcell, Jr. (United States)

Deputy Director General: Narcisa L. Escaler (Philippines)

Washington Office: Suite 1110, 1750 K Street NW., Washington, DC 20006. Phone, 202–862–1826. Fax, 202–862–1879. E-mail, mission@washington.iom.ch
Chief of Mission: Hans-Petter Boe (Norway)

New York Office: Suite 1610, 122 E. 42d Street, New York, NY 10168. Phone, 212–681–7000. Fax, 212–867–5887. E-mail, mission@newyork.iom.ch
Chief of Mission: Andrew Bruce (New Zealand)

Permanent United Nations Observer: Robert G. Paiva (United States)

The International Organization for Migration (IOM), formerly the Intergovernmental Committee for Migration, was created in 1951 at an international migration conference in Brussels sponsored by the United States and Belgium. It was formed outside the United Nations system in order to provide assistance, including health screening and transportation, to refugees as well as to persons not under the protection of the U.N. High Commissioner for Refugees, and to be concerned with international migration issues in general such as the links between migration and development.

As a technical, nonpolitical organization committed to the statement that humane and orderly migration benefits migrants and society, IOM has four strategic objectives:

—to cooperate with its partners in the international community to assist in meeting the operational challenges of migration;

—to advance understanding of migration issues;

—to encourage social and economic development through migration; and

—to work toward effective respect of the human dignity and well-being of migrants.

The Organization plans and carries out refugee migration schemes, programs for returning migrants, and emergency relief activities at the request of its member states and in cooperation with other international organizations, especially U.N. agencies. In addition, it publishes surveys and sponsors conferences on migration trends and issues.

In the United States, IOM carries out certain activities for the U.S. Refugee Admissions Program, facilitates sponsor prepayment for other U.S.-bound immigrants, and operates a limited number of return migration programs. In addition to Washington, DC, and New York, IOM has offices in Chicago, Los Angeles, Miami, and San Francisco.

The Organization comprises 110 states (60 members and 50 observers). They meet once a year in Geneva as the Council, to consider global migration issues and the Organization's work, direction, and budget. Mandatory assessed contributions from member states finance IOM's administrative budget, whereas its operational budget is funded through voluntary contributions. Member states elect the Director General and the Deputy Director General, whose regular terms are 5 years. Several international governmental and nongovernmental organizations are invited to observe and address the IOM Council.

The Organization has observer status at U.N. agencies, the Organization of American States, and other organizations.

Multilateral Investment Guarantee Agency

Headquarters: 1818 H Street NW., Washington, DC 20433. Phone, 202–477–1234

President: James D. Wolfensohn
Executive Vice President: Akira Iida

The Multilateral Investment Guarantee Agency (MIGA), an affiliate of the World Bank, was formally constituted in April 1988.

Its basic purpose is to facilitate the flow of foreign private investment for productive purposes to developing member countries by offering long-term political risk insurance in the areas of expropriation, currency transfer, and war and civil disturbance; and by providing advisory and consultative services. The Agency cooperates with national investment insurance schemes, such as OPIC, and with private insurers.

Organization of American States

General Secretariat: 1889 F Street NW., Washington, DC 20006. Phone, 202–458–3000. Fax, 202–458–3967

Secretary General: César Gaviria
Assistant Secretary General: Christopher Thomas
Executive Secretary for Integral Development: Leonel Zuñiga, *Acting*
Assistant Secretary for Management: James Harding
Assistant Secretary for Legal Affairs: Enrique Lagos

The Organization of American States (OAS) is a regional, intergovernmental organization whose primary purposes are to strengthen the peace and security of the continent; to promote and consolidate representative democracy, with due respect for the principle of nonintervention; to prevent possible causes of difficulties and to conciliate disputes that may arise among the member states; to provide for common action by those states in the event of aggression; to seek the solution of political, juridical, and economic problems that may arise among them; to promote, by cooperative action, their economic, social, and cultural development; and to achieve an effective limitation of conventional weapons that will make it possible to devote the largest amount of resources to the economic and social development of the member states.

With roots dating from 1890, the first OAS Charter was signed in 1948. Three subsequent protocols of amendment, Buenos Aires 1967, Cartagena de Indias 1985, and Washington 1992, gave it its present form. The Protocol of Washington, which entered into force on September 25, 1997, incorporated provisions for the protection of democratically constituted governments and will include among the essential purposes of the Organization the eradication of extreme poverty, which constitutes an obstacle to the full democratic development of the peoples of the hemisphere. A fourth protocol of amendment, the Protocol of Managua 1993, which entered into force on January 29, 1996, established the Inter–American Council for Integral Development (CIDI), which replaces the Inter–American Councils for Economic and Social Affairs and Education, Science and Culture.

The Organization's member states are Argentina, Antigua and Barbuda, Commonwealth of the Bahamas, Barbados, Belize, Bolivia, Brazil, Canada, Chile, Colombia, Costa Rica, Cuba, Commonwealth of Dominica, Dominican Republic, Ecuador, El Salvador, Grenada, Guatemala, Guyana, Haiti, Honduras, Jamaica, Mexico,

Nicaragua, Panama, Paraguay, Peru, St. Kitts and Nevis, St. Lucia, St. Vincent and the Grenadines, Suriname, Trinidad and Tobago, the United States of America, Uruguay, and Venezuela. The present Government of Cuba is excluded from participation by a decision of the Eighth Meeting of Consultation of Ministers of Foreign Affairs in 1962. Thirty-seven non-American countries, as well as the Holy See and the European Union, are permanent observers.

The principal organs of the OAS are:

—the General Assembly, which is normally composed of the foreign ministers of the member states and meets at least once a year to decide the general action and policy of the Organization;

—the Meeting of Consultation of Ministers of Foreign Affairs, which meets on call to consider urgent matters of common interest or threats to the peace and security of the hemisphere;

—the Permanent Council, which meets twice a month at OAS headquarters;

—the Inter-American Council for Integral Development;

—the Inter-American Juridical Committee;

—the Inter-American Commission on Human Rights; and

—the General Secretariat, which is the central and permanent organ, headquartered in Washington, DC.

The Organization has six specialized organizations that handle technical matters of common interest to the American States. It also holds specialized conferences on specific technical matters.

For further information, contact the Director, Department of Public Information, Organization of American States, Seventeenth Street and Constitution Avenue NW., Washington, DC 20006. Phone, 202–458–3760. Fax, 202–458–6421.

United Nations

United Nations, New York, NY 10017. Phone, 212–963–1234

Secretary-General: Kofi A. Annan

United Nations Office at Geneva: Palais des Nations, 1211 Geneva 10, Switzerland

Director-General: Antoine Blanca

United Nations Office at Vienna: Vienna International Centre, P.O. Box 500, A–1400, Vienna, Austria

Director-General: Giorgio Giacomelli

Washington, DC, Office: U.N. Information Centre, Suite 400, 1775 K Street NW., Washington, DC 20006. Phone, 202–331–8670. Fax, 202–331–9191

Director: Joe Sills

The United Nations is an international organization that was set up in accordance with the Charter [1] drafted by governments represented at the Conference on International Organization meeting at San Francisco. The Charter was signed on June 26, 1945, and came into force on October 24, 1945, when the required number of ratifications and accessions had been made by the signatories. Amendments increasing membership of the Security Council and the Economic and Social Council came into effect on August 31, 1965.

The United Nations now consists of 185 member states, of which 51 are founding members.

The purposes of the United Nations set out in the Charter are: to maintain international peace and security; to develop friendly relations among nations; to achieve international cooperation in solving international problems of an economic, social, cultural, or humanitarian character and in promoting respect for human rights; and to be a center for harmonizing the actions of nations in the attainment of these common ends.

The principal organs of the United Nations are:

General Assembly All states that are members of the United Nations are members of the General Assembly. Its functions are to consider and discuss any matter within the scope of the Charter of

---

[1] Charter of the United Nations, together with the Statute of the International Court of Justice (Department of State Publication No. 2353, International Organization and Conference Series III, 21), June 26, 1945. Available for sale from the Superintendent of Documents, Government Printing Office, Washington, DC 20402. Phone, 202–512–1800.

the United Nations and to make recommendations to the members of the United Nations and other organs. It approves the budget of the organization, the expenses of which are borne by the members as apportioned by the General Assembly.

The General Assembly may call the attention of the Security Council to situations likely to endanger international peace and security, may initiate studies, and may receive and consider reports from other organs of the United Nations. Under the "Uniting for Peace" resolution adopted by the General Assembly in November 1950, if the Security Council fails to act on an apparent threat to or breach of the peace or act of aggression because of lack of unanimity of its five permanent members, the Assembly itself may take up the matter within 24 hours—in emergency special session—and recommend collective measures, including, in case of a breach of the peace or act of aggression, use of armed force when necessary to maintain or restore international peace and security.

The General Assembly normally meets in regular annual session in September. It also has met in special sessions and emergency special sessions.

Security Council   The Security Council consists of 15 members, of which 5—the People's Republic of China, France, Russia, the United Kingdom, and the United States of America—are permanent members and are elected each year. The 10 nonpermanent members are elected for 2-year terms by the General Assembly. The primary responsibility of the Security Council is to act on behalf of the members of the United Nations in maintenance of international peace and security. Measures that may be employed by the Security Council are outlined in the Charter.

The Security Council, together with the General Assembly, also elects the judges of the International Court of Justice and makes a recommendation to the General Assembly on the appointment of the Secretary-General of the organization.

The Security Council first met in London on January 17, 1946, and is so organized as to be able to function continuously.

Economic and Social Council   This organ is responsible, under the authority of the General Assembly, for the economic and social programs of the United Nations. Its functions include making or initiating studies, reports, and recommendations on international economic, social, cultural, educational, health, and related matters; promoting respect for and observance of human rights and fundamental freedoms for all; calling international conferences and preparing draft conventions for submission to the General Assembly on matters within its competence; negotiating agreements with the specialized agencies and defining their relationship with the United Nations; coordinating the activities of the specialized agencies; and consulting with nongovernmental organizations concerned with matters within its competence. The Council consists of 54 members of the United Nations elected by the General Assembly for 3-year terms; 18 are elected each year.

The Council usually holds two regular sessions a year. It has also held a number of special sessions.

Trusteeship Council   The Trusteeship Council was initially established to consist of any member states that administered trust territories, permanent members of the Security Council that did not administer trust territories, and enough other nonadministering countries elected by the General Assembly for 3-year terms to ensure that membership would be equally divided between administering and nonadministering members. Under authority of the General Assembly, the Council considered reports from members administering trust territories, examined petitions from trust territory inhabitants, and provided for periodic inspection visits to trust territories.

With the independence of Palau, the last remaining U.N. trust territory, the Trusteeship Council formally suspended operations after nearly half a century.

The council will henceforth meet only on an extraordinary basis, as the need may arise.

International Court of Justice   The International Court of Justice is the principal judicial organ of the United Nations. It has its seat at The Hague, The Netherlands. All members of the United Nations are *ipso facto* parties to the Statute of the Court. Nonmembers of the United Nations may become parties to the Statute of the Court on conditions prescribed by the General Assembly on the recommendation of the Security Council.

The jurisdiction of the Court comprises all cases that the parties refer to it and all matters specially provided for in the Charter of the United Nations or in treaties and conventions in force.

The Court consists of 15 judges known as "members" of the Court. They are elected for 9-year terms by the General Assembly and the Security Council, voting independently, and may be reelected.

Secretariat   The Secretariat consists of a Secretary-General and "such staff as the Organization may require." The Secretary-General, who is appointed by the General Assembly on the recommendation of the Security Council, is the chief administrative officer of the United Nations. He acts in that capacity for the General Assembly, the Security Council, the Economic and Social Council, and the Trusteeship Council. Under the Charter, the Secretary-General "may bring to the attention of the Security Council any matter that in his opinion may threaten the maintenance of international peace and security."

SELECTED BILATERAL ORGANIZATIONS

International Boundary Commission, United States and Canada

United States Section: Suite 100, 1250 23d Street NW., Washington, DC 20037. Phone, 202–736–9100.

Canadian Section: Room 571, 615 Booth Street, Ottawa, ON K1A 0E9. Phone, 613–992–1294.

International Boundary and Water Commission, United States and Mexico

United States Section: Suite C–310, 4171 North Mesa Street, El Paso, TX 79902. Phone, 915–832–4100.

Mexican Section: No. 2180, Avenida Universidad, Ciudad Juárez, Chihuahua, Mexico 32310; or P.O. Box 10525, El Paso, TX 79995. Phone, 011–52–161–37363.

International Joint Commission—United States and Canada

United States Section: Suite 100, 1250 23d Street NW., Washington, DC 20440. Phone, 202–736–9000. Fax, 202–736–9015.

Canadian Section: 100 Metcalfe Street, Ottawa, ON K1P 5M1. Phone, 613–995–2984. Fax, 613–993–5583.

Regional Office: 100 Ouellette Avenue, Windsor, ON N9A 6T3; or P.O. Box 32869, Detroit MI 48232. Phone, 519–257–6700 or 313–226–2170. Fax, 519–257–6740.

Joint Mexican-United States Defense Commission

United States Section: Suite 509, 1111 Jefferson Davis Highway, Arlington, VA 22202. Phone, 703–604–0482 or 703–604–0483.

Mexican Section: 1911 Pennsylvania Avenue NW., Mexican Embassy, Sixth Floor, Washington, DC 20006. Phone, 202–728–1748.

Permanent Joint Board on Defense—United States and Canada

United States Section: Suite 511, 1111 Jefferson Davis Highway, Arlington, VA 22202. Phone, 703–604–0488. Fax, 703–604–0486.

Canadian Section: National Defense Headquarters, 125 Sussex Drive, Ottawa, ON K1A 0G2. Phone, 613–992–5457.

Appendices

APPENDIX A: Commonly Used Abbreviations and Acronyms

AARCC   Alternative Agricultural Research and Commercialization Corporation

ABMC   American Battle Monuments Commission

ACDA   United States Arms Control and Disarmament Agency

ACF   Administration for Children and Families

ACYF   Administration on Children, Youth, and Families

ADA   Americans with Disabilities Act of 1990

ADB   Asian Development Bank

ADD   Administration on Developmental Disabilities

AFAA   Air Force Audit Agency

AFBCMR   Air Force Board for Correction of Military Records

AFCARA   Air Force Civilian Appellate Review Agency

AFDB   African Development Bank

AFDC   Aid to Families with Dependent Children

AFDF   African Development Fund

AFSC   Armed Forces Staff College

AGRICOLA   Agricultural Online Access

AHCPR   Agency for Health Care Policy and Research

AmeriCorps NCCC   AmeriCorps*National Civilian Community Corps

AMS   Agricultural Marketing Service

Amtrak   National Railroad Passenger Corporation

ANA   Administration for Native Americans

AOA   Administration on Aging

APHIS   Animal and Plant Health Inspection Service

ARC   Appalachian Regional Commission

ARS   Agricultural Research Service

ATF   Bureau of Alcohol, Tobacco, and Firearms

ATSDR   Agency for Toxic Substances and Disease Registry

BEA   Bureau of Economic Analysis

BIA   Bureau of Indian Affairs

BIC   Business Information Center (SBA)

BJA   Bureau of Justice Assistance

BJS   Bureau of Justice Statistics

BLM   Bureau of Land Management

BLS   Bureau of Labor Statistics

BTS   Bureau of Transportation Statistics

BVA   Board of Veterans' Appeals

C^3I Command, Control, Communications, and Intelligence

C^4 Command, Control, Communications, and Computers

C⁴I	Command, Control, Communications, Computers, and Intelligence
CALS	Continuous Acquisition and Life-Cycle Support
CBO	Congressional Budget Office
CCC	Commodity Credit Corporation
CDBG	Community Development Block Grant
CDC	Centers for Disease Control and Prevention
CEA	Council of Economic Advisers
CEOS	Child Exploitation and Obscenity Section (Justice)
CEQ	Council on Environmental Quality
CFA	Commission of Fine Arts
CFR	*Code of Federal Regulations*
CFTC	Commodity Futures Trading Commission
CIA	Central Intelligence Agency
CITES	Convention on International Trade in Endangered Species of Wild Fauna and Flora
CNO	Chief of Naval Operations
COPS	Office of Community Oriented Policing Services (Justice)
CPSC	Consumer Product Safety Commission
CRS	Congressional Research Service
CSAP	Center for Substance Abuse Prevention
CSAT	Center for Substance Abuse Treatment
CSE	Office of Child Support Enforcement
CSREES	Cooperative State Research, Education, and Extension Service
CSS	Central Security Service
DA	Department of the Army
DARPA	Defense Advanced Research Projects Agency
DCAA	Defense Contract Audit Agency
DCMC	Defense Contract Management Command
DEA	Drug Enforcement Administration
DIA	Defense Intelligence Agency
DISA	Defense Information Systems Agency
DLA	Defense Logistics Agency
DLSA	Defense Legal Services Agency
DOC	Department of Commerce
DOD	Department of Defense
DOE	Department of Energy
DOL	Department of Labor
DOT	Department of Transportation
DSS	Defense Security Service
DSWA	Defense Special Weapons Agency
DTSA	Defense Technology Security Administration
EDA	Economic Development Administration
EEOC	Equal Employment Opportunity Commission
EO	Executive order
EOUSA	Executive Office for United States Attorneys
EPA	Environmental Protection Agency
ERS	Economic Research Service
Ex-Im Bank	Export-Import Bank of the United States
FAA	Federal Aviation Administration
Fannie Mae	Federal National Mortgage Association
Farmer Mac	Federal Agricultural Mortgage Corporation
FAS	Foreign Agricultural Service
FBI	Federal Bureau of Investigation
FCC	Federal Communications Commission
FDA	Food and Drug Administration
FDIC	Federal Deposit Insurance Corporation
FEB's	Federal Executive Boards
FEC	Federal Election Commission
FEDRIP	Federal Research in Progress Database

FEMA	Federal Emergency Management Agency	HRSA	Health Resources and Services Administration
FERC	Federal Energy Regulatory Commission	HUD	Department of Housing and Urban Development
FFB	Federal Financing Bank	HUMINT	Defense Human Intelligence Service
FHA	Federal Housing Administration		
FHWA	Federal Highway Administration	IAF	Inter-American Foundation
FIA	Federal Insurance Administration	IBRD	International Bank for Reconstruction and Development
FICO	Financing Corporation	IDB	Inter-American Development Bank
FIRS	Federal Information Relay Service		
FLRA	Federal Labor Relations Authority	IDCA	United States International Development Cooperation Agency
FMC	Federal Maritime Commission	IFC	International Finance Corporation
FMCS	Federal Mediation and Conciliation Service	IHA's	Indian Housing Authorities
FMS	Financial Management Service	IHS	Indian Health Service
FNCS	Food, Nutrition, and Consumer Services	ILAB	Bureau of International Labor Affairs
FNMA	Federal National Mortgage Association	ILO	International Labor Organization
FNS	Food and Nutrition Service	IMF	International Monetary Fund
FOIA	Freedom of Information Act	IMLS	Institute of Museum and Library Services
FR	*Federal Register*	INF	Intermediate-range nuclear forces
FRS	Federal Reserve System		
FSA	Farm Service Agency	INS	Immigration and Naturalization Service
FSIS	Food Safety and Inspection Service		
FSS	Federal Supply Service	INTERPOL	International Criminal Police Organization
FTC	Federal Trade Commission	IOM	International Organization for Migration
FWS	Fish and Wildlife Service		
GAO	General Accounting Office	IRMC	Information Resources Management College
GATT	General Agreement on Tariffs and Trade	IRS	Internal Revenue Service
Ginnie Mae	Government National Mortgage Association	ISOO	Information Security Oversight Office
GIPSA	Grain Inspection, Packers, and Stockyards Administration	ITA	International Trade Administration
		JAG	Judge Advocate General
GNMA	Government National Mortgage Association	JCS	Joint Chiefs of Staff
GPO	Government Printing Office	LMI	Office of One-Stop/Labor Market Information (Labor)
GSA	General Services Administration	MA	Maritime Administration
HCFA	Health Care Financing Administration	MASINT	Central Measurement and Signals Intelligence Office
HHS	Department of Health and Human Services	MBDA	Minority Business Development Agency

MIGA	Multilateral Investment Guarantee Agency	NSA	National Security Agency
MMS	Minerals Management Service	NSC	National Security Council
MSHA	Mine Safety and Health Administration	NSF	National Science Foundation
MSPB	Merit Systems Protection Board	NTIA	National Telecommunications and Information Administration
NARA	National Archives and Records Administration	NTID	National Technical Institute for the Deaf
NASA	National Aeronautics and Space Administration	NTIS	National Technical Information Service (Commerce)
NASS	National Agricultural Statistics Service		
NATO	North Atlantic Treaty Organization	NTSB	National Transportation Safety Board
NCPC	National Capital Planning Commission	OAS	Organization of American States
NCRR	National Center for Research Resources	OCC	Office of the Comptroller of the Currency (Treasury)
NCS	National Cemetery System	OCS	Officer Candidate School
NCUA	National Credit Union Administration	OECD	Organization for Economic Cooperation and Development
NEA	National Endowment for the Arts	OGE	Office of Government Ethics
NEH	National Endowment for the Humanities	OMB	Office of Management and Budget
NHI	National Highway Institute	OPIC	Overseas Private Investment Corporation
NHPRC	National Historical Publications and Records Commission	OPM	Office of Personnel Management
NHTSA	National Highway Traffic Safety Administration	ORR	Office of Refugee Resettlement
NIH	National Institutes of Health	OSC	Office of Special Counsel
NIJ	National Institute of Justice	OSDBU	Office of Small and Disadvantaged Business Utilization (Commerce)
NIMA	National Imagery and Mapping Agency	OSHA	Occupational Safety and Health Administration
NIMH	National Institute of Mental Health	OSHRC	Occupational Safety and Health Review Commission
NIST	National Institute of Standards and Technology	OSM	Office of Surface Mining Reclamation and Enforcement
NLM	National Library of Medicine	OTS	Office of Thrift Supervision
NLRB	National Labor Relations Board	OWBO	Office of Women's Business Ownership
NOAA	National Oceanic and Atmospheric Administration	PBGC	Pension Benefit Guaranty Corporation
NPS	National Park Service	PBS	Public Buildings Service
NRC	Nuclear Regulatory Commission	PCC	Panama Canal Commission
NRCS	Natural Resources Conservation Service	PHA's	Public Housing Agencies
		PHS	Public Health Service

POW/MP	Prisoner of War/Missing Personnel	TPCC	Trade Promotion Coordinating Committee
PRC	Postal Rate Commission	TVA	Tennessee Valley Authority
PSC	Program Support Center (Health and Human Services)	U.N.	United Nations [1]
PTO	Patent and Trademark Office	UNESCO	United Nations Educational, Scientific and Cultural Organization
PWBA	Pension and Welfare Benefits Administration	UNHCR	United Nations High Commissioner for Refugees Program
RHS	Rural Housing Service		
RICO	Racketeer Influenced and Corrupt Organizations	UNICEF	United Nations Children's Fund (formerly United Nations International Children's Emergency Fund)
RIT	Rochester Institute of Technology		
RMA	Risk Management Agency (Agriculture)	UNICOR	Federal Prison Industries, Inc.
ROTC	Reserve Officer Training Corps	USA	United States Army
RRB	Railroad Retirement Board	USAF	United States Air Force
RSPA	Research and Special Programs Administration (Transportation)	USAID	United States Agency for International Development
RTB	Rural Telephone Bank	U.S.C.	United States Code
RUS	Rural Utilities Service	USCG	United States Coast Guard
SAIF	Savings Association Insurance Fund	USDA	United States Department of Agriculture
SAMHSA	Substance Abuse and Mental Health Services Administration	USFA	United States Fire Administration
SBA	Small Business Administration	USGS	United States Geological Survey
SEC	Securities and Exchange Commission	USIA	United States Information Agency
SITES	Smithsonian Institution Traveling Exhibition Service	USITC	United States International Trade Commission
SSA	Social Security Administration	USMC	United States Marine Corps
SSI	Supplemental Security Income Program	USN	United States Navy
SSS	Selective Service System	VA	Department of Veterans Affairs
START	Strategic Arms Reduction Treaty	VETS	Veterans' Employment and Training Service
Stat.	United States Statutes at Large	VISTA	Volunteers in Service to America
TASC	Transportation Administrative Service Center		
TDA	Trade and Development Agency		

[1] Acronyms for other U.N. agencies can be found under *Selected Multilateral Organizations* in the preceding text.

VOA   Voice of America
WHO   World Health
      Organization
WIC   Special supplemental
      food program for
      Women, Infants, and
      Children

WNET Women's Network for
      Entrepreneurial Training
      (SBA)
WTO   World Trade
      Organization
YCC   Youth Conservation
      Corps

APPENDIX B: Federal Executive Agencies Terminated, Transferred, or Changed in Name Subsequent to March 4, 1933

NOTE: Italicized terms indicate obsolete agencies, organizations, and entities. In most instances, explanatory remarks are written at those terms elsewhere in this appendix. Dates prior to March 4, 1933, are included to provide additional information about the agencies.

This appendix is indexed in a format considered to be useful to the reader. Entries are carried at the most significant term in their titles, or when there is more than one significant term, the entry is carried at the first significant term. Thus, **Bureau of the Budget** is found at **Budget, Bureau of the,** and **Annual Assay Commission** is found at **Assay Commission, Annual.** Reader comments on the format are encouraged and should be sent to the address shown on page iv of the *Manual.*

Accounts, Bureau of Functions transferred to *Bureau of Government Financial Operations* by Treasury Order 229 of Jan. 14, 1974.

Acquisition, Office of Under Secretary of Defense for Renamed Office of Under Secretary of Defense for Acquisition and Technology by act of Nov. 30, 1993 (107 Stat. 1728).

ACTION Established by Reorg. Plan No. 1 of 1971 (5 U.S.C. app.), effective July 1, 1971. Reorganized by act of Oct. 1, 1973 (87 Stat. 405). Functions relating to SCORE and ACT programs transferred to Small Business Administration by EO 11871 of July 18, 1975 (40 FR 30915). Functions exercised by the Director of ACTION prior to Mar. 31, 1995, transferred to the Corporation for National and Community Service (107 Stat. 888 and Proclamation 6662 of Apr. 4, 1994 (57 FR 16507)).

Acts of Congress See **State Department**

Administrative Conference of the United States Established by act of Aug. 30, 1964 (78 Stat. 615). Terminated by act of Nov. 19, 1995 (109 Stat. 480).

Advanced Research Projects Agency See Defense Advanced Research Projects Agency

Advisory Board, Commission, Committee. *See other part of title*

Aeronautical Board Organized in 1916 by agreement of *War* and Navy Secretaries. Placed under supervision of President by military order of July 5, 1939. Dissolved by Defense Secretary's letter of July 27, 1948, and functions transferred to *Munitions Board* and *Research and Development Board.* Military order of July 5, 1939, revoked by military order of Oct. 18, 1948.

Aeronautics, Bureau of Established in Navy Department by act of July 12, 1921 (42 Stat. 140). Abolished by act of Aug. 18, 1959 (73 Stat. 395)

and functions transferred to *Bureau of Naval Weapons.*

Aeronautics, National Advisory Committee for Established by act of Mar. 3, 1915 (38 Stat. 930). Terminated by act of July 29, 1958 (72 Stat. 432), and functions transferred to National Aeronautics and Space Administration, established by same act.

Aeronautics, Office of Renamed Office of Aeronautics and Space Transportation Technology by Administrator's order of Feb. 24, 1997.

Aeronautics Administration, Civil See **Aeronautics Authority, Civil**

Aeronautics Authority, Civil Established under act of June 23, 1938 (52 Stat. 973). Renamed *Civil Aeronautics Board* and Administrator transferred to Commerce Department by Reorg. Plan Nos. III and IV of 1940, effective June 30, 1940. Office of Administrator designated *Civil Aeronautics Administration* by Department Order 52 of Aug. 29, 1940. *Administration* transferred to *Federal Aviation Agency* by act of Aug. 23, 1958 (72 Stat. 810). Functions of *Board* under act of Aug. 23, 1958 (72 Stat. 775), transferred to National Transportation Safety Board by act of Oct. 15, 1966 (80 Stat. 931). Functions of *Board* terminated or transferred—effective in part Dec. 31, 1981; in part Jan. 1, 1983; and in part Jan. 1, 1985—by act of Aug. 23, 1958 (92 Stat. 1744). Most remaining functions transferred to Transportation Secretary, remainder to U.S. Postal Service. Termination of *Board* finalized by act of Oct. 4, 1984 (98 Stat. 1703).

Aeronautics Board, Civil See **Aeronautics Authority, Civil**

Aeronautics Branch Established in Commerce Department to carry out provisions of act of May 20, 1926 (44 Stat. 568). Renamed *Bureau of Air Commerce* by Secretary's administrative order of July

1, 1934. Personnel and property transferred to *Civil Aeronautics Authority* by EO 7959 of Aug. 22, 1938.

Aeronautics and Space Council, National
Established by act of July 29, 1958 (72 Stat. 427). Abolished by Reorg. Plan No. 1 of 1973, effective June 30, 1973.

Aging, Administration on Established by *Health, Education, and Welfare Secretary* on Oct. 1, 1965, to carry out provisions of act of July 14, 1965 (79 Stat. 218). Reassigned to *Social and Rehabilitation Service* by Department reorganization of Aug. 15, 1967. Transferred to Office of Assistant Secretary for Human Development by Secretary's order of June 15, 1973. Transferred to the Office of the Secretary of Health and Human Services by Secretary's reorganization notice dated Apr. 15, 1991.

Aging, Federal Council on Established by Presidential memorandum of Apr. 2, 1956. Reconstituted at Federal level by Presidential letter of Mar. 7, 1959, to *Health, Education, and Welfare Secretary*. Abolished by EO 11022 of May 15, 1962, which established *President's Council on Aging*.

Aging, Office of Established by *Health, Education, and Welfare Secretary* June 2, 1955, as *Special Staff on Aging*. Terminated Sept. 30, 1965, and functions assumed by Administration on Aging.

Aging, President's Council on Established by EO 11022 of May 14, 1962. Terminated by EO 11022, which was revoked by EO 12379 of Aug. 17, 1982.

Agricultural Adjustment Administration
Established by act of May 12, 1933 (48 Stat. 31). Consolidated into *Agricultural Conservation and Adjustment Administration* as *Agricultural Adjustment Agency*, Agriculture Department, by EO 9069 of Feb. 23, 1942. Grouped with other agencies to form *Food Production Administration* by EO 9280 of Dec. 5, 1942. Transferred to *War Food Administration* by EO 9322 of Mar. 26, 1943. Administration terminated by EO 9577 of June 29, 1945, and functions transferred to Agriculture Secretary. Transfer made permanent by Reorg. Plan No. 3 of 1946, effective July 16, 1946. Functions of *Agricultural Adjustment Agency* consolidated with *Production and Marketing Administration* by Secretary's Memorandum 1118 of Aug. 18, 1945.

Agricultural Adjustment Agency *See* **Agricultural Adjustment Administration**

Agricultural Advisory Commission, National
Established by EO 10472 of July 20, 1953. Terminated Feb. 4, 1965, on resignation of members.

Agricultural Chemistry and Engineering, Bureau of *See* **Agricultural Engineering, Bureau of**

Agricultural Conservation and Adjustment Administration Established by EO 9069 of Feb. 23, 1942, consolidating *Agricultural Adjustment Agency, Sugar Agency, Federal Crop Insurance Corporation,* and *Soil Conservation Service*. Consolidated into *Food Production Administration* by EO 9280 of Dec. 5, 1942.

Agricultural Conservation Program Service
Established by Agriculture Secretary Jan. 21, 1953, from part of *Production and Marketing Administration*. Merged with *Commodity Stabilization Service* by Secretary's Memorandum 1446, supp. 2, of Apr. 19, 1961.

Agricultural Developmental Service, International
Established by Agriculture Secretary's memorandum of July 12, 1963. Functions and delegations of authority transferred to Foreign Agricultural Service by Secretary's memorandum of Mar. 28, 1969. Functions transferred by Secretary to *Foreign Economic Development Service* Nov. 8, 1969.

Agricultural Economics, Bureau of Established by act of May 11, 1931 (42 Stat. 532). Functions transferred to other units of Agriculture Department, including *Consumer and Marketing Service* and Agricultural Research Service, under Secretary's Memorandum 1320, supp. 4, of Nov. 2, 1953.

Agricultural Engineering, Bureau of Established by act of Feb. 23, 1931 (46 Stat. 1266). Merged with *Bureau of Chemistry and Soils* by Secretarial order of Oct. 16, 1938, to form *Bureau of Agricultural Chemistry and Engineering*.

Agricultural and Industrial Chemistry, Bureau of
Bureau of Chemistry and *Bureau of Soils*, created in 1901, combined into *Bureau of Chemistry and Soils* by act of Jan. 18, 1927 (44 Stat. 976). Soils units transferred to other agencies of Agriculture Department and remaining units of *Bureau of Chemistry and Soils* and *Bureau of Agricultural Engineering* consolidated with *Bureau of Agricultural Chemistry and Engineering* by Secretary's order of Oct. 16, 1938. In February 1943 agricultural engineering research made part of *Bureau of Plant Industry, Soils, and Agricultural Engineering,* and organization for continuing agricultural chemistry research relating to crop utilization named *Bureau of Agricultural and Industrial Chemistry,* in accordance with *Research Administration* Memorandum 5 issued pursuant to EO 9069 of Feb. 23, 1942, and in conformity with Secretary's Memorandums 960 and 986. Functions transferred to *Agricultural Research Service* under Secretary's Memorandum 1320, supp. 4, of Nov. 2, 1953.

Agricultural Library, National Established by Agriculture Secretary's Memorandum 1496 of Mar. 23, 1962. Consolidated into *Science and Education Administration* by Secretary's order of Jan. 24, 1978. Reestablished as National Agricultural Library by Secretary's order of June 16, 1981. Became part of Agricultural Research Service in 1994 under Department of Agriculture reorganization.

Agricultural Marketing Administration Established by EO 9069 of Feb. 23, 1942, consolidating *Surplus Marketing Administration, Agricultural Marketing Service,* and *Commodity Exchange Administration*. *Division of Consumers' Counsel* transferred to *Administration* by Secretary's memorandum of Feb. 28, 1942. Consolidated into *Food Distribution Administration* in Agriculture Department by EO 9280 of Dec. 5, 1942.

Agricultural Marketing Service Established by Agriculture Secretary pursuant to act of June 30,

1939 (53 Stat. 939). Merged into *Agricultural Marketing Administration* by EO 9069 of Feb. 23, 1942. Renamed *Consumer and Marketing Service* by Secretary's Memorandum 1567, supp. 1, of Feb. 8, 1965. Reestablished as Agricultural Marketing Service by Agriculture Secretary on Apr. 2, 1972, under authority of Reorg. Plan No. 2 of 1953 (67 Stat. 633).

Agricultural Relations, Office of Foreign   *See* **Agricultural Service, Foreign**

Agricultural Research Administration   Established by EO 9069 of Feb. 23, 1942. Superseded by Agricultural Research Service.

Agricultural Research Service   Established by Agriculture Secretary's Memorandum 1320, supp. 4, of Nov. 2, 1953. Consolidated into *Science and Education Administration* by Secretary's order of Jan. 24, 1978. Reestablished as Agricultural Research Service by Secretarial order of June 16, 1981.

Agricultural Service, Foreign   Established by act of June 5, 1930 (46 Stat. 497). Economic research and agricultural attaché activities administered by *Foreign Agricultural Service Division, Bureau of Agricultural Economics,* until June 29, 1939. Transferred by Reorg. Plan No. II of 1939, effective July 1, 1939, from Agriculture Department to State Department. Economic research functions of *Division* transferred to *Office of Foreign Agricultural Relations* June 30, 1939. Functions of *Office* transferred to Foreign Agricultural Service Mar. 10, 1953. Agricultural attachés placed in Agriculture Department by act of Aug. 28, 1954 (68 Stat. 908).

Agricultural Stabilization and Conservation Service   Established June 5, 1961, by the Secretary of Agriculture under authority of revised statutes (5 U.S.C. 301) and Reorg. Plan No. 2 of 1953 (5 U.S.C. app.). Abolished and functions assumed by the *Farm Service Agency* by Secretary's Memorandum 1010–1 dated Oct. 20, 1994 (59 FR 60297, 60299).

Agricultural Statistics Division   Transferred to *Bureau of Agricultural Economics* by EO 9069 of Feb. 23, 1942.

Agriculture, Division of   *See* **Farm Products, Division of**

Air Commerce, Bureau of   *See* **Aeronautics Branch**

Air Coordinating Committee   Established Mar. 27, 1945, by interdepartmental memorandum; formally established by EO 9781 of Sept. 19, 1946. Terminated by EO 10883 of Aug. 11, 1960, and functions transferred for liquidation to *Federal Aviation Agency.*

Air Force Management Engineering Agency   Established in 1975 in Air Force as separate operating unit. Made subordinate unit of Air Force Military Personnel Center (formerly Air Force Manpower and Personnel Center) in 1978. Reestablished as separate operating unit of Air Force, effective Mar. 1, 1985, by Secretarial order.

Air Force Manpower and Personnel Center   Certain functions transferred on activation of Air Force Management Engineering Agency, which was made

separate operating unit from Air Force Manpower and Personnel Center (later Air Force Military Personnel Center) in April 1985 by general order of Chief of Staff.

Air Force Medical Service Center   Renamed Air Force Office of Medical Support by Program Action Directive 85–1 of Mar. 6, 1985, approved by Air Force Vice Chief of Staff.

Air Mail, Bureau of   Established in Interstate Commerce Commission to carry out provisions of act of June 12, 1934 (48 Stat. 933). Personnel and property transferred to *Civil Aeronautics Authority* by EO 7959 of Aug. 22, 1938.

Air Patrol, Civil   Established in *Civilian Defense Office* by Administrative Order 9 of Dec. 8, 1941. Transferred to *War Department* as auxiliary of Army Air Forces by EO 9339 of Apr. 29, 1943. Transferred to Air Force Department by Defense Secretary's order of May 21, 1948. Established as civilian auxiliary of U.S. Air Force by act of May 26, 1948 (62 Stat. 274).

Air Safety Board   Established by act of June 23, 1938 (52 Stat. 973). Functions transferred to *Civil Aeronautics Board* by Reorg. Plan No. IV of 1940, effective June 30, 1940.

Airways Modernization Board   Established by act of Aug. 14, 1957 (71 Stat. 349). Transferred to *Federal Aviation Agency* by EO 10786 of Nov. 1, 1958.

Alaska, Board of Road Commissioners for   Established in *War Department* by act of Jan. 27, 1905 (33 Stat. 616). Functions transferred to Interior Department by act of June 30, 1932 (47 Stat. 446), and delegated to *Alaska Road Commission.* Functions transferred to Commerce Department by act of June 29, 1956 (70 Stat. 377), and terminated by act of June 25, 1959 (73 Stat. 145).

Alaska, Federal Field Committee for Development Planning in   Established by EO 11182 of Oct. 2, 1964. Abolished by EO 11608 of July 19, 1971.

Alaska, Federal Reconstruction and Development Planning Commission for   Established by EO 11150 of Apr. 2, 1964. Abolished by EO 11182 of Oct. 2, 1964, which established *President's Review Committee for Development Planning in Alaska* and *Federal Field Committee for Development Planning in Alaska.*

Alaska, President's Review Committee for Development Planning in   Established by EO 11182 of Oct. 2, 1964. Superseded by *Federal Advisory Council on Regional Economic Development* established by EO 11386 of Dec. 28, 1967. EO 11386 revoked by EO 12553 of Feb. 25, 1986.

Alaska Communication System   Operational responsibility vested in Army Secretary by act of May 26, 1900 (31 Stat. 206). Transferred to Air Force Secretary by Defense Secretary's reorganization order of May 24, 1962.

Alaska Engineering Commission   *See* **Alaska Railroad**

Alaska Game Commission Established by act of Jan. 13, 1925 (43 Stat. 740). Expired Dec. 31, 1959, pursuant to act of July 7, 1958 (72 Stat. 339).

Alaska International Rail and Highway Commission Established by act of Aug. 1, 1956 (70 Stat. 888). Terminated June 30, 1961, under terms of act.

Alaska Power Administration Established by Interior Secretary in 1967. Transferred to Energy Department by act of Aug. 4, 1977 (91 Stat. 578).

Alaska Railroad Built pursuant to act of Mar. 12, 1914 (38 Stat. 305), which created *Alaska Engineering Commission.* Placed under Interior Secretary by EO 2129 of Jan. 26, 1915, and renamed Alaska Railroad by EO 3861 of June 8, 1923. Authority to regulate tariffs granted to Interstate Commerce Commission by EO 11107 of Apr. 25, 1963. Authority to operate Railroad transferred to Transportation Secretary by act of Oct. 15, 1966 (80 Stat. 941), effective Apr. 1, 1967. Railroad purchased by State of Alaska, effective Jan. 5, 1985.

Alaska Road Commission *See* **Alaska, Board of Road Commissioners for**

Alcohol, Bureau of Industrial Established by act of May 27, 1930 (46 Stat. 427). Consolidated into *Bureau of Internal Revenue* by EO 6166 of June 10, 1933. Consolidation deferred until May 11, 1934, by EO 6639 of Mar. 10, 1934. Order also transferred to Internal Revenue Commissioner certain functions imposed on Attorney General by act of May 27, 1930, with relation to enforcement of criminal laws concerning intoxicating liquors remaining in effect after repeal of 18th amendment; personnel of, and appropriations for, *Bureau of Industrial Alcohol;* and necessary personnel and appropriations of *Bureau of Prohibition,* Justice Department.

Alcohol, Commissioner of Industrial Office created in Treasury Department by act of May 27, 1930 (46 Stat. 427). Abolished by EO 6639 of Mar. 10, 1934.

Alcohol, Drug Abuse, and Mental Health Administration Established by *Health, Education, and Welfare Secretary* by act of May 21, 1972 (88 Stat. 134). Redesignated as an agency of the Public Health Service from the *National Institute of Mental Health* Sept. 25, 1973, by Secretary of Health, Education, and Welfare. Functions transferred to Health and Human Services Department by act of Oct. 17, 1979 (93 Stat. 695). Established as an agency of the Public Health Service by act of Oct. 27, 1986 (100 Stat. 3207–106). Renamed Substance Abuse and Mental Health Services Administration by act of July 10, 1992 (106 Stat. 325).

Alcohol Abuse and Alcoholism, National Institute on Established within the National Institute of Mental Health, *Health, Education, and Welfare Department* by act of Dec. 31, 1970 (84 Stat. 1848). Removed from within the National Institute of Mental Health and made an entity within the Alcohol, Drug Abuse, and Mental Health Administration by act of May 14, 1974 (88 Stat. 1356). Functions transferred to Health and Human Services Department by act of Oct. 17, 1979 (93 Stat. 695). (*See also* act of Oct. 27, 1986; 100 Stat.

3207–106.) Abolished by act of July 10, 1992 (106 Stat. 331). Reestablished by act of July 10, 1992 (106 Stat. 359).

Alcohol Administration, Federal *See* **Alcohol Control Administration, Federal**

Alcohol Control Administration, Federal Established by EO 6474 of Dec. 4, 1933. Abolished Sept. 24, 1935, on induction into office of Administrator, *Federal Alcohol Administration,* as provided in act of Aug. 29, 1935 (49 Stat. 977). Abolished by Reorg. Plan No. III of 1940, effective June 30, 1940, and functions consolidated with activities of Internal Revenue Service.

Alexander Hamilton Bicentennial Commission Established by act of Aug. 20, 1954 (68 Stat. 746). Terminated Apr. 30, 1958.

Alien Property, Office of Transferred to Civil Division, Justice Department, by Attorney General Order 249–61 of Sept. 1, 1961. Abolished by EO 11281 of May 13, 1966, and foreign funds control functions transferred to Office of Foreign Assets Control, Treasury Department. Remaining functions continued by Civil Division, Justice Department. Remaining functions abolished by act of Aug. 23, 1988 (102 Stat. 1370).

Alien Property Custodian Appointed by President Oct. 22, 1917, under authority of act of Oct. 6, 1917 (40 Stat. 415). Office transferred to *Alien Property Division,* Justice Department, by EO 6694 of May 1, 1934. Powers vested in President by act delegated to Attorney General by EO 8136 of May 15, 1939. Authority vested in Attorney General by EO's 6694 and 8136 transferred by EO 9142 of Apr. 21, 1942, to *Office of Alien Property Custodian, Office for Emergency Management,* as provided for by EO 9095 of Mar. 11, 1942.

Alien Property Custodian, Office of Established in *Office for Emergency Management* by EO 9095 of Mar. 11, 1942. Terminated by EO 9788 of Oct. 14, 1946, and functions transferred to Justice Department. Transfer made permanent by Reorg. Plan No. 1 of 1947, effective July 1, 1947.

Alien Property Division *See* **Alien Property Custodian**

American Republics, Office for Coordination of Commercial and Cultural Relations between the Established by *Council of National Defense* order approved by President Aug. 16, 1940. Succeeded by *Office of the Coordinator of Inter-American Affairs, Office for Emergency Management,* established by EO 8840 of July 30, 1941. Renamed *Office of Inter-American Affairs* by EO 9532 of Mar. 23, 1945. Information functions transferred to State Department by EO 9608 of Aug. 31, 1945. Terminated by EO 9710 of Apr. 10, 1946, and functions transferred to State Department, functioning as *Institute of Inter-American Affairs.* Transferred to *Foreign Operations Administration* by Reorg. Plan No. 7, effective Aug. 1, 1953.

American Revolution Bicentennial Administration *See* **American Revolution Bicentennial Commission**

American Revolution Bicentennial Commission
Established by act of July 4, 1966 (80 Stat. 259).
American Revolution Bicentennial Administration
established by act of Dec. 11, 1973 (87 Stat. 697),
to replace *Commission. Administration* terminated
June 30, 1977, pursuant to terms of act. Certain
continuing functions transferred to Interior Secretary
by EO 12001 of June 29, 1977.

American Studies, Office of   Renamed American
Studies Program by Smithsonian Institution
administrative order in 1990.

American Workplace, Office of the   Established by
Labor Secretary's Order No. 2–93 of July 21, 1993.
Terminated due to Congressional budget phaseout of
appropriation.

Anacostia Neighborhood Museum   Renamed
Anacostia Museum by Smithsonian Institution
announcement of Apr. 3, 1987.

Animal Industry, Bureau of   Established in
Agriculture Department by act of May 29, 1884 (23
Stat. 31). Functions transferred to Agricultural
Research Service by Secretary's Memorandum 1320,
supp. 4, of Nov. 2, 1953.

Apprenticeship, Federal Committee on   Previously
known as *Federal Committee on Apprentice
Training*, established by EO 6750–C of June 27,
1934. Functioned as part of *Division of Labor
Standards*, Labor Department, pursuant to act of
Aug. 16, 1937 (50 Stat. 664). Transferred to *Office
of Administrator, Federal Security Agency*, by EO
9139 of Apr. 18, 1942. Transferred to *Bureau of
Training, War Manpower Commission*, by EO 9247
of Sept. 17, 1942. Returned to Labor Department by
EO 9617 of Sept. 19, 1945.

Architect, Office of the Supervising   *See
Construction Branch*

Archive of Folksong   Renamed Archive of Folk
Culture by administrative order of Deputy Librarian
of Congress, effective Sept. 21, 1981.

Archives, Office of the National   Established in the
National Archives and Records Administration.
Reorganized by Archivist under Notice 96–260,
Sept. 23, 1996, effective Jan. 6, 1997. Functions
restructured and transferred to Office of Records
Services—Washington, DC.

Archives Council, National   Established by act of
June 19, 1934 (48 Stat. 1122). Transferred to
General Services Administration by act of June 30,
1949 (63 Stat. 378). Terminated on establishment of
Federal Records Council by act of Sept. 5, 1950 (64
Stat. 583).

Archives Establishment, National   *Office of
Archivist of the U.S.* and *National Archives* created
by act of June 19, 1934 (48 Stat. 1122). Transferred
to General Services Administration by act of June
30, 1949 (63 Stat. 381), and incorporated as
National Archives and Records Service by order of
General Services Administrator, together with
functions of *Division of the Federal Register,
National Archives Council, National Historical
Publications Commission*, National Archives Trust
Fund Board, *Trustees of the Franklin D. Roosevelt*

Library, and Administrative Committee of the Federal
Register. Transferred from General Services
Administration to National Archives and Records
Administration by act of Oct. 19, 1984 (98 Stat.
2283), along with certain functions of Administrator
of General Services transferred to Archivist of the
United States, effective Apr. 1, 1985.

Archives and Records Service, National   *See
Archives Establishment, National*

Archives Trust Fund Board, National   *See Archives
Establishment, National*

Area Redevelopment Administration   Established
May 8, 1961, by Commerce Secretary pursuant to
act of May 1, 1961 (75 Stat. 47) and Reorg. Plan
No. 5 of 1950, effective May 24, 1950. Terminated
Aug. 31, 1965, by act of June 30, 1965 (79 Stat.
195). Functions transferred to Economic
Development Administration in Commerce
Department by Department Order 4–A, effective
Sept. 1, 1965.

Arlington Memorial Amphitheater Commission
Established by act of Mar. 4, 1921 (41 Stat. 1440).
Abolished by act of Sept. 2, 1960 (74 Stat. 739), and
functions transferred to Defense Secretary.

Arlington Memorial Bridge Commission
Established by act of Mar. 4, 1913 (37 Stat. 885;
D.C. Code (1951 ed.) 8–158). Abolished by EO
6166 of June 10, 1933, and functions transferred to
*Office of National Parks, Buildings, and
Reservations.*

Armed Forces Medical Library   Founded in 1836 as
Library of the Surgeon General's Office, U.S. Army.
Later known as *Army Medical Library*, then *Armed
Forces Medical Library* in 1952. Personnel and
property transferred to National Library of Medicine
established in Public Health Service by act of Aug.
3, 1956 (70 Stat. 960).

Armed Forces Museum Advisory Board, National
Established by act of Aug. 30, 1961 (75 Stat. 414).
Functions discontinued due to lack of funding.

Armed Services Renegotiation Board   Established
by Defense Secretary's directive of July 19, 1948.
Abolished by Defense Secretary's letter of Jan. 18,
1952, and functions transferred to *Renegotiation
Board.*

Army Communications Command, U.S.   Renamed
U.S. Army Information Systems Command by
Department General Order No. 26 of July 25, 1984.

**Army Materiel Development and Readiness
Command, U.S.**   Renamed U.S. Army Materiel
Command by Department General Order No. 28 of
Aug. 15, 1984.

Army and Navy, Joint Board   Placed under
direction of President by military order of July 5,
1939. Abolished Sept. 1, 1947, by joint letter of
Aug. 20, 1947, to President from Secretaries of *War*
and Navy.

Army and Navy Staff College   Established Apr. 23,
1943, and operated under Joint Chiefs of Staff.

Redesignated the National War College, effective July 1, 1946.

Army Specialist Corps   Established in *War Department* by EO 9078 of Feb. 26, 1942. Abolished by *War Secretary* Oct. 31, 1942, and functions merged into central *Officer Procurement Service.*

Arthritis, Diabetes, and Digestive and Kidney Diseases, National Institute of   See **Arthritis, Metabolism, and Digestive Diseases, National Institute of**

Arthritis, Metabolism, and Digestive Diseases, National Institute of   Renamed *National Institute of Arthritis, Diabetes, and Digestive and Kidney Diseases* by Secretary's order of June 15, 1981, pursuant to act of Dec. 19, 1980 (94 Stat. 3184). Renamed National Institute of Diabetes and Digestive and Kidney Diseases and National Institute of Arthritis and Musculoskeletal and Skin Diseases by act of Nov. 20, 1985 (99 Stat. 820).

Arts, Advisory Committee on the   Established under authority of act of Sept. 20, 1961 (75 Stat. 527). Terminated July 1973 by act of Oct. 6, 1972. Formally abolished by Reorg. Plan No. 2 of 1977, effective Apr. 1, 1978.

Arts, National Council on the   Established in Executive Office of the President by act of Sept. 3, 1964 (78 Stat. 905). Transferred to National Foundation on the Arts and the Humanities by act of Sept. 29, 1965 (79 Stat. 845).

Assay Commission, Annual   Established initially by act of Apr. 2, 1792 (1 Stat. 250) and by act of Feb. 12, 1873 (Revised Statute sec. 3647; 17 Stat. 432). Terminated and functions transferred to Treasury Secretary by act of Mar. 14, 1980 (94 Stat. 98).

Assistance, Bureau of Public   Renamed *Bureau of Family Services* by order of *Health, Education, and Welfare Secretary,* effective Jan. 1, 1962. Functions redelegated to *Social and Rehabilitation Service* by Secretary's reorganization of Aug. 15, 1967.

Assistance Coordinating Committee, Adjustment   Established by act of Jan. 3, 1975 (88 Stat. 2040). Inactive since 1981.

Assistance Payments Administration   Established by *Health, Education, and Welfare Secretary's* reorganization of Aug. 15, 1967. Transferred by *Secretary's* reorganization of Mar. 8, 1977 (42 FR 13262), from *Social and Rehabilitation Service* to Social Security Administration.

Athletics, Interagency Committee on International   Established by EO 11117 of Aug. 13, 1963. Terminated by EO 11515 of Mar. 13, 1970.

Atlantic-Pacific Interoceanic Canal Study Commission   Established by act of Sept. 22, 1964 (78 Stat. 990). Terminated Dec. 1, 1970, pursuant to terms of act.

Atomic Energy Commission   Established by act of Aug. 1, 1946 (60 Stat. 755). Abolished by act of Oct. 11, 1974 (88 Stat. 1237) and functions transferred to *Energy Research and Development Administration* and Nuclear Regulatory Commission.

Aviation, Interdepartmental Committee on Civil International   Established by Presidential letter of June 20, 1935. Terminated on organization of *Civil Aeronautics Authority.*

Aviation Agency, Federal   Established by act of Aug. 23, 1958 (72 Stat. 731). Transferred to Transportation Secretary by act of Oct. 15, 1966 (80 Stat. 931). *Agency* reestablished as Federal Aviation Administration by act of Jan 12, 1983 (96 Stat. 2416).

Aviation Commission, Federal   Established by act of June 12, 1934 (48 Stat. 938). Terminated Feb. 1, 1935, under provisions of act.

Beltsville Research Center   Established to operate with other agencies of Agriculture Department under *Agricultural Research Administration.* Consolidated into *Agricultural Research Administration,* Agriculture Department, by EO 9069 of Feb. 23, 1942.

Biological Service, National   Established in the Interior Department in 1995 by Secretarial order. Transferred to U.S. Geological Survey as new Biological Resources Division by Secretarial Order No. 3202, Sept. 30, 1996.

Biological Survey, Bureau of   Established by Secretary's order July 1, 1885, as part of *Division of Entomology,* Agriculture Department. Made separate bureau by act of Apr. 23, 1904 (33 Stat. 276). Transferred to Interior Department by Reorg. Plan No. II of 1939, effective July 1, 1939. Consolidated with *Bureau of Fisheries* into *Fish and Wildlife Service* by Reorg. Plan No. III of 1940, effective June 30, 1940.

Biological Survey, National   Established in the Interior Department by Secretarial Order 3173 of Sept. 29, 1993. Renamed *National Biological Service* by Secretarial order in 1995.

Blind, Inc., American Printing House for the   Established in 1858 as privately owned institution in Louisville, KY. Functions of Treasury Secretary, except that relating to perpetual trust funds, transferred to *Federal Security Agency* by Reorg. Plan No. II of 1939, effective July 1, 1939. Functions performed by *Health, Education, and Welfare Department* transferred to Education Department.

Blind-made Products, Committee on Purchases of   Established by act of June 25, 1938 (52 Stat. 1196). Renamed *Committee for Purchase of Products and Services of the Blind and Other Severely Handicapped* by act of June 23, 1971 (85 Stat. 77). Renamed *Committee for Purchase from the Blind and Other Severely Handicapped* by act of July 25, 1974 (88 Stat. 392). Renamed Committee for Purchase From People Who Are Blind or Severely Disabled by act of Oct. 29, 1992 (106 Stat. 4486).

Blind and Other Severely Handicapped, Committee for Purchase of Products and Services of the   See **Blind-made Products, Committee on Purchases of**

Blockade and Supply Division Established by State departmental order of Aug. 27, 1943, in *Office of Foreign Economic Coordination. Office* abolished by departmental order of Nov. 6, 1943, pursuant to EO 9380 of Sept. 25, 1943, which established *Foreign Economic Administration.*

Board. *See other part of title*

Bond and Spirits Division Established as *Taxes and Penalties Unit,* as announced by Assistant to Attorney General in departmental circular of May 25, 1934, pursuant to EO 6639 of May 10, 1934. Abolished by administrative order of October 1942, and functions transferred to Tax, Claims, and Criminal Divisions, Justice Department.

Bonneville Power Administration Established by Interior Secretary pursuant to act of Aug. 20, 1937 (50 Stat. 731). Transferred to Energy Department by act of Aug. 4, 1977 (91 Stat. 578).

Boston National Historic Sites Commission Established by joint resolution of June 16, 1955 (69 Stat. 137). Terminated June 16, 1960, by act of Feb. 19, 1957 (71 Stat. 4).

Brazil-U.S. Defense Commission, Joint Established in May 1942 by agreement between the U.S. and Brazil. Terminated in September 1977 at direction of Brazilian Government.

Broadcast Bureau Merged with *Cable Television Bureau* to form Mass Media Bureau by Federal Communications Commission order, effective Nov. 30, 1982.

Broadcast Intelligence Service, Foreign *See* **Broadcast Monitoring Service, Foreign**

Broadcast Monitoring Service, Foreign Established in Federal Communications Commission by Presidential directive of Feb. 26, 1941. Renamed *Foreign Broadcast Intelligence Service* by FCC order of July 28, 1942. Transferred to *War Department* by Secretarial order of Dec. 30, 1945. Act of May 3, 1945 (59 Stat. 110), provided for liquidation 60 days after Japanese armistice. Transferred to *Central Intelligence Group* Aug. 5, 1946, and renamed *Foreign Broadcast Information Service.*

Budget, Bureau of the Established by act of June 10, 1921 (42 Stat. 20), in Treasury Department under immediate direction of President. Transferred to Executive Office of the President by Reorg. Plan No. I of 1939, effective July 1, 1939. Reorganized by Reorg. Plan No. 2 of 1970, effective July 1, 1970, and renamed Office of Management and Budget.

Buildings Administration, Public Established as part of *Federal Works Agency* by Reorg. Plan No. I of 1939, effective July 1, 1939. Abolished by act of June 30, 1949 (63 Stat. 380), and functions transferred to General Services Administration.

Buildings Branch, Public Organized in *Procurement Division,* established in Treasury Department by EO 6166 of June 10, 1933. Consolidated with *Branch of Buildings Management,* National Park Service, to form *Public Buildings Administration, Federal Works Agency,* under Reorg. Plan No. I of 1939, effective July 1, 1939.

Buildings Commission, Public Established by act of July 1, 1916 (39 Stat. 328). Abolished by EO 6166 of June 10, 1933, and functions transferred to *Office of National Parks, Buildings, and Reservations,* Interior Department. Functions transferred to *Public Buildings Administration, Federal Works Agency,* under Reorg. Plan No. I of 1939, effective July 1, 1939.

Buildings Management, Branch of Functions of National Park Service (except those relating to monuments and memorials) consolidated with *Public Buildings Branch, Procurement Division,* Treasury Department, to form *Public Buildings Administration, Federal Works Agency,* in accordance with Reorg. Plan No. I of 1939, effective July 1, 1939.

Buildings and Public Parks of the National Capital, Office of Public Established by act of Feb. 26, 1925 (43 Stat. 983), by consolidation of *Office of Public Buildings and Grounds* under Chief of Engineers, U.S. Army, and *Office of Superintendent of State, War, and Navy Department Buildings.* Abolished by EO 6166 of June 10, 1933, and functions transferred to *Office of National Parks, Buildings, and Reservations,* Interior Department.

Bureau. *See other part of title*

Business, Cabinet Committee on Small Established by Presidential letter of May 31, 1956. Dissolved January 1961.

Business Administration, Domestic and International *See* **Business and Defense Services Administration**

Business Cooperation, Division of Established in *National Recovery Administration* by EO 7075 of June 15, 1935. Transferred to Commerce Department by EO 7252 of Dec. 21, 1935. By same order, functions of *Division* ordered terminated by Apr. 1, 1936. *Committee of Industrial Analysis* created by EO 7323 of Mar. 21, 1936, to complete work of *Division.*

Business and Defense Services Administration Established by Commerce Secretary Oct. 1, 1953, and operated under Department Organization Order 40-1. Abolished by Department Organization Order 40-1A of Sept. 15, 1970, and functions transferred to *Bureau of Domestic Commerce.* Functions transferred to *Domestic and International Business Administration,* effective Nov. 17, 1972. *Administration* terminated by Secretary's order of Dec. 4, 1977, and functions assumed by *Industry and Trade Administration.*

Business Economics, Office of Established by Commerce Secretary Jan. 17, 1946. Renamed *Office of Economic Analysis* Dec. 1, 1953. Transferred to *Social and Economic Statistics Administration* along with Bureau of the Census and renamed Bureau of Economic Analysis on Jan. 1, 1972.

Business Operations, Bureau of International Established by Commerce Secretary Aug. 8, 1961, by Departmental Orders 173 and 174. Abolished by Departmental Order 182 of Feb. 1, 1963, which established *Bureau of International Commerce.*

Functions transferred to *Domestic and International Business Administration*, effective Nov. 17, 1972.

Cable Television Bureau   Merged with *Broadcast Bureau* by Federal Communications Commission order to form Mass Media Bureau, effective Nov. 30, 1982.

California Debris Commission   Established by act of Mar. 1, 1893 (27 Stat. 507). Abolished by act of Nov. 17, 1986 (100 Stat. 4229), and functions transferred to Interior Secretary.

Canal Zone Government   Established by act of Aug. 24, 1912 (37 Stat. 561). Abolished by act of Sept. 27, 1979 (93 Stat. 454).

Capital Housing Authority, National   Established by act of June 12, 1934 (48 Stat. 930). Made agency of District of Columbia government by act of Dec. 24, 1973 (87 Stat. 779), effective July 1, 1974.

Capital Park Commission, National   Established by act of June 6, 1924 (43 Stat. 463). *National Capital Park and Planning Commission* named successor by act of Apr. 30, 1926 (44 Stat. 374). Functions transferred to National Capital Planning Commission by act of July 19, 1952 (66 Stat. 781).

Capital Park and Planning Commission, National   *See* **Capital Park Commission, National**

Capital Regional Planning Council, National   Established by act of July 19, 1952 (66 Stat. 785). Terminated by Reorg. Plan No. 5 of 1966, effective Sept. 8, 1966.

Capital Transportation Agency, National   Established by act of July 14, 1960 (74 Stat 537). Authorized to establish rapid rail transit system by act of Sept. 8, 1965 (79 Stat. 663). Functions transferred to Washington Metropolitan Area Transit Authority by EO 11373 of Sept. 20, 1967.

Career Executive Board   Established by EO 10758 of Mar. 4, 1958. Terminated July 1, 1959, and EO 10758 revoked by EO 10859 of Feb. 5, 1960.

Caribbean Organization   Act of June 30, 1961 (75 Stat. 194), provided for acceptance by President of Agreement for the Establishment of the Caribbean Organization, signed at Washington, June 21, 1960. Article III of Agreement provided for termination of *Caribbean Commission*, authorized by Agreement signed Oct. 30, 1946, on first meeting of Caribbean Council, governing body of *Organization*. Terminated, effective Dec. 31, 1965, by resolution adopted by Council.

Cemeteries and Memorials in Europe, National   Supervision transferred from *War Department* to American Battle Monuments Commission by EO 6614 of Feb. 26, 1934, which transfer was deferred to May 21, 1934, by EO 6690 of Apr. 25, 1934.

Cemeteries and Parks, National   *War Department* functions regarding National Cemeteries and Parks located in continental U.S. transferred to *Office of National Parks, Buildings, and Reservations,* Interior Department, by EO 6166 of June 10, 1933.

Censorship, Office of   Established by EO 8985 of Dec. 19, 1941. Terminated by EO 9631 of Sept. 28, 1945.

Censorship Policy Board   Established by EO 8985 of Dec. 19, 1941. Terminated by EO 9631 of Sept. 28, 1945.

Census, Bureau of the   *See* **Census Office**

Census Office   Established temporarily within the Interior Department in accordance with act of Mar. 3, 1899. Established as a permanent office by act of Mar. 6, 1902. Transferred from Interior Department to *Department of Commerce and Labor* by act of Feb. 14, 1903. Remained in Commerce Department under provisions of Reorganization Plan No. 5 of May 24, 1950, effective May 24, 1950.

Center.   *See other part of title*

Central.   *See other part of title*

Chemistry and Soils, Bureau of   *See* **Agricultural and Industrial Chemistry, Bureau of**

Chesapeake Bay Center for Environmental Studies   Established in 1965 in Annapolis, MD, as part of Smithsonian Institution by Secretarial order. Merged with *Radiation Biology Laboratory* by Secretarial Order July 1, 1983, to form Smithsonian Environmental Research Center.

Child Development, Office of   *See* **Children's Bureau**

Child Support Enforcement, Office of   Established in *Health, Education, and Welfare Department* by act of Jan. 4, 1975 (88 Stat. 2351). Replaced by Family Support Administration.

Children's Bureau   Established by act of Apr. 9, 1912 (37 Stat. 79). Placed in Labor Department by act of Mar. 4, 1913 (37 Stat. 737). Transferred, with exception of child labor functions, to *Social Security Administration, Federal Security Agency,* by Reorg. Plan No. 2 of 1946, effective July 16, 1946. Continued under *Administration* when *Agency* functions assumed by *Health, Education, and Welfare Department.* Reassigned to *Welfare Administration* by Department reorganization of Jan. 28, 1963. Reassigned to *Social and Rehabilitation Service* by Department reorganization of Aug. 15, 1967. Reassigned to *Office of Child Development* by Department reorganization order of Sept. 17, 1969.

China, U.S. Court for   Established by act of June 30, 1906 (34 Stat. 814). Transferred to Justice Department by EO 6166 of June 10, 1933, effective Mar. 2, 1934. Act of June 30, 1906, repealed effective Sept. 1, 1948 (62 Stat. 992).

Christopher Columbus Quincentenary Jubilee Commission   Established by act of Aug. 7, 1984 (98 Stat. 1257). Terminated pursuant to terms of act.

Civil defense.   *See* **Defense**

Civil Rights, Commission on   Established by act of Sept. 9, 1957 (71 Stat. 634). Terminated in 1983 and reestablished by act of Nov. 30, 1983 (97 Stat. 1301). Renamed United States Commission on Civil Rights by act of Nov. 2, 1994 (108 Stat. 4683).

Civil Service Commission, U.S.   Established by act of Jan. 16, 1883 (22 Stat. 403). Redesignated as Merit Systems Protection Board and functions transferred to Board and Office of Personnel Management by Reorg. Plan No. 2 of 1978, effective Jan. 1, 1979.

Civil War Centennial Commission   Established by act of Sept. 7, 1957 (71 Stat. 626). Terminated May 1, 1966, pursuant to terms of act.

Civilian Conservation Corps   Established by act of June 28, 1937 (50 Stat. 319). Made part of *Federal Security Agency* by Reorg. Plan No. I of 1939, effective July 1, 1939. Liquidation provided for by act of July 2, 1942 (56 Stat. 569), not later than June 30, 1943.

Civilian Health and Medical Program of the United States, Office of   Established as field activity in Department of Defense in 1974. Functions consolidated into the TRICARE Management Activity in November 1997 by Defense Reform Initiative.

Civilian Production Administration   Established by EO 9638 of Oct. 4, 1945. Consolidated with other agencies to form *Office of Temporary Controls, Office for Emergency Management,* by EO 9809 of Dec. 12, 1946.

Civilian Service Awards Board, Distinguished   Established by EO 10717 of June 27, 1957. Terminated by EO 12014 of Oct. 19, 1977, and functions transferred to *U.S. Civil Service Commission.*

Claims, U.S. Court of   Established Feb. 25, 1855 (10 Stat. 612). Abolished by act of Apr. 2, 1982 (96 Stat. 26) and trial jurisdiction transferred to *U.S. Claims Court* and appellate functions merged with those of *U.S. Court of Customs and Patent Appeals* to form U.S. Court of Appeals for the Federal Circuit. *U.S. Claims Court* renamed U.S. Court of Federal Claims by act of Oct. 29, 1992 (106 Stat. 4516).

Claims Commission of the United States, International   Established in State Department by act of Mar. 10, 1950 (64 Stat. 12). Abolished by Reorg. Plan No. 1 of 1954, effective July 1, 1954, and functions transferred to Foreign Claims Settlement Commission of the United States.

Claims Settlement Commission of the United States, Foreign   Established by Reorg. Plan No. 1 of 1954, effective July 1, 1954. Transferred to Justice Department by act of Mar. 14, 1980 (94 Stat. 96).

Clark Sesquicentennial Commission, George Rogers   Established by Public Resolution 51 (45 Stat. 723). Expenditures ordered administered by Interior Department by EO 6166 of June 10, 1933.

Classification Review Committee, Interagency   Established by EO 11652 of Mar. 8, 1972. Abolished by EO 12065 of June 28, 1978.

Clemency Board, Presidential   Established in Executive Office of the President by EO 11803 of Sept. 16, 1974. Final recommendations submitted to President Sept. 15, 1975, and *Board* terminated by EO 11878 of Sept. 10, 1975.

Coal Commission, National Bituminous   Established under authority of act of Aug. 30, 1935 (49 Stat. 992). Abolished by Reorg. Plan No. II of 1939, effective July 1, 1939, and functions transferred to *Bituminous Coal Division,* Interior Department.

Coal Consumers' Counsel, Office of the Bituminous   Established by act of Apr. 11, 1941 (55 Stat. 134), renewing provisions of act of Apr. 23, 1937 (50 Stat. 72) for 2 years to continue functions of *Consumers' Counsel Division,* Interior Department. Functions continued by acts of Apr. 24, 1943 (57 Stat. 68), and May 21, 1943 (57 Stat. 82). Terminated Aug. 24, 1943.

Coal Division, Bituminous   Established July 1, 1939, by Interior Secretary's Order 1394 of June 16, 1939, as amended by Order 1399, of July 5, 1939, pursuant to act of Apr. 3, 1939 (53 Stat. 562) and Reorg. Plan No. II of 1939, effective July 1, 1939. Administered functions vested in *National Bituminous Coal Commission* by act of Apr. 23, 1937 (50 Stat. 72). Act extended to Aug. 24, 1943, on which date it expired.

Coal Labor Board, Bituminous   Established by act of July 12, 1921 (42 Stat. 140). Abolished as result of U.S. Supreme Court decision, May 18, 1936, in case of *Carter* v. *Carter Coal Company et al.*

Coal Leasing Planning and Coordination, Office of   Established Mar. 22, 1978, by Interior Departmental Manual Release 2075. Abolished Aug. 4, 1981, by Departmental Manual Release 2342.

Coal Mine Safety Board of Review, Federal   Established by act of July 16, 1952 (66 Stat. 697). Inactive after Mar. 30, 1970, pursuant to act of Dec. 30, 1969 (83 Stat. 803).

Coal Mines Administration   Established by Interior Secretary July 1, 1943. Abolished by Secretary's Order 1977 of Aug. 16, 1944, as amended by Order 1982 of Aug. 31, 1944, and functions assumed by *Solid Fuels Administration for War. Administration* reestablished in Interior Department by EO 9728 of May 21, 1946. Terminated June 30, 1947, by act of Mar. 27, 1942 (56 Stat. 176).

Coal Research, Office of   Established in Interior Department by act of July 7, 1960 (74 Stat. 336). Functions transferred to *Energy Research and Development Administration* by act of Oct. 11, 1974 (88 Stat. 1237).

Coast and Geodetic Survey   *See* **Coast Survey**

Coast Guard, U.S.   Transferred from Treasury Department to Navy Department by EO 8929 of Nov. 1, 1941. Returned to Treasury Department by EO 9666 of Dec. 28, 1945. Transferred to Transportation Department by act of Oct. 15, 1966 (80 Stat. 931).

Coast Survey   Established by act of Feb. 10, 1807 (2 Stat. 413). Redesignated as *Coast and Geodetic Survey* by act of June 20, 1878 (20 Stat. 206). Transferred to *Environmental Science Services Administration* by Reorg. Plan No. 2 of 1965, effective July 13, 1965.

Codification Board Established by act of June 19, 1937 (50 Stat. 304). Abolished by Reorg. Plan No. II of 1939, effective July 1, 1939, and functions transferred to *Division of the Federal Register.*

Coinage, Joint Commission on the Established by act of July 23, 1965 (79 Stat. 258). Expired Jan. 4, 1975, pursuant to act of Oct. 6, 1972 (88 Stat. 776).

Collection of Fine Arts, National Established within Smithsonian Institution by act of Mar. 24, 1937 (50 Stat. 51). Renamed National Museum of American Art in Smithsonian Institution by act of Oct. 13, 1980 (94 Stat. 1884).

Columbia Institution for the Instruction of the Deaf and Dumb, and the Blind Established by act of Feb. 16, 1857 (11 Stat. 161). Renamed *Columbia Institution for the Instruction of the Deaf and Dumb* by act of Feb. 23, 1865 (13 Stat. 436). Renamed *Columbia Institution for the Deaf* by act of Mar. 4, 1911 (36 Stat. 1422). Renamed *Gallaudet College* by act of June 18, 1954 (68 Stat. 265). Functions of *Health, Education, and Welfare Department* transferred to Education Department by act of Oct. 17, 1979 (93 Stat. 695). Renamed Gallaudet University by act of Aug. 4, 1986 (100 Stat. 781).

Commander in Chief, U.S. Fleet, and Chief of Naval Operations Duties of two positions prescribed by EO 8984 of Dec. 18, 1941. Combined under one officer by EO 9096 of Mar. 12, 1942.

Commerce, Bureau of Domestic *See* **Business and Defense Services Administration**

Commerce, Bureau of Foreign Established by Commerce Secretary Oct. 12, 1953, by Reorg. Plan No. 5 of 1950, effective May 24, 1950. Abolished by department order of Aug. 7, 1961, and functions vested in *Bureau of International Programs* and *Bureau of International Business Operations.*

Commerce, Bureau of Foreign and Domestic Established by act of Aug. 23, 1912 (37 Stat. 407). Functions reassigned to other offices of Commerce Department due to internal reorganizations.

Commerce, Bureau of International *See* **Business Operations, Bureau of International**

Commerce Department, Solicitor for Transferred from Justice Department to Commerce Department by EO 6166 of June 10, 1933.

Commerce Service, Foreign Established in *Bureau of Foreign and Domestic Commerce,* Commerce Department, by act of Mar. 3, 1927 (44 Stat. 1394). Transferred to State Department as part of Foreign Service by Reorg. Plan No. II of 1939, effective July 1, 1939.

Commercial Company, U.S. Established Mar. 27, 1942, as subsidiary of *Reconstruction Finance Corporation.* Transferred to *Office of Economic Warfare* by EO 9361 of July 15, 1943. *Office* consolidated into *Foreign Economic Administration* by EO 9380 of Sept. 25, 1943. Functions returned to *Corporation* by EO 9630 of Sept. 27, 1945, until June 30, 1948.

Commercial Policy, Executive Committee on Established by Presidential letter of Nov. 11, 1933, to Secretary of State. Abolished by EO 9461 of Aug. 7, 1944.

Commercial Services, Office of Foreign Established by Commerce Secretary Feb. 1, 1963, and operated under Department Organization Order 40–4. Abolished Sept. 15, 1970, by Department Organization Order 40–2A and functions transferred to Bureau of International Commerce.

Commercial Standards Division Transferred with *Division of Simplified Trade Practice* from *National Bureau of Standards* to Commerce Secretary by Reorg. Plan No. 3 of 1946, effective July 16, 1946, to permit reassignment to *Office of Domestic Commerce.* Functions transferred to *National Bureau of Standards* by Commerce Department Order 90, June 7, 1963, pursuant to Reorg. Plan No. 5 of 1950, effective May 24, 1950.

Commission. *See other part of title*

Committee. *See also other part of title*

Committee Management Secretariat Established in Office of Management and Budget Jan. 5, 1973, by act of Oct. 6, 1972 (86 Stat. 772). Functions transferred to General Services Administrator by Reorg. Plan No. 1 of 1977, effective Apr. 1, 1978. Reassigned to *National Archives and Records Service* by GSA order of Feb. 22, 1979. Transferred in Archives to Office of the Federal Register by GSA order of Oct. 14, 1980. Transferred to Office of the Archivist of the United States by GSA order of Sept. 24, 1982. Reassigned to Office of Program Initiatives, GSA, by GSA order of May 18, 1984. Transferred to Office of Management Services, GSA, by GSA order of Apr. 7, 1986.

Commodities Corporation, Federal Surplus *See* **Relief Corporation, Federal Surplus**

Commodity Credit Corporation Organized by EO 6340 of Oct. 16, 1933, and managed in close affiliation with *Reconstruction Finance Corporation.* Transferred to Agriculture Department by Reorg. Plan No. I of 1939, effective July 1, 1939.

Commodity Exchange Administration *See* **Grain Futures Administration**

Commodity Exchange Authority *See* **Grain Futures Administration**

Commodity Exchange Commission Established by act of Sept. 21, 1922 (42 Stat. 998). Functions transferred to Commodity Futures Trading Commission by act of Oct. 23, 1974 (88 Stat. 1414).

Commodity Stabilization Service Established Nov. 2, 1953, by Secretary's Memorandum 1320, supp. 4. Renamed Agricultural Stabilization and Conservation Service by Secretary's Memorandum 1458 of June 14, 1961, effective June 5, 1961.

Communication Agency, International *See* **Information Agency, U.S.**

Communications Program, Joint Tactical Combined with *Joint Interoperability of the Tactical Command and Control Systems Programs* to form

Joint Tactical Command, Control, and Communications Agency in July 1984, pursuant to Defense Department Directive 5154.28.

Community Development Corporation   Established in Housing and Urban Development Department by act of Dec. 31, 1970 (84 Stat. 1791). Renamed *New Community Development Corporation* by act of Aug. 22, 1974 (88 Stat. 725). Abolished Nov. 30, 1983, by act of Nov. 30, 1983 (97 Stat. 1238), and functions transferred to Assistant Secretary for Community Planning and Development, Housing and Urban Development Department.

Community Development Corporation, New   *See* **Community Development Corporation**

Community Facilities, Bureau of   Established in 1945 by *Federal Works Administrator.* Transferred by act of June 30, 1949 (63 Stat. 380), to General Services Administration, functioning as *Community Facilities Service.* Certain functions transferred to various agencies, including Interior Department, *Housing and Home Finance Agency,* and *Federal Security Agency* by Reorg. Plans Nos. 15, 16, and 17 of 1950, effective May 24, 1950.

Community Facilities Administration   Established in *Housing and Home Finance Agency* by Administrator's Organizational Order 1 of Dec. 23, 1954. Terminated by act of Sept. 9, 1965 (79 Stat. 667), and functions transferred to Housing and Urban Development Department.

Community Organization, Committee on   Established in *Office of Defense Health and Welfare Services* Sept. 10, 1941. Functions transferred to *Federal Security Agency* by EO 9338 of Apr. 29, 1943.

Community Relations Service   Established in Commerce Department by act of July 2, 1964 (78 Stat. 241). Transferred to Justice Department by Reorg. Plan No. 1 of 1966, effective Apr. 22, 1966.

Community Service, Commission on National and   Established by act of Nov. 16, 1990 (104 Stat. 3168). Abolished by act of Sept. 21, 1993, and functions vested in the Board of Directors or the Executive Director prior to Oct. 1, 1993, transferred to the Corporation for National and Community Service (107 Stat. 873, 888).

Community Services, Office of   Established in Health and Human Services Department by act of Aug. 13, 1981 (95 Stat. 516). Replaced by Family Support Administration.

Community Services Administration   Established by act of Jan. 4, 1975 (88 Stat. 2291) as successor to *Office of Economic Opportunity.* Abolished as independent agency through repeal of act of Aug. 20, 1964 (except titles VIII and X of such act) by act of Aug. 13, 1981 (95 Stat. 519).

Community Services Administration   Functions concerning Legal Services Program transferred to Legal Services Corporation by act of July 25, 1974 (88 Stat. 389). Renamed *Public Services Administration* by Health, Education, and Welfare departmental notice of Nov. 3, 1976. Transferred to

Office of Human Development by Secretary's reorganization of Mar. 8, 1977 (42 FR 13262).

Community War Services   Established in *Office of the Administrator* under EO 9338 of Apr. 29, 1943, and *Federal Security Agency* order. Terminated Dec. 31, 1946, by act of July 26, 1946 (60 Stat. 695).

Conciliation Service, U.S.   Established by act of Mar. 4, 1913 (37 Stat. 738). Functions transferred to Federal Mediation and Conciliation Service, established by act of June 23, 1947 (61 Stat. 153).

Conference on Security and Cooperation in Europe   Renamed Organization for Security and Cooperation in Europe by EO 13029, Dec. 3, 1996 (61 FR 64591).

Conservation and Renewable Energy Office   Renamed Energy Efficiency and Renewable Energy Office by Assistant Secretary's memorandum of Mar. 3, 1993.

Consolidated Farm Service Agency   Established by act of Oct. 13, 1994 (108 Stat. 3214). Renamed Farm Service Agency (61 FR 1109), effective Jan. 16, 1996.

Constitution, Commission on the Bicentennial of the United States   Established by act of Sept. 29, 1983, as amended (97 Stat. 722). Terminated by act of Dec. 3, 1991 (105 Stat. 1232).

Constitution, transfer of functions   *See* **Statutes at Large and other matters**

Construction, Collective Bargaining Committee in   Established by EO 11849 of Apr. 1, 1975. Inactive since Jan. 7, 1976. Formally abolished by EO 12110 of Dec. 28, 1978.

Construction, Equipment and Repairs, Bureau of   Established in Navy Department by act of Aug. 31, 1842 (5 Stat. 579). Abolished by act of July 5, 1862 (12 Stat. 510), and functions distributed among *Bureau of Equipment and Recruiting, Bureau of Construction and Repair,* and *Bureau of Steam Engineering.*

Construction Branch   Established in Treasury Department in 1853 and designated *Bureau of Construction* under control of *Office of Supervising Architect* by Sept. 30, 1855. *Office* incorporated into *Public Buildings Branch, Procurement Division,* by EO 6166 of June 10, 1933. Transferred to *Federal Works Agency* by Reorg. Plan No. I of 1939, effective July 1, 1939, when *Public Buildings Branch of Procurement Division, Bureau of Buildings Management,* National Park Service, Interior Department—so far as latter concerned with operation of public buildings for other departments or agencies—and *U.S. Housing Corporation* consolidated with *Public Buildings Administration, Federal Works Agency.*

Construction Industry Stabilization Committee   Established by EO 11588 of Mar. 29, 1971. Abolished by EO 11788 of June 18, 1974.

Construction and Repair, Bureau of   Established by act of July 5, 1862 (12 Stat. 510), replacing *Bureau of Construction, Equipment and Repairs.* Abolished by act of June 20, 1940 (54 Stat. 492), and functions transferred to *Bureau of Ships.*

Consumer Advisory Council Established by EO 11136 of Jan. 3, 1964. *Office of Consumer Affairs* established in Executive Office of the President by EO 11583 of Feb. 24, 1971, and Council reestablished in *Office.*

Consumer Affairs, Office of Established by EO 11583 of Feb. 24, 1971. Transferred to *Health, Education, and Welfare Department* by EO 11702 of Jan. 25, 1973.

Consumer Affairs Staff, National Business Council for Established in Commerce Department by departmental organization order of Dec. 16, 1971. Terminated by departmental order of Dec. 6, 1973, due to lack of funding.

Consumer agencies Consumer agencies of *National Emergency Council* and *National Recovery Administration* reorganized and functions transferred, together with those of *Consumers' Advisory Board, NRA,* and *Cabinet Committee on Price Policy,* to *Consumers' Division, NRA,* by EO 7120 of July 30, 1935. *Division* transferred to Labor Department by EO 7252 of Dec. 21, 1935. Transferred to *Division of Consumers' Counsel, Agricultural Adjustment Administration,* Agriculture Department, by Labor Secretary's letter of Aug. 30, 1938, to Agriculture Secretary. Continued as *Consumer Standards Project* until June 30, 1941. Research on consumer standards continued by *Consumer Standards Section, Consumers' Counsel Division,* transferred to *Agricultural Marketing Administration* by administrative order of Feb. 28, 1942. Other project activities discontinued.

Consumer Cooperative Bank, National Established by act of Aug. 20, 1978 (92 Stat. 499). Removed from mixed-ownership, Government corporation status by acts of Sept. 13, 1982 (96 Stat. 1062) and Jan. 12, 1983 (96 Stat. 2478).

Consumer Interests, President's Committee on Established by EO 11136 of Jan. 3, 1964. Abolished by EO 11583 of Feb. 24, 1971.

Consumer and Marketing Service Established by Agriculture Secretary Feb. 2, 1965. Renamed Agricultural Marketing Service Apr. 2, 1972, by Secretary's order and certain functions transferred to Animal and Plant Health Inspection Service.

Consumers' Counsel Established in *National Bituminous Coal Commission* by act of Aug. 30, 1935 (49 Stat. 993). Office abolished by Reorg. Plan No. II of 1939, effective July 1, 1939, and functions transferred to Office of Solicitor, Interior Department, to function as *Consumers' Counsel Division* under direction of Interior Secretary. Functions transferred to *Office of the Bituminous Coal Consumers' Counsel* June 1941 by act of Apr. 11, 1941 (55 Stat. 134).

Consumers' Counsel Division *See* **Consumers' Counsel**

Consumers' Counsel, Division of Established by act of May 12, 1933 (48 Stat. 31). Transferred by order of Agriculture Secretary from *Agricultural Adjustment*

Administration to supervision of *Director of Marketing,* effective Feb. 1, 1940. Transferred to *Agricultural Marketing Administration* by administrative order of Feb. 28, 1942.

Consumers' Problems, Adviser on *See* **Consumer agencies**

Contract Committee Government *See* **Contract Compliance, Committee on Government**

Contract Compliance, Committee on Government Established by EO 10308 of Dec. 3, 1951. Abolished by EO 10479 of Aug. 13, 1953, which established successor *Government Contract Committee.* Abolished by EO 10925 of Mar. 6, 1961, and records and property transferred to *President's Committee on Equal Employment Opportunity.*

Contract Settlement, Office of Established by act of July 1, 1944 (58 Stat. 651). Transferred to *Office of War Mobilization and Reconversion* by act of Oct. 3, 1944 (58 Stat. 785). Terminated by EO 9809 of Dec. 12, 1946, and Reorg. Plan No. 1 of 1947, effective July 1, 1947, and functions transferred to Treasury Department. Functions transferred to General Services Administration by act of June 30, 1949 (63 Stat. 380).

Contract Settlement Advisory Board Established by act of July 1, 1944 (58 Stat. 651). Transferred to Treasury Department by EO 9809 of Dec. 12, 1946, and by Reorg. Plan No. 1 of 1947, effective July 1, 1947. Transferred to General Services Administration by act of June 30, 1949 (63 Stat. 380) and established as *Contract Review Board.* Renamed Board of Contract Appeals in 1961 by Administrator's order. Board established as independent entity within General Services Administration Feb. 27, 1979, pursuant to act of Nov. 1, 1978 (92 Stat. 2383).

Contract Settlement Appeal Board, Office of Established by act of July 1, 1944 (58 Stat. 651). Transferred to Treasury Department by EO 9809 of Dec. 12, 1946, and by Reorg. Plan No. 1 of 1947, effective July 1, 1947. Functions transferred to General Services Administration by act of June 30, 1949 (63 Stat. 380). Abolished by act of July 14, 1952 (66 Stat. 627).

Contract Termination Board, Joint Established Nov. 12, 1943, by *Director of War Mobilization.* Functions assumed by *Office of Contract Settlement.*

Contracts Division, Public Established in Labor Department to administer act of June 30, 1936 (49 Stat. 2036). Consolidated with Wage and Hour Division by Secretarial order of Aug. 21, 1942. Absorbed by Wage and Hour Division by Secretarial order of May 1971.

Cooperation Administration, International Established by State Department Delegation of Authority 85 of June 30, 1955, pursuant to EO 10610 of May 9, 1955. Abolished by act of Sept. 4, 1961 (75 Stat. 446), and functions redelegated to Agency for International Development pursuant to Presidential letter of Sept. 30, 1961, and EO 10973 of Nov. 3, 1961.

Cooperative State Research Service Established in the Department of Agriculture. Incorporated into Cooperative State, Research, Education, and Extension Service under Department of Agriculture reorganization in 1995.

Coordinating Service, Federal *Office of Chief Coordinator* created by Executive order promulgated in *Bureau of the Budget* Circular 15, July 27, 1921, and duties enlarged by other *Bureau* circulars. Abolished by EO 6166 of June 10, 1933. Contract form, Federal traffic, and surplus property functions transferred to *Procurement Division* by order of Treasury Secretary, approved by President Oct. 9, 1933, issued pursuant to EO's 6166 of June 10, 1933, and 6224 of July 27, 1933.

Copyright Royalty Tribunal Established as an independent entity within the legislative branch by act of Oct. 19, 1976 (90 Stat. 2594). Abolished by act of Dec. 17, 1993 (107 Stat. 2304), and functions transferred to copyright arbitration royalty panels.

Copyrighted Works, National Commission on New Technological Uses of Established by act of Dec. 31, 1974 (88 Stat. 1873). Terminated Sept. 29, 1978, pursuant to terms of act.

Corporate Payments Abroad, Task Force on Questionable Established by Presidential memorandum of Mar. 31, 1976. Terminated Dec. 31, 1976, pursuant to terms of memorandum.

Corporation, Federal Facilities Established in Treasury Department by EO 10539 of June 22, 1954. Placed under supervision of Director appointed by General Services Administrator by EO 10720 of July 11, 1957. Dissolved by act of Aug. 30, 1961 (75 Stat. 418), and functions transferred to Administrator of General Services.

Corregidor-Bataan Memorial Commission Established by act of Aug. 5, 1953 (67 Stat. 366). Terminated May 6, 1967, by act of Dec. 23, 1963 (77 Stat. 477).

Cost Accounting Standards Board Established by act of Aug. 15, 1970 (84 Stat. 796). Terminated Sept. 30, 1980, due to lack of funding. Reestablished by act of Nov. 17, 1988 (102 Stat. 4059).

Cost of Living Council Established by EO 11615 of Aug. 15, 1971. Abolished by EO 11788 of June 18, 1974.

Cotton Stabilization Corporation Organized June 1930 under laws of Delaware by *Federal Farm Board* pursuant to act of June 15, 1929 (46 Stat. 11). Certificate of dissolution filed with Corporation Commission of Delaware Dec. 27, 1934.

Council. *See other part of title*

Counter-. *See other part of title*

Courts Under act of Aug. 7, 1939 (53 Stat. 1223), and revised June 25, 1948 (62 Stat. 913), to provide for administration of U.S. courts, administrative jurisdiction over all continental and territorial courts transferred to Administrative Office of the U.S. Courts, including U.S. courts of appeals and district courts, District Court for the Territory of Alaska, U.S.

District Court for the District of the Canal Zone, District Court of Guam, District Court of the Virgin Islands, Court of Claims, Court of Customs and Patent Appeals, and Customs Courts.

Credit Unions, Bureau of Federal *See* **Credit Union System, Federal**

Credit Union System, Federal Established by act of June 26, 1934 (48 Stat. 1216), to be administered by *Farm Credit Administration.* Transferred to Federal Deposit Insurance Corporation by EO 9148 of Apr. 27, 1942, and Reorg. Plan No. 1 of 1947, effective July 1, 1947. Functions transferred to *Bureau of Federal Credit Unions, Federal Security Agency,* established by act of June 29, 1948 (62 Stat. 1091). Functions transferred to *Health, Education, and Welfare Department* by Reorg. Plan No. 1 of 1953, effective Apr. 11, 1953. Functions transferred to National Credit Union Administration by act of Mar. 10, 1970 (84 Stat. 49).

Crime, National Council on Organized Established by EO 11534 of June 4, 1970. Terminated by EO 12110 of Dec. 28, 1978.

Critical Materials Council, National Established within Executive Office of the President by act of July 31, 1984 (98 Stat. 1250). *Office* abolished in September 1993 due to lack of funding and functions transferred to the Office of Science and Technology Policy.

Crop Production Loan Office Authorized by Presidential letters of July 26, 1918, and July 26, 1919, to Agriculture Secretary. Further authorized by act of Mar. 3, 1921 (41 Stat. 1347). Transferred to Farm Credit Administration by EO 6084 of Mar. 27, 1933.

Cultural Center, National Established in Smithsonian Institution by act of Sept. 2, 1958 (72 Stat. 1698). Renamed John F. Kennedy Center for the Performing Arts by act of Jan. 23, 1964 (78 Stat. 4).

Customs, Bureau of Functions relating to award of numbers to undocumented vessels, vested in *Collectors of Customs,* transferred to Commandant of Coast Guard by EO 9083 of Feb. 27, 1942. Transfer made permanent by Reorg. Plan No. 3 of 1946, effective July 16, 1946. Redesignated U.S. Customs Service by Treasury Department Order 165–23 of Apr. 4, 1973.

Customs Court, U.S. Formerly established as Board of General Appraisers by act of June 10, 1890 (26 Stat. 136). Renamed *U.S. Customs Court* by act of May 26, 1926 (44 Stat. 669). Renamed U.S. Court of International Trade by act of Oct. 10, 1980 (94 Stat. 1727).

Customs and Patent Appeals, U.S. Court of Established by act of Mar. 2, 1929 (45 Stat. 1475). Abolished by act of Apr. 2, 1982 (96 Stat. 28) and functions merged with appellate functions of *U.S. Court of Claims* to form U.S. Court of Appeals for the Federal Circuit.

Dairy Industry, Bureau of *Bureau of Dairying* established in Agriculture Department by act of May 29, 1924 (43 Stat. 243). *Bureau of Dairy Industry* designation first appeared in act of May 11, 1926

(44 Stat. 499). Functions transferred to Agricultural Research Service by Secretary's Memorandum 1320, supp. 4, of Nov. 2, 1953.

Defense, Advisory Commission to the Council of National See **Defense, Council of National**

Defense, Council of National Established by act of Aug. 29, 1916 (39 Stat. 649). *Advisory Commission*—composed of Advisers on Industrial Production, Industrial Materials, Employment, Farm Products, Price Stabilization, Transportation, and Consumer Protection—established by *Council* pursuant to act and approved by President May 29, 1940. *Commission* decentralized by merging divisions with newly created national defense units. Agencies evolved from *Commission,* except *Office of Agricultural War Relations* and *Office of Price Administration,* made units of *Office for Emergency Management. Council* inactive.

Defense, Office of Civilian Established in *Office for Emergency Management* by EO 8757 of May 20, 1941. Terminated by EO 9562 of June 4, 1945.

Defense Administration, Federal Civil Established in *Office for Emergency Management* by EO 10186 of Dec. 1, 1950; subsequently established as independent agency by act of Jan. 12, 1951 (64 Stat. 1245). Functions transferred to *Office of Defense and Civilian Mobilization* by Reorg. Plan No. 1 of 1958, effective July 1, 1958.

Defense Advanced Research Projects Agency Established as a separate agency of the Department of Defense by DOD Directive 5105.41 dated July 25, 1978. Renamed *Advanced Research Projects Agency* by Defense Secretary's order dated July 13, 1993. Reestablished by P.L. 104–106, Feb. 10, 1996 (110 Stat. 406).

Defense Advisory Council, Civil Established by act of Jan. 12, 1951 (64 Stat. 1245). Transferred to *Office of Defense and Civilian Mobilization* by Reorg. Plan No. 1 of 1958, effective July 1, 1958.

Defense Aid Reports, Division of Established in *Office for Emergency Management* by EO 8751 of May 2, 1941. Abolished by EO 8926 of Oct. 28, 1941, which created *Office of Lend-Lease Administration.*

Defense Air Transportation Administration Established Nov. 12, 1951, by Commerce Department Order 137. Abolished by Amendment 3 of Sept. 13, 1962, to Department Order 128 (revised) and functions transferred to *Office of the Under Secretary of Commerce for Transportation.*

Defense Atomic Support Agency Renamed *Defense Nuclear Agency* by General Order No. 1 of July 1, 1971.

Defense Audiovisual Agency Established by Defense Department Directive 5040.1 of June 12, 1979. Abolished by Secretary's memorandum of Apr. 19, 1985, and functions assigned to the military departments.

Defense Audit Service Established by Defense Department directive of Oct. 14, 1976. Abolished by Deputy Secretary's memorandum of Nov. 2, 1982,

and functions transferred to Office of the Inspector General.

Defense Civil Preparedness Agency Functions transferred from Defense Department to Federal Emergency Management Agency by EO 12148 of July 20, 1979.

Defense and Civilian Mobilization Board Established by EO 10773 of July 1, 1938. Redesignated *Civil and Defense Mobilization Board* by act of Aug. 26, 1958 (72 Stat. 861). Abolished by *Office of Emergency Preparedness* Circular 1200.1 of Oct. 31, 1962.

Defense Communications Agency Established by direction of the Secretary of Defense on May 12, 1960. Renamed Defense Information Systems Agency by DOD Directive 5105.19 dated June 25, 1991.

Defense Communications Board Established by EO 8546 of Sept. 24, 1940. Renamed *Board of War Communications* by EO 9183 of June 15, 1942. Abolished by EO 9831 of Feb. 24, 1947, and property transferred to Federal Communications Commission.

Defense Coordinating Board, Civil Established by EO 10611 of May 11, 1955. EO 10611 revoked by EO 10773 of July 1, 1958.

Defense Electric Power Administration Established by Interior Secretary's Order 2605 of Dec. 4, 1950. Abolished June 30, 1953, by Secretary's Order 2721 of May 7, 1953. Reestablished by Departmental Manual Release No. 253 of Aug. 6, 1959. Terminated by Departmental Manual Release No. 1050 of Jan. 10, 1977.

Defense Fisheries Administration Established by Interior Secretary's Order 2605 of Dec. 4, 1950. Abolished June 30, 1953, by Secretary's Order 2722 of May 13, 1953.

Defense Health and Welfare Services, Office of Established by EO 8890 of Sept. 3, 1941. Terminated by EO 9338 of Apr. 29, 1943, and functions transferred to *Federal Security Agency.*

Defense Homes Corporation Incorporated pursuant to President's letter to Treasury Secretary of Oct. 18, 1940. Transferred to *Federal Public Housing Authority* by EO 9070 of Feb. 24, 1942.

Defense Housing Coordination, Division of Established in *Office for Emergency Management* by EO 8632 of Jan. 11, 1941. Functions transferred to *National Housing Agency* by EO 9070 of Feb. 24, 1942.

Defense Housing Coordinator Office established July 21, 1940, by *Advisory Commission to Council of National Defense.* Functions transferred to *Division of Defense Housing Coordination, Office for Emergency Management,* by EO 8632 of Jan. 11, 1941.

Defense Housing Division, Mutual Ownership Established by Administrator of *Federal Works Agency* under provisions of act of June 28, 1941 (55 Stat. 361). Functions transferred to *Federal Public*

Housing Authority, National Housing Agency, by EO 9070 of Feb. 24, 1942.

Defense Investigative Service Established by the Secretary of Defense Jan. 1, 1972. Renamed Defense Security Service in November 1997 by Defense Reform Initiative.

Defense Manpower Administration Established by Labor Secretary by General Order 48, pursuant to EO 10161 of Sept. 9, 1950, and Reorg. Plan No. 6 of 1950, effective May 24, 1950. General Order 48 revoked by General Order 63 of Aug. 25, 1953, which established *Office of Manpower Administration* in Department.

Defense Mapping Agency Established as a Defense Department agency in 1972. Functions transferred to the National Imagery and Mapping Agency by P.L. 104–201, Sept. 23, 1996 (110 Stat. 2677).

Defense Materials Procurement Agency Established by EO 10281 of Aug. 28, 1951. Abolished by EO 10480 of Aug. 14, 1953, and functions transferred to General Services Administration.

Defense Materials Service *See* **Emergency Procurement Service**

Defense Mediation Board, National Established by EO 8716 of Mar. 19, 1941. Terminated on creation of *National War Labor Board, Office for Emergency Management* by EO 9017 of Jan. 12, 1942. Transferred to Labor Department by EO 9617 of Sept. 19, 1945. *Board* terminated by EO 9672 of Dec. 31, 1945, which established *National Wage Stabilization Board* in Labor Department. Terminated by EO 9809 of Dec. 12, 1946, and functions transferred to Labor Secretary and Treasury Department, effective Feb. 24, 1947.

Defense Medical Programs Activity Functions consolidated into the TRICARE Management Activity in November 1997 by Defense Reform Initiative.

Defense Minerals Administration Established by Interior Secretary's Order 2605 of Dec. 4, 1950. Functions assigned to *Defense Materials Procurement Agency.* Functions of exploration for critical and strategic minerals redelegated to Interior Secretary and administered by *Defense Minerals Exploration Administration* by Secretary's Order 2726 of June 30, 1953. Termination of program announced by Secretary June 6, 1958. Certain activities continued in *Office of Minerals Exploration,* Interior Department.

Defense Minerals Exploration Administration *See* **Defense Minerals Administration**

Defense Mobilization, Office of Established in Executive Office of the President by EO 10193 of Dec. 16, 1950. Superseded by *Office of Defense Mobilization* established by Reorg. Plan No. 3 of 1953, effective June 12, 1953, which assumed functions of former *Office, National Security Resources Board,* and critical materials stockpiling functions of Army, Navy, Air Force, and Interior Secretaries and of *Army and Navy Munitions Board.* Consolidated with *Federal Civil Defense Administration* into *Office of Defense and Civilian*

Mobilization by Reorg. Plan No. 1 of 1958, effective July 1, 1958, and offices of Director and Deputy Director terminated.

Defense Mobilization Board Established by EO 10200 of Jan. 3, 1951, and restated in EO 10480 of Aug. 14, 1953. Terminated by EO 10773 of July 1, 1958.

Defense Nuclear Agency Established in 1971. Renamed Defense Special Weapons Agency by DOD Directive 5105.31 of June 14, 1995.

Defense Plant Corporation Established by act of June 25, 1940 (54 Stat. 572). Transferred from *Federal Loan Agency* to Commerce Department by EO 9071 of Feb. 24, 1942. Returned to *Federal Loan Agency* pursuant to act of Feb. 24, 1945 (59 Stat. 5). Dissolved by act of June 30, 1945 (59 Stat. 310), and functions transferred to *Reconstruction Finance Corporation.*

Defense Plants Administration, Small Established by act of July 31, 1951 (65 Stat. 131). Terminated July 31, 1953, by act of June 30, 1953 (67 Stat. 131). Functions relating to liquidation transferred to Small Business Administration by EO 10504 of Dec. 1, 1953.

Defense Production Administration Established by EO 10200 of Jan. 3, 1951. Terminated by EO 10433 of Feb. 4, 1953, and functions transferred to *Office of Defense Mobilization.*

Defense Property Disposal Service Renamed Defense Reutilization and Marketing Service by Defense Logistics Agency General Order 10–85, effective July 1, 1985.

Defense Prisoner of War/Missing in Action Office Established by DOD Directive 5110.10, July 16, 1993. Renamed Defense Prisoner of War/Missing Personnel Office by Defense Secretary's memorandum of May 30, 1996.

Defense Public Works Division Established in *Public Works Administration.* Transferred to *Office of Federal Works Administrator* by administrative order of July 16, 1941. Abolished by administrative order of Mar. 6, 1942, and functions transferred to *Office of Chief Engineer, Federal Works Agency.*

Defense Purchases, Office for the Coordination of National Established by order of *Council of National Defense,* approved June 27, 1940. Order revoked Jan. 7, 1941, and records transferred to Executive Office of the President.

Defense Research Committee, National Established June 27, 1940, by order of *Council of National Defense.* Abolished by order of *Council* June 28, 1941, and reestablished in *Office of Scientific Research and Development* by EO 8807 of June 28, 1941. *Office* terminated by EO 9913 of Dec. 26, 1947, and property and records transferred to *National Military Establishment.*

Defense Resources Committee Established by Administrative Order 1496 of June 15, 1940. Replaced by *War Resources Council* by Administrative Order 1636 of Jan. 14, 1942. Inactive.

Defense Solid Fuels Administration   Established by Interior Secretary's Order 2605 of Dec. 4, 1950. Abolished June 29, 1954, by Secretary's Order 2764.

Defense Stockpile Manager, National   Established by act of Nov. 14, 1986 (100 Stat. 4067). Functions transferred from General Services Administrator to Defense Secretary by EO 12626 of Feb. 25, 1988.

Defense Supplies Corporation   Established under act of June 25, 1940 (54 Stat. 572). Transferred from *Federal Loan Agency* to Commerce Department by EO 9071 of Feb. 24, 1942. Returned to *Federal Loan Agency* by act of Feb. 24, 1945 (59 Stat. 5). Dissolved by act of June 30, 1945 (59 Stat. 310), and functions transferred to *Reconstruction Finance Corporation.*

Defense Supply Agency   Renamed Defense Logistics Agency by DOD Directive 5105.22 of Jan. 22, 1977.

Defense Supply Management Agency   Established in Defense Department by act of July 1, 1952 (66 Stat. 318). Abolished by Reorg. Plan No. 6 of 1953, effective June 30, 1953, and functions transferred to Defense Secretary.

Defense Transport Administration   Established Oct. 4, 1950, by order of Commissioner of *Interstate Commerce Commission* in charge of *Bureau of Service,* pursuant to EO 10161 of Sept. 9, 1950. Terminated by DTA Commissioner's order, effective July 1, 1955, and functions transferred to Bureau of Safety and Service, Interstate Commerce Commission.

Defense Transportation, Office of   Established in *Office for Emergency Management* by EO 8989 of Dec. 18, 1941. Terminated by EO 10065 of July 6, 1949.

Director.   *See other part of title*

Disarmament Administration, U.S.   Established in State Department. Functions transferred to U.S. Arms Control and Disarmament Agency by act of Sept. 26, 1961 (75 Stat. 638).

Disarmament Problems, President's Special Committee on   Established by President Aug. 5, 1955. Dissolved in February 1958.

Disaster Assistance Administration, Federal   Functions transferred from Housing and Urban Development Department to Federal Emergency Management Agency by EO 12148 of July 20, 1979.

Disaster Loan Corporation   Grouped with other agencies to form *Federal Loan Agency* by Reorg. Plan No. I of 1939, effective July 1, 1939. Transferred to Commerce Department by EO 9071 of Feb. 24, 1942. Returned to *Federal Loan Agency* by act of Feb. 24, 1945 (59 Stat. 5). Dissolved by act of June 30, 1945 (59 Stat. 310), and functions transferred to *Reconstruction Finance Corporation.*

Disease Control, Center for   Established within the Public Health Service by *Health, Education, and Welfare Secretary* on July 1, 1973. Renamed *Centers for Disease Control* by Health and Human Services Secretary's notice of Oct. 1, 1980 (45 FR 67772).

Renamed Centers for Disease Control and Prevention by act of Oct. 27, 1992 (106 Stat. 3504).

Displaced Persons Commission   Established by act of June 25, 1948 (62 Stat. 1009). Terminated Aug. 31, 1952, pursuant to terms of act.

District of Columbia   Established by acts of July 16, 1790 (1 Stat. 130), and Mar. 3, 1791. *Corporations of Washington and Georgetown* and *levy court of Washington County* abolished in favor of territorial form of government in 1871. Permanent commission government established July 1, 1878. District Government created as municipal corporation by act of June 11, 1878 (20 Stat. 102). Treated as branch of U.S. Government by various statutory enactments of Congress. District Government altered by Reorg. Plan No. 3 of 1967, effective Nov. 3, 1967. Charter for local government in District of Columbia provided by act of Dec. 24, 1973 (87 Stat. 774).

District of Columbia, Highway Commission of the   Established by act of Mar. 2, 1893 (27 Stat 532). *National Capital Park and Planning Commission* named successor by act of Apr. 30, 1926 (44 Stat. 374). Functions transferred to National Capital Planning Commission by act of July 19, 1952 (66 Stat. 781).

District of Columbia, Reform-School of the   Established by act of May 3, 1876 (19 Stat. 49). Renamed *National Training School for Boys* by act of May 27, 1908 (35 Stat. 380). Transferred to Justice Department by Reorg. Plan No. II of 1939, effective July 1, 1939, to be administered by Director of Bureau of Prisons.

District of Columbia Auditorium Commission   Established by act of July 1, 1955 (69 Stat. 243). Final report submitted to Congress Jan. 31, 1957, pursuant to act of Apr. 27, 1956 (70 Stat. 115).

District of Columbia Redevelopment Land Agency   Established by act of Aug. 2, 1946 (60 Stat. 790). Agency established as instrumentality of District Government by act of Dec. 24, 1973 (87 Stat. 774), effective July 1, 1974.

District of Columbia-Virginia Boundary Commission   Established by act of Mar. 21, 1934 (48 Stat. 453). Terminated Dec. 1, 1935, to which date it had been extended by Public Resolution 9 (49 Stat. 67).

Division.   *See other part of title*

Domestic Council   Established in Executive Office of the President by Reorg. Plan No. 2 of 1970, effective July 1, 1970. Abolished by Reorg. Plan No. 1 of 1977, effective Mar. 26, 1978, and functions transferred to President and staff designated as *Domestic Policy Staff.* Pursuant to EO 12045 of Mar. 27, 1978, *Staff* assisted President in performance of transferred functions. Renamed Office of Policy Development in 1981. Abolished in February 1992 by President's reorganizational statement, effective May 1992.

Domestic Policy Staff   *See* **Domestic Council**

Dominican Customs Receivership   Transferred from *Division of Territories and Island Possessions,*

Interior Department, to State Department by Reorg. Plan No. IV of 1940, effective June 30, 1940.

Drug Abuse, National Institute on Established within the National Institute of Mental Health, *Health, Education, and Welfare Department* by act of Mar. 21, 1972 (86 Stat. 85). Removed from within the National Institute of Mental Health and made an entity within the Alcohol, Drug Abuse, and Mental Health Administration by act of May 14, 1974 (88 Stat. 136). Functions transferred to Health and Human Services Department by act of Oct. 17, 1979 (93 Stat. 695). (*See also* act of Oct. 27, 1986; 100 Stat. 3207–106.) Abolished by act of July 10, 1992 (106 Stat. 331). Reestablished by act of July 10, 1992 (106 Stat. 361).

Drug Abuse, President's Advisory Commission on Narcotic and Established by EO 11076 of Jan. 15, 1963. Terminated November 1963 under terms of order.

Drug Abuse Control, Bureau of Established in Food and Drug Administration, Health and Human Services Department, to carry out functions of act of July 15, 1965 (79 Stat. 226). Functions transferred to *Bureau of Narcotics and Dangerous Drugs,* Justice Department, by Reorg. Plan No. 1 of 1968, effective Apr. 8, 1968. Abolished by Reorg. Plan No. 2 of 1973, effective July 1, 1973, and functions transferred to Drug Enforcement Administration.

Drug Abuse Law Enforcement, Office of Established by EO 11641 of Jan. 28, 1972. Terminated by EO 11727 of July 6, 1973, and functions transferred to Drug Enforcement Administration.

Drug Abuse Policy, Office of Established in Executive Office of the President by act of Mar. 19, 1976 (90 Stat. 242). Abolished by Reorg. Plan No. 1 of 1977, effective Mar. 26, 1978, and functions transferred to President.

Drug Abuse Prevention, Special Action Office for Established by EO 11599 of June 17, 1971, and act of Mar. 21, 1972 (86 Stat. 65). Terminated June 30, 1975, pursuant to terms of act.

Drug Abuse Prevention, Treatment, and Rehabilitation, Cabinet Committee on Established Apr. 27, 1976, by Presidential announcement. Terminated by Presidential memorandum of Mar. 14, 1977.

Drug Law Enforcement, Cabinet Committee for Established Apr. 27, 1976, pursuant to Presidential message to Congress of Apr. 27, 1976. Abolished by Presidential memorandum of Mar. 14, 1977.

Drugs, Bureau of Narcotics and Dangerous *See* **Drug Abuse Control, Bureau of**

Drugs and Biologics, National Center for Renamed *Center for Drugs and Biologics* by Food and Drug Administration notice of Mar. 9, 1984 (49 FR 10166). Reestablished as Center for Drug Evaluation and Research and Center for Biologics Evaluation and Research by Secretary's notice of Oct. 6, 1987 (52 FR 38275).

Drunk Driving, Presidential Commission on Established by EO 12358 of Apr. 14, 1982. Terminated Dec. 31, 1983, by EO 12415 of Apr. 5, 1983.

Dryden Research Center, Hugh L. Formerly separate field installation of National Aeronautics and Space Administration. Made component of Ames Research Center by NASA Management Instruction 1107.5A of Sept. 3, 1981.

Economic ⸝ dministration, Foreign Established in *Office for Emergency Management* by EO 9380 of Sept. 25, 1943. Functions of *Office of Lend-Lease Administration, Office of Foreign Relief and Rehabilitation Operations, Office of Economic Warfare* (together with *U.S. Commercial Company, Rubber Development Corporation, Petroleum Reserves Corporation,* and *Export-Import Bank of Washington* and functions transferred thereto by EO 9361 of July 15, 1943), and foreign economic operations of *Office of Foreign Economic Coordination* transferred to *Administration.* Foreign procurement activities of *War Food Administration* and Commodity Credit Corporation transferred by EO 9385 of Oct. 6, 1943. Terminated by EO 9630 of Sept. 27, 1945, and functions redistributed to State, Commerce, and Agriculture Departments and *Reconstruction Finance Corporation.*

Economic Analysis, Office of *See* **Business Economics, Office of**

Economic Cooperation Administration Established by act of Apr. 3, 1948 (62 Stat. 138). Abolished by act of Oct. 10, 1951 (65 Stat. 373), and functions transferred to *Mutual Security Agency* pursuant to EO 10300 of Nov. 1, 1951.

Economic Coordination, Office of Foreign *See* **Board of Economic Operations**

Economic Defense Board Established by EO 8839 of July 30, 1941. Renamed *Board of Economic Warfare* by EO 8982 of Dec. 17, 1941. *Board* terminated by EO 9361 of July 15, 1943, and *Office of Economic Warfare* established in *Office for Emergency Management. Office of Economic Warfare* consolidated with *Foreign Economic Administration* by EO 9380 of Sept. 25, 1943.

Economic Development, Office of Regional Established by Commerce Secretary Jan. 6, 1966, pursuant to act of Aug. 26, 1965 (79 Stat. 552). Abolished by Department Order 5A, Dec. 22, 1966, and functions vested in Economic Development Administration.

Economic Development Service, Foreign Established by order of Agriculture Secretary Nov. 8, 1969. Abolished by order of Secretary Feb. 6, 1972, and functions transferred to Economic Research Service.

Economic Growth and Stability, Advisory Board on Established by Presidential letter to Congress of June 1, 1953. Superseded by *National Advisory Board on Economic Policy* by Presidential direction Mar. 12, 1961. *Cabinet Committee on Economic Growth* established by President Aug. 21, 1962, to succeed *Board.*

Economic Management Support Center Established by Agriculture Secretary's Memorandum 1836 of Jan. 9, 1974. Consolidated with other Department units into *Economics, Statistics, and Cooperatives Service* by Secretary's Memorandum 1927, effective Dec. 23, 1977.

Economic Operations, Board of Established by State departmental order of Oct. 7, 1941. Abolished by departmental order of June 24, 1943, and functions transferred to *Office of Foreign Economic Coordination* established by same order. *Office* abolished by departmental order of Nov. 6, 1943, pursuant to EO 9380 of Sept. 25, 1943.

Economic Opportunity, Office of Established in Executive Office of the President by act of Aug. 20, 1964 (78 Stat. 508). All OEO programs except three transferred by administrative action to *Health, Education, and Welfare,* Labor, and Housing and Urban Development Departments July 6, 1973. Community Action, Economic Development, and Legal Services Programs transferred to *Community Services Administration* by act of Jan. 4, 1975 (88 Stat. 2310).

Economic Policy, Council on Established by Presidential memorandum of Feb. 2, 1973. Functions absorbed by *Economic Policy Board* Sept. 30, 1974.

Economic Policy, Council on Foreign Established Dec. 22, 1954, by Presidential letter of Dec. 11, 1954. Abolished by President Mar. 12, 1961, and functions transferred to Secretary of State.

Economic Policy, Council on International Established in Executive Office of the President by Presidential memorandum of January 1971. Reestablished by act of Aug. 29, 1972 (86 Stat. 646). Terminated Sept. 30, 1977, on expiration of statutory authority.

Economic Policy, National Advisory Board on See **Economic Growth and Stability, Advisory Board on**

Economic Policy Board, President's Established by EO 11808 of Sept. 30, 1974. Terminated by EO 11975 of Mar. 7, 1977.

Economic Research Service Established by Agriculture Secretary's Memorandum 1446, supp. 1, of Apr. 3, 1961. Consolidated with other Agriculture Department units into *Economics, Statistics, and Cooperatives Service* by Secretary's Memorandum 1927, effective Dec. 23, 1977. Redesignated as Economic Research Service by Secretarial order of Oct. 1, 1981.

Economic Security, Advisory Council on Established by EO 6757 of June 29, 1934. Terminated on approval of act of Aug. 14, 1935 (49 Stat. 620) Aug. 14, 1935.

Economic Security, Committee on Established by EO 6757 of June 29, 1934. Terminated as formal agency in April 1936, as provided in act, but continued informally for some time thereafter.

Economic Stabilization, Office of Established in *Office for Emergency Management* by EO 9250 of Oct. 3, 1942. Terminated by EO 9620 of Sept. 20,

1945, and functions transferred to *Office of War Mobilization and Reconversion.* Reestablished in *Office for Emergency Management* by EO 9699 of Feb. 21, 1946. Transferred by EO 9762 of July 25, 1946, to *Office of War Mobilization and Reconversion.* Consolidated with other agencies to form *Office of Temporary Controls* by EO 9809 of Dec. 12, 1946.

Economic Stabilization Agency Established by EO 10161 of Sept. 9, 1950, and EO 10276 of July 31, 1951. Terminated, except for liquidation purposes, by EO 10434 of Feb. 6, 1953. Liquidation completed Oct. 31, 1953, pursuant to EO 10480 of Aug. 14, 1953.

Economic Stabilization Board Established by EO 9250 of Oct. 3, 1942. Transferred to *Office of War Mobilization and Reconversion* by EO 9620 of Sept. 20, 1945. Returned to *Office of Economic Stabilization* on reestablishment by EO 9699 of Feb. 21, 1946. *Board* returned to *Office of War Mobilization and Reconversion* by EO 9762 of July 25, 1946. Functions terminated by EO 9809 of Dec. 12, 1946.

Economic Warfare, Board of See **Economic Defense Board**

Economic Warfare, Office of See **Economic Defense Board**

Economics, Bureau of Industrial Established by Commerce Secretary Jan. 2, 1980, in conjunction with Reorg. Plan No. 3 of 1979, effective Oct. 1, 1980, and operated under Department Organization Order 35–5B. Abolished at bureau level by Secretarial order, effective Jan. 22, 1984 (49 FR 4538). Industry-related functions realigned and transferred from Under Secretary for Economic Affairs to Under Secretary for International Trade. Under Secretary for Economic Affairs retained units to support domestic macroeconomic policy functions.

Economics, Statistics, and Cooperatives Service Renamed *Economics and Statistics Service* by Agriculture Secretary's Memorandum 2025 of Sept. 17, 1980. Redesignated as Economic Research Service and *Statistical Reporting Service* by Secretarial order of Oct. 1, 1981.

Economy Board, Joint Placed under direction of President by military order of July 5, 1939. Abolished Sept. 1, 1947, by joint letter of Aug. 20, 1947, from Secretaries of *War* and Navy to President.

Education, Federal Board for Vocational Established by act of Feb. 23, 1917 (39 Stat. 929). Functions transferred to Interior Department by EO 6166 of June 10, 1933. Functions assigned to *Commissioner of Education* Oct. 10, 1933. *Office of Education* transferred from Interior Department to *Federal Security Agency* by Reorg. Plan No. I of 1939, effective July 1, 1939. *Board* abolished by Reorg. Plan No. 2 of 1946, effective July 16, 1946.

Education, National Institute of Established by act of June 23, 1972 (86 Stat. 327). Transferred to Office of Educational Research and Improvement,

Education Department, by act of Oct. 17, 1979 (93 Stat. 678), effective May 4, 1980.

Education, Office of Established as independent agency by act of Mar. 2, 1867 (14 Stat. 434). Transferred to Interior Department by act of July 20, 1868 (15 Stat. 106). Transferred to *Federal Security Agency* by Reorg. Plan No. I of 1939, effective July 1, 1939. Functions of *Federal Security Administrator* administered by *Office of Education* relating to student loans and defense-related education transferred to *War Manpower Commission* by EO 9247 of Sept. 17, 1942.

Education, Office of Bilingual Abolished by act of Oct. 17, 1979 (93 Stat. 675), and functions transferred to Office of Bilingual Education and Minority Languages Affairs, Education Department.

Education Beyond the High School, President's Committee on Established by act of July 26, 1956 (70 Stat. 676). Terminated Dec. 31, 1957. Certain activities continued by *Bureau of Higher Education, Office of Education.*

Education Division Established in *Health, Education, and Welfare Department* by act of June 23, 1972 (86 Stat. 327). Functions transferred to Education Department by act of Oct. 17, 1979 (93 Stat. 677).

Education Statistics, National Center for Established in the Office of the Assistant Secretary, Health and Human Services Department, by act of Aug. 21, 1974 (88 Stat. 556). Transferred to the Office of Educational Research and Improvement, Education Department, by act of Oct. 17, 1979 (93 Stat. 678), effective May 4, 1980. Renamed *Center for Education Statistics* by act of Oct. 17, 1986 (100 Stat. 1579). Renamed National Center for Education Statistics by act of Apr. 28, 1988 (102 Stat. 331).

Educational and Cultural Affairs, Bureau of Established by Secretary of State in 1960. Terminated by Reorg. Plan No. 2 of 1977, effective July 1, 1978, and functions transferred to *International Communication Agency*, effective Apr. 1, 1978.

Educational and Cultural Affairs, Interagency Council on International Established Jan. 20, 1964, by Foreign Affairs Manual Circular, under authority of act of Sept. 21, 1961 (75 Stat. 527). Terminated Oct. 1973 following creation of Subcommittee on International Exchanges by National Security Council directive.

Educational Exchange, U.S. Advisory Commission on Established by act of Jan. 27, 1948 (62 Stat. 10). Abolished by act of Sept. 21, 1961 (75 Stat. 538), and superseded by U.S. Advisory Commission on International Educational and Cultural Affairs.

Efficiency, Bureau of Organized under act of Feb. 28, 1916 (39 Stat. 15). Abolished by act of Mar. 3, 1933 (47 Stat. 1519), and records transferred to *Bureau of the Budget.*

Elderly, Committee on Mental Health and Illness of the Established by act of July 29, 1975 (89 Stat. 347). Terminated Sept. 30, 1977.

Electoral votes for President and Vice President, transfer of functions *See* State Department

Electric Home and Farm Authority Incorporated Aug. 1, 1935, under laws of District of Columbia. Designated as U.S. agency by EO 7139 of Aug. 12, 1935. Continued by act of June 10, 1941 (55 Stat. 248). Grouped with other agencies in *Federal Loan Agency* by Reorg. Plan. No. I of 1939, effective July 1, 1939. Functions transferred to Commerce Department by EO 9071 of Feb. 24, 1942. Terminated by EO 9256 of Oct. 13, 1942.

Electric Home and Farm Authority, Inc. Organized Jan. 17, 1934, under laws of State of Delaware by EO 6514 of Dec. 19, 1933. Dissolved Aug. 1, 1935, and succeeded by *Electric Home and Farm Authority.*

Emergency Administration of Public Works, Federal Established by act of June 16, 1933 (48 Stat. 200). Operation continued by subsequent legislation, including act of June 21, 1938 (52 Stat. 816). Consolidated with *Federal Works Agency* as *Public Works Administration* by Reorg. Plan No. I of 1939, effective July 1, 1939. Functions transferred to *Office of Federal Works Administrator* by EO 9357 of June 30, 1943.

Emergency Conservation Work Established by EO 6101 of Apr. 5, 1933. Succeeded by *Civilian Conservation Corps.*

Emergency Council, National Established by EO 6433–A of Nov. 17, 1933. Consolidated with *Executive Council* by EO 6889–A of Oct. 29, 1934. Abolished by Reorg. Plan No. II of 1939, effective July 1, 1939, and functions (except those relating to *Radio Division* and *Film Service*) transferred to Executive Office of the President.

Emergency Council, Office of Economic Adviser to National Established by EO 6240 of Aug. 3, 1933, in connection with *Executive Council*, which later consolidated with *National Emergency Council*. Records and property used in preparation of statistical and economic summaries transferred to *Central Statistical Board* by EO 7003 of Apr. 8, 1935.

Emergency Management, Liaison Officer for Resignation of Liaison Officer for Emergency Management accepted by Presidential letter of Nov. 3, 1943, and no successor appointed. Liaison facilities terminated pursuant to optional provisions of administrative order of Jan. 7, 1941.

Emergency Management, Office for Established in Executive Office of the President by administrative order of May 25, 1940, in accordance with EO 8248 of Sept. 8, 1939. Inactive.

Emergency Mobilization Preparedness Board Established Dec. 17, 1981, by the President. Abolished by Presidential directive of Sept. 16, 1985.

Emergency Planning, Office of Established as successor to *Office of Civil and Defense Mobilization* by act of Sept. 22, 1961 (75 Stat. 630). Renamed *Office of Emergency Preparedness* by act of Oct. 21, 1968 (82 Stat. 1194). Terminated by

Reorg. Plan No. 2 of 1973, effective July 1, 1973, and functions transferred to the Treasury and Housing and Urban Development Departments and General Services Administration.

Emergency Preparedness, Office of   *See* **Emergency Planning, Office of**

Emergency Procurement Service   Established Sept. 1, 1950, by Administrator of General Services. Renamed *Defense Materials Service* Sept. 7, 1956. Functions transferred to *Property Management and Disposal Service* July 29, 1966. *Service* abolished July 1, 1973, and functions transferred to Federal Supply Service, Public Buildings Service, and Federal Property Resources Service.

Emergency Relief Administration, Federal   Established by act of May 12, 1933 (48 Stat. 55). Expired June 30, 1938, having been liquidated by *Works Progress Administrator* pursuant to act of May 28, 1937 (50 Stat. 352).

Employee-Management Relations Program, President's Committee on the Implementation of the Federal   Established by EO 10988 of Jan. 17, 1962. Terminated upon submission of report to President June 21, 1963.

Employees' Compensation, Bureau of   Transferred from *Federal Security Agency* to Labor Department by Reorg. Plan No. 19 of 1950, effective May 24, 1950. Functions absorbed by Employment Standards Administration Mar. 13, 1972.

Employees' Compensation Appeals Board   Transferred from *Federal Security Agency* to Labor Department by Reorg. Plan No. 19 of 1950, effective May 24, 1950.

Employees' Compensation Commission, U.S.   Established by act of Sept. 7, 1916 (39 Stat. 742). Abolished by Reorg. Plan No. 2 of 1946, effective July 16, 1946, and functions transferred to *Federal Security Administrator*.

Employment Board, Fair   Established by *U.S. Civil Service Commission* pursuant to EO 9980 of July 26, 1948. Abolished by EO 10590 of Jan. 18, 1955.

Employment of the Physically Handicapped, President's Committee on   Established by EO 10640 of Oct. 10, 1955, continuing *Committee* established by act of July 11, 1949 (63 Stat. 409). Superseded by President's Committee on Employment of the Handicapped established by EO 10994 of Feb. 14, 1962.

Employment Policy, President's Committee on Government   Established by EO 10590 of Jan. 18, 1955. Abolished by EO 10925 of Mar. 6, 1961, and functions transferred to *President's Committee on Equal Employment Opportunity*.

Employment Practice, Committee on Fair   Established in *Office of Production Management* by EO 8802 of June 25, 1941. Transferred to *War Manpower Commission* by Presidential letter effective July 30, 1942. Committee terminated on establishment of *Committee on Fair Employment Practice, Office for Emergency Management*, by EO

9346 of May 27, 1943. Terminated June 30, 1946, by act of July 17, 1945 (59 Stat. 743).

Employment Security, Bureau of   Transferred from *Federal Security Agency* to Labor Department by Reorg. Plan No. 2 of 1949, effective Aug. 20, 1949. Abolished by Labor Secretary's order of Mar. 14, 1969, and functions transferred to *Manpower Administration*.

Employment Service, U.S.   Established in Labor Department in 1918 by departmental order. Abolished by act of June 6, 1933 (48 Stat. 113), and created as bureau with same name. Functions consolidated with unemployment compensation functions of *Social Security Board, Bureau of Employment Security*, and transferred to *Federal Security Agency* by Reorg. Plan No. I of 1939, effective July 1, 1939. *Service* transferred to *Bureau of Placement, War Manpower Commission*, by EO 9247 of Sept. 17, 1942. Returned to Labor Department by EO 9617 of Sept. 19, 1945. Transferred to *Federal Security Agency* by act of June 16, 1948 (62 Stat. 443), to function as part of *Bureau of Employment Security*, Social Security Administration. *Bureau*, including *U.S. Employment Service*, transferred to Labor Department by Reorg. Plan No. 2 of 1949, effective Aug. 20, 1949. Abolished by reorganization of *Manpower Administration*, effective Mar. 17, 1969, and functions assigned to *U.S. Training and Employment Service*.

Employment Stabilization Board, Federal   Established by act of Feb. 10, 1931 (46 Stat. 1085). Abolished by EO 6166 of June 10, 1933. Abolition deferred by EO 6623 of Mar. 1, 1934, until functions of *Board* transferred to *Federal Employment Stabilization Office*, established in Commerce Department by same order. *Office* abolished by Reorg. Plan No. I of 1939, effective July 1, 1939, and functions transferred from Commerce Department to *National Resources Planning Board*, Executive Office of the President.

Employment Stabilization Office, Federal.   *See* **Employment Stabilization Board, Federal**

Employment and Training, Office of Comprehensive   Established in Labor Department. Terminated due to expiration of authority for appropriations after fiscal year 1982. Replaced by *Office of Employment and Training Programs*.

Employment and Training Programs, Office of   Renamed Office of Job Training Programs by Employment and Training Administration reorganization in Labor Department, effective June 1984.

Endangered Species Scientific Authority   Established by EO 11911 of Apr. 13, 1976. Terminated by act of Dec. 28, 1979 (93 Stat. 1228), and functions transferred to Interior Secretary.

Energy Administration, Federal   Established by act of May 7, 1974 (88 Stat. 96). Assigned additional responsibilities by acts of June 22, 1974 (88 Stat. 246), Dec. 22, 1975 (89 Stat. 871), and Aug. 14, 1976 (90 Stat. 1125). Terminated by act of Aug. 4,

1977 (91 Stat. 577), and functions transferred to Energy Department.

Energy Conservation, Office of Established by Interior Secretarial Order 2953 May 7, 1973. Functions transferred to *Federal Energy Administration* by act of May 7, 1974 (88 Stat. 100).

Energy Data and Analysis, Office of Established by Interior Secretarial Order 2953 of May 7, 1973. Functions transferred to *Federal Energy Administration* by act of May 7, 1974 (88 Stat. 100).

Energy Policy Office Established in Executive Office of the President by EO 11726 of June 29, 1973. Abolished by EO 11775 of Mar. 26, 1974.

Energy Programs, Office of Established by Commerce Department Organization Order 25–7A, effective Sept. 24, 1975. Terminated by act of Aug. 4, 1977 (91 Stat. 581), and functions transferred to Energy Department.

Energy Research and Development Administration Established by act of Oct. 11, 1974 (88 Stat. 1234). Assigned responsibilities by acts of Sept. 3, 1974 (88 Stat. 1069, 1079), Oct. 26, 1974 (88 Stat. 1431), and Dec. 31, 1974 (88 Stat. 1887). Terminated by act of Aug. 4, 1977 (91 Stat. 577), and functions transferred to Energy Department.

Energy Resources Council Established in Executive Office of the President by act of Oct. 11, 1974 (88 Stat. 1233). Establishing authority repealed by act of Aug. 4, 1977 (91 Stat. 608), and *Council* terminated.

Energy Supplies and Resources Policy, Presidential Advisory Committee on Established July 30, 1954, by President. Abolished Mar. 12, 1961, by President and functions transferred to Interior Secretary.

Enforcement Commission, National Established by General Order 18 of *Economic Stabilization Administrator,* effective July 30, 1952. Functions transferred to Director, *Office of Defense Mobilization,* and Attorney General by EO 10494 of Oct. 14, 1953.

Engineering, Bureau of *See* **Steam Engineering, Bureau of**

Entomology, Bureau of *See* **Entomology and Plant Quarantine, Bureau of**

Entomology and Plant Quarantine, Bureau of *Bureau of Entomology* and *Bureau of Plant Quarantine* created by acts of Apr. 23, 1904 (33 Stat. 276), and July 7, 1932 (47 Stat. 640), respectively. Consolidated with disease control and eradication functions of *Bureau of Plant Industry* into *Bureau of Entomology and Plant Quarantine* by act of Mar. 23, 1934 (48 Stat. 467). Functions transferred to Agricultural Research Service by Secretary's Memorandum 1320, supp. 4, of Nov. 2, 1953.

Environment, Cabinet Committee on the *See* **Environmental Quality Council**

Environmental Financing Authority Established by act of Oct. 18, 1972 (86 Stat. 899). Expired June 30, 1975, pursuant to terms of act.

Environmental Quality Council Established by EO 11472 of May 29, 1969. Renamed *Cabinet Committee on the Environment* by EO 11514 of Mar. 5, 1970. EO 11514 terminated by EO 11541 of July 1, 1970.

Environmental Science Services Administration Established in Commerce Department by Reorg. Plan No. 2 of 1965, effective July 13, 1965, by consolidating *Weather Bureau* and *Coast and Geodetic Survey.* Abolished by Reorg. Plan No. 4 of 1970, effective Oct. 3, 1970, and functions transferred to National Oceanic and Atmospheric Administration.

Equal Employment Opportunity, President's Committee on Established by EO 10925 of Mar. 6, 1961. Abolished by EO 11246 of Sept. 24, 1965, and functions transferred to Labor Department and *U.S. Civil Service Commission.*

Equal Opportunity, President's Council on Established by EO 11197 of Feb. 5, 1965. Abolished by EO 11247 of Sept. 24, 1965, and functions transferred to Justice Department.

Equipment, Bureau of Established as *Bureau of Equipment and Recruiting* by act of July 5, 1862 (12 Stat. 510), replacing *Bureau of Construction, Equipment and Repairs.* Designated as *Bureau of Equipment* in annual appropriation acts commencing with fiscal year 1892 (26 Stat. 192) after cognizance over enlisted personnel matters transferred, effective July 1, 1889, to *Bureau of Navigation.* Functions distributed among bureaus and offices in Navy Department by act of June 24, 1910 (61 Stat. 613). Abolished by act of June 30, 1914 (38 Stat. 408).

Ethics, Office of Government Established in the Office of Personnel Management by act of Oct. 26, 1978 (92 Stat. 1862). Changed to independent executive agency status by act of Nov. 3, 1988 (102 Stat. 3031).

European Migration, Intergovernmental Committee for Renamed Intergovernmental Committee for Migration by Resolution 624, passed by Intergovernmental Committee for European Migration Council, effective Nov. 11, 1980.

Evacuation, Joint Committee on *See* **Health and Welfare Aspects of Evacuation of Civilians, Joint Committee on**

Exchange Service, International Established in 1849 in Smithsonian Institution. Renamed Office of Publications Exchange by Secretary's internal directive of Jan. 11, 1985.

Executive Branch of the Government, Commission on Organization of the Established by act of July 7, 1947 (61 Stat. 246). Terminated June 12, 1949, pursuant to terms of act. Second *Commission on Organization of the Executive Branch of the Government* established by act of July 10, 1953 (67 Stat. 142). Terminated June 30, 1955, pursuant to terms of act.

Executive Council Established by EO 6202–A of July 11, 1933. Consolidated with *National Emergency Council* by EO 6889–A of Oct. 29, 1934.

Executive Exchange, President's Commission on
See **Personnel Interchange, President's Commission on**

Executive orders See **State Department**

Executive Organization, President's Advisory Council on Established by President Apr. 5, 1969. Terminated May 7, 1971.

Executives, Active Corps of Established in ACTION by act of Oct. 1, 1973 (87 Stat. 404). Transferred to Small Business Administration by EO 11871 of July 18, 1975.

Exhibits, Supervisor of Established by Interior Department. Abolished in 1941 due to lack of funding.

Export Control, Administrator of Functions delegated to Administrator by Proc. 2413 of July 2, 1940, transferred to *Office of Export Control, Economic Defense Board,* by EO 8900 of Sept. 15, 1941. Renamed *Board of Economic Warfare* by EO 8982 of Dec. 17, 1941. *Board* terminated by EO 9361 of July 15, 1943.

Export Control, Office of See **Export Control, Administrator of**

Export-Import Bank of Washington Organization of District of Columbia banking corporation directed by EO 6581 of Feb. 2, 1934. Certificate of incorporation filed Feb. 12, 1934. Grouped with other agencies to form *Federal Loan Agency* by Reorg. Plan No. I of 1939, effective July 1, 1939. Transferred to Commerce Department by EO 9071 of Feb. 24, 1942. Functions transferred to *Office of Economic Warfare* by EO 9361 of July 15, 1943. Established as permanent independent agency by act of July 31, 1945 (59 Stat. 526). Renamed Export-Import Bank of the U.S. by act of Mar. 13, 1968 (82 Stat. 47).

Export-Import Bank of Washington, DC, Second Authorized by EO 6638 of Mar. 9, 1934. Abolished by EO 7365 of May 7, 1936, and records transferred to *Export-Import Bank of Washington,* effective June 30, 1936.

Export Marketing Service Established by Agriculture Secretary Mar. 28, 1969. Merged with Foreign Agricultural Service by Secretary's memorandum of Dec. 7, 1973, effective Feb. 3, 1974.

Exports and Requirements, Division of Established in *Office of Foreign Economic Coordination* by State Departmental order of Feb. 1, 1943. Abolished by departmental order of Nov. 6, 1943, pursuant to EO 9380 of Sept. 25, 1943.

Extension Service Established by act of May 14, 1914 (38 Stat. 372). Consolidated into *Science and Education Administration* by Secretary's order of Jan. 24, 1978. Reestablished as *Extension Service* by Secretarial order of June 16, 1981. Became part of Cooperative State, Research, Education, and Extension Service under Department of Agriculture's reorganization in 1995.

Facts and Figures, Office of Established in *Office for Emergency Management* by EO 8922 of Oct. 24, 1941. Consolidated with *Office of War Information* in *Office for Emergency Management* by EO 9182 of June 13, 1942.

Family Security Committee Established in *Office of Defense Health and Welfare Services* Feb. 12, 1941, by administrative order. Terminated Dec. 17, 1942.

Family Services, Bureau of See **Assistance, Bureau of Public**

Family Support Administration Established on Apr. 4, 1986, in Health and Human Services Department under authority of section 6 of Reorganization Plan No. 1 of 1953, effective Apr. 11, 1953 (*see also* 51 FR 11641). Merged into Administration for Children and Families by Secretary's reorganization notice dated Apr. 15, 1991.

Farm Board, Federal Established by act of June 15, 1929 (46 Stat. 11). Renamed Farm Credit Administration and certain functions abolished by EO 6084 of Mar. 27, 1933. Administration placed under Agriculture Department by Reorg. Plan No. I of 1939, effective July 1, 1939. Made independent agency in the executive branch of the Government, to be housed in the Agriculture Department, by act of Aug. 6, 1953 (67 Stat. 390). Removed from Agriculture Department by act of Dec. 10, 1971 (85 Stat. 617).

Farm Credit Administration See **Farm Board, Federal**

Farm Loan Board, Federal Established in Treasury Department to administer act of July 17, 1916 (39 Stat. 360). Offices of appointed members of *Board,* except member designated as *Farm Loan Commissioner,* abolished by EO 6084 of Mar. 27, 1933, and *Board* functions transferred to *Farm Loan Commissioner,* subject to jurisdiction and control of Farm Credit Administration. Title changed to *Land Bank Commissioner* by act of June 16, 1933. Abolished by act of Aug. 6, 1953 (67 Stat. 393).

Farm Loan Bureau, Federal Established in Treasury Department under supervision of *Federal Farm Loan Board* and charged with execution of act of July 17, 1916 (39 Stat. 360). Transferred to *Farm Credit Administration* by EO 6084 of Mar. 27, 1933.

Farm Loan Commissioner See **Farm Loan Board, Federal**

Farm Mortgage Corporation, Federal Established by act of Jan. 31, 1934 (48 Stat. 344). Transferred to Agriculture Department by Reorg. Plan No. I of 1939, effective July 1, 1939, to operate under supervision of Farm Credit Administration. Abolished by act of Oct. 4, 1961 (75 Stat. 773).

Farm Products, Division of (Also known as *Division of Agriculture*) Established by *Advisory Commission to Council of National Defense* pursuant to act of Aug. 29, 1916 (39 Stat. 649). *Office of Agricultural Defense Relations* (later known as *Office for Agricultural War Relations*) established in Agriculture Department by Presidential letter of May 5, 1941, which transferred to Agriculture Secretary functions previously assigned to *Division* *of Agriculture.* Functions concerned with food production transferred to *Food Production Administration* and functions concerned with food distribution transferred to *Food Distribution Administration* by EO 9280 of Dec. 5, 1942.

Farm Security Administration *See* **Resettlement Administration**

Farm Service Agency Established by Secretary's Memorandum 1010–1 dated Oct. 20, 1994, under authority of the act of Oct. 13, 1994 (7 U.S.C. 6901), and assumed certain functions of the *Agricultural Stabilization and Conservation Service,* the *Farmers' Home Administration,* and the *Federal Crop Insurance Corporation.* Renamed *Consolidated Farm Service Agency* by Acting Administrator on Dec. 19, 1994.

Farmer Cooperative Service Established by Agriculture Secretary's Memorandum 1320, supp. 4, of Dec. 4, 1953. Consolidated with other Agriculture Department units into *Economics, Statistics, and Cooperatives Service* by Secretary's Memorandum 1927, effective Dec. 23, 1977.

Farmers' Home Administration. *See* **Resettlement Administration**

Federal. *See also other part of title*

Federal Advisory Council Established in *Federal Security Agency* by act of June 6, 1933 (48 Stat. 116). Transferred to Labor Department by Reorg. Plan No. 2 of 1949, effective Aug. 20, 1949.

Federal Crop Insurance Corporation Established by act of Feb. 16, 1938. Consolidated with the *Agricultural Stabilization and Conservation Service* and *Farmers' Home Administration* in 1995 to form the *Farm Service Agency* pursuant to act of Oct. 13, 1994 (108 Stat. 3178).

Federal Grain Inspection Service Established in the Agriculture Department by act of Oct. 21, 1976 (90 Stat. 2868). Abolished by Secretary's Memorandum 1010–1 dated Oct. 20, 1994, and program authority and functions transferred to the Grain Inspection, Packers and Stockyards Administration.

Federal Register, Administrative Committee of the *See* **Archives Establishment, National**

Federal Register, Division of the Established by act of July 26, 1935 (49 Stat. 500). Transferred to General Services Administration as part of *National Archives and Records Service* by act of June 30, 1949 (63 Stat. 381). Renamed Office of the Federal Register by order of General Services Administrator, Feb. 6, 1959. Transferred to National Archives and Records Administration by act of Oct. 19, 1984 (98 Stat. 2283).

Federal Register, Office of the *See* **Federal Register, Division of the**

Federal Reserve Board Renamed Board of Governors of the Federal Reserve System, and Governor and Vice Governor designated as Chairman and Vice Chairman, respectively, of Board by act of Aug. 23, 1935 (49 Stat. 704).

Field Services, Office of Established by Commerce Secretary Feb. 1, 1963, by Department Organization Order 40–3. Terminated by Department Organization Order 40–1A of Sept. 15, 1970, and functions transferred to *Bureau of Domestic Commerce.*

Filipino Rehabilitation Commission Established by act of June 29, 1944 (58 Stat. 626). Inactive pursuant to terms of act.

Film Service, U.S. Established by *National Emergency Council* in September 1938. Transferred to *Office of Education, Federal Security Agency,* by Reorg. Plan No. II of 1939, effective July 1, 1939. Terminated June 30, 1940.

Films, Coordinator of Government Director of *Office of Government Reports* designated *Coordinator of Government Films* by Presidential letter of Dec. 18, 1941. Functions transferred to *Office of War Information* by EO 9182 of June 13, 1942.

Financial Operations, Bureau of Government Renamed Financial Management Service by Treasury Secretary's Order 145–21, effective Oct. 10, 1984.

Fire Administration, U.S. *See* **Fire Prevention and Control Administration, National**

Fire Council, Federal Established by EO 7397 of June 20, 1936. Transferred July 1, 1939, to *Federal Works Agency* by EO 8194 of July 6, 1939, with functions under direction of *Federal Works Administrator.* Transferred with *Federal Works Agency* to General Services Administration by act of June 30, 1949 (63 Stat. 380). Transferred to Commerce Department by EO 11654 of Mar. 13, 1972.

Fire Prevention and Control, National Academy for Established in Commerce Department by act of Oct. 29, 1974 (88 Stat. 1537). Transferred to Federal Emergency Management Agency by Reorg. Plan No. 3 of 1978, effective Apr. 1, 1979.

Fire Prevention and Control Administration, National Renamed U.S. Fire Administration by act of Oct. 5, 1978 (92 Stat. 932). Transferred to Federal Emergency Management Agency by Reorg. Plan No. 3 of 1978, effective Apr. 1, 1979.

Fish Commission, U.S. *Commissioner of Fish and Fisheries* established as head of *U.S. Fish Commission* by joint resolution of Feb. 9, 1871 (16 Stat. 594). *Commission* established as *Bureau of Fisheries* in *Department of Commerce and Labor* by act of Feb. 14, 1903 (32 Stat. 827). Labor Department created by act of Mar. 4, 1913 (37 Stat. 736), and *Bureau* remained in Commerce Department. Transferred to Interior Department by Reorg. Plan No. II of 1939, effective July 1, 1939. Consolidated with *Bureau of Biological Survey* into *Fish and Wildlife Service* by Reorg. Plan No. III of 1940, effective June 30, 1940.

Fish and Wildlife Service Established by Reorg. Plan No. III of 1940, effective June 30, 1940, consolidating *Bureau of Fisheries* and *Bureau of Biological Survey.* Succeeded by U.S. Fish and Wildlife Service.

Fisheries, Bureau of *See* **Fish Commission, U.S.**

Fisheries, Bureau of Commercial Organized in 1959 under U.S. Fish and Wildlife Service, Interior Department. Abolished by Reorg. Plan No. 4 of 1970, effective Oct. 3, 1970, and functions transferred to National Oceanic and Atmospheric Administration.

Fishery Coordination, Office of Established in Interior Department by EO 9204 of July 21, 1942. Terminated by EO 9649 of Oct. 29, 1945.

Flood Indemnity Administration, Federal Established in *Housing and Home Finance Agency* by Administrator's Organizational Order 1, effective Sept. 28, 1956, redesignated as Administrator's Organizational Order 2 on Dec. 7, 1956, pursuant to act of Aug. 7, 1956 (70 Stat. 1078). Abolished by Administrator's Organizational Order 3, effective July 1, 1957, due to lack of funding.

Food, Cost of Living Council Committee on Established by EO 11695 of Jan. 11, 1973. Abolished by EO 11788 of June 18, 1974.

Food, Drug, and Insecticide Administration Established by act of Jan. 18, 1927 (44 Stat. 1002). Renamed Food and Drug Administration by act of May 27, 1930 (46 Stat. 422). Transferred from Agriculture Department to *Federal Security Agency* by Reorg. Plan No. IV of 1940, effective June 30, 1940. Transferred to *Health, Education, and Welfare Department* by Reorg. Plan No. 1 of 1953, effective Apr. 11, 1953.

Food Distribution Administration Established in Agriculture Department by EO 9280 of Dec. 5, 1942, consolidating *Agricultural Marketing Administration, Sugar Agency,* distribution functions of *Office for Agricultural War Relations,* regulatory work of *Bureau of Animal Industry,* and food units of *War Production Board.* Consolidated with other agencies by EO 9322 of Mar. 26, 1943, to form *Administration of Food Production and Distribution.*

Food and Drug Administration *See* **Food, Drug, and Insecticide Administration**

Food Industry Advisory Committee Established by EO 11627 of Oct. 15, 1971. Abolished by EO 11781 of May 1, 1974.

Food and Nutrition Service Established Aug. 8, 1969, by Secretary of Agriculture under authority of 5 U.S.C. 301 and Reorg. Plan No. 2 of 1953 (5 U.S.C. app.). Abolished by Secretary's Memorandum 1010–1 dated Oct. 20, 1994. Functions assumed by Food and Consumer Service.

Food Production Administration Established in Agriculture Department by EO 9280 of Dec. 5, 1942, which consolidated *Agricultural Adjustment Agency,* Farm Credit Administration, *Farm Security Administration,* Federal Crop Insurance Corporation, Soil Conservation Service, and food production activities of *War Production Board, Office of Agricultural War Relations,* and *Division of Farm Management and Costs, Bureau of Agricultural Economics.* Consolidated with other agencies by EO 9322 of Mar. 26, 1943, to form *Administration of Food Production and Distribution.*

Food Production and Distribution, Administration of Established by consolidation of *Food Production Administration, Food Distribution Administration,* Commodity Credit Corporation, and Extension Service, Agriculture Department, by EO 9322 of Mar. 26, 1943, under direction of Administrator, directly responsible to President. Renamed *War Food Administration* by EO 9334 of Apr. 19, 1943. Terminated by EO 9577 of June 29, 1945, and functions transferred to Agriculture Secretary. Transfer made permanent by Reorg. Plan No. 3 of 1946, effective July 16, 1946.

Food Safety and Quality Service Renamed Food Safety and Inspection Service by Agriculture Secretary's memorandum of June 19, 1981.

Foods, Bureau of Renamed Center for Food Safety and Applied Nutrition by Food and Drug Administration notice of Mar. 9, 1984 (49 FR 10166).

Foreign. *See also other part of title*

Foreign Aid, Advisory Committee on Voluntary Established by President May 14, 1946. Transferred from State Department to Director, *Mutual Security Agency,* and later to Director, *Foreign Operations Administration,* by Presidential letter of June 1, 1953.

Foreign Operations Administration Established by Reorg. Plan No. 7 of 1953, effective Aug. 1, 1953, and functions transferred from *Office of Director of Mutual Security, Mutual Security Agency, Technical Cooperation Administration, Institute of Inter-American Affairs.* Abolished by EO 10610 of May 9, 1955, and functions and offices transferred to State and Defense Departments.

Foreign Scholarships, Board of Renamed J. William Fulbright Foreign Scholarship Board by act of Feb. 16, 1990 (104 Stat. 49).

Forest Reservation Commission, National Established by act of Mar. 1, 1911 (36 Stat. 962). Terminated by act of Oct. 22, 1976 (90 Stat. 2961), and functions transferred to Agriculture Secretary.

Forests, Director of Established by Administrative Order 1283 of May 18, 1938. Made part of *Office of Land Utilization,* Interior Department, by Administrative Order 1466 of Apr. 15, 1940.

Freedmen's Hospital Established by act of Mar. 3, 1871 (16 Stat. 506; T. 32 of D.C. Code). Transferred from Interior Department to *Federal Security Agency* by Reorg. Plan No. IV of 1940, effective June 30, 1940.

Fuel Yards Established by act of July 1, 1918 (40 Stat. 672). Transferred from *Bureau of Mines,* Commerce Department, to *Procurement Division,* Treasury Department, by EO 6166 of June 10, 1933, effective Mar. 2, 1934.

Fuels Coordinator for War, Office of Solid *See* **Fuels Administration for War, Solid**

Fuels Corporation, U.S. Synthetic Established by act of June 30, 1980 (94 Stat. 636). Terminated Apr.

18, 1986, by act of Dec. 19, 1985 (99 Stat. 1249), and functions transferred to Treasury Secretary.

Fund-Raising Within the Federal Service, President's Committee on   Established by EO 10728 of Sept. 6, 1957. Abolished by EO 10927 of Mar. 18, 1961, and functions transferred to *U.S. Civil Service Commission*.

Gallaudet College   *See* **Columbia Institution for the Instruction of the Deaf and Dumb, and the Blind**

General Programs, Office of   Renamed Office of Public Programs by the Chairman, National Endowment for the Humanities, in January 1991.

Geographic Board, U.S.   Established by EO 27–A of Sept. 4, 1890. Abolished by EO 6680 of Apr. 17, 1935, and duties transferred to *U.S. Board on Geographical Names*, Interior Department, effective June 17, 1934. *Board* abolished by act of July 25, 1947 (61 Stat. 457), and duties assumed by *Board on Geographic Names*.

Geographical Names, U.S. Board on   *See* **Geographic Board, U.S.**

Geography, Office of   Function of standardizing foreign place names placed in Interior Department conjointly with *Board on Geographic Names* by act of July 25, 1947 (61 Stat. 456). Functions transferred to Defense Department by memorandum of understanding by Interior and Defense Departments and *Bureau of the Budget* Mar. 9, 1968.

Geological Survey   Established in the Interior Department by act of Mar. 3, 1879 (20 Stat. 394). Renamed United States Geological Survey by acts of Nov. 13, 1991 (105 Stat. 1000) and May 18, 1992 (106 Stat. 172).

Germany, Mixed Claims Commission, U.S. and   Established by agreement of Aug. 10, 1922, between U.S. and Germany. Duties extended by agreement of Dec. 31, 1928. Time limit for filing claims expired June 30, 1928. All claims disposed of by Oct. 30, 1939. Terminated June 30, 1941.

Goethals Memorial Commission   Established by act of Aug. 4, 1935 (49 Stat. 743). Placed under jurisdiction of *War Department* by EO 8191 of July 5, 1939.

Government.   *See other part of title*

Grain Futures Administration   Established in Agriculture Department under provisions of act of Sept. 21, 1922 (42 Stat. 998). Superseded by *Commodity Exchange Administration* by order of Secretary, effective July 1, 1936. Consolidated with other agencies into *Commodity Exchange Branch, Agricultural Marketing Administration*, by EO 9069 of Feb. 23, 1942. Functions transferred to Agriculture Secretary by EO 9577 of June 29, 1945. Transfer made permanent by Reorg. Plan No. 3 of 1946, effective July 16, 1946. Functions transferred to *Commodity Exchange Authority* by Secretary's Memorandum 1185 of Jan. 21, 1947. Functions transferred to Commodity Futures Trading Commission by act of Oct. 23, 1974 (88 Stat. 1414).

Grain Stabilization Corporation   Organized as Delaware corporation to operate in connection with *Federal Farm Board* pursuant to act of June 15, 1929 (46 Stat. 11). Terminated by filing of certificate of dissolution with Corporation Commission of State of Delaware Dec. 14, 1935.

Grants and Program Systems, Office of   Abolished and functions transferred to Cooperative State Research Service, Agriculture Department, by Secretarial Memorandum 1020–26 of July 1, 1986.

Grazing Service   Consolidated with *General Land Office* into Bureau of Land Management, Interior Department, by Reorg. Plan No. 3 of 1946, effective July 16, 1946.

Great Lakes Basin Commission   Established by EO 11345 of Apr. 20, 1967. Terminated by EO 12319 of Sept. 9, 1981.

Great Lakes Pilotage Administration   Established in Commerce Department to administer act of June 30, 1960 (74 Stat. 259). Administration of act transferred to Transportation Secretary by act of Oct. 15, 1966 (80 Stat. 931).

Handicapped, National Center on Education Media and Materials for the   Established by agreement between *Health, Education, and Welfare Secretary* and Ohio State University, pursuant to acts of Aug. 20, 1969 (83 Stat. 102) and Apr. 13, 1970 (84 Stat. 187). Authorization deleted by act of Nov. 29, 1975 (89 Stat. 795), and Secretary authorized to enter into agreements with non-Federal organizations to establish and operate centers for handicapped.

Handicapped, National Council on the   Established in *Health, Education, and Welfare Department* by act of Nov. 6, 1978 (92 Stat. 2977). Transferred to Education Department by act of Oct. 17, 1979 (93 Stat. 677). Reorganized as independent agency by act of Feb. 22, 1984 (98 Stat. 26).

Handicapped Employees, Interagency Committee on   Alternately renamed Interagency Committee on Employment of People with Disabilities by EO 12704 of Feb. 26, 1990.

Handicapped Individuals, White House Conference on   Established by act of Dec. 7, 1974 (88 Stat. 1617). Terminated Dec. 30, 1977, pursuant to terms of act.

Handicapped Research, National Institute of   Renamed National Institute on Disability and Rehabilitation Research by act of Oct. 21, 1986 (100 Stat. 1820).

Health, Cost of Living Council Committee on   Established by EO 11695 of Jan. 11, 1973. Abolished by EO 11788 of June 18, 1974.

Health, Education, and Welfare, Department of   Established by Reorganization Plan No. 1 of 1953 (5 U.S.C. app.), effective Apr. 11, 1953. Renamed Health and Human Services Department by act of Oct. 17, 1979 (93 Stat. 695).

Health, Welfare, and Related Defense Activities, Office of the Coordinator of   *Federal Security Administrator* designated as Coordinator of health, welfare, and related fields of activity affecting national defense, including aspects of education under *Federal Security Agency,* by *Council of National Defense,* with approval of President, Nov. 28, 1940. Office of Coordinator superseded by *Office of Defense Health and Welfare Services,* established in *Office for Emergency Services* by EO 8890 of Sept. 3, 1941.

Health Care Technology, National Council on Established by act of July 1, 1944, as amended (92 Stat. 3447). Renamed *Council on Health Care Technology* by act of Oct. 30, 1984 (98 Stat. 2820). Name lowercased by act of Oct. 7, 1985 (99 Stat. 493). Terminated by act of Dec. 19, 1989 (103 Stat. 2205).

Health Facilities, Financing, Compliance, and Conversion, Bureau of Renamed Bureau of Health Facilities by Health and Human Services Department Secretarial order of Mar. 12, 1980 (45 FR 17207).

Health Industry Advisory Committee Established by EO 11695 of Jan. 11, 1973. Abolished by EO 11781 of May 1, 1974.

Health Manpower, Bureau of Renamed Bureau of Health Professions by Health and Human Services Department Secretarial order of Mar. 12, 1980 (45 FR 17207).

Health and Medical Committee Established by *Council of National Defense* order of Sept. 19, 1940. Transferred to *Federal Security Agency* by *Council* order approved by President Nov. 28, 1940. Reestablished in *Office of Defense Health and Welfare Services, Office for Emergency Management,* by EO 8890 of Sept. 3, 1941. *Committee* transferred to *Federal Security Agency* by EO 9338 of Apr. 29, 1943.

Health Resources Administration Established in Public Health Service. Abolished by Health and Human Services Department Secretarial reorganization of Aug. 20, 1982 (47 FR 38409), and functions transferred to Health Resources and Services Administration.

Health Service, Public Originated by act of July 16, 1798 (1 Stat. 605). Transferred from Treasury Department to *Federal Security Agency* by Reorg. Plan No. I of 1939, effective July 1, 1939.

Health Services Administration Established in Public Health Service. Abolished by Health and Human Services Department Secretarial reorganization of Aug. 20, 1982 (47 FR 38409), and functions transferred to Health Resources and Services Administration.

Health Services Industry, Committee on the Established by EO 11627 of Oct. 15, 1971. Abolished by EO 11695 of Jan. 11, 1973.

Health Services and Mental Health Administration Established in Public Health Service Apr. 1, 1968. Abolished by *Health, Education, and Welfare Department* reorganization order and functions transferred to *Centers for Disease Control, Health Resources Administration,* and *Health Services Administration,* effective July 1, 1973.

Health Services Research, National Center for Established by act of July 23, 1974 (88 Stat. 363). Transferred from *Health Resources Administration* to Office of the Assistant Secretary for Health by *Health, Education, and Welfare Department* reorganization, effective Dec. 2, 1977. Renamed *National Center for Health Services Research and Health Care Technology Assessment* by Secretary's order, pursuant to act of Oct. 30, 1984 (98 Stat. 2817). Terminated by act of Dec. 19, 1989 (103 Stat. 2205).

Health Statistics, National Center for Established by act of July 23, 1974 (88 Stat. 363). Transferred from *Health Resources Administration* to Office of the Assistant Secretary for Health by *Health, Education, and Welfare Department* reorganization, effective Dec. 2, 1977. Transferred to *Centers for Disease Control* by Secretary's notice of Apr. 2, 1987 (52 FR 13318).

Health and Welfare Activities, Interdepartmental Committee to Coordinate Appointed by President Aug. 15, 1935, and reestablished by EO 7481 of Oct. 27, 1936. Terminated in 1939.

Health and Welfare Aspects of Evacuation of Civilians, Joint Committee on Established August 1941 as joint committee of *Office of Defense Health and Welfare Services* and *Office of Civilian Defense.* Reorganized in June 1942 and renamed *Joint Committee on Evacuation. Office of Defense Health and Welfare Services* abolished by EO 9388 of Apr. 29, 1943, and functions transferred to *Federal Security Agency. Committee* terminated.

Heart and Lung Institute, National Renamed National Heart, Lung, and Blood Institute by act of Apr. 22, 1976 (90 Stat. 402).

Heritage Conservation and Recreation Service Established by Interior Secretary Jan. 25, 1978. Abolished by Secretarial Order 3060 of Feb. 19, 1981, and functions transferred to National Park Service.

Highway Safety Agency, National Established in Commerce Department by act of Sept. 9, 1966 (80 Stat. 731). Functions transferred to Transportation Department by act of Oct. 15, 1966 (80 Stat. 931). Functions transferred to *National Highway Safety Bureau* by EO 11357 of June 6, 1967. *Bureau* renamed National Highway Traffic Safety Administration by act of Dec. 31, 1970 (84 Stat. 1739).

Highway Safety Bureau, National *See* **Highway Safety Agency, National**

Home Economics, Bureau of Human Nutrition and *See* **Home Economics, Office of**

Home Economics, Office of Renamed *Bureau of Home Economics* by Secretary's Memorandum 436, effective July 1, 1923, pursuant to act of Feb. 26, 1923 (42 Stat. 1289). Redesignated *Bureau of Human Nutrition and Home Economics* February 1943 in accordance with *Research Administration* Memorandum 5 issued pursuant to EO 9069 of Feb. 23, 1942, and in conformity with Secretary's Memorandums 960 and 986. Functions transferred to Agricultural Research Service by Secretary's Memorandum 1320, supp. 4, of Nov. 2, 1953.

Home Loan Bank Administration, Federal *See* **Home Loan Bank Board, Federal**

Home Loan Bank Board *See* **Home Loan Bank Board, Federal**

Home Loan Bank Board, Federal Established by acts of July 22, 1932 (47 Stat. 725), June 13, 1933 (48 Stat. 128), and June 27, 1934 (48 Stat. 1246). Grouped with other agencies to form *Federal Loan Agency* by Reorg. Plan No. I of 1939, effective July 1, 1939. Functions transferred to *Federal Home Loan Bank Administration, National Housing Agency,* by EO 9070 of Feb. 24, 1942. Abolished by Reorg. Plan No. 3, effective July 27, 1947, and functions transferred to *Home Loan Bank Board, Housing and Home Finance Agency.* Renamed *Federal Home Loan Bank Board* and made independent agency by act of Aug. 11, 1955 (69 Stat. 640). Abolished by act of Aug. 9, 1989 (103 Stat. 354, 415), and functions transferred to Office of Thrift Supervision, Resolution Trust Corporation, Federal Deposit Insurance Corporation, and Federal Housing Finance Board.

Home Loan Bank System, Federal Grouped with other agencies to form *Federal Loan Agency* by Reorg. Plan No. I of 1939, effective July 1, 1939. Functions transferred to *Federal Home Loan Bank Administration, National Housing Agency,* by EO 9070 of Feb. 24, 1942. Transferred to *Housing and Home Finance Agency* by Reorg. Plan No. 3 of 1947, effective July 27, 1947.

Home Mortgage Credit Extension Committee, National Voluntary Established by act of Aug. 2, 1954 (68 Stat 638). Terminated Oct. 1, 1965, pursuant to terms of act.

Home Owners' Loan Corporation Established by act of June 13, 1933 (48 Stat. 128), under supervision of *Federal Home Loan Bank Board.* Grouped with other agencies to form *Federal Loan Agency* by Reorg. Plan No. I of 1939, effective July 1, 1939. Transferred to *Federal Home Loan Bank Administration, National Housing Agency,* by EO 9070 of Feb. 24, 1942. Board of Directors abolished by Reorg. Plan No. 3 of 1947, effective July 27, 1947, and functions transferred, for liquidation of assets, to *Home Loan Bank Board, Housing and Home Finance Agency.* Terminated by order of *Home Loan Bank Board Secretary,* effective Feb. 3, 1954, pursuant to act of June 30, 1953 (67 Stat. 121).

Homesteads, Division of Subsistence Established by act of June 16, 1933 (48 Stat. 205). Interior Secretary authorized to administer section 208 of act by EO 6209 of July 21, 1933. *Federal Subsistence Homesteads Corporation* created by Secretary's order of Dec. 2, 1933, and organization incorporated under laws of Delaware. Transferred to *Resettlement Administration* by EO 7041 of May 15, 1935.

Homesteads Corporation, Federal Subsistence *See* **Homesteads, Division of Subsistence**

Hospitalization, Board of Federal Organized Nov. 1, 1921. Designated as advisory agency to *Bureau of the Budget* May 7, 1943. Terminated June 30, 1948, by Director's letter of May 28, 1948.

Housing, President's Committee on Equal Opportunity in Established by EO 11063 of Nov. 20, 1962. Inactive as of June 30, 1968.

Housing Administration, Federal Established by act of June 27, 1934 (48 Stat. 1246). Grouped with other agencies to form *Federal Loan Agency* by Reorg. Plan No. I of 1939, effective July 1, 1939. Functions transferred to *Federal Housing Administration, National Housing Agency,* by EO 9070 of Feb. 24, 1942. Transferred to *Housing and Home Finance Agency* by Reorg. Plan No. 3, effective July 27, 1947. Functions transferred to Housing and Urban Development Department by act of Sept. 9, 1965 (79 Stat. 667).

Housing Administration, Public Established as constituent agency of *Housing and Home Finance Agency* by Reorg. Plan No. 3 of 1947, effective July 27, 1947. Functions transferred to Housing and Urban Development Department by act of Sept. 9, 1965 (79 Stat. 667).

Housing Agency, National Established by EO 9070 of Feb. 24, 1942, to consolidate housing functions relating to *Federal Home Loan Bank Board, Federal Home Loan Bank System, Federal Savings and Loan Insurance Corporation, Home Owners' Loan Corporation, U.S. Housing Corporation, Federal Housing Administration, U.S. Housing Authority, Defense Homes Corporation, Division of Defense Housing Coordination, Central Housing Committee, Farm Security Administration* with respect to nonfarm housing, *Public Buildings Administration, Division of Defense Housing, Mutual Ownership Defense Housing Division, Office of Administrator of Federal Works Agency,* and *War* and *Navy* Departments with respect to housing located off military installations. Agency dissolved on creation of *Housing and Home Finance Agency* by Reorg. Plan No. 3 of 1947, effective July 27, 1947.

Housing Authority, Federal Public Established by EO 9070 of Feb. 24, 1942. Public housing functions of *Federal Works Agency, War* and *Navy* Departments (except housing located on military installations), and *Farm Security Administration* (nonfarm housing) transferred to *Authority,* and *Defense Homes Corporation* administered by *Authority's* Commissioner. Functions transferred to *Public Housing Administration, Housing and Home Finance Agency,* by Reorg. Plan No. 3 of 1947, effective July 27, 1947.

Housing Authority, U.S. Established in Interior Department by act of Sept. 1, 1937 (50 Stat. 888). Transferred to *Federal Works Agency* by Reorg. Plan No. I of 1939, effective July 1, 1939. Transferred to *Federal Public Housing Authority, National Housing Agency,* by EO 9070 of Feb. 24, 1942. Office of Administrator abolished by Reorg. Plan No. 3 of 1947, effective July 27, 1947, and functions transferred to *Public Housing Administration, Housing and Home Finance Agency.*

Housing Corporation, U.S. Incorporated July 10, 1918, under laws of New York. Transferred from Labor Department to Treasury Department by EO

7641 of June 22, 1937. Transferred from Treasury Department to *Public Buildings Administration, Federal Works Agency,* by EO 8186 of June 29, 1939. Functions transferred for liquidation to *Federal Home Loan Bank Administration, National Housing Agency,* by EO 9070 of Feb. 24, 1942. Terminated Sept. 8, 1952, by Secretary, *Home Loan Bank Board.*

Housing Council, National Established in *Housing and Home Finance Agency* by Reorg. Plan No. 3 of 1947, effective July 27, 1947. Terminated by Reorg. Plan No. 4 of 1965, effective July 27, 1965, and functions transferred to President.

Housing Division Established in *Public Works Administration* by act of June 16, 1933 (48 Stat. 195). Functions transferred to *U.S. Housing Authority* by EO 7732 of Oct. 27, 1937.

Housing Expediter, Office of the Established in *Office of War Mobilization and Reconversion* by Presidential letter of Dec. 12, 1945, to *Housing Expediter.* Functions of *Housing Expediter* defined by EO 9686 of Jan. 26, 1946. *Housing Expediter* confirmed in position of *National Housing Administrator* Feb. 6, 1946. *Office of the Housing Expediter* established by act of May 22, 1946 (60 Stat. 208). Functions of *Office* and *National Housing Administrator* segregated by EO 9820 of Jan. 11, 1947. Housing functions of *Civilian Production Administration* transferred to *Office* by EO 9836 of Mar. 22, 1947, effective Apr. 1, 1947. Rent control functions of *Office of Temporary Controls* transferred to *Office* by EO 9841 of Apr. 23, 1947. *Office* terminated by EO 10276 of July 31, 1951, and functions transferred to *Economic Stabilization Agency.*

Housing and Home Finance Agency Established by Reorg. Plan No. 3 of 1947, effective July 27, 1947. Terminated by act of Sept. 9, 1965 (79 Stat. 667), and functions transferred to Housing and Urban Development Department.

Howard University Established by act of Mar. 2, 1867 (14 Stat. 438). Functions of Interior Department transferred to *Federal Security Agency* by Reorg. Plan No. IV of 1940, effective June 30, 1940. Functions of *Health, Education, and Welfare Department* transferred to Education Department by act of Oct. 17, 1979 (93 Stat. 678).

Human Development, Office of Established in *Health, Education, and Welfare Department.* Renamed Office of Human Development Services and component units transferred to or reorganized under new administrations in Office by Secretary's reorganization order of July 26, 1977. Merged into the Administration for Children and Families by Health and Human Services Department Secretary's reorganization notice dated Apr. 15, 1991.

Human Development Services, Office of *See* **Human Development, Office of**

Hydrographic Office Jurisdiction transferred from *Bureau of Navigation* to Chief of Naval Operations by EO 9126 of Apr. 8, 1942, and by Reorg. Plan No. 3 of 1946, effective July 16, 1946. Renamed U.S. Naval Oceanographic Office by act of July 10, 1962 (76 Stat. 154).

Imagery Office, Central Established as a Defense Department agency on May 6, 1992. Functions transferred to National Imagery and Mapping Agency by P.L. 104–201, Sept. 23, 1996 (110 Stat. 2677).

Immigration, Bureau of Established as branch of Treasury Department by act of Mar. 3, 1891 (26 Stat. 1085). Transferred to *Department of Commerce and Labor* by act of Feb. 14, 1903 (34 Stat. 596). Made *Bureau of Immigration and Naturalization* by act of June 29, 1906 (37 Stat. 736). Made separate division after Labor Department created by act of Mar. 4, 1913 (37 Stat. 736). Consolidated into Immigration and Naturalization Service, Labor Department, by EO 6166 of June 10, 1933. Transferred to Justice Department by Reorg. Plan No. V of 1940, effective June 14, 1940.

Immigration, Commissioners of Offices of commissioners of immigration of the several ports created by act of Aug. 18, 1894 (28 Stat. 391). Abolished by Reorg. Plan No. III of 1940, effective June 30, 1940, and functions transferred to *Bureau of Immigration and Naturalization,* Labor Department.

Immigration and Naturalization, Bureau of *See* **Immigration, Bureau of**

Immigration and Naturalization, District Commissioner of Created by act of Aug. 18, 1894 (28 Stat. 391). Abolished by Reorg. Plan No. III of 1940, effective June 30, 1940. Functions administered by Immigration and Naturalization Commissioner, Justice Department, through district immigration and naturalization directors.

Immigration and Naturalization Service *See* **Immigration, Bureau of**

Import Programs, Office of Established by Commerce Secretary Feb. 14, 1971. Functions transferred to *Domestic and International Business Administration,* effective Nov. 17, 1972.

Indian Claims Commission Established by act of Aug. 13, 1946 (60 Stat. 1049). Terminated by act of Oct. 8, 1976 (90 Stat. 1990), and pending cases transferred to *U.S. Court of Claims* Sept. 30, 1978.

Indian Commissioners, Board of Established by section 2039, Revised Statutes. Abolished by EO 6145 of May 25, 1933.

Indian Medical Facilities Functions transferred from Interior Department to *Health, Education, and Welfare Department,* to be administered by Surgeon General of Public Health Service, by act of Aug. 5, 1954 (68 Stat. 674).

Indian Opportunity, National Council on Established by EO 11399 of Mar. 6, 1968. Terminated Nov. 26, 1974, by act of Nov. 26, 1969 (83 Stat. 220).

Indian Policy Review Commission, American Established by act of Jan. 2, 1975 (88 Stat. 1910). Terminated June 30, 1977, pursuant to terms of act.

Industrial Analysis, Committee of   Established by EO 7323 of Mar. 21, 1936. Terminated Feb. 17, 1937.

Industrial Cooperation, Coordinator for   Established by EO 7193 of Sept. 26, 1935. Continued by EO 7324 of Mar. 30, 1936. Terminated June 30, 1937.

Industrial Emergency Committee   Established by EO 6770 of June 30, 1934. Consolidated with *National Emergency Council* by EO 6889–A of Oct. 29, 1934.

Industrial Pollution Control Council Staff, National   Established by Commerce Department Organization Order 35–3 of June 17, 1970. *Staff* abolished by departmental organization order of Sept. 10, 1973. Council inactive.

Industrial Recovery Board, National   Established by EO 6859 of Sept. 27, 1934. Terminated by EO 7075 of June 15, 1935.

Industrial Recovery Board, Special   Established by EO 6173 of June 16, 1933. Functions absorbed by *National Emergency Council* under terms of EO 6513 of Dec. 18, 1933.

Industrial Relations, Office of   Activated in Navy Department Sept. 14, 1945. Superseded June 22, 1966, by creation of *Office of Civilian Manpower Management.*

Industry and Trade Administration   *See* **Business and Defense Services Administration**

Information, Committee for Reciprocity   Established by EO 6750 of June 27, 1934; reestablished by EO 10004 of Oct. 5, 1948, which revoked EO 6750. Superseded by EO 10082 of Oct. 5, 1949; abolished by EO 11075 of Jan. 15, 1963, which revoked EO 10082.

Information, Coordinator of   Established by Presidential order of July 11, 1941. Functions exclusive of foreign information activities transferred by military order of June 13, 1942, to jurisdiction of Joint Chiefs of Staff, *War Department,* as *Office of Strategic Services.* Foreign information functions transferred to *Office of War Information* by EO 9182 of June 13, 1942.

Information, Division of   Established pursuant to Presidential letter of Feb. 28, 1941, to *Liaison Officer, Office of Emergency Management.* Abolished by EO 9182 of June 13, 1942. Functions relating to public information on war effort transferred and consolidated with *Office of War Information,* and publication services relating to specific agencies of OEM transferred to those agencies.

Information, Office of Coordinator of   Transferred, exclusive of foreign information activities, to *Office of War Information* by EO 9182 of June 13, 1942. Designated *Office of Strategic Services* and transferred to jurisdiction of Joint Chiefs of Staff by military order of June 13, 1942. Terminated by EO 9621 of Sept. 20, 1945, and functions distributed to State and *War* Departments.

Information Administration, International   Transferred from State Department to U.S. Information Agency by Reorg. Plan No. 8 of 1953, effective Aug. 1, 1953.

Information Agency, U.S.   Established by Reorg. Plan No. 8 of 1953, effective Aug. 1, 1953. Abolished by Reorg. Plan No. 2 of 1977, effective Apr. 1, 1978; replaced by and functions transferred to *International Communication Agency.* Redesignated U.S. Information Agency by act of Aug. 24, 1982 (96 Stat. 291).

Information and Public Affairs, Office of   Merged with *Office of Intergovernmental Affairs* to form Office of Public and Intergovernmental Affairs by Labor Secretary's Order 1–85 of June 5, 1985.

Information Resources Management, Office of   *See* **Telecommunications Service, Automated Data**

Information Resources Management Service   Established in the General Services Administration. Renamed Information Technology Service in 1995.

Information Security Committee, Interagency   Established by EO 12065 of June 28, 1978. Abolished by EO 12356 of Apr. 2, 1982.

Information Security Oversight Office   Established in General Services Administration by EO 12065 of June 28, 1978. EO 12065 revoked by EO 12356 of Apr. 2, 1982, which provided for continuation of Office.

Information Service, Government   *See* **Information Service, U.S.**

Information Service, Interim International   Established in State Department by EO 9608 of Aug. 31, 1945. Abolished Dec. 31, 1945, pursuant to terms of order.

Information Service, U.S.   Established in March 1934 as division of *National Emergency Council.* Transferred to *Office of Government Reports* by Reorg. Plan No. II of 1939, effective July 1, 1939. Consolidated, along with other functions of *Office,* into *Division of Public Inquiries, Bureau of Special Services, Office of War Information,* by EO 9182 of June 13, 1942. *Bureau of Special Services* renamed *Government Information Service* and transferred to *Bureau of the Budget* by EO 9608 of Aug. 31, 1945. *Service* transferred to *Office of Government Reports* by EO 9809 of Dec. 12, 1946.

Information Technology Service   Established in General Sevices Adminstration. Abolished by General Services Administrative Order No. 5440.492, Aug. 21, 1996, and functions transferred to Federal Telecommunications Service.

Insane, Government Hospital for the   Established by act of Mar. 3, 1855 (10 Stat. 682). Renamed Saint Elizabeths Hospital by act of July 1, 1916 (39 Stat. 309). Transferred from Interior Department to *Federal Security Agency* by Reorg. Plan No. IV of 1940, effective June 30, 1940. Transferred to *Health, Education, and Welfare Department* by Reorg. Plan No. 1 of 1953, effective Apr. 11, 1953. Functions redelegated to National Institute of Mental Health by Secretary's reorganization order of Aug. 9, 1967.

Property and administration transferred to District of Columbia Government by act of Nov. 8, 1984 (98 Stat. 3369).

Installations, Director of Established in Defense Department by act of July 14, 1952 (66 Stat. 625). Abolished by Reorg. Plan No. 6 of 1953, effective June 30, 1953, and functions transferred to Defense Secretary.

Insular Affairs, Bureau of Transferred from *War Department* to *Division of Territories and Island Possessions*, Interior Department, by Reorg. Plan No. II of 1939, effective July 1, 1939.

Insurance Administrator, Federal Established by act of Aug. 1, 1968 (82 Stat. 567). Functions transferred to Federal Emergency Management Agency by Reorg. Plan No. 3 of 1978, effective Apr. 1, 1979.

Integrity and Efficiency, President's Council on Established by EO 12301 of Mar. 26, 1981 (46 FR 19211). Abolished and reestablished by EO 12625 of Jan 27, 1988 (53 FR 2812). Abolished and reestablished by EO 12805 of May 11, 1992 (57 FR 20627).

Intelligence Activities, President's Board of Consultants on Foreign Established by EO 10656 of Feb. 6, 1956. EO 10656 revoked by EO 10938 of May 4, 1961, and *Board* terminated. Functions transferred to President's Foreign Intelligence Advisory Board.

Intelligence Advisory Board, President's Foreign Established by EO 11460 of Mar. 20, 1969. Abolished by EO 11984 of May 4, 1977. Reestablished by EO 12331 of Oct. 20, 1981.

Intelligence Authority, National Established by Presidential directive of Jan. 22, 1946. Terminated on creation of Central Intelligence Agency under National Security Council by act of July 26, 1947 (61 Stat. 497).

Intelligence Group, Central Terminated on creation of Central Intelligence Agency by act of July 26, 1947 (61 Stat. 497).

Inter-American Affairs, Institute of *See* **American Republics, Office for Coordination of Commercial and Cultural Relations between the**

Inter-American Affairs, Office of *See* **American Republics, Office for Coordination of Commercial and Cultural Relations between the**

Inter-American Affairs, Office of the Coordinator of *See* **American Republics, Office for Coordination of Commercial and Cultural Relations between the**

Interagency. *See other part of title*

Interdepartmental. *See also other part of title*

Interdepartmental Advisory Council Established January 1941 to advise *Coordinator of Health, Welfare, and Related Defense Activities.* Terminated on creation of *Office of Defense Health and Welfare Service* Sept. 3, 1941.

Interest and Dividends, Committee on Established by EO 11695 of Jan. 11, 1973. Abolished by EO 11781 of May 1, 1974.

Intergovernmental Affairs, Office of Merged with *Office of Information and Public Affairs* to form Office of Public and Intergovernmental Affairs by Labor Secretary's Order 1–85 of June 5, 1985.

Intergovernmental Relations, Advisory Commission on Established by act of Sept. 24, 1959 (73 Stat. 703). Terminated pursuant to act of Nov. 19, 1995 (109 Stat. 480). Continued in existence by P.L. 104–328, Oct. 19, 1996 (110 Stat. 4004).

Intergovernmental Relations, Commission on Established by act of July 10, 1953 (67 Stat. 145). Final report submitted to Congress by June 30, 1955, pursuant to act of Feb. 7, 1955 (69 Stat. 7).

Intergovernmental Relations, Office of Established by EO 11455 of Feb. 14, 1969. Functions transferred to *Domestic Council* by EO 11690 of Dec. 14, 1972.

Interim Compliance Panel Established by Dec. 30, 1969 (83 Stat. 774). Terminated June 30, 1976, pursuant to terms of act.

Internal Revenue Service Functions relating to alcohol, tobacco, firearms, and explosives transferred to Bureau of Alcohol, Tobacco and Firearms by Treasury departmental order July 1, 1972.

Internal Security Division Established July 9, 1945, by transfer of functions from Criminal Division. Abolished Mar. 22, 1973, and functions transferred to Criminal Division, Justice Department.

International. *See also other part of title*

International Activities, Office of Renamed *Office of Service and Protocol* by Smithsonian Institution Secretary's internal directive of Jan. 11, 1985.

International Development, Agency for Transferred from State Department to U.S. International Development Cooperation Agency by Reorg. Plan No. 2 of 1979, effective Oct. 1, 1979. Continued as agency within IDCA by IDCA Delegation of Authority No. 1 of Oct. 1, 1979.

Interstate Commerce Commission Created by act of Feb. 4, 1887 (24 Stat. 379). Certain functions as cited in act of Oct. 15, 1966 (80 Stat. 931) transferred to Commerce Secretary. Functions relating to railroad and pipeline safety transferred to Federal Railroad Administrator and motor carrier safety to Federal Highway Administrator by act. Abolished by act of Dec. 29, 1995 (109 Stat. 932) and many functions transferred to the newly created Surface Transportation Board within the Department of Transportation.

Investigation, Bureau of Established by act of May 22, 1908 (35 Stat. 235). Functions consolidated with investigative functions of *Bureau of Prohibition, Division of Investigation,* Justice Department, by EO 6166 of June 10, 1933, effective Mar. 2, 1934.

Investigation, Division of   Designated as Federal Bureau of Investigation in Justice Department by act of Mar. 22, 1935 (49 Stat. 77).

Investigation and Research, Board of   Established by act of Sept. 18, 1940 (54 Stat. 952). Extended to Sept. 18, 1944, by Proc. 2559 of June 26, 1942.

Investigations, Division of   Established by administrative order of Apr. 27, 1933. Abolished Jan. 17, 1942, by administrative order and functions transferred to *Branch of Field Examination, General Land Office,* Interior Department.

Investments, Office of Foreign Direct   Established in Commerce Department Jan. 2, 1968, by Departmental Organization Order 25–3 to carry out provisions of EO 11387 of Jan. 1, 1968. Controls on foreign investments terminated Jan. 29, 1974.

Jamestown-Williamsburg-Yorktown National Celebration Commission   Established by act of Aug. 13, 1953 (67 Stat. 576). Terminated upon submission of final report to Congress Mar. 1, 1958.

Joint.   *See also other part of title*

Joint Resolutions of Congress   *See* **State Department**

Judicial Procedure, Commission on International Rules of   Established by act of Sept. 2, 1958 (72 Stat. 1743). Terminated Dec. 31, 1966, by act of Aug. 30, 1964 (78 Stat. 700).

Justice Assistance, Research, and Statistics, Office of   Established in Justice Department by act of Dec. 27, 1979 (93 Stat. 1201). Abolished by act of Oct. 12, 1984 (98 Stat. 2091).

Kennedy, Commission To Report Upon the Assassination of President John F.   Established by EO 11130 of Nov. 29, 1963. Report submitted Sept. 24, 1964, and *Commission* discharged by Presidential letter of same date.

Labor, President's Committee on Migratory   Appointed by Presidential letter of Aug. 26, 1954. Formally established by EO 10894 of Nov. 15, 1960. Terminated Jan. 6, 1964, by Labor Secretary in letter to members, with approval of President.

Labor and Commerce, Department of   Established by act of Feb. 14, 1903 (32 Stat. 825). Reorganized into separate Departments of Labor and Commerce by act of Mar. 4, 1913 (37 Stat. 736).

Labor Department, Solicitor for   Transferred from Justice Department to Labor Department by EO 6166 of June 10, 1933.

Labor-Management Advisory Committee   Established by EO 11695 of Jan. 11, 1973. Abolished by EO 11788 of June 18, 1974.

Labor-Management Policy, President's Advisory Committee on   Established by EO 10918 of Feb. 16, 1961. Abolished by EO 11710 of Apr. 4, 1973.

Labor-Management Relations Services, Office of   Established by Labor Secretary's Order 3–84 of May 3, 1984. Renamed Bureau of Labor-Management

Relations and Cooperative Programs by Secretarial Order 7–84 of Sept. 20, 1984 (49 FR 38374).

Labor-Management Services Administration   *Office of Pension and Welfare Benefit Programs* transferred from *Administration* and constituted as separate unit by Labor Secretary's Order 1–84 of Jan. 20, 1984 (49 FR 4269). Remaining labor-management relations functions reassigned by Labor Secretary's Order 3–84 of May 3, 1984.

Labor Organization, International   Established in 1919 by Treaty of Versailles with U.S. joining in 1934. U.S. membership terminated Nov. 1, 1977, at President's direction.

Labor Relations Council, Federal   Established by EO 11491 of Oct. 29, 1969. Abolished by Reorg. Plan No. 2 of 1978, effective Jan. 1, 1979, and functions transferred to Federal Labor Relations Authority.

Labor Standards, Apprenticeship Section, Division of   Transferred to *Federal Security Agency* by EO 9139 of Apr. 18, 1942, functioning as *Apprentice Training Service.* Transferred to *War Manpower Commission* by EO 9247 of Sept. 17, 1942, functioning in *Bureau of Training.* Returned to Labor Department by EO 9617 of Sept. 19, 1945.

Labor Standards, Bureau of   Established by Labor departmental order in 1934. Functions absorbed by Occupational Safety and Health Administration in May 1971.

Land Bank Commissioner   *See* **Farm Loan Board, Federal**

Land Law Review Commission, Public   Established by act of Sept. 19, 1964 (78 Stat. 982). Terminated Dec. 31, 1970, pursuant to terms of act.

Land Office, General   Consolidated with *Grazing Service* into Bureau of Land Management, Interior Department, by Reorg. Plan No. 3 of 1946, effective July 16, 1946.

Land Office, Office of Recorder of the General   Created in Interior Department by act of July 4, 1836 (5 Stat. 111). Abolished by Reorg. Plan No. III of 1940, effective June 30, 1940, and functions transferred to *General Land Office.*

Land Policy Section   Established in 1934 as part of *Program Planning Division, Agricultural Adjustment Administration.* Personnel taken over by *Resettlement Administration* in 1935.

Land Problems, Committee on National   Established by EO 6693 of Apr. 28, 1934. Abolished by EO 6777 of June 30, 1934.

Land Program, Director of   Basis of program found in act of June 16, 1933 (48 Stat. 200). *Special Board of Public Works* established by EO 6174 of June 16, 1933. Land Program established by *Board* by resolution passed Dec. 28, 1933, and amended July 18, 1934. *Federal Emergency Relief Administration* designated to administer program Feb. 28, 1934. Land Program transferred to *Resettlement Administration* by EO 7028 of Apr. 30, 1935. Functions of *Administration* transferred to Agriculture

Secretary by EO 7530 of Dec. 31, 1936. Land conservation and land-utilization programs administered by *Administration* transferred to *Bureau of Agricultural Economics* by Secretary's Memorandum 733. Administration of land programs placed under Soil Conservation Service by Secretary's Memorandum 785 of Oct. 6, 1938.

Land Use Coordination, Office of Established by Agriculture Secretary's Memorandum 725 of July 12, 1937. Abolished Jan. 1, 1944, by General Departmental Circular 21 and functions administered by *Land Use Coordinator*.

Land Use and Water Planning, Office of Established in Interior Department by Secretarial Order No. 2953 of May 7, 1973. Abolished by Secretarial Order No. 2988 of Mar. 11, 1976.

Law Enforcement Assistance Administration Established by act of June 19, 1968 (82 Stat. 197). Operations closed out by Justice Department due to lack of appropriations and remaining functions transferred to *Office of Justice Assistance, Research, and Statistics.*

Law Enforcement Training Center, Consolidated Federal Renamed Federal Law Enforcement Training Center by Amendment No. 1 of Aug. 14, 1975, to Treasury Department Order 217 (Revision 1).

Legislative Affairs, Office of Renamed Office of Intergovernmental and Legislative Affairs Feb. 24, 1984, by Attorney General's Order 1054–84 (49 FR 10177).

Lend-Lease Administration, Office of Established by EO 8926 of Oct. 28, 1941, to replace *Division of Defense Aid Reports.* Consolidated with *Foreign Economic Administration* by EO 9380 of Sept. 25, 1943.

Lewis and Clark Trail Commission Established by act of Oct. 6, 1964 (78 Stat. 1005). Terminated October 1969 by terms of act.

Lighthouses, Bureau of Established in Commerce Department by act of Aug. 7, 1789 (1 Stat. 53). Consolidated with U.S. Coast Guard by Reorg. Plan No. II of 1939, effective July 1, 1939.

Lincoln Sesquicentennial Commission Established by joint resolution of Sept. 2, 1957 (71 Stat. 587). Terminated Mar. 1, 1960, pursuant to terms of joint resolution.

Liquidation, Director of Established in *Office for Emergency Management* by EO 9674 of Jan. 4, 1946. Terminated by EO 9744 of June 27, 1946.

Liquidation Advisory Committee Established by EO 9674 of Jan. 4, 1946. Terminated by EO 9744 of June 27, 1946.

Loan Agency, Federal Established by Reorg. Plan No. I of 1939, effective July 1, 1939, by consolidating *Reconstruction Finance Corporation*—including subordinate units of *RFC Mortgage Company, Disaster Loan Corporation, Federal National Mortgage Association, Defense Plant Corporation, Defense Homes Corporation, Defense*

Supplies Corporation, Rubber Reserve Company, Metals Reserve Company, and *War Insurance Corporation* (later known as *War Damage Corporation*)—with *Federal Home Loan Bank Board, Home Owners' Loan Corporation, Federal Savings and Loan Insurance Corporation, Federal Housing Administration, Electric Home and Farm Authority,* and *Export-Import Bank of Washington. Federal Home Loan Bank Board, Federal Savings and Loan Insurance Corporation, Home Owners' Loan Corporation, Federal Housing Administration,* and *Defense Homes Corporation* transferred to *National Housing Agency* by EO 9070 of Feb. 24, 1942. *Reconstruction Finance Corporation* and its units (except *Defense Homes Corporation*), *Electric Home and Farm Authority,* and *Export-Import Bank of Washington* transferred to Commerce Department by EO 9071 of Feb. 24, 1942. *RFC* and units returned to *Federal Loan Agency* by act of Feb. 24, 1945 (59 Stat. 5). *Agency* abolished by act of June 30, 1947 (61 Stat. 202), and all property and records transferred to *Reconstruction Finance Corporation.*

Loan Fund, Development Established in *International Cooperation Administration* by act of Aug. 14, 1957 (71 Stat. 355). Created as independent corporate agency by act of June 30, 1958 (72 Stat. 261). Abolished by act of Sept. 4, 1961 (75 Stat. 445), and functions redelegated to Agency for International Development.

Loan Policy Board Established by act of July 18, 1958 (72 Stat. 385). Abolished by Reorg. Plan No. 4 of 1965, effective July 27, 1965, and functions transferred to Small Business Administration.

Longshoremen's Labor Board, National Established in Labor Department by EO 6748 of June 26, 1934. Terminated by Proc. 2120 of Mar. 11, 1935.

Low-Emission Vehicle Certification Board Established by act of Dec. 31, 1970 (84 Stat. 1701). Terminated by act of Mar. 14, 1980 (94 Stat. 98).

Lowell Historic Canal District Commission Established by act of Jan. 4, 1975 (88 Stat. 2330). Expired January 1977 pursuant to terms of act.

Loyalty Review Board Established Nov. 10, 1947, by *U.S. Civil Service Commission,* pursuant to EO 9835 of Mar. 21, 1947. Abolished by EO 10450 of Apr. 27, 1953.

Management Improvement, Advisory Committee on Established by EO 10072 of July 29, 1949. Abolished by EO 10917 of Feb. 10, 1961, and functions transferred to *Bureau of the Budget.*

Management Improvement, President's Advisory Council on Established by EO 11509 of Feb. 11, 1970. Inactive as of June 30, 1973.

Manpower, President's Committee on Established by EO 11152 of Apr. 15, 1964. Terminated by EO 11515 of Mar. 13, 1970.

Manpower Administration Renamed Employment and Training Administration by Labor Secretary's Order 14–75 of Nov. 12, 1975.

Manpower Management, Office of Civilian
Renamed Office of Civilian Personnel by Navy
Secretary's Notice 5430 of Oct. 1, 1976.

Marine Affairs, Office of Established by Interior
Secretary Apr. 30, 1970, to replace *Office of Marine
Resources,* created by Secretary Oct. 22, 1968.
Abolished by Secretary Dec. 4, 1970.

Marine Corps Memorial Commission, U.S.
Established by act of Aug. 24, 1947 (61 Stat. 724).
Terminated by act of Mar. 14, 1980 (94 Stat. 98).

Marine Inspection and Navigation, Bureau of *See*
Navigation and Steamboat Inspection, Bureau of

**Marine Resources and Engineering Development,
National Council on** Established in Executive
Office of the President by act of June 17, 1966 (80
Stat. 203). Terminated Apr. 30, 1971, due to lack of
funding.

Maritime Administration Established in Commerce
Department by Reorg. Plan No. 21 of 1950, effective
May 24, 1950. Transferred to Transportation
Department by act of Aug. 6, 1981 (95 Stat. 151).

Maritime Advisory Committee Established by EO
11156 of June 17, 1964. Terminated by EO 11427
of Sept. 4, 1968.

Maritime Board, Federal *See* **Maritime
Commission, U.S.**

Maritime Commission, U.S. Established by act of
June 29, 1936 (49 Stat. 1985), as successor agency
to *U.S. Shipping Board* and *U.S. Shipping Board
Merchant Fleet Corporation.* Training functions
transferred to Commandant of Coast Guard by EO
9083 of Feb. 27, 1942. Functions further transferred
to *War Shipping Administration* by EO 9198 of July
11, 1942. Abolished by Reorg. Plan No. 21 of 1950,
effective May 24, 1950, which established *Federal
Maritime Board* and *Maritime Administration* as
successor agencies. *Board* abolished, regulatory
functions transferred to Federal Maritime
Commission, and functions relating to subsidization
of merchant marine transferred to Commerce
Secretary by Reorg. Plan No. 7 of 1961, effective
Aug. 12, 1961.

Maritime Labor Board Authorized by act of June
23, 1938 (52 Stat. 968). Mediatory duties abolished
by act of June 23, 1941 (55 Stat. 259); title expired
June 22, 1942.

Marketing Administration, Surplus Established by
Reorg. Plan No. III of 1940, effective June 30, 1940,
consolidating functions vested in *Federal Surplus
Commodities Corporation* and *Division of Marketing
and Marketing Agreements, Agricultural Adjustment
Administration.* Consolidated with other agencies
into *Agricultural Marketing Administration* by EO
9069 of Feb. 23, 1942.

Marketing and Marketing Agreements, Division of
Established in Agriculture Department by act of June
3, 1937 (50 Stat. 246). Consolidated with *Federal
Surplus Commodities Corporation* into *Surplus
Marketing Administration* by Reorg. Plan No. III of
1940, effective June 30, 1940.

Mediation, U.S. Board of Established by act of
May 20, 1926 (44 Stat. 577). Abolished by act of
June 21, 1934 (48 Stat. 1193), and superseded by
National Mediation Board, July 21, 1934.

**Medical Information Systems Program Office, Tri-
Service** Renamed Defense Medical Systems
Support Center by memorandum of Assistant
Defense Secretary (Health Affairs) May 3, 1985.

Medical Services Administration Established by
Health, Education, and Welfare Secretary's
reorganization of Aug. 15, 1967. Transferred from
Social and Rehabilitation Service to Health Care
Financing Administration by Secretary's
reorganization of Mar. 8, 1977 (42 FR 13262).

Medicine and Surgery, Department of Established
in the *Veterans Administration* by act of Sept. 2,
1958 (72 Stat. 1243). Renamed *Veterans Health
Services and Research Administration* in the
Veterans Affairs Department by act of Oct. 25, 1988
(102 Stat. 2640). Renamed Veterans Health
Administration by act of May 7, 1991 (105 Stat.
187).

Memorial Commission, National Established by
Public Resolution 107 of Mar. 4, 1929 (45 Stat.
1699). Terminated by EO 6166 of June 10, 1933,
and functions transferred to *Office of National Parks,
Buildings, and Reservations,* Interior Department.

Mental Health, National Institute of Established by
act of July 3, 1946 (60 Stat. 425). Made entity within
the Alcohol, Drug Abuse, and Mental Health
Administration by act of May 14, 1974 (88 Stat.
135). Functions transferred to Health and Human
Services Department by act of Oct. 17, 1979 (93
Stat. 695). (*See also* act of Oct. 27, 1986; 100 Stat.
3207–106.) Abolished by act of July 10, 1992 (106
Stat. 331). Reestablished by act of July 10, 1992
(106 Stat. 364).

Metals Reserve Company Established June 28,
1940, by act of Jan. 22, 1932 (47 Stat. 5).
Transferred from *Federal Loan Agency* to Commerce
Department by EO 9071 of Feb. 24, 1942. Returned
to *Federal Loan Agency* by act of Feb. 24, 1945 (59
Stat. 5). Dissolved by act of June 30, 1945 (59 Stat.
310), and functions transferred to *Reconstruction
Finance Corporation.*

Metric Board, U.S. Established by act of Dec. 23,
1975 (89 Stat. 1007). Terminated Oct. 1, 1982, due
to lack of funding.

**Mexican-American Affairs, Interagency Committee
on** Established by Presidential memorandum of
June 9, 1967. Renamed *Cabinet Committee on
Opportunities for Spanish-Speaking People* by act of
Dec. 30, 1969 (83 Stat. 838). Terminated Dec. 30,
1974, pursuant to terms of act.

Mexican Claims Commission, American
Established by act of Dec. 18, 1942 (56 Stat. 1058).
Terminated Apr. 4, 1947, by act of Apr. 3, 1945 (59
Stat. 59).

Mexican Claims Commission, Special Established
by act of Apr. 10, 1935 (49 Stat. 149). Terminated
by EO 7909 of June 15, 1938.

Mexico Commission for Border Development and Friendship, U.S.-   Established through exchange of notes of Nov. 30 and Dec. 3, 1966, between U.S. and Mexico. Terminated Nov. 5, 1969.

Micronesian Claims Commission   Established by act of July 1, 1971 (85 Stat. 92). Terminated Aug. 3, 1976, pursuant to terms of act.

Migration, Intergovernmental Committee for European   Renamed Intergovernmental Committee for Migration by Resolution 624, passed by *Intergovernmental Committee for European Migration Council,* effective Nov. 11, 1980.

Migration, International Committee for   Created in 1951. Renamed International Organization for Migration pursuant to article 29, paragraph 2, of the ICM constitution, effective Nov. 14, 1989.

Migratory Bird Conservation Commission   Chairmanship transferred from Agriculture Secretary to Interior Secretary by Reorg. Plan No. II of 1939, effective July 1, 1939.

Military Air Transport Service   Renamed *Military Airlift Command* in U.S. Air Force by HQ MATS/ MAC Special Order G–164 of Jan. 1, 1966.

Military Airlift Command   Inactivated June 1, 1992.

Military Appeals, United States Court of   Established under Article I of the Constitution of the United States pursuant to act of May 5, 1950, as amended. Renamed United States Court of Appeals for the Armed Forces by act of Oct. 5, 1994 (108 Stat. 2831).

Military Establishment, National   Established as executive department of the Government by act of July 26, 1947 (61 Stat. 495). Designated Department of Defense by act of Aug. 10, 1949 (63 Stat. 579).

Military Purchases, Interdepartmental Committee for Coordination of Foreign and Domestic   Informal liaison committee created on Presidential notification of Dec. 6, 1939, to Treasury and *War* Secretaries and Acting Navy Secretary. Committee dissolved in accordance with Presidential letter to Treasury Secretary Apr. 14, 1941, following approval of act of Mar. 11, 1941 (55 Stat. 31).

Military Renegotiation Policy and Review Board   Established by directive of Defense Secretary July 19, 1948. Abolished by Defense Secretary's letter of Jan. 18, 1952, which transferred functions to *Renegotiation Board.*

Military Sea Transportation Service   Renamed Military Sealift Command in U.S. Navy by COMSC notice of Aug. 1, 1970.

Militia Bureau   Established in 1908 as *Division of Militia Affairs, Office of War Secretary.* Superseded in 1933 by National Guard Bureau.

Mine Health and Safety Academy, National   Transferred from Interior Department to Labor Department by act of July 25, 1979 (93 Stat. 111).

Minerals Exploration, Office of   Established by act of Aug. 21, 1958 (72 Stat. 700). Functions

transferred to *Geological Survey* by Interior Secretary's Order 2886 of Feb. 26, 1965.

Minerals Mobilization, Office of   Established by Interior Secretary pursuant to act of Sept. 8, 1950 (64 Stat. 798) and EO 10574 of Nov. 5, 1954, and by order of *Office of Defense Mobilization.* Succeeded by *Office of Minerals and Solid Fuels* Nov. 2, 1962. *Office of Minerals Policy Development* combined with *Office of Research and Development* in Interior Department May 21, 1976, under authority of Reorg. Plan No. 3 of 1950, to form *Office of Minerals Policy and Research Analysis.* Abolished Sept. 30, 1981, by Secretarial Order 3070 and functions transferred to Bureau of Mines.

Minerals Policy and Research Analysis, Office of   See **Minerals Mobilization, Office of**

Minerals and Solid Fuels, Office of   Established by Interior Secretary Oct. 26, 1962. Abolished and functions assigned to Deputy Assistant Secretary— Minerals and Energy Policy, Office of the Assistant Secretary—Mineral Resources, effective Oct. 22, 1971.

Mines, Bureau of   Established in Interior Department by act of May 16, 1910 (36 Stat. 369). Transferred to Commerce Department by EO 4239 of June 4, 1925. Transferred to Interior Department by EO 6611 of Feb. 22, 1934. Renamed United States Bureau of Mines by act of May 18, 1992 (106 Stat. 172). Terminated pursuant to P.L. 104–99, Jan. 26, 1996 (110 Stat. 32). Certain functions transferred to Secretary of Energy by P.L. 104–134, Apr. 26, 1996 (110 Stat. 1321–167).

Mining Enforcement and Safety Administration   Established by Interior Secretary's Order 2953 of May 7, 1973. Terminated by departmental directive Mar. 9, 1978, and functions transferred to Mine Safety and Health Administration, Labor Department, established by act of Nov. 9, 1977 (91 Stat. 1319).

Minority Business Enterprise, Office of   Renamed Minority Business Development Agency by Commerce Secretarial Order DOO–254A of Nov. 1, 1979.

Mint, Bureau of the   Renamed U.S. Mint by Treasury Secretarial order of Jan. 9, 1984 (49 FR 5020).

Missile Sites Labor Commission   Established by EO 10946 of May 26, 1961. Abolished by EO 11374 of Oct. 11, 1967, and functions transferred to Federal Mediation and Conciliation Service.

Missouri Basin Survey Commission   Established by EO 10318 of Jan. 3, 1952. Final report of *Commission* submitted to President Jan. 12, 1953, pursuant to EO 10329 of Feb. 25, 1952.

Missouri River Basin Commission   Established by EO 11658 of Mar. 22, 1972. Terminated by EO 12319 of Sept. 9, 1981.

Mobilization, Office of Civil and Defense   See **Mobilization, Office of Defense and Civilian**

Mobilization, Office of Defense and Civilian
Established by Reorg. Plan No. 1 of 1958, effective
July 1, 1958. Redesignated as *Office of Civil and
Defense Mobilization* by act of Aug. 26, 1958 (72
Stat. 861), consolidating functions of *Office of
Defense Mobilization* and *Federal Civil Defense
Administration.* Civil defense functions transferred to
Defense Secretary by EO 10952 of July 20, 1961,
and remaining organization redesignated *Office of
Emergency Planning* by act of Sept. 22, 1961 (75
Stat. 630).

Mobilization Policy, National Advisory Board on
Established by EO 10224 of Mar. 15, 1951. EO
10224 revoked by EO 10773 of July 1, 1958.

**Monetary and Financial Problems, National
Advisory Council on International**   Established by
act of July 31, 1945 (59 Stat. 512). Abolished by
Reorg. Plan No. 4 of 1965, effective July 27, 1965,
and functions transferred to President. Functions
assumed by National Advisory Council on
International Monetary and Financial Policies,
established by EO 11269 of Feb. 14, 1966.

Monument Commission, National   Established by
act of Aug. 31, 1954 (68 Stat. 1029). Final report
submitted in 1957, and audit of business completed
September 1964.

**Monuments in War Areas, American Commission
for the Protection and Salvage of Artistic and
Historic**   Established by President June 23, 1943;
announced by Secretary of State Aug. 20, 1943.
Activities assumed by State Department Aug. 16,
1946.

Mortgage Association, Federal National   Chartered
Feb. 10, 1938, by act of June 27, 1934 (48 Stat.
1246). Grouped with other agencies to form *Federal
Loan Agency* by Reorg. Plan No. I of 1939, effective
July 1, 1939. Transferred to Commerce Department
by EO 9071 of Feb. 24, 1942. Returned to *Federal
Loan Agency* by act of Feb. 24, 1945 (59 Stat. 5).
Transferred to *Housing and Home Finance Agency*
by Reorg. Plan No. 22 of 1950, effective July 10,
1950. Rechartered by act of Aug. 2, 1954 (68 Stat.
590) and made constituent agency of *Housing and
Home Finance Agency.* Transferred with functions of
Housing and Home Finance Agency to Housing and
Urban Development Department by act of Sept. 9,
1965 (79 Stat. 667). Made Government-sponsored,
private corporation by act of Aug. 1, 1968 (82 Stat.
536).

Motor Carrier Claims Commission   Established by
act of July 2, 1948 (62 Stat. 1222). Terminated Dec.
31, 1952, by acts of July 11, 1951 (65 Stat. 116),
and Mar. 14, 1952 (66 Stat. 25).

Mount Rushmore National Memorial Commission
Established by act of Feb. 25, 1929 (45 Stat. 1300).
Expenditures ordered administered by Interior
Department by EO 6166 of June 10, 1933.
Transferred to National Park Service, Interior
Department, by Reorg. Plan No. II of 1939, effective
July 1, 1939.

Munitions Board   Established in Defense
Department by act of July 26, 1947 (61 Stat. 499).
Abolished by Reorg. Plan No. 6 of 1953, effective

June 30, 1953, and functions vested in Defense
Secretary.

Munitions Board, Joint Army and Navy   Organized
in 1922. Placed under direction of President by
military order of July 5, 1939. Reconstituted Aug.
18, 1945, by order approved by President.
Terminated on establishment of *Munitions Board* by
act of July 26, 1947 (61 Stat. 505).

Museum of History and Technology, National
Renamed National Museum of American History in
Smithsonian Institution by act of Oct. 13, 1980 (94
Stat. 1884).

Museum Services, Institute of   Established by act of
June 23, 1972 (86 Stat. 327). Transferred to Office
of Educational Research and Improvement,
Education Department, by act of Oct. 17, 1979 (93
Stat. 678), effective May 4, 1980. Transferred to
National Foundation on the Arts and the Humanities
by act of Dec. 23, 1981 (95 Stat. 1414). Functions
transferred to the Institute of Museum and Library
Services by P.L. 104–208, Sept. 30, 1996 (110 Stat.
3009–307).

Narcotics, Bureau of   Established in Treasury
Department by act of June 14, 1930 (46 Stat. 585).
Abolished by Reorg. Plan No. 1 of 1968, effective
Apr. 8, 1968, and functions transferred to *Bureau of
Narcotics and Dangerous Drugs,* Justice Department.

Narcotics, President's Council on Counter-
Renamed President's Drug Policy Council by EO
13023, Nov. 6, 1996 (61 FR 57767).

**Narcotics Control, Cabinet Committee on
International**   Established by Presidential
memorandum of Aug. 17, 1971. Terminated by
Presidential memorandum of Mar. 14, 1977.

National.   *See other part of title*

Naval Material, Office of   Established by act of
Mar. 5, 1948 (62 Stat. 68). Abolished by Defense
Department reorg. order of Mar. 9, 1966, and
functions transferred to Navy Secretary (31 FR 7188).

Naval Material Command   See Naval Material
Support Establishment

Naval Material Support Establishment   Established
by Navy Department General Order 5 of July 1,
1963 (28 FR 7037). Replaced by *Naval Material
Command* pursuant to General Order 5 of Apr. 29,
1966 (31 FR 7188). Functions realigned to form
Office of Naval Acquisition Support, and termination
of *Command* effective May 6, 1985.

Naval Observatory   Jurisdiction transferred from
Bureau of Navigation to Chief of Naval Operations
by EO 9126 of Apr. 8, 1942, and by Reorg. Plan
No. 3 of 1946, effective July 16, 1946.

Naval Oceanography Command   Renamed Naval
Meteorology and Oceanography Command in 1995.

Naval Petroleum and Oil Shale Reserves, Office of
Established by Navy Secretary, as required by law
(70A Stat. 457). Jurisdiction transferred to Energy
Department by act of Aug. 4, 1977 (91 Stat. 581).

Naval Weapons, Bureau of Established by act of Aug. 18, 1959 (73 Stat. 395), to replace *Bureau of Ordnance and Aeronautics.* Abolished by Defense Department reorg. order of Mar. 9, 1966, and functions transferred to Navy Secretary (31 FR 7188), effective May 1, 1966.

Navigation, Bureau of Created by act of July 5, 1884 (23 Stat. 118), as special service under Treasury Department. Transferred to *Department of Commerce and Labor* by act of Feb. 4, 1903 (32 Stat. 825). Consolidated with *Bureau of Navigation and Steamboat Inspection* by act of June 30, 1932 (47 Stat. 415).

Navigation, Bureau of Renamed Bureau of Naval Personnel by act of May 13, 1942 (56 Stat. 276).

Navigation and Steamboat Inspection, Bureau of Renamed *Bureau of Marine Inspection and Navigation* by act of May 27, 1936 (49 Stat. 1380). Functions transferred to *Bureau of Customs,* Treasury Department, and U.S. Coast Guard by EO 9083 of Feb. 28, 1942. Transfer made permanent and *Bureau* abolished by Reorg. Plan. No. 3 of 1946, effective July 16, 1946.

Navy Commissioners, Board of Established by act of Feb. 7, 1815 (3 Stat. 202). Abolished by act of Aug. 31, 1842 (5 Stat. 579).

Navy Department Defense housing functions transferred to *Federal Public Housing Authority, National Housing Agency,* by EO 9070 of Feb. 24, 1942.

Neighborhoods, National Commission on Established by act of Apr. 30, 1977 (91 Stat. 56). Terminated May 4, 1979, pursuant to terms of act.

Neighborhoods, Voluntary Associations and Consumer Protection, Office of Abolished and certain functions transferred to Office of the Assistant Secretary for Housing—Federal Housing Commissioner and Office of the Assistant Secretary for Community Planning and Development. Primary enabling legislation, act of Oct. 31, 1978 (92 Stat. 2119), repealed by act of Aug. 13, 1981 (95 Stat. 398). Abolishment of *Office* and transfer of functions carried out by Housing and Urban Development Secretarial order.

New England River Basins Commission Established by EO 11371 of Sept. 6, 1967. Terminated by EO 12319 of Sept. 9, 1981.

Nicaro Project Responsibility for management of Nicaro nickel producing facilities in Oriente Province, Cuba, transferred from *Office of Special Assistant to the Administrator (Nicaro Project)* to *Defense Materials Service* by General Services Administrator, effective July 7, 1959. Facilities expropriated by Cuban Government and nationalized Oct. 26, 1960.

Northern Mariana Islands Commission on Federal Laws Created by joint resolution of Mar. 24, 1976 (90 Stat. 263). Terminated upon submission of final report in August 1985.

Nursing Research, National Center for Renamed National Institute of Nursing Research by act of June 10, 1993 (107 Stat. 178).

Nutrition Division Functions transferred from *Health, Education, and Welfare Department* to Agriculture Department by EO 9310 of Mar. 3, 1943.

Ocean Mining Administration Established by Interior Secretarial Order 2971 of Feb. 24, 1975. Abolished by Department Manual Release 2273 of June 13, 1980.

Oceanography, Interagency Committee on Established by *Federal Council for Science and Technology* pursuant to EO 10807 of Mar. 13, 1959. Absorbed by *National Council on Marine Resources and Engineering Development* pursuant to Vice Presidential letter of July 21, 1967.

Office. *See also other part of title*

Office Space, President's Advisory Commission on Presidential Established by act of Aug. 3, 1956 (70 Stat. 979). Terminated June 30, 1957, by act of Jan. 25, 1957 (71 Stat. 4).

Official Register Function of preparing *Official Register* vested in Director of the Census by act of Mar. 3, 1925 (43 Stat. 1105). Function transferred to *U.S. Civil Service Commission* by EO 6166 of June 10, 1933. Yearly compilation and publication required by act of Aug. 28, 1935 (49 Stat. 956). Act repealed by act of July 12, 1960 (74 Stat. 427), and last *Register* published in 1959.

Ohio River Basin Commission Established by EO 11578 of Jan. 13, 1971. Terminated by EO 12319 of Sept. 9, 1981.

Oil and Gas, Office of Established by Interior Secretary May 6, 1946, in response to Presidential letter of May 3, 1946. Transferred to *Federal Energy Administration* by act of May 7, 1974 (88 Stat. 100).

Oil Import Administration Established in Interior Department by Proc. 3279 of Mar. 10, 1959. Merged into *Office of Oil and Gas* Oct. 22, 1971.

Oil Import Appeals Board Established by Commerce Secretary Mar. 13, 1959, and made part of Office of Hearings and Appeals Dec. 23, 1971.

Operations Advisory Group Established by EO 11905 of Feb. 18, 1976. Abolished by Presidential Directive No. 2 of Jan. 20, 1977.

Operations Coordinating Board Established by EO 10483 of Sept. 2, 1953, which was superseded by EO 10700 of Feb. 25, 1957. EO 10700 revoked by EO 10920 of Feb. 18, 1961, and *Board* terminated.

Ordnance, Bureau of *See* **Ordnance and Hydrography, Bureau of**

Ordnance and Hydrography, Bureau of Established in Navy Department by act of Aug. 31, 1842 (5 Stat. 579). Replaced under act of July 5, 1862 (12 Stat. 510), by *Bureau of Ordnance* and *Bureau of Navigation.* Abolished by act of Aug. 18, 1959 (73 Stat. 395), and functions transferred to *Bureau of Naval Weapons.*

Organization, President's Advisory Committee on Government   Established by EO 10432 of Jan. 24, 1953. Abolished by EO 10917 of Feb. 10, 1961, and functions transferred to *Bureau of the Budget* for termination.

Organizations Staff, International   Functions merged with Foreign Agricultural Service by Agriculture Secretary's memorandum of Dec. 7, 1973, effective Feb. 3, 1974.

Overseas Private Investment Corporation   Transferred as separate agency to U.S. International Development Cooperation Agency by Reorg. Plan No. 2 of 1979, effective Oct. 1, 1979.

Oversight Board (for the Resolution Trust Corporation)   Established by act of Aug. 9, 1989 (103 Stat. 363). Renamed Thrift Depositor Protection Oversight Board by act of Dec. 12, 1991 (105 Stat. 1767).

Pacific Northwest River Basins Commission   Established by EO 11331 of Mar. 6, 1967. Terminated by EO 12319 of Sept. 9, 1981.

Packers and Stockyards Administration   Established by Agriculture Secretary's Memorandum 1613, supp. 1, of May 8, 1967. Certain functions consolidated into Agricultural Marketing Service by Secretary's Memorandum 1927 of Jan. 15, 1978. Remaining functions incorporated into the Grain Inspection, Packers and Stockyards Administration by Secretary's Memorandum 1010–1 dated Oct. 20, 1994.

Panama Canal   Operation of piers at Atlantic and Pacific terminals transferred to Panama Railroad by EO 7021 of Apr. 19, 1935. Panama Canal reestablished as *Canal Zone Government* by act of Sept. 26, 1950 (64 Stat. 1038).

Panama Canal Company   Established by act of June 29, 1948 (62 Stat. 1076). Abolished and superseded by Panama Canal Commission (93 Stat. 454).

Panama Railroad Company   Incorporated Apr. 7, 1849, by New York State Legislature. Operated under private control until 1881, when original *French Canal Company* acquired most of its stock. *Company* and its successor, *New Panama Canal Company,* operated railroad as common carrier and also as adjunct in attempts to construct canal. In 1904 their shares of stock in *Panama Railroad Company* passed to ownership of U.S. as part of assets of *New Panama Canal Company* purchased under act of June 28, 1902 (34 Stat. 481). Remaining shares purchased from private owners in 1905. *Panama Railroad Company* reincorporated by act of June 29, 1948 (62 Stat. 1075) pursuant to requirements of act of Dec. 6, 1945 (59 Stat. 597). Reestablished as *Panama Canal Company* by act of Sept. 26, 1950 (64 Stat. 1038). Army Secretary directed to discontinue commercial operations of *Company* by Presidential letter of Mar. 29, 1961.

Paperwork, Commission on Federal   Established by act of Dec. 27, 1974 (88 Stat. 1789). Terminated January 1978 pursuant to terms of act.

Park Service, National   Functions in District of Columbia relating to space assignment, site selection for public buildings, and determination of priority in construction transferred to *Public Buildings Administration, Federal Works Agency,* under Reorg. Plan No. I of 1939, effective July 1, 1939.

Park Trust Fund Board, National   Established by act of July 10, 1935 (49 Stat. 477). Terminated by act of Dec. 18, 1967 (81 Stat. 656), and functions transferred to National Park Foundation.

Parks, Buildings, and Reservations, Office of National   Established in Interior Department by EO 6166 of June 10, 1933. Renamed National Park Service by act of Mar. 2, 1934 (48 Stat. 362).

Parole, Board of   Established by act of June 25, 1948 (62 Stat. 854). Abolished by act of Mar. 15, 1976 (90 Stat. 219), and functions transferred to U.S. Parole Commission.

Patent Office   Provisions of first patent act administered by State Department, with authority for granting patents vested in board comprising Secretaries of State and *War* and Attorney General. Board abolished, authority transferred to Secretary of State, and registration system established by act of Feb. 21, 1793 (1 Stat. 318). *Office* made bureau in State Department in October 1802, headed by *Superintendent of Patents. Office* reorganized in 1836 by act of June 4, 1836 (5 Stat. 117) under *Commissioner of Patents. Office* transferred to Interior Department in 1849. *Office* transferred to Commerce Department by EO 4175 of Mar. 17, 1925.

Patents Board, Government   Established by EO 10096 of Jan. 23, 1950. Abolished by EO 10930 of Mar. 24, 1961, and functions transferred to Commerce Secretary.

Pay Board   Established by EO 11627 of Oct. 15, 1971. Abolished by EO 11695 of Jan. 11, 1973.

Peace Corps   Established in State Department by EO 10924 of Mar. 1, 1961, and continued by act of Sept. 22, 1961 (75 Stat. 612), and EO 11041 of Aug. 6, 1962. Functions transferred to ACTION by Reorg. Plan No. 1 of 1971, effective July 1, 1971. Made independent agency in executive branch by act of Dec. 29, 1981 (95 Stat. 1540).

Pennsylvania Avenue, Temporary Commission on   Established by EO 11210 of Mar. 25, 1956. Inactive as of Nov. 15, 1969, due to lack of funding.

Pennsylvania Avenue Development Corporation   Established by act of Oct. 27, 1972 (86 Stat. 1266). Terminated pursuant to P.L. 104–99, Jan. 26, 1996 (110 Stat. 32) and P.L. 104–134, Apr. 26, 1996 (110 Stat. 1321–198). Functions transferred to General Services Administration, National Capital Planning Commission, and National Park Service (61 FR 11308), effective Apr. 1, 1996.

Pension and Welfare Benefit Programs, Office of   *See* **Labor-Management Services Administration**

Pensions, Commissioner of   Provided for by act of Mar. 2, 1833 (4 Stat. 668). Continued by act of Mar. 3, 1835 (4 Stat. 779), and other acts as *Office of the Commissioner of Pensions.* Transferred to Interior Department as bureau by act of Mar. 3, 1849 (9 Stat. 395). Consolidated with other bureaus and agencies into *Veterans Administration* by EO 5398 of July 21, 1930.

Pensions, Office of the Commissioner of *See* **Pensions, Commissioner of**

Perry's Victory Memorial Commission Created by act of Mar. 3, 1919 (40 Stat. 1322). Administration of Memorial transferred to National Park Service by act of June 2, 1936 (49 Stat. 1393). *Commission* terminated by terms of act and membership reconstituted as advisory board to Interior Secretary.

Personal Property, Office of *See* **Supply Service, Federal**

Personnel, National Roster of Scientific and Specialized Established by *National Resources Planning Board* pursuant to Presidential letter of June 18, 1940, to Treasury Secretary. After Aug. 15, 1940, administered jointly by *Board* and *U.S. Civil Service Commission*. Transferred to *War Manpower Commission* by EO 9139 of Apr. 18, 1942. Transferred to Labor Department by EO 9617 of Sept. 19, 1945. Transferred with *Bureau of Employment Security* to *Federal Security Agency* by act of June 16, 1948 (62 Stat. 443). Transferred to Labor Department by Reorg. Plan No. 2 of 1949, effective Aug. 20, 1949, and became inactive. Roster functions transferred to National Science Foundation by act of May 10, 1950 (64 Stat. 154). Reactivated in 1950 as *National Scientific Register* by *Office of Education, Federal Security Agency*, through *National Security Resources Board* grant of funds, and continued by National Science Foundation funds until December 1952, when *Register* integrated into Foundation's National Register of Scientific and Technical Personnel project in Division of Scientific Personnel and Education.

Personnel Administration, Council of Established by EO 7916 of June 24, 1938, effective Feb. 1, 1939. Made unit in *U.S. Civil Service Commission* by EO 8467 of July 1, 1940. Renamed *Federal Personnel Council* by EO 9830 of Feb. 24, 1947. Abolished by act of July 31, 1953 (67 Stat. 300), and personnel and records transferred to *Office of Executive Director, U.S. Civil Service Commission*.

Personnel Council, Federal *See* **Personnel Administration, Council of**

Personnel Interchange, President's Commission on Established by EO 11451 of Jan. 19, 1969. Continued by EO 12136 of May 15, 1979, and renamed *President's Commission on Executive Exchange*. Continued by EO 12493 of Dec. 5, 1984. Abolished by EO 12760 of May 2, 1991.

Personnel Management, Liaison Office for Established by EO 8248 of Sept. 8, 1939. Abolished by EO 10452 of May 1, 1953, and functions transferred to *U.S. Civil Service Commission*.

Petroleum Administration for Defense Established under act of Sept. 8, 1950 (64 Stat. 798) by Interior Secretary's Order 2591 of Oct. 3, 1950, pursuant to EO 10161 of Sept. 9, 1950. Continued by Secretary's Order 2614 of Jan. 25, 1951, pursuant to EO 10200 of Jan. 3, 1951, and PAD Delegation 1 of Jan. 24, 1951. Abolished by Secretary's Order 2755 of Apr. 23, 1954.

Petroleum Administration for War *See* **Petroleum Coordinator for War, Office of**

Petroleum Administrative Board Established Sept. 11, 1933, by Interior Secretary. Terminated Mar. 31, 1936, by EO 7076 of June 15, 1935. Interior Secretary authorized to execute functions vested in President by act of Feb. 22, 1935 (49 Stat. 30) by EO 7756 of Dec. 1, 1937. Secretary also authorized to establish *Petroleum Conservation Division* to assist in administering act. Records of *Petroleum Administrative Board* and *Petroleum Labor Policy Board* housed with *Petroleum Conservation Division, Office of Oil and Gas*, acting as custodian for Interior Secretary.

Petroleum Coordinator for War, Office of Interior Secretary designated *Petroleum Coordinator for National Defense* by Presidential letter of May 28, 1941, and approved *Petroleum Coordinator for War* by Presidential letter of Apr. 20, 1942. *Office* abolished by EO 9276 of Dec. 2, 1942, and functions transferred to *Petroleum Administration for War*, established by same EO. Administration terminated by EO 9718 of May 3, 1946.

Petroleum Labor Policy Board Established by Interior Secretary, as *Administrator of Code of Fair Competition for Petroleum Industry*, on recommendation of Planning and Coordination Committee Oct. 10, 1933. Reorganized by Secretary Dec. 19, 1933, and reorganization confirmed by order of Mar. 8, 1935. Terminated Mar. 31, 1936, when *Petroleum Administrative Board* abolished by EO 7076 of June 15, 1935.

Petroleum Reserves Corporation Established June 30, 1943, by *Reconstruction Finance Corporation*. Transferred to *Office of Economic Warfare* by EO 9360 of July 15, 1943. *Office* consolidated into *Foreign Economic Administration* by EO 9380 of Sept. 25, 1943. Functions transferred to *Reconstruction Finance Corporation* by EO 9630 of Sept. 27, 1945. *RFC's* charter amended Nov. 9, 1945, to change name to *War Assets Corporation*. *Corporation* designated by *Surplus Property Administrator* as disposal agency for all types of property for which *Reconstruction Finance Corporation* formerly disposal agency. Domestic surplus property functions of *Corporation* transferred to *War Assets Administration* by EO 9689 of Jan. 31, 1946. *Reconstruction Finance Corporation Board of Directors* ordered by President to dissolve *War Assets Corporation* as soon after Mar. 25, 1946, as practicable.

Philippine Alien Property Administration Established in *Office for Emergency Management* by EO 9789 of Oct. 14, 1946. Abolished by EO 10254 of June 15, 1951, and functions transferred to Justice Department.

Philippine War Damage Commission Established by act of Apr. 30, 1946 (60 Stat. 128). Terminated Mar. 31, 1951, by act of Sept. 6, 1950 (64 Stat. 712).

Photographic Interpretation Center, National Functions transferred to the National Imagery and Mapping Agency by P.L. 104–201, Sept. 23, 1996 (110 Stat. 2677).

Physical Fitness, Committee on Established in *Office of Federal Security Administrator* by EO 9338 of Apr. 29, 1943. Terminated June 30, 1945.

Physical Fitness, President's Council on *See* **Youth Fitness, President's Council on**

Physician Payment Review Commission Established by act of Apr. 7, 1986 (100 Stat. 190). Terminated by act of Aug. 5, 1997 (111 Stat. 354). Assets, staff, and continuing responsibility for reports transferred to the Medicare Payment Advisory Commission.

Planning Board, National Established by *Administrator of Public Works* July 30, 1933. Terminated by EO 6777 of June 30, 1934.

Plant Industry, Bureau of Established by act of Mar. 2, 1902 (31 Stat. 922). Soil fertility and soil microbiology work of *Bureau of Chemistry and Soils* transferred to *Bureau* by act of May 17, 1935. Soil chemistry and physics and soil survey work of *Bureau of Chemistry and Soils* transferred to *Bureau* by Secretary's Memorandum 784 of Oct. 6, 1938. In February 1943 engineering research of *Bureau of Agricultural Chemistry and Engineering* transferred to *Bureau of Plant Industry, Soils, and Agricultural Engineering* by Research Administration Memorandum 5 issued pursuant to EO 9069 of Feb. 23, 1942, and in conformity with Secretary's Memorandums 960 and 986. Functions transferred to Agricultural Research Service by Secretary's Memorandum 1320, supp. 4, of Nov. 2, 1953.

Plant Industry, Soils, and Agricultural Engineering, Bureau of *See* **Plant Industry, Bureau of**

Plant Quarantine, Bureau of *See* **Entomology and Plant Quarantine, Bureau of**

Policy Development, Office of *See* **Domestic Council**

Post Office Department *See* **Postal Service**

Postal Savings System Established by act of June 25, 1910 (36 Stat. 814). System closed by act of Mar. 28, 1966 (80 Stat. 92).

Postal Service Created July 26, 1775, by Continental Congress. Temporarily established by Congress by act of Sept. 22, 1789 (1 Stat. 70), and continued by subsequent acts. *Post Office Department* made executive department under act of June 8, 1872 (17 Stat. 283). Offices of First, Second, Third, and Fourth Assistant Postmasters General abolished and Deputy Postmaster General and four Assistant Postmasters General established by Reorg. Plan No. 3 of 1949, effective Aug. 20, 1949. Reorganized as U.S. Postal Service in executive branch by act of Aug. 12, 1970 (84 Stat. 719), effective July 1, 1971.

Power Commission, Federal Established by act of June 10, 1920 (41 Stat. 1063). Terminated by act of Aug. 4, 1977 (91 Stat. 578), and functions transferred to Energy Department.

Preparedness, Office of Renamed *Federal Preparedness Agency* by General Services Administrator's order of June 26, 1975.

Preparedness Agency, Federal Functions transferred from General Services Administration to Federal Emergency Management Agency by EO 12148 of July 20, 1979.

Presidential. *See other part of title*

President's. *See other part of title*

Press Intelligence, Division of Established in August 1933. Made division of *National Emergency Council* July 10, 1935. Continued in *Office of Government Reports* by Reorg. Plan No. II of 1939, effective July 1, 1939. Transferred to *Office of War Information* by EO 9182 of June 13, 1942, functioning in *Bureau of Special Services. Office* abolished by EO 9608 of Aug. 31, 1945, and *Bureau* transferred to *Bureau of the Budget.* Upon reestablishment of *Office of Government Reports,* by EO 9809 of Dec. 12, 1946, *Division of Press Intelligence* made unit of *Office.*

Price Administration, Office of Established by EO 8734 of Apr. 11, 1941, combining *Price Division* and *Consumer Division* of *National Defense Advisory Commission.* Renamed *Office of Price Administration* by EO 8875 of Aug. 28, 1941, which transferred *Civilian Allocation Division* to *Office of Production Management.* Consolidated with other agencies into *Office of Temporary Controls* by EO 9809 of Dec. 12, 1946, except *Financial Reporting Division,* transferred to Federal Trade Commission.

Price Commission Established by EO 11627 of Oct. 15, 1971. Abolished by EO 11695 of Jan. 11, 1973.

Price Decontrol Board Established by act of July 25, 1946 (60 Stat. 669). Effective period of act of Jan. 30, 1942 (56 Stat. 23), extended to June 30, 1947, by joint resolution of June 25, 1946 (60 Stat. 664).

Price Stability for Economic Growth, Cabinet Committee on Established by Presidential letter of Jan. 28, 1959. Abolished by Presidential direction Mar. 12, 1961.

Price Stabilization, Office of Established by General Order 2 of *Economic Stabilization Administrator* Jan. 24, 1951. *Director of Price Stabilization* provided for in EO 10161 of Sept. 9, 1950. Terminated Apr. 30, 1953, by EO 10434 of Feb. 6, 1954, and provisions of acts of June 30, 1952 (66 Stat. 296) and June 30, 1953 (67 Stat. 131).

Prices and Costs, Committee on Government Activities Affecting Established by EO 10802 of Jan. 23, 1959. Abolished by EO 10928 of Mar. 23, 1961.

Priorities Board Established by order of *Council of National Defense,* approved Oct. 18, 1940, and by EO 8572 of Oct. 21, 1940. EO 8572 revoked by EO 8629 of Jan. 7, 1941.

Prison Industries, Inc., Federal Established by EO 6917 of Dec. 11, 1934. Transferred to Justice Department by Reorg. Plan No. II of 1939, effective July 1, 1939.

Prison Industries Reorganization Administration
Functioned from Sept. 26, 1935, to Sept. 30, 1940, under authority of act of Apr. 8, 1935 (49 Stat. 115), and of EO's 7194 of Sept. 26, 1935, 7202 of Sept. 28, 1935, and 7649 of June 29, 1937. Terminated due to lack of funding.

Private Sector Programs, Office of   Functions transferred to the Office of Citizen Exchanges within the Bureau of Educational and Cultural Affairs, USIA, by act of Feb. 16, 1990 (104 Stat. 56).

Processing tax   *Agricultural Adjustment Administration's* function of collecting taxes declared unconstitutional by U.S. Supreme Court Jan. 6, 1936. Functions under acts of June 28, 1934 (48 Stat. 1275), Apr. 21, 1934 (48 Stat. 598), and Aug. 24, 1935 (49 Stat. 750) discontinued by repeal of these laws by act of Feb. 10, 1936 (49 Stat. 1106).

Processing Tax Board of Review   Established in Treasury Department by act of June 22, (49 Stat. 1652). Abolished by act of Oct. 21, 1942 (56 Stat. 967).

Proclamations   *See* **State Department**

Procurement, Commission on Government
Established by act of Nov. 26, 1969 (83 Stat. 269). Terminated Apr. 30, 1973, due to expiration of statutory authority.

Procurement and Assignment Service   Established by President Oct. 30, 1941. Transferred from *Office of Defense Health and Welfare Services* to *War Manpower Commission* by EO 9139 of Apr. 18, 1942. Transferred to *Federal Security Agency* by EO 9617 of Sept. 19, 1945, which terminated *Commission.*

Procurement Division   Established in Treasury Department by EO 6166 of June 10, 1933. Renamed *Bureau of Federal Supply* by Treasury Department Order 73 of Nov. 19, 1946, effective Jan. 1, 1947. Transferred to General Services Administration as Federal Supply Service by act of June 30, 1949 (63 Stat. 380).

Procurement Policy, Office of Federal   Established within Office of Management and Budget by act of Aug. 30, 1974 (88 Stat. 97). Abolished due to lack of funding and functions transferred to Office of Management and Budget by act of Oct 28, 1993 (107 Stat. 1236).

Product Standards Policy, Office of   Formerly separate operating unit under Assistant Secretary for Productivity, Technology and Innovation, Commerce Department. Transferred to *National Bureau of Standards* by departmental reorganization order, effective Apr. 27, 1982.

Production Areas, Committee for Congested
Established in Executive Office of the President by EO 9327 of Apr. 7, 1943. Terminated Dec. 31, 1944, by act of June 28, 1944 (58 Stat. 535).

Production Authority, National   Established in Commerce Department Sept. 11, 1950, by EO's 10161 of Sept. 9, 1950, 10193 of Dec. 16, 1950, and 10200 of Jan. 3, 1951. Abolished by Commerce

Secretary's order of Oct. 1, 1953, and functions merged into *Business and Defense Services Administration.*

Production Management, Office of   Established in *Office for Emergency Management* by EO 8629 of Jan. 7, 1941. Abolished by EO 9040 of Jan. 24, 1942, and personnel and property transferred to *War Production Board.*

Production and Marketing Administration
Established by Agriculture Secretary's Memorandum 1118 of Aug. 18, 1945. Functions transferred under Department reorganization by Secretary's Memorandum 1320, supp. 4, of Nov. 2, 1953.

Productivity Council, National   Established by EO 12089 of Oct. 23, 1978. EO 12089 revoked by EO 12379 of Aug. 17, 1982.

Programs, Bureau of International   Established by Commerce Secretary Aug. 8, 1961, by Departmental Orders 173 and 174. Abolished by Departmental Order 182 of Feb. 1, 1963, which established *Bureau of International Commerce.* Functions transferred to *Domestic and International Business Administration,* effective Nov. 17, 1972.

Programs, Office of Public   Established in the National Archives and Records Administration. Reorganized by Archivist under Notice 96–260, Sept. 23, 1996, effective Jan. 6, 1997. Functions restructured and transferred to Office of Records Services—Washington, DC.

Prohibition, Bureau of   Established by act of May 27, 1930 (46 Stat. 427). Investigative functions consolidated with functions of *Bureau of Investigation* into *Division of investigation,* Justice Department, by EO 6166 of June 10, 1933, which set as effective date Mar. 2, 1934, or such later date as fixed by President. All other functions performed by *Bureau of Prohibition* ordered transferred to such division in Justice Department as deemed desirable by Attorney General.

Property, Office of Surplus   Established in *Procurement Division,* Treasury Department, by EO 9425 of Feb. 19, 1944, and act of Oct. 3, 1944 (58 Stat. 765), under general direction of *Surplus Property Board* established by same legislation. Transferred to Commerce Department by EO 9541 of Apr. 19, 1945. Terminated by EO 9643 of Oct. 19, 1945, and activities and personnel transferred to *Reconstruction Finance Corporation.*

Property Administration, Surplus   *See* **War Property Administration, Surplus**

Property Board, Surplus   *See* **War Property Administration, Surplus**

Property Council, Federal   Established by EO 11724 of June 25, 1973, and reconstituted by EO 11954 of Jan. 7, 1977. Terminated by EO 12030 of Dec. 15, 1977.

Property Management and Disposal Service   *See* **Emergency Procurement Service**

Property Office, Surplus   Established in *Division of Territories and Island Possessions,* Interior

Department, under Regulation 1 of *Surplus Property Board,* Apr. 2, 1945. Transferred to *War Assets Administration* by EO 9828 of Feb. 21, 1947.

Property Review Board   Established by EO 12348 of Feb. 25, 1982. EO 12348 revoked by EO 12512 of Apr. 29, 1985.

Prospective Payment Assessment Commission Established by act of Apr. 20, 1983 (97 Stat. 159). Terminated by act of Aug. 5, 1997 (111 Stat. 354). Assets, staff, and continuing responsibility for reports transferred to the Medicare Payment Advisory Commission.

Provisions and Clothing, Bureau of   Established by acts of Aug. 31, 1842 (5 Stat. 579), and July 5, 1862 (12 Stat. 510). Designated *Bureau of Supplies and Accounts* by act of July 19, 1892 (27 Stat. 243). Abolished by Defense Department reorg. order of Mar. 9, 1966, and functions transferred to Navy Secretary (31 FR 7188).

Public.   *See other part of title*

Publications Commission, National Historical Established by act of Oct. 22, 1968 (82 Stat. 1293). Renamed National Historical Publications and Records Commission by act of Dec. 22, 1974 (88 Stat. 1734).

Puerto Rican Hurricane Relief Commission Established by act of Dec. 21, 1928 (45 Stat. 1067). No loans made after June 30, 1934, and *Commission* abolished June 3, 1935, by Public Resolution 22 (49 Stat. 320). Functions transferred to *Division of Territories and Island Possessions,* Interior Department. After June 30, 1946, collection work performed in *Puerto Rico Reconstruction Administration.* Following termination of *Administration,* remaining collection functions transferred to Agriculture Secretary by act of July 11, 1956 (70 Stat. 525).

Puerto Rico, U.S.-Puerto Rico Commission on the Status of   Established by act of Feb. 20, 1964 (78 Stat. 17). Terminated by terms of act.

Puerto Rico Reconstruction Administration Established in Interior Department by EO 7057 of May 28, 1935. Terminated Feb. 15, 1955, by act of Aug. 15, 1953 (67 Stat. 584).

Radiation Biology Laboratory   *See* **Radiation and Organisms, Division of**

Radiation Council, Federal   Established by EO 10831 of Aug. 14, 1959, and act of Sept. 23, 1959 (73 Stat. 688). Abolished by Reorg. Plan No. 3 of 1970, effective Dec. 2, 1970, and functions transferred to Environmental Protection Agency.

Radiation and Organisms, Division of   Established by Secretarial order of May 1, 1929, as part of Smithsonian Astrophysical Observatory. Renamed *Radiation Biology Laboratory* by Secretarial order of Feb. 16, 1965. Merged with *Chesapeake Center for Environmental Studies* by Secretarial order of July 1, 1983, to form Smithsonian Environmental Research Center.

Radio Commission, Federal   Established by act of Feb. 23, 1927 (44 Stat. 1162). Abolished by act of June 19, 1934 (48 Stat. 1102), and functions transferred to Federal Communications Commission.

Radio Division   Established by *National Emergency Council* July 1, 1938. Transferred to *Office of Education, Federal Security Agency,* by Reorg. Plan No. II of 1939, effective July 1, 1939. Terminated June 30, 1940, by terms of act of June 30, 1939 (53 Stat. 927).

Radio Propagation Laboratory, Central   Transferred from *National Bureau of Standards* to *Environmental Science Services Administration* by Commerce Department Order 2–A, effective July 13, 1965.

Radiological Health, National Center for Devices and   Renamed Center for Devices and Radiological Health by Food and Drug Administration notice of Mar. 9, 1984 (49 FR 10166).

Rail Public Counsel, Office of   Established by act of Feb. 5, 1976 (90 Stat. 51). Terminated Dec. 1, 1979, due to lack of funding.

Railroad Administration, U.S.   *See* **Railroads, Director General of**

Railroad and Airline Wage Board   Established by *Economic Stabilization Administrator's* General Order 7 of Sept. 27, 1951, pursuant to act of Sept. 8, 1950 (64 Stat. 816). Terminated Apr. 30, 1953, by EO 10434 of Feb. 6, 1953, and acts of June 30, 1952 (66 Stat. 296), and June 30, 1953 (67 Stat. 131).

Railroads, Director General of   Established under authority of act of Aug. 29, 1916 (39 Stat. 645). Organization of *U.S. Railroad Administration* announced Feb. 9, 1918. Office abolished by Reorg. Plan No. II of 1939, effective July 1, 1939, and functions transferred to Treasury Secretary.

Railway Association, U.S.   Established by act of Jan. 2, 1974 (87 Stat. 985). Terminated Apr. 1, 1987, by act of Oct. 21, 1986 (100 Stat. 1906).

Railway Labor Panel, National   Established by EO 9172 of May 22, 1942. EO 9172 revoked by EO 9883 of Aug. 11, 1947.

Real Estate Board, Federal   Established by EO 8034 of Jan. 14, 1939. Abolished by EO 10287 of Sept. 6, 1951.

Reclamation, Bureau of   *See* **Reclamation Service**

Reclamation Service   Established July 1902 in *Geological Survey* by Interior Secretary, pursuant to act of June 17, 1902 (32 Stat. 388). Separated from Survey in 1907 and renamed *Bureau of Reclamation* June 1923. Power marketing functions transferred to Energy Department by act of Aug. 4, 1977 (91 Stat. 578). *Bureau* renamed *Water and Power Resources Service* by Secretarial Order 3042 of Nov. 6, 1979. Renamed Bureau of Reclamation by Secretarial Order 3064 of May 18, 1981.

Reconciliation Service   Established by Director of Selective Service pursuant to EO 11804 of Sept. 16, 1974. Program terminated Apr. 2, 1980.

Reconstruction Finance Corporation   Established Feb. 2, 1932, by act of Jan. 22, 1932 (47 Stat. 5). Grouped with other agencies to form *Federal Loan Agency* by Reorg. Plan No. I of 1939, effective July 1, 1939. Transferred to Commerce Department by EO 9071 of Feb. 24, 1942. Returned to *Federal Loan Agency* by act of Feb. 24, 1945 (59 Stat. 5). *Agency* abolished by act of June 30, 1947 (61 Stat. 202), and functions assumed by *Corporation*. Functions relating to financing houses or site improvements, authorized by act of Aug. 10, 1948 (61 Stat. 1275), transferred to *Housing and Home Finance Agency* by Reorg. Plan No. 23 of 1950, effective July 10, 1950. *Corporation* Board of Directors, established by act of Jan. 22, 1932 (47 Stat. 5), abolished by Reorg. Plan No. 1 of 1951, effective May 1, 1951, and functions transferred to Administrator and *Loan Policy Board* established by same plan, effective Apr. 30, 1951. Act of July 30, 1953 (67 Stat. 230), provided for *RFC* succession until June 30, 1954, and for termination of its lending powers Sept. 28, 1953. Certain functions assigned to appropriate agencies for liquidation by Reorg. Plan No. 2 of 1954, effective July 1, 1954. *Corporation* abolished by Reorg. Plan No. 1 of 1957, effective June 30, 1957, and functions transferred to *Housing and Home Finance Agency,* General Services Administration, Small Business Administration, and Treasury Department.

Records Administration, Office of   Established in the National Archives and Records Adminstration. Reorganized by Archivist under Notice 96–260, Sept. 23, 1996, effective Jan. 6, 1997. Functions restructured and transferred to Office of Records Services—Washington, DC.

Records Centers, Office of Federal   Established in the National Archives and Records Administration. Reorganized by Archivist under Notice 96–260, Sept. 23, 1996, effective Jan. 6, 1997. Functions restructured and transferred to Office of Regional Records Services.

Records and Information Management, Office of   Functions transferred from *National Archives and Records Service* to *Automated Data and Telecommunications Service* by General Services Administrator's decision, effective Jan. 10, 1982, regionally and Apr. 1, 1982, in Washington, DC.

Recovery Administration, Advisory Council, National   Established by EO 7075 of June 15, 1935. Transferred to Commerce Department by EO 7252 of Dec. 21, 1935, and functions ordered terminated not later than Apr. 1, 1936, by same order. *Committee of Industrial Analysis* created by EO 7323 of Mar. 21, 1936, to complete work of *Council.*

Recovery Administration, National   Established by President pursuant to act of June 16, 1933 (48 Stat. 194). Provisions of title I of act repealed by Public Resolution 26 of June 14, 1935 (49 Stat. 375), and extension of *Administration* in skeletonized form authorized until Apr. 1, 1936. *Office of Administrator, National Recovery Administration,* created by EO 7075 of June 15, 1935. *Administration* terminated by EO 7252 of Dec. 21, 1935, which transferred *Division of Review, Division of Business Corporation,* and *Advisory Council* to Commerce Department for termination of functions by Apr. 1, 1936. *Consumers' Division* transferred to Labor Department by same order.

Recovery Review Board, National   Established by EO 6632 of Mar. 7, 1934. Abolished by EO 6771 of June 30, 1934.

Recreation, Bureau of Outdoor   Established in Interior Department by act of May 28, 1963 (77 Stat. 49). Terminated by Secretary's order of Jan. 25, 1978, and functions assumed by *Heritage Conservation and Recreation Service.*

Recreation and Natural Beauty, Citizens' Advisory Committee on   Established by EO 11278 of May 4, 1966. Terminated by EO 11472 of May 29, 1969.

Recreation and Natural Beauty, President's Council on   Established by EO 11278 of May 4, 1966. Terminated by EO 11472 of May 29, 1969.

Recreation Resources Review Commission, Outdoor   Established by act of June 28, 1958 (72 Stat. 238). Final report submitted to President January 1962 and terminated Sept. 1, 1962.

Regional Action Planning Commissions   Authorized by act of Aug. 26, 1965 (79 Stat. 552). Federal role abolished through repeal by act of Aug. 13, 1981 (95 Stat. 766). At time of repeal, eight commissions—Coastal Plains, Four Corners, New England, Old West Ozarks, Pacific Northwest, Southwest Border, Southwest Border Region, and Upper Great Lakes—affected.

Regional Archives, Office of Special and   Established in the National Archives and Records Adminstration. Reorganized by Archivist under Notice 96–260, Sept. 23, 1996, effective Jan. 6, 1997. Functions restructured and transferred between Office of Records Services—Washington, DC and Office of Regional Records Services.

Regional Councils, Federal   Established by EO 12314 of July 22, 1981. Abolished by EO 12407 of Feb. 22, 1983.

Regional Operations, Executive Director of   Established in Food and Drug Administration by *Health, Education, and Welfare Secretary's* order of May 20, 1971. Merged into Office of Regulatory Affairs by Health and Human Services Secretary's order of Nov. 5, 1984.

Regulatory Council, U.S.   Disbanded by Vice Presidential memorandum of Mar. 25, 1981. Certain functions continued in Regulatory Information Service Center.

Regulatory Relief, Presidential Task Force on   Establishment announced in President's remarks Jan. 22, 1981. Disbanded and functions transferred to Office of Management and Budget in August 1983.

Rehabilitation Services Administration   Functions transferred from *Health, Education, and Welfare Department* to Office of Special Education and Rehabilitative Services, Education Department, by act of Oct. 17, 1979 (93 Stat. 678), effective May 4, 1980.

Relief Corporation, Federal Surplus Organized under powers granted to President by act of June 16, 1933 (48 Stat. 195). Charter granted by State of Delaware Oct. 4, 1933, and amended Nov. 18, 1935, changing name to *Federal Surplus Commodities Corporation* and naming Agriculture Secretary, *Administrator of Agricultural Adjustment Administration,* and *Governor of Farm Credit Administration* as Board of Directors. Continued as agency under Agriculture Secretary by acts of June 28, 1937 (50 Stat. 323) and Feb. 16, 1938 (52 Stat. 38). Consolidated with *Division of Marketing and Marketing Agreements* into *Surplus Marketing Administration* by Reorg. Plan No. III of 1940, effective June 30, 1940. Merged into *Agricultural Marketing Administration* by EO 9069 of Feb. 23, 1942.

Relief and Rehabilitation Operations, Office of Foreign Established in State Department as announced by White House Nov. 21, 1942. Consolidated with *Foreign Economic Administration* by EO 9380 of Sept. 25, 1943.

Renegotiation Board Established by act of Mar. 23, 1951 (65 Stat. 7). Terminated Mar. 31, 1979, by act of Oct. 10, 1978 (92 Stat. 1043).

Rent Advisory Board Established by EO 11632 of Nov. 22, 1971. Abolished by EO 11695 of Jan. 11, 1973.

Rent Stabilization, Office of Established by General Order 9 of *Economic Stabilization Administrator* July 31, 1951, pursuant to act of June 30, 1947 (61 Stat. 193), and EO's 10161 of Sept. 9, 1950, and 10276 of July 31, 1951. Abolished by EO 10475 of July 31, 1953, and functions transferred to *Office of Defense Mobilization. Office of Research and Development* combined with *Office of Minerals Policy Development* in Interior Department May 21, 1976, under authority of Reorg. Plan No. 3 of 1950, effective May 24, 1950, to form *Office of Minerals Policy and Research Analysis.* Abolished Sept. 30, 1981, by Secretarial Order 3070 and functions transferred to *Bureau of Mines.*

Reports, Office of Government Established July 1, 1939, to perform functions of *National Emergency Council* abolished by Reorg. Plan No. II of 1939, effective July 1, 1939. Established as administrative unit of Executive Office of the President by EO 8248 of Sept. 8, 1939. Consolidated with *Office of War Information, Office for Emergency Management,* by EO 9182 of June 13, 1942. Reestablished in Executive Office of the President by EO 9809 of Dec. 12, 1946, which transferred to it functions of *Media Programming Division* and *Motion Picture Division, Office of War Mobilization and Reconversion,* and functions transferred from *Bureau of Special Services, Office of War Information,* to *Bureau of the Budget* by EO 9608 of Aug. 31, 1945. Subsequent to enactment of act of July 30, 1947 (61 Stat. 588), functions of *Office* restricted to advertising and motion picture liaison and operation of library. Terminated June 30, 1948.

Research, Office of University Transferred from *Office of Program Management and Administration,* Research and Special Programs Administration, to Office of Economics, Office of the Assistant Secretary for Policy and International Affairs, under authority of Transportation Department appropriation request for FY 1985, effective Oct. 1, 1984.

Research and Development Board Established in Defense Department by act of July 26, 1947 (61 Stat. 499). Abolished by Reorg. Plan No. 6 of 1953, effective June 30, 1953, and functions vested in Defense Secretary.

Research and Development Board, Joint Established June 6, 1946, by charter of Secretaries of War and Navy. Terminated on creation of *Research and Development Board* by act of July 26, 1947 (61 Stat. 506).

Research and Intelligence Service, Interim Established in State Department by EO 9621 of Sept. 20, 1945. Abolished Dec. 31, 1945, pursuant to terms of order.

Research Resources, Division of Established in National Institutes of Health, Health and Human Services Department. Renamed National Center for Research Resources by Secretarial notice of Feb. 23, 1990 (55 FR 6455) and act of June 10, 1993 (107 Stat. 178).

Research Service, Cooperative State Established by Agriculture Secretary's Memorandum 1462, supp. 1, of Aug. 31, 1961. Consolidated into *Science and Education Administration* by Secretary's order of Jan. 24, 1978. Reestablished as Cooperative State Research Service by Secretarial order of June 16, 1981.

Research and Service Division, Cooperative Functions transferred to Agriculture Secretary in *Farmer Cooperative Service* by act of Aug. 6, 1953 (67 Stat. 390).

Resettlement Administration Established by EO 7027 of Apr. 30, 1935. Functions transferred to Agriculture Department by EO 7530 of Dec. 31, 1936. Renamed *Farm Security Administration* by Secretary's Memorandum 732 of Sept. 1, 1937. Abolished by act of Aug. 14, 1946 (60 Stat. 1062) and functions incorporated into the *Farmers' Home Administration,* effective Jan. 1, 1947. *Farmers' Home Administration* abolished, effective Dec. 27, 1994, under authority of Secretary's Memorandum 1010–1 dated Oct. 20, 1994 (59 FR 66441). Functions assumed by the *Consolidated Farm Service Agency* and the *Rural Housing and Community Development Service.*

Resolution Trust Corporation Established by act of Aug. 9, 1989 (103 Stat. 369). Board of Directors of the Corporation abolished by act of Dec. 12, 1991 (105 Stat. 1769). Corporation functions terminated pursuant to act of Dec. 17, 1993 (107 Stat. 2369).

Resources Board and Advisory Committee, National Established by EO 6777 of June 30, 1934. Abolished by EO 7065 of June 7, 1935, and functions transferred to *National Resources Committee.*

Resources Committee, National Established by EO 7065 of June 7, 1935. Abolished by Reorg. Plan No. I of 1939, effective July 1, 1939, and functions transferred to *National Resources Planning Board* in

Executive Office of the President. *Board* terminated by act of June 26, 1943 (57 Stat. 169).

Resources Planning Board, National *See* **Resources Committee, National**

Retired Executives, Service Corps of Established in *ACTION* by act of Oct. 1, 1973 (87 Stat. 404). Transferred to Small Business Administration by EO 11871 of July 18, 1975.

Retraining and Reemployment Administration Established by EO 9427 of Feb. 24, 1944, and act of Oct. 3, 1944 (58 Stat. 788). Transferred from *Office of War Mobilization and Reconversion* to Labor Department by EO 9617 of Sept. 19, 1945. Terminated pursuant to terms of act.

Revenue Sharing, Office of Established by Treasury Secretary to administer programs authorized by acts of Oct. 20, 1972 (86 Stat. 919), and July 22, 1976 (90 Stat. 999). Transferred from Office of the Secretary to Assistant Secretary (Domestic Finance) by Treasury Department Order 242, rev. 1, of May 17, 1976.

Review, Division of Established in *National Recovery Administration* by EO 7075 of June 15, 1935. Transferred to Commerce Department by EO 7252 of Dec. 21, 1935, and functions terminated Apr. 1, 1936. *Committee of Industrial Analysis* created by EO 7323 of Mar. 21, 1936, to complete work of *Division*.

RFC Mortgage Company Organized under laws of Maryland Mar. 14, 1935, pursuant to act of Jan. 22, 1932 (47 Stat. 5). Grouped with other agencies to form *Federal Loan Agency* by Reorg. Plan No. I of 1939, effective July 1, 1939. Transferred to Commerce Department by EO 9071 of Feb. 24, 1942. Returned to *Federal Loan Agency* by act of Feb. 24, 1945 (59 Stat. 5). Assets and liabilities transferred to *Reconstruction Finance Corporation* by act of June 30, 1947 (61 Stat. 207).

River Basins, Neches, Trinity, Brazos, Colorado, Guadalupe, San Antonio, Nueces, and San Jacinto, and Intervening Areas, U.S. Study Commission on Established by act of Aug. 28, 1958 (72 Stat. 1058). Terminated June 30, 1962.

River Basins, Savannah, Altamaha, Saint Marys, Apalachicola-Chattahoochee, and Perdido-Escambia, and Intervening Areas, U.S. Study Commission on Established by act of Aug. 28, 1958 (72 Stat. 1090). Terminated Dec. 23, 1962.

Road Inquiry, Office of Established by Agriculture Secretary under authority of act of Aug. 8, 1894 (28 Stat. 264). Federal aid for highways to be administered by Agriculture Secretary through *Office of Public Roads and Rural Engineering* authorized by act of July 11, 1916 (39 Stat. 355), known as *Bureau of Public Roads* after July 1918. Transferred to *Federal Works Agency* by Reorg. Plan No. I of 1939, effective July 1, 1939, and renamed *Public Roads Administration.* Transferred to General Services Administration as *Bureau of Public Roads* by act of June 30, 1949 (63 Stat. 380). Transferred to Commerce Department by Reorg. Plan No. 7 of 1949, effective Aug. 20, 1949. Transferred to Transportation Secretary by act of Oct. 15, 1966 (80

Stat. 931), and functions assigned to Federal Highway Administration.

Roads, Bureau of Public *See* **Road Inquiry, Office of**

Roads Administration, Public *See* **Road Inquiry, Office of**

Roads and Rural Engineering, Office of Public *See* **Road Inquiry, Office of**

Rock Creek and Potomac Parkway Commission Established by act of Mar. 14, 1913 (37 Stat. 885). Abolished by EO 6166 of June 10, 1933, and functions transferred to *Office of National Parks, Buildings, and Reservations,* Interior Department.

Roosevelt Centennial Commission, Theodore Established by joint resolution of July 28, 1955 (69 Stat. 383). Terminated Oct. 27, 1959, pursuant to terms of act.

Roosevelt Library, Franklin D. Functions assigned to National Park Service by Reorg. Plan No. 3 of 1946, effective July 16, 1946, transferred to General Services Administration by Reorg. Plan No. 1 of 1963, effective July 27, 1963.

Roosevelt Library, Trustees of the Franklin D. Established by joint resolution of July 18, 1939 (53 Stat. 1063). Transferred to General Services Administration by act of June 30, 1949 (63 Stat. 381). Abolished by act of Mar. 5, 1958 (72 Stat. 34), and Library operated by *National Archives and Records Service,* General Services Administration.

Roosevelt Memorial Commission, Franklin Delano Established by joint resolution of Aug. 11, 1955 (69 Stat. 694). Terminated by act of Nov. 14, 1997 (111 Stat. 1601).

Rubber Development Corporation Establishment announced Feb. 20, 1943, by Commerce Secretary. Organized under laws of Delaware as subsidiary of *Reconstruction Finance Corporation.* Assumed all activities of *Rubber Reserve Company* relating to development of foreign rubber sources and procurement of rubber therefrom. Functions transferred to *Office of Economic Warfare* by EO 9361 of July 15, 1943. *Office* consolidated into *Foreign Economic Administration* by EO 9380 of Sept. 25, 1943. *Office* returned to *Reconstruction Finance Corporation* by EO 9630 of Sept. 27, 1945. Certificate of incorporation expired June 30, 1947.

Rubber Producing Facilities Disposal Commission Established by act of Aug. 7, 1953 (67 Stat. 408). Functions transferred to *Federal Facilities Corporation* by EO 10678 of Sept. 20, 1956.

Rubber Reserve Company Established June 28, 1940, under act of Jan. 22, 1932 (47 Stat. 5). Transferred from *Federal Loan Agency* to Commerce Department by EO 9071 of Feb. 24, 1942. Returned to *Federal Loan Agency* by act of Feb. 24, 1945 (59 Stat. 5). Dissolved by act of June 30, 1945 (59 Stat. 310), and functions transferred to *Reconstruction Finance Corporation.*

Rural Areas Development, Office of Established by Agriculture Secretary's memorandum in 1961 (revised Sept. 21, 1962). Renamed *Rural Community Development Service* by Secretary's Memorandum 1570 of Feb. 24, 1965. .

Rural Business and Cooperative Development Service Established within Agriculture Department by Secretary's Memorandum 1020–34 dated Dec. 31, 1991. Renamed Rural Business-Cooperative Service (61 FR 2899), effective Jan. 30, 1996.

Rural Community Development Service Established by Agriculture Secretary's Memorandum 1570 of Feb. 25, 1965, to supersede *Office of Rural Areas Development.* Abolished Feb. 2, 1970, by Secretary's Memorandum 1670 of Jan. 30, 1970, and functions transferred to other agencies in department.

Rural Development Administration Established within Agriculture Department by Secretary's Memorandum 1020–34 dated Dec. 31, 1991. Abolished Dec. 27, 1994 (59 FR 66441) under authority of Secretary's Memorandum 1010–1 dated Oct. 20, 1994. Functions assumed by the Rural Business and Cooperative Development Service.

Rural Development Committee *See* **Rural Development Program, Committee for**

Rural Development Policy, Office of Established initially as *Office of Rural Development Policy Management and Coordination,* Farmers Home Administration, by Agriculture Secretary's Memorandum 1020–3 of Oct. 26, 1981. Abolished in 1986 due to lack of funding.

Rural Development Program, Committee for Established by EO 10847 of Oct. 12, 1959. Abolished by EO 11122 of Oct. 16, 1963, which established *Rural Development Committee. Committee* superseded by EO 11307 of Sept. 30, 1966, and functions assumed by Agriculture Secretary.

Rural Development Service Established by Agriculture Secretarial order in 1973. Functions transferred to *Office of Rural Development Coordination and Planning, Farmers Home Administration,* by Secretarial order in 1978.

Rural Electrification Administration Established by EO 7037 of May 11, 1935. Functions transferred by EO 7458 of Sept. 26, 1936, to *Rural Electrification Administration* established by act of May 20, 1936 (49 Stat. 1363). Transferred to Agriculture Department by Reorg. Plan No. II of 1939, effective July 1, 1939. Abolished by Secretary's Memorandum 1010–1 dated Oct. 20, 1994, and functions assumed by Rural Utilities Service.

Rural Housing and Community Development Service Established by act of Oct. 13, 1994 (108 Stat. 3219). Renamed Rural Housing Service (61 FR 2899), effective Jan. 30, 1996.

Rural Rehabilitation Division Established April 1934 by act of May 12, 1933 (48 Stat. 55). Functions transferred to *Resettlement Administration* by *Federal Emergency Relief Administrator's* order of June 19, 1935.

Saint Elizabeths Hospital *See* **Insane, Government Hospital for the**

Saint Lawrence Seaway Development Corporation Established by act of May 13, 1954 (68 Stat. 92). Commerce Secretary given direction of general policies of *Corporation* by EO 10771 of June 20, 1958. Transferred to Transportation Department by act of Oct. 15, 1966 (80 Stat. 931).

Salary Stabilization, Office of *See* **Salary Stabilization Board**

Salary Stabilization Board Established May 10, 1951, by *Economic Stabilization Administrator's* General Order 8. Stabilization program administered by *Office of Salary Stabilization.* Terminated Apr. 30, 1953, by EO 10434 of Feb. 6, 1953, and acts of June 30, 1952 (66 Stat. 296), and June 30, 1953 (67 Stat. 131).

Sales Manager, Office of the General Established by Agriculture Secretary Feb. 29, 1976. Consolidated with Foreign Agricultural Service by Secretary's Memorandum 2001 of Nov. 29, 1979.

Savings Bonds, Interdepartmental Committee for the Voluntary Payroll Savings Plan for the Purchase of U.S. Established by EO 11532 of June 2, 1970. Superseded by EO 11981 of Mar. 29, 1977, which established Interagency Committee for the Purchase of U.S. Savings Bonds.

Savings and Loan Advisory Council, Federal Established by act of Oct. 6, 1972 (86 Stat. 770). Continued by act of Dec. 26, 1974 (88 Stat. 1739). Terminated by act of Aug. 9, 1989 (103 Stat. 422).

Savings and Loan Insurance Corporation, Federal Established by act of June 27, 1934 (48 Stat. 1246). Grouped with other agencies to form *Federal Loan Agency* by Reorg. Plan No. I of 1939, effective July 1, 1939. Transferred to *Federal Home Loan Bank Administration, National Housing Agency,* by EO 9070 of Feb. 24, 1942. Board of Trustees abolished by Reorg. Plan No. 3 of 1947, effective July 27, 1947, and functions transferred to *Home Loan Bank Board.* Abolished by act of Aug. 9, 1989 (103 Stat. 354).

Savings Bonds Division, United States Established by Departmental Order 62 of Dec. 26, 1945, as successor to the War and Finance Division, War Savings Staff, and Defense Savings Staff. Functions transferred to Bureau of Public Debt by Departmental Order 101–05 of May 11, 1994, and *Division* renamed Savings Bond Marketing Office.

Science, Engineering, and Technology, Federal Coordinating Council for Established by act of May 11, 1976 (90 Stat. 471). Abolished by Reorg. Plan No. 1 of 1977, effective Feb. 26, 1978, and functions transferred to President. Functions redelegated to Director of the Office of Science and Technology Policy and Federal Coordinating Council for Science, Engineering, and Technology, established by EO 12039 of Feb. 24, 1978.

Science, Engineering, and Technology Panel, Intergovernmental Established by act of May 11, 1976 (90 Stat. 465). Abolished by Reorg. Plan No. 1 of 1977, effective Feb. 26, 1978, and functions transferred to President. Functions redelegated to Director of Office of Science and Technology Policy by EO 12039 of Feb. 24, 1978, which established Intergovernmental Science, Engineering, and Technology Advisory Panel.

Science Advisory Committee, President's
Established by President Apr. 20, 1951, and reconstituted Nov. 22, 1957. Terminated with *Office of Science and Technology,* effective July 1, 1973.

Science Exhibit-Century 21 Exposition, U.S.
Established Jan. 20, 1960, by Commerce Department Order 167. Abolished by revocation of order on June 5, 1963.

Science and Technology, Federal Council for   *See* **Scientific Research and Development, Interdepartmental Committee on**

Science and Technology, Office of   Established by Reorg. Plan No. 2 of 1962, effective June 8, 1962. *Office* abolished by Reorg. Plan No. 1 of 1973, effective June 30, 1973, and functions transferred to National Science Foundation.

Science and Technology, President's Committee on
Established by act of May 11, 1976 (90 Stat. 468). Abolished by Reorg. Plan No. 1 of 1977, effective Feb. 26, 1978, and functions transferred to President.

Scientific and Policy Advisory Committee
Established by act of Sept. 26, 1961 (75 Stat. 631). Terminated Apr. 30, 1996 under terms of act.

Scientific Research and Development, Interdepartmental Committee on   Established by EO 9912 of Dec. 24, 1947. EO 9912 revoked by EO 10807 of Mar. 13, 1959, which established *Federal Council for Science and Technology.* Abolished by act of May 11, 1976 (90 Stat. 472).

Scientific Research and Development, Office of
Established in *Office for Emergency Management* by EO 8807 of June 28, 1941. Terminated by EO 9913 of Dec. 26, 1947, and property transferred to *National Military Establishment* for liquidation.

Scientists and Engineers, National Committee for the Development of   Established by President Apr. 3, 1956. Renamed *President's Committee on Scientists and Engineers* May 7, 1957. Final report submitted Dec. 17, 1958, and expired Dec. 31, 1958.

Scientists and Engineers, President's Committee on
See **Scientists and Engineers, National Committee for the Development of**

Screw Thread Commission, National   Established by act of July 18, 1918 (40 Stat. 912). Terminated by EO 6166 of June 10, 1933, and records transferred to Commerce Department, effective Mar. 2, 1934. Informal Interdepartmental Screw Thread Committee established on Sept. 14, 1939, consisting of *War,* Navy, and Commerce Department representatives.

Security, Commission on Government   Established by act of Aug. 9, 1955 (69 Stat. 595). Terminated Sept. 22, 1957, pursuant to terms of act.

Security, Office of the Director for Mutual   *See* **Security Agency, Mutual**

Security Agency, Federal   Established by Reorg. Plan No. I of 1939, effective July 1, 1939, grouping under one administration *Office of Education, Public Health Service, Social Security Board, U.S. Employment Service, Civilian Conservation Corps,* and *National Youth Administration.* Abolished by Reorg. Plan No. 1 of 1953, effective Apr. 11, 1953, and functions and units transferred to *Health, Education, and Welfare Department.*

Security Agency, Mutual   Established and continued by acts of Oct. 10, 1951 (65 Stat. 373) and June 20, 1952 (66 Stat. 141). *Agency* and *Office of Director for Mutual Security* abolished by Reorg. Plan No. 7 of 1953, effective Aug. 1, 1953, and functions transferred to *Foreign Operations Administration,* established by same plan.

Security and Individual Rights, President's Commission on Internal   Established by EO 10207 of Jan. 23, 1951. Terminated by EO 10305 of Nov. 14, 1951.

Security Resources Board, National   Established by act of July 26, 1947 (61 Stat. 499). Transferred to Executive Office of the President by Reorg. Plan No. 4 of 1949, effective Aug. 20, 1949. Functions of *Board* transferred to Chairman and *Board* made advisory to him by Reorg. Plan No. 25 of 1950, effective July 10, 1950. Functions delegated by Executive order transferred to *Office of Defense Mobilization* by EO 10438 of Mar. 13, 1953. *Board* abolished by Reorg. Plan No. 3 of 1953, effective June 12, 1953, and remaining functions transferred to *Office of Defense Mobilization.*

Security Training Commission, National
Established by act of June 19, 1951 (65 Stat. 75). Expired June 30, 1957, pursuant to Presidential letter of Mar. 25, 1957.

Seed Loan Office   Authorized by Presidential letters of July 26, 1918, and July 26, 1919, to Agriculture Secretary. Further authorized by act of Mar. 3, 1921 (41 Stat. 1347). Office transferred to Farm Credit Administration by EO 6084 of Mar. 27, 1933.

Selective Service Appeal Board, National
Established by EO 9988 of Aug. 20, 1948. Inactive as of Apr. 11, 1975.

Selective Service Records, Office of   *See* **Selective Service System**

Selective Service System   Established by act of Sept. 16, 1940 (54 Stat. 885). Placed under jurisdiction of *War Manpower Commission* by EO 9279 of Dec. 5, 1942, and designated *Bureau of Selective Service.* Designated Selective Service System, separate agency, by EO 9410 of Dec. 23, 1943. Transferred for liquidation to *Office of Selective Service Records* established by act of Mar. 31, 1947 (61 Stat. 31). Transferred to Selective Service System by act of June 24, 1948 (62 Stat. 604).

Self-Help Development and Technical Development, Office of   Established in *National Consumer Cooperative Bank* by act of Aug. 20, 1978 (92 Stat. 499). Abolished by act of Aug. 13,

1981 (95 Stat. 437), and assets transferred to Consumer Cooperative Development Corporation, Commerce Department, Dec. 30, 1982.

Services, Bureau of Special   *See* **Office of War Information**

Services, Division of Central Administrative Established by *Liaison Officer for Emergency Management* pursuant to Presidential letter of Feb. 28, 1941. Terminated by EO 9471 of Aug. 25, 1944, and functions discontinued or transferred to constituent agencies of *Office for Emergency Management* and other agencies.

Shipbuilding Stabilization Committee Originally organized by *National Defense Advisory Commission* in 1940. Established August 1942 by *War Production Board*. Transferred to Labor Department from *Civilian Production Administration*, successor agency to *Board*, by EO 9656 of Nov. 15, 1945. Terminated June 30, 1947.

Shipping Board, U.S. Established by act of Sept. 7, 1916 (39 Stat. 729). Abolished by EO 6166 of June 10, 1933, and functions, including those with respect to *U.S. Shipping Board Merchant Fleet Corporation*, transferred to *U.S. Shipping Board Bureau*, Commerce Department, effective Mar. 2, 1934. Separation of employees deferred until Sept. 30, 1933, by EO 6245 of Aug. 9, 1933. Functions assumed by *U.S. Maritime Commission* Oct. 26, 1936, pursuant to act of June 29, 1936 (49 Stat. 1985).

Shipping Board Bureau, U.S.   *See* **Shipping Board, U.S.**

Shipping Board Emergency Fleet Corporation, U.S. Established Apr. 16, 1917, under authority of act of Sept. 7, 1916 (39 Stat. 729). Renamed *U.S. Shipping Board Merchant Fleet Corporation* by act of Feb. 11, 1927 (44 Stat. 1083). Terminated Oct. 26, 1936, under provisions of act of June 29, 1936 (49 Stat. 1985), and functions transferred to *U.S. Maritime Commission*.

Shipping Board Merchant Fleet Corporation, U.S. *See* **Shipping Board Emergency Fleet Corporation, U.S.**

Ships, Bureau of Established by act of June 20, 1940 (54 Stat. 493), to replace *Bureau of Engineering* and *Bureau of Construction and Repair*. Abolished by Defense Department reorg. order of Mar. 9, 1966, and functions transferred to Navy Secretary (31 FR 7188).

Simpson Historical Research Center, Albert F. Renamed Headquarters USAF Historical Research Center by Defense Secretary's special order of Dec. 16, 1983.

Smithsonian Symposia and Seminars, Office of Renamed Office of Interdisciplinary Studies by Smithsonian Institution announcement of Mar. 16, 1987.

Social Development Institute, Inter-American Established by act of Dec. 30, 1969 (83 Stat. 821). Renamed Inter-American Foundation by act of Feb. 7, 1972 (86 Stat. 34).

Social Protection, Committee on Established in *Office of Defense Health and Welfare Services* by administrative order June 14, 1941. Functions transferred to *Federal Security Agency* by EO 9338 of Apr. 29, 1943.

Social and Rehabilitation Service Established by *Health, Education, and Welfare Secretary's* reorganization of Aug. 15, 1967. Abolished by Secretary's reorganization of Mar. 8, 1977 (42 FR 13262), and constituent units—*Medical Services Administration, Assistance Payments Administration, Office of Child Support Enforcement, and Public Services Administration*—transferred.

Social Security Administration   *See* **Social Security Board**

Social Security Board Established by act of Aug. 14, 1935 (49 Stat. 620). Incorporated into *Federal Security Agency* by Reorg. Plan No. I of 1939, effective July 1, 1939. *Social Security Board* abolished and Social Security Administration established by Reorg. Plan No. 2 of 1946 (5 U.S.C. app.), effective July 16, 1946, and functions of the *Board* transferred to *Federal Security Administrator*. Social Security Administration transferred from the *Federal Security Agency* by Reorganization Plan No. 1 of 1953 (5 U.S.C. app.), effective Apr. 11, 1953, to the *Department of Health, Education, and Welfare*. Social Security Administration became an independent agency in the executive branch by act of Aug. 15, 1994 (108 Stat. 1464), effective Mar. 31, 1995.

Soil Conservation Service   *See* **Soil Erosion Service**

Soil Erosion Service Established in Interior Department following allotment made Aug. 25, 1933. Transferred to Agriculture Department by Interior Secretary's administrative order of Mar. 25, 1935. Made *Soil Conservation Service* by order of Agriculture Secretary, Apr. 27, 1935, pursuant to provisions of act of Apr. 27, 1935 (49 Stat. 163). Certain functions of *Soil Conservation Service* under jurisdiction of Interior Department transferred from Agriculture Department to Interior Department by Reorg. Plan No. IV of 1940, effective June 30, 1940. *Soil Conservation Service* abolished by act of Oct. 13, 1994 (108 Stat. 3225) and functions assumed by the Natural Resources Conservation Service.

Soils, Bureau of   *See* **Agricultural and Industrial Chemistry, Bureau of** and **Plant Industry, Bureau of**

Solicitor General, Office of Assistant Established in Justice Department by act of June 16, 1933 (48 Stat. 307). Terminated by Reorg. Plan No. 2 of 1950, effective May 24, 1950.

Southeastern Power Administration Established by Interior Secretary in 1943 to carry out functions under act of Dec. 22, 1944 (58 Stat. 890). Transferred to Energy Department by act of Aug. 4, 1977 (91 Stat. 578).

Southwestern Power Administration Established by Interior Secretary in 1943 to carry out functions under act of Dec. 22, 1944 (58 Stat. 890). Transferred to Energy Department by act of Aug. 4, 1977 (91 Stat. 578).

Space Access and Technology, Office of
Established in the National Aeronautics and Space
Adminstration. Abolished by Administrator's order of
Feb. 24, 1997.

Space Communications, Office of   Established in
the National Aeronautics and Space Administration.
Abolished by Administrator's order of Feb. 24, 1997.

Space Science, Office of   See **Space and Terrestrial
Applications, Office of**

Space Science Board   Renamed Space Studies
Board by authority of the National Research
Council, National Academy of Sciences, effective
May 8, 1989.

Space Station, Office of   Established in the National
Aeronautics and Space Administration. Abolished in
1990 and remaining functions transferred to the
Office of Space Flight.

Space Technology Laboratories, National
Renamed John C. Stennis Space Center by EO
12641 of May 20, 1988.

Space and Terrestrial Applications, Office of
Combined with *Office of Space Science* to form
Office of Space Science and Applications by
National Aeronautics and Space Administrator's
announcement of Sept. 29, 1981.

Space Tracking and Data Systems, Office of
Renamed Office of Space Operations by National
Aeronautics and Space Administrator's
announcement of Jan. 9, 1987.

Space Transportation Operations, Office of
Combined with *Office of Space Transportation
Systems* to form Office of Space Transportation
Systems, National Aeronautics and Space
Administration, effective July 1982.

Space Transportation Systems, Office of   See **Space
Transportation Operations, Office of**

**Spanish-Speaking People, Cabinet Committee on
Opportunities for**   See **Mexican-American Affairs,
Interagency Committee on**

Special.   *See other part of title*

Specifications Board, Federal   Established by
Bureau of the Budget Circular 42 of Oct. 10, 1921.
Transferred from *Federal Coordinating Service* to
Procurement Division by Treasury Secretary's order
of Oct. 9, 1933. *Board* superseded by *Federal
Specifications Executive Committee*, set up by
Director of Procurement under Circular Letter 106 of
July 16, 1935.

Sport Fisheries and Wildlife, Bureau of   Established
in Interior Department by act of Aug. 8, 1956 (70
Stat. 1119). *Bureau* replaced by U.S. Fish and
Wildlife Service pursuant to act of Apr. 22, 1974 (88
Stat. 92).

Standards, National Bureau of   See **Weights and
Measures, Office of Standard**

State Department   Duty of Secretary of State of
procuring copies of all statutes of the States, as
provided for in act of Sept. 28, 1789 (R.S. 206),
abolished by Reorg. Plan No. 20 of 1950, effective
May 24, 1950. Functions of numbering, editing, and
distributing proclamations and Executive orders
transferred from State Department to *Division of the
Federal Register, National Archives,* by EO 7298 of
Feb. 18, 1936. Duty of Secretary of State of
publishing Executive proclamations and treaties in
newspapers in District of Columbia, provided for in
act of July 31, 1876 (19 Stat. 105), abolished by
Reorg. Plan No. 20 of 1950, effective May 24, 1950.
Functions concerning publication of U.S. Statutes at
Large, acts and joint resolutions in pamphlet form
known as slip laws, and amendments to the
Constitution; electoral votes for President and Vice
President; and Territorial papers transferred from
State Department to General Services Administrator
by Reorg. Plan No. 20 of 1950. (*See also* **Archives
Establishment, National**)

State and Local Cooperation, Division of
Established by *Advisory Commission to Council of
National Defense* Aug. 5, 1940. Transferred to
Office of Civilian Defense.

**State and Local Government Cooperation,
Committee on**   Established by EO 11627 of Oct 15,
1971. Abolished by EO 11695 of Jan. 11, 1973.

State Technical Services, Office of   Established by
Commerce Secretary Nov. 19, 1965, pursuant to act
of Sept. 14, 1965 (79 Stat. 697). Abolished by
Secretary, effective June 30, 1970.

Statistical Board, Central   Organized Aug. 9, 1933,
by EO 6225 of July 27, 1933. Transferred to *Bureau
of the Budget* by Reorg. Plan No. I of 1939, effective
July 1, 1939. Expired July 25, 1940, and functions
taken over by *Division of Statistical Standards,
Bureau of the Budget.*

Statistical Committee, Central   Established by act of
July 25, 1935 (49 Stat. 498). Abolished by Reorg.
Plan No. I of 1939, effective July 1, 1939, and
functions transferred to *Bureau of the Budget.*

Statistical Policy Coordination Committee
Established by EO 12013 of Oct. 7, 1977. Abolished
by EO 12318 of Aug. 21, 1981.

Statistical Reporting Service   Established by
Agriculture Secretary's Memorandum 1446, supp. 1,
part 3, of 1961. Consolidated with other
departmental units into *Economics, Statistics, and
Cooperatives Service* by Secretary's Memorandum
1927, effective Dec. 23, 1977. Redesignated as
Statistical Reporting Service by Secretary's order of
Oct. 1, 1981. Renamed National Agricultural
Statistics Service.

Statistics Administration, Social and Economic
Established Jan. 1, 1972, by Commerce Secretary.
Terminated by Commerce Department Organization
Order 10–2, effective Aug. 4, 1975 (40 FR 42765).
Bureau of Economic Analysis and Bureau of the
Census restored as primary operating units of
Commerce Department by Organization Orders 35–
1A and 2A, effective Aug. 4, 1975.

Statutes at Large   See **State Department**

Statutes of the States   See **State Department**

Steam Engineering, Bureau of Established in Navy Department by act of July 5, 1862 (12 Stat. 510). Redesignated as *Bureau of Engineering* by act of June 4, 1920 (41 Stat. 828). Abolished by act of June 20, 1940 (54 Stat. 492), and functions transferred to *Bureau of Ships.*

Steamboat Inspection Service President authorized to appoint *Service* by act of June 28, 1838 (5 Stat. 252). Treasury Secretary authorized to establish boards of local inspectors at enumerated ports throughout the U.S. by act of Feb. 28, 1871 (16 Stat. 440). Authority to appoint boards of local inspectors delegated to *Secretary of Commerce and Labor* by act of Mar. 4, 1905 (33 Stat. 1026). Consolidated with *Bureau of Navigation and Steamboat Inspection* by act of June 30, 1932 (47 Stat. 415).

Stock Catalog Board, Federal Standard Originated by act of Mar. 2, 1929 (45 Stat. 1461). Transferred from *Federal Coordinating Service* to *Procurement Division* by Treasury Secretary's order of Oct. 9, 1933.

Strategic Defense Initiative Organization Established in 1986 as a separate agency of the Department of Defense. Renamed Ballistic Missile Defense Organization by Deputy Secretary's memorandum in May 1993.

Strategic Services, Office of *See* **Information, Office of Coordinator of**

Subversive Activities Control Board Established by act of Sept. 23, 1950 (64 Stat. 987). Terminated June 30, 1973, due to lack of funding.

Sugar Division Created by act of May 12, 1933 (48 Stat. 31), authorized by act of Sept. 1, 1937 (50 Stat. 903). Taken from *Agricultural Adjustment Administration* and made independent division of Agriculture Department by Secretary's Memorandum 783, effective Oct. 16, 1938. Placed under *Agricultural Conservation and Adjustment Administration* by EO 9069 of Feb. 23, 1942, functioning as *Sugar Agency.* Functions transferred to *Food Distribution Administration* by EO 9280 of Dec. 5, 1942.

Sugar Rationing Administration Established by Agriculture Secretary's Memorandum 1190 of Mar. 31, 1947, under authority of act of Mar. 31, 1947 (61 Stat. 35). Terminated Mar. 31, 1948, on expiration of authority.

Supplies and Accounts, Bureau of *See* **Provisions and Clothing, Bureau of**

Supplies and Shortages, National Commission on Established by act of Sept. 30, 1974 (88 Stat. 1168). Terminated Mar. 31, 1977, pursuant to terms of act.

Supply, Bureau of Federal *See* **Procurement Division**

Supply, Office of Renamed Office of Procurement and Property by Smithsonian Institution announcement of Nov. 4, 1986.

Supply Committee, General Established by act of June 17, 1910 (36 Stat. 531). Abolished by EO 6166 of June 10, 1933, effective Mar. 2, 1934, and functions transferred to *Procurement Division,* Treasury Department.

Supply Priorities and Allocations Board Established in *Office for Emergency Management* by EO 8875 of Aug. 28, 1941. Abolished by EO 9024 of Jan. 16, 1942, and functions transferred to *War Production Board.*

Supply Service, Federal Renamed *Office of Personal Property* by General Services Administration order, effective Sept. 28, 1982; later renamed *Office of Federal Supply and Services* by GSA order of Jan. 22, 1983; then redesignated Federal Supply Service.

Surveys and Maps, Federal Board of *See* **Surveys and Maps of the Federal Government, Board of**

Surveys and Maps of the Federal Government, Board of Established by EO 3206 of Dec. 30, 1919. Renamed *Federal Board of Surveys and Maps* by EO 7262 of Jan. 4, 1936. Abolished by EO 9094 of Mar. 10, 1942, and functions transferred to Director, *Bureau of the Budget.*

Space System Development, Office of Established in the National Aeronautics and Space Administration. Renamed Office of Space Access and Technology in 1995.

Tariff Commission, U.S. Established by act of Sept. 8, 1916 (39 Stat. 795). Renamed U.S. International Trade Commission by act of Jan. 3, 1975 (88 Stat. 2009).

Tax Appeals, Board of Established as an independent agency within the executive branch by act of June 2, 1924 (43 Stat. 336). Continued by acts of Feb. 26, 1926 (44 Stat. 105) and Feb. 10, 1939 (53 Stat. 158). Renamed *Tax Court of the United States* by act of Aug. 16, 1954 (68A Stat. 879). Renamed United States Tax Court by act of Dec. 30, 1969 (83 Stat. 730).

Technical Cooperation Administration Transferred from State Department to *Mutual Security Agency* by EO 10458 of June 1, 1953. Transferred to *Foreign Operations Administration* by Reorg. Plan No. 7 of 1953, effective Aug. 1, 1953.

Technical Services, Office of Designated unit of Office of the Commerce Secretary by Department Order 179, July 23, 1962. Functions transferred to *National Bureau of Standards* by Order 90 of Jan. 30, 1964.

Technology Assessment, Office of Created by act of Oct. 13, 1972 (86 Stat. 797). Office inactive as of Sept. 30, 1995.

Technology, Automation, and Economic Progress, National Commission on Established by act of Aug. 19, 1964 (78 Stat. 463). Terminated January 1966 pursuant to terms of act.

Telecommunications Advisor to the President Established in Executive Office of the President by EO 10297 of Oct. 9, 1951. EO 10297 revoked by EO 10460 of June 16, 1953, and functions transferred to Director of *Office of Defense Mobilization.*

Telecommunications Management, Director of
Established in *Office of Emergency Planning* by EO 10995 of Feb. 16, 1962. Assignment of radio frequencies delegated to Government agencies and foreign diplomatic establishments by EO 11084 of Feb. 16, 1963. Abolished by Reorg. Plan No. 1 of 1970, effective Apr. 20, 1970.

Telecommunications Policy, Office of Established in Executive Office of the President by Reorg. Plan No. 1 of 1970, effective Apr. 20, 1970. Abolished by Reorg. Plan No. 1 of 1977, effective Mar. 26, 1978, and certain functions transferred to President with all other functions transferred to Commerce Department.

Telecommunications Service, Automated Data
Renamed *Office of Information Resources Management* by General Services Administration order of Aug. 17, 1982. Later renamed Information Resources Management Service.

Temporary Controls, Office of Established in *Office for Emergency Management* by EO 9809 of Dec. 12, 1946, consolidating *Office of War Mobilization and Reconversion, Office of Economic Stabilization, Office of Price Administration,* and *Civilian Production Administration.* Functions with respect to Veterans' Emergency Housing Program transferred to *Housing Expediter* by EO 9836 of Mar. 22, 1947. Functions with respect to distribution and price of sugar products transferred to Agriculture Secretary by act of Mar. 31, 1947 (61 Stat. 36). Office terminated by EO 9841 of Apr. 23, 1947, and remaining functions redistributed.

Temporary Emergency Court of Appeals
Established by act of Dec. 22, 1971 (85 Stat. 749). Abolished by act of Oct. 29, 1992, effective Apr. 30, 1993 (106 Stat. 4507). Court's jurisdiction and pending cases transferred to the United States Court of Appeals for the Federal Circuit.

Territorial Affairs, Office of Established by Interior Secretarial Order 2951 of Feb. 6, 1973. Abolished by Departmental Manual Release 2270 of June 6, 1980, and functions transferred to Office of Assistant Secretary for Territorial and International Affairs.

Territorial papers *See* **State Department**

Territories, Office of Established by Interior Secretary July 28, 1950. Functions reassigned to *Deputy Assistant Secretary for Territorial Affairs* in *Office of the Assistant Secretary—Public Land Management,* Interior Department, by Secretarial Order 2942, effective July 1, 1971.

Terrorism, Cabinet Committee To Combat
Established by Presidential memorandum of Sept. 25, 1972. Terminated by National Security Council memorandum of Sept. 16, 1977.

Textile Industry, Board of Inquiry for the Cotton
Established by EO 6840 of Sept. 5, 1934. Abolished by EO 6858 of Sept. 26, 1934.

Textile National Industrial Relations Board
Established by administrative order of June 28, 1934. Abolished by EO 6858 of Sept. 26, 1934, which created *Textile Labor Relations Board* in connection with Labor Department. *Board* terminated July 1,

1937, and functions absorbed by *U.S. Conciliation Service,* Labor Department.

Textile National Industrial Relations Board, Cotton
Established by original Code of Fair Competition for the Cotton Textile Industry, as amended July 10, 1934. Abolished by EO 6858 of Sept. 26, 1934.

Textile Work Assignment Board, Cotton
Amendments to Code of Fair Competition for Cotton Textile Industry approved by EO 6876 of Oct. 16, 1934, and *Cotton Textile Work Assignment Board* appointed by *Textile Labor Relations Board. Board* expired June 15, 1935.

Textile Work Assignment Board, Silk Appointed by *Textile Labor Relations Board* following President's approval of amendments to Code of Fair Competition for Silk Textile Industry by EO 6875 of Oct. 16, 1934. Terminated June 15, 1935.

Textile Work Assignment Board, Wool Established by EO 6877 of Oct. 16, 1934. Terminated June 15, 1935.

Textiles, Office of Established by Commerce Secretary Feb. 14, 1971. Functions transferred to *Domestic and International Business Administration,* effective Nov. 17, 1972.

Trade, Special Adviser to the President on Foreign
Established by EO 6651 of Mar. 23, 1934. Terminated on expiration of *National Recovery Administration.*

Trade Administration, International *See* **Business and Defense Services Administration**

Trade Agreements, Interdepartmental Committee on
Established by Secretary of State in 1934 and reestablished by EO 9832 of Feb. 25, 1947. Abolished by EO 11075 of Jan. 15, 1963.

Trade and Development Program Established by act of Sept. 4, 1961, as amended (88 Stat. 1804). Designated separate entity within the U.S. International Development Cooperation Agency by act of Sept. 4, 1961, as amended (102 Stat. 1329). Renamed Trade and Development Agency by act of Oct. 28, 1992 (106 Stat. 3657).

Trade Expansion Act Advisory Committee
Established by EO 11075 of Jan. 15, 1963. Abolished by EO 11846 of Mar. 27, 1975, and records transferred to Trade Policy Committee established by same EO.

Trade Negotiations, Office of the Special Representative for Renamed Office of the U.S. Trade Representative by EO 12188 of Jan. 4, 1980.

Trade Policy Committee Established by EO 10741 of Nov. 25, 1957. Abolished by EO 11075 of Jan. 15, 1963.

Traffic Safety, President's Committee for
Established by Presidential letter of Apr. 14, 1954. Continued by EO 10858 of Jan. 13, 1960. Abolished by EO 11382 of Nov. 28, 1967.

Traffic Safety Agency, National Established in Commerce Department by act of Sept. 9, 1966 (80 Stat. 718). Activity transferred to Transportation

Department by act of Oct. 15, 1966 (80 Stat. 931).
Responsibility placed in *National Highway Safety
Bureau* by EO 11357 of June 6, 1967.

Training and Employment Service, U.S.   Established
in *Manpower Administration,* Labor Department,
Mar. 17, 1969. Abolished by Secretary's letter of
Dec. 6, 1971, and functions assigned to *Office of
Employment Development Programs* and *U.S.
Employment Service.*

Training School for Boys, National   *See* **District of
Columbia, Reform-School of the**

Transportation, Federal Coordinator of   Established
by act of June 16, 1933 (48 Stat. 211). Expired June
16, 1936, under provisions of Public Resolution 27
(49 Stat. 376).

Transportation, Office of   Established in Agriculture
Department by Secretary's Memorandum 1966 dated
Dec. 12, 1978. Abolished by Secretary's
Memorandum 1030–25 dated Dec. 28, 1990.

Transportation and Communications Service
Established by General Services Administrator Oct.
19, 1961. Abolished by Administrator's order,
effective July 15, 1972. Motor equipment,
transportation, and public utilities responsibilities
assigned to Federal Supply Service;
telecommunications function assigned to *Automated
Data Telecommunications Service.*

Transportation and Public Utilities Service
Abolished by General Services Administration order
of Aug. 17, 1982. Functions transferred to various
GSA organizations.

Transportation Safety Board, National   Established
in Transportation Department by act of Oct. 15,
1966 (80 Stat. 935). Abolished by act of Jan. 3, 1975
(88 Stat. 2156), which established independent
National Transportation Safety Board.

Travel Service, U.S.   Replaced by *U.S. Travel and
Tourism Administration,* Commerce Department,
pursuant to act of Oct. 16, 1981 (95 Stat. 1014).

Travel and Tourism Adminstration, U.S.
Established by act of Oct. 16, 1981 (95 Stat. 1014).
Abolished by P.L. 104–288, Oct. 11, 1996 (110 Stat.
3407).

Travel and Tourism Advisory Board   Established by
act of Oct. 16, 1981 (95 Stat. 1017). Abolished by
P.L. 104–288, Oct. 11, 1996 (110 Stat. 3407).

**Treasury, Office of the Assistant Secretary of the—
Electronics and Information Technology**
Established by Secretary's Order 114–1 of Mar. 14,
1983. Abolished by Secretary's Order 114–3 of May
17, 1985, and functions transferred to Office of the
Assistant Secretary for Management. Certain
provisions effective Aug. 31, 1985 (50 FR 23573).

Treasury, Solicitor of the   Position established
when certain functions of *Solicitor of the Treasury*
transferred to Justice Department by EO 6166 of
June 10, 1933. *Solicitor of the Treasury* transferred
from Justice Department to Treasury Department by
same order. *Office of Solicitor of the Treasury*
abolished by act of May 10, 1934 (48 Stat. 758),
and functions transferred to General Counsel,
Treasury Department.

Treasury Secretary, Assistant   Office abolished by
Reorg. Plan No. III of 1940, effective June 30, 1940,
and functions transferred to Fiscal Assistant
Secretary, Treasury Department.

Treaties   *See* **State Department**

Typhus Commission, U.S. of America   Established
in *War Department* by EO 9285 of Dec. 24, 1942.
Abolished June 30, 1946, by EO 9680 of Jan. 17,
1946.

U.S.   *See other part of title*

**Uniformed Services University of the Health
Sciences, School of Medicine of the**   Renamed F.
Edward Hébert School of Medicine by act of Sept.
24, 1983 (97 Stat. 704).

**United Nations Educational, Scientific and Cultural
Organization**   U.S. membership in UNESCO
authorized by act of July 30, 1946 (60 Stat. 712).
Announcement of U.S. intention to withdraw made
Dec. 28, 1983, in accordance with UNESCO
constitution. Official U.S. withdrawal effective Dec.
31, 1984, by Secretary of State's letter of Dec. 19,
1984. U.S. maintains status as observer mission in
UNESCO.

United States Court of Military Appeals
Established under Article I of the Constitution of the
United States pursuant to act of May 5, 1950, as
amended (10 U.S.C. 867). Renamed United States
Court of Appeals for the Armed Forces by act of
Oct. 5, 1995 (108 Stat. 2831).

Upper Mississippi River Basin Commission
Established by EO 11659 of Mar. 22, 1972.
Terminated by EO 12319 of Sept. 9, 1981.

Urban Affairs, Council for   Established in Executive
Office of the President by EO 11452 of Jan. 23,
1969. Terminated by EO 11541 of July 1, 1970.

Urban Mass Transportation Administration
Functions regarding urban mass transportation
established in the Department of Housing and Urban
Development by act of July 9, 1964 (78 Stat. 302).
Most functions transferred to Transportation
Department by Reorg. Plan No. 2 of 1968, effective
June 30, 1968 (82 Stat. 1369), and joint
responsibility assigned to Transportation and
Housing and Urban Development Departments for
functions relating to research, technical studies, and
training. Transportation and Housing and Urban
Development Under Secretaries agreed in November
1969 that Transportation Department should be
focal point for urban mass transportation grant
administration; at which time functions transferred to
the Department of Transportation. Renamed Federal
Transit Administration by act of Dec. 18, 1991 (105
Stat. 2088).

Urban Renewal Administration   Established in
Housing and Home Finance Agency by
Administrator's Organizational Order 1 of Dec. 23,
1954. Functions transferred to Housing and Urban
Development Department by act of Sept. 9, 1965
(78 Stat. 667), and *Administration* terminated.

Utilization and Disposal Service   Established July 1, 1961, by Administrator of General Services and assigned functions of Federal Supply Service and Public Buildings Service. Functions transferred to *Property Management and Disposal Service* July 29, 1966.

Veterans Administration   Legal work in defense of suits against the U.S. arising under act of June 7, 1924 (43 Stat. 607), transferred to Justice Department by EO 6166 of June 10, 1933. Transfer deferred to Sept. 10, 1933, by EO 6222 of July 27, 1933. Established as an independent agency under the President by Executive Order 5398 of July 21, 1930, in accordance with the act of July 3, 1930 (46 Stat. 1016) and the act of Sept. 2, 1958 (72 Stat. 1114). Made an executive department in the executive branch and redesignated Veterans Affairs Department by act of Oct. 25, 1988 (102 Stat. 2635).

Veterans Education Appeals Board   *See* **Veterans Tuition Appeals Board**

Veterans Employment Service   Renamed Veterans' Employment and Training Service by Labor Secretary's Order 4–83 of Mar. 24, 1983 (48 FR 14092).

Veterans Health Administration   *See* **Medicine and Surgery, Department of**

Veterans Health Services and Research Administration   *See* **Medicine and Surgery, Department of**

Veterans Placement Service Board   Established by act of June 22, 1944 (58 Stat. 293). Abolished by Reorg. Plan No. 2 of 1949, effective Aug. 20, 1949, and functions transferred to Labor Secretary.

Veterans Tuition Appeals Board   Established by act of Aug. 24, 1949 (63 Stat. 654). Functions assumed by *Veterans Education Appeals Board* established by act of July 13, 1950 (64 Stat. 336). *Board* terminated by act of Aug. 28, 1957 (71 Stat. 474).

Veterinary Medicine, Bureau of   Established in Food and Drug Administration, *Health, Education, and Welfare Department.* Renamed Center for Veterinary Medicine by FDA notice of Mar. 9, 1984 (49 FR 10166).

Virgin Islands   Public works programs under act of Dec. 20, 1944 (58 Stat. 827), transferred from General Services Administrator to Interior Secretary by Reorg. Plan No. 15 of 1950, effective May 24, 1950.

Virgin Islands Company   Established in 1934. Reincorporated as Government corporation by act of June 30, 1949 (63 Stat. 350). Program terminated June 30, 1965, and *Corporation* dissolved July 1, 1966.

Virgin Islands Corporation   *See* **Virgin Islands Company**

Visitor Facilities Advisory Commission, National   Established by act of Mar. 12, 1968 (82 Stat. 45). Expired Jan. 5, 1975, pursuant to act of Oct. 6, 1972 (86 Stat. 776).

Vocational Rehabilitation, Office of   Established to administer provisions of act of July 6, 1943 (57 Stat. 374). Other duties delegated by acts of Aug. 3, 1954 (68 Stat. 652), Nov. 8, 1965 (79 Stat. 1282), July 12, 1960 (74 Stat. 364), and July 10, 1954 (68 Stat. 454). Redesignated *Vocational Rehabilitation Administration* Jan. 28, 1963. Made component of newly created *Social and Rehabilitation Service* as *Rehabilitation Services Administration* by Health, Education, and Welfare Department reorganization of Aug. 15, 1967.

Vocational Rehabilitation Administration   *See* **Vocational Rehabilitation, Office of**

Voluntary Citizen Participation, State Office of   Renamed State Office of Voluntarism in ACTION by notice of Apr. 18, 1986 (51 FR 13265), effective May 18, 1986.

Volunteer Service, International, Secretariat for   Established in 1962 by International Conference on Middle Level Manpower called by President. Terminated Mar. 31, 1976, due to insufficient funding.

Volunteers in Service to America   Established by act of Nov. 8, 1966 (80 Stat. 1472). Service administered by *Office of Economic Opportunity* and functions transferred to ACTION by Reorg. Plan No. 1 of 1971, effective July 1, 1971.

Wage Adjustment Board   Established May 29, 1942, by Labor Secretary at Presidential direction of May 14, 1942, to accomplish purpose of act of Mar. 3, 1931 (46 Stat. 1494), as amended by acts of Aug. 30, 1935 (49 Stat. 1011), and Jan. 30, 1942 (56 Stat. 23). Disbanded on termination of *National Wage Stabilization Board.*

Wage and Price Stability, Council on   Established in Executive Office of the President by act of Aug. 24, 1974 (88 Stat. 750). Abolished by EO 12288 of Jan. 29, 1981. Funding ceased beyond June 5, 1981, by act of June 5, 1981 (95 Stat. 74), and authorization for appropriations repealed by act of Aug. 13, 1981 (95 Stat. 432).

Wage and Price Stability Program   *See* **Wage and Price Stability, Council on**

Wage Stabilization Board   Established by EO 10161 of Sept. 9, 1950. Reconstituted by EO 10377 of July 25, 1952. Terminated Apr. 30, 1953, by EO 10434 of Feb. 6, 1953, and acts of June 30, 1952 (66 Stat. 296), and June 30, 1953 (67 Stat. 131).

Wage Stabilization Board, National   *See* **Defense Mediation Board, National**

Wallops Flight Center, Wallops Island, VA   Formerly separate field installation of National Aeronautics and Space Administration. Made component of Goddard Space Flight Center by NASA Management Instruction 1107.10A of Sept. 3, 1981.

War, Solid Fuels Administration for   Established in Interior Department by EO 9332 of Apr. 19, 1943. Absorbed *Office of Solid Fuels Coordinator for War* (originally established as *Office of Solid Fuels Coordinator for National Defense*) pursuant to

Presidential letter of Nov. 5, 1941; later changed by Presidential letter of May 25, 1942. Terminated by EO 9847 of May 6, 1947.

War Assets Administration   Established in *Office for Emergency Management* by EO 9689 of Jan. 31, 1946. Functions transferred to *Surplus Property Administration* by Reorg. Plan No. 1 of 1947, effective July 1, 1947, and agency renamed *War Assets Administration.* Abolished by act of June 30, 1949 (63 Stat. 738), and functions transferred for liquidation to General Services Administration.

War Assets Corporation   *See* **Petroleum Reserves Corporation**

War Claims Commission   Established by act of July 3, 1948 (62 Stat. 1240). Abolished by Reorg. Plan No. 1 of 1954, effective July 1, 1954, and functions transferred to Foreign Claims Settlement Commission of the U.S.

War Commodities Division   Established in *Office of Foreign Economic Coordination* by State Departmental Order of Aug. 27, 1943. *Office* abolished by departmental order of Nov. 6, 1943, pursuant to EO 9380 of Sept. 25, 1943, which established *Foreign Economic Administration* in *Office for Emergency Management.*

War Communications, Board of   *See* **Defense Communications Board**

War Contracts Price Adjustment Board   Established by act of Feb. 25, 1944 (58 Stat. 85). Abolished by act of Mar. 23, 1951 (65 Stat. 7), and functions transferred to *Renegotiation Board,* established by same act, and General Services Administrator.

War Damage Corporation   *See* **War Insurance Corporation**

War Department   Established by act of Aug. 7, 1789 (1 Stat. 49), succeeding similar department established prior to adoption of the Constitution. Three military departments—Army; Navy, including naval aviation and U.S. Marine Corps; and Air Force—reorganized under *National Military Establishment* by act of July 26, 1947 (61 Stat. 495).

War Finance Corporation   Established by act of Apr. 5, 1918 (40 Stat. 506). Functions and obligations transferred by Reorg. Plan No. II of 1939, effective July 1, 1939, to Treasury Secretary for liquidation not later than Dec. 31, 1939.

War Food Administration   *See* **Food Production and Distribution, Administration of**

War Information, Office of   Established in *Office of Emergency Management* by EO 9182 of June 13, 1942, consolidating *Office of Facts and Figures; Office of Government Reports; Division of Information, Office for Emergency Management;* and *Foreign Information Service—Outpost, Publications, and Pictorial Branches, Coordinator of Information.* Abolished by EO 9608 of Aug. 31, 1945. *Bureau of Special Services* and functions with respect to review of publications of Federal agencies transferred to *Bureau of the Budget.* Foreign information activities transferred to State Department.

War Insurance Corporation   Established Dec. 13, 1941, by act of June 10, 1941 (55 Stat. 249). Charter filed Mar. 31, 1942. Renamed *War Damage Corporation* by act of Mar. 27, 1942 (56 Stat. 175). Transferred from *Federal Loan Agency* to Commerce Department by EO 9071 of Feb. 24, 1942. Returned to *Federal Loan Agency* by act of Feb. 24, 1945 (59 Stat. 5). *Agency* abolished by act of June 30, 1947 (61 Stat. 202), and functions assumed by *Reconstruction Finance Corporation.* Powers of *War Damage Corporation,* except for purposes of liquidation, terminated as of Jan. 22, 1947.

War Labor Board, National   *See* **Defense Mediation Board, National**

War Manpower Commission   Established in *Office for Emergency Management* by EO 9139 of Apr. 18, 1942. Terminated by EO 9617 of Sept. 19, 1945, and functions, except *Procurement and Assignment Service,* transferred to Labor Department.

War Mobilization, Office of   Established by EO 9347 of May 27, 1943. Transferred to *Office of War Mobilization and Reconversion* by EO 9488 of Oct. 3, 1944.

War Mobilization and Reconversion, Office of   Established by act of Oct. 3, 1944 (58 Stat. 785). Consolidated with other agencies by EO 9809 of Dec. 12, 1946, to form *Office of Temporary Controls.* Media Programming Division and *Motion Picture Division* transferred to *Office of Government Reports,* reestablished by same order. Certain other functions transferred to President and Commerce Secretary.

War Mobilization and Reconversion Advisory Board, Office of   Established by act of Oct. 3, 1944 (58 Stat. 788). Transferred to *Office of Temporary Controls* by EO 9809 of Dec. 12, 1946.

War Plants Corporation, Smaller   Established by act of June 11, 1942 (56 Stat. 351). Functions transferred by EO 9665 of Dec. 27, 1945, to *Reconstruction Finance Corporation* and Commerce Department. Abolished by act of June 30, 1947 (61 Stat. 202), and functions transferred for liquidation to General Services Administration by Reorg. Plan No. 1 of 1957, effective July 1, 1957.

War and Post War Adjustment Policies, Advisory Unit on   Established in *Office of War Mobilization* by Presidential direction Nov. 6, 1943. Report submitted Feb. 15, 1944, and Unit Director and Assistant Director submitted letter to Director of *War Mobilization* ending their work May 12, 1944.

War Production Board   Established in *Office for Emergency Management* by EO 9024 of Jan. 16, 1942. *Board* terminated and successor agency, *Civilian Production Administration,* established by EO 9638 of Oct. 4, 1945.

War Property Administration, Surplus   Established in *Office of War Mobilization* by EO 9425 of Feb. 19, 1944. Terminated on establishment of *Surplus Property Board* by act of Oct. 3, 1944 (58 Stat. 768). *Surplus Property Administration* established in *Office of War Mobilization and Reconversion* by act of Sept. 18, 1945 (59 Stat. 533), and *Board* abolished. Domestic functions of *Administration* merged into

War Assets Corporation, Reconstruction Finance Corporation, by EO 9689 of Jan. 31, 1946. Foreign functions transferred to State Department by same order. Transfers made permanent by Reorg. Plan No. 1 of 1947, effective July 1, 1947.

War Refugee Board   Established in Executive Office of the President by EO 9417 of Jan. 22, 1944. Terminated by EO 9614 of Sept. 14, 1945.

War Relations, Agricultural, Office for   *See* **Farm Products, Division of**

War Relief Agencies, President's Committee on Established by Presidential letter of Mar. 13, 1941. *President's War Relief Control Board* established by EO 9205 of July 25, 1942, to succeed *Committee.* Board terminated by EO 9723 of May 14, 1946, and functions transferred to State Department.

War Relief Control Board, President's   *See* **President's Committee on War Relief Agencies**

War Relocation Authority   Established in *Office for Emergency Management* by EO 9102 of Mar. 18, 1942. Transferred to Interior Department by EO 9423 of Feb. 16, 1944. Terminated by EO 9742 of June 25, 1946.

War Resources Board   Established in August 1939 as advisory committee to work with *Joint Army and Navy Munitions Board.* Terminated by President Nov. 24, 1939.

War Resources Council   *See* **Defense Resources Committee**

War Shipping Administration   Established in *Office for Emergency Management* by EO 9054 Feb. 7, 1942. Terminated by act of July 8, 1946 (60 Stat. 501), and functions transferred to *U.S. Maritime Commission,* effective Sept. 1, 1946.

Water, Office of Saline   Established to perform functions vested in Interior Secretary by act of July 29, 1971 (85 Stat. 159). Merged with *Office of Water Resources Research* to form *Office of Water Research and Technology* by Secretary's Order 2966 of July 26, 1974.

Water Commission, National   Established by act of Sept. 26, 1968 (82 Stat. 868). Terminated Sept. 25, 1973, pursuant to terms of act.

Water Policy, Office of   Established by Interior Department Manual Release 2374 of Dec. 29, 1981, under authority of Assistant Secretary. Abolished by Secretarial Order No. 3096 of Oct. 19, 1983, and functions transferred to *Geological Survey* and *Office of Policy Analysis.*

Water Pollution Control Administration, Federal Established under *Health, Education, and Welfare Secretary* by act of Oct. 2, 1965 (79 Stat. 903). Transferred to Interior Department by Reorg. Plan No. 2 of 1966, effective May 10, 1966. Renamed *Federal Water Quality Administration* by act of Apr. 3, 1970. Abolished by Reorg. Plan No. 3 of 1970, effective Dec. 2, 1970, and functions transferred to Environmental Protection Agency.

Water and Power Resources Service   Renamed Bureau of Reclamation May 18, 1981, by Interior Secretarial Order 3064.

Water Quality Administration, Federal   *See* **Water Pollution Control Administration, Federal**

Water Research and Technology, Office of Established by Interior Secretarial Order 2966 of July 26, 1974. Abolished by Secretarial order of Aug. 25, 1982, and functions transferred to Bureau of Reclamation, Geological Survey, and *Office of Water Policy.*

Water Resources Council   Established by act of July 22, 1965 (89 Stat 575). Inactive as of Oct. 1, 1982.

Water Resources Research, Office of   Established to perform functions vested in Interior Secretary by act of July 17, 1964 (78 Stat. 329). Merged with *Office of Saline Water* to form *Office of Water Research and Technology* by Secretary's Order 2966 of July 26, 1974.

Watergate Special Prosecution Force   Established by Attorney General order, effective May 25, 1973. Terminated by Attorney General order, effective June 20, 1977.

Waterways Corporation, Inland   Incorporated under act of June 3, 1924 (43 Stat. 360). Transferred from *War Department* to Commerce Department by Reorg. Plan No. II of 1939, effective July 1, 1939. *Corporation* sold to *Federal Waterways Corporation* under contract of July 24, 1953. Renamed *Federal Barge Lines, Inc.* Liquidated by act of July 19, 1963 (77 Stat. 81).

Weather Bureau   Established in Agriculture Department by act of Oct. 1, 1890 (26 Stat. 653). Transferred to Commerce Department by Reorg. Plan No. IV of 1940, effective June 30, 1940. Functions transferred to *Environmental Science Services Administration* by Reorg. Plan No. 2 of 1965, effective July 13, 1965.

Weather Control, Advisory Committee on Established by act of Aug. 13, 1953 (67 Stat. 559). Act of Aug. 28, 1957 (71 Stat. 426), provided for termination by Dec. 31, 1957.

Weights and Measures, Office of Standard Renamed *National Bureau of Standards* by act of Mar. 3, 1901 (31 Stat. 1449). *Bureau* transferred from Treasury Department to *Department of Commerce and Labor* by act of Feb. 14, 1903 (32 Stat. 825). *Bureau* established within the Department of Commerce by act of Mar. 4, 1913 (37 Stat. 736). Renamed National Institute of Standards and Technology by act of Aug. 23, 1988 (102 Stat. 1827).

Welfare Administration   Established by *Health, Education, and Welfare Secretary's* reorganization of Jan. 28, 1963. Components consisted of *Bureau of Family Services, Children's Bureau, Office of Juvenile Delinquency and Youth Development,* and *Cuban Refugee Staff.* These functions reassigned to *Social and Rehabilitation Service* by Department reorganization of Aug. 15, 1967.

Wilson Memorial Commission, Woodrow
Established by act of Oct. 4, 1961 (75 Stat. 783).
Terminated on submittal of final report to President
and Congress Sept. 29, 1966.

**Women, Interdepartmental Committee on the
Status of**   Established by EO 11126 of Nov. 1,
1963. Terminated by EO 12050 of Apr. 4, 1978.

Women, President's Commission on the Status of
Established by EO 10980 of Dec. 14, 1961.
Submitted final report to President Oct. 11, 1963.

Women's Army Auxiliary Corps   Established by act
of May 14, 1942 (56 Stat. 278). Repealed in part
and superseded by act of July 1, 1943 (57 Stat. 371),
which established *Women's Army Corps. Corps*
abolished by Defense Secretary Apr. 24, 1978,
pursuant to provisions of 10 U.S.C. 125A.

Women's Business Enterprise Division   Renamed
Office of Women's Business Enterprise by Small
Business Administrator's reorganization, effective
Aug. 19, 1981. Renamed Office of Women's
Business Ownership Aug. 19, 1982.

Women's Reserve   Established in U.S. Coast Guard
by act of Nov. 23, 1942 (56 Stat. 1020).

**Women's Year, 1975, National Commission on the
Observance of International**   Established by EO
11832 of Jan. 9, 1975. Continued by act of Dec. 23,
1975 (89 Stat. 1003). Terminated Mar. 31, 1978,
pursuant to terms of act.

Wood Utilization, National Committee on
Established by Presidential direction in 1925.
Abolished by EO 6179–B of June 16, 1933.

Work Projects Administration   *See* **Works Progress
Administration**

Work-Training Programs, Bureau of   Abolished by
reorganization of *Manpower Administration* and
functions assigned to *U.S. Training and Employment
Service*, effective Mar. 17, 1969.

**Working Life, Productivity and Quality of, National
Center for**   Established by act of Nov. 28, 1975 (89
Stat. 935). Authorized appropriations expired Sept.
30, 1978, and functions assumed by *National
Productivity Council.*

Works, Advisory Committee on Federal Public
Established by President Oct. 5, 1955. Abolished by
President Mar. 12, 1961, and functions assigned to
Bureau of the Budget.

Works Administration, Federal Civil   Established by
EO 6420–B of Nov. 9, 1933. Function of
employment expired March 1934. Function of
settling claims continued under *Works Progress
Administration.*

Works Administration, Public   *See* **Emergency
Administration of Public Works, Federal**

Works Agency, Federal   Established by Reorg. Plan
No. I of 1939, effective July 1, 1939. Functions

relating to defense housing transferred to *Federal
Public Housing Authority, National Housing Agency,*
by EO 9070 of Feb. 24, 1942. Abolished by act of
June 30, 1949 (63 Stat. 380), and functions
transferred to General Services Administration.

Works Emergency Housing Corporation, Public
Established by EO 6470 of Nov. 29, 1933.
Incorporated under laws of State of Delaware.
Abolished and liquidated as of Aug. 14, 1935, by
filing of certificate of surrender of corporate rights.

Works Emergency Leasing Corporation, Public
Incorporated Jan. 3, 1934, under laws of Delaware
by direction of Administrator of Public Works.
Terminated with filed certificate of dissolution with
secretary of state of Delaware Jan. 2, 1935.

Works Progress Administration   Established by EO
7034 of May 6, 1935, and continued by subsequent
yearly emergency relief appropriation acts. Renamed
Work Projects Administration by Reorg. Plan No. I
of 1939, effective July 1, 1939, which provided for
consolidation of *Works Progress Administration* into
Federal Works Agency. Transferred by President to
Federal Works Administrator Dec. 4, 1942.

Works, Special Board of Public   *See* **Land Program,
Director of**

Yards and Docks, Bureau of   Established by acts of
Aug. 31, 1842 (5 Stat. 579), and July 5, 1862 (12
Stat. 510). Abolished by Defense Department reorg.
order of Mar. 9, 1966, and functions transferred to
Navy Secretary (31 FR 7188).

Youth Administration, National   Established in
Works Progress Administration by EO 7086 of June
26, 1935. Transferred to *Federal Security Agency* by
Reorg. Plan No. I of 1939, effective July 1, 1939.
Transferred to *Bureau of Training, War Manpower
Commission*, by EO 9247 of Sept. 17, 1942.
Terminated by act of July 12, 1943 (57 Stat. 539).

**Youth Crime, President's Committee on Juvenile
Delinquency and**   Established by EO 10940 of May
11, 1961. Terminated by EO 11529 of Apr. 24,
1970.

Youth Fitness, President's Council on   Established
by EO 10673 of July 16, 1956. Renamed *President's
Council on Physical Fitness* by EO 11074 of Jan. 8,
1963. Renamed President's Council on Physical
Fitness and Sports by EO 11398 of Mar. 4, 1968.

Youth Opportunity, President's Council on
Established by EO 11330 of Mar. 5, 1967. Inactive
as of June 30, 1971; EO 11330 revoked by EO
12379 of Aug. 17, 1982.

Youth Programs, Office of   Established in Interior
Department by Secretarial Order No. 2985 of Jan. 7,
1965. Functions moved to Office of Historically
Black College and University Programs and Job
Corps, Office of the Secretary, by Departmental
Manual Release 2788 of Mar. 22, 1988.

APPENDIX C: Agencies Appearing in the Code of Federal Regulations

NOTE: This section contains an alphabetical listing of agencies appearing in the *Code of Federal Regulations* (CFR). The listing was revised as of April 1, 1998.

Agency	CFR Title, Subtitle or Chapter
ACTION	45, XII
Administrative Committee of the Federal Register	1, I
Advanced Research Projects Agency	32, I
Advisory Commission on Intergovernmental Relations	5, VII
Advisory Committee on Federal Pay	5, IV
Advisory Council on Historic Preservation	36, VIII
African Development Foundation	22, XV
Federal Acquisition Regulation	48, 57
Agency for International Development, United States	22, II
Federal Acquisition Regulation	48, 7
Agricultural Marketing Service	7, I, IX, X, XI
Agricultural Research Service	7, V
Agriculture Department	
Agricultural Marketing Service	7, I, IX, X, XI
Agricultural Research Service	7, V
Animal and Plant Health Inspection Service	7, III; 9, I
Chief Financial Officer, Office of	7, XXX
Commodity Credit Corporation	7, XIV
Cooperative State Research, Education, and Extension Service	7, XXXIV
Economic Research Service	7, XXXVII
Energy, Office of	7, XXIX
Environmental Quality, Office of	7, XXXI
Farm Service Agency	7, VII, XVIII
Federal Acquisition Regulation	48, 4
Federal Crop Insurance Corporation	7, IV
Food and Consumer Service	7, II
Food Safety and Inspection Service	9, III
Foreign Agricultural Service	7, XV
Forest Service	36, II
Grain Inspection, Packers and Stockyards Administration	7, VIII; 9, II
Information Resources Management, Office of	7, XXVII
Inspector General, Office of	7, XXVI
National Agricultural Library	7, XLI
National Agricultural Statistics Service	7, XXXVI
Natural Resources Conservation Service	7, VI
Operations, Office of	7, XXVIII
Rural Business-Cooperative Service	7, XVIII, XLII
Rural Development Administration	7, XLII
Rural Housing Service	7, XVIII, XXXV
Rural Telephone Bank	7, XVI
Rural Utilities Service	7, XVII, XVIII, XLII
Secretary of Agriculture, Office of	7, Subtitle A
Transportation, Office of	7, XXXIII
World Agricultural Outlook Board	7, XXXVIII
Air Force Department	32, VII
Federal Acquisition Regulation Supplement	48, 53
Alaska Natural Gas Transportation System, Office of the Federal Inspector	10, XV
Alcohol, Tobacco and Firearms, Bureau of	27, I

Agency	CFR Title, Subtitle or Chapter
Mine Safety and Health Administration	30, I
Minerals Management Service	30, II
Mines, Bureau of	30, VI
Minority Business Development Agency	15, XIV
Miscellaneous Agencies	1, IV
Monetary Offices	31, I
National Aeronautics and Space Administration	5, LIX; 14, V
Federal Acquisition Regulation	48, 18
National Agricultural Library	7, XLI
National Agricultural Statistics Service	7, XXXVI
National Archives and Records Administration	5, LXVI; 36, XII
Information Security Oversight Office	32, XX
National Bureau of Standards	15, II
National Capital Planning Commission	1, IV
National Commission for Employment Policy	1, IV
National Commission on Libraries and Information Science	45, XVII
National and Community Service, Corporation for	45, XXV
National Council on Disability	34, XII
National Credit Union Administration	12, VII
National Drug Control Policy, Office of	21, III
National Foundation on the Arts and the Humanities	45, XI
National Highway Traffic Safety Administration	23, II, III; 49, V
National Imagery and Mapping Agency	32, I
National Indian Gaming Commission	25, III
National Institute for Literacy	34, XI
National Institute of Standards and Technology	15, II
National Labor Relations Board	5, LXI; 29, I
National Marine Fisheries Service	50, II, IV
National Mediation Board	29, X
National Oceanic and Atmospheric Administration	15, IX; 50, II, III, IV, VI
National Park Service	36, I
National Railroad Adjustment Board	29, III
National Railroad Passenger Corporation (AMTRAK)	49, VII
National Science Foundation	5, XLIII; 45, VI
Federal Acquisition Regulation	48, 25
National Security Council	32, XXI
National Security Council and Office of Science and Technology Policy	47, II
National Telecommunications and Information Administration	15, XXIII; 47, III
National Transportation Safety Board	49, VIII
National Weather Service	15, IX
Natural Resources Conservation Service	7, VI
Navajo and Hopi Indian Relocation, Office of	25, IV
Navy Department	32, VI
Federal Acquisition Regulation	48, 52
Neighborhood Reinvestment Corporation	24, XXV
Northeast Dairy Compact Commission	7, XIII
Nuclear Regulatory Commission	5, XLVIII; 10, I
Federal Acquisition Regulation	48, 20
Occupational Safety and Health Administration	29, XVII
Occupational Safety and Health Review Commission	29, XX
Offices of Independent Counsel	28, VI
Operations Office	7, XXVIII
Overseas Private Investment Corporation	5, XXXIII; 22, VII
Panama Canal Commission	48, 35
Panama Canal Regulations	35, I
Patent and Trademark Office	37, I
Payment From a Non-Federal Source for Travel Expenses	41, 304
Payment of Expenses Connected With the Death of Certain Employees	41, 303
Peace Corps	22, III
Pennsylvania Avenue Development Corporation	36, IX
Pension and Welfare Benefits Administration	29, XXV
Pension Benefit Guaranty Corporation	29, XL
Personnel Management, Office of	5, I, XXXV; 45, VIII
Federal Acquisition Regulation	48, 17
Federal Employees Group Life Insurance Federal Acquisition Regulation	48, 21

NAME INDEX

NOTE: Separate listings of Senators and Representatives can be found beginning on pages 32 and 34, respectively. Any other references to said persons can be found in this index.

Auten, John H.—442
Autin, John—157
Awantang, Felix—704
Ayele, Moges—408
Ayers, Troy—430
Azama, Rod—684
Azcuenaga, Mary L.—565

B

Babbitt, Bruce—308, 502, 602
Babbitt, George T., Jr.—189
Babbitt, Harriet C.—582, 699
Babbitts, Larry—387
Babcock, Mary L.—268
Baca, Edward D.—186, 197
Baca, Joseph F.—743
Baca, Polly B.—581
Baca, Sylvia V.—309
Bachiller, R.M.—212
Bachman, Ronald G.—387
Bachner, Jane H.—409
Bachula, Gary R.—149
Bacon, John—485
Bacon, Kenneth H.—174
Baden, Larry—607
Baebel, Emilie M.—442
Baer, Gregory A.—441
Baer, William J.—565
Baerwald, Thomas J.—622
Baffa, John H.—478
Bahl, Barry T.—488
Bailey, Betty L.—510
Bailey, Chester V.—522
Bailey, Judith—565
Bailey, Kevin J.—446
Bailey, Liz—173
Baird, Iain S.—146
Baird, Richard D.—659
Baird, Ronald—164
Baity, William—442
Baker, Becky—604
Baker, C. Steven—570
Baker, D. James—148
Baker, Edward L.—266
Baker, Elaine L.—544
Baker, Howard H., Jr.—725
Baker, James R.—110
Baker, John—693
Baker, Jon A.—492
Baker, Jonathan B.—565
Baker, Michael C.—488
Baker, Richard L.—555
Baker, S.H.—211
Balderston, Kris M.—91
Baldock, Bobby R.—72
Balducchi, Deborah K.—660
Baldwin, Hattie P.—692
Baldwin, Jeffrey—458
Baldwin, Robert N.—743
Baldwin, Wendy—269
Balinskas, James A.—587
Ball, Theresa—374
Ballantyne, Harry C.—679
Ballantyne, Janet—704
Ballard, Ernesta—713
Ballard, Joe N.—197
Ballentine, Roger—93
Balsanek, Thomas G.—477
Balsiger, James W.—162
Baltar, Jorge—486
Baltay, Maureen S.—475
Baltz, Richard—489
Balutis, Alan P.—145
Bangart, Richard L.—632
Bange, Gerald—110
Banko, Tony—607

Banks, Cecil—495
Banks, Samuel—446
Banque, Robert T.—443
Banscher, Roland—725
Baquet, Charles R., III—649
Barajas, Phyllis—245
Baratz, Max—197
Barbash, Barry P.—660
Barbee-Fletcher, Sharon—653
Barber, Edwin L.—443
Barberesi, Raymond R.—412
Barbor, K.E.—211
Barca, Peter—677, 678
Barclay, George N.—572
Barile, Vincent L.—477
Bark, Dennis L.—744
Barkan, Joel W.—158
Barker, Barry M.—486
Barker, Betty L.—146
Barkett, Rosemary—73
Barksdale, James C.—677
Barksdale, Rhesa H.—71
Barlow, Elizabeth T.—144
Barlow, Ralph M.—533
Barnes, Beverly—92
Barnes, C. Richard—554, 555
Barnes, Devereaux—512
Barnes, Donald G.—510
Barnes, Janet L.—641
Barnes, Jeffrey S.—487
Barnes, Paul D.—679
Barnett, Judith—147
Barnett, Stewart—209
Barr, John, III—248
Barr, Mari R.—309
Barr, Michael—441
Barr, Robert E.—449
Barram, David J.—571, 602
Barranca, Nicholas F.—713
Barrett, John W., Jr.—499
Barrett, Lake H.—253
Barrett, Lawrence—669
Barrett, Thomas J.—406
Barringer, Martha M.—657
Barris, Mark R.—399
Barron, William G., Jr.—369
Barry, Camille—271
Barry, Donald J.—308
Barry, Marion S., Jr.—602
Barshefsky, Charlene—106
Bartanowicz, Robert—423
Bartell, Michael E.—660
Bartholow, Steven A.—657
Bartning, Delores de la Torre—524
Barton, William R.—571
Baseman, Leroy T.—185
Basham, W. Ralph—447
Bashaw, Peter A.—413
Baskir, Lawrence M.—196
Bass, David—628
Basso, David L.—615
Basso, Peter J.—405
Batchelder, Alice M.—71
Bates, Melinda—92
Bates, Sandra N.—572
Batliner, Terrence S.—475
Batres, Alfonso R.—476
Battaglini, J.R.—208
Battey, James F., Jr.—270
Battey, Phil—535
Battocchi, Ronald S.—628
Batts, Linda—447
Batts, Walter—268
Baucom, Thomas—446
Baucom, William—705
Bauer, Frank—141
Bauer, Norman W.—487

Bauerlein, Joan W.—407
Bauerlein, Robert D.—184
Baugh, Charles R.—463
Baum, Robert L.—309
Baumgaertner, Martin W.—584
Bavis, John—617
Baxter, Gregory—384
Baxter, Thomas C., Jr.—559
Bay, Ann—727
Bay, Donald—109
Baylen, James L.—605
Bayless, David B.—665
Bazar, Kenneth—380
Bazzle, Diane N.—509
Beach, Milo C.—726
Beale, James R.—185
Beale, Richard E., Jr.—226
Beals, Theodore F.—476
Beam, Clarence Arlen—72
Bean, Robert—444
Bear, Dinah—95
Beatty, Robert H., Jr.—555
Beaulieu, David—245
Beaulieu, Phyllis—503
Beaven, Vida—270
Bechtol, Lisa S.—474
Beck, Mary Coutts—97
Beckenbaugh, Scot—555
Becker, Charles—157
Becker, Edward R.—70
Beckley, Sandra—484, 486
Beebe, Cora Prifold—450
Beecher, Donna D.—641
Beecher, William M.—632
Beeman, Josiah H.—399
Beene, J. Paul—462, 463
Beers, Rand—391
Begala, Kathleen P.—500
Begala, Paul—91
Belaga, Julie D.—524
Belger, Monte R.—406
Belisle, Philip—461
Bell, Gary—449
Bell-Goodrich, Sharon—487, 488
Bell, Hubert T., Jr.—632
Bell, Linda—608
Bellardo, Lewis J.—594
Belles, Gail—477
Bellmore, Teresa—678
Belton, Linda W.—475
Belz, James K.—713
Benages, James—379
Benavides, Fortunado P.—71
Benedict, Lawrence N.—398
Beneke, Patricia J.—308
Benken, Eric—186
Bennett, David L.—406
Bennett, Donna D.—572
Benoit, Jeffrey R.—163
Benowitz, Stephen C.—270
Bensey, Roger L.—110
Benson, B. Allan—615
Bentivoglio, John—328
Bentley, Bill—503
Benton, David—445
Benz, Charity—383
Berek, Judy—268
Berenson, Robert—268
Berg, Lisa—94
Berg, Olena—368
Bergdoll, Thomas—678
Berger, Samuel R.—91, 96
Bergman, Charles—186
Berkenwald, Carl—586
Berkowitz, Francine—727
Berkowsky, Pamela—173
Bernard, Eddie N.—164

AGENCY/SUBJECT INDEX

NOTE: This index does not include material appearing in Appendices A–C.

859

RECENT CHANGES

Personnel actions brought to the attention of *Manual* editors June 2–August 1, 1998

Page	Position	Action

U.S. Courts of Appeals

70	U.S. Circuit Judge for the Second Circuit	Rosemary S. Pooler confirmed June 2.
70	U.S. Circuit Judge for the Second Circuit	Robert D. Sack confirmed June 15.
72	U.S. Circuit Judge for the Eighth Circuit	John D. Kelly confirmed July 31, vice Frank J. Magill.
72	U.S. Circuit Judge for the Ninth Circuit	Kim McLean Wardlaw confirmed July 31.

White House Office

91	Counselor to the President and Special Envoy for the Americas	Thomas F. McClarty III resigned (effective June 30).

Office of Management and Budget

99	Director	Jacob J. Lew confirmed July 31.
99	Administrator, Office of Federal Procurement Policy	Deidre A. Lee confirmed July 30.

Office of Science and Technology Policy

105	Assistant to the President for Science and Technology and Director	Neal F. Lane confirmed July 31, vice John H. Gibbons.
105	Associate Director for Environment	Rosina M. Bierbaum confirmed July 30.

Agriculture Department

110	General Counsel	Charles R. Rawls confirmed July 31.

Commerce Department

144	Assistant Secretary for Legislative and Intergovernmental Affairs	Deborah K. Kilmer confirmed July 31.
147	Assistant Secretary for Trade Development	Michael J. Copps confirmed June 26.
147	Assistant Secretary and Director General of the U.S. and Foreign Commercial Service	Awilda R. Marquez confirmed June 26.
149	Deputy Assistant Secretary and Deputy Commissioner of Patents and Trademarks	Q. Todd Dickinson confirmed June 18.

Defense Department

173	Director, Defense Research and Engineering	Hans Mark confirmed June 9.

Air Force Department

184	Assistant Secretary of the Air Force (Manpower, Reserve Affairs, Installations, and Environment)	Ruby B. DeMesme confirmed July 30, vice Rodney A. Coleman.
186	Chief, National Guard Bureau	Lt. Gen. Russell C. Davis, USAF, confirmed July 30, vice Lt. Gen. Edward D. Baca, USA.

Army Department

195	Secretary of the Army	Louis Caldera confirmed June 24.
195	Assistant Secretary of the Army (Civil Works)	Joseph W. Westphal confirmed June 9.
195	Assistant Secretary of the Army (Installations, Logistics, and Environment)	Mahlon Apgar IV confirmed June 9.

RECENT CHANGES—Continued
Personnel actions brought to the attention of *Manual* editors June 2–August 1, 1998

Page	Position	Action
195	Assistant Secretary of the Army (Manpower and Reserve Affairs)	Patrick T. Henry confirmed July 30.
197	Chief, National Guard Bureau	Lt. Gen. Russell C. Davis, USAF, confirmed July 30, vice Lt. Gen. Edward D. Baca, USA.

Navy Department

209	Assistant Secretary of the Navy (Manpower and Reserve Affairs)	Carolyn H. Becraft confirmed July 30, vice Bernard S. Rostker.

Energy Department

253	Secretary	Bill Richardson confirmed July 31, vice Federico Peña.
253	General Counsel	Mary Anne Sullivan confirmed June 25.

Interior Department

308	Assistant Secretary for Fish and Wildlife and Parks	Donald J. Barry confirmed June 25.

Justice Department

329	Assistant Attorney General, Criminal Division	James K. Robinson confirmed June 15.

Labor Department

368	Assistant Secretary for Employment and Training	Raymond L. Bramucci confirmed July 30.

State Department

398	U.S. Ambassador to Armenia	Michael C. Lemmon confirmed June 26, vice Peter Tomsen.
398	U.S. Ambassador to The Bahamas	Arthur L. Schechter confirmed July 31, vice Sidney Williams.
398	U.S. Ambassador to Belgium	Paul L. Cejas confirmed June 26, vice Alan J. Blinken.
398	U.S. Ambassador to Chile	John O'Leary confirmed June 26, vice Gabriel Guerra-Mondragon.
398	U.S. Ambassador to Denmark	Richard N. Swett confirmed July 31, vice Edward E. Elson.
398	U.S. Ambassador to Eritrea	William D. Clarke confirmed June 26.
398	U.S. Ambassador to Finland	Eric S. Edelman confirmed June 26.
398	U.S. Ambassador to Gambia	George W.B. Haley confirmed June 26, vice Gerald W. Scott.
398	U.S. Ambassador to Georgia	Kenneth S. Yalowitz confirmed June 26, vice William H. Courtney.
398	U.S. Ambassador to Latvia	James H. Holmes confirmed July 31, vice Larry C. Napper.
398	U.S. Ambassador to Lebanon	David M. Satterfield confirmed July 31, vice Richard H. Jones.
398	U.S. Ambassador to Lesotho	Katherine Hubay Peterson confirmed June 26, vice Bismarck Myrick.
398	U.S. Ambassador to Madagascar	Shirley E. Barnes confirmed June 26.
398	U.S. Ambassador to Mexico	Jeffrey Davidow confirmed June 26.
399	U.S. Ambassador to Moldova	Rudolf V. Perina confirmed June 26, vice John T. Stewart.
399	U.S. Ambassador to The Netherlands	Cynthia P. Schneider confirmed June 26, vice K. Terry Dornbush.
399	U.S. Ambassador to Oman	John B. Craig confirmed July 31, vice Frances D. Cook.
399	U.S. Ambassador to Pakistan	William B. Milam confirmed July 31, vice Thomas W. Simons, Jr.
399	U.S. Ambassador to Slovenia	Nancy Halliday Ely-Raphel confirmed June 26, vice Victor Jackovich.
399	U.S. Ambassador to Spain	Edward L. Romero confirmed June 23.
399	U.S. Ambassador to Tanzania	Charles R. Stith confirmed June 26.